The Broadview Anthology of

BRITISH LITERATURE

The Twentieth Century and Beyond: Volume 6A, From 1900 to World War II

The Broadview Anthology of British Literature

The Broadview Anthology of

BRITISH LITERATURE

The Twentieth Century and Beyond: Volume 6A, From 1900 to World War II

GENERAL EDITORS

Joseph Black, University of Massachusetts
Leonard Conolly, Trent University
Kate Flint, Rutgers University
Isobel Grundy, University of Alberta
Don LePan, Broadview Press
Roy Liuzza, University of Tennessee
Jerome J. McGann, University of Virginia
Anne Lake Prescott, Barnard College
Barry V. Qualls, Rutgers University
Claire Waters, University of California, Davis

broadview press

LIBRARY AND ARCHIVES CANADA CATALOGUING IN PUBLICATION

The Broadview anthology of British literature / general editors, Joseph Black ... [et al].

Includes bibliographical references and index.
Contents: v.1. The Medieval period. —v.2. The Renaissance and the early seventeenth century. —v. 3. The Restoration and the eighteenth century.—v.4. The age of romanticism.—v.5. The Victorian era.—v.6A. The twentieth century and beyond: from 1900 to World War II.—v.6B. The twentieth century and beyond: from 1945 to the twenty-first century.

ISBN 1-55111-609-x (v.1), —ISBN 1-55111-610-3 (v.2), —ISBN 1-55111-611-1 (v.3), —ISBN 1-55111-612-x (v.4),— ISBN 1-55111-613-8 (v.5),—ISBN 978-1-55111-923-6 (v.6A),—ISBN 978-1-55111-924-3 (v.6B)

1. English literature. I. Black, Joseph Laurence, 1962–

PR1109.B77   2006   820.8   C2006-900091-3

Broadview Press is an independent, international publishing house, incorporated in 1985. Broadview believes in shared ownership, both with its employees and with the general public; since the year 2000 Broadview shares have traded publicly on the Toronto Venture Exchange under the symbol BDP.

We welcome comments and suggestions regarding any aspect of our publications—please feel free to contact us at the addresses below or at broadview@broadviewpress.com.

North America
PO Box 1243,
Peterborough, Ontario
Canada K9J 7H5

2215 Kenmore Ave.,
Buffalo, NY, USA 14207
Tel: (705) 743-8990;
Fax: (705) 743-8353
email: customerservice@broadviewpress.com

UK, Ireland, and continental Europe
NBN International
Estover Road
Plymouth
UK PL6 7PY
Tel: +44 (0) 1752 202301;
Fax: +44 (0) 1752 202331;
Fax Order Line: +44 (0) 1752 202333;
Cust Ser: enquiries@nbninternational.com
Orders: orders@nbninternational.com

Australia and New Zealand
UNIREPS,
University of New South Wales
Sydney, NSW, 2052
Australia
Tel: 61 2 9664 0999;
Fax: 61 2 9664 5420
email: info.press@unsw.edu.au

www. broadviewpress.com
Broadview Press acknowledges the financial support of the Government of Canada through the Book Publishing Industry Development Program (BPIDP) for our publishing activities.

Cover design by Lisa Brawn

PRINTED IN CANADA

CONTRIBUTING EDITORS AND WRITERS

MANAGING EDITOR	Don LePan
EDITORIAL COORDINATOR	Jennifer McCue
DEVELOPMENTAL EDITOR	Laura Cardiff
ASSISTANT DEVELOPMENTAL EDITOR	Melissa Goertzen
GENERAL ACADEMIC AND TEXTUAL EDITORS	Colleen Franklin, Morgan Rooney
DESIGN COORDINATOR	Kathryn Brownsey

CONTRIBUTING EDITORS

Katherine O. Acheson
Sandra Bell
Emily Bernhard Jackson
Joseph Black
Robert Boenig
Michael Calabrese
Laura Cardiff
Noel Chevalier
Mita Choudhury
Thomas J. Collins
Leonard Conolly
Dianne Dugaw
Michael Faletra
Christina Fitzgerald
Stephen Glosecki

Amanda Goldrick-Jones
John Holmes
Michael Keefer
Scott Kleinman
Gary Kuchar
Don LePan
Roy Liuzza
Marie Loughlin
D.L. Macdonald
Anne McWhir
Tobias Menely
David Oakleaf
Jude Polsky
Anne Lake Prescott
Joyce Rappaport

Herbert Rosengarten
Jason Rudy
Peter Sabor
Janice Schroeder
Geoffrey Sill
Emily Steiner
David Swain
Andrew Taylor
Peggy Thompson
Fred Waage
Craig Walker
Claire Waters
James Winny

CONTRIBUTING WRITERS

Laura Cardiff
Jude Polsky
Victoria Abboud
Steven Alvarez
Balaka Basu
Lopamudra Basu
Jane Beal
Rachel Beatty
Jennifer Beauvais
Rachel Bennett
Emily Bernhard Jackson
Rebecca Blasco
Julie Brennan
Andrew Bretz
Emily Cargan
Mia Chen
Adrienne Eastwood
Wendy Eberle-Sinatra
Peter Enman
Jamie Ferguson

Louise Geddes
Alina Gharabegian
Jane Grove
Isobel Grundy
Dorothy Hadfield
Camille Isaacs
Erik Isford
Andrea Jones
Stephanie King
Don LePan
Anna Lepine
John McIntyre
Susan McNeil-Bindon
Pia Mukherji
Carrie Nartkler
Byron Nelson
Kenna Olsen
Seamus O'Malley
Kendra O'Neal Smith
Allisandra Paschkowiak

Laura Pellerine
Jason Rudy
Anne Salo
Janice Schroeder
Karen Selesky
Carrie Shanafelt
Nicole Shukin
James Soderholm
Anne Sorbie
Martha Stoddard-Holmes
Jenna Stook
Candace Taylor
Yevgeniya Traps
David van Belle
Shari Watling
Matthew Williams
bj Wray
Nicole Zylstra

LAYOUT AND TYPESETTING

Kathryn Brownsey   Susan Chamberlain

ILLUSTRATION FORMATTING AND ASSISTANCE

Cheryl Baldwin   Lisa Brawn

PRODUCTION COORDINATORS

Barbara Conolly   Leonard Conolly   Judith Earnshaw

PERMISSIONS COORDINATORS

Emily Cargan   Katie Dole   Jennifer Elsayed
Chris Griffin   Amy Nimegeer

PROOFREADERS

Jennifer Bingham   Lynn Fraser   Lynn Neufeld
Martin Boyne   Anne Hodgetts   Morgan Rooney
Lucy Conolly   Amy Neufeld   Kerry Taylor

EDITORIAL ADVISORS

Rachel Ablow, University of Rochester
Joan Beal, University of Sheffield
Donald Beecher, Carleton University
Rita Bode, Trent University
Susan Brown, University of Guelph
Catherine Burroughs, Wells College
Elizabeth Campbell, Oregon State University
Margaret Case, Ohio Northern University
William Christmas, San Francisco State
    University
Nancy Cirillo, University of Illinois, Chicago
Angelo Costanzo, Professor Emeritus,
    Shippensburg University
David Cowart, University of South Carolina
Alex Dick, University of British Columbia
Len Diepeveen, Dalhousie University
Daniel Fischlin, University of Guelph
Robert Forman, St. John's University
Barbara Gates, University of Delaware
Chris Gordon-Craig, University of Alberta
Stephen Guy-Bray, University of British
    Columbia
Elizabeth Hodgson, University of British
    Columbia

John Holmes, University of Reading
Peter Jeffrey, Princeton University
Michael Keefer, University of Guelph
Gordon Kipling, University of California,
    Los Angeles
William Liston, Ball State University
Peter Mallios, University of Maryland
Kirsteen McCue, University of Glasgow
Rod Michell, Thompson Rivers University
Byron Nelson, West Virginia University
Michael North, University of California,
    Los Angeles
Anna C. Patchias, formerly of the University of
    Virginia, Charlottesville
Alex Pettit, University of Northern Texas
John Pollock, San Jose State University
Jason Rudy, University of Maryland
Carol Senf, Georgia Tech
Sharon Smulders, Mount Royal College
Marni Stanley, Malaspina University-College
Goran Stanivukovic, St. Mary's University
Roderick Watson, University of Stirling
Julian Yates, University of Delaware

CONTENTS

VOLUME A, FROM 1900 TO WORLD WAR II

APPENDICES

Preface

A Fresh Approach

To those with some awareness of the abundance of fresh material and lively debate in the field of English Studies in recent generations, it may seem surprising that this abundance has not been more fully reflected in the number of available anthologies. Thirty years ago there were two comprehensive anthologies designed for courses surveying British Literature: *The Norton Anthology of English Literature* and one alternative. In recent years there have been still two choices available—the *Norton* and one alternative. Over that time span *The Longman Anthology of British Literature* replaced *The Oxford Anthology of English Literature* in the role of "alternative," but there has been no expansion in range of available choices to match the expansion of content and of approach that has characterized the discipline itself. The number of available handbooks and guides to writing has multiplied steadily (to the point where there are literally hundreds of available choices), while the number of comprehensive anthologies of British literature has remained at two.

For those of us who have been working for the past three years on *The Broadview Anthology of British Literature*, it is not difficult to understand why. The very expansion of the discipline has made the task of assembling and editing an anthology that fully and vibrantly reflects the ways in which the British literary tradition is studied and taught an extraordinarily daunting one. The sheer amount of work involved is enormous, but so too is the amount of expertise that needs to be called on. With that background very much in mind, we have charted a new course in the preparation of *The Broadview Anthology of British Literature*. Rather than dividing up the work among a relatively small number of academics, and asking each of them to handle on their own the work of choosing, annotating, and preparing introductions to texts in their own areas of specialization, we have involved a large number of contributors in the process (as the pages following the

title page to this volume attest), and encouraged a high degree of collaboration at every level. First and foremost have been the distinguished academics who have served as our General Editors for the project, but in all there have literally been hundreds of people involved at various stages in researching, drafting headnotes or annotations, reviewing material, editing material, and finally carrying out the work of designing and typesetting the texts and other materials. That approach has allowed us to draw on a diverse range of talent, and to prepare a large anthology with unusual speed. It has also facilitated the maintenance of a high degree of consistency. Material has been reviewed and revised in-house at Broadview, by outside editors (chief among them Colleen Franklin, an academic with a wide-ranging background and also a superb copy editor), by a variety of academics with an extraordinarily diverse range of backgrounds and academic specialities, and by our team of General Editors for the project as a whole. The aim has been not only to ensure accuracy but also to make sure that the same standards are applied throughout the anthology to matters such as extent and coverage in author introductions, level of annotation, tone of writing, and student accessibility.

Our General Editors have throughout taken the lead in the process of making selections for the anthology. Along the way we have been guided by several core principles. We have endeavored to provide a selection that is broadly representative, while also being mindful of the importance of choosing texts that have the capacity to engage readers' interest today. We have for the most part made it a policy to include long works in their entirety or not at all; readers will find complete in these pages works such as *Utopia*, *Confessions of an English Opium Eater*, *In Memoriam* and *A Room of One's Own* that are often excerpted in other anthologies. Where inexpensive editions of works are available in our series of paperback Broadview Editions, we have often decided to omit them here, on the grounds that those wishing to teach one or more such works may easily order them in a combination package with the anthology; on these grounds we have decided against including *Frankenstein*, *Pride and Prejudice*, or *Heart of Darkness*. (For both Mary Shelley and Jane Austen we have made exceptions to our general policy regarding excerpts, however, including selections from *The Last Man* to represent Shelley and the first four chapters of *Pride and Prejudice*, together with a complete shorter work, *Lady Susan*, to represent Austen.)

Any discussion of what is distinctive about *The Broadview Anthology of British Literature* must focus above all on the contents. In every volume of the anthology there is material that is distinctive and fresh—including not only selections by lesser-known writers but also less familiar selections from canonical writers. The anthology takes a fresh approach too to a great many canonical texts. The first volume of the anthology includes not only Roy Liuzza's translation of *Beowulf* (widely acclaimed as the most engaging and reliable translation available), but also new translations by Liuzza of many other works of Old English poetry and prose. Also included in the first volume of the anthology are a new verse translation of *Judith* by Stephen Glosecki, and new translations by Claire Waters of several of the *Lais* of Marie de France. The second volume includes *King Lear* not only in the full Folio version but also with three key scenes from the Quarto version; readers are thus invited to engage first-hand with the question of how textual issues may substantially affect larger issues of meaning. And so on through all six volumes.

In a number of these cases the distinctive form of the anthology facilitates the presentation of content in an engaging and practical fashion. Notably, the adoption of a two-column format allows for some translations (the Marie de France *Lais*, the James Winny translation of *Sir Gawain and the Green Knight*) to be presented in parallel column format alongside the original texts, allowing readers to experience something of the flavor of the original, while providing convenient access to an accessible translation. Similarly, scenes from the Quarto version of *King Lear* are presented alongside the comparable sections of the Folio text, and passages from four translations of the Bible are laid out parallel to each other for ready comparison.

The large trim-size, two-column format also allows for greater flexibility in the presentation of visual materials. Throughout we have aimed to make this an anthology that is fully alive to the connections between literary and visual culture, from the discussion of the CHI-RHO page of the Lindisfarne Gospels in the first volume of the anthology (and the accompanying color illustration) to the inclusion in Volume 6 of a number of selections (including Graham Greene's "The Basement Room," Hanif Kureishi's "My Son the Fanatic," Tom Stoppard's "Professional Foul," and several skits from "Monty Python's Flying Circus") that may be discussed in connection with film or television versions. Along the way appear several full-page illustrations from the Ellesmere manuscript of Chaucer's *Canterbury Tales* and illustrations to a wide variety of other works, from *Robinson Crusoe* and *Gulliver's Travels* to *A Christmas Carol* and *The Road to Wigan Pier*.

CONTEXTUAL MATERIALS

Visual materials are also an important component of the background materials that form an important part of the anthology. These materials are presented in two ways. Several "Contexts" sections on particular topics or themes appear in each volume of the anthology, presented independent of any particular text or author. These include broadly based groupings of material on such topics as "Religion and Spiritual Life," "Print Culture," "India and the Orient," "The Abolition of Slavery," "The New Art of Photography," and "The End of Empire." The groups of "In Context" materials each relate to a particular text or author. They range from the genealogical tables provided as a supplement to *Beowulf*; to materials on "The Eighteenth-Century Sexual Imagination" (presented in conjunction with Haywood's *Fantomina*); to a selection of materials relating to the Peterloo massacre (presented in conjunction with Percy Shelley's "The Mask of Anarchy"); to materials on "'The Vilest Scramble for Loot' in Central Africa" (presented in conjunction with Conrad's "An Outpost of Progress"). For the most part these contextual materials are, as the word suggests, included with a view to setting texts in their broader literary, historical, and cultural contexts; in some cases, however, the materials included in "Contexts" sections are themselves literary works of a high order. The autobiographical account by Eliza M. of nineteenth-century life in Cape Town, for example (included in the section in Volume 5 on "Race and Empire"), is as remarkable for its literary qualities as it is for the light it sheds on the realities of colonial life. In the inclusion of texts such as these, as well as in other ways, the anthology aims to encourage readers to explore the boundaries of the literary and the non-literary, and the issue of what constitutes a "literary text."

WOMEN'S PLACE

A central element of the broadening of the canon of British literature in recent generations has of course been a great increase in the attention paid to texts by women writers. As one might expect from a publisher that has played an important role in making neglected works by women writers widely available, this anthology reflects the broadening of the canon quantitatively, by including a substantially larger number of women writers than have earlier anthologies of British literature. But it also reflects this broadening in other ways. In many anthologies of literature (anthologies of British literature, to be sure, but also anthologies of literature of a variety of other sorts) women writers are set somewhat apart, referenced in introductions and headnotes only in relation to issues of gender, and treated as important only for the fact of their being women writers. *The Broadview Anthology* strenuously resists such segregation; while women writers are of course discussed in relation to gender issues, their texts are also presented and discussed alongside those by men in a wide variety of other contexts, including seventeenth-century religious and political controversies, the abolitionist movement and World War I pacifism. Texts by women writers are front and center in the discussion of the development of realism in nineteenth-century fiction. And when it comes to the twentieth century, both Virginia Woolf and Dorothy Richardson are included alongside James Joyce as practitioners of groundbreaking modernist narrative techniques.

"BRITISH," "ENGLISH," "IRISH," "SCOTTISH," "WELSH," "OTHER"

The broadening of English Studies, in conjunction with the expansion and subsequent contraction of British power and influence around the world, has considerably complicated the issue of exactly how inclusive anthologies should be. In several respects this anthology (like its two main competitors) is significantly more inclusive than its title suggests, including a number of non-British writers whose works connect in important ways with the traditions of British literature. We have endeavored first of all to portray the fluid and multilingual reality of the medieval period through the inclusion not only of works in Old and Middle English but also, where other cultures interacted with the nascent "English" language and "British" culture, works in Latin, in French, and in Welsh. In later periods the word "British" becomes deeply problematic in different respects, but on balance we have preferred it to the only obvious alternative, "English." There are several objections to the latter in this context. Perhaps most obviously, "English" excludes authors or texts not only from Ireland but also from Scotland and from Wales, both of which retain to this day cultures quite distinct from that of the English. "English literature," of course, may also be taken to mean "literature written in English," but since the anthology does not cover *all* literature written in English (most obviously in excluding American literature), the ambiguity would not in this case be helpful.

The inclusion of Irish writers presents a related but even more tangled set of issues. At the beginning of the period covered by the six volumes of this anthology we find works, such as the *Book of Kells*, that may have been created in what is now England, in what is now Scotland, in what is now Ireland—or in some combination of these. Through most of the seventeenth, eighteenth, and nineteenth centuries almost the whole of Ireland was under British control—but for the most part unwillingly. In the period covered in the last of the six volumes Ireland was partitioned, with Northern Ireland becoming a part of the United Kingdom and the

Republic of Ireland declared independent of Britain on 6 December 1921. Less than two months earlier, James Joyce had completed *Ulysses*, which was first published as a complete work the following year (in Paris, not in Britain). It would be obviously absurd to regard Joyce as a British writer up to just before the publication of *Ulysses*, and an Irish writer thereafter. And arguably he and other Irish writers should never be regarded as British, whatever the politics of the day. If on no other grounds than their overwhelming influence on and connection to the body of literature written in the British Isles, however, we have included Irish writers—among them Swift, Sheridan, Wilde, Shaw, Beckett, Bowen, Muldoon, and Heaney as well as Joyce —throughout this anthology. We have also endeavored to give a real sense in the introductions to the six volumes of the anthology, in the headnotes to individual authors, and in the annotations to the texts themselves, of the ways in which the histories and the cultures of England, Ireland, Scotland and Wales, much as they interact with one another, are also distinct.

Also included in this anthology are texts by writers from areas that are far removed geographically from the British Isles but that are or have been British possessions. Writers such as Mary Rowlandson, Olaudah Equiano, and Phillis Wheatley are included, as they spent all or most of their lives living in what were then British colonial possessions. Writers who came of age in an independent United States, on the other hand, are not included, unless (like T.S. Eliot) they subsequently put down roots in Britain and became important British literary figures. Substantial grey areas, of course, surround such issues. One might well argue, for example, that Henry James merits inclusion in an anthology of British literature, or that W.H. Auden and Thom Gunn are more American poets than British ones. But the chosen subject matter of James's work has traditionally been considered to mark him as having remained an American writer, despite having spent almost two-thirds of his life in England. And both Auden and Gunn so clearly made a mark in Britain before crossing the Atlantic that it would seem odd to exclude them from these pages on the grounds of their having lived the greater part of their adult lives in America. One of our competitors includes Sylvia Plath in their anthology of British literature; Plath lived in England for only five of her thirty years, though, and her poetry is generally agreed to have more in common with the traditions of Lowell, Merwin and Sexton than with the currents of British poetry in the 1950s and '60s.

As a broad principle, we have been open to the inclusion of twentieth and twenty-first century work in English not only by writers from the British Isles but also by writers from British possessions overseas, and by writers from countries that were once British possessions and have remained a part of the British Commonwealth. In such cases we have often chosen selections that relate in one way or another to the tradition of British literature and the British colonial legacy. Of the Judith Wright poems included here, several relate to her coming to terms with the British colonial legacy in Australia; similarly, both the Margaret Atwood and the Alice Munro selections include work in which these Canadian authors attempt to recreate imaginatively the experience of British emigrants to Canada in the nineteenth century; the Chinua Achebe story in the anthology concerns the divide between British colonial culture and traditional Nigerian culture; and so on. For convenience we have also grouped most of the post-World War II non-British authors together, following the "Contexts: The End of Empire" section. (Other than that, the table of contents for the anthology is arranged chronologically according to the birthdate of each author.)

THE HISTORY OF LANGUAGE, AND OF PRINT CULTURE

Among the liveliest discussions we had at meetings of our General Editors were those concerning the issue of whether or not to bring spelling and punctuation into accord with present-day practice. We finally decided that, in the interests of making the anthology accessible to the introductory student, we should *in most cases* bring spelling and punctuation in line with present-day practice. An important exception has been made for works in which modernizing spelling and punctuation would alter the meaning or the aural and metrical qualities. In practice this means that works before the late sixteenth century tend to be presented either in their original form or in translation, whereas later texts tend to have spelling and punctuation modernized. But where spelling and punctuation choices in later texts are known (or believed on reliable authority) to represent conscious choice on the part of the author rather than simply the common practice of the time, we have in those cases, too, made an exception and retained the original spelling and punctuation. (Among these are texts by Edmund Spenser, by William Cowper, by William Blake, John Clare, and several other poets of the Romantic era, by George Bernard Shaw, and by contemporary figures such as Linton Kwesi Johnson.)

Beyond this, we all agreed that we should provide for readers a real sense of the development of the language and of print culture. To that end we have included in each volume examples of texts in their original form—in some cases through the use of pages shown in facsimile, in others by providing short passages in which spelling and punctuation have not been modernized. A list of these appears near the beginning of each volume of the anthology.

We have also included a section of the history of the language as part of the introduction to each volume. And throughout the anthology we include materials—visual as well as textual—relating to the history of print culture.

A Dynamic and Flexible Anthology

Almost all major book publishing projects nowadays are accompanied by an adjunct website, and most large-scale anthologies are accompanied by websites that provide additional background materials in electronic form. The website component of this anthology, on the other hand, is precisely that—a *component* of the anthology itself. The notion of a website of this sort grew organically out of the process of trying to winnow down the contents of the anthology to a manageable level—the point at which all the material to be included would fit within the covers of bound books that would not be overwhelmingly heavy. And we simply could not do it. After we had made a very substantial round of cuts we were still faced with a table of contents in which each volume was at least 200 or 300 pages longer than our agreed-upon maximum. Our solution was not to try to cut anything more, but rather to select a range of material to be made available in a website component of the anthology. This material is in every way produced according to the same high standards of the material in the bound books; the editorial standards, the procedures for annotation, the author introductions, and the page design and layout—all are the same. The texts on the web, in short, are not "extra" materials; they are an integral part of the full anthology. In accordance with that principle, we have been careful to include a wide range of texts by lesser-known writers within the bound books, and a number of texts by canonical writers within the web component of the anthology.

The latter may be used in a variety of ways. Most obviously, readings from the web component are available to any purchaser of the book. Instructors who adopt *The Broadview Anthology of British Literature* as a course text are also granted permission to reproduce any web material for which Broadview holds copyright in a supplementary coursepack. An alternative for instructors who want to "create their own" anthology is to provide the publisher with a list of desired table of contents; Broadview will then make available to students through their university bookstore a custom-made coursepack with precisely those materials included. Other options are available too. Volumes of the anthology itself may of course be shrink-wrapped together at special prices in any desired combination. They may also (for a modest additional charge) be combined in a shrink-wrapped package with one or more of the over 200 volumes in the Broadview Editions series.

We anticipate that over the years the web-based component of the anthology will continue to grow—every year there will be a greater choice of web-based texts in the anthology. And every year too we anticipate additional web "extras" (discussed below). But we never foresee a day when the web will be the only option; we expect physical books always to remain central to Broadview's approach to publishing.

The Broadview List

One of the reasons we have been able to bring a project of this sort to fruition in such a relatively short time is that we have been able to draw on the resources of the full Broadview list: the many titles in the Broadview Editions series, and also the considerable range of other Broadview anthologies. As the contributors' pages and the permissions acknowledgments pages indicate, a number of Broadview authors have acted as contributing editors to this volume, providing material from other volumes that has been adapted to suit the needs of the present anthology; we gratefully acknowledge their contribution.

As it has turned out, the number of cases where we have been able to draw on the resources of the Broadview list in the full sense, using in these pages texts and annotations in very much the same form in which they appear elsewhere, has been relatively small; whether because of an issue such as the level of textual modernization or one of style of annotation, we have more often than not ended up deciding that the requirements of this anthology were such that we could not use material from another Broadview source as-is. But even in these cases we often owe a debt of gratitude to the many academics who have edited outstanding editions and anthologies for Broadview. For even where we have not drawn directly from them, we have often been inspired by them— inspired to think of a wider range of texts as possibilities than we might otherwise have done, inspired to think of contextual materials in places where we might otherwise not have looked, inspired by the freshness of approach that so many of these titles exemplify.

EDITORIAL PROCEDURES AND CONVENTIONS, APPARATUS

The in-house set of editorial guidelines for *The Broadview Anthology of British Literature* now runs to over 40 pages, covering everything from conventions for the spacing of marginal notes, to the use of small caps for the abbreviations CE and BCE, to the approach we have adopted to references in author headnotes to name changes. Perhaps the most important core principle in the introductions to the various volumes, in the headnotes for each author, in the introductions in "Contexts" sections, and in annotations throughout the anthology, is to endeavor to provide a sufficient amount of information to enable students to read and interpret these texts, but without making evaluative judgements or imposing particular interpretations. In practice that is all a good deal more challenging than it sounds; it is often extremely difficult to describe why a particular author is considered to be important without using language that verges on the interpretive or the evaluative. But it is fine line that we have all agreed is worth trying to walk; we hope that readers will find that the anthology achieves an appropriate balance.

ANNOTATION: It is also often difficult to make judgments as to where it is appropriate to provide an explanatory annotation for a word or phrase. Our policy as been to annotate where we feel it likely that most first- or second-year students are likely to have difficulty understanding the denotative meaning. (We have made it a practice not to provide notes discussing connotative meanings.) But in practice the vocabularies and levels of verbal facility of first- and second-year students may vary enormously, both from institution to institution and within any given college or university class. On the whole, we provide somewhat more annotation than our competitors, and somewhat less interpretation. Again, we hope that readers will find that the anthology has struck a appropriate balance.

THE ETHICS AND POLITICS OF ANNOTATION: On one issue regarding annotation we have felt that principles are involved that go beyond the pedagogical. Most anthologies of British literature allow many words or phrases of a racist, sexist, anti-Semitic, or homophobic nature either to pass entirely without comment, or to be glossed with apologist comments that leave the impression that such comments were excusable in the past, and may even be unobjectionable in the present. Where derogatory comments about Jewish people and money-lending are concerned, for example, anthologies often leave the impression that money-lending was a pretty unsavory practice that Jewish people entered by choice; it has been all too rare to provide readers with any sense of the degree to which English society consistently discriminated against Jews, expelling them entirely for several centuries, requiring them to wear physical marks identifying their Jewish status, prohibiting them from entering most professions, and so on. *The Broadview*

Anthology endeavors in such cases, first of all, not to allow such words and phrases to pass without comment; and second, to gloss without glossing over.

DATES: We make it a practice to include the date when a work was first made public, whether publication in print or, in the case of dramatic works, made public through the first performance of the play. Where that date is known to differ substantially from the date of composition, a note to this effect is included in parentheses. With medieval works, where there is no equivalent to the "publication" of later eras, where texts often vary greatly from one manuscript copy to another, and where knowledge as to date of original composition is usually imprecise, the date that appears at the end of each work is an estimate of the date of the work's origin in the written form included in the anthology. Earlier oral or written versions are of course in some cases real possibilities.

TEXTS: Where translations appear in this anthology, a note at the bottom of the first page indicates what translation is being used. Similar notes also address overall textual issues where choice of copy text is particularly significant. Reliable editions of all works are listed in the bibliography for the anthology, which is included as part of the website component rather than in the bound books, to facilitate ready revision. (In addition to information as to reliable editions, the bibliography provides for each author and for each of the six periods a select lists of important or useful historical and critical works.) Copyright information for texts not in the public domain, however, is provided within the bound books in a section listing Permissions Acknowledgments.

INTRODUCTIONS: In addition to the introductory headnotes for each author included in the anthology, each "Contexts" section includes a substantial introduction, and each volume includes an introduction to the period as a whole. These introductions to the six volumes of the anthology endeavor to provide a sense not only of the broad picture of literary developments in the period, but also of the historical, social, and political background, and of the cultural climate. Readers should be cautioned that, while there is inevitably some overlap

between information presented here and information presented in the author headnotes, an effort has been made to avoid such repetition as much as possible; the general introduction to each period should thus be read in conjunction with the author headnotes. The general introductions aim not only to provide an overview of ways in which texts and authors included in these pages may connect with one another, but also to give readers a sense of connection with a range of other writers and texts of the period.

READING POETRY: For much of the glossary and for the "Reading Poetry" section that appears as part of the appendices to each volume we have drawn on the superb material prepared by Herbert Rosengarten and Amanda Goldrick-Jones for *The Broadview Anthology of Poetry*; this section provides a concise but comprehensive introduction to the study of poetry. It includes discussions of diction, imagery, poetic figures, and various poetic forms, as well as offering an introduction to prosody.

MAPS: Also appearing within each of the bound books are maps especially prepared for this anthology, including, for each volume, a map of Britain showing towns and features of relevance during the pertinent period; a map showing the counties of Britain and of Ireland; maps both of the London area and of the inner city; and world maps indicating the locations of some of the significant places referenced in the anthology, and for later volumes showing the extent of Britain's overseas territories.

GLOSSARY: Some other anthologies of British literature include both glossaries of terms and essays introducing students to various political and religious categories in British history. Similar information is included in *The Broadview Anthology of British Literature*, but we have adopted a more integrated approach, including political and religious terms along with literary ones in a convenient general glossary. While we recognize that "googling" for information of this sort is often the student's first resort (and we recognize too the value of searching the web for the wealth of background reference information available there), we also recognize that information culled from the Internet is often far from reliable; it is our intent, through this glossary, through our introductions and headnotes, and through the wealth of accessible annotation in the anthology, to provide as part of the anthology a reliable core of information in the most convenient and accessible form possible.

OTHER MATERIALS: A chart of Monarchs and Prime Ministers is also provided within these pages. A range of other adjunct materials may be accessed through *The Broadview Anthology of British Literature* website. "Texts and Contexts" charts for each volume provide a convenient parallel reference guide to the dates of literary texts and historical developments. "Money in Britain" provides a thumbnail sketch of the world of pounds, shillings, and pence, together with a handy guide to estimating the current equivalents of monetary values from earlier eras. And the website offers, too, a variety of aids for the student and the instructor. An up-to-date list of these appears on the site.

ACKNOWLEDGMENTS

The names of those on the Editorial Board that shaped this anthology appear on the title page, and those of the many who contributed directly to the writing, editing, and production of the project on the following two pages. Special acknowledgment should go to Jennifer McCue, who as Editorial Coordinator has been instrumental in tying together all the vast threads of this project and in making it a reality; to Laura Cardiff and Jude Polsky, who have carried larger loads than any others in drafting introductory materials and annotations, and who have done so with great skill and unfailing grace; to Kathryn Brownsey, who has been responsible for design and typesetting, and has continued to do a superb job and to maintain her good spirits even when faced with near-impossible demands; to Colleen Franklin, for the range of her scholarship as well as for her keen eye as our primary copy editor for the entire project; to Emily Cargan, Jennifer Elsayed and Amy Nimegeer who have together done superb work on the vast job of clearing permissions for the anthology; and to Michelle Lobkowicz and Anna Del Col, who have ably and enthusiastically taken the lead with marketing matters.

The academic members of the Advisory Editorial Board and all of us in-house at Broadview owe an enormous debt of gratitude to the hundreds of academics who have offered assistance at various stages of this project. In particular we would like to express our appreciation and our thanks to the following:

Rachel Ablow, University of Rochester
Bryan Alexander, Middlebury College
Sharon Alker, Whitman College
James Allard, Brock University
Laurel Amtower, San Diego State University
Rob Anderson, Oakland University
Christopher Armitage, University of North Carolina, Chapel Hill
Clinton Atchley, Henderson State University
John Baird, University of Toronto
William Baker, Northern Illinois University
Karen Bamford, Mount Allison University
John Batchelor, University of Newcastle
Lynn Batten, University of California, Los Angeles
Alexandra Bennett, Northern Illinois University
John Beynon, California State University, Fresno
Robert E. Bjork, Arizona State University
Rita Bode, Trent University
Robert Boenig, Texas A & M University
Rick Bowers, University of Alberta
David Brewer, Ohio State University

William Brewer, Appalachian State University
Susan Brown, University of Guelph
Sylvia Brown, University of Alberta
Sheila Burgar, University of Victoria
Catherine Burroughs, Wells College
Rebecca Bushnell, University of Pennsylvania
Michael Calabrese, California State University
Elizabeth Campbell, Oregon State University
Cynthia Caywood, University of San Diego
Jane Chance, Rice University
Ranita Chatterjee, California State University, Northridge
Nancy Cirillo, University of Illinois, Chicago
Eric Clarke, University of Pittsburgh
Jeanne Clegg, University of Aquila, Italy
Thomas J. Collins, University of Western Ontario
Kevin Cope, Louisiana State University
David Cowart, University of South Carolina
Catherine Craft-Fairchild, University of St. Thomas
Carol Davison, University of Windsor
Alex Dick, University of British Columbia

Len Diepeveen, Dalhousie University
Mary Dockray-Miller, Lesley College
Frank Donoghue, Ohio State University
Chris Downs, Saint James School
Julie Early, University of Alabama, Huntsville
Siân Echard, University of British Columbia
Garrett Epp, University of Alberta
Daniel Fischlin, University of Guelph
Verlyn Flieger, University of Maryland
Robert Forman, St. John's University
Lorcan Fox, University of British Columbia
Roberta Frank, Yale University
Jeff Franklin, University of Colorado, Denver
Maria Frawley, George Washington University
Mark Fulk, Buffalo State College
Andrew Galloway, Cornell University
Michael Gamer, University of Pennsylvania
Barbara Gates, University of Delaware
Daniel Gonzalez, University of New Orleans
Jan Gorak, University of Denver
Chris Gordon-Craig, University of Alberta
Ann-Barbara Graff, Georgia Tech University
Michael Griffin, formerly of Southern Illinois
    University
Elisabeth Gruner, University of Richmond
Stephen Guy-Bray, University of British Columbia
Ruth Haber, Worcester State College
Dorothy Hadfield, University of Guelph
Margaret Hadley, University of Calgary
Robert Hampson, Royal Holloway University of
    London
Michael Hanly, Washington State University
Lila Harper, Central Washington State University
Joseph Harris, Harvard University
Anthony Harrison, North Carolina State University
Douglas Hayes, Winona State University
Jennifer Hellwarth, Allegheny University
Peter Herman, San Diego State University
Kathy Hickock, Iowa State University
John Hill, US Naval Academy
Thomas Hill, Cornell University
Elizabeth Hodgson, University of British Columbia
Joseph Hornsby, University of Alabama
Scott Howard, University of Denver
Tara Hyland-Russell, St. Mary's College

Catherine Innes-Parker, University of Prince Edward
    Island
Jacqueline Jenkins, University of Calgary
John Johansen, University of Alberta
Richard Juang, Susquehanna University
Michael Keefer, University of Guelph
Sarah Keefer, Trent University
Jon Kertzer, University of Calgary
Helen Killoran, Ohio University
Gordon Kipling, University of California, Los Angeles
Anne Klinck, University of New Brunswick
Elizabeth Kraft, University of Georgia
Mary Kramer, University of Massachusetts, Lowell
Linda Leeds, Bellevue Community College
Mary Elizabeth Leighton, University of Victoria
William Liston, Ball State University
Sharon Locy, Loyola Marymount University
Ross MacKay, Malaspina University-College
Peter Mallios, University of Maryland
Arnold Markley, Penn State University
Pamela McCallum, University of Calgary
Kristen McDermott, Central Michigan University
John McGowan, University of North Carolina
Thomas McLean, University of Otago, New Zealand
Susan McNeill-Bindon, University of Alberta
Rod Michell, Thompson Rivers University
Kitty Millett, San Francisco State University
Richard Moll, University of Western Ontario
Monique Morgan, McGill University
Lucy Morrison, Salisbury University
Byron Nelson, West Virginia University
Carolyn Nelson, West Virginia University
Claudia Nelson, Southwest Texas State University
Holly Faith Nelson, Trinity Western University
John Niles, University of Wisconsin, Madison
Michael North, University of California, Los Angeles
Mary Anne Nunn, Central Connecticut State University
David Oakleaf, University of Calgary
Tamara O'Callaghan, Northern Kentucky University
Karen Odden, Assistant Editor for *Victorian Literature
    and Culture* (formerly of University of Wisconsin,
    Milwaukee)
Erika Olbricht, Pepperdine University
Patrick O'Malley, Georgetown University
Patricia O'Neill, Hamilton College

Delilah Orr, Fort Lewis College
Cynthia Patton, Emporia State University
Russell Perkin, St. Mary's University
Marjorie G. Perloff, Stanford University
Summer Pervez, University of Ottawa
John Peters, University of North Texas
Alexander Pettit, University of North Texas
Jennifer Phegley, The University of Missouri,
    Kansas City
John Pollock, San Jose State University
Mary Poovey, New York University
Gautam Premnath, University of Massachusetts, Boston
Regina Psaki, University of Oregon
Katherine Quinsey, University of Windsor
Geoff Rector, University of Ottawa
Margaret Reeves, Atkinson College, York University
Cedric Reverand, University of Wyoming
Gerry Richman, Suffolk University
David Robinson, University of Arizona
Laura Rotunno, Pennsylvania State University, Altoona
Nicholas Ruddick, University of Regina
Jason Rudy, University of Maryland
Donelle Ruwe, Northern Arizona University
Michelle Sauer, Minot State University
SueAnn Schatz, Lock Haven University of Pennsylvania
Dan Schierenbeck, Central Missouri State University
Norbert Schürer, California State University,
    Long Beach
David Seed, University of Liverpool
Karen Selesky, University College of the Fraser Valley
Carol Senf, Georgia Tech University
Judith Slagle, East Tennessee State University
Sharon Smulders, Mount Royal College
Malinda Snow, Georgia State University
Goran Stanivukovic, St. Mary's University
Richard Stein, University of Oregon

Eric Sterling, Auburn University Montgomery
James Stokes, University of Wisconsin, Stevens Point
Mary-Ann Stouck, Simon Fraser University
Nathaniel Strout, Hamilton College
Lisa Surridge, University of Victoria
Beth Sutton-Ramspeck, Ohio State University
Nanora Sweet, University of Missouri, St. Louis
Dana Symons, Simon Fraser University
Andrew Taylor, University of Ottawa
Elizabeth Teare, University of Dayton
Doug Thorpe, University of Saskatchewan
Jane Toswell, University of Western Ontario
Kim Trainor, University of British Columbia
Herbert Tucker, University of Virginia
John Tucker, University of Victoria
Mark Turner, King's College, University of London
Eleanor Ty, Wilfrid Laurier University
Deborah Tyler-Bennett, Loughborough University
Kirsten Uszkalo, University of Alberta
Lisa Vargo, University of Saskatchewan
Gina Luria Walker, New School, New York City
Kim Walker, Victoria University of Wellington
Miriam Wallace, New College of Florida
Hayden Ward, West Virginia State University
Ruth Wehlau, Queen's University
Lynn Wells, University of Regina
Chris Willis, Birkbeck University of London
Lisa Wilson, SUNY College at Potsdam
Anne Windholz, Augustana College
Susan Wolfson, Princeton University
Kenneth Womack, Pennsylvania State University
Carolyn Woodward, University of New Mexico
Julia Wright, Wilfrid Laurier University
Julian Yates, University of Delaware
Arlene Young, University of Manitoba
Lisa Zeitz, University of Western Ontario

THE EARLY TWENTIETH CENTURY:
FROM 1900 TO WORLD WAR II

The first half of the twentieth century saw a fracturing of almost every aspect of British life. At the beginning of the century, Queen Victoria, monarch for 63 years, still reigned over a nation that had become the world's greatest economic and political power. Over the course of the nineteenth century, the industrial revolution had transformed the economy and Great Britain had become "factory to the world." Despite a high level of religious anxiety among the educated classes of the late Victorian period, the established church retained its authority over a God-fearing society. The working class was not always contented with its lot—and with reason—but the class hierarchy remained extraordinarily stable. So, too, did gender roles; a small minority of women was pressing to be given the vote, but they were regarded as extremists by the vast majority of the population. Expressions of sexuality were tightly circumscribed, and the possibility of having an orientation other than heterosexual was unmentioned (except for occasional veiled references to difficulties or scandals "of the Oscar Wilde sort.") And the British Empire had reached its zenith. The vast dominions of Canada and Australia had become semi-autonomous (in 1867 and 1901 respectively), but overwhelmingly their people were proud to call themselves British subjects. Despite a lively debate in the latter half of the nineteenth century as to whether Britain's imperial ambitions were truly benefitting either the colonizers or the colonized, the majority of British citizens were not "little Englanders" looking to reduce Britain's overseas commitments; they were pleased that British rule extended over all of India, a very large part of Africa, and a considerable amount of the rest of the world. England was seen by the English, in the words of the popular poet W.E. Henley, as the "Chosen daughter of the Lord." Britain had certainly not been immune to change in the second half the nineteenth century—indeed, many of the lines along which twentieth-century society would fracture were in place in the late Victorian era. Political and ideological strains that would shake class structure were already forming; categories of gender and sexuality were already becoming far less stable than they had been a decade or two earlier; and the "Aesthetes" had begun in the 1890s to break free of characteristically Victorian patterns of anxiety over the religious, the moral, and the aesthetic. But for most British people the world in 1900 seemed recognizably the same world as that of 1850, and Britain held a central place within it.

By 1950 that world had been distinctly altered. The four years of World War I had resulted in the deaths of millions and had had a catastrophic effect on the nation's spirit; the great economic depression of the 1930s had bred poverty and despair; the seven years of World War II had threatened Britain's survival and left the nation exhausted, even in victory; and immediately in its wake, with Britain still physically and emotionally devastated, had begun a new war, a "Cold War" against the Soviet Union. Exhausted by these struggles, Britain in 1950 had lost its place as the world's leading power to the United States. Daily life had been radically altered by the radio, the telephone, and the automobile. Church-going was in decline, and the nation was well on its way to becoming a secular society. Though Britain remained more class-conscious than North America or Australia, the class structure itself had seen great change; only the wealthy had servants, and all social classes partook of the same culture to an unprecedented extent. The Labour Party government of Clement Attlee, elected in 1945 in a clean break from Winston Churchill and the glorious but conservative path that he represented, had for five years been building a welfare state; this was Britain's first avowedly socialist government. "Votes for women"—to most minds a far-fetched notion in 1900—had in 1950 been a reality for over 30 years; women had done "men's work" during two long world wars, and were starting to wonder if winning the vote might represent the beginning rather than the end of the struggle for gender equality. Much

King Edward VII.

The streets of London decorated for the Coronation of Edward VII, 1902.

of Britain was as repressed sexually as it had been in 1900—but more and more people were starting to see the awkwardness that surrounded sexual matters as an obstacle to be overcome rather than as the expression of a necessary and appropriate sense of modesty. And the sun was rapidly setting on the British Empire. The dominions were now fully independent and beginning to drift away from the mother country culturally; India had been partitioned in 1947 into two independent nations; and in Britain's African and Caribbean possessions the stirrings of unrest that would lead to independence had already begun. In literature Britain had in the years between 1900 and 1950 undergone the Modernist revolution.[1] The sometimes fractured, some-

times free-flowing approaches to form that the poetry of T.S. Eliot, the plays of Samuel Beckett, and the prose fiction of James Joyce and Virginia Woolf represented had not been taken up by the majority of writers. Yet many serious writers in 1950 were aware of the expanded possibilities of literary form that modernism had revealed—and many wrote with a sense that the world was not the ordered and coherent whole that it had been widely assumed to be at the dawn of the twentieth century.

THE EDWARDIAN PERIOD

If it is true to say that the first half of the twentieth century may be characterized as a period in which the old Britain and the old world broke apart, it is also true that much of that fracturing did not begin to be readily visible until the years after 1910. 1910 was marked by the death of Edward VII, but more significantly this was the time of the first explosions of Modernism—Cubism in painting, Imagism in poetry, in music such ground-breaking works as Stravinsky's *The Rite of Spring* (1913). With these began the fracturing of form that would become a dominant theme in the cultural history of much of the rest of the century. With 1914 came the

[1] "Modernist" and "Modernism" are commonly used as umbrella terms to describe a wide range of inter-connected intellectual and aesthetic developments of the first half of the twentieth century that occurred in France, Italy, the United States and other areas as well as in Britain. A connecting thread is that expressions of Modernism tend to shun the linear, the decorative, and the sentimental. They tend too towards the presentation of reality fractured into its component pieces—and conversely, towards a rejection of aesthetic traditions through which reality is represented through the construction of conventionally unified wholes, through a single point of view, or through a single, unbroken narrative. Modernism is discussed more fully both later in this introduction and in a separate "Contexts" section elsewhere in this volume.

outbreak of World War I, and with 1915 and 1916—the years of the gruesomely drawn-out battles of Ypres and of the Somme—came a more visceral sense of fracturing as the full horror of the war's unprecedented carnage began to sink home.

The deaths of Victoria in 1901 and of her son Edward nine years later have often been seen as defining moments in the change from the Victorian to the modern world. Edwardian Britain liked to see itself as highly distinct from its Victorian predecessor. And certainly there were some changes; architectural style became rather less ornate, for example, and social style rather less formal. But at its core the Edwardian era was as much a continuation from the Victorian one as a break with it. Established religion, a hierarchy of social class, a largely inflexible set of attitudes towards gender roles, a complacent confidence in Britain's dominant position in the world—all these remained largely unchanged.

In some respects a "Victorian" sense of Empire carried on into the 1920s and 1930s. Here Queen Mary (wife of George V) is shown visiting the Burma pavilion at the British Empire Exhibition, London, 1924. Though some complained that the Exhibition's strongly patriotic flavor was excessively self-congratulatory, it was highly popular with most Londoners.

A sternwheel steamer and trading canoes at Okopedi on the Eyong River, Nigeria, 1909. Nigeria was among the last British possessions to be governed through a trading company; in 1900, control was transferred from the Royal Niger Company to the government, and the territory became the Protectorate of Southern Nigeria. The Niger Company continued as the leading trading entity in the region.

In the literary world Victorian traditions were being carried forward by novelists such as George Moore and Arnold Bennett, dramatists such as Arthur Wing Pinero, and poets such as Robert Bridges and W.E. Henley, the immensely popular author of "Invictus" and "Pro Rege Nostro" ("England, My England"). And even much of the literature that we now think of as recognizably modern may as readily be seen as connecting with that of the late Victorian era as anticipating the later literature of the century. The prose fiction of Joseph Conrad, for example, with its laying bare of the dark corners of the human soul (and of the dark realities of colonialism), touches the nerves of the reader in ways that we think of as distinctively modern. Indeed, the cry "that was no more than a breath" of the dying ivory agent

Kurtz in Conrad's *Heart of Darkness* (1899, 1902)— "The horror! The horror!"—is often regarded as a defining expression of the anguish that came to be felt as characteristic of the twentieth century. And some of Conrad's narrative techniques break ground that would become heavily tilled in the twentieth century; through layering of viewpoints (stories within stories, multiple narrators) Conrad found ways to create a narrative density that at once intensifies and destabilizes the reader's experience of the events being recounted. But Conrad was an extraordinary innovator, not a revolutionary; however original, the threads of most of his fiction are still woven through a storytelling art that draws on the conventions of fiction writing that held sway through the nineteenth century—conventions of realism through which implausible coincidences or exotic adventures could be made believable to the reader. As a *New York Times* reviewer put it in 1903, "the adventures he describes are little short of miraculous and are laid among scenes wholly alien to commonplace life, [but] they are wrought into a tissue of truth so firm and so tough as to resist the keenest scepticism…. Not even his Kurtz, the man of impenetrable darkness of soul, is either a bloodless or an incredible figure."

The novelist E.M. Forster is recognizably an author of the twentieth century in his treatment not only of the sexual (see below for a discussion of his novel *Maurice*) but also of the spiritual; his approach to the spiritual realities that transcend everyday life connects to the work of later twentieth-century writers such as Elizabeth Bowen, Graham Greene, and Kazuo Ishiguro. And in some stylistic respects (notably, the shifting, ironic narrative voice of *A Passage to India* [1924]), his fiction has affinities with modernism. But the texture of his work—most notably of the novels *A Room With a View* (1908) and *Howard's End* (1910)—is woven of nuances of social interaction and of subtle modulations of feeling, and relates at least as strongly to the conventions of Victorian realism as it does to those of Modernism. Forster is above all a social novelist, whose work recognizably connects with the traditions of his nineteenth-century predecessors.

Much of H.G. Wells's fiction was forward-looking in a more precise sense. Beginning in 1895 with the publication of *The Time Machine*, and continuing with *The Island of Dr. Moreau* (1896), *The Invisible Man* (1897), and *The War of the Worlds* (1898), Wells had founded the genre of science fiction as we still know it today. He continued in this vein in the new century with such works as *The First Men in Moon* (1901) and *The War in the Air* (1908). But in the style of his fiction Wells, too, was a traditional storyteller. And, though he is remembered today primarily for his science fiction, he wrote in a vein of social comedy with at least as much frequency, and with even greater success in his own lifetime. *Love and Mr. Lewisham* (1900), *Kipps: The Story of a Simple Soul* (1905), and *The History of Mr. Polly* (1910) are comic novels that draw on Wells's own struggles in painting an entertaining but strongly critical picture of the English social class system.

Like many writers of the time—playwright George Bernard Shaw perhaps most prominent among them— Wells became a committed socialist in the early years of the twentieth century. The chief vehicle of socialist response in Britain at the time was the Fabian society, founded in 1884 to promote *evolutionary* socialism (thus disavowing violent class struggle). The Fabian Society, led by Shaw, Sidney Webb, and Beatrice Potter Webb, was instrumental in forming the Labour Representation Committee in 1900; that committee, with substantial input as well from the Trades Union Congress, transformed itself into a political party in 1906, and over the course of the next generation the Labour Party managed to displace the Liberal Party as the main political alternative to Britain's Conservative Party. *Mrs Warren's Profession* is among the earliest of a long series of plays that give dramatic life to Shaw's progressive views; among its most memorable successors are *Major Barbara* (1905) and *Pygmalion* (1913). Shaw continued to write for the stage well into the 1920s (and lived until 1950), but he too expressed a powerful sense of change more in the content of his work than in its form. And other writers of the Edwardian era—including novelists and dramatists of thoroughly modern views such as Sarah Grand, Ella Hepworth Dixon, and Cicely Hamilton (all of whom expressed their strong feminist views through their work), for the most part structured their texts in traditional ways.

Wyndham Lewis, *Workshop*, c. 1915. The Canadian-born writer and artist Wyndham Lewis (1882–1957) lived largely in England from 1908 onwards. In the period 1912–15 he was a leader among those painters variously described as Futurist, Cubist, and "Vorticist"—the last of these a term that Lewis himself coined. (See the Contexts section on "Modernism" in this volume for more on this topic.) Though his writing—like that of Pound and others in their circle—is tainted by anti-Semitism, misogyny, and, in Lewis's case, venomous portrayals of homosexuals, Lewis is unquestionably a figure central to British Modernism. *Workshop* is one of the works that extend furthest his vision of harsh lines and fragmented shapes conveying a sense of the modern city, and of modernity itself.

World War I recruiting poster used in Ireland, c. 1915.

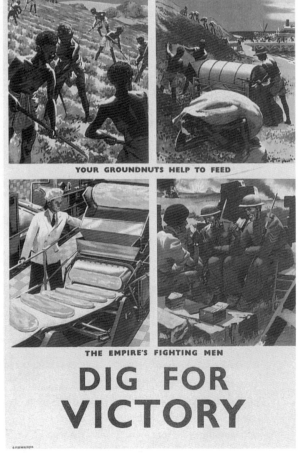

"Dig for Victory" poster,
distributed in Britain's West African colonies, 1940.

A bombed street in London, 1940. The photographer is unknown.

Sirkka-Liisa Konttinen, *Kendal Street, 1969*. A member of the Amber collective, between 1969 and 1983 Finnish-born Konttinen documented the life and eventual demolition of Byker, a terraced community in Newcastle upon Tyne in northern England. In 2003 she and Amber returned to document the Byker Wall Estate that replaced it.

Bill Brandt, *The Lambeth Walk*, 1936. This photo, originally published in the illustrated weekly magazine *Picture Post*, was taken in the Bethnal Green area of London. The girl performs a dance popular at the time.

Members of a slum-dwelling family in London, c. 1913. Though Britain was the world's wealthiest nation, the poor often lived in appalling conditions of hardship.

David Lloyd George, 1906. Lloyd George was a leading advocate of the interests of the working class in the early years of the century. As Chancellor of the Exchequer, he introduced the "Peoples' Budget" of 1909, calling for new taxes on the better-off to pay for measures to improve the lot of the poor, including an old age pension. The Old Age Pensions Act was resisted so strongly by the House of Lords that the Liberal Government acted to reduce the power of the House; both that Act and the Parliament Act, which established the supremacy of the House of Commons, became law in 1911. Lloyd George was also responsible for the National Insurance Act (1911), which provided some protection for workers who lost earnings through illness or unemployment.

Workers share a paper to read the news during the General Strike of 1926. The condition of the working class had improved somewhat by the 1920s, but in some sectors—notably coal mining— efforts were being made to roll back improvements in wages and working conditions. The 1926 General Strike in support of the coal miners lasted nine days.

THE WORLD WARS

As Lord Earl Grey, the British Foreign Secretary, watched the streetlights being lit from his office window one evening just before the outbreak of war in August 1914, he is famously reported to have remarked to a friend, "The lamps are going out all over Europe; we shall not see them lit again in our lifetime." At the time such thinking went against the grain; at the outset of the "Great War," many in England firmly expected their soldiers to be home before Christmas. But over the next thirty years many came to believe that the moment at which the First World War broke out had heralded nothing less than the collapse of civilization as it had long been known. At the outset of the Second World War in 1940, George Orwell adopted this vein of apocalyptic pessimism in his long essay "Inside the Whale":

The war of 1914–1918 was only a heightened moment in an almost continuous crisis. At this date it hardly needs a war to bring home to us the disintegration of our society and the increasingly helplessness of all decent people.... While I have been writing this book another European war has broken out. It will either last several years and tear western civilization to pieces, or it will end inconclusively and prepare the way for yet another war that will do the job once and for all.

Western civilization has proved to be rather more resilient than Orwell had feared, but his view of the period beginning in 1914 as "an almost continuous crisis" is now widely shared by historians; increasingly the two world wars of the twentieth century are being seen as part of a continuum. From more than one angle this makes sense. In both wars, Britain and her Empire/ Commonwealth allies, joined belatedly by the United States, were fighting against a militaristic and expansionist Germany. In both wars much of the rest of the world was drawn in to the conflict, though there was no parallel in World War I to the crucial importance of the Pacific theater and the struggle between the Allies and Japan in World War II.

The two wars are also linked through a chain of causation. Though all authorities agree that both wars had multiple causes, it is also universally agreed that one vitally important cause of the Second World War was the decision by the allies after World War I to demand reparations—a decision that had the effect in the short term of crippling Germany economically—and that had the even more pernicious effect over the longer term of so embittering the German people as to make a majority highly receptive to Hitler's appeals to nationalism, expansionism, anti-Semitism, and hate. The British economist John Maynard Keynes had been among those prescient enough to foresee the problem early on. In his chapter on "Europe after the Treaty" in *The Economic Consequences of the Peace* (1919), he summarized the matter with blunt eloquence:

This chapter must be one of pessimism. The treaty includes no provisions for the economic rehabilitation of Europe—nothing to make the defeated ... into good neighbours, nothing to stabilise the new states of Europe; ... Nor does it promote in any way a compact of economic solidarity amongst the Allies themselves ... It is an extraordinary fact that the fundamental economic problem of a Europe starving and disintegrating before their eyes, was the one question in which it was impossible to arouse the interest of the Four [powers that imposed the peace treaty].

Hitler's eventual rise to power, then, was partly fueled by the hardships imposed on the Germans by the Allies at the conclusion of World War I.

The Western Front in World War I, 1915.

If there are similarities and connections between the two world wars, there are also important differences. There are differences in the way the wars were fought, to start with—the trench warfare, stagnation and machine gun carnage of World War I contrasts with the tanks, submarines, airplanes, and bombs of World War II. There is usually also agreed to be a substantial difference in the moral context in which the two wars were fought. Many have suggested that ethically there

Londoners sleeping in the Elephant and Castle underground station during the bombing raids of 1940. These raids, popularly referred to as "the Blitz," were intended by the Nazis to "soften up" the English in preparation for a German invasion. Though much of London (and of other cities) was destroyed, the efforts of the British Air Force against superior numbers in what came to be known as the "Battle of Britain" were highly successful, and Hitler eventually decided against attempting an invasion of the British Isles; only the two Channel Islands fell to the Nazi forces. The Battle of Britain during the Blitz subsequently became a defining event in the British national consciousness.

was little to choose between the two sides in World War I—that the essential nature of the conflict was simply a power struggle between Britain and Germany as co-aggressors. And it has often (and rightly) been suggested that the tangle of old world alliances that existed prior to the First World War did much to facilitate the sort of stumbling into war that occurred in the wake of the assassination of Archduke Franz Ferdinand of Austria on 28 June 1914. In fact there probably was to some degree a legitimate moral case to be made on the side of Britain at the outset of World War I—much as the jingoism of the time on all sides may now strike us as repulsive. There is no question, though, that the moral imperative that lay behind the Allies' decision to go to war with Germany in 1939 was far stronger than it was at any time during World War I. Nazi atrocities against the Jews had in 1939 not yet reached their full extent, but already Hitler had shown that he was a dictator willing to persecute minorities ruthlessly and to invade neighboring countries on the flimsiest of pretexts.

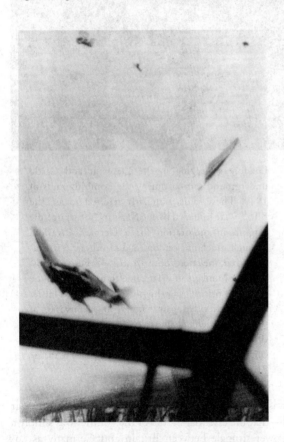

This image of the 1940 Battle of Britain was taken from the cockpit of a German fighter plane. It shows a British Hurricane fighter with its left wing torn off; the wing is visible in the top right of the photo, and the pilot, parachuting to safety, is seen in the top left.

World War II, then, was driven far more persuasively than was the first by a moral imperative, and there was thus much less of a disconnect than there had been in World War I between idealistic calls for sacrifice and the reality as it was sensed by the ordinary soldier; few looked at Nazi Germany in the autumn of 1939 with the detached tone that the poet W.H. Auden famously adopted in "September 1, 1939" in seeking to explain the phenomenon of Hitler, the "psychopathic god": "Those to whom evil is done / Do evil in return." To most it seemed clear that both in the case of Hitler as an individual and in the case of the people of Nazi Germany as a whole, the evil that was being done was far disproportionate to whatever evil had been committed against them. (Even today, many who admire Auden's poem as an affirmation of the humane in the face of the more basely human and in the face of war as a general proposition find the feelings the poem expresses odd or inappropriate in the moral context of World War II.)

A crucial difference between the experience of World War I and II was that in World War II the horrors of war had less shock value. Paul Fussell, whose *The Great War and Modern Memory* is a landmark study of the connections between wartime experience and literature, was a soldier himself in World War II; by the time of World War II, as he put it, "we didn't need to be told by people like Remarqué [author of *All Quiet on the Western Front*] and Siegfried Sassoon how nasty war was. We knew that already, and we just had to pursue it in a sort of controlled despair. It didn't have the ironic shock value of the Great War." It should perhaps not surprise us, then, that the body of serious literature that arose *directly* from the experience of World War II turned out to be slighter than the body of such literature that emerged during and after World War I. Certainly works such as Robert Graves's *Goodbye to All That*, Siegfried Sassoon's *Memoirs of an Infantry Officer*, David Jones's *In Parenthesis*, and the poetry of Wilfred Owen, Isaac Rosenberg and others all seem to have secured a place in the canon of British literature, whereas few if any works emerging directly out of the combat experience of World War II have staked such a claim. Indeed, Auden's "September 1, 1939" and Virginia Woolf's *Between the Acts* are among the few works still widely read from that time on themes that relate to the experience of the war even tangentially.

Two aspects of the 1939–45 conflict have come to be seen as defining elements of twentieth-century experience. The first of these was the planned extermination of an entire people—the event that resulted in the murder of approximately six million Jews (as well as significant numbers of other groups deemed "undesirables" by the Nazis, notably homosexuals and Roma), and that has come to be known as "The Holocaust." The second is the use of the atomic bomb against Japan by the United States in 1945—and the consequent dawning among the world's population of an awareness that humans now had the capacity to destroy the entire human race. From those most horrific aspects of World War II has emerged a literature that will surely be lasting (including the works of Primo Levi, the diaries of Anne Frank, John Hersey's *Hiroshima*)—but few if any of its most important works are by British writers.

Brighton Rock (1938), Graham Greene's "entertainment" about the lives of young British gangsters, was first issued in a Penguin paperback in 1943. The price of 2 shillings is equivalent to a little over £3 in 2006 UK currency.

THIS IS A WARTIME BOOK

THIS POCKET BOOK INCLUDES EVERY WORD CONTAINED IN THE ORIGINAL, HIGHER-PRICED EDITION. IT IS PRINTED FROM BRAND-NEW PLATES MADE FROM COMPLETELY RESET, LARGE, CLEAR, EASY-TO-READ TYPE, AND IS PRODUCED IN FULL COMPLIANCE WITH THE GOVERN-MENT'S REGULATIONS FOR CONSERVING PAPER AND OTHER ESSENTIAL MATERIALS.

F-I

Printed in Canada

Notice from copyright page of a 1945 printing of the paperback edition of Mazo de la Roche's *Jalna*, one volume of the family saga that has remained extraordinarily popular from its publication in 1927.

As in World War I, however, there was a rich body of literary work produced in Britain during World War II that was not directly *about* the war. Works of this sort in the years 1914–18 includes T.S. Eliot's *Prufrock and Other Observations* (1917) and James Joyce's *Portrait of an Artist as a Young Man* (1916).[1] In the years 1939–45, the list of such works is both long and remarkably diverse, and include the exuberant verse of Dylan Thomas's *The Map of Love* (1939); Eliot's *Four Quartets* (which he regarded as his finest work); many of Auden's finest lyrics, including "Lay Your Sleeping Head, My Love," "Musee des Beaux Arts," and "Song (As I Walked Out One Evening)" (all first published in 1940); the bubbling hilarity of Noel Coward's play about the afterlife, *Blithe Spirit* (1942); the memorably self-deprecating and socially observant light comedy of Monica Dickens's memoir *One Pair of Hands* (1939); now-classic memoirs by Vera Brittain (*Testament of Friendship*, 1940) and Flora Thompson (*Lark Rise to Candleford*, 1940); Joyce Cary's novel of the memorable

---

[1] See below under "Modernism" for a discussion of these authors.

artist and outsider Gulley Jimson, *The Horse's Mouth* (1944); Graham Greene's tragic novel of a disillusioned "whisky priest" in revolutionary Mexico, *The Power and the Glory* (1940); and two very different but equally devastating fictional treatments of the horrors of totalitarian communism, Arthur Koestler's grim novel of the suffering endured by a "deviationist," *Darkness at Noon* (1940), and Orwell's fable of a collectivist society that comes to be based on the principle that "all animals are equal, but some are more equal than others," *Animal Farm* (1945). In writing the following comments in 1940 about the literature of World War I, Orwell clearly also had World War II in mind:

> In 1917 there was nothing a thinking and sensitive person could do, except remain human, if possible. ... By simply staying aloof and keeping in touch with pre-war emotions, Eliot [in publishing *Prufrock* in 1917] was carrying on the human heritage.... So different from bayonet drill! After the bombs and the food queues and the recruiting posters, a human voice! What a relief!

MARX, EINSTEIN, FREUD, AND MODERNISM

Several towering figures in the intellectual and cultural life of the twentieth century played a key part in shaping the world view according to which human life was subject to forces over which, individually, humans could have little control, and of which they would often be entirely unaware. The first of these figures—Karl Marx—died 17 years before the end of the nineteenth century. But his vision of economic forces and class struggles saturated with historical inevitability continued to shape political and social attitudes (as well as a good many literary ones) throughout the twentieth century. An intellectual underpinning derived from Marx is, to a large extent, what differentiates the attitudes of social realist writers such as Shaw, Wells, and George Gissing from those of predecessors such as Charles Dickens and Elizabeth Gaskell. Much as Dickens and Gaskell had deplored the conditions of inequality that beset Victorian Britain, they believed that the actions and the goodwill of individual human beings could ameliorate social problems. The approach of 1890s and early

twentieth-century socially progressive writers, in contrast, derived largely from the Marxist view that individuals are typically caught in a web of large social and economic forces over which they have no control; that class oppression is a systemic matter; and that mass struggle and political action (rather than appeals to the higher natures of the ruling classes) are the appropriate means of bringing about a better world. Thus for Shaw, for example, the "fundamental condition of the existence" of prostitution was that "a large class of women are more highly paid and better treated as prostitutes than they would be as respectable women." The activist writer and publisher Nancy Cunard was equally alert to the interactions of class, gender, money—and race. Author of some of a number of important essays on colonialism (and publisher of such key modernist works as Samuel Beckett's *Whoroscope* and Pound's *Cantos*), Cunard spoke of the British Empire in unvarnished terms of class and race as few had before: when writing in *Negro* of the system of British rule in Jamaica, for example, she understood it clearly as having been purposefully structured as "white at the top, mulatto in the centre and back at the bottom of the economic and social scale" so as to rule by dividing "the peoples of African and semi-African descent."[1]

If the socially progressive literature of the early twentieth century had intellectual underpinnings derived largely from Marx, the intellectual underpinnings of twentieth-century modernist literature are intimately connected with the ideas of physicist Albert Einstein, of philosophers of language such as Bertrand Russell, and of the psychoanalyst Sigmund Freud. Einstein's paper, "The Electrodynamics of Moving Bodies" (1905), later to become known as his Special Theory of Relativity, posited that both time and motion are not absolute but rather relative to the observer. In the same year he completed his thesis on "A New Determination of Molecular Dimension," a major step forward in the development of quantum theory in which he postulated (among other things) that light was

---

[1] *The activist ... descent* Cunard was greatly assisted in these endeavors by George Padmore (1902–59), a Trinidadian-born writer and activist who later lived in the United States and in Britain and who played an important role in various progressive causes in the 1930s. A strong pan-Africanist, Padmore eventually became personal advisor to Kwame Nkrumah, Ghana's first President.

both waves and tiny particles of light quanta, or photons. Much as they may have been imperfectly understood, the broad outlines of Einstein's theories became widely disseminated in subsequent years, and clearly contributed to a growing sense of a world that was being discovered to be in a far less stable form that it had been thought.

New language-based trends in analytic philosophy were also undermining certainties. The ideas developed by Gottlieb Frege, Bertrand Russell, and Ludwig Wittgenstein in the late nineteenth and early twentieth century had the effect of destabilizing what had been thought of as largely fixed relationships between words and meanings. The focus of these philosophers was on analysing the content of what we mean when we make statements, whether they be statements referring to objects in the "real" world or statements involving claims of a more abstract sort. They endeavored to design symbolic systems that could convey meaning more reliably than words, for their work suggested that relationships between a word and a presumed referent were exceedingly complex and inherently unstable; Wittgenstein's work, in particular, suggested that it was in the nature of language for words to float largely free of fixed referents in any world of "objective truth." Indeed, Wittgenstein suggested in his groundbreaking 1921 work *Tractatus Logico-Philosophicus* that "Language disguises thought. So much so, that from the outward form of the clothing it is impossible to infer the form of the thought beneath it, because the outward form of the clothing is not designed to reveal the form of the body, but for entirely different purposes."

The perceived unreliability and instability of language and of meaning affected the realm of ethics as much as it did those of metaphysics and epistemology, and from about 1910 onward, moral relativism was a subject of lively debate. (G.E. Moore's *Ethics*, an influential attempt to hold such relativism at bay, was published in 1912; T.S. Eliot read a paper on "The Relativity of the Moral Judgement" in the Cambridge rooms of his friend Bertrand Russell in 1915.) Russell became famous as a result of his pacifism (for which he was jailed in 1918), his efforts to undermine the authority of Christianity over Western society, and his challenge to societal constrictions on sexual behavior. But the changes that he helped to bring about to the foundations of analytic philosophy may have been even more revolutionary—and more influential in the literary realm—than his shocking views on social issues.

Just as important as the work of Marx, Einstein, or the philosophers of language to the intellectual shape of the twentieth century was that of several explorers of the human psyche. Of these, pride of place is traditionally accorded to Sigmund Freud, an Austrian psychiatrist who advanced revolutionary notions of the importance and complexity of sexuality in the human psyche, and of the importance of the unconscious in human thought and behavior. Both notions had an enormous effect on twentieth-century intellectual life in general and on imaginative literature in particular, as writers sought ways to represent sexuality as a much more central element of human experience than had been the habit of the Victorians, and sought ways in which to represent the richness of the human unconscious.[1]

Another key pioneer in the study of the human mind was the American William James (brother of novelist Henry James). Among James's most important contributions was his conceptualization of the fluidity of consciousness. James entitled a chapter in his *Principles of Psychology* (1892) "The Stream of Consciousness," beginning by observing that "within each personal consciousness states are always changing" and that "each personal consciousness is sensibly continuous." The connections between the ideas of James and twentieth-century literary developments are not difficult to discern. Most obviously, the "stream of consciousness" technique of prose fiction that features so prominently in core Modernist texts such as Dorothy Richardson's *Pilgrimage* (1915–67), Virginia Woolf's *Mrs. Dalloway* (1925), and James Joyce's *Ulysses* (1922) represents a

---

[1] Though Freud's important work began in the 1890s, he began to become well-known in the English-speaking world only after 1910, with the publication of a series of lectures he had given at Clark University in the United States on *The Origin and Development of Psychoanalysis*. Of his most important works, *The Interpretation of Dreams* (1900) was translated in 1913, *The Psychopathology of Everyday Life* (1901) in 1914; soon after his work came to the attention of the Bloomsbury Group in England, and both Leonard Woolf and Lytton Strachey wrote reviews of or commentaries on Freud's work. (In the 1920s the Woolfs' Hogarth Press became for a time the leading publisher of English translations of Freud's work.)

new form of realism that is psychological rather than social in character. These writers aim at an increased awareness of the ways in which the mind associates freely, in which "irrelevant" thoughts may connect with repressed impulses or emotions that are central to the psyche, and in which unpredictable but meaningful details are constantly jostling together with the quotidian.

A similar apparent disconnectedness is also an obvious feature of Modernist poetry—most obviously in the disjunctions that characterize many of the poems of Ezra Pound and T.S. Eliot. To be sure, many have argued persuasively that a unity both of thought and of feeling emerges from the extended allusive density of poems such as *The Waste Land*. But it is abundantly clear that any such unity is very different in character from the unity that emerges, say, from a defining long poem of the Victorian period such as Tennyson's *In Memoriam*, just as whatever unity emerges from Joyce's *Ulysses* is very different in character from that of the classic realism of Victorian novels such as George Eliot's *Middlemarch* or Anthony Trollope's *The Way We Live Now*.

Less frequently discussed is the modernity of Eliot's later poetry—most notably, *The Four Quartets* (1935–43), an extended poetic expression of the search for meaning and truth in a context of instability. Much as the poem is infused with the Anglo-Catholicism to which Eliot had converted in 1927, it is also deeply colored by the sorts of destabilizing awareness that were so central to the habits of thought that came to the fore in the first half of the twentieth century. The poet continually struggles to conceptualize the movements of time, but finds that

> Words strain,
> Crack, and sometimes break, under the burden,
> Under the tension, slip, slide, perish,
> Decay with imprecision, will not stay in place,
> Will not stay still.

Samuel Beckett, one of the first to appreciate that most disconnected of all Joyce's works, *Finnegan's Wake* (1939), became the last great figure of Modernist literature. It was Beckett, above all, who pioneered the expression in action of the psychological insights of Modernism and the despair that so often accompanied

them. It is perhaps the case that "action" should here be put in quotation marks, however, for Beckett's plays—perhaps most notably *Waiting For Godot* (1952), *Krapp's Last Tape* (1958), and *Endgame* (1957)—are informed by an unprecedented awareness of the degree to which a *lack* of action may be as expressive as action, just as silences may be as expressive as words. Beckett extended the Modernist project in his prose fiction as well as in his plays—and in French as well as in English through to the 1970s; it is perhaps due more to his influence than that of any of the other great figures of Modernism that ripples from the Modernist tradition have continued to radiate in British literature even into the twenty-first century.

A common tendency is to assume that what is aesthetically revolutionary will substantially overlap with what is politically revolutionary (or at least with what is progressive). In fact there is no necessary connection between the two—and, indeed, a striking feature of twentieth-century Modernism is that many of its key figures were politically conservative or even reactionary.[1] During his lifetime, T.S. Eliot was probably almost as influential for his political, religious, and cultural conservatism as he was for his revolutionary aesthetic. Writer and artist Wyndham Lewis, whose concept of Vorticism was for a time central to the intellectual currents of Modernism, embraced political views that could fairly be characterized as reactionary rather than conservative. Ezra Pound, for his part, who was even more revolutionary than Eliot in his Modernist aesthetic, ended even further to the right politically—notoriously lending his support to the fascist cause, and calling for the extermination of Jews during World War II. Eliot and Pound were also far from progressive in their attitudes on gender and sex; many have suggested that a dark sense of sexuality is a fundamental aspect of Eliot's world view—and almost as many have suggested that a disturbing element of misogyny lurks not far below the surface of much of his writing (his early writing in particular).

---

[1] The roots of this conservatism are in part in various nineteenth-century political and ideological developments—especially a strain of ultra-conservatism in France that developed in the second half of the century and that connects both with Pound and the Symbolists and with twentieth-century fascisms.

Leading modernist women writers, by contrast, more often combined the freedom of modernist forms with progressive, unconventional, or even revolutionary political and social views. The futurist poet Mina Loy, for example, was a strong feminist and decidedly left of center politically; Nancy Cunard was a pioneer of left-of-center class analysis as well as of modernist publishing; and Virginia Woolf, though she rarely shared the unqualified sense of political conviction that came to motivate her husband Leonard (who ran for Parliament as a Labour Party candidate in 1920), was herself not only a powerful voice for feminism but also a Labour Party member and a supporter of a variety of socialist and progressive causes.

It was Woolf who famously assigned a specific point in time to the great change that Modernism represented: "on or about December 1910," she commented in a 1924 essay (excerpted in the "Modernism" Contexts section in this volume), "human character changed." She was, of course, exaggerating for effect; few in her era were more acutely aware of how erratically change may occur, and of the ways in which the characteristics of one era may extend into the next. In that connection it is worth reminding ourselves that, much as the Modernism of Eliot, Joyce, and Woolf has come to take on the character of the defining spirit of British literature in the 1910s and 1920s, its centrality was far from obvious at the time. For every admirer of the Cubist paintings of Picasso and Braque, there were many who reacted with contempt or ridicule. For every gallery-goer who was stirred by the modernist sculptures of Jacob Epstein (such as the young colonial P.K. Page, as recounted in her poem "Ecce Homo"), there were many chuckling over the way in which such sculpture was lampooned in the pages of the satirical magazine *Punch*. And for every dedicated reader of *The Waste Land* or *To the Lighthouse* there were dozens of readers of the ballads of Robert Service, and of the traditionally structured novels of Arnold Bennett and John Galsworthy. Not until 1948 and 1969 respectively were T.S. Eliot and Samuel Beckett awarded the Nobel Prize for literature; the only British writers to receive the award before 1940 were Rudyard Kipling (1907), W.B. Yeats (1923), George Bernard Shaw (1925), and Galsworthy (1932).

Illustration by Ernest H. Shepard from the chapter "The Further Adventures of Toad" in Kenneth Grahame's *The Wind in the Willows* (1908). The early decades of the twentieth century are remembered for the dawn of Modernism, but they were also something of a golden age for children's literature; in addition to Grahame's work, Sir J.M. Barrie's *Peter Pan* (1906), Lucy Maud Montgomery's *Anne of Green Gables* (1908), and A.A. Milne's *Winnie the Pooh* (1926) and *The House at Pooh Corner* (1928) all remain popular classics.

THE PLACE OF WOMEN

As well as being a central figure of Modernism in the British literary tradition, Woolf is central to what is arguably the most important historical development of the twentieth century, the attempt to free women from the dense network of social, economic, and legal restrictions that had always ensured male dominance and control. If *To the Lighthouse* (1927) and *Mrs. Dalloway* (1925), with their psychological realism, are key documents of Modernism, *A Room of One's Own* (1929) is a key document of the struggle by women in the twentieth century for full equality. Woolf's call for change, and also her evocation of personal experience in a male-dominated social and literary milieu, continue to resonate with readers in the present century.

Illustration accompanying the article "Presentation Day at London University," by "A Lady Graduate" in *The Girl's Own Paper*, July 1898. The University of London had begun to admit women as full degree students at the undergraduate level in 1878, but it was not until the 1920s that Oxford and Cambridge followed suit, even at the undergraduate level.

As the twentieth century opened women were still second-class citizens in almost every respect—unable to vote, subject to a variety of employment limitations, restricted for the most part from higher education, and restricted too in myriad intangible ways by social nuance and convention. Oppression in the workplace in the context of the industrial revolution has long been widely acknowledged; at least as pervasive in the late nineteenth and early twentieth centuries was the exploitation of retail workers, as the Report of the Royal Commission on Labour detailed:

> The maximum salary in addition to board and lodging ever paid to women in the shop working 70 3/4 hours was stated at 35 to 40 shillings [equivalent

to roughly £200 in 2006]; in the other shops 30 shillings was stated as the maximum salary ever given. The girls declared that they had nothing to complain of, except the long hours of work and the short time allowed for meals, which had seriously affected their health. No one closed earlier than 11:00 p.m. on Saturdays, 9:30 on Fridays, and 9:00 on Mondays, Tuesdays, and Wednesdays, beginning in each case at 8:30 a.m.

For decades, those in the suffrage movement and other women's groups struggled to bring change. In 1903, Emmeline Pankhurst, together with others frustrated with the pace of change and with the "lady-like" tone of the protests by other women's groups, formed The Women's Social and Political Union, taking as their motto "Deeds Not Words." As Pankhurst recalled in 1914,

> From the very first, in those early London days, when … we were few in numbers and very poor in purse, we made the public aware of the woman suffrage movement as it had never been before. We adopted Salvation Army methods and went out into the highways and byways after converts.

Real change finally began to take effect just before the end of the war in 1918, with the Representation of the People Act granting the vote to all men over the age of 21 and to women over the age of 30 who also met one or more of several restrictive criteria regarding marital status and property.[1] (Not until 1928 were all such restrictions lifted and all women over 21 granted the franchise.) The London *Times* provided a (doubtless oversimplified) summary of the effect of the war on the suffrage movement in an article on the occasion of the 1930 commemoration by Prime Minister Stanley Baldwin of a statue of Pankhurst:

> The World War came. In the twinkling of an eye … the militant suffragettes laid aside their banners.

---

[1] Two "Contexts" sections elsewhere in this volume ("War and Revolution" and "Gender and Sexual Orientation") document the events of World War I and the ways in which they hastened the move towards equality.

They put on their overalls and went into the factory and into the field; they were nursing, they made munitions, and they endured sacrifices with the men, and the effective opposition to the movement melted in the furnace of the War.

The success of the suffrage movement and the change in the role women played in the workplace were the most dramatic gender-related changes during this period, but there were many other important developments; as a "Contexts" section elsewhere in this volume discusses, the era was also characterized by changing notions regarding gender and education, contraception and reproductive technology, and the nature of masculinity.

The arrest of Emmeline Pankhurst during a suffragette demonstration near Buckingham Palace, 1914.

Sylvia Pankhurst (daughter of suffragette leader Emmeline Pankhurst) painting the slogan "Votes for Women" on the front of the Women's Social Defence League offices in London, 1912.

Women's contingent to the 1930 "Hunger March," a demonstration in London's Hyde Park.

AVANT-GARDE AND MASS CULTURE

The concept of the avant-garde, of a tiny minority far in advance of the popular taste in culture (or of the majority view politically) came into its own in the twentieth century. No doubt it may have resonated with particular force simply because of the degree to which cultural activity was being extended to "the masses"; with primary education having been made compulsory in Britain through the Education Act of 1870, the twentieth century was the first in which the vast majority of British people were fully literate. The expansion of libraries had helped to spread the habit of reading through the nineteenth century, and with the publishing industry's shift in the 1890s away from "triple deckers" intended for purchase by libraries and toward one-volume novels of modest length aimed at individual buyers, the habit of book-buying began to spread at a comparable rate. In the early years of the century, publishers introduced series of relatively affordable hardcover editions of literary classics, aimed at a broad popular market (chief among them the Everyman's Library series from Dent and the World's Classics series from Oxford University Press).

The British film industry was competitive with that of the United States in the 1920s and early 1930s. In this 1920s photograph a scene from the (now lost) film *The Thrill* is being shot on a beach near Brighton.

THE PUBLISHERS OF *EVERYMAN'S LIBRARY* WILL BE PLEASED TO SEND FREELY TO ALL APPLICANTS A LIST OF THE PUBLISHED AND PROJECTED VOLUMES TO BE COMPRISED UNDER THE FOLLOWING THIRTEEN HEADINGS:

TRAVEL ❦ SCIENCE ❦ FICTION
THEOLOGY & PHILOSOPHY
HISTORY   CLASSICAL
FOR YOUNG PEOPLE
ESSAYS ❦ ORATORY
POETRY & DRAMA
BIOGRAPHY
REFERENCE
ROMANCE

IN FOUR STYLES OF BINDING: CLOTH, FLAT BACK, COLOURED TOP; LEATHER, ROUND CORNERS, GILT TOP; LIBRARY BINDING IN CLOTH, & QUARTER PIGSKIN

LONDON: J. M. DENT & SONS, LTD.
NEW YORK: E. P. DUTTON & CO.

Preliminary advertising page from *Captain Cook's Voyages of Discovery*, one of the Everyman's Library volumes published in 1906, the year the series was founded. Eventually its list grew to include over 1,000 titles.

An even more revolutionary step came in 1936, with the introduction of Penguin Books' series of affordable paperback editions. "The Penguin books are splendid value for sixpence," wrote George Orwell in reviewing Penguin's third batch of ten titles, "so splendid that if the other publishers had any sense they could combine against them and suppress them. [If instead] the other publishers follow suit, the result may be a flood of cheap reprints which will cripple the lending libraries ... and check the output of new novels." Within a few years the paperback novel had indeed become ubiquitous in British society, but with none of the disastrous effects Orwell had feared; the size of the market for books had been expanded sufficiently by the arrival of the paperback to more than compensate authors and publishers for the lower revenue per copy sold.

Along with the spread of a mass literary culture—and the spread as well of the cinema and of radio—came huge social and cultural changes. If Modernism was a cultural movement concentrated in a small elite, modernity swept through every corner of society in the 1920s and 1930s. The social and cultural attitudes of the late Victorian age may have persisted through to the end of the Edwardian era, but within 10

World War I and the years that followed brought huge changes in women's fashion, with shorter skirts and dresses and more freedom of movement. This photograph, from the 1920s, shows two London models.

years "Victorian" had become a synonym for "stuffy and old fashioned." The book that set the tone more than any other was Lytton Strachey's *Eminent Victorians* (1918), a series of biographical essays on four leading members of Victorian society (Henry Edward Cardinal Manning, Florence Nightingale, Matthew Arnold, and General Charges George Gordon). Strachey's work is often characterized as "satirical," but "irreverent" is perhaps a better adjective. He writes in a breezy, brilliant, style, but he is interested in the depths of human emotion as well as the surfaces. He pokes fun at his subjects, to be sure, but he is more interested in exploring the workings of what he sees as pretension,

hypocrisy, ambition, and self-deception than he is in ridiculing them. Here is how Strachey begins his essay on Florence Nightingale:

> Everyone knows the popular conception of Florence Nightingale. The saintly, self-sacrificing woman, the delicate maiden of high degree who threw aside the pleasures of a life of ease to succour the afflicted, the Lady with the Lamp, gliding through the horrors of the hospital at Scutari, and consecrating with the radiance of her goodness the dying soldier's couch— the vision is familiar to all. But the truth was different. The Miss Nightingale of fact was not as facile fancy painted her. She worked in another fashion, and towards another end; she moved under the stress of an impetus which finds no place in the popular imagination. A Demon possessed her. Now demons, whatever else they may be, are full of interest. And so it happens that in the real Miss Nightingale there was more that was interesting than in the legendary one; there was also less that was agreeable.

The deft touch of Strachey's satire became simplified and coarsened in the ridicule popularly directed at Victorian styles—and, in particular, at Victorian attitudes towards sexuality—as an emerging mass society sought to define itself against the backdrop of supposed Victorian narrowness and prudery. The reaction may have been overdone, and certainly the characterization of the Victorians was simplistic, but there could be no doubt that the short skirts, jazz music, and sexual attitudes of the 1920s and 1930s were as far removed from those of only fifteen or twenty years before as those of 1905 or 1910 had been from the attitudes and styles of a full century earlier. Virginia Woolf's recollections of a Bloomsbury scene from the 1920s in which Woolf, her sister Vanessa Bell, and her husband Clive Bell are together in the drawing room at 46 Gordon Square give something of the flavor of the time:

> Suddenly the door opened and the long and sinister figure of Mr. Lytton Strachey stood on the threshold. He pointed a finger at a stain on Vanessa's white dress.
> "Semen?" he said.

Can one really say it? I thought and we burst out laughing. With that one word all barriers of reticence and reserve went down. ... So there was now nothing that one could not say, nothing that one could not do, at 46 Gordon Square.

A larger excerpt from Woolf's recollections of this and related incidents appears in the "Contexts" section "Gender and Sexuality" elsewhere in this volume. As that section also makes clear, few places in Britain in the 1920s and 1930s had left Victorian conventions of respectability so firmly behind as had 46 Gordon Square; few others had travelled so far in the same direction, or so fast, as had the "bohemians" of the Bloomsbury Group.

Indeed, the literary portrayal even of heterosexual love (let alone of homosexuality) remained largely off limits through to the 1960s. A litmus test was D.H. Lawrence's *Lady Chatterley's Lover*, which was published in 1928, but with certain passages, which were considered objectionable on account of their sexual content, removed. Not until 1960, after a high profile court case, was the unexpurgated text of the novel (by today's standards still far from explicit in its portrayal of sexuality) finally published. Despite such strictures, however, change was occurring throughout society, and "Victorian" attitudes seemed to many to be part of the distant past.

Two women, outside a London bookshop, holding copies of the newly-published paperback edition of *Lady Chatterley's Lover* (1960).

A commuter chooses *Lady Chatterley's Lover* over *The Times*, London, 1960.

SEXUAL ORIENTATION

The number of leading writers in the first half of the twentieth century who acknowledged a same-sex sexual orientation, at least among their circle of friends, was probably greater than it had been in any previous era of British history—certainly greater than at any time since the early years of the seventeenth century. The list of writers and intellectuals who are now known to have been gay, lesbian, or bisexual includes not only W.H. Auden and Christopher Isherwood, but also A.E. Housman, Nancy Cunard, E.M. Forster, Radclyffe Hall, John Maynard Keynes, Lytton Strachey, Sylvia Townsend-Warner, and a number of others.

It should be emphasized here that sexual identities are far from being stable, trans-historical categories. As a "Contexts" section elsewhere in this volume details, notions of and attitudes towards same-sex orientation were in flux throughout the late nineteenth and early twentieth centuries. Until well into the second half of the twentieth century, however (interestingly, at about the time that the word gay began to be used to identify those with a same-sex sexual orientation), there was little or no tolerance of same-sex sexuality in most sectors of society. As Auden and his friend and sometime literary collaborator Isherwood tacitly recognized when they moved to the United States, Britain in the 1920s and 1930s was even less ready than was America to openly acknowledge the legitimacy of same-sex relationships. Famously, the novelist and playwright Oscar Wilde had been tried and imprisoned in 1895 for "acts of gross indecency," and homosexuality continued to be widely regarded (in a somewhat contradictory fashion) both as a sin and as a disease throughout the first half of the century. E.M. Forster's novel on the theme of homosexual love, *Maurice*, which was not published until after his death in 1971, but which he had completed in 1914, gives a strong sense of the reality. When Maurice, having realized that "he loved men and had always loved them," confesses to his doctor that he is "an unspeakable of the Oscar Wilde sort," he is met with disgust and denial:

> "Rubbish, rubbish!…Now listen to me, Maurice, never let that evil hallucination, that temptation from the devil, occur to you again."
>
> The voice impressed him; was not science speaking?
>
> "Who put that lie into your head? You whom I see and know to be a decent fellow! We'll never mention it again. No—I'll not discuss. I'll not discuss. The worst thing I could do for you is to discuss it."

Maurice eventually does accept his sexual identity, but not before a further consultation, this one with a Mr. Lasker-Jones, who claims a fifty-per cent rate of "cure" by means of hypnotism for what he terms "congenital homosexuality."

If male homosexuality remained "unspeakable" through much of this period, female homosexuality remained for many unimaginable. In 1921 the British Parliament debated adding "acts of gross indecency between women" to the list of acts prohibited in the criminal statutes, but elected not to do so for fear of advertising homosexuality to "innocent" women. A few years later Hall's novel *The Well of Loneliness* was the occasion for the greatest literary storm of the era, over its alleged "obscenity." The novel recounts the story of a young woman named Stephen (whose parents had hoped for and expected a boy, and gone forward with the planned name regardless when the baby turned out to be a girl), and the romantic relationships she forms with other women. That the book could have been deemed obscene is astonishing to many readers today. In many ways the book is striking for the sense of normalcy it evokes as to the quotidian aspects of love:

> And now for the first time the old house was home. Mary went quickly from room to room humming a little tune as she did so, feeling that she saw with a new understanding the intimate objects that filled those rooms—were they not Stephen's? Every now and again she must pause to touch them because they were Stephen's.

Even when the novel's prose becomes effusive over the physical and spiritual aspects of the union, the most specific suggestions of the expression of sexual love between two women are passages such as the following: "Stephen bent down and kissed Mary's hands very humbly, for now she could find no words any more … and that night they were not divided."

Radclyffe Hall, c. 1920.

Such effusive attestations of the rapturous purity of unions at once physical and spiritual as one finds in *Maurice* and *The Well of Loneliness* may seem unexceptionable today, and even at the time many people were supportive; *The Well of Loneleiness* was published to a generally favorable reception in the press. In the view of *The Sunday Times*, Hall's novel was written "with distinction, with a lively sense of characterization, and with a feeling for the background of her subject which makes her work delightful reading. And, first and last, she has courage and honesty." *The Daily Herald* asserted that there was "nothing pornographic" in the book:

> The evil minded will seek in vain in these pages for any stimulant to sexual excitement. The lustful [figures] of popular fiction may continue their sadistic course unchecked in those pornographic novels which are sold by the million, but Miss Radclyffe Hall has entirely ignored these crude and violent figures of sexual melodrama. She has given to English literature a profound and moving study of a profound and moving problem.

The Daily Express was the lone dissenter; a 19 August 1928 article headed "A Book That Must Be Suppressed" accused the novel of "devastating young souls" with its story of "sexual inversion and perversion." It seems probable that the *Express* represented popular feeling at the time more accurately than did the *Sunday Times* or the *Daily Herald*; soon after the *Express* article appeared, the Home Office advised the publishers to discontinue publication, and the police then charged the publishers under the 1857 Obscene Publications Act. Despite the support of dozens of high-profile authors and intellectuals, the magistrate Sir Charles Biron ruled against *The Well of Loneliness*:

> Unfortunately these women exist, and the book asks that their existence and vices should be recognised and tolerated, and not treated with condemnation, as they are at present by all decent people. This being the tenor of the book I have no hesitation in saying it is an ... offence against public decency, and an obscene libel, and I shall order it to be destroyed.

The inevitable focus of history on landmark cases such as those of Oscar Wilde and *The Well of Loneliness* has to a considerable degree sensationalized and darkened our sense of late nineteenth- and early twentieth-century life outside the heterosexual mainstream. That it could be a dark and depressing existence there can be no doubt—the pessimism that Forster expressed even as late as 1960 ("police prosecutions will continue ...") is surely understandable. But, as documents such as the letters exchanged between Strachey and Keynes attest, it could also be one of self-assured candour, zestful comedy, and a wholehearted enjoyment of life. "Our time will come," declared Strachey, speaking confidently in an 8 April 1906 letter to Keynes of the situation of homosexuals in Britain, "about a hundred years hence." A hundred years later it is beginning to seem that Strachey's optimism may have been at least as well founded as Forster's more pessimistic view.

A young boy sings nationalist songs to a crowd outside Mountjoy Prison, Dublin, where an Irish Republican Army prisoner is about to be executed (1921).

IRELAND

If a remarkable amount of memorable literature emerged in Britain from the years of turmoil between the two World Wars in the first half of the twentieth century, the same statement could be made of Ireland, as the Irish endured the state of turmoil that remained a constant throughout the first half of the century. The fiction of James Joyce and the plays of Samuel Beckett have already been mentioned as central to the evolution of Modernist literature. The other important Irish literary work of the period includes J.M. Synge's vivid portrayals of the elemental life of the Aran Islanders on the coast of western Ireland in plays such as *Riders of the Sea* (1904) and *The Playboy of the Western World* (1907); the plays of Lady Augusta Gregory; the sweeping expressiveness of Sean O'Casey's great dramas *Juno and the Paycock* (1924) and *The Plough and the Stars* (1926); and the extraordinary range of the poetry of William Butler Yeats from the 1890s through the 1930s—lyrical, Romantic, Symbolist, mystical, political, Existential, and perhaps above all, passionate.

To this list should be added the plays of George Bernard Shaw, who was born in Dublin and lived there for the first twenty years of his life. Shaw has often been called the most important dramatist in English after Shakespeare; he was a socially committed writer who understood, as he puts it in the "Preface" to his 1905 play *Major Barbara*, that "it is difficult to make people realise that an evil is an evil." Shaw *was* able to make people realize such things, not only through effective polemic but also (and more memorably) through the sparkling wit of his plays. Shaw's important work extends from brilliantly biting works of the 1890s and early 1900s such as *Mrs. Warren's Profession*, *Arms and the Man*, and *Major Barbara* (on the topics of prostitution, militaristic attitudes, and religion and social reform, respectively); to *Pygmalion* (1912), a satire of attitudes toward social class and its expression through language, on which the 1950s musical *My Fair Lady* was based; to the epic historical drama *Saint Joan* (1923).

Cover, *Major Barbara: A Screen Version*, Penguin, 1945. This early "film tie-in" publication (number 500 in the Penguin series) was still in the standard early Penguin format; not until the 1960s did it become common for book publishers to employ a different cover design in such situations.

If the Irish Shaw is arguably the greatest "British" dramatist of the twentieth century, one of the greatest "British" writers of the 1890s, Oscar Wilde, had also been born and raised in Ireland before moving to London. Indeed, many have judged the literary outpouring from Irish writers during the period 1890–1960 to amount to a more important body of work than the entire literature of Britain over the same period—despite the fact that the combined population of England, Scotland, and Wales, at almost 50 million, was more than ten times that of Ireland.

But how are Britain and Ireland to be defined? Here matters become tangled, for during this period Ireland, for centuries a predominantly Catholic (and mostly unwilling) component of the United Kingdom, finally achieved the status of an independent republic. In the process, however, it became geographically split, with several largely Protestant counties of Northern Ireland remaining a political unit of the United Kingdom.

The Irish had been treated as second-class citizens throughout the centuries of English rule over Ireland. But the hardships they endured in the nineteenth century were particularly severe; the potato famine of 1845–51 alone is estimated to have killed almost a million Irish—almost 10 per cent of the population. By the 1880s and 1890s political pressure in Ireland for radical change had become extremely powerful. And there was pressure for cultural change too; the Celtic Revival (also known as the Irish Literary revival), begun in 1896 by Irishmen and women such as Yeats and Lady Augusta Gregory, was remarkably successful both in increasing appreciation for the traditions of Irish culture and in encouraging the creation of new works in those traditions.

In the late nineteenth century, too, many in England became more sympathetic to Irish aspirations. In an effort to end the long history of oppression and resistance in British-controlled Ireland, Liberal governments twice introduced bills providing for one form or another of "Home Rule" (the term used to refer to limited Irish self-government) in the British House of Commons. The second of these was passed by the House of Commons but defeated in the Conservative-dominated House of Lords. In 1912, another Home Rule Bill was passed, and again the House of Lords rejected it. But now the rules had been changed; as a result of the previous year's Parliament Act, a veto by the House of Lords retained force for only three years. As the date in 1914 approached when the veto was due to expire and Home Rule would thus come into effect, tension rose to such a pitch that many felt civil war to be a real possibility. Substantial areas of the north of Ireland that had been forcibly settled by the English in earlier eras were now staunchly Protestant and vowed resistance to any government order to allow an Ireland dominated by "Papists" to become independent of Britain. And since Protestants from Ulster, in the north of Ireland, were heavily represented in the British army's

contingent of troops stationed in Ireland, the military could not be relied on to carry out orders. With the onset of World War I, however, the implementation of the Home Rule Bill was postponed until after the war—and in a fateful move, Prime Minister Herbert Asquith promised that the British government would never force Ulster Protestants to accept Home Rule involuntarily.

Given the long history of vetoes and postponements—and given that the promised self-government in any case was to bring only a limited independence from Britain—it is unsurprising that Irish nationalists were impatient. On Easter Monday, 1916, rebels stormed public buildings in Dublin and proclaimed a republic. In the struggle, as Yeats famously wrote in "Easter, 1916," the Irish were "transformed utterly" and "a terrible beauty" was born. The uprising was brutally suppressed, but the nationalist Sinn Fein continued to wage a guerrilla opposition to British rule. Yet another Home Rule Bill was passed in 1920, providing for six counties of Ulster to be partitioned at independence, and the remainder of the island to remain a part of the British Empire but to be granted Dominion status (parallel to that of Canada, Australia, New Zealand, and South Africa) as the Irish Free State. That limited form of independence came into effect in 1922, but many Irish Republicans refused to accept any form of subservience to the British Crown, and the Irish Republican Army continued a clandestine struggle. In 1937 a new constitution changed the status of the country to that of a sovereign state within the British Commonwealth—a status sufficiently independent of Britain that Ireland was able to remain neutral in World War II—and in 1949 an Irish Republic was finally proclaimed, with the nation withdrawing from the Commonwealth. But the long struggle was still not fully over; tensions within Northern Ireland would continue to haunt Britain into the twenty-first century.

An understanding of the politics and religion of Ireland is essential background for an understanding of Irish history—and Irish literary history—during this period. But it gives little sense of the daily reality of Catholics and Protestants who lived largely in isolation from each other, Catholics overwhelmingly the majority in Ireland, Protestants forming the majority in Northern

Ireland. The novelist Elizabeth Bowen, who was raised mainly in Dublin in an Irish Protestant family (she "was taught to say 'Church of Ireland,' not 'Protestant'") later described her experiences in *Seven Winters: Memories of a Dublin Childhood* (1943):

> It was not until the end of those seven winters that I understood that we Protestants were a minority, and that the unquestioned rules of our being came, in fact, from the closeness of a minority world. … I took the existence of Roman Catholics for granted but met few and was not interested in them. They were, simply, "the others," whose world lay alongside ours but never touched. As to the difference between the two religions, I was too discreet to ask questions—if I wanted to know. This appeared to share a delicate, awkward aura with those two other differences—of sex, of class. So quickly in a child's mind does prudery seed itself and make growth that I remember, even, an almost sexual shyness on the subject of Roman Catholics. I walked with hurried steps and averted cheek past porticos of churches that were "not ours," uncomfortably registering in my nostrils the pungent, unlikely smell [of incense] that came round curtains, through swinging doors.

IDEOLOGY AND ECONOMICS IN THE 1930S AND 1940S

How do ideologies differ from ideas? In part they are simply sets of ideas, but the question goes beyond that: an ideology is a systematic set of beliefs that is shared widely, and that prescribes a program of political action in association with those beliefs. In the twentieth century, such ideologies as communism, socialism, fascism, and liberalism all exerted enormous power. The central concepts of liberal democracy took shape in the nineteenth century, and by the end of the twentieth century had spread to much of the world. But for much of the twentieth century they were powerfully challenged by those of other ideologies: socialism (and its relative, communism) and fascism.

Fascism is identified as an ideology of the far right and it has indeed often co-existed with capitalist economic structures. But the strength of its appeal is—like that of communism—collectivist in nature. As the official name of the Nazi party in Germany (the National Socialist Party) suggests, fascism is "socialist" in its appeal to the egalitarian instincts of the populace. But whereas socialism and communism are (in theory at least) internationalist, appealing to the fellow-feeling of humans *as humans*, fascism appeals strongly to nationalist feeling—to the instinct of the population to pull together *as a nation*. More broadly, the egalitarian ideals of fascist societies are never inclusive; the nation defines itself not only against other nations, but typically also against a backdrop of a perceived "other" within its midst. Whether the "other" be immigrants, those of a different skin color, those of a different religion, or a group such as the Jews that is defined by race, culture, and religion, the otherness is typically used as a focal point for the defining the nation's identity, and for lending intensity to the ideological allegiance of the fascist core.

Nazi authorities affix a poster to a shop as part of their campaign of persecution, 1935. The sign reads "Buy nothing from Jews!"

If fascism weirdly approaches socialism from one direction, communism departs from socialist ideals in another. Socialist ideals are above all those of fairness and equality in a society in which government is prepared to intervene consistently on behalf of the greater good—to control capitalism, in socialism's weaker version (social democracy), or to replace it with a system of government ownership of the means of production on behalf of the entire population, in the full-fledged socialist model. Such ideals are built on foundations very similar to those of communist ideology, but the differences turn out in practice to be crucial. Perhaps the most important difference is that communist ideology—especially as it attained full force in the twentieth century—embodied the paradoxical notion that an elite could act as the "vanguard" for the masses, and that a "dictatorship of the proletariat" could reasonably act on behalf of all the people, without the people in practice having a direct say in who was to govern, or how. With the benefit of hindsight, it seems obvious that such an ideology was likely to result in almost as much oppression and cruelty as was the ideology of fascism. But in a Russia that had been laboring under the inequalities of a semi-feudal system, or indeed in Depression-era North America or Great Britain, when the engines of capitalism seemed to be merciless and unrestrained by government, to many communism seemed the only realistic path toward a society that would be both more free and more fair for all citizens.

The greatest ideological struggles of the first half the century were unquestionably those that unfolded in Russia in 1917 and in Germany and Italy in the 1930s, but an ideologically charged climate was a worldwide reality. In some ways, the twentieth-century ideological tapestry may be seen in sharpest focus in the context of the Spanish Civil War (1936-39). Under the banner of those fighting for the Republican cause were liberals, socialists, communists, and anarchists—all ranged against the fascist forces of Generalissimo Francisco Franco. As George Orwell details in his account of the ideological and physical battles of the war, *Homage to Catalonia* (1938), the Spanish Civil War became a battleground not only between democracy and fascism, but also between the various factions on the Republican side, with idealism all too often being trumped by self-interest or by the dictates of outside governments lending support. In the end, the Communist government of the Soviet Union was as reluctant as were the capitalist governments of Britain or the United States to stand in the way of the anticipated "stable" government that the fascist General Franco represented.

The Spanish Civil War is often regarded as central to 1930s intellectual currents, and certainly the degree to which intellectuals from Britain (and indeed, from throughout the western world) rallied to the Republican side was remarkable. Sylvia Townsend Warner was among the leading British writers in Spain during the war; as she reported in a 1937 magazine article, the conflict was extraordinary not least of all for the bond that grew up between intellectuals and common citizens: "It is unusual for writers to hear words such as 'Here come the Intellectuals' spoken by working-class people and common soldiers in tones of kindliness and enthusiasm."

Others spoke out not only against fascism but against all forms of militarism—and against war itself. Notably, Virginia Woolf's polemic *Three Guineas* (1938) inquired into the role that women could play in the prevention of war, concluding that war is not merely a public issue—that, rather, "the public and the private worlds are inseparably connected; that the tyrannies and servilities of the one are the tyrannies and servilities of the other."

Even before the Spanish Civil War became a focal point for literature and politics, literature in the 1930s had become more highly political than that of the 1920s. Writers such as Auden (in his early work), Christopher Isherwood, C. Day Lewis, Louis MacNeice, Stephen Spender, and Edward Upward were all, in the view of MacNeice in his *Modern Poetry* (1932), "unlike Yeats and Eliot ... emotionally partisan":

> Yeats [in the 1930s] proposed to turn his back on desire and hatred; Eliot sat back and watched other people's emotions with ennui and ironical self-pity. ... The whole poetry, on the other hand, of Auden, Spender, and Day Lewis implies that they have desires and hatreds of their own and, further, that they think some things *ought* to be desired and others hated.

Many of these writers joined or were sympathetic to the Communist Party through much of the 1930s. In the later twentieth century it would have been unimaginable for most of the important writers of a generation to be sympathetic to "the Party," as it came to be called, but in the early 1930s the brutality of Soviet communism under Stalin was not yet public knowledge—and the mainstream parties in Britain (Labour as well as the Conservatives) were dealing timorously and ineffectively with an economic downturn of unprecedented severity.

A young woman takes aim during target practice, Spain, 1936.

The Great Depression that began late in 1929 and lasted until the outbreak of war ten years later was a worldwide phenomenon—and one exacerbated in Britain (as in North America) by the determination of governments not to go into debt in order to provide support for the unemployed and otherwise impoverished, or to invest in getting the economy moving. Individuals, too, reacted with fear, and strove to increase their savings, thereby contributing to what British economist John Maynard Keynes termed "the paradox of thrift": when people saved rather than spending what little they had, they further reduced the demand for goods, which in turn led to further reductions in production, more unemployment, lower wages for those still working—and so the cycle continued. By the end of 1930, some 20% of the British workforce was unemployed, and by the mid-1930s it was estimated that a quarter of the population had been reduced to a subsistence diet.

Keynes—an important figure in the Bloomsbury Group, and something of a cultural icon as well as one of the most important twentieth-century economists—broke new ground with his arguments for government intervention in the economy—recommending both that governments intervene to control inflation and that they act to "even out" the imbalances of the economic cycle by spending more during downturns. Conservatives argued that such imbalances would right themselves in the long run in any case, and should not be tampered with; Keynes's response was that "the long run is a misleading guide to current affairs. In the long run we are all dead." It was not until after World War II, though, that governments in Britain and elsewhere adopted Keynes's prescriptions for smoothing out the business cycle; although economic conditions improved somewhat in the south of Britain in the late 1930s, it was not until the war that economic growth resumed throughout the country.

A turn toward the political left is to be expected during any severe and prolonged economic downturn; given that the Great Depression was more severe and prolonged a downturn than any in the twentieth century, it is unsurprising that writers and intellectuals moved further to the left politically during the 1930s than at any other time during the century. But why did they embrace, in such large numbers, the relatively rigid doctrines of the Communist Party? As Orwell looked back in 1940, he took the view that the ideological coloring of the intellectual life of the 1930s had been as broadly connected to cultural as it had been to economic trends:

> By 1930 ... the debunking of western civilization had reached its climax.... How many of the values by which our grandfathers lived could now be taken seriously? Patriotism, religion, the Empire, the family, the sanctity of marriage, the Old School Tie, birth, breeding, honour, discipline—anyone of ordinary education could turn the whole lot of them inside out in three minutes. But what do you achieve, after all, by getting rid of such primal things as patriotism and religion? You have not necessarily gotten rid of the need for something to believe in.... It is significant that [those intellectuals who did embrace religion in these years] went almost invariably to the Roman Church.... They went, that is, to the church with a world-wide organization, the

one with a rigid discipline, the one with power and prestige behind it. … I do not think one need look farther than this for the reason the young writers of the thirties flocked into or towards the Communist Party. It was simply something to believe in. Here was a church, an army, an orthodoxy, a discipline.

With World War II, however, another form of discipline inevitably took hold; even though Britain and the United States became allies, the ties between the British and American intellectual communities and the Soviet Communist Party steadily loosened. With the beginning of the "Cold War" between the West and the USSR immediately following the end of World War II (and a new sense of purpose in the Labour Party under Clement Attlee), the link between British intellectuals and the Communist Party had for the most part come to an end.

THE LITERATURE OF THE 1930S AND 1940S

George Orwell may be seen as one of the writers who most fully expresses the ideological conflicts over socialism, communism, fascism, and liberal democracy that were at the heart of so much of twentieth-century life. His earlier works detail the appalling toll that capitalism was exacting on the working class. In *Down and Out in Paris and London* (1933), he recounts from personal experience the reality of the life of a vagrant, and of the life of the lowest of workers in the Paris hotel and restaurant industry. In *The Road to Wigan Pier* (1937), Orwell details the hardships of miners in the north of England, and of the working class population throughout the country. Orwell was an avowed socialist; ironically enough, however, the two works for which he remains best known have often been portrayed as attacks on socialism; they are both novels in which he attacks the corruption of socialist ideals under Soviet-style communism. *Animal Farm* is a fable that shows the ways in which power may readily be seized by the most powerful and unprincipled in a "collectivist" system; *1984* is a futurist view of a society in which "Big Brother" controls people's minds as much as their actions.

Like Orwell's *1984*, Aldous Huxley's *Brave New World* (1932) is a dystopia in which the State effectively controls the minds of its citizens, who are convinced that they are expressing human potential to its fullest.

Another writer of central importance to twentieth-century literature who was initially defined against a backdrop of ideology is the poet W.H. Auden. Auden first became famous as a political poet, particularly with his memorable call to arms against fascism in "Spain, 1937": "But today the struggle." Auden quickly became disenchanted with political polemic, however, not least of all his own. He became disillusioned with the Republican side in the Spanish Civil War after witnessing the persecution of Catholic priests by members of the Republican army, and after traveling through China in the wake of the 1937–38 Nanking Massacre he became convinced that violence is a disease that lurks within every human heart. "The act of taking sides," he became convinced, "spelled out the death of free culture and the triumph … of its enemies." Auden's poetic response to the outbreak of World War II, "September 1, 1939," was famously equivocal, the emphasis being placed on the expiration of the 1930s—dubbed by Auden "a low, dishonest decade"—rather than on the imminence of the fascist threat to freedom.

"Spain, 1937" and "September 1, 1939" were among those poems that Auden refused to allow to be printed in later volumes of his poetry. Even in the 1930s, his work was extraordinarily diverse, and more and more as the years went by his name became paired with that of T.S. Eliot; after the death of Yeats in 1939, Eliot and Auden were almost universally regarded as the leading poets of the day. But the two may in more than one respect be seen as polar opposites. Whereas Eliot had moved permanently from the United States to England as a young man, Auden moved permanently from Britain to New York to 1939. Eliot's first marriage had failed in the face of the mental illness of his wife, Vivienne; she was eventually confined in a mental institution, and Eliot embraced the stiff collar traditions of Church and of respectable society with ever-greater conviction. Auden's marriage to novelist Thomas Mann's daughter Erica also ended, but it could hardly have been said to have "failed," since it had been entered into only to protect Erica from persecution at the hands of the Nazis. Auden made no secret of his same-sex sexual orientation (at a time when it took considerable courage to do so), and felt stifled by the society of which Eliot was a pillar; he moved in 1939 to New York, where he soon entered into a lifelong relationship with the poet Chester Kallman, and where his rumpled figure became a quiet fixture on the literary scene. If Eliot was a central figure of Modernism, Auden's connections to the forms of Modernism were more tenuous. His skill with poetic forms was extraordinarily wide ranging, but unlike Eliot he kept returning to accentual-syllabic meters, and to the use of rhyme.

The explosive sexuality of D.H. Lawrence's fiction has been touched on above. If sexual love was one of the great themes of his work, the other was surely the corrosive effect that the British class system exerted on human relationships. In the 1930s that became a theme more and more widely taken up by novelists, in works such as Henry Green's *Living* (1929), Walter Greenwood's *Love on the Dole* (1933), and J.B. Priestley's *Angel Pavement* (1930). With the notable exception of the novels and stories of Edward Upward, however, expressions of outrage against the capitalist order of things tended to be fewer in number and milder in tone in the prose fiction of the time than they were in its poetry.

Somerset Maugham's *The Razor's Edge* (1944), a novel of romance and spirituality, became one of the twentieth century's bestselling novels both in Britain and in North America. It was issued in paperback editions on both sides of the Atlantic in 1946. Pocket Books, which had followed Penguin's lead and introduced mass market paperbacks into the United States in 1941, published the American paperback edition (shown here).

At least as numerous and at least as popular in Britain during this era were fiction writers of a more conservative political stripe, including Somerset Maugham, with his tightly crafted novels and short stories; Evelyn Waugh, with his bitingly satirical novels; and P.G. Wodehouse, with his more light-hearted brand of satirical fiction. Many have seen an inherent conservatism, too, in what was then a new genre of popular fiction, the detective novel. The genre saw few if any worthy successors to Sir Arthur Conan Doyle's nineteenth-century creation, Sherlock Holmes, until Agatha Christie introduced her detective Hercule Poirot and the equally astute Jane Marple to readers in the late 1920s and 1930s. Together with the Father Brown novels of the Catholic conservative G. K. Chesterton,

Christie's works founded an enduring tradition of English mystery novels.

The revolutionary experiments of Modernism that are so central to the literary history of the 1910s and 1920s were for the most part not extended in the following decades. To this generalization, David Jones's *In Parenthesis* (1937) is a notable exception; written partly in prose, partly in free verse, Jones's epic of the World War I bears the unmistakable stamp of Modernism. And some other authors continued to experiment with literary form. Henry Green's *Living*, for example, is written with an economy of expression that mirrors the economies of the working-class life it depicts, with articles and nouns frequently omitted from the normal syntactical flow. But most fiction writers of the period adopted a traditional approach to narrative, and even T. S. Eliot seemed to be backing away from Modernism with his ritualized play *Murder in the Cathedral* (1935)—and, following World War II, with a series of drawing room comedies.

From the late 1930s well into the 1970s one of the leading figures of British literature was unquestionably Graham Greene. Greene exploded onto the literary scene in 1938 with the publication of *Brighton Rock,* a tautly written exploration of the seediness and cruelty that lurked not far below the surface of much of British life. In subsequent novels, perhaps most notable among them *The Power and the Glory* (1940) and *The Heart of the Matter* (1948), Greene went on to explore the same qualities in human life generally. The setting of Greene's novels might be colonial Africa, rural Mexico, or war-torn London, but it is always recognizably "Greeneland"; always in the background is a sense of anguished Catholicism tinged with a bleak sense of despair.

LITERATURE AND EMPIRE

No matter how widely Greene's geographical imagination ranged, the human souls he was interested in exploring were mostly those of white males from the Western world. Other British writers of the time, however, were beginning to reach for an understanding of the world that would take fuller account of the lives and the souls of those who lived under British rule in Africa, India, and much of the rest of the world. The essays of Nancy Cunard, along with those of Orwell, expressed a wide-ranging understanding of the mechanisms of Imperial rule, and of the reality of life for many who suffered under it. In fiction, the novelist Joyce Cary broke new ground with his *Mr. Johnson* (1939), a comic novel with a Nigerian clerk as its protagonist. The novel represents the Nigerian in ways that are bound to make today's reader wince. Yet it also gives expression to a specifically Nigerian sense of humor, and conveys a genuinely sympathetic understanding of the situation both of Johnson and of Nigerians generally under British rule. *Mr. Johnson* is a long way from the literature of the last few decades of the twentieth century in its approach to colonial and multi-cultural realities (let alone the debates of the late twentieth century over "appropriation of voice"). Yet in a very real sense it marks a step forward for British literature in the possibilities it demonstrates for the British imagination of connecting with the rest of the world. In a very direct sense there is also a connection between *Mr. Johnson* and the explosion of African literature later in the century (in the first half of the century exceedingly few African writers were published). As Chinua Achebe later recalled, reading the Cary novel was one of the things that led him to become a writer; "in spite of [Cary's] ability, in spite of his sympathy and understanding, he could not get under the skin of his African. They just did not communicate. And I felt if a good [English white] writer could make this mess perhaps we ought to try our hand."

The twentieth century had begun for Britain with a war in South Africa that had ended with a Pyrrhic victory. In a struggle against white colonists of Dutch background (Afrikaaners, or "Boers") that came to involve the Zulus and other native populations, the superior firepower of the British prevailed—but not without the adoption of a variety of brutally oppressive measures as the British struggled to control a guerrilla campaign by the Afrikaaners. At the time, the war seemed an extension of the British struggle against the Afrikaaners that had been continuing on and off for more than fifty years—and, as with previous conflicts, this one resulted in an expansion of the size of the British Empire. The war aroused objections to the

Imperial project to an unprecedented degree, however; more than a century later, it is difficult not to see in it a foreshadowing of the loss of Empire. The brutalities in which the British allowed themselves to engage as they struggled to assert control seem a foretaste of the struggles against the Independence Movement in India in the 1930s and 1940s that would end with the independence of India in 1947, and of the struggles in Kenya and elsewhere in Africa in the 1950s that could be resolved only through the independence of those colonies. In one of his most famous speeches during the dark days of the Battle of Britain in 1940, Prime Minister Winston Churchill alluded to the possibility of the British Empire lasting for "a thousand years." Even then its foundations had crumbled, and within another 20 years the edifice of Empire would be almost entirely dismantled.

The English Language in the Early Twentieth Century

Many trends in the development of the English language that had begun in the nineteenth century or earlier continued through the first half of the twentieth. Punctuation became simpler: whereas, for example, it remained common in Britain through to the end of the nineteenth century and into the twentieth to precede a dash with a comma, by mid-century the norm was always to use one or the other, never both. Long periodic sentences had been on the decline through most of the nineteenth century, and this trend continued into the twentieth; on both sides of the Atlantic, sentences became shorter. Paragraphs also became shorter. To these generalizations, however, there were significant exceptions. With the growth of universities and the expansion of business, government, and political bureaucracies came an increase in academic, administrative, and political jargon of the sort of which Orwell complained in his famous essay "Politics and the English Language" (1946). While the majority of people (including most writers of fiction) were using shorter sentences, in other quarters writers were, in Orwell's words, "gumming together long strips of words which have already been set in order by someone else, and making the results presentable by sheer humbug."

In the twentieth century spelling was largely stable on both sides of the Atlantic; though shortened forms of some of the more archaic spellings in standard English became common in down-market forms of advertising, particularly in the United States (*thru, donut*), even there few of these came close to displacing the longer traditional forms. Conventions for marking direct speech also stabilized on both sides of the Atlantic, with the British using single quotation marks and the Canadians adopting the American convention of using double quotation marks.

Vocabulary, of course, continued to expand, with many new coinages entering the language as the result of new developments in science and technology. Interestingly, Britain and the United States developed largely separate terminologies regarding that most influential of twentieth century developments in technology, the automobile; in Britain cars run on *petrol*, the engine is under the *bonnet*, the luggage goes in the *boot*, and you drive on the *motorway*—without much noise unless there is a hole in your *silencer*. In numerous other areas in which new coinages were necessary, British usage developed as quite distinct from that in the United States—from television *presenters* (hosts); to *breeze block* construction (concrete block), to battery-powered *torches* (flashlights), to *Wellingtons* (rubber boots), to *hire purchase plans* (instalment plans), British English remained distinct from American English. (Former British possessions such as Canada and Australia partook of both in forming their own national patterns.)

Perhaps the greatest structural shift in English in the first half of the twentieth century was the simplification or elimination of forms marking the subjunctive mood. In constructions such as "If I were to travel through time I would…," for example, the old subjunctive form came to be largely replaced by the simple past form of the verb ("If I traveled through time I would …").

Throughout the nineteenth century, the spread of literacy and of mass transportation led to a steady decrease in the distinctiveness of the various dialects of English spoken in Britain, and in the distinctiveness of regional accents. That movement toward standardization continued in the twentieth century, with radio and television as its new vehicles. In 1922, the government set up the BBC (at first the initials stood for British

Broadcasting Company, but the name was soon changed to British Broadcasting Corporation), and it remained the dominant force in British radio—and, from the 1950s on, British television—for most of the century. In 1926, John Reith, the BBC's managing director, created an Advisory Committee on Spoken English, chaired by Robert Bridges, then the Poet Laureate, with the task of making recommendations to facilitate a standard of pronunciation over the air. Reith specifically asked that the committee seek a "style or quality of English that would not be laughed at in any part of the country." In practice, the standardized pronunciations recommended by the committee—which remained largely mandatory for announcers until 1989—were broadly similar to the pronunciations taught in the nation's elite "public" schools (see the glossary at the back of this volume for a discussion of this term) in southern England. Indeed, the three terms "public school pronunciation," "BBC pronunciation," and "Received Standard Pronunciation" (a term introduced by Henry Cecil Wyld in the early twentieth century to denote "the form which … is heard with practically no variation among speakers of the better class all over the country") are all roughly synonymous. Despite the ongoing trend towards standardization of speech in the twentieth century, however, the varieties of British English remained extraordinarily diverse throughout the century—so much so that someone from London could at century's end still have great difficulty understanding the accent of a Glaswegian or a "Geordie" (a native of the Newcastle area).

History of the Language and of Print Culture

In an effort to provide for readers a direct sense of the development of the language and of print culture, examples of texts in their original form, of illustrations, and of other materials related to book culture have been provided in each volume. A list of these within the present volume, arranged chronologically, appears below. An overview of developments in the history of language during the first half of the century appears on pages lxiii to lxiv; material on developments in the history of language since World War II appears on pages 621, 628-29, and 631-33; and a "Contexts" section on "Power, Politics, and the Book" appears as part of the website component of the anthology.

Illustrations from Henry Morgan Stanley, *In Darkest Africa*, pp. 90–91.

Advertising page from a volume in Everyman's Library, p. l.

John Macrae, autograph copy of "In Flanders Fields," p. 127.

A Soldier's Own Diary, pages for November 4–10, 1917, p, 134.

"Why Women Get Into Parliament," Cartoon, *Daily Mirror*, p. 303.

"Up, Clerks, and At 'Em," Cartoon, *Daily Mirror*, p. 310.

Cover of Penguin edition of Graham Greene's *Brighton Rock*, p. xliii.

Cover of Pan edition of Graham Greene's *Journey Without Maps*, color insert pages.

"Wartime Book" notice from the copyright page of a 1945 printing of Mazo de la Roche's *Jalna*, p. xliii.

Cover of Penguin edition of Bernard Shaw's *Major Barbara: A Screen Version*, p. lv.

Cover of Pocket Book edition of Somerset Maugham's *The Razor's Edge*, p. lxi.

Photographs of readers of the 1960 Penguin edition of D.H. Lawrence's *Lady Chatterley's Lover*, soon after publication, p. lii.

Cover of Minerva paperback edition of Roddy Doyle's *The Van*, color insert pages.

Cover, *Political Spider* (African Writers Series), p. 621.

Still from the Peter Brook film of William Golding's *Lord of the Flies* (used as the cover image for the 1963 Educational Edition), p. 622.

Cover, 1994 Broadview edition of Wilkie Collins's *The Evil Genius*, p. 625.

Cover of Kazuo Ishiguro's *Never Let Me Go*, color insert pages.

Thomas Hardy
1840 — 1928

Thomas Hardy, novelist and poet, was born in 1840 in Dorset, which was to become the setting of much of his fiction. A frail child, he did not attend the local school until the age of eight. His ill health did foster in him, however, a love of reading. In his walks in the area, Hardy also came into contact with the local farmers and laborers, whose hardship and poverty deeply touched him. At the age of 15, he was apprenticed to a local architect, a career that would sustain him until he became established as a writer.

In 1862 Hardy moved to London to work with another architect. Always driven, he would rise at five in the morning to complete three or four hours of reading—in Homer, the Greek Testament, the Renaissance poets —before going in to the office. On his return from work, he would often stay up reading and writing until midnight. It was during this time that he began writing poetry and short stories. Although he submitted many pieces to various magazines and the editors often wrote that he showed promise, his work was consistently rejected. The hectic schedule that Hardy was following caused his health to deteriorate, and he was forced to return to the countryside in 1867 to recuperate. In Dorchester, he worked as an architect during the day, writing in his spare time. It was in the course of his employment that he met his first wife, Emma Gifford. He had been sent to St. Juliot to draw plans for a church restoration, and Emma was the sister-in-law of the rector. The two struck up a close friendship and Emma was very supportive of his writing. With Emma's encouragement, Hardy published his first novel, *Desperate Remedies* (1871). The novel, which has much in common with sensation fiction, a popular sub-genre of the 1860s, met with mixed reviews, but he continued writing and *Under the Greenwood Tree*, published in 1872, brought him popular acclaim.

In his early novels Hardy began to include real places from the Dorset area, renamed Wessex—and to be praised for his portrayal of the countryside and the people of the region. *A Pair of Blue Eyes* appeared in 1873, and mirrored his own courtship with Emma. The two were married in 1874. That year also saw the publication of *Far from the Madding Crowd*, the first of what are now regarded as his classic novels. It depicts the life and loves of Bathsheba Everdene, and provides a convincing portrait of rural life. The novel also includes one of Hardy's "fallen women": the case of Fanny Robin, who is seduced and eventually dies in a workhouse, shocked many readers. Despite this, the novel was very popular, and allowed him to give up his architectural work and concentrate solely on writing.

The Return of the Native, published in 1878, was also very successful. All of Hardy's novels were by now appearing in serialized form in monthly family magazines—a development that affected both the way that he wrote and the content of his fiction. Like most serialized writers, Hardy incorporated a steady flow of incidents in his novels; he was catering to an audience that needed to be encouraged to keep reading and buy the next issue. The "family" nature of the magazines often led his editors (one of whom was Leslie Stephen, the father of Virginia Woolf) to caution him to tone down the racier scenes and rewrite large sections. Because of the strict morality that dominated editorial policy, for example, Hardy could not state explicitly that some of his characters might have been involved in extra-marital activities. Instead, such situations are written vaguely and readers are left to decide for themselves whether or not something illicit has taken place.

Censure of Hardy's depiction of "immoral" subject matter reached its peak with the publication of his next two major novels, *Tess of the D'Urbervilles* (1891) and *Jude the Obscure* (1895). In the first of these, Tess is raped by and bears an illegitimate child to Alec D'Urberville. Both the "seduction" itself and Tess's attempt to have the illegitimate child baptized shocked readers of the time. Tess eventually marries Angel Clare but is forced back into a relationship with D'Urberville when Clare discovers the truth about her past and abandons her. Her husband eventually forgives her, but she kills D'Urberville and is hanged for it. Hardy rewrote many of the novel's explicit or controversial sections for serialization in *Longman's Magazine*, but when the novel was published as a complete volume the controversial sections were restored.

From the mid 1890s, Hardy concentrated on composing poetry, continuing in a different genre the portrayal of the Wessex region he had made famous in the novels. *Wessex Poems* appeared in 1898, *Satires of Circumstance* in 1914, and *Moments of Vision* in 1917. Hardy's poems form a body of work strongly rooted in the physical details of place—but even more than that, one strongly rooted in the past. Hardy often borrows from traditional poetic forms (such as the ballad), and he often employs archaic diction. In subject matter, too, the poems tend to be strongly rooted in the past—more often than not a very personal past, with love and the loss of love being recalled by the speaker; in very many of Hardy's poems an elegiac tone is pervasive.

Hardy's poetry is sometimes discussed as constituting a reaction to modernism; perhaps it would be more accurate to think of it standing as a strong counterweight to modernism. Certainly the strong simplicity and emotional resonance of his poetry have exerted a strong influence on the works of many subsequent poets (Philip Larkin perhaps most prominent among them). So too has Hardy's formal approach. His rhythms, his rhymes, and the way in which he varies quantity are all tightly controlled and finely modulated; the extraordinary degree of technical accomplishment in much of Hardy's poetry does not call attention to itself, and is perhaps all the more impressive for so often being unobtrusive.

Hardy's reputation continues to rest on his lyrics and ballads—most of them tightly compact works. His most ambitious poetic work is much longer; *The Dynasts* is an extraordinary epic poem set in the Napoleonic Wars. It was published in three parts between 1903 and 1908.

The death of Emma in 1912, and Hardy's subsequent remorse over their relationship, resulted in some of his finest poetry, which appeared in *Satires of Circumstance* (1914). Hardy remarried in 1914; his second wife, Florence, is listed as the author of a two-volume biography of Hardy that appeared in 1928 and 1930, but it has since been established that Hardy wrote the work himself. Hardy was awarded the Order of Merit in 1910 and the Gold Medal of the Royal Society of Literature in 1912. When he died in 1928, his body was buried in Poets' Corner of Westminster Abbey, but his heart was buried with Emma in Stinsford, in southern England.

⌘ ⌘ ⌘

Hap°   *chance*

If but some vengeful god would call to me
From up the sky, and laugh: "Thou suffering thing,

Know that thy sorrow is my ecstasy,
That thy love's loss is my hate's profiting!"

Then would I bear it, clench myself, and die,
Steeled by the sense of ire unmerited;

Half-eased in that a Powerfuller than I
Had willed and meted° me the tears I shed.   *allotted*

But not so. How arrives it joy lies slain,
10 And why unblooms the best hope ever sown?
—Crass Casualty obstructs the sun and rain,
And dicing Time for gladness casts a moan....
These purblind Doomsters[1] had as readily strown
Blisses about my pilgrimage as pain.
—1898 (WRITTEN 1866)

Neutral Tones

We stood by a pond that winter day,
    And the sun was white, as though chidden of God,
And a few leaves lay on the starving sod;
    —They had fallen from an ash, and were gray.

5   Your eyes on me were as eyes that rove
Over tedious riddles of years ago;
And some words played between us to and fro
    On which lost the more by our love.

The smile on your mouth was the deadest thing
10 Alive enough to have strength to die;
And a grin of bitterness swept thereby
    Like an ominous bird a-wing …

Since then, keen° lessons that love deceives,   *sharp*
And wrings with wrong, have shaped to me
15 Your face, and the God-curst sun, and a tree,
    And a pond edged with grayish leaves.
—1898 (WRITTEN 1867)

The Darkling° Thrush   *in the dark*

I leant upon a coppice gate[2]
    When Frost was spectre-grey,
And Winter's dregs made desolate
The weakening eye of day.

5   The tangled bine[3]-stems scored the sky
    Like strings of broken lyres,
And all mankind that haunted nigh
    Had sought their household fires.

The land's sharp features seemed to be
10   The Century's corpse outleant,[4]
His crypt the cloudy canopy,
The wind his death-lament.
The ancient pulse of germ and birth
Was shrunken hard and dry,
15 And every spirit upon earth
    Seemed fervorless as I.

At once a voice arose among
The bleak twigs overhead
In a full-hearted evensong
20 Of joy illimited;
An aged thrush, frail, gaunt, and small,
    In blast-beruffled plume,[5]
Had chosen thus to fling his soul
    Upon the growing gloom.

25 So little cause for carolings
    Of such ecstatic sound
Was written on terrestrial things
    Afar or nigh around,
That I could think there trembled through
30   His happy good-night air
Some blessed Hope, whereof he knew
    And I was unaware.
—1901 (WRITTEN 31 DECEMBER 1900)

The Ruined Maid

"O'Melia, my dear, this does everything crown![6]
    Who could have supposed I should meet you
    in Town?"

---

1 *purblind Doomsters* Half-blind judges.

2 *coppice gate* Gate leading to a thicket or small forest.

3 *bine* Hop, a climbing plant.

4 *The Century's corpse outleant* I.e., as if the century were leaning out of its coffin.

5 *plume* I.e., feathers.

6 *this does everything* This surpasses everything.

And whence such fair garments, such prosperi-ty?"—
"O didn't you know I'd been ruined?" said she.

5 —"You left us in tatters, without shoes or socks,
Tired of digging potatoes, and spudding up docks;[1]
And now you've gay bracelets and bright feathers three!"—
"Yes: that's how we dress when we're ruined," said she.

—"At home in the barton° you said 'thee' and 'thou,'   barnyard
10 And 'thik oon,' and 'theäs oon,' and 't'other'; but now
Your talking quite fits 'ee for high compa-ny!"—
"Some polish is gained with one's ruin," said she.

—"Your hands were like paws then, your face blue
     and bleak
But now I'm bewitched by your delicate cheek,
15 And your little gloves fit as on any la-dy!"—
"We never do work when we're ruined," said she.

—"You used to call home-life a hag-ridden dream,
And you'd sigh, and you'd sock;[2] but at present you seem
To know not of megrims° or melancho-ly!"—   depression
20 "True. One's pretty lively when ruined," said she.

—"I wish I had feathers, a fine sweeping gown,
And a delicate face, and could strut about Town!"—
"My dear—a raw country girl, such as you be,
Cannot quite expect that. You ain't ruined," said she.
—1901 (WRITTEN 1866)

A Broken Appointment

You did not come.
And marching Time drew on, and wore me numb.—
Yet less for loss of your dear presence there
Than that I thus found lacking in your make
5 That high compassion which can overbear
Reluctance for pure lovingkindness' sake
Grieved I, when, as the hope-hour stroked its sum,
     You did not come.

---

[1] *spudding up docks* Uprooting weeds.

[2] *sock* Mouth your displeasure.

You love not me,
10 And love alone can lend you loyalty;
—I know and knew it. But, unto the store
Of human deeds divine in all but name,
Was it not worth a little hour or more
To add yet this: Once you, a woman, came
15 To soothe a time-torn man; even though it be
     You love not me?
—1902

Shut out that Moon

Close up the casement, draw the blind,
     Shut out that stealing moon,
She wears too much the guise she wore
     Before our lutes were strewn
5 With years-deep dust, and names we read
     On a white stone were hewn.

Step not out on the dew-dashed lawn
     To view the Lady's Chair,
Immense Orion's glittering form,
10   The Less and Greater Bear:[3]
Stay in; to such sights we were drawn
     When faded ones were fair.

Brush not the bough for midnight scents
     That come forth lingeringly,
15 And wake the same sweet sentiments
     They breathed to you and me
When living seemed a laugh, and love
     All it was said to be.

Within the common lamp-lit room
20   Prison my eyes and thought;
Let dingy details crudely loom,
     Mechanic° speech be wrought: low, vulgar
Too fragrant was Life's early bloom,
     Too tart the fruit it brought!
—1909

---

[3] *Lady's Chair ... Greater Bear* Constellations.

The Convergence of the Twain

(Lines on the Loss of the "Titanic")[1]

I

In a solitude of the sea
Deep from human vanity,
And the Pride of Life that planned her, stilly couches she.

2

Steel chambers, late the pyres
5   Of her salamandrine fires,[2]
Cold currents thrid,[3] and turn to rhythmic tidal lyres.

3

Over the mirrors meant
To glass the opulent
The sea-worm crawls—grotesque, slimed, dumb, indifferent.

4

10   Jewels in joy designed
To ravish the sensuous mind
Lie lightless, all their sparkles bleared and black and blind.

5

Dim moon-eyed fishes near
Gaze at the gilded gear
15   And query: "What does this vaingloriousness down here?" …

6

Well: while was fashioning
This creature of cleaving wing,
The Immanent Will[4] that stirs and urges everything

7

Prepared a sinister mate
20   For her—so gaily great—
A Shape of Ice, for the time far and dissociate.

8

And as the smart ship grew
In stature, grace, and hue,
In shadowy silent distance grew the Iceberg too.

9

25   Alien they seemed to be:
No mortal eye could see
The intimate welding of their later history,

10

Or sign that they were bent
By paths coincident
30   On being anon twin halves of one august event,

11

Till the Spinner of the Years
Said "Now!" And each one hears,
And consummation comes, and jars two hemispheres.
—1914

Channel Firing[5]

That night your great guns, unawares,
Shook all our coffins as we lay,
And broke the chancel[6] window-squares,
We thought it was the Judgment-day

5   And sat upright. While drearisome
Arose the howl of wakened hounds:
The mouse let fall the altar-crumb,
The worms drew back into the mounds,

---

[1] *the "Titanic"* At the time the largest ship ever built, the ocean liner *Titanic* had been described as unsinkable, but on its maiden voyage in 1912 it collided with an iceberg; over 1,400 people drowned when it sank.

[2] *salamandrine fires* According to mythology, salamanders are able to survive any heat.

[3] *thrid* Thread.

[4] *The Immanent Will* The force that pervades and determines human existence.

[5] *Channel Firing* In the months leading up to the First World War both the British and the German navies practised firing in the English Channel. (This poem was written in April 1914; the First World War began in August of the same year.)

[6] *chancel* Eastern part of a church, used by those who officiate at services.

The glebe[1] cow drooled. Till God called, "No;
10   It's gunnery practice out at sea
Just as before you went below;
The world is as it used to be:

"All nations striving strong to make
Red war yet redder. Mad as hatters[2]
15   They do no more for Christés° sake   Christ's
Than you who are helpless in such matters.

"That this is not the judgment-hour
For some of them's a blessed thing,
For if it were they'd have to scour
20   Hell's floor for so much threatening. …

"Ha, ha. It will be warmer when
I blow the trumpet (if indeed
I ever do; for you are men,
And rest eternal sorely need)."

25   So down we lay again. "I wonder,
Will the world ever saner be,"
Said one, "than when He sent us under
In our indifferent century!"

And many a skeleton shook his head.
30   "Instead of preaching forty year,"
My neighbour Parson Thirdly said,
"I wish I had stuck to pipes and beer."

Again the guns disturbed the hour,
Roaring their readiness to avenge,
35   As far inland as Stourton Tower,
And Camelot, and starlit Stonehenge.[3]
    —1914

---

[1] *glebe* Field, especially a field belonging to a church.

[2] *Mad as hatters* Makers of felt hats in the late 18th and early 19th century frequently went insane as a result of breathing in mercury compounds used in the manufacture of the hats.

[3] *Stourton Tower … Stonehenge* Stourton Tower was built to commemorate the victory of King Alfred over the Danes; Camelot was the site of King Arthur's court; Stonehenge is the famous prehistoric stone monument near Salisbury.

The Voice

Woman much missed, how you call to me, call to me,
   Saying that now you are not as you were
When you had changed from the one who was all to me,
   But as at first, when our day was fair.

5   Can it be you that I hear? Let me view you, then,
   Standing as when I drew near to the town
Where you would wait for me: yes, as I knew you then,
   Even to the original air-blue gown!

Or is it only the breeze, in its listlessness
10   Travelling across the wet mead° to me here,   *meadow*
   You being ever dissolved to wan wistlessness,
   Heard no more again far or near?

      Thus I; faltering forward,
      Leaves around me falling,
15   Wind oozing thin through the thorn from norward,
      And the woman calling.
—1914 (WRITTEN DECEMBER 1912)

Transformations

Portion of this yew[4]
   Is a man my grandsire knew,
Bosomed here at its foot:
This branch may be his wife,
5   A ruddy human life
Now turned to a green shoot.

These grasses must be made
Of her who often prayed,
Last century, for repose;
10   And the fair girl long ago
Whom I vainly tried to know
May be entering this rose.

So, they are not underground,
But as nerves and veins abound

---

[4] *yew* Traditionally, yew trees have been planted beside churches and near graveyards.

15 In the growths of upper air,
And they feel the sun and rain,
And the energy again
That made them what they were!
—1915

In Time of "The Breaking of Nations"[1]

1

Only a man harrowing clods
   In a slow silent walk
With an old horse that stumbles and nods
   Half asleep as they stalk.

2

5 Only thin smoke without flame
   From the heaps of couch-grass;
Yet this will go onward the same
   Though Dynasties pass.

3

Yonder a maid and her wight[2]
10   Come whispering by:
War's annals will fade into night
   Ere their story die.
   —1916

The Photograph

The flame crept up the portrait line by line
   As it lay on the coals in the silence of night's profound,
      And over the arm's incline,
And along the marge of the silkwork superfine,
5 And gnawed at the delicate bosom's defenceless round.

Then I vented a cry of hurt, and averted my eyes;
The spectacle was one that I could not bear,
      To my deep and sad surprise;

But, compelled to heed, I again looked furtivewise
10 Till the flame had eaten her breasts, and mouth, and hair.

"Thank God, she is out of it now!" I said at last,
In a great relief of heart when the thing was done
      That had set my soul aghast,
And nothing was left of the picture unsheathed from
   the past
15 But the ashen ghost of the card it had figured on.

She was a woman long hid amid packs of years,
She might have been living or dead; she was lost to
   my sight,
      And the deed that had nigh drawn tears
Was done in a casual clearance of life's arrears;
20 But I felt as if I had put her to death that night! …

—Well; she knew nothing thereof did she survive,
And suffered nothing if numbered among the dead;
      Yet—yet—if on earth alive
Did she feel a smart, and with vague strange anguish
   strive?
25 If in heaven, did she smile at me sadly and shake her
   head?
   —1917

During Wind and Rain

They sing their dearest songs—
   He, she, all of them—yea,
Treble and tenor and bass,
   And one to play;
5 With the candles mooning each face.…
   Ah, no; the years O!
How the sick leaves reel down in throngs!

They clear the creeping moss—
   Elders and juniors—aye,
10 Making the pathways neat
   And the garden gay;
And they build a shady seat.…
   Ah, no; the years, the years;
See, the white storm-birds wing across.

---

[1] *In Time of "The Breaking of Nations"*   See Jeremiah 51.20: "Thou art my battleaxe and weapons of war: for with thee will I break in pieces the nations.…"

[2] *wight*   I.e., man.

15 They are blithely breakfasting all—
Men and maidens—yea,
Under the summer tree,
    With a glimpse of the bay,
While pet fowl come to the knee. ...
20   Ah, no; the years O!
And the rotten rose is ript from the wall.

They change to a high new house,
He, she, all of them—aye,
Clocks and carpets and chairs
25   On the lawn all day,
And brightest things that are theirs. ...
    Ah, no; the years, the years;
Down their carved names the rain-drop ploughs.
—1917

The Oxen

Christmas Eve, and twelve of the clock.
    "Now they are all on their knees,"[1]
An elder said as we sat in a flock
    By the embers in hearthside ease.

5 We pictured the meek mild creatures where
    They dwelt in their strawy pen,
Nor did it occur to one of us there
    To doubt they were kneeling then.

So fair a fancy few would weave
10   In these years! Yet, I feel,
If someone said on Christmas Eve,
    "Come; see the oxen kneel,

In the lonely barton° by yonder coomb°   *barnyard* / *valley*
    Our childhood used to know,"
15 I should go with him in the gloom,
    Hoping it might be so.
—1917

Going and Staying

1

The moving sun-shapes on the spray,
    The sparkles where the brook was flowing,
Pink faces, plightings, moonlit May—
These were the things we wished would stay;
5   But they were going.

2

Seasons of blankness as of snow,
The silent bleed of a world decaying,
The moan of multitudes in woe—
These were the things we wished would go;
10   But they were staying.

3

Then we looked closelier at Time,
And saw his ghostly arms revolving
To sweep off woeful things with prime,
Things sinister with things sublime
15   Alike dissolving.
—1920

---

[1] *Now they are all on their knees* It was once widely believed that oxen would kneel at the appointed time on Christmas every year in imitation of the ox in the manger kneeling when Christ was born.

In Context

Hardy's Reflections on the Writing of Poetry

The Life of Thomas Hardy, published under the name of his second wife, Florence Hardy, was later discovered to have been written by Hardy himself. When this third-person autobiography discusses Hardy's poetic career in relation to his fiction writing, the author reveals his sensitivity to suggestions that he had taken up poetry only as a result of the reaction against his later novels:

> In the early weeks of this year [1899] the poems were reviewed in the customary periodicals—mostly in a friendly tone, even in a tone of respect, and with praise for many pieces in the volume; though by some critics not without umbrage at Hardy's having taken the liberty to adopt another vehicle of expression than prose fiction without consulting them....
>
> Almost all the fault-finding was, in fact, based on the one great antecedent conclusion that an author who has published prose first, and that largely, must necessarily express himself badly in verse, no reservation being added to except cases in which he may have published prose for temporary or compulsory reasons, or prose of a poetical kind, or have written verse first of all, or for a long time intermediately. ... In the present case, although it was shown that many of the verses had been written before their author dreamt of novels, the critics' view was very little affected that he had "at the eleventh hour," as they untruly put it, taken up a hitherto uncared-for art.

A few pages on, the account is again at pains to emphasize the purity of Hardy's motives in abandoning prose fiction and devoting himself to poetry:

> When one considers how he might have made himself a man of affluence by taking the current of popularity as it served, writing "best sellers," and ringing changes upon the novels he had already written, his bias towards poetry must have been instinctive and disinterested.

Hardy includes few reflections on the nature of his own poetry, but he does take issue with Wordsworth's famous strictures against poetic diction, asserting that Wordsworth "should have put the matter somewhat like this: in works of *passion and sentiment* (not 'imagination and sentiment') the language of verse is the language of prose. In works of *fancy* (or *imagination*), 'poetic diction' (of the real kind) is proper, and even necessary." Here and there Hardy also makes interesting comments on the origin of particular poems. Here, for example, are his remarks concerning "In Time of 'The Breaking of Nations'":

> I believe it would be said by people who knew me well that I have a faculty (perhaps not uncommon) for burying an emotion in my heart or brain for forty years, and exhuming it at the end of that time as fresh as when interred. For instance, the poem entitled "The Breaking of Nations" contains a feeling that moved me in 1870, during the Franco-Prussian war, when I chanced to be looking at such an agricultural incident in Cornwall. But I did not write the verses till during the war with Germany of 1914, and onwards.

BERNARD SHAW
1856 – 1950

Considered by many to be the greatest dramatist of his age, George Bernard Shaw was at times revered by, at times alienated from, the London society he criticized through his plays. A committed socialist, Shaw often used his plays to expound his views on the rights of women, on numerous social injustices, or on the deleterious effects of capitalism. In some cases he treated topics (such as prostitution and religion) in ways that caused his plays to be banned in England for many years, but Shaw himself always remained in the public eye. In the end he wrote more than 50 plays, and was awarded the Nobel Prize for Literature, the prize money for which he directed be used for the translation of Swedish works into English. He is the only Nobel laureate to have won an Academy Award (for his screenplay *Pygmalion*). The adjective "Shavian" was coined to describe his witty dialogue and epigrams.

Shaw was born into somewhat shabby gentility in Dublin in 1856, the son of a failing corn merchant and alcoholic father and a music teacher and singer mother. Shaw spent a great deal of time with the servants, one of whom exposed him to the realities of working-class life in Dublin when she was supposed to be taking him for air. The poverty and hardship he saw, and the ragtag characters with whom he came into contact, stayed with him for life and greatly influenced his later work. He and his two older sisters had a governess for their early education, but neither parent showed a particular interest in their children's formal education. As a result, Shaw flitted from school to school, attending irregularly; he finally gave it all up at age 15 to work as a clerk in a land surveyor's office. One of his duties was to collect rent from poor tenants. Shaw hated his work, but it provided fodder for his plays, the first of which, *Widowers' Houses* (1892), dealt with slum landlords. It was also during this time that Shaw dropped the "George" from his name, and became known as Bernard Shaw.

In 1876 Shaw moved to London to join his mother, who had moved there in 1873 with her music teacher. For the next nine years, Shaw honed his writing skills, building a successful career as a music and art critic. It was also during this time that he began to develop his creative writing. From 1879 to 1883 Shaw wrote five novels, none of which was published at the time. (Shaw eventually gave up writing novels; he said he had come to dislike the form, and called it clumsy and unreal.) From 1891 onward, Shaw dedicated himself to work as a playwright. His family background—a music-filled home, a mother who had been a performer—had helped foster a love of the stage, and he had become particularly interested in theater while still in Dublin, where he had frequented the Theatre Royal.

From 1891 to 1903 Shaw wrote 12 plays, some of which had very short runs in London, while others premiered in America (e.g., *The Devil's Disciple*) or Germany (*Caesar and Cleopatra*). By 1898 he was earning enough in royalties from his plays to be financially secure; it was also in that year that he married Charlotte Payne Townshend, a marriage that brought still greater financial stability.

Shaw created several categories for his plays: his *Plays Unpleasant* engage with various social issues. In addition to *Widowers' Houses*, these include *The Philanderer* (1905) and *Mrs. Warren's Profession*

(1902), which explored the topic of prostitution and was banned from public performance in England for 30 years. His next set of plays, *Plays Pleasant*, received better reviews and gave him his first commercial successes. These plays include *Candida*, *Arms and the Man*, *The Man of Destiny*, and *You Never Can Tell*. He termed various of his other plays "Comedies," "Chronicles," and "Political Extravaganzas." During Shaw's lifetime his most highly acclaimed plays included *Man and Superman* (1905), *Major Barbara* (1905), *Pygmalion* (1913), *Heartbreak House* (1920), and *Saint Joan* (1923). Throughout his long career Shaw remained very involved in the production of his plays, often arranging the casting, direction, and staging.

In awarding Shaw the Nobel Prize for 1925, the selection committee commended him for his "work which is marked by both idealism and humanity, its stimulating satire often being infused with a singular poetic beauty." He was offered a knighthood in 1926, but declined it, as he did many other honors. Shaw died in 1950, after falling from a tree he had been pruning. Throughout his life he had remained an eccentric, distinguished not only by his literary reputation but also by his vegetarianism, his discordant political views (he opposed Britain's involvement in World War I), and odd clothing (he wore an unbleached wool suit through much of his life for its perceived health benefits). In almost every way Shaw was an original.

⌘ ⌘ ⌘

Mrs. Warren's Profession

A Note on the Text of Mrs. Warren's Profession

Mrs. Warren's Profession was first published in 1898 in volume 1 (*Plays Unpleasant*) of *Plays Pleasant and Unpleasant*, in London by Grant Richards, and in Chicago and New York by Herbert S. Stone. The other plays in *Plays Unpleasant* were *Widowers' Houses* and *The Philanderer*. The first separate edition of *Mrs. Warren's Profession* was published in London by Grant Richards in 1902 in an identical text, but with a new preface by Shaw and photographs of the Stage Society production of 5–6 January 1902. Shaw revised *Mrs. Warren's Profession* for the *Plays Unpleasant* volume (1930) of *The Works of Bernard Shaw: Collected Edition*, published in London by Constable between 1930 and 1938. This was the text of *Mrs. Warren's Profession* used for *Bernard Shaw: Collected Plays with Their Prefaces* published in seven volumes by Max Reinhardt between 1970 and 1974 under the editorial supervision of Dan H. Laurence, and subsequently by Penguin Books, again under the editorial supervision of Dan H. Laurence. The definitive Penguin text is the copytext for the Broadview edition on which the text printed here is based.

Shaw made numerous revisions in the 1898 text for the 1930 edition. Many are relatively minor, but those that suggest significant changes in Shaw's thinking about a character or situation are recorded here in footnotes in this edition.

Shaw had strong opinions on matters of spelling, punctuation, and typography. He retained some archaic spellings (e.g. *shew* for *show*), and dropped the "u" in "our" spellings such as *honor*, *labor*, and *neighbor*. He preferred to reserve the use of italics for stage directions and descriptions of settings and characters (which are detailed and elaborate for the benefit of readers who might never have the opportunity of seeing his plays), electing to indicate emphasis of a word by spacing the letters (e.g., d e a r for *dear*, v e r y for *very*). He had no choice but to use italics for stressing *I*, and he sometimes chose to use small capital letters for stressing some words (e.g., ME for *me*).

Shaw disliked the apostrophe, believing it to be redundant (and ugly) in most instances. He eliminated it whenever he could (e.g., in *Ive, youve, thats, werent, dont, wont*), though it was necessary to retain it where its omission might cause confusion (e.g. *I'll, it's, he'll*).

For some readers Shaw's rationale for these practices is unconvincing, and the idiosyncrasies are irritating. They are, however, Shaw's clear preferences, and serve if nothing else as a frequent reminder of his nonconformity—the essence of the man and his work—and have, therefore, been retained in this anthology.

⌘ ⌘ ⌘

Mrs. Warren's Profession [1]

ACT 1

(*Summer afternoon in a cottage garden on the eastern slope of a hill a little south of Haslemere*[2] *in Surrey. Looking up the hill, the cottage is seen in the left hand corner of the garden, with its thatched roof and porch, and a large lattice*[3] *window to the left of the porch. A paling*[4] *completely shuts in the garden, except for a gate on the right. The common rises uphill beyond the paling to the sky line. Some folded canvas garden chairs are leaning against the side bench in the porch. A lady's bicycle is propped against the wall, under the window. A little to the right of the porch a hammock is slung from two posts. A big canvas umbrella, stuck in the ground, keeps the sun off the hammock, in which a young lady lies reading and making notes, her head towards the cottage and her feet towards the gate. In front of the hammock, and within reach of her hand, is a common kitchen chair, with a pile of serious-looking books and a supply of writing paper on it.*

A gentleman walking on the common comes into sight from behind the cottage. He is hardly past middle age, with something of the artist about him, unconventionally but carefully dressed and clean-shaven except for a moustache, with an eager susceptible face and very amiable and considerate manners. He has silky black hair, with waves of grey and white in it. His eyebrows are white, his moustache black. He seems not certain of his way. He looks over the paling; takes stock of the place; and sees the young lady.)

THE GENTLEMAN. (*Taking off his hat.*) I beg your pardon. Can you direct me to Hindhead View—Mrs Alison's?

THE YOUNG LADY. (*Glancing up from her book.*) This is
5   Mrs Alison's. (*She resumes her work.*)

THE GENTLEMAN.   Indeed! Perhaps—may I ask are you Miss Vivie Warren?

THE YOUNG LADY. (*Sharply, as she turns on her elbow to get a good look at him.*) Yes.

10 THE GENTLEMAN. (*Daunted and conciliatory.*) I'm afraid I appear intrusive. My name is Praed.[5] (*Vivie at once throws her books upon the chair, and gets out of the hammock.*) Oh, pray dont[6] let me disturb you.

VIVIE. (*Striding to the gate and opening it for him.*) Come
15 in, Mr. Praed. (*He comes in.*) Glad to see you. (*She proffers her hand and takes his with a resolute and hearty grip. She is an attractive specimen of the sensible, able, highly-educated young middle-class Englishwoman. Age 22. Prompt, strong, confident, self-possessed. Plain business-like
20 dress, but not dowdy. She wears a chatelaine*[7] *at her belt, with a fountain pen and a paper knife among its pendants.*)

---

[1] *Mrs. Warren's Profession* Shaw took the name of Mrs. Warren from Warren Street, near one of his early London homes in Fitzroy Square, Bloomsbury. Mrs. Warren's profession—prostitution—is never explicitly identified in the play.

[2] *Haslemere* Market town about 40 miles southwest of London.

[3] *lattice* Divided by strips into square or diamond-shaped sections.

[4] *paling* Fence.

[5] *Praed* Praed's name is perhaps an allusion to Winthrop Mackworth Praed (1802–39), a Cambridge-educated politician and poet. His portrait hung in the National Gallery in London. Praed St. is just north of Hyde Park in west-central London.

[6] *dont* Shaw often omits the apostrophe in contractions such as "dont," "Ive," and "doesnt." See above, "A Note on the Text."

[7] *chatelaine* Set of short chains attached to a woman's belt used for carrying small items (such as Vivie's fountain pen and paper knife).

PRAED. Very kind of you indeed, Miss Warren. (*She shuts the gate with a vigorous slam. He passes in to the middle of the garden, exercising his fingers, which are slightly numbed by her greeting.*) Has your mother arrived?

VIVIE. (*Quickly, evidently scenting aggression.*) Is she coming?

PRAED. (*Surprised.*) Didnt you expect us?

VIVIE. No.

PRAED. Now, goodness me, I hope Ive not mistaken the day. That would be just like me, you know. Your mother arranged that she was to come down from London and that I was to come over from Horsham[1] to be introduced to you.

VIVIE. (*Not at all pleased.*) Did she? Hm! My mother has rather a trick of taking me by surprise—to see how I behave myself when she's away, I suppose. I fancy I shall take my mother very much by surprise one of these days, if she makes arrangements that concern me without consulting me beforehand. She hasnt come.

PRAED. (*Embarrassed.*) I'm really very sorry.

VIVIE. (*Throwing off her displeasure.*) It's not your fault, Mr Praed, is it? And I'm very glad youve come. You are the only one of my mother's friends I have ever asked her to bring to see me.

PRAED. (*Relieved and delighted.*) Oh, now this is really very good of you, Miss Warren!

VIVIE. Will you come indoors; or would you rather sit out here and talk?

PRAED. It will be nicer out here, dont you think?

VIVIE. Then I'll go and get you a chair. (*She goes to the porch for a garden chair.*)

PRAED. (*Following her.*) Oh, pray, pray! Allow me. (*He lays hands on the chair.*)

VIVIE. (*Letting him take it.*) Take care of your fingers, theyre rather dodgy things, those chairs. (*She goes across to the chair with the books on it; pitches them into the hammock; and brings the chair forward with one swing.*)

PRAED. (*Who has just unfolded his chair.*) Oh, now do let me take that hard chair. I like hard chairs.

VIVIE. So do I. Sit down, Mr Praed. (*This invitation she gives with genial peremptoriness, his anxiety to please her*

clearly striking her as a sign of weakness of character on his part. But he does not immediately obey.*)

PRAED. By the way, though, hadnt we better go to the station to meet your mother?

VIVIE. (*Coolly.*) Why? She knows the way.

PRAED. (*Disconcerted.*) Er—I suppose she does. (*He sits down.*)

VIVIE. Do you know, you are just like what I expected. I hope you are disposed to be friends with me.

PRAED. (*Again beaming.*) Thank you, my d e a r[2] Miss Warren: thank you. Dear me! I'm so glad your mother hasnt spoilt you!

VIVIE. How?

PRAED. Well, in making you too conventional. You know, my dear Miss Warren, I am a born anarchist. I hate authority. It spoils the relations between parent and child: even between mother and daughter. Now I was always afraid that your mother would strain her authority to make you very conventional. It's such a relief to find that she hasnt.

VIVIE. Oh! have I been behaving unconventionally?

PRAED. Oh no: oh dear no. At least not conventionally unconventionally, you understand. (*She nods and sits down. He goes on, with a cordial outburst.*) But it was so charming of you to say that you were disposed to be friends with me! You modern young ladies are splendid: perfectly splendid!

VIVIE. (*Dubiously.*) Eh? (*Watching him with dawning disappointment as to the quality of his brains and character.*)

PRAED. When I was your age, young men and women were afraid of each other: there was no good fellowship. Nothing real. Only gallantry copied out of novels, and as vulgar and affected as it could be. Maidenly reserve! gentlemanly chivalry! always saying no when you meant yes! simple purgatory[3] for shy and sincere souls.

VIVIE. Yes, I imagine there must have been a frightful waste of time. Especially women's time.

PRAED. Oh, waste of life, waste of everything. But things are improving. Do you know, I have been in a positive state of excitement about meeting you ever

---

[1] *Horsham* Market town about 38 miles southwest of London (about 15 miles east of Haslemere).

[2] *d e a r* The spacing between letters is Shaw's way of indicating an emphasis on the word. See above, "A Note on the Text."

[3] *purgatory* In Catholic doctrine, a place for spiritual cleansing of the dead before entry to heaven.

since your magnificent achievements at Cambridge: a thing unheard of in my day. It was perfectly splendid, your tieing with the third wrangler.[1] Just the right place, you know. The first wrangler is always a dreamy, morbid fellow, in whom the thing is pushed to the length of a disease.

VIVIE.   It doesnt pay. I wouldnt do it again for the same money!

PRAED.   (*Aghast.*) The same money!

VIVIE.   I did it for £50.[2]

PRAED.   Fifty pounds!

VIVIE.   Yes. Fifty pounds. Perhaps you dont know how it was. Mrs Latham, my tutor at Newnham,[3] told my mother that I could distinguish myself in the mathematical tripos[4] if I went in for it in earnest. The papers were full just then of Phillipa Summers[5] beating the senior wrangler. You remember about it, of course.

PRAED.   (*Shakes his head energetically*) !!!

VIVIE.   Well anyhow she did: and nothing would please my mother but that I should do the same thing. I said flatly it was not worth my while to face the grind since I was not going in for teaching; but I offered to try for fourth wrangler or thereabouts for £50. She closed with me at that, after a little grumbling; and I was better than my bargain. But I wouldnt do it again for that. £200 would have been better near the mark.

PRAED.   (*Much damped.*) Lord bless me! Thats a very practical way of looking at it.

VIVIE.   Did you expect to find me an unpractical person?

PRAED.   But surely its practical to consider not only the work these honors cost, but also the culture they bring.

VIVIE.   Culture! My dear Mr Praed: do you know what the mathematical tripos means? It means grind, grind, grind for six to eight hours a day at mathematics, and nothing but mathematics. I'm supposed to know something about science; but I know nothing except the mathematics it involves. I can make calculations for engineers, electricians, insurance companies, and so on; but I know next to nothing about engineering or electricity or insurance. I dont even know arithmetic well. Outside mathematics, lawn-tennis, eating, sleeping, cycling, and walking, I'm a more ignorant barbarian than any woman could possibly be who hadnt gone in for the tripos.

PRAED.   (*Revolted.*) What a monstrous, wicked, rascally system! I knew it! I felt at once that it meant destroying all that makes womanhood beautiful.

VIVIE.   I dont object to it on that score in the least. I shall turn it to very good account, I assure you.

PRAED.   Pooh! in what way?

VIVIE.   I shall set up chambers[6] in the City, and work at actuarial calculations and conveyancing.[7] Under cover of that I shall do some law, with one eye on the Stock Exchange all the time. Ive come down here by myself to read law: not for a holiday, as my mother imagines. I hate holidays.

PRAED.   You make my blood run cold. Are you to have no romance, no beauty in your life?

VIVIE.   I dont care for either, I assure you.

PRAED.   You cant mean that.

VIVIE.   Oh yes I do. I like working and getting paid for it. When I'm tired of working, I like a comfortable chair, a cigar, a little whisky, and a novel with a good detective story in it.

PRAED.   (*Rising in a frenzy of repudiation.*) I dont believe it. I am an artist; and I cant believe it: I refuse to believe

---

[1] *wrangler* Wranglers were those who achieved a first-class honors degree in mathematics at Cambridge. Vivie had placed equal third among the wranglers in her year. The top student was designated senior wrangler.

[2] *£50* It would have taken most working-class women in England at this time two years to earn this amount.

[3] *Newnham* Newnham College was founded as a women's college of Cambridge University in 1871. The first Cambridge college for women, Girton, was founded in 1869. All other colleges of the University admitted men only.

[4] *tripos* The Tripos was (and is) the honors course at Cambridge, so-called because of the medieval tradition of the candidate sitting on a three-legged stool.

[5] *Phillipa Summers* Allusion to Philippa Fawcett, daughter of Henry Fawcett (1833–84), Professor of Political Economy at Cambridge and Liberal Member of Parliament, and Millicent Fawcett (1847–1929), leader of the women's suffrage movement and strong proponent of women's education at Cambridge. Philippa Fawcett gained the highest mark in the mathematical tripos in June 1890 (*The Times*, 9 June 1890), the first woman to do so.

[6] *chambers* Law office.

[7] *conveyancing* Vivie will specialize as an actuary (compiling and analyzing statistics to calculate insurance risks and premiums) and a conveyancer (transferring ownership of property).

it. It's only that you havnt discovered yet what a wonderful world art can open up to you.

VIVIE. Yes I have. Last May I spent six weeks in London with Honoria Fraser. Mamma thought we were doing a round of sightseeing together; but I was really at Honoria's chambers in Chancery Lane[1] every day, working away at actuarial calculations for her, and helping her as well as a greenhorn could. In the evenings we smoked and talked, and never dreamt of going out except for exercise. And I never enjoyed myself more in my life. I cleared all my expenses, and got initiated into the business without a fee into the bargain.

PRAED. But bless my heart and soul, Miss Warren, do you call that discovering art?

VIVIE. Wait a bit. That wasnt the beginning. I went up to town on an invitation from some artistic people in Fitzjohn's Avenue:[2] one of the girls was a Newnham chum. They took me to the National Gallery —[3]

PRAED. (*Approving.*) Ah!! (*He sits down, much relieved.*)

VIVIE. (*Continuing.*) —to the Opera—

PRAED. (*Still more pleased.*) Good!

VIVIE. —and to a concert where the band played all the evening: Beethoven and Wagner[4] and so on. I wouldnt go through that experience again for anything you could offer me. I held out for civility's sake until the third day; and then I said, plump out, that I couldnt stand anymore of it, and went off to Chancery Lane. Now you know the sort of perfectly splendid modern young lady I am. How do you think I shall get on with my mother?

PRAED. (*Startled.*) Well, I hope—er—

VIVIE. It's not so much what you hope as what you believe, that I want to know.

PRAED. Well, frankly, I am afraid your mother will be a little disappointed. Not from any shortcoming on your part, you know: I dont mean that. But you are so different from her ideal.

VIVIE. Her what?!

PRAED. Her ideal.

VIVIE. Do you mean her ideal of ME?

PRAED. Yes.

VIVIE. What on Earth is it like?

PRAED. Well, you must have observed, Miss Warren, that people who are dissatisfied with their own bringing-up generally think that the world would be all right if everybody were to be brought up quite differently. Now your mother's life has been—er—I suppose you know—

VIVIE. Dont suppose anything, Mr Praed. I hardly know my mother. Since I was a child I have lived in England, at school or college, or with people paid to take charge of me. I have been boarded out all my life. My mother has lived in Brussels or Vienna and never let me go to her. I only see her when she visits England for a few days. I dont complain: it's been very pleasant; for people have been very good to me; and there has always been plenty of money to make things smooth. But dont imagine I know anything about my mother. I know far less than you do.

PRAED. (*Very ill at ease.*) In that case—(*He stops, quite at a loss. Then, with a forced attempt at gaiety.*) But what nonsense we are talking! Of course you and your mother will get on capitally. (*He rises, and looks abroad at the view.*) What a charming little place you have here!

VIVIE. (*Unmoved.*) Rather a violent change of subject, Mr Praed. Why wont my mother's life bear being talked about?

PRAED. Oh, you really musnt say that. Isnt it natural that I should have a certain delicacy in talking to my old friend's daughter about her behind her back? You and she will have plenty of opportunity of talking about it when she comes.

VIVIE. No: s h e wont talk about it either. (*Rising.*) However, I daresay you have good reasons for telling me nothing. Only, mind this, Mr Praed. I expect there will be a battle royal when my mother hears of my Chancery Lane project.

PRAED. (*Ruefully.*) I'm afraid there will.

VIVIE. Well, I shall win because I want nothing but my fare to London to start there to-morrow earning my

---

[1] *Chancery Lane* Street in west-central London, the location of many legal offices and related businesses.

[2] *Fitzjohn's Avenue* Street in the fashionable district of Hampstead, northwest of central London.

[3] *National Gallery* Founded in 1824, the National Gallery moved to its current location on the north side of Trafalgar Square in 1838. The Gallery holds one of the world's finest collections of European paintings. Shaw was a frequent visitor.

[4] *Beethoven and Wagner* German composers Ludwig van Beethoven (1770–1827) and Wilhelm Richard Wagner (1813–83) were Shaw's favorite composers.

own living by devilling[1] for Honoria. Besides, I have no mysteries to keep up; and it seems she has. I shall use that advantage over her if necessary.

PRAED. (*Greatly shocked.*) Oh no! No, pray. Youd not do such a thing.

VIVIE. Then tell me why not.

PRAED. I really cannot. I appeal to your good feeling. (*She smiles at his sentimentality.*) Besides, you may be too bold. Your mother is not to be trifled with when she's angry.

VIVIE. You can't frighten me, Mr Praed. In that month at Chancery Lane I had opportunities of taking the measure of one or two women v e r y like my mother. You may back me to win. But if I hit harder in my ignorance than I need, remember that it is you who refuse to enlighten me. Now, let us drop the subject. (*She takes her chair and replaces it near the hammock with the same vigorous swing as before.*)

PRAED. (*Taking a desperate resolution.*) One word, Miss Warren. I had better tell you. It's very difficult; but –

(*Mrs Warren and Sir George Crofts arrive at the gate. Mrs Warren is between 40 and 50, formerly pretty, showily dressed in a brilliant hat and a gay blouse fitting tightly over her bust and flanked by fashionable sleeves. Rather spoilt and domineering, and decidedly vulgar, but, on the whole, a genial and fairly presentable old blackguard[2] of a woman.*

Crofts is a tall powerfully-built man of about 50, fashionably dressed in the style of a young man. Nasal voice, reedier than might be expected from his strong frame. Clean-shaven bulldog jaws, large flat ears, and thick neck: gentlemanly combination of the most brutal types of city man, sporting man, and man about town.)

VIVIE. Here they are. (*Coming to them as they enter the garden.*) How do, mater?[3] Mr Praed's been here this half hour waiting for you.

MRS WARREN. Well, if youve been waiting, Praddy, it's your own fault: I thought youd have had the gumption[4] to know I was coming by the 3:10 train. Vivie: put your hat on, dear: youll get sunburnt. Oh, I forgot to introduce you. Sir George Crofts: my little Vivie.

(*Crofts advances to Vivie with his most courtly manner. She nods, but makes no motion to shake hands.*)

CROFTS. May I shake hands with a young lady whom I have known by reputation very long as the daughter of one of my oldest friends?

VIVIE. (*Who has been looking him up and down sharply.*) If you like. (*She takes his tenderly proffered hand and gives it a squeeze that makes him open his eyes; then turns away and says to her mother*) Will you come in, or shall I get a couple more chairs? (*She goes into the porch for the chairs.*)

MRS WARREN. Well, George, what do you think of her?

CROFTS. (*Ruefully.*) She has a powerful fist. Did you shake hands with her, Praed?

PRAED. Yes: it will pass off presently.

CROFTS. I hope so. (*Vivie reappears with two more chairs. He hurries to her assistance.*) Allow me.

MRS WARREN. (*Patronizingly.*) Let Sir George help you with the chairs, dear.

VIVIE. (*Pitching them into his arms.*) Here you are. (*She dusts her hands and turns to Mrs Warren.*) Youd like some tea, wouldnt you?

MRS WARREN. (*Sitting in Praed's chair and fanning herself.*) I'm dying for a drop to drink.

VIVIE. I'll see about it. (*She goes into the cottage.*)

(*Sir George has by this time managed to unfold a chair and plant it beside Mrs Warren, on her left. He throws the other on the grass and sits down, looking dejected and rather foolish, with the handle of his stick in his mouth. Praed, still very uneasy, fidgets about the garden on their right.*)

MRS WARREN. (*To Praed, looking at Crofts.*) Just look at him, Praddy: he looks cheerful, dont he? He's been worrying my life out these three years to have that little

---

[1] *devilling* Serve as a barrister's (i.e., lawyer's) junior assistant.

[2] *blackguard* Person characterized by dishonorable behavior; here used by Shaw more as a term of endearment. In the 1898 text Mrs. Warren is still "good-looking" (not just "formerly pretty"), and she is not described as "decidedly vulgar."

[3] *mater* Latin: mother. University slang.

[4] *gumption* Common sense.

girl of mine shewn to him; and now that Ive done it, he's quite out of countenance. (*Briskly.*) Come! Sit up, George; and take your stick out of your mouth. (*Crofts sulkily obeys.*)

310 PRAED. I think, you know—if you dont mind my saying so—that we had better get out of the habit of thinking of her as a little girl. You see she has really distinguished herself; and I'm not sure, from what I have seen of her, that she is not older than any of us.

315 MRS WARREN. (*Greatly amused.*) Only listen to him, George! Older than any of us! Well, she h a s been stuffing you nicely with her importance.

PRAED. But young people are particularly sensitive about being treated in that way.

320 MRS WARREN. Yes; and young people have to get all that nonsense taken out of them, and a good deal more besides. Dont you interfere, Praddy: I know how to treat my own child as well as you do. (*Praed, with a grave shake of his head, walks up the garden with his hands*

325 *behind his back. Mrs Warren pretends to laugh, but looks after him with perceptible concern. Then she whispers to Crofts.*) Whats the matter with him? What does he take it like that for?

CROFTS. (*Morosely.*) Youre afraid of Praed.

330 MRS WARREN. What! Me! Afraid of dear old Praddy! Why, a fly wouldnt be afraid of him.

CROFTS. Youre afraid of him.

MRS WARREN. (*Angry.*) I'll trouble you to mind your own business, and not try any of your sulks on me. I'm

335 not afraid of y o u, anyhow. If you cant make yourself agreeable, youd better go home. (*She gets up, and, turning her back on him, finds herself face to face with Praed.*) Come, Praddy, I know it was only your tender-heartedness. Youre afraid I'll bully her.

340 PRAED. My dear Kitty: you think I'm offended. Dont imagine that: pray dont. But you know I often notice things that escape you; and though you never take my advice, you sometimes admit afterwards that you ought to have taken it.

345 MRS WARREN. Well, what do you notice now?

PRAED. Only that Vivie is a grown woman. Pray, Kitty, treat her with every respect.

MRS WARREN. (*With genuine amazement.*) Respect! Treat my own daughter with respect! What next, pray!

350 VIVIE. (*Appearing at the cottage door and calling to Mrs Warren.*) Mother: will you come to my room before tea?

MRS WARREN. Yes, dearie. (*She laughs indulgently at Praed's gravity, and pats him on the cheek as she passes him on her way to the porch.*) Dont be cross, Praddy. (*She*

355 *follows Vivie in to the cottage.*)

CROFTS. (*Furtively.*) I say, Praed.

PRAED. Yes.

CROFTS. I want to ask you a rather particular question.

PRAED. Certainly. (*He takes Mrs Warren's chair and sits*

360 *close to Crofts.*)

CROFTS. Thats right: they might hear us from the window. Look here: did Kitty ever tell you who that girl's father is?

PRAED. Never.

365 CROFTS. Have you any suspicion of who it might be?

PRAED. None.

CROFTS. (*Not believing him.*) I know, of course, that you perhaps might feel bound not to tell if she had said anything to you. But it's very awkward to be uncertain

370 about it now that we shall be meeting the girl every day. We wont exactly know how we ought to feel towards her.

PRAED. What difference can that make? We take her on her own merits. What does it matter who her father

375 was?

CROFTS. (*Suspiciously.*) Then you know who he was?

PRAED. (*With a touch of temper.*) I said no just now. Did you not hear me?

CROFTS. Look here, Praed. I ask you as a particular

380 favor. If you d o know (*Movement of protest from Praed.*)—I only say, if you know, you might at least set my mind at rest about her. The fact is, I feel attracted.

PRAED. (*Sternly.*) What do you mean?

CROFTS. Oh, dont be alarmed: it's quite an innocent

385 feeling. Thats what puzzles me about it. Why, for all I know I might be her father.

PRAED. You! Impossible!

CROFTS. (*Catching him up cunningly.*) You know for certain that I'm not?

390 PRAED. I know nothing about it, I tell you, anymore than you. But really, Crofts—oh no, it's out of the question. Theres not the least resemblance.

CROFTS.   As to that, theres no resemblance between her and her mother that I can see. I suppose she's not y o u r daughter, is she?

395 PRAED.   (*Rising indignantly.*) Really, Crofts—!

CROFTS.   No offence, Praed. Quite allowable as between two men of the world.

PRAED.   (*Recovering himself with an effort and speaking gently and gravely.*) Now listen to me, my dear Crofts.
400 (*He sits down again.*)   I have nothing to do with that side of Mrs Warren's life, and never had. She has never spoken to me about it; and of course I have never spoken to her about it. Your delicacy will tell you that a handsome woman needs some friends who are
405 not—well, not on that footing with her. The effect of her own beauty would become a torment to her if she could not escape from it occasionally. You are probably on much more confidential terms with Kitty than I am.
410 Surely you can ask her the question yourself.

CROFTS.   I h a v e asked her, often enough. But she's so determined to keep the child all to herself that she would deny that it ever had a father if she could. (*Rising.*) I'm thoroughly uncomfortable about it, Praed.

415 PRAED.   (*Rising also.*) Well, as you are, at all events, old enough to be her father, I dont mind agreeing that we both regard Miss Vivie in a parental way, as a young girl whom we are bound to protect and help. What do you say?

420 CROFTS.   (*Aggressively.*) I'm no older than you, if you come to that.

PRAED.   Yes you are, my dear fellow: you were born old. I was born a boy: Ive never been able to feel the assurance of a grown-up man in my life. (*He folds his
425 chair and carries it to the porch.*)

MRS WARREN.   (*Calling from within the cottage.*) Prad-dee! George! Tea-ea-ea-ea!

CROFTS.   (*Hastily.*) She's calling us. (*He hurries in.*)

(*Praed shakes his head bodingly, and is following Crofts when he is hailed by a young gentleman who has just appeared on the common, and is making for the gate. He is pleasant, pretty, smartly dressed, cleverly good-for-nothing, not long turned 20, with a charming voice and agreeably disrespectful manners. He carries a light sporting magazine rifle.[1])*

THE YOUNG GENTLEMAN.   Hallo! Praed!

430 PRAED.   Why, Frank Gardner! (*Frank comes in and shakes hands cordially.*) What on earth are you doing here?

FRANK.   Staying with my father.

PRAED.   The Roman father?[2]

435 FRANK.   He's rector here. I'm living with my people this autumn for the sake of economy. Things came to a crisis in July: the Roman father had to pay my debts. He's stony broke in consequence; and so am I. What are you up to in these parts? Do you know the people here?

440 PRAED.   Yes: I'm spending the day with a Miss Warren.

FRANK.   (*Enthusiastically.*) What! Do you know Vivie? Isnt she a jolly girl? I'm teaching her to shoot with this (*putting down the rifle*). I'm so glad she knows you: youre just the sort of fellow she ought to know. (*He
445 smiles, and raises the charming voice almost to a singing tone as he exclaims.*) It's e v e r so jolly to find you here, Praed.

PRAED.   I'm an old friend of her mother. Mrs Warren brought me over to make her daughter's acquaintance.

450 FRANK.   The mother! Is s h e here?

PRAED.   Yes: inside, at tea.

MRS WARREN.   (*Calling from within.*) Prad-dee-ee-ee-eee! The tea-cake'll be cold.

PRAED.   (*Calling.*) Yes, Mrs Warren. In a moment. Ive
455 just met a friend here.

MRS WARREN.   A what?

PRAED.   (*Louder.*) A friend.

MRS WARREN.   Bring him in.

PRAED.   (*To Frank.*) Will you accept the invitation?

460 FRANK.   (*Incredulous, but immensely amused.*) Is that Vivie's mother?

PRAED.   Yes.

FRANK.   By Jove! What a lark! Do you think she'll like me?

465 PRAED.   Ive no doubt youll make yourself popular as usual. Come in and try. (*Moving toward the house.*)

---

[1]   *magazine rifle* Automatic rifle.

[2]   *Roman father* This might be thought to suggest that Frank's father is a Catholic priest, but he is in fact a clergyman of the Church of England. It is more likely an ironic reference to supposed "Roman" qualities of strictness and integrity.

FRANK. Stop a bit. (*Seriously.*) I want to take you into my confidence.

PRAED. Pray dont. It's only some fresh folly, like the
470 barmaid at Redhill.[1]

FRANK.   Its ever so much more serious than that. You say youve only just met Vivie for the first time?

PRAED. Yes.

FRANK. (*Rhapsodically.*) Then you can have no idea
475 what a girl she is. Such character! Such sense! And her cleverness! Oh, my eye, Praed, but I can tell you she is clever! And—need I add?—she loves me.

CROFTS. (*Putting his head out of the window.*) I say, Praed: what are you about? Do come along. (*He
480 disappears.*)

FRANK. Hallo! Sort of chap that would take a prize at a dog show, aint he? Who's he?

PRAED. Sir George Crofts, an old friend of Mrs Warren's. I think we had better come in.

(*On their way to the porch they are interrupted by a call from the gate. Turning, they see an elderly clergyman looking over it.*)

485 THE CLERGYMAN. (*Calling.*) Frank!

FRANK. Hallo! (*To Praed.*) The Roman father. (*To The Clergyman.*) Yes, gov'nor: all right: presently. (*To Praed.*) Look here, Praed: youd better go in to tea. I'll join you directly.

490 PRAED. Very good. (*He goes into the cottage.*)

(*The Clergyman remains outside the gate, with his hands on the top of it. The Rev. Samuel Gardner, a beneficed[2] clergyman of the Established Church,[3] is over 50. Externally he is pretentious, booming, noisy, important. Really he is that obsolescent social phenomenon the fool of the family dumped on the Church by his father the patron, clamorously asserting himself as father and clergyman without being able to command respect in either capacity.*)

REV. S. Well, sir. Who are your friends here, if I may ask?

FRANK. Oh, it's all right, gov'nor! Come in.

REV. S. No, sir; not until I know whose garden I am
495 entering.

FRANK. It's all right. It's Miss Warren's.

REV. S. I have not seen her at church since she came.

FRANK. Of course not: she's a third wrangler. Ever so intellectual. Took a higher degree than you did; so why
500 should she go to hear you preach?

REV. S. Dont be disrespectful, sir.

FRANK. Oh, it dont matter: nobody hears us. Come in. (*He opens the gate, unceremoniously pulling his father with it into the garden.*) I want to introduce you to her. Do
505 you remember the advice you gave me last July, gov'nor?

REV. S. (*Severely.*) Yes. I advised you to conquer your idleness and flippancy, and to work your way into an honorable profession and live on it and not upon me.

FRANK. No: thats what you thought of afterwards. What
510 you actually said was that since I had neither brains nor money, I'd better turn my good looks to account by marrying somebody with both. Well, look here, Miss Warren has brains: you cant deny that.

REV. S. Brains are not everything.

515 FRANK. No, of course not: theres the money—

REV. S. (*Interrupting him austerely.*) I was not thinking of money sir. I was speaking of higher things. Social position, for instance.

FRANK. I dont care a rap about that.

520 REV. S. But I do, sir.

FRANK. Well, nobody wants y o u to marry her. Anyhow, she has what amounts to a high Cambridge degree;[4] and she seems to have as much money as she wants.

525 REV. S. (*Sinking into a feeble vein of humor.*) I greatly doubt whether she has as much money as you will want.

FRANK. Oh, come: I havnt been so very extravagant. I live ever so quietly; I dont drink; I dont bet much; and I never go regularly on the razzle-dazzle as you did when
530 you were my age.

---

[1] *Redhill* Small town about 25 miles south of London. Frank's "folly" with the barmaid is not further explained, but it hints at the nature of his pre-Vivie relationships.

[2] *beneficed* Supported by the church (with house and salary).

[3] *Established Church* Church of England.

[4] *Cambridge degree* Vivie has not actually been awarded a degree by Cambridge, only, as Frank says, "what amounts to one." Although women were allowed to attend lectures and sit examinations at Cambridge in the nineteenth century, they were not awarded degrees until 1921.

REV. S. (*Booming hollowly.*) Silence, sir.

FRANK.   Well, you told me yourself, when I was making ever such an ass of myself about the barmaid at Redhill, that you once offered a woman £50 for the letters you
535   wrote to her when—

REV. S. (*Terrified.*) Sh-sh-sh, Frank, for Heaven's sake! (*He looks around apprehensively. Seeing no one within earshot he plucks up courage to boom again, but more subduedly.*) You are taking an ungentlemanly advantage
540   of what I confided to you for your own good, to save you from an error you would have repented all your life long. Take warning by your father's follies, sir; and dont make them an excuse for your own.

FRANK.   Did you ever hear the story of the Duke of
545   Wellington and his letters?

REV. S.   No, sir; and I dont want to hear it.

FRANK.   The old Iron Duke didnt throw away £50: not he. He just wrote: "Dear Jenny: publish and be damned! Yours affectionately, Wellington." Thats what you
550   should have done.[1]

REV. S. (*Piteously.*) Frank, my boy: when I wrote those letters I put myself into that woman's power. When I told you about them I put myself, to some extent, I am sorry to say, in your power. She refused my money with
555   these words, which I shall never forget. "Knowledge is power," she said; "and I never sell power." Thats more than twenty years ago; and she has never made use of her power or caused me a moment's uneasiness. You are behaving worse to me than she did, Frank.

560   FRANK.   Oh yes I dare say! Did you ever preach at her the way you preach at me every day?

REV. S. (*Wounded almost to tears.*) I leave you, sir. You are incorrigible. (*He turns toward the gate.*)

FRANK. (*Utterly unmoved.*) Tell them I shant be home
565   to tea, will you, gov'nor, like a good fellow? (*He moves towards the cottage door and is met by Praed and Vivie coming out.*)

VIVIE. (*To Frank.*) Is that your father, Frank? I do so want to meet him.

570   FRANK.   Certainly. (*Calling after his father.*) Gov'nor. Youre wanted. (*The parson turns at the gate, fumbling nervously at his hat. Praed crosses the garden to the opposite side, beaming in anticipation of civilities.*) My father: Miss Warren.

575   VIVIE. (*Going to The Clergyman. and shaking his hand.*) Very glad to see you here, Mr Gardner. (*Calling to the cottage.*) Mother: come along: youre wanted.

(*Mrs Warren appears on the threshold, and is immediately transfixed recognizing The Clergyman.*)

VIVIE. (*Continuing.*) Let me introduce —

MRS WARREN. (*Swooping on the Reverend Samuel.*)
580   Why, it's Sam Gardner, gone into the church! Well, I never! Dont you know us, Sam? This is George Crofts, as large as life and twice as natural. Dont you remember me?

REV. S. (*Very red.*) I really—er—

585   MRS WARREN.   Of course you do. Why, I have a whole album of your letters still: I came across them only the other day.

REV. S. (*Miserably confused.*) Miss Vavasour,[2] I believe.

MRS WARREN. (*Correcting him quickly in a loud*
590   *whisper.*) Tch! Nonsense! Mrs Warren: Don't you see my daughter there?

ACT 2

(*Inside the cottage after nightfall. Looking eastward from within instead of westward from without, the latticed window, with its curtains drawn, is now seen in the middle of the front wall of the cottage, with the porch door to the left of it. In the left-hand side wall is the door leading to the kitchen. Farther back against the same wall is a dresser with a candle and matches on it, and Frank's rifle standing beside them, with the barrel resting in the plate-rack. In the centre a table stands with a lighted lamp on it. Vivie's books and writing materials are on a table to the right of the window, against the wall. The fireplace is on the right*

---

[1]   *Thats what you should have done*   Arthur Wellesley, 1st Duke of Wellington (1769–1852), defeated Napoleon at Waterloo in 1815. He later served as Prime Minister, 1828–30. His comment "Publish and be damned" was in response to a blackmail letter concerning a London courtesan well-known to Wellington. Wellington's iron-fisted discipline in military matters caused him to be known as the Iron Duke.

[2]   *Miss Vavasour*   Name used by Mrs Warren at the time the Reverend Samuel knew her. A vavasour was a medieval vassal owing allegiance to a great lord.

with a settle:[1] *there is no fire. Two of the chairs are set right and left of the table.*

The cottage door opens, shewing a fine starlit night without; and Mrs Warren, her shoulders wrapped in a shawl borrowed from Vivie, enters, followed by Frank, who throws his cap on the window seat. She has had enough of walking, and gives a gasp of relief as she unpins her hat; takes it off; sticks the pin through the crown; and puts it on the table.)

MRS WARREN. O Lord! I dont know which is the worst of the country, the walking or the sitting at home with nothing to do. I could do with a whisky and soda now very well, if only they had such a thing in this place.

5 FRANK. Perhaps Vivie's got some.

MRS WARREN. Nonsense! What would a young girl like her be doing with such things! Never mind: it dont matter. I wonder how she passes her time here! I'd a good deal rather be in Vienna.

10 FRANK. Let me take you there. (*He helps her to take off her shawl, gallantly giving her shoulders a very perceptible squeeze*[2] *as he does so.*)

MRS WARREN. Ah! would you? I'm beginning to think youre a chip of the old block.[3]

15 FRANK. Like the gov'nor, eh? (*He hangs the shawl on the nearest chair and sits down.*)

MRS WARREN. Never you mind. What do you know about such things? Youre only a boy. (*She goes to the hearth, to be farther from temptation.*)

20 FRANK. Do come to Vienna with me. It'd be ever such larks.

MRS WARREN. No, thank you. Vienna is no place for you—at least not until youre a little older. (*She nods at him to emphasize this piece of advice. He makes a mock-*
25 *piteous face, belied by his laughing eyes. She looks at him; then comes back to him.*) Now, look here, little boy. (*Taking his face in her hands and turning it up to her.*) I know you through and through by your likeness to your father, better than you know yourself. Dont you go

30 taking any silly ideas into your head about me. Do you hear?

FRANK. (*Gallantly wooing her with his voice.*) Cant help it, my dear Mrs Warren: it runs in the family.

(*She pretends to box his ears; then looks at the pretty laughing upturned face for a moment, tempted. At last she kisses him, and immediately turns away, out of patience with herself.*)

35 MRS WARREN. There! I shouldnt have done that. I a m wicked. Never mind, my dear: it's only a motherly kiss. Go and make love to Vivie.

FRANK. So I have.

MRS WARREN. (*Turning on him with a sharp note of*
40 *alarm in her voice.*) What!

FRANK. Vivie and I are ever such chums.

MRS WARREN. What do you mean? Now see here: I wont have any young scamp tampering with my little girl. Do you hear? I wont have it.

45 FRANK. (*Quite unabashed.*) My dear Mrs Warren: dont you be alarmed. My intentions are honorable: ever so honorable; and your little girl is jolly well able to take care of herself. She dont need looking after half so much as her mother. She aint so handsome, you know.

50 MRS WARREN. (*Taken aback by his assurance.*) Well, you have got a nice healthy two inches thick of cheek all over you. I dont know where you got it. Not from your father, anyhow.

CROFTS. (*In the garden.*) The gipsies, I suppose?

55 REV. S. (*Replying.*) The broomsquires[4] are far worse.

MRS WARREN. (*To Frank.*) Sh-sh! Remember! youve had your warning.

(*Crofts and the Reverend Samuel come in from the garden, the Clergyman continuing his conversation as he enters.*)

REV. S. The perjury at the Winchester assizes is deplorable.[5]

---

[1] *settle* A wooden bench with high back and arms, and a box or draw under the seat.

[2] *squeeze* In the 1898 text Frank's "*very perceptible squeeze*" is "*the most delicate possible little caress.*"

[3] *chip of the old block* "Chip *off* the old block" is relatively recent usage. "Chip *of* the old block" was standard in Shaw's time.

[4] *broomsquires* Itinerant makers and vendors of brooms made from a bunch of heather or twigs.

[5] *Winchester assizes* Courts of law held periodically in Winchester, as in other counties in England, for the administering of civil and criminal justice. Shaw may have had a particular case in mind, but it has not been traced. The line does not appear in the 1898 text.

60 MRS WARREN. Well? what became of you two? And wheres Praddy and Vivie?

CROFTS. (*Putting his hat on the settle and his stick in the chimney corner.*) They went up the hill. We went to the village. I wanted a drink. (*He sits down on the settle,* 65 *putting his legs up along the seat.*)

MRS WARREN. We she oughtnt go off like that without telling me. (*To Frank.*) Get your father a chair, Frank: where are your manners? (*Frank springs up and gracefully offers his father his chair; then takes another from the wall* 70 *and sits down at the table, in the middle, with his father on his right and Mrs Warren on his left.*) George: where are you going to stay tonight? You cant stay here. And whats Praddy going to do?

CROFTS. Gardner'll put me up.

75 MRS WARREN. Oh, no doubt youve taken care of yourself! But what about Praddy?

CROFTS. Dont know. I suppose he can sleep at the inn.

MRS WARREN. Havnt you room for him, Sam?

REV. S. Well—er—you see, as rector here, I am not free 80 to do as I like. Er—what is Mr Praed's social position?

MRS WARREN. Oh, he's all right: he's an architect. What an old stick-in-the-mud you are, Sam!

FRANK. Yes, it's all right, gov'nor. He built that place down in Wales for the Duke. Caernarvon Castle they 85 call it. You must have heard of it. (*He winks with lightning smartness at Mrs Warren, and regards his father blandly.*)

REV. S. Oh, in that case, of course we shall only be too happy. I suppose he knows the Duke personally.

90 FRANK. Oh, ever so intimately! We can stick him in Georgina's old room.

MRS WARREN. Well, thats settled. Now if only those two would only come in and let us have supper. Theyve no right to stay out after dark like this.

95 CROFTS. (*Aggressively.*) What harm are they doing you?

MRS WARREN. Well, harm or not, I dont like it.

FRANK. Better not wait for them, Mrs Warren. Praed will stay out as long as possible. He has never known before what it is to stray over the heath on a summer 100 night with my Vivie.

CROFTS. (*Sitting up in some consternation.*) I say, you know! Come!

REV. S. (*Rising, startled out of his professional manner into real force and sincerity.*) Frank, once for all, it's out of the question. Mrs Warren will tell you that it's not to be 105 thought of.

CROFTS. Of course not.

FRANK. (*With enchanting placidity.*) Is that so, Mrs Warren?

110 MRS WARREN. (*Reflectively.*) Well, Sam, I dont know. If the girl wants to get married, no good can come of keeping her unmarried.

REV. S. (*Astounded.*) But married to h i m!—your daughter to my son! Only think: it's impossible.

115 CROFTS. Of course it's impossible. Dont be a fool, Kitty.

MRS WARREN. (*Nettled.*) Why not? Isnt my daughter good enough for your son?

REV. S. But surely, my dear Mrs Warren, you know the 120 reasons—

MRS WARREN. (*Defiantly.*) I know no reasons. If you know any, you can tell them to the lad, or to the girl, or to your congregation, if you like.

REV. S. (*Collapsing helplessly into his chair.*) You know 125 very well that I couldnt tell anyone the reasons. But my boy will believe me when I tell him there a r e reasons.

FRANK. Quite right, Dad: he will. But has your boy's conduct ever been influenced by your reasons?

CROFTS. You cant marry her; and thats all about it. (*He* 130 *gets up and stands on the hearth, with his back to the fireplace, frowning determinedly.*)

MRS WARREN. (*Turning on him sharply.*) What have you got to do with it, pray?

FRANK. (*With his prettiest lyrical cadence.*) Precisely what 135 I was going to ask myself, in my own graceful fashion.

CROFTS. (*To Mrs Warren.*) I suppose you dont want to marry the girl to a man younger than herself and without either a profession or twopence to keep her on. Ask Sam, if you dont believe me. (*To the parson.*) How 140 much more money are you going to give him?

REV. S. Not another penny. He has had his patrimony and he spent the last of it in July. (*Mrs Warren's face falls.*)

CROFTS. (*Watching her.*) There! I told you. (*He resumes* 145 *his place on the settle and puts his legs on the seat again, as if the matter were finally disposed of.*)

FRANK. (*Plaintively.*) This is ever so mercenary. Do you suppose Miss Warren's going to marry for money? If we love one another—

150 MRS WARREN. Thank you. Your love's a pretty cheap commodity, my lad. If you have no means of keeping a wife, that settles it: you cant have Vivie.

FRANK. (*Much amused.*) What do y o u say, gov'nor, eh?

REV. S. I agree with Mrs Warren.

155 FRANK. And good old Crofts has already expressed his opinion.

CROFTS. (*Turning angrily on his elbow.*) Look here: I want none of y o u r cheek.

FRANK. (*Pointedly.*) I'm e v e r so sorry to surprise you,
160 Crofts, but you allowed yourself the liberty of speaking to me like a father a moment ago. One father is enough, thank you.

CROFTS. (*Contemptuously.*) Yah! (*He turns away again.*)

FRANK. (*Rising.*) Mrs Warren: I cannot give my Vivie
165 up, even for your sake.

MRS WARREN. (*Muttering.*) Young scamp!

FRANK. (*Continuing.*) And as you no doubt intend to hold out other prospects to her, I shall lose no time in placing my case before her. (*They stare at him, and he
170 begins to declaim gracefully*)

> He either fears his fate too much,
> Or his deserts are small,
> That dares not put it to the touch
> To gain or lose it all.[1]

(*The cottage door opens whilst he is reciting; and Vivie and Praed come in. He breaks off. Praed puts his hat on the dresser. There is an immediate improvement in the company's behavior. Crofts takes down his legs from the settle and pulls himself together as Praed joins him at the fireplace. Mrs Warren loses her ease of manner and takes refuge in querulousness.*)[2]

175 MRS WARREN. Wherever have you been, Vivie?

VIVIE. (*Taking off her hat and throwing it carelessly on the table.*) On the hill.

MRS WARREN. Well, you shouldnt go off like that without letting me know. How could I tell what had
180 become of you? And night coming on too!

VIVIE. (*Going to the door of the kitchen and opening it, ignoring her mother.*) Now, about supper? (*All rise except Mrs Warren.*) We shall be rather crowded in here, I'm afraid.

185 MRS WARREN. Did you hear what I said, Vivie?

VIVIE. (*Quietly.*) Yes, mother. (*Reverting to the supper difficulty.*) How many are we? (*Counting.*) One, two, three, four, five, six. Well, two will have to wait until the rest are done: Mrs Alison has only plates and knives
190 for four.

PRAED. Oh, it doesnt matter about me. I—

VIVIE. You have had a long walk and are hungry, Mr Praed: you shall have your supper at once. I can wait myself. I want one person to wait with me. Frank: are
195 you hungry?

FRANK. Not the least in the world. Completely off my peck,[3] in fact.

MRS WARREN. (*To Crofts.*) Neither are you, George. You can wait.

200 CROFTS. Oh, hang it, Ive eaten nothing since tea-time. Cant Sam do it?

FRANK. Would you starve my poor father?

REV. S. (*Testily.*) Allow me to speak for myself, sir. I am perfectly willing to wait.

205 VIVIE. (*Decisively.*) Theres no need. Only two are wanted. (*She opens the door of the kitchen.*) Will you take my mother in, Mr Gardner. (*The parson takes Mrs Warren; and they pass into the kitchen. Praed and Crofts follow. All except Praed clearly disapprove of the
210 arrangement, but do not know how to resist it. Vivie stands at the door looking in at them.*) Can you squeeze past to that corner, Mr Praed: it's a rather tight fit. Take care of your coat against the white-wash: thats right. Now, are you all comfortable?

215 PRAED. (*Within.*) Quite, thank you.

MRS WARREN. (*Within.*) Leave the door open, dearie. (*Vivie frowns; but Frank checks her with a gesture, and steals to the cottage door, which he softly sets wide open.*) Oh Lor, what a draught! Youd better shut it, dear.

---

[1] *He either ... all* From "My Dear and Only Love," a poem by the Scottish soldier and writer James Graham, Marquess of Montrose (1612–50). Frank slightly misquotes. "He either fears his fate too much, / Or his deserts are small, / That puts it not unto the touch / To win or lose it all."

[2] *querulousness* Petulance.

---

[3] *off my peck* Not hungry.

(*Vivie shuts it with a slam,*[1] *and then, noting with disgust that her mother's hat and shawl are lying about, takes them tidily to the window seat, whilst Frank noiselessly shuts the cottage door.*)

220 FRANK. (*Exulting.*) Aha! Got rid of em. Well, Vivvums: what do you think of my governor?

VIVIE. (*Preoccupied and serious.*) Ive hardly spoken to him. He doesnt strike me as being a particularly able person.

225 FRANK. Well, you know, the old man is not altogether such a fool as he looks. You see, he was shoved into the church rather; and in trying to live up to it he makes a much bigger ass of himself than he really is. I dont dislike him as much as you might expect. He means

230 well. How do you think youll get on with him?

VIVIE. (*Rather grimly.*) I dont think my future life will be much concerned with him, or with any of that old circle of my mother's, except perhaps Praed. (*She sits down on the settle.*) What do you think of my mother?

235 FRANK. Really and truly?

VIVIE. Yes, really and truly.

FRANK. Well, she's ever so jolly. But she's rather a caution,[2] isnt she? And Crofts! oh, my eye, Crofts! (*He sits beside her.*)

240 VIVIE. What a lot, Frank!

FRANK. What a crew!

VIVIE. (*With intense contempt for them.*) If I thought that *I* was like that—that I was going to be a waster, shifting along from one meal to another with no purpose, and

245 no character, and no grit in me, I'd open an artery and bleed to death without one moment's hesitation.

FRANK. Oh no, you wouldnt. Why should they take any grind when they can afford not to? I wish I had their luck. No: what I object to is their form. It isnt the thing:

250 it's slovenly, ever so slovenly.

VIVIE. Do you think your form will be any better when youre as old as Crofts, if you dont work?

FRANK. Of course I do. Ever so much better. Vivvums musnt lecture: her little boy is incorrigible. (*He attempts*

255 *to take her face caressingly in his hands.*)

---

[1] *with a slam* In the 1898 text Vivie merely shuts the door "*promptly.*"

[2] *a caution* Eccentric person; a "bit of a character."

VIVIE. (*Striking his hands down sharply.*) Off with you: Vivvums is not in a humor for petting her little boy this evening. (*She rises and comes forward to the other side of the room.*)

260 FRANK. (*Following her.*) How unkind!

VIVIE. (*Stamping at him.*) Be serious. I'm serious.

FRANK. Good. Let us talk learnedly. Miss Warren: do you know that all the most advanced thinkers are agreed that half the diseases of modern civilization are due to

265 starvation of the affections in the young. Now, I—

VIVIE. (*Cutting him short.*) You are very tiresome. (*She opens the inner door.*) Have you room for Frank there? He's complaining of starvation.

MRS WARREN. (*Within.*) Of course there is (*Clatter of*

270 *knives and glasses as she moves the things on the table.*) Here! theres room now beside me. Come along, Mr Frank.

FRANK. Her little boy will be ever so even with his Vivvums for this. (*He passes into the kitchen.*)

275 MRS WARREN. (*Within.*) Here, Vivie: come on you too, child. You must be famished. (*She enters, followed by Crofts, who holds the door open for Vivie with marked deference. She goes out without looking at him; and shuts the door after her.*) Why, George, you cant be done:

280 youve eaten nothing. Is there anything wrong with you?

CROFTS. Oh, all I wanted was a drink. (*He thrusts his hands in his pockets, and begins prowling around the room, restless and sulky.*)

MRS WARREN. Well, I like enough to eat. But a little of

285 that cold beef and cheese and lettuce goes a long way. (*With a sigh of only half repletion she sits down lazily on the settle.*)

CROFTS. What do you go encouraging that young pup for?

290 MRS WARREN. (*On the alert at once.*) Now see here, George: what are you up to about that girl? Ive been watching your way of looking at her. Remember: I know you and what your looks mean.

CROFTS. Theres no harm in looking at her, is there?

295 MRS WARREN. I'd put you out and pack you back to London pretty soon if I saw any of your nonsense. My girl's little finger is more to me than any of your body and soul. (*Crofts receives this with a sneering grin. Mrs Warren, flushing a little at her failure to impose on him in*

300 *the character of a theatrically devoted mother, adds in a*

lower key.) Make your mind easy: the young pup has no more chance than you have.

CROFTS.   Maynt a man take an interest in a girl?

MRS WARREN.   Not a man like you.

305 CROFTS.   How old is she?

MRS WARREN.   Never you mind how old she is.

CROFTS.   Why do you make such a secret of it?

MRS WARREN.   Because I choose.

CROFTS.   Well, I'm not fifty yet; and my property is as 310 good as ever it was—

MRS WARREN.   (*Interrupting him.*) Yes, because youre as stingy as youre vicious.

CROFTS.   (*Continuing.*) And a baronet[1] isnt to be picked up every day. No other man in my position would put 315 up with you for a mother-in-law. Why shouldnt she marry me?

MRS WARREN.   You!

CROFTS.   We three could live together quite comfortably: I'd die before her and leave her a bouncing widow 320 with plenty of money. Why not? It's been growing in my mind all the time Ive been walking with that fool inside there.

MRS WARREN.   (*Revolted.*) Yes: it's the sort of thing that w o u l d grow in your mind.

(*He halts in his prowling; and the two look at one another, she steadfastly, with a sort of awe behind her contemptuous disgust: he stealthily, with a carnal gleam in his eye and a loose grin.*)

325 CROFTS.   (*Suddenly becoming anxious and urgent as he sees no sign of sympathy in her.*) Look here, Kitty: youre a sensible woman: you neednt put on any moral airs. I'll ask no more questions; and you need answer none. I'll settle the whole property on her; and if you want a 330 cheque for yourself on the wedding day, you can name any figure you like—in reason.

MRS WARREN.   So it's come to that with you, George, like all the other worn-out old creatures!

CROFTS.   (*Savagely.*) Damn you!

(*Before she can retort[2] the door of the kitchen is opened; and the voices of the others are heard returning. Crofts, unable to recover his presence of mind, hurries out of the cottage. The Clergyman appears at the kitchen door.*)

335 REV. S.   (*Looking around.*) Where is Sir George?

MRS WARREN.   Gone out to have a pipe. (*The Clergyman takes his hat from the table, and joins Mrs Warren at the fireside. Meanwhile Vivie comes in, followed by Frank, who collapses into the nearest chair with an air 340 of extreme exhaustion. Mrs Warren looks round at Vivie and says, with her affectation of maternal patronage ever more forced than usual.*) Well, dearie, have you had a good supper?

VIVIE.   You know what Mrs Alison's suppers are. (*She 345 turns to Frank and pets him.*) Poor Frank! was all the beef gone? did it get nothing but bread and cheese and ginger beer? (*Seriously, as if she had done quite enough trifling for one evening.*) Her butter is really awful. I must get some down from the stores.

350 FRANK.   Do, in Heaven's name!

(*Vivie goes to the writing-table and makes a memorandum to order the butter. Praed comes in from the kitchen, putting up his handkerchief, which he has been using as a napkin.*)

REV. S.   Frank, my boy: it is time for us to be thinking of home. Your mother does not know yet that we have visitors.

PRAED.   I'm afraid we're giving trouble.

355 FRANK.   (*Rising.*) Not the least in the world: my mother will be delighted to see you. She's a genuinely intellectual artistic woman; and she sees nobody here from one year's end to another except the gov'nor; so you can imagine how jolly dull it pans out for her. (*To 360 his father.*) Y o u r e not intellectual or artistic: are you pater? So take Praed home at once; and I'll stay here and entertain Mrs Warren. Youll pick up Crofts in the garden. He'll be excellent company for the bull-pup.[3]

PRAED.   (*Taking his hat from the dresser, and coming close*

---

[1]   *baronet* The lowest of Britain's hereditary titles, established in 1611. It confers a knighthood, however: hence, *Sir* George Crofts. His wife would be titled *Lady* Crofts.

[2]   *Before she can retort* In the 1898 text Mrs Warren is given more time: "*She rises and turns fiercely on him.*"

[3]   *bull-pup* Sarcastic reference to Praed. He's not a bull-*dog*.

365 *to Frank.*) Come with us, Frank. Mrs Warren has not
seen Miss Vivie for a long time; and we have prevented
them from having a moment together yet.

FRANK. (*Quite softened and looking at Praed with
romantic admiration.*) Of course. I forgot. Ever so
370 thanks for reminding me. Perfect gentleman, Praddy.
Always were. My ideal through life. (*He rises to go, but
pauses a moment between the two older men, and puts his
hand on Praed's shoulder.*) Ah, if you had only been my
father instead of this unworthy old man! (*He puts his
375 other hand on his father's shoulder.*)

REV. S.   (*Blustering.*) Silence, sir, silence: you are profane.

MRS WARREN.   (*Laughing heartily.*) You should keep
him in better order, Sam. Goodnight. Here: take
George his hat and stick with my compliments.

380 REV. S.   (*Taking them.*) Goodnight. (*They shake hands. As
he passes Vivie he shakes hands with her also and bids her
goodnight. Then, in booming command, to Frank.*) Come
along, sir, at once. (*He goes out.*)

MRS WARREN.   Byebye, Praddy.

385 PRAED.   Byebye, Kitty.

(*They shake hands affectionately and go out together, she
accompanying him to the garden gate.*)

FRANK.   (*To Vivie.*) Kissums?

VIVIE.   (*Fiercely.*) No. I hate you.[1] (*She takes a couple of
books and some paper from the writing-table, and sits
down with them at the middle table, at the end next the
390 fireplace.*)

FRANK.   (*Grimacing.*) Sorry. (*He goes for his cap and rifle.
Mrs Warren returns. He takes her hand.*) Goodnight,
d e a r Mrs Warren. (*He kisses her hand.[2] She snatches it
away, her lips tightening, and looks more than half disposed
395 to box his ears. He laughs mischievously and runs off,
clapping-to[3] the door behind him.*)

MRS WARREN.   (*Resigning herself to an evening of
boredom now that the men are gone.*) Did you ever in
your life hear anyone rattle on so? Isnt he a tease? (*She

400 sits at the table.*) Now that I think of it, dearie, dont you
go encouraging him. I'm sure he's a regular good-for-
nothing.

VIVIE.   (*Rising to fetch more books.*) I'm afraid so. Poor
Frank! I shall have to get rid of him; but I shall feel sorry
405 for him, though he's not worth it. That man Crofts does
not seem to me to be good for much either: is he? (*She
throws the books on the table rather roughly.*)

MRS WARREN.   (*Galled by Vivie's indifference.*)[4] What do
you know of men, child, to talk that way about them?
410 Youll have to make up your mind to see a good deal of
Sir George Crofts, as he's a friend of mine.

VIVIE.   (*Quite unmoved.*) Why? (*She sits down and opens
a book.*) Do you expect that we shall be much together?
You and I, I mean?

415 MRS WARREN.   (*Staring at her.*) Of course: until youre
married. Youre not going back to college again.

VIVIE.   Do you think my way of life would suit you? I
doubt it.

MRS WARREN.   Y o u r way of life! What do you mean?

420 VIVIE.   (*Cutting a page[5] of her book with the paper knife on
her chatelaine.*) Has it really never occurred to you,
mother, that I have a way of life like other people?

MRS WARREN.   What nonsense is this youre trying to
talk? Do you want to shew your independence, now that
425 youre a great little person at school? Dont be a fool, child.

VIVIE.   (*Indulgently.*) Thats all you have to say on the
subject, is it, mother?

MRS WARREN.   (*Puzzled, then angry.*) Dont you keep on
asking me questions like that. (*Violently.*) Hold your
430 tongue. (*Vivie works on, losing no time, and saying
nothing.*) You and your way of life, indeed! What next?
(*She looks at Vivie again. No reply.*) Your way of life will
be what I please, so it will. (*Another pause.*) Ive been
noticing these airs in you ever since you got that tripos
435 or whatever you call it. If you think I'm going to put up
with them youre mistaken; and the sooner you find it
out, the better. (*Muttering.*) All I have to say on the
subject, indeed! (*Again rising her voice angrily.*) Do you
know who youre speaking to, Miss?

440 VIVIE.   (*Looking across at her without raising her head

---

[1]   *I hate you* In the 1898 text Frank "*silently begs a kiss,*" and
receives in return from Vivie "*a stern glance,*" rather than her fierce
comment.

[2]   *kisses her hand* In the 1898 text Frank "*squeezes*" Mrs. Warren's
hand.

[3]   *clapping-to* Slamming.

[4]   *Vivie's indifference* In the 1898 text Mrs. Warren is galled by
Vivie's "*cool tone,*" rather than her indifference.

[5]   *Cutting a page* Books were sold with their pages uncut, that is, as
folded by the binder.

from her book.) No. Who are you? What are you?

MRS WARREN. (*Rising breathless.*) You young imp!

VIVIE. Everybody knows my reputation, my social standing, and the profession I intend to pursue. I know nothing about you. What is that way of life which you invite me to share with you and Sir George Crofts, pray?

MRS WARREN. Take care. I shall do something I'll be sorry for after, and you too.

VIVIE. (*Putting aside her books with cool decision.*) Well, let us drop the subject until you are better able to face it. (*Looking critically at her mother.*) You want some good walks and a little lawn tennis to set you up. You are shockingly out of condition: you were not able to manage twenty yards uphill today without stopping to pant; and your wrists are mere rolls of fat. Look at mine. (*She holds out her wrists.*)

MRS WARREN. (*After looking at her helplessly, begins to whimper.*) Vivie—

VIVIE. (*Springing up sharply.*) Now pray dont begin to cry. Anything but that. I really cannot stand whimpering. I will go out of the room if you do.

MRS WARREN. (*Piteously.*) Oh, my darling, how can you be so hard on me? Have I no rights over you as your mother?

VIVIE. A r e you my mother?

MRS WARREN. (*Appalled.*) A m I your mother! Oh, Vivie!

VIVIE. Then where are our relatives? my father? our family friends? You claim the rights of a mother: the right to call me fool and child; to speak to me as no woman in authority over me at college dare speak to me; to dictate my way of life; and to force on me the acquaintance of a brute whom any one can see to be the most vicious sort of London man about town. Before I give myself the trouble to resist such claims, I may as well find out whether they have any real existence.

MRS WARREN. (*Distracted, throwing herself on her knees.*) Oh no, no. Stop, stop. I a m your mother, I swear it. Oh, you cant mean to turn on me—my own child! it's not natural. You believe me, dont you? Say you believe me.

VIVIE. Who was my father?

MRS WARREN. You dont know what youre asking. I cant tell you.

VIVIE. (*Determinedly.*) Oh yes you can, if you like. I have a right to know; and you know very well that I have that right. You can refuse to tell me, if you please; but if you do you will see the last of me tomorrow morning.

MRS WARREN. Oh, it's too horrible to hear you talk like that. You wouldnt—you c o u l d n t leave me.

VIVIE. (*Ruthlessly.*) Yes, without a moment's hesitation, if you trifle with me about this. (*Shivering with disgust.*) How can I feel sure that I may not have the contaminated blood of that brutal waster in my veins?

MRS WARREN. No, no. On my oath it's not he, nor any of the rest that you have ever met. I'm certain of that, at least.

(*Vivie's eyes fasten sternly on her mother as the significance of this flashes on her.*)

VIVIE. (*Slowly.*) You are certain of that, at l e a s t. Ah! You mean that that is all you are certain of. (*Thoughtfully.*) I see. (*Mrs Warren buries her face in her hands.*) Dont do that, mother: you know you dont feel it a bit. (*Mrs Warren takes down her hands and looks up deplorably at Vivie, who takes out her watch and says*) Well, that is enough for tonight. At what hour would you like breakfast? Is half-past eight too early for you?

MRS WARREN. (*Wildly.*) My God, what sort of woman are you?

VIVIE. (*Coolly.*) The sort the world is mostly made of, I should hope. Otherwise I dont understand how it gets its business done. Come (*taking her mother by the wrist, and pulling her up pretty resolutely*): pull yourself together. Thats right.

MRS WARREN. (*Querulously.*) Youre very rough with me, Vivie.

VIVIE. Nonsense. What about bed? It's past ten.

MRS WARREN. (*Passionately.*) Whats the use of my going to bed? Do you think I could sleep?

VIVIE. Why not? I shall.

MRS WARREN. You! youve no heart. (*She suddenly breaks out vehemently in her natural tongue—the dialect of a woman of the people—with all her affectations of maternal authority and conventional manners gone, and an overwhelming inspiration of true conviction and scorn in her.*) Oh, I wont bear it: I wont put up with the injustice of it. What right have you to set yourself up

above m e like this? You boast of what you are to
me—to me, who gave you the chance of being what you
are. What chance had I? Shame on you for a bad
daughter and a stuck-up prude!

VIVIE. (*Sitting down with a shrug,*[1] *no longer confident; for
her replies, which have sounded sensible and strong to her
so far, now begin to ring rather woodenly and even
priggishly against the new tone of her mother.*) Dont think
for a moment I set myself up against you in any way.
You attacked me with the conventional authority of a
mother: I defended myself with the conventional
superiority of a respectable woman. Frankly, I am not
going to stand any of your nonsense; and when you
drop it I shall not expect you to stand any of mine. I
shall always respect your right to your own opinions and
your own way of life.

MRS WARREN. My own opinions and my own way of
life! Listen to her talking! Do you think I was brought
up like you? able to pick and choose my own way of life?
Do you think I did what I did because I liked it, or
thought it right, or wouldnt rather have gone to college
and been a lady if I'd had the chance?

VIVIE. Everybody has some choice, mother. The poorest
girl alive may not be able to choose between being
Queen of England or Principal of Newnham; but she
can choose between ragpicking and flowerselling,
according to her taste. People are always blaming their
circumstances for what they are. I dont believe in
circumstances. The people who get on this world are the
people who get up and look for the circumstances they
want, and, if they cant find them, make them.

MRS WARREN. Oh, it's easy to talk, very easy, isnt it?
Here! would you like to know what m y circumstances
were?

VIVIE. Yes: you had better tell me. Wont you sit down?

MRS WARREN. Oh, I'll sit down: dont you be afraid.
(*She plants her chair farther forward with brazen energy,
and sits down. Vivie is impressed in spite of herself.*) D'you
know what your gran'mother was?

VIVIE. No.

MRS WARREN. No, you dont. I do. She called herself a
widow and had a fried-fish shop down by the Mint,[2]
and kept herself and four daughters out of it. Two of us
were sisters: that was me and Liz; and we were both
good-looking and well made. I suppose our father was
a well-fed man: mother pretended he was a gentleman;
but I dont know. The other two were only half sisters:
undersized, ugly, starved looking, hard working, honest
poor creatures: Liz and I would have half-murdered
them if mother hadnt half-murdered u s to keep our
hands off them. They were the respectable ones. Well,
what did they get by their respectability? I'll tell you.
One of them worked in a whitelead factory[3] twelve
hours a day for nine shillings a week until she died of
lead poisoning. She only expected to get her hands a
little paralyzed; but she died. The other was always held
up to us as a model because she married a Government
laborer in the Deptford victualling yard,[4] and kept his
room and the three children neat and tidy on eighteen
shillings a week—until he took to drink. That was
worth being respectable for, wasnt it?

VIVIE. (*Now thoughtfully attentive.*) Did you and your
sister think so?

MRS WARREN. Liz didnt, I can tell you: she had more
spirit. We both went to a church school—that was part
of the ladylike airs we gave ourselves to be superior to
the children that knew nothing and went nowhere—
and we stayed there until Liz went out one night and
never came back. I know the schoolmistress thought I'd
soon follow her example; for the clergyman was always
warning me that Lizzie'd end by jumping off Waterloo
Bridge.[5] Poor fool: that was all he knew about it! But I
was more afraid of the whitelead factory than I was of

---

[1] *with a shrug* In the 1898 text Vivie is still "*cool and determined*"
at this point.

[2] *the Mint* The Royal Mint is the official manufacturer of British
coinage. In Shaw's time it was located in working-class East End
London. It moved in 1968 to its present location in Llantrisant,
South Wales.

[3] *whitelead factory* Whitelead is a mixture of lead carbonate and
hydrated lead oxide used as a white pigment in paint.

[4] *Deptford victualling yard* The Royal Victualling Yard—for
providing supplies and provisions for the Royal Navy—was established at Deptford (on the River Thames) in 1742.

[5] *Waterloo Bridge* Waterloo Bridge connects Victoria Embankment
with Waterloo on the south bank of the Thames in London. The
original bridge (built in 1817) was demolished in 1936 and replaced
with the present structure.

the river; and so would you have been in my place. That clergyman got me a situation as scullery[1] maid in a temperance restaurant[2] where they sent out for anything you liked. Then I was waitress; and then I went to the bar at Waterloo station:[3] fourteen hours a day serving drinks and washing glasses for four shillings a week and my board. That was considered a great promotion for me. Well, one cold, wretched night, when I was so tired I could hardly keep myself awake, who should come up for a half of scotch[4] but Lizzie, in a long fur cloak, elegant and comfortable, with a lot of sovereigns[5] in her purse.

VIVIE. (Grimly.) My aunt Lizzie!

MRS WARREN. Yes; and a very good aunt to have, too. She's living down at Winchester[6] now, close to the cathedral, one of the most respectable ladies there. Chaperones girls at the county ball, if you please. No river for Liz, thank you! You remind me of Liz a little: she was a first-rate business woman—saved money from the beginning—never let herself look too like what she was—never lost her head or threw away a chance. When she saw I'd grown up good-looking she said to me across the bar "What are you doing there, you little fool? wearing out your health and your appearance for other people's profit!" Liz was saving money then to take a house for herself in Brussels; and she thought we two could save faster than one. So she lent me some money and gave me a start; and I saved steadily and first paid her back, and then went into business with her as her partner. Why shouldnt I have done it? The house in Brussels was real high class: a much better place for a woman to be in than the factory where Anne Jane got poisoned. None of our girls were ever treated as I was treated in the scullery of that temperance place, or at the Waterloo bar, or at home. Would you have had me stay in them and become a worn-out old drudge before I was

forty?

VIVIE. (Intensely interested by this time.) No, but why did you choose that business? Saving money and good management will succeed in any business.

MRS WARREN. Yes, saving money. But where can a woman get the money to save in any other business? Could you save out of four shillings a week and keep yourself dressed as well? Not you. Of course, if youre a plain woman and cant earn anything more; or if you have a turn for music, or the stage, or newspaper-writing: thats different. But neither Liz nor I had any turn for such things: all we had was our appearance and our turn for pleasing men. Do you think we were such fools as to let other people trade in our good looks by employing us as shopgirls, or barmaids, or waitresses, when we could trade in them ourselves and get all the profits instead of starvation wages? Not likely.

VIVIE. You were certainly quite justified—from the business point of view.

MRS WARREN. Yes; or any other point of view. What is any respectable girl brought up to do but to catch some rich man's fancy and get the benefit of his money by marrying him?—as if a marriage ceremony could make any difference in the right or wrong of the thing! Oh, the hypocrisy of the world makes me sick! Liz and I had to work and save and calculate just like other people; elseways[7] we should be as poor as any good-for-nothing drunken waster of a woman that thinks her luck will last forever. (With great energy.) I despise such people: theyve no character; and if theres a thing I hate in a woman, it's want of character.

VIVIE. Come now, mother: Frankly! Isn't it part of what you call character in a woman that she should greatly dislike such a way of making money?

MRS WARREN. Why, of course. Everybody dislikes having to work and make money; but they have to do it all the same. I'm sure Ive often pitied a poor girl, tired out and in low spirits, having to try to please some man that she doesnt care two straws for—some half-drunken fool that thinks he's making himself agreeable when he's teasing and worrying and disgusting a woman so that hardly any money could pay her for putting up with it. But she has to bear with disagreeables and take the

---

[1] *scullery* Small room adjacent to the kitchen used mainly for washing dishes.

[2] *temperance restaurant* Restaurant that does not serve alcohol.

[3] *Waterloo station* Then, and now, one of London's principal railway stations.

[4] *half of scotch* Large glass of Scotch whisky.

[5] *sovereigns* Gold coins worth £1.

[6] *Winchester* City about 65 miles southwest of London.

[7] *elseways* Otherwise.

rough with the smooth, just like a nurse in a hospital or anyone else. It's not work that any woman would do for pleasure, goodness knows; though to hear the pious people talk you would suppose it was a bed of roses.

VIVIE.   Still, you consider it worth while. It pays.

MRS WARREN.   Of course it's worth while to a poor girl, if she can resist temptation and is good-looking and well conducted and sensible. It's far better than any other employment open to her. I always thought that oughtnt to be. It c a n t be right, Vivie, that there shouldnt be better opportunities for women. I stick to that: it's wrong. But it's so, right or wrong; and a girl must make the best of it. But of course it's not worth while for a lady. If you took to it youd be a fool; but I should have been a fool if I'd taken to anything else.

VIVIE.   (More and more deeply moved.) Mother: suppose we were both as poor as you were in those wretched old days, are you quite sure that you wouldnt advise me to try the Waterloo bar, or marry a laborer, or even go into the factory?

MRS WARREN.   (Indignantly.) Of course not. What sort of mother do you take me for! How could you keep your self-respect in such starvation and slavery? And whats a woman worth? whats life worth? without self-respect! Why am I independent and able to give my daughter a first-rate education, when other women that had just as good opportunities are in the gutter? Because I always knew how to respect myself and control myself. Why is Liz looked up to in a cathedral town? The same reason. Where would we be now if we'd minded the clergyman's foolishness? Scrubbing floors for one and sixpence a day and nothing to look forward to but the workhouse infirmary.[1] Dont you be led astray by people who dont know the world, my girl. The only way for a woman to provide for herself decently is for her to be good to some man that can afford to be good to her. If she's in his own station of life, let her make him marry her; but if she's far beneath him she cant expect it: why should she? it wouldnt be for her own happiness. Ask

any lady in London society that has daughters; and she'll tell you the same, except that I tell you straight and she'll tell you crooked. Thats all the difference.

VIVIE.   (Fascinated, gazing at her.) My dear mother: you are a wonderful woman: you are stronger than all England. And are you really and truly not one wee bit doubtful—or—or—ashamed?

MRS WARREN.   Well, of course, dearie, it's only good manners to be ashamed of it: it's expected from a woman. Women have to pretend to feel a great deal that they dont feel. Liz used to be angry with me for plumping out the truth about it. She used to say that when every woman could learn enough from what was going on in the world before her eyes, there was no need to talk about it to her. But then Liz was such a perfect lady! She had the true instinct of it; while I was always a bit of a vulgarian. I used to be so pleased when you sent me your photos to see that you were growing up like Liz: youve just her ladylike, determined way. But I cant stand saying one thing when everyone knows I mean another. Whats the use in such hypocrisy? If people arrange the world that way for women, there's no good pretending it's arranged the other way. No: I never was a bit ashamed really. I consider I had a right to be proud of how we managed everything so respectably, and never had a word against us, and how the girls were so well taken care of. Some of them did very well: one of them married an ambassador. But of course now I darent talk about such things: whatever would they think of us! (She yawns.) Oh dear! I do believe I'm getting sleepy after all. (She stretches herself lazily, thoroughly relieved by her explosion, and placidly ready for her night's rest.)

VIVIE.   I believe it is I who will not be able to sleep now. (She goes to the dresser and lights the candle. Then she extinguishes the lamp, darkening the room a good deal.) Better let in some fresh air before locking up. (She opens the cottage door, and finds that it is a broad moonlight.) What a beautiful night! Look! (She draws aside the curtains of the window. The landscape is seen bathed in the radiance of the harvest moon rising over Blackdown.[2])

MRS WARREN.   (With a perfunctory glance of the scene.) Yes, dear; but take care you dont catch your death of

---

[1]   workhouse infirmary Workhouses, which supported the sick and the indigent, had existed in England since the early seventeenth century. The Poor Law Amendment Act of 1834 limited assistance to the able-bodied poor and made conditions as uncomfortable as possible. Most workhouses had their own infirmaries where rudimentary medical help was provided. Workhouses were phased out in England by about 1930.

[2]   Blackdown Prominent hill about three miles south of Haslemere.

cold from the night air.

VIVIE. (*Contemptuously.*) Nonsense.

MRS WARREN. (*Querulously.*) Oh yes: everything I say
765 is nonsense, according to you.

VIVIE. (*Turning to her quickly.*) No: really that is not so,
mother. You have got completely the better of me
tonight, though I intended it to be the other way. Let us
be good friends now.

770 MRS WARREN. (*Shaking her head a little ruefully.*) So it
has been the other way. But I suppose I must give in to
it. I always got the worst of it from Liz; and now I
suppose it'll be the same with you.

VIVIE. Well, never mind. Come: goodnight, dear old
775 mother. (*She takes her mother in her arms.*)

MRS WARREN. (*Fondly.*) I brought you up well, didnt I,
dearie?

VIVIE. You did.

MRS WARREN. And youll be good to your poor old
780 mother for it, wont you?

VIVIE. I will, dear. (*Kissing her.*) Goodnight.

MRS WARREN. (*With unction.*) Blessings on my own
dearie darling! a mother's blessing!

(*She embraces her daughter protectingly, instinctively
looking upward for divine sanction.*)

ACT 3

(*In the Rectory garden next morning, with the sun shining
from a cloudless sky. The garden wall has a five-barred
wooden gate, wide enough to admit a carriage, in the
middle. Beside the gate hangs a bell on a coiled spring,
communicating with a pull outside. The carriage drive
comes down the middle of the garden and then swerves to
its left, where it ends in a little gravelled circus[1] opposite the
Rectory porch. Beyond the gate is seen the dusty high road,
parallel with the wall, bounded on the farther side by a
strip of turf and an unfenced pine wood. On the lawn,
between the house and the drive, is a clipped yew tree, with
a garden bench in its shade. On the opposite side the garden
is shut in by a box hedge; and there is a sundial on the turf,
with an iron chair near it. A little path leads off through*
the box hedge, behind the sundial.

*Frank, seated on the chair near the sundial, on which
he has placed the morning papers, is reading The Standard.[2]
His father comes from the house, red-eyed and shivery, and
meets Frank's eye with misgiving.*)

FRANK. (*Looking at his watch.*) Half-past eleven. Nice
hour for a rector to come down to breakfast!

REV. S. Dont mock, Frank: dont mock. I am a
little—er—(*Shivering.*)—

5 FRANK. Off color?

REV. S. (*Repudiating the expression.*) No, sir: u n w e l l
this morning. Wheres your mother?

FRANK. Dont be alarmed: she's not here. Gone to town
by the 11.13 with Bessie. She left several messages for
10 you. Do you feel equal to receiving them now, or shall
I wait til you have breakfasted?

REV. S. I h a v e breakfasted, sir. I am surprised at your
mother going to town when we have people staying
with us. Theyll think it very strange.

15 FRANK. Possibly she has considered that. At all events,
if Crofts is going to stay here, and you are going to sit
up every night with him until four, recalling the
incidents of your fiery youth, it is clearly my mother's
duty, as a prudent housekeeper, to go up to the stores
20 and order a barrel of whisky and a few hundred
siphons.[3]

REV. S. I did not observe that Sir George drank
excessively.

FRANK. You were not in a condition to, gov'nor.

25 REV. S. Do you mean to say that I—?

FRANK. (*Calmly.*) I never saw a beneficed clergyman less
sober. The anecdotes you told about your past career
were so awful that I really dont think Praed would have
passed the night under your roof if it hadnt been for the
30 way my mother and he took to one another.

REV. S. Nonsense, sir. I am Sir George Crofts' host. I
must talk to him about something; and he has only one
subject. Where is Mr Praed now?

FRANK. He is driving my mother and Bessie to the
35 station.

---

[1] *circus* Circular driveway.

[2] *The Standard* A leading London daily newspaper, first published
in 1827.

[3] *siphons* Bottles of soda (to mix with the whisky).

REV. S. Is Crofts up yet?

FRANK. Oh, long ago. He hasnt turned a hair: he's in much better practice than you. He has kept it up ever since, probably. He's taken himself off somewhere to smoke.

(*Frank resumes his paper. The parson turns disconsolately towards the gate; then comes back irresolutely.*)

REV. S. Er—Frank.

FRANK. Yes.

REV. S. Do you think the Warrens will expect to be asked here after yesterday afternoon?

FRANK. Theyve been asked already.

REV. S. (*Appalled.*) What!!!

FRANK. Crofts informed us at breakfast that you told him to bring Mrs Warren and Vivie over here today, and to invite them to make this house their home. My mother then found she must go to town by the 11.13 train.

REV. S. (*With despairing vehemence.*) I never gave any such invitation. I never thought of such a thing.

FRANK. (*Compassionately.*) How do you know, gov'nor, what you said and thought last night?

PRAED. (*Coming in through the hedge.*) Good morning.

REV. S. Good morning. I must apologize for not having met you at breakfast. I have a touch of—of—

FRANK. Clergyman's sore throat, Praed. Fortunately not chronic.

PRAED. (*Changing the subject.*) Well, I must say your house is in a charming spot here. Really most charming.

REV. S. Yes: it is indeed. Frank will take you for a walk, Mr Praed, if you like. I'll ask you to excuse me: I must take the opportunity to write my sermon while Mrs Gardner is away and you are all amusing yourself. You wont mind, will you?

PRAED. Certainly not. Dont stand on the slightest ceremony with me.

REV. S. Thank you. I'll—er—er—(*He stammers his way to the porch and vanishes into the house.*)

PRAED. Curious thing it must be writing a sermon every week.

FRANK. Ever so curious, if he did it. He buys em. He's gone for some soda water.

PRAED. My dear boy: I wish you would be more respectful to your father. You know you can be so nice when you like.

FRANK. My dear Praddy: you forget that I have to live with the governor. When two people live together—it dont matter whether theyre father and son or husband and wife or brother and sister—they cant keep up the polite humbug thats so easy for ten minutes on an afternoon call. Now the governor, who unites to many admirable domestic qualities the irresoluteness of a sheep and the pompousness and aggressiveness of a jackass—

PRAED. No, pray, pray, my dear Frank, remember! He is your father.

FRANK. I give him due credit for that. (*Rising and flinging down his paper.*) But just imagine his telling Crofts to bring the Warrens over here! He must have been ever so drunk. You know, my dear Praddy, my mother wouldnt stand Mrs Warren for a moment. Vivie mustnt come here until she has gone back to town.

PRAED. But your mother doesnt know anything about Mrs Warren, does she? (*He picks up the paper and sits down to read it.*)

FRANK. I dont know. Her journey to town looks as if she did. Not that my mother would mind in the ordinary way: she has stuck like a brick to lots of women who had got into trouble. But they were all nice women. Thats what makes the real difference. Mrs Warren, no doubt, has her merits; but she's ever so rowdy; and my mother simply wouldnt put up with her. So—hallo! (*This exclamation is provoked by the reappearance of the clergyman, who comes out of the house in haste and dismay.*)

REV. S. Frank: Mrs Warren and her daughter are coming across the heath with Crofts: I saw them from the study windows. What am I to say about your mother?

FRANK. Stick on your hat and go out and say how delighted you are to see them; and that Frank's in the garden; and that mother and Bessie have been called to the bedside of a sick relative, and were ever so sorry that they couldnt stop; and that you hope Mrs Warren slept well; and—and—say any blessed thing except the truth, and leave the rest to Providence.

REV. S. But how are we to get rid of them afterwards?

FRANK. Theres no time to think of that now. Here! (*He*

bounds into the house.)

REV. S.   He's so impetuous. I dont know what to do with him, Mr Praed.

125 FRANK.   (*Returning with a clerical felt hat, which he claps on his father's head.*) Now: off with you. (*Rushing him through the gate.*) Praed and I'll wait here, to give the thing an unpremeditated air. (*The clergyman, dazed but obedient, hurries off.*)

130 FRANK.   We must get the old girl back to town somehow, Praed. Come! Honestly, dear Praddy, do you like seeing them together?

PRAED.   Oh, why not?

FRANK.   (*His teeth on edge.*) Dont it make your flesh
135 creep ever so little? that wicked old devil, up to every villainy under the sun, I'll swear, and Vivie—ugh!

PRAED.   Hush, pray. Theyre coming.

(*The clergyman and Crofts are seen coming along the road, followed by Mrs Warren and Vivie walking affectionately together.*)

FRANK.   Look: she actually has her arm round the old
140 woman's waist. It's her right arm: she began it. She's gone sentimental, by God! Ugh! ugh! Now do you feel the creeps? (*The clergyman opens the gate; and Mrs Warren and Vivie pass him and stand in the middle of the garden looking at the house. Frank, in an ecstasy of
145 dissimulation, turns gaily to Mrs Warren, exclaiming*) Ever so delighted to see you, Mrs Warren. This quiet old rectory garden becomes you perfectly.

MRS WARREN.   Well, I never! Did you hear that, George? He says I look well in a quiet old rectory
150 garden.

REV. S.   (*Still holding the gate for Crofts who loafs through it, heavily bored.*) You look well everywhere, Mrs Warren.

FRANK.   Bravo, gov'nor! Now look here: lets have a treat
155 before lunch. First lets see the church. Everyone has to do that. It's a regular old thirteenth century church, you know: the gov'nor's ever so fond of it, because he got up a restoration fund and had it completely rebuilt six years ago. Praed will be able to shew its points.

160 PRAED.   (*Rising.*) Certainly, if the restoration has left any to shew.

REV. S.   (*Mooning[1] hospitably at them.*) I shall be pleased, I'm sure, if Sir George and Mrs Warren really care about it.

165 MRS WARREN.   Oh, come along and get it over.

CROFTS.   (*Turning back towards the gate.*) Ive no objection.

REV. S.   Not that way. We go through the fields, if you dont mind. Round here. (*He leads the way by the little
170 path through the box hedge.*)

CROFTS.   Oh, all right. (*He goes with the parson.*)

(*Praed follows with Mrs Warren. Vivie does not stir: she watches them until they have gone, with all the lines of purpose in her face marking it strongly.*)

FRANK.   Aint you coming?

VIVIE.   No. I want to give you a warning, Frank. You were making fun of my mother just now when you said
175 that about the rectory garden. That is barred in the future. Please treat my mother with as much respect as you treat your own.

FRANK.   My dear Viv: she wouldnt appreciate it: the two cases require different treatment. But what on earth has
180 happened to you? Last night we were perfectly agreed as to your mother and her set. This morning I find you attitudinizing sentimentally with your arm round your parent's waist.

VIVIE.   (*Flushing.*) Attitudinizing!

185 FRANK.   That was how it struck me. First time I ever saw you do a second-rate thing.

VIVIE.   (*Controlling herself.*) Yes, Frank: there has been a change; but I dont think it a change for the worse. Yesterday I was a little prig.

190 FRANK.   And today?

VIVIE.   (*Wincing; then looking at him steadily.*) Today I know my mother better than you do.

FRANK.   Heaven forbid!

VIVIE.   What do you mean?

195 FRANK.   Viv: theres a freemasonry among thoroughly immoral people that you know nothing of. Youve too much character. T h a t s the bond between your mother and me: thats why I know her better than youll ever know her.

---

[1] *mooning*   Listlessly, without energy (he has a hangover).

VIVIE.   You are wrong: you know nothing about her. If you knew the circumstances against which my mother had to struggle—

FRANK.   (*Adroitly finishing the sentence for her.*) I should know why she is what she is, shouldnt I? What difference would that make? Circumstances or no circumstances, Viv, you wont be able to stand your mother.

VIVIE.   (*Very angrily.*) Why not?

FRANK.   Because she's an old wretch, Viv. If you ever put your arm round her waist in my presence again, I'll shoot myself there and then as a protest against an exhibition which revolts me.

VIVIE.   Must I choose between dropping your acquaintance and dropping my mother's?

FRANK.   (*Gracefully.*) That would put the old lady at ever such a disadvantage. No, Viv; your infatuated little boy will have to stick to you in any case. But he's all the more anxious that you shouldnt make mistakes. It's no use, Viv: your mother's impossible. She may be a good sort; but she's a bad lot, a very bad lot.

VIVIE.   (*Hotly.*) Frank—! (*He stands his ground. She turns away and sits down on the bench under the yew tree, struggling to recover her self-command. Then she says*) Is she to be deserted by all the world because she's what you call a bad lot? Has she no right to live?

FRANK.   No fear of that, Viv: she wont ever be deserted. (*He sits on the bench beside her.*)

VIVIE.   But I am to desert her, I suppose.

FRANK.   (*Babyishly, lulling her and making love to her with his voice.*) Musnt go live with her. Little family group of mother and daughter wouldnt be a success. Spoil o u r little group.

VIVIE.   (*Falling under the spell.*) What little group?

FRANK.   The babes in the wood: Vivie and little Frank. (*He nestles against her like a weary child.*) Lets go and get covered up with leaves.

VIVIE.   (*Rhythmically, rocking him like a nurse.*) Fast asleep, hand in hand, under the trees.

FRANK.   The wise little girl with her silly little boy.

VIVIE.   The dear little boy with his dowdy little girl.

FRANK.   Ever so peaceful, and relieved from the imbecility of the little boy's father and the questionableness of the little girl's—

VIVIE.   (*Smothering the word against her breast.*) Sh-sh-sh- sh! little girl wants to forget all about her mother. (*They are silent for some moments, rocking one another. Then Vivie wakes up with a shock, exclaiming*) What a pair of fools we are! Come: sit up. Gracious! your hair. (*She smooths it.*) I wonder do all grown up people play in that childish way when nobody is looking. I never did it when I was a child.

FRANK.   Neither did I. You are my first playmate. (*He catches her hand to kiss it, but checks himself to look round first. Very unexpectedly, he sees Crofts emerging from the box hedge.*)[1] Oh damn!

VIVIE.   Why damn, dear?

FRANK.   (*Whispering.*) Sh! Heres this brute Crofts. (*He sits farther away from her with an unconcerned air.*)

CROFTS.   Could I have a few words with you, Miss Vivie?

VIVIE.   Certainly.

CROFTS.   (*To Frank.*) Youll excuse me, Gardner. Theyre waiting for you in the church, if you dont mind.

FRANK.   (*Rising.*) Anything to oblige you, Crofts— except church. If you should happen to want me, Vivvums, ring the gate bell. (*He goes into the house with unruffled suavity.*)

CROFTS.   (*Watching him with a crafty air as he disappears, and speaking to Vivie with an assumption of being on privileged terms with her.*) Pleasant young fellow that, Miss Vivie. Pity he has no money, isnt it?

VIVIE.   Do you think so?

CROFTS.   Well, whats he to do? No profession. No property. Whats he good for?

VIVIE.   I realize his disadvantages, Sir George.

CROFTS.   (*A little taken aback at being so precisely interpreted.*) Oh, it's not that. But while we're in this world, we're in it; and money's money. (*Vivie does not answer.*) Nice day, isnt it?

VIVIE.   (*With scarcely veiled contempt for this effort at conversation.*) Very.

CROFTS.   (*With brutal good humor, as if he liked her pluck.*) Well, thats not what I came to say. (*Sitting down beside her.*) Now listen, Miss Vivie I'm quite aware that I'm not a young lady's man.

VIVIE.   Indeed, Sir George?

---

[1] At this point in the 1898 text Vivie says: "Dont be rude to him, Frank. I particularly want to be polite to him. It will please my mother."

CROFTS.   No; and to tell you the honest truth I dont want to be either. But when I say a thing I mean it; when I feel a sentiment I feel it in earnest; and what I value I pay hard money for. Thats the sort of man I am.

VIVIE.   It does you great credit, I'm sure.

CROFTS.   Oh, I dont mean to praise myself. I have my faults, Heaven knows: no man is more sensible of[1] that than I am. I know I'm not perfect; thats one of the advantages of being a middle-aged man; for I'm not a young man, and I know it. But my code is a simple one, and, I think, a good one. Honor between man and man; fidelity between man and woman; and no cant about this religion or that religion, but an honest belief that things are making for good on the whole.

VIVIE.   (With biting irony.) "A power, not ourselves, that makes for righteousness,"[2] eh?

CROFTS.   (Taking her seriously.) Oh certainly. Not ourselves, of course. You understand what I mean. Well, now as to practical matters. You may have an idea that I have flung my money about; but I havnt: I'm richer today than when I first came into the property. Ive used my knowledge of the world to invest my money in ways that other men have overlooked; and whatever else I may be, I'm a safe man from the money point of view.

VIVIE.   It's very kind of you to tell me all this.

CROFTS.   Oh well, come, Miss Vivie: you neednt pretend you dont see what I'm driving at. I want to settle down with a Lady Crofts. I suppose you think me very blunt, eh?

VIVIE.   Not at all: I am much obliged to you for being so definite and business-like. I quite appreciate the offer: the money, the position, L a d y C r o f t s and so on. But I think I will say no, if you dont mind. I'd rather not. (She rises, and strolls across to the sundial to get out of his immediate neighborhood.)

CROFTS.   (Not at all discouraged, and taking advantage of the additional room left him on the seat to spread himself comfortably, as if a few preliminary refusals were part of the inevitable routine of courtship.) I'm in no hurry. It was only just to let you know in case young Gardner should try to trap you. Leave the question open.

VIVIE.   (Sharply.) My no is final. I wont go back from it.

(Crofts is not impressed. He grins; leans forward with his elbows on his knees to prod with his stick at some unfortunate insect in the grass; and looks cunningly at her. She turns away impatiently.)

CROFTS.   I'm a good deal older than you. Twenty-five years: quarter of a century. I shant live forever; and I'll take care that you shall be well off when I'm gone.

VIVIE.   I am proof against even that inducement, Sir George. Dont you think youd better take your answer? There is not the slightest chance of my altering it.

CROFTS.   (Rising, after a final slash at a daisy, and coming nearer to her.) Well, no matter. I could tell you some things that would change your mind fast enough; but I wont, because I'd rather win you by honest affection. I was a good friend to your mother: ask her whether I wasnt. She'd never have made the money that paid for your education if it hadnt been for my advice and help, not to mention the money I advanced her. There are not many men who would have stood by her as I have. I put not less than £40,000 into it, from first to last.

VIVIE.   (Staring at him.) Do you mean to say you were my mother's business partner?

CROFTS.   Yes. Now just think of all the trouble and the explanations it would save if we were to keep the whole thing in the family, so to speak. Ask your mother whether she'd like to have to explain all her affairs to a perfect stranger.

VIVIE.   I see no difficulty, since I understand that the business is wound up, and the money invested.

CROFTS.   (Stopping short, amazed.) Wound up! Wind up a business thats paying 35 per cent in the worst years! Not likely. Who told you that?

VIVIE.   (Her color quite gone.) Do you mean that it is still—? (She stops abruptly, and puts her hand on the sundial to support herself. Then she gets quickly to the iron chair and sits down.) What business are you talking about?

CROFTS.   Well, the fact is it's not what would be considered exactly a high-class business in my set—the county set, you know—o u r set it will be if you think better of my offer. Not that theres any mystery about it: dont think that. Of course you know by your mother's

---

[1]   sensible of   Aware of.

[2]   A power ... righteousness   Matthew Arnold, Literature and Dogma (1873), chapter 8: "The eternal not ourselves that makes for righteousness."

being in it that it's perfectly straight and honest. Ive known her for many years; and I can say of her that she'd cut off her hands sooner than touch anything that was not what it ought to be. I'll tell you all about it if you like. I dont know whether youve found in travelling how hard it is to find a really comfortable private hotel.

VIVIE. (*Sickened, averting her face.*) Yes: go on.

CROFTS. Well, thats all it is. Your mother has a genius for managing such things. Weve got two in Brussels, one in Ostend, one in Vienna and two in Budapest.[1] Of course there are others besides ourselves in it: but we hold most of the capital; and your mother's indispensable as managing director. Youve noticed, I dare say, that she travels a good deal. But you see you cant mention such things in society. Once let out the word hotel and everybody says you keep a public-house. You wouldnt like people to say that of your mother, would you? Thats why we're so reserved about it. By the way, youll keep it to yourself, wont you? Since its been a secret so long, it had better remain so.

VIVIE. And this is the business you invite me to join you in?

CROFTS. Oh, no. My wife shant be troubled with business. Youll not be in it more than youve always been.

VIVIE. *I* always been! What do you mean?

CROFTS. Only that youve always lived on it. It paid for your education and the dress you have on your back. Dont turn up your nose at business, Miss Vivie; where would your Newnhams and Girtons be without it?

VIVIE. (*Rising, almost beside herself.*) Take care. I know what this business is.

CROFTS. (*Starting, with a suppressed oath.*) Who told you?

VIVIE. Your partner. My mother.

CROFTS. (*Black with rage.*) The old—

VIVIE. Just so.

(*He swallows the epithet and stands for a moment swearing and raging foully to himself. But he knows that his cue is to be sympathetic. He takes refuge in generous indignation.*)

CROFTS. She ought to have had more consideration for you. *I*'d never have told you.

VIVIE. I think you would probably have told me when we were married: it would have been a convenient weapon to break me in with.

CROFTS. (*Quite sincerely.*) I never intended that. On my word as a gentleman I didnt.

(*Vivie wonders at him. Her sense of the irony of his protest cools and braces her. She replies with contemptuous self-possession.*)

VIVIE. It does not matter. I suppose you understand that when we leave here today our acquaintance ceases.

CROFTS. Why? Is it for helping your mother?

VIVIE. My mother was a very poor woman who had no reasonable choice but to do as she did. You were a rich gentleman; and you did the same for the sake of 35 per cent. You are a pretty common sort of scoundrel, I think. That is my opinion of you.

CROFTS. (*After a stare: not at all displeased, and much more at his ease on these frank terms than on their former ceremonious ones.*) Ha! ha! ha! ha! Go it, little missie, go it; it doesnt hurt me and it amuses you. Why the devil shouldnt I invest my money that way? I take the interest on my capital like other people: I hope you dont think I dirty my own hands with the work. Come! you wouldnt refuse the acquaintance of my mother's cousin the Duke of Belgravia[2] because some of the rents he gets are earned in queer ways. You wouldnt cut the Archbishop of Canterbury,[3] I suppose, because the Ecclesiastical Commissioners[4] have a few publicans and sinners among their tenants. Do you remember your Crofts scholarship at Newnham? Well, that was founded by my brother the M.P. He gets his 22 per cent out of a factory with 600 girls in it, and not one of them

---

[1] In the 1898 text the count of brothels is slightly different: two in Brussels, one in Berlin, one in Vienna, and two in Budapest.

[2] *Belgravia* Belgravia was (and is) a fashionable and expensive residential area of London. The title "Duke of Belgravia" is fictitious.

[3] *Archbishop of Canterbury* The Archbishop of Canterbury in office at the time that Shaw was writing *Mrs. Warren's Profession* was Edward White Benson (1829–96), Archbishop from 1882 to his death.

[4] *Ecclesiastical Commissioners* A body established in 1836 to buy, sell, and manage land and property and oversee other business operations for the Church of England. It consisted of leading ecclesiastics, politicians, and judges.

435 getting wages enough to live on. How d'ye suppose they manage when they have no family to fall back on? Ask your mother. And do you expect me to turn my back on 35 per cent when all the rest are pocketing what they can, like sensible men? No such fool! If youre going to

440 pick and choose your acquaintances on moral principles, youd better clear out of this country, unless you want to cut yourself out of all decent society.

VIVIE. (*Conscience stricken*.) You might go on to point out that I myself never asked where the money I spent

445 came from. I believe I am just as bad as you.

CROFTS. (*Greatly reassured*.) Of course you are; and a very good thing too! What harm does it do after all? (*Rallying her jocularly*.) So you dont think me such a scoundrel now you come to think it over. Eh?

450 VIVIE. I have shared profits with you; and I admitted you just now to the familiarity of knowing what I think of you.

CROFTS. (*With serious friendliness*.) To be sure you did. You wont find me a bad sort: I dont go in for being

455 superfine intellectually: but Ive plenty of honest human feeling; and the old Crofts breed comes out in a sort of instinctive hatred of anything low, in which I'm sure youll sympathize with me. Believe me, Miss Vivie, the world isnt such a bad place as the croakers[1] make out. As

460 long as you dont fly openly in the face of society, society doesnt ask any inconvenient questions; and it makes precious short work of the cads who do. There are no secrets better kept than the secrets everybody guesses. In the class of people I can introduce you to, no lady or

465 gentleman would so far forget themselves as to discuss my business affairs or your mother's. No man can offer you a safer position.

VIVIE. (*Studying him curiously*.) I suppose you really think youre getting on famously with me.

470 CROFTS. Well, I hope I may flatter myself that you think better of me than you did at first.

VIVIE. (*Quietly*.)[2] I hardly find you worth thinking about at all now. When I think of the society that tolerates you, and the laws that protect you! when I

475 think of how helpless nine out of ten young girls would

---

[1] *croakers* Those who speaks dismally, forebodingly.

[2] *quietly* The 1898 text specifies that Vivie speaks to Crofts "*almost gently, but with intense conviction.*"

be in the hands of you and my mother! the unmentionable woman and her capitalist bully—

CROFTS. (*Livid*.) Damn you!

VIVIE. You need not. I feel among the damned already.

(*She raises the latch of the gate to open it and go out. He follows her and puts his hand heavily on the top bar to prevent its opening.*)

480 CROFTS. (*Panting with fury*.) Do you think I'll put up with this from you, you young devil?

VIVIE. (*Unmoved*.) Be quiet. Some one will answer the bell. (*Without flinching a step she strikes the bell with the back of her hand. It clangs harshly; and he starts back

485 involuntarily. Almost immediately Frank appears at the porch with his rifle.*)

FRANK. (*With cheerful politeness*.) Will you have the rifle, Viv; or shall I operate?

VIVIE. Frank: have you been listening?

490 FRANK. (*Coming down into the garden*.) Only for the bell, I assure you; so that you shouldnt have to wait. I think I shewed great insight into your character, Crofts..

CROFTS. For two pins I'd take that gun from you and break it across your head.

495 FRANK. (*Stalking him cautiously*.) Pray dont. I'm ever so careless in handling firearms. Sure to be a fatal accident, with a reprimand from the coroner's jury for my negligence.

VIVIE. Put the rifle away, Frank; it's quite unnecessary.

500 FRANK. Quite right, Viv. Much more sportsmanlike to catch him in a trap. (*Crofts, understanding the insult, makes a threatening movement.*) Crofts: there are fifteen cartridges in the magazine here; and I am a dead shot at the present distance and at an object of your size.

505 CROFTS. Oh, you neednt be afraid. I'm not going to touch you.

FRANK. Ever so magnanimous of you under the circumstances! Thank you!

CROFTS. I'll just tell you this before I go. It may interest

510 you, since youre so fond of one another. Allow me, Mr Frank, to introduce you to your half-sister, the eldest daughter of the Reverend Samuel Gardner. Miss Vivie: your half-brother. Good morning. (*He goes out through the gate along the road.*)

515 FRANK. (*After a pause of stupefaction, raising the rifle.*)

Youll testify before the coroner that its an accident, Viv. (*He takes aim at the retreating figure of Crofts. Vivie seizes the muzzle and pulls it round against her breast.*)

VIVIE. Fire now. You may.

520 FRANK. (*Dropping his end of the rifle hastily.*) Stop! take care. (*She lets it go. It falls on the turf.*) Oh, youve given your little boy such a turn. Suppose it had gone off! ugh! (*He sinks on the garden seat overcome.*)

VIVIE. Suppose it had: do you think it would not have
525 been a relief to have some sharp physical pain tearing through me?

FRANK. (*Coaxingly.*) Take it ever so easy, dear Viv. Remember: even if the rifle scared that fellow into telling the truth for the first time in his life, that only
530 makes us the babes in the wood in earnest. (*He holds out his arms to her.*) Come and be covered up with leaves again.

VIVIE. (*With a cry of disgust.*) Ah, not that, not that. You make all my flesh creep.

535 FRANK. Why, whats the matter?

VIVIE. Goodbye. (*She makes for the gate.*)

FRANK. (*Jumping up.*) Hallo! Stop! Viv! Viv! (*She turns in the gateway.*) Where are you going to? Where shall we find you?

540 VIVIE. At Honoria Fraser's chambers, 67 Chancery Lane, for the rest of my life. (*She goes off quickly in the opposite direction to that taken by Crofts.*)

FRANK. But I say—wait dash it! (*He runs after her.*)

ACT 4

(*Honoria Fraser's chambers in Chancery Lane. An office at the top of New Stone Buildings, with a plate-glass window, distempered[1] walls, electric light, and a patent stove.[2] Saturday afternoon. The chimneys of Lincoln's Inn[3] and the western sky beyond are seen through the window. There is a double writing table in the middle of the room, with a* cigar box, ash pans,[4] *and a portable electric reading lamp almost snowed up in heaps of papers and books. This table has knee holes and chairs right and left and is very untidy. The clerk's desk, closed and tidy, with its high stool, is against the wall, near a door communicating with the inner rooms. In the opposite wall is the door leading to the public corridor. Its upper panel is of opaque glass, lettered in black on the outside,* Fraser and Warren. *A baize screen hides the corner between this door and the window.*

Frank, in a fashionable light-colored coaching suit, with his stick, gloves, and white hat in his hands, is pacing up and down the office. Somebody tries the door with a key.)

FRANK. (*Calling.*) Come in. It's not locked.

(*Vivie comes in, in her hat and jacket. She stops and stares at him.*)

VIVIE. (*Sternly.*) What are you doing here?

FRANK. Waiting to see you. Ive been here for hours. Is this the way you attend to your business? (*He puts his hat
5 and stick on the table, and perches himself with a vault on the clerk's stool looking at her with every appearance of being in a specially restless, teasing, flippant mood.*)

VIVIE. Ive been away exactly twenty minutes for a cup of tea. (*She takes off her hat and jacket and hangs them up
10 behind the screen.*) How did you get in?

FRANK. The staff had not left when I arrived. He's gone to play cricket on Primrose Hill.[5] Why dont you employ a woman, and give your sex a chance?

VIVIE. What have you come for?

15 FRANK. (*Springing off the stool and coming close to her.*) Viv: lets go and enjoy the Saturday half-holiday somewhere, like the staff. What do you say to Richmond,[6] and then a music hall,[7] and a jolly supper?

VIVIE. Cant afford it. I shall put in another six hours
20 work before I go to bed.

---

[1] *distempered* Painted.

[2] *patent stove* Open stove.

[3] *Lincoln's Inn* One of four (Lincoln's Inn, Gray's Inn, Inner Temple, Middle Temple) institutions, all located in London, that have exercised the exclusive right since the Middle Ages of admitting barristers (lawyers) to the bar (i.e., to practise law). Lincoln's Inn is located just off Chancery Lane, near to Honoria Fraser's chambers.

[4] *ash pans* I.e., ashtrays.

[5] *Primrose Hill* Parkland area northwest of central London, frequently visited by Shaw.

[6] *Richmond* Town on the Thames, a few miles southwest of central London.

[7] *music hall* Music halls were popular places of entertainment in Victorian England, featuring songs, comedy, dances, and novelty acts.

FRANK.   Cant afford it, cant we? Aha! Look here. (*He takes out a handful of sovereigns and makes them chink.*) Gold, Viv: gold!

VIVIE.   Where did you get it?

25 FRANK.   Gambling, Viv: gambling. Poker.

VIVIE.   Pah! It's meaner than stealing it. No: I'm not coming. (*She sits down to work at the table, with her back to the glass door, and begins turning over the papers.*)

FRANK.   (*Remonstrating piteously.*) But, my dear Viv, I 30 want to talk to you ever so seriously.

VIVIE.   Very well: sit down in Honoria's chair and talk here. I like ten minutes chat after tea. (*He murmurs.*) No use groaning: I'm inexorable. (*He takes the opposite seat disconsolately.*) Pass that cigar box, will you?

35 FRANK.   (*Pushing the cigar box across.*) Nasty womanly habit. Nice men dont do it any longer.

VIVIE.   Yes: they object to the smell in the office; and weve had to take to cigarets. See! (*She opens the box and takes out a cigaret, which she lights. She offers him one; but 40 he shakes his head with a wry face. She settles herself comfortably in her chair, smoking.*) Go ahead.

FRANK.   Well, I want to know what youve done—what arrangements youve made.

VIVIE.   Everything was settled twenty minutes after I 45 arrived here. Honoria has found the business too much for her this year; and she was on the point of sending for me and proposing partnership when I walked in and told her I hadnt a farthing[1] in the world. So I installed myself and packed her off for a fortnight's holiday. 50 What happened at Haslemere when I left?

FRANK.   Nothing at all. I said you had gone to town on particular business.

VIVIE.   Well?

FRANK.   Well, either they were too flabbergasted to say 55 anything, or else Crofts had prepared your mother. Anyhow, she didnt say anything; and Crofts didnt say anything; and Praddy only stared. After tea they got up and went; and Ive not seen them since.

VIVIE.   (*Nodding placidly with one eye on a wreath of 60 smoke.*) Thats all right.

FRANK.   (*Looking round disparagingly.*) Do you intend to stick in this confounded place?

---

[1] *farthing* A bronze coin, the smallest denomination of British currency (one quarter of a penny). The farthing was withdrawn from circulation in 1961.

VIVIE.   (*Blowing the wreath decisively away, and sitting straight up.*) Yes. These two days have given me back all 65 my strength and self-possession. I will never take a holiday again as long as I live.

FRANK.   (*With a very wry face.*) Mps! You look quite happy. And as hard as nails.

VIVIE.   (*Grimly.*) Well for me that I am!

70 FRANK.   (*Rising.*) Look here, Viv: we must have an explanation. We parted the other day under a complete misunderstanding. (*He sits on the table, close to her.*)

VIVIE.   (*Putting away the cigaret.*) Well: clear it up.

FRANK.   You remember what Crofts said?

75 VIVIE.   Yes.

FRANK.   That revelation was supposed to bring about a complete change in the nature of our feeling for one another. It placed us on the footing of brother and sister.

80 VIVIE.   Yes.

FRANK.   Have you ever had a brother?

VIVIE.   No.

FRANK.   Then you dont know what being brother and sister feels like? Now I have lots of sisters; and the 85 fraternal feeling is quite familiar to me. I assure you my feeling for you is not the least in the world like it. The girls will go their way; I will go mine; and we shant care if we never see one another again. Thats brother and sister. But as to you, I cant be easy if I have to pass a 90 week without seeing you. Thats not brother and sister. It's exactly what I felt an hour before Crofts made his revelation. In short, dear Viv, it's love's young dream.

VIVIE.   (*Bitingly.*) The same feeling, Frank, that brought your father to my mother's feet. Is that it?

95 FRANK.   (*So revolted that he slips off the table for a moment.*) I very strongly object, Viv, to have my feelings compared to any which the Reverend Samuel is capable of harboring; and I object still more to a comparison of you to your mother. (*Resuming his perch.*) Besides, I 100 dont believe the story. I have taxed my father with it, and obtained from him what I consider tantamount to a denial.

VIVIE.   What did he say?

FRANK.   He said he was sure there must be some 105 mistake.

VIVIE.   Do you believe him?

FRANK.   I am prepared to take his word as against

Crofts'.

VIVIE. Does it make any difference? I mean in your imagination or conscience; for of course it makes no real difference.

FRANK. (*Shaking his head.*) None whatever to m e.

VIVIE. Nor to me.

FRANK. (*Staring.*) But this is ever so surprising! (*He goes back to his chair.*) I thought our whole relations were altered in your imagination and conscience, as you put it, the moment those words were out of that brute's muzzle.

VIVIE. No: it was not that. I didnt believe him. I only wish I could.

Frank. Eh?

VIVIE. I think brother and sister would be a very suitable relation for us.

FRANK. You really mean that?

VIVIE. Yes. It's the only relation I care for, even if we could afford any other. I mean that.

FRANK. (*Raising his eyebrows like one on whom a new light has dawned, and rising with quite an effusion of chivalrous sentiment.*) My dear Viv: why didnt you say so before? I am ever so sorry for persecuting you. I understand, of course.

VIVIE. (*Puzzled.*) Understand what?

FRANK. Oh, I'm not a fool in the ordinary sense: only in the Scriptural sense of doing all the things the wise man declared to be folly, after trying them himself on the most extensive scale.[1] I see I am no longer Vivvum's little boy. Dont be alarmed: I shall never call you Vivvums again—at least unless you get tired of your new little boy, whoever he may be.

VIVIE. My new little boy!

FRANK. (*With conviction.*) Must be a new little boy. Always happens that way. No other way, in fact.

VIVIE. None that you know of, fortunately for you.

(*Someone knocks at the door.*)

FRANK. My curse upon yon caller, whoe'er he be!

VIVIE. It's Praed. He's going to Italy and wants to say goodbye. I asked him to call this afternoon. Go and let him in.

---

[1] *extensive scale* Perhaps a reference to Solomon's comments on folly throughout the Book of Proverbs.

FRANK. We can continue our conversation after his departure for Italy. I'll stay him out. (*He goes to the door and opens it.*) How are you, Praddy? Delighted to see you. Come in.

(*Praed, dressed for travelling, comes in, in high spirits.*)

PRAED. How do you do, Miss Warren? (*She presses his hand cordially, though a certain sentimentality in his high spirits jars on her.*) I start in an hour from the Holborn Viaduct.[2] I wish I could persuade you to try Italy.

VIVIE. What for?

PRAED. Why, to saturate yourself with beauty and romance, of course.

(*Vivie, with a shudder, turns her chair to the table, as if the work waiting for her there were a support to her. Praed sits opposite to her. Frank places a chair near Vivie, and drops lazily and carelessly into it, talking at her over his shoulder.*)

FRANK. No use, Praddy. Viv is a little Philistine.[3] She is indifferent to my romance, and insensible to my beauty.

VIVIE. Mr Praed: once for all, there is no beauty and no romance in life for me. Life is what it is; and I am prepared to take it as it is.

PRAED. (*Enthusiastically.*) You will not say that if you come with me to Verona and on to Venice. You will cry with delight at living in such a beautiful world.

FRANK. This is most eloquent, Praddy. Keep it up.

PRAED. Oh, I assure you *I* have cried—I shall cry again, I hope—at fifty! At your age, Miss Warren, you would not need to go so far as Verona. Your spirits would absolutely fly up at the mere sight of Ostend. You would be charmed with the gaiety, the vivacity, the happy air of Brussels.

VIVIE. (*Springing up with an exclamation of loathing.*) Agh!

PRAED. (*Rising.*) Whats the matter?

---

[2] *Holborn Viaduct* The Holborn Viaduct opened in London in 1869 as a route for trains over the valley of the Fleet River (which had been covered over since the middle of the eighteenth century).

[3] *Philistine* From the historical Philistines, enemies of the Israelites; the modern sense of the word denotes someone hostile or indifferent to culture and the arts.

FRANK.   (*Rising.*) Hallo, Viv!

VIVIE.   (*To Praed, with deep reproach.*) Can you find no better example of your beauty and romance than Brussels to talk to me about?

PRAED.   (*Puzzled.*) Of course it's very different from Verona. I dont suggest for a moment that—

VIVIE.   (*Bitterly.*) Probably the beauty and romance come to much the same in both places.

PRAED.   (*Completely sobered and much concerned.*) My dear Miss Warren: I—(*Looking inquiringly at Frank.*) Is anything the matter?

FRANK.   She thinks your enthusiasm frivolous, Praddy. She's had ever such a serious call.[1]

VIVIE.   (*Sharply.*) Hold your tongue, Frank. Dont be silly.

FRANK.   (*Sitting down.*) Do you call this good manners, Praed?

PRAED.   (*Anxious and considerate.*) Shall I take him away, Miss Warren? I feel sure we have disturbed you at your work.

VIVIE.   Sit down: I'm not ready to go back to work yet. (*Praed sits.*) You both think I have an attack of nerves. Not a bit of it. But there are two subjects I want dropped, if you dont mind. One of them (*To Frank.*) is love's young dream in any shape or form: the other (*To Praed.*) is the romance and beauty of life, especially Ostend and the gaiety of Brussels. You are welcome to any illusions you have left on these subjects: I have none. If we three are to remain friends, I must be treated as a woman of business, permanently single (*To Frank.*) and permanently unromantic (*To Praed.*).

FRANK.   I shall also remain permanently single until you change your mind. Praddy: change the subject. Be eloquent about something else.

PRAED.   (*Diffidently.*) I'm afraid theres nothing else in the world I c a n talk about. The Gospel of Art is the only one I can preach. I know Miss Warren is a great devotee of the Gospel of Getting On; but we cant discuss that without hurting your feelings, Frank, since you are determined not to get on.

FRANK.   Oh, dont mind my feelings. Give me some improving advice by all means: it does me ever so much good. Have another try to make a successful man of me,

Viv. Come: lets have it all: energy, thrift, foresight, self-respect, character. Dont you hate people who have no character, Viv?

VIVIE.   (*Wincing.*) Oh, stop, stop: let us have no more of that horrible cant. Mr Praed: if there are really only those two gospels in the world, we had better all kill ourselves; for the same taint is in both, through and through.

FRANK.   (*Looking critically at her.*) There is a touch of poetry about you today, Viv, which has hitherto been lacking.

PRAED.   (*Remonstrating.*) My dear Frank: arnt you a little unsympathetic?

VIVIE.   (*Merciless to herself.*) No: it's good for me. It keeps me from being sentimental.

FRANK.   (*Bantering her.*) Checks your strong natural propensity that way, dont it?

VIVIE.   (*Almost hysterically.*) Oh yes: go on: dont spare me. I was sentimental for one moment in my life—beautifully sentimental—by moonlight; and now—

FRANK.   (*Quickly.*) I say, Viv: take care. Dont give yourself away.

VIVIE.   Oh, do you think Mr Praed does not know all about my mother? (*Turning on Praed.*) You had better have told me that morning, Mr Praed. You are very old fashioned in your delicacies, after all.

PRAED.   Surely it is you who are a little old fashioned in your prejudices, Miss Warren. I feel bound to tell you, speaking as an artist, and believing that the most intimate human relationships are far beyond and above the scope of the law, that though I know that your mother is an unmarried woman, I do not respect her the less on that account. I respect her more.

FRANK.   (*Airily.*) Hear! Hear!

VIVIE.   (*Staring at him.*) Is that a l l you know?

PRAED.   Certainly that is all.

VIVIE.   Then you neither of you know anything. Your guesses are innocence itself compared to the truth.

PRAED.   (*Rising, startled and indignant, and preserving his politeness with an effort.*) I hope not. (*More empathetically.*) I hope not, Miss Warren.

FRANK.   (*Whistles.*) Whew!

VIVIE.   You are not making it easy for me to tell you, Mr Praed.

---

[1]   *call* I.e., divine prompting to service.

PRAED.   (*His chivalry drooping before their conviction.*) If there i s anything worse—that is, anything else—are you sure you are right to tell us, Miss Warren?

VIVIE.   I am sure that if I had the courage I should spend the rest of my life in telling everybody—stamping and branding it into them until they all felt their part in its abomination as I feel mine. There is nothing I despise more than the wicked convention that protects these things by forbidding a woman to mention them. And yet I cant tell you. The two infamous words[1] that describe what my mother is are ringing in my ears and struggling on my tongue; but I cant utter them: the shame of them is too horrible for me. (*She buries her face in her hands. The two men, astonished, stare at one another and then at her. She raises her head again desperately and snatches a sheet of paper and a pen.*) Here: let me draft you a prospectus.

FRANK.   Oh, she's mad. Do you hear, Viv? mad. Come! pull yourself together.

VIVIE.   You shall see. (*She writes.*) "Paid up capital: not less than £40,000 standing in the name of Sir George Crofts, Baronet, the chief shareholder. Premises at Brussels, Ostend, Vienna and Budapest. Managing director: Mrs Warren"; and now dont let us forget her qualifications: the two words. (*She writes the words and pushes the paper to them.*) There! Oh no: dont read it: dont! (*She snatches it back and tears it to pieces; then seizes her head in her hands and hides her face on the table.*)

(*Frank, who has watched the writing over her shoulder, and opened his eyes very widely at it, takes a card from his pocket; scribbles the two words on it; and silently hands it to Praed, who reads it with amazement, and hides it hastily in his pocket.*)

FRANK.   (*Whispering tenderly.*) Viv, dear: thats all right. I read what you wrote: so did Praddy. We understand. And we remain, as this leaves us at present, yours ever so devotedly.

PRAED.   We do indeed, Miss Warren. I declare you are the most splendidly courageous woman I ever met.

(*This sentimental compliment braces Vivie. She throws it away from her with an impatient shake, and forces herself to stand up, though not without some support from the table.*)

FRANK.   Dont stir, Viv, if you dont want to. Take it easy.

VIVIE.   Thank you. You can always depend on me for two things: not to cry and not to faint. (*She moves a few steps toward the door of the inner room, and stops close to Praed to say*) I shall need much more courage than that when I tell my mother that we have come to the parting of the ways. Now I must go into the next room for a moment to make myself neat again, if you dont mind.

PRAED.   Shall we go away?

VIVIE.   No: I'll be back presently. Only for a moment. (*She goes into the other room, Praed opening the door for her.*)

PRAED.   What an amazing revelation! I'm extremely disappointed in Crofts: I am indeed.

FRANK.   I'm not in the least. I feel he's perfectly accounted for at last. But what a facer[2] for me, Praddy! I cant marry her now.

PRAED.   (*Sternly.*) Frank! (*The two look at one another, Frank unruffled, Praed deeply indignant.*) Let me tell you, Gardner, that if you desert her now you will behave very despicably.

FRANK.   Good old Praddy! Ever chivalrous! But you mistake: it's not the moral aspect of the case: it's the money aspect. I really cant bring myself to touch the old woman's money now.

PRAED.   And was that what you were going to marry on?

FRANK.   What else? *I* havnt any money, nor the smallest turn for making it. If I married Viv now she would have to support me; and I should cost her more than I am worth.

PRAED.   But surely a clever bright fellow like you can make something by your own brains.

FRANK.   Oh yes, a little. (*He takes out his money again.*) I made all that yesterday in an hour and a half. But I made it in a highly speculative business. No, dear Praddy: even if Bessie and Georgina[3] marry millionaires

---

1   *two infamous words* Having read the page proofs of *Mrs Warren's Profession* in July 1897, actress Ellen Terry asked Shaw what the "two infamous words" were. Shaw replied, "Prostitute and Procuress."

2   *facer* A blow in the face (figuratively); a sudden difficulty.

3   *Bessie and Georgina* Frank's sisters. In the 1898 text Bessie is Jessie, and Frank has other (unnamed) sisters.

335 and the governor dies after cutting them off with a shilling,[1] I shall have only four hundred a year. And he wont die until he's three score and ten.[2] He hasnt originality enough. I shall be on short allowance for the next twenty years. No short allowance for Viv, if I can 340 help it. I withdraw gracefully and leave the field to the guilded youth of England. So thats settled. I shant worry her about it: I'll just send her a little note after we're gone. She'll understand.

PRAED. (*Grasping his hand.*) Good fellow, Frank! I heartily 345 beg your pardon. But must you never see her again?

FRANK.   Never see her again! Hang it all, be reasonable. I shall come along as often as possible, and be her brother. I can n o t understand the absurd consequences you romantic people expect from the most ordinary 350 transactions. (*A knock at the door.*) I wonder who this is. Would you mind opening the door? If it's a client it will look more respectable than if I appeared.

PRAED. Certainly. (*He goes to the door, and opens it. Frank sits down in Vivie's chair to scribble a note.*) My 355 dear Kitty: come in: come in.

(*Mrs Warren comes in, looking apprehensively round for Vivie. She has done her best to make herself matronly and dignified. The brilliant hat is replaced by a sober bonnet, and the gay blouse covered by a costly black silk mantle. She is pitiably anxious and ill at ease: evidently panic-stricken.*)

MRS WARREN. (*To Frank.*) What! Y o u r e here, are you?

FRANK. (*Turning in his chair from his writing, but not* 360 *rising.*) Here, and charmed to see you. You come like a breath of spring.

MRS WARREN. Oh, get out with your nonsense. (*In a low voice.*) Wheres Vivie?

(*Frank points expressively to the door of the inner room, but says nothing.*)

MRS WARREN. (*Sitting down suddenly and almost*

---

[1] *shilling* A shilling was one-twentieth part of £1 in the British currency system prior to decimilization in 1971.

[2] *three score and ten* From Psalms 90.10: "The days of our years are three-score years and ten ..." I.e., the number of years traditionally allotted to human beings.

365 *beginning to cry.*) Praddy: wont she see me, dont you think?

PRAED. My dear Kitty: dont distress yourself. Why should she not?

MRS WARREN. Oh, you never can see why not: youre 370 too innocent.[3] Mr Frank: did she say anything to you?

FRANK. (*Folding his note.*) She m u s t see you, if (*very expressively*) you wait til she comes in.

MRS WARREN. (*Frightened.*) Why shouldnt I wait?

(*Frank looks quizzically at her; puts his note carefully on the ink bottle, so that Vivie cannot fail to find it when next she dips her pen; then rises and devotes his attention to her.*)

FRANK. My dear Mrs Warren: suppose you were a 375 sparrow—ever so tiny and pretty a sparrow hopping in the roadway—and you saw a steam roller coming in your direction, would you wait for it?

MRS WARREN. Oh, dont bother me with your sparrows. What did she run away from the Haslemere like that 380 for?

FRANK. I'm afraid she'll tell you if you rashly await her return.

MRS WARREN. Do you want me to go away?

FRANK. No: I always want you to stay. But I a d v i s e 385 you to go away.

MRS WARREN. What! And never see her again!

FRANK. Precisely.

MRS WARREN. (*Crying again.*) Praddy: dont let him be cruel to me. (*She hastily checks her tears and wipes her* 390 *eyes.*) She'll be so angry if she sees Ive been crying.

FRANK. (*With a touch of real compassion in his airy tenderness.*) You know that Praddy is the soul of kindness, Mrs Warren. Praddy: what do y o u say? Go or stay?

395 PRAED. (*To Mrs Warren.*) I really should be very sorry to cause you unnecessary pain; but I think perhaps you had better not wait. The fact is—(*Vivie is heard at the inner door.*)

FRANK. Sh! Too late. She's coming.

400 MRS WARREN. Dont tell her I was crying. (*Vivie comes in. She stops gravely on seeing Mrs Warren, who greets her with hysterical cheerfulness.*) Well, dearie. So here you are

---

[3] *too innocent* In the 1898 text Praed is "too amiable."

at last.

VIVIE.   I am glad you have come. I want to speak to you.
405   You said you were going, Frank, I think.

FRANK.   Yes. Will you come with me, Mrs Warren? What do you say to a trip to Richmond, and the theatre in the evening? There is safety in Richmond. No steam roller there.

410   VIVIE.   Nonsense, Frank. My mother will stay here.

MRS WARREN.   (*Scared.*) I dont know: perhaps I'd better go. We're disturbing you at your work.

VIVIE.   (*With quiet decision.*) Mr Praed: please take Frank away. Sit down, mother. (*Mrs Warren obeys helplessly.*)

415   PRAED.   Come, Frank. Goodbye, Miss Vivie.

VIVIE.   (*Shaking hands.*) Goodbye. A pleasant trip.

PRAED.   Thank you: thank you. I hope so.

FRANK.   (*To Mrs Warren.*) Goodbye: youd ever so much better have taken my advice. (*He shakes hands with her.*
420   *Then airily to Vivie.*) Byebye, Viv.

VIVIE.   Goodbye. (*He goes out gaily without shaking hands with her.*)

PRAED.   (*Sadly.*) Goodbye, Kitty.

MRS WARREN.   (*Snivelling.*) —oobye!

(*Praed goes. Vivie, composed and extremely grave, sits down in Honoria's chair, and waits for her mother to speak. Mrs Warren, dreading a pause, loses no time in beginning.*)

425   MRS WARREN.   Well, Vivie, what did you go away like that for without saying a word to me? How could you do such a thing! And what have you done to poor George? I wanted him to come with me; but he shuffled out of it. I could see that he was quite afraid of you.
430   Only fancy: he wanted me not to come. As if (*Trembling.*) I should be afraid of you, dearie. (*Vivie's gravity deepens.*) But of course I told him it was all settled and comfortable between us, and that we were on the best of terms. (*She breaks down.*) Vivie: whats the meaning of
435   this? (*She produces a commercial envelope, and fumbles at the enclosure with trembling fingers.*) I got it from the bank this morning.

VIVIE.   It is my month's allowance. They sent it to me as usual the other day. I simply sent it back to be placed to
440   your credit, and asked them to send you the lodgment receipt.[1] In future I shall support myself.

MRS WARREN.   (*Not daring to understand.*) Wasnt it enough? Why didnt you tell me? (*With a cunning gleam in her eye.*) I'll double it: I was intending to double it.
445   Only let me know how much you want.

VIVIE.   You know very well that that has nothing to do with it. From this time I go my own way in my own business and among my own friends. And you will go yours. (*She rises.*) Goodbye.

450   MRS WARREN.   (*Rising, appalled.*) Goodbye?

VIVIE.   Yes: Goodbye. Come: dont let us make a useless scene: you understand perfectly well. Sir George Crofts has told me the whole business.

MRS WARREN.   (*Angrily.*) Silly old—(*She swallows an*
455   *epithet, and turns white at the narrowness of her escape from uttering it.*)

VIVIE.   Just so.

MRS WARREN.   He ought to have his tongue cut out. But I thought it was ended: you said you didnt mind.

460   VIVIE.   (*Steadfastly.*) Excuse me: I d o mind.

MRS WARREN.   But I explained—

VIVIE.   You explained how it came about. You did not tell me that it is still going on. (*She sits.*)

(*Mrs Warren, silenced for a moment, looks forlornly at Vivie, who waits, secretly hoping that the combat is over. But the cunning expression comes back into Mrs Warren's face; and she bends across the table, sly and urgent, half whispering.*)

MRS WARREN.   Vivie: do you know how rich I am?

465   VIVIE.   I have no doubt you are very rich.

MRS WARREN.   But you dont know all that that means: youre too young. It means a new dress every day; it means theatres and balls every night; it means having the pick of all the gentlemen in Europe at your feet; it
470   means a lovely house and plenty of servants; it means the choicest of eating and drinking; it means everything you like, everything you want, everything you can think of. And what are you here? A mere drudge, toiling and moiling[2] early and late for your bare living and two
475   cheap dresses a year. Think over it. (*Soothingly.*) Youre shocked, I know. I can enter into your feelings; and I think they do you credit; but trust me, nobody will

---

[1]   *lodgment receipt*   Deposit receipt.

[2]   *toiling and moiling*   Working extremely hard.

blame you: you may take my word for that. I know what young girls are; and I know youll think better of it when youve turned it over in your mind.

VIVIE.   So thats how it's done, is it? You must have said all that to many a woman, mother, to have it so pat.

MRS WARREN.   (*Passionately.*) What harm am I asking you to do? (*Vivie turns away contemptuously. Mrs Warren continues desperately.*) Vivie: listen to me: you dont understand: youve been taught wrong on purpose: you dont know what the world is really like.

VIVIE.   (*Arrested.*) Taught wrong on purpose! What do you mean?

MRS WARREN.   I mean that youre throwing away all your chances for nothing. You think that people are what they pretend to be: that the way you were taught at school and college to think right and proper is the way things really are. But it's not: it's all only a pretence, to keep the cowardly slavish common run of people quiet. Do you want to find that out, like other women, at forty when youve thrown yourself away and lost your chances; or wont you take it in good time now from your own mother, that loves you and swears to you that it's truth: gospel truth? (*Urgently.*) Vivie: the big people, the clever people, the managing people, all know it. They do as I do, and think what I think. I know plenty of them. I know them to speak to, to introduce you to, to make friends of for you. I dont mean anything wrong: thats what you dont understand: your head is full of ignorant ideas about me. What do the people that taught you know about life or about people like me? When did they ever meet me, or speak to me, or let anyone tell them about me? the fools! Would they ever have done anything for you if I hadnt paid them? Havnt I told you that I want you to be respectable? Havnt I brought you up to be respectable? And how can you keep it up without my money and my influence and Lizzie's friends? Cant you see that youre cutting your own throat as well as breaking my heart in turning your back on me?

VIVIE.   I recognize the Crofts philosophy of life, mother. I heard it all from him that day at the Gardners'.

MRS WARREN.   You think I want to force that played-out old sot on you! I dont, Vivie: on my oath I dont.

VIVIE.   It would not matter if you did: you would not succeed. (*Mrs Warren winces, deeply hurt by the implied indifference towards her affectionate intention. Vivie, neither understanding this nor concerning herself about it, goes on calmly.*) Mother: you dont at all know the sort of person I am. I dont object to Crofts more than to any other coarsely built man of his class. To tell you the truth, I rather admire him for being strongminded enough to enjoy himself in his own way and make plenty of money instead of living the usual shooting, hunting, dining-out, tailoring, loafing life of his set merely because all the rest do it. And I'm perfectly aware that if I'd been in the same circumstances as my aunt Liz, I'd have done exactly what she did. I dont think I'm more prejudiced or straightlaced than you: I think I'm less. I'm certain I'm less sentimental. I know very well that fashionable morality is all a pretence, and that if I took your money and devoted the rest of my life to spending it fashionably, I might be as worthless and vicious and the silliest woman could possibly want to be without having a word said to me about it. But I dont want to be worthless. I shouldnt enjoy trotting about the park to advertise my dressmaker and carriage builder, or being bored at the opera to shew off a shopwindowful of diamonds.

MRS WARREN.   (*Bewildered.*) But—

VIVIE.   Wait a moment. Ive not done. Tell me why you continue your business now that you are independent of it. Your sister, you told me, has left all that behind her. Why dont you do the same?

MRS WARREN.   Oh, it's all very easy for Liz: she likes good society, and has the air of being a lady. Imagine m e in a cathedral town! Why, the very rooks in the trees would find me out even if I could stand the dulness of it. I must have work and excitement, or I should go melancholy mad. And what else is there for me to do? The life suits me: I'm fit for it and not for anything else. If I didnt do it, somebody else would; so I dont do any real harm by it. And then it brings in money; and I like making money. No: it's no use: I cant give it up—not for anybody. But what need you know about it? I'll never mention it. I'll keep Crofts away. I'll not trouble you much: you see I have to be constantly running about from one place to another. Youll be quit of me altogether when I die.

VIVIE.   No: I am my mother's daughter. I am like you: I must have work, and must make more money than I spend. But my work is not your work, and my way not your way. We must part. It will not make much difference to us: instead of meeting one another for perhaps a few months in twenty years, we shall never meet: thats all.

MRS WARREN. (*Her voice stifled in tears.*) Vivie: I meant to have been more with you: I did indeed.

VIVIE. It's no use, mother: I am not to be changed by a few cheap tears and entreaties any more than you are, I daresay.

MRS WARREN. (*Wildly.*) Oh, you call a mother's tears cheap.

VIVIE. They cost you nothing; and you ask me to give you the peace and quietness of my whole life in exchange for them. What use would my company be to you if you could get it? What have we two in common that could make either of us happy together?

MRS WARREN. (*Lapsing recklessly into her dialect.*) We're mother and daughter. I want my daughter. Ive a right to you. Who is to care for me when I'm old? Plenty of girls have taken to me like daughters and cried at leaving me; but I let them all go because I had you to look forward to. I kept myself lonely for you. Youve no right to turn on me now and refuse to do your duty as daughter.

VIVIE. (*Jarred and antagonized by the echo of the slums in her mother's voice.*) My duty as a daughter! I thought we should come to that presently. Now once for all, mother, you want a daughter and Frank wants a wife. I dont want a mother; and I dont want a husband. I have spared neither Frank nor myself in sending him about his business. Do you think I will spare y o u?

MRS WARREN. (*Violently.*) Oh, I know the sort you are: no mercy for yourself or anyone else. *I* know. My experience has done that for me anyhow: I can tell the pious, canting, hard, selfish woman when I meet her. Well, keep yourself to yourself: *I* dont want you. But listen to this. Do you now what I would do with you if you were a baby again? aye, as sure as theres a Heaven above us.

VIVIE. Strangle me, perhaps.

MRS WARREN. No: I'd bring you up to be a real daughter to me, and not what you are now, with your pride and your prejudices and the college education you stole from me: yes, stole: deny it if you can: what was it but stealing? I'd bring you up in my own house, I would.

VIVIE. (*Quietly.*) In one of your own houses.

MRS WARREN. (*Screaming.*) Listen to her! listen to how she spits on her mother's grey hairs! Oh, may you live to have your own daughter tear and trample on you as you have trampled on me. And you will: you will. No woman ever had luck with a mother's curse on her.

VIVIE. I wish you wouldnt rant, mother. It only hardens me. Come: I suppose I am the only young woman you ever had in your power that you did good to. Dont spoil it all now.

MRS WARREN. Yes, Heaven forgive me, it's true; and you are the only one that ever turned on me. Oh, the injustice of it! the injustice! the injustice! I always wanted to be a good woman. I tried honest work; and I was slave-driven until I cursed the day I ever heard of honest work. I was a good mother; and because I made my daughter a good woman she turns me out as if I was a leper. Oh, if I only had my life to live over again! I'd talk to that lying clergyman in the school. From this time forth, so help me Heaven in my last hour, I'll do wrong and nothing but wrong. And I'll prosper on it.

VIVIE. Yes: it's better to choose your line and go through with it. If I had been you, mother, I might have done as you did: but I should not have lived one life and believed in another. You are a conventional woman at heart. That is why I am bidding you goodbye now. I am right, am I not?

MRS WARREN. (*Taken aback.*) Right to throw away all my money?

VIVIE. No: right to get rid of you! I should be a fool not to. Isnt that so?

MRS WARREN. (*Sulkily.*) Oh well, yes, if you come to that, I suppose you are. But Lord help the world if everybody took to doing the right thing! And now I'd better go than stay where I'm not wanted. (*She turns to the door.*)

VIVIE. (*Kindly.*) Wont you shake hands?

MRS WARREN. (*After looking at her fiercely for a moment with a savage impulse to strike her.*) No, thank you. Goodbye.

VIVIE. (*Matter-of-factly.*) Goodbye. (*Mrs Warren goes out, slamming the door behind her. The strain on Vivie's face relaxes; her grave expression breaks up into one of joyous content; her breath goes out in a half sob, half laugh* of intense relief. *She goes buoyantly to her place at the writing-table; pushes the electric lamp out of the way; pulls over a great sheaf of papers; and is in the act of dipping her pen in the ink when she finds Frank's note. She opens it unconcernedly and reads it quickly, giving a little laugh at some quaint turn of expression in it.*) And goodbye, Frank. (*She tears the note up and tosses the pieces into the waste paper basket without a second thought. Then she goes at her work with a plunge, and soon becomes absorbed in its figures.*)

—1898, 1930

Joseph Conrad
1857 – 1924

Joseph Conrad has long been recognized as one of the twentieth century's greatest writers of fiction in English—an extraordinary fact given that English was his third language, and that a significant portion of his early adult life was spent in nautical, rather than literary, pursuits. He did not become a British citizen until he was almost 30 years old, and did not begin his career as an author until he was almost 40. Yet in spite of his status as an outsider to the vibrant literary circles of late nineteenth-century British society, Conrad soon established himself as one of the finest literary craftsmen of his

age. Initially many regarded him as an able seaman who simply turned his colorful experiences into material for his novels; it soon became evident that Joseph Conrad was an exceptional writer whose work demonstrated a careful and deliberate attention to political, psychological, and social nuances.

Joseph Conrad was born Jozef Teodor Konrad Nalecz Korzeniowski on 3 December 1857, in Poland (then under Russian rule). His parents, Apollo and Evalina, were members of the educated, landed gentry who opposed Czarist Russian control in Poland. Apollo was arrested for revolutionary conspiracy, and, in 1862, the family was exiled to Vologda in northern Russia and forced to endure years of hardship and illness; Conrad's mother died in 1865 and his father in 1868.

Following the death of his parents, Conrad came under the guardianship of his maternal uncle in Kraków, Poland; he spent much of the next few years reading translations of Shakespeare, Dickens, and Victor Hugo. Yet Conrad seemed to dislike school life; he was bored and restless. At the age of fifteen, he expressed his desire to go to sea. He spent the next two years pressing his family for permission against strong opposition. His pleas were eventually heard, and in 1874, nearing his seventeenth birthday, Conrad traveled to Marseilles and joined the French merchant navy.

From 1874 to 1877, Conrad made a number of voyages to Martinique and the West Indies aboard French ships, where he quickly acquired great skill as a sailor. During these years he spent time engaged in illicit gunrunning on behalf of the Carlist Royalists in Spain. In 1878, due to huge debts acquired through smuggling and gambling, Conrad shot himself in the chest. He long claimed that this injury was the result of a duel, rather than what seems to have been a suicide attempt. Whatever the case, Conrad recovered from his injury and escaped his creditors by joining the British merchant navy. Knowing just a few words in English, Conrad began to learn the language in voyages between the ports of Lowescroft and Newcastle, aboard a coal schooner.

Over the next sixteen years, Conrad traveled to Australia, South America, India, Borneo, and the South Pacific in the service of the British merchant navy. In 1886, he achieved several important milestones: he received his certificate as a master mariner, became a British citizen, and changed his name to Joseph Conrad. In 1888, Conrad was given his only sea command as captain of the *Otago*; he spent the next 15 months journeying from Bangkok to Singapore, about the Malay Archipelago, and to Australia and Mauritius. Conrad would later use his experiences aboard the *Otago* as inspiration for *The Secret Sharer*. In 1890 he took a steamboat up the Congo River to take command of a

Belgian steamer—a journey that was an unmitigated disaster and yet would form the template for his best known work, *Heart of Darkness*. It was also while in the Congo that Conrad contracted malaria, the effects of which would plague him for years. In ill health and with his interest in writing increasing steadily, Conrad retired from seafaring and settled permanently in England in 1894; his first published novel was *Almayer's Folly* in 1895. He would dedicate the rest of his life to literary pursuits, writing prolifically until his death of a heart attack, near Canterbury, in 1924.

Conrad wrote 13 novels, two volumes of memoirs, and 28 short stories, but suffered from persistent doubts as to the quality of his creative output and from constant financial pressure. His experiences at sea form the background for many of his stories; his major interest is the profound moral and psychological ambiguities of the human experience. In *Lord Jim* (1900) he explores the concept of personal honor by presenting the hero's history as a life spent in atonement for an act of cowardice as a young marine officer. In *The Nigger of the "Narcissus"* (1897), Conrad shows how a single black seaman's plight affects the morale of an entire ship's crew. In *Heart of Darkness* (1902), Conrad revisits his own terrifying journey to the Congo as he explores the extent of human corruptibility.

In his later works, Conrad shifted his attention away from the sea and toward the complexities of politics. With *Nostromo* (1904), he explored the effects of politics and "material interests" on human relationships and the futility of human attempts at change. *The Secret Agent* (1906) concerns an anarchist bomb plot in London, and *Under Western Eyes* (1911) presents a story of betrayal and a search for redemption amidst antigovernment violence in Czarist Russia.

Conrad has long been considered a master of English prose—an extraordinary feat for a man who was twenty-one years of age before he began speaking a word of English. In part, however, his distanced relationship with the language may have helped free him to make English prose do new things. Words are carefully chosen for their evocative and symbolic functions and his often poetic prose style seems to float free of local idiosyncrasies.

Like much of Conrad's work, *The Secret Sharer* (1912) reflects his own personal experience—in this case, his experience as a new captain aboard the *Otago,* when he felt like an interloper aboard his own ship. The story features a *doppelgänger,* in the character of Leggatt; in addition to being a real character and contributor to the events of the story, Leggatt functions as the Captain's second self or alter ego. The work may be best viewed in the context of the late nineteenth- and early twentieth-century preoccupation with the unconscious and "true self." Like much of Conrad's work, it displays a tendency to regard society and the individual in terms of dualisms: good and evil, savagery and civilization, emotion and intellect. But whereas for many others of the time such dualisms fostered simplistic habits of thought, in Conrad's work they give rise to complexity and ambiguity.

In the "Preface" to *The Nigger of the "Narcissus,"* Conrad outlined his aims as an artist. The "Preface" was written a few months after finishing the work itself, and first appeared in the 1898 version of the book, at a time when Conrad had fully dedicated himself to his writing and found himself (in his own words) "done with the sea."

⌘ ⌘ ⌘

An Outpost of Progress

I

There were two white men in charge of the trading station. Kayerts, the chief, was short and fat; Carlier, the assistant, was tall, with a large head and a very broad trunk perched upon a long pair of thin legs. The third man on the staff was a Sierra Leone nigger,[1] who maintained that his name was Henry Price. However, for some reason or other, the natives down the river had given him the name of Makola, and it stuck to him through all his wanderings about the country. He spoke English and French with a warbling accent, wrote a beautiful hand, understood bookkeeping, and cherished in his innermost heart the worship of evil spirits. His wife was a negress from Loanda,[2] very large and very noisy. Three children rolled about in sunshine before the door of his low, shed-like dwelling. Makola, taciturn and impenetrable, despised the two white men. He had charge of a small clay storehouse with a dried-grass roof, and pretended to keep a correct account of beads, cotton cloth, red kerchiefs, brass wire, and other trade goods it contained. Besides the storehouse and Makola's hut, there was only one large building in the cleared ground of the station. It was built neatly of reeds, with a verandah on all the four sides. There were three rooms in it. The one in the middle was the living-room, and had two rough tables and a few stools in it. The other two were the bedrooms for the white men. Each had a bedstead and a mosquito net for all furniture. The plank floor was littered with the belongings of the white men; open half-empty boxes, torn wearing apparel, old boots; all the things dirty, and all the things broken, that accumulate mysteriously round untidy men. There was also another dwelling-place some distance away from the buildings. In it, under a tall cross much out of the perpendicular, slept the man who had seen the beginning of all this; who had planned and had watched the construction of this outpost of progress. He had been, at home, an unsuccessful painter who, weary of pursuing fame on an empty stomach, had gone out there

through high protections. He had been the first chief of that station. Makola had watched the energetic artist die of fever in the just finished house with his usual kind of "I told you so" indifference. Then, for a time, he dwelt alone with his family, his account books, and the Evil Spirit that rules the lands under the equator. He got on very well with his god. Perhaps he had propitiated him by a promise of more white men to play with, by and by. At any rate the director of the Great Trading Company, coming up in a steamer that resembled an enormous sardine box with a flat-roofed shed erected on it, found the station in good order, and Makola as usual quietly diligent. The director had the cross put up over the first agent's grave, and appointed Kayerts to the post. Carlier was told off as second in charge. The director was a man ruthless and efficient, who at times, but very imperceptibly, indulged in grim humour. He made a speech to Kayerts and Carlier, pointing out to them the promising aspect of their station. The nearest trading-post was about three hundred miles away. It was an exceptional opportunity for them to distinguish themselves and to earn percentages on the trade. This appointment was a favour done to beginners. Kayerts was moved almost to tears by his director's kindness. He would, he said, by doing his best, try to justify the flattering confidence, &c, &c. Kayerts had been in the Administration of the Telegraphs, and knew how to express himself correctly. Carlier, an ex-non-commissioned officer of cavalry in an army guaranteed from harm by several European Powers, was less impressed. If there were commissions to get, so much the better; and, trailing a sulky glance over the river, the forests, the impenetrable bush that seemed to cut off the station from the rest of the world, he muttered between his teeth, "We shall see, very soon."

Next day, some bales of cotton goods and a few cases of provisions having been thrown on shore, the sardine-box steamer went off, not to return for another six months. On the deck the director touched his cap to the two agents, who stood on the bank waving their hats, and turning to an old servant of the Company on his passage to headquarters, said, "Look at those two imbeciles. They must be mad at home to send me such specimens. I told those fellows to plant a vegetable garden, build new storehouses and fences, and construct

---

[1] *nigger* The use of derogatory racial terms in literature remained common until the 1930s.

[2] *Loanda* Capital of Angola (also Luanda).

a landing-stage. I bet nothing will be done! They won't know how to begin. I always thought the station on this river useless, and they just fit the station!"

"They will form themselves there," said the old stager with a quiet smile.

"At any rate, I am rid of them for six months," retorted the director.

The two men watched the steamer round the bend, then, ascending arm in arm the slope of the bank, returned to the station. They had been in this vast and dark country only a very short time, and as yet always in the midst of other white men, under the eye and guidance of their superiors. And now, dull as they were to the subtle influences of surroundings, they felt themselves very much alone, when suddenly left unassisted to face the wilderness; a wilderness rendered more strange, more incomprehensible by the mysterious glimpses of the vigorous life it contained. They were two perfectly insignificant and incapable individuals, whose existence is only rendered possible through the high organization of civilized crowds. Few men realize that their life, the very essence of their character, their capabilities and their audacities, are only the expression of their belief in the safety of their surroundings. The courage, the composure, the confidence; the emotions and principles; every great and every insignificant thought belongs not to the individual but to the crowd: to the crowd that believes blindly in the irresistible force of its institutions and of its morals, in the power of its police and of its opinion. But the contact with pure unmitigated savagery, with primitive nature and primitive man, brings sudden and profound trouble into the heart. To the sentiment of being alone of one's kind, to the clear perception of the loneliness of one's thoughts, of one's sensations—to the negation of the habitual, which is safe, there is added the affirmation of the unusual, which is dangerous; a suggestion of things vague, uncontrollable, and repulsive, whose discomposing intrusion excites the imagination and tries the civilized nerves of the foolish and the wise alike.

Kayerts and Carlier walked arm in arm, drawing close to one another as children do in the dark; and they had the same, not altogether unpleasant, sense of danger which one half suspects to be imaginary. They chatted persistently in familiar tones. "Our station is prettily situated," said one. The other assented with enthusiasm, enlarging volubly on the beauties of the situation. Then they passed near the grave. "Poor devil!" said Kayerts. "He died of fever, didn't he?" muttered Carlier, stopping short. "Why," retorted Kayerts, with indignation, "I've been told that the fellow exposed himself recklessly to the sun. The climate here, everybody says, is not at all worse than at home, as long as you keep out of the sun. Do you hear that, Carlier? I am chief here, and my orders are that you should not expose yourself to the sun!" He assumed his superiority jocularly, but his meaning was serious. The idea that he would, perhaps, have to bury Carlier and remain alone, gave him an inward shiver. He felt suddenly that this Carlier was more precious to him here, in the centre of Africa, than a brother could be anywhere else. Carlier, entering into the spirit of the thing, made a military salute and answered in a brisk tone, "Your orders shall be attended to, chief!" Then he burst out laughing, slapped Kayerts on the back and shouted, "We shall let life run easily here! Just sit still and gather in the ivory those savages will bring. This country has its good points, after all!" They both laughed loudly while Carlier thought: That poor Kayerts; he is so fat and unhealthy. It would be awful if I had to bury him here. He is a man I respect." … Before they reached the verandah of their house they called one another "my dear fellow."

The first day they were very active, pottering about with hammers and nails and red calico, to put up curtains, make their house habitable and pretty; resolved to settle down comfortably to their new life. For them an impossible task. To grapple effectually with even purely material problems requires more serenity of mind and more lofty courage than people generally imagine. No two beings could have been more unfitted for such a struggle. Society, not from any tenderness, but because of its strange needs, had taken care of those two men, forbidding them all independent thought, all initiative, all departure from routine; and forbidding it under pain of death. They could only live on condition of being machines. And now, released from the fostering care of men with pens behind the ears, or of men with gold lace on the sleeves, they were like those lifelong prisoners who, liberated after many years, do not know what use to make of their freedom. They did not know what use to make of their faculties, being both, through want of practice, incapable of independent thought.

At the end of two months Kayerts often would say, "If it was not for my Melie, you wouldn't catch me here." Melie was his daughter. He had thrown up his post in the Administration of the Telegraphs, though he had been for seventeen years perfectly happy there, to earn a dowry for his girl. His wife was dead, and the child was being brought up by his sisters. He regretted the streets, the pavements, the cafés, his friends of many years; all the things he used to see, day after day; all the thoughts suggested by familiar things—the thoughts effortless, monotonous, and soothing of a Government clerk; he regretted all the gossip, the small enmities, the mild venom, and the little jokes of Government offices. "If I had had a decent brother-in-law," Carlier would remark, "a fellow with a heart, I would not be here." He had left the army and had made himself so obnoxious to his family by his laziness and impudence, that an exasperated brother-in-law had made superhuman efforts to procure him an appointment in the Company as a second-class agent. Having not a penny in the world he was compelled to accept this means of livelihood as soon as it became quite clear to him that there was nothing more to squeeze out of his relations. He, like Kayerts, regretted his old life. He regretted the clink of sabre and spurs on a fine afternoon, the barrack-room witticisms, the girls of garrison towns; but, besides, he had also a sense of grievance. He was evidently a much ill-used man. This made him moody, at times. But the two men got on well together in the fellowship of their stupidity and laziness. Together they did nothing, absolutely nothing, and enjoyed the sense of idleness for which they were paid. And in time they came to feel something resembling affection for one another.

They lived like blind men in a large room, aware only of what came in contact with them (and of that only imperfectly), but unable to see the general aspect of things. The river, the forest, all the great land throbbing with life, were like a great emptiness. Even the brilliant sunshine disclosed nothing intelligible. Things appeared and disappeared before their eyes in an unconnected and aimless kind of way. The river seemed to come from nowhere and flow nowhither. It flowed through a void. Out of that void, at times, came canoes, and men with spears in their hands would suddenly crowd the yard of the station. They were naked, glossy black, ornamented with snowy shells and glistening brass wire, perfect of limb. They made an uncouth babbling noise when they spoke, moved in a stately manner, and sent quick, wild glances out of their startled, never-resting eyes. Those warriors would squat in long rows, four or more deep, before the verandah, while their chiefs bargained for hours with Makola over an elephant tusk. Kayerts sat on his chair and looked down on the proceedings, understanding nothing. He stared at them with his round blue eyes, called out to Carlier, "Here, look! look at that fellow there—and that other one, to the left. Did you ever see such a face? Oh, the funny brute!"

Carlier, smoking native tobacco in a short wooden pipe, would swagger up twirling his moustaches, and surveying the warriors with haughty indulgence, would say—

"Fine animals. Brought any bone? Yes? It's not any too soon. Look at the muscles of that fellow—third from the end. I wouldn't care to get a punch on the nose from him. Fine arms, but legs no good below the knee. Couldn't make cavalry men of them." And after glancing down complacently at his own shanks, he always concluded: "Pah! Don't they stink! You, Makola! Take that herd over to the fetish" (the storehouse was in every station called the fetish, perhaps because of the spirit of civilization it contained) "and give them up some of the rubbish you keep there. I'd rather see it full of bone than full of rags."

Kayerts approved.

"Yes, yes! Go and finish that palaver[1] over there, Mr. Makola. I will come round when you are ready, to weigh the tusk. We must be careful." Then turning to his companion: "This is the tribe that lives down the river; they are rather aromatic. I remember, they had been once before here. D'ye hear that row? What a fellow has got to put up with in this dog of a country! My head is split."

Such profitable visits were rare. For days the two pioneers of trade and progress would look on their empty courtyard in the vibrating brilliance of vertical sunshine. Below the high bank, the silent river flowed on glittering and steady. On the sands in the middle of

---

[1]   *palaver* Discussion (particularly one concerning matters of trade).

the stream, hippos and alligators sunned themselves side by side. And stretching away in all directions, surrounding the insignificant cleared spot of the trading post, immense forests, hiding fateful complications of fantastic life, lay in the eloquent silence of mute greatness. The two men understood nothing, cared for nothing but for the passage of days that separated them from the steamer's return. Their predecessor had left some torn books. They took up these wrecks of novels, and, as they had never read anything of the kind before, they were surprised and amused. Then during long days there were interminable and silly discussions about plots and personages. In the centre of Africa they made acquaintance of Richelieu and of d'Artagnan, of Hawk's Eye and of Father Goriot,[1] and of many other people. All these imaginary personages became subjects for gossip as if they had been living friends. They discounted their virtues, suspected their motives, decried their successes; were scandalized at their duplicity or were doubtful about their courage. The accounts of crimes filled them with indignation, while tender or pathetic passages moved them deeply. Carlier cleared his throat and said in a soldierly voice, "What nonsense!" Kayerts, his round eyes suffused with tears, his fat cheeks quivering, rubbed his bald head, and declared, "This is a splendid book. I had no idea there were such clever fellows in the world." They also found some old copies of a home paper. That print discussed what it was pleased to call "Our Colonial Expansion" in high-flown language. It spoke much of the rights and duties of civilization, of the sacredness of the civilizing work, and extolled the merits of those who went about bringing light, and faith and commerce to the dark places of the earth. Carlier and Kayerts read, wondered, and began to think better of themselves. Carlier said one evening, waving his hand about, "In a hundred years, there will be perhaps a town here. Quays, and warehouses, and barracks, and—and— billiard-rooms. Civilization, my boy, and virtue—and all. And then, chaps will read that two good fellows, Kayerts and Carlier, were the first civilized men to live

in this very spot!" Kayerts nodded, "Yes, it is a consolation to think of that." They seemed to forget their dead predecessor; but, early one day, Carlier went out and replanted the cross firmly. "It used to make me squint whenever I walked that way," he explained to Kayerts over the morning coffee. "It made me squint, leaning over so much. So I just planted it upright. And solid, I promise you! I suspended myself with both hands to the cross-piece. Not a move. Oh, I did that properly."

At times Gobila came to see them. Gobila was the chief of the neighbouring villages. He was a gray-headed savage, thin and black, with a white cloth round his loins and a mangy panther skin hanging over his back. He came up with long strides of his skeleton legs, swinging a staff as tall as himself, and, entering the common room of the station, would squat on his heels to the left of the door. There he sat, watching Kayerts, and now and then making a speech which the other did not understand. Kayerts, without interrupting his occupation, would from time to time say in a friendly manner: "How goes it, you old image?" and they would smile at one another. The two whites had a liking for that old and incomprehensible creature, and called him Father Gobila. Gobila's manner was paternal, and he seemed really to love all white men. They all appeared to him very young, indistinguishably alike (except for stature), and he knew that they were all brothers, and also immortal. The death of the artist, who was the first white man whom he knew intimately, did not disturb this belief, because he was firmly convinced that the white stranger had pretended to die and got himself buried for some mysterious purpose of his own, into which it was useless to inquire. Perhaps it was his way of going home to his own country? At any rate, these were his brothers, and he transferred his absurd affection to them. They returned it in a way. Carlier slapped him on the back, and recklessly struck off matches for his amusement. Kayerts was always ready to let him have a sniff at the ammonia bottle. In short, they behaved just like that other white creature that had hidden itself in a hole in the ground. Gobila considered them attentively. Perhaps they were the same being with the other—or one of them was. He couldn't decide—clear up that mystery; but he remained always very friendly. In consequence of that friendship the women of Gobila's

---

[1] *of … Goriot* Cardinal Richelieu and d'Artagnan appear as characters in Alexandre Dumas' *The Three Musketeers* (1844); Hawkeye is a character in James Fenimore Cooper's "Leatherstocking Novels" (1823–41); Father Goriot is the protagonist in Honoré de Balzac's 1834 novel *Père Goriot*.

village walked in single file through the reedy grass, bringing every morning to the station, fowls, and sweet potatoes, and palm wine, and sometimes a goat. The Company never provisions the stations fully, and the agents required those local supplies to live. They had them through the good-will of Gobila, and lived well. Now and then one of them had a bout of fever, and the other nursed him with gentle devotion. They did not think much of it. It left them weaker, and their appearance changed for the worse. Carlier was hollow-eyed and irritable. Kayerts showed a drawn, flabby face above the rotundity of his stomach, which gave him a weird aspect. But being constantly together, they did not notice the change that took place gradually in their appearance, and also in their dispositions. Five months passed in that way.

Then, one morning, as Kayerts and Carlier, lounging in their chairs under the verandah, talked about the approaching visit of the steamer, a knot of armed men came out of the forest and advanced towards the station. They were strangers to that part of the country. They were tall, slight, draped classically from neck to heel in blue fringed cloths, and carried percussion muskets over their bare right shoulders. Makola showed signs of excitement, and ran out of the storehouse (where he spent all his days) to meet these visitors. They came into the courtyard and looked about them with steady, scornful glances. Their leader, a powerful and determined-looking negro with bloodshot eyes, stood in front of the verandah and made a long speech. He gesticulated much, and ceased very suddenly.

There was something in his intonation, in the sounds of the long sentences he used, that startled the two whites. It was like a reminiscence of something not exactly familiar, and yet resembling the speech of civilized men. It sounded like one of those impossible languages which sometimes we hear in our dreams.

"What lingo is that?" said the amazed Carlier. "In the first moment I fancied the fellow was going to speak French. Anyway, it is a different kind of gibberish to what we ever heard."

"Yes," replied Kayerts. "Hey, Makola, what does he say? Where do they come from? Who are they?"

But Makola, who seemed to be standing on hot bricks, answered hurriedly, "I don't know. They come from very far. Perhaps Mrs. Price will understand. They are perhaps bad men."

The leader, after waiting for a while, said something sharply to Makola, who shook his head. Then the man, after looking round, noticed Makola's hut and walked over there. The next moment Mrs. Makola was heard speaking with great volubility. The other strangers—they were six in all—strolled about with an air of ease, put their heads through the door of the storeroom, congregated round the grave, pointed understandingly at the cross, and generally made themselves at home.

"I don't like those chaps—and, I say, Kayerts, they must be from the coast; they've got firearms," observed the sagacious Carlier.

Kayerts also did not like those chaps. They both, for the first time, became aware that they lived in conditions where the unusual may be dangerous, and that there was no power on earth outside of themselves to stand between them and the unusual. They became uneasy, went in and loaded their revolvers. Kayerts said, "We must order Makola to tell them to go away before dark."

The strangers left in the afternoon, after eating a meal prepared for them by Mrs. Makola. The immense woman was excited, and talked much with the visitors. She rattled away shrilly, pointing here and there at the forests and at the river. Makola sat apart and watched. At times he got up and whispered to his wife. He accompanied the strangers across the ravine at the back of the station-ground, and returned slowly looking very thoughtful. When questioned by the white men he was very strange, seemed not to understand, seemed to have forgotten French—seemed to have forgotten how to speak altogether. Kayerts and Carlier agreed that the nigger had had too much palm wine.

There was some talk about keeping a watch in turn, but in the evening everything seemed so quiet and peaceful that they retired as usual. All night they were disturbed by a lot of drumming in the villages. A deep, rapid roll near by would be followed by another far off—then all ceased. Soon short appeals would rattle out here and there, then all mingle together, increase, become vigorous and sustained, would spread out over the forest, roll through the night, unbroken and ceaseless, near and far, as if the whole land had been one immense drum booming out steadily an appeal to heaven. And through the deep and tremendous noise sudden yells that resembled snatches of songs from a madhouse darted shrill and high in discordant jets of sound which seemed to rush far above the earth and drive all peace from under the stars.

Carlier and Kayerts slept badly. They both thought they had heard shots fired during the night—but they could not agree as to the direction. In the morning Makola was gone somewhere. He returned about noon with one of yesterday's strangers, and eluded all Kayerts' attempts to close with him: had become deaf apparently. Kayerts wondered. Carlier, who had been fishing off the bank, came back and remarked while he showed his catch, "The niggers seem to be in a deuce of a stir; I wonder what's up. I saw about fifteen canoes cross the river during the two hours I was there fishing." Kayerts, worried, said, "Isn't this Makola very queer today?" Carlier advised, "Keep all our men together in case of some trouble."

2

There were ten station men who had been left by the Director. Those fellows, having engaged themselves to the Company for six months (without having any idea of a month in particular and only a very faint notion of time in general), had been serving the cause of progress for upwards of two years. Belonging to a tribe from a very distant part of the land of darkness and sorrow, they did not run away, naturally supposing that as wandering strangers they would be killed by the inhabitants of the country; in which they were right. They lived in straw huts on the slope of a ravine overgrown with reedy grass, just behind the station buildings. They were not happy, regretting the festive incantations, the sorceries, the human sacrifices of their own land; where they also had parents, brothers, sisters, admired chiefs, respected magicians, loved friends, and other ties supposed generally to be human. Besides, the rice rations served out by the Company did not agree with them, being a food unknown to their land, and to which they could not get used. Consequently they were unhealthy and miserable. Had they been of any other tribe they would have made up their minds to die—for nothing is easier to certain savages than suicide—and so

have escaped from the puzzling difficulties of existence. But belonging, as they did, to a warlike tribe with filed teeth, they had more grit, and went on stupidly living through disease and sorrow. They did very little work, and had lost their splendid physique. Carlier and Kayerts doctored them assiduously without being able to bring them back into condition again. They were mustered every morning and told off to different tasks—grass-cutting, fence-building, tree-felling, &c, &c, which no power on earth could induce them to execute efficiently. The two whites had practically very little control over them.

In the afternoon Makola came over to the big house and found Kayerts watching three heavy columns of smoke rising above the forests. "What is that?" asked Kayerts. "Some villages burn," answered Makola, who seemed to have regained his wits. Then he said abruptly: "We have got very little ivory; bad six months' trading. Do you like get a little more ivory?"

"Yes," said Kayerts, eagerly. He thought of percentages which were low.

"Those men who came yesterday are traders from Loanda who have got more ivory than they can carry home. Shall I buy? I know their camp."

"Certainly," said Kayerts. "What are those traders?"

"Bad fellows," said Makola, indifferently. "They fight with people, and catch women and children. They are bad men, and got guns. There is a great disturbance in the country. Do you want ivory?"

"Yes," said Kayerts. Makola said nothing for a while. Then: "Those workmen of ours are no good at all," he muttered, looking round. "Station in very bad order, sir. Director will growl. Better get a fine lot of ivory, then he say nothing."

"I can't help it; the men won't work," said Kayerts. "When will you get that ivory?"

"Very soon," said Makola. "Perhaps tonight. You leave it to me, and keep indoors, sir. I think you had better give some palm wine to our men to make a dance this evening. Enjoy themselves. Work better tomorrow. There's plenty palm wine—gone a little sour."

Kayerts said "yes," and Makola, with his own hands, carried big calabashes to the door of his hut. They stood there till the evening, and Mrs. Makola looked into every one. The men got them at sunset. When Kayerts and Carlier retired, a big bonfire was flaring before the men's huts. They could hear their shouts and drumming. Some men from Gobila's village had joined the station hands, and the entertainment was a great success.

In the middle of the night, Carlier waking suddenly, heard a man shout loudly; then a shot was fired. Only one. Carlier ran out and met Kayerts on the verandah. They were both startled. As they went across the yard to call Makola, they saw shadows moving in the night. One of them cried, "Don't shoot! It's me, Price." Then Makola appeared close to them. "Go back, go back, please," he urged, "you spoil all." "There are strange men about," said Carlier. "Never mind; I know," said Makola. Then he whispered, "All right. Bring ivory. Say nothing! I know my business." The two white men reluctantly went back to the house, but did not sleep. They heard footsteps, whispers, some groans. It seemed as if a lot of men came in, dumped heavy things on the ground, squabbled a long time, then went away. They lay on their hard beds and thought: "This Makola is invaluable." In the morning Carlier came out, very sleepy, and pulled at the cord of the big bell. The station hands mustered every morning to the sound of the bell. That morning nobody came. Kayerts turned out also, yawning. Across the yard they saw Makola come out of his hut, a tin basin of soapy water in his hand. Makola, a civilized nigger, was very neat in his person. He threw the soapsuds skilfully over a wretched little yellow cur he had, then turning his face to the agent's house, he shouted from the distance, "All the men gone last night!"

They heard him plainly, but in their surprise they both yelled out together: "What!" Then they stared at one another. "We are in a proper fix now," growled Carlier. "It's incredible!" muttered Kayerts. "I will go to the huts and see," said Carlier, striding off. Makola coming up found Kayerts standing alone.

"I can hardly believe it," said Kayerts, tearfully. "We took care of them as if they had been our children."

"They went with the coast people," said Makola after a moment of hesitation.

"What do I care with whom they went—the ungrateful brutes!" exclaimed the other. Then with sudden suspicion, and looking hard at Makola, he added: "What do you know about it?"

Makola moved his shoulders, looking down on the ground. "What do I know? I think only. Will you come and look at the ivory I've got there? It is a fine lot. You never saw such."

He moved towards the store. Kayerts followed him mechanically, thinking about the incredible desertion of the men. On the ground before the door of the fetish lay six splendid tusks.

"What did you give for it?" asked Kayerts, after surveying the lot with satisfaction.

"No regular trade," said Makola. "They brought the ivory and gave it to me. I told them to take what they most wanted in the station. It is a beautiful lot. No station can show such tusks. Those traders wanted carriers badly, and our men were no good here. No trade, no entry in books; all correct."

Kayerts nearly burst with indignation. "Why!" he shouted, "I believe you have sold our men for these tusks!" Makola stood impassive and silent. "I—I—will—I," stuttered Kayerts. "You fiend!" he yelled out.

"I did the best for you and the Company," said Makola, imperturbably. "Why you shout so much? Look at this tusk."

"I dismiss you! I will report you—I won't look at the tusk. I forbid you to touch them. I order you to throw them into the river. You—you!"

"You very red, Mr. Kayerts. If you are so irritable in the sun, you will get fever and die—like the first chief!" pronounced Makola impressively.

They stood still, contemplating one another with intense eyes, as if they had been looking with effort across immense distances. Kayerts shivered. Makola had meant no more than he said, but his words seemed to Kayerts full of ominous menace! He turned sharply and went away to the house. Makola retired into the bosom of his family; and the tusks, left lying before the store, looked very large and valuable in the sunshine.

Carlier came back on the verandah. "They're all gone, hey?" asked Kayerts from the far end of the common room in a muffled voice. "You did not find anybody?"

"Oh, yes," said Carlier, "I found one of Gobila's people lying dead before the huts—shot through the body. We heard that shot last night."

Kayerts came out quickly. He found his companion staring grimly over the yard at the tusks, away by the store. They both sat in silence for a while. Then Kayerts related his conversation with Makola. Carlier said nothing. At the midday meal they ate very little. They hardly exchanged a word that day. A great silence seemed to lie heavily over the station and press on their lips. Makola did not open the store; he spent the day playing with his children. He lay full-length on a mat outside his door, and the youngsters sat on his chest and clambered all over him. It was a touching picture. Mrs. Makola was busy cooking all day as usual. The white men made a somewhat better meal in the evening. Afterwards, Carlier smoking his pipe strolled over to the store; he stood for a long time over the tusks, touched one or two with his foot, even tried to lift the largest one by its small end. He came back to his chief, who had not stirred from the verandah, threw himself in the chair and said—

"I can see it! They were pounced upon while they slept heavily after drinking all that palm wine you've allowed Makola to give them. A put-up job! See? The worst is, some of Gobila's people were there, and got carried off too, no doubt. The least drunk woke up, and got shot for his sobriety. This is a funny country. What will you do now?"

"We can't touch it, of course," said Kayerts.

"Of course not," assented Carlier.

"Slavery is an awful thing," stammered out Kayerts in an unsteady voice.

"Frightful—the sufferings," grunted Carlier with conviction.

They believed their words. Everybody shows a respectful deference to certain sounds that he and his fellows can make. But about feelings people really know nothing. We talk with indignation or enthusiasm; we talk about oppression, cruelty, crime, devotion, self-sacrifice, virtue, and we know nothing real beyond the words. Nobody knows what suffering or sacrifice mean—except, perhaps the victims of the mysterious purpose of these illusions.

Next morning they saw Makola very busy setting up in the yard the big scales used for weighing ivory. By and by Carlier said: "What's that filthy scoundrel up to?" and lounged out into the yard. Kayerts followed.

They stood watching. Makola took no notice. When the balance was swung true, he tried to lift a tusk into the scale. It was too heavy. He looked up helplessly without a word, and for a minute they stood round that balance as mute and still as three statues. Suddenly Carlier said: "Catch hold of the other end, Makola—you beast!" and together they swung the tusk up. Kayerts trembled in every limb. He muttered, "I say! O! I say!" and putting his hand in his pocket found there a dirty bit of paper and the stump of a pencil. He turned his back on the others, as if about to do something tricky, and noted stealthily the weights which Carlier shouted out to him with unnecessary loudness. When all was over Makola whispered to himself: "The sun's very strong here for the tusks." Carlier said to Kayerts in a careless tone: "I say, chief, I might just as well give him a lift with this lot into the store."

As they were going back to the house Kayerts observed with a sigh: "It had to be done." And Carlier said: "It's deplorable, but, the men being Company's men the ivory is Company's ivory. We must look after it." "I will report to the Director, of course," said Kayerts. "Of course; let him decide," approved Carlier.

At midday they made a hearty meal. Kayerts sighed from time to time. Whenever they mentioned Makola's name they always added to it an opprobrious epithet. It eased their conscience. Makola gave himself a half-holiday, and bathed his children in the river. No one from Gobila's villages came near the station that day. No one came the next day, and the next, nor for a whole week. Gobila's people might have been dead and buried for any sign of life they gave. But they were only mourning for those they had lost by the witchcraft of white men, who had brought wicked people into their country. The wicked people were gone, but fear remained. Fear always remains. A man may destroy everything within himself, love and hate and belief, and even doubt; but as long as he clings to life he cannot destroy fear: the fear, subtle, indestructible, and terrible, that pervades his being; that tinges his thoughts; that lurks in his heart; that watches on his lips the struggle of his last breath. In his fear, the mild old Gobila offered extra human sacrifices to all the Evil Spirits that had taken possession of his white friends. His heart was heavy. Some warriors spoke about burning and killing, but the cautious old savage dissuaded them. Who could foresee the woe those mysterious creatures, if irritated, might bring? They should be left alone. Perhaps in time they would disappear into the earth as the first one had disappeared. His people must keep away from them, and hope for the best.

Kayerts and Carlier did not disappear, but remained above on this earth, that, somehow, they fancied had become bigger and very empty. It was not the absolute and dumb solitude of the post that impressed them so much as an inarticulate feeling that something from within them was gone, something that worked for their safety, and had kept the wilderness from interfering with their hearts. The images of home; the memory of people like them, of men that thought and felt as they used to think and feel, receded into distances made indistinct by the glare of unclouded sunshine. And out of the great silence of the surrounding wilderness, its very hopelessness and savagery seemed to approach them nearer, to draw them gently, to look upon them, to envelop them with a solicitude irresistible, familiar, and disgusting.

Days lengthened into weeks, then into months. Gobila's people drummed and yelled to every new moon, as of yore, but kept away from the station. Makola and Carlier tried once in a canoe to open communications, but were received with a shower of arrows, and had to fly back to the station for dear life. That attempt set the country up and down the river into an uproar that could be very distinctly heard for days. The steamer was late. At first they spoke of delay jauntily, then anxiously, then gloomily. The matter was becoming serious. Stores were running short. Carlier cast his lines off the bank, but the river was low, and the fish kept out in the stream. They dared not stroll far away from the station to shoot. Moreover, there was no game in the impenetrable forest. Once Carlier shot a hippo in the river. They had no boat to secure it, and it sank. When it floated up it drifted away, and Gobila's people secured the carcass. It was the occasion for a national holiday, but Carlier had a fit of rage over it and talked about the necessity of exterminating all the niggers before the country could be made habitable. Kayerts mooned about silently; spent hours looking at the portrait of his Melie. It represented a little girl with long bleached tresses and a rather sour face. His legs

were much swollen, and he could hardly walk. Carlier, undermined by fever, could not swagger any more, but kept tottering about, still with a devil-may-care air, as became a man who remembered his crack regiment. He had become hoarse, sarcastic, and inclined to say unpleasant things. He called it "being frank with you." They had long ago reckoned their percentages on trade, including in them that last deal of "this infamous Makola." They had also concluded not to say anything about it. Kayerts hesitated at first—was afraid of the Director.

"He has seen worse things done on the quiet," maintained Carlier, with a hoarse laugh. "Trust him! He won't thank you if you blab. He is no better than you or me. Who will talk if we hold our tongues? There is nobody here."

That was the root of the trouble! There was nobody there; and being left there alone with their weakness, they became daily more like a pair of accomplices than like a couple of devoted friends. They had heard nothing from home for eight months. Every evening they said, "Tomorrow we shall see the steamer." But one of the Company's steamers had been wrecked, and the Director was busy with the other, relieving very distant and important stations on the main river. He thought that the useless station, and the useless men, could wait. Meantime Kayerts and Carlier lived on rice boiled without salt, and cursed the Company, all Africa, and the day they were born. One must have lived on such diet to discover what ghastly trouble the necessity of swallowing one's food may become. There was literally nothing else in the station but rice and coffee; they drank the coffee without sugar. The last fifteen lumps Kayerts had solemnly locked away in his box, together with a half-bottle of Cognac, "in case of sickness," he explained. Carlier approved. "When one is sick," he said, "any little extra like that is cheering."

They waited. Rank grass began to sprout over the courtyard. The bell never rang now. Days passed, silent, exasperating, and slow. When the two men spoke, they snarled; and their silences were bitter, as if tinged by the bitterness of their thoughts.

One day after a lunch of boiled rice, Carlier put down his cup untasted, and said: "Hang it all! Let's have a decent cup of coffee for once. Bring out that sugar,

Kayerts!"

"For the sick," muttered Kayerts, without looking up.

"For the sick," mocked Carlier. "Bosh! ... Well! I am sick."

"You are no more sick than I am, and I go without," said Kayerts in a peaceful tone.

"Come! out with that sugar, you stingy old slave-dealer."

Kayerts looked up quickly. Carlier was smiling with marked insolence. And suddenly it seemed to Kayerts that he had never seen that man before. Who was he? He knew nothing about him. What was he capable of? There was a surprising flash of violent emotion within him, as if in the presence of something undreamt-of, dangerous, and final. But he managed to pronounce with composure—

"That joke is in very bad taste. Don't repeat it."

"Joke!" said Carlier, hitching himself forward on his seat. "I am hungry—I am sick—I don't joke! I hate hypocrites. You are a hypocrite. You are a slave-dealer. I am a slave-dealer. There's nothing but slave-dealers in this cursed country. I mean to have sugar in my coffee today, anyhow!"

"I forbid you to speak to me in that way," said Kayerts with a fair show of resolution.

"You!—What?" shouted Carlier, jumping up.

Kayerts stood up also. "I am your chief," he began, trying to master the shakiness of his voice.

"What?" yelled the other. "Who's chief? There's no chief here. There's nothing here: there's nothing but you and I. Fetch the sugar—you pot-bellied ass."

"Hold your tongue. Go out of this room," screamed Kayerts. "I dismiss you—you scoundrel!"

Carlier swung a stool. All at once he looked dangerously in earnest. "You flabby, good-for-nothing civilian—take that!" he howled.

Kayerts dropped under the table, and the stool struck the grass inner wall of the room. Then, as Carlier was trying to upset the table, Kayerts in desperation made a blind rush, head low, like a cornered pig would do, and over-turning his friend, bolted along the verandah, and into his room. He locked the door, snatched his revolver, and stood panting. In less than a minute Carlier was kicking at the door furiously, howling, "If

you don't bring out that sugar, I will shoot you at sight, like a dog. Now then—one—two—three. You won't? I will show you who's the master."

Kayerts thought the door would fall in, and scrambled through the square hole that served for a window in his room. There was then the whole breadth of the house between them. But the other was apparently not strong enough to break in the door, and Kayerts heard him running round. Then he also began to run laboriously on his swollen legs. He ran as quickly as he could, grasping the revolver, and unable yet to understand what was happening to him. He saw in succession Makola's house, the store, the river, the ravine, and the low bushes; and he saw all those things again as he ran for the second time round the house. Then again they flashed past him. That morning he could not have walked a yard without a groan.

And now he ran. He ran fast enough to keep out of sight of the other man.

Then as, weak and desperate, he thought, "Before I finish the next round I shall die," he heard the other man stumble heavily, then stop. He stopped also. He had the back and Carlier the front of the house, as before. He heard him drop into a chair cursing, and suddenly his own legs gave way, and he slid down into a sitting posture with his back to the wall. His mouth was as dry as a cinder, and his face was wet with perspiration—and tears. What was it all about? He thought it must be a horrible illusion; he thought he was dreaming; he thought he was going mad! After a while he collected his senses. What did they quarrel about? That sugar! How absurd! He would give it to him—didn't want it himself. And he began scrambling to his feet with a sudden feeling of security. But before he had fairly stood upright, a common-sense reflection occurred to him and drove him back into despair. He thought: If I give way now to that brute of a soldier, he will begin this horror again tomorrow—and the day after—every day—raise other pretensions, trample on me, torture me, make me his slave—and I will be lost! Lost! The steamer may not come for days—may never come. He shook so that he had to sit down on the floor again. He shivered forlornly. He felt he could not, would not move any more. He was completely distracted by the sudden perception that the position was without issue—that death and life had in a moment become equally difficult and terrible.

All at once he heard the other push his chair back; and he leaped to his feet with extreme facility. He listened and got confused. Must run again! Right or left? He heard footsteps. He darted to the left, grasping his revolver, and at the very same instant, as it seemed to him, they came into violent collision. Both shouted with surprise. A loud explosion took place between them; a roar of red fire, thick smoke; and Kayerts, deafened and blinded, rushed back thinking: I am hit—it's all over. He expected the other to come round—to gloat over his agony. He caught hold of an upright of the roof—"All over!" Then he heard a crashing fall on the other side of the house, as if somebody had tumbled headlong over a chair—then silence. Nothing more happened. He did not die. Only his shoulder felt as if it had been badly wrenched, and he had lost his revolver. He was disarmed and helpless! He waited for his fate. The other man made no sound. It was a stratagem. He was stalking him now! Along what side? Perhaps he was taking aim this very minute!

After a few moments of an agony frightful and absurd, he decided to go and meet his doom. He was prepared for every surrender. He turned the corner, steadying himself with one hand on the wall; made a few paces, and nearly swooned. He had seen on the floor, protruding past the other corner, a pair of turned-up feet. A pair of white naked feet in red slippers. He felt deadly sick, and stood for a time in profound darkness. Then Makola appeared before him, saying quietly: "Come along, Mr. Kayerts. He is dead." He burst into tears of gratitude; a loud, sobbing fit of crying. After a time he found himself sitting in a chair and looking at Carlier, who lay stretched on his back. Makola was kneeling over the body.

"Is this your revolver?" asked Makola, getting up.

"Yes," said Kayerts; then he added very quickly, "He ran after me to shoot me—you saw!"

"Yes, I saw," said Makola. "There is only one revolver; where's his?"

"Don't know," whispered Kayerts in a voice that had become suddenly very faint.

"I will go and look for it," said the other, gently. He made the round along the verandah, while Kayerts sat

still and looked at the corpse. Makola came back empty-handed, stood in deep thought, then stepped quietly into the dead man's room, and came out directly with a revolver, which he held up before Kayerts. Kayerts shut his eyes. Everything was going round. He found life more terrible and difficult than death. He had shot an unarmed man.

After meditating for a while, Makola said softly, pointing at the dead man who lay there with his right eye blown out—

"He died of fever." Kayerts looked at him with a stony stare. "Yes," repeated Makola, thoughtfully, stepping over the corpse, "I think he died of fever. Bury him tomorrow."

And he went away slowly to his expectant wife, leaving the two white men alone on the verandah.

Night came, and Kayerts sat unmoving on his chair. He sat quiet as if he had taken a dose of opium. The violence of the emotions he had passed through produced a feeling of exhausted serenity. He had plumbed in one short afternoon the depths of horror and despair, and now found repose in the conviction that life had no more secrets for him: neither had death! He sat by the corpse thinking; thinking very actively, thinking very new thoughts. He seemed to have broken loose from himself altogether. His old thoughts, convictions, likes and dislikes, things he respected and things he abhorred, appeared in their true light at last! Appeared contemptible and childish, false and ridiculous. He revelled in his new wisdom while he sat by the man he had killed. He argued with himself about all things under heaven with that kind of wrong-headed lucidity which may be observed in some lunatics. Incidentally he reflected that the fellow dead there had been a noxious beast anyway; that men died every day in thousands; perhaps in hundreds of thousands—who could tell?—and that in the number, that one death could not possibly make any difference; couldn't have any importance, at least to a thinking creature. He, Kayerts, was a thinking creature. He had been all his life, till that moment, a believer in a lot of nonsense like the rest of mankind—who are fools; but now he thought! He knew! He was at peace; he was familiar with the highest wisdom! Then he tried to imagine himself dead, and Carlier sitting in his chair watching him; and his attempt met with such unexpected success, that in a very few moments he became not at all sure who was dead and who was alive. This extraordinary achievement of his fancy startled him, however, and by a clever and timely effort of mind he saved himself just in time from becoming Carlier. His heart thumped, and he felt hot all over at the thought of that danger. Carlier! What a beastly thing! To compose his now disturbed nerves—and no wonder!—he tried to whistle a little. Then, suddenly, he fell asleep, or thought he had slept; but at any rate there was a fog, and somebody had whistled in the fog.

He stood up. The day had come, and a heavy mist had descended upon the land: the mist penetrating, enveloping, and silent; the morning mist of tropical lands; the mist that clings and kills; the mist white and deadly, immaculate and poisonous. He stood up, saw the body, and threw his arms above his head with a cry like that of a man who, waking from a trance, finds himself immured forever in a tomb. "*Help! … My God!*"

A shriek inhuman, vibrating and sudden, pierced like a sharp dart the white shroud of that land of sorrow. Three short, impatient screeches followed, and then, for a time, the fog-wreaths rolled on, undisturbed, through a formidable silence. Then many more shrieks, rapid and piercing, like the yells of some exasperated and ruthless creature, rent the air. Progress was calling to Kayerts from the river. Progress and civilization and all the virtues. Society was calling to its accomplished child to come, to be taken care of, to be instructed, to be judged, to be condemned; it called him to return to that rubbish heap from which he had wandered away, so that justice could be done.

Kayerts heard and understood. He stumbled out of the verandah, leaving the other man quite alone for the first time since they had been thrown there together. He groped his way through the fog, calling in his ignorance upon the invisible heaven to undo its work. Makola flitted by in the mist, shouting as he ran—

"Steamer! Steamer! They can't see. They whistle for the station. I go ring the bell. Go down to the landing, sir. I ring."

He disappeared. Kayerts stood still. He looked upwards; the fog rolled low over his head. He looked round like a man who has lost his way, and he saw a dark smudge, a cross-shaped stain, upon the shifting purity of the mist. As he began to stumble towards it, the station bell rang in a tumultuous peal its answer to the impatient clamour of the steamer.

The Managing Director of the Great Civilizing Company (since we know that civilization follows trade) landed first, and incontinently lost sight of the steamer. The fog down by the river was exceedingly dense; above, at the station, the bell rang unceasing and brazen.

The Director shouted loudly to the steamer:

"There is nobody down to meet us; there may be something wrong, though they are ringing. You had better come, too!"

And he began to toil up the steep bank. The captain and the engine-driver of the boat followed behind. As they scrambled up the fog thinned, and they could see their Director a good way ahead. Suddenly they saw him start forward, calling to them over his shoulder: "Run! Run to the house! I've found one of them. Run, look for the other!"

He had found one of them! And even he, the man of varied and startling experience, was somewhat discomposed by the manner of this finding. He stood and fumbled in his pockets (for a knife) while he faced Kayerts, who was hanging by a leather strap from the cross! He had evidently climbed the grave, which was high and narrow, and after tying the end of the strap to the arm, had swung himself off. His toes were only a couple of inches above the ground; his arms hung stiffly down; he seemed to be standing rigidly at attention, but with one purple cheek playfully posed on the shoulder. And, irreverently, he was putting out a swollen tongue at his Managing Director.

—1897

The Preface to *The Nigger of the "Narcissus"*[1]
[The Task of the Artist]

A work that aspires, however humbly, to the condition of art should carry its justification in every line. And art itself may be defined as a single-minded attempt to render the highest kind of justice to the visible universe, by bringing to light the truth, manifold and one, underlying its every aspect. It is an attempt to find in its forms, in its colours, in its light, in its shadows, in the aspects of matter and in the facts of life, what of each is fundamental, what is enduring and essential—their one illuminating and convincing quality—the very truth of their existence. The artist, then, like the thinker or the scientist, seeks the truth and makes his appeal. Impressed by the aspect of the world the thinker plunges into ideas, the scientist into facts—whence, presently, emerging they make their appeal to those qualities of our being that fit us best for the hazardous enterprise of living. They speak authoritatively to our common-sense, to our intelligence, to our desire of peace or to our desire of unrest; not seldom to our prejudices, sometimes to our fears, often to our egoism—but always to our credulity. And their words are heard with reverence, for their concern is with weighty matters: with the cultivation of our minds and the proper care of our bodies; with the attainment of our ambitions; with the perfection of the means and the glorification of our precious aims.

It is otherwise with the artist.

Confronted by the same enigmatical spectacle the artist descends within himself, and in that lonely region of stress and strife, if he be deserving and fortunate, he finds the terms of his appeal. His appeal is made to our less obvious capacities: to that part of our nature which, because of the warlike conditions of existence, is necessarily kept out of sight within the more resisting and hard qualities—like the vulnerable body within the steel armour. His appeal is less loud, more profound, less

distinct, more stirring—and sooner forgotten. Yet its effect endures for ever. The changing wisdom of successive generations discards ideas, questions facts, demolishes theories. But the artist appeals to that part of our being which is not dependent on wisdom: to that in us which is a gift and not an acquisition—and, therefore, more permanently enduring. He speaks to our capacity for delight and wonder, to the sense of mystery surrounding our lives; to our sense of pity, and beauty, and pain; to the latent feeling of fellowship with all creation—and to the subtle but invincible, conviction of solidarity that knits together the loneliness of innumerable hearts: to the solidarity in dreams, in joy, in sorrow, in aspirations, in illusions, in hope, in fear, which binds men to each other, which binds together all humanity—the dead to the living and the living to the unborn.

It is only some such train of thought, or rather of feeling, that can in a measure explain the aim of the attempt, made in the tale which follows, to present an unrestful episode in the obscure lives of a few individuals out of all the disregarded multitude of the bewildered, the simple and the voiceless. For, if there is any part of truth in the belief confessed above, it becomes evident that there is not a place of splendour or a dark corner of the earth that does not deserve, if only a passing glance of wonder and pity. The motive, then, may be held to justify the matter of the work; but this preface, which is simply an avowal of endeavour, cannot end here—for the avowal is not yet complete.

Fiction—if it at all aspires to be art—appeals to temperament. And in truth it must be, like painting, like music, like all art, the appeal of one temperament to all the other innumerable temperaments whose subtle and resistless power endows passing events with their true meaning, and creates the moral, the emotional atmosphere of the place and time. Such an appeal, to be effective, must be an impression conveyed through the senses; and, in fact, it cannot be made in any other way, because temperament, whether individual or collective, is not amenable to persuasion. All art, therefore, appeals primarily to the senses, and the artistic aim when expressing itself in written words must also make its appeal through the senses, if its high desire is to reach the secret spring of responsive emotions. It must strenuously aspire to the plasticity of sculpture, to the colour

---

[1] *Preface ... Narcissus* Conrad's novella *The Nigger of the "Narcissus"* was first published in *The New Review* in 1897. Conrad added the preface when it came out in book form in 1898. The novella deals with the death of a black seaman aboard a merchant ship called the *Narcissus*. Conrad had served as first mate on a ship bearing that name in 1883.

of painting, and to the magic suggestiveness of music—which is the art of arts. And it is only through complete, unswerving devotion to the perfect blending of form and substance; it is only through an unremitting, never-discouraged care for the shape and ring of sentences that an approach can be made to plasticity, to colour; and the light of magic suggestiveness may be brought to play for an evanescent instant over the commonplace surface of words: of the old, old words, worn thin, defaced by ages of careless usage.

The sincere endeavour to accomplish that creative task, to go as far on that road as his strength will carry him, to go undeterred by faltering, weariness or reproach, is the only valid justification for the worker in prose. And if his conscience is clear, his answer to those who, in the fulness of a wisdom which looks for immediate profit, demand specifically to be edified, consoled, amused; who demand to be promptly improved, or encouraged, or frightened, or shocked, or charmed, must run thus:—My task which I am trying to achieve is, by the power of the written word, to make you hear, to make you feel—it is, before all, to make you *see*. That—and no more, and it is everything. If I succeed, you shall find there according to your deserts: encouragement, consolation, fear, charm—all you demand; and, perhaps, also that glimpse of truth for which you have forgotten to ask.

To snatch in a moment of courage, from the remorseless rush of time, a sapping phase of life is only the beginning of the task. The task approached in tenderness and faith is to hold up unquestioningly, without choice and without fear, the rescued fragment before all eyes and in the light of a sincere mood. It is to show its vibration, its colour, its form; and through its movement, its form, and its colour, reveal the substance of its truth—disclose its inspiring secret: the stress and passion within the core of each convincing moment. In a single-minded attempt of that kind, if one be deserving and fortunate, one may perchance attain to such clearness of sincerity that at last the presented vision of regret or pity, of terror or mirth, shall awaken in the hearts of the beholders that feeling of unavoidable solidarity; of the solidarity in mysterious origin, in toil, in joy, in hope, in uncertain fate, which binds men to each other and all mankind to the visible world.

It is evident that he who, rightly or wrongly, holds by the convictions expressed above cannot be faithful to any one of the temporary formulas of his craft. The enduring part of them—the truth which each only imperfectly veils—should abide with him as the most precious of his possessions, but they all: Realism, Romanticism, Naturalism, even the unofficial sentimentalism (which, like the poor, is exceedingly difficult to get rid of);[1] all these gods must, after a short period of fellowship, abandon him—even on the very threshold of the temple—to the stammerings of his conscience and to the outspoken consciousness of the difficulties of his work. In that uneasy solitude the supreme cry of Art for Art, even, loses the exciting ring of its apparent immorality. It sounds far off. It has ceased to be a cry, and is heard only as a whisper, often incomprehensible, but at times, and faintly, encouraging.

Sometimes, stretched at ease in the shade of a roadside tree, we watch the motions of a labourer in a distant field, and after a time, begin to wonder languidly as to what the fellow may be at. We watch the movements of his body, the waving of his arms, we see him bend down, stand up, hesitate, begin again. It may add to the charm of an idle hour to be told the purpose of his exertions. If we know he is trying to lift a stone, to dig a ditch, to uproot a stump, we look with a more real interest at his efforts; we are disposed to condone the jar of his agitation upon the restfulness of the landscape; and even, if in a brotherly frame of mind, we may bring ourselves to forgive his failure. We understood his object, and, after all, the fellow has tried, and perhaps he had not the strength, and perhaps he had not the knowledge. We forgive, go on our way—and forget.

And so it is with the workman of art. Art is long and life is short,[2] and success is very far off. And thus, doubtful of strength to travel so far, we talk a little about the aim—the aim of art, which, like life itself, is inspiring, difficult—obscured by mists. It is not in the clear logic of a triumphant conclusion; it is not in the unveiling of one of those heartless secrets which are called the Laws of Nature. It is not less great, but only more

---

[1] *like the poor ... get rid of* The reference is to John 12.8: "for the poor always you have with you."

[2] *Art is long and life is short* The Latin proverb *ars longa, vita brevis* derives from a saying of the Greek physician Hippocrates.

difficult.

To arrest, for the space of a breath, the hands busy about the work of the earth, and compel men entranced by the sight of distant goals to glance for a moment at the surrounding vision of form and colour, of sunshine and shadows; to make them pause for a look, for a sigh, for a smile—such is the aim, difficult and evanescent, and reserved only for a very few to achieve. But sometimes, by the deserving and the fortunate, even that task is accomplished. And when it is accomplished—behold! —all the truth of life is there: a moment of vision, a sigh, a smile—and the return to an eternal rest.

—1898

The Secret Sharer

I

On my right hand there were lines of fishing stakes resembling a mysterious system of half-submerged bamboo fences, incomprehensible in its division of the domain of tropical fishes, and crazy of aspect as if abandoned forever by some nomad tribe of fishermen now gone to the other end of the ocean; for there was no sign of human habitation as far as the eye could reach. To the left a group of barren islets, suggesting ruins of stone walls, towers, and blockhouses, had its foundations set in a blue sea that itself looked solid, so still and stable did it lie below my feet; even the track of light from the westering sun shone smoothly, without that animated glitter which tells of an imperceptible ripple. And when I turned my head to take a parting glance at the tug which had just left us anchored outside the bar, I saw the straight line of the flat shore joined to the stable sea, edge to edge, with a perfect and un-marked closeness, in one leveled floor half brown, half blue under the enormous dome of the sky. Corresponding in their insignificance to the islets of the sea, two small clumps of trees, one on each side of the only fault in the impeccable joint, marked the mouth of the river Meinam[1] we had just left on the first preparatory stage

of our homeward journey; and, far back on the inland level, a larger and loftier mass, the grove surrounding the great Paknam pagoda,[2] was the only thing on which the eye could rest from the vain task of exploring the monotonous sweep of the horizon. Here and there gleams as of a few scattered pieces of silver marked the windings of the great river; and on the nearest of them, just within the bar, the tug steaming right into the land became lost to my sight, hull and funnel and masts, as though the impassive earth had swallowed her up without an effort, without a tremor. My eye followed the light cloud of her smoke, now here, now there, above the plain, according to the devious curves of the stream, but always fainter and farther away, till I lost it at last behind the miter-shaded hill of the great pagoda. And then I was left alone with my ship, anchored at the head of the Gulf of Siam.[3]

She floated at the starting point of a long journey, very still in an immense stillness, the shadows of her spars[4] flung far to the eastward by the setting sun. At that moment I was alone on her decks. There was not a sound in her—and around us nothing moved, nothing lived, not a canoe on the water, not a bird in the air, not a cloud in the sky. In this breathless pause at the threshold of a long passage we seemed to be measuring our fitness for a long and arduous enterprise, the appointed task of both our existences to be carried out, far from all human eyes, with only sky and sea for spectators and for judges.

There must have been some glare in the air to interfere with one's sight, because it was only just before the sun left us that my roaming eyes made out beyond the highest ridges of the principal islet of the group something which did away with the solemnity of perfect solitude. The tide of darkness flowed on swiftly; and with tropical suddenness a swarm of stars came out above the shadowy earth, while I lingered yet, my hand resting lightly on my ship's rail as if on the shoulder of a trusted friend. But, with all that multitude of celestial

---

[1] *the river Meinam*   Conrad may have been referring to the Chao Phraya river in the city of Samut Prakan, Thailand. Located just south of Bangkok, Samut Prakan is a port city on the Gulf of Thailand.

[2] *Paknam pagoda*   Located in Samut Prakan, the Phra Samut Chedi pagoda was originally built in the middle of the river. Today it adjoins the west bank due to silt accumulation.

[3] *Siam*   Thailand.

[4] *spars*   Mast attachments securing the sail; also called booms or gaffs.

bodies staring down at one, the comfort of quiet communion with her was gone for good. And there were also disturbing sounds by this time—voices, footsteps forward; the steward flitted along the main-deck, a busily ministering spirit; a hand bell tinkled urgently under the poop deck[1]…

I found my two officers waiting for me near the supper table, in the lighted cuddy.[2] We sat down at once, and as I helped the chief mate, I said:

"Are you aware that there is a ship anchored inside the islands? I saw her mastheads above the ridge as the sun went down."

He raised sharply his simple face, overcharged by a terrible growth of whisker, and emitted his usual ejaculations: "Bless my soul, sir! You don't say so!"

My second mate was a round-cheeked, silent young man, grave beyond his years, I thought; but as our eyes happened to meet I detected a slight quiver on his lips. I looked down at once. It was not my part to encourage sneering on board my ship. It must be said, too, that I knew very little of my officers. In consequence of certain events of no particular significance, except to myself, I had been appointed to the command only a fortnight before. Neither did I know much of the hands forward. All these people had been together for eighteen months or so, and my position was that of the only stranger on board. I mention this because it has some bearing on what is to follow. But what I felt most was my being a stranger to the ship; and if all the truth must be told, I was somewhat of a stranger to myself. The youngest man on board (barring the second mate), and untried as yet by a position of the fullest responsibility, I was willing to take the adequacy of the others for granted. They had simply to be equal to their tasks; but I wondered how far I should turn out faithful to that ideal conception of one's own personality every man sets up for himself secretly.

Meantime the chief mate, with an almost visible effect of collaboration on the part of his round eyes and frightful whiskers, was trying to evolve a theory of the anchored ship. His dominant trait was to take all things

into earnest consideration. He was of a painstaking turn of mind. As he used to say, he "liked to account to himself" for practically everything that came in his way, down to a miserable scorpion he had found in his cabin a week before. The why and the wherefore of that scorpion—how it got on board and came to select his room rather than the pantry (which was a dark place and more what a scorpion would be partial to), and how on earth it managed to drown itself in the inkwell of his writing desk—had exercised him infinitely. The ship within the islands was much more easily accounted for; and just as we were about to rise from table he made his pronouncement. She was, he doubted not, a ship from home lately arrived. Probably she drew too much water to cross the bar except at the top of spring tides. Therefore she went into that natural harbour to wait for a few days in preference to remaining in an open roadstead.

"That's so," confirmed the second mate, suddenly, in his slightly hoarse voice. "She draws over twenty feet. She's the Liverpool ship *Sephora* with a cargo of coal. Hundred and twenty-three days from Cardiff."

We looked at him in surprise.

"The tugboat skipper told me when he came on board for your letters, sir," explained the young man. "He expects to take her up the river the day after tomorrow."

After thus overwhelming us with the extent of his information he slipped out of the cabin. The mate observed regretfully that he "could not account for that young fellow's whims." What prevented him telling us all about it at once, he wanted to know.

I detained him as he was making a move. For the last two days the crew had had plenty of hard work, and the night before they had very little sleep. I felt painfully that I—a stranger—was doing something unusual when I directed him to let all hands turn in without setting an anchor watch. I proposed to keep on deck myself till one o'clock or thereabouts. I would get the second mate to relieve me at that hour.

"He will turn out the cook and the steward at four," I concluded, "and then give you a call. Of course at the slightest sign of any sort of wind we'll have the hands up and make a start at once."

He concealed his astonishment. "Very well, sir." Outside the cuddy he put his head in the second mate's

---

[1] *poop deck* Highest and aftermost deck on a ship.

[2] *cuddy* Small ship-board cabin.

door to inform him of my unheard-of caprice to take a five hours' anchor watch on myself. I heard the other raise his voice incredulously—"What? The Captain himself?" Then a few more murmurs, a door closed, then another. A few moments later I went on deck.

My strangeness, which had made me sleepless, had prompted that unconventional arrangement, as if I had expected in those solitary hours of the night to get on terms with the ship of which I knew nothing, manned by men of whom I knew very little more. Fast alongside a wharf, littered like any ship in port with a tangle of unrelated things, invaded by unrelated shore people, I had hardly seen her yet properly. Now, as she lay cleared for sea, the stretch of her main-deck seemed to me very find under the stars. Very fine, very roomy for her size, and very inviting. I descended the poop and paced the waist, my mind picturing to myself the coming passage through the Malay Archipelago, down the Indian Ocean, and up the Atlantic. All its phases were familiar enough to me, every characteristic, all the alternatives which were likely to face me on the high seas— everything!... except the novel responsibility of command. But I took heart from the reasonable thought that the ship was like other ships, the men like other men, and that the sea was not likely to keep any special surprises expressly for my discomfiture.

Arrived at that comforting conclusion, I bethought myself of a cigar and went below to get it. All was still down there. Everybody at the after end of the ship was sleeping profoundly. I came out again on the quarter-deck, agreeably at ease in my sleeping suit on that warm breathless night, barefooted, a glowing cigar in my teeth, and, going forward, I was met by the profound silence of the fore end of the ship. Only as I passed the door of the forecastle, I heard a deep, quiet, trustful sigh of some sleeper inside. And suddenly I rejoiced in the great security of the sea as compared with the unrest of the land, in my choice of that untempted life presenting no disquieting problems, invested with an elementary moral beauty by the absolute straightforwardness of its appeal and by the singleness of its purpose.

The riding light in the forerigging burned with a clear, untroubled, as if symbolic, flame, confident and bright in the mysterious shades of the night. Passing on my way aft along the other side of the ship, I observed that the rope side ladder, put over, no doubt, for the master of the tug when he came to fetch away our letters, had not been hauled in as it should have been. I became annoyed at this, for exactitude in some small matters is the very soul of discipline. Then I reflected that I had myself peremptorily dismissed my officers from duty, and by my own act had prevented the anchor watch being formally set and things properly attended to. I asked myself whether it was wise ever to interfere with the established routine of duties even from the kindest of motives. My action might have made me appear eccentric. Goodness only knew how that absurdly whiskered mate would "account" for my conduct, and what the whole ship thought of that informality of their new captain. I was vexed with myself.

Not from compunction certainly, but, as it were mechanically, I proceeded to get the ladder in myself. Now a side ladder of that sort is a light affair and comes in easily, yet my vigorous tug, which should have brought it flying on board, merely recoiled upon my body in a totally unexpected jerk. What the devil!... I was so astounded by the immovableness of that ladder that I remained stockstill, trying to account for it to myself like that imbecile mate of mine. In the end, of course, I put my head over the rail.

The side of the ship made an opaque belt of shadow on the darkling glassy shimmer of the sea. But I saw at once something elongated and pale floating very close to the ladder. Before I could form a guess a faint flash of phosphorescent light, which seemed to issue suddenly from the naked body of a man, flickered in the sleeping water with the elusive, silent play of summer lightning in a night sky. With a gasp I saw revealed to my stare a pair of feet, the long legs, a broad livid back immersed right up to the neck in a greenish cadaverous glow. One hand, awash, clutched the bottom rung of the ladder. He was complete but for the head. A headless corpse! The cigar dropped out of my gaping mouth with a tiny plop and a short hiss quite audible in the absolute stillness of all things under heaven. At that I suppose he raised up his face, a dimly pale oval in the shadow of the ship's side. But even then I could only barely make out down there the shape of his black-haired head. However, it was enough for the horrid, frost-bound sensation which had gripped me about the chest to pass off. The moment of vain exclamations was past, too. I only climbed on the spare spar and leaned over the rail as far as I could, to bring my eyes nearer to that mystery floating alongside.

As he hung by the ladder, like a resting swimmer, the sea lightning played about his limbs at every stir; and he appeared in it ghastly, silvery, fishlike. He remained as mute as a fish, too. He made no motion to get out of the water, either. It was inconceivable that he should not attempt to come on board, and strangely troubling to suspect that perhaps he did not want to. And my first words were prompted by just that troubled incertitude.

"What's the matter?" I asked in my ordinary tone, speaking down to the face upturned exactly under mine.

"Cramp," it answered, no louder. Then slightly anxious, "I say, no need to call anyone."

"I was not going to," I said.

"Are you alone on deck?"

"Yes."

I had somehow the impression that he was on the point of letting go the ladder to swim away beyond my ken—mysterious as he came. But, for the moment, this being appearing as if he had risen from the bottom of the sea (it was certainly the nearest land to the ship) wanted only to know the time. I told him. And he, down there, tentatively:

"I suppose your captain's turned in?"

"I am sure he isn't," I said.

He seemed to struggle with himself, for I heard something like the low, bitter murmur of doubt. "What's the good?" His next words came out with a hesitating effort.

"Look here, my man. Could you call him out quietly?"

I thought the time had come to declare myself.

"I am the captain."

I heard a "By Jove!" whispered at the level of the water. The phosphorescence flashed in the swirl of the water all about his limbs, his other hand seized the ladder.

"My name's Leggatt."

The voice was calm and resolute. A good voice. The self-possession of that man had somehow induced a corresponding state in myself. It was very quietly that I remarked:

"You must be a good swimmer."

"Yes. I've been in the water practically since nine o'clock. The question for me now is whether I am to let go this ladder and go on swimming till I sink from exhaustion, or—to come on board here."

I felt this was no mere formula of desperate speech, but a real alternative in the view of a strong soul. I should have gathered from this that he was young; indeed, it is only the young who are ever confronted by such clear issues. But at the time it was pure intuition on my part. A mysterious communication was established already between us two—in the face of that silent, darkened tropical sea. I was young, too; young enough to make no comment. The man in the water began suddenly to climb up the ladder, and I hastened away from the rail to fetch some clothes.

Before entering the cabin I stood still, listening in the lobby at the foot of the stairs. A faint snore came through the closed door of the chief mate's room. The second mate's door was on the hook, but the darkness in there was absolutely soundless. He, too, was young and could sleep like a stone. Remained the steward, but he was not likely to wake up before he was called. I got a sleeping suit out of my room and, coming back on deck, saw the naked man from the sea sitting on the main hatch, glimmering white in the darkness, his elbows on his knees and his head in his hands. In a moment he had concealed his damp body in a sleeping suit of the same gray-stripe pattern as the one I was wearing and followed me like my double on the poop. Together we moved right aft, barefooted, silent.

"What is it?" I asked in a deadened voice, taking the lighted lamp out of the binnacle,[1] and raising it to his face.

"An ugly business."

He had rather regular features; a good mouth; light eyes under somewhat heavy, dark eyebrows; a smooth, square forehead; no growth on his cheeks; a small, brown mustache, and a well-shaped, round chin. His expression was concentrated, meditative, under the inspecting light of the lamp I held up to his face; such as a man thinking hard in solitude might wear. My sleeping suit was just right for his size. A well-knit

---

[1] *binnacle* Box, or stand, containing a compass and lantern.

young fellow of twenty-five at most. He caught his lower lip with the edge of white, even teeth.

"Yes," I said, replacing the lamp in the binnacle. The warm, heavy tropical night closed upon his head again.

"There's a ship over there," he murmured.

"Yes, I know. The *Sephora*. Did you know of us?"

"Hadn't the slightest idea. I am the mate of her—" He paused and corrected himself. "I should say I *WAS*."

"Aha! Something wrong?"

"Yes. Very wrong indeed. I've killed a man."

"What do you mean? Just now?"

"No, on the passage. Weeks ago. Thirty-nine south. When I say a man—"

"Fit of temper," I suggested, confidently.

The shadowy, dark head, like mine, seemed to nod imperceptibly above the ghostly gray of my sleeping suit. It was, in the night, as though I had been faced by my own reflection in the depths of a somber and immense mirror.

"A pretty thing to have to own up to for a Conway boy," murmured my double, distinctly.

"You're a Conway boy?"

"I am," he said, as if startled. Then, slowly… "Perhaps you too—"

It was so; but being a couple of years older I had left before he joined. After a quick interchange of dates a silence fell; and I thought suddenly of my absurd mate with his terrific whiskers and the "Bless my soul—you don't say so" type of intellect. My double gave me an inkling of his thoughts by saying: "My father's a parson in Norfolk. Do you see me before a judge and jury on that charge? For myself I can't see the necessity. There are fellows that an angel from heaven—And I am not that. He was one of those creatures that are just simmering all the time with a silly sort of wickedness. Miserable devils that have no business to live at all. He wouldn't do his duty and wouldn't let anybody else do theirs. But what's the good of talking! You know well enough the sort of ill-conditioned snarling cur—"

He appealed to me as if our experiences had been as identical as our clothes. And I knew well enough the pestiferous danger of such a character where there are no means of legal repression. And I knew well enough also that my double there was no homicidal ruffian. I did not think of asking him for details, and he told me the

story roughly in brusque, disconnected sentences. I needed no more. I saw it all going on as though I were myself inside that other sleeping suit.

"It happened while we were setting a reefed foresail,[1] at dusk. Reefed foresail! You understand the sort of weather. The only sail we had left to keep the ship running; so you may guess what it had been like for days. Anxious sort of job, that. He gave me some of his cursed insolence at the sheet. I tell you I was overdone with this terrific weather that seemed to have no end to it. Terrific, I tell you—and a deep ship. I believe the fellow himself was half crazed with funk. It was no time for gentlemanly reproof, so I turned round and felled him like an ox. He up and at me. We closed just as an awful sea made for the ship. All hands saw it coming and took to the rigging, but I had him by the throat, and went on shaking him like a rat, the men above us yelling, 'Look out! look out!' Then a crash as if the sky had fallen on my head. They say that for over ten minutes hardly anything was to be seen of the ship— just the three masts and a bit of the forecastle head and of the poop all awash driving along in a smother of foam. It was a miracle that they found us, jammed together behind the forebitts. It's clear that I meant business, because I was holding him by the throat still when they picked us up. He was black in the face. It was too much for them. It seems they rushed us aft together, gripped as we were, screaming 'Murder!' like a lot of lunatics, and broke into the cuddy. And the ship running for her life, touch and go all the time, any minute her last in a sea fit to turn your hair gray only a-looking at it. I understand that the skipper, too, started raving like the rest of them. The man had been deprived of sleep for more than a week, and to have this sprung on him at the height of a furious gale nearly drove him out of his mind. I wonder they didn't fling me overboard after getting the carcass of their precious shipmate out of my fingers. They had rather a job to separate us, I've been told. A sufficiently fierce story to make an old judge and a respectable jury sit up a bit. The first thing I heard when I came to myself was the maddening howling of that endless gale, and on that the voice of the old man. He was hanging on to my bunk, staring into

---

[1] *reefed fore sail*   The sail set furthest forward; also known as the jib. A reefed sail has been tied back to reduce the sail area.

my face out of his sou'wester.[1]

"'Mr. Leggatt, you have killed a man. You can act no longer as chief mate of this ship.'"

His care to subdue his voice made it sound monotonous. He rested a hand on the end of the skylight to steady himself with, and all that time did not stir a limb, so far as I could see. "Nice little tale for a quiet tea party," he concluded in the same tone.

One of my hands, too, rested on the end of the skylight; neither did I stir a limb, so far as I knew. We stood less than a foot from each other. It occurred to me that if old "Bless my soul—you don't say so" were to put his head up the companion and catch sight of us, he would think he was seeing double, or imagine himself come upon a scene of weird witchcraft; the strange captain having a quiet confabulation by the wheel with his own gray ghost. I became very much concerned to prevent anything of the sort. I heard the other's soothing undertone.

"My father's a parson in Norfolk," it said. Evidently he had forgotten he had told me this important fact before. Truly a nice little tale.

"You had better slip down into my stateroom now," I said, moving off stealthily. My double followed my movements; our bare feet made no sound; I let him in, closed the door with care, and, after giving a call to the second mate, returned on deck for my relief.

"Not much sign of any wind yet," I remarked when he approached.

"No, sir. Not much," he assented, sleepily, in his hoarse voice, with just enough deference, no more, and barely suppressing a yawn.

"Well, that's all you have to look out for. You have got your orders."

"Yes, sir."

I paced a turn or two on the poop and saw him take up his position face forward with his elbow in the ratlines of the mizzen[2] rigging before I went below. The mate's faint snoring was still going on peacefully. The cuddy lamp was burning over the table on which stood a vase with flowers, a polite attention from the ship's

provision merchant—the last flowers we should see for the next three months at the very least. Two bunches of bananas hung from the beam symmetrically, one on each side of the rudder casing. Everything was as before in the ship—except that two of her captain's sleeping suits were simultaneously in use, one motionless in the cuddy, the other keeping very still in the captain's stateroom.

It must be explained here that my cabin had the form of the capital letter L, the door being within the angle and opening into the short part of the letter. A couch was to the left, the bed place to the right; my writing desk and the chronometers' table faced the door. But anyone opening it, unless he stepped right inside, had no view of what I call the long (or vertical) part of the letter. It contained some lockers surmounted by a bookcase; and a few clothes, a thick jacket or two, caps, oilskin coat, and such like, hung on hooks. There was at the bottom of that part a door opening into my bathroom, which could be entered also directly from the saloon. But that way was never used.

The mysterious arrival had discovered the advantage of this particular shape. Entering my room, lighted strongly by a big bulkhead lamp swung on gimbals above my writing desk, I did not see him anywhere till he stepped out quietly from behind the coats hung in the recessed part.

"I heard somebody moving about, and went in there at once," he whispered.

I, too, spoke under my breath.

"Nobody is likely to come in here without knocking and getting permission."

He nodded. His face was thin and the sunburn faded, as though he had been ill. And no wonder. He had been, I heard presently, kept under arrest in his cabin for nearly seven weeks. But there was nothing sickly in his eyes or in his expression. He was not a bit like me, really; yet, as we stood leaning over my bed place, whispering side by side, with our dark heads together and our backs to the door, anybody bold enough to open it stealthily would have been treated to the uncanny sight of a double captain busy talking in whispers with his other self.

"But all this doesn't tell me how you came to hang on to our side ladder," I inquired, in the hardly audible

---

[1] *sou'wester* Waterproof, often oilskin, hat with a wide slanting brim that is longer in back than in front.

[2] *mizzen* The shorter mast behind the main mast aboard a ketch or yawl.

murmurs we used, after he had told me something more of the proceedings on board the *Sephora* once the bad weather was over.

"When we sighted Java Head I had had time to think all those matters out several times over. I had six weeks of doing nothing else, and with only an hour or so every evening for a tramp on the quarter-deck."

He whispered, his arms folded on the side of my bed place, staring through the open port. And I could imagine perfectly the manner of this thinking out—a stubborn if not a steadfast operation; something of which I should have been perfectly incapable.

"I reckoned it would be dark before we closed with the land," he continued, so low that I had to strain my hearing near as we were to each other, shoulder touching shoulder almost. "So I asked to speak to the old man. He always seemed very sick when he came to see me—as if he could not look me in the face. You know, that foresail saved the ship. She was too deep to have run long under bare poles. And it was I that managed to set it for him. Anyway, he came. When I had him in my cabin—he stood by the door looking at me as if I had the halter round my neck already—I asked him right away to leave my cabin door unlocked at night while the ship was going through Sunda Straits.[1] There would be the Java coast within two or three miles, off Angier Point. I wanted nothing more. I've had a prize for swimming my second year in the Conway."

"I can believe it," I breathed out.

"God only knows why they locked me in every night. To see some of their faces you'd have thought they were afraid I'd go about at night strangling people. Am I a murdering brute? Do I look it? By Jove! If I had been he wouldn't have trusted himself like that into my room. You'll say I might have chucked him aside and bolted out, there and then—it was dark already. Well, no. And for the same reason I wouldn't think of trying to smash the door. There would have been a rush to stop me at the noise, and I did not mean to get into a confounded scrimmage. Somebody else might have got killed—for I would not have broken out only to get chucked back, and I did not want any more of that work. He refused, looking more sick than ever. He was

afraid of the men, and also of that old second mate of his who had been sailing with him for years—a gray-headed old humbug; and his steward, too, had been with him devil knows how long—seventeen years or more—a dogmatic sort of loafer who hated me like poison, just because I was the chief mate. No chief mate ever made more than one voyage in the *Sephora*, you know. Those two old chaps ran the ship. Devil only knows what the skipper wasn't afraid of (all his nerve went to pieces altogether in that hellish spell of bad weather we had)—of what the law would do to him—of his wife, perhaps. Oh, yes! she's on board. Though I don't think she would have meddled. She would have been only too glad to have me out of the ship in any way. The 'brand of Cain' business, don't you see. That's all right. I was ready enough to go off wandering on the face of the earth—and that was price enough to pay for an Abel of that sort. Anyhow, he wouldn't listen to me. 'This thing must take its course. I represent the law here.' He was shaking like a leaf. 'So you won't?' 'No!' 'Then I hope you will be able to sleep on that,' I said, and turned my back on him. 'I wonder that *you* can,' cries he, and locks the door.

"Well after that, I couldn't. Not very well. That was three weeks ago. We have had a slow passage through the Java Sea; drifted about Carimata for ten days. When we anchored here they thought, I suppose, it was all right. The nearest land (and that's five miles) is the ship's destination; the consul would soon set about catching me; and there would have been no object in bolding to these islets there. I don't suppose there's a drop of water on them. I don't know how it was, but tonight that steward, after bringing me my supper, went out to let me eat it, and left the door unlocked. And I ate it—all there was, too. After I had finished I strolled out on the quarter-deck. I don't know that I meant to do anything. A breath of fresh air was all I wanted, I believe. Then a sudden temptation came over me. I kicked off my slippers and was in the water before I had made up my mind fairly. Somebody heard the splash and they raised an awful hullabaloo. 'He's gone! Lower the boats! He's committed suicide! No, he's swimming.' Certainly I was swimming. It's not so easy for a swimmer like me to commit suicide by drowning. I landed on the nearest islet before the boat left the ship's side. I

---

[1] *Sunda Straits* Located between the islands of Sumatra and Java in Indonesia.

heard them pulling about in the dark, hailing, and so on, but after a bit they gave up. Everything quieted down and the anchorage became still as death. I sat down on a stone and began to think. I felt certain they would start searching for me at daylight. There was no place to hide on those stony things—and if there had been, what would have been the good? But now I was clear of that ship, I was not going back. So after a while I took off all my clothes, tied them up in a bundle with a stone inside, and dropped them in the deep water on the outer side of that islet. That was suicide enough for me. Let them think what they liked, but I didn't mean to drown myself. I meant to swim till I sank—but that's not the same thing. I struck out for another of these little islands, and it was from that one that I first saw your riding light. Something to swim for. I went on easily, and on the way I came upon a flat rock a foot or two above water. In the daytime, I dare say, you might make it out with a glass from your poop. I scrambled up on it and rested myself for a bit. Then I made another start. That last spell must have been over a mile."

His whisper was getting fainter and fainter, and all the time he stared straight out through the porthole, in which there was not even a star to be seen. I had not interrupted him. There was something that made comment impossible in his narrative, or perhaps in himself; a sort of feeling, a quality, which I can't find a name for. And when he ceased, all I found was a futile whisper: "So you swam for our light?"

"Yes—straight for it. It was something to swim for. I couldn't see any stars low down because the coast was in the way, and I couldn't see the land, either. The water was like glass. One might have been swimming in a confounded thousand-feet deep cistern with no place for scrambling out anywhere; but what I didn't like was the notion of swimming round and round like a crazed bullock before I gave out; and as I didn't mean to go back…No. Do you see me being hauled back, stark naked, off one of these little islands by the scruff of the neck and fighting like a wild beast? Somebody would have got killed for certain, and I did not want any of that. So I went on. Then your ladder—"

"Why didn't you hail the ship?" I asked, a little louder.

He touched my shoulder lightly. Lazy footsteps came right over our heads and stopped. The second mate had crossed from the other side of the poop and might have been hanging over the rail for all we knew.

"He couldn't hear us talking—could he?" My double breathed into my very ear, anxiously.

His anxiety was in answer, a sufficient answer, to the question I had put to him. An answer containing all the difficulty of that situation. I closed the porthole quietly, to make sure. A louder word might have been overheard.

"Who's that?" he whispered then.

"My second mate. But I don't know much more of the fellow than you do."

And I told him a little about myself. I had been appointed to take charge while I least expected anything of the sort, not quite a fortnight ago. I didn't know either the ship or the people. Hadn't had the time in port to look about me or size anybody up. And as to the crew, all they knew was that I was appointed to take the ship home. For the rest, I was almost as much of a stranger on board as himself, I said. And at the moment I felt it most acutely. I felt that it would take very little to make me a suspect person in the eyes of the ship's company.

He had turned about meantime; and we, the two strangers in the ship, faced each other in identical attitudes.

"Your ladder—" he murmured, after a silence. "Who'd have thought of finding a ladder hanging over at night in a ship anchored out here! I felt just then a very unpleasant faintness. After the life I've been leading for nine weeks, anybody would have got out of condition. I wasn't capable of swimming round as far as your rudder chains. And, lo and behold! there was a ladder to get hold of. After I gripped it I said to myself, 'What's the good?' When I saw a man's head looking over I thought I would swim away presently and leave him shouting—in whatever language it was. I didn't mind being looked at. I—I liked it. And then you speaking to me so quietly—as if you had expected me—made me hold on a little longer. It had been a confounded lonely time—I don't mean while swimming. I was glad to talk a little to somebody that didn't belong to the *Sephora*. As to asking for the captain, that was a mere impulse. It could have been no use, with all the ship knowing about me and the other people pretty certain to be round here in the morning. I don't know—I wanted to be seen, to talk with somebody, before I went on. I don't know what I would have said.... 'Fine night, isn't it?' or something of the sort."

"Do you think they will be round here presently?" I asked with some incredulity.

"Quite likely," he said, faintly.

He looked extremely haggard all of a sudden. His head rolled on his shoulders.

"H'm. We shall see then. Meantime get into that bed," I whispered. "Want help? There."

It was a rather high bed place with a set of drawers underneath. This amazing swimmer really needed the lift I gave him by seizing his leg. He tumbled in, rolled over on his back, and flung one arm across his eyes. And then, with his face nearly hidden, he must have looked exactly as I used to look in that bed. I gazed upon my other self for a while before drawing across carefully the two green serge curtains which ran on a brass rod. I thought for a moment of pinning them together for greater safety, but I sat down on the couch, and once there I felt unwilling to rise and hunt for a pin. I would do it in a moment. I was extremely tired, in a peculiarly intimate way, by the strain of stealthiness, by the effort of whispering and the general secrecy of this excitement. It was three o'clock by now and I had been on my feet since nine, but I was not sleepy; I could not have gone to sleep. I sat there, fagged out, looking at the curtains, trying to clear my mind of the confused sensation of being in two places at once, and greatly bothered by an exasperating knocking in my head. It was a relief to discover suddenly that it was not in my head at all, but on the outside of the door. Before I could collect myself the words "Come in" were out of my mouth, and the steward entered with a tray, bringing in my morning coffee. I had slept, after all, and I was so frightened that I shouted, "This way! I am here, steward," as though he had been miles away. He put down the tray on the table next the couch and only then said, very quietly, "I can see you are here, sir." I felt him give me a keen look, but I dared not meet his eyes just then. He must have wondered why I had drawn the curtains of my bed before going to sleep on the couch. He went out, hooking the door open as usual.

I heard the crew washing decks above me. I knew I would have been told at once if there had been any wind. Calm, I thought, and I was doubly vexed. Indeed, I felt dual more than ever. The steward reappeared suddenly in the doorway. I jumped up from the couch so quickly that he gave a start.

"What do you want here?"

"Close your port, sir—they are washing decks."

"It is closed," I said, reddening.

"Very well, sir." But he did not move from the doorway and returned my stare in an extraordinary, equivocal manner for a time. Then his eyes wavered, all his expression changed, and in a voice unusually gentle, almost coaxingly:

"May I come in to take the empty cup away, sir?"

"Of course!" I turned my back on him while he popped in and out. Then I unhooked and closed the door and even pushed the bolt. This sort of thing could not go on very long. The cabin was as hot as an oven, too. I took a peep at my double, and discovered that he had not moved, his arm was still over his eyes; but his chest heaved; his hair was wet; his chin glistened with perspiration. I reached over him and opened the port.

"I must show myself on deck," I reflected.

Of course, theoretically, I could do what I liked, with no one to say nay to me within the whole circle of the horizon; but to lock my cabin door and take the key away I did not dare. Directly I put my head out of the companion I saw the group of my two officers, the second mate barefooted, the chief mate in long India-rubber boots, near the break of the poop, and the steward halfway down the poop ladder talking to them eagerly. He happened to catch sight of me and dived, the second ran down on the main-deck shouting some order or other, and the chief mate came to meet me, touching his cap.

There was a sort of curiosity in his eye that I did not like. I don't know whether the steward had told them that I was "queer" only, or downright drunk, but I know the man meant to have a good look at me. I watched him coming with a smile which, as he got into point-blank range, took effect and froze his very whiskers. I did not give him time to open his lips.

"Square the yards by lifts and braces before the hands go to breakfast."

It was the first particular order I had given on board that ship; and I stayed on deck to see it executed, too. I had felt the need of asserting myself without loss of time. That sneering young cub got taken down a peg or two on that occasion, and I also seized the opportunity of having a good look at the face of every foremast man as they filed past me to go to the after braces. At breakfast time, eating nothing myself, I presided with such frigid dignity that the two mates were only too glad to escape from the cabin as soon as decency permitted; and all the time the dual working of my mind distracted me almost to the point of insanity. I was constantly watching myself, my secret self, as dependent on my actions as my own personality, sleeping in that bed, behind that door which faced me as I sat at the head of the table. It was very much like being mad, only it was worse because one was aware of it.

I had to shake him for a solid minute, but when at last he opened his eyes it was in the full possession of his senses, with an inquiring look.

"All's well so far," I whispered. "Now you must vanish into the bathroom."

He did so, as noiseless as a ghost, and then I rang for the steward, and facing him boldly, directed him to tidy up my stateroom while I was having my bath—"and be quick about it." As my tone admitted of no excuses, he said, "Yes, sir," and ran off to fetch his dustpan and brushes. I took a bath and did most of my dressing, splashing, and whistling softly for the steward's edification, while the secret sharer of my life stood drawn up bolt upright in that little space, his face looking very sunken in daylight, his eyelids lowered under the stern, dark line of his eyebrows drawn together by a slight frown.

When I left him there to go back to my room the steward was finishing dusting. I sent for the mate and engaged him in some insignificant conversation. It was, as it were, trifling with the terrific character of his whiskers; but my object was to give him an opportunity for a good look at my cabin. And then I could at last shut, with a clear conscience, the door of my stateroom and get my double back into the recessed part. There was nothing else for it. He had to sit still on a small folding stool, half smothered by the heavy coats hanging there. We listened to the steward going into the bathroom out of the saloon, filling the water bottles there, scrubbing the bath, setting things to rights, whisk, bang, clatter—out again into the saloon—turn the key—click. Such was my scheme for keeping my second self invisible. Nothing better could be contrived under the circumstances. And there we sat; I at my writing desk ready to appear busy with some papers, he behind me out of sight of the door. It would not have been prudent to talk in daytime; and I could not have stood the excitement of that queer sense of whispering to myself. Now and then, glancing over my shoulder, I saw him far back there, sitting rigidly on the low stool, his bare feet close together, his arms folded, his head hanging on his breast—and perfectly still. Anybody would have taken him for me.

I was fascinated by it myself. Every moment I had to glance over my shoulder. I was looking at him when a voice outside the door said:

"Beg pardon, sir."

"Well!" … I kept my eyes on him, and so when the voice outside the door announced, "There's a ship's boat coming our way, sir," I saw him give a start—the first movement he had made for hours. But he did not raise his bowed head.

"All right. Get the ladder over."

I hesitated. Should I whisper something to him? But what? His immobility seemed to have been never disturbed. What could I tell him he did not know already?… Finally I went on deck.

2

The skipper of the *Sephora* had a thin red whisker all round his face, and the sort of complexion that goes with hair of that colour; also the particular, rather smeary shade of blue in the eyes. He was not exactly a showy figure; his shoulders were high, his stature but middling—one leg slightly more bandy than the other. He shook hands, looking vaguely around. A spiritless tenacity was his main characteristic, I judged. I behaved with a politeness which seemed to disconcert him. Perhaps he was shy. He mumbled to me as if he were ashamed of what he was saying; gave his name (it was something like Archbold—but at this distance of years I hardly am sure), his ship's name, and a few other particulars of that sort, in the manner of a criminal making a reluctant and doleful confession. He had had terrible weather on the passage out—terrible—terrible — wife aboard, too.

By this time we were seated in the cabin and the steward brought in a tray with a bottle and glasses. "Thanks! No." Never took liquor. Would have some water, though. He drank two tumblerfuls. Terrible thirsty work. Ever since daylight had been exploring the islands round his ship.

"What was that for—fun?" I asked, with an appearance of polite interest.

"No!" He sighed. "Painful duty."

As he persisted in his mumbling and I wanted my double to hear every word, I hit upon the notion of informing him that I regretted to say I was hard of hearing.

"Such a young man, too!" he nodded, keeping his smeary blue, unintelligent eyes fastened upon me. "What was the cause of it—some disease?" he inquired, without the least sympathy and as if he thought that, if so, I'd got no more than I deserved.

"Yes; disease," I admitted in a cheerful tone which seemed to shock him. But my point was gained, because he had to raise his voice to give me his tale. It is not worth while to record his version. It was just over two months since all this had happened, and he had thought so much about it that he seemed completely muddled as to its bearings, but still immensely impressed.

"What would you think of such a thing happening on board your own ship? I've had the *Sephora* for these fifteen years. I am a well-known shipmaster."

He was densely distressed—and perhaps I should have sympathized with him if I had been able to detach my mental vision from the unsuspected sharer of my cabin as though he were my second self. There he was on the other side of the bulkhead, four or five feet from us, no more, as we sat in the saloon. I looked politely at Captain Archbold (if that was his name), but it was the other I saw, in a gray sleeping suit, seated on a low stool, his bare feet close together, his arms folded, and every word said between us falling into the ears of his dark head bowed on his chest.

"I have been at sea now, man and boy, for seven-and-thirty years, and I've never heard of such a thing happening in an English ship. And that it should be my

ship. Wife on board, too."

I was hardly listening to him.

"Don't you think," I said, "that the heavy sea which, you told me, came aboard just then might have killed the man? I have seen the sheer weight of a sea kill a man very neatly, by simply breaking his neck."

"Good God!" he uttered, impressively, fixing his smeary blue eyes on me. "The sea! No man killed by the sea ever looked like that." He seemed positively scandalized at my suggestion. And as I gazed at him certainly not prepared for anything original on his part, he advanced his head close to mine and thrust his tongue out at me so suddenly that I couldn't help starting back.

After scoring over my calmness in this graphic way he nodded wisely. If I had seen the sight, he assured me, I would never forget it as long as I lived. The weather was too bad to give the corpse a proper sea burial. So next day at dawn they took it up on the poop, covering its face with a bit of bunting; he read a short prayer, and then, just as it was, in its oilskins and long boots, they launched it amongst those mountainous seas that seemed ready every moment to swallow up the ship herself and the terrified lives on board of her.

"That reefed foresail saved you," I threw in.

"Under God—it did," he exclaimed fervently. "It was by a special mercy, I firmly believe, that it stood some of those hurricane squalls."

"It was the setting of that sail which—" I began.

"God's own hand in it," he interrupted me. "Nothing less could have done it. I don't mind telling you that I hardly dared give the order. It seemed impossible that we could touch anything without losing it, and then our last hope would have been gone."

The terror of that gale was on him yet. I let him go on for a bit, then said, casually—as if returning to a minor subject:

"You were very anxious to give up your mate to the shore people, I believe?"

He was. To the law. His obscure tenacity on that point had in it something incomprehensible and a little awful; something, as it were, mystical, quite apart from his anxiety that he should not be suspected of "countenancing any doings of that sort." Seven-and-thirty virtuous years at sea, of which over twenty of immaculate command, and the last fifteen in the Sephora, seemed to have laid him under some pitiless obligation.

"And you know," he went on, groping shame-facedly amongst his feelings, "I did not engage that young fellow. His people had some interest with my owners. I was in a way forced to take him on. He looked very smart, very gentlemanly, and all that. But do you know—I never liked him, somehow. I am a plain man. You see, he wasn't exactly the sort for the chief mate of a ship like the *Sephora*."

I had become so connected in thoughts and impressions with the secret sharer of my cabin that I felt as if I, personally, were being given to understand that I, too, was not the sort that would have done for the chief mate of a ship like the *Sephora*. I had no doubt of it in my mind.

"Not at all the style of man. You understand," he insisted, superfluously, looking hard at me.

I smiled urbanely. He seemed at a loss for a while.

"I suppose I must report a suicide."

"Beg pardon?"

"Suicide! That's what I'll have to write to my owners directly I get in."

"Unless you manage to recover him before tomorrow," I assented, dispassionately… "I mean, alive."

He mumbled something which I really did not catch, and I turned my ear to him in a puzzled manner. He fairly bawled:

"The land—I say, the mainland is at least seven miles off my anchorage."

"About that."

My lack of excitement, of curiosity, of surprise, of any sort of pronounced interest, began to arouse his distrust. But except for the felicitous pretense of deafness I had not tried to pretend anything. I had felt utterly incapable of playing the part of ignorance properly, and therefore was afraid to try. It is also certain that he had brought some ready-made suspicions with him, and that he viewed my politeness as a strange and unnatural phenomenon. And yet how else could I have received him? Not heartily! That was impossible for psychological reasons, which I need not state here. My only object was to keep off his inquiries. Surlily? Yes, but surliness might have provoked a point-blank question. From its novelty to him and from its nature, punctilious courtesy was the manner best calculated to restrain the man. But there was the danger of his breaking through my defense bluntly. I could not, I think, have met him by a direct lie, also for psychological (not moral) reasons. If he had only known how afraid I was of his putting my feeling of identity with the other to the test! But, strangely enough—(I thought of it only afterwards)—I believe that he was not a little disconcerted by the reverse side of that weird situation, by something in me that reminded him of the man he was seeking—suggested a mysterious similitude to the young fellow he had distrusted and disliked from the first.

However that might have been, the silence was not very prolonged. He took another oblique step.

"I reckon I had no more than a two-mile pull to your ship. Not a bit more."

"And quite enough, too, in this awful heat," I said.

Another pause full of mistrust followed. Necessity, they say, is mother of invention, but fear, too, is not barren of ingenious suggestions. And I was afraid he would ask me point-blank for news of my other self.

"Nice little saloon, isn't it?" I remarked, as if noticing for the first time the way his eyes roamed from one closed door to the other. "And very well fitted out, too. Here, for instance," I continued, reaching over the back of my seat negligently and flinging the door open, "is my bathroom."

He made an eager movement, but hardly gave it a glance. I got up, shut the door of the bathroom, and invited him to have a look round, as if I were very proud of my accommodation. He had to rise and be shown round, but he went through the business without any raptures whatever.

"And now we'll have a look at my stateroom," I declared, in a voice as loud as I dared to make it, crossing the cabin to the starboard side with purposely heavy steps.

He followed me in and gazed around. My intelligent double had vanished. I played my part.

"Very convenient—isn't it?"

"Very nice. Very comf … " He didn't finish and went out brusquely as if to escape from some unrighteous wiles of mine. But it was not to be. I had been too frightened not to feel vengeful; I felt I had him on the run, and I meant to keep him on the run. My polite insistence must have had something menacing in it, because he gave in suddenly. And I did not let him off a single item; mate's room, pantry, storerooms, the very sail locker which was also under the poop—he had to look into them all. When at last I showed him out on the quarter-deck he drew a long, spiritless sigh, and mumbled dismally that he must really be going back to his ship now. I desired my mate, who had joined us, to see to the captain's boat.

The man of whiskers gave a blast on the whistle which he used to wear hanging round his neck, and yelled, "*Sephora's* away!" My double down there in my cabin must have heard, and certainly could not feel more relieved than I. Four fellows came running out from somewhere forward and went over the side, while my own men, appearing on deck too, lined the rail. I escorted my visitor to the gangway ceremoniously, and nearly overdid it. He was a tenacious beast. On the very ladder he lingered, and in that unique, guiltily conscientious manner of sticking to the point:

"I say … you … you don't think that—"

I covered his voice loudly:

"Certainly not … I am delighted. Good-by."

I had an idea of what he meant to say, and just saved myself by the privilege of defective hearing. He was too shaken generally to insist, but my mate, close witness of that parting, looked mystified and his face took on a thoughtful cast. As I did not want to appear as if I wished to avoid all communication with my officers, he had the opportunity to address me.

"Seems a very nice man. His boat's crew told our chaps a very extraordinary story, if what I am told by the steward is true. I suppose you had it from the captain, sir?"

"Yes. I had a story from the captain."

"A very horrible affair—isn't it, sir?"

"It is."

"Beats all these tales we hear about murders in Yankee ships."

"I don't think it beats them. I don't think it resembles them in the least."

"Bless my soul—you don't say so! But of course I've no acquaintance whatever with American ships, not I so I couldn't go against your knowledge. It's horrible enough for me…. But the queerest part is that those fellows seemed to have some idea the man was hidden aboard here. They had really. Did you ever hear of such a thing?"

"Preposterous—isn't it?"

We were walking to and fro athwart the quarter-deck. No one of the crew forward could be seen (the day was Sunday), and the mate pursued:

"There was some little dispute about it. Our chaps took offense. 'As if we would harbour a thing like that,' they said. 'Wouldn't you like to look for him in our coal-hole?' Quite a tiff. But they made it up in the end. I suppose he did drown himself. Don't you, sir?"

"I don't suppose anything."

"You have no doubt in the matter, sir?"

"None whatever."

I left him suddenly. I felt I was producing a bad impression, but with my double down there it was most trying to be on deck. And it was almost as trying to be below. Altogether a nerve-trying situation. But on the whole I felt less torn in two when I was with him. There was no one in the whole ship whom I dared take into my confidence. Since the hands had got to know his story, it would have been impossible to pass him off for anyone else, and an accidental discovery was to be dreaded now more than ever….

The steward being engaged in laying the table for dinner, we could talk only with our eyes when I first went down. Later in the afternoon we had a cautious try at whispering. The Sunday quietness of the ship was against us; the stillness of air and water around her was against us; the elements, the men were against us—everything was against us in our secret partnership; time itself—for this could not go on forever. The very trust in Providence was, I suppose, denied to his guilt. Shall I confess that this thought cast me down very much? And as to the chapter of accidents which counts for so much in the book of success, I could only hope that it was closed. For what favourable accident could be expected?

"Did you hear everything?" were my first words as soon as we took up our position side by side, leaning over my bed place.

He had. And the proof of it was his earnest whisper, "The man told you he hardly dared to give the order."

I understood the reference to be to that saving foresail.

"Yes. He was afraid of it being lost in the setting."

"I assure you he never gave the order. He may think he did, but he never gave it. He stood there with me on the break of the poop after the main topsail blew away, and whimpered about our last hope—positively whimpered about it and nothing else—and the night coming on! To hear one's skipper go on like that in such weather was enough to drive any fellow out of his mind. It worked me up into a sort of desperation. I just took it into my own hands and went away from him, boiling, and—But what's the use telling you? YOU know!... Do you think that if I had not been pretty fierce with them I should have got the men to do anything? Not it! The bo's'n[1] perhaps? Perhaps! It wasn't a heavy sea—it was a sea gone mad! I suppose the end of the world will be something like that; and a man may have the heart to see it coming once and be done with it— but to have to face it day after day—I don't blame anybody. I was precious little better than the rest. Only—I was an officer of that old coal wagon, anyhow—"

"I quite understand," I conveyed that sincere assurance into his ear. He was out of breath with whispering; I could hear him pant slightly. It was all very simple. The same strung-up force which had given twenty-four men a chance, at least, for their lives, had, in a sort of recoil, crushed an unworthy mutinous existence.

But I had no leisure to weigh the merits of the matter—footsteps in the saloon, a heavy knock. "There's enough wind to get under way with, sir." Here was the call of a new claim upon my thoughts and even upon my feelings.

"Turn the hands up," I cried through the door. "I'll be on deck directly."

I was going out to make the acquaintance of my ship. Before I left the cabin our eyes met—the eyes of the only two strangers on board. I pointed to the recessed part where the little campstool awaited him and laid my finger on my lips. He made a gesture—somewhat vague—a little mysterious, accompanied by a faint smile, as if of regret.

This is not the place to enlarge upon the sensations of a man who feels for the first time a ship move under his feet to his own independent word. In my case they were not unalloyed. I was not wholly alone with my command; for there was that stranger in my cabin. Or rather, I was not completely and wholly with her. Part of me was absent. That mental feeling of being in two places at once affected me physically as if the mood of secrecy had penetrated my very soul. Before an hour had elapsed since the ship had begun to move, having occasion to ask the mate (he stood by my side) to take a compass bearing of the pagoda, I caught myself reaching up to his ear in whispers. I say I caught myself, but enough had escaped to startle the man. I can't describe it otherwise than by saying that he shied. A grave, preoccupied manner, as though he were in possession of some perplexing intelligence, did not leave him henceforth. A little later I moved away from the rail to look at the compass with such a stealthy gait that the helmsman noticed it—and I could not help noticing the unusual roundness of his eyes. These are trifling instances, though it's to no commander's advantage to be suspected of ludicrous eccentricities. But I was also more seriously affected. There are to a seaman certain words, gestures, that should in given conditions come as naturally, as instinctively as the winking of a menaced eye. A certain order should spring on to his lips without thinking; a certain sign should get itself made, so to speak, without reflection. But all unconscious alertness had abandoned me. I had to make an effort of will to recall myself back (from the cabin) to the conditions of the moment. I felt that I was appearing an irresolute commander to those people who were watching me more or less critically.

And, besides, there were the scares. On the second day out, for instance, coming off the deck in the afternoon (I had straw slippers on my bare feet) I stopped at the open pantry door and spoke to the steward. He was doing something there with his back to me. At the sound of my voice he nearly jumped out of his skin, as the saying is, and incidentally broke a cup.

"What on earth's the matter with you?" I asked, astonished.

He was extremely confused. "Beg your pardon, sir. I made sure you were in your cabin."

"You see I wasn't."

[1] *bo's'n* Boatswain (petty officer in charge of ship's rigging, sails, anchors, and deck crew).

"No, sir. I could have sworn I had heard you moving in there not a moment ago. It's most extraordinary … very sorry, sir."

I passed on with an inward shudder. I was so identified with my secret double that I did not even mention the fact in those scanty, fearful whispers we exchanged. I suppose he had made some slight noise of some kind or other. It would have been miraculous if he hadn't at one time or another. And yet, haggard as he appeared, he looked always perfectly self-controlled, more than calm—almost invulnerable. On my suggestion he remained almost entirely in the bathroom, which, upon the whole, was the safest place. There could be really no shadow of an excuse for anyone ever wanting to go in there, once the steward had done with it. It was a very tiny place. Sometimes he reclined on the floor, his legs bent, his head sustained on one elbow. At others I would find him on the campstool, sitting in his gray sleeping suit and with his cropped dark hair like a patient, unmoved convict. At night I would smuggle him into my bed place, and we would whisper together, with the regular footfalls of the officer of the watch passing and repassing over our heads. It was an infinitely miserable time. It was lucky that some tins of fine preserves were stowed in a locker in my stateroom; hard bread I could always get hold of; and so he lived on stewed chicken, *paté de foie gras*, asparagus, cooked oysters, sardines—on all sorts of abominable sham delicacies out of tins. My early-morning coffee he always drank; and it was all I dared do for him in that respect.

Every day there was the horrible maneuvering to go through so that my room and then the bathroom should be done in the usual way. I came to hate the sight of the steward, to abhor the voice of that harmless man. I felt that it was he who would bring on the disaster of discovery. It hung like a sword over our heads.

The fourth day out, I think (we were then working down the east side of the Gulf of Siam, tack for tack, in light winds and smooth water)—the fourth day, I say, of this miserable juggling with the unavoidable, as we sat at our evening meal, that man, whose slightest movement I dreaded, after putting down the dishes ran up on deck busily. This could not be dangerous. Presently he came down again; and then it appeared that he had remembered a coat of mine which I had thrown over a

rail to dry after having been wetted in a shower which had passed over the ship in the afternoon. Sitting stolidly at the head of the table I became terrified at the sight of the garment on his arm. Of course he made for my door. There was no time to lose.

"Steward," I thundered. My nerves were so shaken that I could not govern my voice and conceal my agitation. This was the sort of thing that made my terrifically whiskered mate tap his forehead with his forefinger. I had detected him using that gesture while talking on deck with a confidential air to the carpenter. It was too far to hear a word, but I had no doubt that this pantomime could only refer to the strange new captain.

"Yes, sir," the pale-faced steward turned resignedly to me. It was this maddening course of being shouted at, checked without rhyme or reason, arbitrarily chased out of my cabin, suddenly called into it, sent flying out of his pantry on incomprehensible errands, that accounted for the growing wretchedness of his expression.

"Where are you going with that coat?"

"To your room, sir."

"Is there another shower coming?"

"I'm sure I don't know, sir. Shall I go up again and see, sir?"

"No! never mind."

My object was attained, as of course my other self in there would have heard everything that passed. During this interlude my two officers never raised their eyes off their respective plates; but the lip of that confounded cub, the second mate, quivered visibly.

I expected the steward to hook my coat on and come out at once. He was very slow about it; but I dominated my nervousness sufficiently not to shout after him. Suddenly I became aware (it could be heard plainly enough) that the fellow for some reason or other was opening the door of the bathroom. It was the end. The place was literally not big enough to swing a cat in. My voice died in my throat and I went stony all over. I expected to hear a yell of surprise and terror, and made a movement, but had not the strength to get on my legs. Everything remained still. Had my second self taken the poor wretch by the throat? I don't know what I could have done next moment if I had not seen the steward come out of my room, close the door, and then stand quietly by the sideboard.

"Saved," I thought. "But, no! Lost! Gone! He was gone!"

I laid my knife and fork down and leaned back in my chair. My head swam. After a while, when sufficiently recovered to speak in a steady voice, I instructed my mate to put the ship round at eight o'clock himself.

"I won't come on deck," I went on. "I think I'll turn in, and unless the wind shifts I don't want to be disturbed before midnight. I feel a bit seedy."

"You did look middling bad a little while ago," the chief mate remarked without showing any great concern.

They both went out, and I stared at the steward clearing the table. There was nothing to be read on that wretched man's face. But why did he avoid my eyes, I asked myself. Then I thought I should like to hear the sound of his voice.

"Steward!"

"Sir!" Startled as usual.

"Where did you hang up that coat?"

"In the bathroom, sir." The usual anxious tone. "It's not quite dry yet, sir."

For some time longer I sat in the cuddy. Had my double vanished as he had come? But of his coming there was an explanation, whereas his disappearance would be inexplicable ... I went slowly into my dark room, shut the door, lighted the lamp, and for a time dared not turn round. When at last I did I saw him standing bolt-upright in the narrow recessed part. It would not be true to say I had a shock, but an irresistible doubt of his bodily existence flitted through my mind. Can it be, I asked myself, that he is not visible to other eyes than mine? It was like being haunted. Motionless, with a grave face, he raised his hands slightly at me in a gesture which meant clearly, "Heavens! what a narrow escape!" Narrow indeed. I think I had come creeping quietly as near insanity as any man who has not actually gone over the border. That gesture restrained me, so to speak.

The mate with the terrific whiskers was now putting the ship on the other tack. In the moment of profound silence which follows upon the hands going to their stations I heard on the poop his raised voice: "Hard alee!"[1] and the distant shout of the order repeated on the main-deck. The sails, in that light breeze, made but a faint fluttering noise. It ceased. The ship was coming round slowly: I held my breath in the renewed stillness of expectation; one wouldn't have thought that there was a single living soul on her decks. A sudden brisk shout, "Mainsail haul!" broke the spell, and in the noisy cries and rush overhead of the men running away with the main brace we two, down in my cabin, came together in our usual position by the bed place.

He did not wait for my question. "I heard him fumbling here and just managed to squat myself down in the bath," he whispered to me. "The fellow only opened the door and put his arm in to hang the coat up. All the same—"

"I never thought of that," I whispered back, even more appalled than before at the closeness of the shave, and marveling at that something unyielding in his character which was carrying him through so finely. There was no agitation in his whisper. Whoever was being driven distracted, it was not he. He was sane. And the proof of his sanity was continued when he took up the whispering again.

"It would never do for me to come to life again."

It was something that a ghost might have said. But what he was alluding to was his old captain's reluctant admission of the theory of suicide. It would obviously serve his turn—if I had understood at all the view which seemed to govern the unalterable purpose of his action.

"You must maroon me as soon as ever you can get amongst these islands off the Cambodge[2] shore," he went on.

"Maroon you! We are not living in a boy's adventure tale," I protested. His scornful whispering took me up.

"We aren't indeed! There's nothing of a boy's tale in this. But there's nothing else for it. I want no more. You don't suppose I am afraid of what can be done to me? Prison or gallows or whatever they may please. But you don't see me coming back to explain such things to an old fellow in a wig and twelve respectable tradesmen, do you? What can they know whether I am guilty or not—or of *what* I am guilty, either? That's my affair. What

---

[1] *Hard alee* "Hard a lee" (meaning "hard towards the leeward side") is the command given when a ship comes about.

[2] *Cambodge* Cambodia.

does the Bible say? 'Driven off the face of the earth.' Very well, I am off the face of the earth now. As I came at night so I shall go."

"Impossible!" I murmured. "You can't."

"Can't? … Not naked like a soul on the Day of Judgment. I shall freeze on to this sleeping suit. The Last Day is not yet—and … you have understood thoroughly. Didn't you?"

I felt suddenly ashamed of myself. I may say truly that I understood—and my hesitation in letting that man swim away from my ship's side had been a mere sham sentiment, a sort of cowardice.

"It can't be done now till next night," I breathed out. "The ship is on the off-shore tack and the wind may fail us."

"As long as I know that you understand," he whispered. "But of course you do. It's a great satisfaction to have got somebody to understand. You seem to have been there on purpose." And in the same whisper, as if we two whenever we talked had to say things to each other which were not fit for the world to hear, he added, "It's very wonderful."

We remained side by side talking in our secret way—but sometimes silent or just exchanging a whispered word or two at long intervals. And as usual he stared through the port. A breath of wind came now and again into our faces. The ship might have been moored in dock, so gently and on an even keel she slipped through the water, that did not murmur even at our passage, shadowy and silent like a phantom sea.

At midnight I went on deck, and to my mate's great surprise put the ship round on the other tack. His terrible whiskers flitted round me in silent criticism. I certainly should not have done it if it had been only a question of getting out of that sleepy gulf as quickly as possible. I believe he told the second mate, who relieved him, that it was a great want of judgment. The other only yawned. That intolerable cub shuffled about so sleepily and lolled against the rails in such a slack, improper fashion that I came down on him sharply.

"Aren't you properly awake yet?"

"Yes, sir! I am awake."

"Well, then, be good enough to hold yourself as if you were. And keep a lookout. If there's any current we'll be closing with some islands before daylight."

The east side of the gulf is fringed with islands, some solitary, others in groups. On the blue background of the high coast they seem to float on silvery patches of calm water, arid and gray, or dark green and rounded like clumps of evergreen bushes, with the larger ones, a mile or two long, showing the outlines of ridges, ribs of gray rock under the dark mantle of matted leafage. Unknown to trade, to travel, almost to geography, the manner of life they harbour is an unsolved secret. There must be villages—settlements of fishermen at least—on the largest of them, and some communication with the world is probably kept up by native craft. But all that forenoon, as we headed for them, fanned along by the faintest of breezes, I saw no sign of man or canoe in the field of the telescope I kept on pointing at the scattered group.

At noon I have no orders for a change of course, and the mate's whiskers became much concerned and seemed to be offering themselves unduly to my notice. At last I said:

"I am going to stand right in. Quite in—as far as I can take her."

The stare of extreme surprise imparted an air of ferocity also to his eyes, and he looked truly terrific for a moment.

"We're not doing well in the middle of the gulf," I continued, casually. "I am going to look for the land breezes tonight."

"Bless my soul! Do you mean, sir, in the dark amongst the lot of all them islands and reefs and shoals?"

"Well—if there are any regular land breezes at all on this coast one must get close inshore to find them, mustn't one?"

"Bless my soul!" he exclaimed again under his breath. All that afternoon he wore a dreamy, contemplative appearance which in him was a mark of perplexity. After dinner I went into my stateroom as if I meant to take some rest. There we two bent our dark heads over a half-unrolled chart lying on my bed.

"There," I said. "It's got to be Koh-ring. I've been looking at it ever since sunrise. It has got two hills and a low point. It must be inhabited. And on the coast opposite there is what looks like the mouth of a biggish river—with some towns, no doubt, not far up. It's the best chance for you that I can see."

"Anything. Koh-ring let it be."

He looked thoughtfully at the chart as if surveying chances and distances from a lofty height—and following with his eyes his own figure wandering on the blank land of Cochin-China, and then passing off that piece of paper clean out of sight into uncharted regions. And it was as if the ship had two captains to plan her course for her. I had been so worried and restless running up and down that I had not had the patience to dress that day. I had remained in my sleeping suit, with straw slippers and a soft floppy hat. The closeness of the heat in the gulf had been most oppressive, and the crew were used to seeing me wandering in that airy attire.

"She will clear the south point as she heads now," I whispered into his ear. "Goodness only knows when, though, but certainly after dark. I'll edge her in to half a mile, as far as I may be able to judge in the dark—"

"Be careful," he murmured, warningly—and I realized suddenly that all my future, the only future for which I was fit, would perhaps go irretrievably to pieces in any mishap to my first command.

I could not stop a moment longer in the room. I motioned him to get out of sight and made my way on the poop. That unplayful cub had the watch. I walked up and down for a while thinking things out, then beckoned him over.

"Send a couple of hands to open the two quarter-deck ports," I said, mildly.

He actually had the impudence, or else so forgot himself in his wonder at such an incomprehensible order, as to repeat:

"Open the quarter-deck ports! What for, sir?"

"The only reason you need concern yourself about is because I tell you to do so. Have them open wide and fastened properly."

He reddened and went off, but I believe made some jeering remark to the carpenter as to the sensible practice of ventilating a ship's quarter-deck. I know he popped into the mate's cabin to impart the fact to him because the whiskers came on deck, as it were by chance, and stole glances at me from below—for signs of lunacy or drunkenness, I suppose.

A little before supper, feeling more restless than ever, I rejoined, for a moment, my second self. And to find

him sitting so quietly was surprising, like something against nature, inhuman.

I developed my plan in a hurried whisper.

"I shall stand in as close as I dare and then put her round. I will presently find means to smuggle you out of here into the sail locker, which communicates with the lobby. But there is an opening, a sort of square for hauling the sails out, which gives straight on the quarter-deck and which is never closed in fine weather, so as to give air to the sails. When the ship's way is deadened in stays and all the hands are aft at the main braces you will have a clear road to slip out and get overboard through the open quarter-deck port. I've had them both fastened up. Use a rope's end to lower yourself into the water so as to avoid a splash—you know. It could be heard and cause some beastly complication."

He kept silent for a while, then whispered, "I understand."

"I won't be there to see you go," I began with an effort. "The rest … I only hope I have understood, too."

"You have. From first to last"—and for the first time there seemed to be a faltering, something strained in his whisper. He caught hold of my arm, but the ringing of the supper bell made me start. He didn't though; he only released his grip.

After supper I didn't come below again till well past eight o'clock. The faint, steady breeze was loaded with dew; and the wet, darkened sails held all there was of propelling power in it. The night, clear and starry, sparkled darkly, and the opaque, lightless patches shifting slowly against the low stars were the drifting islets. On the port bow there was a big one more distant and shadowily imposing by the great space of sky it eclipsed.

On opening the door I had a back view of my very own self looking at a chart. He had come out of the recess and was standing near the table.

"Quite dark enough," I whispered.

He stepped back and leaned against my bed with a level, quiet glance. I sat on the couch. We had nothing to say to each other. Over our heads the officer of the watch moved here and there. Then I heard him move quickly. I knew what that meant. He was making for the companion; and presently his voice was outside my door.

"We are drawing in pretty fast, sir. Land looks rather close."

"Very well," I answered. "I am coming on deck directly."

I waited till he was gone out of the cuddy, then rose. My double moved too. The time had come to exchange our last whispers, for neither of us was ever to hear each other's natural voice.

"Look here!" I opened a drawer and took out three sovereigns. "Take this anyhow. I've got six and I'd give you the lot, only I must keep a little money to buy some fruit and vegetables for the crew from native boats as we go through Sunda Straits."

He shook his head.

"Take it," I urged him, whispering desperately. "No one can tell what—"

He smiled and slapped meaningly the only pocket of the sleeping jacket. It was not safe, certainly. But I produced a large old silk handkerchief of mine, and tying the three pieces of gold in a corner, pressed it on him. He was touched, I supposed, because he took it at last and tied it quickly round his waist under the jacket, on his bare skin.

Our eyes met; several seconds elapsed, till, our glances still mingled, I extended my hand and turned the lamp out. Then I passed through the cuddy, leaving the door of my room wide open…"Steward!"

He was still lingering in the pantry in the greatness of his zeal, giving a rub-up to a plated cruet stand the last thing before going to bed. Being careful not to wake up the mate, whose room was opposite, I spoke in an undertone.

He looked round anxiously. "Sir!"

"Can you get me a little hot water from the galley?"

"I am afraid, sir, the galley fire's been out for some time now."

"Go and see."

He flew up the stairs.

"Now," I whispered, loudly, into the saloon—too loudly, perhaps, but I was afraid I couldn't make a sound. He was by my side in an instant—the double captain slipped past the stairs—through a tiny dark passage…a sliding door. We were in the sail locker, scrambling on our knees over the sails. A sudden thought struck me. I saw myself wandering barefooted,

bareheaded, the sun beating on my dark poll. I snatched off my floppy hat and tried hurriedly in the dark to ram it on my other self. He dodged and fended off silently. I wonder what he thought had come to me before he understood and suddenly desisted. Our hands met gropingly, lingered united in a steady, motionless clasp for a second…No word was breathed by either of us when they separated.

I was standing quietly by the pantry door when the steward returned.

"Sorry, sir. Kettle barely warm. Shall I light the spirit lamp?"

"Never mind."

I came out on deck slowly. It was now a matter of conscience to shave the land as close as possible—for now he must go overboard whenever the ship was put in stays. Must! There could be no going back for him. After a moment I walked over to leeward and my heart flew into my mouth at the nearness of the land on the bow. Under any other circumstances I would not have held on a minute longer. The second mate had followed me anxiously.

I looked on till I felt I could command my voice.

"She will weather," I said then in a quiet tone.

"Are you going to try that, sir?" he stammered out incredulously.

I took no notice of him and raised my tone just enough to be heard by the helmsman.

"Keep her good full."

"Good full, sir."

The wind fanned my cheek, the sails slept, the world was silent. The strain of watching the dark loom of the land grow bigger and denser was too much for me. I had shut my eyes—because the ship must go closer. She must! The stillness was intolerable. Were we standing still?

When I opened my eyes the second view started my heart with a thump. The black southern hill of Koh-ring seemed to hang right over the ship like a towering fragment of everlasting night. On that enormous mass of blackness there was not a gleam to be seen, not a sound to be heard. It was gliding irresistibly towards us and yet seemed already within reach of the hand. I saw the vague figures of the watch grouped in the waist, gazing in awed silence.

"Are you going on, sir?" inquired an unsteady voice

at my elbow.

I ignored it. I had to go on.

"Keep her full. Don't check her way. That won't do now," I said warningly.

"I can't see the sails very well," the helmsman answered me, in strange, quavering tones.

Was she close enough? Already she was, I won't say in the shadow of the land, but in the very blackness of it, already swallowed up as it were, gone too close to be recalled, gone from me altogether.

"Give the mate a call," I said to the young man who stood at my elbow as still as death. "And turn all hands up."

My tone had a borrowed loudness reverberated from the height of the land. Several voices cried out together: "We are all on deck, sir."

Then stillness again, with the great shadow gliding closer, towering higher, without a light, without a sound. Such a hush had fallen on the ship that she might have been a bark of the dead floating in slowly under the very gate of Erebus.[1]

"My God! Where are we?"

It was the mate moaning at my elbow. He was thunderstruck, and as it were deprived of the moral support of his whiskers. He clapped his hands and absolutely cried out, "Lost!"

"Be quiet," I said, sternly.

He lowered his tone, but I saw the shadowy gesture of his despair. "What are we doing here?"

"Looking for the land wind."

He made as if to tear his hair, and addressed me recklessly.

"She will never get out. You have done it, sir. I knew it'd end in something like this. She will never weather, and you are too close now to stay. She'll drift ashore before she's round. O my God!"

I caught his arm as he was raising it to batter his poor devoted head, and shook it violently.

"She's ashore already," he wailed, trying to tear himself away.

"Is she? … Keep good full there!"

"Good full, sir," cried the helmsman in a frightened, thin, childlike voice.

I hadn't let go the mate's arm and went on shaking it. "Ready about, do you hear? You go forward"— shake—"and stop there"—shake—"and hold your noise"—shake—"and see these head-sheets properly overhauled"—shake, shake—shake.

And all the time I dared not look towards the land lest my heart should fail me. I released my grip at last and he ran forward as if fleeing for dear life.

I wondered what my double there in the sail locker thought of this commotion. He was able to hear everything—and perhaps he was able to understand why, on my conscience, it had to be thus close—no less. My first order "Hard alee!" re-echoed ominously under the towering shadow of Koh-ring as if I had shouted in a mountain gorge. And then I watched the land intently. In that smooth water and light wind it was impossible to feel the ship coming-to. No! I could not feel her. And my second self was making now ready to ship out and lower himself overboard. Perhaps he was gone already…?

The great black mass brooding over our very mastheads began to pivot away from the ship's side silently. And now I forgot the secret stranger ready to depart, and remembered only that I was a total stranger to the ship. I did not know her. Would she do it? How was she to be handled?

I swung the mainyard and waited helplessly. She was perhaps stopped, and her very fate hung in the balance, with the black mass of Koh-ring like the gate of the everlasting night towering over her taffrail.[2] What would she do now? Had she way on her yet? I stepped to the side swiftly, and on the shadowy water I could see nothing except a faint phosphorescent flash revealing the glassy smoothness of the sleeping surface. It was impossible to tell—and I had not learned yet the feel of my ship. Was she moving? What I needed was something easily seen, a piece of paper, which I could throw overboard and watch. I had nothing on me. To run down for it I didn't dare. There was no time. All at once my strained, yearning stare distinguished a white object floating within a yard of the ship's side. White on the black water. A phosphorescent flash passed under it. What was that thing?… I recognized my own floppy

---

[1] *Erebus* In classical myth, a place of darkness between earth and Hades, the underworld.

[2] *taffrail* Stern rail.

hat. It must have fallen off his head … and he didn't bother. Now I had what I wanted—the saving mark for my eyes. But I hardly thought of my other self, now gone from the ship, to be hidden forever from all friendly faces, to be a fugitive and a vagabond on the earth, with no brand of the curse on his sane forehead to stay a slaying hand … too proud to explain.

And I watched the hat—the expression of my sudden pity for his mere flesh. It had been meant to save his homeless head from the dangers of the sun. And now—behold—it was saving the ship, by serving me for a mark to help out the ignorance of my strangeness. Ha! It was drifting forward, warning me just in time that the ship had gathered sternaway.

"Shift the helm," I said in a low voice to the seaman standing still like a statue.

The man's eyes glistened wildly in the binnacle light as he jumped round to the other side and spun round the wheel.

I walked to the break of the poop. On the overshadowed deck all hands stood by the forebraces waiting for my order. The stars ahead seemed to be gliding from right to left. And all was so still in the world that I heard the quiet remark, "She's round," passed in a tone of intense relief between two seamen.

"Let go and haul."

The foreyards ran round with a great noise, amidst cheery cries. And now the frightful whiskers made themselves heard giving various orders. Already the ship was drawing ahead. And I was alone with her. Nothing! no one in the world should stand now between us, throwing a shadow on the way of silent knowledge and mute affection, the perfect communion of a seaman with his first command.

Walking to the taffrail, I was in time to make out, on the very edge of a darkness thrown by a towering black mass like the very gateway of Erebus—yes, I was in time to catch an evanescent glimpse of my white hat left behind to mark the spot where the secret sharer of my cabin and of my thoughts, as though he were my second self, had lowered himself into the water to take his punishment: a free man, a proud swimmer striking out for a new destiny.

—1912

from *Some Reflections on the Loss of the Titanic*

Years ago I remember overhearing two genuine shellbacks[1] of the old type commenting on a ship's officer, who, if not exactly incompetent, did not commend himself to their severe judgment of accomplished sailor-men. Said one, resuming and concluding the discussion in a funnily judicial tone:

"The Board of Trade must have been drunk when they gave him his certificate."

I confess that this notion of the Board of Trade as an entity having a brain which could be overcome by the fumes of strong liquor charmed me exceedingly. For then it would have been unlike the limited companies of which some exasperated wit has once said that they had no souls to be saved and no bodies to be kicked, and thus were free in this world and the next from all the effective sanctions of conscientious conduct. But, unfortunately, the picturesque pronouncement overheard by me was only a characteristic sally of an annoyed sailor. The Board of Trade is composed of bloodless departments. It has no limbs and no physiognomy, or else at the forthcoming inquiry it might have paid to the victims of the *Titanic* disaster the small tribute of a blush. I ask myself whether the Marine Department of the Board of Trade did really believe, when they decided to shelve the report on equipment for a time, that a ship of 45,000 tons, that *any* ship, could be made practically indestructible by means of watertight bulkheads? It seems incredible to anybody who had ever reflected upon the properties of material, such as wood or steel. You can't, let builders say what they like, make a ship of such dimensions as strong proportionately as a much smaller one. The shocks our old whalers had to stand amongst the heavy floes in Baffin's Bay were perfectly staggering, notwithstanding the most skilful handling, and yet they lasted for years. The *Titanic,* if one may believe the last reports, has only scraped against a piece of ice which, I suspect, was not an enormously bulky and comparatively easily seen berg, but the low edge of a floe—and sank. Leisurely enough, God knows—and here the advantage of bulkheads

---

[1] *shellbacks* Hardened sailors.

comes in—for time is a great friend, a good helper —though in this lamentable case these bulkheads served only to prolong the agony of the passengers who could not be saved. But she sank, causing, apart from the sorrow and the pity of the loss of so many lives, a sort of surprised consternation that such a thing should have happened at all. Why? You build a 45,000 ton hotel of thin steel plates to secure the patronage of, say, a couple of thousand rich people (for if it had been for the emigrant trade alone, there would have been no such exaggeration of mere size), you decorate it in the style of the Pharaohs or in the Louis Quinze style—I don't know which—and to please the aforesaid fatuous handful of individuals, who have more money than they know what to do with, and to the applause of two continents, you launch that mass with 2,000 people on board at twenty-one knots across the sea—a perfect exhibition of the modern blind trust in mere material and appliances. And then this happens. General uproar. The blind trust in material and appliances has received a terrible shock. I will say nothing of the credulity which accepts any statement which specialists, technicians, and office-people are pleased to make, whether for purposes of gain or glory. You stand there astonished and hurt in your profoundest sensibilities. But what else under the circumstances could you expect?

For my part I could much sooner believe in an unsinkable ship of 3,000 tons than in one of 40,000 tons. It is one of those things that stand to reason. You can't increase the thickness of scantling and plates indefinitely. And the mere weight of this bigness is an added disadvantage. In reading the reports, the first reflection which occurs to one is that, if that luckless ship had been a couple of hundred feet shorter, she would have probably gone clear of the danger. But then, perhaps, she could not have had a swimming bath and a French cafe. That, of course, is a serious consideration. I am well aware that those responsible for her short and fatal existence ask us in desolate accents to believe that if she had hit end on she would have survived. "Which, by a sort of coy implication, seems to mean that it was all the fault of the officer of the watch (he is dead now) for trying to avoid the obstacle. We shall have presently, in deference to commercial and industrial interests, a new kind of seamanship. A very new and "progressive"

kind. If you see anything in the way, by no means try to avoid it; smash at it full tilt. And then—and then only you shall see the triumph of material, of clever contrivances, of the whole box of engineering tricks in fact, and cover with glory a commercial concern of the most unmitigated sort, a great Trust, and a great shipbuilding yard, justly famed for the super-excellence of its material and workmanship. Unsinkable! See? I told you she was unsinkable, if only handled in accordance with the new seamanship. Everything's in that. And, doubtless, the Board of Trade, if properly approached, would consent to give the needed instructions to its examiners of Masters and Mates. Behold the examination-room of the future. Enter to the grizzled examiner a young man of modest aspect: "Are you well up in modern seamanship?" "I hope so, sir." "H'm, let's see You are at night on the bridge in charge of a 150,000 tons ship, with a motor track, organ-loft, etc., etc., with a full cargo of passengers, a full crew of 1,500 cafe waiters, two sailors and a boy, three collapsible boats as per Board of Trade regulations, and going at your three-quarter speed of, say, about forty knots. You perceive suddenly right ahead, and close to, something that looks like a large ice-floe. What would you do?" "Put the helm amidships." "Very well. Why?" "In order to hit end on." "On what grounds should you endeavour to hit end on?" "Because we are taught by our builders and masters that the heavier the smash, the smaller the damage, and because the requirements of material should be attended to."

And so on and so on. The new seamanship: when in doubt try to ram fairly—whatever's before you. Very simple. If only the *Titanic* had rammed that piece of ice (which was *not* a monstrous berg) fairly, every puffing paragraph would have been vindicated in the eyes of the credulous public which pays. But would it have been? Well, I doubt it. I am well aware that in the 'eighties the steamship *Arizona,* one of the "greyhounds of the ocean" in the jargon of that day, did run bows on against a very unmistakable iceberg, and managed to get into port on her collision bulkhead. But the *Arizona* was not, if I remember rightly, 5,000 tons register, let alone 45,000, and she was not going at twenty knots per hour. I can't be perfectly certain at this distance of time, but her sea-speed could not have been more than fourteen at the outside. Both these facts made for safety. And, even if she had been engined to go twenty knots, there would not have been behind that speed the enormous mass, so difficult to check in its impetus, the terrific weight of which is bound to do damage to itself or others at the slightest contact.

I assure you it is not for the vain pleasure of talking about my own poor experiences, but only to illustrate my point, that I will relate here a very unsensational little incident I witnessed now rather more than twenty years ago in Sydney, N.S.W. Ships were beginning then to grow bigger year after year, though, of course, the present dimensions were not even dreamt of. I was standing on the Circular Quay with a Sydney pilot watching a big mail steamship of one of our best-known companies being brought alongside. We admired her lines, her noble appearance, and were impressed by her size as well, though her length, I imagine, was hardly half that of the *Titanic*.

She came into the Cove (as that part of the harbour is called), of course very slowly, and at some hundred feet or so short of the quay she lost her way. That quay was then a wooden one, a fine structure of mighty piles and stringers bearing a roadway—a thing of great strength. The ship, as I have said before, stopped moving when some hundred feet from it. Then her engines were rung on slow ahead, and immediately rung off again. The propeller made just about five turns, I should say. She began to move, stealing on, so to speak, without a ripple; coming alongside with the utmost gentleness. I went on looking her over, very much interested, but the man with me, the pilot, muttered under his breath: "Too much, too much." His exercised judgment had warned him of what I did not even suspect. But I believe that neither of us was exactly prepared for what happened. There was a faint concussion of the ground under our feet, a groaning of piles, a snapping of great iron bolts, and with a sound of ripping and splintering, as when a tree is blown down by the wind, a great strong piece of wood, a baulk of squared timber, was displaced several feet as if by enchantment. I looked at my companion in amazement. "I could not have believed it," I declared. "No," he said. "You would not have thought she would have cracked an egg—eh?"

I certainly wouldn't have thought that. He shook his

head, and added: "Ah! These great, big things, they want some handling."

Some months afterwards I was back in Sydney. The same pilot brought me in from sea. And I found the same steamship, or else another as like her as two peas, lying at anchor not far from us. The pilot told me she had arrived the day before, and that he was to take her alongside to-morrow. I reminded him jocularly of the damage to the quay. "Oh!" he said, "we are not allowed now to bring them in under their own steam. We are using tugs."

A very wise regulation. And this is my point—that size is to a certain extent an element of weakness. The bigger the ship, the more delicately she must be handled. Here is a contact which, in the pilot's own words, you wouldn't think could have cracked an egg; with the astonishing result of something like eighty feet of good strong wooden quay shaken loose, iron bolts snapped, a baulk of stout timber splintered. Now, suppose that quay had been of granite (as surely it is now)—or, instead of the quay, if there had been, say, a North Atlantic fog there, with a full-grown iceberg in it, awaiting the gentle contact of a ship groping its way along blindfold? Something would have been hurt, but it would not have been the iceberg.

Apparently, there is a point in development when it ceases to be a true progress—in trade, in games, in the marvellous handiwork of men, and even in their demands and desires and aspirations of the moral and mental kind. There is a point when progress, to remain a real advance, must change slightly the direction of its line. But this is a wide question. What I wanted to point out here is—that the old *Arizona,* the marvel of her day, was proportionately stronger, handier, better equipped, than this triumph of modern naval architecture, the loss of which, in common parlance, will remain the sensation of this year. The clatter of the presses has been worthy of the tonnage, of the preliminary paeans of triumph round that vanished hull, of the reckless statements, and elaborate descriptions of its ornate splendour. A great babble of news (and what sort of news too, good heavens!) and eager comment has arisen around this catastrophe, though it seems to me that a less strident note would have been more becoming in the presence of so many victims left struggling on the sea, of lives miserably thrown away for nothing, or worse than nothing: for false standards of achievement, to satisfy a vulgar demand of a few moneyed people for a banal hotel luxury—the only one they can understand—and because the big ship pays, in one way or another: in money or in advertising value.

It is in more ways than one a very ugly business, and a mere scrape along the ship's side, so slight that, if reports are to be believed, it did not interrupt a card party in the gorgeously fitted (but in chaste style) smoking-room—or was it in the delightful French cafe —is enough to bring on the exposure. All the people on board existed under a sense of false security. How false, it has been sufficiently demonstrated. And the fact which seems undoubted, that some of them actually were reluctant to enter the boats, when told to do so, shows the strength of that falsehood. Incidentally, it shows also the sort of discipline on board these ships, the sort of hold kept on the passengers in the face of the

unforgiving sea. These people seemed to imagine it an optional matter: whereas the order to leave the ship should be an order of the sternest character, to be obeyed unquestioningly and promptly by every one on board, with men to enforce it at once, and to carry it out methodically and swiftly. And it is no use to say it cannot be done, for it can. It has been done. The only requisite is manageableness of the ship herself and of the numbers she carries on board. That is the great thing which makes for safety. A commander should be able to hold his ship and everything on board of her in the hollow of his hand, as it were. But with the modern foolish trust in material, and with those floating hotels, this has become impossible. A man may do his best, but he cannot succeed in a task which from greed, or more likely from sheer stupidity, has been made too great for anybody's strength.

—1921

The Titanic being towed out for sea trial, 1912.

IN CONTEXT

"The Vilest Scramble for Loot" in Central Africa

Conrad does not state the exact location in which "An Outpost of Progress" takes place; the nationality of Kayerts and Carlier is not specified, and the origin of various groups of indigenous peoples is indicated only through phrases such as "from a very distant part of the land of darkness and sorrow." It seems clear, however, that in writing the story he drew extensively on his experiences in the Belgian Congo in 1890. At that time what is now the Democratic Republic of the Congo was the personal preserve of King Leopold II of Belgium—though with macabre irony the territory bore the official title of the Congo Free State. Under Leopold there was little pretense of bringing "civilization" to the local populace in the fashion that it was often imposed in other colonial contexts—through education and religious indoctrination. There was some missionary activity, but almost all interaction with the native peoples was nakedly commercial and brutally oppressive. Though slavery was officially illegal, the local people were often slaves in all but name; they had taxes imposed upon them, were often forced to provide labor free of charge, and were subject to mutilation and death at the first sign of disobedience. The Belgians led the way in these practices, but they were not alone; American, British, Dutch, French, and Portuguese companies were all licensed to trade in the region, and all did so on roughly similar terms. From East Africa came Arab traders in slaves and ivory (the notorious Tippu Tib most prominent among them).

Just south of the Congo Free State lay the Portuguese colony of Angola, where the level of cruelty (both by the Portuguese towards the native African population and by African groups towards others) was not far removed from that in the Congo itself. The Angolan port of Luanda, some 200 miles south of the mouth of the Congo River (also known as the Lualaba River), was in the late nineteenth century a thriving city, exporting timber, coffee, and cotton as well as ivory.

During Conrad's journey through the Congo, a Belgian commercial agent named Alphonse Kayerts traveled with him on the steamer *Roi de Belges* as it sailed between Stanley Pool and Stanley Falls. The captain of another steamer traveling in the area, the *Lualaba*, was named Carlier. The Belgians spoke French, whereas the colonial language of Angola was Portuguese—a Romance language with Latin roots, like French. In "An Outpost of Progress" Kayerts and Carlier never discover where the group of strangers comes from. Their possession of firearms is taken as evidence that they come "from the coast," but they are evidently not Arab traders; their leader is described as "a powerful and determined-looking negro." It is notable that the language of the group strikes the two at the station as strangely familiar.

The following materials document some aspects of the late nineteenth- and early twentieth-century horrors in the Congo region.

from William G. Stairs, *Diaries* (1887)

Stairs, a Canadian military man, traveled the Congo with Henry Morgan Stanley on Stanley's "Emin Pasha" expedition of 1887–89, visiting many of the same areas through which Conrad traveled less than three years later.

16 April 1887

... I met a very nice chap today on the road, in charge of some of the Sanford expedition porters, carrying machinery and parts of the hull of a steamer up-river for trading purposes on the upper waters of the Congo and its branches. He asked me to breakfast and gave me two eggs as a present, which was a most acceptable gift under such circumstances as we are placed in. All these fellows and the officers of the Congo Free State travel from place to place like lords: they have the very best of tinned goods of all sorts—jams, bacon, oatmeal, tea, coffee, condensed milk, tinned fish, besides fruits, and whatever else the country yields. They generally have three or four native boys as servants, carry swell tents and beds, and generally do themselves up well. In fact, I know one or two officers of the CFS [Congo Free State] who get carried about by porters wherever they go. These Belgian officers are very hospitable to us as we pass by the different stations, but they appear to us to be the wrong sort of men to have as agents of a young state such as this is. They seem to lack energy and push, to be too fond of staying indoors at the stations and as a rule are very ignorant of the country above [Stanley] Pool. ...

31 May 1887

... We have now seen the whole of the working of the Congo Independent State. We have seen how it treats the different trading houses under its jurisdiction. We have also seen a fair portion of the country it governs and the natives under its charge. Our unanimous opinion is that the state, as now constructed, is one huge mistake. It was originally intended to be a *free state*, open to all, welcoming all honest trade, countenancing all open dealings with the natives and doing its best to establish postal and other communication between its different stations. Instead of this, what does really exist? A Congo *independent state*, open as regards its officials to all Belgians, is continually at variance with all the trading houses—English, Dutch, French, and Portuguese alike—hindering instead of aiding trade, and absolutely ignoring the importance of even a rough track with bush bridges on such a thoroughfare as that between Mataddi and Stanley Pool.

Certainly the Congo Independent State is a huge unwieldy mistake (as managed at present), worked purely in the interests of the King of the Belgians, who takes the best of care that outside influence is excluded and apparently imagines that some day this place will form a safe deposit for Belgian capital and manufactures. ...

from Henry Morgan Stanley, Speech given to the Lotus Club, New York (27 November 1886)

... After I had written my book, *Through the Dark Continent*, I began to lecture, using these words: "I have passed through a land watered by the largest river of the African continent, and that land knows no owner. A word to the wise is sufficient. You have cloths and hardware and glassware and gunpowder and these millions of natives have ivory and gums and rubber and dyestuffs, and in barter there is good profit." [Applause.]

The King of the Belgians commissioned me to go to that country. My expedition when we started from the coast numbered 300 colored people and fourteen Europeans. We returned with 3,000 trained black men and 300 Europeans. The first sum allowed me was $50,000 a year, but it has ended at something like $700,000 a year. Thus, you see, the progress of civilization. We found the Congo, having only canoes. Today there are eight steamers. It was said at first that King Leopold was a dreamer. He dreamed he could unite the barbarians of Africa into a confederacy and call it the Free State, but on February 25, 1885, the Powers of Europe and America also ratified an act, recognizing the territories acquired by us to be the free and independent State of the Congo. ...

from Henry Morgan Stanley, *In Darkest Africa* (1890)

... [T]he bandits fling themselves upon a settlement without mercy to obtain the largest share of loot, of children, flocks, poultry, and ivory.

All this would be clearly beyond their power if they possessed no gunpowder. Not a mile beyond their settlements would the Arabs and their followers dare venture. It is more than likely that if gunpowder was prohibited entry into Africa there would be a general and quick migration to the sea of all Arabs from inner Africa, as the native Chiefs would be immeasurably stronger than any combination of Arabs armed with spears. What possible chance could Tippu Tib, Abed bin Salim, Ugarrowwa and Kilonga-Longa have against the Basongora and Bakusu? How could the Arabs of Ujiji resist the Wajiji and Warundi, or how could those of Unyamyembé live among the bowmen and spearmen of Unyanrwezi?

There is only one remedy for these wholesale devastations of African aborigines, and that is the solemn combination of England, Germany, France, Portugal, South and East Africa, and Congo State against the introduction of gunpowder into any part of the Continent except for the use of their own agents, soldiers, and employees, or seizing upon every tusk of ivory brought out, as there is not a single piece nowadays which has been gained lawfully. Every tusk, piece and scrap in the possession of an Arab trader has been steeped and dyed in blood. Every pound weight has cost the life of a man, woman, or child, for every five pounds a hut has been burned, for every two tusks a whole village has been destroyed, every twenty tusks have been obtained at the price of a district with all its people,

Attacking an Elephant in the Ituri River. (Illustration from *In Darkest Africa*.)

Our Landing at Yambuya. (Illustration by A. Forestter, from *In Darkest Africa.*)

villages, and plantations. It is simply incredible that, because ivory is required for ornaments or billiard games, the rich heart of Africa should be laid waste at this late year of the nineteenth century, signalized as it has been by so much advance, that populations, tribes, and nations should be utterly destroyed. Whom after all does this bloody seizure of ivory enrich? Only a few dozens of half-castes, Arab and Negro, who, if due justice were dealt to them, should be made to sweat out the remainder of their piratical lives in the severest penal servitude. ...

from Joseph Chamberlain, Speech to the House of Commons (6 August 1901)

... It is a question [of native labour] which has engaged my most careful attention in connection with West Africa and other Colonies. To listen to the right honourable gentleman, you would almost think that it would be a good thing for the native to be idle. I think it is a good thing for him to be industrious; and by every means in our power we must teach him to work. ... No people ever have lived in the world's history who would not work. In the interests of the natives all over Africa, we have to teach them to work.

from Roger Casement, *Congo Report* (1903)

The Concession Companies, I believe, account for the armed men in their service on the ground that their factories and agents must be protected against the possible violence of the rude forest dwellers with whom they deal; but this legitimate need for safeguarding European establishments does not suffice to account for the presence, far from those establishments, of large numbers of armed men quartered throughout the native villages, and who exercise upon their surroundings an influence far from protective. The explanation offered me of this state of things was that, as the "impositions" laid upon the natives were regulated by law, and were calculated on the scale of public labour the Government had a right to require of the people, the collection of these "impositions" had to be strictly enforced. ...

Ivory Collecting, Congo. Photo by Alice Harris, c. 1900–04.

A.E. HOUSMAN
1859 – 1936

During his lifetime, A.E. Housman published only two slim volumes of poetry, *A Shropshire Lad* and *Last Poems*. Yet his poems were widely read by both popular and academic audiences, and these two books continue to receive substantial critical attention. In 1996, as part of the festivities commemorating the centenary of the publication of *A Shropshire Lad*, a window in the Poets' Corner of Westminster Abbey was dedicated to Housman. Tom Stoppard's play about Housman, *The Invention of Love*, was produced at the National Theatre, London, in 1997, and debuted in the United States in the winter of 1999–2000.

Although Housman is now known primarily for his poetry, he considered his life's work to be classical scholarship. By the time he was appointed Professor of Latin at Cambridge, Housman had published 99 classical papers, the first volume of his edition of Manilius, an edition of Juvenal, and an edition of Ovid's *Ibis*. In a testimony to Housman's scholarly writings, T.S. Eliot commented in 1933 that Housman "is one of the few living masters of English prose."

The eldest of seven children, Alfred Edward Housman was born on 26 March 1859 to Sarah Jane Williams, a clergyman's daughter, and Edward Housman, a lawyer. As a young child, Housman took great pleasure in words, and was writing verse by the age of eight. He frequently directed the younger children in playacting and wrote out a family magazine that he circulated among friends and relatives. His happy childhood at the family home in Bromsgrove, Worcestershire was dramatically interrupted by the news, in 1869, that his mother had breast cancer. In a sad coincidence, she died on 26 March 1871, on Housman's twelfth birthday. During his wife's illness, Edward Housman began to drink heavily; the family maintained respectable appearances but his drinking worsened, as did their financial situation.

In 1870, a scholarship enabled Housman to enter Bromsgrove School as a day-boy. He was serious and quiet, nicknamed "Mouse" by his classmates, but also a gifted student, winning prizes for English verse, freehand drawing, French, and Latin and Greek verse. These successes resulted in a scholarship to study Classics at St. John's College, Oxford, in 1877 where Housman initially excelled, passing the required second-year examinations with First Class Honours. During this time, his poetry began to be published by *Waifs and Strays*, an Oxford magazine. In 1880, Housman moved out of the college buildings to share a residence with A.W. Pollard and Moses Jackson. Some biographers have argued that Jackson was the love of Housman's life; if so, however, his feelings were apparently never reciprocated. Housman's Oxford career ended in disappointment when, in May 1881, he failed the final set of examinations required of undergraduates. Housman returned to Oxford in 1882 so that he could take another exam and receive the lesser "pass" degree.

With his father's health in decline and the family finances in a shambles, Housman passed the Civil Service exam in June 1882 in order to qualify himself for employment. Shortly after, he accepted a position as clerk in the Patent Office in London, where Moses Jackson also worked. Housman toiled for ten years in the Patent Office, all the while continuing his study of Classics by reading in the evenings at the British Museum. His first scholarly article appeared in 1882 in the *Journal of Philology*; during his time at the Patent Office he would publish 25 essays, although many of his colleagues were unaware of his scholarly pursuits. By 1892, when Housman applied for the position of Professor of Latin at University College, London, he was a well-respected classical scholar with an international reputation.

Housman's first book of poetry, *A Shropshire Lad*, has never been out of print. The manuscript was originally rejected by the Macmillan publishing company, as well as several others, and Housman published it at his own expense with the firm of Kegan Paul in 1896. Housman composed most of the poems in *A Shropshire Lad* in the wake of two deaths—that of his friend Adalbert Jackson in 1892, and that of his father in 1894. Coincidentally, the period of the poems' composition was also the period of Oscar Wilde's trial and conviction under the Labouchere Amendment that outlawed homosexuality in England. Housman carefully guarded his own sexuality in his life and his work, no doubt aware that he would have risked prison and exile if he had chosen to express himself openly. Several modern critics have pointed to the ways in which Housman expresses same-sex love through various poetic codes, and certainly he left ample scope for a broader public to read his poems as expressing a love that was entirely conventional. In form, Housman tends to choose straightforward iambic rhythms and simple rhymes, and in its subject matter his poetry returns again and again to themes of loss, of pastoral beauty, of idealized (and often unrequited) love, and of patriotism. Much as Housman was an intellectual in his approach to classical literature—meticulous in his scholarship, and scathing in his criticism of those less careful or competent—he was fundamentally a Romantic in his own poetry; he argued in his essay *The Name and Nature of Poetry* (1933) that poetry should appeal more to the emotions than to the intellect, and his own work embodies that belief. It was an approach that went against the grain of the intellectual currents of modernism, but that was entirely in line with early twentieth-century popular sentiment.

A Shropshire Lad was followed, in 1922, by the publication of *Last Poems*. As with Housman's first book of poetry, this new collection immediately found a wide audience. In 1921, after nineteen years as Professor of Latin at University College, Housman was appointed Professor of Latin at Trinity College, Cambridge, and for the next 25 years he occupied the Kennedy Chair in Latin. On 24 April 1936, Housman gave his last lecture at Cambridge, and six days later he died. After Housman's death, his brother Laurence produced *More Poems* from the finished poems contained within Housman's notebooks. Many of these pieces, as well as *Additional Poems*, published in Laurence's biography of his brother, contain explicitly homosexual material that Housman dared not publish within his lifetime. (The propriety of publishing poems that Housman had, in his will, instructed his brother to destroy has been extensively debated by biographers and scholars.)

⌘⌘⌘

Loveliest of Trees

Loveliest of trees, the cherry now
Is hung with bloom along the bough,
And stands about the woodland ride
Wearing white for Eastertide.

5 Now, of my threescore years and ten,
Twenty will not come again,
And take from seventy springs a score,
It only leaves me fifty more.

And since to look at things in bloom
10 Fifty springs are little room,
About the woodlands I will go
To see the cherry hung with snow.
—1896

To an Athlete Dying Young

The time you won your town the race
We chaired you through the market-place;
Man and boy stood cheering by,
And home we brought you shoulder-high.

5   Today, the road all runners come,
Shoulder-high we bring you home,
And set you at your threshold down,
Townsman of a stiller town.

Smart lad, to slip betimes away
10 From fields where glory does not stay,
And early though the laurel[1] grows
It withers quicker than the rose.

Eyes the shady night has shut
Cannot see the record cut,°   *broken*
15 And silence sounds no worse than cheers
After earth has stopped the ears:

Now you will not swell the rout°   *group*
Of lads that wore their honours out,
Runners whom renown outran
20 And the name died before the man.

So set, before its echoes fade,
The fleet foot on the sill of shade,
And hold to the low lintel[2] up
The still-defended challenge-cup.

25 And round that early laurelled head
Will flock to gaze the strengthless dead
And find unwithered on its curls
The garland briefer than a girl's.
　　　—1896

---

[1] *laurel* Evergreen bush or tree whose branches were used to crown victorious athletes in ancient Greece.

[2] *lintel* Horizontal support beam, often running across a doorway or window.

Terence, This Is Stupid Stuff

"Terence,[3] this is stupid stuff:
You eat your victuals fast enough;
There can't be much amiss, 'tis clear,
To see the rate you drink your beer.
5   But oh, good Lord, the verse you make,
It gives a chap the belly-ache.
The cow, the old cow, she is dead;
It sleeps well, the hornèd head:
We poor lads, 'tis our turn now
10 To hear such tunes as killed the cow.
Pretty friendship 'tis to rhyme
Your friends to death before their time
Moping melancholy mad:
Come, pipe a tune to dance to, lad."

15 Why, if 'tis dancing you would be,
There's brisker pipes than poetry.
Say, for what were hop-yards[4] meant,
Or why was Burton built on Trent?[5]
Oh many a peer[6] of England brews
20 Livelier liquor than the Muse,[7]
And malt does more than Milton can
To justify God's ways to man.[8]
Ale, man, ale's the stuff to drink
For fellows whom it hurts to think:
25 Look into the pewter pot°   *mug*
To see the world as the world's not.
And faith, 'tis pleasant till 'tis past:
The mischief is that twill not last.

---

[3] *Terence* This poem is from Housman's *The Shropshire Lad* (originally titled *The Poems of Terence Hearsay*), a series of poems that tell the story of a central character, Terence Hearsay, who leaves his hometown and moves to London.

[4] *hop-yards* Or hop-gardens: areas of land upon which hops are grown.

[5] *Burton ... Trent* Burton-on-Trent, a town in East Staffordshire, is the historical center of the British brewing industry. Brewing was first begun there by Benedictine monks in the eleventh century.

[6] *peer* Member of the British nobility. Brewers were among those raised to the peerage, and were thus referred to as "beer barons."

[7] *Muse* One of nine Greek goddesses of arts and learning; here, the source of poetic inspiration.

[8] *Milton ... man* Cf. John Milton's *Paradise Lost* (1667), Book 1.26.

Oh I have been to Ludlow[1] fair
30 And left my necktie God knows where,
And carried half-way home, or near,
Pints and quarts of Ludlow beer:
Then the world seemed none so bad,
And I myself a sterling lad;
35 And down in lovely muck I've lain,
Happy till I woke again.
Then I saw the morning sky:
Heigho, the tale was all a lie;
The world, it was the old world yet,
40 I was I, my things were wet,
And nothing now remained to do
But begin the game anew.

Therefore, since the world has still
Much good, but much less good than ill,
45 And while the sun and moon endure
Luck's a chance, but trouble's sure,
I'd face it as a wise man would,
And train for ill and not for good.
'Tis true the stuff I bring for sale
50 Is not so brisk a brew as ale:
Out of a stem that scored the hand
I wrung it in a weary land.
But take it: if the smack is sour,
The better for the embittered hour;
55 It should do good to heart and head
When your soul is in my soul's stead;
And I will friend you, if I may,
In the dark and cloudy day.

There was a king reigned in the East:
60 There, when kings will sit to feast,
They get their fill before they think
With poisoned meat and poisoned drink.
He gathered all that springs to birth
From the many-venomed earth;
65 First a little, thence to more,
He sampled all her killing store;
And easy, smiling, seasoned sound,

Sate the king when healths went round.
They put arsenic in his meat
70 And stared aghast to watch him eat;
They poured strychnine in his cup
And shook to see him drink it up:
They shook, they stared as white's their shirt:
Them it was their poison hurt.
75 —I tell the tale that I heard told.
Mithridates, he died old.[2]
—1896

The Chestnut Casts His Flambeaux[3]

The chestnut casts his flambeaux, and the flowers
   Stream from the hawthorn in the wind away,
The doors clap to, the pane is blind with showers.
   Pass me the can,[4] lad; there's an end of May.

5 There's one spoilt spring to scant° our mortal lot,   *reduce*
   One season ruined of our little store.
May will be fine next year as like as not:
   Oh ay, but then we shall be twenty-four.

We for a certainty are not the first
10   Have sat in taverns while the tempest hurled
Their hopeful plans to emptiness, and cursed
   Whatever brute and blackguard[5] made the world.

It is in truth iniquity on high
15   To cheat our sentenced souls of aught they crave,
And mar the merriment as you and I
   Fare on our long fool's-errand to the grave.

Iniquity it is; but pass the can.
   My lad, no pair of kings our mothers bore;

---

[1] *Ludlow* Market town in Shropshire.

[2] *There was ... died old* According to Pliny's *Natural History*, Mithridates, king of Pontus from approximately 114 to 63 BCE, gradually built up a tolerance to all known poisons by ingesting a small amount of each daily, starting in childhood.

[3] *Flambeaux* French: torch or candlestick. The horse chestnut is known for its long, upright clusters (or "candles") of flowers, usually white in color with a reddish tinge.

[4] *can* I.e., of beer; mug or tankard.

[5] *blackguard* Scoundrel.

20 Our only portion is the estate of man:
        We want the moon, but we shall get no more.

    If here today the cloud of thunder lours[1]
        Tomorrow it will hie° on far behests;°   *hasten / commands*
    The flesh will grieve on other bones than ours
25   Soon, and the soul will mourn in other breasts.

    The troubles of our proud and angry dust
        Are from eternity, and shall not fail.
    Bear them we can, and if we can we must.
        Shoulder the sky, my lad, and drink your ale.
    —1922

Epitaph on an Army of Mercenaries[2]

These, in the day when heaven was falling,
    The hour when earth's foundations fled,
Followed their mercenary calling
    And took their wages and are dead.

5   Their shoulders held the sky suspended;
        They stood, and earth's foundations stay;
    What God abandoned, these defended,
        And saved the sum of things for pay.
    —1922

---

[1] *lours* Looks dark and ominous.

[2] *Epitaph … Mercenaries* Housman published this poem in *The Times* on 31 October 1917, the third anniversary of the First Battle of Ypres, in order to honor the bravery of the professional soldiers who fought and died in the battle.

EDWARD THOMAS
1878 – 1917

During his lifetime Edward Thomas gained a reputation as a skilled critic, reviewer, and prose writer, but today he is best known for the body of poetry he produced in the last two years of life. Those 150 poems now occupy an important place in twentieth-century poetry, alongside those of poets such as Wilfred Owen, Isaac Rosenberg, and Siegfried Sassoon—who, like Thomas, fought in World War I—and as a forerunner to poets such as W.H. Auden and Philip Larkin, who admired his combination of traditional lyric forms and occasionally archaic diction with a modern sensibility.

Thomas was born in London to Welsh parents, and his family's frequent trips to Wales, as well as vacations in rural England, fueled a love of the countryside that came to have a central place in his

writing. At eighteen he published his first work, *The Woodland Life* (1897), a collection of essays on his country wanderings that imitates the style of Victorian naturalist Richard Jefferies, whom Thomas greatly admired. Encouraged in his literary ambitions by literary critic James Ashcroft Noble (whose daughter, Helen, Thomas married in 1899), Thomas chose writing as his profession, in the face of his father's disapproval.

Having completed a degree in history, Thomas and his growing family moved among a variety of country cottages, where he struggled to earn a living writing reviews, literary, criticism, essays, guidebooks, and other long prose works. He churned out several more "country books," among them *The Heart of England* (1906) and *The South Country* (1909), the essays of which mix observation, portrait, autobiography, anecdote, and literary criticism. Meanwhile, his clear, precise style and intelligent observations earned him a reputation as a discerning critic, and his reviews were widely cited. He had a knack for recognizing promising poets, and was among the first to extol the poetic virtues of D.H. Lawrence, Thomas Hardy, and W.B. Yeats. His skill in poetic analysis was evident in his extended studies of literary figures such as Charles Algernon Swinburne (1912), Walter Pater (1913), and John Keats (1916); these were considered his most important works during his lifetime. Thomas also tried his hand at novel-writing and enjoyed some success, but he generally felt himself to be a "doomed hack" during these years.

1913 brought a turning point in Thomas's literary career. First, he wrote an enthusiastic review of the work of Robert Frost (then a virtually unknown American poet) and, with his praise, launched the poet's career in Britain and then in the United States. Frost sought out the anonymous reviewer's friendship and soon convinced Thomas that there was poetry latent in his prose writing. While reading Frost's own poetry and that of his contemporaries, Thomas was able to discover his own poetic voice. Meanwhile, the beginning of World War I brought Thomas's vision of England into sharper focus: he observed the reactions of his countrymen and considered the war's potential effects on his beloved countryside, on the natural order, and on rural lifestyles and culture, which were already being lost to industrialization and urban growth. In his reverence for natural beauty and his simple poetic style, he is sometimes compared to Frost, though elements of his highly personalized voice and intense vision are clearly unique, and were obviously developed through many years of prose writing. Whereas Thomas's prose style was sometimes seen as long-winded or overly ornate, his poems are, as he said, "quintessences of the best parts of my prose books."

In 1915, after months of deliberating, Thomas joined the Artists' Rifles, and in 1916 he volunteered for overseas service. He was killed in the battle of Arras in France in April 1917. He saw *Six Poems* (1916) published under the pseudonym Edward Eastaway (Thomas feared reviewers would unfairly dismiss his poems if he published under his own name), but his remaining work was published posthumously. *Poems* (1917), also published under his pseudonym, was being produced when he died, and *Last Poems* (1918) and *Collected Poems* (1920) appeared later under his own name.

Thomas is often thought of as a war poet, despite the fact that only one of his poems, "This Is No Case of Petty Right or Wrong," deals directly with World War I. Instead, his poems show war as merely one manifestation of the evils plaguing human civilization. He sees war as exacerbating the dislocations of modernity and describes rural communities as victims of economic change. Throughout his work a melancholy, meditative tone predominates, as the poet explores a sense of solitude and isolation. This portrayal of individual alienation continues to have resonance for readers today.

⌘ ⌘ ⌘

Tears

It seems I have no tears left. They should have
  fallen—
Their ghosts, if tears have ghosts, did fall—that day
When twenty hounds streamed by me, not yet
    combed out
But still all equals in their rage of gladness
5   Upon the scent, made one, like a great dragon
In Blooming Meadow that bends towards the sun
And once bore hops: and on that other day
When I stepped out from the double-shadowed Tower
Into an April morning, stirring and sweet
10   And warm. Strange solitude was there and silence.
A mightier charm than any in the Tower
Possessed the courtyard. They were changing guard,
Soldiers in line, young English countrymen,
Fair-haired and ruddy, in white tunics. Drums
15   And fifes were playing "The British Grenadiers."[1]
The men, the music piercing that solitude
And silence, told me truths I had not dreamed,
And have forgotten since their beauty passed.
—1917

The Owl

Downhill I came, hungry, and yet not starved;
  Cold, yet had heat within me that was proof
Against the North wind; tired, yet so that rest
Had seemed the sweetest thing under a roof.

5   Then at the inn I had food, fire, and rest,
Knowing how hungry, cold, and tired was I.
All of the night was quite barred out except
An owl's cry, a most melancholy cry

Shaken out long and clear upon the hill,
10   No merry note, nor cause of merriment,
But one telling me plain what I escaped
And others could not, that night, as in I went.

And salted was my food, and my repose,
Salted and sobered, too, by the bird's voice
15   Speaking for all who lay under the stars,
Soldiers and poor, unable to rejoice.
—1917

---

[1] *The British Grenadiers* Marching song about the Brigade of Guards, an infantry unit.

Rain

Rain, midnight rain, nothing but the wild rain
On this bleak hut, and solitude, and me
Remembering again that I shall die
And neither hear the rain nor give it thanks
5 For washing me cleaner than I have been
Since I was born into this solitude.
Blessed are the dead that the rain rains upon:[1]
But here I pray that none whom once I loved
Is dying tonight or lying still awake
10 Solitary, listening to the rain,
Either in pain or thus in sympathy
Helpless among the living and the dead,
Like a cold water among broken reeds,
Myriads of broken reeds all still and stiff,
15 Like me who have no love which this wild rain
Has not dissolved except the love of death,
If love it be towards what is perfect and
Cannot, the tempest tells me, disappoint.
—1917

---

[1] *Blessed are ... upon* Proverbial.

SIEGFRIED SASSOON
1886 – 1967

Siegfried Sassoon gained his reputation during and after World War I as a poet who stridently protested the war. Shocked by the realities of the front, he transformed his horror and disgust into accusatory, didactic verse meant to confront those at home with the atrocities of war.

Sassoon was born into a wealthy merchant family, and his privileged upbringing that included horseback riding, fox hunting, a Cambridge education, and London socializing left him little prepared for war. Having decided to become a poet, however, he found that because he was without ambition or direction in life his poetry lacked passion. On the morning that war was declared, he enlisted.

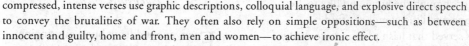

When Sassoon was first commissioned into the Royal Welch Fusiliers, his poetry was neither satirical nor disillusioned; like many young poets of the day, he gave voice to patriotic sentiments. His perception changed dramatically after surviving the Battle of the Somme on 1 July 1916—the day on which 19,000 British men were killed and 38,000 wounded. Sassoon distinguished himself with his fierce courage in this battle—earning himself a Military Cross (which he later threw away) and the nickname "Mad Jack"—but the experience purged him of any romantic notions as to the glory of war.

In a new, starkly realistic voice, Sassoon attacked commanding officers, Church and State, and all those back home who were ignorant of or indifferent to the conditions of war. His compressed, intense verses use graphic descriptions, colloquial language, and explosive direct speech to convey the brutalities of war. They often also rely on simple oppositions—such as between innocent and guilty, home and front, men and women—to achieve ironic effect.

In April 1917, Sassoon was sent home to recover from a sniper wound. There he drafted his famous public protest, published in *The Times* on 31 July 1917, in which he declared that the war had become a mere matter of "aggression and conquest" and that it was being deliberately prolonged. Sassoon was saved from prison only by the intervention of his friend Robert Graves, a fellow poet and Welch Fusilier, who testified that Sassoon was shell-shocked. Eager to avoid making a martyr of Sassoon, a medical board sent him to Edinburgh's Craiglockhart War Hospital instead.

While at Craiglockhart (where he met Wilfred Owen, another poet), Sassoon began to experiment with longer, dramatic-narrative poems that evoked the physical details of the trench. He was declared fit for active duty in 1918, but was on the front lines only a month before he received a shot in the head that sent him back to England for good. His war poems were published—to little critical acclaim—in *The Old Huntsman* (1917) and *Counter-Attack and Other Poems* (1918). After the war, Sassoon continued to launch vociferous poetic salvos, now directed against the Allies' vindictive treatment of Germany and the British government's neglect of returned soldiers. Gradually, however, anger subsided into disillusionment with and alienation from a world he could not change.

Sassoon retreated into his own memories, beginning a six-volume autobiography that took nearly twenty years to complete. The first three volumes, *Memoirs of a Fox-Hunting Man* (1928), *Memoirs of an Infantry Officer* (1930), and *Sherston's Progress* (1936), revisit the past under the guise of a fictional persona, George Sherston, while the second three, *The Old Century and Seven More Years* (1938), *The Weald of Youth* (1942), and *Siegfried's Journey: 1916–1920* (1945) are autobiography. In all six of these volumes, however, Sassoon noticeably distanced himself from his most traumatic experiences as he attempted to deal with the war and its after-effects. Sassoon's posthumously published diaries make clear exactly how much he had omitted, including the turbulent events surrounding his marriage in 1933, the birth of his son George in 1936, the dissolution of his marriage in 1941, and a long period of anguish over his homosexuality.

Sassoon continued to write, but he published most of his later poetry collections privately. He felt his work was frequently misunderstood, particularly as his religious faith increased and he became a self-proclaimed "religious poet" in the years preceding his conversion to Roman Catholicism in 1957. After this point Sassoon wrote very little poetry, and he spent the remainder of his life in relative seclusion at his home in Wiltshire, where he died in 1967.

⌘ ⌘ ⌘

They

The Bishop tells us: "When the boys come back
    They will not be the same; for they'll have fought
In a just cause: they lead the last attack
On Anti-Christ; their comrades' blood has bought
5 New right to breed an honourable race,
They have challenged Death and dared him face to face."
"We're none of us the same!" the boys reply.
"For George lost both his legs; and Bill's stone blind;
Poor Jim's shot through the lungs and like to die;
10 And Bert's gone syphilitic: you'll not find
A chap who's served that hasn't found *some* change."
And the Bishop said: "The ways of God are strange!"
    —1917 (WRITTEN 31 OCTOBER 1916)

Glory of Women

You love us when we're heroes, home on leave,
    Or wounded in a mentionable place.
You worship decorations; you believe
That chivalry redeems the war's disgrace.
5 You make us shells. You listen with delight,
By tales of dirt and danger fondly thrilled.
You crown our distant ardours while we fight,

And mourn our laurelled memories when we're killed.
You can't believe that British troops "retire"
10 When hell's last horror breaks them, and they run,
Trampling the terrible corpses—blind with blood.
O German mother dreaming by the fire,
While you are knitting socks to send your son
His face is trodden deeper in the mud.
    —1918 (WRITTEN 1917)

Everyone Sang

Everyone suddenly burst out singing;
    And I was filled with such delight
As prisoned birds must find in freedom,
Winging wildly across the white
5 Orchards and dark-green fields; on—on—and out of
    sight.

Everyone's voice was suddenly lifted;
And beauty came like the setting sun:
My heart was shaken with tears; and horror
Drifted away ... O, but Everyone
10 Was a bird; and the song was wordless; the singing
    will never be done.
    —1919

from *Memoirs of an Infantry Officer*[1]

On July the first, the weather, after an early morning mist, was of the kind commonly called heavenly. Down in our frowsty[2] cellar we breakfasted at six, unwashed and apprehensive. Our table, appropriately enough, was an empty ammunition box. At six-forty-five the final bombardment began, and there was nothing for us to do except sit round our candle until the tornado ended. For more than forty minutes the air vibrated and the earth rocked and shuddered. Through the sustained uproar the tap and rattle of machine-guns could be identified; but except for the whistle of bullets no retaliation came our way until a few 5.9 shells[3] shook the roof of our dugout. Barton and I sat speechless, deafened and stupefied by the seismic state of affairs, and when he lit a cigarette the match flame staggered crazily. Afterwards I asked him what he had been thinking about. His reply was "Carpet slippers and Kettle-holders." My own mind had been working in much the same style, for during that cannonading cataclysm the following refrain was running in my head:

They come as a boon and a blessing to men,
The Something, the Owl, and the Waverley Pen.[4]

For the life of me I couldn't remember what the first one was called. Was it the Shakespeare? Was it the Dickens? Anyhow it was an advertisement which I'd often seen in smoky railway stations. Then the bombardment lifted and lessened, our vertigo abated, and we looked at one another in dazed relief. Two brigades of our division were now going over the top on our right. Our brigade was to attack "when the main assault had reached its final objective." In our fortunate role of privileged spectators Barton and I went up the stairs to see what we could from Kingston Road Trench. We left

Jenkins crouching in a corner, where he remained most of the day. His haggard blinking face haunts my memory. He was an example of the paralysing effect which such an experience could produce on a nervous system sensitive to noise, for he was a good officer both before and afterwards. I felt no sympathy for him at the time, but I do now. From the support-trench, which Barton called "our opera box," I observed as much of the battle as the formation of the country allowed, the rising ground on the right making it impossible to see anything of the attack towards Mametz. A small shiny black notebook contains my pencilled particulars, and nothing will be gained by embroidering them with afterthoughts. I cannot turn my field-glasses on to the past....

7.45. The barrage is now working to the right of Fricourt and beyond. I can see the 21st Division advancing about three-quarters of a mile away on the left and a few Germans coming to meet them, apparently surrendering. Our men in small parties (not extended in line) go steadily on to the German front-line. Brilliant sunshine and a haze of smoke drifting along the landscape. Some Yorkshires[5] a little way below on the left, watching the show and cheering as if at a football match. The noise almost as bad as ever.

9.30. Came back to dug-out and had a shave. 21st Division still going across the open, apparently without casualties. The sunlight flashes on bayonets as the tiny figures move quietly forward and disappear beyond mounds of trench debris. A few runners come back and ammunition parties go across. Trench-mortars[6] are knocking hell out of Sunken Road Trench and the ground where the Manchesters will attack soon. Noise not so bad now and very little retaliation.

9.50. Fricourt half-hidden by clouds of drifting smoke, blue, pinkish and grey. Shrapnel bursting in small bluish-white puffs with tiny flashes. The birds seem bewildered; a lark begins to go up and then flies feebly along, thinking better of it. Others flutter above the trench with querulous cries, weak on the wing. I can

---

[1] *from ... Officer* The following excerpt, which describes the beginning of the Battle of the Somme in 1916, is taken from Section 4, Chapter 2, entitled "Battle."

[2] *frowsty* Musty; stale or unpleasant smelling.

[3] *5.9 shells* 5.9-caliber shells.

[4] *They come ... Pen* This then-popular slogan of MacNiven and Cameron, Ltd. (a producer of pen nibs) advertises three types of nibs: the Pickwick (the missing term) the Owl, and the Waverley.

[5] *Yorkshires* I.e., men belonging to one of the battalions of the Yorkshire Regiment that fought at the Battle of the Somme.

[6] *Trench-mortars* Small mortars used to propel bombs into enemy trenches.

see seven of our balloons,[1] on the right. On the left our men still filing across in twenties and thirties. Another huge explosion in Fricourt and a cloud of brown-pink smoke. Some bursts are yellowish.

10.5. I can see the Manchesters down in New Trench, getting ready to go over. Figures filing down the trench. Two of them have gone out to look at our wire gaps![2] Have just eaten my last orange.... I am staring at a sunlit picture of Hell, and still the breeze shakes the yellow weeds, and the poppies glow under Crawley Ridge where some shells fell a few minutes ago. Manchesters are sending forward some scouts. A bayonet glitters. A runner comes back across the open to their Battalion Headquarters, close here on the right. 21st Division still trotting along the sky line toward La Boisselle. Barrage going strong to the right of Contalmaison Ridge. Heavy shelling toward Mametz.

12.15. Quieter the last two hours. Manchesters still waiting. Germans putting over a few shrapnel shells. Silly if I got hit! Weather cloudless and hot. A lark singing confidently overhead.

1.30. Manchesters attack at 2.30. Mametz and Montauban reported taken. Mametz consolidated.

2.30. Manchesters left New Trench and apparently took Sunken Road Trench, bearing rather to the right. Could see about 400. Many walked casually across with sloped arms. There were about forty casualties on the left (from machine-gun in Fricourt). Through my glasses I could see one man moving his left arm up and down as he lay on his side; his face was a crimson patch. Others lay still in the sunlight while the swarm of figures disappeared over the hill. Fricourt was a cloud of pinkish smoke. Lively machine-gun fire on the far side of the hill. At 2.50 no one to be seen in No Man's Land except the casualties (about   half-way across). Our dug-out shelled again since 2.30.

5.0. I saw about thirty of our A Company crawl across to Sunken Road from New Trench. Germans put a few big shells on the cemetery and traversed Kingston Road with machine-gun. Manchester wounded still out

there. Remainder of A Company went across—about 100 altogether. Manchesters reported held up in Bois Français Support. Their Colonel went across and was killed.

8.0. Staff Captain of our brigade has been along. Told Barton that Seventh Division has reached its objectives with some difficulty, except on this brigade front. Manchesters are in trouble, and Fricourt attack has failed. Several hundred prisoners brought in on our sector.

9.30. Our A Company holds Rectangle and Sunken Road. Jenkins gone off in charge of a carrying-party.[3] Seemed all right again. C Company now reduced to six runners, two stretcher-bearers, Company-Sergeant-Major, signallers, and Barton's servant. Flook away on carrying-party. Sky cloudy westward. Red sunset. Heavy gunfire on the left.

2.30. (Next afternoon.) Adjutant[4] has just been up here, excited, optimistic, and unshaven. He went across last night to ginger up A Company who did very well, thanks to the bombers. About 40 casualties; only 4 killed. Fricourt and Rose Trench occupied this morning without resistance. I am now lying out in front of our trench in the long grass, basking in sunshine where yesterday there were bullets. Our new front-line on the hill is being shelled. Fricourt is full of troops wandering about in search of souvenirs. The village was a ruin and is now a dust heap. A gunner (Forward Observation Officer) has just been along here with a German helmet in his hand. Said Fricourt is full of dead; he saw one officer lying across a smashed machine-gun with his head bashed in—"a fine looking chap," he said, with some emotion, which rather surprised me.

8.15. Queer feeling, seeing people moving about freely between here and Fricourt. Dumps being made. Shacks and shelters being put up under skeleton trees and all sorts of transport arriving at Cemetery Cross Roads. We stay here till to-morrow morning. Feel a bit of a fraud.

—1930 (WRITTEN 1916)

---

[1] *balloons* As a defense against hostile aircrafts, troops set up a series of connected balloons attached to long wire cables.

[2] *wire gaps* Holes made in the protective barbed wire by enemy shells.

[3] *carrying-party* Party sent to deliver supplies.

[4] *Adjutant* Military officer whose role is to communicate the orders of superior officers.

RUPERT BROOKE
1887 – 1915

In his 26 April 1915 commemoration of Rupert Brooke in *The Times*, Winston Churchill wrote that Brooke's voice had been "more able to do justice to the nobility of our youth in arms engaged in the present war, than any other." Of Brooke himself he declared, "he was all that one would wish England's noblest sons to be." Famous for his five war sonnets—particularly "The Soldier," which is inscribed on his memorial plaque at the Rugby School Chapel—Brooke became a national legend during World War I when he died shortly after publishing a collection of patriotic, idealistic poems celebrating England and the war.

Born on 3 August 1887, Brooke was the son of a housemaster at Rugby (the renowned boys' boarding school, located in Rugby, Warwickshire). He attended Rugby, where he excelled as an academic and an athlete. He was popular, charismatic, and, by all accounts, extraordinarily good looking. In 1906 he won a scholarship to study Classics at King's College, Cambridge, but later switched to English to pursue his interest in poetry. At Cambridge he soon earned a place for himself among the intellectual elite, which included John Maynard Keynes and Lytton Strachey (both of whom later became members of the influential "Bloomsbury Group"), and Edward Marsh (later appointed private secretary to Churchill at the Admiralty).

Brooke wrote copious amounts of poetry while at school, and in 1911 he published his first volume, *Poems 1911*. "The Old Vicarage, Grantchester," printed in *Poetry Review* in 1912, won him that journal's prize for the year's best poem. In 1912 Brooke and Marsh conceived of *Georgian Poetry*, an anthology whose mandate would be to publish new and innovative English poetry. Marsh acted as senior editor of the anthology and covered its costs, while Brooke assumed responsibility for publicity. Contributors—referred to as "Georgian poets"—included Brooke, W.H. Davies, Walter de la Mare, Lascelles Abercrombie, and D.H. Lawrence. In place of the ornate, elevated diction of the late Victorians, these poets proposed to write in plain, concrete language and to offer sharp, detailed descriptions. The Georgians' commitment to realism, their fresh approach to the pastoral, and their pro-English sentiments had considerable influence: many war poets made use of the Georgians' techniques—and a number of others reacted against their use of these techniques in their portrayals of war.

When the war broke out, Brooke secured a commission as an officer in the Royal Naval Division. In October 1914 this division was sent to Antwerp. Though he saw no action there, it was from this experience that Brooke composed his five war sonnets. Their highly publicized release occurred only days before he died of blood poisoning on his way to Gallipoli in March 1915.

Perhaps inevitably, given his limited exposure to battle, Brooke's poems focus on his own thoughts and experiences and provide little sense of the vast brutalities of the Great War. Brooke's "begloried sonnets," as Isaac Rosenberg called them, have since been criticized for their sentimentality and their failure to depict the realities of warfare. The romanticism of these poems, however, marks so striking a departure from the witty, irreverent tone of his earlier works as to convince many that, had he lived, Brooke's poetry would have continued to shift its ground, and would have moved beyond idealism to a more critical approach to combat.

In 1915 the British public was only beginning to assimilate the horror that was unfolding across the English Channel; Rupert Brooke helped a shocked and grieving public articulate their reactions to the conflict. His poems' nostalgia for an innocent, unspoiled England (which Brooke, with his blond good looks and life of gilded privilege, seemed to embody) gave voice to national sentiment. Meanwhile, his articulation of the concept of an innate and indestructible Englishness (which he had died to defend) encouraged patriotism and helped boost wartime morale. As a result, Brooke continues to occupy at least as important a position in Britain's history as he does in its literary history.

⌘⌘⌘

Clouds

Down the blue night the unending columns press
In noiseless tumult, break and wave and flow,
    Now tread the far South, or lift rounds of snow
Up to the white moon's hidden loveliness.
5 Some pause in their grave wandering comradeless,
    And turn with profound gesture vague and slow,
    As who would pray good for the world, but know
Their benediction empty as they bless.

They say that the Dead die not, but remain
10   Near to the rich heirs of their grief and mirth.
        I think they ride the calm mid-heaven, as these,
In wise majestic melancholy train,
        And watch the moon, and the still-raging seas,
    And men, coming and going on the earth.
—1913

The Dead

Blow out, you bugles, over the rich Dead!
    There's none of these so lonely and poor of old,
    But, dying, has made us rarer gifts than gold.
These laid the world away; poured out the red
5 Sweet wine of youth; gave up the years to be
    Of work and joy, and that unhoped serene,
    That men call age; and those who would have been,
Their sons, they gave, their immortality.

Blow, bugles, blow! They brought us, for our dearth,
10   Holiness, lacked so long, and Love, and Pain.
Honour has come back, as a king, to earth,
    And paid his subjects with a royal wage;
And Nobleness walks in our ways again;
    And we have come into our heritage.
—1914

The Soldier

If I should die, think only this of me:
    That there's some corner of a foreign field
That is forever England. There shall be
    In that rich earth a richer dust concealed;
5 A dust whom England bore, shaped, made aware,
    Gave, once, her flowers to love, her ways to roam,
A body of England's, breathing English air,
    Washed by the rivers, blest by suns of home.

And think, this heart, all evil shed away,
10   A pulse in the Eternal mind, no less
        Gives somewhere back the thoughts by
            England given,
Her sights and sounds; dreams happy as her day;
    And laughter, learnt of friends; and gentleness,
        In hearts at peace, under an English heaven.
—1915

Isaac Rosenberg
1890 – 1918

Ironically, Isaac Rosenberg's reputation as a poet rests on a handful of poems he considered marginal to his *oeuvre*. Known primarily as a "war poet" and frequently discussed alongside Wilfred Owen, Rupert Brooke, Siegfried Sassoon, and Robert Graves, he is a prominent figure in any examination of World War I poetry. However, Rosenberg neither supported the war nor sought it as a primary topic for his writing. Upon enlisting, he declared, "I am determined that this war, with all its powers for devastation, shall not master my poeting." Unfortunately, he was killed on the Western Front and his last poems—his most skillfully developed and sophisticated—have the war as their topic.

Born in Bristol on 25 November 1890, Rosenberg was the son of Jewish refugees from Russia. Rosenberg's family struggled to make a living in England, and when he was seven they moved to London's East End in the hopes of improving their circumstances. At fourteen, Rosenberg apprenticed as an engraver, taking night classes in art and writing poetry in his spare time. Eventually he was able to study art full time at the Slade School of Art, but his passion for poetry soon eclipsed his earlier love of painting.

He devoted himself to achieving success as a poet with remarkable determination, distributing his works in pamphlets published at his own expense. The first, *Night and Day*, was published in 1912, followed in 1915 by *Youth* and then by the verse play *Moses* in 1916. These pamphlets remained his only publications until "Marching Song" and "Break of Day in the Trenches" were published in *Poetry* in 1916, and "Koelue" appeared in the anthology *Georgian Poetry* in 1917. Rosenberg received some encouragement and financial support from Edward Marsh, the editor of *Georgian Poetry*, but his background distanced him from Marsh and the anthology's other contributors, all of whom were from the upper classes and had been educated at Cambridge or Oxford. Rosenberg's poems drew from his knowledge of Yiddish and the Old Testament rather than a classical education; alluded to Hebrew myths rather than Celtic; and dealt with Jewish and Babylonian history rather than Greek or Roman. In form, imagery, and rhythm his poems were unlike those of his contemporaries.

After the war broke out, Rosenberg found it increasingly difficult to find the work necessary to supplement his family's income. After months of deliberation, he decided in late 1915 to enlist, despite "the immorality of joining with no patriotic convictions," in order to provide his mother with a military allowance. Once on the Western Front, he remained on or near the line until he was killed in a German offensive on 1 April 1918.

Rosenberg's war poems are frequently described as "raw." Their direct, simple language, their sense of immediacy and involvement (many of the poems' speakers participate directly in the war), and their strongly visual descriptions of the horrors of battle all convey an elemental sense of war. Yet Rosenberg did not limit his work to an emotional or personal reaction. Instead, he fused experience with evaluation and analysis. The look and feel of the battlefield is portrayed, yet the details of conflict are also explored in a larger context; in "Break of Day," for example, the plight of the soldier is explored in relation to the world of nature.

At the time of Rosenberg's death and for some time afterward, his poetry had little impact. His work was rediscovered by the poets of World War II, whose conceptions of war often approximated his own, and since then the originality of his voice has been increasingly appreciated.

⌘ ⌘ ⌘

Break of Day in the Trenches

The darkness crumbles away.
It is the same old druid[1] Time as ever,
Only a live thing leaps my hand,
A queer sardonic rat,
5   As I pull the parapet's[2] poppy
To stick behind my ear.
Droll rat, they would shoot you if they knew
Your cosmopolitan sympathies.
Now you have touched this English hand
10   You will do the same to a German
Soon, no doubt, if it be your pleasure
To cross the sleeping green between.
It seems you inwardly grin as you pass
Strong eyes, fine limbs, haughty athletes,
15   Less chanced than you for life,
Bonds to the whims of murder,
Sprawled in the bowels of the earth,
The torn fields of France.
What do you see in our eyes
20   At the shrieking iron and flame
Hurled through still heavens?
What quaver—what heart aghast?
Poppies whose roots are in man's veins
Drop, and are ever dropping;
25   But mine in my ear is safe—
Just a little white with the dust.
                    —1916

Dead Man's Dump

The plunging limbers[3] over the shattered track
Racketed with their rusty freight,
Stuck out like many crowns of thorns,
And the rusty stakes like sceptres old
5   To stay the flood of brutish men
Upon our brothers dear.

The wheels lurched over sprawled dead
But pained them not, though their bones crunched,
Their shut mouths made no moan.
10   They lie there huddled, friend and foeman,
Man born of man, and born of woman,
And shells go crying over them
From night till night and now.

Earth has waited for them,
15   All the time of their growth
Fretting for their decay:
Now she has them at last!
In the strength of their strength
Suspended—stopped and held.

20   What fierce imaginings their dark souls lit?
Earth! have they gone into you?
Somewhere they must have gone,
And flung on your hard back
Is their soul's sack,
25   Emptied of God-ancestralled essences.
Who hurled them out? Who hurled?

---

[1] *druid* Member of an ancient Celtic order in Gaul and Britain. Druids often figure in Irish and Welsh legend as magicians, sorcerers, and soothsayers.

[2] *parapet* Defence of earth in front of a military trench.

---

[3] *limbers* Two-wheeled carriages that hold guns or ammunition chests.

None saw their spirits' shadow shake the grass,
Or stood aside for the half-used life to pass
Out of those doomed nostrils and the doomed mouth,
30   When the swift iron burning bee
Drained the wild honey of their youth.

What of us who, flung on the shrieking pyre,
Walk, our usual thoughts untouched,
Our lucky limbs as on ichor[1] fed,
35   Immortal seeming ever?
Perhaps when the flames beat loud on us,
A fear may choke in our veins
And the startled blood may stop.

The air is loud with death,
40   The dark air spurts with fire,
The explosions ceaseless are.
Timelessly now, some minutes past,
These dead strode time with vigorous life,
Till the shrapnel called "An end!"
45   But not to all. In bleeding pangs
Some borne on stretchers dreamed of home,
Dear things, war-blotted from their hearts.

A man's brains splattered on
A stretcher-bearer's face;
50   His shook shoulders slipped their load,
But when they bent to look again
The drowning soul was sunk too deep
For human tenderness.

They left this dead with the older dead,
55   Stretched at the crossroads.

Burnt black by strange decay
Their sinister faces lie;
The lid over each eye,
The grass and coloured clay
60   More motion have than they,
Joined to the great sunk silences.

Here is one not long dead;
His dark hearing caught our far wheels,
And the choked soul stretched weak hands
65   To reach the living word the far wheels said,
The blood-dazed intelligence beating for light,
Crying through the suspense of the far torturing wheels
Swift for the end to break,
Or the wheels to break,
70   Cried as the tide of the world broke over his sight.

Will they come? Will they ever come?
Even as the mixed hoofs of the mules,
The quivering-bellied mules,
And the rushing wheels all mixed
75   With his tortured upturned sight.
So we crashed round the bend,
We heard his weak scream,
We heard his very last sound,
And our wheels grazed his dead face.
—1922

Louse Hunting

Nudes—stark and glistening,
Yelling in lurid glee. Grinning faces
And raging limbs
Whirl over the floor one fire.
5   For a shirt verminously busy
Yon soldier tore from his throat, with oaths
Godhead might shrink at, but not the lice.
And soon the shirt was aflare
Over the candle he'd lit while we lay.

10   Then we all sprang up and stript
To hunt the verminous brood.
Soon like a demons' pantomime
The place was raging.
See the silhouettes agape,
15   See the gibbering shadows
Mixed with the battled arms on the wall.

---

[1] *ichor* Ethereal fluid that, according to Greek mythology, flowed in the veins of the immortal gods.

See gargantuan hooked fingers
Pluck in supreme flesh
To smutch supreme littleness.
20 See the merry limbs in hot Highland fling[1]
Because some wizard vermin
Charmed from the quiet this revel
When our ears were half lulled
By the dark music
25 Blown from Sleep's trumpet.
       —1922

Returning, We Hear the Larks

Sombre the night is.
And though we have our lives, we know
What sinister threat lurks there.

Dragging these anguished limbs, we only know
5   This poison-blasted track opens on our camp—
On a little safe sleep.

But hark! joy—joy—strange joy.
Lo! heights of night ringing with unseen larks.
Music showering on our upturned list'ning faces.

10 Death could drop from the dark
As easily as song—
But song only dropped,
Like a blind man's dreams on the sand

By dangerous tides,
15 Like a girl's dark hair for she dreams no ruin lies there,
Or her kisses where a serpent hides.
       —1922

---

[1] *Highland fling* Scottish dance in which the arms and legs are
moved vigorously.

WILFRED OWEN
1893 — 1918

Wilfred Owen's humane responses to World War I, his compassionate depictions of the suffering that war engendered, and his critique of nationalism challenged the imperialist rhetoric of honor, glory, and patriotic duty, prompting Dylan Thomas later to declare him "a poet of all times, all places, and all wars."

Owen was the first-born son and of Thomas Owen and Susan Shaw of Shropshire, and the favorite of his mother, who hoped to see him become a clergyman. When Owen left school in 1911 he took a post as lay assistant to the Vicar of Dunsden, who would help him prepare for his university entrance exam in exchange for parish work. Owen, however, became increasingly critical of the Church's response to the suffering of the poor, and found his passion for poetry eclipsed his religious faith. He left the vicarage and, having failed to win a university scholarship, departed for France to work as a private tutor.

Though Owen had little intention of joining up when war broke out, pressure to do so increased as the fighting continued. In 1915 he returned to England, enlisted in the Artists' Rifles, and was commissioned lieutenant in the Manchester Regiment. Owen crossed the channel in December of 1916 to join his men on the Somme, where he began recording his impressions in letters and poems immediately. His use of a pastoral mode owed much to the influence of Keats, but his powerful descriptions of death, wounded bodies, and the weapons of war, which coupled startling images and shifting angles of vision, subverted the traditional pastoral. Owen also developed his own approach to rhyme, in which half rhymes (pararhymes) and assonance featured prominently. This gave his poetry a discordant, mournful quality that echoed his pessimistic warnings of further suffering to come, and helped create haunting elegies for the generation he shows being slaughtered like cattle in "Anthem for Doomed Youth" (1920).

Owen had been at the front only four months when a shell exploded a few feet from his head, resulting in his nearly being buried alive. A few weeks later he was removed to Craiglockhart War Hospital, outside Edinburgh, and treated for shell shock. There he met Siegfried Sassoon, another war poet whose stridently satirical poetry Owen greatly admired. It was during this time, while recovering from his trauma, that Owen wrote most of his poems. The influence of Sassoon is evident in his more didactic work, such as "Dulce et Decorum Est" (1920), which uses graphic descriptions of the battlefield and powerful direct speech to attack the classic dictum that it is sweet and fitting to die for one's country.

In his expressions of pity for his fellow soldiers, Owen occasionally fell into the trap of romanticizing death and sacrifice for which he criticized both Church and State, at times portraying soldiers as Christ-figures crucified by those in charge. The men of his poems, regardless of nationality, are usually victims passively laying down their lives, never killing. Several of Owen's strongest poems—such as "Strange Meeting" (1920)—attempt to confront and explore these contradictions.

Owen faced a similar incongruity in his own attitude towards war. Though he opposed the fighting in principle, he was glad to be able to return to the front in August 1918 and to resume serving with his men in battle. He was, he said, "a conscientious objector with a very seared conscience." Owen was killed less than three months after returning to his regiment—only a week before the war's end—while leading an offensive on the banks of the Sambre Canal.

⌘ ⌘ ⌘

Arms and the Boy

Let the boy try along this bayonet-blade
How cold steel is, and keen with hunger of blood;
Blue with all malice, like a madman's flash;
And thinly drawn with famishing for flesh.

5   Lend him to stroke these blind, blunt bullet-heads
Which long to nuzzle in the hearts of lads,
Or give him cartridges of fine zinc teeth,
Sharp with the sharpness of grief and death.

For his teeth seem for laughing round an apple.
10   There lurk no claws behind his fingers supple;
And God will grow no talons at his heels,
Nor antlers through the thickness of his curls.
—1920

Dulce et Decorum Est[1]

Bent double, like old beggars under sacks,
Knock-kneed, coughing like hags, we cursed
        through sludge,
Till on the haunting flares we turned our backs,
And towards our distant rest began to trudge.
5   Men marched asleep. Many had lost their boots,
But limped on, blood-shod. All went lame, all blind;
Drunk with fatigue; deaf even to the hoots
Of gas-shells dropping softly behind.

Gas! GAS! Quick, boys!—An ecstasy of fumbling,
10   Fitting the clumsy helmets just in time,
But someone still was yelling out and stumbling
And flound'ring like a man in fire or lime—
Dim, through the misty panes[2] and thick green light,
As under a green sea, I saw him drowning.

15   In all my dreams before my helpless sight
He plunges at me, guttering, choking, drowning.

If in some smothering dreams, you too could pace
Behind the wagon that we flung him in,
And watch the white eyes writhing in his face,
20   His hanging face, like a devil's sick of sin;
If you could hear, at every jolt, the blood
Come gargling from the froth-corrupted lungs,
Bitter as the cud
Of vile, incurable sores on innocent tongues,—
25   My friend, you would not tell with such high zest
To children ardent for some desperate glory,
The old Lie: Dulce et decorum est
Pro patria mori.
—1920

Anthem for Doomed Youth

What passing-bells for these who die as cattle?
Only the monstrous anger of the guns.
Only the stuttering rifles' rapid rattle
Can patter out their hasty orisons.°   prayers
5   No mockeries for them from prayers or bells,
Nor any voice of mourning save the choirs,—

---

[1] *Dulce et Decorum Est* Owen's poem takes its title from a famous line from the Roman poet Horace's *Odes* (3.2): "Dulce et decorum est pro patria mori" (Latin: "Sweet and fitting it is to die for one's country").

[2] *panes* Visors of the gas masks.

The shrill, demented choirs of wailing shells;
And bugles calling for them from sad shires.

What candles may be held to speed them all?
10 Not in the hands of boys, but in their eyes
Shall shine the holy glimmers of good-byes.
The pallor of girls' brows shall be their pall;[1]
Their flowers the tenderness of silent minds,
And each slow dusk a drawing-down of blinds.
—1920

Strange Meeting

It seemed that out of battle I escaped
Down some profound dull tunnel, long since
    scooped
Through granites which titanic wars had groined.
Yet also there encumbered sleepers groaned,
5 Too fast in thought or death to be bestirred.
Then, as I probed them, one sprang up, and stared
With piteous recognition in fixed eyes,
Lifting distressful hands as if to bless.
And by his smile, I knew that sullen hall,
10 By his dead smile I knew we stood in Hell.
With a thousand pains that vision's face was grained;
Yet no blood reached there from the upper ground,
And no guns thumped, or down the flues made moan.
"Strange friend," I said, "here is no cause to mourn."
15 "None," said the other, "save the undone years,
The hopelessness. Whatever hope is yours,
Was my life also; I went hunting wild
After the wildest beauty in the world,
Which lies not calm in eyes, or braided hair,
20 But mocks the steady running of the hour,
And if it grieves, grieves richlier than here.
For of my glee might many men have laughed,
And of my weeping something had been left,
Which must die now. I mean the truth untold,
25 The pity of war, the pity war distilled.
Now men will go content with what we spoiled.
Or, discontent, boil bloody, and be spilled.
They will be swift with swiftness of the tigress,

None will break ranks, though nations trek from progress.
30 Courage was mine, and I had mystery,
Wisdom was mine, and I had mastery;
To miss the march of this retreating world
Into vain citadels that are not walled.
Then, when much blood had clogged their chariot-
    wheels,
35 I would go up and wash them from sweet wells,
Even with truths that lie too deep for taint.
I would have poured my spirit without stint
But not through wounds; not on the cess° of war.   bog
Foreheads of men have bled where no wounds were.
40 I am the enemy you killed, my friend.
I knew you in this dark; for so you frowned
Yesterday through me as you jabbed and killed.
I parried; but my hands were loath and cold.
Let us sleep now...."
—1920

Futility

Move him into the sun—
Gently its touch awoke him once,
At home, whispering of fields half-sown.
Always it woke him, even in France,
5 Until this morning and this snow.
If anything might rouse him now
The kind old sun will know.

Think how it wakes the seeds—
Woke once the clays of a cold star.
10 Are limbs, so dear achieved, are sides
Full-nerved, still warm, too hard to stir?
Was it for this the clay grew tall?
—O what made fatuous sunbeams toil
To break earth's sleep at all?
—1920

---

[1] *pall* Cloth spread over a coffin, hearse, or tomb.

Letters

TO SUSAN OWEN
Sunday, 7 January 1917
[2nd Manchester Regt., B.E.F.[1]]

My dear dear Mother,

It is afternoon. We had an inspection to make from 9 to 12 this morning. I have wandered into a village cafe where they gave me writing paper. We made a redoubtable march yesterday from the last camp to this. The awful state of the roads and the enormous weight carried was too much for scores of men. Officers also carried full packs, but I had a horse part of the way.

It was beginning to freeze through the rain when we arrived at our tents. We were at the mercy of the cold, and, being in health, I never suffered so terribly as yesterday afternoon. I am really quite well, but have sensations kindred to being seriously ill.

As I was making my damp bed, I heard the guns for the first time. It was a sound not without a certain sublimity. They woke me again at 4 o'clock.

We are two in a tent. I am with the Lewis gun[2] officer. We begged stretchers from the doctor to sleep on. Our servant brings our food to us in our tents. This would not be so bad but for lack of water, and the intense damp cold.

I have had to censor letters by the hundred lately. They don't make inspiring reading.

This morning I have been reading trench standing orders to my platoon. (Verb. Sap.)[3]

Needless to say I show a cheerier face to them than I wear in writing this letter; but I must not disguise from you the fact that we are at one of the worst parts of the line.

I have lost no possessions so far; but have acquired a pair of boots and a map case (presents). And of course my valise is heavier by much dirt.

I want a compass really more than field glasses.
My address is

2nd Manchester Regt.
B.E.F.

I have not a word from England since I left.

I can't tell you any more facts. I have no fancies and no feelings.

Positively they went numb with my feet.

Love is not quenched, except the unenduring flickerings thereof. By your love, O Mother, O Home, I am protected from fatigue of life and the keen spiritual cold.

Your own W.E.O.

TO SUSAN OWEN
10 January 1917
[2nd Manchester Regt., B.E.F.]

My own Mother,

I was censoring letters all afternoon. After tea commenced a big commotion among my friendly neighbours the Howitzers, in the midst of which I wrote a distracted note to Leslie,[4] but the concussion[5] blew out my candle so many times that I lost heart.

I am kept pretty busy, though there is only a short "parade." The men do practically nothing all day but write letters; but officers have frequent meetings over schemes, maps, instructions, and a thousand cares.

Yesterday I took a tour into the line which we shall occupy. Our little party was shelled going up across the open country. It was not at all frightful and only one 4.7[6] got anywhere near, falling plump in the road, but quite a minute after we had passed the spot. I tell you these things because *afterwards* they will sound less exciting. If I leave all my exploits for recitation after the war without mentioning them now, they will be appearing bomb-shell-bastic.

Now I am not so uncomfortable as last week, for my new servant, who has been a chemist's assistant, has

---

1   *B.E.F.*   British Expeditionary Force.

2   *Lewis gun*   Early form of light machine gun, designed in 1911 by U.S. Army Colonel Isaac Newton Lewis.

3   *Verb. Sap.*   Short for the Latin phrase "Verbum sapienti sat est," meaning "a word is sufficient for a wise person." The expression is used in place of a full explanation, implying that the reader can infer the rest, or can understand the reason for the writer's reticence.

4   *Leslie*   Owen's cousin, Leslie Gunston.

5   *concussion*   Violent shaking.

6   *4.7*   I.e., a 4.7 inch shell, one of the standard sizes of shells used in World War I.

turned out not only clean & smart, but enterprising and inventive. He keeps a jolly fire going; and thieves me wood with much cunning.

My company commander (A Company) has been out here since the beginning: 'tis a gentleman and *an original* (!)

Next in command is Heydon, whom I greatly like, and once revered as the assistant adjutant at Witley & Oswestry.

Then come I, for the remaining subalterns are junior. I chose No. 3 Platoon. I was posted to 2, but one day I took No. 3 in tow when its officer left, because I liked the look of the men.

Even as they prophesied in the Artists,[1] I have to take a close interest in feet, and this very day I knelt down with a candle and watched each man perform his anointment with whale oil; praising the clean feet, but not reviling the unclean.

As a matter of fact, my servant and one other are the only non-verminous bodies in the platoon; not to say lice-ntious.

Today's letters were rather interesting. The Daddys' letters are specially touching, and the number of xxx to sisters and mothers weigh more in heaven than Victoria Crosses.[2] The Victoria Cross! I covet it not. Is it not *Victorian*? yah! pah!

I am not allowed to send a sketch, but you must know I am transformed now, wearing a steel helmet, buff jerkin of leather, rubber-waders up to the hips, & gauntlets. But for the rifle, we are exactly like Cromwellian Troopers.[3] The waders are of course indispensable. In 2½ miles of trench which I waded yesterday there was not one inch of dry ground. There is a mean depth of 2 feet of water.

It seems an era since Christmas Day, and goose,[4] carols, Dickens,[5] & mistletoe.

Assuming the war lasts another year I should get leave twice, or three times, for we get it, or should get it every 3 months.

Be sure to have no chloride of lime in the house. Our water is overdosed with it enough to poison us. But in the Mess we can get Perrier, fortunately.

You need not ask where I am. I have told you as far as I can. These things I need
  (1) small pair nail scissors
  (2) celluloid hair-pin box from Boots[6] (9d.) with tightfitting lid, & containing boracic powder
  (3) Players Navy Cut[7]
  (4) Ink pellets
  (5) Sweets (!!) (We shall not be in touch with Supplies by day)
Have no anxiety. I cannot do a better thing or be in a righter place. Yet I am not sainted therefore, and so I beg you to annoy ——, for my wicked pleasure.

W.E.O. xxx

TO SUSAN OWEN
Tuesday: 16 January 1917
[2nd Manchester Regt., B.E.F.]

My own sweet Mother,

I am sorry you have had about 5 days letterless. I hope you had my two letters "posted" since you wrote your last, which I received tonight. I am bitterly disappointed that I never got one of yours.

I can see no excuse for deceiving you about these last 4 days. I have suffered seventh hell.

I have not been at the front.

I have been in front of it.

---

[1] *Artists* The Artists' Rifles, the volunteer corps into which Owen had first enlisted. During World War I it was established as an Officers Training Corps, and it attracted mainly educated young men from public schools and universities.

[2] *Victoria Crosses* The highest British military decorations awarded for bravery.

[3] *Cromwellian Troopers* I.e., early modern soldiers.

[4] *goose* Traditional Christmas dinner in the UK.

[5] *Dickens* British novelist Charles Dickens wrote, among many other stories and novels, annual Christmas stories (e.g., *A Christmas Carol*).

[6] *Boots* British drugstore chain.

[7] *Players Navy Cut* Brand of cigarettes.

I held an advanced post, that is, a "dug-out" in the middle of no man's land.[1]

We had a march of 3 miles over shelled road then nearly 3 along a flooded trench. After that we came to where the trenches had been blown flat out and had to go over the top. It was of course dark, too dark, and the ground was not mud, not sloppy mud, but an octopus of sucking clay, 3, 4, and 5 feet deep, relieved only by craters full of water. Men have been known to drown in them. Many stuck in the mud & only got on by leaving their waders, equipment, and in some cases their clothes.

High explosives were dropping all around out, and machine guns spluttered every few minutes. But it was so dark that even the German flares did not reveal us.

Three quarters dead, I mean each of us 3/4 dead, we reached the dugout, and relieved the wretches therein. I then had to go forth and find another dug-out for a still more advanced post where I left 18 bombers. I was responsible for other posts on the left but there was a junior officer in charge.

My dug-out held 25 men tight packed. Water filled it to a depth of 1 or 2 feet, leaving say 4 feet of air.

One entrance had been blown in & blocked.

So far, the other remained.

The Germans knew we were staying there and decided we shouldn't.

Those fifty hours were the agony of my happy life.

Every ten minutes on Sunday afternoon seemed an hour.

I nearly broke down and let myself drown in the water that was now slowly rising over my knees.

Towards 6 o'clock, when, I suppose, you would be going to church, the shelling grew less intense and less accurate: so that I was mercifully helped to do my duty and crawl, wade, climb and flounder over no man's land to visit my other post. It took me half an hour to move about 150 yards.

I was chiefly annoyed by our own machine guns from behind. The seeng-seeng-seeng of the bullets reminded me of Mary's[2] canary. On the whole I can support the canary better.

In the platoon on my left the sentries over the dug-out were blown to nothing. One of these poor fellows was my first servant whom I rejected. If I had kept him he would have lived, for servants don't do sentry duty. I kept my own sentries half way down the stairs during the more terrific bombardment. In spite of this one lad was blown down and, I am afraid, blinded.

This was my only casualty.

The officer of the left platoon has come out completely prostrated and is in hospital.

I am now as well, I suppose, as ever.

I allow myself to tell you all these things because I am never going back to this awful post. It is the worst the Manchesters have ever held; and we are going back for a rest.

I hear that the officer who relieved me left his 3 Lewis guns behind when he came out. (He had only 24 hours in). He will be court-martialled.

In conclusion, I must say that if there is any power whom the soldiery execrate more than another it is that of our distinguished countryman....

Don't pass round these sheets but have portions typed for Leslie etc. My previous letter to you has just been returned. It will be too heavy to include in this.

Your very own Wilfred x

TO COLIN OWEN[3]

2 March 1917
B Coy Dug-Out

My dearest Colin,

This is the first time I have written from a dug-out. I am in a French one now. We have straw to sleep on, but it is pretty lousy—after the poilus![4]

There is a gas-alarm on just now, but I don't really expect it. The air is too still. Just this moment, and since I sat down, a tremendous artillery strafe[5] has opened up. We all remark to each other that it seems there is a war on. I went up to the front line with a Fatigue Party for

---

[1]   *no man's land*   Terrain between the two armies.

[2]   *Mary*   Owen's younger sister (1896–1956).

[3]   *Colin Owen*   Wilfred's youngest brother, who was then sixteen.

[4]   *poilus*   French common soldiers. From the French "poilu," meaning "hairy."

[5]   *strafe*   Assault.

digging. Let me tell you in confidence that I was for the first time a target.* I ran over the top to get to the head of the party in the trench, & stood a moment to shout an order, when a bullet went Ping, a good 3 ft. over my silly head.

Next day. Where you see the * I left off because the order came "Stand to Arms!" What a commotion! We half expected an attack, but nothing happened. I have no paper to write more, but this letter should be interesting circumstantially.

Dearest love to you, sweet my brother.

W.E.O.

You *must* disinfect your hands, whether sore or not, after stables.

TO SUSAN OWEN

[?16] May 1917
41st Stationary Hospital

My own dear Mother,

Just had yours of Sat. evening and was astonished to apprehend that the Great Shadow is creeping on towards Colin. What will he be next birthday,[1] seventeen?

I wrote him a wholesome bit of realism in that last letter, as well as a fantasy in the language of the Auth. Ver. of 1611.[2] I have changed my mind and see no reason why you should not have that letter and that fantasia. It was on the model of Leslie's "Throw her down. So they threw her down. And he said Throw her down again. And they threw her down again. And they gathered up of the fragments that remained, etc."

I did it without any reference to the Book, of course; and without any more detraction from reverence, than, say, is the case when a bishop uses modern slang to relate a biblical story. I simply employed seventeenth century English, and was carried away with it.

Incidentally, I think the big number of texts which jogged up in my mind in half-an-hour bears witness to

a goodly store of them in my being. It is indeed so; and I am more and more Christian as I walk the unchristian ways of Christendom. Already I have comprehended a light which never will filter into the dogma of any national church: namely that one of Christ's essential commands was: Passivity at any price! Suffer dishonour and disgrace; but never resort to arms. Be bullied, be outraged, be killed; but do not kill. It may be a chimerical and an ignominious principle, but there it is. It can only be ignored: and I think pulpit professionals are ignoring it very skilfully and successfully indeed.

Have you seen what ridiculous figures Frederick & Arthur Wood[3] are cutting? If they made the Great Objection,[4] I should admire them. They have not the courage.

To begin with I think it was puny of Fritz to deny his name. They are now getting up a petition, mentioning their "unique powers," "invaluable work," and so on, and wish to carry on their work from 82 Mortimer St. W. as usual. I do not recollect Christ's office address in Jerusalem, but in any case I don't think He spent much time there.

St. Paul's business premises, if I remember, were somewhat cramped, not to say confined.

But I must not malign these brethren because I do not know their exact apologia.

And am I not myself a conscientious objector with a very seared conscience?

The evangelicals have fled from a few candles, discreet incense, serene altars, mysterious music, harmonious ritual to powerful electric-lighting, overheated atmosphere, palm-tree platforms, grand pianos, loud and animated music, extempore ritual; but I cannot see that they are any nearer to the Kingdom.

Christ is literally in no man's land. There men often hear His voice: Greater love hath no man than this, that a man lay down his life—for a friend.

Is it spoken in English only, and French?

I do not believe so.

Thus you see how pure Christianity will not fit in with pure patriotism.

---

[1] *next birthday* Colin would turn seventeen on 24 July.

[2] *Auth. Ver. of 1611* I.e., the authorized version of the King James Bible, first published in 1611.

[3] *Frederick ... Wood* Two traveling evangelists. "Fritz" in the following paragraph is a nickname for "Frederick."

[4] *made the Great Objection* I.e., become conscientious objectors.

I am glad you sent that cutting from Wells' book.[1] I hope you understood it. I did not. Not a word of it can I make sense of. I would rather we did not read this book. Now *The Passionate Friends*[2] I found astounding in its realism but like all the great terrible books it is impossible to "take sides." It is not meant to be a comfortable book; it is discussional; it refuses to ignore the unpleasant.

(This practice of *selective ignorance* is, as I have pointed out, one cause of the war. Christians have deliberately *cut* some of the main teachings of their code.)

At present I am deep in a marvellous work of Hugo's, *The Laughing Man*.[3]

By the same post as your letter came two books from Leslie, by O. Henry.[4]

So I am well set up.

I am marked *for the next evacuation*!!

So glad my oak seedlings are growing. How many are there likely to thrive, out of how many acorns? They have been "dry," you know, for 6 years. Give them every chance.

This countryside is now superb. But from this we are no longer allowed out of the hospital bounds.

Many thanks for *Punch*.[5] Yes, Colin has been very good in writing to me. Keep him up to it. It will do *him* good, don't-you-know! And as for me: they bring me Shropshire,[6] even as yours bring me home.

Expect me—before Christmas.

Your—one and only—Wilfred x

---

[1] *Wells' Book* It is uncertain to which book by H.G. Wells Owen refers, but it may be *God the Invisible King* (1917), referred to again in Owen's letter of 22 August 1917.

[2] *The Passionate Friends* By H.G. Wells (1913).

[3] *Hugo's ... Man* Victor Hugo's *L'homme qui vit* (1869).

[4] *O. Henry* William Sidney Porter (1862–1910), an American journalist and short-story writer.

[5] *Punch* Magazine of humor and satire, 1841–2002.

[6] *Shropshire* County in England that lies on the border of England and Wales.

TO SUSAN OWEN

18 May 1917
[41st Stationary Hospital]

Dearest Mother,

I had the parcel (shirt) last night. Have just awakened—too late to write before the post leaves. Your two letters, with enclosures from Paris, came at the same time. The flowers were quite fresh; & I was very refreshed with them.

No more now. They have just awakened me to know if I have any letters for post!

Your W.E.O. x

TO SUSAN OWEN

23 May 1917
[41st Stationary Hospital]

Dearest Mother,

I wondered why it was such an effort to write the short notes of a day or two ago. I have discovered that I had a temperature of 102.9, so it was not surprising. I am still feverish but on the right side of 100°. I suppose it is trench fever, which has been incubating all this time, but they don't say what it is and I don't think they know.

I have had a wretched enough time, *not from the fever* in myself but from the stew that the whole hospital has got into. A completely new staff from England has taken over. The old people cleared off bag and baggage, bed & bedding, before even the new things arrived. They did put us in some sort of beds, but otherwise they stripped the ward stark, taking even the drugs. There was not left one chair, one mug, one teapot, one rug, one screen. They took the very ashtrays to which indeed they were welcome, for they are not worth a farthing, and I don't smoke.

No, I could no more smoke a cigarette than any unborn chicken. My servant informed me that I had some mangee[7]—as he calls it—in my valise. But it does not tempt me at all.

He will not follow me to the base when—or if—I go.

---

[7] *mangee* Unidentified.

I repeat the new address of this place:

41st Stationary Hospital.

It is quite likely that I shall appear in the casualty list, as neurasthenia[1] is marked W(ound) not S(ick)—not wrongly I think. I know that Capt. Sorrel was mentioned for shock, and that some persons wear gold stripes for neurasthenia!

Many more are worn for bullet grazes which did no more harm than a needle-scratch.

I am afraid it is quite out of the question to find anything for Mary or even to write for today's post.

Yours ever W.E.O. x

The new staff of the hospital will no doubt start unpacking today.

But I shall never get over my indignation at the manner of the relief!

*Pronounced mŭnjy (Lancashire u).

To Susan Owen

22 August 1917
Craiglockhart

My own dear Mother,

I have been waiting for the address. The most momentous news I have for you is my meeting with Sassoon. He was struggling to read a letter from H. G. Wells when I went in. Wells is thinking of coming up here to see him & his doctor, not about Sassoon's state of health, but about Wells' last book you wot of:[2] *God the Invisible King*.

Sassoon talks about as badly as Wells writes; they accord a slurred *suggestion* of words only. Certain old sonnets of mine did not please S. at all. But the "Antaeus" he applauded long & fervently, saying So-and-so would like to read this. And a short lyric, done here, he pronounced perfect work, absolutely charming, etc. etc., & begged I would copy it for him, to show to the powers that be. The last thing he said to me was, "Sweat your guts out writing poetry."

He also warned me against early publishing. He is

himself 30. Looks under 25.

I shall be able to tell you much more when I get home.

Saw Harry Lauder[3] the other day, a sincere, good-hearted man, kept one smiling, but never provided a bursting laugh.

The play finished very successfully. Had to do a little gagging with Pockett because Isaacson missed his cue once & didn't come on when expected; a terrible moment.

Was invited to tea last Sunday by Capt. Mackenzie, whose wife, boy and girl were at the concert. (Verb. Sap.) The children, it seems, like me, and contrived a picnic in which I was to play the principal. But the feeling is not reciprocated and I managed to get out of the picnic.

As I said before I have had enough picnicking to last several lifetimes. I have also a large family: in England, France—and Ireland.

Bobby writes this morning from Co. Clare[4] saying they are having a good time shooting.

The Field Club are going to the zoo this afternoon. I missed the last outing.

I am being forced to repeat my biological paper next Monday.

German is getting on.

Saw Ch. Chaplin again.

Keeping very well, and generally sleeping well. The barraged nights are quite the exception.

I have been asked to continue a class of French which has been started. But I don't feel too inclined.

Am anxious about your weather. Beastly up here *for Holidays*; though I have nothing to complain of; the showers are short; and the mists are delightful. Don't bother about writing till you get back. Forget everything but your new environment.

Forget self in the presence of the sea—I will do all the thinking and remembering of you.

Had a model yacht regatta this morning. Thought how Father would have liked to compete.

Your own Wilfred x

---

[1] *neurasthenia* Disorder of the nerves.

[2] *wot of* Know of.

[3] *Harry Lauder* Scottish comedian and singer (1870–1950).

[4] *Co. Clare* I.e., County Clare, in Ireland.

To Tom Owen

26 August 1917
[Craiglockhart]

My dear Father,

I think this work of Sassoon's will show you to the best possible advantage the tendencies of Modern Poetry. If you don't appreciate these then it's Na-poo.[1] There is nothing better this century can offer you. I've marked the pieces for first reading, and those underlined are specially good. "The Old Huntsman" was put in as a title piece, to catch the hunting-people, and make 'em read the rest.

"The Death-Bed" is a piece of perfect art.

"Morning Express," page 56, is the kind of thing that makes me despair of myself; everyone says, "I could have done that myself!"

Only no one ever did.

Please send me your criticisms.

I am beginning to feel uncomfortably editorial again after a fortnight's rest. Nobody is willing to write about our last concerts, and it looks as if I shall have to fill half the mag.[2] myself, between now & tomorrow.

I *am* glad Colin is with you.

Realizing how impossible it is for me to be there has spoilt my holiday here. I was make-believing that I was a free creature here, but it is only that my chain has been let out a little. I should only hurt myself with tugging at it.

Fondest love to all,

Your W.E.O.

To Mary Owen

Thursday, 29 August 1917
Craiglockhart

My dear Mary,

I was grieved—almost aggrieved—to hear you had had some bad days at Aberystwyth,[3] and I am still waiting to hear you are all right. This cloud, and a great

many other real ones messing about in the heavens and sometimes mooning around the building itself, and generally behaving unbecomingly on the top of us all—and the Russians panicking, and getting out of the war, and ourselves getting deeper and deeper into it, these things, I say, do not make one (eider)— downhearted. So it is not to be wondered at that I was a bit snappy in my editorial, which you shall have in a day or two.

But a word from Sassoon, though he is not a cheery dog himself, makes me cut capers of pleasure.

My dear, except in one or two of my letters (alas!), you will find nothing so perfectly truthfully descriptive of war. Cinemas, cartoons, photographs, tales, plays— Na-poo.

Now you see why I have always extolled poetry.

The "Redeemer," I have been wishing to write every week for the last three years.

Well, it has been done and I have shaken the greater hand that did it.

"The Death-Bed," my dear sister, should be read seven times, and after that, not again, but thought of only.

Here is a very good brooch, a *very* good brooch. Unless you like it much, I shall very likely sneak it again for a model of latter-day design! There is no hint of a board[4] for me yet! I'm going down to make my evening tea now. Just a card will tell me how you & dear Mother are.

Your loving Wilfred

To Susan Owen

4 (or 6) October 1918
In the Field

Strictly private

My darling Mother,

As you must have known both by my silence and from the newspapers which mention this division—and perhaps by other means & senses—I have been in action for some days.

---

[1] *Na-poo* Finished; good for nothing.

[2] *the mag.* Hospital magazine, *The Hydra*, which Owen edited.

[3] *Aberystwyth* Town on the west coast of Wales.

[4] *board* Meeting of hospital authorities, at which Owen's fitness to return to active duty would be determined.

I can find no word to qualify my experiences except the word SHEER. (Curiously enough I find the papers talk about sheer fighting!) It passed the limits of my abhorrence. I lost all my earthly faculties, and fought like an angel.

If I started into detail of our engagement I should disturb the censor and my own rest.

You will guess what has happened when I say I am now commanding the company, and in the line had a boy lance-corporal as my sergeant-major.

With this corporal who stuck to me and shadowed me like your prayers I captured a German machine gun and scores of prisoners.

I'll tell you exactly how another time. I only shot one man with my revolver (at about 30 yards!); The rest I took with a smile. The same thing happened with other parties all along the line we entered.

I have been recommended for the Military Cross;[1] and have recommended every single N.C.O.[2] who was with me!

My nerves are in perfect order.

I came out in order to help these boys—directly by leading them as well as an officer can; indirectly, by watching their sufferings that I may speak of them as well as a pleader can. I have done the first.

Of whose blood lies yet crimson on my shoulder where his head was— and where so lately yours was—I must not now write.

It is all over for a long time. We are marching steadily *back*.

Moreover

The war is nearing an end.

Still,

Wilfred and more than Wilfred

TO SUSAN OWEN
[8 October 1918]
[2nd Manchester Regt.]

It is 5 o'clock this Sunday evening. You will be sitting at tea. I fear you are without news, and a little wondering …

You will understand I could not write—when you think of us for days all but surrounded by the enemy. All one day (after the battle) we could not move from a small trench, though hour by hour the wounded were groaning just outside. Three stretcher-bearers who got up were hit, one after one. I had to order no one to show himself after that, but remembering my own duty, and remembering also my forefathers, the agile Welsh-men of the mountains, I scrambled out myself & felt an exhilaration in baffling the machine guns by quick bounds from cover to cover. After the shells we had been through, and the gas, bullets were like the gentle rain from heaven.[3]

My servant was wounded in the first hour of the attack. My new servant has just gone on leave this afternoon, carrying with him some books & binoculars of mine, with instructions to call on you as he passes through Shrewsbury (to Manchester). This Howarth is a "scratch" servant not my choice; but I rather hope he'll call on you & tell you what he can.

So strange to read your letters again! And so good to hear you are at least trying to keep quite well. Glad you find your help worth accommodating.

Must now write to hosts of parents of missing, etc.

Your W.E.O. x

TO SUSAN OWEN
29 October 1918
[2nd Manchester Regt.]

Dearest Mother,

Through so much marching I have not been able to write for a day or two. I don't want to send field cards in case you suppose they mean in the line. In future, however, a f. card will be no proof that I am actually there.

Last night I slept in a cottage, but in an hour or two we move on: *not* to fight.

Your last letters were the two with the permang & the boric. Many many thanks for sending this so quickly.

Yesterday evening I hear the post corporal fell into

---

[1] *Military Cross*   Decoration for gallantry.

[2] *N.C.O.*   Non-commissioned Officer.

[3] *gentle rain from heaven*   Cf. Portia's "quality of mercy" speech in Shakespeare's *The Merchant of Venice* (4.1.179–200).

a river; I understand the letters are all right; but haven't got any yet.

Howarth came back a day or two ago, but I did not take him back to me. My present one is Pte. Roberts, whom I knew in Scarborough.

The civilians here are a wretched, dirty crawling community, afraid of *us*, some of them, and no wonder after the shelling we gave them 3 weeks go.

Did I tell you that five healthy girls died of fright in one night at the last village? The people in England and France who thwarted a peaceable retirement of the enemy from these areas are therefore now sacrificing aged French peasants and charming French children to our guns. Shells made by women in Birmingham are at this moment burying little children alive not very far from here.

It is rumoured that Austria has really surrendered.[1] The new soldiers cheer when they hear these rumours, but the old ones bite their pipes, and go on cleaning their rifles, unbelieving.

A little gleam of good news I discovered in your note which said already you felt rested by being in bed. I wonder what your diet is? For my next parcel, will Mary please get:

    1 small bottle Tatcho
    1 Oatine
    1 pair cork boot-socks, size 6
    20 Players
    Chocolate

There is a pair of breeches too narrow in the knees left in a drawer. Would Father get the tailor who made my last pair to enlarge the knees? & dispatch to me? I will send a cheque soon. Thank Father very much for his last letter.

The cutting from the *News*, & especially Gardiner's article[2] was appreciated by us all.

Siegfried sent me a little book which he had in France. Offered a job in war propaganda under Beaverbrook[3] he wrote to B's private sec. saying he had no qualifications for such work, except that he had been wounded in the head.

So glad you liked Tolstoy.[4]

All my dearest love, my darling Mother.

W.E.O.

TO SUSAN OWEN
Thursday, 31 October [1918], 6.15 p.m.
[2nd Manchester Regt.]

Dearest Mother,

I will call the place from which I'm now writing "The Smoky Cellar of the Forester's House." I write on the first sheet of the writing pad which came in the parcel yesterday. Luckily the parcel was small, as it reached me just before we moved off to the line. Thus only the paraffin was unwelcome in my pack. My servant & I ate the chocolate in the cold middle of last night, crouched under a draughty tamboo,[5] roofed with planks. I husband[6] the malted milk for tonight & tomorrow night. The handkerchief & socks are most opportune, as the ground is marshy, & I have a slight cold!

So thick is the smoke in this cellar that I can hardly see by a candle 12 ins. away, and so thick are the inmates that I can hardly write for pokes, nudges, & jolts. On my left the Coy. Commander[7] snores on a bench: other officers repose on wire beds behind me. At my right hand, Kellett, a delightful servant of a Coy. in *The Old Days* radiates joy & contentment from pink cheeks and baby eyes. He laughs with a signaler, to whose left ear is glued the receiver; but whose eyes rolling with gaiety show that he is listening with his right ear to a merry corporal, who appears at this distance away (some three feet) nothing [but] a gleam of white teeth & a wheeze of jokes.

Splashing my hand, an old soldier with a walrus moustache peels & drops potatoes into the pot. By him, Keyes, my cook, chops wood; another feeds the smoke

---

[1] *rumoured ... surrendered*   On 3 November 1918 an armistice was signed with the Italians.

[2] *Gardiner's article*   *Daily News* article by the editor, A.G. Gardiner, on possible ways to negotiate final peace terms.

[3] *Beaverbrook*   William Maxwell Aitkin, Lord Beaverbrook (1879–1964), who was Minister of Information.

[4] *Tolstoy*   Russian author Leo Tolstoy (1828–1910).

[5] *tamboo*   Temporary shelter in a trench.

[6] *husband*   Economize; lay by a store of.

[7] *Coy. Commander*   I.e., Company Commander.

with the damp wood.

It is a great life. I am more oblivious than, alas! yourself, dear Mother, of the ghastly glimmering of the guns outside, & the hollow crashing of the shells.

There is no danger down here, or if any, it will be well over before you read these lines.[1]

I hope you are as warm as I am; as serene in your room as I am here; and that you think of me never in bed as resignedly as I think of you always in bed. Of this I am certain you could not be visited by a band of friends half so fine as surround me here.

Ever Wilfred x

—1967 (WRITTEN 1917–18)

---

[1] *no danger ... these lines* In fact Owen was killed five days later; this is his last known letter.

War and Revolution

CONTEXTS

B ritain declared war on Germany on 4 August 1914, and nearly every family in England had lost someone before the Armistice on 11 November 1918. Roughly nine million soldiers died—nearly one in every eight who enlisted. Eighteen million more were wounded. While soldiers and civilians alike began the war filled with idealism, there was little room for glory in the trench warfare that became the dominant mode of conflict during the war. The battle line on the Western Front remained virtually unmoved for three years, with both sides making attempted advancements at great loss of life. The German use of poison gas at the second battle of Ypres (1915), the British landing at Gallipoli (1915), and the British introduction of tanks at the Somme (1916) were all launched in the hope they would lead to a victorious breakthrough–and all ended horrifically. Indeed, the "Great War," as it was called at the time, was characterized from first to last by extreme disillusionment, from the misplaced hope at its outset that the fighting would end by Christmas 1914, to the confidence voiced by Woodrow Wilson (the American President who brought the United States into the war in 1917) that the conflict would lead nations to come together in a new League of Nations that would make this "a war to end all wars." After the war the British people would never again recapture the idealism and firm faith in technology, progress, and traditional values that had been prevalent earlier in the century. In stark contrast to Wilson's optimism, many were persuaded by the war's end that technological progress and failed humanity were driving civilization towards a perpetual state of war. Subsequent years were filled with unrest as the British people struggled to make sense of the sweeping changes war had brought.

The war was certainly unprecedented in its technology—airplanes as well as tanks were used for the first time in warfare, and machine guns facilitated new levels of mass slaughter. And the industrial nature of the war meant that civilians were relied upon nearly as much as soldiers for military success. Morale was thus important almost as much at home as on the front, and artists, photographers, poets, actors and performers became important participants in the manufacture of patriotism. This section opens with a testament to the importance of patriotic poetry during wartime, and a sampling of popular poems and songs. There was little that was heroic or romantic about the daily life of soldiers in the trenches, but through songs such as "I Learned to Wash in Shell-holes" and "It's a Lovely War" soldiers might keep up morale by viewing their deplorable living conditions with humor. ("It's a Lovely War," by J.P. Long and Maurice Scott, became once again widely known after the 1960s stage production *Oh, What a Lovely War!* and the film that took its title from the play's.)

The war was unprecedented too in its geographic scope; the fighting extended into Africa and the Middle East as well as across Europe and into Asia. The British Empire fought as one, with troops from all areas serving under imperial command. Canadian troops were particularly influential at Vimy Ridge, where in April 1917 they forced German troops to retreat from their dominant position on the northern front. Soldiers from Australia and New Zealand were vitally important in offensives at the Somme and Gallipoli, where they sustained heavy losses.

War transformed everyday life and affected every aspect of society. Everyone was at risk, and everyone had a part to play in the war effort. While Victorian society had been characterized by rigid boundaries—between public and private space, between masculine and feminine realms and duties, and between classes—the war forced a sudden breakdown of these categories. After the war they were partially restored, but society was forever transformed. In her essay "The Cordite Makers," Rebecca West (the pen name of Cicily Fairfield) highlights the parallels between the daily lives of soldiers on the home front and that of many women working in the arms industry—particularly in terms of the personal sacrifices that they made and the dangers that they faced.

Ivor Gurney's poem "To His Love" and Vince Palmer's "The Farmer Remembers the Somme," both of which appear below, provide a grim sense of how firm a grip the memory of horror and of loss took upon those who had experienced the fighting at first hand. Less focused on the horror of battle is the excerpt below from poet Robert Graves's *Goodbye to All That*. Graves's description of his war years as an officer in the Royal Welch Fusiliers, is among the most vivid and detailed prose accounts of life on the front. The passage excerpted here gives among other things a clear sense of the stark differences between civilians' and soldiers' perceptions of the war.

If the Great War revolutionized the way in which British people saw the world, it also helped to bring full-scale revolution to Britain's largest ally. The Russian Revolution was the product of many causes, but not the least of these was the hardship and desperation brought on by the war itself. Ultimately, the Revolution proved to be one of the central events of the twentieth century; over the course of the next two generations, the ideological models of Marx and Lenin and the institutional models of Lenin and Stalin would spread through much of the world. The excerpt included in these pages highlights the conflict between communist idealism and totalitarian realism that came to a head almost immediately following the Bolshevik "October Revolution" of 1917.

⌘ ⌘ ⌘

from Anonymous, Introduction to *Songs and Sonnets for England in War Time* (1914)

> The *Songs and Sonnets for England in War Time* anthology was the first of a genre that became common in World War I, the popular anthology of war poetry. The introduction provides a straightforward statement of the rationale for such volumes.

In the stress of a nation's peril, the poet at last comes into his own again, and with clarion call he rouses the sleeping soul of the Empire. Prophet he is, champion and consoler.

If in these later times the poet has been neglected, now in our infinite need, in our pride and our sorrow, he is here to strengthen, comfort and inspire. The poet is vindicated.

What can so nobly uplift the hearts of a people facing war with its unspeakable agony as music and poetry? The sound of martial music steels men's hearts before battle. The sound of martial words inspires human souls to do and to endure. God, His poetry, and His music are the Holy Trinity of war.

… The greatest songs [have not always been those] that have sent men on to victory. Sometimes it has been a modest verse that has found refuge in the heart of the soldier ready for the ultimate sacrifice, cheered on his way by the lilt of a humble song. Who else, indeed, can take the place of a poet?

Recruitment poster for South Australia, 1914.

Recruitment poster for Canada, 1914.

"In Flanders Fields": The Poem and Some Responses

Canadian physician John McCrae's "In Flanders Fields," scribbled in twenty minutes while he was sitting on the back of an ambulance just north of the field of Ypres, remains the most widely recited poem of the war. McCrae, not satisfied with the poem, would have thrown it away, but a fellow officer sent it to London, where it was published by *Punch* (after being rejected by *The Spectator*). The responses to the poem reproduced below are only three of many—a testimony to the strength of emotion the poem evoked in readers. Elizabeth Daryush's more personal description of loss provides a sharp contrast to the two more patriotic poems by Mitchell and Armstrong.

John McCrae, "In Flanders Fields" (1915)

In Flanders Fields the poppies blow
Between the crosses, row on row,
That mark our place; and in the sky
The larks, still bravely singing, fly
5   Scarce heard amid the guns below.

We are the Dead. Short days ago
We lived, felt dawn, saw sunset glow,
Loved and were loved, and now we lie
In Flanders Fields.

10 Take up our quarrel with the foe:
To you from failing hands we throw
The torch; be yours to hold it high.

In Flanders Fields

—

In Flanders fields the poppies grow
Between the crosses, row on row
That mark our place : and in the sky
The larks still bravely singing, fly
Scarce heard amid the guns below.

We are the Dead . Short days ago
We lived, felt dawn, saw sunset glow,
Loved, and were loved, and now we lie
In Flanders fields .

Take up our quarrel with the foe :
To you from failing hands we throw
The torch : be yours to hold it high !
If ye break faith with us who die
We shall not sleep, though poppies grow
In Flanders fields .

John McCrae

An autograph copy of McCrae's famous poem.
Note that in this version he has replaced "blow" with "grow" in the first line.

If ye break faith with us who die
We shall not sleep, though poppies grow
15 In Flanders Fields.

John Mitchell, "Reply to 'In Flanders Fields'" (1916)

Oh! sleep in peace where poppies grow;
The torch your falling hands let go
Was caught by us, again held high,
A beacon light in Flanders sky
5 That dims the stars to those below.
You are our dead, you held the foe,
And ere the poppies cease to blow,
We'll prove our faith in you who lie
In Flanders Fields.

10 Oh! rest in peace, we quickly go
To you who bravely died, and know
In other fields was heard the cry,
For freedom's cause, of you who lie,
So still asleep where poppies grow,
15 In Flanders Fields.

As in rumbling sound, to and fro,
The lightning flashes, sky aglow,
The mighty hosts appear, and high
Above the din of battle cry,
20 Scarce heard amidst the guns below,
Are fearless hearts who fight the foe,
And guard the place where poppies grow.
Oh! sleep in peace, all you who lie
In Flanders Fields.

25 And still the poppies gently blow,
Between the crosses, row on row.
The larks, still bravely soaring high,
Are singing now their lullaby
To you who sleep where poppies grow
30 In Flanders Fields.

German troops in a trench on
the Western Front, 1918.

J.A. Armstrong, "Another Reply to 'In Flanders Fields'" (1916)

In Flanders Fields the cannons boom,
And fitful flashes light the gloom;
While up above, like eagles, fly
The fierce destroyers of the sky;
5 With stains the earth wherein you lie
Is redder than the poppy bloom,
In Flanders Fields.
Sleep on, ye brave! The shrieking shell,
The quaking trench, the startling yell,
10 The fury of the battle hell
Shall wake you not, for all is well;
Sleep peacefully, for all is well.
Your flaming torch aloft we bear,
With burning heart and oath we swear
15 To keep the faith, to fight it through,
To crush the foe, or sleep with you,

In Flanders Fields.
Elizabeth Daryush, "Flanders Fields" (1916)

Here the scented daisy glows
Glorious as the carmined° rose;   *reddened*
Here the hill-top's verdure mean
Fair is with unfading green;
5 Here, where sorrow still must tread,
All her graves are garlanded.

And still, O glad passer-by
Of the fields of agony,
Lower laughter's voice, and bare
10 Thy head in the valley where
Poppies bright and rustling wheat
Are a desert to love's feet.

Anonymous, "I Learned to Wash in Shell-Holes"

I learned to wash in shell-holes and to shave myself in
    tea,
While the fragments of a mirror did a balance on my knee;
I learned to dodge the whizzbangs[1] and the flying lumps
    of lead,
And to keep a foot of earth between the snipers and my
    head.

5 I learned to keep my haversack[2] well filled with
    buckshee[3] food,
To take my army issue and to pinch what else I could;
I learned to cook Maconochie[4] with candle ends and
    string,
With four-by-two[5] and sardine oil and any old darn
    thing.

I learned to use my bayonet according, as you please,
10 For a bread-knife or a chopper or a prong for toasting
    cheese;

---

[1] *whizzbangs* Shells fired by small-caliber, high-velocity German
guns.

[2] *haversack* Stout canvas bag for carrying daily rations.

[3] *buckshee* Extra, spare.

[4] *Maconochie* Tinned vegetable stew (named after its inventor).

[5] *four-by-two* Rag for cleaning the barrel of a rifle.

Shells inscribed by soldiers.

I learned to gather souvenirs that home I hoped to send,
And hump them round for months and months and
    dump them in the end.

I never used to grumble after breakfast in the line
That the eggs were cooked too lightly or the bacon cut
    too fine;
15 I never told the sergeant just exactly what I thought;
I never did a pack-drill[6] for I never quite got caught.
I never stopped a whizzbang though I've stopped a lot
    of mud,
But the one that Fritz[7] sent over with my name on was
    a dud.

J.P Long and Maurice Scott, "Oh! It's a Lovely War"
(1917)

Up to your waist in water, up to your eyes in slush,
Using the kind of language that makes the sergeant
    blush,
Who wouldn't join the army? That's what we all
    enquire.
Don't we pity the poor civilians sitting beside the fire.

---

[6] *pack-drill* Form of drill used as punishment, in which soldiers
had to march in full uniform while carrying a heavy pack.

[7] *Fritz* Nickname for a German soldier.

(Chorus)

5 *Oh, oh, oh it's a lovely war.*
Who wouldn't be a soldier, eh? Oh it's a shame to take the
    pay.
As soon as reveille[1] has gone we feel just as heavy as lead,
But we never get up till the sergeant brings our breakfast up
    to bed.
Oh, oh, oh it's a lovely war.
10 *What do we want with eggs and ham when we've got plum*
    and apple jam?
Form fours. Right turn. How shall we spend the money we
    earn?
Oh, oh, oh it's a lovely war.

When does a soldier grumble? When does he make a
    fuss?
No one is more contented in all the world than us.
15 Oh it's a cushy life, boys, really we love it so:
Once a fellow was sent on leave and simply refused to
    go.

Come to the cookhouse door, boys, sniff at the lovely
    stew.
Who is it says the colonel gets better grub than you?
Any complaints this morning? Do we complain? Not
    we.
20 What's the matter with lumps of onion floating around
    the tea?

from Rebecca West, "The Cordite Makers" (1916)

The world was polished to brightness by an east wind
when I visited the cordite[2] factory, and shone with
hard colours like a German toy-landscape. The marshes
were very green and the scattered waters very blue, and
little white clouds roamed one by one across the sky like
grazing sheep on a meadow. On the hills around stood
elms, and grey churches and red farms and yellow ricks,[3]
painted bright by the sharp sunshine. And very distinct
on the marshes there lay the village which is always full

A ship full of Australian and New Zealand troops on
their way to the Turkish peninsula of Gallipoli in the
summer of 1915. The Gallipoli offensive was disastrous. Winston Churchill (then First Lord of the
Admiralty) had hoped Gallipoli would provide an
alternative to the trench warfare of the sort endured in
Flanders, but the offensive was doomed by poor
planning, insufficient knowledge of the terrain, and an
underestimation of the enemy's strength.

of people, and yet is the home of nothing except death.

In the glare it showed that like so many institutions
of the war it has the disordered and fantastic quality of
a dream. It consists of a number of huts, some like the
government-built cottages for Irish labourers, and some
like the open-air shelters in a sanatorium, scattered over
five hundred acres; they are connected by raised wooden
gangways and interspersed with green mounds and rush
ponds. It is of such vital importance to the State that it
is ringed with barbed-wire entanglements and patrolled
by sentries, and its products must have sent tens of
thousands of our enemies to their death. And it is
inhabited chiefly by pretty young girls clad in a Red-
Riding-Hood fancy dress of khaki and scarlet.

Every morning at six, when the night mist still hangs
over the marshes, 250 of these girls are fetched by a light
railway from their barracks on a hill two miles away.
When I visited the works they had already been at work
for nine hours, and would work for three more. This
twelve-hour shift is longer than one would wish, but it
is not possible to introduce three shifts, since the girls

would find an eight-hour day too light and would complain of being debarred from the opportunity of making more money; and it is not so bad as it sounds, for in these airy and isolated huts there is neither the orchestra of rattling machines nor the sense of a confined area crowded with tired people which make the ordinary factory such a fatiguing place. Indeed, these girls, working in teams of six or seven in those clean and tidy rooms, look as if they were practising a neat domestic craft rather than a deadly domestic process. ...

But how deceptive this semblance of normal life is; what extraordinary work this is for women and how extraordinarily they are doing it, is made manifest in a certain row of huts where the cordite is being pressed through wire mesh. This, in all the world, must be the place where war and grace are closest linked. Without, a strip of garden runs beside the huts, gay with shrubs and formal with a sundial. Within there is a group of girls that composes into so beautiful a picture that one remembers that the most glorious painting in the world, Velasquez's[1] *The Weavers*, shows women working just like this.

One girl stands high on a platform against the wall, filling the cordite paste into one of the two great iron presses, and when she has finished with that she swings round the other one on a swivel with a fine free gesture. The other girls stand round the table laying out the golden cords in graduated sizes from the thickness of rope to the thinness of macaroni, the clear khaki and scarlet of their dresses shining back from the wet floor in a perpetually changing pattern as they move quickly about their work. They look very young in their pretty, childish dresses, and one thinks them good children for working so diligently. And it occurs to one as something incredible that they are now doing the last three hours of a twelve-hour shift.

If one asks the manager whether this zeal can possibly be normal, whether it is not perhaps the result of his presence, one is confronted by the awful phenomenon, beside which a waterspout or a volcano in eruption would be a little thing, of a manager talking about his employees with reverence. It seems that the girls work all day with a fury which mounts to a climax

in the last three hours before the other 250 girls step into their places for the twelve-hour night shift. In these hours spies are sent out to walk along the verandah to see how the teams in the other huts are getting on, and their reports set the girls on to an orgy of competitive industry. Here again it was said that for attention, enthusiasm and discipline, there could not be better workmen than these girls.

There is matter connected with these huts, too, that showed the khaki and scarlet hoods to be no fancy dress, but a military uniform. They are a sign, for they have been dipped in a solution that makes them fireproof, that the girls are ready to face an emergency, which had arisen in those huts only a few days ago. There had been one of those incalculable happenings of which high explosives are so liable, an inflammatory mixture of air with acetone, and the cordite was ignited. Two huts were instantly gutted, and the girls had to walk out through the flame. In spite of the uniform one girl lost a hand. These, of course, are the everyday dangers of the high-explosives factory. There is very little to be feared by our enemies by land, and it is the sentries' grief and despair that their total bag for the eighteen months of their patrol of the marshes consists of one cow.

Surely, never before in modern history can women have lived a life so completely parallel to that of the regular Army. The girls who take up this work sacrifice almost as much as men who enlist; for although they make on an average $30s^2$ a week they are working much harder than most of them, particularly the large number who were formerly domestic servants, would ever have dreamed of working in peacetime. And, although their colony of wooden huts has been well planned by their employers, and is pleasantly administered by the Young Women's Christian Association, it is, so far as severance of home-ties goes, barrack life. For although they are allowed to go home for Sunday, travelling is difficult from this remote village, and the girls are so tired that most of them spend the day in bed.

And there are two things about the cordite village which the State ought never to forget, and which ought to be impressed upon the public mind by the bestowal of military rank upon the girls. First of all there is the

---

[1] *Velasquez* Spanish painter Diego Velásquez (1599–1660).

[2] *s* Shillings.

cold fact that they face more danger every day than any soldier on home defence has seen since the beginning of the war. And secondly, there is the fact—and one wishes it could be expressed in terms of the saving of English and the losing of German life—that it is because of this army of cheerful and disciplined workers that this cordite factory has been able to increase its output since the beginning of the war by something over 1,500 per cent. It was all very well for the Army to demand high explosives, and for Mr. Lloyd George[1] to transmit the demand to industry; in the last resort the matter lay in the hands of the girls in the khaki and scarlet hoods, and the State owes them a very great debt for the way in which they have handled it.

from Francis Marion Beynon, *Aleta Day* (1919)

The following excerpt is from Francis Marion Beynon's autobiographical novel *Aleta Day*, which recounts the heroine's childhood in a small town in Manitoba, Canada, and her subsequent love for a man who enlists when World War I begins. Beynon herself was a journalist known for her feminist views and her pacifism—a stance that lost her her job in 1917. This excerpt, however, expresses the idealism that permeated the nation in the months after the declaration of war, before the realities of trench warfare were realized.

from CHAPTER 24: WAR

Then the war came. It burst like a cloud upon our holidaying world, and set us all a-tremble and a-thrill.

Germany had broken the peace of the world and plunged us into night. Very well, we would collect a few Canadians and send them over and they would settle the matter in a few months and come home, and we would give them a banquet, and allow them to die in the poorhouse, as had been done to the heroes of other wars.

What days those were! An extra[2] every half-hour!

---

[1] *Mr. Lloyd George* David Lloyd George (1863–1945), British Prime Minister.

[2] *extra* Additional issue of a newspaper.

Female workers at a Birmingham airplane factory in September 1918.

War maps in every hand! A half mile towards Paris— gloom for two days! A great ship sunk—gloom for a week! Our hearts were sensitive to suffering then and the death of a hundred thousand men meant something to us. The blood reeked in our nostrils.

Yet for all that we [were] women, old men and cripples, how we did shout our patriotism from the housetops, so that nobody should miss our voice in the great songs.

What days those were!

The even tramp of troops along the streets! The morning call of the bugle! The thrill of an hourly excitement! The awful torment of soul as one read of rivers full of dead bodies. Human bodies! It broke our hearts to read of men with their legs and arms blown off; with their faces shattered to pieces; men who would go on living under the most horrible physical limitations. That was early in the war before we had grown callous to the pain of other human beings.

And yet, mixed with our horror, there was a thrill, a feeling that something had really happened in our time.

What days those were!

Ivor Gurney, "To his Love" (1919)

Ivor Gurney (1890–1937) fought on the Western front from May 1916 to October 1917 (when he was poisoned by gas). He published two collections of war poems, as well as other work, but was increasingly affected by severe mental illness, and in 1922 was certified as insane.

He's gone, and all our plans
  Are useless indeed.
We'll walk no more on Cotswold[1]
  Where the sheep feed
5   Quietly and take no heed.

His body that was so quick
  Is not as you
Knew it, on Severn River
  Under the blue
10   Driving our small boat through.
You would not know him now....
  But still he died
Nobly, so cover him over
  With violets of pride
15   Purple from Severn side.
Cover him, cover him soon!

  And with thick-set
Masses of memoried flowers
  Hide that red wet
20   Thing I must somehow forget.

Vance Palmer, "The Farmer Remembers the Somme" (1920)

Both Vance Palmer (1885–1959), who was better known as a writer of fiction than as a poet, and his wife, Nettie Palmer, a leading critic as well as a poet, played central roles in Australian cultural life from the 1920s through to the 1950s. Vance Palmer joined the Australian Army in 1918, but never saw active service.

Will they never fade or pass!
  The mud, and the misty figures endlessly coming
In file through the foul morass,°   *marsh*
And the grey flood-water lipping the reeds and grass,
5 And the steel wings drumming.

The hills are bright in the sun:
There's nothing changed or marred in the well-known
  places;
When work for the day is done
There's talk, and quiet laughter, and gleams of fun
10 On the old folks' faces.

I have returned to these:
The farm, and the kindly Bush, and the young calves
  lowing;
But all that my mind sees
Is a quaking bog in a mist—stark, snapped trees,
15 and the dark Somme flowing.

---

[1] *Cotswold* Range of hills in western England.

11th Month	NOVEMBER	1917	1917	NOVEMBER	30 Days
4 Sun—22nd after Trinity			8 Th		
5 Mon					
6 Tues—(Last Quarter, 3.5 p.m.			9 Fri		
7 Wed			10 Sat—s. r. 7.10, s. s. 4.18		

NEWLY-DUG TRENCHES. Apart from uniforms, there are times when soldiers have no chance of disguising their whereabouts from an enemy. A hastily-prepared trench may indicate your position more clearly than the brightest accoutrements.

Suppose, as in the sketch on opposite page, you have only just had time to throw up an entrenchment, the newly-turned earth, AA, will stand up in the shape of a very distinct wall against a green background, and so your enemy will quickly "spot" you.

A page from the *Soldier's Own Diary*, copies of which were widely distributed to troops during the war.

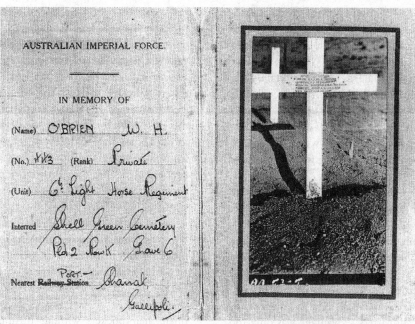

AUSTRALIAN IMPERIAL FORCE.

IN MEMORY OF

(Name) O'BRIEN W. H.

(No.) XX3 (Rank) Private

(Unit) 6ᵗ Light Horse Regiment

Interred Shell Green Cemetery
Plot 2 Row K Grave 6

Nearest Railway Station Anzal,
Gallipoli.

PORT.—

Memorial card for an Australian soldier killed and buried at Gallipoli. After the war, when the process of gathering the remains of soldiers and of constructing cemeteries began, Gallipoli became the final resting place for many New Zealand and Australian soldiers. Because most families could not arrange a visit to their loved one's grave, pictures were supplied to these families upon request.

from Robert Graves, *Good-Bye to All That* (1929, revised 1957)

from CHAPTER 17

We[1] once discussed which were the cleanest troops in trenches, taken by nationalities. We agreed on a descending-order list like this: English and German Protestants; Northern Irish, Welsh and Canadians; Irish and German Catholics; Scots, with certain higher-ranking exceptions; Mohammedan Indians; Algerians; Portuguese; Belgians; French. We put the Belgians and French there for spite; they could not have been dirtier than the Algerians and the Portuguese.

Propaganda reports of atrocities were, it was agreed, ridiculous. We remembered that while the Germans *could* commit atrocities against enemy civilians, Ger-

many itself, except for an early Russian cavalry raid, had never had the enemy on her soil. We no longer believed the highly-coloured accounts of German atrocities in Belgium; knowing the Belgians now at first-hand. By atrocities we meant, specifically, rape, mutilation and torture—not summary shootings of suspected spies, harbourers of spies, *francs-tireurs*,[2] or disobedient local officials. If the atrocity-list had to include the accidental-on-purpose bombing or machine-gunning of civilians from the air, the Allies were now committing as many atrocities as the Germans. French and Belgian civilians had often tried to win our sympathy by exhibiting mutilations of children—stumps of hands and feet, for instance—representing them as deliberate, fiendish atrocities when, as likely as not, they were merely the result of shell-fire. We did not believe rape to be any more common on the German side of the line than on

---

[1] *We* Graves, who was an officer in the Royal Welch Fusiliers, is here recounting his discussions with other British officers.

[2] *francs-tireurs* French: sharp-shooters.

the Allied side. And since a bully-beef diet, fear of death, and absence of wives made ample provision of women necessary in the occupied areas, no doubt the German Army authorities provided brothels in the principal French towns behind the line, as the French did on the Allied side. We did not believe stories of women's forcible enlistment in these establishments. "What's wrong with the voluntary system?" we asked cynically.

As for atrocities against soldiers—where should one draw the line? The British soldier, at first, regarded as atrocious the use of bowie-knives[1] by German patrols. After a time, he learned to use them himself; they were cleaner killing weapons than revolvers or bombs. The Germans regarded as equally atrocious the British Mark VII rifle-bullet, which was more apt to turn on striking than the German bullet. For true atrocities, meaning personal rather than military violations of the code of war, few opportunities occurred—except in the interval between the surrender of prisoners and their arrival (or non-arrival) at Headquarters. Advantage was only too often taken of this opportunity. Nearly every instructor in the Mess could quote specific instances of prisoners having been murdered on the way back. The commonest motives were, it seems, revenge for the death of friends or relatives, jealousy of the prisoner's trip to a comfortable prison camp in England, military enthusiasm, fear of being suddenly overpowered by the prisoners or, more simply, impatience with the escorting job. In any of these cases the conductors would report on arrival at Headquarters that a German shell had killed the prisoners; and no questions would be asked. We had every reason to believe that the same thing happened on the German side, where prisoners, as useless mouths to feed in a country already short of rations, would be even less welcome. None of us had heard of German prisoners being more than threatened at Headquarters to get military information from them. The sort that they could give was not of sufficient importance to make torture worth while; and anyhow, it had been found that, when treated kindly, prisoners were anxious in gratitude to tell as much as they knew. German intelligence officers had probably discovered that too.

The troops with the worst reputation for acts of

violence against prisoners were the Canadians (and later the Australians). The Canadians' motive was said to be revenge for a Canadian found crucified with bayonets through his hands and feet in a German trench. This atrocity had never been substantiated; nor did we believe the story, freely circulated, that the Canadians crucified a German officer in revenge shortly afterwards. How far this reputation for atrocities was deserved, and how far it could be ascribed to the overseas habit of bragging and leg-pulling, we could not decide. At all events, most overseas men, and some British troops, made atrocities against prisoners a boast, not a confession.

Later in the War, I heard two first-hand accounts.

A Canadian-Scot: "They sent me back with three bloody prisoners, you see, and one started limping and groaning, so I had to keep on kicking the sod down the trench. He was an officer. It was getting dark and I felt fed up, so I thought: 'I'll have a bit of a game.' I had them covered with the officer's revolver and made 'em open their pockets without turning round. Then I dropped a Mills bomb[2] in each, with the pin out, and ducked behind a traverse. Bang, bang, bang! No more bloody prisoners. No good Fritzes[3] but dead 'uns."

An Australian: "Well, the biggest lark I had was at Morlancourt, when we took it the first time. There were a lot of Jerries[4] in a cellar, and I said to 'em: 'Come out, you Camarades!' So out they came, a dozen of 'em, with their hands up. 'Turn out your pockets,' I told 'em. They turned 'em out. Watches, and gold and stuff, all dinkum.[5] Then I said: 'Now back to your cellar, you sons of bitches!' For I couldn't be bothered with 'em. When they were all safely down I threw half a dozen Mills bombs in after 'em. I'd got the stuff all right, and we weren't taking prisoners that day."

An old woman at Cardonette on the Somme gave me my first-hand account of large-scale atrocities. I was billeted with her in July 1916. Close to her home, a battalion of French Turcos[6] overtook the rear-guard of

---

[1] *bowie-knives* Curved, double-edged knives of about 15 inches in length.

[2] *Mills bomb* Type of hand grenade made to form shrapnel on explosion.

[3] *Fritzes* Nickname for German soldiers.

[4] *Jerries* Nickname for German soldiers.

[5] *dinkum* Australian slang: genuine, authentic.

[6] *French Turcos* Algerians serving in the French infantry.

a German division retreating from the Marne in September 1914. The Turcos surprised the dead-weary Germans while still marching in column. The old woman went, with gestures, through the pantomime of slaughter, and ended: "*Et enfin, ces animaux leur ont arraché les oreilles et les ont mis à la poche!*"[1] ...

We discussed the continuity of regimental morale. A captain in a Line battalion of a Surrey regiment said: "Our battalion has never recovered from the first Battle of Ypres. What's wrong is that we have a rotten depot. The drafts are bad, and so we get a constant re-infection." He told me one night in our sleeping hut: "In both the last two shows I had to shoot a man of my company to get the rest out of the trench. It was so bloody awful, I couldn't stand it. That's why I applied to be sent down here." This was the truth, not the usual loose talk that one heard at the base. I felt sorrier for him than for any other man I met in France. He deserved a better regiment.

The boast of every good battalion was that it had never lost a trench; both our Line battalions made it—meaning, that they had never been forced out of a trench without recapturing it before the action ended. Capturing a German trench and being unable to hold it for lack of reinforcements did not count; nor did retirement by order from Headquarters, or when the battalion next door had broken and left a flank in the air. And, towards the end of the War, trenches could be honourably abandoned as being wholly obliterated by bombardment, or because not really trenches at all, but a line of selected shell-craters.

We all agreed on the value of arms-drill as a factor in morale. "Arms-drill as it should be done," someone said, "is beautiful, especially when the company feels itself as a single being, and each movement is not a synchronized movement of every man together, but the single movement of one large creature." I used to get big bunches of Canadians to drill: four or five hundred at a time. Spokesmen stepped forward once and asked what sense there was in sloping and ordering arms, and fixing and unfixing bayonets. They said they had come across to fight, and not to guard Buckingham Palace. I told them that in every division of the four in which I had

served—the First, Second, Seventh and Eighth—there had been three different kinds of troops. Those that had guts but were no good at drill; those that were good at drill but had no guts; and those that had guts and were good at drill. These last, for some reason or other, fought by far the best when it came to a show—I didn't know why, and I didn't care. I told them that when they were better at fighting than the Guards they could perhaps afford to neglect their arms-drill.

We often theorized in the Mess about drill. I held that the best drill never resulted from being bawled at by a sergeant-major: that there must be perfect respect between the man who gives the order and the men who carry it out. The test of drill came, I said, when the officer gave an incorrect word of command. If his company could, without hesitation, carry out the order intended or, if the order happened to be impossible, could stand absolutely still, or continue marching, without confusion in the ranks, that was good drill. Some instructors regarded the corporate spirit that resulted from drilling together as leading to loss of initiative in the men drilled.

Others argued that it acted just the other way round: "Suppose a section of men with rifles get isolated from the rest of the company, without an N.C.O.[2] in charge, and meet a machine-gun. Under the stress of danger this section will have that all-one-body feeling of drill, and obey an imaginary word of command. There may be no communication between its members, but there will be a drill movement, with two men naturally opening fire on the machine-gun while the remainder work round, part on the left flank and part on the right; and the final rush will be simultaneous. Leadership is supposed to be the perfection for which drill has been instituted. That's wrong. Leadership is only the first stage. Perfection of drill is communal action. Though drill may seem to be antiquated parade-ground stuff, it's the foundation of tactics and musketry. Parade-ground musketry won all the battles in our regimental histories; this War, which is unlikely to open out, and must end with the collapse, by 'attrition,' of one side or the other, will be won by parade-ground tactics—by the simple drill tactics of small units fighting in limited spaces, and in noise and

---

[1] *Et enfin ... poche* French: And finally, these animals tore off their ears [i.e., the ears of their prisoners] and put them in their pockets.

[2] *N.C.O.* Non-commissioned officer.

confusion so great that leadership is quite impossible." Despite variance on this point we all agreed that regimental pride remained the strongest moral force that kept a battalion going as an effective fighting unit; contrasting it particularly with patriotism and religion.

Patriotism, in the trenches, was too remote a sentiment, and at once rejected as fit only for civilians, or prisoners. A new arrival who talked patriotism would soon be told to cut it out. As "Blighty,"[1] a geographical concept, Great Britain was a quiet, easy place for getting back to out of the present foreign misery; but as a nation it included not only the trench-soldiers themselves and those who had gone home wounded, but the staff, Army Service Corps, lines-of-communication troops, base units, home-service units, and all civilians down to the detested grades of journalists, profiteers, "starred" men exempted from enlistment, conscientious objectors, and members of the Government. The trench-soldier, with this carefully graded caste-system of honour, never considered that the Germans opposite might have built up exactly the same system themselves. He thought of Germany as a nation in arms, a unified nation inspired with the sort of patriotism that he himself despised. He believed most newspaper reports on conditions and sentiments in Germany, though believing little or nothing of what he read about similar conditions and sentiments in England. Yet he never under-rated the German as a soldier. Newspaper libels on Fritz's courage and efficiency were resented by all trench-soldiers of experience.

Hardly one soldier in a hundred was inspired by religious feeling of even the crudest kind. It would have been difficult to remain religious in the trenches even if one had survived the irreligion of the training battalion at home. A regular sergeant at Montagne, a Second Battalion man, had recently told me that he did not hold with religion in time of war. He said that the "niggers" (meaning the Indians) were right in officially relaxing their religious rules while fighting. "And all this damn nonsense, Sir—excuse me, Sir—that we read in the papers, Sir, about how miraculous it is that the wayside crucifixes are always getting shot at, but the figure of our Lord Jesus somehow don't get hurt, it fairly makes me sick, Sir." This was his explanation why, when giving practice fire-orders from the hill-top, he had shouted, unaware that I stood behind him: "Seven hundred, half left, bloke on cross, five rounds, concentrate, FIRE!" And why, for "concentrate," he had humorously substituted "consecrate." His platoon, including the two unusual "Bible-wallahs" whose letters home always began in the same formal way: "Dear Sister in Christ," or "Dear Brother in Christ," blazed away.

Women celebrating on V-day, London, 1918.

from May Wedderburn Cannan, *Grey Ghosts and Voices* (1976)

The following is taken from the autobiography of May Wedderburn Cannan, daughter of the head of the Oxford University Press. During the war Cannan worked at the Press and as a volunteer nurse, participating in the mobilization of the Red Cross. She also went to France to volunteer in a soldiers' canteen in Rouen, an experience she describes in the excerpt below. Cannan gives a sense of the change of attitude—from optimism to cynicism—among both poets and the general public as the war progressed when she explains the popular expression at the time, "Went to the war with Rupert Brooke and came home with Siegfried Sassoon." While Brooke was an idealistic poet whose verse celebrated his country and its cause, Sassoon's verse painted in grim detail the horrors of a war the senseless atrocities of which could not be idealized. After years of trench warfare, the poems of Brooke seemed naive and simplistic to many.

---

[1] *Blighty* England; home.

I suppose it is difficult for anyone to realise now what "France" meant to us. In the Second War I met a young man of the Left who assured me that Rupert Brooke's[1] verse was of no account, phoney, because it was "impossible that anyone should have thought like that." I turned and rent him, saying that he was entitled to his own opinion of Rupert Brooke's verse, but not entitled to say that no one could have thought like that. How could he know how we had thought?—All our hopes and all our loves, and God knew, all our fears, were in France; to get to France, if only to stand on her soil, was something; to share, in however small a way, in what was done there was Heart's Desire.

I asked my Father could I take all my holidays in one and go for four weeks to France—I did not want holidays, I said, but I did want France. It was dark and we were walking home through the confines of Little Clarendon Street; my voice, I knew, shook; he took his pipe out of his mouth, halted his step for a moment and looked down at me. "Ah! France" he said, "France, yes, I think you should go. We'll manage." I stammered thanks and we walked home in silence, understanding each other.

The Canteen was started at Rouen because Lord Brassey's yacht *The Sunbeam* had made two or three journeys there during the shortage of hospital ships bringing wounded home. Lady Mabelle Egerton, his daughter, looking round the desolate railway yards beyond the quays asked the R.T.O.[2] if there was anything that could be done for the troops; drafts going up the line to Railhead, who had to spend a long day there, and sometimes a long night.

He said that the men brought their rations, including tea, but that there was no means of making hot water. (It was long before the days of another war when motorised infantry "brewed up" with their petrol cans) —Could she find some philanthropic person to take on the job? She could find no one—and decided to do it herself, and so the Canteen, later known affectionately

to thousands of the B.E.F. and the New Armies[3] as "the Coffee Shop," was born....

Along the length of railway line ran a row of sheds with huge sliding doors. In the first, and smaller one, was established a boiler room where enormous vats of hot water forever boiled. Beyond, steps led to a room where we ate our own meals when there was time and kept books for anyone who asked for something to read going up the Line. And across the whole of the great sheds ran heavy tables, ours with shelves under which at night held guttering candles and trays for change. Behind were the steaming cauldrons where we washed, (when a draft had left), the unbelievably pink French bowls in which we served coffee.

Coffee had proved more possible to get than tea and to it was added ham sandwiches. We had hundreds of someone's "Handy Hams" enclosed in a kind of scaly protection. In cold weather when we could not peel them we flung them with violence onto the stone floor to crack them; then endlessly we cut slices of ham.

I remember at the end of a long cutting session my left hand could not close itself; it had held the ham steady against the knife for so long, but we did have two machines for cutting bread. Butter in the cold weather was hard and stiff to spread, and when it was hot it dripped.

We were wanted because there had been an epidemic of measles among the staff; one girl had died of pneumonia, and another was home on sick leave—we were gapfillers only, but we were wanted —they needed us....

When the big trains were due in we opened the sliding doors of the sheds, the train doors banged and banged down the long line of the corridors and some 2,000 men would surge in. Barricaded behind our heavy table, and thankful for it when the pressure was heavy or a draft had somehow got hold of some drink, we handed out bowls of coffee and sandwiches, washed dirty bowls till the water in the tall vats was chocolate brown, and served again.

Someone would play the piano; Annie Laurie; Loch Lomond. Blurred lanterns lit the scene as best they might when it rained and our candles in the tills under

---

[1] *Rupert Brooke* Poet (1887–1915) known for his patriotic, idealistic verse. Brooke died of blood poisoning on the way to Gallipoli in 1915.

[2] *R.T.O.* Railroad Transportation Officer.

[3] *B.E.F.* British Expeditionary Force; *New Armies* Forces assembled from the 1914 volunteer recruitment campaign of the Earl of Kitchener, Secretary of State for War.

the tables guttered in the wind. One was hot or horrid cold, harried, dirty, and one's feet ached with the stone floors. When the smaller drafts came one could distinguish faces, and regimental badges; have a word or two. Two men told me with impressment that they were "the New Army, Kitchener's!" I said yes, and we had been expecting them, and thought of the old Army and the T.A.[1] Worried young officers asked one to change a pound note and frowned over getting "25 shillings" (francs) to the pound. Twice I came on an old friend but there was no time save for a brief greeting and a "good bye and good luck."

When the whistle blew they stood to save the King[2] and the roof came off the sheds. Two thousand men, maybe, singing—it was the most moving thing I knew. Then there'd be the thunder of seats pushed back, the stamp of army boots on the pave, and as the train went out they sang Tipperary[3]—

No one seemed to know how the song, written and first sung at Stalybridge in 1912, had become the song of the B.E.F. My brother-in-law, a Mons man,[4] said they did not sing it till they read in the papers that they were—then they learned it! …

That spring I collected such verse as I thought "possible," got my Father to "cast an eye over it," and set forth to see Mr. Blackwell.[5] He had a small office up an uncarpeted stair at the back of the famous bookshop in the Broad.[6] At the last moment my Father said he would come with me. I think that he wanted to make sure that I was not published in any series or involved in any clique.

Mr. Blackwell was, I remember, very kind, but as I was practically blind and deaf with nerves I have a blurred recollection of what happened. We walked up the Broad together afterwards, and, suddenly realising that his ridiculous daughter was struggling with tears, he

stopped dead. "Why are you crying?" "I'm not," I said, using the old formula; "It's all right only I did think he might take it." "But he has!" "Has he?" I asked astounded. "Yes, of course" said my Father, and continuing up the street; "The trouble with you and that young man is that you have both got the Oxford manner so badly you can't understand each other." He seemed amused. As I have never been able to discover what the Oxford manner is I have never known what he meant. …

I was lucky for after the Somme there was a change of heart among poets. Siegfried Sassoon wrote to the Press from France saying that the war was now a war of conquest and without justification,[7] and declared himself to be a conscientious objector. He was rescued from trouble by Robert Graves and his friends who claimed a breakdown. C.E. Montague wrote *Disenchantment* and Wilfred Owen was much influenced by him.[8] A saying went round, "Went to the war with Rupert Brooke and came home with Siegfried Sassoon."

I had much admired some of Sassoon's verse but I was not coming home with him. Someone must go on writing for those who were still convinced of the right of the cause for which they had taken up arms.

The conscription tribunals were often ruthless and sometimes, rather horrible; but by no means always (after all the army did not want unwilling, and therefore bad, soldiers), and, testifying their conscientious objections, persistent defenders of culture and antiwar writers were excused active service and able to do other work. There was a colony of them at Garsington near Oxford where Philip and Lady Ottoline Morrell[9] had their

---

[1] *T.A.* Territorial Army.

[2] *to save the King* I.e., they stood to sing the national anthem, "God Save the King."

[3] *Tipperary* The song "It's a Long Way to Tipperary."

[4] *Mons man* I.e., a man who had fought at the Battle of Mons, in Belgium, the first battle of World War I (23 August 1914).

[5] *Blackwell* The publisher Basil Blackwell (1889–1984).

[6] *bookshop in the Broad* I.e., Blackwell's, Broad Street, Oxford.

[7] *Siegfried Sassoon … justification* Sassoon's letter, in which he condemned the war as a mere matter of "aggression and conquest," was published in *The Times* on 31 July 1917. After his friend and fellow poet Robert Graves testified that Sassoon was suffering from shell-shock, a medical board sent Sassoon to Craiglockhart War Hospital, Edinburgh, rather than to prison.

[8] *C.E. Montague* Journalist and novelist Charles Edward Montague (1867–1928), whose *Disenchantment* comprised a series of articles he had published in the *Manchester Guardian* in 1920 and 1921 on the impact of the war; *Wilfred Owen* War poet (1893–1918).

[9] *Philip and Lady Ottoline Morrell* Solicitor and politician Philip Morrell (1870–1943) and his wife Ottoline (1873–1938), a well-known literary hostess. Both were pacifists, and their Oxford home, Garsington Manor, provided a refuge for conscientious objectors during the war.

home and entertained such people as Middleton Murry, Katherine Mansfield, Lawrence, Bertrand Russell,[1] my cousin Gilbert Cannan and others of the intellectual élite who stayed there talking of art and verse and genius and pure intellect....

from "Proceedings" of the All-Russian Central Executive Committee of Soviets of Workers', Soldiers', and Peasants' Deputies[2] (17 November 1917)

In March of 1917 (February according to the old Julian calendar, which the Russians used until 1918, when they adopted the Gregorian calendar), with Russia suffering from extreme poverty and in the midst of the war against Germany, the autocratic regime of Czar Nicholas II crumbled as troops refused orders to suppress workers' risings in Moscow and St. Petersburg. The Czar was replaced by a provisional government led by Alexander Kerensky, a democratic socialist. In November (October, according to the Julian calendar), a second revolution occurred when the more radical Bolsheviks, led by V.I. Lenin, seized power. Between June 1917 and January of the following year, representatives of councils of workers (or "soviets") met in Petrograd (St. Petersburg). The discussions shed interesting light on the connections between the revolution and World War I and touch on vitally important issues such as the degree to which the new government would tolerate free speech and the ways in which it contemplated interacting with the rest of the world. The way in which many of the issues discussed here were handled by the Communist government would shape a great deal of twentieth-century history.

The speakers in the excerpts below are V.A. Avanesov, soon to become Secretary of the Central Executive Committee of the new government; A. L. Kalegayev and V. A. Karelin, leaders of the Socialist-Revolutionary Party; Soviet representative S.M. Zaks; Vladimir Lenin, leader of the Bolshevik Party (forerunner of the Communist Party, which domi-

nated the country from 1917 until the collapse of the USSR in 1989–91); and Leon Trotsky, Lenin's second-in-command. (Trotsky later broke with Communist Party authorities after Joseph Stalin came to power; he was murdered while living in exile in Mexico.)

AVANESOV. The question of press freedom must be seen in the context of the current political situation in the country as a whole. It seems that no one objects to closure of bourgeois newspapers during an insurrection, when fighting is in progress. If this is so, [we must ask ourselves] whether the struggle is indeed over and the moment has come when we can pass on to a normal mode of life. Having silenced the bourgeois press, [the revolutionary authorities] would be very naive if they were to let slip from their hands such a powerful means of influencing the ideals of all workers, soldiers, and peasants. All these measures are designed to facilitate the creation of a new regime, free from capitalist oppression, in which a socialist press will ensure freedom of speech for all citizens and for all tendencies of thought.

We defend freedom of the press [in principle], but this concept must be divorced from old petty-bourgeois or bourgeois notions of liberty. If the new government has had the strength to abolish private landed property, thereby infringing the rights of the landlords, it would be ridiculous for Soviet power to stand up for antiquated notions about liberty of the press. First the newspapers must be freed from capitalist oppression, just as we have freed the land from the landlords, and then we can promulgate new socialist laws and norms enshrining a liberty that will serve the whole toiling people, and not just capital....

KALEGAYEV. ... [T]here is a profound disagreement between our position and that of the Bolsheviks. [The latter argue:] previously we defended all civil liberties, but now we are prepared to muzzle our opponents. However, one cannot emancipate society from the fetters of capitalism by taking repressive measures against newspapers. Nor is it possible to carve up freedom of the press like a loaf of bread, allocating so much freedom to each group according to the influence exerted by its ideas. When the Bolsheviks talk of poisoning the people's consciousness by the printed word, they

---

[1] *Middleton Murry* Writer and editor John Middleton Murry (1889–1957), husband of author Katherine Mansfield (1888–1923); *Lawrence* Writer D.H. Lawrence (1885–1930); *Bertrand Russell* Philosopher and journalist (1872–1970).

[2] *Proceedings ... Deputies* Translated by H.L. Keep.

are adopting the viewpoint of [the editors of] *Zemsh-china*.[1]

TROTSKY. One should distinguish between the situation during a civil war and the situation once victory is complete. To demand that all repressive measures should be abandoned during a civil war is equivalent to demanding that the war itself should cease. Such a demand could come only from adversaries of the proletariat. Our opponents are not offering us peace. No one can provide a guarantee against [a victory of] the Komilovites.[2] During a civil war it is legitimate to suppress newspapers that support the other side. But when we are finally victorious our attitude toward the press will be analogous to that on freedom of trade. Then we shall naturally move on to a [regular] regime in press matters. In our party press we have for a long time been accustomed to take a non-proprietorial view of press freedom. Measures taken against [suspect] individuals should also be taken against press organs. We should confiscate and socialize printing-presses and stocks of newsprint ... (*Shouts from the floor:* "And Bolshevik ones too?") Yes, all these stocks should be transferred to public ownership. Any group of [workers,] soldiers, or peasants will be able to submit an application for [access to supplies of] newsprint and to a printing-press....

KARELIN. It is a Hottentot[3] morality which holds that it's bad if someone steals my wife but good if I steal someone else's. I say this because Trotsky has been critical of our party. It is surprising that we should hear [such arguments] from a party which itself now enjoys freedom of the press. We cannot have double standards of morality.

But I would rather discuss this question in terms of political expediency. Is it expedient to muzzle the expression of any trend of opinion? History teaches that whenever this is done it only makes such opinions more attractive. Forbidden fruit is sweet. I agree with Trotsky that we have to eliminate capitalist oppression in regard to the press. But the measures [he proposes] are risky. One can attain this objective without muzzling opinion, simply by undertaking a wide range of protective actions in the distribution of material. The [Bolshevik] resolution proposes that parties and groups should have [the right to publish] newspapers in proportion to the number of their supporters, but such calculations will scarcely be practicable. It would be absurd to distribute [opportunities to publish] in proportion to [the strength of various currents of] opinion; this would be like socializing thought itself.

I should make it clear that in advocating freedom of opinion we do not seek to extend it to the weakest sector [in terms of popular support]. Trotsky alleges that we are arguing from the standpoint of capital. I say that whoever puts the question in such terms is arguing from the standpoint of his own ministerial portfolio. Genuine representatives of the people should not be afraid of minority opinions. Such fear betrays an awareness that one's own opinions are weak. "Who wants press freedom?" Trotsky asks. The answer is: everyone who cherishes the [revolutionary] movement of our people....

ZAKS. [I]f we burn our bridges will we not be entirely isolated? After all, we have won precious little support so far. Western Europe is shamefully silent. One can't build socialism by decree and by relying solely upon a single party.

LENIN. The phrase "the west is shamefully silent" is impermissible from the lips of an internationalist.[4] One would have to be blind not to notice the ferment that has gripped the working classes of Germany and the west [in general]. The leaders of the German proletariat, the socialist intelligentsia, consist in main of defensists, as they do everywhere else, but their proletarian followers are prepared to desert them and to respond to our call. The savage discipline that prevails in the German army and navy has not prevented elements opposed [to the war] from taking action. The revolutionary sailors in the German navy, knowing that their enterprise was

---

[1] *Zemshchina* Russian newspaper whose title translates as "lands of the state," i.e., lands where the workers live (as opposed to the *oprichnina*, which was the personal domain of the Tsar).

[2] *Kornilovites* Supporters of General Kornilov, who attempted to replace Kerensky with a military government.

[3] *Hottentot* I.e., ignorant; inferior. (A derogatory term deriving from the name then given to members of a Southwest African people.)

[4] *internationalist* Socialists who supported an international workers' rebellion, and who thought such a movement should take precedence over the war.

doomed to fail, went to meet their fate heroically, in the hope that their sacrifice would awaken the spirit of insurrection among the people. ...

We believe in a revolution in the west. We know that this is inevitable, but of course we can't bring it about to order. Did we know last December what was to happen in February? Did we know for sure in September that next month Russian revolutionary democracy would bring off the greatest overturn in world [history]? We knew that the old government was sitting on a volcano and we could guess from many signs that beneath the surface a great change was occurring in people's ideas. We could feel the electricity in the air, we knew that it would inevitably discharge itself in a purifying storm. But we could not predict the day and hour when the storm would break. It is exactly the same now in the case of Germany. There too the people's sullen discontent is growing and is bound to erupt in the form of a broad mass movement. We cannot decree the revolution, but we can at least help it along. We shall organize fraternization in the trenches and help the western peoples to launch the invincible socialist revolution.

Revolutionary soldiers during the March 1917 uprising in Petrograd.

Vladimir Lenin and Leon Trotsky, c. 1917.

WILLIAM BUTLER YEATS
_1865 – 1939_

In _On Poetry and Poets_ (1957), fellow poet and contemporary T.S. Eliot wrote of William Butler Yeats: "Born into a world in which the doctrine of "Art for Art's Sake" was generally accepted, and living on into one in which art has been asked to be instrumental to social purposes, he held firmly to the right view which is between these, though not in any way a compromise between them, and showed that an artist, by serving his art with entire integrity, is at the same time rendering the greatest service he can to his own nation and to the whole world." In truth, few poets of the twentieth century have contributed as much to the cultural, political, and social framework of their own country, and to English literature in general. An analysis of Yeats's poetry, however, is impossible without understanding the deeply personal and biographical nature of his writing, and Yeats's own endeavor to shape his entire canon of work into a unified body of art.

William Butler Yeats was born in the Dublin suburb of Sandymount on 13 June 1865. His father, John Butler Yeats, had given up law to take up portrait painting, a decision that, though artistically and intellectually stimulating, led to many years of uprooted existence and strained finances for his family. When William was two, the family moved to London, yet much of his childhood was spent moving between schooling in London and retreats to the family home of his mother, Susan Pollexfen, in County Sligo, Ireland. In County Sligo, Yeats would find inspiration in the beauty of the countryside, the local folklore, and Irish tradition. That would remains apparent throughout his lifetime, as evidenced in early poems such as "The Lake Isle of Innisfree" and in later works such as "Under Ben Bulben." In 1880, the family returned permanently to Ireland and settled in Howth, close to Dublin. In 1883, having completed high school, Yeats decided to be an artist and enrolled in the Metropolitan School of Art, but he soon left to pursue his true passion, poetry. His first published poems appeared in the _Dublin University Review_ in 1885. Yeats also capitalized on his burgeoning literary talent and interest in Irish folklore by editing two anthologies, _Poems and Ballads of Young Ireland_ (1888) and _Fairy and Folk Tales of the Irish Peasantry_ (1888). From an early age, Yeats is said to have followed an inner voice that commanded him to "hammer his thoughts into unity."

Also at an early age, influenced by his father's religious skepticism, Yeats developed a strong interest in occultism, folklore, and theosophism, a system of philosophical thought based on the direct and immediate experience of the divine. In 1885 he joined with friends to form the Dublin Hermetic Society, a group devoted to discussion of occult sciences and pseudo-sciences of the day. This group was predominantly influenced by a more famous mystical society, The Theosophical Society, founded in New York by Madame Helena Blavatsky. In 1887, Yeats met with Madame Blavatsky and later joined the Esoteric section of the London chapter of the Theosophical Society. In 1890, Yeats left the Society to join the Hermetic Order of the Golden Dawn, an occult society that drew upon astrology, tarot, kabbala, and Eastern mysticism for its teachings. Throughout his life and career, Yeats would turn to mythology and the occult as tools for developing his own vision of history and imagination.

In his poetry, this vision is evident in an elaborate system of images and symbols that Yeats would continually investigate and refine.

In 1889 Yeats's first collection, *The Wanderings of Oisin and Other Poems*, was published. The collection was well received, but the attention of one reader in particular would be responsible for what Yeats would term "the troubling of my life." The beautiful actress and Irish nationalist Maud Gonne was introduced to Yeats by a mutual friend, John O'Leary, shortly after the collection was published. The meeting marked a fateful moment in the life of Yeats, as Gonne would become his obsession for the next quarter-century, and his poetry would resonate with his love and despair for her in poems such as "Adam's Curse" (1904), "No Second Troy" (1910), and "A Prayer for My Daughter" (1921). Despite remaining intimate with Yeats for many years, Maud Gonne persistently refused to marry him, and added to his turmoil with her marriage to an Irish soldier, John MacBride, in 1903. Yet in spite of the heartache Yeats endured through his relationship with Gonne, she helped inspire him in two new cultural endeavors: the establishment of an Irish national theatre and the development of a public voice for the Irish nationalist movement for independence.

For several years after the publication of *The Wanderings of Oisin and Other Poems*, Yeats continued to gain literary prominence with further collections of poetry and studies of Irish folklore and fairy tales. In 1896 Yeats met Lady Augusta Gregory, a fellow writer and promoter of Irish literature, who invited him to stay in her country house at Coole Park. Through her influence, Yeats became involved in the founding of the Irish National Theatre in 1899. In writing for the theater, Yeats found a new voice for his interest in mythology, mysticism, Irish nationalism, and Maud Gonne. In 1902, Gonne played the title role in Yeats's nationalist play *Cathleen Ni Houlihan*. In 1904, the Irish National Theatre's permanent home, The Abbey Theatre, opened with Yeats's play *On Baile's Strand*. As the Abbey's director and dramatist, Yeats helped develop it into one of the world's leading theaters and, perhaps more importantly to him, into the center of the Irish literary renaissance.

In 1908, eight volumes of Yeats's *Collected Works* were published. Although Yeats was most interested in the Abbey Theatre during this period, this publication by no means heralded the slowdown of his poetic career. On the contrary, as he was becoming a figure of national importance, Yeats began to develop a more public voice in his poetry. Abandoning the more lyrical and self-conscious mode of his earlier poems, Yeats began to trace the growing political upheaval of the period. The publication of *The Green Helmet and Other Poems* in 1910 marks Yeats's transition into the second phase of his poetic career. Where his early poems often offered romantic melancholy and idyllic meditations on pagan themes, the poetry of this second phase became more direct in its analysis of the events and attitudes of the period. As Yeats became embittered by the small-minded nationalism of The Abbey's middle-class audiences, and as he watched with horror the growing violence in the struggle for Irish independence, poems such as "Easter 1916," "Meditations In Time of Civil War," and "Nineteen Hundred and Nineteen" began to reflect his distrust of popular judgement and concern for the future of his country.

At the same time, Yeats continued to develop his complex system of symbolism and esoteric theories regarding the movement of history and human intellect. In 1917, having exhausted his proposals to Maud Gonne and suffered another humiliating refusal by Gonne's daughter Iseult, Yeats married Georgie Hyde-Lees, whom he had met in 1911. On their honeymoon, Hyde-Lees delighted Yeats with her gift for automatic writing (believed by Yeats to be dictated by spirits), and for several years her writings inspired Yeats to refine his symbolic system, as described in his book *A Vision* (1925). Although Yeats's poetry is by no means unintelligible without an understanding of *A Vision*, many of his poems refer directly to the patterns and imagery examined within its pages. According to Yeats, the progress of art and thought is directly interwoven through the spirals, or gyres, of human history, represented in *A Vision* by two interpenetrating cones that make up antithetical cycles of 2000 years. These ideas became increasingly evident in his poetic works, particularly later poems such as "Byzantium" and "Sailing to Byzantium."

In 1922 Yeats was elected Senator of the Irish Free State; a year later, he was awarded the Nobel Prize for Literature, becoming the first Irish writer to receive the award. Yeats continued to produce major poetry well into his later years. As his health began to decline, his poetry took on a defiant tone, reflecting an awareness of his own mortality. Poems of this period, such as "Lapis Lazuli," "The Circus Animals' Desertion," and "Under Ben Bulben," rage against old age while reflecting on his life and body of work. Poems published in *The Tower* (1928), *The Winding Stair* (1933), and *Last Poems* (1939) are thought by many critics to be among his finest.

Following a long period of heart trouble, Yeats died on 28 January 1939, and was buried in Roquebrune, France, where he had been spending the winter. In 1948, his remains were reinterred, as he had wished, in Drumcliff, County Sligo. Also according to his wishes, his epitaph is taken from "Under Ben Bulben": "Cast a cold eye / On life, on death. / Horseman, pass by!"

⌘ ⌘ ⌘

The Lake Isle of Innisfree [1]

I will arise and go now, and go to Innisfree,
And a small cabin build there, of clay and wattles
     made;[2]
Nine bean-rows will I have there, a hive for the honey
     bee,
And live alone in the bee-loud glade.

5   And I shall have some peace there, for peace comes
         dropping slow,
Dropping from the veils of the morning to where the
         cricket sings;
There midnight's all a glimmer, and noon a purple glow,
And evening full of the linnet's° wings.   *small songbird's*

I will arise and go now, for always night and day
10   I hear lake water lapping with low sounds by the shore;
While I stand on the roadway, or on the pavements grey,
I hear it in the deep heart's core.
—1890

When You Are Old [3]

When you are old and gray and full of sleep,
     And nodding by the fire, take down this book,
And slowly read, and dream of the soft look
Your eyes had once, and of their shadows deep;

5   How many loved your moments of glad grace,
And loved your beauty with love false or true,
But one man loved the pilgrim soul in you,
And loved the sorrows of your changing face;

And bending down beside the glowing bars,
10   Murmur, a little sadly, how Love fled
And paced upon the mountains overhead
And hid his face amid a crowd of stars.
—1892

---

[1] *Lake Isle of Innisfree*   A small island in Lough Gill, County Sligo; Innisfree (*Inis Fraoigh* in Gaelic) means "Heather Island."

[2] *wattles*   Poles and reeds interwoven to create a thatched wall or roof.

[3] *When You Are Old*   Based on one of Pierre de Ronsard's (1524–85) *Sonnets pour Hélène*, "*Quand vous serez bien vieille, au soir, à la chandelle*," which translates to: "When you very old, sitting by the candlelight at night."

Who Goes with Fergus?[1]

Who will go drive with Fergus now,
    And pierce the deep wood's woven shade,
And dance upon the level shore?
Young man, lift up your russet brow,
5   And lift your tender eyelids, maid,
And brood on hopes and fear no more.

And no more turn aside and brood
Upon love's bitter mystery;
For Fergus rules the brazen cars,
10 And rules the shadows of the wood,
And the white breast of the dim sea
And all dishevelled wandering stars.
—1893

Adam's Curse [2]

We sat together at one summer's end,
    That beautiful mild woman,[3] your close friend,
And you[4] and I, and talked of poetry.
I said, "A line will take us hours maybe;
5   Yet if it does not seem a moment's thought,
Our stitching and unstitching has been naught.
Better go down upon your marrow-bones
And scrub a kitchen pavement, or break stones
Like an old pauper, in all kinds of weather;
10 For to articulate sweet sounds together
Is to work harder than all these, and yet
Be thought an idler by the noisy set
Of bankers, schoolmasters, and clergymen
The martyrs call the world."

15   And thereupon
That beautiful mild woman for whose sake

There's many a one shall find out all heartache
On finding that her voice is sweet and low
Replied, "To be born woman is to know —
20 Although they do not talk of it at school —
That we must labour to be beautiful."

I said, "It's certain there is no fine thing
Since Adam's fall but needs much labouring.
There have been lovers who thought love should be
25 So much compounded of high courtesy
That they would sigh and quote with learned looks
Precedents out of beautiful old books;
Yet now it seems an idle trade enough."

We sat grown quiet at the name of love;
30 We saw the last embers of daylight die,
And in the trembling blue-green of the sky
A moon, worn as if it had been a shell
Washed by time's waters as they rose and fell
About the stars and broke in days and years.

35 I had a thought for no one's but your ears:
That you were beautiful, and that I strove
To love you in the old high way of love;
That it had all seemed happy, and yet we'd grown
As weary-hearted as that hollow moon.
—1904

No Second Troy [5]

Why should I blame her[6] that she filled my days
    With misery, or that she would of late[7]
Have taught to ignorant men most violent ways,
Or hurled the little streets upon the great,
5   Had they but courage equal to desire?
What could have made her peaceful with a mind
That nobleness made simple as a fire,
With beauty like a tightened bow, a kind
That is not natural in an age like this,

---

[1] *Fergus* Ancient Irish king who gave up his throne in order to spend more time fighting, feasting, and hunting.

[2] *Adam's Curse* Cf. Genesis 3.17–19: Adam was banished from the Garden of Eden for disobeying God and was thereafter cursed to live a life of hard work.

[3] *That beautiful mild woman* The sister of Maud Gonne, prominent Irish activist, Kathleen Pilcher.

[4] *you* Maud Gonne.

[5] *Troy* During the Trojan War, the Greeks besieged and destroyed the city of Troy in an effort to retrieve Helen, who had been abducted by the Trojan, Paris, from her husband, the Greek Menelaus.

[6] *her* Maud Gonne.

[7] *of late* Gonne ceased her political work in 1905.

10 Being high and solitary and most stern?
    Why, what could she have done being what she is?
    Was there another Troy for her to burn?
    —1910

Easter 1916 [1]

I have met them at close of day
Coming with vivid faces
From counter or desk among grey
Eighteenth-century houses.
5   I have passed with a nod of the head
Or polite meaningless words,
Or have lingered awhile and said
Polite meaningless words,
And thought before I had done
10 Of a mocking tale or a gibe
To please a companion
Around the fire at the club,
Being certain that they and I
But lived where motley° is worn: *jester's costume*
15 All changed, changed utterly:
A terrible beauty is born.

That woman's days were spent
In ignorant good-will,
Her nights in argument
20 Until her voice grew shrill. [2]
What voice more sweet than hers
When, young and beautiful,
She rode to harriers?
This man had kept a school

25 And rode our wingèd horse; [3]
This other his helper and friend [4]
Was coming into his force;
He might have won fame in the end,
So sensitive his nature seemed,
30 So daring and sweet his thought.
This other man I had dreamed
A drunken, vainglorious lout. [5]
He had done most bitter wrong
To some who are near my heart,
35 Yet I number him in the song;
He, too, has resigned his part
In the casual comedy;
He, too, has been changed in his turn,
Transformed utterly:
40 A terrible beauty is born.

Hearts with one purpose alone
Through summer and winter seem
Enchanted to a stone
To trouble the living stream.
45 The horse that comes from the road,
The rider, the birds that range
From cloud to tumbling cloud,
Minute by minute they change;
A shadow of cloud on the stream
50 Changes minute by minute;
A horse-hoof slides on the brim,
And a horse plashes within it;
The long-legged moor-hens dive,
And hens to moor-cocks call;
55 Minute by minute they live:
The stone's in the midst of all.

Too long a sacrifice
Can make a stone of the heart.
O when may it suffice?

---

[1] *Easter 1916*   On Easter Monday, 24 April 1916, Irish nationalists instigated an unsuccessful rebellion against the British government (which was then at war with Germany); the Easter rebellion lasted until 29 April. Many of the Irish nationalist leaders were executed that May.

[2] *That woman's ... shrill* Countess Markiewicz, née Constance Gore-Booth (1868–1927), played a central role in the Easter Rebellion; she was arrested and sentenced to death (though the death sentence was later commuted). Yeats later wrote a poem about her and her Irish-nationalist sister, "In Memory of Eva Gore-Booth and Con Markiewicz" (1929).

[3] *This man ... wingèd horse* Pádraic Pearse (1879–1916) founded St. Enda's School near Dublin. He was a leader in the effort to revive the Gaelic language, and wrote both Irish and English poetry; the "wingèd horse" refers to Pegasus, the horse of the Muses.

[4] *This other his helper and friend* Thomas MacDonagh (1878–1916), an Irish poet and playwright who also taught school.

[5] *vainglorious lout* Major John MacBride (1865–1916), estranged husband of Irish nationalist Maud Gonne; their separation just two years after marriage was due in part to his drinking bouts.

60 That is Heaven's part, our part
To murmur name upon name,
As a mother names her child
When sleep at last has come
On limbs that had run wild.
65 What is it but nightfall?
No, no, not night but death;
Was it needless death after all?
For England may keep faith
For all that is done and said.[1]
70 We know their dream; enough
To know they dreamed and are dead;
And what if excess of love
Bewildered them till they died?
I write it out in a verse—
75 MacDonagh and MacBride
And Connolly[2] and Pearse[3]
Now and in time to be,
Wherever green is worn,
Are changed, changed utterly:
80 A terrible beauty is born.
—1916

The Wild Swans at Coole [4]

The trees are in their autumn beauty,
   The woodland paths are dry,
Under the October twilight the water
Mirrors a still sky;
5 Upon the brimming water among the stones
Are nine-and-fifty swans.

The nineteenth autumn[5] has come upon me
Since I first made my count;

I saw, before I had well finished,
10 All suddenly mount
And scatter wheeling in great broken rings
Upon their clamorous wings.

I have looked upon those brilliant creatures,
And now my heart is sore.
15 All's changed since I, hearing at twilight,
The first time on this shore,
The bell-beat of their wings above my head,
Trod with a lighter tread.

Unwearied still, lover by lover,
20 They paddle in the cold
Companionable streams or climb the air;
Their hearts have not grown old;
Passion or conquest, wander where they will,
Attend upon them still.

25 But now they drift on the still water,
Mysterious, beautiful;
Among what rushes will they build,
By what lake's edge or pool
Delight men's eyes, when I awake some day
30 To find they have flown away?
—1917

In Memory of Major Robert Gregory [6]

I

Now that we're almost settled in our house[7]
   I'll name the friends that cannot sup with us
Beside a fire of turf [8] in th' ancient tower,
And having talked to some late hour
5 Climb up the narrow winding stair to bed:
Discoverers of forgotten truth

---

1 *For England … said* England had originally granted Ireland Home Rule in 1913, but then postponed it due to World War I, promising to institute it after the war.

2 *Connolly* James Connolly (1868–1916), Irish Socialist.

3 *MacDonagh … Pearse* All four men were executed for their involvement in the Easter Uprising of 1916.

4 *Coole* Coole Park, County Galway estate of Lady Gregory, friend and patron of Yeats.

5 *nineteenth autumn* Yeats first visited Coole Park in 1897, nineteen years before he wrote this poem.

6 [Yeats's note] Major Robert Gregory [Lady Gregory's only son (1881–1918)], R.F.C. [Royal Flying Corps], M.C. [Military Cross], Legion of Honour, was killed in action on the Italian Front, January 23, 1918.

7 *our house* Yeats had bought a section of Lady Gregory's estate at Coole Park; Thoor Ballylee, an ancient Norman tower situated there, became his home.

8 *turf* Dried peat used for fuel.

Or mere companions of my youth,
All, all are in my thoughts tonight being dead.

2

10 Always we'd have the new friend meet the old
And we are hurt if either friend seem cold,
And there is salt to lengthen out the smart
In the affections of our heart,
And quarrels are blown up upon that head;
15 But not a friend that I would bring
This night can set us quarrelling,
For all that come into my mind are dead.

3

Lionel Johnson[1] comes the first to mind,
That loved his learning better than mankind,
Though courteous to the worst; much falling he
20 Brooded upon sanctity
Till all his Greek and Latin learning seemed
A long blast upon the horn that brought
A little nearer to his thought
A measureless consummation that he dreamed.

4

25 And that enquiring man John Synge[2] comes next,
That dying chose the living world for text
And never could have rested in the tomb
But that, for long travelling, he had come
Towards nightfall upon certain set apart
30 In a most desolate stony place,[3]
Towards nightfall upon a race
Passionate and simple like his heart.

5

And then I think of old George Pollexfen,[4]
In muscular youth well known to Mayo[5] men
35 For horsemanship at meets or at racecourses,
That could have shown how pure-bred horses

And solid men, for all their passion, live
But as the outrageous stars incline
By opposition, square and trine;[6]
40 Having grown sluggish and contemplative.

6

They were my close companions many a year,
A portion of my mind and life, as it were,
And now their breathless faces seem to look
Out of some old picture-book;
45 I am accustomed to their lack of breath,
But not that my dear friend's dear son,
Our Sidney[7] and our perfect man,
Could share in that discourtesy of death.

7

For all things the delighted eye now sees
50 Were loved by him; the old storm-broken trees
That cast their shadows upon road and bridge;
The tower set on the stream's edge;
The ford where drinking cattle make a stir
Nightly, and startled by that sound
55 The water-hen must change her ground;
He might have been your heartiest welcomer.

8

When with the Galway foxhounds he would ride
From Castle Taylor to the Roxborough side
Or Esserkelly plain, few kept his pace;
60 At Mooneen he had leaped a place[8]
So perilous that half the astonished meet
Had shut their eyes; and where was it
He rode a race without a bit?
And yet his mind outran the horses' feet.

---

[1] *Lionel Johnson* English poet and scholar (1867–1902).

[2] *John Synge* Irish playwright (1871–1909), co-director, along with Yeats and Lady Gregory, of the Abbey Theatre.

[3] *set apart ... place* Synge had set some of his plays in the Aran Islands, off the west coast of Ireland.

[4] *George Pollexfen* Yeats's maternal uncle, an astrologer.

[5] *Mayo* County north of Galway.

[6] *opposition, square and trine* Astrological terms used to describe angles between heavenly bodies.

[7] *Sidney* Elizabethan poet Sir Philip Sidney (1554–86), who, like Gregory, was an artist, scholar, and statesman who died young in battle.

[8] *Castle ... Mooneen* Country manors in the County of Galway: Roxborough was Lady Gregory's childhood home; Moneen is beside Esserkelly, which is near Ardrahan in County Galway.

9

65   We dreamed that a great painter had been born
     To cold Clare[1] rock and Galway rock and thorn,
     To that stern colour and that delicate line
     That are our secret discipline
     Wherein the gazing heart doubles her might.
70   Soldier, scholar, horseman, he,
     And yet he had the intensity
     To have published all to be a world's delight.

10

     What other could so well have counselled us
     In all lovely intricacies of a house
75   As he that practised or that understood
     All work in metal or in wood,
     In moulded plaster or in carven stone?
     Soldier, scholar, horseman, he,
     And all he did done perfectly
80   As though he had but that one trade alone.

11

     Some burn faggots,° others may consume   *bundles of twigs*
     The entire combustible world in one small room
     As though dried straw, and if we turn about
     The bare chimney is gone black out
85   Because the work had finished in that flare.
     Soldier, scholar, horseman, he,
     As 'twere all life's epitome,
     What made us dream that he could comb grey hair?

12

     I had thought, seeing how bitter is that wind
90   That shakes the shutter, to have brought to mind
     All those that manhood tried, or childhood loved
     Or boyish intellect approved,
     With some appropriate commentary on each;
     Until imagination brought
95   A fitter welcome; but a thought
     Of that late death took all my heart for speech.
     —1918

Nineteen Hundred and Nineteen[2]

I

Many ingenious lovely things are gone
    That seemed sheer miracle to the multitude,
Protected from the circle of the moon
That pitches common things about. There stood
5   Amid the ornamental bronze and stone
An ancient image made of olive wood —[3]
And gone are Phidias' famous ivories[4]
And all the golden grasshoppers and bees.[5]

We too had many pretty toys when young;
10 A law indifferent to blame or praise,
To bribe or threat; habits that made old wrong
Melt down, as it were wax in the sun's rays;
Public opinion ripening for so long
We thought it would outlive all future days.
15 O what fine thought we had because we thought
That the worst rogues and rascals had died out.

All teeth were drawn, all ancient tricks unlearned,
And a great army but a showy thing;
What matter that no cannon had been turned
20 Into a ploughshare?[6] Parliament and king
Thought that unless a little powder burned
The trumpeters might burst with trumpeting
And yet it lack all glory; and perchance
The guardsmen's drowsy chargers would not prance.

---

[2] *Nineteen Hundred and Nineteen* 1919 was a year of increasing armed confrontation between the Irish Republican Army and the Irish government, which was controlled by Britain.

[3] *ancient…wood* Statue of Athena, patron goddess of Athens, was carved out of the wood of the sacred olive tree and stood on the Acropolis; the statue was later destroyed in a fire.

[4] *Phidias's famous ivories* Phidias (sometimes spelled "Pheidias" or "Phideas," c. 500–c. 432 BCE) was a celebrated Greek sculptor who created an ivory- and gold-encrusted statue of Athena (since destroyed) in the Parthenon.

[5] *golden grasshoppers and bees* Offerings to the gods in the form of golden trinkets; Thucydides wrote of the Athenian custom of tying up a lock of hair with a golden grasshopper.

[6] *no cannon … ploughshare* Cf. Isaiah 2.4: "They shall beat their swords into plowshares … nation shall not lift up sword against nation, neither shall they learn war anymore."

25 Now days are dragon-ridden, the nightmare
Rides upon sleep: a drunken soldiery
Can leave the mother, murdered at her door,
To crawl in her own blood, and go scot-free; *No justice*
The night can sweat with terror as before
30 We pieced our thoughts into philosophy,
And planned to bring the world under a rule,
Who are but weasels fighting in a hole.

He who can read the signs nor sink unmanned
Into the half-deceit of some intoxicant
35 From shallow wits; who knows no work can stand,
Whether health, wealth or peace of mind were spent
On master-work of intellect or hand,
No honour leave its mighty monument,
Has but one comfort left: all triumph would
40 But break upon his ghostly solitude.

But is there any comfort to be found?
Man is in love and loves what vanishes,
What more is there to say? That country round
None dared admit, if such a thought were his,
45 Incendiary or bigot could be found
To burn that stump on the Acropolis,
Or break in bits the famous ivories
Or traffic in the grasshoppers or bees.

2

When Loie Fuller's[1] Chinese dancers enwound
50 A shining web, a floating ribbon of cloth,
It seemed that a dragon of air
Had fallen among dancers, had whirled them round
Or hurried them off on its own furious path;
55 So the Platonic Year[2]
Whirls out new right and wrong,
Whirls in the old instead;
All men are dancers and their tread
Goes to the barbarous clangour of a gong.

---

[1] *Loie Fuller* An American dancer and choreographer (1862–1928); her dancers were Japanese, not Chinese.

[2] *Platonic Year* Full revolution of the constellations in relation to the equinoxes, approximately 26,000 years.

Shelly

3

60 Some moralist or mythological poet
Compares the solitary soul to a swan; *Prometheus Unbound*
I am satisfied with that,
Satisfied if a troubled mirror show it,
Before that brief gleam of its life be gone,
65 An image of its state;
The wings half spread for flight,
The breast thrust out in pride
Whether to play, or to ride
Those winds that clamour of approaching night.

70 A man in his own secret meditation
Is lost amid the labyrinth that he has made
In art or politics;
Some Platonist affirms that in the station
Where we should cast off body and trade
75 The ancient habit sticks,
And that if our works could
But vanish with our breath
That were a lucky death,
For triumph can but mar our solitude.

80 The swan has leaped into the desolate heaven:
That image can bring wildness, bring a rage
To end all things, to end
What my laborious life imagined, even
The half-imagined, the half-written page;
85 O but we dreamed to mend
Whatever mischief seemed
To afflict mankind, but now
That winds of winter blow
Learn that we were crack-pated when we dreamed.

4

90 We, who seven years ago
Talked of honour and of truth,
Shriek with pleasure if we show
The weasel's twist, the weasel's tooth.

5

Come let us mock at the great
95 That had such burdens on the mind
And toiled so hard and late

To leave some monument behind,
Nor thought of the levelling wind.

Come let us mock at the wise;
100 With all those calendars whereon
They fixed old aching eyes,
They never saw how seasons run,
And now but gape at the sun.

Come let us mock at the good
105 That fancied goodness might be gay,
And sick of solitude
Might proclaim a holiday:
Wind shrieked—and where are they?

Mock mockers after that
110 That would not lift a hand maybe
To help good, wise or great
To bar that foul storm out, for we
Traffic in mockery.

6

Violence upon the roads: violence of horses;
115 Some few have handsome riders, are garlanded
On delicate sensitive ear or tossing mane,
But wearied running round and round in their courses
All break and vanish, and evil gathers head:
Herodias' daughters have returned again,[1]
120 A sudden blast of dusty wind and after
Thunder of feet, tumult of images,
Their purpose in the labyrinth of the wind;
And should some crazy hand dare touch a daughter
All turn with amorous cries, or angry cries,
125 According to the wind, for all are blind.
But now wind drops, dust settles; thereupon
There lurches past, his great eyes without thought
Under the shadow of stupid straw-pale locks,
That insolent fiend Robert Artisson[2]

130 To whom the love-lorn Lady Kyteler brought
Bronzed peacock feathers, red combs of her cocks.[3]
—1919

A Prayer for my Daughter [4]

Once more the storm is howling, and half hid
Under this cradle-hood and coverlid
My child sleeps on. There is no obstacle
But Gregory's wood[5] and one bare hill
5 Whereby the haystack- and roof-levelling wind,
Bred on the Atlantic, can be stayed;
And for an hour I have walked and prayed
Because of the great gloom that is in my mind.

I have walked and prayed for this young child an hour
10 And heard the sea-wind scream upon the tower,[6]
And under the arches of the bridge, and scream
In the elms above the flooded stream;
Imagining in excited reverie
That the future years had come,
15 Dancing to a frenzied drum,
Out of the murderous innocence of the sea.

May she be granted beauty and yet not
Beauty to make a stranger's eye distraught,
Or hers before a looking-glass, for such,
20 Being made beautiful overmuch,
Consider beauty a sufficient end,
Lose natural kindness and maybe
The heart-revealing intimacy
That chooses right, and never find a friend.

---

[1] *Herodias' ... again* The reference here is not to the Biblical character (whose daughter was Salomé) but rather to the eponymous witch-goddess of Germanic mythology. Her daughters are associated with violently whirling winds.

[2] [Yeats's note] My last symbol, Robert Artisson, was an evil spirit much run after in Kilkenny at the start of the fourteenth century.

[3] *To whom ... cocks* It was said that Artisson seduced Lady Kyteler, who supposedly sacrificed cocks and peacocks to him and was accused of poisoning her husbands; *combs* Pronounced ridges on cocks' crowns.

[4] *My Daughter* Anne Butler Yeats, born 26 February 1919.

[5] *Gregory's wood* Lady Gregory's wood at Coole Park, her estate in western Ireland.

[6] *tower* Thoor Ballylee, the ancient Norman tower on the land Yeats bought from Lady Gregory in June 1917.

25 Helen[1] being chosen found life flat and dull
And later had much trouble from a fool,
While that great Queen, that rose out of the spray,[2]
Being fatherless could have her way
Yet chose a bandy-leggèd smith[3] for man.
30 It's certain that fine women eat
A crazy salad with their meat
Whereby the Horn of Plenty is undone.

In courtesy I'd have her chiefly learned;
Hearts are not had as a gift but hearts are earned
35 By those that are not entirely beautiful;
Yet many, that have played the fool
For beauty's very self, has charm made wise,
And many a poor man that has roved,
Loved and thought himself beloved,
40 From a glad kindness cannot take his eyes.

May she become a flourishing hidden tree
That all her thoughts may like the linnet be,
And have no business but dispensing round
Their magnanimities of sound,
45 Nor but in merriment begin a chase,
Nor but in merriment a quarrel.
O may she live like some green laurel
Rooted in one dear perpetual place.

My mind, because the minds that I have loved,
50 The sort of beauty that I have approved,
Prosper but little, has dried up of late,
Yet knows that to be choked with hate
May well be of all evil chances chief.
If there's no hatred in a mind
55 Assault and battery of the wind
Can never tear the linnet from the leaf.

An intellectual hatred is the worst,
So let her think opinions are accursed.

Have I not seen the loveliest woman[4] born
60 Out of the mouth of Plenty's horn,
Because of her opinionated mind
Barter that horn and every good
By quiet natures understood
For an old bellows full of angry wind?

65 Considering that, all hatred driven hence,
The soul recovers radical innocence
And learns at last that it is self-delighting,
Self-appeasing, self-affrighting,
And that its own sweet will is Heaven's will;
70 She can, though every face should scowl
And every windy quarter howl
Or every bellows burst, be happy still.

And may her bridegroom bring her to a house
Where all's accustomed, ceremonious;
75 For arrogance and hatred are the wares
Peddled in the thoroughfares.
How but in custom and in ceremony
Are innocence and beauty born?
Ceremony's a name for the rich horn,
80 And custom for the spreading laurel tree.
—1919

An Irish Airman Foresees his Death

I know that I shall meet my fate
Somewhere among the clouds above;
Those that I fight I do not hate
Those that I guard I do not love;
5 My country is Kiltartan Cross,[5]
My countrymen Kiltartan's poor,
No likely end could bring them loss
Or leave them happier than before.
Nor law, nor duty bade me fight,
10 Nor public man, nor cheering crowds,
A lonely impulse of delight
Drove to this tumult in the clouds;

---

1 *Helen*   Wife of Menelaus. She was abducted by Paris, the son of the king of Troy; the Greeks besieged the city for ten years to save her, finally bringing her back to her husband.

2 *that great Queen ... spray*   Aphrodite, the Greek goddess of love, beauty, and fecundity, rose out of the sea at birth.

3 *bandy-leggèd smith*   Hephaestus, god of fire and husband of Aphrodite, was born lame.

4 *loveliest woman*   Maud Gonne, whom Yeats had loved, was an important Irish liberation activist; she married Major John MacBride in 1903.

5 *Kiltartan Cross*   In County Galway, Ireland.

I balanced all, brought all to mind,
The years to come seemed waste of breath,
15   A waste of breath the years behind
In balance with this life, this death.
—1919

The Second Coming [1]

Turning and turning in the widening gyre[2]
The falcon cannot hear the falconer;
Things fall apart; the centre cannot hold;
Mere anarchy is loosed upon the world,
5   The blood-dimmed tide is loosed, and everywhere
The ceremony of innocence is drowned;
The best lack all conviction, while the worst
Are full of passionate intensity.

Surely some revelation is at hand;
10   Surely the Second Coming is at hand.
The Second Coming! Hardly are those words out
When a vast image out of *Spiritus Mundi*[3]
Troubles my sight: somewhere in sands of the desert
A shape with lion body and the head of a man,[4]
15   A gaze blank and pitiless as the sun,
Is moving its slow thighs, while all about it
Reel shadows of the indignant desert birds.
The darkness drops again; but now I know
That twenty centuries of stony sleep
20   Were vexed to nightmare by a rocking cradle,[5]
And what rough beast, its hour come round at last,
Slouches towards Bethlehem to be born?
—1920

---

[1] *The Second Coming*   The return of Christ, as predicted in the New Testament. See Revelation 1.7: "Behold, he cometh with clouds; and every eye shall see him."

[2] *gyre*   Spiral formed from concentric circles.

[3] *Spiritus Mundi*   Universal spirit that houses the images of civilization's past memories and provides divine inspiration for the poet; the human race is a connected whole in the *spiritus mundi*.

[4] *shape … man*   The Egyptian Sphinx.

[5] *rocking cradle*   Cradle of the Christ Child.

Meditations in Time of Civil War

I

Ancestral Houses

Surely among a rich man's flowering lawns,
Amid the rustle of his planted hills,
Life overflows without ambitious pains;
And rains down life until the basin spills,
5   And mounts more dizzy high the more it rains
As though to choose whatever shape it wills
And never stoop to a mechanical
Or servile shape, at others' beck and call.

Mere dreams, mere dreams! Yet Homer had not sung
10   Had he not found it certain beyond dreams
That out of life's own self-delight had sprung
The abounding glittering jet;[6] though now it seems
As if some marvellous empty sea-shell flung
Out of the obscure dark of the rich streams,
15   And not a fountain, were the symbol which
Shadows the inherited glory of the rich.

Some violent bitter man, some powerful man
Called architect and artist in, that they,
Bitter and violent men, might rear in stone
20   The sweetness that all longed for night and day,
The gentleness none there had ever known;
But when the master's buried mice can play,
And maybe the great-grandson of that house,
For all its bronze and marble, 's but a mouse.

25   O what if gardens where the peacock strays
With delicate feet upon old terraces,
Or else all Juno[7] from an urn displays
Before the indifferent garden deities;
O what if levelled lawns and gravelled ways
30   Where slippered Contemplation finds his ease
And Childhood a delight for every sense,
But take our greatness with our violence?
What if the glory of escutcheoned doors,
And buildings that a haughtier age designed,

---

[6] *jet*   Stream of liquid emerging from a fountain.

[7] *Juno*   Roman goddess of marriage and protector of women.

35 The pacing to and fro on polished floors
    Amid great chambers and long galleries, lined
    With famous portraits of our ancestors;
    What if those things the greatest of mankind
    Consider most to magnify, or to bless,
40 But take our greatness with our bitterness?

2
My House

An ancient bridge, and a more ancient tower,
A farmhouse that is sheltered by its wall,
An acre of stony ground,
Where the symbolic rose can break in flower,
45 Old ragged elms, old thorns innumerable,
The sound of the rain or sound
Of every wind that blows;
The stilted water-hen
Crossing stream again
50 Scared by the splashing of a dozen cows;

A winding stair, a chamber arched with stone,
A grey stone fireplace with an open hearth,
A candle written page.
Il Penseroso's Platonist[1] toiled on
55 In some like chamber, shadowing forth
How the daemonic rage
Imagined everything.
Benighted travellers
From markets and from fairs
60 Have seen his midnight candle glimmering.

Two men have founded here. A man-at-arms
Gathered a score of horse and spent his days
In this tumultuous spot,
Where through long wars and sudden night alarms
65 His dwindling score and he seemed castaways
Forgetting and forgot;
And I, that after me
My bodily heirs may find,
To exalt a lonely mind,
70 Befitting emblems of adversity.

---

[1] *Il Penseroso's Platonist* Hermes Trismegistus, a semi-mythical character in Milton's poem, purported to be the author of thousands of Neo-Platonic texts.

3
My Table

Two heavy trestles, and a board
Where Sato's gift, a changeless sword,[2]
By pen and paper lies,
That it may moralise
75 My days out of their aimlessness.
A bit of an embroidered dress
Covers its wooden sheath.
Chaucer had not drawn breath
When it was forged. In Sato's house,
80 Curved like new moon, moon-luminous,
It lay five hundred years.
Yet if no change appears
No moon; only an aching heart
Conceives a changeless work of art.
85 Our learned men have urged
That when and where 'twas forged
A marvellous accomplishment,
In painting or in pottery, went
From father unto son
90 And through the centuries ran
And seemed unchanging like the sword.
Soul's beauty being most adored,
Men and their business took
The soul's unchanging look;
95 For the most rich inheritor,
Knowing that none could pass Heaven's door
That loved inferior art,
Had such an aching heart
That he, although a country's talk
100 For silken clothes and stately walk,
Had waking wits; it seemed
Juno's peacock screamed.[3]

4
My Descendants

Having inherited a vigorous mind

---

[2] *Sato's gift, a changeless sword* Japanese sword given to Yeats by his friend Junzo Sato in 1920.

[3] *Juno's peacock screamed* Peacocks are sacred to Juno, Roman queen of the gods and goddess of childbirth. The peacock was once said to complain to Juno that although he was beautiful, his cry was shrill.

From my old fathers, I must nourish dreams
105 And leave a woman and a man[1] behind
As vigorous of mind, and yet it seems
Life scarce can cast a fragrance on the wind,
Scarce spread a glory to the morning beams,
But the torn petals strew the garden plot;
110 And there's but common greenness after that.

And what if my descendants lose the flower
Through natural declension of the soul,
Through too much business with the passing hour,
Through too much play, or marriage with a fool?
115 May this laborious stair and this stark tower
Become a roofless ruin that the owl
May build in the cracked masonry and cry
Her desolation to the desolate sky.

The Primum Mobile[2] that fashioned us
120 Has made the very owls in circles move;
And I, that count myself most prosperous,
Seeing that love and friendship are enough,
For an old neighbour's[3] friendship chose the house
And decked and altered it for a girl's[4] love,
125 And know whatever flourish and decline
These stones remain their monument and mine.

5
The Road at My Door

An affable Irregular,[5]
A heavily-built Falstaffian[6] man,
Comes cracking jokes of civil war
130 As though to die by gunshot were
The finest play under the sun.

A brown Lieutenant[7] and his men,
Half dressed in national uniform,
Stand at my door, and I complain
135 Of the foul weather, hail and rain,
A pear tree broken by the storm.

I count those feathered balls of soot
The moor-hen guides upon the stream,
To silence the envy in my thought;
140 And turn towards my chamber, caught
In the cold snows of a dream.

6
The Stare's Nest by My Window[8]

The bees build in the crevices
Of loosening masonry, and there
The mother birds bring grubs and flies.
145 My wall is loosening; honey-bees,
Come build in the empty house of the stare.

We are closed in, and the key is turned
On our uncertainty; somewhere
A man is killed, or a house burned,
150 Yet no clear fact to be discerned:
Come build in the empty house of the stare.

A barricade of stone or of wood;
Some fourteen days of civil war;
Last night they trundled down the road
155 That dead young soldier in his blood:
Come build in the empty house of the stare.

We had fed the heart on fantasies,
The heart's grown brutal from the fare;
More substance in our enmities
160 Than in our love; O honey-bees,
Come build in the empty house of the stare.

---

[1] *a woman and a man* Anne and Michael Butler Yeats, Yeats's daughter and son.

[2] *Primum Mobile* Cause of all things; "the first mover."

[3] *an old neighbour* Lady Augusta Gregory.

[4] *a girl's* Georgie Yeats's.

[5] *Irregular* Member of the Irish Republican Army.

[6] *Falstaffian* Resembling the Shakespearean character Sir John Falstaff, known for his girth, roguish joviality, lustfulness, brashness, and fondness for alcohol.

---

[7] *brown Lieutenant* Member of the National Army of England.

[8] [Yeats's note] In the west of Ireland we call a starling a stare, and during the civil war one built a hole in the masonry by my bedroom window.

7
I See Phantoms of Hatred and of the Heart's Fullness and of the Coming Emptiness

I climb to the tower-top and lean upon broken stone,
A mist that is like blown snow is sweeping over all,
Valley, river, and elms, under the light of a moon
165 That seems unlike itself, that seems unchangeable,
A glittering sword out of the east. A puff of wind
And those white glimmering fragments of the mist
        sweep by.
Frenzies bewilder, reveries perturb the mind;
Monstrous familiar images swim to the mind's eye.

170 "Vengeance upon the murderers,"[1] the cry goes up,
"Vengeance for Jacques Molay."[2] In cloud-pale rags,
        or in lace,
The rage-driven, rage-tormented, and rage-hungry
        troop,
Trooper belabouring trooper, biting at arm or at face,
Plunges towards nothing, arms and fingers spreading
        wide
175 For the embrace of nothing; and I, my wits astray
Because of all that senseless tumult, all but cried
For vengeance on the murderers of Jacques Molay.

Their legs long, delicate and slender, aquamarine their
        eyes,
Magical unicorns bear ladies on their backs.[3]
180 The ladies close their musing eyes. No prophecies,
Remembered out of Babylonian almanacs,
Have closed the ladies' eyes, their minds are but a pool
Where even longing drowns under its own excess;
Nothing but stillness can remain when hearts are full
185 Of their own sweetness, bodies of their loveliness.

The cloud-pale unicorns, the eyes of aquamarine,
The quivering half-closed eyelids, the rags of cloud or
        of lace,
Or eyes that rage has brightened, arms it has made lean,
Give place to an indifferent multitude, give place
190 To brazen hawks.[4] Nor self-delighting reverie,
Nor hate of what's to come, nor pity for what's gone,
Nothing but grip of claw, and the eye's complacency,
The innumerable clanging wings that have put out
        the moon.

I turn away and shut the door, and on the stair
195 Wonder how many times I could have proved my
        worth
In something that all others understand or share;
But O! ambitious heart, had such a proof drawn forth
A company of friends, a conscience set at ease,
It had but made us pine the more. The abstract joy,
200 The half-read wisdom of daemonic images,
Suffice the ageing man as once the growing boy.
—1923

Leda and the Swan[5]

A sudden blow: the great wings beating still
Above the staggering girl, her thighs caressed
By the dark webs, her nape caught in his bill,
He holds her helpless breast upon his breast.

5 How can those terrified vague fingers push
The feathered glory from her loosening thighs?
And how can body, laid in that white rush,
But feel the strange heart beating where it lies?

A shudder in the loins engenders there
10 The broken wall, the burning roof and tower

---

[1] [Yeats's note] A cry for vengeance because of the murder of the Grand Master of the Templars seems to me fit symbol for those who labour for hatred, and so for sterility in various kinds. It is said to have been incorporated in the ritual of certain Masonic societies of the eighteenth century, and to have fed class-hatred.

[2] *Jacques Molay* Jacques de Molay, Grand Master of the Order of Knights Templar, was tortured and burned at the stake in 1314 after refusing to confess to heresy.

[3] *Magical unicorns ... backs* In Gustave Moreau's painting *Ladies and Unicorns.*

[4] [Yeats's note] I suppose that I must have put hawks in the fourth stanza because I have a ring with a hawk and a butterfly upon it, to symbolize the straight road of logic, and so of mechanism, and the crooked road of intuition: "For wisdom is a butterfly and not a gloomy bird of prey."

[5] *Leda and the Swan* Zeus came to Leda in the form of a swan and raped her; she then gave birth to Helen of Troy (whose abduction from her husband, King Menelaus, by Paris, initiated the Trojan War) and the twins, Castor and Pollux.

And Agamemnon[1] dead.
                              Being so caught up,
So mastered by the brute blood of the air,
Did she put on his knowledge with his power
Before the indifferent beak could let her drop?
—1924

Among School Children

1

I walk through the long schoolroom questioning;
A kind old nun in a white hood replies;
The children learn to cipher and to sing,
To study reading-books and history,
5   To cut and sew, be neat in everything
In the best modern way—the children's eyes
In momentary wonder stare upon
A sixty-year-old smiling public man.

2

I dream of a Ledaean[2] body, bent
10 Above a sinking fire, a tale that she
Told of a harsh reproof, or trivial event
That changed some childish day to tragedy—
Told, and it seemed that our two natures blent
Into a sphere from youthful sympathy,
15 Or else, to alter Plato's parable,
Into the yolk and white of the one shell.[3]

3

And thinking of that fit of grief or rage
I look upon one child or t'other there
And wonder if she stood so at that age—
20 For even daughters of the swan[4] can share
Something of every paddler's heritage—
And had that colour upon cheek or hair,

And thereupon my heart is driven wild:
She stands before me as a living child.

4

25 Her present image floats into the mind—
Did Quattrocento finger[5] fashion it
Hollow of cheek as though it drank the wind
And took a mess of shadows for its meat?
And I though never of Ledaean kind
30 Had pretty plumage once—enough of that,
Better to smile on all that smile, and show
There is a comfortable kind of old scarecrow.

5

What youthful mother, a shape upon her lap
Honey of generation[6] had betrayed,
35 And that must sleep, shriek, struggle to escape
As recollection or the drug decide,
Would think her son, did she but see that shape
With sixty or more winters on its head,
A compensation for the pang of his birth,
40 Or the uncertainty of his setting forth?

6

Plato thought nature but a spume that plays
Upon a ghostly paradigm of things;[7]
Solider Aristotle played the taws
Upon the bottom of a king of kings;[8]
45 World-famous golden-thighed Pythagoras

---

1   *broken wall ... Agamemnon dead*   Events of the Trojan War.

2   *Ledaean*   Like that of Leda (see note on Leda below).

3   *Plato's parable ... shell*   A speaker in Plato's *Symposium* explains that man was originally both male and female in one form, but was then divided into two; love was the reunion of man with his other half.

4   *daughters of the swan*   Leda, raped by Zeus in the form of a swan, gave birth to Helen of Troy.

5   *Quattrocento finger*   Skillful hand of a fifteenth-century Italian artist.

6   [Yeats's note] I have taken the "honey of generation" from Porphyry's essay on "The Cave of the Nymphs," but find no warrant in Porphyry for considering it the "drug" that destroys the "recollection" of prenatal freedom. [The Neoplatonic philosopher Porphyry (233–c. 304) stated that the pleasure of sexual intercourse, like the sweetness of honey, drugs infants, thereby causing them to forget prenatal bliss before being born into this mortal world.]

7   *Plato ... things*   Plato argued that the appearance of nature was merely an imitation of the real world; therefore, nature itself was unreal, but provided a "ghostly" image of the real "paradigm of things."

8   *Solider ... kings*   Unlike Plato, Aristotle believed that reality took form in the image of nature; therefore, nature was reality itself. Aristotle tutored Alexander the Great, the son of King Philip of Macedonia; *taws* Leather whip.

Fingered upon a fiddle-stick or strings[1]
What a star sang and careless Muses heard:
Old clothes upon old sticks to scare a bird.

7

50 Both nuns and mothers worship images,
But those the candles light are not as those
That animate a mother's reveries,
But keep a marble or a bronze repose.
And yet they too break hearts—O Presences
55 That passion, piety or affection knows,
And that all heavenly glory symbolise—
O self-born mockers of man's enterprise;

8

Labour is blossoming or dancing where
The body is not bruised to pleasure soul,
Nor beauty born out of its own despair,
60 Nor blear-eyed wisdom out of midnight oil.
O chestnut tree, great-rooted blossomer,
Are you the leaf, the blossom, or the bole?°   *trunk*
O body swayed to music, O brightening glance,
How can we know the dancer from the dance?
—1927

Sailing to Byzantium [2]

I

That is no country for old men. The young
In one another's arms, birds in the trees
— Those dying generations — at their song,
The salmon-falls, the mackerel-crowded seas,
5 Fish, flesh, or fowl, commend all summer long

Whatever is begotten, born, and dies.
Caught in that sensual music all neglect
Monuments of unageing intellect.

2

An aged man is but a paltry thing,
10 A tattered coat upon a stick, unless
Soul clap its hands and sing, and louder sing
For every tatter in its mortal dress,
Nor is there singing school but studying
Monuments of its own magnificence;
15 And therefore I have sailed the seas and come
To the holy city of Byzantium.

3

O sages standing in God's holy fire
As in the gold mosaic of a wall,
Come from the holy fire, perne in a gyre,[3]
20 And be the singing-masters of my soul.
Consume my heart away; sick with desire
And fastened to a dying animal
It knows not what it is; and gather me
Into the artifice of eternity.

4

25 Once out of nature I shall never take
My bodily form from any natural thing,
But such a form as Grecian goldsmiths make
Of hammered gold and gold enamelling
To keep a drowsy Emperor awake;
30 Or set upon a golden bough to sing[4]
To lords and ladies of Byzantium
Of what is past, or passing, or to come.
—1927

---

[1] *golden-thighed ... strings* Pythagoras, a Greek philosopher of the sixth century BCE, developed a theory of the mathematical regularity of the universe and the mathematical origins of musical harmony. He was said to have a golden thigh.

[2] *Byzantium* Ancient city eventually renamed Constantinople (now Istanbul), capital of the Eastern Roman Empire. In *A Vision*, Yeats envisioned Byzantium as a center for artists: "The painter, the mosaic worker, the worker in gold and silver, the illuminator of sacred books were almost impersonal, almost perhaps without the consciousness of individual design, absorbed in their subject matter and that the vision of a whole people."

[3] *perne in a gyre* Rotate in a spiral; the literal definition of "perne" is bobbin.

[4] [Yeats's note] I have read somewhere that in the Emperor's palace at Byzantium was a tree made of gold and silver, and artificial birds that sang.

The Tower [1]

I

What shall I do with this absurdity—
O heart, O troubled heart—this caricature,
Decrepit age that has been tied to me
As to a dog's tail?
                              Never had I more
5   Excited, passionate, fantastical
Imagination, nor an ear and eye
That more expected the impossible—
No, not in boyhood when with rod and fly,
10 Or the humbler worm, I climbed Ben Bulben's[2] back
And had the livelong summer day to spend.
It seems that I must bid the Muse go pack,
Choose Plato and Plotinus[3] for a friend
Until imagination, ear and eye,
15 Can be content with argument and deal
In abstract things; or be derided by
A sort of battered kettle at the heel.

2

I pace upon the battlements and stare
On the foundations of a house, or where
20 Tree, like a sooty finger, starts from the earth;
And send imagination forth
Under the day's declining beam, and call
Images and memories
From ruin or from ancient trees,
25 For I would ask a question of them all.

Beyond that ridge lived Mrs. French, and once
When every silver candlestick or sconce
Lit up the dark mahogany and the wine,
A serving-man, that could divine
30 That most respected lady's every wish,

Ran and with the garden shears
Clipped an insolent farmer's ears
And brought them in a little covered dish.[4]

Some few remembered still when I was young
35 A peasant girl commended by a song,
Who'd lived somewhere upon that rocky place,
And praised the colour of her face,
And had the greater joy in praising her,
Remembering that, if walked she there,
40 Farmers jostled at the fair
So great a glory did the song confer.

And certain men, being maddened by those rhymes,
Or else by toasting her a score of times,
Rose from the table and declared it right
45 To test their fancy by their sight;
But they mistook the brightness of the moon
For the prosaic light of day—
Music had driven their wits astray—
And one was drowned in the great bog of Cloone.[5]

50 Strange, but the man who made the song was blind;
Yet, now I have considered it, I find
That nothing strange; the tragedy began
With Homer that was a blind man,
And Helen has all living hearts betrayed.[6]
55 O may the moon and sunlight seem
One inextricable beam,
For if I triumph I must make men mad.

And I myself created Hanrahan[7]
And drove him drunk or sober through the dawn

---

[1]   [Yeats's note] The persons mentioned are associated by legend, story and tradition with the neighbourhood of Thoor Ballylee or Ballylee Castle [the "tower" in which Yeats lived], where the poem was written.

[2]   *Ben Bulben* Mountain in County Sligo; Yeats is buried within sight of the mountain at Drumcliff Churchyard.

[3]   [Yeats's note] When I wrote the lines about Plato and Plotinus I forgot that it is something in our own eyes that makes us see them as all transcendence.

[4]   [Yeats's note] Mrs. French lived at Peterswell in the eighteenth century and was related to Sir Jonah Barrington, who described the incident of the ears and the trouble that came of it. [Jonah Barrington's description appears in his book of local history, *Personal Sketches of His Own Time*.]

[5]   [Yeats's note] The peasant beauty and the blind poet are Mary Hynes and [Anthony] Raftery, and the incident of the man drowned in Cloone Bog [County Galway] is recorded in my *Celtic Twilight*.

[6]   *Homer ... betrayed* Helen of Troy was the gorgeous daughter of the Greek god Zeus and his mortal lover Leda; the ten-year Trojan War was fought over her. The story of the Trojan war is told in Homer's *Iliad*.

[7]   *Hanrahan* Red Hanrahan, a character in Yeats's prose and poetry.

60 From somewhere in the neighbouring cottages.
    Caught by an old man's juggleries
    He stumbled, tumbled, fumbled to and fro
    And had but broken knees for hire
    And horrible splendour of desire;
65 I thought it all out twenty years ago:[1]

    Good fellows shuffled cards in an old bawn;° *fortified pasture*
    And when that ancient ruffian's turn was on
    He so bewitched the cards under his thumb
    That all but the one card became
70 A pack of hounds and not a pack of cards,
    And that he changed into a hare.
    Hanrahan rose in frenzy there
    And followed up those baying creatures towards—

    O towards I have forgotten what—enough!
75 I must recall a man that neither love
    Nor music nor an enemy's clipped ear
    Could, he was so harried, cheer;
    A figure that has grown so fabulous
    There's not a neighbour left to say
80 When he finished his dog's day:
    An ancient bankrupt master of this house.

    Before that ruin came, for centuries,
    Rough men-at-arms, cross-gartered to the knees
    Or shod in iron, climbed the narrow stairs,
85 And certain men-at-arms there were
    Whose images, in the Great Memory stored,
    Come with loud cry and panting breast
    To break upon a sleeper's rest
    While their great wooden dice beat on the board.[2]

90 As I would question all, come all who can;
    Come old, necessitous, half-mounted man;
    And bring beauty's blind rambling celebrant;
    The red man the juggler sent
    Through God-forsaken meadows; Mrs. French,

95 Gifted with so fine an ear;
    The man drowned in a bog's mire,
    When mocking Muses chose the country wench.

    Did all old men and women, rich and poor,
    Who trod upon these rocks or passed this door,
100 Whether in public or in secret rage
    As I do now against old age?
    But I have found an answer in those eyes
    That are impatient to be gone;
    Go therefore; but leave Hanrahan,
105 For I need all his mighty memories.

    Old lecher with a love on every wind,
    Bring up out of that deep considering mind
    All that you have discovered in the grave,
    For it is certain that you have
110 Reckoned up every unforeknown, unseeing
    Plunge, lured by a softening eye,
    Or by a touch or a sigh,
    Into the labyrinth of another's being;

    Does the imagination dwell the most
115 Upon a woman won or woman lost?
    If on the lost, admit you turned aside
    From a great labyrinth out of pride,
    Cowardice, some silly over-subtle thought
    Or anything called conscience once;
120 And that if memory recur, the sun's
    Under eclipse and the day blotted out.

                        3
    It is time that I wrote my will;
    I choose upstanding men
    That climb the streams until
125 The fountain leap, and at dawn
    Drop their cast at the side
    Of dripping stone; I declare
    They shall inherit my pride,
    The pride of people that were
130 Bound neither to Cause nor to State,
    Neither to slaves that were spat on,
    Nor to the tyrants that spat,

---

[1] [Yeats's note] Hanrahan's pursuit of the phantom hare and hounds
is from my *Stories of Red Hanrahan*.

[2] [Yeats's note] The ghosts have been seen at their game of dice in
what is now my bedroom, and the old bankrupt man lived about a
hundred years ago. According to one legend he could only leave the
Castle upon a Sunday because of his creditors, and according to
another he hid in the secret passage.

The people of Burke and of Grattan[1]
That gave, though free to refuse—
135 Pride, like that of the morn,
When the headlong light is loose,
Or that of the fabulous horn,[2]
Or that of the sudden shower
When all streams are dry,
140 Or that of the hour
When the swan must fix his eye
Upon a fading gleam,
Float out upon a long
Last reach of glittering stream
145 And there sing his last song.[3]
And I declare my faith:
I mock Plotinus' thought
And cry in Plato's teeth,
Death and life were not
150 Till man made up the whole,
Made lock, stock and barrel
Out of his bitter soul,
Aye, sun and moon and star, all,
And further add to that
155 That, being dead, we rise,
Dream and so create
Translunar Paradise.
I have prepared my peace
With learned Italian things
160 And the proud stones of Greece,
Poet's imaginings
And memories of love,
Memories of the words of women,
All those things whereof
165 Man makes a superhuman
Mirror-resembling dream.

As at the loophole there

The daws° chatter and scream,   *crows*
And drop twigs layer upon layer.
170 When they have mounted up,
The mother bird will rest
On their hollow top,
And so warm her wild nest.

I leave both faith and pride
175 To young upstanding men
Climbing the mountain-side,
That under bursting dawn
They may drop a fly;
Being of that metal made
180 Till it was broken by
This sedentary trade.

Now shall I make my soul,
Compelling it to study
In a learned school
185 Till the wreck of body,
Slow decay of blood,
Testy delirium
Or dull decrepitude,
Or what worse evil come—
190 The death of friends, or death
Of every brilliant eye
That made a catch in the breath—
Seem but the clouds of the sky
When the horizon fades;
195 Or a bird's sleepy cry
Among the deepening shades.
—1927

---

1 *Burke*   Edmund Burke (1729–97), political writer and statesman;
Grattan   Henry Grattan (1746–1820), Protestant Member of the
Irish House of Commons, who opposed efforts to unite Ireland with
Great Britain. Both men supported Catholic relief and emancipa-
tion.

2 *fabulous horn*   Horn of Plenty.

3 [Yeats's note] I have unconsciously echoed one of the loveliest
lyrics of our time—Mr. Sturge Moore's "Dying Swan." I often
recited it during an American lecturing tour, which explains the
theft.

A Dialogue of Self and Soul

I

My Soul. I summon to the winding ancient stair;
Set all your mind upon the steep ascent,
Upon the broken, crumbling battlement,
Upon the breathless starlit air,
5 Upon the star that marks the hidden pole;
Fix every wandering thought upon
That quarter where all thought is done:
Who can distinguish darkness from the soul?

My Self. The consecrated blade upon my knees
10   Is Sato's ancient blade,[1] still as it was,
Still razor-keen, still like a looking-glass
Unspotted by the centuries;
That flowering, silken, old embroidery, torn
From some court-lady's dress and round
15   The wooden scabbard bound and wound
Can, tattered, still protect, faded adorn.

My Soul. Why should the imagination of a man
Long past his prime remember things that are
Emblematical of love and war?
20   Think of ancestral night that can,
If but imagination scorn the earth
And intellect is wandering
To this and that and t'other thing,
Deliver from the crime of death and birth.

25   *My Self.* Montashigi,[2] third of his family, fashioned it
Five hundred years ago, about it lie
Flowers from I know not what embroidery—
Heart's purple—and all these I set
For emblems of the day against the tower
30   Emblematical of the night,
And claim as by a soldier's right
A charter to commit the crime once more.

My Soul. Such fullness in that quarter overflows
And falls into the basin of the mind
35   That man is stricken deaf and dumb and blind,
For intellect no longer knows
Is from the *Ought,* or *Knower* from the *Known*—
That is to say, ascends to Heaven;
Only the dead can be forgiven;
40   But when I think of that my tongue's a stone.

2

My Self. A living man is blind and drinks his drop.
What matter if the ditches are impure?
What matter if I live it all once more?
Endure that toil of growing up;
45   The ignominy of boyhood; the distress

Of boyhood changing into man;
The unfinished man and his pain
Brought face to face with his own clumsiness;

The finished man among his enemies?—
50   How in the name of Heaven can he escape
That defiling and disfigured shape
The mirror of malicious eyes
Casts upon his eyes until at last
He thinks that shape must be his shape?
55   And what's the good of an escape
If honour find him in the wintry blast?

I am content to live it all again
And yet again, if it be life to pitch
Into the frog-spawn of a blind man's ditch,
60   A blind man battering blind men;
Or into that most fecund ditch of all,
The folly that man does
Or must suffer, if he woos
A proud woman not kindred of his soul.

65   I am content to follow to its source
Every event in action or in thought;
Measure the lot; forgive myself the lot!
When such as I cast out remorse
So great a sweetness flows into the breast
70   We must laugh and we must sing,
We are blest by everything,
Everything we look upon is blest.
—1929

Byzantium[3]

The unpurged images of day recede;
The Emperor's drunken soldiery are abed;
Night resonance recedes, night walkers'[4] song

---

[1]   *Sato's ancient blade*   Japanese sword given to Yeats in 1920 by his friend Junzo Sato.

[2]   *Montashigi*   Swordmaker.

[3]   *Byzantium*   Constantinople (today, Istanbul); Yeats recorded "the subject for a poem" in his diary of 1930: "Describe Byzantium as it is in the system towards the end of the first Christian millennium… Flames at the street corners where the soul is purified, birds of hammered gold singing in the golden trees, in the harbour [dolphins] offering their backs to the wailing dead that they may carry them to Paradise."

[4]   *night walkers*   Prostitutes.

After great cathedral gong;[1]
A starlit or a moonlit dome disdains
All that man is,
All mere complexities,
The fury and the mire of human veins.

Before me floats an image, man or shade,
Shade more than man, more image than a shade;
For Hades'[2] bobbin° bound in mummy-cloth   *spool*
May unwind the winding path;
A mouth that has no moisture and no breath
Breathless mouths may summon;
I hail the superhuman;
I call it death-in-life and life-in-death.[3]

Miracle, bird or golden handiwork,
More miracle than bird or handiwork,
Planted on the star-lit golden bough,
Can like the cocks of Hades crow,[4]
Or, by the moon embittered, scorn aloud
In glory of changeless metal
Common bird or petal
And all complexities of mire or blood.

At midnight on the Emperor's pavement flit
Flames that no faggot feeds, nor steel has lit,
Nor storm disturbs, flames begotten of flame,
Where blood-begotten spirits come
And all complexities of fury leave,
Dying into a dance,
An agony of trance,
An agony of flame that cannot singe a sleeve.

Astraddle on the dolphin's mire and blood,[5]
Spirit after spirit! The smithies break the flood,
The golden smithies of the Emperor!
Marbles of the dancing floor
Break bitter furies of complexity,
Those images that yet
Fresh images beget,
That dolphin-torn, that gong-tormented sea.
—1930

For Anne Gregory [6]

"Never shall a young man,
    Thrown into despair
By those great honey-coloured
Ramparts at your ear,
Love you for yourself alone
And not your yellow hair."

"But I can get a hair-dye
And set such colour there,
Brown, or black, or carrot,
That young men in despair
May love me for myself alone
And not my yellow hair."

"I heard an old religious man
But yesternight declare
That he had found a text to prove
That only God, my dear,
Could love you for yourself alone
And not your yellow hair."
—1932

---

[1] *great cathedral* Church of St. Sophia, built in Byzantium by the emperor Justinian I in 532–37.

[2] *Hades* Greek god of the underworld.

[3] *death-in-life and life-in-death* Cf. Tennyson's "Tears, Idle Tears," 20: "O Death in Life" and Coleridge's *The Rime of the Ancient Mariner* 3.193: "The Nightmare LIFE-IN-DEATH was she."

[4] *the cocks of Hades crow* Because cocks symbolized rebirth and resurrection, they appeared on Roman tombstones as a sign of the continuation of human life.

[5] *Astraddle … blood* According to Neoplatonism, dolphins symbolize the soul in transition, as they transport the recently departed to the Islands of the Blest.

[6] *Anne Gregory* Granddaughter of Lady Gregory, well-known figure of the Irish literary revival and close friend of Yeats.

Crazy Jane Talks with the Bishop

I met the Bishop on the road
And much said he and I.
"Those breasts are flat and fallen now,
Those veins must soon be dry;
5   Live in a heavenly mansion,
Not in some foul sty."

"Fair and foul are near of kin,
And fair needs foul," I cried.
"My friends are gone, but that's a truth
10   Nor grave nor bed denied,
Learned in bodily lowliness
And in the heart's pride.

"A woman can be proud and stiff
When on love intent;
15   But Love has pitched his mansion in
The place of excrement;
For nothing can be sole or whole
That has not been rent."
                                    —1933

Lapis Lazuli [1]
(*For Harry Clifton*) [2]

I have heard that hysterical women say
They are sick of the palette and fiddle-bow,
Of poets that are always gay,
For everybody knows or else should know
5   That if nothing drastic is done
Aeroplane and Zeppelin [3] will come out,

Pitch like King Billy bomb-balls [4] in
Until the town lie beaten flat.

All perform their tragic play,
10   There struts Hamlet, there is Lear,
That's Ophelia, that Cordelia; [5]
Yet they, should the last scene be there,
The great stage curtain about to drop,
If worthy their prominent part in the play,
15   Do not break up their lines to weep.
They know that Hamlet and Lear are gay;
Gaiety transfiguring all that dread.
All men have aimed at, found and lost;
Black out; Heaven blazing into the head:
20   Tragedy wrought to its uttermost.
Though Hamlet rambles and Lear rages,
And all the drop-scenes drop at once
Upon a hundred thousand stages,
It cannot grow by an inch or an ounce.

25   On their own feet they came, or on shipboard,
Camel-back, horse-back, ass-back, mule-back,
Old civilisations put to the sword.
Then they and their wisdom went to rack:
No handiwork of Callimachus, [6]
30   Who handled marble as if it were bronze,
Made draperies that seemed to rise
When sea-wind swept the corner, stands;
His long lamp-chimney shaped like the stem
Of a slender palm, stood but a day;
35   All things fall and are built again,
And those that build them again are gay.

---

[1]   *Lapis Lazuli*   Yeats received a carving made of lapis lazuli (semiprecious blue stone) on his birthday, 13 June 1935. Yeats described the stone in a letter to Dorothy Wellesley (English poet and friend): "Ascetic, pupil, hard stone, eternal theme of the sensual east. The heroic cry in the midst of despair. But no, I am wrong, the east has its solutions always and therefore knows nothing of tragedy. It is we, not the east, that must raise the heroic cry."

[2]   *Harry Clifton*   Yeats's apprentice, who gave the elder poet a gift made of lapis lazuli for his seventieth birthday.

[3]   *Zeppelin*   German airship used to bomb London during World War I; in 1938 another war with Germany seemed imminent.

[4]   *King Billy bomb-balls*   King William III (William of Orange) overcame the soldiers of the deposed king James II at the Battle of the Boyne in Ireland, 1690. An anonymous ballad describes the fight: "King William he threw his bomb-balls in, / And set them on fire." Also a nickname for Kaiser Wilhelm, German emperor and king of Prussia during World War I.

[5]   *There struts … Cordelia*   References to tragedies by Shakespeare: *Hamlet* tells the story of the death of Ophelia, beloved of Prince Hamlet, and then of Hamlet himself; *King Lear* tells of the death first of Lear's daughter Cordelia, then of Lear himself.

[6]   *Callimachus*   Greek sculptor of the fifth century BCE.

Two Chinamen, behind them a third,
Are carved in lapis lazuli,
Over them flies a long-legged bird,
40   A symbol of longevity;
The third, doubtless a serving-man,
Carries a musical instrument.

Every discoloration of the stone,
Every accidental crack or dent,
45   Seems a water-course or an avalanche,
Or lofty slope where it still snows
Though doubtless plum or cherry-branch
Sweetens the little half-way house
Those Chinamen climb towards, and I
50   Delight to imagine them seated there;
There, on the mountain and the sky,
On all the tragic scene they stare.
One asks for mournful melodies;
Accomplished fingers begin to play.
55   Their eyes mid many wrinkles, their eyes,
Their ancient, glittering eyes, are gay.
          —1938

The Circus Animals' Desertion

1

I sought a theme and sought for it in vain,
I sought it daily for six weeks or so.
Maybe at last, being but a broken man,
I must be satisfied with my heart, although
5   Winter and summer till old age began
My circus animals were all on show,
Those stilted boys, that burnished chariot,[1]
Lion and woman and the Lord knows what.

2

What can I but enumerate old themes?
10   First that sea-rider Oisín[2] led by the nose

Through three enchanted islands, allegorical dreams,
Vain gaiety, vain battle, vain repose,
Themes of the embittered heart, or so it seems,
That might adorn old songs or courtly shows;
15   But what cared I that set him on to ride,
I, starved for the bosom of his faery bride?

And then a counter-truth filled out its play,
The Countess Cathleen[3] was the name I gave it;
She, pity-crazed, had given her soul away,
20   But masterful Heaven had intervened to save it.
I thought my dear must her own soul destroy,
So did fanaticism and hate enslave it,
And this brought forth a dream and soon enough
This dream itself had all my thought and love.

25   And when the Fool and Blind Man stole the bread
Cuchulain fought the ungovernable sea;[4]
Heart-mysteries there, and yet when all is said
It was the dream itself enchanted me:
Character isolated by a deed
30   To engross the present and dominate memory.
Players and painted stage took all my love,
And not those things that they were emblems of.

3

Those masterful images because complete
Grew in pure mind, but out of what began?
35   A mound of refuse or the sweepings of a street,
Old kettles, old bottles, and a broken can,
Old iron, old bones, old rags, that raving slut[5]
Who keeps the till. Now that my ladder's gone,

---

[1] *Those stilted ... chariot* Yeats may be alluding to the ancient Irish heroes of his first works; the chariot may refer to the carriage built on the stage of his play, *The Unicorn from the Stars* (1908).

[2] *Oisín* Irish warrior of Yeats's *The Wanderings of Oisín* (1889); Oisín is led by the fairy, Niamh, to three islands—called Delight, Many Fears, Forgetfulness—purported to be paradisiacal. When he

returns to Ireland 150 years later he finds his friends dead and his country converted to Christianity.

[3] *The Countess Cathleen* Play written by Yeats in 1892; an Irish countess, modeled on the Irish activist Maud Gonne, sells her soul to the devil to save the starving peasantry, but in the end is saved by God for her magnanimous motives.

[4] *And when ... sea* In Yeats's play *On Baile's Strand* (1904), Cuchulain goes mad after he discovers that he has killed his own son. He runs out to the sea to fight the waves; meanwhile, the fool and the blind man steal bread from the ovens of the townspeople watching Cuchulain's sea-battle.

[5] *slut* Foul or unkempt woman. (Here the word has no connotation of sexual looseness.)

I must lie down where all the ladders start,
40   In the foul rag-and-bone shop of the heart.
      —1939

Under Ben Bulben[1]

Swear by what the sages spoke
Round the Mareotic Lake[2]
That the Witch of Atlas[3] knew,
Spoke and set the cocks a-crow.
5 Swear by those horsemen, by those women
Complexion and form prove superhuman,
That pale, long-visaged company
That air an immortality
Completeness of their passions won;
10 Now they ride the wintry dawn[4]
Where Ben Bulben sets the scene.
Here's the gist of what they mean.

2

Many times man lives and dies
Between his two eternities,
15 That of race and that of soul,
And ancient Ireland knew it all.
Whether man die in his bed
Or the rifle knocks him dead,
A brief parting from those dear
20 Is the worst man has to fear.
Though grave-diggers' toil is long,
Sharp their spades, their muscles strong,
They but thrust their buried men
Back in the human mind again.

3

25 You that Mitchel's prayer have heard,
"Send war in our time, O Lord!"[5]
Know that when all words are said
And a man is fighting mad,
Something drops from eyes long blind,
30 He completes his partial mind,
For an instant stands at ease,
Laughs aloud, his heart at peace.
Even the wisest man grows tense
With some sort of violence
35 Before he can accomplish fate,
Know his work or choose his mate.

4

Poet and sculptor, do the work,
Nor let the modish painter shirk
What his great forefathers did.
40 Bring the soul of man to God,
Make him fill the cradles right.
Measurement began our might:
Forms a stark Egyptian thought,[6]
Forms that gentler Phidias[7] wrought.
45 Michelangelo[8] left a proof
On the Sistine Chapel roof,
Where but half-awakened Adam
Can disturb globe-trotting Madam
Till her bowels are in heat,
50 Proof that there's a purpose set
Before the secret working mind:
Profane perfection of mankind.
Quattrocento[9] put in paint

---

1 *Ben Bulben*   Mountain in County Sligo; Yeats is buried within sight of the mountain at Drumcliff Churchyard.

2 *Mareotic Lake*   Lake Mareotis, south of Alexandria in Egypt, was associated with the Christian Neoplatonists and the rise of Christian monasticism.

3 *the Witch of Atlas*   Cf. Percy Bysshe Shelley's poem "The Witch of Atlas": "By Moeris and the Mareotid lakes / ... / The shadows of the massy temples lie, / And never are erased—but tremble ever" (505–15).

4 *those horsemen ... wintry dawn*   The Sidhe, the fairy people of ancient Irish mythology, who were said to ride through the country on the wind.

5 *Mitchel's prayer ... O Lord*   John Mitchel (1815–75) was an Irish nationalist imprisoned for his activism; in *Jail Journal* he wrote: "Give us war in our time, O Lord!," a play on the Book of Common Prayer's "Give us peace in our time, O Lord."

6 *stark Egyptian thought*   Possibly that of Plotinus, Egyptian philosopher of the third century BCE who founded Neoplatonism.

7 *Phidias*   Greek sculptor of the fifth century BCE.

8 *Michelangelo*   Michelangelo Buonarroti (1475–1564), Italian Renaissance artist.

9 *Quattrocentro*   Fifteenth century; by extension, the Italian Renaissance art for which the century is famous.

On backgrounds for a God or Saint
55   Gardens where a soul's at ease;
Where everything that meets the eye,
Flowers and grass and cloudless sky,
Resemble forms that are or seem
When sleepers wake and yet still dream,
60   And when it's vanished still declare,
With only bed and bedstead there,
That heavens had opened.
    Gyres[1] run on;
When that greater dream had gone
65   Calvert and Wilson, Blake and Claude,[2]
Prepared a rest for the people of God,[3]
Palmer's phrase,[4] but after that
Confusion fell upon our thought.

5

Irish poets, learn your trade,
70   Sing whatever is well made,
Scorn the sort now growing up
All out of shape from toe to top,

Their unremembering hearts and heads
Base-born products of base beds.
75   Sing the peasantry, and then
Hard-riding country gentlemen,
The holiness of monks, and after
Porter-drinkers' randy laughter;
Sing the lords and ladies gay
80   That were beaten into the clay
Through seven heroic centuries;
Cast your mind on other days
That we in coming days may be
Still the indomitable Irishry.

6

85   Under bare Ben Bulben's head
In Drumcliff churchyard Yeats is laid.
An ancestor[5] was rector there
Long years ago, a church stands near,
By the road an ancient cross.
90   No marble, no conventional phrase;
On limestone quarried near the spot
By his command these words are cut:
    Cast a cold eye
    On life, on death.
95   *Horseman, pass by!*[6]
——1939

---

[1] *Gyres* Spirals formed from concentric circles.

[2] *Calvert* Edward Calvert (1799–1883), English wood-engraver and painter, a follower of William Blake; *Wilson* Richard Wilson (1714– 82), English landscape painter; *Blake* William Blake (1757–1827), English poet and artist; *Claude* Claude Lorrain (1600–82), French landscape artist.

[3] *a rest ... God* From Hebrews 4.9: "There remaineth therefore a rest to the people of God."

[4] *Palmer's phrase* Samuel Palmer (1805–81), an English artist, used the phrase from Hebrews to describe Blake's illustrations as "a drawing aside of the fleshly curtain, and the glimpse which all the most holy, studious saints and sages have enjoyed, of the rest which remains to the people of God."

[5] *An ancestor* Yeats's great-grandfather, the Reverend John Yeats (1774–1846).

[6] *Cast ... pass by* Initially buried in France, where he died, Yeats was reinterred at Drumcliff Churchyard in 1948; on his tombstone are engraved these final lines.

In Context

Yeats on Poetic Inspiration

As Yeats explains in the excerpt below from "The Symbolism of Poetry," he believed that philosophy or criticism had the capacity to evoke the "most startling inspiration" for poets.

from "The Symbolism of Poetry" (1900)

"Symbolism, as seen in the writers of our day, would have no value if it were not seen also, under one disguise or another, in every great imaginative writer," writes Mr. Arthur Symons in *The Symbolist Movement in Literature*, a subtle book which I cannot praise as I would, because it has been dedicated to me; and he goes on to show how many profound writers have in the last few years sought for a philosophy of poetry in the doctrine of symbolism, and how even in countries where it is almost scandalous to seek for any philosophy of poetry, new writers are following them in their search. We do not know what the writers of ancient times talked of among themselves, and one bull is all that remains of Shakespeare's talk, who was on the edge of modern times; and the journalist is convinced, it seems, that they talked of wine and women and politics, but never about their art, or never quite seriously about their art. He is certain that no one, who had a philosophy of his art or a theory of how he should write, has ever made a work of art, that people have no imagination who do not write without forethought and afterthought as he writes his own articles. He says this with enthusiasm, because he has heard it at so many comfortable dinner tables, where someone had mentioned through carelessness, or foolish zeal, a book whose difficulty had offended indolence, or a man who had not forgotten that beauty is an accusation. These formulas and generalisations, in which a hidden sergeant has drilled the ideas of journalists and through them the ideas of all but all the modern world, have created in their turn a forgetfulness like that of soldiers in battle, so that journalists and their readers have forgotten, among many like events, that Wagner[1] spent seven years arranging and explaining his ideas before he began his most characteristic music; that opera, and with it modern music, arose from certain talks at the house of one Giovanni Bardi[2] of Florence; and that the Pleiade[3] laid the foundations of modern French literature with a pamphlet. Goethe[4] has said, "a poet needs all philosophy, but he must keep it out of his work," though that is not always necessary; and almost certainly no great art, outside England, where journalists are more powerful and ideas less plentiful than elsewhere, has arisen without a great criticism, for its herald or its interpreter and protector, and it may be for this reason that great art, now that vulgarity has armed itself and multiplied itself, is perhaps dead in England.

All writers, all artists of any kind, in so far as they have had any philosophical or critical power, perhaps just in so far as they have been deliberate artists at all, have had some philosophy, some criticism of their art; and it has often been this philosophy, or this criticism, that has evoked their most startling inspiration, calling into outer life some portion of the divine life, or of the buried reality, which could alone extinguish in the emotions what their philosophy or their criticism would

---

[1]   *Wagner*   German composer Richard Wagner (1813–83).

[2]   *Giovanni Bardi*   Musician, scholar, and aristocrat (1534–1612).

[3]   *Pleiade*   Group of seven ancient Greek poets.

[4]   *Goethe*   Johann Wolfgang von Goethe, German author who wrote the dramatic poem *Faust* (1749–1832).

extinguish in the intellect. They have sought for no new thing, it may be, but only to understand and to copy the pure inspiration of early times, but because the divine life wars upon our outer life, and must needs change its weapons and its movements as we change ours, inspiration has come to them in beautiful startling shapes. The scientific movement brought with it a literature, which was always tending to lose itself in externalities of all kinds, in opinion, in declamation, in picturesque writing, in word painting, or in what Mr. Symons has called an attempt "to build in brick and mortar inside the covers of a book"; and now writers have begun to dwell upon the element of evocation, of suggestion, upon what we call the symbolism in great writers.

The sources of inspiration for Yeats were many and varied. The inspiration for "The Lake Isle of Innisfree," for example, was a chance association as the poet was walking along Fleet Street in Central London:

from "Four Years" (1921)

I had various women friends on whom I would call towards five o'clock mainly to discuss my thoughts that I could not bring to a man without meeting some competing thought, but partly because their tea and toast saved my pennies for the bus ride home; but with women, apart from their intimate exchanges of thought, I was timid and abashed. I was sitting on a seat in front of the British Museum feeding pigeons when a couple of girls sat near and began enticing my pigeons away, laughing and whispering to one another, and I looked straight in front of me, very indignant, and presently went into the museum without turning my head towards them. Since then I have often wondered if they were pretty or merely very young. Sometimes I told myself very adventurous love stories with myself for hero, and at other times I planned out a life of lonely austerity, and at other times mixed the ideals and planned a life of lonely austerity mitigated by periodical lapses. I had still the ambition, formed in Sligo[1] in my teens, of living in imitation of Thoreau on Innisfree, a little island in Lough Gill, and when walking through Fleet Street very homesick I heard a little tinkle of water and saw a fountain in a shop window which balanced a little ball upon its jet, and began to remember lake water. From the sudden remembrance came my poem Innisfree, my first lyric with anything in its rhythm of my own music. I had begun to loosen rhythm as an escape from rhetoric and from that emotion of the crowd that rhetoric brings, but I only understood vaguely and occasionally that I must for my special purpose use nothing but the common syntax. A couple of years later I would not have written that first line with its conventional archaism—"Arise and go"—nor the inversion in the last stanza.

A crucially important moment in the growth of Yeats as a poet was the forging of an extraordinary form of creative collaboration with his wife Georgie (or "George," as Yeats called her). The images Yeats gleaned through George's "automatic writing" evidently played a vital role in providing raw material for Yeats's poetry from the late teens through the 1920s and 1930s. In his introduction to *A Vision* (1925), Yeats tells the story of how that collaboration began.

---

[1] *Sligo* County in Ireland.

from "Introduction" to *A Vision* (1925)

The other day Lady Gregory said to me: "You are a much better educated man than you were ten years ago and much more powerful in argument." And I put *The Tower* and *The Winding Stair* into evidence to show that my poetry has gained in self possession and power. I owe this change to an incredible experience.

2

On the afternoon of October 24th 1917, four days after my marriage, my wife surprised me by attempting automatic writing.[1] What came in disjointed sentences, in almost illegible writing, was so exciting, sometimes so profound, that I persuaded her to give an hour or two day after day to the unknown writer, and after some half dozen such hours offered to spend what remained of life explaining and piecing together those scattered sentences. "No," was the answer, "we have come to give you metaphors for poetry." The unknown writer took his theme at first from my just published *Per Amica Silentia Lunae*.[2] I had made a distinction between the perfection that is from a man's combat with himself and that which is from a combat with circumstance, and upon this simple distinction he built up an elaborate classification of men according to their more or less complete expression of one type or the other. He supported his classification by a series of geometrical symbols and put these symbols in an order that answered the question in my essay as to whether some prophet could not prick upon the calendar the birth of a Napoleon or a Christ. A system of symbolism, strange to my wife and to myself, certainly awaited expression, and when I asked how long that would take I was told years. Sometimes when my mind strays back to those first days I remember that Browning's Paracelsus[3] did not obtain the secret until he had written his spiritual history at the bidding of his Byzantine teacher, that before initiation Wilhelm Meister[4] read his own history written by another, and I compare my *Per Amica* to those histories.

3

When the automatic writing began we were in a hotel on the edge of Ashdown Forest, but soon returned to Ireland and spent much of 1918 at Glendalough, at Rosses Point, at Coole Park, at a house near it, at Thoor Ballylee,[5] always more or less solitary, my wife bored and fatigued by her almost daily task and I thinking and talking of little else. Early in 1919 the communicator of the moment—they were constantly changed— said they would soon change the method from the written to the spoken word as that would fatigue her less, but the change did not come for some months. I was on a lecturing tour in America to earn a roof for Thoor Ballylee when it came. We had one of those little sleeping compartments in a train, with two berths, and were somewhere in Southern California. My wife, who had been asleep for some minutes, began to talk in her sleep, and from that on almost all communications came in that way. My teachers did not seem to speak out of her sleep but as if from above it, as though it were a tide upon which they floated. A chance word spoken

---

[1] *automatic writing* Automatism, a practice of Spiritualism, in which spirits express themselves through the hands of the living. Both William and Georgie Yeats were involved in Spiritualism and the occult.

[2] *Per Amica Silentia Lunae* Published in 1918, Yeats's book contained both poetic and mystical writings defining his system of spirituality and its link to creativity.

[3] *Browning's Paracelcus* Robert Browning wrote a poem about Philippus Aureolus Paracelsus (1493–1541), Swiss physician, alchemist, and author of numerous works on the occult, who believed in the unlimited power of the imagination.

[4] *Wilhelm Meister* From the book *Wilhelm Meister's Travels* by Johann Wolfgang von Goethe.

[5] *Thoor Ballylee* The Yeats's summer home, a castle in County Galway.

before she fell asleep would sometimes start a dream that broke in upon the communications, as if from below, to trouble or overwhelm, as when she dreamed she was a cat lapping milk or a cat curled up asleep and therefore dumb. The cat returned night after night, and once when I tried to drive it away by making the sound one makes when playing at being a dog to amuse a child, she awoke trembling, and the shock was so violent that I never dared repeat it. It was plain therefore that, though the communicators' critical powers were awake, hers slept, or that she was aware of the idea the sound suggested but not of the sound.

4

Whenever I received a certain signal (I will explain what it was later), I would get pencil and paper ready. After they had entranced my wife suddenly when sitting in a chair, I suggested that she must always be lying down before they put her to sleep. They seemed ignorant of our surroundings and might have done so at some inconvenient time or place; once when they had given their signal in a restaurant they explained that because we had spoken of a garden they had thought we were in it. Except at the start of a new topic, when they would speak or write a dozen sentences unquestioned, I had always to question, and every question to rise out of a previous answer and to deal with their chosen topic. My questions must be accurately worded, and, because they said their thought was swifter than ours, asked without delay or hesitation. I was constantly reproved for vague or confused questions, yet I could do no better, because, though it was plain from the first that their exposition was based upon a single geometrical conception, they kept me from mastering that conception. They shifted ground whenever my interest was at its height, whenever it seemed that the next day must reveal what, as I soon discovered, they were determined to withhold until all was upon paper. November 1917 had been given to an exposition of the twenty-eight typical incarnations or phases and to the movements of their *Four Faculties*, and then on December 6th a cone or gyre had been drawn and related to the soul's judgment after death;[1] and then just as I was about to discover that incarnations and judgment alike implied cones or gyres, one within the other, turning in opposite directions, two such cones were drawn and related neither to judgment nor to incarnations but to European history. They drew their first symbolical map of that history, and marked upon it the principal years of crisis, early in July 1918, some days before the publication of the first German edition of Spengler's *Decline of the West*,[2] which, though founded upon a different philosophy, gives the same years of crisis and draws the same general conclusions, and then returned to the soul's judgment. I believe that they so changed their theme because, had I grasped their central idea, I would have lacked the patience and the curiosity to follow their application of it, preferring some hasty application of my own. They once told me not to speak of any part of the system, except of the incarnations which were almost fully expounded, because if I did the people I talked to would talk to other people, and the communicators would mistake that misunderstanding for their own thought.

---

[1] *twenty-eight… death* Astrology was part of Yeats's belief system; hence his concern with the moon's cycles. The *Four Faculties*—or forces within a person's consciousness—and the symbol of the cone or gyre are also important features of the system.

[2] *Spengler's… West* In his book, Oswald Spengler outlined a cross-cultural pattern of behavior throughout history and suggested that all aspects (art, politics, religion, etc.) of cultures have similar underlying principles.

IN CONTEXT

The Struggle for Irish Independence

The leaders of the Easter Rebellion, the failed Irish nationalist uprising of 1916, issued the following document, written and read by Pádraic Pearse, upon their occupation of the Dublin General Post Office. (For an overview of historical developments, see the Introduction to this volume, pp. LV–LVII.)

Poblacht na h-Eireann[1] / *Proclamation of the Irish Republic* (Easter 1916)

THE PROVISIONAL GOVERNMENT OF THE IRISH REPUBLIC TO THE PEOPLE OF IRELAND

Irishmen and Irishwomen:

In the name of God and of the dead generations from which she receives her old tradition of nationhood, Ireland, through us, summons her children to her flag and strikes for her freedom. Having organised and trained her manhood through her secret revolutionary organisation, the Irish Republican Brotherhood, and through her open military organisations, the Irish Volunteers and the Irish Citizen Army, having patiently perfected her discipline, having resolutely waited for the right moment to reveal itself, she now seizes that moment, and, supported by her exiled children in America and by gallant allies in Europe, but relying in the first on her own strength, she strikes in full confidence of victory.

We declare the right of the people of Ireland to the ownership of Ireland, and to the unfettered control of Irish destinies, to be sovereign and indefeasible. The long usurpation of that right by a foreign people and government has not extinguished the right, nor can it ever be extinguished except by the destruction of the Irish people. In every generation the Irish have asserted their right to national freedom and sovereignty; six times during the past three hundred years they have asserted it in arms. Standing on that fundamental right and again asserting it in arms in the face of the world, we hereby proclaim the Irish Republic as a Sovereign Independent State, and we pledge our lives and the lives of our comrades-in-arms to the cause of its freedom, of its welfare, and of its exaltation among the nations.

The Irish Republic is entitled to, and hereby claims, the allegiance of every Irishman and Irishwoman. The Republic guarantees religious and civil liberty, equal rights and equal opportunities to all its citizens, and declares its resolve to pursue the happiness and prosperity of the whole nation and of all its parts, cherishing all the children of the nation equally, and oblivious of the differences carefully fostered by an alien government, which have divided a minority from the majority in the past.

Until our arms have brought the opportune moment for the establishment of a permanent National Government, representative of the whole people of Ireland and elected by the suffrages of all her men and women, the Provisional Government, hereby constituted, will administer the civil and military affairs of the Republic in trust for the people.

We place the cause of the Irish Republic under the protection of the Most High God, Whose blessing we invoke upon our arms, and we pray that no one who serves that cause will dishonor it by

---

[1]   *Poblacht na h-Eireann*   Irish Republic.

cowardice, inhumanity, or rapine.[1] In this supreme hour the Irish nation must, by its valour and discipline and by the readiness of its children to sacrifice themselves for the common good, prove itself worthy of the august destiny to which it is called.

Signed on Behalf of the Provisional Government,

Thomas J. Clarke,
Sean MacDiarmada,
Thomas MacDonagh,
P.H. Pearse,
Eamonn Ceannt,
James Connolly,
Joseph Plunkett.

Pádraic Pearse, Statement (1916)

Pádraic Pearse (1879–1916) was a poet and politician who fought for Irish independence. He was one of the leaders of the failed Easter Rebellion of 1916, in which Irish nationalists took arms against British rule. Pearse was taken prisoner during the uprising and was executed by a firing squad soon after delivering this statement.

The following is the substance of what I said when asked today by the President of the Court-Martial at Richmond Barracks whether I had anything to say in my defence:

I desire, in the first place, to repeat what I have already said in letters to General Maxwell and Brigadier General Lowe. My object in agreeing to an unconditional surrender was to prevent the further slaughter of the civil population of Dublin and to save the lives of our gallant fellows, who, having made for six days a stand unparalleled in military history, were now surrounded, and in the case of those under the immediate command of H.Q., without food. I fully understand now, as then, that my own life is forfeit to British law, and I shall die very cheerfully if I can think that the British Government, as it has already shown itself strong, will now show itself magnanimous enough to accept my single life in forfeiture and to give a general amnesty to the brave men and boys who have fought at my bidding.

In the second place, I wish it to be understood that any admissions I make here are to be taken as involving myself alone. They do not involve and must not be used against anyone who acted with me, not even those who may have set their names to documents with me. (The Court assented to this.)

I admit that I was Commandant-General Commanding-in-Chief of the forces of the Irish Republic which have been acting against you for the past week, and that I was President of the Provisional Government. I stand over all my acts and words done or spoken, in these capacities. When I was a child of ten I went on my bare knees by my bedside one night and promised God that I should devote my life to an effort to free my country. I have kept the promise. I have helped to organize, to arm, to train, and to discipline my fellow countrymen to the sole end that, when the time came, they might fight for Irish freedom. The time, as it seemed to me, did come, and we went into the fight. I am glad we did, we seem to have lost, but we have not lost. To refuse to fight would have been to lose, to fight is to win; we have kept faith with the past, and handed on a tradition to the future. I repudiate the assertion of the prosecutor that I sought to aid and abet England's enemy. Germany is no more to me than England is. I asked and accepted German aid in the shape of arms

[1] *rapine* Robbery.

and an expeditionary force; we neither asked for nor accepted German gold, nor had any traffic with Germany but what I state. My object was to win Irish freedom. We struck the first blow ourselves, but I should have been glad of an ally's aid.

I assume that I am speaking to Englishmen who value their freedom and who profess to be fighting for the freedom of Belgium and Serbia; believe that we too love freedom and desire it. To us it is more desirable than anything in the world. If you strike us down now we shall rise again and renew the fight; you cannot conquer Ireland, you cannot extinguish the Irish passion for freedom; if our deed has not been sufficient to win freedom, then our children will win it by a better deed.

DOROTHY RICHARDSON
1873 – 1957

Twentieth-century novelist Dorothy Richardson produced only one novel during the course of her writing career, but that novel, *Pilgrimage*, consists of 13 volumes in which she undertook no less ambitious a project than the reworking of the conventions of fiction and the reinventing of language. *Pilgrimage* is credited with being the first English example of what became known as stream of consciousness style—the setting down in writing of the full flow of a character's thoughts and perceptions (Richardson preferred the term "interior monologue"). Though readers from the time of the novel's publication to the present day have accused it of being dull, obscure, and inconsequential, Richardson's single-minded pursuit of her uncompromisingly experimental style resulted in a novel that influenced such writers as Virginia Woolf, May Sinclair, and Katherine Mansfield; in fact, it can be said that it influenced the course of twentieth-century fiction.

Born into genteel poverty, Richardson lived with her family until she was 17, when she left home to work as a tutor-governess in Germany and England, and then as a dental receptionist in Bloomsbury. While living in London she immersed herself in the literary and political societies of her day, attending meetings of groups as diverse as the Quakers, Anarchists, Zionists, Suffragettes, and Fabians. During this time she also met novelist H.G. Wells, on whom the character of Hypo Wilson in *Pilgrimage* is modeled, and with whom she formed a close personal and professional relationship.

Encouraged by Wells, Richardson left her dental job in 1907 to make her living as a translator and writer. She contributed hundreds of columns, reviews, and literary sketches to a variety of journals, including *The Dental Record, The Saturday Review, Crank, The Open Road,* and the avant-garde film journal *Close Up.* She also wrote a number of poems and short stories and several non-fiction works, including *The Quakers Past and Present* (1914) and *John Austen and the Inseparables* (1930). Through her writing she supported herself and her husband, artist Alan Odle, whom she married in 1917.

In 1912 Richardson began *Pointed Roofs* (1915), the first of the 13 volumes (referred to as "chapters" by Richardson) of *Pilgrimage*. *Pilgrimage* details the impact of urban life on Miriam Henderson (an alter-ego of Richardson), who struggles to free herself from the stereotypical female roles of Victorian England. The unusual form of the novel is perhaps best described by Virginia Woolf, who declared upon reading it, "There is no word, such as romance or realism, to cover, even roughly, the works of Miss Dorothy Richardson … She has invented a sentence we might call the psychological sentence of the feminine gender." In her writing, Richardson rejected the traditional framework of the realist novel, which she felt "dramatized life misleadingly" with its events devised to form a plot, climax, and resolution. Richardson believed this conventional form privileged traditionally "masculine" qualities: logic, dualistic thinking, hierarchical categorization, emphasis on external appearances, and a tendency to analyze and compartmentalize. Not only did fiction of this sort neglect the more "feminine" values of imagination, intuition, and relational abilities, as

Richardson saw it; it also tended to misrepresent female experience and to ignore what she saw as the heart of all experience—the perceiving, reflecting mind.

Pilgrimage, therefore, was an attempt to provide what Richardson called the "feminine equivalent of the current masculine realism"—a form that would give precedence to these previously ignored experiences and values and would embody the flow of "being." Richardson confined the reality of her novel to the subjective reality of Miriam's perception and strove to make her writing style inseparable from her character's consciousness. Much of *Pointed Roofs* is made up of dialogue or sentences written with conventional grammar and syntax, but even in this first "chapter" Richardson employs prose that is virtually unpunctuated, with brief, half-formulated phrases linked by ellipses. The style, designed to access the depths of Miriam's consciousness, to envelop the vague shapes of her thoughts, and to imitate the random succession of her impressions, is more widely used in later "chapters." Though Richardson called this prose "feminine" because of the qualities it embodied, she did not see it as being in any way limited to writing by or about women.

Richardson worked on her novel for the remainder of her life; the last volume, *March Moonlight* (1967), was found among her papers after her death in 1957. There is no formal conclusion to *Pilgrimage*, which stops at a point midway through Miriam's life.

⌘ ⌘ ⌘

About Punctuation

Only to patient reading will come forth the charm concealed in ancient manuscripts. Deep interest there must be, or sheer necessity, to keep eye and brain at their task of scanning a text that moves along unbroken, save by an occasional full-stop. But the reader who persists finds presently that his task is growing easier. He is winning familiarity with the writer's style, and is able to punctuate unconsciously as he goes.... It is at this point that he begins to be aware of the charm that has been sacrificed by the systematic separation of phrases. He finds himself *listening*. Reading through the ear as well as through the eye. And while in any way of reading the ear plays its part, unless it is most cunningly attacked it co-operates, in our modern way, scarcely at all. It is left behind. For as light is swifter than sound so is the eye swifter than the ear. But in the slow, attentive reading demanded by unpunctuated texts, the faculty of hearing has its chance, is enhanced until the text *speaks* itself. And it is of this enhancement that the strange lost charm is born. Quite modest matter, read thus, can arouse and fuse the faculties of mind and heart.

Only the rarest of modern prose can thus arouse and affect. Only now and again, today, is there any strict and vital relationship between the reader and what he reads.

Most of our reading is a superficial swift gathering, as we loll on the borderland between inertia and attention, of the matter of a text. An easygoing collaboration, with the reader's share reduced to the minimum. So much the better, it may be said. Few books, ancient or modern, are worth a whole self. Very few can call us forth to yield all we are and suffer change. Yet it is not to be denied that the machinery of punctuation and type, while lifting burdens from reader and writer alike and perfectly serving the purposes of current exchange, have also, on the whole, devitalized the act of reading; have tended to make it less organic, more mechanical.

There is no discourtesy, since punctuation has come to be regarded as invariable, in calling it part of the machinery of book production. An invisible part. For so long as it conforms to rule punctuation is invisible. After the school years it is invisible; its use, for most people, as unconscious as the act of breathing. Most of us were taught punctuation exactly as we were taught rule of three.[1] Even if we were given some sense of the time-value of the stop and its subdivisions, the thing that came first and last, the fun of the game, was the invariability of the rules. And so charming is convention, so

---

[1]   *rule of three* In arithmetic, the rule for finding the fourth term when three are given and the fourth must have the same ratio to the third as the second has to the first.

exhilarating a deliberate conformity to tradition, that it is easy to forget that the sole aim of law is liberty; in this case, liberty to express.

It is not very long since an English gentleman's punctuation was as romantic as his spelling. The formal law was strictly observed only by scholars. Not until lately have infringements, by the ordinary, been regarded as signs of ill-breeding. And in high places there have always been those who have honoured the rules in the breach, without rebuke. Sterne,[1] for example, joyously broke them all, and it has been accounted unto him for righteousness. Beside him stands Rabelais,[2] wielding form as Pantaloon wields his bladder. Were they perhaps castigated for their liberties by the forgotten orthodox of the period? Or is it that the stickler for stereotyped punctuation makes his first appearance in our own time? Why, in either case, have Mr. Wells's[3] experiments, never going further than a reinforcement of the full-stop and a free use of the dash, been dragged into the market-place and lynched, while the wholesale depredations of Sterne and Rabelais are merely affectionately hugged? Is it because their rows and rows of dots, their stars, and their paragraphs built of a single word are so very often a libidinous digging of the reader's ribs? Because their stars wink? It is noteworthy that so long as his dots were laughter Mr. Wells was not called over the coals for mannerism. There was no trouble until those signs were used to italicize an idea or drive home a point; until they became pauses for reflection, by the reader. From that time onwards there have been, amongst his opponents, those who take refuge in attack on his method. Scorn of the dot and the dash has come forward to play its part in the business of answering Mr. Wells. Sterne and Rabelais and the earlier Wells, genially aware of the reader and with nothing to fear from him, offer open hospitality on their pages, space, while their wit detonates, for the responsive beat of the reader's own consciousness. The later Wells, usually the prey of dismay, anger or despair, handles the resources of the printed page almost exclusively as missiles, aimed full at the intelligence alone.

Of the value of punctuation and, particularly, of its value as pacemaker for the reader's creative consciousness, no one has had a keener sense than Mr. Henry James.[4] No one has more sternly, or more cunningly, secured the collaboration of the reader. Along his prose not even the most casual can succeed in going at top-speed. Short of the casting off of burdens, the deep breath, the headlong plunge, the sustained steady swimming, James gives nothing at all. To complete renunciation he offers the recreative repose that is the result of open-eyed concentration. As aesthetic exercise, with its peculiar joys and edifications, the prose of James keeps its power, even for those in utmost revolt against his vision, indefinitely. It is a spiritual Swedish Drill. Gently, painlessly, without shock or weariness, as he carries us unhasting, unresting, over his vast tracts of statement, we learn to stretch attention to the utmost. And to the utmost James tested, suspending from the one his wide loops, and from the other his deep-hung garlands of expression, the strength of the comma and the semi-colon. He never broke a rule. With him, punctuation, neither made, nor created, nor begotten, but proceeding directly from its original source in life, stands exactly where it was at its first discovery. His text, for one familiar with it, might be reduced, without increase of the attention it demands, to the state of the unpunctuated scripts of old time. So rich and splendid is the fabric of sound he weaves upon the appointed loom, that his prose, chanted to his punctuation, in an unknown tongue, would serve as well as a mass—in D minor.

Yet even James, finding within bonds all the freedom he desired, did not quite escape the police. Down upon almost his last written words came the iron hand of Mr. Crosland, sternly, albeit most respectfully, recommending a strait-jacket in the shape of full-stops to be borrowed—from Mr. Bart Kennedy.[5] Whose stops are shouts. A pleasant jest. Relieving no doubt a long felt desire for the presence in Mr. James of a little ginger.

---

[1] *Sterne* Novelist Laurence Sterne (1713–68).

[2] *Rabelais* French writer François Rabelais, author of the comic sixteenth-century masterpiece *Gargantua and Pantagruel*, in which Pantaloon is a character.

[3] *Mr. Wells* British writer H.G. Wells (1866–1946).

[4] *Henry James* American novelist (1843–1916).

[5] *Down upon ... Kennedy* The references are to British poets Thomas William Hodgson Crosland (1865–1924) and Bart Kennedy (1861–1930).

But Crosland is austere. Sternly, with no intervals for laughter, he drags us headlong, breathless, belaboured, from jest to jest with never a smile or pause. It is his essential compactness that makes him a so masterly sonneteer. His sonnets gleam, now like metalled ships, now like jewels. Prose, in his sense, might be written like a sonnet. First the form, a well-balanced distribution of stops for each paragraph, and then the text. An interesting experiment.

As interesting as that now on trial in a prose that is a conscious protest against everything that has been done to date by the hand of talent at work upon inspiration. But the dadaists,[1] in so far as they are paying to law the loud tribute of anarchy, are the counterparts of the strictly orthodox.

Meanwhile, for those who stand between purists and rebels, the rules of punctuation are neither sacred, nor execrable, nor quite absolute. No waving of the tablets of the law has been able to arrest organic adaptation. The test of irregularities is their effectiveness. Verbless phrases flanked by full-stops,[2] the use of *and* at the beginning of a sentence, and kindred effective irregularities, are safe servants, for good, in the cause of the written word. And always there has been a certain variability in the use of the comma. As the shortest breath of punctuation it is allowed, without controversy, to wander a little.

Yet the importance of the comma cannot be exaggerated. It is the angel, or the devil, amongst the stops. In prose, everything turns upon its use. Misplaced, it destroys sense more readily than either of its fellows. For while their wanderings are heavy-footed, either at once obvious, or easily traceable, the comma plays its pranks unobtrusively. Used discreetly, it clears meaning and sets both tone and pace. And it possesses a charm denied to other stops. Innocence, punctuating at the bidding of a prompting from within, has the comma for its darling. Spontaneous commas are as delightful in their way as spontaneous spelling; as delightful as the sharp breath drawn by a singing child in the middle of a word.

Experiment with the comma, as distinct from recourse to its recognised variability, is to be found,

since the stereotyping of the rules, only here and there and takes one form: its exclusion from sequences of adjectives. This exclusion suggests an awareness of the power of the comma as a holder-up, a desire to allow adjectives to converge, in the mind of the reader, as swiftly as possible upon their object. But one would expect to find, together with such awareness, discrimination. And, so far as I know, the exclusion of the comma when it is practised at all, is unvarying; the possibilities are missed as surely here, as they are in conformity to the letter of the law.

The use of the comma, whether between phrases or in sequences of adjectives, is best regulated by the consideration of its time-value. If, for example, we read:—

"Tom went singing at the top of his voice up the stairs at a run that ended suddenly on the landing in a collision with the sweep,"

we are brought sensibly nearer to sharing the incident than if we read:—

"Tom went, singing at the top of his voice, up the stairs, at a run that ended, suddenly, on the landing, in a collision with the sweep."

Conversely, if we read:—

"Tom stupid with fatigue fearing the worst staggered without word or sign of greeting into the room,

we are further off than in reading:—

"Tom, stupid with fatigue, fearing the worst, staggered, without word or sign of greeting, into the room."

Even more obvious is the time-value of the comma in sequences of adjectives:—

"Suave low-toned question-begging excuses"

bears the same meaning as:—

---

[1] *dadaists* Followers of an artistic and literary movement, Dada, that was characterized by a rebellion against convention and reason.

[2] *full-stops* Periods.

"Suave, low-toned, question-begging excuses."

But the second is preferable.

"Huge soft bright pink roses"

may be written:—

"Huge, soft, bright, pink roses."

But the first wins.

It is a good plan, in the handling of phrases, to beware of pauses when appealing mainly to the eye, and to cherish them when appealing to reflection. With sequences of single words, and particularly of adjectives, when the values are concrete, reinforcing each other, accumulating without modification or contradiction upon a single object of sight, the comma is an obstruction. When the values are abstract, qualifying each other and appealing to reflection, or to vision, or to both vision and reflection at once, the comma is essential. If there is a margin of uncertainty, any possibility of ambiguity or misapprehension, it is best, no matter what is sacrificed of elasticity or of swiftness, to load up with commas. Or the reader may pay tax. And it is dangerous in these days of hurried readings to ask for the re-scanning even of a single phrase.

But there is woe in store, unless he be a prince of proof-readers, for the writer who varies his punctuation. The kindly hands that regulate his spelling will regulate also his use of stops; and, since hands are human, they will regulate irregularly. The result, when the author has altered the alterations, also irregularly, sometimes reading punctuation on to the page when it is not there—is chaos.

—1924

Journey to Paradise

When we are lords at last of earth and sea and the spell of the wild shall have retreated to the stars, the charm of coasts will remain, the ancient charm of land and sea in relationship. It is a thing inexorable even by villas, even in a world imagined as edged along the whole of its coastlines by promenades, villa-fringed. And indeed, wild coast, now so rapidly diminishing, was, for the majority, until the present century, until the coming of motors, even in England almost unknown. There was the ocean, across which brave people ventured for diversion or for business. And there was the seaside, certain known strands, frequented in the proper season. The interspaces were legendary, matter for travellers' tales. And a visit to even the best known and most easily accessible resort was an enterprise fraught with so many perils that every book of household management offered a little homily on the subject of sea air—a substance only less redoubtable than night air—and a discourse on the dangers of bathing. To the end of my days, though I have shed more of this lore than I can recall, I shall know just how long one should acclimatise before venturing into the water, how long to remain therein, the best restoratives to take on mergence, and the number of minutes that may safely be spent in resting before the sharp walk that is essential to survival from the ordeal.

From our earliest years my sister and I were familiar with every detail of the ritual, discussed, no doubt, each summer in advance by our parents and nurses, and serving, I fancy, with them no less than with ourselves only as an enhancement of the coming adventure. It is certain that once we had arrived they were immediately forgotten. Bathing, which began on the first morning, I remember as an exciting and tiresome interruption of entrancements, of building and dyke making, shell gathering, shrimping, wading or mere ecstatic pattering about to the movement of sea and sky and cliffs. It was exciting because that quaint Quaker invention, the bathing machine,[1] rattled across the sands at a tremendous pace, and it was happiness, while being unrobed, to stand on the bench in the dark enclosure and watch through the tiny square of window the outside brilliance racing by. Bathing was tiresome because the hands of the huge bathing women who stood about in the shallows and cut short private enterprise by dipping us one by one turn and turn about beneath the advancing

---

[1] *that quaint … machine* Small enclosure pulled across the beach by horses, in which bathers could enjoy the beach or change in privacy. Quaker Benjamin Beale invented an awning which would extend from the machine into the water.

waves were large and red and very hard. The interruption over we immediately followed our own devices, though I remember that there were, if no restoratives, at least buns, incomparable brown sun-hot new buns, to allay the worst pangs of a most ferocious hunger.

To this day when in London I prepare for a swift rush to the coast I know that I am going, not casually to the sea, but marvellously to the seaside; the seaside that is one place and has no name. The place that was seaside to me in my childhood, being in South Devon, had a rich and lovely name, a name that my father, with a touch of jocular patronage, used to speak in the West Country fashion, and my childish condemnation of his pose was in reality a resentment of any naming of my heaven. I know now how unjust I was, that the young man, ancient to me, who doughtily, summer after summer, carried his offspring the long day's journey to the far west, took refuge in the local speech because he, too, was shy of naming the unnameable. He, too, was going to the seaside. And I can appreciate, knowing that although seaside is one and indescribable, there are shores and shores, the excellence of his choice. For though today I love the pale and narrow sea that tumbles heavily upon the Sussex coast, the fresh little sea dancing in the east wind off Norfolk, the green Atlantic rollers that break against the Cornish cliffs, and many another stretch of our island waters, each one brings between-whiles the nostalgia of my own seaside, of the fine, fine shingles of the Devon beaches, the recurrent sound of them under the tide, the infinitely refreshing hiss and wash as they are lifted and dragged backwards by the waves, and the echoes of this sound in the red caves and tunnels. For years I knew no other coast. Did not know that there were cliffless beaches of grey pebble, pallid in unbroken sunlight, and waves that retired soundlessly over sands of muddy grey. The first sight of such pebbles and such sands seemed heartbreak.

And I have seen Devon triumph, seen her coast a lifetime of other coasts.

My seaside is no longer the seaside that I knew. But the pier and promenade that have usurped the places of the old stone jetty and the sea wall have not changed the sound of the sea in the coves nor dimmed the beauty of the innumerable shells washed up there. A handful of shingle still yields cowries,[1] the small tooled shapes that were nuggets in dross to my eager hands, minutely heavy, sea wet and pinky brown in their fine ribbings along the spine, paling to where the lips curl inwards, ivory white.

But it was not of these things that I thought when into endless summer, into a garden whose boundaries were as yet unknown, there came the news of the great journey, but rather of the dazzling spaces of sunlit salty air above the little town and of the way sound echoed through it fresh and free. Morning sounds, the blithe barking of a dog upon the shore, the shrill high voice of the fishwife announcing my incomparable seaside breakfast, and later the sounds of donkeys trotting and of people hurrying to the beach on silent rubbered feet to laughter and the clinking of little buckets. The air above the small town behind the cliffs held always some echoes, and this for me was its deepest charm, haunting me while I conned over[2] with my sisters the joys to come. Nothing could fully banish its enchantment, neither the childish squabblings that at home could fill the universe with darkness, nor the first misery of scorched legs nor even the recurrent tragedy of bedtime. And though each day I was lost in the joy of the strong red cliffs, the happy wash and ripple of the waves, the shapes and colours of the lovely things to be seen and handled in rock pools, my best bliss came down upon me away from the shore. All that made seaside was fused and distilled within the dazzling air above the open space where our house stood in the mainway of the townlet, a wide road divided by narrow ribbons of green lawn that ran each side of a stone-rimmed torrent broken every few yards by a steeply gushing fall. I felt both pity and contempt for these tame sweet waters. Yet it was in passing over the little bridge that spanned their gentle rush to the sea, in hearing the plash and murmur of their cascades go up into the sky, that I tasted the deepest of my joy.

Early on a summer morning we would start from the outskirts of our little Berkshire town. Unfamiliar shadow under the home gables and strange quiet in park and marketplace, I remember no family, no incident of departure, only the sense of known things passing away,

---

[1]   *cowries* Gastropods with oval-shaped, porcelain-like shells.

[2]   *conned over* Studied carefully.

and then, it seemed at once, the being roused from sleep in the midst of the fearful adventure of Paddington.[1] I knew not then that Paddington was the aristocrat of the London termini with proud traditions and a leisurely staff. To me it was inferno; chaos with but one refuge, perhaps undiscoverable, the seaside train. The regulation Paddington train with its well-hung coaches panelled in ivory and brown, rolling smoothly westwards at the bidding of a decorously low-voiced bell-toned whistle, was, I thought, a vehicle kept in state for its glorious mission. Paddington has changed but little. The many buffets, the automatic machines and other modernities crowding the platforms accommodate themselves to its atmosphere. The staff, including the smallest newspaper boy, is still courtly. And the turn of the wheel that was bringing back mahogany and repp[2] has restored to the Great Western rolling stock its Victorian garb of chocolate and cream to delight the eye of survivors.

Paddington and piled luggage, and my family suddenly present. My mother, in sprigged muslin and dustcloak[3] and small round hat tilted nosewards from piled hair, disquietingly anxious and dependent. My sisters in sprigged cotton and reefers, their flushed faces framed by monstrous "zulu" hats,[4] kept for the seaside and most miserable in the wearing, with a poke that hit the sky and was brought plastering down over the ears by means of a tight bridle of elastic cutting, when new, unmercifully across beneath the chin. A torment now banished for ever. It had its compensations. You could, for instance, at unobserved moments, by the simple device of working the elastic to the tip of your chin, become a mounted policeman—a painful process causing the coarse straw to scrape the tender parts of your hot ears, and dangerous unless you preserved a policemanlike immobility. Usually you did not, and the

elastic slid and leapt, to come, with a cutting sting, tightly to rest under your nose.

My father on these occasions was less tranquil than the terminus, though quite as stately. Circumstances were exacting. All of us, including my mother and the servants, reduced to eager and not always mute helplessness, were pendant upon his omniscience, excited, frightened, and, but for him, lost utterly. His to carry us through not only without help, but hampered by the humiliating necessity of parting with some of the finer shades of the composure inseparable from the bearing of the travelling English gentleman. This bearing was his by nature and by the grace of an almost religious cultivation. But the travelling English gentleman of his day clothed his composure in frieze and deerstalker,[5] and though on these holiday flittings high summer seems always to have blazed, my father, whenever exposed to the vulgar gaze, bore these articles upon his tall and slender form. The long frieze, it is true, hung open, revealing the cool silky alpaca that lay beneath. But the weather and the occasion tyrannised. Useless to deny it—the English gentleman was flustered. Small wonder that my mother, goddess omnipotent, became almost one of ourselves, shared our torment: the certainty that the train would elude us. Small wonder, indeed, that my father shepherded the forlorn group into a waiting-room and forbade the opening of its door until he should reappear. To this day the inside of a waiting room recalls to me that fearful interval. Its terrifying length, the pictures of disaster that filled the small space so closely surrounded by large suggestive sounds. And its end was not the least of its fearfulness. The door would open quickly, not upon a stranger or a porter, but upon the dreaded form of my father, upon his voice, urgent. It was now or never. And the pilgrimage that ended in the security of our reserved carriage was made always in the certainty that this time it was to be never, that we alone amongst the small throng of travellers were doomed by some miracle to miss our heaven.

Once we were safely in the charm descended. Joy was secure. My mother, tearful with relief, would take up her twofold task of sympathy with our happiness and the protection of my father from disturbance. There

---

[1] *Paddington* Paddington Station was opened in 1854 as the London terminal of the Great Western Railway, which ran to Bristol, Wales, and the west. The station later became the birthplace of the London Underground railway. The spectacular building has an iron-girder roof covering the train-shed and is attached to the Great Western Hotel.

[2] *repp* Fabric with a corded surface.

[3] *sprigged muslin* Muslin, a lightweight cotton fabric, decorated with an embroidered, woven, or stamped patterns; *dustcloak* Cloak worn to protect one's clothes from dust.

[4] *"zulu" hats* Wide-brimmed hats made of straw.

[5] *frieze* Type of coarse woolen cloth; *deerstalker* Style of tight-fitting, low-crowned hat.

was, however, an interval of licence lasting from the moment he stood up to free himself from his outer garments until he was ensconced, having for a while unbent to share our celebrations, sideways in his corner with his Times.[1]

But the act of keeping comparatively still brought its own rewards. One could hear the faithful rumbling of the wheels, set now to hymn tunes sung quickly, and now, while the train sped rocking, and the telegraph wires, running together, refused to be counted, to a song of its own, the wordless, exultant beating, it seemed, of life itself. And the great events of the day came in the silence to life between memory and anticipation, blossomed in pictures upon the air vibrating to the song of the train. And suddenly there would be Basingstoke. Just a name, standing for a moment on its board on a platform and presently gone. Always for me it was the remotest point of our journey through unknown worlds, and always it filled me with a longing to escape the life I knew. I would look at the faces about me averted towards the platform, and wonder if they too knew where we were—on the borderland of what strange enchantment. … After we had passed I suffered loss, as if something of me, alighting there, had been caught up into a state of being that knew no more of seaside and of home.

Quite different was faraway Exeter, "Xturr, Xturr," the porters would say conversationally. In high, fresh air. The first breath of the air that stood above the little seaside town. And these porters, because they breathed it, were different from other porters. Belonging to the world of seaside, they looked happy and serene, as if, though always there, they knew quite well where they were. But these happy porters stood in the distance at the end of the long day. The sound of the wheels would begin to tell of the long, long hours, and presently, unawares, I was wakening from deep sleep to see the brown hamper open for lunch, to feel older by a long day past, and blissful, waking up after a party, to find another party just begun.

By the time far Exeter was reached we children were knowingly weary. And Exeter, with its message of the sea's nearness, was trial—the last trial of the day; a repetition in miniature of the agonies of Paddington. Like Paddington it was large, and, though comparatively

mild and gentle, still important and awe-inspiring. To my childish imagination it was purely in a spirit of respect for its manner and its size that the train waited so long there. It was at Exeter, too, that the sternest of my grandmothers joined us. She was to the smaller of us little more than an apparition. Once at the seaside she disappeared, doubtless preferring the quiet of independent lodgings to the turmoil of our enchanted house. I cannot remember that she took any part in our life by the shore. Only from time to time came the reminder that somewhere in the bright scene Grannie was abiding. It was the only solemn thought that touched me during the length of our stay. And the conviction —arising in my mind if for long enough I stood staring at the cascading waters beyond our door—that I was, in the opinion of everyone but this laughing stream, a very naughty girl—was cheerful compared to any reflection on Grannie's sojourning. The first intimation of her coming was the departure of my father into the unknown. Once more we were left to anxious helplessness, to the certainty of disaster. Relief would come at last with the sound of Grannie's voice—the high, staccato, wavering voice of deafness and old age, crazing my childish nerves with the imagined horror of a soundless world, chilling me with the fear that the train, having stood so long, would move on while she was being got in. There she would stand, black-robed and towering between her black-robed maid and one of ours, my father behind, and my mother, all anxious helpfulness, inside the carriage door.

But when at last she was arranged within there was compensation for this large, dark presence with its terribly chanting voice. When the speechless greetings were over and my parents had communicated with her by means of repeated shoutings into the mouthpiece of the long tube hanging, a sinuous black garland, across the carriage, she would, before finally folding her hands to sit with eyes contemplative upon each of us in turn, extract and distribute—acid drops. The real lemon drops, that vanished with the application of modern chemistry to lollipops. They were strong. They contained the pure juice of the lemon and the cane, were satisfyingly sweet and acidly refreshing. They were also a noble size, square and thick and with deep bevelled edges. They lasted. But they were slippery. And if, their

---

[1] *Times* Prominent British newspaper.

first charm exhausted, the return of weariness brought a sudden collapse, they slipped and lodged, four-square, halfway down, and the end of the journey was sharp pangs, pangs lessening and ending at last in forgetfulness, till lifting arms were there, and the window and the sea where the train tunnels its way in and out of the red cliffs along its edge. A strange, forbidding sea, ghostly in fading light, as in the morning things that been ghostly. An eternity, a child's whole day with unfamiliar lateness added, had gone to the making of a journey that now takes a few hours. But the days to come were perhaps the richer for the joys and agonies of that tremendous preliminary.

—1928

"Foreword" to *Pilgrimage*

Although the translation of the impulse behind his youthful plan for a tremendous essay on *Les Forces humaines* makes for the population of his great cluster of novels with types rather than with individuals, the power of a sympathetic imagination, uniting him with each character in turn, gives to every portrait the quality of a faithful self-portrait, and his treatment of backgrounds, contemplated with an equally passionate interest and themselves, indeed, individual and unique, would alone qualify Balzac[1] to be called the father of realism.

Less deeply concerned with the interplay of human forces, his first English follower portrays with complete fidelity the lives and adventures of inconspicuous people, and for a while, when in the English literary world it began its career as a useful label, realism was synonymous with Arnold Bennett.[2]

But whereas both Balzac and Bennett, while representing, the one in regard to a relatively concrete and coherent social system, the other in regard to a society already showing signs of disintegration, the turning of the human spirit upon itself, may be called realists by

nature and unawares, their immediate successors possess an articulate creed.[3] They believe themselves to be substituting, for the telescopes of the writers of romance whose lenses they condemn as both rose-coloured and distorting, mirrors of plain glass.

By 1911, though not yet quite a direct supply of documentary material for the dossiers of the *cause célèbre*, Man versus conditions impeached as the authors of his discontent, realist novels are largely explicit satire and protest, and every form of conventionalized human association is being arraigned by biographical and autobiographical novelists.[4]

Since all these novelists happened to be men, the present writer, proposing at this moment to write a novel and looking round for a contemporary pattern, was faced with the choice between following one of her regiments and attempting to produce a feminine equivalent of the current masculine realism. Choosing the latter alternative, she presently set aside, at the bidding of a dissatisfaction that revealed its nature without supplying any suggestion as to the removal of its cause, a considerable mass of manuscript. Aware, as she wrote, of the gradual falling away of the preoccupations that for a while had dictated the briskly moving script, and of the substitution, for these inspiring preoccupations, of a stranger in the form of contemplated reality having for the first time in her experience its own say, and apparently justifying those who acclaim writing as the surest means of discovering the truth about one's own thoughts and beliefs, she had been at the same time increasingly tormented, not only by the failure, of this now so independently assertive reality, adequately to appear within the text, but by its revelation, whencesoever focused, of a hundred faces, any one of which, the moment it was entrapped within the close mesh of direct statement, summoned its fellows to disqualify it.

---

[1] *Balzac* Honoré de Balzac, French journalist and novelist (1799–1850) whose great masterpiece, *La Comédie humaine*, comprises over 90 novels and short stories and includes over 2000 characters from nearly all classes and professions of society.

[2] *Arnold Bennett* English novelist (1897–1931).

[3] *their immediate … creed* Richardson probably had in mind, among others, Somerset Maugham, John Galsworthy, and H.G. Wells as successors to Bennett and Balzac.

[4] *By 1911 … novelists* In the year 1911, Wells published his essay on "The Contemporary Novel," which declared "We are going to write about it all. We are going to write about business and finance and politics and precedence and pretentiousness and decorum and indecorum, until a thousand pretences and ten thousand impostures shrivel in the cold, clear air of our elucidations…. Before we have done, we will have all life within the scope of the novel."

In 1913, the opening pages of the attempted chronicle became the first chapter of "Pilgrimage," written to the accompaniment of a sense of being upon a fresh pathway, an adventure so searching and, sometimes, so joyous as to produce a longing for participation; not quite the same as a longing for publication, whose possibility, indeed, as the book grew, receded to vanishing point.

To a publisher, nevertheless, at the bidding of Mr. J.D. Beresford, the book was ultimately sent. By the time it returned, the second chapter was partly written and the condemned volume, put away and forgotten, would have remained in seclusion but for the persistence of the same kind friend, who acquired and sent it to Edward Garnett, then reading for Messrs Duckworth. In 1915, the covering title being at the moment in use elsewhere, it was published as "Pointed Roofs."

The lonely track, meanwhile, had turned out to be a populous highway. Amongst those who had simultaneously entered it, two figures[1] stood out. One a woman mounted upon a magnificently caparisoned charger, the other a man walking, with eyes devoutly closed, weaving as he went a rich garment of new words wherewith to clothe the antique dark material of his engrossment.

News came from France of one Marcel Proust, said to be producing an unprecedentedly profound and opulent reconstruction of experience focused from within the mind of a single individual, and, since Proust's first volume had been published and several others written by 1913, the France of Balzac now appeared to have produced the earliest adventurer.

Finally, however, the role of pathfinder was declared to have been played by a venerable gentleman, a charmed and charming high priest of nearly all the orthodoxies, inhabiting a softly lit enclosure he mistook, until 1914, for the universe, and celebrated by evolving, for the accommodation of his vast tracts of urbane commentary, a prose style demanding, upon the first reading, a perfection of sustained concentration akin to that which brought it forth, and bestowing, again upon the first reading, the recreative delights peculiar to this form of spiritual exercise.

And while, indeed, it is possible to claim for Henry James, keeping the reader incessantly watching the conflict of human forces through the eye of a single observer, rather than taking him, before the drama begins, upon a tour amongst the properties, or breaking in with descriptive introductions of the players as one by one they enter his enclosed resounding chamber where no plant grows and no mystery pours in from the unheeded stars, a far from inconsiderable technical influence, it was nevertheless not without a sense of relief that the present writer recently discovered, in "Wilhelm Meister,"[2] the following manifesto:

> In the novel, reflections and incidents should be featured; in drama, character and action. The novel must proceed slowly, and the thought-processes of the principal figure must, by one device or another, hold up the development of the whole. ... The hero of the novel must be acted upon, or, at any rate, not himself the principal operator. ... Grandison, Clarissa, Pamela, the Vicar of Wakefield, and Tom Jones himself,[3] even where they are not acted upon, are still retarding personalities and all the incidents are, in a certain measure, modelled according to their thoughts.

Phrases began to appear, formulae devised to meet the exigencies of literary criticism. "The Stream of Consciousness" lyrically led the way, to be gladly welcomed by all who could persuade themselves of the possibility of comparing consciousness to a stream. Its transatlantic successors, "Interior Monologue" and "Slow-motion Photography," may each be granted a certain technical applicability leaving them, to this extent, unhampered by the defects of their qualities.

Lives in plenty have been devoted to the critic's exacting art and a lifetime might be spent in engrossed contemplation of the movements of its continuous ballet. When the dancers tread living boards, the boards will sometimes be heard to groan. The present writer groans, gently and resignedly, beneath the reiterated tap-tap accusing her of feminism, of failure to perceive the value of the distinctively masculine

---

1   *two figures*   Virginia Woolf and James Joyce.

2   *Wilhelm Meister*   German writer and philosopher Johann Wolfgang van Goethe's novel *Wilhelm Meister's Apprenticeship* (1795–96).

3   *Grandison ... himself*   Protagonists of Samuel Richardson's *History of Sir Charles Grandison* (1753–54), *Clarisa* (1747–48), and *Pamela; or, Virtue Rewarded* (1740); Oliver Goldsmith's *The Vicar of Wakefield* (1766); and Henry Fielding's *The History of Tom Jones, A Foundling* (1749).

intelligence, of pre-War sentimentality, of post-War Freudianity. But when her work is danced upon for being unpunctuated and therefore unreadable, she is moved to cry aloud. For here is truth.

Feminine prose, as Charles Dickens and James Joyce have delightfully shown themselves to be aware, should properly be unpunctuated, moving from point to point without formal obstructions. And the author of "Pilgrimage" must confess to an early habit of ignoring, while writing, the lesser of the stereotyped system of signs, and, further, when finally sprinkling in what appeared to be necessary, to a small unconscious departure from current usage. While meeting approval, first from the friend who discovered and pointed it out to her, then from an editor who welcomed the article she wrote to elucidate and justify it,[1] and, recently,

by the inclusion of this article in a text-book for students of journalism and its translation into French, the small innovation, in further complicating the already otherwise sufficiently complicated task of the official reader, helped to produce the chaos for which she is justly reproached.

For the opportunity, afforded by the present publishers, of eliminating this source of a reputation for creating avoidable difficulties, and of assembling the scattered chapters of "Pilgrimage" in their proper relationship, the author desires here to express her gratitude and, further, to offer to all those readers who have persisted in spite of every obstacle, a heart-felt apology.

—1938

---

[1] *the article ... it*   "About Punctuation," first published in *Adelphi* 1.1 (April 1924).

E.M. FORSTER
1879 – 1970

When E.M. Forster died on 7 June 1970 he was widely acknowledged as one of the great figures of English literature. King's College, Cambridge, had recognized Forster's role in English literature by appointing him an Honorary Fellow in 1946. In 1953, Queen Elizabeth II paid tribute to Forster's creative talent by awarding him the Order of Merit, Britain's highest honor for artistic achievement. Forster's place in the twentieth-century literary pantheon was undercut on two fronts in the 1960s, however. To the avant-garde, his traditional approach to narrative and to the creation of character was out of step with a period that put a premium on the experimental; so too was his fine sense of social nuance and delicacy of touch. And to some others—in a time when homophobia was prevalent—the revelation of Forster's homosexuality was a further alienating factor. More recently, however, Forster's work has received renewed critical attention. Five film versions of Forster's novels have exposed his work to an international audience.

Known as Morgan throughout his life, Forster was born in London on New Year's Day 1879. His

father, Edward Morgan Llewellyn Forster, died of consumption less than two years after Morgan's birth. He was brought up by his mother, Alice ("Lily") Whichelo Forster and various aunts, including his great-aunt, Marianne Thornton, whose biography he would later write. Forster had a rich and close relationship with his mother, and her death in 1945 was a profound loss. Forster spent much of his childhood at Rooksnest, a house in Hertfordshire, England that he nostalgically evoked in his fourth novel, *Howards End* (1910). In 1893, Forster and his mother moved to Tonbridge, where he attended Tonbridge School. Forster's unhappiness at the school is vividly portrayed in his representation of the Sawston School in *The Longest Journey* (1907), his second novel.

Forster flourished during his years of study at Cambridge (1897–1901) and he later described the university, in *Goldsworthy Lowes Dickinson* (1934), as a place where "people and books reinforced each other, intelligence joined hands with affection, speculation became a passion, and discussion was made profound by love." Forster was elected to the Cambridge Apostles, a secret society that fostered discussion of controversial topics, including sexuality. Many of the friendships he cultivated with his fellow Apostles—several of whom became closely associated with the Bloomsbury Group—lasted until the end of his life. At Cambridge—where in the 1930s it was more possible than anywhere else in England for gay intellectuals to feel at home—he fell in love with a fellow undergraduate, Hugh Meredith, the model for Clive Durham in Forster's posthumously published novel *Maurice* (1971).

After graduating, Forster decided to travel. He and his mother spent a year in Italy and Austria that proved invaluable in fostering his creative energy. Forster explains in his introduction to *Collected Short Stories* (1948) that his first story, "The Story of a Panic," came to him as a kind of epiphany while traveling through Italy with his mother: "I took a walk near Ravello. I sat down in a valley, a few miles above the town, and suddenly the first chapter of the story rushed in to my mind as if it had waited for me there. I received it as an entity and wrote it out as soon as I returned to the hotel." The intense creative inspiration associated with travel and new geographical locations is in evidence in many of Forster's works. In particular, his travels in India—as a tourist in 1912 and as the private secretary to the Maharajah of Dewas in 1921—provided the material for his fifth novel, *A Passage to India* (1924).

In his most significant novels—*A Room With a View* (1908), *Howard's End*, and *A Passage to India*—Forster managed to combine in a fashion unique to his generation an extraordinary alertness to the nuances of social class, to the particularities of individuals within the social milieu, the human condition in general, and to overarching spiritual issues. If at times Forster's prose may have felt the strain as he grasped for a spiritual as well as a social or psychological reality, those moments are few and far between; Forster remains among the most readable and interesting twentieth-century writers of fiction.

In 1930, Forster fell in love with Bob Buckingham, a police constable in London. Their relationship was complicated by Buckingham's marriage in 1932, but eventually Forster and Buckingham's new wife May established a close friendship. Buckingham frequently accompanied Forster on his travels, and the Buckinghams named their son, Morgan, in honor of his godfather. In 1970, when Forster suffered the last of several strokes in his rooms at Cambridge, he was brought to the Buckinghams' home, where he died.

Forster was a prominent public intellectual, whose belief in freedom of expression led him vigorously to protest the suppression of Radclyffe Hall's lesbian novel *The Well of Loneliness* (1928) and to testify as a defense witness in the obscenity trial of D.H. Lawrence's *Lady Chatterley's Lover* (1960). As the first president of the National Council of Civil Liberties (1934), he was a vocal critic of England's Sedition Bill and succeeded in discrediting the legislation. Forster's commitment to civil liberties had a highly personal resonance; until 1967, homosexuality acts were considered criminal offences in England. Not surprisingly, during his lifetime Forster did not wish to risk publishing *Maurice*, a novel dealing with homosexual themes that had a happy ending. The novel, completed in 1914 and periodically revised until 1960, was finally published in 1971, a year after Forster's death.

In addition to fiction, Forster's inspiration found outlets in several other creative forms: he recorded over 130 broadcasts for the British Broadcasting Corporation, the vast majority of them promoting English literature (1928–1960); he co-authored, with Eric Crozier, the libretto for Benjamin Britten's opera *Billy Budd* (1951); he published several works of travel writing, including *Alexandria: A History and a Guide* (1922) and *The Hill of Devi* (1953); he gathered his reviews and essays into two collections, *Aspects of the Novel* (1927) and *Two Cheers for Democracy* (1951); and he wrote biographies of his great-aunt, *Marianne Thornton* (1956), and his Cambridge mentor, *Goldsworthy Lowes Dickinson* (1934).

⌘ ⌘ ⌘

The Road from Colonus

I

For no very intelligible reason, Mr. Lucas had hurried ahead of his party. He was perhaps reaching the age at which independence becomes valuable, because it is so soon to be lost. Tired of attention and consideration, he liked breaking away from the younger members to ride by himself, and to dismount unassisted. Perhaps he also relished that more subtle pleasure of being kept waiting for lunch, and of telling the others on their arrival that it was of no consequence.

So, with childish impatience, he battered the animal's sides with his heels, and made the muleteer bang it with a thick stick and prick it with a sharp one, and jolted down the hillsides through clumps of flowering shrubs and stretches of anemones and asphodel, till he heard the sound of running water, and came in sight of the group of plane trees where they were to have their meal.

Even in England those trees would have been remarkable, so huge were they, so interlaced, so magnificently clothed in quivering green. And here in Greece they were unique, the one cool spot in that hard brilliant landscape, already scorched by the heat of an April sun. In their midst was hidden a tiny Khan or country inn, a frail mud building with a broad wooden balcony in which sat an old woman spinning, while a small brown pig, eating orange peel, stood beside her. On the wet earth below squatted two children, playing some primaeval game with their fingers; and their mother, none too clean either, was messing with some rice inside. As Mrs. Forman would have said, it was all very Greek, and the fastidious Mr. Lucas felt thankful that they were bringing their own food with them, and should eat it in the open air.

Still, he was glad to be there—the muleteer had helped him off—and glad that Mrs. Forman was not there to forestall his opinions—glad even that he should not see Ethel for quite half an hour. Ethel was his youngest daughter, still unmarried. She was unselfish and affectionate, and it was generally understood that she was to devote her life to her father, and be the comfort of his old age. Mrs. Forman always referred to her as Antigone,[1] and Mr. Lucas tried to settle down to the role of Oedipus, which seemed the only one that public opinion allowed him.

He had this in common with Oedipus, that he was growing old. Even to himself it had become obvious. He had lost interest in other people's affairs, and seldom attended when they spoke to him. He was fond of talking himself but often forgot what he was going to say, and even when he succeeded, it seldom seemed worth the effort. His phrases and gestures had become stiff and set, his anecdotes, once so successful, fell flat, his silence was as meaningless as his speech. Yet he had led a healthy, active life, had worked steadily, made money, educated his children. There was nothing and no one to blame: he was simply growing old.

At the present moment, here he was in Greece, and one of the dreams of his life was realized. Forty years ago he had caught the fever of Hellenism, and all his life he had felt that could he but visit that land, he would not have lived in vain. But Athens had been dusty, Delphi wet, Thermopylae flat, and he had listened with amazement and cynicism to the rapturous exclamations of his companions. Greece was like England: it was a man who was growing old, and it made no difference whether that man looked at the Thames or the Eurotas. It was his last hope of contradicting that logic of experience, and it was failing.

Yet Greece had done something for him, though he did not know it. It had made him discontented, and there are stirrings of life in discontent. He knew that he was not the victim of continual ill-luck. Something great was wrong, and he was pitted against no mediocre or accidental enemy. For the last month a strange desire had possessed him to die fighting.

"Greece is the land for young people," he said to himself as he stood under the plane trees, "but I will enter into it, I will possess it. Leaves shall be green again, water shall be sweet, the sky shall be blue. They were so forty years ago, and I will win them back. I do mind being old, and I will pretend no longer."

He took two steps forward, and immediately cold waters were gurgling over his ankle.

"Where does the water come from?" he asked himself. "I do not even know that." He remembered that all the hillsides were dry; yet here the road was suddenly covered with flowing streams.

He stopped still in amazement, saying: "Water out of a tree—out of a hollow tree? I never saw nor thought of that before."

For the enormous plane that leant towards the Khan was hollow—it had been burnt out for charcoal—and from its living trunk there gushed an impetuous spring, coating the bark with fern and moss, and flowing over the mule track to create fertile meadows beyond. The simple country folk had paid to beauty and mystery such tribute as they could, for in the rind of the tree a shrine was cut, holding a lamp and a little picture of the Virgin, inheritor of the Naiad's and Dryad's[2] joint

---

[1] *Antigone*   Daughter of King Oedipus and his mother, Jocasta. In his play *Oedipus at Colonus*, the Greek dramatist Sophocles (496–06 BCE) tells how Oedipus, after stabbing out his own eyes and being banished from Thebes by his sons (who have assumed the throne), wanders for several years, accompanied only by his daughter, Antigone. The two finally arrive at Colonus, outside of Athens, where the King of Athens welcomes them.

[2] *Naiad and Dryad*   Name for a water and a wood nymph, respectively.

abode.

"I never saw anything so marvellous before," said Mr. Lucas. "I could even step inside the trunk and see where the water comes from."

For a moment he hesitated to violate the shrine. Then he remembered with a smile his own thought—"the place shall be mine; I will enter it and possess it"—and leapt almost aggressively on to a stone within.

The water pressed up steadily and noiselessly from the hollow roots and hidden crevices of the plane, forming a wonderful amber pool ere it spilt over the lip of bark on to the earth outside. Mr. Lucas tasted it and it was sweet, and when he looked up the black funnel of the trunk he saw sky which was blue, and some leaves which were green; and he remembered, without smiling, another of his thoughts.

Others had been before him—indeed he had a curious sense of companionship. Little votive offerings to the presiding Power were fastened on to the bark—tiny arms and legs and eyes in tin, grotesque models of the brain or the heart—all tokens of some recovery of strength or wisdom or love. There was no such thing as the solitude of nature, for the sorrows and joys of humanity had pressed even into the bosom of a tree. He spread out his arms and steadied himself against the soft charred wood, and then slowly leant back, till his body was resting on the trunk behind. His eyes closed, and he had the strange feeling of one who is moving, yet at peace— the feeling of the swimmer, who, after long struggling with chopping seas, finds that after all the tide will sweep him to his goal.

So he lay motionless, conscious only of the stream below his feet, and that all things were a stream, in which he was moving.

He was aroused at last by a shock—the shock of an arrival perhaps, for when he opened his eyes, something unimagined, indefinable, had passed over all things, and made them intelligible and good.

There was meaning in the stoop of the old woman over her work, and in the quick motions of the little pig, and in her diminishing globe of wool. A young man came singing over the streams on a mule, and there was beauty in his pose and sincerity in his greeting. The sun made no accidental patterns upon the spreading roots of the trees, and there was intention in the nodding clumps of asphodel, and in the music of the water. To Mr. Lucas, who, in a brief space of time, had discovered not only Greece, but England and all the world and life, there seemed nothing ludicrous in the desire to hang within the tree another votive offering—a little model of an entire man.

"Why, here's papa, playing at being Merlin."

All unnoticed they had arrived—Ethel, Mrs. Forman, Mr. Graham, and the English-speaking dragoman.[1] Mr. Lucas peered out at them suspiciously. They had suddenly become unfamiliar, and all that they did seemed strained and coarse.

"Allow me to give you a hand," said Mr. Graham, a young man who was always polite to his elders.

Mr. Lucas felt annoyed. "Thank you, I can manage perfectly well by myself," he replied. His foot slipped as he stepped out of the tree, and went into the spring.

"Oh papa, my papa!" said Ethel, "what are you doing? Thank goodness I have got a change for you on the mule."

She tended him carefully, giving him clean socks and dry boots, and then sat him down on the rug beside the lunch basket, while she went with the others to explore the grove.

They came back in ecstasies, in which Mr. Lucas tried to join. But he found them intolerable. Their enthusiasm was superficial, commonplace, and spasmodic. They had no perception of the coherent beauty that was flowering around them. He tried at least to explain his feelings, and what he said was:

"I am altogether pleased with the appearance of this place. It impresses me very favourably. The trees are fine, remarkably fine for Greece, and there is something very poetic in the spring of clear running water. The people too seem kindly and civil. It is decidedly an attractive place."

Mrs. Forman upbraided him for his tepid praise.

"Oh, it is a place in a thousand!" she cried, "I could live and die here! I really would stop if I had not to be back at Athens! It reminds me of the Colonus of Sophocles."

"Well, *I* must stop," said Ethel. "I positively must."

"Yes, do! You and your father! Antigone and Oedipus. Of course you must stop at Colonus!"

---

[1] *dragoman* Interpreter.

Mr. Lucas was almost breathless with excitement. When he stood within the tree, he had believed that his happiness would be independent of locality. But these few minutes' conversation had undeceived him. He no longer trusted himself to journey through the world, for old thoughts, old wearinesses might be waiting to rejoin him as soon as he left the shade of the planes, and the music of the virgin water. To sleep in the Khan with the gracious, kind-eyed country people, to watch the bats flit about within the globe of shade, and see the moon turn the golden patterns into silver—one such night would place him beyond relapse, and confirm him for ever in the kingdom he had regained. But all his lips could say was: "I should be willing to put in a night here."

"You mean a week, papa! It would be sacrilege to put in less."

"A week then, a week," said his lips, irritated at being corrected, while his heart was leaping with joy. All through lunch he spoke to them no more, but watched the place he should know so well, and the people who would so soon be his companions and friends. The inmates of the Khan only consisted of an old woman, a middle-aged woman, a young man and two children, and to none of them had he spoken, yet he loved them as he loved everything that moved or breathed or existed beneath the benedictory shade of the planes.

"*En route!*" said the shrill voice of Mrs. Forman. "Ethel! Mr. Graham! The best of things must end."

"Tonight," thought Mr. Lucas, "they will light the little lamp by the shrine. And when we all sit together on the balcony, perhaps they will tell me which offerings they put up."

"I beg your pardon, Mr. Lucas," said Graham, "but they want to fold up the rug you are sitting on."

Mr. Lucas got up, saying to himself: "Ethel shall go to bed first, and then I will try to tell them about my offering too—for it is a thing I must do. I think they will understand if I am left with them alone."

Ethel touched him on the cheek. "Papa! I've called you three times. All the mules are here."

"Mules? What mules?"

"Our mules. We're all waiting. Oh, Mr. Graham, do help my father on."

"I don't know what you're talking about, Ethel."

"My dearest papa, we must start. You know we have to get to Olympia tonight."

Mr. Lucas in pompous, confident tones replied: "I always did wish, Ethel, that you had a better head for plans. You know perfectly well that we are putting in a week here. It is your own suggestion."

Ethel was startled into impoliteness. "What a perfectly ridiculous idea. You must have known I was joking. Of course I meant I wished we could."

"Ah! if we could only do what we wished!" sighed Mrs. Forman, already seated on her mule.

"Surely," Ethel continued in calmer tones, "you didn't think I meant it."

"Most certainly I did. I have made all my plans on the supposition that we are stopping here, and it will be extremely inconvenient, indeed, impossible for me to start."

He delivered this remark with an air of great conviction, and Mrs. Forman and Mr. Graham had to turn away to hide their smiles.

"I am sorry I spoke so carelessly; it was wrong of me. But, you know, we can't break up our party, and even one night here would make us miss the boat at Patras."

Mrs. Forman, in an aside, called Mr. Graham's attention to the excellent way in which Ethel managed her father.

"I don't mind about the Patras boat. You said that we should stop here, and we are stopping."

It seemed as if the inhabitants of the Khan had divined in some mysterious way that the altercation touched them. The old woman stopped her spinning, while the young man and the two children stood behind Mr. Lucas, as if supporting him.

Neither arguments nor entreaties moved him. He said little, but he was absolutely determined, because for the first time he saw his daily life aright. What need had he to return to England? Who would miss him? His friends were dead or cold. Ethel loved him in a way, but, as was right, she had other interests. His other children he seldom saw. He had only one other relative, his sister Julia, whom he both feared and hated. It was no effort to struggle. He would be a fool as well as a coward if he stirred from the place which brought him happiness and peace.

At last Ethel, to humour him, and not disinclined to

air her modern Greek, went into the Khan with the astonished dragoman to look at the rooms. The woman inside received them with loud welcomes, and the young man, when no one was looking, began to lead Mr. Lucas' mule to the stable.

"Drop it, you brigand!" shouted Graham, who always declared that foreigners could understand English if they chose. He was right, for the man obeyed, and they all stood waiting for Ethel's return.

She emerged at last, with close-gathered skirts, followed by the dragoman bearing the little pig, which he had bought at a bargain.

"My dear papa, I will do all I can for you, but stop in that Khan—no."

"Are there—fleas?" asked Mrs. Forman.

Ethel intimated that "fleas" was not the word.

"Well, I'm afraid that settles it," said Mrs. Forman, "I know how particular Mr. Lucas is."

"It does not settle it," said Mr. Lucas. "Ethel, you go on. I do not want you. I don't know why I ever consulted you. I shall stop here alone."

"That is absolute nonsense," said Ethel, losing her temper. "How can you be left alone at your age? How would you get your meals or your bath? All your letters are waiting for you at Patras. You'll miss the boat. That means missing the London operas, and upsetting all your engagements for the month. And as if you could travel by yourself!"

"They might knife you," was Mr. Graham's contribution. The Greeks said nothing; but whenever Mr. Lucas looked their way, they beckoned him towards the Khan. The children would even have drawn him by the coat, and the old woman on the balcony stopped her almost completed spinning, and fixed him with mysterious appealing eyes. As he fought, the issue assumed gigantic proportions, and he believed that he was not merely stopping because he had regained youth or seen beauty or found happiness, but because in that place and with those people a supreme event was awaiting him which would transfigure the face of the world. The moment was so tremendous that he abandoned words and arguments as useless, and rested on the strength of his mighty unrevealed allies: silent men, murmuring water, and whispering trees. For the whole place called with one voice, articulate to him, and

his garrulous opponents became every minute more meaningless and absurd. Soon they would be tired and go chattering away into the sun, leaving him to the cool grove and the moonlight and the destiny he foresaw.

Mrs. Forman and the dragoman had indeed already started, amid the piercing screams of the little pig, and the struggle might have gone on indefinitely if Ethel had not called in Mr. Graham.

"Can you help me?" she whispered. "He is absolutely unmanageable."

"I'm no good at arguing—but if I could help you in any other way"—and he looked down complacently at his well-made figure.

Ethel hesitated. Then she said: "Help me in any way you can. After all, it is for his good that we do it."

"Then have his mule led up behind him."

So when Mr. Lucas thought he had gained the day, he suddenly felt himself lifted off the ground, and sat sideways on the saddle, and at the same time the mule started off at a trot. He said nothing, for he had nothing to say, and even his face showed little emotion as he felt the shade pass and heard the sound of the water cease. Mr. Graham was running at his side, hat in hand, apologizing.

"I know I had no business to do it, and I do beg your pardon awfully. But I do hope that some day you too will feel that I was—damn!"

A stone had caught him in the middle of the back. It was thrown by the little boy, who was pursuing them along the mule track. He was followed by his sister, also throwing stones.

Ethel screamed to the dragoman, who was some way ahead with Mrs. Forman, but before he could rejoin them, another adversary appeared. It was the young Greek, who had cut them off in front, and now dashed down at Mr. Lucas' bridle. Fortunately Graham was an expert boxer, and it did not take him a moment to beat down the youth's feeble defence, and to send him sprawling with a bleeding mouth into the asphodel. By this time the dragoman had arrived, the children, alarmed at the fate of their brother, had desisted, and the rescue party, if such it is to be considered, retired in disorder to the trees.

"Little devils!" said Graham, laughing with triumph. "That's the modern Greek all over. Your father meant money if he stopped, and they consider we were taking it out of their pocket."

"Oh, they are terrible—simply savages! I don't know how I shall ever thank you. You've saved my father."

"I only hope you didn't think me brutal."

"No," replied Ethel with a little sigh. "I admire strength."

Meanwhile the cavalcade reformed, and Mr. Lucas, who, as Mrs. Forman said, bore his disappointment wonderfully well, was put comfortably on to his mule. They hurried up the opposite hillside, fearful of another attack, and it was not until they had left the eventful place far behind that Ethel found an opportunity to speak to her father and ask his pardon for the way she had treated him.

"You seemed so different, dear father, and you quite frightened me. Now I feel that you are your old self again."

He did not answer, and she concluded that he was not unnaturally offended at her behaviour.

By one of those curious tricks of mountain scenery, the place they had left an hour before suddenly reappeared far below them. The Khan was hidden under the green dome, but in the open there still stood three figures, and through the pure air rose up a faint cry of defiance or farewell.

Mr. Lucas stopped irresolutely, and let the reins fall from his hand.

"Come, father dear," said Ethel gently.

He obeyed, and in another moment a spur of the hill hid the dangerous scene for ever.

2

It was breakfast time, but the gas was alight, owing to the fog. Mr. Lucas was in the middle of an account of a bad night he had spent. Ethel, who was to be married in a few weeks, had her arms on the table, listening.

"First the door bell rang, then you came back from the theatre. Then the dog started, and after the dog the cat. And at three in the morning a young hooligan passed by singing. Oh yes: then there was the water gurgling in the pipe above my head."

"I think that was only the bath water running away," said Ethel, looking rather worn.

"Well, there's nothing I dislike more than running

water. It's perfectly impossible to sleep in the house. I shall give it up. I shall give notice next quarter. I shall tell the landlord plainly, 'The reason I am giving up the house is this: it is perfectly impossible to sleep in it.' If he says—says—well, what has he got to say?"

"Some more toast, father?"

"Thank you, my dear." He took it, and there was an interval of peace.

But he soon recommenced. "I'm not going to submit to the practising next door as tamely as they think. I wrote and told them so—didn't I?"

"Yes," said Ethel, who had taken care that the letter should not reach. "I have seen the governess, and she has promised to arrange it differently. And Aunt Julia hates noise. It will sure to be all right."

Her aunt, being the only unattached member of the family, was coming to keep house for her father when she left him. The reference was not a happy one, and Mr. Lucas commenced a series of half articulate sighs, which was only stopped by the arrival of the post.

"Oh, what a parcel!" cried Ethel. "For me! What can it be! Greek stamps. This is most exciting!"

It proved to be some asphodel bulbs, sent by Mrs. Forman from Athens for planting in the conservatory.

"Doesn't it bring it all back! You remember the asphodels, father. And all wrapped up in Greek newspapers. I wonder if I can read them still. I used to be able to, you know."

She rattled on, hoping to conceal the laughter of the children next door—a favourite source of querulousness at breakfast time.

"Listen to me! 'A rural disaster.' Oh, I've hit on something sad. But never mind. 'Last Tuesday at Plataniste, in the province of Messenia, a shocking tragedy occurred. A large tree'—aren't I getting on well?—'blew down in the night and'—wait a minute—oh, dear! 'crushed to death the five occupants of the little Khan there, who had apparently been sitting in the balcony. The body of Maria Rhomaides, the aged proprietress, and of her daughter, aged forty-six, were easily recognizable, whereas that of her grandson'—oh, the rest is really too horrid; I wish I had never tried it, and what's more I feel to have heard the name Plataniste before. We didn't stop there, did we, in the spring?"

"We had lunch," said Mr. Lucas, with a faint

expression of trouble on his vacant face. "Perhaps it was where the dragoman bought the pig."

"Of course," said Ethel in a nervous voice. "Where the dragoman bought the little pig. How terrible!"

"Very terrible!" said her father, whose attention was wandering to the noisy children next door. Ethel suddenly started to her feet with genuine interest.

"Good gracious!" she exclaimed. "This is an old paper. It happened not lately but in April—the night of Tuesday the eighteenth—and we—we must have been there in the afternoon."

"So we were," said Mr. Lucas. She put her hand to her heart, scarcely able to speak.

"Father, dear father, I must say it: you wanted to stop there. All those people, those poor half savage people, tried to keep you, and they're dead. The whole place, it says, is in ruins, and even the stream has changed its course. Father, dear, if it had not been for me, and if Arthur had not helped me, you must have been killed."

Mr. Lucas waved his hand irritably. "It is not a bit of good speaking to the governess, I shall write to the landlord and say, 'The reason I am giving up the house is this: the dog barks, the children next door are intolerable, and I cannot stand the noise of running water.'"

Ethel did not check his babbling. She was aghast at the narrowness of the escape, and for a long time kept silence. At last she said: "Such a marvellous deliverance does make one believe in Providence."

Mr. Lucas, who was still composing his letter to the landlord, did not reply.

—1911

from *What I Believe*

I do not believe in Belief. But this is an Age of Faith, and there are so many militant creeds that, in self-defence, one has to formulate a creed of one's own. Tolerance, good temper, and sympathy are no longer enough in a world which is rent by religious and racial persecution, in a world where ignorance rules, and Science, who ought to have ruled, plays the subservient pimp. Tolerance, good temper, and sympathy—they are

what matter really, and if the human race is not to collapse they must come to the front before long. But for the moment they are not enough, their action is no stronger than a flower, battered beneath a military jackboot. They want stiffening, even if the process coarsens them. Faith, to my mind, is a stiffening process, a sort of mental starch, which ought to be applied as sparingly as possible. I dislike the stuff. I do not believe in it, for its own sake, at all. Herein I probably differ from most people, who believe in Belief, and are only sorry they cannot swallow even more than they do. My law-givers are Erasmus and Montaigne,[1] not Moses and St. Paul. My temple stands not upon Mount Moriah but in that Elysian Field[2] where even the immoral are admitted. My motto is: "Lord, I disbelieve—help thou my unbelief."

I have, however, to live in an Age of Faith—the sort of epoch I used to hear praised when I was a boy. It is extremely unpleasant really. It is bloody in every sense of the word. And I have to keep my end up in it. Where do I start?

With personal relationships. Here is something comparatively solid in a world full of violence and cruelty. Not absolutely solid, for Psychology has split and shattered the idea of a "Person," and has shown that there is something incalculable in each of us, which may at any moment rise to the surface and destroy our normal balance. We don't know what we are like. We can't know what other people are like. How, then, can we put any trust in personal relationships, or cling to them in the gathering political storm? In theory we cannot. But in practice we can and do. Though A is not unchangeably A, or B unchangeably B, there can still be love and loyalty between the two. For the purpose of living one has to assume that the personality is solid, and the "self" is an entity, and to ignore all contrary evidence. And since to ignore evidence is one of the characteristics of faith, I certainly can proclaim that I believe in personal relationships.

---

[1] *Erasmus* Humanist scholar Desiderius Erasmus (c. 1467–1536); *Montaigne* French essayist Michel de Montaigne (1533–92).

[2] *Mount Moriah* Biblical name for the hill of East Jerusalem that was supposedly the site of Solomon's temple; *Elysian Field* In Greek mythology, the place where those favored by the gods reside after death.

Starting from them, I get a little order into the contemporary chaos. One must be fond of people and trust them if one is not to make a mess of life, and it is therefore essential that they should not let one down. They often do. The moral of which is that I must, myself, be as reliable as possible, and this I try to be. But reliability is not a matter of contract—that is the main difference between the world of personal relationships and the world of business relationships. It is a matter for the heart, which signs no documents. In other words, reliability is impossible unless there is a natural warmth. Most men possess this warmth, though they often have bad luck and get chilled. Most of them, even when they are politicians, *want* to keep faith. And one can, at all events, show one's own little light here, one's own poor little trembling flame, with the knowledge that it is not the only light that is shining in the darkness, and not the only one which the darkness does not comprehend. Personal relations are despised today. They are regarded as bourgeois luxuries, as products of a time of fair weather which is now past, and we are urged to get rid of them, and to dedicate ourselves to some movement or cause instead. I hate the idea of causes, and if I had to choose between betraying my country and betraying my friend I hope I should have the guts to betray my country. Such a choice may scandalize the modern reader, and he may stretch out his patriotic hand to the telephone at once and ring up the police. It would not have shocked Dante,[1] though. Dante places Brutus and Cassius in the lowest circle of Hell because they had chosen to betray their friend Julius Caesar rather than their country Rome. Probably one will not be asked to make such an agonizing choice. Still, there lies at the back of every creed something terrible and hard for which the worshipper may one day be required to suffer, and there is even a terror and a hardness in this creed of personal relationships, urbane and mild though it sounds. Love and loyalty to an individual can run counter to the claims of the State. When they do—down with the State, say I, which means that the State would down me.

This brings me along to Democracy, "Even love, the beloved Republic, That feeds upon freedom and lives."[2] Democracy is not a beloved Republic really, and never will be. But it is less hateful than other contemporary forms of government, and to that extent it deserves our support. It does start from the assumption that the individual is important, and that all types are needed to make a civilization. It does not divide its citizens into the bossers and the bossed—as an efficiency-regime tends to do. The people I admire most are those who are sensitive and want to create something or discover something, and do not see life in terms of power, and such people get more of a chance under a democracy than elsewhere. They found religions, great or small, or they produce literature and art, or they do disinterested scientific research, or they may be what is called "ordinary people," who are creative in their private lives, bring up their children decently, for instance, or help their neighbours. All these people need to express themselves; they cannot do so unless society allows them liberty to do so, and the society which allows them most liberty is a democracy.

Democracy has another merit. It allows criticism, and if there is not public criticism there are bound to be hushed-up scandals. That is why I believe in the press, despite all its lies and vulgarity, and why I believe in Parliament. Parliament is often sneered at because it is a Talking Shop.[3] I believe in it *because* it is a talking shop. I believe in the Private Member who makes himself a nuisance. He gets snubbed and is told that he is cranky or ill-informed, but he does expose abuses which would otherwise never have been mentioned, and very often an abuse gets put right just by being mentioned. Occasionally, too, a well-meaning public official starts losing his head in the cause of efficiency, and thinks himself God Almighty. Such officials are particularly frequent in the Home Office. Well, there will be questions about them in Parliament sooner or later, and then they will have to mind their steps. Whether Parliament is either a representative body or an

---

[1] *Dante* Italian poet Dante Alighieri (1265–1321), author of the famous epic poem *The Divine Comedy*, to which Forster refers here.

[2] *Even ... lives* From Algernon Charles Swinburne's "Hertha" (1871), line 190.

[3] *Talking Shop* I.e., a place of idle talk. A derogatory term commonly applied to Parliament, and particularly to the House of Commons.

efficient one is questionable, but I value it because it criticizes and talks, and because its chatter gets widely reported.

So two cheers for Democracy: one because it admits variety, and two because it permits criticism. Two cheers are quite enough: there is no occasion to give three. Only Love the Beloved Republic deserves that.

What about Force, though? While we are trying to be sensitive and advanced and affectionate and tolerant, an unpleasant question pops up: does not all society rest upon force? If a government cannot count upon the police and the army, how can it hope to rule? And if an individual gets knocked on the head or sent to a labour camp, of what significance are his opinions?

This dilemma does not worry me as much as it does some. I realize that all society rests upon force. But all the great creative actions, all the decent human relations, occur during the intervals when force has not managed to come to the front. These intervals are what matter. I want them to be as frequent and as lengthy as possible, and I call them "civilization." Some people idealize force and pull it into the foreground and worship it, instead of keeping it in the background as long as possible. I think they make a mistake, and I think that their opposites, the mystics, err even more when they declare that force does not exist. I believe that it exists, and that one of our jobs is to prevent it from getting out of its box. It gets out sooner or later, and then it destroys us and all the lovely things which we have made. But it is not out all the time, for the fortunate reason that the strong are so stupid. ...

So that is what I feel about force and violence. It is, alas! the ultimate reality on this earth, but it does not always get to the front. Some people call its absences "decadence"; I call them "civilization" and find in such interludes the chief justification for the human experiment. I look the other way until fate strikes me. Whether this is due to courage or to cowardice in my own case I cannot be sure. But I know that, if men had not looked the other way in the past, nothing of any value would survive. The people I respect most behave as if they were immortal and as if society was eternal. Both assumptions are false: both of them must be accepted as true if we are to go on eating and working and loving, and are to keep open a few breathing-holes

for the human spirit. No millennium seems likely to descend upon humanity; no better and stronger League of Nations will be instituted; no form of Christianity and no alternative to Christianity will bring peace to the world or integrity to the individual; no "change of heart" will occur. And yet we need not despair, indeed, we cannot despair; the evidence of history shows us that men have always insisted on behaving creatively under the shadow of the sword; that they have done their artistic and scientific and domestic stuff for the sake of doing it, and that we had better follow their example under the shadow of the aeroplanes. Others, with more vision or courage than myself, see the salvation of humanity ahead, and will dismiss my conception of civilization as paltry, a sort of tip-and-run game. Certainly it is presumptuous to say that we *cannot* improve, and that Man, who has only been in power for a few thousand years, will never learn to make use of his power. All I mean is that, if people continue to kill one another as they do, the world cannot get better than it is, and that, since there are more people than formerly, and their means for destroying one another superior, the world may well get worse. What is good in people—and consequently in the world—is their insistence on creation, their belief in friendship and loyalty for their own sakes; and, though Violence remains and is, indeed, the major partner in this muddled establishment, I believe that creativeness remains too, and will always assume direction when violence sleeps. So, though I am not an optimist, I cannot agree with Sophocles[1] that it were better never to have been born. And although, like Horace,[2] I see no evidence that each batch of births is superior to the last, I leave the field open for the more complacent view. This is such a difficult moment to live in, one cannot help getting gloomy and also a bit rattled, and perhaps short-sighted.

In search of a refuge, we may perhaps turn to hero-worship. But here we shall get no help, in my opinion. Hero-worship is a dangerous vice, and one of the minor merits of a democracy is that it does not encourage it, or produce that unmanagable type of citizen known as the Great Man. It produces instead different kinds of small men—a much finer achievement. But people who

[1] *Sophocles*   Greek dramatist (496–406 BCE).

[2] *Horace*   Roman poet (65–8 BCE).

cannot get interested in the variety of life, and cannot make up their own minds, get discontented over this, and they long for a hero to bow down before and to follow blindly. It is significant that a hero is an integral part of the authoritarian stock-in-trade today. An efficiency-regime cannot be run without a few heroes stuck about it to carry off the dullness—much as plums have to be put into a bad pudding to make it palatable. One hero at the top and a smaller one each side of him is a favourite arrangement, and the timid and the bored are comforted by the trinity, and, bowing down, feel exalted and strengthened.

No, I distrust Great Men. They produce a desert of uniformity around them and often a pool of blood too, and I always feel a little man's pleasure when they come a cropper.[1] Every now and then one reads in the newspapers some such statement as: "The *coup d'état* appears to have failed, and Admiral Toma's whereabouts is at present unknown." Admiral Toma had probably every qualification for being a Great Man—an iron will, personal magnetism, dash, flair, sexlessness—but fate was against him, so he retires to unknown whereabouts instead of parading history with his peers. He fails with a completeness which no artist and no lover can experience, because with them the process of creation is itself an achievement, whereas with him the only possible achievement is success.

I believe in aristocracy, though—if that is the right word, and if a democrat may use it. Not an aristocracy of power, based upon rank and influence, but an aristocracy of the sensitive, the considerate, and the plucky. Its members are to be found in all nations and classes, and all through the ages, and there is a secret understanding between them when they meet. They represent the true human tradition, the one permanent victory of our queer race over cruelty and chaos. Thousands of them perish in obscurity, a few are great names. They are sensitive for others as well as for themselves, they are considerate without being fussy, their pluck is not swankiness but the power to endure, and they can take a joke. I give no examples—it is risky to do that—but the reader may as well consider whether this is the type of person he would like to meet and to be, and whether (going further with me) he would

prefer that this type should *not* be an ascetic one. I am against asceticism myself. I am with the old Scotsman who wanted less chastity and more delicacy. I do not feel that my aristocrats are a real aristocracy if they thwart their bodies, since bodies are the instruments through which we register and enjoy the world. Still, I do not insist. This is not a major point. It is clearly possible to be sensitive, considerate, and plucky and yet be an ascetic too, and if anyone possesses the first three qualities I will let him in! On they go—an invincible army, yet not a victorious one. The aristocrats, the elect, the chosen, the Best People—all the words that describe them are false, and all attempts to organize them fail. Again and again Authority, seeing their value, has tried to net them and to utilize them as the Egyptian Priesthood or the Christian Church or the Chinese Civil Service or the Group Movement, or some other worthy stunt. But they slip through the net and are gone; when the door is shut, they are no longer in the room; their temple, as one of them[2] remarked, is the holiness of the Heart's affections, and their kingdom, though they never possess it, is the wide-open world!

With this type of person knocking about, and constantly crossing one's path if one has eyes to see or hands to feel, the experiment of earthly life cannot be dismissed as a failure. But it may well be hailed as a tragedy, the tragedy being that no device has been found by which these private decencies can be transmitted to public affairs. As soon as people have power they go crooked and sometimes dotty as well, because the possession of power lifts them into a region where normal honesty never pays. For instance, the man who is selling newspapers outside the Houses of Parliament can safely leave his papers to go for a drink, and his cap beside them: anyone who takes a paper is sure to drop a copper into the cap. But the men who are inside the Houses of Parliament—they cannot trust one another like that, still less can the Government they compose trust other governments. No caps upon the pavement here, but suspicion, treachery, and armaments. The more highly public life is organized the lower does its morality sink; the nations of today behave to each other

---

[1]   *come a cropper*   I.e., fail badly.

[2]   *one of them*   John Keats (1795–1821), who said " I am certain of nothing but the holiness of the heart's affection and the truth of imagination."

worse than they ever did in the past, they cheat, rob, bully and bluff, make war without notice, and kill as many women and children as possible; whereas primitive tribes were at all events restrained by taboos. It is a humiliating outlook—though the greater the darkness, the brighter shine the little lights, reassuring one another, signalling: "Well, at all events, I'm still here. I don't like it very much, but how are you?" Unquenchable lights of my aristocracy! Signals of the invincible army! "Come along—anyway, let's have a good time while we can." I think they signal that too.

The Saviour of the future—if ever he comes—will not preach a new Gospel. He will merely utilize my aristocracy, he will make effective the goodwill and the good temper which are already existing. In other words, he will introduce a new technique. In economics, we are told that if there was a new technique of distribution there need be no poverty, and people would not starve in one place while crops were being ploughed under in another. A similar change is needed in the sphere of morals and politics. The desire for it is by no means new; it was expressed, for example, in theological terms by Jacopone da Todi[1] over six hundred years ago. "Ordena questo amore, tu che m'ami," he said; "O thou who lovest me—set this love in order." His prayer was not granted, and I do not myself believe that it ever will be, but here, and not through a change of heart, is our probable route. Not by becoming better, but by ordering and distributing his native goodness, will Man shut up Force, into its box, and so gain time to explore the universe and to set his mark upon it worthily. At present he only explores it at odd moments, when Force is looking the other way, and his divine creativeness appears as a trivial by-product, to be scrapped as soon as the drums beat and the bombers hum.

Such a change, claim the orthodox, can only be made by Christianity, and will be made by it in God's good time: man always has failed and always will fail to organize his own goodness, and it is presumptuous of him to try. This claim—solemn as it is—leaves me cold.

I cannot believe that Christianity will ever cope with the present world-wide mess, and I think that such influence as it retains in modern society is due to the money behind it, rather than to its spiritual appeal. It was a spiritual force once, but the indwelling spirit will have to be restated if it is to calm the waters again, and probably restated in a non-Christian form. Naturally a lot of people, and people who are not only good but able and intelligent, will disagree here; they will vehemently deny that Christianity has failed, or they will argue that its failure proceeds from the wickedness of men, and really proves its ultimate success. They have Faith, with a large F. My faith has a very small one, and I only intrude it because these are strenuous and serious days, and one likes to say what one thinks while speech is comparatively free; it may not be free much longer.

The above are the reflections of an individualist and a liberal who has found liberalism crumbling beneath him and at first felt ashamed. Then, looking around, he decided there was no special reason for shame, since other people, whatever they felt, were equally insecure. And as for individualism—there seems no way of getting off this, even if one wanted to. The dictator-hero can grind down his citizens till they are all alike, but he cannot melt them into a single man. That is beyond his power. He can order them to merge, he can incite them to mass-antics, but they are obliged to be born separately, and to die separately, and, owing to these unavoidable termini, will always be running off the totalitarian rails. The memory of birth and the expectation of death always lurk within the human being, making him separate from his fellows and consequently capable of intercourse with them. Naked I came into the world, naked I shall go out of it![2] And a very good thing too, for it reminds me that I am naked under my shirt, whatever its colour.

—1938

---

[1] *Jacopone da Todi* Italian poet (c. 1230–1306).

[2] *Naked ... it* See Ecclesiastes 5.15: "As he came forth of his mother's womb, naked shall he return to go as he came, and shall take nothing of his labor, which he may carry away in his hand."

P.G. WODEHOUSE
1881 – 1975

P.G. Wodehouse (Pelham Grenville, known to his friends as "Plum") wrote ninety-two comic novels—and in so doing did much to define the popular view of England during the Edwardian era and the 1920s. He also wrote eighteen plays and thirty-five musicals during his prolific career; he still holds the record for having the most concurrent shows on Broadway (five, in 1917). Of these, the best were based in a world he knew first-hand, the world of the privileged. They told stories of young aristocrats, adventurous young men, and ingenious young women.

Wodehouse was educated in an English boarding school while his parents lived in Hong Kong. His father, a magistrate, rarely came back to England and as a result, Plum spent breaks from school in the homes of aunts or the manor houses of his school-mates. Later, when his father returned to England because of health problems, Wodehouse took a job as a bank clerk. He spent his evenings writing, and his early stories focused on boarding-school life. He sold his first story in 1901, accepted a part-time job as a humor columnist, and never looked back. To date, his novels have sold over fifty million copies.

He traveled to New York for the first time in the spring of 1904, at the age of twenty-two. He returned to England after a month, suddenly finding that his short sojourn had done wonders for his freelance reputation. Soon after, he began creating comedic characters and novels in which he interpreted America for the English and the English for American audiences. He developed a good ear for dialogue, and the rhythms of his characters' speech capture the popular idiom of the era. Wodehouse's reputation rests above all on his series of "Jeeves" novels, which had their origin in a 1915 *Saturday Evening Post* story. These novels feature the feckless aristocrat Bertie Wooster and his butler, the unflappable Jeeves. The image they created was of an England in which the concept of everyone knowing his or her proper place might be a source of amusement, but never one of contempt. Even as the old social order of aristocrats and servants was in fact crumbling, the Jeeves novels lent light-hearted support to the old institutions—and became something of an institution themselves.

Wodehouse spent much of the 1910s and 1920s working as a theater critic for a new magazine called *Vanity Fair*, and then as a lyricist with the composer Jerome Kern and his writing partner Guy Bolton. Together they largely transformed the traditional musical, which had been based until then on the nineteenth-century operetta, featuring comedic performances set in exotic locations. The musical plays of Kern, Bolton, and Wodehouse tended to be set in contemporary culture, to have complex musical scores, and to feature ordinary people. Also in contrast to earlier musicals, the lyrics of the songs in these musicals were a fundamental part of the plot, and were used to communicate the central conflict.

In the 1930s, as the Depression took hold, it became more difficult for many British readers to take a light-hearted view of aristocratic privilege, and Wodehouse's novels became much less popular in his native land. He purchased a villa in Le Touquet, France, and was living there in 1940 when the Germans made their advance through Belgium and into France. He was placed under house arrest, and then spent time in several prisons. Released in 1941, he made five broadcasts from Berlin, recounting the story of his internment and poking fun at the Germans, the Belgians, and the British. Many in Britain were outraged and Parliament even considered trying him for treason, but George Orwell argued persuasively that the naive Plum was simply an innocent victim of the German desire to appease America, where Wodehouse was a huge celebrity.

Wodehouse avoided any formal charge of treason, but this incident plagued him for the rest of his life. After the war, he returned to New York. During his long retirement, he moved to Remesberg, a village in the Hamptons, where he died on Valentine's Day, 1975. The Queen knighted him just two weeks before his death.

⌘ ⌘ ⌘

Honeysuckle Cottage

"Do you believe in ghosts?" asked Mr. Mulliner abruptly. I weighed the question thoughtfully. I was a little surprised, for nothing in our previous conversation had suggested the topic.

"Well," I replied, "I don't like them, if that's what you mean. I was once butted by one as a child."

"Ghosts. Not goats."

"Oh, ghosts? Do I believe in ghosts?"

"Exactly."

"Well, yes—and no."

"Let me put it another way," said Mr. Mulliner, patiently. "Do you believe in haunted houses? Do you believe that it is possible for a malign influence to envelop a place and work a spell on all who come within its radius?"

I hesitated.

"Well, no—and yes."

Mr. Mulliner sighed a little. He seemed to be wondering if I was always as bright as this.

"Of course," I went on, "one has read stories. Henry James's *Turn of The Screw*…"

"I am not talking about fiction."

"Well, in real life—Well, look here, I once, as a matter of fact, did meet a man who knew a fellow …"

"My distant cousin James Rodman spent some weeks in a haunted house," said Mr. Mulliner, who, if he has a fault, is not a very good listener. "It cost him five thousand pounds. That is to say, he sacrificed five thousand pounds by not remaining there. Did you ever," he asked, wandering, it seemed to me, from the subject, "hear of Leila J. Pinckney?"

Naturally I had heard of Leila J. Pinckney. Her death some years ago has diminished her vogue, but at one time it was impossible to pass a book-shop or a railway bookstall without seeing a long row of her novels. I have never myself actually read any of them, but I knew that in her particular line of literature, the Squashily Sentimental, she had always been regarded by those entitled to judge as pre-eminent. The critics usually headed their reviews of her stories with the words:

ANOTHER PINCKNEY

or sometimes, more offensively:

ANOTHER PINCKNEY ! ! !

And once, dealing with, I think, *The Love Which Prevails,* the literary expert of the *Scrutinizer* had compressed his entire critique into the single phrase "Oh, God!"

"Of course," I said. "But what about her?"

"She was James Rodman's aunt."

"Yes?"

"And when she died James found that she had left him five thousand pounds and the house in the country where she had lived for the last twenty years of her life."

"A very nice little legacy."

"Twenty years," repeated Mr. Mulliner. "Grasp that, for it has a vital bearing on what follows. Twenty years, mind you, and Miss Pinckney turned out two novels and twelve short stories regularly every year besides a monthly page of Advice to Young Girls in one of the magazines. That is to say, forty of her novels and no fewer than two hundred and forty of her short stories were written under the roof of Honeysuckle Cottage."

"A pretty name."

"A nasty, sloppy name," said Mr. Mulliner severely, "which should have warned my distant cousin James from the start. Have you a pencil and a piece of paper?" He scribbled for a while, poring frowningly over columns of figures. "Yes," he said, looking up, "if my calculations are correct, Leila J. Pinckney wrote in all a matter of nine million one hundred and forty thousand words of glutinous sentimentality at Honeysuckle Cottage, and it was a condition of her will that James should reside there for six months in every year. Failing to do this, he was to forfeit the five thousand pounds."

"It must be great fun making a freak will," I mused. "I often wish I was rich enough to do it."

"This was not a freak will. The conditions are perfectly understandable. James Rodman was a writer of sensational mystery stories, and his aunt Leila had always disapproved of his work. She was a great believer in the influence of environment, and the reason why she inserted that clause in her will was that she wished to compel James to move from London to the country. She considered that living in London hardened him and made his outlook on life sordid. She often asked him if he thought it quite nice to harp so much on sudden death and blackmailers with squints. Surely, she said, there were enough squinting blackmailers in the world without writing about them.

"The fact that Literature meant such different things to these two had, I believe, caused something of a coolness between them, and James had never dreamed that he would be remembered in his aunt's will. For he had never concealed his opinion that Leila J. Pinckney's style of writing revolted him, however dear it might be to her enormous public. He held rigid views on the art of the novel, and always maintained that an artist with a true reverence for his craft should not descend to gooey love stories, but should stick austerely to revolvers, cries in the night, missing papers, mysterious Chinamen and dead bodies—with or without gash in throat. And not even the thought that his aunt had

dandled him on her knee as a baby could induce him to stifle his literary conscience to the extent of pretending to enjoy her work. First, last and all the time, James Rodman had held the opinion—and voiced it fearlessly—that Leila J. Pinckney wrote bilge.

"It was a surprise to him, therefore, to find that he had been left this legacy. A pleasant surprise, of course. James was making quite a decent income out of the three novels and eighteen short stories which he produced annually, but an author can always find a use for five thousand pounds. And, as for the cottage, he had actually been looking about for a little place in the country at the very moment when he received the lawyer's letter. In less than a week he was installed at his new residence."

James's first impressions of Honeysuckle Cottage were, he tells me, wholly favourable. He was delighted with the place. It was a low, rambling, picturesque old house with funny little chimneys and a red roof, placed in the middle of the most charming country. With its oak beams, its trim garden, its trilling birds and its rose-hung porch, it was the ideal spot for a writer. It was just the sort of place, he reflected whimsically, which his aunt had loved to write about in her books. Even the apple-cheeked old housekeeper who attended to his needs might have stepped straight out of one of them.

It seemed to James that his lot had been cast in pleasant places. He had brought down his books, his pipes and his golf-clubs, and was hard at work finishing the best thing he had ever done. *The Secret Nine* was the title of it; and on the beautiful summer afternoon on which this story opens he was in the study, hammering away at his typewriter, at peace with the world. The machine was running sweetly, the new tobacco he had bought the day before was proving admirable, and he was moving on all six cylinders to the end of a chapter.

He shoved in a fresh sheet of paper, chewed his pipe thoughtfully for a moment, then wrote rapidly:

"For an instant Lester Gage thought that he must have been mistaken. Then the noise came again, faint but unmistakable—a soft scratching on the outer panel.

"His mouth set in a grim line. Silently, like a panther, he made one quick step to the desk, noiselessly opened a drawer, drew out his automatic. After that affair of the poisoned needle, he was taking no chances. Still in dead silence, he tiptoed to the door; then, flinging it suddenly open, he stood there, his weapon poised.

"On the mat stood the most beautiful girl he had ever beheld. A veritable child of Faerie. She eyed him for a moment with a saucy smile; then with a pretty, roguish look of reproof shook a dainty forefinger at him.

'I believe you've forgotten me, Mr. Gage!' she fluted with a mock severity which her eyes belied."

James stared at the paper dumbly. He was utterly perplexed. He had not had the slightest intention of writing anything like this. To begin with, it was a rule with him, and one which he never broke, to allow no girls to appear in his stories. Sinister landladies, yes, and naturally any amount of adventuresses with foreign accents, but never under any pretext what may be broadly described as girls. A detective story, he maintained, should have no heroine. Heroines only held up the action and tried to flirt with the hero when he should have been busy looking for clues, and then went and let the villain kidnap them by some childishly simple trick. In his writing, James was positively monastic.

And yet here was this creature with her saucy smile and her dainty forefinger horning in at the most important point in the story. It was uncanny.

He looked once more at his scenario. No, the scenario was all right.

In perfectly plain words it stated that what happened when the door opened was that a dying man fell in and after gasping, "The beetle! Tell Scotland Yard that the blue beetle is—" expired on the hearth-rug, leaving Lester Gage not unnaturally somewhat mystified. Nothing whatever about any beautiful girls.

In a curious mood of irritation, James scratched out the offending passage, wrote in the necessary corrections and put the cover on the machine. It was at this point that he heard William whining.

The only blot on this paradise which James had so far been able discover was the infernal dog, William. Belonging nominally to the gardener, on the very first morning he had adopted James by acclamation, and he maddened and infuriated James. He had a habit of coming and whining under the window when James was at work. The latter would ignore this as long as he could; then, when the thing became insupportable, would bound out of his chair, to see the animal standing on the gravel, gazing expectantly up at him with a stone in his mouth. William had a weak-minded passion for chasing stones; and on the first day James, in a rash spirit of camaraderie, had flung one for him. Since then James had thrown no more stones; but he had thrown any number of other solids, and the garden was littered with objects ranging from match boxes to a plaster statuette of the young Joseph prophesying before Pharaoh.[1] And still William came and whined, an optimist to the last.

The whining, coming now at a moment when he felt irritable and unsettled, acted on James much as the scratching on the door had acted on Lester Gage. Silently, like a panther, he made one quick step to the mantelpiece, removed from it a china mug bearing the legend A Present From Clacton-on-Sea, and crept to the window.

And as he did so a voice outside said, "Go away, sir, go away!" and there followed a short, high-pitched bark which was certainly not William's. Will was a mixture of Airedale, setter, bull-terrier, and mastiff; and when in vocal mood, favoured the mastiff side of his family.

James peered out. There on the porch stood a girl in blue. She held in her arms a small fluffy white dog, and she was endeavouring to foil the upward movement toward this of the blackguard[2] William. William's mentality had been arrested some years before at the point where he imagined that everything in the world had been created for him to eat. A bone, a boot, a steak, the back wheel of a bicycle—it was all one to William. If it was there he tried to eat it. He had even made a plucky attempt to devour the remains of the young Joseph prophesying before Pharaoh. And it was perfectly plain now that he regarded the curious wriggling object in the girl's arms purely in the light of a snack to keep body and soul together till dinner-time.

"William!" bellowed James.

William looked courteously over his shoulder with eyes that beamed with the pure light of a life's devotion,

---

[1] *Joseph ... Pharaoh*   See Genesis 41.14–40.

[2] *blackguard*   Scoundrel.

wagged the whiplike tail which he had inherited from his bull-terrier ancestor and resumed his intent scrutiny of the fluffy dog.

"Oh, please!" cried the girl. "This great rough dog is frightening poor Toto."

The man of letters and the man of action do not always go hand in hand, but practice had made James perfect in handling with a swift efficiency any situation that involved William. A moment later that canine moron, having received the present from Clacton in the short ribs, was scuttling round the corner of the house, and James had jumped through the window and was facing the girl.

She was an extraordinarily pretty girl. Very sweet and fragile she looked as she stood there under the honeysuckle with the breeze ruffling a tendril of golden hair that strayed from beneath her coquettish little hat. Her eyes were very big and very blue, her rose-tinted face becomingly flushed. All wasted on James, though. He disliked all girls, and particularly the sweet, droopy type.

"Did you want to see somebody?" he asked stiffly.

"Just the house," said the girl, "if it wouldn't be giving any trouble. I do so want to see the room where Miss Pinckney wrote her books. This is where Leila J. Pinckney used to live, isn't it?"

"Yes; I am her nephew. My name is James Rodman."

"Mine is Rose Maynard."

James led the way into the house, and she stopped with a cry of delight on the threshold of the morning-room.

"Oh, how too perfect!" she cried. "So this was her study?"

"Yes."

"What a wonderful place it would be for you to think in if you were a writer too."

James held no high opinion of women's literary taste, but nevertheless he was conscious of an unpleasant shock.

"I am a writer," he said coldly. "I write detective stories."

"I—I'm afraid"—she blushed—"I'm afraid I don't often read detective stories."

"You no doubt prefer," said James, still more coldly, "the sort of thing my aunt used to write."

"Oh, I love her stories!" cried the girl, clasping her hands ecstatically. "Don't you?"

"I cannot say that I do."

"What?"

"They are pure apple sauce," said James sternly; "just nasty blobs of sentimentality, thoroughly untrue to life."

The girl stared.

"Why, that's just what's so wonderful about them, their trueness to life! You feel they might all have happened. I don't understand what you mean."

They were walking down the garden now. James held the gate open for her and she passed through into the road.

"Well, for one thing," he said, "I decline to believe that a marriage between two young people is invariably preceded by some violent and sensational experience in which they both share."

"Are you thinking of *Scent o' the Blossom,* where Edgar saves Maud from drowning?"

"I am thinking of every single one of my aunt's books." He looked at her curiously. He had just got the solution of a mystery which had been puzzling him for some time. Almost from the moment he had set eyes on her she had seemed somehow strangely familiar. It now suddenly came to him why it was that he disliked her so much. "Do you know," he said, "you might be one of my aunt's heroines yourself? You're just the sort of girl she used to love to write about."

Her face lit up.

"Oh, do you really think so?" She hesitated. "Do you know what I have been feeling ever since I came here? I've been feeling that you are exactly like one of Miss Pinckney's heroes."

"No, I say, really!" said James, revolted.

"Oh, but you are! When you jumped through that window it gave me quite a start. You were so exactly like Claude Masterton in *Heather o' the Hills.*"

"I have not read *Heather o' the Hills,*" said James with a shudder.

"He was very strong and quiet, with deep, dark, sad eyes."

James did not explain that his eyes were sad because her society gave him a pain in the neck. He merely laughed scornfully.

"So now, I suppose," he said, "a car will come and knock you down and I shall carry you gently into the house and lay you—Look out!" he cried.

It was too late. She was lying in a little huddled heap at his feet. Round the corner a large automobile had come bowling, keeping with an almost affected precision to the wrong side of the road. It was now receding into the distance, the occupant of the tonneau,[1] a stout red-faced gentleman in a fur coat, leaning out over the back. He had bared his head—not, one fears, as a pretty gesture of respect and regret, but because he was using his hat to hide the number plate.

The dog Toto was unfortunately uninjured.

James carried the girl gently into the house and laid her on the sofa in the morning-room. He rang the bell and the apple-cheeked housekeeper appeared.

"Send for the doctor," said James. "There has been an accident."

The housekeeper bent over the girl.

"Eh, dearie, dearie!" she said. "Bless her sweet pretty face!"

The gardener, he who technically owned William, was routed out from among the young lettuces and told to fetch Doctor Brady. He separated his bicycle from William, who was making a light meal off the left pedal, and departed on his mission. Doctor Brady arrived and in due course he made his report.

"No bones broken, but a number of nasty bruises. And, of course, the shock. She will have to stay here for some time, Rodman. Can't be moved."

"Stay here! But she can't! It isn't proper."

"Your housekeeper will act as a chaperone."

The doctor sighed. He was a stolid-looking man of middle age with side whiskers.

"A beautiful girl, that, Rodman," he said.

"I suppose so," said James.

"A sweet, beautiful girl. An elfin child."

"A what?" cried James, starting.

This imagery was very foreign to Doctor Brady as he knew him. On the only previous occasion on which they had had any extended conversation, the doctor had talked exclusively about the effect of too much protein on the gastric juices.

"An elfin child; a tender, fairy creature. When I was

looking at her just now, Rodman, I nearly broke down. Her little hand lay on the coverlet like some white lily floating on the surface of a still pool, and her dear, trusting eyes gazed up at me."

He pottered off down the garden, still babbling, and James stood staring after him blankly. And slowly, like some cloud athwart a summer sky, there crept over James's heart the chill shadow of a nameless fear.

It was about a week later that Mr. Andrew McKinnon, the senior partner in the well-known firm of literary agents, McKinnon & Gooch, sat in his office in Chancery Lane, frowning thoughtfully over a telegram. He rang the bell.

"Ask Mr. Gooch to step in here." He resumed his study of the telegram. "Oh, Gooch," he said when his partner appeared, "I've just had a curious wire from young Rodman. He seems to want to see me very urgently."

Mr. Gooch read the telegram.

"Written under the influence of some strong mental excitement," he agreed. "I wonder why he doesn't come to the office if he wants to see you so badly."

"He's working very hard, finishing that novel for Prodder & Wiggs. Can't leave it, I suppose. Well, it's a nice day. If you will look after things here I think I'll motor down and let him give me lunch."

As Mr. McKinnon's car reached the crossroads a mile from Honeysuckle Cottage, he was aware of a gesticulating figure by the hedge. He stopped the car.

"Morning, Rodman."

"Thank God you've come!" said James. It seemed to Mr. McKinnon that the young man looked paler and thinner. "Would you mind walking the rest of the way? There's something I want to speak to you about."

Mr. McKinnon alighted; and James, as he glanced at him, felt cheered and encouraged by the very sight of the man. The literary agent was a grim, hard-bitten person, to whom, when he called at their offices to arrange terms, editors kept their faces turned so that they might at least retain their back collar studs. There was no sentiment in Andrew McKinnon. Editresses of society papers practised their blandishments on him in vain, and many a publisher had waked screaming in the

---

[1] *tonneau* Rear seating compartment.

night, dreaming that he was signing a McKinnon contract.

"Well, Rodman," he said, "Prodder & Wiggs have agreed to our terms. I was writing to tell you so when your wire arrived. I had a lot of trouble with them, but it's fixed at twenty per cent, rising to twenty-five, and two hundred pounds advance royalties on the day of publication."

"Good!" said James absently. "Good! McKinnon, do you remember my aunt, Leila J. Pinckney?"

"Remember her? Why, I was her agent all her life."

"Of course. Then you know the sort of tripe she wrote."

"No author," said Mr. McKinnon reprovingly, "who pulls down a steady twenty thousand pounds a year writes tripe."

"Well anyway, you know her stuff."

"Who better?"

"When she died she left me five thousand pounds and her house, Honeysuckle Cottage. I'm living there now. McKinnon, do you believe in haunted houses?"

"No."

"Yet I tell you solemnly that Honeysuckle Cottage is haunted!"

"By your aunt?" said Mr. McKinnon, surprised.

"By her influence. There's a malignant spell over the place; a sort of miasma[1] of sentimentalism. Everybody who enters it succumbs."

"Tut-tut! You mustn't have these fancies."

"They aren't fancies."

"You aren't seriously meaning to tell me—"

"Well, how do you account for this? That book you were speaking about, which Prodder & Wiggs are to publish—*The Secret Nine*. Every time I sit down to write it a girl keeps trying to sneak in."

"Into the room?"

"Into the story."

"You don't want a love interest in your sort of book," said Mr. McKinnon, shaking his head. "It delays the action."

"I know it does. And every day I have to keep shooing this infernal female out. An awful girl, McKinnon. A soppy, soupy, treacly, drooping girl with a roguish smile. This morning she tried to butt in on the scene where Lester Gage is trapped in the den of the mysterious leper."

"No!"

"She did, I assure you. I had to rewrite three pages before I could get her out of it. And that's not the worst. Do you know, McKinnon, that at this moment I am actually living the plot of a typical Leila J. Pinckney novel in just the setting she always used! And I can see the happy ending coming nearer every day! A week ago a girl was knocked down by a car at my door and I've had to put her up, and every day I realise more clearly that sooner or later I shall ask her to marry me."

"Don't do it," said Mr. McKinnon, a stout bachelor. "You're too young to marry."

"So was Methuselah,[2]" said James, a stouter. "But all the same I know I'm going to do it. It's the influence of this awful house weighing upon me. I feel like an eggshell in a maelstrom. I am being sucked in by a force too strong for me to resist. This morning I found myself kissing her dog!"

"No!"

"I did! And I loathe the little beast. Yesterday I got up at dawn and plucked a nosegay of flowers for her, wet with the dew."

"Rodman!"

"It's a fact. I laid them at her door and went downstairs kicking myself all the way. And there in the hall was the apple-cheeked housekeeper regarding me archly. If she didn't murmur 'Bless their sweet young hearts!' my ears deceived me."

"Why don't you pack up and leave?"

"If I do I lose the five thousand pounds."

"Ah!" said Mr. McKinnon.

"I can understand what has happened. It's the same with all haunted houses. My aunt's subliminal ether vibrations have woven themselves into the texture of the place, creating an atmosphere which forces the ego of all who come in contact with it to attune themselves to it. It's either that or something to do with the fourth dimension."

Mr. McKinnon laughed scornfully.

"Tut-tut!" he said again. "This is pure imagination. What has happened is that you've been working too

---

[1] *miasma* Noxious haze.

[2] *Methuselah* According to Genesis 5.27, Methuselah lived to be 969 years old.

hard. You'll see this precious atmosphere of yours will have no effect on me."

"That's exactly why I asked you to come down. I hoped you might break the spell."

"I will that," said Mr. McKinnon jovially.

The fact that the literary agent spoke little at lunch caused James no apprehension. Mr. McKinnon was ever a silent trencherman.[1] From time to time James caught him stealing a glance at the girl, who was well enough to come down to meals now, limping pathetically; but he could read nothing in his face. And yet the mere look of his face was a consolation. It was so solid, so matter of fact, so exactly like an unemotional coconut.

"You've done me good," said James with a sigh of relief, as he escorted the agent down the garden to his car after lunch. "I felt all along that I could rely on your rugged common sense. The whole atmosphere of the place seems different now."

Mr. McKinnon did not speak for a moment. He seemed to be plunged in thought.

"Rodman," he said, as he got into his car, "I've been thinking over that suggestion of yours of putting a love interest into *The Secret Nine*. I think you're wise. The story needs it. After all, what is there greater in the world than love? Love—love—aye, it's the sweetest word in the language. Put in a heroine and let her marry Lester Gage."

"If," said James grimly, "she does succeed in worming her way in she'll jolly well marry the mysterious leper. But look here, I don't understand—"

"It was seeing that girl that changed me," proceeded Mr. McKinnon. And as James stared at him aghast, tears suddenly filled his hard-boiled eyes. He openly snuffled. "Aye, seeing her sitting there under the roses, with all that smell of honeysuckle and all. And the birdies singing so sweet in the garden and the sun lighting up her bonny face. The puir[2] wee lass!" he muttered, dabbing at his eyes. "The puir bonny wee lass! Rodman," he said, his voice quivering, "I've decided that we're being hard on Prodder & Wiggs. Wiggs has had sickness in his home lately. We mustn't be hard on a man who's had sickness in his home, hey, laddie? No, no! I'm going to take back that contract and alter it to a flat twelve per cent and no advance royalties."

"What!"

"But you shan't lose by it, Rodman. No, no, you shan't lose by it, my manny. I am going to waive my commission. The puir bonny wee lass!"

The car rolled off down the road. Mr. McKinnon, seated in the back, was blowing his nose violently.

"This is the end!" said James.

It is necessary at this point to pause and examine James Rodman's position with an unbiased eye. The average man, unless he puts himself in James's place, will be unable to appreciate it. James, he will feel, was making a lot of fuss about nothing. Here he was, drawing daily closer and closer to a charming girl with big blue eyes, and surely rather to be envied than pitied.

But we must remember that James was one of Nature's bachelors. And no ordinary man, looking forward dreamily to a little home of his own with a loving wife putting out his slippers and changing the gramophone records, can realise the intensity of the instinct for self-preservation which animates Nature's bachelors in times of peril.

James Rodman had a congenital horror of matrimony. Though a young man, he had allowed himself to develop a great many habits which were as the breath of life to him; and these habits, he knew instinctively, a wife would shoot to pieces within a week of the end of the honeymoon.

James liked to breakfast in bed; and, having breakfasted, to smoke in bed and knock the ashes out on the carpet. What wife would tolerate this practice?

James liked to pass his days in a tennis shirt, grey flannel trousers and slippers. What wife ever rests until she has inclosed her husband in a stiff collar, tight boots and a morning suit and taken him with her to *thés musicales*?[3]

These and a thousand other thoughts of the same kind flashed through the unfortunate young man's mind as the days went by, and every day that passed seemed to draw him nearer to the brink of the chasm. Fate appeared to be taking a malicious pleasure in making things as difficult for him as possible. Now that the girl was well enough to leave her bed, she spent her

---

[1] *trencherman* Eater.

[2] *puir* Scottish dialect for "poor."

[3] *thés musicales* French: musical teas, social events featuring musical recitals at which tea is served.

time sitting in a chair on the sun-sprinkled porch, and James had to read to her—and poetry, at that; and not the jolly, wholesome sort of poetry the boys are turning out nowadays, either—good, honest stuff about sin and gas-works and decaying corpses—but the old-fashioned kind with rhymes in it, dealing almost exclusively with love. The weather, moreover, continued superb. The honeysuckle cast its sweet scent on the gentle breeze; the roses over the porch stirred and nodded; the flowers in the garden were lovelier than ever; the birds sang their little throats sore. And every evening there was a magnificent sunset. It was almost as if Nature were doing it on purpose.

At last James intercepted Doctor Brady as he was leaving after one of his visits and put the thing to him squarely:

"When is that girl going?"

The doctor patted him on the arm.

"Not yet, Rodman," he said in a low, understanding voice. "No need to worry yourself about that. Mustn't be moved for days and days and days—I might almost say weeks and weeks and weeks."

"Weeks and weeks!" cried James.

"And weeks," said Doctor Brady. He prodded James roguishly in the abdomen.

"Good luck to you, my boy, good luck to you," he said.

It was some small consolation to James that the mushy physician immediately afterward tripped over William on his way down the path and broke his stethoscope. When a man is up against it like James every little helps.

He was walking dismally back to the house after this conversation when he was met by the apple-cheeked housekeeper.

"The little lady would like to speak to you, sir," said the apple-cheeked exhibit, rubbing her hands.

"Would she?" said James hollowly.

"So sweet and pretty she looks, sir—oh, sir, you wouldn't believe! Like a blessed angel sitting there with her dear eyes all a-shining."

"Don't do it!" cried James with extraordinary vehemence. "Don't do it!"

He found the girl propped up on the cushions and thought once again how singularly he disliked her. And

yet, even as he thought this, some force against which he had to fight madly was whispering to him, "Go to her and take that little hand! Breathe into that little ear the burning words that will make that little face turn away crimsoned with blushes!" He wiped a bead of perspiration from his forehead and sat down.

"Mrs. Stick-in-the-Mud—what's her name?—says you want to see me."

The girl nodded.

"I've had a letter from Uncle Henry. I wrote to him as soon as I was better and told him what had happened, and he is coming here tomorrow morning."

"Uncle Henry?"

"That's what I call him, but he's really no relation. He is my guardian. He and daddy were officers in the same regiment, and when daddy was killed, fighting on the Afghan frontier, he died in Uncle Henry's arms and with his last breath begged him to take care of me."

James started. A sudden wild hope had waked in his heart. Years ago, he remembered, he had read a book of his aunt's entitled *Rupert's Legacy*, and in that book—

"I'm engaged to marry him," said the girl quietly.

"Wow!" shouted James.

"What?" asked the girl, startled.

"Touch of cramp," said James. He was thrilling all over. That wild hope had been realised.

"It was daddy's dying wish that we should marry," said the girl.

"And dashed sensible of him, too; dashed sensible," said James warmly.

"And yet," she went on, a little wistfully, "I sometimes wonder—"

"Don't!" said James. "Don't! You must respect daddy's dying wish. There's nothing like daddy's dying wish; you can't beat it. So he's coming here tomorrow, is he? Capital, capital. To lunch, I suppose? Excellent! I'll run down and tell Mrs. Who-Is-It to lay in another chop."

It was with a gay and uplifted heart that James strolled the garden and smoked his pipe next morning. A great cloud seemed to have rolled itself away from him. Everything was for the best in the best of all possible worlds. He had finished *The Secret Nine* and shipped it off to Mr. McKinnon, and now as he strolled there was shaping itself in his mind a corking plot about a man with only half a face who lived in a secret den and terrorised London with a series of shocking murders. And what made them so shocking was the fact that each of the victims, when discovered, was found to have only half a face too. The rest had been chipped off, presumably by some blunt instrument.

The thing was coming out magnificently, when suddenly his attention was diverted by a piercing scream. Out of the bushes fringing the river that ran beside the garden burst the apple-cheeked housekeeper.

"Oh, sir! Oh, sir! Oh, sir!"

"What is it?" demanded James irritably.

"Oh, sir! Oh, sir! Oh, sir!"

"Yes, and then what?"

"The little dog, sir! He's in the river!"

"Well, whistle him to come out."

"Oh, sir, do come quick! He'll be drowned!"

James followed her through the bushes, taking off his coat as he went. He was saying to himself, "I will not rescue this dog. I do not like the dog. It is high time he had a bath, and in any case it would be much simpler to stand on the bank and fish for him with a rake. Only an ass out of a Leila J. Pinckney book would dive into a beastly river to save—"

At this point he dived. Toto, alarmed by the splash, swam rapidly for the bank, but James was too quick for him. Grasping him firmly by the neck, he scrambled ashore and ran for the house, followed by the housekeeper.

The girl was seated on the porch. Over her there bent the tall soldierly figure of a man with keen eyes and greying hair. The housekeeper raced up.

"Oh, miss! Toto! In the river! He saved him! He plunged in and saved him!"

The girl drew a quick breath.

"Gallant, damme![1] By Jove! By gad! Yes, gallant, by George!" exclaimed the soldierly man.

The girl seemed to wake from a reverie.

"Uncle Henry, this is Mr. Rodman. Mr. Rodman, my guardian, Colonel Carteret."

"Proud to meet you, sir," said the colonel, his honest blue eyes glowing as he fingered his short crisp moustache. "As fine a thing as I ever heard of, damme!"

"Yes, you are brave—brave," the girl whispered.

"I am wet—wet," said James, and went upstairs to change his clothes.

When he came down for lunch, he found to his relief that the girl had decided not to join them, and Colonel Carteret was silent and preoccupied. James, exerting himself in his capacity of host, tried him with the weather, golf, India, the Government, the high cost of living, first-class cricket, the modern dancing craze, and murderers he had met, but the other still preserved that strange, absent-minded silence. It was only when the meal was concluded and James had produced cigarettes that he came abruptly out of his trance.

"Rodman," he said, "I should like to speak to you."

"Yes?" said James, thinking it was about time.

"Rodman," said Colonel Carteret, "or rather, George—I may call you George?" he added, with a sort of wistful diffidence that had a singular charm.

"Certainly," replied James, "if you wish it. Though my name is James."

"James, eh? Well, well, it amounts to the same thing, eh, what, damme, by gad?" said the colonel with a momentary return of his bluff soldierly manner. "Well, then, James, I have something that I wish to say to you. Did Miss Maynard—did Rose happen to tell you anything about myself in—er—in connection with herself?"

"She mentioned that you and she were engaged to be married."

The colonel's tightly drawn lips quivered.

"No longer," he said.

"What?"

"No, John, my boy."

"James."

"No, James, my boy, no longer. While you were upstairs changing your clothes she told me—breaking down, poor child, as she spoke—that she wished our engagement to be at an end."

James half rose from the table, his cheeks blanched.

"You don't mean that!" he gasped.

Colonel Carteret nodded. He was staring out of the window, his fine eyes set in a look of pain.

"But this is nonsense!" cried James. "This is absurd! She—she mustn't be allowed to chop and change like this. I mean to say, it—it isn't fair—"

"Don't think of me, my boy."

---

[1] *damme* Shortened form of "damn me."

"I'm not—I mean, did she give any reason?"

"Her eyes did."

"Her eyes did?"

"Her eyes, when she looked at you on the porch, as you stood there—young, heroic—having just saved the life of the dog she loves. It is you who have won that tender heart, my boy."

"Now, listen," protested James, "you aren't going to sit there and tell me that a girl falls in love with a man just because he saves her dog from drowning?"

"Why, surely," said Colonel Carteret, surprised. "What better reason could she have?" He sighed. "It is the old, old story, my boy. Youth to youth. I am an old man. I should have known—I should have fore-seen—yes, youth to youth."

"You aren't a bit old."

"Yes, yes."

"No, no."

"Yes, yes."

"Don't keep on saying yes, yes!" cried James, clutch-ing at his hair. "Besides, she wants a steady old buffer[1]—a steady, sensible man of medium age—to look after her."

Colonel Carteret shook his head with a gentle smile. "This is mere quixotry,[2] my boy. It is splendid of you to take this attitude; but no, no."

"Yes, yes."

"No, no." He gripped James's hand for an instant, then rose and walked to the door. "That is all I wished to say, Tom."

"James."

"James. I just thought that you ought to know how matters stood. Go to her, my boy, go to her, and don't let any thought of an old man's broken dream keep you from pouring out what is in your heart. I am an old soldier, lad, an old soldier. I have learned to take the rough with the smooth. But I think—I think I will leave you now. I—I should—should like to be alone for a while. If you need me you will find me in the raspberry bushes."

He had scarcely gone when James also left the room. He took his hat and stick and walked blindly out of the garden, he knew not whither. His brain was numbed. Then, as his powers of reasoning returned, he told himself that he should have foreseen this ghastly thing. If there was one type of character over which Leila J. Pinckney had been wont to spread herself, it was the pathetic guardian who loves his ward but relinquishes her to the younger man. No wonder the girl had broken off the engagement. Any elderly guardian who allowed himself to come within a mile of Honeysuckle Cottage was simply asking for it. And then, as he turned to walk back, a dull defiance gripped James. Why, he asked, should he be put upon in this manner? If the girl liked to throw over this man, why should he be the goat?

He saw his way clearly now. He just wouldn't do it, that was all. And if they didn't like it they could lump it.

Full of a new fortitude, he strode in at the gate. A tall, soldierly figure emerged from the raspberry bushes and came to meet him.

"Well?" said Colonel Carteret.

"Well?" said James defiantly.

"Am I to congratulate you?"

James caught his keen blue eye and hesitated. It was not going to be so simple as he had supposed.

"Well—er—" he said.

Into the keen blue eyes there came a look that James had not seen there before. It was the stern, hard look which—probably—had caused men to bestow upon this old soldier the name of Cold-Steel Carteret.

"You have not asked Rose to marry you?"

"Er—no; not yet."

The keen blue eyes grew keener and bluer.

"Rodman," said Colonel Carteret in a strange, quiet voice, "I have known that little girl since she was a tiny child. For years she has been all in all to me. Her father died in my arms and with his last breath bade me see that no harm came to his darling. I have nursed her through mumps, measles—aye, and chicken-pox—and I live but for her happiness." He paused, with a signifi-cance that made James's toes curl. "Rodman," he said, "do you know what I would do to any man who trifled with that little girl's affections?" He reached in his hip pocket and an ugly-looking revolver glittered in the sunlight. "I would shoot him like a dog."

"Like a dog?" faltered James.

---

[1] *buffer* Fellow.

[2] *quixotry* Idealism, in the manner of Don Quixote, the chivalric protagonist of Cervantes's novel of that name (1605–15).

"Like a dog," said Colonel Carteret. He took James's arm and turned him towards the house. "She is on the porch. Go to her. And if—" He broke off. "But tut!" he said in a kindlier tone. "I am doing you an injustice, my boy. I know it."

"Oh, you are," said James fervently.

"Your heart is in the right place."

"Oh, absolutely," said James.

"Then go to her, my boy. Later on you may have something to tell me. You will find me in the strawberry beds."

It was very cool and fragrant on the porch. Overhead, little breezes played and laughed among the roses. Somewhere in the distance sheep bells tinkled, and in the shrubbery a thrush was singing its evensong.

Seated in her chair behind a wicker table laden with tea things, Rose Maynard watched James as he shambled up the path.

"Tea's ready," she called gaily. "Where is Uncle Henry?" A look of pity and distress flitted for a moment over her flower-like face. "Oh, I—I forgot," she whispered.

"He is in the strawberry beds," said James in a low voice.

She nodded unhappily.

"Of course, of course. Oh, why is life like this?" James heard her whisper.

He sat down. He looked at the girl. She was leaning back with closed eyes, and he thought he had never seen such a little squirt in his life. The idea of passing his remaining days in her society revolted him. He was stoutly opposed to the idea of marrying anyone; but if, as happens to the best of us, he ever were compelled to perform the wedding glide, he had always hoped it would be with some lady golf champion who would help him with his putting, and thus, by bringing his handicap down a notch or two, enable him to save something from the wreck, so to speak. But to link his lot with a girl who read his aunt's books and liked them; a girl who could tolerate the presence of the dog Toto; a girl who clapped her hands in pretty, childish joy when she saw a nasturtium in bloom—it was too much. Nevertheless, he took her hand and began to speak.

"Miss Maynard—Rose—"

She opened her eyes and cast them down. A flush had come into her cheeks. The dog Toto at her side sat up and begged for cake, disregarded.

"Let me tell you a story. Once upon a time there was a lonely man who lived in a cottage all by himself—"

He stopped. Was it James Rodman who was talking this bilge?

"Yes?" whispered the girl.

"—but one day there came to him out of nowhere a little fairy princess. She—"

He stopped again, but this time not because of the sheer shame of listening to his own voice. What caused him to interrupt his tale was the fact that at this moment the tea-table suddenly began to rise slowly in the air, tilting as it did so a considerable quantity of hot tea on to the knees of his trousers.

"Ouch!" cried James, leaping.

The table continued to rise, and then fell sideways, revealing the homely countenance of William, who, concealed by the cloth, had been taking a nap beneath it. He moved slowly forward, his eyes on Toto. For many a long day William had been desirous of putting to the test, once and for all, the problem of whether Toto was edible or not. Sometimes he thought yes, at other times no. Now seemed an admirable opportunity for a definite decision. He advanced on the object of his experiment, making a low whistling noise through his nostrils, not unlike a boiling kettle. And Toto, after one long look of incredulous horror, tucked his shapely tail between his legs and, turning, raced for safety. He had laid a course in a bee-line for the open garden gate, and William, shaking a dish of marmalade off his head a little petulantly, galloped ponderously after him. Rose Maynard staggered to her feet.

"Oh, save him!" she cried.

Without a word James added himself to the procession. His interest in Toto was but tepid. What he wanted was to get near enough to William to discuss with him that matter of the tea on his trousers. He reached the road and found that the order of the runners had not changed. For so small a dog, Toto was moving magnificently. A cloud of dust rose as he skidded round the corner. William followed. James followed William.

And so they passed Farmer Birkett's barn, Farmer Giles's cow shed, the place where Farmer Willetts's pigsty used to be before the big fire, and the Bunch of Grapes public house, Jno. Biggs propr., licensed to sell tobacco, wines and spirits. And it was as they were turning down the lane that leads past Farmer Robinson's chicken run that Toto, thinking swiftly, bolted abruptly into a small drain pipe.

"William!" roared James, coming up at a canter. He stopped to pluck a branch from the hedge and swooped darkly on.

William had been crouching before the pipe, making a noise like a bassoon into its interior; but now he rose and came beamingly to James. His eyes were aglow with chumminess and affection; and placing his forefeet on James's chest, he licked him three times on the face in rapid succession. And as he did so, something seemed to snap in James. The scales seemed to fall from James's eyes. For the first time he saw William as he really was, the authentic type of dog that saves his master from a frightful peril. A wave of emotion swept over him.

"William!" he muttered. "William!"

William was making an early supper off a half brick he had found in the road. James stooped and patted him fondly.

"William," he whispered, "you knew when the time had come to change the conversation, didn't you, old boy!" He straightened himself. "Come, William," he said. "Another four miles and we reach Meadowsweet Junction. Make it snappy and we shall just catch the up express, first stop London."

William looked up into his face and it seemed to James that he gave a brief nod of comprehension and approval. James turned. Through the trees to the east he could see the red roof of Honeysuckle Cottage, lurking like some evil dragon in ambush. Then, together, man and dog passed silently into the sunset.

That (concluded Mr. Mulliner) is the story of my distant cousin James Rodman. As to whether it is true, that, of course, is an open question. I, personally, am of the opinion that it is. There is no doubt that James did go to live at Honeysuckle Cottage and, while there, underwent some experience which has left an ineradicable mark upon him. His eyes today have that unmistakable look which is to be seen only in the eyes of confirmed bachelors whose feet have been dragged to the very brink of the pit and who have gazed at close range into the naked face of matrimony.

And, if further proof be needed, there is William. He is now James's inseparable companion. Would any man be habitually seen in public with a dog like William unless he had some solid cause to be grateful to him—unless they were linked together by some deep and imperishable memory? I think not. Myself, when I observe William coming along the street, I cross the road and look into a shop window till he has passed. I am not a snob, but I dare not risk my position in Society by being seen talking to that curious compound.

Nor is the precaution an unnecessary one. There is about William a shameless absence of appreciation of class distinctions which recalls the worst excesses of the French Revolution.[1] I have seen him with these eyes chivvy[2] a pomeranian belonging to a Baroness in her own right from near the Achilles Statue to within a few yards of the Marble Arch.[3]

And yet James walks daily with him in Piccadilly. It is surely significant.

—1925

---

[1] *which ... Revolution* Reference to speech by Lady Bracknell in Act One of Oscar Wilde's *The Importance of Being Earnest* (1895).

[2] *chivvy* Harass.

[3] *Achilles ... Arch* Two locations in London's Hyde Park.

Virginia Woolf
1882 – 1941

A towering figure in the history of twentieth-century feminist thought, Virginia Woolf also occupies a central place in the development of the twentieth-century novel. Woolf, along with contemporaries such as James Joyce and Dorothy Richardson, rejected the traditional conventions of fiction, which included narrative coherence, omniscient narration, and emphasis on external settings and events. Instead, she explored the everyday, internal lives of her characters in a style—often called stream-of-consciousness—that mimics the flow of her characters' thoughts. In her fiction and essays alike, she examined the ways in which social roles and values are constructed and the effects these have on the lives and interactions of individuals.

Virginia Woolf was born Adeline Virginia Stephen, the third child of an illustrious, upper-middle-class London family. Her father, Leslie Stephen, a philosopher and literary critic, was primarily known as editor of the *Dictionary of National Biography* and President of the London Library. Her mother, born Julia Jackson, had been married into the Duckworth publishing family, and then married Stephen some time after the death of her first husband. Deeply connected to Victorian literary circles, the Stephen family included among its friends Henry James, Matthew Arnold, and George Eliot. From childhood, Woolf was drawn to a literary career, and her father in particular encouraged her, as she says, "to read what one liked because one liked it, never to pretend to admire what one did not. ... To write in the fewest possible words, as clearly as possible, exactly what one meant."

Surrounded by her father's impressive library, Woolf immersed herself in the study of languages and literary classics. While her brothers Thoby and Adrian went to public schools and eventually to university at Cambridge, Woolf and her sister Vanessa were educated at home by their father and private tutors. The lack of formal education for women would become a pervasive issue in Woolf's novels and later essays such as *A Room of One's Own* (1929) and *Three Guineas* (1938). A frequent exploration into the emotional effects of death in her later writing would also stem from Woolf's youthful experience. In 1895, her mother died of influenza; a few months later, at the age of thirteen, Woolf suffered a mental breakdown, symptoms of which included hearing voices, avoiding food, and experiencing extreme anxiety. Her mother's death was followed by that of her beloved half-sister and maternal substitute, Stella Duckworth, in childbirth, and then by that of her father, from cancer, in 1904. A second breakdown resulted. These breakdowns were harbingers of Woolf's lifelong struggle with manic and depressive episodes, which were generally brought about by stress—such as the emotional and mental anxiety that accompanied the completion of a book.

Despite Woolf's emotional turmoil in the year following her father's death, the event freed her from her family's inhibiting influence and facilitated her emergence amongst London's intelligentsia. With an unsigned review, she received her first publication in *The Guardian*, and against her extended family's attempts to introduce her into polite society, Woolf and several of her siblings moved to the Bloomsbury area of London. There they began associating with her brother Thoby's Cambridge friends, and what began as a social gathering of casual friends for drinks and conversation eventually came to be known as the Bloomsbury Group, a cultural circle bound together by an intense interest in current literary, philosophical, artistic, sexual, and political issues. Its members included novelist E.M. Forster, biographer and essayist Lytton Strachey, painter Duncan Grant, art critics Roger Fry and Clive Bell (the future husband of Woolf's sister Vanessa), economist John Maynard Keynes, and political theorist Leonard Woolf. Although Thoby Stephen died of typhoid in 1906, the group continued to meet throughout Woolf's lifetime. It attracted a certain amount of controversy as a result of the new ideas (particularly concerning sexuality) and frank artistic expression it fostered, and also because of the class snobbery it was perceived to exhibit (to the extent that the word *Bloomsbury* later became widely used to connote an insular and patronizing aestheticism).

In 1912, Virginia Stephen married Leonard Woolf, who throughout her life provided her with the time, encouragement, and emotional support necessary for her to continue writing as she alternated between periods of stability and intense productivity and episodes of immobilizing emotional collapse. In 1915, *The Voyage Out*, Woolf's first major novel, was published, introducing her readers for the first time to the character of Clarissa Dalloway, whom Woolf would make central to her later novel *Mrs. Dalloway* (1925). *The Voyage Out* and its successor, *Night and Day* (1919), are Woolf's most conventional works.

In 1917, Woolf and her husband Leonard bought a hand press and established Hogarth Press at their London home, intending to publish their own works and those of their friends. The Hogarth Press soon became a highly successful enterprise, publishing the early works of authors such as E.M. Forster, Katherine Mansfield, and T.S. Eliot, as well as English translations of the works of Sigmund Freud.

Woolf's 1922 novel, *Jacob's Room*, based on the life and death of Woolf's brother Thoby, represented a stylistic breakthrough for her. In this novel, she tried an entirely different approach, ignoring much of the framework of external events and descriptions present in her earlier work. In this novel, she said, there was "no scaffolding; scarcely a brick to be seen; all crepuscular." By 1925, Woolf had completed *Mrs. Dalloway*, the culmination of many years' experimentation with narrative technique. Originally titled *The House*, *Mrs. Dalloway* takes place in a twenty-four hour period in London, and explores the subjectivities of characters who never meet, but whose observations, experiences, and memories reveal a curious kinship between them. Describing her new method of characterization, Woolf said, "I dig out beautiful caves behind my characters.... The idea is that the caves shall connect and each come to daylight at the present moment."

In Woolf's next novel, *To the Lighthouse* (1927), Woolf further developed her stream-of-consciousness style, relying heavily on imagery and rich symbolism to convey meaning. Divided into three distinct parts that take place against the backdrop of ordinary domestic events, the novel experiments with the passage of time through the consciousness of its various characters. By alternating between various viewpoints, Woolf demonstrates how rare, tenuous, and fleeting the moments of real connection between people are.

In 1929, Woolf's best-known work of non-fiction was published. Originally constructed as lecture notes for talks to be given at Newnham and Girton Colleges at Cambridge, the work was expanded and published as *A Room of One's Own*. The essay, which has become a foundational text of literary feminism, explores the traditional barriers and prejudices faced by women writers. At the core of Woolf's argument is her conclusion that a woman must have financial independence and privacy (a room of her own) if she is to write fiction successfully. In presenting the concept of the androgynous mind, Woolf also provides insight into her own literary process. As defined by Woolf, the successful author of whatever sex must possess the ability to draw creative forces from all facets of his or her emotional and intellectual being—regardless of whether these facets are traditionally classified as "masculine" or "feminine." To do so, the author must move beyond any awareness of his or her own gender role as dictated by social customs; as Woolf says, "It is fatal for anyone who writes to think of their sex." In her novel of the previous year, *Orlando*, Woolf had celebrated what she saw as the androgynous creative mind of her friend Vita Sackville-West. Subtitled *A Biography*, *Orlando* plays overtly with the form of genre as Woolf follows her main character—who is able to change sex as the times and his or her desires demanded—across several hundred years of British history.

For the next twelve years, Woolf continued to pursue more radical experiments with form while developing her ideas about writing, genre, and gender roles in numerous essays (most of which are collected in two volumes of her *Common Readers*). Woolf's next novel, *The Waves* (1931), is a poem-novel written "to a rhythm and not to a plot" that focuses on the mutability of life. In 1938, Woolf extended the feminist critique of male privilege begun in *A Room of One's Own* with *Three Guineas*, which implicitly links the values of patriarchal society with those of fascism. Less popular at the time than its predecessor, *Three Guineas*, and the pacifism is advocates, have found a more receptive audience in the later twentieth and early twenty-first centuries.

Just as *The Waves* sought to combine poetry and the novel, Woolf described her 1937 work, *The Years*, as an "essay-novel," and her final novel, *Between the Acts* (1941), is something of a drama-novel, focusing on the audience reception of an amateur pageant that takes place as the threat of war is imminent. Woolf herself, discouraged by the progress of World War II and its implications for herself and her Jewish husband, and dreading the critical reception this work would receive, faced another emotional breakdown. Before she could complete the revisions of *Between the Acts*, she began to feel mental illness engulf her. She composed a note to her husband explaining that she felt that this time she would not recover, filled her pockets with stones, and drowned herself in the River Ouse near her home.

Throughout her lifetime, Woolf was offered numerous honors, all of which she refused because of her avowed contempt for patriarchal society. After declining an honorary degree from Manchester University, she wrote in her diary, "It is an utterly corrupt society …, and I will take nothing that it can give me." She did not want to be condescended to or used as a "token woman." Nevertheless, the honors continued to be offered, and, after her death, the loss of her unique vision and style were greatly mourned. She has since been hailed as a pioneer of the modernist novel, a central early figure in the development of feminist theory, and a central figure in the twentieth-century world of letters. Her personal diaries and letters, published posthumously in several volumes, provide unique insight into her aims as an artist and her intellectual development in a remarkable literary and artistic milieu.

⌘ ⌘ ⌘

Monday or Tuesday

Monday or Tuesday, a collection of eight short stories accompanied by four wood-cut illustrations by Vanessa Bell, was the only collection of short fiction that Virginia Woolf ever published. First published by the newly-established Hogarth Press, the book was the only one of her books never to be reprinted, although Leonard Woolf did publish six of the stories (all but "A Society" and "Blue & Green") in *A Haunted House and Other Short Stories*, a collection of Virginia Woolf's short fiction that he released in 1944, after her death. The full text of all

eight stories of *Monday or Tuesday* are reprinted below.

A Haunted House

Whatever hour you woke there was a door shutting. From room to room they went, hand in hand, lifting here, opening there, making sure—a ghostly couple.

"Here we left it," she said. And he added, "Oh, but here too!" "It's upstairs," she murmured. "And in the garden," he whispered "Quietly," they said, "or we shall wake them."

But it wasn't that you woke us. Oh, no. "They're looking for it; they're drawing the curtain," one might say, and so read on a page or two. "Now they've found it," one would be certain, stopping the pencil on the margin. And then, tired of reading, one might rise and see for oneself, the house all empty, the doors standing open, only the wood pigeons bubbling with content and the hum of the threshing machine sounding from the farm. "What did I come in here for? What did I want to find?" My hands were empty. "Perhaps it's upstairs then?" The apples were in the loft. And so down again, the garden still as ever, only the book had slipped into the grass.

But they had found it in the drawing room. Not that one could ever see them. The window panes reflected apples, reflected roses; all the leaves were green in the glass. If they moved in the drawing room, the apple only turned its yellow side. Yet, the moment after, if the door was opened, spread about the floor, hung upon the walls, pendant from the ceiling—what? My hands were empty. The shadow of a thrush crossed the carpet; from the deepest wells of silence the wood pigeon drew its bubble of sound. "Safe, safe, safe," the pulse of the house beat softly. "The treasure buried; the room ..." the pulse stopped short. Oh, was that the buried treasure?

A moment later the light had faded. Out in the garden then? But the trees spun darkness for a wandering beam of sun. So fine, so rare, coolly sunk beneath the surface the beam I sought always burnt behind the glass. Death was the glass; death was between us; coming to the woman first, hundreds of years ago, leaving the house, sealing all the windows; the rooms were darkened. He left it, left her, went North, went East, saw the stars turned in the Southern sky; sought the house, found it dropped beneath the Downs. "Safe, safe, safe," the pulse of the house beat gladly. "The treasure yours."

The wind roars up the avenue. Trees stoop and bend this way and that. Moonbeams splash and spill wildly in the rain. But the beam of the lamp falls straight from the window. The candle burns stiff and still. Wandering through the house, opening the windows, whispering not to wake us, the ghostly couple seek their joy.

"Here we slept," she says. And he adds, "Kisses without number." "Waking in the morning—" "Silver between the trees—" "Upstairs—" "In the garden—" "When summer came—" "In winter snowtime—" The doors go shutting far in the distance, gently knocking like the pulse of a heart.

Nearer they come; cease at the doorway. The wind falls, the rain slides silver down the glass. Our eyes darken; we hear no steps beside us; we see no lady spread her ghostly cloak. His hands shield the lantern. "Look," he breathes. "Sound asleep. Love upon their lips."

Stooping, holding their silver lamp above us, long they look and deeply. Long they pause. The wind drives straightly; the flame stoops slightly. Wild beams of moonlight cross both floor and wall, and, meeting, stain the faces bent; the faces pondering; the faces that search the sleepers and seek their hidden joy.

"Safe, safe, safe," the heart of the house beats proudly. "Long years—" he sighs. "Again you found me." "Here," she murmurs, "sleeping; in the garden reading; laughing, rolling apples in the loft. Here we left our treasure—" Stooping, their light lifts the lids upon my eyes. "Safe! safe! safe!" the pulse of the house beats wildly. Waking, I cry "Oh, is this your buried treasure? The light in the heart.

A Society

This is how it all came about. Six or seven of us were sitting one day after tea. Some were gazing across the street into the windows of a milliner's shop where the light still shone brightly upon scarlet feathers and golden slippers. Others were idly occupied in building little towers of sugar upon the edge of the tea tray. After a time, so far as I can remember, we drew round the fire and began as usual to praise men—how strong, how noble, how brilliant, how courageous, how beautiful they were—how we envied those who by hook or by crook managed to get attached to one for life—when Poll, who had said nothing, burst into tears. Poll, I must tell you, has always been queer. For one thing her father was a strange man. He left her a fortune in his will, but on condition that she read all the books in the London Library. We comforted her as best we could; but we knew in our hearts how vain it was. For though we like her, Poll is no beauty; leaves her shoe laces untied; and must have been thinking, while we praised men, that not one of them would ever wish to marry her. At last she dried her tears. For some time we could make nothing of what she said. Strange enough it was in all conscience. She told us that, as we knew, she spent most of her time in the London Library, reading. She had begun, she said, with English literature on the top floor; and was steadily working her way down to *The Times* on the bottom. And now half, or perhaps only a quarter, way through a terrible thing had happened. She could read no more. Books were not what we thought them. "Books," she cried, rising to her feet and speaking with an intensity of desolation which I shall never forget, "are for the most part unutterably bad!"

Of course we cried out that Shakespeare wrote books, and Milton and Shelley.

"Oh, yes," she interrupted us. "You've been well taught, I can see. But you are not members of the London Library." Here her sobs broke forth anew. At length, recovering a little, she opened one of the pile of books which she always carried about with her—"From a Window" or "In a Garden," or some such name as that it was called, and it was written by a man called Benton or Henson, or something of that kind. She read the first few pages. We listened in silence. "But that's not a book," someone said. So she chose another. This time it was a history, but I have forgotten the writer's name. Our trepidation increased as she went on. Not a word of it seemed to be true, and the style in which it was written was execrable.

"Poetry! Poetry!" we cried, impatiently. "Read us poetry!"

I cannot describe the desolation which fell upon us as she opened a little volume and mouthed out the verbose, sentimental foolery which it contained.

"It must have been written by a woman," one of us urged. But no. She told us that it was written by a young man, one of the most famous poets of the day. I leave you to imagine what the shock of the discovery was. Though we all cried and begged her to read no more, she persisted and read us extracts from the *Lives of the Lord Chancellors*. When she had finished, Jane, the eldest and wisest of us, rose to her feet and said that she for one was not convinced.

"Why," she asked, "if men write such rubbish as this, should our mothers have wasted their youth in bringing them into the world?"

We were all silent; and, in the silence, poor Poll could be heard sobbing out, "Why, why did my father teach me to read?"

Clorinda was the first to come to her senses. "It's all our fault," she said. "Every one of us knows how to read. But no one, save Poll, has ever taken the trouble to do it. I, for one, have taken it for granted that it was a woman's duty to spend her youth in bearing children. I venerated my mother for bearing ten; still more my grandmother for bearing fifteen; it was, I confess, my own ambition to bear twenty. We have gone on all these ages supposing that men were equally industrious, and that their works were of equal merit. While we have borne the children, they, we supposed, have borne the books and the pictures. We have populated the world. They have civilized it. But now that we can read, what prevents us from judging the results? Before we bring another child into the world we must swear that we will find out what the world is like."

So we made ourselves into a society for asking questions. One of us was to visit a man-of-war; another was to hide herself in a scholar's study; another was to attend a meeting of business men; while all were to read books, look at pictures, go to concerts, keep our eyes open in the streets, and ask questions perpetually. We were very young. You can judge of our simplicity when I tell you that before parting that night we agreed that the objects of life were to produce good people and good books. Our questions were to be directed to finding out how far these objects were now attained by men. We vowed solemnly that we would not bear a single child until we were satisfied.

Off we went then, some to the British Museum; others to the King's Navy; some to Oxford; others to Cambridge; we visited the Royal Academy and the Tate;[1] heard modern music in concert rooms, went to the Law Courts, and saw new plays. No one dined out without asking her partner certain questions and carefully noting his replies. At intervals we met together and compared our observations. Oh, those were merry meeting! Never have I laughed so much as I did when Rose read her notes upon "Honour" and described how

---

[1]   *Royal Academy and the Tate*   Two London art galleries.

she had dressed herself as an Ethiopian Prince and gone aboard one of His Majesty's ships.[1] Discovering the hoax, the Captain visited her (now disguised as a private gentleman) and demanded that honour should be satisfied. "But how?" she asked. "How?" he bellowed. "With the cane of course!" Seeing that he was beside himself with rage and expecting that her last moment had come, she bent over and received, to her amazement, six light taps upon the behind. "The honour of the British Navy is avenged!" he cried, and, raising herself, she saw him with the sweat pouring down his face holding out a trembling right hand. "Away!" she exclaimed, striking an attitude and imitating the ferocity of his own expression, "My honour has still to be satisfied!" "Spoken like a gentleman!" he returned, and fell into profound thought. "If six strokes avenge the honour of the King's Navy," he mused, "how many avenge the honour of a private gentleman?" He said he would prefer to lay the case before his brother officers. She replied haughtily that she could not wait. He praised her sensibility. "Let me see," he cried suddenly, "did your father keep a carriage?" "No," she said. "Or a riding horse?" "We had a donkey," she bethought her, "which drew the mowing machine." At this his face lighted. "My mother's name—" she added. "For God's sake, man, don't mention your mother's name!" he shrieked, trembling like an aspen and flushing to the roots of his hair, and it was ten minutes at least before she could induce him to proceed. At length he decreed that if she gave him four strokes and a half in the small of the back at a spot indicated by himself (the half conceded, he said, in recognition of the fact that her great grandmother's uncle was killed at Trafalgar) it was his opinion that her honour would be as good as new. This was done; they retired to a restaurant; drank two bottles of wine for which he insisted upon paying; and parted with protestations of eternal friendship.

Then we had Fanny's account of her visit to the Law Courts. At her first visit she had come to the conclusion that the Judges were either made of wood or were impersonated by large animals resembling man who had been trained to move with extreme dignity, mumble,

and nod their heads. To test her theory she had liberated a handkerchief of bluebottles[2] at the critical moment of a trial, but was unable to judge whether the creatures gave signs of humanity for the buzzing of the flies induced so sound a sleep that she only woke in time to see the prisoners led into the cells below. But from the evidence she brought we voted that it is unfair to suppose that the Judges are men.

Helen went to the Royal Academy, but when asked to deliver her report upon the pictures she began to recite from a pale blue volume, "O! for the touch of a vanished hand and the sound of a voice that is still.[3] Home is the hunter, home from the hill.[4] He gave his bridle reins a shake.[5] Love is sweet, love is brief.[6] Spring, the fair spring, is the year's pleasant King.[7] O! to be in England now that April's there.[8] Men must work and women must weep.[9] The path of duty is the way to glory—"[10] We could listen to no more of this gibberish.

"We want no more poetry!" we cried.

"Daughters of England!" she began, but here we pulled her down, a vase of water getting spilt over her in the scuffle.

"Thank God!" she exclaimed, shaking herself like a dog. "Now I'll roll on the carpet and see if I can't brush off what remains of the Union Jack. Then perhaps—" here she rolled energetically. Getting up she began to explain to us what modern pictures are like when Castalia stopped her.

"What is the average size of a picture?" she asked. "Perhaps two feet by two and a half," she said. Castalia made notes while Helen spoke, and when she had done,

---

[2] *bluebottles* Bluebottle flies, which have large, bluish bodies.

[3] *O … is still* Alfred, Lord Tennyson, "Break, Break, Break" (1842).

[4] *Home is … hill* Robert Louis Stevenson, *Underwoods*, "Requiem" XXI (1887).

[5] *He gave … shake* Robert Burns, "'It was a' for our Rightful King" (1796).

[6] *Love is … brief* Cf. Algernon Charles Swinburne, "Hymn to Proserpine" (1866).

[7] *Spring the … King* Thomas Nashe, "Spring" (1600).

[8] *O … April's there* Robert Browning, "Home-Thoughts from Abroad" (1845).

[9] *Men must … weep* Charles Kingsley, "The Three Fishers" (1851).

[10] *The path … glory* Alfred, Lord Tennyson, "Ode on the Death of the Duke of Wellington" (1852).

and we were trying not to meet each other's eyes, rose and said, "At your wish I spent last week at Oxbridge,[1] disguised as a charwoman. I thus had access to the rooms of several Professors and will now attempt to give you some idea—only," she broke off, "I can't think how to do it. It's all so queer. These Professors," she went on, "live in large houses built round grass plots each in a kind of cell by himself. Yet they have every convenience and comfort. You have only to press a button or light a little lamp. Their papers are beautifully filed. Books abound. There are no children or animals, save half a dozen stray cats and one aged bullfinch—a cock. I remember," she broke off, "an Aunt of mine who lived at Dulwich and kept cactuses. You reached the conservatory through the double drawing-room, and there, on the hot pipes, were dozens of them, ugly, squat, bristly little plants each in a separate pot. Once in a hundred years the Aloe flowered, so my Aunt said. But she died before that happened—" We told her to keep to the point. "Well," she resumed, "when Professor Hobkin was out, I examined his life work, an edition of Sappho.[2] It's a queer looking book, six or seven inches thick, not all by Sappho. Oh, no. Most of it is a defence of Sappho's chastity, which some German had denied, and I can assure you the passion with which these two gentlemen argued, the learning they displayed, the prodigious ingenuity with which they disputed the use of some implement which looked to me for all the world like a hairpin astounded me; especially when the door opened and Professor Hobkin himself appeared. A very nice, mild, old gentleman, but what could *he* know about chastity?" We misunderstood her.

"No, no," she protested, "he's the soul of honour I'm sure—not that he resembled Rose's sea captain in the least. I was thinking rather of my Aunt's cactuses. What could *they* know about chastity?"

Again we told her not to wander from the point,—did the Oxbridge professors help to produce good people and good books?—the objects of life.

"There!" she exclaimed. "It never struck me to ask. It never occurred to me that they could possibly produce anything."

"I believe," said Sue, "that you made some mistake. Probably Professor Hobkin was a gynecologist. A scholar is a very different sort of man. A scholar is overflowing with humour and invention—perhaps addicted to wine, but what of that?—a delightful companion, generous, subtle, imaginative—as stands to reason. For he spends his life in company with the finest human beings that have ever existed."

"Hum," said Castalia. "Perhaps I'd better go back and try again."

Some three months later it happened that I was sitting alone when Castalia entered. I don't know what it was in the look of her that so moved me; but I could not restrain myself, and, dashing across the room, I clasped her in my arms. Not only was she very beautiful; she seemed also in the highest spirits. "How happy you look!" I exclaimed, as she sat down.

"I've been at Oxbridge," she said.

"Asking questions?"

"Answering them," she replied.

"You have not broken our vows?" I said anxiously, noticing something about her figure.

"Oh, the vow," she said casually. "I'm going to have a baby, if that's what you mean. You can't imagine," she burst out, "how exciting, how beautiful, how satisfying—"

"What is?" I asked.

"To—to—answer questions," she replied in some confusion. Whereupon she told me the whole of her story. But in the middle of an account which interested and excited me more than anything I had ever heard, she gave the strangest cry, half whoop, half holloa—

"Chastity! Chastity! Where's my chastity!" she cried. "Help Ho! The scent bottle!"

There was nothing in the room but a cruet containing mustard, which I was about to administer when she recovered her composure.

"You should have thought of that three months ago," I said severely.

"True," she replied. "There's not much good in thinking of it now. It was unfortunate, by the way, that my mother had me called Castalia."[3]

---

[1] *Oxbridge* Term for the universities of Oxford and Cambridge, considered together.

[2] *Sappho* Ancient Greek lyric poet from the island of Lesbos.

[3] *Castalia* According to Greek mythology, the nymph of the prophetic Castalian spring who threw herself into the water when pursued by the god Apollo.

"Oh, Castalia, your mother—" I was beginning when she reached for the mustard pot.

"No, no, no," she said, shaking her head. "If you'd been a chaste woman yourself you would have screamed at the sight of me—instead of which you rushed across the room and took me in your arms. No, Cassandra.[1] We are neither of us chaste." So we went on talking.

Meanwhile the room was filling up, for it was the day appointed to discuss the results of our observations. Everyone, I thought, felt as I did about Castalia. They kissed her and said how glad they were to see her again. At length, when we were all assembled, Jane rose and said that it was time to begin. She began by saying that we had now asked questions for over five years, and that though the results were bound to be inconclusive—here Castalia nudged me and whispered that she was not so sure about that. Then she got up, and, interrupting Jane in the middle of a sentence, said:

"Before you say any more, I want to know—am I to stay in the room? Because," she added, "I have to confess that I am an impure woman."

Everyone looked at her in astonishment.

"You are going to have a baby?" asked Jane.

She nodded her head.

It was extraordinary to see the different expressions on their faces. A sort of hum went through the room, in which I could catch the words "impure," "baby," "Castalia," and so on. Jane, who was herself considerably moved, put it to us:

"Shall she go? Is she impure?"

Such a roar filled the room as might have been heard in the street outside.

"No! No! No! Let her stay! Impure? Fiddlesticks!" Yet I fancied that some of the youngest, girls of nineteen or twenty, held back as if overcome with shyness. Then we all came about her and began asking questions, and at last I saw one of the youngest, who had kept in the background, approach shyly and say to her:

"What is chastity then? I mean is it good, or is it bad, or is it nothing at all?" She replied so low that I could not catch what she said.

"You know I was shocked," said another, "for at least

ten minutes."

"In my opinion," said Poll, who was growing crusty from always reading in the London Library, "chastity is nothing but ignorance—a most discreditable state of mind. We should admit only the unchaste to our society. I vote that Castalia shall be our President."

This was violently disputed.

"It is as unfair to brand women with chastity as with unchastity," said Poll. "Some of us haven't the opportunity either. Moreover, I don't believe Cassy herself maintains that she acted as she did from a pure love of knowledge."

"He is only twenty-one and divinely beautiful," said Cassy, with a ravishing gesture.

"I move," said Helen, "that no one be allowed to talk of chastity or unchastity save those who are in love."

"Oh, bother," said Judith, who had been enquiring into scientific matters, "I'm not in love and I'm longing to explain my measures for dispensing with prostitutes and fertilizing virgins by Act of Parliament."

She went on to tell us of an invention of hers to be erected at Tube[2] stations and other public resorts, which, upon payment of a small fee, would safeguard the nation's health, accommodate its sons, and relieve its daughters. Then she had contrived a method of preserving in sealed tubes the germs of future Lord Chancellors "or poets or painters or musicians," she went on, "supposing, that is to say, that these breeds are not extinct, and that women still wish to bear children—"

"Of course we wish to bear children!" cried Castalia, impatiently. Jane rapped the table.

"That is the very point we are met to consider," she said. "For five years we have been trying to find out whether we are justified in continuing the human race. Castalia has anticipated our decision. But it remains for the rest of us to make up our minds."

Here one after another of our messengers rose and delivered their reports. The marvels of civilisation far exceeded our expectations, and, as we learnt for the first time how man flies in the air, talks across space, penetrates to the heart of an atom, and embraces the universe in his speculations, a murmur of admiration burst from our lips.

"We are proud," we cried, "that our mothers sacri-

---

[1] *Cassandra* In Greek mythology, the clairvoyant daughter of Priam (the king of Troy) who was cursed by Apollo, as punishment for a betrayal, so her prophesies would never be believed.

[2] *Tube* Subway.

ficed their youth in such a cause as this!" Castalia, who had been listening intently, looked prouder than all the rest. Then Jane reminded us that we had still much to learn, and Castalia begged us to make haste. On we went through a vast tangle of statistics. We learnt that England has a population of so many millions, and that such and such a proportion of them is constantly hungry and in prison; that the average size of a working man's family is such, and that so great a percentage of women die from maladies incident to childbirth. Reports were read of visits to factories, shops, slums, and dockyards. Descriptions were given of the Stock Exchange, of a gigantic house of business in the City, and of a Government Office. The British Colonies were now discussed, and some account was given of our rule in India, Africa, and Ireland. I was sitting by Castalia and I noticed her uneasiness.

"We shall never come to any conclusion at all at this rate," she said. "As it appears that civilisation is so much more complex than we had any notion, would it not be better to confine ourselves to our original enquiry? We agreed that it was the object of life to produce good people and good books. All this time we have been talking of aeroplanes, factories, and money. Let us talk about men themselves and their arts, for that is the heart of the matter."

So the diners out stepped forward with long slips of paper containing answers to their questions. These had been framed after much consideration. A good man, we had agreed, must at any rate be honest, passionate, and unworldly. But whether or not a particular man possessed those qualities could only be discovered by asking questions, often beginning at a remote distance from the centre. Is Kensington a nice place to live in? Where is your son being educated—and your daughter? Now please tell me, what do you pay for your cigars? By the way, is Sir Joseph a baronet or only a knight? Often it seemed that we learnt more from trivial questions of this kind than from more direct ones. "I accepted my peerage," said Lord Bunkum, "because my wife wished it." I forget how many titles were accepted for the same reason. "Working fifteen hours out of the twenty-four, as I do—" ten thousand professional men began.

"No, no, of course you can neither read nor write. But why do you work so hard?" "My dear lady, with a

growing family—" "But *why* does your family grow?" Their wives wished that too, or perhaps it was the British Empire. But more significant than the answers were the refusals to answer. Very few would reply at all to questions about morality and religion, and such answers as were given were not serious. Questions as to the value of money and power were almost invariably brushed aside, or pressed at extreme risk to the asker. "I'm sure," said Jill, "that if Sir Harley Tightboots hadn't been carving the mutton when I asked him about the capitalist system he would have cut my throat. The only reason why we escaped with our lives over and over again is that men are at once so hungry and so chivalrous. They despise us too much to mind what we say."

"Of course they despise us," said Eleanor. "At the same time how do you account for this—I made enquiries among the artists. Now, no woman has ever been an artist, has she, Polls?"

"Jane–Austen–Charlotte–Brontë–George–Eliot,"[1] cried Poll, like a man crying muffins in a back street.

"Damn the woman!" someone exclaimed. "What a bore she is!"

"Since Sappho there has been no female of first rate—" Eleanor began, quoting from a weekly newspaper.

"It's now well known that Sappho was the somewhat lewd invention of Professor Hobkin," Ruth interrupted.

"Anyhow, there is no reason to suppose that any woman ever has been able to write or ever will be able to write," Eleanor continued. "And yet, whenever I go among authors they never cease to talk to me about their books. Masterly! I say, or Shakespeare himself! (for one must say something) and I assure you, they believe me."

"That proves nothing," said Jane. "They all do it. Only," she sighed, "it doesn't seem to help *us* much. Perhaps we had better examine modern literature next. Liz, it's your turn."

Elizabeth rose and said that in order to prosecute her enquiry she had dressed as a man and been taken for a reviewer.

"I have read new books pretty steadily for the past five years," said she. "Mr. Wells is the most popular living writer; then comes Mr. Arnold Bennett; then Mr.

---

[1] *Jane … Eliot* Novelists Jane Austen (1775–1817), Charlotte Brontë (1816–45), and George Eliot (pseudonym of Marian Evans, 1819–1880).

Compton Makenzie; Mr. McKenna and Mr. Walpole may be bracketed together."[1] She sat down.

"But you've told us nothing!" we expostulated. "Or do you mean that these gentlemen have greatly surpassed Jane-Eliot and that English fiction is—where's that review of yours? Oh, yes, 'safe in their hands.'"

"Safe, quite safe," she said, shifting uneasily from foot to foot. "And I'm sure that they give away even more than they receive."

We were all sure of that. "But," we pressed her, "do they write good books?"

"Good books?" she said, looking at the ceiling "You must remember," she began, speaking with extreme rapidity, "that fiction is the mirror of life. And you can't deny that education is of the highest importance, and that it would be extremely annoying, if you found yourself alone at Brighton late at night, not to know which was the best boarding house to stay at, and suppose it was a dripping Sunday evening—wouldn't it be nice to go to the Movies?"

"But what has that got to do with it?" we asked.

"Nothing—nothing—nothing whatever," she replied.

"Well, tell us the truth," we bade her.

"The truth? But isn't it wonderful," she broke off—"Mr. Chitter has written a weekly article for the past thirty years upon love or hot buttered toast and has sent all his sons to Eton—"

"The truth!" we demanded.

"Oh, the truth," she stammered, "the truth has nothing to do with literature," and sitting down she refused to say another word.

It all seemed to us very inconclusive.

"Ladies, we must try to sum up the results," Jane was beginning, when a hum, which had been heard for some time through the open window, drowned her voice.

"War! War! War! Declaration of War!" men were shouting in the street below. We looked at each other in horror. "What war?" we cried. "What war?" We remembered, too late, that we had never thought of sending anyone to the House of Commons. We had forgotten all about it. We turned to Poll, who had reached the history shelves in the London Library, and asked her to enlighten us.

"Why," we cried, "do men go to war?"

"Sometimes for one reason, sometimes for another," she replied calmly. "In 1760, for example—" The shouts outside drowned her words. "Again in 1797—in 1804—It was the Austrians in 1866—1870 was the Franco-Prussian—In 1900 on the other hand—"

"But it's now 1914!" we cut her short.

"Ah, I don't know what they're going to war for now," she admitted.

* * *

The war was over and peace was in process of being signed,[2] when I once more found myself with Castalia in the room where our meetings used to be held. We began idly turning over the pages of our old minute books. "Queer," I mused, "to see what we were thinking five years ago." "We are agreed," Castalia quoted, reading over my shoulder, "that it is the object of life to produce good people and good books." We made no comment upon that. "A good man is at any rate honest, passionate and unworldly." "What a woman's language!" I observed. "Oh, dear," cried Castalia, pushing the book away from her, "what fools we were! It was all Poll's father's fault," she went on. "I believe he did it on purpose—that ridiculous will, I mean, forcing Poll to read all the books in the London Library. If we hadn't learnt to read," she said bitterly, "we might still have been bearing children in ignorance and that I believe was the happiest life after all. I know what you're going to say about war," she checked me, "and the horror of bearing children to see them killed, but our mothers did it, and their mothers, and their mothers before them. And they didn't complain. They couldn't read. I've done my best," she sighed, "to prevent my little girl from learning to read, but what's the use? I caught Ann only yesterday with a newspaper in her hand and she was beginning to ask me if it was 'true.' Next she'll ask me whether Mr. Lloyd George is a good man, then whether Mr. Arnold Bennett is a good novelist, and finally whether I believe in God. How can I bring my daughter up to believe in nothing?" she demanded.

[1] *Mr. Wells* H.G Wells (1866–1946); *Mr. Arnold Bennett* 1867–1931; *Mr. Compton Mackenzie* 1883–1972; *Mr. McKenna* Andrew McKenna (1833–72); *Mr. Walpole* Horace Walpole (1717–97).

[2] *peace … signed* The Treaty of Versailles was signed on 28 June 1919 and took effect on 10 January 1920.

"Surely you could teach her to believe that a man's intellect is, and always will be, fundamentally superior to a woman's?" I suggested. She brightened at this and began to turn over our old minutes again. "Yes," she said, "think of their discoveries, their mathematics, their science, their philosophy, their scholarship—" and then she began to laugh, "I shall never forget old Hobkin and the hairpin," she said, and went on reading and laughing and I thought she was quite happy, when suddenly she drew the book from her and burst out, "Oh, Cassandra, why do you torment me? Don't you know that our belief in man's intellect is the greatest fallacy of them all?" "What?" I exclaimed. "Ask any journalist, schoolmaster, politician or public house keeper in the land and they will all tell you that men are much cleverer than women." "As if I doubted it," she said scornfully. "How could they help it? Haven't we bred them and fed and kept them in comfort since the beginning of time so that they may be clever even if they're nothing else? It's all our doing!" she cried. "We insisted upon having intellect and now we've got it. And it's intellect," she continued, "that's at the bottom of it. What could be more charming than a boy before he has begun to cultivate his intellect? He is beautiful to look at; he gives himself no airs; he understands the meaning of art and literature instinctively; he goes about enjoying his life and making other people enjoy theirs. Then they teach him to cultivate his intellect. He becomes a barrister, a civil servant, a general, an author, a professor. Every day he goes to an office. Every year he produces a book. He maintains a whole family by the products of his brain—poor devil! Soon he cannot come into a room without making us all feel uncomfortable; he condescends to every woman he meets, and dares not tell the truth even to his own wife; instead of rejoicing our eyes we have to shut them if we are to take him in our arms. True, they console themselves with stars of all shapes, ribbons of all shades, and incomes of all sizes—but what is to console us? That we shall be able in ten years' time to spend a weekend at Lahore? Or that the least insect in Japan has a name twice the length of its body? Oh, Cassandra, for Heaven's sake let us devise a method by which men may bear children! It is our only chance. For unless we provide them with some innocent occupation we shall get neither good people nor good books; we shall perish beneath the fruits of their unbridled activity; and not a human being will survive to know that there once was Shakespeare!"

"It is too late," I replied. "We cannot provide even for the children that we have."

"And then you ask me to believe in intellect," she said.

While we spoke, man were crying hoarsely and wearily in the street, and, listening, we heard that the Treaty of Peace had just been signed. The voices died away. The rain was falling and interfered no doubt with the proper explosion of the fireworks.

"My cook will have bought the *Evening News*," said Castalia, "and Ann will be spelling it out over her tea. I must go home."

"It's no good—not a bit of good," I said. "Once she knows how to read there's only one thing you can teach her to believe in—and that is herself."

"Well, that would be a change," sighed Castalia.

So we swept up the papers of our Society, and, though Ann was playing with her doll very happily, we solemnly made her a present of the lot and told her we had chosen her to be President of the Society of the future—upon which she burst into tears, poor little girl.

MONDAY OR TUESDAY

Lazy and indifferent, shaking space easily from his wings, knowing his way, the heron passes over the church beneath the sky. White and distant, absorbed in itself, endlessly the sky covers and uncovers, moves and remains. A lake? Blot the shores of it out! A mountain? Oh, perfect—the sun gold on its slopes. Down that falls. Ferns then, or white feathers, for ever and ever—

Desiring truth, awaiting it, laboriously distilling a few words, for ever desiring—(a cry starts to the left, another to the right. Wheels strike divergently. Omnibuses conglomerate in conflict)—for ever desiring—(the clock asseverates with twelve distinct strokes that it is midday; light sheds gold scales; children swarm)—for ever desiring truth. Red is the dome; coins hang on the trees; smoke trails from the chimneys; bark, shout, cry "Iron for sale"—and truth?

Radiating to a point men's feet and women's feet,

black or gold-encrusted—(This foggy weather—Sugar? No, thank you—The commonwealth of the future) —the firelight darting and making the room red, save for the black figures and their bright eyes, while outside a van discharges, Miss Thingummy drinks tea at her desk, and plate-glass preserves fur coats—

Flaunted, leaf-light, drifting at corners, blown across the wheels, silver-splashed, home or not home, gathered, scattered, squandered in separate scales, swept up, down, torn, sunk, assembled—and truth?

Now to recollect by the fireside on the white square of marble. From ivory depths words rising shed their blackness, blossom and penetrate. Fallen the book; in the flame, in the smoke, in the momentary sparks—or now voyaging, the marble square pendant, minarets beneath and the Indian seas, while space rushes blue and stars glint—truth? content with closeness?

Lazy and indifferent the heron returns; the sky veils her stars; then bares them.

AN UNWRITTEN NOVEL

Such an expression of unhappiness was enough by itself to make one's eyes slide above the paper's edge to the poor woman's face—insignificant without that look, almost a symbol of human destiny with it. Life's what you see in people's eyes; life's what they learn, and, having learnt it, never, though they seek to hide it, cease to be aware of—what? That life's like that, it seems. Five faces opposite—five mature faces—and the knowledge in each face. Strange, though, how people want to conceal it! Marks of reticence are on all those faces: lips shut, eyes shaded, each one of the five doing something to hide or stultify his knowledge. One smokes; another reads; a third checks entries in a pocket book; a fourth stares at the map of the line framed opposite; and the fifth—the terrible thing about the fifth is that she does nothing at all. She looks at life. Ah, but my poor, unfortunate woman, do play the game—do, for all our sakes, conceal it!

As if she heard me, she looked up, shifted slightly in her seat and sighed. She seemed to apologise and at the same time to say to me, "If only you knew!" Then she looked at life again. "But I do know," I answered silently, glancing at *The Times* for manners' sake. "I know the whole business. 'Peace between Germany and the Allied Powers was yesterday officially ushered in at Paris—Signor Nitti, the Italian Prime Minister—a passenger train at Doncaster was in collision with a goods train...' We all know—*The Times* knows—but we pretend we don't." My eyes had once more crept over the paper's rim. She shuddered, twitched her arm queerly to the middle of her back and shook her head. Again I dipped into my great reservoir of life. "Take what you like," I continued, "births, deaths, marriages, Court Circular, the habits of birds, Leonardo da Vinci, the Sandhills murder, high wages and the cost of living—oh, take what you like," I repeated, "it's all in *The Times*!" Again with infinite weariness she moved her head from side to side until, like a top exhausted with spinning, it settled on her neck.

The Times was no protection against such sorrow as hers. But other human beings forbade intercourse. The best thing to do against life was to fold the paper so that it made a perfect square, crisp, thick, impervious even to life. This done, I glanced up quickly, armed with a shield of my own. She pierced through my shield; she gazed into my eyes as if searching any sediment of courage at the depths of them and damping it to clay. Her twitch alone denied all hope, discounted all illusion.

So we rattled through Surrey and across the border into Sussex. But with my eyes upon life I did not see that the other travellers had left, one by one, till, save for the man who read, we were alone together. Here was Three Bridges station. We drew slowly down the platform and stopped. Was he going to leave us? I prayed both ways—I prayed last that he might stay. At that instant he roused himself, crumpled his paper contemptuously, like a thing done with, burst open the door, and left us alone.

The unhappy woman, leaning a little forward, palely and colourlessly addressed me—talked of stations and holidays, of brothers at Eastbourne, and the time of year, which was, I forget now, early or late. But at last looking from the window and seeing, I knew, only life, she breathed, "Staying away—that's the drawback of it—" Ah, now we approached the catastrophe, "My sister-in-law"—the bitterness of her tone was like lemon on cold steel, and speaking, not to me, but to herself, she muttered, "nonsense, she would say—that's what they all say," and while she spoke she fidgeted as though the skin on her back were as a plucked fowl's in a poulterer's shop-window.

"Oh, that cow!" she broke off nervously, as though the great wooden cow in the meadow had shocked her and saved her from some indiscretion. Then she shuddered, and then she made the awkward angular movement that I had seen before, as if, after the spasm, some spot between the shoulders burnt or itched. Then again she looked the most unhappy woman in the world, and I once more reproached her, though not with the same conviction, for if there were a reason, and if I knew the reason, the stigma was removed from life.

"Sisters-in-law," I said—

Her lips pursed as if to spit venom at the word; pursed they remained. All she did was to take her glove and rub hard at a spot on the window-pane. She rubbed as if she would rub something out for ever—some stain, some indelible contamination. Indeed, the spot remained for all her rubbing, and back she sank with the shudder and the clutch of the arm I had come to expect. Something impelled me to take my glove and rub my window. There, too, was a little speck on the glass. For all my rubbing it remained. And then the spasm went through me; I crooked my arm and plucked at the middle of my back. My skin, too, felt like the damp chicken's skin in the poulterer's shop-window; one spot between the shoulders itched and irritated, felt clammy, felt raw. Could I reach it? Surreptitiously I tried. She saw me. A smile of infinite irony, infinite sorrow, flitted and faded from her face. But she had communicated, shared her secret, passed her poison; she would speak no more. Leaning back in my corner, shielding my eyes from her eyes, seeing only the slopes and hollows, greys and purples, of the winter's landscape, I read her message, deciphered her secret, reading it beneath her gaze.

Hilda's the sister-in-law. Hilda? Hilda? Hilda Marsh—Hilda the blooming, the full bosomed, the matronly. Hilda stands at the door as the cab draws up, holding a coin. "Poor Minnie, more of a grasshopper than ever—old cloak she had last year. Well, well, with too children these days one can't do more. No, Minnie, I've got it; here you are, cabby—none of your ways with me. Come in, Minnie. Oh, I could carry you, let alone

your basket!" So they go into the dining-room. "Aunt Minnie, children." Slowly the knives and forks sink from the upright. Down they get (Bob and Barbara), hold out hands stiffly; back again to their chairs, staring between the resumed mouthfuls. [But this we'll skip; ornaments, curtains, trefoil china plate, yellow oblongs of cheese, white squares of biscuit—skip—oh, but wait! Half-way through luncheon one of those shivers; Bob stares at her, spoon in mouth. "Get on with your pudding, Bob"; but Hilda disapproves. "Why *should* she twitch?" Skip, skip, till we reach the landing on the upper floor; stairs brass-bound; linoleum worn; oh, yes! little bedroom looking out over the roofs of Eastbourne—zigzagging roofs like the spines of caterpillars, this way, that way, striped red and yellow, with blue-black slating.] Now, Minnie, the door's shut; Hilda heavily descends to the basement; you unstrap the straps of your basket, lay on the bed a meagre nightgown, stand side by side furred felt slippers. The looking-glass—no, you avoid the looking-glass. Some methodical disposition of hat-pins. Perhaps the shell box has something in it? You shake it; it's the pearl stud there was last year—that's all. And then the sniff, the sigh, the sitting by the window. Three o'clock on a December afternoon; the rain drizzling; one light low in the skylight of a drapery emporium; another high in a servant's bedroom—this one goes out. That gives her nothing to look at. A moment's blankness—then, what are you thinking? (Let me peep across at her opposite; she's asleep or pretending it; so what would she think about sitting at the window at three o'clock in the afternoon? Health, money, bills, her God?) Yes, sitting on the very edge of the chair looking over the roofs of Eastbourne, Minnie Marsh prays to Gods. That's all very well; and she may rub the pane too, as though to see God better; but what God does she see? Who's the God of Minnie Marsh, the God of the back streets of Eastbourne, the God of three o'clock in the afternoon? I, too, see roofs, I see sky; but, oh, dear—this seeing of Gods! More like President Kruger than Prince Albert[1]— that's the best I can do for him; and I see him on a

---

[1] *President Kruger* Paulus Kruger (1825–1904), who led the Boers in the 1880 rebellion against Britain and then became president of the Transvaal; *Prince Albert* Husband of Queen Victoria (1819–61).

chair, in a black frock-coat, not so very high up either; I can manage a cloud or two for him to sit on; and then his hand trailing in the cloud holds a rod, a truncheon is it?—black, thick, thorned—a brutal old bully—Minnie's God! Did he send the itch and the patch and the twitch? Is that why she prays? What she rubs on the window is the stain of sin. Oh, she committed some crime!

I have my choice of crimes. The woods flit and fly—in summer there are bluebells; in the opening there, when Spring comes, primroses. A parting, was it, twenty years ago? Vows broken? Not Minnie's! … She was faithful. How she nursed her mother! All her savings on the tombstone—wreaths under glass—daffodils in jars. But I'm off the track. A crime… They would say she kept her sorrow, suppressed her secret—her sex, they'd say—the scientific people. But what flummery to saddle *her* with sex! No—more like this. Passing down the streets of Croydon twenty years ago, the violet loops of ribbon in the draper's window spangled in the electric light catch her eye. She lingers—past six. Still by running she can reach home. She pushes through the glass swing door. It's sale-time. Shallow trays brim with ribbons. She pauses, pulls this, fingers that with the raised roses on it—no need to choose, no need to buy, and each tray with its surprises. "We don't shut till seven," and then it *is* seven. She runs, she rushes, home she reaches, but too late. Neighbours—the doctor—baby brother—the kettle—scalded—hospital—dead—or only the shock of it, the blame? Ah, but the detail matters nothing! It's what she carries with her; the spot, the crime, the thing to expiate, always there between her shoulders.

"Yes," she seems to nod to me, "it's the thing I did."

Whether you did, or what you did, I don't mind; it's not the thing I want. The draper's window looped with violet—that'll do; a little cheap perhaps, a little commonplace—since one has a choice of crimes, but then so many (let me peep across again—still sleeping, or pretending sleep! white, worn, the mouth closed—a touch of obstinacy, more than one would think—no hint of sex)—so many crimes aren't *your* crime; your crime was cheap; only the retribution solemn; for now the church door opens, the hard wooden pew receives her; on the brown tiles she kneels; every day, winter, summer, dusk, dawn (here she's at it) prays. All her sins fall, fall, for ever fall. The spot receives them. It's raised, it's red, it's burning. Next she twitches. Small boys point. "Bob at lunch to-day"—But elderly women are the worst.

Indeed now you can't sit praying any longer. Kruger's sunk beneath the clouds—washed over as with a painter's brush of liquid grey, to which he adds a tinge of black—even the tip of the truncheon gone now. That's what always happens! Just as you've seen him, felt him, someone interrupts. It's Hilda now.

How you hate her! She'll even lock the bathroom door overnight, too, though it's only cold water you want, and sometimes when the night's been bad it seems as if washing helped. And John at breakfast—the children—meals are worst, and sometimes there are friends—ferns don't altogether hide 'em—they guess, too; so out you go along the front, where the waves are grey, and the papers blow, and the glass shelters green and draughty, and the chairs cost tuppence—too much—for there must be preachers along the sands. Ah, that's a nigger—that's a funny man—that's a man with parakeets—poor little creatures! Is there no one here who thinks of God?—just up there, over the pier, with his rod—but no—there's nothing but grey in the sky or if it's blue the white clouds hide him, and the music—it's military music—and what they are fishing for? Do they catch them? How the children stare! Well, then home a back way—"Home a back way!" The words have meaning; might have been spoken by the old man with whiskers—no, no, he didn't really speak; but everything has meaning—placards leaning against doorways—names above shop-windows—red fruit in baskets—women's heads in the hairdresser's—all say "Minnie Marsh!" But here's a jerk. "Eggs are cheaper!" That's what always happens! I was heading her over the waterfall, straight for madness, when, like a flock of dream sheep, she turns t'other way and runs between my fingers. Eggs are cheaper. Tethered to the shores of the world, none of the crimes, sorrows, rhapsodies, or insanities for poor Minnie Marsh; never late for luncheon; never caught in a storm without a mackintosh; never utterly unconscious of the cheapness of eggs. So she reaches home—scrapes her boots.

Have I read you right? But the human face—the human face at the top of the fullest sheet of print holds more, withholds more. Now, eyes open, she looks out; and in the human eye—how d'you define it?—there's a break—a division—so that when you've grasped the stem the butterfly's off—the moth that hangs in the evening over the yellow flower--move, raise your hand, off, high, away. I won't raise my hand. Hang still, then, quiver, life, soul, spirit, whatever you are of Minnie Marsh—I, too, on my flower—the hawk over the down—alone, or what were the worth of life? To rise; hang still in the evening, in the midday; hang still over the down. The flicker of a hand—off, up! then poised again. Alone, unseen; seeing all so still down there, all so lovely. None seeing, none caring. The eyes of others our prisons; their thoughts our cages. Air above, air below. And the moon and immortality… Oh, but I drop to the turf! Are you down too, you in the corner, what's your name—woman—Minnie Marsh; some such name as that? There she is, tight to her blossom; opening her hand-bag, from which she takes a hollow shell—an egg—who was saying that eggs were cheaper? You or I? Oh, it was you who said it on the way home, you remember, when the old gentleman, suddenly opening his umbrella—or sneezing was it? Anyhow, Kruger went, and you came "home a back way," and scraped your boots. Yes. And now you lay across your knees a pocket-handkerchief into which drop little angular fragments of eggshell—fragments of a map—a puzzle. I wish I could piece them together! If you would only sit still. She's moved her knees—the map's in bits again. Down the slopes of the Andes the white blocks of marble go bounding and hurtling, crushing to death a whole troop of Spanish muleteers, with their con-voy—Drake's[1] booty, gold and silver. But to return—

To what, to where? She opened the door, and, putting her umbrella in the stand—that goes without saying; so, too, the whiff of beef from the basement; dot, dot, dot. But what I cannot thus eliminate, what I must, head down, eyes shut, with the courage of a battalion and the blindness of a bull, charge and disperse are, indubitably, the figures behind the ferns, commercial travellers. There I've hidden them all this time in the hope that somehow they'd disappear, or better still

emerge, as indeed they must, if the story's to go on gathering richness and rotundity, destiny and tragedy, as stories should, rolling along with it two, if not three, commercial travellers and a whole grove of aspidistra. "The fronds of the aspidistra only partly concealed the commercial traveller—" Rhododendrons would conceal him utterly, and into the bargain give me my fling of red and white, for which I starve and strive; but rhodo-dendrons in Eastbourne—in December—on the Marshes' table—no, no, I dare not; it's all a matter of crusts and cruets, frills and ferns. Perhaps there'll be a moment later by the sea. Moreover, I feel, pleasantly pricking through the green fretwork and over the glacis[2] of cut glass, a desire to peer and peep at the man opposite—one's as much as I can manage. James Moggridge is it, whom the Marshes call Jimmy? [Minnie, you must promise not to twitch till I've got this straight]. James Moggridge travels in—shall we say buttons?—but the time's not come for bringing *them* in—the big and the little on the long cards, some peacock-eyed, others dull gold; cairngorms[3] some, and others coral sprays—but I say the time's not come. He travels, and on Thursdays, his Eastbourne day, takes his meals with the Marshes. His red face, his little steady eyes—by no means altogether commonplace—his enormous appetite (that's safe; he won't look at Minnie till the bread's swamped the gravy dry), napkin tucked diamond-wise—but this is primitive, and, whatever it may do the reader, don't take me in. Let's dodge to the Moggridge household, set that in motion. Well, the family boots are mended on Sundays by James himself. He reads *Truth*. But his passion? Roses—and his wife a retired hospital nurse—interesting—for God's sake let me have one woman with a name I like! But no; she's of the unborn children of the mind, illicit, none the less loved, like my rhododendrons. How many die in every novel that's written—the best, the dearest, while Mog-gridge lives. It's life's fault. Here's Minnie eating her egg at the moment opposite and at t'other end of the line—are we past Lewes?—there must be Jimmy—or what's her twitch for?

There must be Moggridge—life's fault. Life imposes her laws; life blocks the way; life's behind the fern; life's

---

[1] *Drake* Sir Francis Drake (c. 1540–96), English privateer and slave trader who was second-in-command of the English Fleet in the battle against the Spanish Armada.

[2] *glacis* Sloping bank.

[3] *cairngorms* Precious, wine-colored stones.

the tyrant; oh, but not the bully! No, for I assure you I come willingly; I come wooed by Heaven knows what compulsion across ferns and cruets, table splashed and bottles smeared. I come irresistibly to lodge myself somewhere on the firm flesh, in the robust spine, wherever I can penetrate or find foothold on the person, in the soul, of Moggridge the man. The enormous stability of the fabric; the spine tough as whalebone, straight as oaktree; the ribs radiating branches; the flesh taut tarpaulin; the red hollows; the suck and regurgitation of the heart; while from above meat falls in brown cubes and beer gushes to be churned to blood again—and so we reach the eyes. Behind the aspidistra[1] they see something: black, white, dismal; now the plate again; behind the aspidistra they see an elderly woman; "Marsh's sister, Hilda's more my sort;" the tablecloth now. "Marsh would know what's wrong with Morris…" talk that over; cheese has come; the plate again; turn it round—the enormous fingers; now the woman opposite. "Marsh's sister—not a bit like Marsh; wretched, elderly female… You should feed your hens… God's truth, what's set her twitching? Not what I said? Dear, dear, dear! these elderly women. Dear, dear!"

[Yes, Minnie; I know you've twitched, but one moment—James Moggridge].

"Dear, dear, dear!" How beautiful the sound is! like the knock of a mallet on seasoned timber, like the throb of the heart of an ancient whaler when the seas press thick and the green is clouded. "Dear, dear!" what a passing bell for the souls of the fretful to soothe them and solace them, lap them in linen, saying, "So long. Good luck to you!" and then, "What's your pleasure?" for though Moggridge would pluck his rose for her, that's done, that's over. Now what's the next thing? "Madam, you'll miss your train," for they don't linger.

That's the man's way; that's the sound that reverberates; that's St. Paul's and the motor-omnibuses. But we're brushing the crumbs off. Oh, Moggridge, you won't stay? You must be off? Are you driving through Eastbourne this afternoon in one of those little carriages? Are you the man who's walled up in green cardboard boxes, and sometimes has the blinds down, and sometimes sits so solemn staring like a sphinx, and

always there's a look of the sepulchral, something of the undertaker, the coffin, and the dusk about horse and driver? Do tell me—but the doors slammed. We shall never meet again. Moggridge, farewell!

Yes, yes, I'm coming. Right up to the top of the house. One moment I'll linger. How the mud goes round in the mind—what a swirl these monsters leave, the waters rocking, the weeds waving and green here, black there, striking to the sand, till by degrees the atoms reassemble, the deposit sifts itself, and again through the eyes one sees clear and still, and there comes to the lips some prayer for the departed, some obsequy for the souls of those one nods to, the people one never meets again.

James Moggridge is dead now, gone for ever. Well, Minnie—"I can face it no longer." If she said that—(Let me look at her. She is brushing the eggshell into deep declivities). She said it certainly, leaning against the wall of the bedroom, and plucking at the little balls which edge the claret-coloured curtain. But when the self speaks to the self, who is speaking?—the entombed soul, the spirit driven in, in, in to the central catacomb; the self that took the veil and left the world—a coward perhaps, yet somehow beautiful, as it flits with its lantern restlessly up and down the dark corridors. "I can bear it no longer," her spirit says. "That man at lunch—Hilda—the children." Oh, heavens, her sob! It's the spirit wailing its destiny, the spirit driven hither, thither, lodging on the diminishing carpets—meagre footholds—shrunken shreds of all the vanishing universe—love, life, faith, husband, children, I know not what splendours and pageantries glimpsed in girlhood. "Not for me—not for me."

But then—the muffins, the bald elderly dog? Bead mats I should fancy and the consolation of underlinen. If Minnie Marsh were run over and taken to hospital, nurses and doctors themselves would exclaim…. There's the vista and the vision—there's the distance—the blue blot at the end of the avenue, while, after all, the tea is rich, the muffin hot, and the dog—"Benny, to your basket, sir, and see what mother's brought you!" So, taking the glove with the worn thumb, defying once more the encroaching demon of what's called going in holes, you renew the fortifications, threading the grey wool, running it in and out.

---

[1] *aspidistra* Type of common house plant; in discussions of twentieth-century English life, it is often used as a symbol of common middle-class respectability.

Running it in and out, across and over, spinning a web through which God himself—hush, don't think of God! How firm the stitches are! You must be proud of your darning. Let nothing disturb her. Let the light fall gently, and the clouds show an inner vest of the first green leaf. Let the sparrow perch on the twig and shake the raindrop hanging to the twig's elbow.... Why look up? Was it a sound, a thought? Oh, heavens! Back again to the thing you did, the plate glass with the violet loops? But Hilda will come. Ignominies, humiliations, oh! Close the breach.

Having mended her glove, Minnie Marsh lays it in the drawer. She shuts the drawer with decision. I catch sight of her face in the glass. Lips are pursed. Chin held high. Next she laces her shoes. Then she touches her throat. What's your brooch? Mistletoe or merry-thought?[1] And what is happening? Unless I'm much mistaken, the pulse's quickened, the moment's coming, the threads are racing, Niagara's ahead. Here's the crisis! Heaven be with you! Down she goes. Courage, courage! Face it, be it! For God's sake don't wait on the mat now! There's the door! I'm on your side. Speak! Confront her, confound her soul!

"Oh, I beg your pardon! Yes, this is Eastbourne. I'll reach it down for you. Let me try the handle." [But, Minnie, though we keep up pretences, I've read you right—I'm with you now.]

"That's all your luggage?"

"Much obliged, I'm sure."

(But why do you look about you? Hilda won't come to the station, nor John; and Moggridge is driving at the far side of Eastbourne.)

"I'll wait by my bag, ma'am, that's safest. He said he'd meet me.... Oh, there he is! That's my son."

So they walk off together.

Well, but I'm confounded.... Surely, Minnie, you know better! A strange young man.... Stop! I'll tell him—Minnie!—Miss Marsh!—I don't know though. There's something queer in her cloak as it blows. Oh, but it's untrue, it's indecent.... Look how he bends as they reach the gateway. She finds her ticket. What's the joke? Off they go, down the road, side by side.... Well, my world's done for! What do I stand on? What do I know? That's not Minnie. There never was Moggridge.

Who am I? Life's bare as bone.

And yet the last look of them—he stepping from the kerb and she following him round the edge of the big building brims me with wonder—floods me anew. Mysterious figures! Mother and son. Who are you? Why do you walk down the street? Where to-night will you sleep, and then, to-morrow? Oh, how it whirls and surges—floats me afresh! I start after them. People drive this way and that. The white light splutters and pours. Plate-glass windows. Carnations; chrysanthemums. Ivy in dark gardens. Milk carts at the door. Wherever I go, mysterious figures, I see you, turning the corner, mothers and sons; you, you, you. I hasten, I follow. This, I fancy, must be the sea. Grey is the landscape; dim as ashes; the water murmurs and moves. If I fall on my knees, if I go through the ritual, the ancient antics, it's you, unknown figures, you I adore; if I open my arms, it's you I embrace, you I draw to me—adorable world!

THE STRING QUARTET

Well, here we are, and if you cast your eye over the room you will see that Tubes[2] and trams and omnibuses, private carriages not a few, even, I venture to believe, landaus with bays[3] in them, have been busy at it, weaving threads from one end of London to the other. Yet I begin to have my doubts—

If indeed it's true, as they're saying, that Regent Street is up, and the Treaty signed,[4] and the weather not cold for the time of year, and even at that rent not a flat to be had, and the worst of influenza its after effects; if I bethink me of having forgotten to write about the leak in the larder, and left my glove in the train; if the ties of blood require me, leaning forward, to accept cordially the hand which is perhaps offered hesitatingly—

"Seven years since we met!"

"The last time in Venice."

"And where are you living now?"

"Well, the late afternoon suits me the best, though, if it weren't asking too much—"

---

[1] *merry-thought* Bird's wishbone.

[2] *Tubes* Subways.

[3] *landaus* Four-wheeled carriages; *bays* Bay windows.

[4] *Treaty* The Treaty of Versailles was signed on 28 June 1919 and took effect on 10 January 1920.

"But I knew you at once!"

"Still, the war made a break—"

If the mind's shot through by such little arrows, and—for human society compels it—no sooner is one launched than another presses forward; if this engenders heat and in addition they've turned on the electric light; if saying one thing does, in so many cases, leave behind it a need to improve and revise, stirring besides regrets, pleasures, vanities, and desires—if it's all the facts I mean, and the hats, the fur boas, the gentlemen's swallow-tail coats, and pearl tie-pins that come to the surface—what chance is there?

Of what? It becomes every minute more difficult to say why, in spite of everything, I sit here believing I can't now say what, or even remember the last time it happened.

"Did you see the procession?"

"The King looked cold."

"No, no, no. But what was it?"

"She's bought a house at Malmesbury."

"How lucky to find one!"

On the contrary, it seems to me pretty sure that she, whoever she may be, is damned, since it's all a matter of flats and hats and sea gulls, or so it seems to be for a hundred people sitting here well dressed, walled in, furred, replete. Not that I can boast, since I too sit passive on a gilt chair, only turning the earth above a buried memory, as we all do, for there are signs, if I'm not mistaken, that we're all recalling something, furtively seeking something. Why fidget? Why so anxious about the sit of cloaks; and gloves—whether to button or unbutton? Then watch that elderly face against the dark canvas, a moment ago urbane and flushed; now taciturn and sad, as if in shadow. Was it the sound of the second violin tuning in the ante-room? Here they come; four black figures, carrying instruments, and seat themselves facing the white squares under the downpour of light; rest the tips of their bows on the music stand; with a simultaneous movement lift them; lightly poise them, and, looking across at the player opposite, the first violin counts one, two, three—

Flourish, spring, burgeon, burst! The pear tree on the top of the mountain. Fountains jet; drops descend. But the waters of the Rhone flow swift and deep, race under the arches, and sweep the trailing water leaves, washing shadows over the silver fish, the spotted fish rushed down by the swift waters, now swept into an eddy where—it's difficult this—conglomeration of fish all in a pool; leaping, splashing, scraping sharp fins; and such a boil of current that the yellow pebbles are churned round and round, round and round—free now, rushing downwards, or even somehow ascending in exquisite spirals into the air; curled like thin shavings from under a plane; up and up…. How lovely goodness is in those who, stepping lightly, go smiling through the world! Also in jolly old fishwives, squatted under arches, oh scene old women, how deeply they laugh and shake and rollick, when they walk, from side to side, hum, hah!

"That's an early Mozart, of course—"

"But the tune, like all his tunes, makes one despair—I mean hope. What do I mean? That's the worst of music! I want to dance, laugh, eat pink cakes, yellow cakes, drink thin, sharp wine. Or an indecent story, now—I could relish that. The older one grows the more one likes indecency. Hall, hah! I'm laughing. What at? You said nothing, nor did the old gentleman opposite…. But suppose—suppose—Hush!"

The melancholy river bears us on. When the moon comes through the trailing willow boughs, I see your face, I hear your voice and the bird singing as we pass the osier bed. What are you whispering? Sorrow, sorrow. Joy, joy. Woven together, like reeds in moonlight. Woven together, inextricably commingled, bound in pain and strewn in sorrow—crash!

The boat sinks. Rising, the figures ascend, but now leaf thin, tapering to a dusky wraith, which, fiery tipped, draws its twofold passion from my heart. For me it sings, unseals my sorrow, thaws compassion, floods with love the sunless world, nor, ceasing, abates its tenderness but deftly, subtly, weaves in and out until in this pattern, this consummation, the cleft ones unify; soar, sob, sink to rest, sorrow and joy.

Why then grieve? Ask what? Remain unsatisfied? I say all's been settled; yes; laid to rest under a coverlet of rose leaves, falling. Falling. Ah, but they cease. One rose leaf, falling from an enormous height, like a little parachute dropped from an invisible balloon, turns, flutters waveringly. It won't reach us.

"No, no. I noticed nothing. That's the worst of music—these silly dreams. The second violin was late, you say?"

"There's old Mrs. Munro, feeling her way out—blinder each year, poor woman—on this slippery floor."

Eyeless old age, grey-headed Sphinx … There she stands on the pavement, beckoning, so sternly, the red omnibus.

"How lovely! How well they play! How—how—how!"

The tongue is but a clapper. Simplicity itself. The feathers in the hat next me are bright and pleasing as a child's rattle. The leaf on the plane-tree flashes green through the chink in the curtain. Very strange, very exciting.

"How—how—how!" Hush!

These are the lovers on the grass.

"If, madam, you will take my hand—"

"Sir, I would trust you with my heart. Moreover, we have left our bodies in the banqueting hall. Those on the turf are the shadows of our souls."

"Then these are the embraces of our souls." The lemons nod assent. The swan pushes from the bank and floats dreaming into mid stream.

"But to return. He followed me down the corridor, and, as we turned the corner, trod on the lace of my petticoat. What could I do but cry 'Ah!' and stop to finger it? At which he drew his sword, made passes as if he were stabbing something to death, and cried, 'Mad! Mad! Mad!' Whereupon I screamed, and the Prince, who was writing in the large vellum book in the oriel window, came out in his velvet skull-cap and furred slippers, snatched a rapier from the wall—the King of Spain's gift, you know—on which I escaped, flinging on this cloak to hide the ravages to my skirt—to hide… But listen! the horns!"

The gentleman replies so fast to the lady, and she runs up the scale with such witty exchange of compliment now culminating in a sob of passion, that the words are indistinguishable though the meaning is plain enough—love, laughter, flight, pursuit, celestial bliss—all floated out on the gayest ripple of tender endearment—until the sound of the silver horns, at first far distant, gradually sounds more and more distinctly, as if seneschals were saluting the dawn or proclaiming ominously the escape of the lovers… The green garden, moonlit pool, lemons, lovers, and fish are all dissolved in the opal sky, across which, as the horns are joined by trumpets and supported by clarions there rise white arches firmly planted on marble pillars… Tramp and trumpeting. Clang and clangour. Firm establishment. Fast foundations. March of myriads. Confusion and chaos trod to earth. But this city to which we travel has neither stone nor marble; hangs enduring; stands unshakable; nor does a face, nor does a flag greet or welcome. Leave then to perish your hope; droop in the desert my joy; naked advance. Bare are the pillars; auspicious to none; casting no shade; resplendent; severe. Back then I fall, eager no more, desiring only to go, find the street, mark the buildings, greet the apple-woman, say to the maid who opens the door: A starry night.

"Good night, good night. You go this way?"

"Alas. I go that."

BLUE & GREEN

GREEN

The pointed fingers of glass hang downwards. The light slides down the glass, and drops a pool of green. All day long the ten fingers of the lustre drop green upon the marble. The feathers of parakeets—their harsh cries—sharp blades of palm trees—green, too; green needles glittering in the sun. But the hard glass drips on to the marble; the pools hover above the desert sand; the camels lurch through them; the pools settle on the marble; rushes edge them; weeds clog them; here and there a white blossom; the frog flops over; at night the stars are set there unbroken. Evening comes, and the shadow sweeps the green over the mantelpiece; the ruffled surface of ocean. No ships come; the aimless waves sway beneath the empty sky. It's night; the needles drip blots of blue. The green's out.

BLUE

The snub-nosed monster rises to the surface and spouts through his blunt nostrils two columns of water, which, fiery-white in the centre, spray off into a fringe of blue beads. Strokes of blue line the black tarpaulin of his hide. Slushing the water through mouth and nostrils he sinks, heavy with water, and the blue closes over him dowsing the polished pebbles of his eyes. Thrown upon the beach he lies, blunt, obtuse, shedding dry blue scales. Their metallic blue stains the rusty iron on the beach. Blue are the ribs of the wrecked rowing boat. A wave rolls beneath the blue bells. But the cathedral's different, cold, incense laden, faint blue with the veils of madonnas.

KEW GARDENS

From the oval-shaped flower-bed there rose perhaps a hundred stalks spreading into heart-shaped or tongue-shaped leaves half way up and unfurling at the tip red or blue or yellow petals marked with spots of colour raised upon the surface; and from the red, blue or yellow gloom of the throat emerged a straight bar, rough with gold dust and slightly clubbed at the end. The petals were voluminous enough to be stirred by the summer breeze, and when they moved, the red, blue, and yellow lights passed one over the other, staining an inch of the brown earth beneath with a spot of the most intricate colour. The light fell either upon the smooth grey back of a pebble, or the shell of a snail with its brown circular veins, or, falling into a raindrop, it expanded with such intensity of red, blue, and yellow the thin walls of water that one expected them to burst and disappear. Instead, the drop was left in a second silver grey once more, and the light now settled upon the flesh of a leaf, revealing the branching thread of fibre beneath the surface, and again it moved on and spread its illumination in the vast green spaces beneath the dome of the heart-shaped and tongue-shaped leaves. Then the breeze stirred rather more briskly overhead and the colour was flashed into the air above, into the eyes of the men and women who walk in Kew Gardens in July.

The figures of these men and women straggled past the flower-bed with a curiously irregular movement not unlike that of the white and blue butterflies who crossed the turf in zig-zag flights from bed to bed. The man was about six inches in front of the woman, strolling carelessly, while she bore on with greater purpose, only turning her head now and then to see that the children were not too far behind. The man kept this distance in front of the woman purposely, though perhaps unconsciously, for he wanted to go on with his thoughts.

"Fifteen years ago I came here with Lily," he thought. "We sat somewhere over there by a lake, and I begged her to marry me all through the hot afternoon. How the dragon-fly kept circling round us: how clearly I see the dragon-fly and her shoe with the square silver buckle at the toe. All the time I spoke I saw her shoe and when it moved impatiently I knew without looking up what she was going to say: the whole of her seemed to be in her shoe. And my love, my desire, were in the dragon-fly; for some reason I thought that if it settled there, on that leaf, the broad one with the red flower in the middle of it, if the dragonfly settled on the leaf she would say 'Yes' at once. But the dragon-fly went round and round: it never settled anywhere—of course not, happily not, or I shouldn't be walking here with Eleanor and the children—Tell me, Eleanor, d'you ever think of the past?"

"Why do you ask, Simon?"

"Because I've been thinking of the past. I've been thinking of Lily, the woman I might have married … Well, why are you silent? Do you mind my thinking of the past?"

"Why should I mind, Simon? Doesn't one always think of the past, in a garden with men and women lying under the trees? Aren't they one's past, all that remains of it, those men and women, those ghosts lying under the trees … one's happiness, one's reality?"

"For me, a square silver shoe-buckle and a dragon-fly—"

"For me, a kiss. Imagine six little girls sitting before their easels twenty years ago, down by the side of a lake, painting the water-lilies, the first red water-lilies I'd ever seen. And suddenly a kiss, there on the back of my neck. And my hand shook all the afternoon so that I couldn't paint. I took out my watch and marked the hour when I would allow myself to think of the kiss for five minutes only—it was so precious—the kiss of an old grey-haired woman with a wart on her nose, the mother of all my kisses all my life. Come Caroline, come Hubert."

They walked on past the flower-bed, now walking four abreast, and soon diminished in size among the trees and looked half transparent as the sunlight and shade swam over their backs in large trembling irregular patches.

In the oval flower-bed the snail, whose shell had been stained red, blue and yellow for the space of two minutes or so, now appeared to be moving very slightly in its shell, and next began to labour over the crumbs of loose earth which broke away and rolled down as it passed over them. It appeared to have a definite goal in front of it, differing in this respect from the singular high-stepping angular green insect who attempted to cross in front of it, and waited for a second with its antennae trembling as if in deliberation, and then stepped off as rapidly and strangely in the opposite direction. Brown cliffs with deep green lakes in the hollows, flat blade-like trees that waved from root to tip, round boulders of grey stone, vast crumpled surfaces of a thin crackling texture—all these objects lay across the snail's progress between one stalk and another to his goal. Before he had decided whether to circumvent the arched tent of a dead leaf or to breast it there came past the bed the feet of other human beings.

This time they were both men. The younger of the two wore an expression of perhaps unnatural calm; he raised his eyes and fixed them very steadily in front of him while his companion spoke, and directly his companion had done speaking he looked on the ground again and sometimes opened his lips only after a long pause and sometimes did not open them at all. The elder man had a curiously uneven and shaky method of walking, jerking his hand forward and throwing up his head abruptly, rather in the manner of an impatient carriage horse tired of waiting outside a house; but in the man these gestures were irresolute and pointless. He talked almost incessantly; he smiled to himself and again began to talk, as if the smile had been an answer. He was talking about spirits—the spirits of the dead, who, according to him, were even now telling him all sorts of odd things about their experiences in Heaven.

"Heaven was known to the ancients as Thessaly, William, and now, with this war, the spirit matter is rolling between the hills like thunder." He paused, seemed to listen, smiled, jerked his head and continued:—

"You have a small electric battery and a piece of rubber to insulate the wire—isolate?—insulate?—well,

we'll skip the details, no good going into details that wouldn't be understood—and in short the little machine stands in any convenient position by the head of the bed, we will say, on a neat mahogany stand. All arrangements being properly fixed by workmen under my direction, the widow applies her ear and summons the spirit by sign as agreed. Women! Widows! Women in black—"

Here he seemed to have caught sight of a woman's dress in the distance, which in the shade looked a purple black. He took off his hat, placed his hand upon his heart, and hurried towards her muttering and gesticulating feverishly. But William caught him by the sleeve and touched a flower with the tip of his walking-stick in order to divert the old man's attention. After looking at it for a moment in some confusion the old man bent his ear to it and seemed to answer a voice speaking from it, for he began talking about the forests of Uruguay which he had visited hundreds of years ago in company with the most beautiful young woman in Europe. He could be heard murmuring about forests of Uruguay blanketed with the wax petals of tropical roses, nightingales, sea beaches, mermaids and women drowned at sea, as he suffered himself to be moved on by William, upon whose face the look of stoical patience grew slowly deeper and deeper.

Following his steps so closely as to be slightly puzzled by his gestures came two elderly women of the lower middle class, one stout and ponderous, the other rosy-cheeked and nimble. Like most people of their station[1] they were frankly fascinated by any signs of eccentricity betokening a disordered brain, especially in the well-to-do; but they were too far off to be certain whether the gestures were merely eccentric or genuinely mad. After they had scrutinised the old man's back in silence for a moment and given each other a queer, sly look, they went on energetically piecing together their very complicated dialogue:

"Nell, Bert, Lot, Cess, Phil, Pa, he says, I says, she says, I says, I says, I says—"

"My Bert, Sis, Bill, Grandad, the old man, sugar,
　　Sugar, flour, kippers, greens
　　Sugar, sugar, sugar."

The ponderous woman looked through the pattern of

---

[1] *their station* I.e., their position in English society.

falling words at the flowers standing cool, firm and upright in the earth, with a curious expression. She saw them as a sleeper waking from a heavy sleep sees a brass candlestick reflecting the light in an unfamiliar way, and closes his eyes and opens them, and seeing the brass candlestick again, finally starts broad awake and stares at the candlestick with all his powers. So the heavy woman came to a standstill opposite the oval-shaped flower-bed, and ceased even to pretend to listen to what the other woman was saying. She stood there letting the words fall over her, swaying the top part of her body slowly backwards and forwards, looking at the flowers. Then she suggested that they should find a seat and have their tea.

The snail had now considered every possible method of reaching his goal without going round the dead leaf or climbing over it. Let alone the effort needed for climbing a leaf, he was doubtful whether the thin texture which vibrated with such an alarming crackle when touched even by the tip of his horns would bear his weight; and this determined him finally to creep beneath it, for there was a point where the leaf curved high enough from the ground to admit him. He had just inserted his head in the opening and was taking stock of the high brown roof and was getting used to the cool brown light when two other people came past outside on the turf. This time they were both young, a young man and a young woman. They were both in the prime of youth, or even in that season which precedes the prime of youth, the season before the smooth pink folds of the flower have burst their gummy case, when the wings of the butterfly, though fully grown, are motionless in the sun.

"Lucky it isn't Friday," he observed.

"Why? D'you believe in luck?"

"They make you pay sixpence on Friday."

"What's sixpence anyway? Isn't it worth sixpence?"

"What's 'it'—what do you mean by 'it'?"

"O anything—I mean—you know what I mean."

Long pauses came between each of these remarks: they were uttered in toneless and monotonous voices. The couple stood still on the edge of the flower-bed, and together pressed the end of her parasol deep down into the soft earth. The action and the fact that his hand rested on the top of hers expressed their feelings in a strange way, as these short insignificant words also

expressed something, words with short wings for their heavy body of meaning, inadequate to carry them far and thus alighting awkwardly upon the very common objects that surrounded them and were to their inexperienced touch so massive: but who knows (so they thought as they pressed the parasol into the earth) what precipices aren't concealed in them, or what slopes of ice don't shine in the sun on the other side? Who knows? Who has ever seen this before? Even when she wondered what sort of tea they gave you at Kew, he felt that something loomed up behind her words, and stood vast and solid behind them; and the mist very slowly rose and uncovered—O Heavens,—what were those shapes?—little white tables, and waitresses who looked first at her and then at him; and there was a bill that he would pay with a real two shilling piece, and it was real, all real, he assured himself, fingering the coin in his pocket, real to everyone except to him and to her; even to him it began to seem real; and then—but it was too exciting to stand and think any longer, and he pulled the parasol out of the earth with a jerk and was impatient to find the place where one had tea with other people, like other people.

"Come along, Trissie; it's time we had our tea."

"Wherever does one have one's tea?" she asked with the oddest thrill of excitement in her voice, looking vaguely round and letting herself be drawn on down the grass path, trailing her parasol, turning her head this way and that way, forgetting her tea, wishing to go down there and then down there, remembering orchids and cranes among wild flowers, a Chinese pagoda and a crimson-crested bird; but he bore her on.

Thus one couple after another with much the same irregular and aimless movement passed the flower-bed and were enveloped in layer after layer of green-blue vapour, in which at first their bodies had substance and a dash of colour, but later both substance and colour dissolved in the green-blue atmosphere. How hot it was! So hot that even the thrush chose to hop, like a mechanical bird, in the shadow of the flowers, with long pauses between one movement and the next; instead of rambling vaguely the white butterflies danced one above another, making with their white shifting flakes the outline of a shattered marble column above the tallest flowers; the glass roofs of the palm house shone as if a whole market full of shiny green umbrellas had opened in the sun; and in the drone of the aeroplane the voice of the summer sky murmured its fierce soul. Yellow and black, pink and snow white, shapes of all these colours, men, women, and children, were spotted for a second upon the horizon, and then, seeing the breadth of yellow that lay upon the grass, they wavered and sought shade beneath the trees, dissolving like drops of water in the yellow and green atmosphere, staining it faintly with red and blue. It seemed as if all gross and heavy bodies had sunk down in the heat motionless and lay huddled upon the ground, but their voices went wavering from them as if they were flames lolling from the thick waxen bodies of candles. Voices, yes, voices, wordless voices, breaking the silence suddenly with such depth of contentment, such passion of desire, or, in the voices of children, such freshness of surprise; breaking the silence? But there was no silence; all the time the motor omnibuses were turning their wheels and changing their gear; like a vast nest of Chinese boxes all of wrought steel turning ceaselessly one within another the city murmured; on the top of which the voices cried aloud and the petals of myriads of flowers flashed their colours into the air.

THE MARK ON THE WALL

Perhaps it was the middle of January in the present year that I first looked up and saw the mark on the wall. In order to fix a date it is necessary to remember what one saw. So now I think of the fire; the steady film of yellow light upon the page of my book; the three chrysanthemums in the round glass bowl on the mantelpiece. Yes, it must have been the winter time, and we had just finished our tea, for I remember that I was smoking a cigarette when I looked up and saw the mark on the wall for the first time. I looked up through the smoke of my cigarette and my eye lodged for a moment upon the burning coals, and that old fancy of the crimson flag flapping from the castle tower came into my mind, and I thought of the cavalcade of red knights riding up the side of the black rock. Rather to my relief the sight of the mark interrupted the fancy, for it is an old fancy, an automatic fancy, made as a child perhaps. The mark was a small round mark, black upon the white wall, about six or seven inches above the mantel-

piece.

How readily our thoughts swarm upon a new object, lifting it a little way, as ants carry a blade of straw so feverishly, and then leave it… .If that mark was made by a nail, it can't have been for a picture, it must have been for a miniature—the miniature of a lady with white powdered curls, powder-dusted cheeks, and lips like red carnations. A fraud of course, for the people who had this house before us would have chosen pictures in that way—an old picture for an old room. That is the sort of people they were— very interesting people, and I think of them so often, in such queer places, because one will never see them again, never know what happened next. They wanted to leave this house because they wanted to change their style of furniture, so he said, and he was in process of saying that in his opinion art should have ideas behind it when we were torn asunder, as one is torn from the old lady about to pour out tea and the young man about to hit the tennis ball in the back garden of the suburban villa as one rushes past in the train.

But as for that mark, I'm not sure about it; I don't believe it was made by a nail after all; it's too big, too round, for that. I might get up, but if I got up and looked at it, ten to one I shouldn't be able to say for certain; because once a thing's done, no one ever knows how it happened. Oh! dear me, the mystery of life! The inaccuracy of thought! The ignorance of humanity! To show how very little control of our possessions we have—what an accidental affair this living is after all our civilization—let me just count over a few of the things lost in our lifetime, beginning, for that seems always the most mysterious of losses—what cat would gnaw, what rat would nibble—three pale blue canisters of bookbinding tools? Then there were the bird cages, the iron hoops, the steel skates, the Queen Anne coal-scuttle, the bagatelle board,[1] the hand organ—all gone, and jewels too. Opals and emeralds, they lie about the roots of turnips. What a scraping paring affair it is to be sure! The wonder is that I've any clothes on my back, that I sit surrounded by solid furniture at this moment. Why, if one wants to compare life to anything, one must liken it to being blown through the Tube[2] at fifty miles an

---

[1] *bagatelle board* Playing surface for a game similar to billiards.

[2] *Tube* Nickname for the London Underground, the system of subway lines that underlies the city of London.

hour—landing at the other end without a single hairpin in one's hair! Shot out at the feet of God entirely naked! Tumbling head over heels in the asphodel[1] meadows like brown paper parcels pitched down a shoot in the post office! With one's hair flying back like the tail of a racehorse. Yes, that seems to express the rapidity of life, the perpetual waste and repair; all so casual, all so haphazard....

But after life. The slow pulling down of thick green stalks so that the cup of the flower, as it turns over, deluges one with purple and red light. Why, after all, should one not be born there as one is born here, helpless, speechless, unable to focus one's eyesight, groping at the roots of the grass, at the toes of the Giants? As for saying which are trees, and which are men and women, or whether there are such things, that one won't be in a condition to do for fifty years or so. There will be nothing but spaces of light and dark, intersected by thick stalks, and rather higher up perhaps, rose-shaped blots of an indistinct colour—dim pinks and blues—which will, as time goes on, become more definite, become—I don't know what....

And yet the mark on the wall is not a hole at all. It may even be caused by some round black substance, such as a small rose leaf, left over from the summer, and I, not being a very vigilant housekeeper—look at the dust on the mantelpiece, for example, the dust which, so they say, buried Troy three times over, only fragments of pots utterly refusing annihilation, as one can believe.

The tree outside the window taps very gently on the pane ... I want to think quietly, calmly, spaciously, never to be interrupted, never to have to rise from my chair, to slip easily from one thing to another, without any sense of hostility, or obstacle. I want to sink deeper and deeper, away from the surface, with its hard separate facts. To steady myself, let me catch hold of the first idea that passes ... Shakespeare ... Well, he will do as well as another. A man who sat himself solidly in an arm-chair, and looked into the fire, so—A shower of ideas fell perpetually from some very high Heaven down through his mind. He leant his forehead on his hand, and people, looking in through the open door—for this

scene is supposed to take place on a summer's evening—But how dull this is, this historical fiction! It doesn't interest me at all. I wish I could hit upon a pleasant track of thought, a track indirectly reflecting credit upon myself, for those are the pleasantest thoughts, and very frequent even in the minds of modest mouse-coloured people, who believe genuinely that they dislike to hear their own praises. They are not thoughts directly praising oneself; that is the beauty of them; they are thoughts like this:

"And then I came into the room. They were discussing botany. I said how I'd seen a flower growing on a dust heap on the site of an old house in Kingsway. The seed, I said, must have been sown in the reign of Charles the First. What flowers grew in the reign of Charles the First?" I asked—(but I don't remember the answer). Tall flowers with purple tassels to them perhaps. And so it goes on. All the time I'm dressing up the figure of myself in my own mind, lovingly, stealthily, not openly adoring it, for if I did that, I should catch myself out, and stretch my hand at once for a book in self-protection. Indeed, it is curious how instinctively one protects the image of oneself from idolatry or any other handling that could make it ridiculous, or too unlike the original to be believed in any longer. Or is it not so very curious after all? It is a matter of great importance. Suppose the looking-glass smashes, the image disappears, and the romantic figure with the green of forest depths all about it is there no longer, but only that shell of a person which is seen by other people—what an airless, shallow, bald, prominent world it becomes! A world not to be lived in. As we face each other in omnibuses and underground railways we are looking into the mirror; that accounts for the vagueness, the gleam of glassiness, in our eyes. And the novelists in future will realise more and more the importance of these reflections, for of course there is not one reflection but an almost infinite number; those are the depths they will explore, those the phantoms they will pursue, leaving the description of reality more and more out of their stories, taking a knowledge of it for granted, as the Greeks did and Shakespeare perhaps—but these generalisations are very worthless. The military sound of the word is enough. It recalls leading articles, cabinet ministers—a whole class of things indeed which as a child one thought the thing

---

[1] *asphodel* Genus of liliaceous flowers; said to cover the Elysian fields, the paradise where (according to Greek mythology) the blessed would reside after death.

itself, the standard thing, the real thing, from which one could not depart save at the risk of nameless damnation. Generalisations bring back somehow Sunday in London, Sunday afternoon walks, Sunday luncheons, and also ways of speaking of the dead, clothes, and habits—like the habit of sitting all together in one room until a certain hour, although nobody liked it. There was a rule for everything. The rule for tablecloths at that particular period was that they should be made of tapestry with little yellow compartments marked upon them, such as you may see in photographs of the carpets in the corridors of the royal palaces. Tablecloths of a different kind were not real tablecloths. How shocking, and yet how wonderful it was to discover that these real things, Sunday luncheons, Sunday walks, country houses, and tablecloths were not entirely real, were indeed half phantoms, and the damnation which visited the disbeliever in them was only a sense of illegitimate freedom. What now takes the place of those things I wonder, those real standard things? Men perhaps, should you be a woman; the masculine point of view which governs our lives, which sets the standard, which establishes Whitaker's Table of Precedency,[1] which has become, I suppose, since the war half a phantom to many men and women, which soon, one may hope, will be laughed into the dustbin where the phantoms go, the mahogany sideboards and the Landseer prints,[2] Gods and Devils, Hell and so forth, leaving us all with an intoxicating sense of illegitimate freedom—if freedom exists. ...

In certain lights that mark on the wall seems actually to project from the wall. Nor is it entirely circular. I cannot be sure, but it seems to cast a perceptible shadow, suggesting that if I ran my finger down that strip of the wall it would, at a certain point, mount and descend a small tumulus, a smooth tumulus like those barrows on the South Downs[3] which are, they say, either tombs or camps. Of the two I should prefer them to be tombs, desiring melancholy like most English people, and finding it natural at the end of a walk to think of

the bones stretched beneath the turf ... There must be some book about it. Some antiquary[4] must have dug up those bones and given them a name ... What sort of a man is an antiquary, I wonder? Retired Colonels for the most part, I daresay, leading parties of aged labourers to the top here, examining clods of earth and stone, and getting into correspondence with the neighbouring clergy, which, being opened at breakfast time, gives them a feeling of importance, and the comparison of arrowheads necessitates cross-country journeys to the country towns, an agreeable necessity both to them and to their elderly wives, who wish to make plum jam or to clean out the study, and have every reason for keeping that great question of the camp or the tomb in perpetual suspension, while the Colonel himself feels agreeably philosophic in accumulating evidence on both sides of the question. It is true that he does finally incline to believe in the camp; and, being opposed, indites a pamphlet which he is about to read at the quarterly meeting of the local society when a stroke lays him low, and his last conscious thoughts are not of wife or child, but of the camp and that arrowhead there, which is now in the case at the local museum, together with the foot of a Chinese murderess, a handful of Elizabethan nails, a great many Tudor clay pipes, a piece of Roman pottery, and the wine-glass that Nelson drank out of—proving I really don't know what.

No, no, nothing is proved, nothing is known. And if I were to get up at this very moment and ascertain that the mark on the wall is really—what shall I say?—the head of a gigantic old nail, driven in two hundred years ago, which has now, owing to the patient attrition of many generations of housemaids, revealed its head above the coat of paint, and is taking its first view of modern life in the sight of a white-walled fire-lit room, what should I gain? Knowledge? Matter for further speculation? I can think sitting still as well as standing up. And what is knowledge? What are our learned men save the descendants of witches and hermits who crouched in caves and in woods brewing herbs, interrogating shrew-mice and writing down the language of the stars? And the less we honour them as our superstitions dwindle and our respect for beauty and health of mind increases ... Yes, one could imagine a

---

[1] *Table of Precedency* Table in *Whitaker's Almanac* that illustrates the hierarchy of the various ranks of the British social order.

[2] *Landseer prints* Edwin Henry Landseer (1802–73) produced paintings and engravings of animals.

[3] *South Downs* Range of chalk hills in southeastern England; *barrows* Mounds of earth or stone.

[4] *antiquary* Collector of antiquities, usually a non-professional.

very pleasant world. A quiet spacious world, with the flowers so red and blue in the open fields. A world without professors or specialists or house-keepers with the profiles of policemen, a world which one could slice with one's thought as a fish slices the water with his fin, grazing the stems of the water-lilies, hanging suspended over nests of white sea eggs.... How peaceful it is down here, rooted in the centre of the world and gazing up through the grey waters, with their sudden gleams of light, and their reflections—if it were not for Whitaker's Almanack—if it were not for the Table of Precedency!

I must jump up and see for myself what that mark on the wall really is—a nail, a rose-leaf, a crack in the wood?

Here is Nature once more at her old game of self-preservation. This train of thought, she perceives, is threatening mere waste of energy, even some collision with reality, for who will ever be able to lift a finger against Whitaker's Table of Precedency? The Archbishop of Canterbury is followed by the Lord High Chancellor; the Lord High Chancellor is followed by the Archbishop of York. Everybody follows somebody, such is the philosophy of Whitaker; and the great thing is to know who follows whom. Whitaker knows, and let that, so Nature counsels, comfort you, instead of enraging you; and if you can't be comforted, if you must shatter this hour of peace, think of the mark on the wall.

I understand Nature's game—her prompting to take action as a way of ending any thought that threatens to excite or to pain. Hence, I suppose, comes our slight contempt for men of action—men, we assume, who don't think. Still, there's no harm in putting a full stop to one's disagreeable thoughts by looking at a mark on the wall.

Indeed, now that I have fixed my eyes upon it, I feel that I have grasped a plank in the sea; I feel a satisfying sense of reality which at once turns the two Archbishops and the Lord High Chancellor to the shadows of shades. Here is something definite, something real. Thus, waking from a midnight dream of horror, one hastily turns on the light and lies quiescent, worshipping the chest of drawers, worshipping solidity, worshipping reality, worshipping the impersonal world which is proof of some existence other than ours. That is what one wants to be sure of.... Wood is a pleasant thing to think about. It comes from a tree; and trees grow, and

we don't know how they grow. For years and years they grow, without paying any attention to us, in meadows, in forests, and by the side of rivers—all things one likes to think about. The cows swish their tails beneath them on hot afternoons; they paint rivers so green that when a moorhen dives one expects to see its feathers all green when it comes up again. I like to think of the fish balanced against the stream like flags blown out; and of water-beetles slowly raising domes of mud upon the bed of the river. I like to think of the tree itself: first the close dry sensation of being wood; then the grinding of the storm; then the slow, delicious ooze of sap. I like to think of it, too, on winter's nights standing in the empty field with all leaves close-furled, nothing tender exposed to the iron bullets of the moon, a naked mast upon an earth that goes tumbling, tumbling all night long. The song of birds must sound very loud and strange in June; and how cold the feet of insects must feel upon it, as they make laborious progresses up the creases of the bark, or sun themselves upon the thin green awning of the leaves, and look straight in front of them with diamond-cut red eyes.... One by one the fibres snap beneath the immense cold pressure of the earth, then the last storm comes and, falling, the highest branches drive deep into the ground again. Even so, life isn't done with; there are a million patient, watchful lives still for a tree, all over the world, in bedrooms, in ships, on the pavement, lining rooms, where men and women sit after tea, smoking cigarettes. It is full of peaceful thoughts, happy thoughts, this tree. I should like to take each one separately—but something is getting in the way.... Where was I? What has it all been about? A tree? A river? The Downs? Whitaker's Almanack? The fields of asphodel? I can't remember a thing. Everything's moving, falling, slipping, vanishing.... There is a vast upheaval of matter. Someone is standing over me and saying—

"I'm going out to buy a newspaper."

"Yes?"

"Though it's no good buying newspapers.... Nothing ever happens. Curse this war; God damn this war! ... All the same, I don't see why we should have a snail on our wall."

Ah, the mark on the wall! It was a snail.

—1921

Mrs. Dalloway in Bond Street

Mrs. Dalloway said she would buy the gloves herself. Big Ben was striking as she stepped out into the street. It was eleven o'clock and the unused hour was fresh as if issued to children on a beach. But there was something solemn in the deliberate swing of the repeated strokes; something stirring in the murmur of wheels and the shuffle of footsteps.

No doubt they were not all bound on errands of happiness. There is much more to be said about us than that we walk the streets of Westminster. Big Ben too is nothing but steel rods consumed by rust were it not for the care of H.M.'s Office of Works. Only for Mrs. Dalloway the moment was complete; for Mrs. Dalloway June was fresh. A happy childhood—and it was not to his daughters only that Justin Parry had seemed a fine fellow (weak of course on the Bench); flowers at evening, smoke rising; the caw of rooks falling from ever so high, down down through the October air—there is nothing to take the place of childhood. A leaf of mint brings it back: or a cup with a blue ring.

Poor little wretches, she sighed, and pressed forward. Oh, right under the horses' noses, you little demon! and there she was left on the kerb stretching her hand out, while Jimmy Dawes grinned on the further side.

A charming woman, poised, eager, strangely white-haired for her pink cheeks, so Scope Purvis, C. B.,[1] saw her as he hurried to his office. She stiffened a little, waiting for Durtnall's van to pass. Big Ben struck the tenth; struck the eleventh stroke. The leaden circles dissolved in the air. Pride held her erect, inheriting, handing on, acquainted with discipline and with suffering. How people suffered, how they suffered, she thought, thinking of Mrs. Foxcroft at the Embassy last night decked with jewels, eating her heart out, because that nice boy was dead, and now the old Manor House (Durtnall's van passed) must go to a cousin.

"Good morning to you!" said Hugh Whitbread raising his hat rather extravagantly by the china shop, for they had known each other as children. "Where are you off to?"

"I love walking in London," said Mrs. Dalloway. "Really it's better than walking in the country!"

"We've just come up," said Hugh Whitbread. "Unfortunately to see doctors."

"Milly?" said Mrs. Dalloway, instantly compassionate.

"Out of sorts," said Hugh Whitbread. "That sort of thing. Dick all right?"

"First rate!" said Clarissa.

Of course, she thought, walking on, Milly is about my age—fifty—fifty-two. So it is probably that, Hugh's manner had said so, said it perfectly—dear old Hugh, thought Mrs. Dalloway, remembering with amusement, with gratitude, with emotion, how shy, like a brother—one would rather die than speak to one's brother—Hugh had always been, when he was at Oxford, and came over, and perhaps one of them (drat the thing!) couldn't ride. How then could women sit in Parliament? How could they do things with men? For there is this extraordinarily deep instinct, something inside one; you can't get over it; it's no use trying; and men like Hugh respect it without our saying it, which is what one loves, thought Clarissa, in dear old Hugh.

She had passed through the Admiralty Arch and saw at the end of the empty road with its thin trees Victoria's white mound,[2] Victoria's billowing motherliness, amplitude and homeliness, always ridiculous, yet how sublime, thought Mrs. Dalloway, remembering Kensington Gardens and the old lady in horn spectacles and being told by Nanny to stop dead still and bow to the Queen. The flag flew above the Palace. The King and Queen were back then. Dick had met her at lunch the other day—a thoroughly nice woman. It matters so much to the poor, thought Clarissa, and to the soldiers. A man in bronze stood heroically on a pedestal with a gun on her left hand side—the South African war. It matters, thought Mrs. Dalloway walking towards Buckingham Palace. There it stood four-square, in the broad sunshine, uncompromising, plain. But it was character, she thought; something inborn in the race; what Indians respected. The Queen went to hospitals, opened bazaars—the Queen of England, thought Clarissa, looking at the Palace. Already at this hour a motor car passed out at the gates; soldiers saluted; the

---

[1]   *C.B.*   Companion of the Bath. The Order of the Bath is an order of chivalry conferred by the sovereign of England.

[2]   *Victoria's white mound*   Monument to Queen Victoria at the entrance to Buckingham Palace.

gates were shut. And Clarissa, crossing the road, entered the Park,[1] holding herself upright.

June had drawn out every leaf on the trees. The mothers of Westminster with mottled breasts gave suck to their young. Quite respectable girls lay stretched on the grass. An elderly man, stooping very stiffly, picked up a crumpled paper, spread it out flat and flung it away. How horrible! Last night at the Embassy Sir Dighton had said, "If I want a fellow to hold my horse, I have only to put up my hand." But the religious question is far more serious than the economic, Sir Dighton had said, which she thought extraordinarily interesting, from a man like Sir Dighton. "Oh, the country will never know what it has lost," he had said, talking of his own accord, about dear Jack Stewart.

She mounted the little hill lightly. The air stirred with energy. Messages were passing from the Fleet to the Admiralty. Piccadilly and Arlington Street and the Mall[2] seemed to chafe the very air in the Park and lift its leaves hotly, brilliantly, upon waves of that divine vitality which Clarissa loved. To ride; to dance; she had adored all that. Or going long walks in the country, talking, about books, what to do with one's life, for young people were amazingly priggish—oh, the things one had said! But one had conviction. Middle age is the devil. People like Jack'll never know that, she thought; for he never once thought of death, never, they said, knew he was dying. And now can never mourn—how did it go?—a head grown grey … From the contagion of the world's slow stain[3] … have drunk their cup a round or two before.[4] … From the contagion of the world's slow stain! She held herself upright.

But how Jack would have shouted! Quoting Shelley, in Piccadilly! "You want a pin," he would have said. He hated frumps. "My God Clarissa! My God Clarissa!"—

she could hear him now at the Devonshire House[5] party, about poor Sylvia Hunt in her amber necklace and that dowdy old silk. Clarissa held herself upright for she had spoken aloud and now she was in Piccadilly, passing the house with the slender green columns, and the balconies; passing club windows full of newspapers; passing old Lady Burdett-Coutts's house where the glazed white parrot used to hang; and Devonshire House, without its gilt leopards; and Claridge's,[6] where she must remember Dick wanted her to leave a card on Mrs. Jepson or she would be gone. Rich Americans can be very charming. There was St. James's Palace; like a child's game with bricks; and now—she had passed Bond Street—she was by Hatchard's book shop. The stream was endless—endless—endless. Lords, Ascot, Hurlingham—what was it? What a duck, she thought, looking at the frontispiece of some book of memoirs spread wide in the bow window, Sir Joshua perhaps or Romney;[7] arch, bright, demure; the sort of girl—like her own Elizabeth—the only real sort of girl. And there was that absurd book, Soapy Sponge,[8] which Jim used to quote by the yard; and Shakespeare's Sonnets. She knew them by heart. Phil and she had argued all day about the Dark Lady, and Dick had said straight out at dinner that night that he had never heard of her. Really, she had married him for that! He had never read Shakespeare! There must be some little cheap book she could buy for Milly—Cranford[9] of course! Was there ever anything so enchanting as the cow in petticoats? If only people had that sort of humour, that sort of self-respect now, thought Clarissa, for she remembered the broad pages; the sentences ending; the characters—how one talked about them as if they were real. For all the great things one must go to the past, she thought. From the contagion of the world's slow stain … Fear no more the heat

---

[1] *the Park* St. James's Park, London.

[2] *the Mall* Walk bordered by trees in St. James's Park.

[3] *how did it … stain* See Percy Shelley's "Adonais" (1821): "From the contagion of the world's slow stain / He is secure, and now can never mourn. / A heart grown cold, a head grown grey in vain" (lines 356–58).

[4] *have drunk … before* See Edward Fitzgerald's *The Rubáiyát of Omar Khayyám* (1859): "Lo! some we loved, the loveliest and best / That Time and Fate of all their Vintage prest / Have drunk their Cup a Round or two before / And one by one crept silently to Rest."

[5] *Devonshire House* London home of the Duke of Devonshire.

[6] *Claridge's* Claridge's Hotel.

[7] *Sir Joshua … Romney* Sir Joshua Reynolds (1723–92) and George Romney (1734–1802), English painters.

[8] *Soapy Sponge* The nickname of the protagonist of R.S. Surtees's novel *Mr. Sponge's Sporting Tour* (1853).

[9] *Cranford* Novel by Elizabeth Gaskell (1853). In the book, Miss Betsy Barker dresses her cow in grey flannel after a fall into a lime pit removes all its hair.

o' the sun.[1] ... And now can never mourn, can never mourn, she repeated, her eyes straying over the window; for it ran in her head; the test of great poetry; the moderns had never written anything one wanted to read about death, she thought; and turned.

Omnibuses joined motor cars; motor cars vans; vans taxicabs, taxicabs motor cars—here was an open motor car with a girl, alone. Up till four, her feet tingling, I know, thought Clarissa, for the girl looked washed out, half asleep, in the corner of the car after the dance. And another car came; and another. No! No! No! Clarissa smiled good-naturedly. The fat lady had taken every sort of trouble, but diamonds! orchids! at this hour of the morning! No! No! No! The excellent policeman would, when the time came, hold up his hand. Another motor car passed. How utterly unattractive! Why should a girl of that age paint black round her eyes? And a young man, with a girl, at this hour, when the country—The admirable policeman raised his hand and Clarissa acknowledging his sway, taking her time, crossed, walked towards Bond Street; saw the narrow crooked street, the yellow banners; the thick notched telegraph wires stretched across the sky.

A hundred years ago her great-great-grandfather, Seymour Parry, who ran away with Conway's daughter, had walked down Bond Street. Down Bond Street the Parrys had walked for a hundred years, and might have met the Dalloways (Leighs on the mother's side) going up. Her father got his clothes from Hill's. There was a roll of cloth in the window, and here just one jar on a black table, incredibly expensive; like the thick pink salmon on the ice block at the fishmonger's. The jewels were exquisite—pink and orange stars, paste, Spanish, she thought, and chains of old gold; starry buckles, little brooches which had been worn on sea-green satin by ladies with high head-dresses. But no good looking! One must economise. She must go on past the picture dealer's where one of the odd French pictures hung, as if people had thrown confetti—pink and blue—for a joke. If you had lived with pictures (and it's the same with books and music) thought Clarissa, passing the

Aeolian Hall, you can't be taken in by a joke.

The river of Bond Street was clogged. There, like a Queen at a tournament, raised, regal, was Lady Bexborough. She sat in her carriage, upright, alone, looking through her glasses. The white glove was loose at her wrist. She was in black, quite shabby, yet, thought Clarissa, how extraordinarily it tells, breeding, self-respect, never saying a word too much or letting people gossip; an astonishing friend; no one can pick a hole in her after all these years, and now, there she is, thought Clarissa, passing the Countess who waited powdered, perfectly still, and Clarissa would have given anything to be like that, the mistress of Clarefield, talking politics, like a man. But she never goes anywhere, thought Clarissa, and it's quite useless to ask her, and the carriage went on and Lady Bexborough was borne past like a Queen at a tournament, though she had nothing to live for and the old man is failing and they say she is sick of it all, thought Clarissa and the tears actually rose to her eyes as she entered the shop.

"Good morning," said Clarissa in her charming voice. "Gloves," she said with her exquisite friendliness and putting her bag on the counter began, very slowly, to undo the buttons. "White gloves," she said. "Above the elbow," and she looked straight into the shop-woman's face—but this was not the girl she remembered? She looked quite old. "These really don't fit," said Clarissa. The shop-girl looked at them. "Madame wears bracelets?" Clarissa spread out her fingers. "Perhaps it's my rings." And the girl took the grey gloves with her to the end of the counter.

Yes, thought Clarissa, if it's the girl I remember, she's twenty years older .... There was only one other customer, sitting sideways at the counter, her elbow poised, her bare hand drooping, vacant; like a figure on a Japanese fan, thought Clarissa, too vacant perhaps, yet some men would adore her. The lady shook her head sadly. Again the gloves were too large. She turned round the glass. "Above the wrist," she reproached the grey-headed woman; who looked and agreed.

They waited; a clock ticked; Bond Street hummed, dulled, distant; the woman went away holding gloves. "Above the wrist," said the lady, mournfully, raising her voice. And she would have to order chairs, ices, flowers, and cloak-room tickets, thought Clarissa. The people

---

[1] *Fear ... sun* From Shakespeare's *Cymbeline*, 4.2: "Fear no more the heat o' the sun / Nor the furious winter's rages / Thou thy worldly task hast done / Home art gone, and ta'en thy wages / Golden lads and girls all must / As chimney-sweepers, come to dust."

she didn't want would come; the others wouldn't. She would stand by the door. They sold stockings—silk stockings. A lady is known by her gloves and her shoes, old Uncle William used to say. And through the hanging silk stockings quivering silver she looked at the lady, sloping shouldered, her hand drooping, her bag slipping, her eyes vacantly on the floor. It would be intolerable if dowdy women came to her party! Would one have liked Keats[1] if he had worn red socks? Oh, at last—she drew into the counter and it flashed into her mind:

"Do you remember before the war you had gloves with pearl buttons?"

"French gloves, Madame?"

"Yes, they were French," said Clarissa. The other lady rose very sadly and took her bag, and looked at the gloves on the counter. But they were all too large—always too large at the wrist.

"With pearl buttons," said the shop-girl, who looked ever so much older. She split the lengths of tissue paper apart on the counter. With pearl buttons, thought Clarissa, perfectly simple—how French!

"Madame's hands are so slender," said the shop-girl, drawing the glove firmly, smoothly, down over her rings. And Clarissa looked at her arm in the looking-glass. The glove hardly came to the elbow. Were there others half an inch longer? Still it seemed tiresome to bother her—perhaps the one day in the month, thought Clarissa, when it's an agony to stand. "Oh, don't bother," she said. But the gloves were brought.

"Don't you get fearfully tired," she said in her charming voice, "standing? When d'you get your holiday?"

"In September, Madame, when we're not so busy."

When we're in the country thought Clarissa. Or shooting. She has a fortnight at Brighton. In some stuffy lodging. The landlady takes the sugar. Nothing would be easier than to send her to Mrs. Lumley's right in the country (and it was on the tip of her tongue). But then she remembered how on their honeymoon Dick had shown her the folly of giving impulsively. It was much more important, he said, to get trade with China. Of course he was right. And she could feel the girl wouldn't like to be given things. There she was in her place. So was Dick. Selling gloves was her job. She had her own

sorrows quite separate, "and now can never mourn, can never mourn," the words ran in her head. "From the contagion of the world's slow stain," thought Clarissa holding her arm stiff, for there are moments when it seems utterly futile (the glove was drawn off leaving her arm flecked with powder)—simply one doesn't believe, thought Clarissa, any more in God.

The traffic suddenly roared; the silk stockings brightened. A customer came in.

"White gloves," she said, with some ring in her voice that Clarissa remembered.

It used, thought Clarissa, to be so simple. Down down through the air came the caw of the rooks. When Sylvia died, hundreds of years ago, the yew hedges looked so lovely with the diamond webs in the mist before early church. But if Dick were to die tomorrow, as for believing in God—no, she would let the children choose, but for herself, like Lady Bexborough, who opened the bazaar, they say, with the telegram in her hand—Roden, her favourite, killed—she would go on. But why, if one doesn't believe? For the sake of others, she thought, taking the glove in her hand. The girl would be much more unhappy if she didn't believe.

"Thirty shillings," said the shop-woman. "No, pardon me Madame, thirty-five. The French gloves are more."

For one doesn't live for oneself, thought Clarissa.

And then the other customer took a glove, tugged it, and it split.

"There!" she exclaimed.

"A fault of the skin," said the grey-headed woman hurriedly. "Sometimes a drop of acid in tanning. Try this pair, Madame."

"But it's an awful swindle to ask two pound ten!"

Clarissa looked at the lady; the lady looked at Clarissa.

"Gloves have never been quite so reliable since the war," said the shop-girl, apologising, to Clarissa.

But where had she seen the other lady?—elderly, with a frill under her chin; wearing a black ribbon for gold eyeglasses; sensual, clever, like a Sargent[2] drawing. How one can tell from a voice when people are in the habit, thought Clarissa, of making other people—"It's a shade too tight," she said—obey. The shop-woman

---

[1] *Keats*   John Keats (1795–1821), English Romantic poet.

[2] *Sargent painting*   John Singer Sargent (1856–1925), the celebrated American artist, was (and is) known for his portraits of women of fashion.

went off again. Clarissa was left waiting. Fear no more she repeated, playing her finger on the counter. Fear no more the heat o' the sun. Fear no more she repeated. There were little brown spots on her arm. And the girl crawled like a snail. Thou thy worldly task hast done. Thousands of young men had died that things might go on. At last! Half an inch above the elbow; pearl buttons; five and a quarter. My dear slow coach, thought Clarissa, do you think I can sit here the whole morning? Now you'll take twenty-five minutes to bring me my change!

There was a violent explosion in the street outside. The shop-women cowered behind the counters. But Clarissa, sitting very upright, smiled at the other lady. "Miss Anstruther!" she exclaimed.

—1923

from *On Re-reading Novels*[1]

So there are to be new editions of Jane Austen and the Brontës and George Meredith.[2] Left in trains, forgotten in lodging-houses, thumbed and tattered to destruction, the old ones have served their day, and for the new-comers in their new houses there are to be new editions and new readings and new friends. It speaks very well for the Georgians. It is still more to the credit of the Victorians. In spite of the mischief-makers, the grandchildren, it seems, get along very nicely with the grandparents; and the sight of their concord points inevitably to the later breach between the generations, a breach more complete than the other, and perhaps more momentous. The failure of the Edwardians, comparative yet disastrous—that is a question which waits to be discussed. How the year 1860 was a year of empty cradles; how the reign of Edward the Seventh[3] was barren of poet, novelist, or critic; how it followed that the Georgians read Russian novels in translations;

how they benefited and suffered; how different a story we might have told today had there been living heroes to worship and destroy—all this we find significant in view of the new editions of the old books. The Georgians, it seems, are in the odd predicament of turning for solace and guidance not to their parents who are alive, but to their grandparents who are dead. And so, as likely as not, we shall be faced one of these days by a young man reading Meredith for the first time.

He has bought *Harry Richmond*[4] and he is in the middle of it, and he is obviously annoyed when they come and ask him for his ticket. Is he not enviable? And what was it like, reading *Harry Richmond* for the first time? Let us try to remember. The book begins with a statue who turns out be a man, and there is a preposterous adventurer, somehow descended from the Royal family, and there is a scene at a dinner-party, and a fire, and a dashing, impetuous girl, and a handsome manly boy, and England in June at night, and stars and rivers and love-making and gallantry. In short, the young man ought to be enjoying himself, and one of these days we will read *Harry Richmond* again. But there are difficulties to be faced. We do not mean that Meredith is said (perhaps not so truly) to be under a cloud. In our climate that is inevitable. But we mean that to read a novel for the second time is far more of an undertaking than to read it for the first. To rush it breathlessly through does very well for a beginning. But that is not the way to read finally; and somehow or other these fat Victorian volumes, these *Vanity Fairs, Copperfields, Richmonds*, and *Adam Bedes*[5] must be read finally, if we are to do them justice—must be read as one reads *Hamlet*, as a whole. But, then, one reads *Hamlet* in the four hours between dinner and bedtime. It is not beyond human endurance to read it from first to last, in and out, and, so far as our faculties permit, as a whole. *Hamlet* may change; we know, indeed, that *Hamlet* will change; but tonight *Hamlet* is ours. And for that reason, too, we hesitate before reading *Harry Richmond* again. Tonight *Harry Richmond* will not be ours. We shall have broken off a tantalising fragment; days may pass before

---

[1] *On Re-reading Novels* An essay published in the *Times Literary Supplement*, 20 July 1922. Woolf later revised this essay; the later version was published in her *Collected Essays*, volume 2 (1966). The text reproduced here is that of the original published version.

[2] *So there ... Meredith* New editions of the novels of Jane Austen (1775–1817); Charlotte (1816–45), Emily (1818–48), and Anne (1829–49) Brontë; and George Meredith (1828–1909) were all released that year—the latter by Constable, the others by J.M. Dent.

[3] *the reign ... Seventh* From 1901 to 1910.

[4] *Harry Richmond* George Meredith's novel *The Adventures of Harry Richmond* (1870–71).

[5] *Vanity Fair* 1847–48 novel by W.M. Thackeray; *Copperfield* David Copperfield (1849–50), by Charles Dickens; *Adam Bede* 1859 novel by Charles Dickens.

we can add to it. Meanwhile the plan is lost; the book pours to waste; we blame ourselves; we abuse the author; nothing is more exasperating and dispiriting. Better leave the Victorian novelists to crumble on the shelves and be bolted whole by schoolboys. Let us confine ourselves to apt quotations from Mrs. Gamp, and find Hartfield on the map.[1] Let us call Jane Austen "Jane," and debate for ever which curate Emily Brontë loved. But the business of reading novels is beyond us, and there is nothing more melancholy than the sight of so many fine brains irrevocably expressed in the one form which makes them for ever inaccessible. So, instead of reading *Harry Richmond*, we will envy the young man opposite and wish Defoe and Fanny Burney[2] at the bottom of the sea. They were the parents of the modern novel, and their burden is heavy.

Some such mood of exasperation and bewilderment, of violence, yet of remorse, is abroad at present among those common readers whom Dr. Johnson respected, for it is by them, he said, that "must be finally decided all claim to poetical honours."[3] It bodes ill for fiction if the commons of letters vote against it, so let us lay bare our dilemma without caring overmuch if we say some foolish things and many vague ones. To begin with, we have obviously got it into our heads that there is a right way to read, and that is to read straight through and grasp the book entire. The national habit has been formed by the drama, and the drama has always recognised the fact that human beings cannot sit for more than five hours at a stretch in front of a stage. And on top of that we are by temperament and tradition poetic. There still lingers among us the belief that poetry is the senior branch of the service. If we have an hour to spend we feel that we lay it out to better advantage with Keats than with Macaulay.[4] And so perhaps we come to novels

neither knowing the right way to read them nor very much caring to acquire it. We ask one thing and they give us another. They are so long, so dull, so badly written; and, after all, one has life enough on one's hands already without living it all over again between dinner and bedtime in prose. Such are the stock complaints, and they lose nothing of their acrimony if with the same breath we have to admit that we owe more to Tolstoy, Dostoevsky, and Hardy than we can measure; that if we wish to recall our happier hours they would be those Conrad has given us and Henry James;[5] and that to have seen a young man bolting Meredith whole recalls the pleasure of so many first readings that we are even ready to venture a second. Only with these contrary impulses at work it will be a hazardous affair. Not again shall we be floated over on the tide of careless rapture. The pleasure we shall now look for will lie not so obviously on the surface; and we shall find ourselves hard pressed to make out what is the lasting quality, if such there be, which justifies these long books about modern life in prose. The collective reading of generations which has set us at the right angle for reading plays has not yet shaped our attitude to fiction. That *Hamlet* is a work of art goes without saying; but that *Harry Richmond* is a work of art has to be said for the first time.

Some months ago Mr. Percy Lubbock applied himself to answer some of these questions in *The Craft of Fiction*,[6] a book which is likely to have much influence upon readers, and may perhaps eventually reach the critics and writers. To say that it is the best book on the subject is probably true; but it is more to the point to say that it is the only one. He has attempted a task which has never been properly attempted, and has tentatively explored a field of inquiry which it is astonishing to find almost untilled. The subject is vast and the book short, but it will be our fault, not Mr. Lubbock's, if we talk as vaguely about novels in the future as we have done in the past. For example, do we say that we cannot read *Harry Richmond* twice? We are led by Mr. Lubbock to suspect that it was our first reading that was to blame. A strong but vague emotion, two or three

[1] *Mrs. Gamp* Character in Charles Dickens's *The Life and Adventures of Martin Chuzzlewit*; *Hartfield* Name of the country house in which Emma, the heroine of Jane Austen's novel of that name (1816) lives.

[2] *Defoe ... Burney* Novelists Daniel Defoe (1660–1731) and Frances Burney (1752–1840).

[3] *Dr. Johnson* Author, biographer, and lexicographer Samuel Johnson (1709–84). The quote is from his *Lives of the English Poets* (1779–81), "Gray."

[4] *Keats* Poet John Keats (1795–1821); *Macaulay* Historian and poet Thomas Babington Macaulay (1800–59).

[5] *Tolstoy ... Henry James* Novelists Leo Tolstoy (1828–1910), Fyodor Dostoevsky (1821–81), Thomas Hardy (1840–1928), Joseph Conrad (1857–1924), and Henry James (1843–1916).

[6] *Mr. Percy ... Fiction* Percy Lubbock (1879–1965), *The Craft of Fiction* was published by Jonathan Cape in 1921.

characters, half a dozen scattered scenes—if that is all that *Harry Richmond* means to us, the fault lies, perhaps, not with Meredith, but with ourselves. Did we read the book as he meant it to be read, or did we not reduce it to chaos through our own incompetency? Novels, above all other books, we are reminded, bristle with temptations. We identify ourselves with this person or with that. We fasten upon the character or scene which is congenial. We swing our imaginations capriciously from spot to spot. We compare the world of fiction with the real world and judge it by the same standards. Undoubtedly we do all this, and easily find excuses for so doing. "But meanwhile the book, the thing he made, lies imprisoned in the volume, and our glimpse of it was too fleeting, it seems, to leave us with a lasting knowledge of its form."[1] That is the point. There is something lasting that we can lay hands on. There is, Mr. Lubbock argues, such a thing as the book itself. We should read at arm's length from the distractions we have named. We must receive impressions, but we must relate them to each other as the author intended; and we can only do his bidding by making ourselves acquainted with his method. When we have shaped our impressions, as the author would have us, we are then in a position to perceive the form itself, and it is this which endures, however mood or fashion may change....

Now, as Mr. Lubbock laments, the criticism of fiction is in its infancy, and its language, though not all of one syllable, is baby language. This word "form," of course, comes from the visual arts, and for our part we wish that he could have seen his way to do without it. It is confusing. The form of the novel differs from the dramatic form—that is true; we can, if we choose, say that we see the difference in our mind's eyes. But can we see that the form of *The Egoist*[2] differs from the form of *Vanity Fair*. We do not raise the question in order to stickle for accuracy where most words are provisional, many metaphorical, and some on trial for the first time. The question is not one of words only. It goes deeper than that, into the very process of reading itself. Here we have Mr. Lubbock telling us that the book itself is equivalent to its form, and seeking with admirable subtlety and lucidity to trace out those methods by which novelists build up the final and enduring structure of their books.....[3]

The "book itself is not form which you see, but emotion which you feel, and the more intense the writer's feeling the more exact without slip or chink its expressions in words." And whenever Mr. Lubbock talks of form it is as if something were interposed between us and the book as we know it. We feel the presence of an alien substance which requires to be visualised imposing itself upon emotions which we feel naturally, and name simply, and range in final order by feeling their right relations to each other. Thus we have reached our conception of "Un Coeur Simple" by working from the emotion outwards, and, the reading over, there is nothing to be seen; there is everything to be felt. And only when the emotion is feeble and the workmanship excellent can we separate what is felt from the expression and remark, for example, what excellence of form.... The point is worth labouring, not simply to substitute one word for another, but to insist, among all this talk of methods, that both in writing and in reading it is the emotion that must come first.

Still, we have only made a beginning, and a very dangerous one at that. To snatch an emotion and luxuriate in it and tire of it and throw it away is as dissipating in literature as in life. Yet, if we wring this pleasure from Flaubert, the most austere of writers, there is no limit to be put upon the intoxicating effects of Meredith and Dickens and Dostoevsky, of Scott[4] and Charlotte Brontë. Or, rather, there is a limit, and we have found it over and over again in the extremes of satiety and distrust. If we are to read them a second time, we must somehow discriminate. Emotion is our material; but what do we mean by emotion? How many different kinds of emotion are there not in one short story, of how many qualities, and composed of how many different elements? And, therefore, to get our emotion directly, and for ourselves, is only the first step. We must go on to test it and riddle it with questions. If

---

[1] *But meanwhile ... its form*   See *The Craft of Fiction* chapter 1.

[2] *The Egoist*   1879 novel by George Meredith.

[3] ...   In the excised passage, Woolf outlines the process of a first and second reading of French novelist Gustave Flaubert's short story "Un Coeur Simple" (1877). She explains that emotions and various, unconnected impressions one has upon a first reading can, on a second reading, be arranged, controlled, and developed into more acute observations about "why the story was written."

[4] *Scott*   Scottish novelist Sir Walter Scott (1771–1832).

nothing survives, well and good; if something remains, all the better. The resolution is admirable; the only difficulty is how to enforce it. Did we thus wish to examine our impressions of some new play or poem, there are many dead, and five or six living, critics at whose command we cheerfully revise our views. But when it is fiction, and fiction hot from the press, far from accepting the judgement of any living critic or the applause or neglect of the public, we are forced, after comparing half a dozen judgements, each based on a different conception of the art or on no conception at all, either to do the work for ourselves or to conclude that for some mysterious reason the work cannot be done. There may be something so emotional in fiction that the critics inevitably lose their heads. There may be something so unamenable to discipline in the art itself that it is hopeless either to judge it by the old standards or to devise new ones afresh. But now—at last—Mr. Lubbock applies his Röntgen rays.[1] The voluminous lady submits to examination. The flesh, the finery, even the smile and witchery, together with the umbrellas and brown paper parcels which she has collected on her long and toilsome journey, dissolve and disappear; the skeleton alone remains. It is surprising. It is even momentarily shocking. Our old familiar friend has vanished. But, after all, there is something satisfactory in bone—one can grasp it.

In other words, by concentrating on the novelist's method Mr. Lubbock draws our attention to the solid and enduring thing to which we can hold fast when we attack a novel for the second time. Here is something to which we can turn and turn again, and with each clearer view of it our understanding of the whole becomes more definite. Here is something removed (as far as may be) from the influence of our fluctuating and private emotions. The novelist's method is simply his device for expressing his emotion; but if we discover how that effect is produced we shall undoubtedly deepen the impression. Let us put it to the proof, since words are misleading. It is essential in "Un Coeur Simple" that we should feel the lapse of time; the incidents are significant because they are scattered so sparsely over so long a stretch of years, and the effect must be given in a few short pages. So Flaubert introduces a number of people

for no purpose, as we think; but later we hear that they are now all dead, and we realise then for how long Félicité herself has lived. To realise that is to enforce the effect. It fastens our attention upon the story as a work of art, and gives us such a prise on it as we have already, thanks to their more rigid technique, upon drama and poetry, but have to contrive for fiction, afresh, each time we open a book.

But that is one detail in a short story. Can we sharpen our impressions of a long and crowded novel in the same way? Can we make out that the masters — Tolstoy and Flaubert, and Dickens, and Henry James, and Meredith—expressed by methods which we can trace and understand the enormous mass and the myriad detail of their books? If so the novel, the voluminous Victorian novel, is capable of being read, as we read *Hamlet*, as a whole. And the novelists, children of instinct, purveyors of illusion and distraction at the cheapest rates quoted in literature, are of the blood royal all the same. That is the conclusion to which Mr. Lubbock certainly brings us by means of an argument which is at once fascinating and strangely unfamiliar. We have been along the road so often and have wasted so many matches looking for sign-posts in dark corners. We must have been aware that a novelist, before he can persuade us that his world is real and his people alive, must solve certain questions and acquire certain skill. But until Mr. Lubbock pierced through the flesh and made us look at the skeleton we were almost ready to believe that nothing was needed but genius and ink. The novelists themselves have done little to open our eyes. They have praised the genius and blamed the ink, but they have never, with two famous exceptions, invited us in to see the process at work. Yet obviously there must be a process, and it is at work always and in every novel. The simplest story begins more often than not, as Mr. Lubbock points out, by the use of three different methods: the scene, the retrospect, the summary. And our innocence is gauged by the fact that though we swallow them daily it is with our eyes tight shut. Names have to be found and methods defined now for the first time.

No writer, indeed, has so many methods at his disposal as a novelist. He can put himself at any point of view; he can to some extent combine several different views. He can appear in person, like Thackeray; or

---

[1] *Röntgen rays*   X rays (which were discovered by R.W. Röntgen).

disappear (never perhaps completely), like Flaubert. He can state the facts, like Defoe, or give the thought without the fact, like Henry James. He can sweep the widest horizons, like Tolstoy, or seize upon one old apple-woman and her basket, like Tolstoy again. Where there is every freedom there is every licence; and the novel, open-armed, free to all comers, claims more victims than the other forms of literature all put together. But let us look at the victors. We are tempted, indeed, to look at them a great deal more closely than space allows. For they too look different if you watch them at work. There is Thackeray always taking measures to avoid a scene, and Dickens (save in *David Copperfield*) invariably seeking one. There is Tolstoy dashing into the midst of his story without staying to lay foundations, and Balzac[1] laying foundations so deep that the story itself seems never to begin. But we must check the desire to see where Mr. Lubbock's criticism would lead us in reading particular books. The general view is more striking, and a general view is to be had....

For from that vantage ground the art of fiction can be seen, not clearly indeed, but in a new proportion. We may speak of infancy, of youth, and of maturity. We may say that Scott is childish and Flaubert by comparison a grown man. We may go on to say that the vigour and splendour of youth almost outweigh the more deliberate virtues of maturity. And then we may pause upon the significance of "almost," and wonder whether, perhaps, it has not some bearing upon our reluctance to read the Victorians twice. The gigantic, sprawling books still seem to reverberate the yawns and lamentations of their makers. To build a castle, sketch a profile, fire off a poem, reform a workhouse, or pull down a prison were occupations more congenial to the writers, or more befitting their manhood, than to sit chained at a desk scribbling novels for a simple-minded public. The genius of Victorian fiction seems to be making its magnificent best of an essentially bad job. But it is never possible to say of Henry James that he is making the best of a bad job. In all the long stretch of *The Wings of the Dove* and *The Ambassadors*[2] there is not a hint of a yawn, not a sign of condescension. The novel is his job.

It is the appropriate form for what he has to say. It wins a beauty from that fact—a fine and noble beauty—which it has never worn before. And now at last (so we seem to see) the novel is a form distinct from any other. It will not burden itself with other people's relics. It will choose to say whatever it says best. Flaubert will take for his subject an old maid and a stuffed parrot. Henry James will find all he needs round a tea-table in a drawing room. The nightingales and roses are banished—or at least the nightingale sounds strange against the traffic, and the roses in the light of the arc lamps are not quite so red. There are new combinations of old material, and the novel, when it is used for the sake of its qualities and not for the sake of its defects, enforces fresh aspects of the perennial story.

Mr. Lubbock prudently carries his survey no farther than the novels of Henry James. But already the years have mounted up. We may expect the novel to change and develop as it is explored by the most vigorous minds of a very complex age. What have we not, indeed, to expect from M. Proust[3] alone? But if he will listen to Mr. Lubbock, the common reader will refuse to sit any longer open-mouthed in passive expectation. That is to encourage the charlatan to shock us and the conjuror to play us tricks. We must press close on his heels, and so bring to bear upon the novelist who spins his books in solitude the pressure of an audience. The pressure of an audience will not reduce the novel to a play which we can read through in the four hours between dinner and bedtime. But it will encourage the novelist to find out—and that is all we ask of him—what it is that he means and how best to show it us.

—1921

from *How It Strikes a Contemporary*[4]

In the first place a contemporary can scarcely fail to be struck by the fact that two critics at the same table at the same moment will pronounce completely different

[1] *Balzac* Honoré de Balzac (1799–1850), French novelist.

[2] *The Wings ... Ambassadors* Novels by Henry James, published in 1902 and 1903, respectively.

[3] *M. Proust* Novelist Marcel Proust (1871–1922).

[4] *How It ... Contemporary* An essay published in the *Times Literary Supplement* of 5 April 1923. Woolf later revised and re-published the essay in *The Common Reader*, volume 1. The text reproduced here is that of the original published version.

opinions about the same book. Here, on the right, it is declared a masterpiece of English prose; on the left, simultaneously, a mere mass of waste paper which, if the fire could survive it, should be thrown upon the flames. Yet both critics are in agreement about Milton and about Keats.[1] They display an exquisite sensibility and have undoubtedly a genuine enthusiasm. It is only when they discuss the work of contemporary writers that they inevitably come to blows. The book in question, which is at once a lasting contribution to English literature and a mere farrago of pretentious mediocrity, was published about two months ago. That is the explanation; that is why they differ.

The explanation is a strange one. It is equally disconcerting to the reader who wishes to take his bearings in the chaos of contemporary literature and to the writer who has a natural desire to know whether his own work, produced with infinite pains and in almost utter darkness, is likely to burn for ever among the fixed luminaries of English letters or, on the contrary, to put out the fire. But if we identify ourselves with the reader and explore his dilemma first, our bewilderment is short-lived enough. The same thing has happened so often before. We have heard the doctors disagreeing about the new and agreeing about the old twice a year on the average, in spring and autumn, ever since Robert Elsmere, or was it Stephen Phillips,[2] somehow pervaded the atmosphere, and there was the disagreement among grown-up people about them. It would be much more marvellous, and indeed much more upsetting, if, for a wonder, both gentlemen agreed, pronounced Blank's book an undoubted masterpiece, and thus faced us with the necessity of deciding whether we should back their judgement to the extent of ten and sixpence. Both are critics of reputation; the opinions tumbled out so spontaneously here will be starched and stiffened into columns of sober prose which will uphold the dignity of letters in England and America.

It must be some innate cynicism, then, some ungenerous distrust of contemporary genius, which determines us automatically as the talk goes on that, were they to agree—which they show no signs of doing—half a guinea is altogether too large a sum to squander upon contemporary enthusiasms, and the case will be met quite adequately by a card to the library. Still the question remains, and let us put it boldly to the critics themselves. Is there no guidance nowadays for a reader who yields to none in reverence for the dead, but is tormented by the suspicion that reverence for the dead is vitally connected with understanding of the living? After a rapid survey both critics are agreed that there is unfortunately no such person. For what is their own judgement worth where new books are concerned? Certainly not ten and sixpence. And from the stores of their experience they proceed to bring forth terrible examples of past blunders; crimes of criticism which, if they had been committed against the dead and not against the living, would have lost them their jobs and imperilled their reputations. The only advice they can offer is to respect one's own instincts, to follow them fearlessly and, rather than submit them to the control of any critic or reviewer alive, to check them by reading and reading again the masterpieces of the past.

Thanking them humbly, we cannot help reflecting that it was not always so. Once upon a time, we must believe, there was a rule, a discipline, which controlled the great republic of readers in a way which is now unknown. That is not to say that the great critic—the Dryden, the Johnson, the Coleridge, the Arnold[3]—was an impeccable judge of contemporary work, whose verdicts stamped the book indelibly and saved the reader the trouble of reckoning the value for himself. The mistakes of these great men about their own contemporaries are too notorious to be worth recording. But the mere fact of their existence had a centralising influence. That alone, it is not fantastic to suppose, would have controlled the disagreements of the dinner-table and given to random chatter about some book just out an authority now entirely to seek. The diverse schools would have debated as hotly as ever, but at the back of every reader's mind would have been the consciousness that there was at least one man who kept the main principles of literature closely in view: who, if you had

---

[1] *Milton ... Keats* Poets John Milton (1608–74) and John Keats (1795–1821).

[2] *Robert Elsmere*   1888 best-selling novel by Mrs. Humphrey Ward; *Stephen Phillips* Dramatic poet (1864–1915).

[3] *Dryden ... Arnold* Authors and literary critics John Dryden (1631–1700), Samuel Johnson (1709–84), Samuel Taylor Coleridge (1772–1834), and Matthew Arnold (1822–88).

taken to him some eccentricity of the moment, would have brought it into touch with permanence and tethered it by his own authority in the contrary blasts of praise and blame. But when it comes to the making of a critic, Nature must be generous and Society ripe. The scattered dinner-tables of the modern world, the chase and eddy of the various currents which compose the Society of our time, could only be dominated by a giant of fabulous dimensions. And where is even the very tall man whom we have the right to expect? Critics, of course, abound. But the too frequent result of their able and industrious pens is a desiccation of the living tissues of literature into a network of little bones Nowhere shall we find the downright vigour of Dryden, or Keats with his fine and natural bearing, or Flaubert[1] and his fanaticism, or Coleridge, above all, brewing in his head the whole of poetry and letting issue now and then one of those profound general statements which are caught up by the mind when hot with the friction of reading as if they were of the soul of the book itself.

And to all this, too, the critics, generously, agree. A great critic, they say, is the rarest of beings. But should one miraculously appear, how should we maintain him, on what should we feed him? Great critics, if they are not themselves great poets, are bred from the profusion of the age. And our age is meagre to the verge of destitution. There is no name which dominates the rest, no master in whose workshop the young are proud to serve apprenticeship. Mr. Hardy has long since withdrawn from the arena, and there is something exotic about the genius of Mr. Conrad[2] which makes him not so much an influence as an idol, honoured and admired, but aloof and apart. As for the rest, though they are many and vigorous and in the full flood of creative activity, there is none whose influence can seriously affect his contemporaries, or penetrate beyond our day to that not very distant future which it pleases us to call immortality. If we make a century our test, and ask how much of the work produced in these days in England will be in existence then, we shall have to answer not merely that we cannot agree upon the same book, but that we are more than doubtful whether such a book there is. It is an age of fragments. A few stanzas, a few pages, a

chapter here and there, the beginning of this novel, the end of that, are equal to the best of any age or author. But can we go to posterity with a sheaf of loose pages, or ask the readers of those days, with the whole of literature before them, to sift our enormous rubbish heaps for our tiny pearls? To such questions it is fitting that a writer should reply; yet with what conviction?

At first the weight of pessimism seems sufficient to bear down all opposition. It is a lean age, we repeat, with much to justify its poverty; but, frankly, if we pit one century against another the comparison seems overwhelmingly against us.

… Picking and choosing, we select now this, now that, hold it up for display, hear it defended or derided, and finally have to meet the objection that even so we are only agreeing with the critics that it is an age incapable of sustained effort, littered with fragments, and not seriously to be compared with the age that went before.

But it is just when opinions universally prevail and we have added lip service to their authority that we become sometimes most keenly conscious that we do not believe a word that we are saying. It is a barren and exhausted age, we repeat; we must look back with envy to the past. Meanwhile it is one of the first fine days of spring. Life is not altogether lacking in colour. The telephone, which interrupts the most serious conversations, has a romance of its own. And the random talk of people who have no chance of immortality and thus can speak their minds out has a setting, often, of lights, streets, houses, human beings, beautiful or grotesque, which will weave itself into the moment for ever. But this is life; the talk is about literature. We must try to disentangle the two, and justify the rash revolt of optimism against the superior plausibility, the finer distinction, of pessimism. In one sense, of course, optimism is universal. No one would seriously choose to go back a hundred years. There is something about the present with all its trivialities which we would not exchange for the past, however august—just as an instinct, blind but essential to the conduct of life, makes every tramp prefer to be himself rather than any king, or hero, or millionaire of them all. And modern literature in spite of its imperfections has the same hold on us, the same endearing quality of being part of ourselves, of being the globe in which we are and not the globe

---

[1]   *Flaubert*   French writer Gustave Flaubert (1821–80).

[2]   *Mr. Conrad*   Novelist Joseph Conrad (1857–1924).

which we look upon respectfully from outside. Nor has any generation more need than ours to cherish its contemporaries. We are sharply cut off from our predecessors. A shift in the scale—the war, the sudden slip of masses held in position for ages—has shaken the fabric from top to bottom, alienated us from the past and made us perhaps too vividly conscious of the present. Every day we find ourselves doing, saying, or thinking things that would have been impossible to our fathers. And we feel the differences which have not been noted far more keenly than the resemblances which have been very perfectly expressed. New books lure us to read them partly in the hope that they will reflect this rearrangement of our attitude—these scenes, thoughts, and apparently fortuitous groupings of incongruous things which impinge upon us with so keen a sense of novelty—and, as literature does, give it back into our keeping, whole and comprehended. Here indeed there is every reason for optimism. No age can have been more rich than ours in writers determined to give expression to the differences which separate them from the past and not to the resemblances which connect them with it. It would be invidious to mention names, but the most casual reader dipping into poetry, into fiction, into biography can hardly fail to be impressed by the courage, the sincerity, in a word by the widespread originality of our time. But our exhilaration is strangely curtailed. Book after book leaves us with the same sense of promise unachieved, of intellectual poverty, of brilliance which has been snatched from life but not transmuted into literature. Much of what is best in contemporary work has the appearance of being noted under pressure, taken down in a bleak shorthand which preserves with astonishing brilliance the movements and expressions of the figures as they pass across the screen. But the flash is soon over, and there remains with us a profound dissatisfaction. The irritation is as acute as the pleasure was intense.

Now, of course, is the time to correct these extremes of opinion by consulting, as the critics advise, the masterpieces of the past. We feel ourselves indeed driven to them, impelled not by calm judgement but by some imperious need to anchor our instability upon their security. But, honestly, the shock of the comparison between past and present is at first disconcerting.

Undoubtedly there is a dullness in great books. There is an unabashed tranquillity in page after page of Wordsworth and Scott and Miss Austen[1] which is sedative to the verge of somnolence. Opportunities occur and they neglect them. Shades and subtleties accumulate and they ignore them. They seem deliberately to refuse to gratify those senses which are stimulated so briskly by the moderns; the senses of sight, of sound, of touch—above all, the sense of personality vibrating with perceptions which, since they are not generalised, but have their centre in some particular person at some precise moment, serve to make that person and that moment vivid to the utmost extreme. There is little of all this in the works of Wordsworth and Scott and Jane Austen. From what, then, arises that sense of security which gradually, delightfully, and completely overcomes us? It is the power of their belief—their conviction, that imposes itself upon us. In Wordsworth, the philosophic poet, this is obvious enough. But it is equally true of the careless Scott, who scribbled masterpieces to build castles before breakfast, and of the modest maiden lady who wrote furtively and quietly simply to give pleasure. In both there is the same natural conviction that life is of a certain quality. They have their judgement of conduct. They know the relations of human beings towards each other and towards the universe. Neither of them probably has a word to say about the matter outright. But everything depends on it. Only believe, we find ourselves saying, and all the rest will come of itself. Only believe, to take a very simple instance which the recent publication of *The Watsons*[2] brings to mind, that a nice girl will instinctively try to soothe the feelings of a boy who has been snubbed at a dance, and then, if you believe it implicitly and unquestioningly, you will not only make people a hundred years later feel the same thing, but will make them feel it as literature. For certainty of that kind is the condition which makes it possible to write. To believe that your impressions hold good for others is to be released from the cramp and confinement of personality. It is to be free, as Scott was

---

[1]   *Wordsworth* Poet William Wordsworth (1770–1850); *Scott* Scottish novelist Sir Walter Scott (1771–1832); *Miss Austen* Novelist Jane Austen (1775–1817).

[2]   *The Watsons* 1871 novel by Jane Austen that was republished by Leonard Parsons in 1923.

free, to explore with a vigour which still holds us spell-bound the whole world of adventure and romance. It is also the first step in that mysterious process in which Jane Austen was so great an adept. The little grain of experience being selected, believed in, and set outside herself, could be put precisely in its place, and she was then free to make it, by a process which never yields its secret to the analyst, into that complete statement which is literature.

So, then, our contemporaries afflict us because they have ceased to believe. The most sincere of them will only tell us what it is that happens to himself. They cannot make a world, because they are not free of other human beings. They cannot tell stories, because they do not believe that stories are true. They cannot generalise. They depend on their senses and emotions, whose testimony is trustworthy, rather than on their intellects, whose message is obscure. And they have perforce to deny themselves the use of some of the most powerful and some of the most exquisite of the weapons of their craft. Set down at a fresh angle of the eternal prospect, they can only whip out their notebooks and record with agonised intensity the flying gleams, which light on what? and the transitory splendours, which may perhaps compose nothing whatever. The critics may well declare that if the age is indeed like this—and our vision is determined, of course, by our place at the table—then the risks of judging contemporary work are greater than ever before. There is every excuse for them if they are wide of the mark; and no doubt it would be better to retreat, as Matthew Arnold advised, from the burning ground of the present, "of which the estimates are so often not only personal, but personal with passion,"[1] to the safe tranquillity of the past. But the note of pessimism jars. It is true that the writer of the present day must renounce his hope of making that complete statement which we call a masterpiece. He must be content to be a taker of notes. But if notebooks are perishable volumes, he may reflect that they are, after all, the stuff from which the masterpieces of the future are made. Truth, again, to speak in the manner of the myth-makers, has always been thus volatile, sometimes coming quietly into the open and suffering herself to be looked at, at others flying averted and obscured. But if she is the truth then we do well to watch for her most brief apparitions; and the sight of her will convince us that she is always the same, from Chaucer even to Mr. Conrad. The difference is on the surface; the continuity in the depths.

As for the critic, whose task it is to pass judgement on the books of the moment, let him think of them as the anonymous activities of free craftsmen working under the lash of no master, but obscurely, with ardour, and in the interest of a greater writer who is not yet born. Let him therefore be generous of encouragement, but chary of bestowing wreaths which fade and coronets which fall off. Let him see the present in relation to the future. Let him, in short, slam the door upon the cosy company where butter is plentiful and sugar cheap, and emulate rather that gaunt aristocrat, Lady Hester Stanhope,[2] who kept a milk-white horse in her stable in readiness for the Messiah, and was forever scanning the mountain tops, impatiently, but with confidence, for the first signs of His approach.

—1921

Modern Fiction

In making any survey, even the freest and loosest, of modern fiction, it is difficult not to take it for granted that the modern practice of the art is somehow an improvement upon the old. With their simple tools and primitive materials, it might be said, Fielding did well and Jane Austen even better,[3] but compare their opportunities with ours! Their masterpieces certainly have a strange air of simplicity. And yet the analogy between literature and the process, to choose an example, of making motor cars scarcely holds good beyond the first glance. It is doubtful whether in the course of the centuries, though we have learnt much about making machines, we have learnt anything about making literature. We do not come to write better; all that we

[1] *of which ... passion* From T.H. Ward, ed., *The English Poets*, volume 1.

[2] *Lady Hester Stanhope* An eccentric who was an occasional topic of Woolf's writing. (See, for example, her essays "Lady Hester Stanhope" and "The Eccentrics.")

[3] *Fielding ... better* Henry Fielding (1707–54) and Jane Austen (1775–1817), British novelists.

can be said to do is to keep moving, now a little in this direction, now in that, but with a circular tendency should the whole course of the track be viewed from a sufficiently lofty pinnacle. It need scarcely be said that we make no claim to stand, even momentarily, upon that vantage ground. On the flat, in the crowd, half blind with dust, we look back with envy to those happier warriors, whose battle is won and whose achievements wear so serene an air of accomplishment that we can scarcely refrain from whispering that the fight was not so fierce for them as for us. It is for the historian of literature to decide; for him to say if we are now beginning or ending or standing in the middle of a great period of prose fiction, for down in the plain little is visible. We only know that certain gratitudes and hostilities inspire us; that certain paths seem to lead to fertile land, others to the dust and the desert; and of this perhaps it may be worth while to attempt some account.

Our quarrel, then, is not with the classics, and if we speak of quarrelling with Mr. Wells, Mr. Bennett, and Mr. Galsworthy,[1] it is partly that by the mere fact of their existence in the flesh their work has a living, breathing, everyday imperfection which bids us take what liberties with it we choose. But it is also true that, while we thank them for a thousand gifts, we reserve our unconditional gratitude for Mr. Hardy, for Mr. Conrad, and in a much lesser degree for the Mr. Hudson of *The Purple Land, Green Mansions,* and *Far Away and Long Ago*.[2] Mr. Wells, Mr. Bennett, and Mr. Galsworthy have excited so many hopes and disappointed them so persistently that our gratitude largely takes the form of thanking them for having shown us what they might have done but have not done; what we certainly could not do, but as certainly, perhaps, do not wish to do. No single phrase will sum up the charge or grievance which we have to bring against a mass of work so large in its

volume and embodying so many qualities, both admirable and the reverse. If we tried to formulate our meaning in one word we should say that these three writers are materialists. It is because they are concerned not with the spirit but with the body that they have disappointed us, and left us with the feeling that the sooner English fiction turns its back upon them, as politely as may be, and marches, if only into the desert, the better for its soul. Naturally, no single word reaches the centre of three separate targets. In the case of Mr. Wells it falls notably wide of the mark. And yet even with him it indicates to our thinking the fatal alloy in his genius, the great clod of clay that has got itself mixed up with the purity of his inspiration. But Mr. Bennett is perhaps the worst culprit of the three, inasmuch as he is by far the best workman. He can make a book so well constructed and solid in its craftsmanship that it is difficult for the most exacting of critics to see through what chink or crevice decay can creep in. There is not so much as a draught between the frames of the windows, or a crack in the boards. And yet—if life should refuse to live there? That is a risk which the creator of *The Old Wives' Tale*, George Cannon, Edwin Clayhanger,[3] and hosts of other figures, may well claim to have surmounted. His characters live abundantly, even unexpectedly, but it remains to ask how do they live, and what do they live for? More and more they seem to us, deserting even the well-built villa in the Five Towns,[4] to spend their time in some softly padded first-class railway carriage, pressing bells and buttons innumerable; and the destiny to which they travel so luxuriously becomes more and more unquestionably an eternity of bliss spent in the very best hotel in Brighton. It can scarcely be said of Mr. Wells that he is a materialist in the sense that he takes too much delight in the solidity of his fabric. His mind is too generous in its sympathies to allow him to spend much time in making things shipshape and substantial. He is a materialist from sheer goodness of heart, taking upon his shoulders the work that ought to have been discharged by Government officials, and in the plethora

---

[1] *Mr. Wells ... Galsworthy* H.G. Wells (1866–1946), Arnold Bennett (1867–1931), and John Galsworthy (1867–1933), three popular novelists at the time.

[2] *Mr. Hardy ... Ago* Thomas Hardy (1840–1928), author of *Tess of the D'Urbervilles* and *Jude the Obscure*; Joseph Conrad (1857–1924), author of *Heart of Darkness*; William Henry Hudson (1841–1922), Argentinean author and naturalist who lived in London. *The Purple Land* and *Green Mansions* are romances set in Argentina, and *Far Away and Long Ago* is an account of Hudson's early life in Argentina.

[3] *Geroge ... Clayhanger* Characters from Bennett's novels *The Roll-Call* and *Clayhanger*.

[4] *the Five Towns* Five towns in Staffordshire that comprise the center of England's pottery industry and that provide the setting for many of Bennett's novels.

of his ideas and facts scarcely having leisure to realise, or forgetting to think important, the crudity and coarseness of his human beings. Yet what more damaging criticism can there be both of his earth and of his Heaven than that they are to be inhabited here and hereafter by his Joans and his Peters? Does not the inferiority of their natures tarnish whatever institutions and ideals may be provided for them by the generosity of their creator? Nor, profoundly though we respect the integrity and humanity of Mr. Galsworthy, shall we find what we seek in his pages.

If we fasten, then, one label on all these books, on which is one word materialists, we mean by it that they write of unimportant things; that they spend immense skill and immense industry making the trivial and the transitory appear the true and the enduring.

We have to admit that we are exacting, and, further, that we find it difficult to justify our discontent by explaining what it is that we exact. We frame our question differently at different times. But it reappears most persistently as we drop the finished novel on the crest of a sigh—Is it worth while? What is the point of it all? Can it be that, owing to one of those little deviations which the human spirit seems to make from time to time, Mr. Bennett has come down with his magnificent apparatus for catching life just an inch or two on the wrong side? Life escapes; and perhaps without life nothing else is worth while. It is a confession of vagueness to have to make use of such a figure as this, but we scarcely better the matter by speaking, as critics are prone to do, of reality. Admitting the vagueness which afflicts all criticism of novels, let us hazard the opinion that for us at this moment the form of fiction most in vogue more often misses than secures the thing we seek. Whether we call it life or spirit, truth or reality, this, the essential thing, has moved off, or on, and refuses to be contained any longer in such ill-fitting vestments as we provide. Nevertheless, we go on perseveringly, conscientiously, constructing our two and thirty chapters after a design which more and more ceases to resemble the vision in our minds. So much of the enormous labour of proving the solidity, the likeness to life, of the story is not merely labour thrown away but labour misplaced to the extent of obscuring and blotting out the light of the conception. The writer seems constrained, not by

his own free will but by some powerful and unscrupulous tyrant who has him in thrall, to provide a plot, to provide comedy, tragedy, love interest, and an air of probability embalming the whole so impeccable that if all his figures were to come to life they would find themselves dressed down to the last button of their coats in the fashion of the hour. The tyrant is obeyed; the novel is done to a turn. But sometimes, more and more often as time goes by, we suspect a momentary doubt, a spasm of rebellion, as the pages fill themselves in the customary way. Is life like this? Must novels be like this?

Look within and life, it seems, is very far from being "like this." Examine for a moment an ordinary mind on an ordinary day. The mind receives a myriad impressions—trivial, fantastic, evanescent, or engraved with the sharpness of steel. From all sides they come, an incessant shower of innumerable atoms; and as they fall, as they shape themselves into the life of Monday or Tuesday, the accent falls differently from of old; the moment of importance came not here but there; so that, if a writer were a free man and not a slave, if he could write what he chose, not what he must, if he could base his work upon his own feeling and not upon convention, there would be no plot, no comedy, no tragedy, no love interest or catastrophe in the accepted style, and perhaps not a single button sewn on as the Bond Street tailors would have it. Life is not a series of gig lamps symmetrically arranged; life is a luminous halo, a semitransparent envelope surrounding us from the beginning of consciousness to the end. Is it not the task of the novelist to convey this varying, this unknown and uncircumscribed spirit, whatever aberration or complexity it may display, with as little mixture of the alien and external as possible? We are not pleading merely for courage and sincerity; we are suggesting that the proper stuff of fiction is a little other than custom would have us believe it.

It is, at any rate, in some such fashion as this that we seek to define the quality which distinguishes the work of several young writers, among whom Mr. James Joyce[1] is the most notable, from that of their predecessors. They attempt to come closer to life, and to preserve more sincerely and exactly what interests and moves them, even if to do so they must discard most of the

---

[1] *Mr. James Joyce* James Joyce (1882–1941), Irish novelist.

conventions which are commonly observed by the novelist. Let us record the atoms as they fall upon the mind in the order in which they fall, let us trace the pattern, however disconnected and incoherent in appearance, which each sight or incident scores upon the consciousness. Let us not take it for granted that life exists more fully in what is commonly thought big than in what is commonly thought small. Any one who has read *The Portrait of the Artist as a Young Man* or, what promises to be a far more interesting work, *Ulysses*,[1] now appearing in the *Little Review*, will have hazarded some theory of this nature as to Mr. Joyce's intention. On our part, with such a fragment before us, it is hazarded rather than affirmed; but whatever the intention of the whole, there can be no question but that it is of the utmost sincerity and that the result, difficult or unpleasant as we may judge it, is undeniably important. In contrast with those whom we have called materialists, Mr. Joyce is spiritual; he is concerned at all costs to reveal the flickerings of that innermost flame which flashes its messages through the brain, and in order to preserve it he disregards with complete courage whatever seems to him adventitious, whether it be probability, or coherence, or any other of these signposts which for generations have served to support the imagination of a reader when called upon to imagine what he can neither touch nor see. The scene in the cemetery,[2] for instance, with its brilliancy, its sordidity, its incoherence, its sudden lightning flashes of significance, does undoubtedly come so close to the quick of the mind that, on a first reading at any rate, it is difficult not to acclaim a masterpiece. If we want life itself, here surely we have it. Indeed, we find ourselves fumbling rather awkwardly if we try to say what else we wish, and for what reason a work of such originality yet fails to compare, for we must take high examples, with *Youth* or *The Mayor of Casterbridge*.[3] It fails because of the comparative poverty of the writer's mind, we might say simply and have done with it. But it is possible to press a little further and wonder whether we may not refer our sense of being in a bright yet narrow room, confined and shut in, rather than enlarged and set free, to some limitation imposed by the method as well as by the mind. Is it the method that inhibits the creative power? Is it due to the method that we feel neither jovial nor magnanimous, but centred in a self which, in spite of its tremor of susceptibility, never embraces or creates what is outside itself and beyond? Does the emphasis laid, perhaps didactically, upon indecency, contribute to the effect of something angular and isolated? Or is it merely that in any effort of such originality it is much easier, for contemporaries especially, to feel what it lacks than to name what it gives? In any case it is a mistake to stand outside examining "methods." Any method is right, every method is right, that expresses what we wish to express, if we are writers; that brings us closer to the novelist's intention if we are readers. This method has the merit of bringing us closer to what we were prepared to call life itself; did not the reading of *Ulysses* suggest how much of life is excluded or ignored, and did it not come with a shock to open *Tristram Shandy* or even *Pendennis*[4] and be by them convinced that there are not only other aspects of life, but more important ones into the bargain.

However this may be, the problem before the novelist at present, as we suppose it to have been in the past, is to contrive means of being free to set down what he chooses. He has to have the courage to say that what interests him is no longer "this" but "that": out of "that" alone must he construct his work. For the moderns "that," the point of interest, lies very likely in the dark places of psychology. At once, therefore, the accent falls a little differently; the emphasis is upon something hitherto ignored; at once a different outline of form becomes necessary, difficult for us to grasp, incomprehensible to our predecessors. No one but a modern, no one perhaps but a Russian, would have felt the interest of the situation which Tchekov[5] has made into the short story which he calls "Gusev."[6] Some Russian soldiers lie ill on board a ship which is taking them back to Russia. We are given a few scraps of their talk and some of their thoughts; then one of them dies

---

[1] [Woolf's note]   Written in April, 1919.

[2] *The scene … cemetery*   In the "Hades" section of *Ulysses*.

[3] *Youth … Casterbridge*   By Joseph Conrad and Thomas Hardy, respectively.

[4] *Tristram … Pendennis*   Novels by Laurence Sterne (1713–68) and William Makepeace Thackeray (1811–68), respectively.

[5] *Tchekov*   Russian playwright and short story writer Anton Chekhov (1860–1904).

[6] *"Gusev"*   Published in 1890.

and is carried away; the talk goes on among the others for a time, until Gusev himself dies, and looking "like a carrot or a radish" is thrown overboard. The emphasis is laid upon such unexpected places that at first it seems as if there were no emphasis at all; and then, as the eyes accustom themselves to twilight and discern the shapes of things in a room we see how complete the story is, how profound, and how truly in obedience to his vision Tchekov has chosen this, that, and the other, and placed them together to compose something new. But it is impossible to say "this is comic," or "that is tragic," nor are we certain, since short stories, we have been taught, should be brief and conclusive, whether this, which is vague and inconclusive, should be called a short story at all.

The most elementary remarks upon modern English fiction can hardly avoid some mention of the Russian influence, and if the Russians are mentioned one runs the risk of feeling that to write of any fiction save theirs is waste of time. If we want understanding of the soul and heart where else shall we find it of comparable profundity? If we are sick of our own materialism the least considerable of their novelists has by right of birth a natural reverence for the human spirit. "Learn to make yourself akin to people . . . . But let this sympathy be not with the mind—for it is easy with the mind—but with the heart, with love towards them." In every great Russian writer we seem to discern the features of a saint, if sympathy for the sufferings of others, love towards them, endeavour to reach some goal worthy of the most exacting demands of the spirit constitute saintliness. It is the saint in them which confounds us with a feeling of our own irreligious triviality, and turns so many of our famous novels to tinsel and trickery. The conclusions of the Russian mind, thus comprehensive and compassionate, are inevitably, perhaps, of the utmost sadness. More accurately indeed we might speak of the inconclusive-ness of the Russian mind. It is the sense that there is no answer, that if honestly examined life presents question after question which must be left to sound on and on after the story is over in hopeless interrogation that fills us with a deep, and finally it may be with a resentful, despair. They are right perhaps; unquestionably they see further than we do and without our gross impediments of vision. But perhaps we see

something that escapes them, or why should this voice of protest mix itself with our gloom? The voice of protest is the voice of another and an ancient civilisation which seems to have bred in us the instinct to enjoy and fight rather than to suffer and understand. English fiction from Sterne to Meredith[1] bears witness to our natural delight in humour and comedy, in the beauty of earth, in the activities of the intellect, and in the splendour of the body. But any deductions that we may draw from the comparison of two fictions so immeasurably far apart are futile save indeed as they flood us with a view of the infinite possibilities of the art and remind us that there is no limit to the horizon, and that nothing—no "method," no experiment, even of the wildest—is forbidden, but only falsity and pretence. "The proper stuff of fiction" does not exist; everything is the proper stuff of fiction, every feeling, every thought; every quality of brain and spirit is drawn upon; no perception comes amiss. And if we can imagine the art of fiction come alive and standing in our midst, she would undoubtedly bid us break her and bully her, as well as honour and love her, for so her youth is renewed and her sovereignty assured.

—1925

from *A Room of One's Own*[2]

CHAPTER I

But, you may say, we asked you to speak about women and fiction—what has that got to do with a room of one's own? I will try to explain. When you asked me to speak about women and fiction I sat down on the banks of a river and began to wonder what the words meant. They might mean simply a few remarks about Fanny Burney; a few more about Jane Austen; a tribute to the Brontës and a sketch of Haworth Parson-

---

[1] *Meredith* George Meredith, novelist and poet (1828–1909).

[2] [Woolf's note] This essay is based upon two papers read to the Arts Society at Newnham and the Odtaa at Girton in October 1928. The papers were too long to be read in full, and have since been altered and expanded. [Newnham and Girton are women's colleges at Cambridge University, and Odtaa (an acronym for "One Damn Thing After Another") was a literary society whose name was taken from John Masefield's 1926 novel of that title.]

age under snow; some witticisms if possible about Miss Mitford; a respectful allusion to George Eliot; a reference to Mrs. Gaskell and one would have done.[1] But at second sight the words seemed not so simple. The title women and fiction might mean, and you may have meant it to mean, women and what they are like; or it might mean women and the fiction that they write; or it might mean women and the fiction that is written about them; or it might mean that somehow all three are inextricably mixed together and you want me to consider them in that light. But when I began to consider the subject in this last way, which seemed the most interesting, I saw that it had one fatal drawback. I should never be able to come to a conclusion. I should never be able to fulfil what is, I understand, the first duty of a lecturer—to hand you after an hour's discourse a nugget of pure truth to wrap up between the pages of your notebooks and keep on the mantel-piece for ever. All I could do was to offer you an opinion upon one minor point—a woman must have money and a room of her own if she is to write fiction; and that, as you will see, leaves the great problem of the true nature of woman and the true nature of fiction unsolved. I have shirked the duty of coming to a conclusion upon these two questions—women and fiction remain, so far as I am concerned, unsolved problems. But in order to make some amends I am going to do what I can to show you how I arrived at this opinion about the room and the money. I am going to develop in your presence as fully and freely as I can the train of thought which led me to think this. Perhaps if I lay bare the ideas, the prejudices, that lie behind this statement you will find that they have some bearing upon women and some upon fiction. At any rate, when a subject is highly controversial—and any question about sex is that—one cannot hope to tell the truth. One can only show how one came to hold whatever opinion one does hold. One can only give one's audience the chance of drawing their own conclusions as they observe the limitations, the prejudices, the idiosyncrasies of the speaker. Fiction here is likely to contain more truth than fact. Therefore I propose, making use of all the liberties and licences of a novelist, to tell you the story of the two days that preceded my coming here—how, bowed down by the weight of the subject which you have laid upon my shoulders, I pondered it, and made it work in and out of my daily life. I need not say that what I am about to describe has no existence; Oxbridge is an invention; so is Fernham;[2] "I" is only a convenient term for somebody who has no real being. Lies will flow from my lips, but there may perhaps be some truth mixed up with them; it is for you to seek out this truth and to decide whether any part of it is worth keeping. If not, you will of course throw the whole of it into the wastepaper basket and forget all about it.

Here then was I (call me Mary Beton, Mary Seton, Mary Carmichael[3] or by any name you please—it is not a matter of any importance) sitting on the banks of a river a week or two ago in fine October weather, lost in thought. That collar I have spoken of, women and fiction, the need of coming to some conclusion on a subject that raises all sorts of prejudices and passions, bowed my head to the ground. To the right and left bushes of some sort, golden and crimson, glowed with the colour, even it seemed burnt with the heat, of fire. On the further bank the willows wept in perpetual lamentation, their hair about their shoulders. The river reflected whatever it chose of sky and bridge and burning tree, and when the undergraduate had oared his boat through the reflections they closed again, completely, as if he had never been. There one might have sat the clock round lost in thought. Thought—to call it by a prouder name than it deserved—had let its line down into the stream. It swayed, minute after minute, hither and thither among the reflections and the weeds, letting the water lift it and sink it, until—you know the little

[1] *Fanny Burney* (1752–1840) Novelist, diarist, and dramatist; *Haworth Parsonage* The family home of novelists Charlotte (1816–55), Emily (1818–48), and Anne (1820–49) Brontë; *Miss Mitford* Mary Russell Mitford (1787–1855), poet; *George Eliot* Pseudonym of Marian Evans (1810–65), author of many novels, including *The Mill on the Floss* (1860) and *Adam Bede* (1959); *Elizabeth Gaskell* Novelist (1810–65), author of *Cranford* and *Mary Barton*.

[2] *Oxbridge* Amalgamation of the names of the Universities of Oxford and Cambridge, a term used to describe the two collectively; *Fernham* Woolf combines characteristics of Newnham and Girton in her description of this fictional college.

[3] *Mary Beton ... Carmichael* See the "Ballad of Mary Hamilton," in which the companions of Mary, Queen of Scots were "Mary Beton and Mary Seton, / Mary Carmichael and me."

tug—the sudden conglomeration of an idea at the end of one's line: and then the cautious hauling of it in, and the careful laying of it out? Alas, laid on the grass how small, how insignificant this thought of mine looked; the sort of fish that a good fisherman puts back into the water so that it may grow fatter and be one day worth cooking and eating. I will not trouble you with that thought now, though if you look carefully you may find it for yourselves in the course of what I am going to say.

But however small it was, it had, nevertheless, the mysterious property of its kind—put back into the mind, it became at once very exciting, and important; and as it darted and sank, and flashed hither and thither, set up such a wash and tumult of ideas that it was impossible to sit still. It was thus that I found myself walking with extreme rapidity across a grass plot. Instantly a man's figure rose to intercept me. Nor did I at first understand that the gesticulations of a curious-looking object, in a cut-away coat and evening shirt, were aimed at me. His face expressed horror and indignation. Instinct rather than reason came to my help; he was a Beadle;[1] I was a woman. This was the turf; there was the path. Only the Fellows and Scholars are allowed here; the gravel is the place for me. Such thoughts were the work of a moment. As I regained the path the arms of the Beadle sank, his face assumed its usual repose, and though turf is better walking than gravel, no very great harm was done. The only charge I could bring against the Fellows and Scholars of whatever the college might happen to be was that in protection of their turf, which has been rolled for 300 years in succession, they had sent my little fish into hiding.

What idea it had been that had sent me so audaciously trespassing I could not now remember. The spirit of peace descended like a cloud from heaven, for if the spirit of peace dwells anywhere, it is in the courts and quadrangles of Oxbridge on a fine October morning. Strolling through those colleges past those ancient halls the roughness of the present seemed smoothed away; the body seemed contained in a miraculous glass cabinet through which no sound could penetrate, and the mind, freed from any contact with facts (unless one trespassed on the turf again), was at liberty to settle down upon whatever meditation was in harmony with the moment. As chance would have it, some stray memory of some old essay about revisiting Oxbridge in the long vacation brought Charles Lamb[2] to mind—Saint Charles, said Thackeray,[3] putting a letter of Lamb's to his forehead. Indeed, among all the dead (I give you my thoughts as they came to me), Lamb is one of the most congenial; one to whom one would have liked to say, Tell me then how you wrote your essays? For his essays are superior even to Max Beerbohm's,[4] I thought, with all their perfection, because of that wild flash of imagination, that lightning crack of genius in the middle of them which leaves them flawed and imperfect, but starred with poetry. Lamb then came to Oxbridge perhaps a hundred years ago. Certainly he wrote an essay—the name escapes me—about the manuscript of one of Milton's poems which he saw here. It was *Lycidas* perhaps, and Lamb wrote how it shocked him to think it possible that any word in *Lycidas* could have been different from what it is. To think of Milton changing the words in that poem seemed to him a sort of sacrilege. This led me to remember what I could of *Lycidas* and to amuse myself with guessing which word it could have been that Milton had altered, and why. It then occurred to me that the very manuscript itself which Lamb had looked at was only a few hundred yards away, so that one could follow Lamb's footsteps across the quadrangle to that famous library[5] where the treasure is kept. Moreover, I recollected, as I put this plan into execution, it is in this famous library that the manuscript of Thackeray's *Esmond* is also preserved. The critics often say that *Esmond* is Thackeray's most perfect novel. But the affectation of the style, with its imitation of the eighteenth century, hampers one, so far as I remember; unless indeed the eighteenth-century style was natural to Thackeray—a fact that one might prove by looking at the manuscript and seeing whether the alterations were

---

[1] *Beadle* Minor church or college official.

[2] *Charles Lamb* English essayist (1775–1834). The essay referred to later in this paragraph is "Oxford in the Vacation" (1820).

[3] *Thackeray* William Makepeace Thackeray, English novelist (1811–1863).

[4] *Max Beerbohm* English parodist, essayist, and cartoonist (1872–1956).

[5] *that famous library* The manuscript of Milton's *Lycidas* held by the library of Trinity College, Cambridge.

for the benefit of the style or of the sense. But then one would have to decide what is style and what is meaning, a question which—but here I was actually at the door which leads into the library itself. I must have opened it, for instantly there issued, like a guardian angel barring the way with a flutter of black gown instead of white wings, a deprecating, silvery, kindly gentleman, who regretted in a low voice as he waved me back that ladies are only admitted to the library if accompanied by a Fellow of the College or furnished with a letter of introduction.

That a famous library has been cursed by a woman is a matter of complete indifference to a famous library. Venerable and calm, with all its treasures safe locked within its breast, it sleeps complacently and will, so far as I am concerned, so sleep for ever. Never will I wake those echoes, never will I ask for that hospitality again, I vowed as I descended the steps in anger. Still an hour remained before luncheon, and what was one to do? Stroll on the meadows? Sit by the river? Certainly it was a lovely autumn morning; the leaves were fluttering red to the ground; there was no great hardship in doing either. But the sound of music reached my ear. Some service or celebration was going forward. The organ complained magnificently as I passed the chapel door. Even the sorrow of Christianity sounded in that serene air more like the recollection of sorrow than sorrow itself; even the groanings of the ancient organ seemed lapped in peace. I had no wish to enter had I the right, and this time the verger[1] might have stopped me, demanding perhaps my baptismal certificate, or a letter of introduction from the Dean. But the outside of these magnificent buildings is often as beautiful as the inside. Moreover, it was amusing enough to watch the congregation assembling, coming in and going out again, busying themselves at the door of the chapel like bees at the mouth of a hive. Many were in cap and gown; some had tufts of fur on their shoulders; others were wheeled in bath-chairs;[2] others, though not past middle age, seemed creased and crushed into shapes so singular that one was reminded of those giant crabs and crayfish who heave with difficulty across the sand of an aquarium. As

I leant against the wall the University indeed seemed a sanctuary in which are preserved rare types which would soon be obsolete if left to fight for existence on the pavement of the Strand.[3] Old stories of old deans and old dons came back to mind, but before I had summoned up courage to whistle—it used to be said that at the sound of a whistle old Professor —— instantly broke into a gallop—the venerable congregation had gone inside. The outside of the chapel remained. As you know, its high domes and pinnacles can be seen, like a sailing-ship always voyaging never arriving, lit up at night and visible for miles, far away across the hills.[4] Once, presumably, this quadrangle with its smooth lawns, its massive buildings, and the chapel itself was marsh too, where the grasses waved and the swine rootled.[5] Teams of horses and oxen, I thought, must have hauled the stone in wagons from far countries, and then with infinite labour the grey blocks in whose shade I was now standing were poised in order one on top of another, and then the painters brought their glass for the windows, and the masons were busy for centuries up on that roof with putty and cement, spade and trowel. Every Saturday somebody must have poured gold and silver out of a leathern purse into their ancient fists, for they had their beer and skittles[6] presumably of an evening. An unending stream of gold and silver, I thought, must have flowed into this court perpetually to keep the stones coming and the masons working; to level, to ditch, to dig and to drain. But it was then the age of faith, and money was poured liberally to set these stones on a deep foundation, and when the stones were raised, still more money was poured in from the coffers of kings and queens and great nobles to ensure that hymns should be sung here and scholars taught. Lands were granted; tithes were paid. And when the age of faith was over and the age of reason had come, still the same flow of gold and silver went on; fellowships were founded; lectureships endowed; only the gold and silver

---

[1] *verger* Church attendant.

[2] *bath-chairs* Large chairs on wheels for invalids, so named for Bath, an English spa city, and retreat for ill and elderly people.

[3] *the Strand* Busy street in London that runs parallel to the northern bank of the Thames.

[4] *As you ... hills* Description of the chapel of King's College, Cambridge, which was built from 1446 to 1547.

[5] *rootled* Rooted about.

[6] *skittles* Game resembling bowling. The expression "all beer and skittles" denotes pure enjoyment.

flowed now, not from the coffers of the king, but from the chests of merchants and manufacturers, from the purses of men who had made, say, a fortune from industry, and returned, in their wills, a bounteous share of it to endow more chairs, more lectureships, more fellowships in the university where they had learnt their craft. Hence the libraries and laboratories; the observatories; the splendid equipment of costly and delicate instruments which now stands on glass shelves, where centuries ago the grasses waved and the swine rooted. Certainly, as I strolled round the court, the foundation of gold and silver seemed deep enough; the pavement laid solidly over the wild grasses. Men with trays on their heads went busily from staircase to staircase. Gaudy blossoms flowered in window-boxes. The strains of the gramophone blared out from the rooms within. It was impossible not to reflect—the reflection whatever it may have been was cut short. The clock struck. It was time to find one's way to luncheon.

It is a curious fact that novelists have a way of making us believe that luncheon parties are invariably memorable for something very witty that was said, or for something very wise that was done. But they seldom spare a word for what was eaten. It is part of the novelist's convention not to mention soup and salmon and ducklings, as if soup and salmon and ducklings were of no importance whatsoever, as if nobody ever smoked a cigar or drank a glass of wine. Here, however, I shall take the liberty to defy that convention and to tell you that the lunch on this occasion began with soles, sunk in a deep dish, over which the college cook had spread a counterpane of the whitest cream, save that it was branded here and there with brown spots like the spots on the flanks of a doe. After that came the partridges, but if this suggests a couple of bald, brown birds on a plate you are mistaken. The partridges, many and various, came with all their retinue of sauces and salads, the sharp and the sweet, each in its order; their potatoes, thin as coins but not so hard; their sprouts, foliated as rosebuds but more succulent. And no sooner had the roast and its retinue been done with than the silent serving-man, the Beadle himself perhaps in a milder manifestation, set before us, wreathed in napkins, a confection which rose all sugar from the waves. To call it pudding and so relate it to rice and tapioca would be an insult. Meanwhile the wineglasses had flushed yellow and flushed crimson; had been emptied; had been filled. And thus by degrees was lit, halfway down the spine, which is the seat of the soul, not that hard little electric light which we call brilliance, as it pops in and out upon our lips, but the more profound, subtle and subterranean glow, which is the rich yellow flame of rational intercourse. No need to hurry. No need to sparkle. No need to be anybody but oneself. We are all going to heaven and Vandyck is of the company[1]—in other words, how good life seemed, how sweet its rewards, how trivial this grudge or that grievance, how admirable friendship and the society of one's kind, as, lighting a good cigarette, one sunk among the cushions in the window-seat.

If by good luck there had been an ashtray handy, if one had not knocked the ash out of the window in default, if things had been a little different from what they were, one would not have seen, presumably, a cat without a tail. The sight of that abrupt and truncated animal padding softly across the quadrangle changed by some fluke of the subconscious intelligence the emotional light for me. It was as if some one had let fall a shade. Perhaps the excellent hock[2] was relinquishing its hold. Certainly, as I watched the Manx cat pause in the middle of the lawn as if it too questioned the universe, something seemed lacking, something seemed different. But what was lacking, what was different, I asked myself, listening to the talk. And to answer that question I had to think myself out of the room, back into the past, before the war indeed, and to set before my eyes the model of another luncheon party held in rooms not very far distant from these; but different. Everything was different. Meanwhile the talk went on among the guests, who were many and young, some of this sex, some of that; it went on swimmingly, it went on agreeably, freely, amusingly. And as it went on I set it against the background of that other talk, and as I matched the two together I had no doubt that one was the descendant, the legitimate heir of the other. Nothing was changed;

[1] *We are all ... company*   These were said to be the last words of English portrait and landscape painter Thomas Gainsborough (1727–88); *Vandyck*   Sir Anthony Van Dyck (1599–1641), portrait artist.

[2] *hock*   I.e., Hochheimer, a German white wine.

nothing was different save only—here I listened with all my ears not entirely to what was being said, but to the murmur or current behind it. Yes, that was it—the change was there. Before the war at a luncheon party like this people would have said precisely the same things but they would have sounded different, because in those days they were accompanied by a sort of humming noise, not articulate, but musical, exciting, which changed the value of the words themselves. Could one set that humming noise to words? Perhaps with the help of the poets one could. A book lay beside me and, opening it, I turned casually enough to Tennyson. And here I found Tennyson was singing:

> There has fallen a splendid tear
>   From the passion-flower at the gate.
> She is coming, my dove, my dear;
>   She is coming, my life, my fate;
> The red rose cries, "She is near, she is near;"
>   And the white rose weeps, "She is late;"
> The larkspur listens, "I hear, I hear;"
>   And the lily whispers, "I wait." [1]

Was that what men hummed at luncheon parties before the war? And the women?

> My heart is like a singing bird
>   Whose nest is in a water'd shoot;
> My heart is like an apple tree
>   Whose boughs are bent with thick-set fruit;
> My heart is like a rainbow shell
>   That paddles in a halcyon sea;
> My heart is gladder than all these
>   Because my love is come to me. [2]

Was that what women hummed at luncheon parties before the war?

There was something so ludicrous in thinking of people humming such things even under their breath at luncheon parties before the war that I burst out laughing, and had to explain my laughter by pointing at the Manx cat, who did look a little absurd, poor beast, without a tail, in the middle of the lawn. Was he really

born so, or had he lost his tail in an accident? The tailless cat, though some are said to exist in the Isle of Man, is rarer than one thinks. It is a queer animal, quaint rather than beautiful. It is strange what a difference a tail makes—you know the sort of things one says as a lunch party breaks up and people are finding their coats and hats.

This one, thanks to the hospitality of the host, had lasted far into the afternoon. The beautiful October day was fading and the leaves were falling from the trees in the avenue as I walked through it. Gate after gate seemed to close with gentle finality behind me. Innumerable beadles were fitting innumerable keys into well-oiled locks; the treasure-house was being made secure for another night. After the avenue one comes out upon a road—I forget its name—which leads you, if you take the right turning, along to Fernham. But there was plenty of time. Dinner was not till half-past seven. One could almost do without dinner after such a luncheon. It is strange how a scrap of poetry works in the mind and makes the legs move in time to it along the road. Those words—

> There has fallen a splendid tear
>   From the passion-flower at the gate.
> She is coming, my dove, my dear—

sang in my blood as I stepped quickly along towards Headingley. And then, switching off into the other measure, I sang, where the waters are churned up by the weir:

> My heart is like a singing bird
>   Whose nest is in a water'd shoot;
> My heart is like an apple tree ....

What poets, I cried aloud, as one does in the dusk, what poets they were!

In a sort of jealousy, I suppose, for our own age, silly and absurd though these comparisons are, I went on to wonder if honestly one could name two living poets now as great as Tennyson and Christina Rossetti were then. Obviously it is impossible, I thought, looking into those foaming waters, to compare them. The very reason why the poetry excites one to such abandonment, such rapture, is that it celebrates some feeling that one used to have (at luncheon parties before the war perhaps), so

---

[1] *There has ... wait*   from Alfred, Lord Tennyson's "Maud" (1855), 1.22.10.

[2] *My heart ... me*   The opening stanza of Christina Rossetti's "A Birthday" (1861).

that one responds easily, familiarly, without troubling to check the feeling, or to compare it with any that one has now. But the living poets express a feeling that is actually being made and torn out of us at the moment. One does not recognize it in the first place; often for some reason one fears it; one watches it with keenness and compares it jealously and suspiciously with the old feeling that one knew. Hence the difficulty of modern poetry; and it is because of this difficulty that one cannot remember more than two consecutive lines of any good modern poet. For this reason—that my memory failed me—the argument flagged for want of material. But why, I continued, moving on towards Headingley, have we stopped humming under our breath at luncheon parties? Why has Alfred ceased to sing

> She is coming, my dove, my dear?

Why has Christina ceased to respond

> My heart is gladder than all these
> Because my love is come to me?

Shall we lay the blame on the war? When the guns fired in August 1914, did the faces of men and women show so plain in each other's eyes that romance was killed? Certainly it was a shock (to women in particular with their illusions about education, and so on) to see the faces of our rulers in the light of the shell-fire. So ugly they looked—German, English, French—so stupid. But lay the blame where one will, on whom one will, the illusion which inspired Tennyson and Christina Rossetti to sing so passionately about the coming of their loves is far rarer now than then. One has only to read, to look, to listen, to remember. But why say "blame"? Why, if it was an illusion, not praise the catastrophe, whatever it was, that destroyed illusion and put truth in its place? For truth … those dots mark the spot where, in search of truth, I missed the turning up to Fernham. Yes indeed, which was truth and which was illusion, I asked myself. What was the truth about these houses, for example, dim and festive now with their red windows in the dusk, but raw and red and squalid, with their sweets and their boot-laces, at nine o'clock in the morning? And the willows and the river and the gardens that run down to the river, vague now with the mist stealing over

them, but gold and red in the sunlight—which was the truth, which was the illusion about them? I spare you the twists and turns of my cogitations, for no conclusion was found on the road to Headingley, and I ask you to suppose that I soon found out my mistake about the turning and retraced my steps to Fernham.

As I have said already that it was an October day, I dare not forfeit your respect and imperil the fair name of fiction by changing the season and describing lilacs hanging over garden walls, crocuses, tulips and other flowers of spring. Fiction must stick to facts, and the truer the facts the better the fiction—so we are told. Therefore it was still autumn and the leaves were still yellow and falling, if anything, a little faster than before, because it was now evening (seven twenty-three to be precise) and a breeze (from the southwest to be exact) had risen. But for all that there was something odd at work:

> My heart is like a singing bird
> Whose nest is in a water'd shoot;
> My heart is like an apple tree
> Whose boughs are bent with thick-set fruit—

perhaps the words of Christina Rossetti were partly responsible for the folly of the fancy—it was nothing of course but a fancy—that the lilac was shaking its flowers over the garden walls, and the brimstone butterflies were scudding hither and thither, and the dust of the pollen was in the air. A wind blew, from what quarter I know not, but it lifted the half-grown leaves so that there was a flash of silver grey in the air. It was the time between the lights when colours undergo their intensification and purples and golds burn in window-panes like the beat of an excitable heart; when for some reason the beauty of the world revealed and yet soon to perish (here I pushed into the garden, for, unwisely, the door was left open and no beadles seemed about), the beauty of the world which is so soon to perish, has two edges, one of laughter, one of anguish, cutting the heart asunder. The gardens of Fernham lay before me in the spring twilight, wild and open, and in the long grass, sprinkled and carelessly flung, were daffodils and bluebells, not orderly perhaps at the best of times, and now wind-blown and waving as they tugged at their roots. The windows of the building, curved like ships' windows among generous waves of red brick, changed from lemon to silver under the flight of the quick spring clouds. Somebody was in a hammock, somebody, but in this light they were phantoms only, half guessed, half seen, raced across the grass—would no one stop her?—and then on the terrace, as if popping out to breathe the air, to glance at the garden, came a bent figure, formidable yet humble, with her great forehead and her shabby dress—could it be the famous scholar, could it be J —— H ——[1] herself? All was dim, yet intense too, as if the scarf which the dusk had flung over the garden were torn asunder by star or sword—the flash of some terrible reality leaping, as its way is, out of the heart of the spring. For youth—

Here was my soup. Dinner was being served in the great dining-hall. Far from being spring it was in fact an evening in October. Everybody was assembled in the big dining-room. Dinner was ready. Here was the soup. It was a plain gravy soup. There was nothing to stir the fancy in that. One could have seen through the transparent liquid any pattern that there might have been on the plate itself. But there was no pattern. The plate was plain. Next came beef with its attendant greens and potatoes—a homely trinity, suggesting the rumps of cattle in a muddy market, and sprouts curled and yellowed at the edge, and bargaining and cheapening, and women with string bags on Monday morning. There was no reason to complain of human nature's daily food, seeing that the supply was sufficient and coal-miners doubtless were sitting down to less. Prunes and custard followed. And if any one complains that prunes, even when mitigated by custard, are an uncharitable vegetable (fruit they are not), stringy as a miser's heart and exuding a fluid such as might run in misers' veins who have denied themselves wine and warmth for eighty years and yet not given to the poor, he should reflect that there are people whose charity embraces even the prune. Biscuits and cheese came next, and here the water-jug was liberally passed round, for it is the nature of biscuits to be dry, and these were biscuits to the core. That was all. The meal was over. Everybody scraped their chairs back; the swing-doors swung violently to and fro; soon the hall was emptied of every sign of food and made ready no doubt for breakfast next morning. Down corridors and up staircases the youth of England went banging and singing. And was it for a guest, a stranger (for I had no more right here in Fernham than in Trinity or Somerville or Girton or Newnham or Christchurch[2]), to say, "The dinner was not good," or to say (we were now, Mary Seton and I, in her sitting-room), "Could we not have dined up here alone?" for if I had said anything of the kind I should have been prying and searching into the secret economies of a house which to the stranger wears so fine a front of gaiety and courage. No, one could say nothing of the sort. Indeed, conversation for a moment flagged. The human frame being what it is, heart, body and brain all mixed together, and not contained in separate compartments as they will be no doubt in another million years, a good dinner is of great importance to good talk. One cannot think well, love well, sleep well, if one has not dined well. The lamp in the spine does not light on beef and prunes. We are all *probably* going to heaven, and Vandyck is, we *hope*, to meet us round the next corner—that is the dubious and qualifying state of mind that beef and prunes at the end of the day's work breed between them. Happily my friend, who taught science, had a cupboard where there was a squat bottle and little glasses—(but there should have been sole and partridge to begin with)—so that we were able to draw up to the fire and repair some of the damages of the day's living. In a minute or so we were slipping freely in and out among all those objects of curiosity and interest which form in the mind in the absence of a particular person, and are naturally to be discussed on coming together again—how somebody has married, another has not; one thinks this, another that; one has improved out of all knowledge, the other most amazingly gone to the bad—with all those speculations upon human nature and the character of the amazing world we live in which spring naturally from such beginnings. While these things were being said, however, I became shamefacedly aware of a current setting in of its own accord and carrying everything forward to an end of its own. One might be talking of Spain or Portugal, or book or racehorse, but the real interest of whatever was said was none of those things, but a scene of masons on a high

---

[1] *J——H——* Jane Harrison (1850–1928), cultural anthropologist and archaeologist who was a Fellow at Newnham College.

[2] *Trinity ... Christchurch* Somerville and Christchurch are colleges at Oxford, while Trinity, Girton, and Newnham are Cambridge colleges.

roof some five centuries ago. Kings and nobles brought treasure in huge sacks and poured it under the earth. This scene was for ever coming alive in my mind and placing itself by another of lean cows and a muddy market and withered greens and the stringy hearts of old men—these two pictures, disjointed and disconnected and nonsensical as they were, were for ever coming together and combating each other and had me entirely at their mercy. The best course, unless the whole talk was to be distorted, was to expose what was in my mind to the air, when with good luck it would fade and crumble like the head of the dead king when they opened the coffin at Windsor. Briefly, then, I told Miss Seton about the masons who had been all those years on the roof of the chapel, and about the kings and queens and nobles bearing sacks of gold and silver on their shoulders, which they shovelled into the earth; and then how the great financial magnates of our own time came and laid cheques and bonds, I suppose, where the others had laid ingots and rough lumps of gold. All that lies beneath the colleges down there, I said; but this college, where we are now sitting, what lies beneath its gallant red brick and the wild unkempt grasses of the garden? What force is behind the plain china off which we dined, and (here it popped out of my mouth before I could stop it) the beef, the custard and the prunes?

Well, said Mary Seton, about the year 1860—Oh, but you know the story, she said, bored, I suppose, by the recital. And she told me—rooms were hired. Committees met. Envelopes were addressed. Circulars were drawn up. Meetings were held; letters were read out; so-and-so has promised so much; on the contrary, Mr. —— won't give a penny. The *Saturday Review* has been very rude. How can we raise a fund to pay for offices? Shall we hold a bazaar? Can't we find a pretty girl to sit in the front row? Let us look up what John Stuart Mill[1] said on the subject. Can any one persuade the editor of the —— to print a letter? Can we get Lady —— to sign it? Lady —— is out of town. That was the way it was done, presumably, sixty years ago, and it was a prodigious effort, and a great deal of time was spent on it. And it was only after a long struggle and with the

utmost difficulty that they got thirty thousand pounds together.[2] So obviously we cannot have wine and partridges and servants carrying tin dishes on their heads, she said. We cannot have sofas and separate rooms. "The amenities," she said, quoting from some book or other, "will have to wait."[3]

At the thought of all those women working year after year and finding it hard to get two thousand pounds together, and as much as they could do to get thirty thousand pounds, we burst out in scorn at the reprehensible poverty of our sex. What had our mothers been doing then that they had no wealth to leave us? Powdering their noses? Looking in at shop windows? Flaunting in the sun at Monte Carlo? There were some photographs on the mantel-piece. Mary's mother—if that was her picture—may have been a wastrel[4] in her spare time (she had thirteen children by a minister of the church), but if so her gay and dissipated life had left too few traces of its pleasures on her face. She was a homely body; an old lady in a plaid shawl which was fastened by a large cameo; and she sat in a basket-chair, encouraging a spaniel to look at the camera, with the amused, yet strained expression of one who is sure that the dog will move directly the bulb is pressed. Now if she had gone into business; had become a manufacturer of artificial silk or a magnate on the Stock Exchange; if she had left two or three hundred thousand pounds to Fernham, we could have been sitting at our ease tonight and the subject of our talk might have been archaeology, botany, anthropology, physics, the nature of the atom, mathematics, astronomy, relativity, geography. If only Mrs. Seton and her mother and her mother before her had learnt the great art of making money and had left their money, like their fathers and their grandfathers before them, to found fellowships and lectureships and prizes and scholarships appropriated to the use of their

---

[1] *John Stuart Mill* English philosopher and economist (1806–73) who was interested in the status and treatment of women; author of *The Subjection of Women*.

[2] [Woolf's note] "We are told that we ought to ask for 30,000 at least…. It is not a large sum, considering that there is to be but one college of this sort for Great Britain, Ireland, and the Colonies, and considering how easy it is to raise immense sums for boys' schools. But considering how few people really wish women to be educated, it is a good deal."—Lady Stephen, *Life of Miss Emily Davies*.

[3] [Woolf's note] "Every penny which could be scraped together was set aside for building, and the amenities had to be postponed." –R. Strachey, *The Cause*.

[4] *wastrel* Spendthrift.

own sex, we might have dined very tolerably up here alone off a bird and a bottle of wine; we might have looked forward without undue confidence to a pleasant and honourable lifetime spent in the shelter of one of the liberally endowed professions. We might have been exploring or writing; mooning about the venerable places of the earth; sitting contemplative on the steps of the Parthenon, or going at ten to an office and coming home comfortably at half-past four to write a little poetry. Only, if Mrs. Seton and her like had gone into business at the age of fifteen, there would have been—that was the snag in the argument—no Mary. What, I asked, did Mary think of that? There between the curtains was the October night, calm and lovely, with a star or two caught in the yellowing trees. Was she ready to resign her share of it and her memories (for they had been a happy family, though a large one) of games and quarrels up in Scotland, which she is never tired of praising for the fineness of its air and the quality of its cakes, in order that Fernham might have been endowed with fifty thousand pounds or so by a stroke of the pen? For, to endow a college would necessitate the suppression of families altogether. Making a fortune and bearing thirteen children—no human being could stand it. Consider the facts, we said. First there are nine months before the baby is born. Then the baby is born. Then there are three or four months spent in feeding the baby. After the baby is fed there are certainly five years spent in playing with the baby. You cannot, it seems, let children run about the streets. People who have seen them running wild in Russia say that the sight is not a pleasant one. People say, too, that human nature takes its shape in the years between one and five. If Mrs. Seton, I said, had been making money, what sort of memories would you have had of games and quarrels? What would you have known of Scotland, and its fine air and cakes and all the rest of it? But it is useless to ask these questions, because you would never have come into existence at all. Moreover, it is equally useless to ask what might have happened if Mrs. Seton and her mother and her mother before her had amassed great wealth and laid it under the foundations of college and library, because, in the first place, to earn money was impossible for them, and in the second, had it been possible, the law denied them the right to possess what money they earned. It is only for the last forty-eight years that Mrs. Seton has had a penny of her own.[1] For all the centuries before that it would have been her husband's property—a thought which, perhaps, may have had its share in keeping Mrs. Seton and her mothers off the Stock Exchange. Every penny I earn, they may have said, will be taken from me and disposed of according to my husband's wisdom—perhaps to found a scholarship or to endow a fellowship in Balliol or Kings,[2] so that to earn money, even if I could earn money, is not a matter that interests me very greatly. I had better leave it to my husband.

At any rate, whether or not the blame rested on the old lady who was looking at the spaniel, there could be no doubt that for some reason or other our mothers had mismanaged their affairs very gravely. Not a penny could be spared for "amenities"; for partridges and wine, beadles and turf, books and cigars, libraries and leisure. To raise bare walls out of the bare earth was the utmost they could do.

So we talked standing at the window and looking, as so many thousands look every night, down on the domes and towers of the famous city beneath us. It was very beautiful, very mysterious in the autumn moonlight. The old stone looked very white and venerable. One thought of all the books that were assembled down there; of the pictures of old prelates and worthies hanging in the panelled rooms; of the painted windows that would be throwing strange globes and crescents on the pavement; of the tablets and memorials and inscriptions; of the fountains and the grass; of the quiet rooms looking across the quiet quadrangles. And (pardon me the thought) I thought, too, of the admirable smoke and drink and the deep armchairs and the pleasant carpets: of the urbanity, the geniality, the dignity which are the offspring of luxury and privacy and space. Certainly our mothers had not provided us with anything comparable to all this—our mothers who found it difficult to scrape together thirty thousand pounds, our mothers who bore thirteen children to ministers of religion at St. Andrews.

---

[1] *It is … own* Reference to the Married Women's Property Acts of 1870 and 1882, which allowed married women the same rights to their property that single women enjoyed.

[2] *Balliol or Kings* Two colleges, the first at Oxford and the second at Cambridge.

So I went back to my inn, and as I walked through the dark streets I pondered this and that, as one does at the end of the day's work. I pondered why it was that Mrs. Seton had no money to leave us; and what effect poverty has on the mind; and what effect wealth has on the mind; and I thought of the queer old gentlemen I had seen that morning with tufts of fur upon their shoulders; and I remembered how if one whistled one of them ran; and I thought of the organ booming in the chapel and of the shut doors of the library; and I thought how unpleasant it is to be locked out; and I thought how it is worse perhaps to be locked in; and, thinking of the safety and prosperity of the one sex and of the poverty and insecurity of the other and of the effect of tradition and of the lack of tradition upon the mind of a writer, I thought at last that it was time to roll up the crumpled skin of the day, with its arguments and its impressions and its anger and its laughter, and cast it into the hedge. A thousand stars were flashing across the blue wastes of the sky. One seemed alone with an inscrutable society. All human beings were laid asleep—prone, horizontal, dumb. Nobody seemed stirring in the streets of Oxbridge. Even the door of the hotel sprang open at the touch of an invisible hand—not a boots[1] was sitting up to light me to bed, it was so late.

Chapter 2

The scene, if I may ask you to follow me, was now changed. The leaves were still falling, but in London now, not Oxbridge; and I must ask you to imagine a room, like many thousands, with a window looking across people's hats and vans and motor-cars to other windows, and on the table inside the room a blank sheet of paper on which was written in large letters WOMEN AND FICTION, but no more. The inevitable sequel to lunching and dining at Oxbridge seemed, unfortunately, to be a visit to the British Museum. One must strain off what was personal and accidental in all these impressions and so reach the pure fluid, the essential oil of truth. For that visit to Oxbridge and the luncheon and the dinner had started a swarm of questions. Why did men drink wine and women water? Why was one

sex so prosperous and the other so poor? What effect has poverty on fiction? What conditions are necessary for the creation of works of art?—a thousand questions at once suggested themselves. But one needed answers, not questions; and an answer was only to be had by consulting the learned and the unprejudiced, who have removed themselves above the strife of tongue and the confusion of body and issued the result of their reasoning and research in books which are to be found in the British Museum. If truth is not to be found on the shelves of the British Museum, where, I asked myself, picking up a notebook and a pencil, is truth?

Thus provided, thus confident and enquiring, I set out in the pursuit of truth. The day, though not actually wet, was dismal, and the streets in the neighbourhood of the Museum were full of open coal-holes, down which sacks were showering; four-wheeled cabs were drawing up and depositing on the pavement corded boxes containing, presumably, the entire wardrobe of some Swiss or Italian family seeking fortune or refuge or some other desirable commodity which is to be found in the boarding-houses of Bloomsbury[2] in the winter. The usual hoarse-voiced men paraded the streets with plants on barrows. Some shouted; others sang. London was like a workshop. London was like a machine. We were all being shot backwards and forwards on this plain foundation to make some pattern. The British Museum was another department of the factory. The swing-doors swung open; and there one stood under the vast dome, as if one were a thought in the huge bald forehead which is so splendidly encircled by a band of famous names. One went to the counter; one took a slip of paper; one opened a volume of the catalogue, and .... the five dots here indicate five separate minutes of stupefaction, wonder, and bewilderment. Have you any notion of how many books are written about women in the course of one year? Have you any notion how many are written by men? Are you aware that you are, perhaps, the most discussed animal in the universe? Here had I come with a notebook and pencil proposing to spend a morning reading, supposing that at the end of the morning I should have transferred the truth to my

---

[1] *boots* I.e., hotel servant, because one of a servant's chores was to clean the guests' boots.

[2] *Bloomsbury* Area of London in which the British Museum is located and in which many of Woolf's circle (known collectively as "The Bloomsbury Group") lived.

notebook. But I should need to be a herd of elephants, I thought, and a wilderness of spiders, desperately referring to the animals that are reputed longest lived and most multitudinously eyed, to cope with all this. I should need claws of steel and beak of brass even to penetrate the husk. How shall I ever find the grains of truth embedded in all this mass of paper, I asked myself, and in despair began running my eye up and down the long list of titles. Even the names of the books gave me food for thought. Sex and its nature might well attract doctors and biologists; but what was surprising and difficult of explanation was the fact that sex—woman, that is to say—also attracts agreeable essayists, light-fingered novelists, young men who have taken the M.A. degree; men who have taken no degree; men who have no apparent qualification save that they are not women. Some of these books were, on the face of it, frivolous and facetious; but many, on the other hand, were serious and prophetic, moral and hortatory. Merely to read the titles suggested innumerable schoolmasters, innumerable clergymen mounting their platforms and pulpits and holding forth with a loquacity which far exceeded the hour usually allotted to such discourse on this one subject. It was a most strange phenomenon; and apparently—here I consulted the letter M—one confined to male sex. Women do not write books about men—a fact that I could not help welcoming with relief, for if I had first to read all that men have written about women, then all that women have written about men, the aloe that flowers once in a hundred years would flower twice before I could set pen to paper. So, making a perfectly arbitrary choice of a dozen volumes or so, I sent my slips of paper to lie in the wire tray, and waited in my stall, among the other seekers for the essential oil of truth.

What could be the reason, then, of this curious disparity, I wondered, drawing cart-wheels on the slips of paper provided by the British taxpayer for other purposes. Why are women, judging from this catalogue, so much more interesting to men than men are to women? A very curious fact it seemed, and my mind wandered to picture the lives of men who spend their time in writing books about women; whether they were old or young, married or unmarried, red-nosed or humpbacked—anyhow, it was flattering, vaguely, to feel oneself the object of such attention, provided that it was not entirely bestowed by the crippled and the in-firm—so I pondered until all such frivolous thoughts were ended by an avalanche of books sliding down on to the desk in front of me. Now the trouble began. The student who has been trained in research at Oxbridge has no doubt some method of shepherding his question past all distractions till it runs into its answer as a sheep runs into its pen. The student by my side, for instance, who was copying assiduously from a scientific manual was, I felt sure, extracting pure nuggets of the essential ore every ten minutes or so. His little grunts of satisfaction indicated so much. But if, unfortunately, one has had no training in a university, the question far from being shepherded into its pen flies like a frightened flock hither and thither, helter-skelter, pursued by a whole pack of hounds. Professors, schoolmasters, sociologists, clergymen, novelists, essayists, journalists, men who had no qualification save that they were not women, chased my simple and single question—Why are women poor?—until it became fifty questions; until the fifty questions leapt frantically into mid-stream and were carried away. Every page in my notebook was scribbled over with notes. To show the state of mind I was in, I will read you a few of them, explaining that the page was headed quite simply, WOMEN AND POVERTY, in block letters; but what followed was something like this:

> *Condition in Middle Ages of,*
> *Habits in the Fiji Islands of,*
> *Worshipped as goddesses by,*
> *Weaker in moral sense than,*
> *Idealism of,*
> *Greater conscientiousness of,*
> *South Sea Islanders, age of puberty among,*
> *Attractiveness of,*
> *Offered as sacrifice to,*
> *Small size of brain of,*
> *Profounder sub-consciousness of,*
> *Less hair on the body of,*
> *Mental, moral and physical inferiority of,*
> *Love of children of,*
> *Greater length of life of,*
> *Weaker muscles of,*
> *Strength of affections of,*
> *Vanity of,*
> *Higher education of,*

Shakespeare's opinion of,
Lord Birkenhead's[1] opinion of,
Dean Inge's[2] opinion of,
La Bruyère's[3] opinion of,
Dr. Johnson's[4] opinion of,
Mr. Oscar Browning's[5] opinion of, …

Here I drew breath and added, indeed, in the margin, Why does Samuel Butler[6] say, "Wise men never say what they think of women?" Wise men never say anything else apparently. But, I continued, leaning back in my chair and looking at the vast dome in which I was a single but by now somewhat harassed thought, what is so unfortunate is that wise men never think the same thing about women. Here is Pope:

Most women have no character at all.[7]

And here is La Bruyère:

Les femmes sont extrêmes; elles sont meilleures ou
pires que les hommes—[8]

a direct contradiction by keen observers who were contemporary. Are they capable of education or incapable? Napoleon thought them incapable. Dr. Johnson thought the opposite.[9] Have they souls or have they not

souls? Some savages say they have none. Others, on the contrary, maintain that women are half divine and worship them on that account.[10] Some sages hold that they are shallower in the brain; others that they are deeper in the consciousness. Goethe[11] honoured them; Mussolini[12] despises them. Wherever one looked men thought about women and thought differently. It was impossible to make head or tail of it all, I decided, glancing with envy at the reader next door who was making the neatest abstracts, headed often with an A or a B or a C, while my own notebook rioted with the wildest scribble of contradictory jottings. It was distressing, it was bewildering, it was humiliating. Truth had run through my fingers. Every drop had escaped.

I could not possibly go home, I reflected, and add as a serious contribution to the study of women and fiction that women have less hair on their bodies than men, or that the age of puberty among the South Sea Islanders is nine—or is it ninety?—even the handwriting had become in its distraction indecipherable. It was disgraceful to have nothing more weighty or respectable to show after a whole morning's work. And if I could not grasp the truth about W. (as for brevity's sake I had come to call her) in the past, why bother about W. in the future? It seemed pure waste of time to consult all those gentlemen who specialise in woman and her effect on whatever it may be—politics, children, wages, morality—numerous and learned as they are. One might as well leave their books unopened.

But while I pondered I had unconsciously, in my listlessness, in my desperation, been drawing a picture where I should, like my neighbour, have been writing a conclusion. I had been drawing a face, a figure. It was the face and the figure of Professor von X. engaged in writing his monumental work entitled *The Mental, Moral, and Physical Inferiority of the Female Sex.* He was

---

[1] *Lord Birkenhead* Frederick Elwin Smith, Earl of Birkenhead, who was Lord Chancellor from 1919 to 1922 and an opponent of women's suffrage.

[2] *Dean Inge* William Ralph Inge, Dean of St. Paul's Cathedral from 1911 to 1934.

[3] *La Bruyère* Jean de La Bruyère, French essayist and moralist (1645–1696).

[4] *Dr. Johnson* Samuel Johnson (1709–84), British lexicographer, critic, poet, and essayist.

[5] *Mr. Oscar Browning* History lecturer at King's College, Cambridge (1837–1923).

[6] *Samuel Butler* Nineteenth-century English author (1835–1902).

[7] *Most … all* From the opening of English poet and satirist Alexander Pope's Epistle 2, "To a Lady" from his *Moral Essays:* "Nothing so true as what you once let fall, / 'Most women have no character at all.'"

[8] *Les … hommes* "Women are extreme: they are better or worse than men." From La Bruyère's *Les Caractères* (1688).

[9] [Woolf's note] "'Men know that women are an overmatch for them, and therefore they choose the weakest or the most ignorant. If they did not think so, they never would be afraid of women knowing as much as themselves.' … In justice to the sex, I think it

but candid to acknowledge that, in a subsequent conversation, he told me that he was serious in what he said."—Boswell, *The Journal of a Tour to the Hebrides.*

[10] [Woolf's note] "The ancient Germans believed that there was something holy in women, and accordingly consulted them as oracles."—Frazer, *Golden Bough.*

[11] *Goethe* German writer Johann Wolfgang van Goethe (1749–1832).

[12] *Mussolini* Benito Mussolini (1833–1945), Italian Fascist dictator.

not in my picture a man attractive to women. He was heavily built; he had a great jowl; to balance that he had very small eyes; he was very red in the face. His expression suggested that he was labouring under some emotion that made him jab his pen on the paper as if he were killing some noxious insect as he wrote, but even when he had killed it that did not satisfy him; he must go on killing it; and even so, some cause for anger and irritation remained. Could it be his wife, I asked, looking at my picture. Was she in love with a cavalry officer? Was the cavalry officer slim and elegant and dressed in astrachan?[1] Had he been laughed at, to adopt the Freudian theory, in his cradle by a pretty girl? For even in his cradle the professor, I thought, could not have been an attractive child. Whatever the reason, the professor was made to look very angry and very ugly in my sketch, as he wrote his great book upon the mental, moral and physical inferiority of women. Drawing pictures was an idle way of finishing an unprofitable morning's work. Yet it is in our idleness, in our dreams, that the submerged truth sometimes comes to the top. A very elementary exercise in psychology, not to be dignified by the name of psycho-analysis, showed me, on looking at my notebook, that the sketch of the angry professor had been made in anger. Anger had snatched my pencil while I dreamt. But what was anger doing there? Interest, confusion, amusement, boredom—all these emotions I could trace and name as they succeeded each other throughout the morning. Had anger, the black snake, been lurking among them? Yes, said the sketch, anger had. It referred me unmistakably to the one book, to the one phrase, which had roused the demon; it was the professor's statement about the mental, moral and physical inferiority of women. My heart had leapt. My cheeks had burnt. I had flushed with anger. There was nothing specially remarkable, however foolish, in that. One does not like to be told that one is naturally the inferior of a little man—I looked at the student next me—who breathes hard, wears a ready-made tie, and has not shaved this fortnight. One has certain foolish vanities. It is only human nature, I reflected, and began drawing cart-wheels and circles over the angry professor's face till he looked like a burning bush or a flaming comet—anyhow, an apparition without human semblance or significance. The professor was nothing now but a faggot[2] burning on the top of Hampstead Heath.[3] Soon my own anger was explained and done with; but curiosity remained. How explain the anger of the professors? Why were they angry? For when it came to analysing the impression left by these books there was always an element of heat. This heat took many forms; it showed itself in satire, in sentiment, in curiosity, in reprobation. But there was another element which was often present and could not immediately be identified. Anger, I called it. But it was anger that had gone underground and mixed itself with all kinds of other emotions. To judge from its odd effects, it was anger disguised and complex, not anger simple and open.

Whatever the reason, all these books, I thought, surveying the pile on the desk, are worthless for my purposes. They were worthless scientifically, that is to say, though humanly they were full of instruction, interest, boredom, and very queer facts about the habits of the Fiji Islanders. They had been written in the red light of emotion and not in the white light of truth. Therefore they must be returned to the central desk and restored each to his own cell in the enormous honeycomb. All that I had retrieved from that morning's work had been the one fact of anger. The professors—I lumped them together thus—were angry. But why, I asked myself, having returned the books, why, I repeated, standing under the colonnade among the pigeons and the prehistoric canoes, why are they angry? And, asking myself this question, I strolled off to find a place for luncheon. What is the real nature of what I call for the moment their anger? I asked. Here was a puzzle that would last all the time that it takes to be served with food in a small restaurant somewhere near the British Museum. Some previous luncher had left the lunch edition of the evening paper on a chair, and, waiting to be served, I began idly reading the headlines. A ribbon of very large letters ran across the page. Somebody had made a big score in South Africa. Lesser ribbons an-

---

[1] *astrachan*   I.e., astrakhan, wool of very young lambs.

[2] *faggot*   Bundle of sticks for fuel.

[3] *Hampstead Heath*   Natural area in north London and the highest point in the city.

nounced that Sir Austen Chamberlain was at Geneva.[1] A meat axe with human hair on it had been found in a cellar. Mr. Justice —— commented in the Divorce Courts upon the Shamelessness of Women. Sprinkled about the paper were other pieces of news. A film actress had been lowered from a peak in California and hung suspended in mid-air. The weather was going to be foggy. The most transient visitor to this planet, I thought, who picked up this paper could not fail to be aware, even from this scattered testimony, that England is under the rule of a patriarchy. Nobody in their senses could fail to detect the dominance of the professor. His was the power and the money and the influence. He was the proprietor of the paper and its editor and sub-editor. He was the Foreign Secretary and the Judge. He was the cricketer; he owned the race-horses and the yachts. He was the director of the company that pays two hundred per cent to its shareholders. He left millions to charities and colleges that were ruled by himself. He suspended the film actress in mid-air. He will decide if the hair on the meat axe is human; he it is who will acquit or convict the murderer, and hang him, or let him go free. With the exception of the fog he seemed to control everything. Yet he was angry. I knew that he was angry by this token. When I read what he wrote about women I thought, not of what he was saying, but of himself. When an arguer argues dispassionately he thinks only of the argument; and the reader cannot help thinking of the argument too. If he had written dispassionately about women, had used indisputable proofs to establish his argument and had shown no trace of wishing that the result should be one thing rather than another, one would not have been angry either. One would have accepted the fact, as one accepts the fact that a pea is green or a canary yellow. So be it, I should have said. But I had been angry because he was angry. Yet it seemed absurd, I thought, turning over the evening paper, that a man with all this power should be angry. Or is anger, I wondered, somehow, the familiar, the attendant sprite on power? Rich people, for example, are often angry because they suspect that the poor want to seize their wealth. The professors, or patriarchs, as it

might be more accurate to call them, might be angry for that reason partly, but partly for one that lies a little less obviously on the surface. Possibly they were not "angry" at all; often, indeed, they were admiring, devoted, exemplary in the relations of private life. Possibly when the professor insisted a little too emphatically upon the inferiority of women, he was concerned not with their inferiority, but with his own superiority. That was what he was protecting rather hot-headedly and with too much emphasis, because it was a jewel to him of the rarest price. Life for both sexes—and I looked at them, shouldering their way along the pavement—is arduous, difficult, a perpetual struggle. It calls for gigantic courage and strength. More than anything, perhaps, creatures of illusion as we are, it calls for confidence in oneself. Without self-confidence we are as babes in the cradle. And how can we generate this imponderable quality, which is yet so invaluable, most quickly? By thinking that other people are inferior to oneself. By feeling that one has some innate superiority—it may be wealth, or rank, a straight nose, or the portrait of a grandfather by Romney[2]—for there is no end to the pathetic devices of the human imagination—over other people. Hence the enormous importance to a patriarch who has to conquer, who has to rule, of feeling that great numbers of people, half the human race indeed, are by nature inferior to himself. It must indeed be one of the chief sources of his power. But let me turn the light of this observation on to real life, I thought. Does it help to explain some of those psychological puzzles that one notes in the margin of daily life? Does it explain my astonishment the other day when Z, most humane, most modest of men, taking up some book by Rebecca West[3] and reading a passage in it, exclaimed, "The arrant feminist! She says that men are snobs!" The exclamation, to me so surprising—for why was Miss West an arrant feminist for making a possibly true if uncomplimentary statement about the other sex?—was not merely the cry of wounded vanity; it was a protest against some infringement of his power to believe in himself. Women have served all these centuries as

---

[2] *Romney* George Romney, eighteenth-century British painter and portraitist.

[3] *Rebecca West* Assumed name of Cecily Isabel Andrews (1892–1983), English novelist, critic, and journalist.

[1] *Sir Austin Chamberlain* Statesman, member of the British House of Commons and Secretary of State of Foreign Affairs from 1924 to 1929; *Geneva* Location of the League of Nations headquarters.

looking-glasses possessing the magic and delicious power of reflecting the figure of man at twice its natural size. Without that power probably the earth would still be swamp and jungle. The glories of all our wars would be unknown. We should still be scratching the outlines of deer on the remains of mutton bones and bartering flints for sheepskins or whatever simple ornament took our unsophisticated taste. Supermen and Fingers of Destiny would never have existed. The Czar and the Kaiser would never have worn their crowns or lost them. Whatever may be their use in civilised societies, mirrors are essential to all violent and heroic action. That is why Napoleon and Mussolini both insist so emphatically upon the inferiority of women, for if they were not inferior, they would cease to enlarge. That serves to explain in part the necessity that women so often are to men. And it serves to explain how restless they are under her criticism; how impossible it is for her to say to them this book is bad, this picture is feeble, or whatever it may be, without giving far more pain and rousing far more anger than a man would do who gave the same criticism. For if she begins to tell the truth, the figure in the looking-glass shrinks; his fitness for life is diminished. How is he to go on giving judgement, civilising natives, making laws, writing books, dressing up and speechifying at banquets, unless he can see himself at breakfast and at dinner at least twice the size he really is? So I reflected, crumbling my bread and stirring my coffee and now and again looking at the people in the street. The looking-glass vision is of supreme importance because it charges the vitality; it stimulates the nervous system. Take it away and man may die, like the drug fiend deprived of his cocaine. Under the spell of that illusion, I thought, looking out of the window, half the people on the pavement are striding to work. They put on their hats and coats in the morning under its agreeable rays. They start the day confident, braced, believing themselves desired at Miss Smith's tea party; they say to themselves as they go into the room, I am the superior of half the people here, and it is thus that they speak with that self-confidence, that self-assurance, which have had such profound consequences in public life and lead to such curious notes in the margin of the private mind.

But these contributions to the dangerous and fascinating subject of the psychology of the other sex—it is one, I hope, that you will investigate when you have five hundred a year of your own—were interrupted by the necessity of paying the bill. It came to five shillings and ninepence. I gave the waiter a ten-shilling note and he went to bring me change. There was another ten-shilling note in my purse; I noticed it, because it is a fact that still takes my breath away—the power of my purse to breed ten-shilling notes automatically. I open it and there they are. Society gives me chicken and coffee, bed and lodging, in return for a certain number of pieces of paper which were left me by an aunt, for no other reason than that I share her name.

My aunt, Mary Beton, I must tell you, died by a fall from her horse when she was riding out to take the air in Bombay. The news of my legacy reached me one night about the same time that the act was passed that gave votes to women. A solicitor's letter fell into the post-box and when I opened it I found that she had left me five hundred pounds a year for ever. Of the two—the vote and the money—the money, I own, seemed infinitely the more important. Before that I had made my living by cadging odd jobs from newspapers, by reporting a donkey show here or a wedding there; I had earned a few pounds by addressing envelopes, reading to old ladies, making artificial flowers, teaching the alphabet to small children in a kindergarten. Such were the chief occupations that were open to women before 1918. I need not, I am afraid, describe in any detail the hardness of the work, for you know perhaps women who have done it; nor the difficulty of living on the money when it was earned, for you may have tried. But what still remains with me as a worse infliction than either was the poison of fear and bitterness which those days bred in me. To begin with, always to be doing work that one did not wish to do, and to do it like a slave, flattering and fawning, not always necessarily perhaps, but it seemed necessary and the stakes were too great to run risks; and then the thought of that one gift which it was death to hide—a small one but dear to the possessor—perishing and with it myself, my soul—all this became like a rust eating away the bloom of the spring, destroying the tree at its heart. However, as I say, my aunt died; and whenever I change a ten-shilling note a little of that rust and corrosion is rubbed off; fear and bitterness go. Indeed, I thought, slipping the silver into my purse, it is remarkable, remembering the bitterness of those days, what a change of temper a fixed income will bring about. No force in the world can take from me my five hundred pounds. Food, house, and clothing are mine for ever. Therefore not merely do effort and labour cease, but also hatred and bitterness. I need not hate any man; he cannot hurt me. I need not flatter any man; he has nothing to give me. So imperceptibly I found myself adopting a new attitude towards the other half of the human race. It was absurd to blame any class or any sex, as a whole. Great bodies of people are never responsible for what they do. They are driven by instincts which are not within their control. They too, the patriarchs, the professors, had endless difficulties, terrible drawbacks to contend with. Their education had been in some ways as faulty as my own. It had bred in them defects as great. True, they had money and power, but only at the cost of harbouring in their breasts an eagle, a vulture, for ever tearing the liver out and plucking at the lungs—the instinct for possession, the rage for acquisition which drives them to desire other people's fields and goods perpetually; to make frontiers and flags; battleships and poison gas; to offer up their own lives and their children's lives. Walk through the Admiralty Arch[1] (I had reached that monument), or any other avenue given up to trophies and cannon, and reflect upon the kind of glory celebrated there. Or watch in the spring sunshine the stockbroker and the great barrister going indoors to make money and more money and more money when it is a fact that five hundred pounds a year will keep one alive in the sunshine. These are unpleasant instincts to harbour, I reflected. They are bred of the conditions of life; of the lack of civilisation, I thought, looking at the statue of the Duke of Cambridge, and in particular at the feathers in his cocked hat, with a fixity that they have scarcely ever received before. And, as I realised these drawbacks, by degrees fear and bitterness modified themselves into pity and toleration; and then in a year or two, pity and toleration went, and the greatest release of all came, which is freedom to think of things in themselves. That building,

for example, do I like it or not? Is that picture beautiful or not? Is that in my opinion a good book or a bad? Indeed my aunt's legacy unveiled the sky to me, and substituted for the large and imposing figure of a gentleman, which Milton recommended for my perpetual adoration,[2] a view of the open sky.

So thinking, so speculating, I found my way back to my house by the river. Lamps were being lit and an indescribable change had come over London since the morning hour. It was as if the great machine after labouring all day had made with our help a few yards of something very exciting and beautiful—a fiery fabric flashing with red eyes, a tawny monster roaring with hot breath. Even the wind seemed flung like a flag as it lashed the houses and rattled the hoardings.

In my little street, however, domesticity prevailed. The house painter was descending his ladder; the nursemaid was wheeling the perambulator carefully in and out back to nursery tea; the coal-heaver was folding his empty sacks on top of each other; the woman who keeps the green-grocer's shop was adding up the day's takings with her hands in red mittens. But so engrossed was I with the problem you have laid upon my shoulders that I could not see even these usual sights without referring them to one centre. I thought how much harder it is now than it must have been even a century ago to say which of these employments is the higher, the more necessary. Is it better to be a coal-heaver or a nursemaid; is the charwoman[3] who has brought up eight children of less value to the world than the barrister who has made a hundred thousand pounds? It is useless to ask such questions; for nobody can answer them. Not only do the comparative values of charwomen and lawyers rise and fall from decade to decade, but we have no rods with which to measure them even as they are at the moment. I had been foolish to ask my professor to furnish me with "indisputable proofs" of this or that in his argument about women. Even if one could state the value of any one gift at the moment, those values will change; in a century's time very possibly they will have changed completely. Moreover, in a hundred years, I

---

1 *Admiralty Arch*   Triple arch leading from Trafalgar Square into the Mall in London, forming part of the ceremonial approach to Buckingham Palace.

2 *gentleman ... adoration*   In *Paradise Lost* (1667), Milton suggests that man (Adam) was formed "for God only" and woman (Eve) "for God in him" (4.299).

3 *charwoman*   Cleaning woman.

thought, reaching my own doorstep, women will have ceased to be the protected sex. Logically they will take part in all the activities and exertions that were once denied them. The nursemaid will heave coal. The shopwoman will drive an engine. All assumptions founded on the facts observed when women were the protected sex will have disappeared—as, for example (here a squad of soldiers marched down the street), that women and clergymen and gardeners live longer than other people. Remove that protection, expose them to the same exertions and activities, make them soldiers and sailors and engine-drivers and dock labourers, and will not women die off so much younger, so much quicker, than men that one will say, "I saw a woman today," as one used to say, "I saw an aeroplane." Anything may happen when womanhood has ceased to be a protected occupation, I thought, opening the door. But what bearing has all this upon the subject of my paper, Women and Fiction? I asked, going indoors.

CHAPTER 3

It was disappointing not to have brought back in the evening some important statement, some authentic fact. Women are poorer than men because—this or that. Perhaps now it would be better to give up seeking for the truth, and receiving on one's head an avalanche of opinion hot as lava, discoloured as dish-water. It would be better to draw the curtains; to shut out distractions; to light the lamp; to narrow the enquiry and to ask the historian, who records not opinions but facts, to describe under what conditions women lived, not throughout the ages, but in England, say in the time of Elizabeth.

For it is a perennial puzzle why no woman wrote a word of that extraordinary literature when every other man, it seemed, was capable of song or sonnet. What were the conditions in which women lived, I asked myself; for fiction, imaginative work that is, is not dropped like a pebble upon the ground, as science may be; fiction is like a spider's web, attached ever so lightly perhaps, but still attached to life at all four corners. Often the attachment is scarcely perceptible; Shakespeare's plays, for instance, seem to hang there complete by themselves. But when the web is pulled askew, hooked up at the edge, torn in the middle, one remem-

bers that these webs are not spun in mid-air by incorporeal creatures, but are the work of suffering human beings, and are attached to grossly material things, like health and money and the houses we live in.

I went, therefore, to the shelf where the histories stand and took down one of the latest, Professor Trevelyan's *History of England*.[1] Once more I looked up Women, found "position of," and turned to the pages indicated. "Wife-beating," I read, "was a recognised right of man, and was practised without shame by high as well as low.... Similarly," the historian goes on, "the daughter who refused to marry the gentleman of her parents' choice was liable to be locked up, beaten and flung about the room, without any shock being inflicted on public opinion. Marriage was not an affair of personal affection, but of family avarice, particularly in the 'chivalrous' upper classes.... Betrothal often took place while one or both of the parties was in the cradle, and marriage when they were scarcely out of the nurses' charge." That was about 1470, soon after Chaucer's time. The next reference to the position of women is some two hundred years later, in the time of the Stuarts. "It was still the exception for women of the upper and middle class to choose their own husbands, and when the husband had been assigned, he was lord and master, so far at least as law and custom could make him. Yet even so," Professor Trevelyan concludes, "neither Shakespeare's women nor those of authentic seventeenth-century memoirs, like the Verneys and the Hutchinsons,[2] seem wanting in personality and character." Certainly, if we consider it, Cleopatra must have had a way with her; Lady Macbeth, one would suppose, had a will of her own; Rosalind, one might conclude, was an attractive girl.[3] Professor Trevelyan is speaking

---

[1] *Professor ... England* George Macaulay Trevelyan's *History of England* (1929).

[2] *Verneys* The *Memoirs of the Verney Family* (published 1892) is a family history that records, as one of its authors boasted, "an ordinary gentleman's family of the higher class" consisting of "good average specimens of hundreds of men or women of their age." *Hutchinsons* Lucy Hutchinson's *Memoirs of the Life of Colonel Hutchinson* (published 1806) detailed the life of her husband, John Hutchinson, and his experiences in the civil war.

[3] *Cleopatra ... girl* Cleopatra, Lady Macbeth, and Rosalind are the heroines of Shakespeare's *Antony and Cleopatra*, *Macbeth*, and *As You Like It*, respectively.

no more than the truth when he remarks that Shakespeare's women do not seem wanting in personality and character. Not being a historian, one might go even further and say that women have burnt like beacons in all the works of all the poets from the beginning of time—Clytemnestra, Antigone, Cleopatra, Lady Macbeth, Phedre, Cressida, Rosalind, Desdemona, the Duchess of Malfi, among the dramatists;[1] then among the prose writers: Millamant, Clarissa, Becky Sharp, Anna Karenina, Emma Bovary, Madame de Guermantes[2]—the names flock to mind, nor do they recall women "lacking in personality and character." Indeed, if woman had no existence save in the fiction written by men, one would imagine her a person of the utmost importance; very various; heroic and mean; splendid and sordid; infinitely beautiful and hideous in the extreme; as great as a man, some think even greater.[3] But this is woman in fiction. In fact, as Professor Trevelyan points out, she was locked up, beaten and flung about the room.

A very queer, composite being thus emerges. Imaginatively she is of the highest importance; practically she

[1] *Clytemnestra ... dramatists* Heroines from Aeschylus's *Agamemnon*; Sophocles's *Antigone*; Shakespeare's *Antony and Cleopatra* and *Macbeth*; Racine's *Phèdre*; Shakespeare's *Troilus and Cressida*, *As You Like It*, and *Othello*; and Webster's *The Duchess of Malfi*.

[2] *then ... Guermantes* Characters from, respectively, Congreve's *Way of the World*; Richardson's *Clarissa*; Thackeray's *Vanity Fair*; Tolstoy's *Anna Karenina*; Flaubert's *Madame Bovary*; and Proust's *À la recherche du temps perdu*.

[3] [Woolf's note] "It remains a strange and almost inexplicable fact that in Athena's city, where women were kept in almost Oriental suppression as odalisques or drudges, the stage should yet have produced figures like Clytemnestra and Cassandra, Atossa and Antigone, Phèdra and Medea, and all the other heroines who dominate play after play of the 'misogynist' Euripides. But the paradox of this world where in real life a respectable woman could hardly show her face alone in the street, and yet on the stage woman equals or surpasses man, has never been satisfactorily explained. In modern tragedy the same predominance exists. At all events, a very cursory survey of Shakespeare's work (similarly with Webster, though not with Marlowe or Jonson) suffices to reveal how this dominance, this initiative of women, persists from Rosalind to Lady Macbeth. So too in Racine; six of his tragedies bear their heroines' names; and what male characters of his shall we set against Hermione and Andromaque, Bérénice and Roxane, Phèdre and Athalie? So again with Ibsen; what men shall we match with Solveig and Nora, Hedda and Hilda Wangel and Rebecca West?"—F.L. Lucas, *Tragedy*, pp. 114–15.

is completely insignificant. She pervades poetry from cover to cover; she is all but absent from history. She dominates the lives of kings and conquerors in fiction; in fact she was the slave of any boy whose parents forced a ring upon her finger. Some of the most inspired words, some of the most profound thoughts in literature fall from her lips; in real life she could hardly read, could scarcely spell, and was the property of her husband.

It was certainly an odd monster that one made up by reading the historians first and the poets afterwards—a worm winged like an eagle; the spirit of life and beauty in a kitchen chopping up suet. But these monsters, however amusing to the imagination, have no existence in fact. What one must do to bring her to life was to think poetically and prosaically at one and the same moment, thus keeping in touch with fact—that she is Mrs. Martin, aged thirty-six, dressed in blue, wearing a black hat and brown shoes; but not losing sight of fiction either—that she is a vessel in which all sorts of spirits and forces are coursing and flashing perpetually. The moment, however, that one tries this method with the Elizabethan woman, one branch of illumination fails; one is held up by the scarcity of facts. One knows nothing detailed, nothing perfectly true and substantial about her. History scarcely mentions her. And I turned to Professor Trevelyan again to see what history meant to him. I found by looking at his chapter headings that it meant—"The Manor Court and the Methods of Open-field Agriculture ... The Cistercians and Sheep-farming ... The Crusades ... The University ... The House of Commons ... The Hundred Years' War ... The War of the Roses ... The Renaissance Scholars ... The Dissolution of the Monasteries ... Agrarian and Religious Strife ... The Origin of English Sea-power ... The Armada ... " and so on. Occasionally an individual woman is mentioned, an Elizabeth, or a Mary; a queen or a great lady. But by no possible means could middle-class women with nothing but brains and character at their command have taken part in any one of the great movements which, brought together, constitute the historian's view of the past. Nor shall we find her in any collection of anecdotes. Aubrey[4] hardly mentions her. She never writes her own life and scarcely keeps a diary;

[4] *Aubrey* John Aubrey (1626–97), writer and antiquary known for his *Brief Lives*, a collection of short, informal biographies.

there are only a handful of her letters in existence. She left no plays or poems by which we can judge her. What one wants, I thought—and why does not some brilliant student at Newnham or Girton supply it?—is a mass of information; at what age did she marry; how many children had she as a rule; what was her house like; had she a room to herself; did she do the cooking; would she be likely to have a servant? All these facts lie somewhere, presumably, in parish registers and account books; the life of the average Elizabethan woman must be scattered about somewhere, could one collect it and make a book of it. It would be ambitious beyond my daring, I thought, looking about the shelves for books that were not there, to suggest to the students of those famous colleges that they should re-write history, though I own that it often seems a little queer as it is, unreal, lopsided; but why should they not add a supplement to history? calling it, of course, by some inconspicuous name so that women might figure there without impropriety? For one often catches a glimpse of them in the lives of the great, whisking away into the background, concealing, I sometimes think, a wink, a laugh, perhaps a tear. And, after all, we have lives enough of Jane Austen; it scarcely seems necessary to consider again the influence of the tragedies of Joanna Baillie[1] upon the poetry of Edgar Allen Poe; as for myself, I should not mind if the homes and haunts of Mary Russell Mitford[2] were closed to the public for a century at least. But what I find deplorable, I continued, looking about the bookshelves again, is that nothing is known about women before the eighteenth century. I have no model in my mind to turn about this way and that. Here I am asking why women did not write poetry in the Elizabethan age, and I am not sure how they were educated; whether they were taught to write; whether they had sitting-rooms to themselves; how many women had children before they were twenty-one; what, in short, they did from eight in the morning till eight at night. They had no money evidently; according to Professor

Trevelyan they were married whether they liked it or not before they were out of the nursery, at fifteen or sixteen very likely. It would have been extremely odd, even upon this showing, had one of them suddenly written the plays of Shakespeare, I concluded, and I thought of that old gentleman, who is dead now, but was a bishop, I think, who declared that it was impossible for any woman, past, present, or to come, to have the genius of Shakespeare. He wrote to the papers about it. He also told a lady who applied to him for information that cats do not as a matter of fact go to heaven, though they have, he added, souls of a sort. How much thinking those old gentlemen used to save one! How the borders of ignorance shrank back at their approach! Cats do not go to heaven. Women cannot write the plays of Shakespeare.

Be that as it may, I could not help thinking, as I looked at the works of Shakespeare on the shelf, that the bishop was right at least in this; it would have been impossible, completely and entirely, for any woman to have written the plays of Shakespeare in the age of Shakespeare. Let me imagine, since facts are so hard to come by, what would have happened had Shakespeare had a wonderfully gifted sister, called Judith, let us say. Shakespeare himself went, very probably—his mother was an heiress—to the grammar school, where he may have learnt Latin—Ovid, Virgil, and Horace—and the elements of grammar and logic. He was, it is well known, a wild boy who poached rabbits, perhaps shot a deer, and had, rather sooner than he should have done, to marry a woman in the neighbourhood, who bore him a child rather quicker than was right. That escapade sent him to seek his fortune in London. He had, it seemed, a taste for the theatre; he began by holding horses at the stage door. Very soon he got work in the theatre, became a successful actor, and lived at the hub of the universe, meeting everybody, knowing everybody, practising his art on the boards, exercising his wits in the streets, and even getting access to the palace of the queen. Meanwhile his extraordinarily gifted sister, let us suppose, remained at home. She was as adventurous, as imaginative, as agog to see the world as he was. But she was not sent to school. She had no chance of learning grammar and logic, let alone of reading Horace and Virgil. She picked up a book now and then, one of her

---

[1] *Joanna Baillie* Romantic English poet and dramatist (1787–1865).

[2] *Mary Russell Mitford* Poet, novelist, and playwright whose correspondence with notable authors, including Elizabeth Barrett Browning, Charles Lamb, and Harriet Martineau, provides insight into the literary world of the early nineteenth century.

brother's perhaps, and read a few pages. But then her parents came in and told her to mend the stockings or mind the stew and not moon about with books and papers. They would have spoken sharply but kindly, for they were substantial people who knew the conditions of life for a woman and loved their daughter—indeed, more likely than not she was the apple of her father's eye. Perhaps she scribbled some pages up in an apple loft on the sly, but was careful to hide them or set fire to them. Soon, however, before she was out of her teens, she was to be betrothed to the son of a neighbouring wool-stapler.[1] She cried out that marriage was hateful to her, and for that she was severely beaten by her father. Then he ceased to scold her. He begged her instead not to hurt him, not to shame him in this matter of her marriage. He would give her a chain of beads or a fine petticoat, he said; and there were tears in his eyes. How could she disobey him? How could she break his heart? The force of her own gift alone drove her to it. She made up a small parcel of her belongings, let herself down by a rope one summer's night and took the road to London. She was not seventeen. The birds that sang in the hedge were not more musical than she was. She had the quickest fancy, a gift like her brother's, for the tune of words. Like him, she had a taste for the theatre. She stood at the stage door; she wanted to act, she said. Men laughed in her face. The manager—a fat, loose-lipped man—guffawed. He bellowed something about poodles dancing and women acting[2]—no woman, he said, could possibly be an actress. He hinted—you can imagine what. She could get no training in her craft. Could she even seek her dinner in a tavern or roam the streets at midnight? Yet her genius was for fiction and lusted to feed abundantly upon the lives of men and women and the study of their ways. At last—for she was very young, oddly like Shakespeare the poet in her face, with the same grey eyes and rounded brows—at last Nick Greene the actor-manager took pity on her; she found herself with child by that gentleman and

so—who shall measure the heat and violence of the poet's heart when caught and tangled in a woman's body?—killed herself one winter's night and lies buried at some cross-roads where the omnibuses now stop outside the Elephant and Castle.[3]

That, more or less, is how the story would run, I think, if a woman in Shakespeare's day had had Shakespeare's genius. But for my part, I agree with the deceased bishop, if such he was—it is unthinkable that any woman in Shakespeare's day should have had Shakespeare's genius. For genius like Shakespeare's is not born among labouring, uneducated, servile people. It was not born in England among the Saxons and the Britons. It is not born today among the working classes. How, then, could it have been born among women whose work began, according to Professor Trevelyan, almost before they were out of the nursery, who were forced to it by their parents and held to it by all the power of law and custom? Yet genius of a sort must have existed among women as it must have existed among the working classes. Now and again an Emily Brontë or a Robert Burns blazes out and proves its presence. But certainly it never got itself on to paper. When, however, one reads of a witch being ducked, of a woman possessed by devils, of a wise woman selling herbs, or even of a very remarkable man who had a mother, then I think we are on the track of a lost novelist, a suppressed poet, of some mute and inglorious Jane Austen,[4] some Emily Brontë who dashed her brains out on the moor or mopped and mowed about the highways crazed with the torture that her gift had put her to. Indeed, I would venture to guess that Anon, who wrote so many poems without signing them, was often a woman. It was a woman Edward Fitzgerald,[5] I think, suggested who made the ballads and the folk-songs, crooning them to her children, beguiling her spinning with them, or the length of the winter's night.

---

[1] *wool-stapler* Dealer in wool.

[2] *He ... acting* Reference to Samuel Johnson's infamous statement, recorded by Boswell, that "a woman's preaching is like a dog's walking on its hinder legs. It is not done well; but you are surprised to find it done at all" (James Boswell, *Life of Samuel Johnson*, 31 July 1763).

[3] *lies buried ... Castle* It was common practice to bury victims of suicide at crossroads. The Elephant and Castle was a pub located south of the Thames.

[4] *some ... Austen* See Thomas Gray, "Elegy Written in a Country Church-Yard" (1751): "Some mute and inglorious Milton here may rest" (line 59).

[5] *Edward Fitzgerald* Author of *The Rubáiyát of Omar Khayyám* (1859).

This may be true or it may be false—who can say?—but what is true in it, so it seemed to me, reviewing the story of Shakespeare's sister as I had made it, is that any woman born with a great gift in the sixteenth century would certainly have gone crazed, shot herself, or ended her days in some lonely cottage outside the village, half witch, half wizard, feared and mocked at. For it needs little skill in psychology to be sure that a highly gifted girl who had tried to use her gift for poetry would have been so thwarted and hindered by other people, so tortured and pulled asunder by her own contrary instincts, that she must have lost her health and sanity to a certainty. No girl could have walked to London and stood at a stage door and forced her way into the presence of actor-managers without doing herself a violence and suffering an anguish which may have been irrational—for chastity may be a fetish invented by certain societies for unknown reasons—but were none the less inevitable. Chastity had then, it has even now, a religious importance in a woman's life, and has so wrapped itself round with nerves and instincts that to cut it free and bring it to the light of day demands courage of the rarest. To have lived a free life in London in the sixteenth century would have meant for a woman who was poet and playwright a nervous stress and dilemma which might well have killed her. Had she survived, whatever she had written would have been twisted and deformed, issuing from a strained and morbid imagination. And undoubtedly, I thought, looking at the shelf where there are no plays by women, her work would have gone unsigned. That refuge she would have sought certainly. It was the relic of the sense of chastity that dictated anonymity to women even so late as the nineteenth century. Currer Bell, George Eliot, George Sand,[1] all the victims of inner strife as their writings prove, sought ineffectively to veil themselves by using the name of a man. Thus they did homage to the convention, which if not implanted by the other sex was liberally encouraged by them (the chief glory of a woman is not to be talked of, said Pericles,[2] himself a much-talked-of man), that publicity in women

is detestable. Anonymity runs in their blood. The desire to be veiled still possesses them. They are not even now as concerned about the health of their fame as men are, and, speaking generally, will pass a tombstone or a signpost without feeling an irresistible desire to cut their names on it, as Alf, Bert, or Chas. must do in obedience to their instinct, which murmurs if it sees a fine woman go by, or even a dog, Ce chien est à moi.[3] And, of course, it may not be a dog, I thought, remembering Parliament Square, the Sièges Allée[4] and other avenues; it may be a piece of land or a man with curly black hair. It is one of the great advantages of being a woman that one can pass even a very fine negress without wishing to make an Englishwoman of her.

That woman, then, who was born with a gift of poetry in the sixteenth century, was an unhappy woman, a woman at strife against herself. All the conditions of her life, all her own instincts, were hostile to the state of mind which is needed to set free whatever is in the brain. But what is the state of mind that is most propitious to the act of creation, I asked. Can one come by any notion of the state that furthers and makes possible that strange activity? Here I opened the volume containing the Tragedies of Shakespeare. What was Shakespeare's state of mind, for instance, when he wrote *Lear* and *Antony and Cleopatra?* It was certainly the state of mind most favourable to poetry that there has ever existed. But Shakespeare himself said nothing about it. We only know casually and by chance that he "never blotted a line."[5] Nothing indeed was ever said by the artist himself about his state of mind until the eighteenth century perhaps. Rousseau[6] perhaps began it. At any rate, by the nineteenth century self-consciousness had developed so far that it was the habit for men of letters to describe their minds in confessions and autobiographies. Their lives also were written, and their letters were printed after their deaths. Thus, though we do not know what Shakespeare went through when he wrote *Lear*, we do know what Carlyle went through when he

---

[1] *Currer ... Sand* Male pseudonyms under which female authors Charlotte Brontë, Mary Anne Evans, and Amandine Dupin published.

[2] *Pericles* Athenian statesman (d. 429 BCE).

[3] *Ce ... moi* French: this dog is mine.

[4] *Sièges Allée* Victory Avenue, in Berlin.

[5] *never ... line* Ben Jonson, *Timber:* "I remember, the players have often mentioned it as an honour to Shakespeare that in his writing (whatsoever he penned) he never blotted out a line."

[6] *Rousseau* French philosopher Jean-Jacques Rousseau (1712–87).

wrote the *French Revolution*; what Flaubert went through when he wrote *Madame Bovary*; what Keats was going through when he tried to write poetry against the coming of death and the indifference of the world.[1]

And one gathers from this enormous modern literature of confession and self-analysis that to write a work of genius is almost always a feat of prodigious difficulty. Everything is against the likelihood that it will come from the writer's mind whole and entire. Generally material circumstances are against it. Dogs will bark; people will interrupt; money must be made; health will break down. Further, accentuating all these difficulties and making them harder to bear is the world's notorious indifference. It does not ask people to write poems and novels and histories; it does not need them. It does not care whether Flaubert finds the right word or whether Carlyle scrupulously verifies this or that fact. Naturally, it will not pay for what it does not want. And so the writer, Keats, Flaubert, Carlyle, suffers, especially in the creative years of youth, every form of distraction and discouragement. A curse, a cry of agony, rises from those books of analysis and confession. "Mighty poets in their misery dead"[2]—that is the burden of their song. If anything comes through in spite of all this, it is a miracle, and probably no book is born entire and uncrippled as it was conceived.

But for women, I thought, looking at the empty shelves, these difficulties were infinitely more formidable. In the first place, to have a room of her own, let alone a quiet room or a sound-proof room, was out of the question, unless her parents were exceptionally rich or very noble, even up to the beginning of the nineteenth century. Since her pin money, which depended on the good will of her father, was only enough to keep her clothed, she was debarred from such alleviations as came even to Keats or Tennyson or Carlyle, all poor men, from a walking tour, a little journey to France, from the separate lodging which, even if it were miserable enough, sheltered them from the claims and tyran-

nies of their families. Such material difficulties were formidable; but much worse were the immaterial. The indifference of the world which Keats and Flaubert and other men of genius have found so hard to bear was in her case not indifference but hostility. The world did not say to her as it said to them, Write if you choose; it makes no difference to me. The world said with a guffaw, Write? What's the good of your writing? Here the psychologists of Newnham and Girton might come to our help, I thought, looking again at the blank spaces on the shelves. For surely it is time that the effect of discouragement upon the mind of the artist should be measured, as I have seen a dairy company measure the effect of ordinary milk and Grade A milk upon the body of the rat. They set two rats in cages side by side, and of the two one was furtive, timid, and small, and the other was glossy, bold, and big. Now what food do we feed women as artists upon? I asked, remembering, I suppose, that dinner of prunes and custard. To answer that question I had only to open the evening paper and to read that Lord Birkenhead[3] is of opinion—but really I am not going to trouble to copy out Lord Birkenhead's opinion upon the writing of women. What Dean Inge[4] says I will leave in peace. The Harley Street[5] specialist may be allowed to rouse the echoes of Harley Street with his vociferations without raising a hair on my head. I will quote, however, Mr. Oscar Browning, because Mr. Oscar Browning was a great figure in Cambridge at one time, and used to examine the students at Girton and Newnham. Mr. Oscar Browning was wont to declare "that the impression left on his mind, after looking over any set of examination papers, was that, irrespective of the marks he might give, the best woman was intellectually the inferior of the worst man." After saying that Mr. Browning went back to his rooms—and it is this sequel that endears him and makes him a human figure of some bulk and majesty—he went back to his rooms and found a stable-boy lying on the sofa—"a mere skeleton, his cheeks were cavernous and sallow, his teeth were black, and he did not appear to have the full use of his limbs. ... 'That's Arthur' [said

---

[1] *we do ... world*   Philosopher Thomas Carlyle provided this autobiographical information in his *Reminiscences* (1881), while French novelist Gustave Flaubert and English Romantic poet John Keats wrote extensively about their writing experiences in their letters.

[2] *Mighty ... dead*   William Wordsworth, *Resolution and Independence* (1807).

[3] *Lord Birkenhead*   Lord Chancellor from 1919 to 1922.

[4] *Dean Inge*   Dean of St. Paul's Cathedral, London.

[5] *Harley Street*   Street upon which many of the most highly regarded or fashionable medical practices were located.

Mr. Browning]. 'He's a dear boy really and most high-minded.'"[1] The two pictures always seem to me to complete each other. And happily in this age of biography the two pictures often do complete each other, so that we are able to interpret the opinions of great men not only by what they say, but by what they do.

But though this is possible now, such opinions coming from the lips of important people must have been formidable enough even fifty years ago. Let us suppose that a father from the highest motives did not wish his daughter to leave home and become writer, painter or scholar. "See what Mr. Oscar Browning says," he would say; and there was not only Mr. Oscar Browning; there was the *Saturday Review*; there was Mr. Greg—the "essentials of a woman's being," said Mr. Greg[2] emphatically, "are that *they are supported by, and they minister to, men*"—there was an enormous body of masculine opinion to the effect that nothing could be expected of women intellectually. Even if her father did not read out loud these opinions, any girl could read them for herself; and the reading, even in the nineteenth century, must have lowered her vitality, and told profoundly upon her work. There would always have been that assertion—you cannot do this, you are incapable of doing that—to protest against, to overcome. Probably for a novelist this germ is no longer of much effect; for there have been women novelists of merit. But for painters it must still have some sting in it; and for musicians, I imagine, is even now active and poisonous in the extreme. The woman composer stands where the actress stood in the time of Shakespeare. Nick Greene, I thought, remembering the story I had made about Shakespeare's sister, said that a woman acting put him in mind of a dog dancing. Johnson repeated the phrase two hundred years later of women preaching. And here, I said, opening a book about music, we have the very words used again in this year of grace, 1928, of women who try to write music. "Of Mlle. Germaine Tailleferre one can only repeat Dr. Johnson's dictum concerning a woman preacher, transposed into terms of music. 'Sir, a woman's composing is like a dog's walking on his hind

legs. It is not done well, but you are surprised to find it done at all.'"[3] So accurately does history repeat itself.

Thus, I concluded, shutting Mr. Oscar Browning's life and pushing away the rest, it is fairly evident that even in the nineteenth century a woman was not encouraged to be an artist. On the contrary, she was snubbed, slapped, lectured, and exhorted. Her mind must have been strained and her vitality lowered by the need of opposing this, of disproving that. For here again we come within range of that very interesting and obscure masculine complex which has had so much influence upon the woman's movement; that the deep-seated desire, not so much that *she* shall be inferior as that *he* shall be superior, which plants him wherever one looks, not only in front of the arts, but barring the way to politics too, even when the risk to himself seems infinitesimal and the suppliant humble and devoted. Even Lady Bessborough,[4] I remembered, with all her passion for politics, must humbly bow herself and write to Lord Granville Leveson-Gower: "... notwithstanding all my violence in politics and talking so much on that subject, I perfectly agree with you that no woman has any business to meddle with that or any other serious business, farther than giving her opinion (if she is ask'd)." And so she goes on to spend her enthusiasm where it meets with no obstacle whatsoever upon that immensely important subject, Lord Granville's maiden speech in the House of Commons. The spectacle is certainly a strange one, I thought. The history of men's opposition to women's emancipation is more interesting perhaps than the story of that emancipation itself. An amusing book might be made of it if some young student at Girton or Newnham would collect examples and deduce a theory—but she would need thick gloves on her hands, and bars to protect her of solid gold.

But what is amusing now, I recollected, shutting Lady Bessborough, had to be taken in desperate earnest once. Opinions that one now pastes in a book labelled cock-a-doodle-dum and keeps for reading to select audiences on summer nights once drew tears, I can

---

[1]   *Mr. Oscar Browning ... high-minded*   Oscar Browning (1837–1923), history lecturer at King's College, Cambridge.

[2]   *Mr. Greg*   Probably W.H. Greg, a well-known journalist of the era.

[3]   [Woolf's note]   *A Survey of Contemporary Music*, Cecil Gray, p.246.

[4]   *Lady Bessborough*   Henrietta Elizabeth, daughter of the first Earl Spencer, later Lady Bessborough (1761–1821). Lady Bessborough had an affair with Lord Granville.

assure you. Among your grandmothers and great-grandmothers there were many that wept their eyes out. Florence Nightingale shrieked aloud in her agony.[1] Moreover, it is all very well for you, who have got yourselves to college and enjoy sitting-rooms—or is it only bed-sitting-rooms?—of your own to say that genius should disregard such opinions; that genius should be above caring what is said of it. Unfortunately, it is precisely the men or women of genius who mind most what is said of them. Remember Keats. Remember the words he had cut on his tombstone.[2] Think of Tennyson; think—but I need hardly multiply instances of the undeniable, if very unfortunate, fact that it is the nature of the artist to mind excessively what is said about him. Literature is strewn with the wreckage of men who have minded beyond reason the opinions of others.

And this susceptibility of theirs is doubly unfortunate, I thought, returning again to my original enquiry into what state of mind is most propitious for creative work, because the mind of an artist, in order to achieve the prodigious effort of freeing whole and entire the work that is in him, must be incandescent, like Shakespeare's mind, I conjectured, looking at the book which lay open at *Antony and Cleopatra*. There must be no obstacle in it, no foreign matter unconsumed.

For though we say that we know nothing about Shakespeare's state of mind, even as we say that, we are saying something about Shakespeare's state of mind. The reason perhaps why we know so little of Shakespeare—compared with Donne or Ben Jonson or Milton—is that his grudges and spites and antipathies are hidden from us. We are not held up by some "revelation" which reminds us of the writer. All desire to protest, to preach, to proclaim an injury, to pay off a score, to make the world the witness of some hardship or grievance was fired out of him and consumed. Therefore his poetry flows from him free and unimpeded. If ever a human being got his work expressed completely, it was Shakespeare. If ever a mind was incandescent, unimpeded, I thought, turning again to the bookcase, it was Shakespeare's mind.

---

[1] [Woolf's note] *See Cassandra*, by Florence Nightingale, printed in *The Cause*, by R. Strachey.

[2] *Remember ... tombstone* "Here lies one whose name was writ in water."

from *A Sketch of the Past*[3]

—I begin: the first memory.

This was of red and purple flowers on a black ground—my mother's dress; and she was sitting either in a train or in an omnibus, and I was on her lap. I therefore saw the flowers she was wearing very close; and can still see purple and red and blue, I think, against the black; they must have been anemones, I suppose. Perhaps we were going to St. Ives;[4] more probably, for from the light it must have been evening, we were coming back to London. But it is more convenient artistically to suppose that we were going to St. Ives, for that will lead to my other memory, which also seems to be my first memory, and in fact it is the most important of all my memories. If life has a base that it stands upon, if it is a bowl that one fills and fills and fills—then my bowl without a doubt stands upon this memory. It is of lying half asleep, half awake, in bed in the nursery at St. Ives. It is of hearing the waves breaking, one, two, one, two, and sending a splash of water over the beach; and then breaking, one, two, one, two, behind a yellow blind. It is of hearing the blind draw its little acorn[5] across the floor as the wind blew the blind out. It is of lying and hearing this splash and seeing this light, and feeling, it is almost impossible that I should be here; of feeling the purest ecstasy I can conceive.

I could spend hours trying to write that as it should be written, in order to give the feeling which is even at this moment very strong in me. But I should fail (unless I had some wonderful luck); I dare say I should only succeed in having the luck if I had begun by describing Virginia herself.

Here I come to one of the memoir writer's difficulties—one of the reasons why, though I read so many, so many are failures. They leave out the person to whom

---

[3] *A Sketch of the Past* An essay that was published as part of *Moments of Being* (1976), a collection of Woolf's autobiographical writings the title of which has its origins in this excerpt. This essay is structured in the style of a diary or journal, and with each entry Woolf uses the present as a springboard from which to explore the past. This entry was composed on 18 April 1939.

[4] *St. Ives* Town in Cornwall at which Woolf's family spent holidays. It is the setting of Woolf's novel *To The Lighthouse*.

[5] *acorn* I.e., acorn-shaped bead on the end of a curtain pull.

things happened. The reason is that it is so difficult to describe any human being. So they say. "This is what happened"; but they do not say what the person was like to whom it happened. And the events mean very little unless we know first to whom they happened. Who was I then? Adeline Virginia Stephen, the second daughter of Leslie and Julia Prinsep Stephen, born on 25th January 1882, descended from a great many people, some famous, others obscure; born into a large connection, born not of rich parents, but of well-to-do parents, born into a very communicative, literate, letter writing, visiting, articulate, late nineteenth century world; so that I could if I liked to take the trouble, write a great deal here not only about my mother and father but about uncles and aunts, cousins, and friends. But I do not know how much of this, or what part of this, made me feel what I felt in the nursery at St. Ives. I do not know how far I differ from other people. That is another memoir writer's difficulty. Yet to describe oneself truly one must have some standard of comparison; was I clever, stupid, good looking, ugly, passionate, cold—? Owing partly to the fact that I was never at school, never competed in any way with children of my own age, I have never been able to compare my gifts and defects with other people's. But of course there was one external reason for the intensity of this first impression: the impression of the waves and the acorn on the blind; the feeling, as I describe it sometimes to myself, of lying in a grape and seeing through a film of semi-transparent yellow—it was due partly to the many months we spent in London. The change of nursery was a great change. And there was the long train journey; and the excitement. I remember the dark; the lights; the stir of the going up to bed.

But to fix my mind upon the nursery—it had a balcony; there was a partition, but it joined the balcony of my father's and mother's bedroom. My mother would come out onto her balcony in a white dressing gown. There were passion flowers growing on the wall; they were great starry blossoms, with purple streaks, and large green buds, part empty, part full.

If I were a painter I should paint these first impressions in pale yellow, silver, and green. There was the pale yellow blind; the green sea; and the silver of the passion flowers. I should make a picture that was globular; semi-transparent. I should make a picture of curved petals; of shells; of things that were semi-transparent; I should make curved shapes, showing the light through, but not giving a clear outline. Everything would be large and dim; and what was seen would at the same time be heard; sounds would come through this petal or leaf—sounds indistinguishable from sights. Sound and sight seem to make equal parts of these first impressions. When I think of the early morning in bed I also hear the caw of rooks falling from a great height. The sound seems to fall through an elastic, gummy air; which holds it up; which prevents it from being sharp and distinct. The quality of the air above Talland House[1] seemed to suspend sound, to let it sink down slowly, as if it were caught in a blue gummy veil. The rooks cawing is part of the waves breaking—one, two, one, two—and the splash as the wave drew back and then it gathered again, and I lay there half awake, half asleep, drawing in such ecstasy as I cannot describe.

The next memory—all these colour-and-sound memories hang together at St. Ives—was much more robust; it was highly sensual. It was later. It still makes me feel warm; as if everything were ripe; humming; sunny; smelling so many smells at once; and all making a whole that even now makes me stop—as I stopped then going down to the beach; I stopped at the top to look down at the gardens. They were sunk beneath the road. The apples were on a level with one's head. The gardens gave off a murmur of bees; the apples were red and gold; there were also pink flowers; and grey and silver leaves. The buzz, the croon, the smell, all seemed to press voluptuously against some membrane; not to burst it; but to hum round one such a complete rapture of pleasure that I stopped, smelt; looked. But again I cannot describe that rapture. It was rapture rather than ecstasy.

The strength of these pictures—but sight was always then so much mixed with sound that picture is not the right word—the strength anyhow of these impressions makes me again digress. Those moments—in the nursery, on the road to the beach—can still be more real than the present moment. This I have just tested. For I got up and crossed the garden. Percy was digging the asparagus bed; Louie was shaking a mat in front of the

---

[1]   *Talland House*   Name of the Stephens's summer house.

bedroom door.[1] But I was seeing them through the sight I saw here—the nursery and the road to the beach. At times I can go back to St. Ives more completely than I can this morning. I can reach a state where I seem to be watching things happen as if I were there. That is, I suppose, that my memory supplies what I had forgotten, so that it seems as if it were happening independently, though I am really making it happen. In certain favourable moods, memories—what one has forgotten—come to the top. Now if this is so, is it not possible—I often wonder—that things we have felt with great intensity have an existence independent of our minds; are in fact still in existence? And if so, will it not be possible, in time, that some device will be invented by which we can tap them? I see it—the past—as an avenue lying behind; a long ribbon of scenes, emotions. There at the end of the avenue still, are the garden and the nursery. Instead of remembering here a scene and there a sound, I shall fit a plug into the wall; and listen in to the past. I shall turn up August 1890. I feel that strong emotion must leave its trace; and it is only a question of discovering how we can get ourselves again attached to it, so that we shall be able to live our lives through from the start.

But the peculiarity of these two strong memories is that each was very simple. I am hardly aware of myself, but only of the sensation. I am only the container of the feeling of ecstasy, of the feeling of rapture. Perhaps this is characteristic of all childhood memories; perhaps it accounts for their strength. Later we add to feelings much that makes them more complex; and therefore less strong; or if not less strong, less isolated, less complete. But instead of analysing this, here is an instance of what I mean—my feeling about the looking-glass in the hall.

There was a small looking-glass in the hall at Talland House. It had, I remember, a ledge with a brush on it. By standing on tiptoe I could see my face in the glass. When I was six or seven perhaps, I got into the habit of looking at my face in the glass. But I only did this if I was sure that I was alone. I was ashamed of it. A strong feeling of guilt seemed naturally attached to it. But why was this so? One obvious reason occurs to me—Vanessa[2] and I were both what was called tomboys; that is, we played cricket, scrambled over rocks, climbed trees, were

said not to care for clothes and so on. Perhaps therefore to have been found looking in the glass would have been against our tomboy code. But I think that my feeling of shame went a great deal deeper. I am almost inclined to drag in my grandfather—Sir James, who once smoked a cigar, liked it, and so threw away his cigar and never smoked another. I am almost inclined to think that I inherited a streak of the puritan, of the Clapham Sect.[3] At any rate, the looking-glass shame has lasted all my life, long after the tomboy phase was over. I cannot now powder my nose in public. Everything to do with dress—to be fitted, to come into a room wearing a new dress—still frightens me; at least makes me shy, self-conscious, uncomfortable. "Oh to be able to run, like Julian Morrell, all over the garden in a new dress," I thought not many years ago at Garsington;[4] when Julian undid a parcel and put on a new dress and scampered round and round like a hare. Yet femininity was very strong in our family. We were famous for our beauty—my mother's beauty, Stella's[5] beauty, gave me as early as I can remember, pride and pleasure. What then gave me this feeling of shame, unless it were that I inherited some opposite instinct? My father was spartan, ascetic, puritanical. He had I think no feeling for pictures; no ear for music; no sense of the sound of words. This leads me to think that my—I would say "our" if I knew enough about Vanessa, Thoby and Adrian[6]—but how little we know even about brothers and sisters—this leads me to think that my natural love for beauty was checked by some ancestral dread. Yet this did not prevent me from feeling ecstasies and raptures spontaneously and intensely and without any shame or the least sense of guilt, so long as they were disconnected with my own body. I thus detect another element in the

---

[1] *Percy* The Stephens's gardener; *Louie* The housekeeper.

[2] *Vanessa* Woolf's older sister; later Vanessa Bell.

[3] *Clapham Sect* Group of wealthy English social reformers based in the town of Clapham. Its members, mostly evangelical Anglicans, devoted their time and money to worthy Christian causes, primarily the abolition of slavery. Woolf's grandfather, James Stephen, married Jane Catherine Venn, whose father and grandfather, John and Henry Venn, were the rector and curate of Clapham.

[4] *Julian Morrell* The daughter of Philip Morrell, a member of Parliament, and Ottoline Morrell, prominent member of literary society; *Garsington* Morrell family home.

[5] *Stella* Stella Duckworth, Woolf's half-sister. Stella's brother Gerald is mentioned later in this paragraph.

[6] *Thoby and Adrian* Woolf's brothers.

shame which I had in being caught looking at myself in the glass in the hall. I must have been ashamed or afraid of my own body. Another memory, also of the hall, may help to explain this. There was a slab outside the dining room door for standing dishes upon. Once when I was very small Gerald Duckworth lifted me onto this, and as I sat there he began to explore my body. I can remember the feel of his hand going under my clothes; going firmly and steadily lower and lower. I remember how I hoped that he would stop; how I stiffened and wriggled as his hand approached my private parts. But it did not stop. His hand explored my private parts too. I remember resenting, disliking it—what is the word for so dumb and mixed a feeling? It must have been strong, since I still recall it. This seems to show that a feeling about certain parts of the body; how they must not be touched; how it is wrong to allow them to be touched; must be instinctive. It proves that Virginia Stephen was not born on the 25th January 1882, but was born many thousands of years ago; and had from the very first to encounter instincts already acquired by thousands of ancestresses in the past.

And this throws light not merely on my own case, but upon the problem that I touched on the first page; why it is so difficult to give any account of the person to whom things happen. The person is evidently immensely complicated. Witness the incident of the looking-glass. Though I have done my best to explain why I was ashamed of looking at my own face I have only been able to discover some possible reasons; there may be others; I do not suppose that I have got at the truth; yet this is a simple incident; and it happened to me personally; and I have no motive for lying about it. In spite of all this, people write what they call "lives" of other people; that is, they collect a number of events, and leave the person to whom it happened unknown. Let me add a dream; for it may refer to the incident of the looking-glass. I dreamt that I was looking in a glass when a horrible face—the face of an animal—suddenly showed over my shoulder. I cannot be sure if this was a dream, or if it happened. Was I looking in the glass one day when something in the background moved, and seemed to me alive? I cannot be sure. But I have always remembered the other face in the glass, whether it was a dream or a fact, and that it frightened me.

These then are some of my first memories. But of course as an account of my life they are misleading, because the things one does not remember are as important; perhaps they are more important. If I could remember one whole day I should be able to describe, superficially at least, what life was like as a child. Unfortunately, one only remembers what is exceptional. And there seems to be no reason why one thing is exceptional and another not. Why have I forgotten so many things that must have been, one would have thought, more memorable than what I do remember? Why remember the hum of bees in the garden going down to the beach, and forget completely being thrown naked by father into the sea? (Mrs. Swanwick says she saw that happen.)[1]

This leads to a digression, which perhaps may explain a little of my own psychology; even of other people's. Often when I have been writing one of my so-called novels I have been baffled by this same problem; that is, how to describe what I call in my private shorthand—"non-being." Every day includes much more non-being than being. Yesterday for example, Tuesday the 18th of April, was it happened a good day; above the average in "being." It was fine; I enjoyed writing these first pages; my head was relieved of the pressure of writing about Roger;[2] I walked over Mount Misery[3] and along the river; and save that the tide was out, the country, which I notice very closely always, was coloured and shaded as I like—there were the willows, I remember, all plumy and soft green and purple against the blue. I also read Chaucer with pleasure; and began a book—the memoirs of Madame de la Fayette—which interested me. These separate moments of being were however embedded in many more moments of non-being. I have already forgotten what Leonard and I talked about at lunch; and at tea; although it was a good day the goodness was embedded in a kind of nondescript cotton wool. This is always so. A great part of

[1]   *Mrs. Swanwick ... happen*   In her autobiography, *I Have Been Young* (1935), Helena Sickert Swanwich, who became acquainted with Leslie Stephen at St. Ives, remembers watching "with delight his naked babies running around the beach or being towed into the sea between his legs."

[2]   *Roger*   Woolf was working on *Roger Fry: A Biography*, which was published in 1940.

[3]   *Mount Misery*   The nickname given to two cottages located between Piddinghow and Southease in the Ouse River valley.

every day is not lived consciously. One walks, eats, sees things, deals with what has to be done; the broken vacuum cleaner; ordering dinner; writing orders to Mabel;[1] washing; cooking dinner; bookbinding. When it is a bad day the proportion of non-being is much larger. I had a slight temperature last week; almost the whole day was non-being. The real novelist can somehow convey both sorts of being. I think Jane Austen can; and Trollope; perhaps Thackeray and Dickens and Tolstoy. I have never been able to do both. I tried—in *Night and Day*; and in *The Years*. But I will leave the literary side alone for the moment.

As a child then, my days, just as they do now, contained a large proportion of this cotton wool, this non-being. Week after week passed at St. Ives and nothing made any dint upon me. Then, for no reason that I know about, there was a sudden violent shock; something happened so violently that I have remembered it all my life. I will give a few instances. The first: I was fighting with Thoby on the lawn. We were pommelling each other with our fists. Just as I raised my fist to hit him, I felt: why hurt another person? I dropped my hand instantly, and stood there, and let him beat me. I remember the feeling. It was a feeling of hopeless sadness. It was as if I became aware of something terrible; and of my own powerlessness. I slunk off alone, feeling horribly depressed. The second instance was also in the garden at St. Ives. I was looking at the flower bed by the front door; "That is the whole," I said. I was looking at a plant with a spread of leaves; and it seemed suddenly plain that the flower itself was a part of the earth; that a ring enclosed what was the flower; and that was the real flower; part earth; part flower. It was a thought I put away as being likely to be very useful to me later. The third case was also at St. Ives. Some people called Valpy had been staying at St. Ives, and had left. We were waiting at dinner one night, when somehow I overheard my father or my mother say that Mr. Valpy had killed himself. The next thing I remember is being in the garden at night and walking on the path by the apple tree. It seemed to me that the apple tree was connected with the horror of Mr. Valpy's suicide. I could not pass it. I stood there looking at the grey-green creases of the bark—it was a moonlit night—in a trance

of horror. I seemed to be dragged down, hopelessly, into some pit of absolute despair from which I could not escape. My body seemed paralysed.

These are three instances of exceptional moments. I often tell them over, or rather they come to the surface unexpectedly. But now that for the first time I have written them down, I realise something that I have never realised before. Two of these moments ended in a state of despair. The other ended, on the contrary, in a state of satisfaction. When I said about the flower "That is the whole," I felt that I had made a discovery. I felt that I had put away in my mind something that I should go back, to turn over and explore. It strikes me now that this was a profound difference. It was the difference in the first place between despair and satisfaction. This difference I think arose from the fact that I was quite unable to deal with the pain of discovering that people hurt each other; that a man I had seen had killed himself. The sense of horror held me powerless. But in the case of the flower I found a reason; and was thus able to deal with the sensation. I was not powerless. I was conscious—if only at a distance—that I should in time explain it. I do not know if I was older when I saw the flower than I was when I had the other two experiences. I only know that many of these exceptional moments brought with them a peculiar horror and a physical collapse; they seemed dominant; myself passive. This suggests that as one gets older one has a greater power through reason to provide an explanation; and that this explanation blunts the sledge-hammer force of the blow. I think this is true, because though I still have the peculiarity that I receive these sudden shocks, they are now always welcome; after the first surprise, I always feel instantly that they are particularly valuable. And so I go on to suppose that the shock-receiving capacity is what makes me a writer. I hazard the explanation that a shock is at once in my case followed by the desire to explain it. I feel that I have had a blow; but it is not, as I thought as a child, simply a blow from an enemy hidden behind the cotton wool of daily life; it is or will become a revelation of some order; it is a token of some real thing behind appearances; and I make it real by putting it into words. It is only by putting it into words that I make it whole; this wholeness means that it has lost its power to hurt me; it gives me, perhaps because

---

[1] *Mabel* The Woolfs's maid.

by doing so I take away the pain, a great delight to put the severed parts together. Perhaps this is the strongest pleasure known to me. It is the rapture I get when in writing I seem to be discovering what belongs to what; making a scene come right; making a character come together. From this I reach what I might call a philosophy; at any rate it is a constant idea of mine; that behind the cotton wool is hidden a pattern; that we—I mean all human beings—are connected with this; that the whole world is a work of art; that we are parts of the work of art. *Hamlet* or a Beethoven quartet is the truth about this vast mass that we call the world. But there is no Shakespeare, there is no Beethoven; certainly and emphatically there is no God; we are the words; we are the music; we are the thing itself. And I see this when I have a shock.

This intuition of mine—it is so instinctive that it seems given to me, not made by me—has certainly given its scale to my life ever since I saw the flower in the bed by the front door at St. Ives. If I were painting myself I should have to find some—rod, shall I say—something that would stand for the conception. It proves that one's life is not confined to one's body and what one says and does; one is living all the time in relation to certain background rods or conceptions. Mine is that there is a pattern hid behind the cotton wool. And this conception affects me every day. I prove this, now, by spending the morning writing, when I might be walking, running a shop, or learning to do something that will be useful if war comes. I feel that by writing I am doing what is far more necessary than anything else.

All artists I suppose feel something like this. It is one of the obscure elements in life that has never been much discussed. It is left out in almost all biographies and autobiographies, even of artists. Why did Dickens spend his entire life writing stories? What was his conception? I bring in Dickens partly because I am reading *Nicholas Nickleby* at the moment; also partly because it struck me, on my walk yesterday, that these moments of being of mine were scaffolding in the background; were the invisible and silent part of my life as a child. But in the foreground there were of course people; and these people were very like characters in Dickens. They were caricatures; they were very simple; they were immensely alive. They could be made with three strokes of the pen,

if I could do it. Dickens owes his astonishing power to make characters alive to the fact that he saw them as a child sees them; as I saw Mr. Wolstenholme, C.B. Clarke, and Mr. Gibbs.

I name these three people because they all died when I was a child. Therefore they have never been altered. I see them exactly as I saw them then. Mr. Wolstenholme was a very old gentleman who came every summer to stay with us. He was brown; he had a beard and very small eyes in fat cheeks; and he fitted into a brown wicker beehive chair as if it had been his nest. He used to sit in this beehive chair smoking and reading. He had only one characteristic—that when he ate plum tart he spurted the juice through his nose so that it made a purple stain on his grey moustache. This seemed enough to cause us perpetual delight. We called him "The Woolly One." By way of shading him a little I remember that we had to be kind to him because he was not happy at home; that he was very poor, yet once gave Thoby half a crown; that he had a son who was drowned in Australia; and I know too that he was a great mathematician. He never said a word all the time I knew him. But he still seems to me a complete character; and whenever I think of him I begin to laugh.

Mr. Gibbs was perhaps less simple. He wore a tie ring; had a bald, benevolent head; was dry; neat; precise; and had folds of skin under his chin. He made father groan—"why can't you go—why can't you go?" And he gave Vanessa and myself two ermine skins, with slits down the middle out of which poured endless wealth—streams of silver. I also remember him lying in bed, dying; husky; in a night shirt; and showing us drawings by Retzsch.[1] The character of Mr. Gibbs also seems to me complete and amuses me very much.

As for C.B. Clarke, he was an old botanist; and he said to my father "All you young botanists like Osmunda."[2] He had an aunt aged eighty who went for a walking tour in the New Forest. That is all—that is all I have to say about these three old gentlemen. But how real they were! How we laughed at them! What an immense part they played in our lives!

—1979 (WRITTEN 1939–40)

---

[1] *Retzsch* Friedrich Retzsch (1779–1857), German engraver of the early nineteenth century.

[2] *Osmunda* Genus of fern.

IN CONTEXT

Woolf and Bloomsbury[1]

Virginia Woolf was a central figure in a group of talented and influential friends that came to be known as the "Bloomsbury Group" after the part of London in which many of them lived. In addition to Woolf and her husband Leonard, the group included Woolf's sister Vanessa Bell, historian and intellectual Lytton Strachey, economist John Maynard Keynes, artist Duncan Grant, art critic Roger Fry, and novelist E.M. Forster. On the fringes of the group were such other leading figures as T.S. Eliot; since many of the group's central figures were widely connected, the social circle that revolved around Bloomsbury was a large one. As Eliot put it after she died, Woolf "was the center not merely of an esoteric group, but of the literary life of London.... With the death of Virginia Woolf, a whole pattern of culture is broken."[2]

Vanessa Bell, *Virginia Woolf*, 1912.

The Woolfs were publishers as well as writers; small though it was, Hogarth Press published several of the most important books of the era, including Eliot's *Poems*, Katherine Mansfield's *Prelude*, and the first English edition of several of Sigmund Freud's works, as well as Woolf's own fiction. One of their friends, John Lehman, has given a good sense of the press's physical operations:

---

[1] *Woolf and Bloomsbury*   Unless otherwise specified, all quotes are from *Recollections of Virginia Woolf*, edited by Joan Russell Noble (1972).

[2] *was the ... broken*   From T.S. Eliot's obituary of Woolf in *Horizon*, May 1941, 313–16.

The Hogarth Press was named after Hogarth house in Richmond where [the Woolfs] were living when they began printing and publishing. In 1924 they moved to No. 52 Tavistock Square in Bloomsbury. Leonard and Virginia lived upstairs, and the activities of the Press were concentrated in the basement—a rather ramshackle basement, as was the case with any of the old Bloomsbury houses. The front room, looking on to the square, was the general office, in which there were as a rule not more than two or three girls at work, whose business it was to deal with the order, make out the invoices, pack up the books and handle the general correspondence. Leading out of the basement front room was a longish, dark corridor, piled with binders' packets of recently published books. On one side was the former scullery, in which Leonard had installed the treadle[1] printing press, still used for occasional small and special books.

Of Woolf herself, many have left vivid recollections—many of them touching on the strong sense of *joie de vivre* that she often radiated. In the context of the frequent depression that she experienced this may seem surprising, but the accounts are too numerous to be doubted. For Clive Bell, a sense of fun is the most lasting impression left by Woolf:[2]

> Writing was her passion and her joy and her poison. Yet, I repeat, hers was a happy nature. … My children, from the time they were old enough to enjoy anything beyond their animal satisfactions, enjoyed beyond anything a visit from Virginia: "Virginia's coming, what fun we shall have." That is what they said and felt when they were children and went on saying and feeling to the end. And so said all of us. So said everyone who knew her. … She might be divinely witty or outrageously fanciful; she might retail village gossip or tell stories of her London friends; always she was indescribably entertaining.

Bell also speaks of how Woolf sometimes "grew angry and lashed out" when she suspected she was being condescended to. She often felt resentful of "the way in which men, as she thought, patronized women, especially women who were attempting to create works of art or succeed in what were once considered manly professions. Assuredly Virginia did not wish to be a man, or to be treated as a man: she wished to be treated as an equal—just possibly as a superior."

Others describe a similar mixture in Woolf's personality. According to the novelist Elizabeth Bowen, Woolf could be "awfully naughty," even "fiendish." "She could say things about people, all in a flash, which remained with one. Fleetingly malicious, rather than outright cruel." Bowen also recalled a streak of superciliousness: "I was reminded sometimes of 'The Lord thy God is a jealous God: Thou shalt have no other God but me.' There was a touch of that about her." But, like Bell, Bowen recalls more strongly her exuberant and joyful spirit: "I was aware, one could not but be aware, of an undertow often of sadness, of melancholy, of great fear. But the main impression was of a creature of laughter and movement. … And her laughter was entrancing, it was outrageous laughter, almost like a child's laughter." Bowen has also likened Woolf's inquisitiveness to that of a child:

> She wanted to know all the details of people's lives. … She would say to anybody, to me, or anyone to whom she was talking, "Now what did you do, *exactly* what did you do? … You say you went to a party, where was it, who was there, what were they wearing?" Or, "You walked down the street, now *why* did you walk down the street? Who were you with? What did you see? Did you see a cat, did you see a dog?" It was that sort of inquisitiveness—almost

---

[1] *treadle* Lever worked by the foot.

[2] *Clive Bell … Woolf* All Clive Bell's recollections are from his *Old Friends: Personal Recollections* (1956).

childish. I never knew her to probe *deeply* into anything, and I don't know whether she really took much interest in people's affairs of the heart or not. … Past a point, her own imagination took over.

Bowen is one of many to have remarked on Woolf's intensity as a writer; another is E.M. Forster. As he put it when comparing her to many of her contemporaries, "she liked writing with an intensity which few writers have attained or desired":

> Most of them write with half an eye on their royalties, half an eye on their critics, and a third half eye on improving the world, which leaves them with only half an eye for the task on which she concentrated her entire vision. She would not look elsewhere, and her circumstances combined with her temperament to focus her. Money she had not to consider, because she possessed a private income, and though financial independence is not always a safeguard against commercialism, it was in her case.

Anonymous, *Virginia Woolf and T.S. Eliot*, 1920s.

Even those who were not always sympathetic to Woolf or to Bloomsbury recognized that her approach both to those around her and to the craft of writing was in many respects extraordinary. The poet Stephen Spender was among those who sniped at Bloomsbury, calling it a "clique" rather than a group, and suggesting that Woolf "moved in a very limited social world." Yet even he felt obliged to remark on the "undiluted purity of one of those uncorrupted natures which seem set aside from the world for a special task by a strange conjunction of fortune and misfortune."[1] With Woolf, he ventured, "style, form, and material are indivisible."

---

[1] *undiluted ... misfortune* This and the following quote are from Stephen Spender's obituary of Woolf in the *Listener*, 10 April 1941, 533.

IN CONTEXT

Woolf as Writer

The following selections from Woolf's diaries and from contemporary reviews of her work provide a direct sense of Bloomsbury, of Woolf's consciousness of herself as a social being and as a writer, and of the different reactions that her work prompted.

from Virginia Woolf, *A Writer's Diary*

Monday, May 12th [1919]

We are in the thick of our publishing season; Murry, Eliot[1] and myself are in the hands of the public this morning. For this reason, perhaps, I feel slightly but decidedly depressed. I read a bound copy of *Kew Gardens* through; having put off the evil task until it was complete. The result is vague. It seems to me slight and short; I don't see how the reading of it impressed Leonard so much. According to him it is the best short piece I have done yet; and this judgment led me to read the *Mark on the Wall* and I found a good deal of fault with that. As Sydney Waterlow[2] once said, the worst of writing is that one depends so much upon praise. I feel rather sure that I shall get none for this story; and I shall mind a little. Unpraised, I find it hard to start writing in the morning; but the dejection lasts only 30 minutes, and once I start I forget all about it. One should aim, seriously, at disregarding ups and downs; a compliment here, silence there; Murry and Eliot ordered, and not me; the central fact remains stable, which is the fact of my own pleasure in the art. And these mists of the spirit have other causes, I expect; though they are deeply hidden. There is some ebb and flow of the tide of life which accounts for it; though what produces either ebb or flow I'm not sure.

Tuesday, June 10th [1919]

I must use up the fifteen minutes before dinner in going on again, in order to make up the great gap. We are just in from the Club; from ordering a reprint of the *Mark on the Wall* at the Pelican Press; and from tea with James.[3] His news is that Maynard[4] in disgust at the peace terms has resigned, kicked the dust of office off him and is now an academic figure at Cambridge. But I must really sing my own praises, since I left off at the point when we came back from Asheham[5] to find the hall table stacked, littered, with orders for *Kew Gardens*. They strewed the sofa and we opened them intermittently through dinner and quarrelled, I'm sorry to say, because we were both excited, and opposite tides of excitement coursed in us, and they were blown to waves by the critical blast of

---

[1]   *Murry*   Writer and editor John Middleton Murry (1889–1957), husband of Katherine Mansfield; *Eliot*   Poet T.S. Eliot (1888–1965).

[2]   *Sydney Waterlow*   Printer (1822–1906).

[3]   *James*   James Strachey (1887–1967), psychoanalyst and translator of Freud's works, which were published by the Hogarth Press.

[4]   *Maynard*   John Maynard Keynes (1883–1946), an economist who was the chief Treasury representative at the Peace Conference at Versailles. He resigned from the Treasury in May 1919, horrified at the excessive reparations that the Allies demanded from Germany.

[5]   *Asheham*   House in East Sussex that Leonard and Virginia rented, and at which they spent many holidays and weekends.

Charleston. All these orders—150 about, from shops and private people—come from a review in the *Lit. Sup.* presumably by Logan,[1] in which as much praise was allowed me as I like to claim. And 10 days ago I was stoically facing complete failure! The pleasure of success was considerably damaged, first by our quarrel, and second by the necessity of getting some 90 copies ready, cutting covers, printing labels, glueing backs, and finally despatching, which used up all spare time and some not spare till this moment. ....

Tuesday, May 11th [1920]

It is worth mentioning, for future reference, that the creative power which bubbles so pleasantly in beginning a new book[2] quiets down after a time, and one goes on more steadily. Doubts creep in. Then one becomes resigned. Determination not to give in, and the sense of an impending shape keep one at it more than anything. I'm a little anxious. How am I to bring off this conception? Directly one gets to work one is like a person walking, who has seen the country stretching out before. I want to write nothing in this book that I don't enjoy writing. Yet writing is always difficult.

Wednesday, June 23rd [1920]

I was struggling, at this time, to say honestly that I don't think Conrad's[3] last book a good one. I have said it. It is painful (a little) to find fault there, where almost solely, one respects. I can't help suspecting the truth to be that he never sees anyone who knows good writing from bad, and then being a foreigner, talking broken English, married to a lump of a wife, he withdraws more and more into what he once did well, only piles it on higher and higher, until what can one call it but stiff melodrama. I would not like to find *The Rescue* signed Virginia Woolf. But will anyone agree with this? Anyhow nothing shakes my opinion of a book. Nothing—nothing. Only perhaps if it's the book of a young person—or of a friend—no, even so, I think myself infallible. ...

Friday, April 8th [1921]

... One wants, as Roger[4] said very truly yesterday, to be kept up to the mark; that people should be interested and watch one's work. What depresses me is the thought that I have ceased to interest people—at the very moment when, by the help of the press, I thought I was becoming more myself. One does *not* want an established reputation, such as I think I was getting, as one of our leading female novelists. I have still, of course, to gather in all the private criticism, which is the real test.[5] When I have weighed this I shall be able to say whether I am "interesting" or obsolete. Anyhow, I feel quite alert enough to stop, if I'm obsolete. I shan't become a machine, unless a machine for grinding articles. As I write, there rises somewhere in my head that queer and very pleasant sense of something which I want to write; my own point of view. I wonder, though, whether this feeling that I write for half a dozen instead of 1500 will pervert this?—make me eccentric—no, I think not. But, as I said, one must face the despicable vanity which is at the root of all this niggling and haggling. I think the only prescription for me is to have a thousand interests—if one is damaged, to be able instantly to let

---

[1] *review ... Logan*   The review, published 29 May 1919, was not by Logan Pearsall Smith, as Woolf believed, but by Harold Child, a frequent contributor to the *Times Literary Supplement.*

[2] *a new book*   Woolf was just beginning to write *Jacob's Room* (1922).

[3] *Conrad*   Novelist Joseph Conrad (1857–1924), whose novel *The Rescue* was published that year.

[4] *Roger*   Painter and art critic Roger Fry (1866–1934), a member of the Bloomsbury group. Woolf published a biography of Fry in 1940.

[5] *I have ... test*   Woolf refers to criticism of *Monday or Tuesday*, which had just been released. Woolf was discouraged by a review of the book in *The Times* which she described as "complimentary enough, but quite unintelligent. ... They don't see that I'm after something interesting."

my energy flow into Russian, or Greek, or the press, or the garden, or people, or some activity disconnected with my own writing.

Sunday, May 12th [1929]

Here, having just finished what I call the final revision of *Women and Fiction*[1] so that L.[2] can read it after tea, I stop; surfeited. And the pump, which I was so sanguine as to think ceased, begins again. About *Women and Fiction* I am not sure—a brilliant essay?—I daresay: it has much work in it, many opinions boiled down into a kind of jelly, which I have stained red as far as I can. But I am eager to be off—to write without any boundary coming slick in one's eyes: here my public has been too close; facts; getting them malleable, easily yielding to each other.

Wednesday, October 23rd [1929]

As it is true—I write only for an hour, then rush back feeling I cannot keep my brain on that spin any more—then typewrite, and am done by 12. I will here sum up my impressions before publishing *A Room of One's Own*. It is a little ominous that Morgan[3] won't review it. It makes me suspect that there is a shrill feminine tone in it which my intimate friends will dislike. I forecast, then, that I shall get no criticism, except of the evasive jocular kind, from Lytton,[4] Roger, and Morgan; that the press will be kind and talk of its charm and sprightliness; also I shall be attacked for a feminist and hinted at for a Sapphist;[5] Sybil[6] will ask me to luncheon; I shall get a good many letters from young women. I am afraid it will not be taken seriously. Mrs. Woolf is so accomplished a writer that all she says makes easy reading … this very feminine logic … a book to be put in the hands of girls. I doubt that I mind very much. The Moths; but I think it is to be waves,[7] is trudging along; and I have that to refer to, if I am damped by the other. It is a trifle, I shall say; so it is; but I wrote it with ardour and conviction.

from E.M. Forster, "Review of 'Kew Gardens'" (*Daily News*, July 31, 1919)

Flowers and Men
In "The Mark on the Wall" there is, as Mrs. Woolf sadly points out, a moral of a sort; she is a poor housekeeper, or the mark would not be there. But it is impossible to extract any moral from "Kew Gardens." It is vision unalloyed. Or, rather, there are two visions which gradually draw together (as when one adjusts field-glasses), until they grow unforgettably bright and become one. Flowers and men are the two items at which Mrs. Woolf is looking, and, at first, they seem strongly contrasted. The flowers are down in their bed with a snail, the men, erect and sentient, are strolling past with their womenkind, and the possibility of tea. And the men sometimes look at the flowers, whereas the

---

[1] *Women and Fiction* Woolf's early title for *A Room of One's Own* (1929).

[2] *L.* Leonard Woolf.

[3] *Morgan* Novelist and literary critic E.M. Forster (1879–1970), a peripheral member of the Bloomsbury group who had reviewed several of Woolf's previous works. Woolf always took particular note of his comments. Woolf has added in the magin, "He wrote yesterday, 3 Dec. and said he very much liked it."

[4] *Lytton* Critic and biographer Lytton Strachey (1880–1932), a member of the Bloomsbury group.

[5] *Sapphist* I.e., a lesbian (after Sappho, the famous ancient Greek poet of Lesbos whose love poems are thought to be addressed to women).

[6] *Sybil* Lady Colefax (1874–1950), a society hostess who won fame in London when she organized a charity poetry reading, chaired by Edmund Gosse, at which T.S. Eliot and Aldous Huxley, among others, read.

[7] *The Moths … waves* Woolf's original title for *The Waves* (1931) was *The Moths*.

flowers never look at the men. But as the story goes on this difference becomes terribly unimportant, and at the end the flowers, if anyone, have the upper hand. They win not in any allegorical sense—Mrs. Woolf is no pantheist. Their victory is over the eye: they cause us to see men also as petals or coloured blobs that loom and dissolve in the green blue atmosphere of Kew. One cannot quote from this extraordinary story, because it is constructed with such care that the fun and the beauty—and there is much of both—depend for their main effect on their position in the general scheme. But those who like it will like it very much, and those who do not like it are to be pitied.

They are to be pitied, but not to be despised. Mrs. Woolf's art is of a very unusual type, and one realises that quite good critics, especially of the academic kind, may think it insignificant. It has no moral, no philosophy, nor has it what is usually understood by Form. It aims deliberately at aimlessness, at long loose sentences, that sway and meander; it is opposed to tensity and intensity, and willingly reveals the yawn and the gape. Most writers seem to be so solemn even when being funny; they are so anxious to express their devotion to their art, and they frown when we do not attend to their jokes. Mrs. Woolf, though she doubtless welcomes attention, is very careful to make no bid for it. She only says, "Oh, here is something that I have seen," and then strays forward. Forward it is, but those who are blind to the newer developments of English prose may not think so, and may complain at the end that the authoress has left them where she found them. Which is, no doubt, exactly what she would wish to do.

The stories are not to be had through the booksellers. Those who would experiment in them should write to the Hogarth Press, Richmond.

from unsigned "Review of 'Kew Gardens,'" (*Times Literary Supplement*, April 7, 1921)

Two of the stories in Virginia Woolf's new book, *Monday or Tuesday*, have been published before. "Kew Gardens" and "The Mark on the Wall" are already on the shelves of those who collect Hogarth Press books, and in the memories of those who follow Mrs. Woolf's writings. The piece which gives its title to the new volume, *Monday or Tuesday*, is an example of the "unrepresentational" art which is creeping across from painting to see what it can make of words. It sounds beautiful; it suggests beautiful, or at least life-full things—the heron flying, the busy street, the fire-lit room, and others. The trouble with it is that even this sort of art cannot empty itself altogether of intellectual content. One sentence seems to "mean"—that is, to represent—something; the intrusion of this representation makes the next sentence, or the other portions of the same sentence, "mean" nothing. We complain of Monday or Tuesday, not that it means too little that is intelligible to the plain mind, but that it cannot help meaning too much for its purpose. Prose may "aspire to the condition of music";[1] it cannot reach it.

Some measure of this objection applies to "Blue and Green," though there the aim is different; and Mrs. Woolf does perfectly in a few lines what J. A. Symonds[2] once did imperfectly (and spread thin) over many pages....

---

[1] *aspire ... music* Reference to Walter Pater's famous statement that "all arts aspire to the condition of music" in *The Renaissance* (1873).

[2] *J. A. Symonds* Writer John Addington Symonds (1840–1893).

from W.L. Courtney, "Review of *Jacob's Room*" (*Daily Telegraph*, November 10, 1922)

In estimating the tendencies of a particular era in literature it is well to take extreme cases. We recognise that there are certain distinctive peculiarities about modern novels. But in order to make sure of the fact we need only take up a book like *Jacob's Room*, by Mrs. Virginia Woolf. Even so, we shall be a little perplexed, for sometimes—perhaps oftener than not—we do not quite understand what the authoress is driving at, nor are we in a position to feel certain that she achieves the results at which she aims. One thing is clear. Instead of a straightforward narrative dealing with certain characters, with the interactions of those characters on one another, and with the destiny which carries them to their appointed end, we have a perfectly different art form. There is no particular story to tell, unless, indeed, you can gather some kind of story out of the piecemeal references to personages and things. But what does emerge is the constant activity, the perpetual reaction of a sensitive mind upon the impressions which come through the senses—so that an event or a character is not viewed as it is, but only as steeped in the consciousness of the author. That is the great and decisive difference between an older art-method and a later, and sometimes the contrast is a little embarrassing. The old craving for a plot still remains in our unregenerate breasts, and when all that we receive in compensation for what we have lost is the attitude of Mrs. Virginia Woolf towards her creations—or rather, perhaps, a theory of life as interpreted by a clever observer—there must inevitably be some confusion and a mixture of mere narration with the intrusions and philosophisings of a superior mind. Anything like an objective creation becomes impossible. By an objective creation I mean the portrayal of a particular thing, person, or incident as it exists in itself. Flaubert[1] thought that that was the only right way of writing a novel, and hence his theory—driven hard by a man who consciously lived his life apart from others—was the absolute exclusion of the author's personality from the written page. Mrs. Woolf confidently chatters as though she were seated in an armchair playing with her puppets. It is she who gives them life. It is she who imparts to them such character as they are allowed to possess. They talk well because the author of their being talks well. They say clever things, not as from their own mouths, but as prompted by their creator. And if their creator appears to be a clever and original woman, her creations have the stamp of real life. But does she really care for them? Is she enamoured of her puppets? I wonder. ...

---

[1] *Flaubert* French novelist Gustave Flaubert (1821–80).

Gender and Sexual Orientation
CONTEXTS

In the twentieth century, questions about the nature of women and of femininity were at the forefront of public attention. Women's biology, emotional nature, and familial and social roles were all matters of interest, not only as a result of the suffrage campaign, but also because of the wider struggle of feminists for better education and equal social and political opportunities. Women were appearing in public, demonstrating, giving speeches, campaigning, and being more assertive and independent than ever before. Large numbers of women also entered the workforce during both World Wars, and many were loathe to leave it when the men returned. At work they often did what had been categorized as "men's work," wore masculine clothing, and were thus perceived as "unfeminine."

Many twentieth-century debates focused on the differences between gender, a socially-defined category, and sex, a category determined by physical characteristics. That men and women were biologically different nobody could dispute, but to what extent should this difference dictate their roles? Would women truly be "unsexed" (as Grant Allen claims below) if they left the home to participate in the public sphere? Cecily Hamilton's essay *Marriage as a Trade*, also excerpted here, makes very clear that, historically, there had been little difference between a woman's reproductive function and her profession—much to the detriment of women and of society. While men were free to choose a variety of lifestyles—without sacrificing their status as men—women were told that they were not really "women" unless they married and had children.

But more and more women were choosing to do just that; or, if they did marry and have children, they were also seeking some form of participation in the public sphere. In the early twentieth century, the suffrage campaign was the primary focus of female activists, as Emmeline Pankhurst discusses in the excerpt below from her autobiography. Many men—including some in Parliament—felt the idea of female suffrage was nothing short of absurd. There was also widespread concern that female suffrage would further blur the dividing line between men and women, a line that was largely seen as natural and indisputable. If women could move into the political sphere, this would, in effect, threaten the traditional realm and definition of masculinity.

The nature of masculinity was not as heavily contested during this period as that of femininity, and—as the exchange between George Orwell and Frank Richard over "Boys' Weeklies," excerpted below, illustrates—many male paradigms were resistant to change. As the twentieth century advanced, however, a number of different ideas were advanced concerning the appearance of the "modern man" like (many of them created by filmmakers). There was also considerable insecurity surrounding masculinity throughout this period, particularly during the Great Depression of the 1930s. After World War I unemployment became more persistent and pervasive. The government took measures to provide assistance for unemployed people, including unemployment insurance and benefits, but this increased the strain on the nation's already tight budget, and the measures were controversial; many felt that those who relied upon such government benefits were not fulfilling their basic responsibilities as "breadwinners." At the same time, modern women could be seen breaking new ground in many spheres of employment, further challenging the idea of the male breadwinner.

Investigations into the nature of sexuality and sexual orientation added another dimension to debates over sex and gender. In the excerpt below from *The Classic Slum*, Robert Roberts recalls that the trial of Oscar Wilde for homosexuality in the late nineteenth century had a lingering effect. For years many members of the lower classes used the term "oscarwile" as a synonym for "homosexual." The association of homosexual men with effeminacy was a common one at the time, and trials of famous homosexuals such as Wilde seemed to prove the existence of "feminine" men. In the early twentieth century, homosexuality was for the first time a topic not only of discussion but of serious scientific inquiry, as the selections by Havelock Ellis and Edward Carpenter that are included in this section indicate. Studies of homosexual individuals (or any others who seemed to transgress the norms of their gender) led some researchers to call into question the validity of existing sexual categories. Perhaps these people were actually members of a third sex, one that was somehow halfway between the existing male and female categories. One of the first German scientists to put forward this theory, the German "sexologist" Richard Krafft-Ebing, described "inverts" (as homosexuals were then commonly known) as suffering from a sort of psychic androgyny: they were men trapped in women's bodies, or women trapped in men's. Krafft-Ebing believed such beings were degenerate or abnormal, and believed they could be identified by anatomical deformities.

Many theorists who followed Krafft-Ebing took a more positive view of this intermediate sex. Edward Carpenter and Havelock Ellis (both of whose works are excerpted below) took pains to indicate that a number of extremely gifted, artistic individuals surely belonged to the "third sex"—that is, even if they were not homosexual, they exhibited characteristics traditionally thought of as belonging to the other gender. But, these authors wondered, if there were such things as "masculine" and feminine" characteristics, perhaps every person contained a mixture of the two; thus even the most womanly woman might have elements of the masculine in her, or vice versa. This is the theory that Virginia Woolf's narrator seems to advocate in the excerpt below from *Orlando*, in which the title character miraculously changes sex midway through the book, nevertheless retaining the same personality.

As the excerpt from Woolf's memoirs illustrates vividly, attitudes towards sexuality were changing dramatically in some sectors of society. But if the intellectual community was beginning by the middle of the twentieth century to be more open to what would by century's end be termed the gay and lesbian community, the general populace was slow to follow. It was not until 1967 that same-sex sexual activity was decriminalized in Great Britain; even in 1960, as E.M. Forster attests in his "Terminal Note" to *Maurice*, the public harbored considerable loathing for the thought of homosexuality. Attitudes towards (and understanding of) sexual behavior among heterosexuals were also often resistant to change. Marie Stopes, in her 1918 treatise on marriage, *Married Love*, attempted to bridge the communication gap between men and women and facilitate the formation of happy relationships. As the illustration reproduced below from the *Daily Express* makes clear, many modern women were more independent and self-confident, and they were looking for friendship and both intellectual and physical companionship. The popular press (which was becoming more attuned to female readers) was increasingly filled with relationship advice, much of which warned husbands and fathers that they needed to be more involved with domestic responsibilities. As Robert Roberts demonstrates in the excerpt below from *The Classic Slum*, however, many working-class men struggled with unemployment and thus felt that their masculinity was already threatened; refusing to help out in the home was one of the only ways in which they felt that they could maintain any sense of dignity.

⌘ ⌘ ⌘

from Edward Carpenter, *Love's Coming of Age* (1896)

The ideas set out in the chapter excerpted here from *Love's Coming of Age* were expanded in Edward Carpenter's 1908 work *The Intermediate Sex*, which was widely read both in England and North America, and influenced a number of writers, including E.M. Forster, Siegfried Sassoon, Robert Graves, and D.H. Lawrence.

"THE INTERMEDIATE SEX"

In late years (and since the arrival of the New Woman[1] amongst us) many things in the relation of men and women to each other have altered, or at any rate become clearer. The growing sense of equality in habits and customs—university studies, art, music, politics, etc.—all these things have brought about a rapprochement between the sexes. If the modern woman is a little more masculine in some ways than her predecessor, the modern man (it is to be hoped), while by no means effeminate, is a little more sensitive in temperament and artistic in feeling than the original John Bull.[2] It is beginning to be recognised that the sexes do not or should not normally form two groups hopelessly isolated in habit and feeling from each other, but that they rather represent the two poles of one group—which is the human race; so that while certainly the extreme specimens at either pole are vastly divergent, there are great numbers in the middle region who (though differing corporeally as men and women), are by emotion and temperament very near to each other. We all know women with a strong dash of the masculine temperament, and we all know men whose almost feminine sensibility and intuition seem to belie their bodily form. Nature, it might appear, in mixing the elements which go to compose each individual, does not always keep her two groups of ingredients—which

represent the two sexes—properly apart, but often throws them crosswise in a somewhat baffling manner, now this way and now that; yet wisely, we must think—for if a severe distinction of elements were always maintained, the two sexes would soon drift into far latitudes and absolutely cease to understand each other. As it is, there are some remarkable and (we think) indispensable types of character, in whom there is such a union or balance of the feminine and masculine qualities that these people become to a great extent the interpreters of men and women to each other.

There is another point which has become clearer of late. For as people are beginning to see that the sexes form in a certain sense a continuous group, so they are beginning to see that Love and Friendship—which have been so often set apart from each other as things distinct—are in reality closely related and shade imperceptibly into each other. Women are beginning to demand that Marriage shall mean Friendship as well as Passion; that a comrade-like Equality shall be included in the word Love; and it is recognised that from the one extreme of a "Platonic" friendship (generally between persons of the same sex) up to the other extreme of passionate love (generally between persons of opposite sex) no hard and fast line can at any point be drawn effectively separating the different kinds of attachment. We know, in fact, of Friendships so romantic in sentiment that they verge into love; we know of Loves so intellectual and spiritual that they hardly dwell in the sphere of Passion.

A moment's thought will show that the general conceptions indicated above—if anywhere near the truth—point to an immense diversity of human temperament and character in matters relating to sex and love; but though such diversity has probably always existed, it has only in comparatively recent times become a subject of study.

More than thirty years ago, however, an Austrian writer, K.H. Ulrichs, drew attention in a series of pamphlets (*Memnon, Ara Spei, Inclusa,* etc.) to the existence of a class of people who strongly illustrate the above remarks, and with whom specially this paper is concerned. He pointed out that there were people born in such a position—as it were on the dividing line between the sexes—that while belonging distinctly to

---

[1] *New Woman* Phrase coined by Sarah Grand (1854–1943) in her essay "The New Aspect of the Woman Question" (1894) to express the values—principally social, political, and educational equality with men, as well as economic independence—of many women of her generation.

[2] *John Bull* Name used to refer to Englishmen collectively, or to a typical English gentleman.

one sex as far as their bodies are concerned, they may be said to belong *mentally* and *emotionally* to the other; that there were men, for instance, who might be described as of feminine soul enclosed in a male body (*anima muliebris in corpore virili inclusa*), or in other cases, women whose definition would be just the reverse. And he maintained that this doubleness of nature was to a great extent proved by the special direction of their love-sentiment. For in such cases, as indeed might be expected, the (apparently) masculine person instead of forming a love-union with a female tended to contract romantic friendships with one of his own sex; while the apparently feminine would, instead of marrying in the usual way, devote herself to the love of another feminine.

People of this kind (i.e., having this special variation of the love-sentiment) he called Urnings;[1] and though we are not obliged to accept his theory about the cross-wise connection between "soul" and "body," since at best these words are somewhat vague and indefinite; yet his work was important because it was one of the first attempts, in modern times, to recognise the existence of what might be called an Intermediate sex, and to give at any rate some explanation of it.

… Formerly it was assumed, as a matter of course, that the type was merely a result of disease and degeneration; but now with the examination of the actual facts it appears that, on the contrary, many are fine, healthy specimens of their sex, muscular and well-developed in body, of powerful brain, high standard of conduct, and with nothing abnormal or morbid[2] of any kind observable in their physical structure or constitution…. It is also worth noticing that it is now acknowledged that even in the most healthy cases the special affectional temperament of the "Intermediate" is, as a rule, ineradicable; so much so that when (as in not a few instances) such men and women, from social or other considerations, have forced themselves to marry, and even have children, they have still not been able to overcome their own bias, or the leaning after all of their life-attachment to some friend of their own sex.…

As indicated then already, in bodily structure there is, as a rule, nothing to distinguish the subjects of our discussion from ordinary men and women; but if we take the general mental characteristics it appears from almost universal testimony that the male tends to be of a rather gentle, emotional disposition—with defects, if such exist, in the direction of subtlety, evasiveness, timidity, vanity, etc.; while the female is just the opposite—fiery, active, bold and truthful, with defects running to brusqueness and coarseness. Moreover, the mind of the former is generally intuitive and instinctive in its perceptions, with more or less of artistic feeling; while the mind of the latter is more logical, scientific, and precise than usual with the normal woman. So marked indeed are these general characteristics that sometimes by means of them (though not an infallible guide) the nature of the boy or girl can be detected in childhood, before full development has taken place; and needless to say, it may often be very important to be able to do this.

… [T]he extreme specimens—as in most cases of extremes—are not particularly attractive, sometimes quite the reverse. In the male of this kind we have a distinctly effeminate type, sentimental, lackadaisical, mincing in gait and manners, something of a chatterbox, skilful at the needle and in woman's work, sometimes taking pleasure in dressing in woman's clothes; his figure not unfrequently betraying a tendency towards the feminine, large at the hips, supple, not muscular, the face wanting in hair, the voice inclined to be high-pitched, etc.; while his dwelling-room is orderly in the extreme, even natty, and choice of decoration and perfume. His affection too is often feminine in character, clinging, dependent and jealous, as of one desiring to be loved almost more than to love.

On the other hand, as the extreme type of the homogenic female, we have a rather markedly aggressive person, of strong passions, masculine manners and movements, practical in the conduct of life, sensuous rather than sentimental in love, often untidy, and *outré*[3] in attire; her figure muscular, her voice rather low in pitch; her dwelling-room decorated with sporting-scenes, pistols, etc., and not without a suspicion of the fragrant weed[4] in the atmosphere; while her love (generally to rather soft and feminine specimens of her own sex) is often a sort of furor, similar to the ordinary

---

[1] *Urnings* From *Uranus*, heaven.

[2] *morbid* Diseased; unhealthy.

[3] *outré* French: extreme; unorthodox.

[4] *fragrant weed* I.e., tobacco.

masculine love, and at times almost uncontrollable.

These are types which, on account of their salience, everyone will recognise more or less. Naturally, when they occur, they excite a good deal of attention, and it is not an uncommon impression that most persons of the homogenic nature belong to either one or other of these classes. But in reality, of course, these extreme developments are rare, and for the most part the temperament in question is embodied in men and women of quite normal and unsensational exterior. ...

I have now sketched—very briefly and inadequately it is true—both the extreme types and the more healthy types of the "Intermediate" man and woman: types which can be verified from history and literature, though more certainly and satisfactorily perhaps from actual life around us. And unfamiliar though the subject is, it begins to appear that it is one which modern thought and science will have to face. Of the latter and more normal types it may be said that they exist, and have always existed, in considerable abundance, and from that circumstance alone there is a strong probability that they have their place and purpose. As pointed out there is no particular indication of morbidity about them, unless the special nature of their love-sentiment be itself accounted morbid; and in the alienation of the sexes from each other, of which complaint is so often made today, it must be admitted that they do much to fill the gap.

The instinctive artistic nature of the male of this class, his sensitive spirit, his wavelike emotional temperament, combined with hardihood of intellect and body; and the frank, free nature of the female, her masculine independence and strength wedded to thoroughly feminine grace of form and manner; may be said to give them both, through their double nature, command of life in all its phases, and a certain freemasonry[1] of the secrets of the two sexes which may well favor their function as reconcilers and interpreters. Certainly it is remarkable that some of the world's greatest leaders and artists have been dowered either wholly or in part with the Uranian temperament—as in the cases of Michael Angelo, Shakespeare, Marlowe,[2] Alexander the Great,

Julius Caesar, or, among women, Christine of Sweden, Sappho the poetess,[3] and others.

from Havelock Ellis, *Sexual Inversion* (1897)

> Havelock Ellis (1859–1939) was Britain's most prominent sex theorist at the turn of the century. *Sexual Inversion*, the second volume of Ellis's seven-volume *Studies in the Psychology of Sex* was labeled obscene by British courts (which had criminalized male homosexuality in 1885.) The volume was widely read and discussed, however, and earned him the friendship of other would-be sex reformers such as Margaret Sanger, a pioneer advocate for birth control. Ellis continued to oppose discrimination against homosexuals, and he received letters throughout his life from readers seeking advice on their own problems and experiences.

from CHAPTER 3: SEXUAL INVERSION IN MEN

From time to time we read letters in the newspapers denouncing public schools[4] as "hot-beds of vice," and one anonymous writer remarks that "some of our public schools almost provoke the punishment of the cities of the Plain."[5] But these actions are rarely or never submitted to accurate investigation. The physicians and masters of public school who are in a position to study the matter usually possess no psychological training, and appear to view homosexuality with too much disgust to care to pay any careful attention to it. What knowledge they possess they keep to themselves, for it is considered to be in the interests of public schools that these things should be hushed up. When anything very scandalous occurs one or two lads are expelled, to their own grave and, perhaps, life-long injury, and without benefit to

---

[1] *freemasonry* Here, instinctive sympathy.

[2] *Marlowe* English dramatist and poet Christopher Marlowe (1564-93).

[3] *Christine of Sweden* Maria Christina Alexandra (1626–89), daughter of Gustavus II and Queen Regnant of Sweden between 1632 and 1654; *Sappho the poetess* The celebrated sixth-century BCE Greek poet Sappho, who wrote love lyrics to women.

[4] *public schools* I.e., private, fee-paying schools.

[5] *cities of the Plain* The Biblical cities of Sodom, Gomorrah, Admah, Zeboiim, and Zoar. According to Genesis 19, all except the latter were destroyed by God when He incinerated Sodom because of the immorality of its inhabitants.

those who remain, whose awakening sexual life rarely receives intelligent sympathy....

Max Dessoir came to the conclusion that "an undifferentiated sexual feeling is normal, on the average, during the first years of puberty—i.e., from 13 to 15 in boys and from 12 to 14 in girls—while in later years it must be regarded as pathological."... How far the sexual instinct may be said to be undifferentiated in early puberty as regards sex is a little doubtful. It is comparatively undifferentiated, but except in rare cases it is not absolutely undifferentiated.

We have to admit, however, that, in the opinion of the latest physiologists of sex, such as Castle, Heape, and Marshall, each sex contains the latent characters of the other or recessive sex. Each sex is latent in the other, and each, as it contains the characters of both sexes (and can transmit those of the recessive sex) is latently hermaphrodite. A homosexual tendency may thus be regarded as simply the psychical manifestation of special characters of the recessive sex, susceptible of being evolved under changed circumstances, such as may occur near puberty, and associated with changed metabolism.

In recent years Freud has accepted and developed the conception of the homosexual strain as normal in early life. Thus, in 1905, in his "Bruchstück einer Hysterie-Analyse"..., Freud regards it as a well-known fact that boys and girls at puberty normally show plain signs of the existence of a homosexual tendency. Under favourable circumstances this tendency is overcome, but when a happy heterosexual love is not established it remains liable to reappear under the influence of an appropriate stimulus. In the neurotic these homosexual germs are more highly developed. "I have never carried through any psychoanalysis of a man or a woman," Freud states, "without discovering a very significant homosexual tendency."... The normality of a homosexual element in early life may be said to be accepted by most psychoanalysts, even of the schools that are separated from Freud. Stekel would go farther, and regards various psychic sexual anomalies as signs of a concealed bisexual tendency; psychic impotence, the admiration of men for masculine women and of women for feminine men, various forms of fetichism—they are all masks of homosexuality....

from Chapter 4: Sexual Inversion in Women

Homosexuality is not less common in women than in men....A Catholic confessor, a friend tells me, informed him that for one man who acknowledges homosexual practices there are three women. For the most part feminine homosexuality runs everywhere a parallel course to masculine homosexuality and is found under the same conditions. It is as common in girls as in boys; it has been found, under certain conditions, to abound among women in colleges and convents and prisons, as well as under the ordinary conditions of society....

Moreover, inversion is as likely to be accompanied by high intellectual ability in a woman as in a man. The importance of a clear conception of inversion is indeed in some respects, under present social conditions, really even greater in the case of women than of men. For if, as has sometimes been said of our civilization, "this is a man's world," the large proportion of able women inverts, whose masculine qualities render it comparatively easy for them to adopt masculine avocations, becomes a highly significant fact.

It has been noted of distinguished women in all ages and in all fields of activity that they have frequently displayed some masculine traits....

It must also be said that in literature homosexuality in women has furnished a much more frequent motive to the artist than homosexuality in men. Among the Greeks, indeed, homosexuality in women seldom receives literary consecration, and in the revival of the classical spirit at the Renaissance it was still chiefly in male adolescents ... that the homosexual ideal found expression. After that date male inversion was for a long period rarely touched in literature, save briefly and satirically, while inversion in women becomes a subject which might be treated in detail and even with complacence. Many poets and novelists, especially in France, might be cited in evidence.

from Chapter 5: The Nature of Sexual Inversion

All avocations are represented among inverts....There are, however, certain avocations to which inverts seem especially called. One of the chief of these is literature. The apparent predominance of physicians is easily explicable. The frequency with which literature is represented is probably more genuine. Here, indeed, inverts seem to find the highest degree of success and reputation. At least half a dozen of my subjects are successful men of letters, and I could easily add others by going outside the group of Histories included in this study. They especially cultivate those regions of *belles-lettres* which lie on the borderland between prose and verse. Though they do not usually attain much eminence in poetry, they are often very accomplished writers of verse. They may be attracted to history, but rarely attempt tasks of great magnitude, involving much patient labor, though to this rule there are exceptions. Pure science seems to have relatively little attraction for the homosexual.

from Grant Allen, "Woman's Place in Nature," (*Forum*, May 1889)

Novelist and essayist Grant Allen (1848–99) was a supporter of extending women's rights and of improving their educational opportunities, but he was a firm believer that marriage and childbearing were a woman's primary responsibilities. Here Allen responds to an article written by American sociologist Lester F. Ward, who believed in equal education for women. Ward argued that the progress of the human race depends on the elevation of women, because in the natural world the female sex, as the bearer of the young, is primary.

Instead of its being true, as Professor Ward emphatically puts it, that "woman is the race," I believe it to be true that she is very much less the race than man; that she is, indeed, not even half the race at present, but rather a part of it told specially off for the continuance of the species.... She is the sex sacrificed to reproductive necessities. Let us look the question, as a biological problem, frankly in the face....The actual truth is that the cases where the females constitute in a certain sense the race, occur mostly among the lower animals; that among the higher animals the superiority and relative importance of the male is distinctly marked; and that in man, the highest of all, the superiority and necessity of the male is most marked of any, so much so that almost

all the practical life of the race is carried on by men alone, and most of all in the highest human communities.... All the vast gains of our race in its progress toward civilization have been gains made for the most part by men alone. ...

In mammals ... the habit of gestation and the suckling of the young make the burden of sex much heavier on the female. In man this tendency reaches its highest development; the long period of gestation and suckling, the helpless infancy, and the slow childhood compel the mothers to be almost wholly devoted to reproductive and nursing functions, while the fathers look rather after the food, shelter, and clothing of the family. Hence, for the most part the males have built up human civilization and have made the great functionally-acquired gains in human faculty, while the females have acted as mere passive transmitters of these male acquisitions.... Able women there are no doubt; but the things that produce and beget ability—commerce, manufacture, art, invention—are and have always been almost entirely in male hands.

In man, therefore, I would confidently assert, as biological fact, the males are the race....All that is distinctively human is man—the field, the ship, the mine, the workshop; all that is truly woman is merely reproductive—the home, the nursery, the schoolroom. There are women, to be sure, who inherit much of male faculty, and some of these prefer to follow male avocations; but in so doing they for the most part unsex themselves; they fail to perform satisfactorily their maternal functions.

from Cicely Hamilton, *Marriage as a Trade* (1909)

Novelist Cecily Hamilton (1872–1952) devoted her life to improving women's options for employment and financial security. She was a leading campaigner for women's rights and a popular public speaker on female suffrage; she also, in both her writing and her speeches, attempted to encourage women to have a greater sense of self-worth, and to regard themselves as valuable members of society, outside the home as well as in it. Her treatise *Marriage as a Trade* outlines her strong views on women and economics, and her disgust with the traditional Edwardian marriage, which seemed to many women little better than a tyranny to which they were forced to submit.

By a woman ... I understand an individual human being whose life is her own concern; whose worth, in my eyes (worth being an entirely personal matter) is in no way advanced or detracted from by the accident of marriage; who does not rise in my estimation by reason of a purely physical capacity for bearing children, or sink in my estimation through a lack of that capacity. I am quite aware, of course, that her life, in many cases, will have been moulded to a great extent by the responsibilities of marriage and the care of children; just as I am aware that the lives of most of the men with whom I am acquainted have been moulded to a great extent by the trade or profession by which they earn their bread. But my judgment of her and appreciation of her are a personal judgment and appreciation, having nothing to do with her actual or potential relations, sexual or maternal, with other people. In short, I never think of her either as a wife or as a mother—I separate the woman from her attributes. To me she is an entity in herself....

It is hardly necessary to point out that the mental attitude of the average man towards woman is something quite different from this. It is a mental attitude reminding one of that of the bewildered person who could not see the wood for the trees. To him the accidental factor in woman's life is the all-important and his conception of her has never got beyond her attributes—and certain only of these. As far as I can make out, he looks upon her as something having a definite and necessary physical relation to man; without that definite and necessary relation she is, as the cant phrase goes, "incomplete."...

To support life it is necessary to have access to the fruits of the earth, either directly—as in the case of the agriculturist—or indirectly, and through a process of exchange as the price of work done in other directions. And in this process of exchange woman, as compared with her male fellow-worker, has always been at a disadvantage. The latter, even where direct access to the earth was denied to him, has usually been granted some measure of choice as to the manner in which he would pay for the necessities the earth produced for him—that

is to say, he was permitted to select the trade by which he earned his livelihood. From woman, who has always been far more completely excluded from direct access to the necessities of life, who has often been barred, both by law and by custom, from the possession of property, one form of payment was demanded, and one only. It was demanded of her that she should enkindle and satisfy the desire of the male, who would thereupon admit her to such share of the property he possessed or earned as should seem good to him. In other words, she exchanged, by the ordinary process of barter, possession of her person for the means of existence.

Whether such a state of things is natural or unnatural I do not pretend to say; but it is, I understand, peculiar to women, having no exact counterpart amongst the females of other species. Its existence, at any rate, justifies us in regarding marriage as essentially (from the woman's point of view) a commercial or trade undertaking....

If it be granted that marriage is, as I have called it, essentially a trade on the part of woman—the exchange of her person for the means of subsistence—it is legitimate to inquire into the manner in which that trade is carried on, and to compare the position of the worker in the matrimonial with the position of the worker in any other market. Which brings us at once to the fact—arising from the compulsory nature of the profession—that it is carried on under disadvantages unknown and unfelt by those who earn their living by other methods. For the regulations governing compulsory service—the institution of slavery and the like—are always framed, not in the interests of the worker, but in the interests of those who impose his work upon him. The regulations governing exchange and barter in the marriage market, therefore, are necessarily framed in the interests of the employer—the male.

... Freedom of bargaining to the best advantage, permitted as a matter of course to every other worker, is denied to her. It is, of course, claimed and exercised by the prostitute class—a class which has pushed to its logical conclusion the principle that woman exists by virtue of a wage paid her in return for the possession of her person; but it is interesting to note that the "unfortunate" enters the open market with the hand of the law extended threateningly above her head. The fact is curious if inquired into: since the theory that woman should live by physical attraction of the opposite sex has never been seriously denied, but rather insisted upon, by men, upon what principle is solicitation, or open offer of such attraction, made a legal offence? (Not because the woman is a danger to the community, since the male sensualist is an equal source of danger.) Only, apparently, because the advance comes from the wrong side. I speak under correction, but cannot, unaided, light upon any other explanation; and mine seems to be borne out by the fact that, in other ranks of life, custom, like the above-mentioned law, strenuously represses any open advance on the part of the woman. So emphatic, indeed, is this unwritten law, that one cannot help suspecting that it was needful it should be emphatic, lest woman, adapting herself to her economic position, should take the initiative in a matter on which her livelihood depended, and deprive her employer not only of the pleasure of the chase, but of the illusion that their common bargain was as much a matter of romance and volition on her part as on his....

With women the endeavour to approximate to a single type has always been compulsory. It is ridiculous to suppose that nature, who never makes two blades of grass alike, desired to turn out indefinite millions of women all cut to the regulation pattern of wifehood: that is to say, all home-loving, charming, submissive, industrious, unintelligent, tidy, possessed with a desire to please, well-dressed, jealous of their own sex, self-sacrificing, cowardly, filled with a burning desire for maternity, endowed with a talent for cooking, narrowly uninterested in the world outside their own gates, and capable of sinking their own identity and interests in the interests and identity of a husband. I imagine that very few women naturally unite in their single persons these characteristics of the class wife; but, having been relegated from birth upwards to the class wife, they had to set to work, with or against the grain, to acquire some semblance of those that they knew were lacking....

[T]he trade of marriage is, by its very nature, an isolated trade, permitting of practically no organization or common action amongst the workers; and consequently the marriage-trained woman (and nearly all women are marriage-trained—or perhaps it would be more correct to say marriage expectant) enters industrial life with no tradition of such organization and common action behind her....

Woman's intercourse with her kind has been much more limited in extent, and very often purely and narrowly social in character. Until comparatively recent years it was unusual for women to form one of a large body of persons working under similar conditions and conscious of similar interests. It is scarcely to be wondered at that the modern system of industrialism with its imperative need for co-operation and common effort should have found her—thanks to her training—unprepared and entirely at a disadvantage.

... A good many causes have combined to bring about the sweating of women customary in most, if not all, departments of the labour market; but it seems to me that not the least of those causes is the long-established usage of regarding the work of a wife in the home as valueless from the economic point of view—a thing to be paid for (if paid for at all) by occasional gushes of sentiment. Woman and wife being, according to masculine ideas, interchangeable terms, it follows that, since the labour of a wife is valueless from the economic point of view, the labour of any woman is valueless. Naturally enough, this persistent undervaluing of her services has had its effect upon woman herself; having been taught for generations that she must expect nothing but the lowest possible wage for her work, she finds considerable difficulty in realizing that it is worth more—and undersells her male competitor. Thereupon angry objections on the part of the male competitor, who fails to realize that cheap female labour is one of the inevitable results of the complete acceptance by woman of the tradition of her own inferiority to himself....

The habit of judging a woman entirely by externals—appearance, dress, and manners—is not confined to the man who is in search of a wife. ("Judging" is, perhaps, the wrong phrase to use—it is, rather, a habit of resigning judgment so as to fall completely under the influence of externals.) It is very general amongst all classes of male employers, and its result is, it seems to me, a serious bar to efficiency in women's work. It pays better in the marriage market to be attractive than to be efficient, and in a somewhat lesser degree the same rule holds good in certain other departments of women's labour....

One result of the assumption that every woman is provided with the necessaries of life by a husband, father, or other male relative is that the atmosphere which surrounds the working-woman is considerably more chilling than that which surrounds the working-man. His right to work is recognized; hers is not. He is more or less helped, stimulated, and encouraged to work; she is not. On the contrary, her entry into the paid labour market is often discouraged and resented. The difference is, perhaps, most clearly marked in those middle-class families where sons and daughters alike have no expectation of independence by inheritance, but where money, time, and energy are spent in the anxious endeavour to train and find suitable openings for the sons, and the daughters left to shift for themselves and find openings as they can. The young man begins his life in an atmosphere of encouragement and help; the young woman in one of discouragement, or, at best, of indifference....

If humanity had only been created in order to reproduce its kind, we might still be dodging cave-bears in the intervals of grubbing up roots with our nails. It is not only the children who matter: there is the world into which they are born. ... [T]hose women who are proving by their lives that marriage is not a necessity for them, that maternity is not a necessity for them, are preparing a heritage of fuller humanity for the daughters of others—who will be daughters of their own in the spirit, if not in the flesh. The home of the future will be more of an abiding-place and less of a prison because they have made it obvious that, so far as many women are concerned, the home can be done without; and if the marriage of the future is what it ought to be—a voluntary contract on both sides—it will be because they have proved the right of every woman to refuse it if she will, by demonstrating that there are other means of earning a livelihood than bearing children and keeping house. It is the woman without a husband to support her, the woman who has no home but such as she makes for herself by her own efforts, who is forcing a reluctant masculine generation to realize that she is something more than the breeding factor of the race. By her very existence she is altering the male conception of her sex.

Female Suffrage

The first piece included in this section is an anonymous poem written by one of the many women imprisoned in London's Holloway Prison during March and April of 1912. Like many of these suffragettes, the poem's speaker has been jailed for window-breaking. "Suffragettes" was a term that originated in 1906 to differentiate the militant members of the Women's Social and Political Union (WSPU) from more moderate "suffragists." Also below is an excerpt from the autobiography of Emmeline Pankhurst, who started the WSPU and who was arrested many times for her militant activities. The WSPU's mission was to campaign for votes for women on the same terms they were granted to men; its motto was "Deeds, not Words." Much as the WSPU suffragettes were comparatively militant, however, they still relied upon means that did not threaten human life—for example, cutting telephone wires, burning or bombing empty buildings, throwing stones, and breaking windows. Once in jail, many of these women, including Pankhurst, continued their protests through hunger strikes. Pankhurst, however, called a temporary suspension of militant activities at the outbreak of World War I and requested all her followers to support the war effort. By 1917 it appeared that women would soon be granted the vote. In February 1918 royal assent was given to the Representation of the People Act, which gave the vote to any women over thirty who were householders, wives of householders, or graduates from universities. In July 1928 a new law granted all women over twenty-one voting rights on equal terms with men.

Anonymous, ["There Was a Small Woman Called G"] (1912)

There was a small woman called G,
Who smashed two big windows at B—
They sent her to jail, her fate to bewail,
For votes must be kept, must be kept for the male.

5 They asked that small woman called G,
Why she smashed those big windows at B—

She made a long speech, then made her defence,
But it wasn't no use, their heads were so dense;
They just hummed the refrain, although it is stale—
10   Votes must be kept, must be kept for the male.

They sent her to H for six months and a day,
In the coach Black Maria[1] she went sadly away;
But she sang in this strain, as it jolted and rumbled,
We will have the vote, we will not be humbled.
15   We must have the vote by hill and by dale,
Votes shall not alone be kept for the male.

"When Women Get into Parliament," *Daily Mirror*, 30 November 1918. The caption below this picture reads "Will they, in firm maternal manner, soothe the mere male legislator and teach him how to behave? There appears to be some fear amongst male politicians that their feminine rivals will completely control them."

---

[1] *Black Maria* Vehicle for transporting prisoners.

from Emmeline Pankhurst, *My Own Story* (1914)

Emmeline Pankhurst's husband, Dr. Richard Pankhurst (whom she mentions below), was a radical lawyer and advocate for women's rights. It was after her husband's unexpected death in 1898, a devastating blow to her, that Pankhurst formed the WSPU. She also toured the United States and Canada several times, speaking on women's issues and on her attempts to gain the vote for women in England. When the bill was passed in 1928 giving the vote to all women over 21, Prime Minister Stanley Baldwin unveiled a statue of Pankhurst in Victoria Tower Gardens, near the Houses of Parliament.

I was between eighteen and nineteen when I finally returned from school in Paris and took my place in my father's home as a finished young lady. I sympathised with and worked for the woman-suffrage movement, and came to know Dr. Pankhurst, whose work for woman suffrage had never ceased. It was Dr. Pankhurst who drafted the first enfranchisement bill, known as the Women's Disabilities Removal Bill, and introduced into the House of Commons in 1870 by Jacob Bright. The bill advanced to its second reading by a majority vote of thirty-three, but it was killed in committee by Mr. Gladstone's[2] peremptory orders. Dr. Pankhurst, as I have already said, with another distinguished barrister, Lord Coleridge, acted as counsel for the Manchester women, who tried in 1868 to be placed on the register as voters. He also drafted the bill giving married women absolute control over their property and earnings, a bill which became law in 1882.[3] My marriage with Dr. Pankhurst took place in 1879.

I think we cannot be too grateful to the group of men and women who, like Dr. Pankhurst, in those early days lent the weight of their honoured names to the suffrage movement in the trials of its struggling youth. These men did not wait until the movement became popular, nor did they hesitate until it was plain that women were roused to the point of revolt. They worked all their lives with those who were organising, educating,

---

[2] *Gladstone* William Gladstone, who was British Prime Minister on four separate occasions (1868–74, 1880–85, 1886, and 1892–94).

[3] *He also … 1882* The Married Women's Property Act.

and preparing for the revolt which was one day to come. Unquestionably those pioneer men suffered in popularity for their feminist views. Some of them suffered financially, some politically. Yet they never wavered.

My married life lasted through nineteen happy years. Often I have heard the taunt that suffragists are women who have failed to find any normal outlet for their emotions, and are therefore soured and disappointed beings. This is probably not true of any suffragist, and it is most certainly not true of me....

Gladstone was an implacable foe of woman suffrage. He believed that women's work and politics lay in service to men's parties. One of the shrewdest acts of Mr. Gladstone's career was his disruption of the suffrage organisation in England. He accomplished this by substituting "something just as good," that something being Women's Liberal Associations. Beginning in 1881 in Bristol, these associations spread rapidly through the country and, in 1887, became a National Women's Liberal Federation. The promise of the Federation was that by allying themselves with men in party politics, women would soon earn the right to vote. The avidity with which the women swallowed this promise, left off working for themselves, and threw themselves into the men's work was amazing....

I am told that women in America have recently allied themselves with political parties, believing, just as we did, that such action would break down opposition to suffrage by showing the men that women possess political ability, and that politics is work for women as well as men. Let them not be deceived. I can assure the American women that our long alliance with the great parties, our devotion to party programmes, our faithful work at elections, never advanced the suffrage cause one step....

The foundation of our policy is opposition to a Government who refuse votes to women. To support by word or deed a Government hostile to woman suffrage is simply to invite them to go on being hostile. We oppose the Liberal Party because it is in power. We would oppose a Unionist government if it were in power and were opposed to woman suffrage. We say to women that as long as they remain in the ranks of the Liberal Party they give their tacit approval to the Government's anti-suffrage policy. We say to Members of Parliament that as long as they support any of the Government's policies they give their tacit approval to the anti-suffrage policy. We call upon all sincere suffragists to leave the Liberal Party until women are given votes on equal terms with men. We call upon all voters to vote against Liberal candidates until the Liberal Government does justice to women....

The contention of the old-fashioned suffragists, and of the politicians as well, has always been that an educated public opinion will ultimately give votes to women without any great force being exerted in behalf of the reform. We agree that public opinion must be educated, but we contend that even an educated public opinion is useless unless it is vigorously utilised. The keenest weapon is powerless unless it is courageously wielded. In the year 1906 there was an immensely large public opinion in favour of woman suffrage. But what good did that do the cause? We called upon the public for a great deal more than sympathy. We called upon it to demand of the Government to yield to public opinion and give women votes. And we declared that we would wage war, not only on all anti-suffrage forces, but on all neutral and non-active forces. Every man with a vote was considered a foe to woman suffrage unless he was prepared to be actively a friend.

Militant suffragette Emily Davidson was hit by King George V's horse in 1913 at the Epsom Derby after running onto the racecourse waving banners of the WSPU. She suffered a skull fracture and died of the injury five days later. It is not clear whether she intended to become a martyr to the cause, but her fellow suffragettes honored her as one.

from Marie Stopes, *Married Love* (1918)

Marie Stopes's best-selling treatise on marriage, *Married Love*, was based on her own sexological research, on an analysis of her own experiences and feelings concerning sexuality, and on her exposure to the ideas of American birth control campaigner Margaret Sanger. Stopes (1880-1958) later became an active birth control advocate herself, and her later works deal more explicitly with the topic (which is only mentioned briefly in *Married Love*). Here she focuses on the practical problems, both physical and emotional, that many couples face. Stopes herself claimed to have married in complete ignorance of the physical details of sex, and she sought an annulment to her 1910 marriage to Canadian botanist Reginald Gates, claiming that the marriage had never been consummated.

AUTHOR'S PREFACE

More than ever today are happy homes needed. It is my hope that this book may serve the State by adding to their numbers. Its object is to increase the joys of marriage, and to show how much sorrow may be avoided.

The only secure basis for a present-day State is the welding of its units in marriage; but there is rottenness and danger at the foundations of the State if many of the marriages are unhappy. Today, particularly in the middle classes in this country, marriage is far less really happy than its surface appears. Too many who marry expecting joy are bitterly disappointed; and the demand for "freedom" grows; while those who cry aloud are generally unaware that it is more likely to have been their own ignorance than the "marriage-bond" which was the origin of their unhappiness.

It is never *easy* to make marriage a lovely thing; and it is an achievement beyond the powers of the selfish, or the mentally cowardly. Knowledge is needed and, as things are at present, knowledge is almost unobtainable by those who are most in want of it.

The problems of the sex-life are infinitely complex, and for their solution urgently demand both sympathy and scientific research.

I have some things to say about sex, which, so far as I am aware, have not yet been said, things which seem to be of profound importance to men and women who hope to make their marriages beautiful. ...

MARRIED LOVE

It has become a tradition of our social life that the ignorance of woman about her own body and that of her future husband is a flower-like innocence. And to such an extreme is this sometimes pushed, that not seldom is a girl married unaware that married life will bring her into physical relations with her husband fundamentally different from those with her brother. When she discovers the true nature of his body, and learns the part she has to play as a wife, she may refuse utterly to agree to her husband's wishes. I know one pair of which the husband, chivalrous and loving, had to wait years before his bride recovered from the shock of the discovery of the meaning of marriage and was able to allow him a natural relation. There have been not a few brides whom the horror of the first night of marriage with a man less considerate has driven to suicide or insanity.

That girls can reach a marriageable age without some knowledge of the realities of marriage would seem incredible were it not a fact. One highly educated lady intimately known to me told me that when she was about eighteen she suffered many months of agonising apprehension that she was about to have a baby because a man had snatched a kiss from her lips at a dance. And another girl told me she also not only suffered in the same way mentally, but that this fear of the results of a mere kiss so affected her that menstruation was suppressed for months.

When girls so brought up are married it is a *rape* for the husband to insist on his "marital rights" at once. It will be difficult or impossible for such a bride ever after to experience the joys of sex-union, for such a beginning must imprint upon her consciousness the view that the man's animal nature dominates him. ...

It should be realised that a man does not woo and win a woman once for all when he marries her: *he must woo her before every separate act of coitus*, for each act corresponds to a marriage as other creatures know it. Wild animals are not so foolish as man; a wild animal does not unite with his female without the wooing characteristics of his race, whether by stirring her by a display of his strength in fighting another male, or by exhibiting his beautiful feathers or song. And he must not forget that the wild animals are assisted by nature; they generally only woo just at the season when the female is beginning to feel natural desire. But man, who wants his mate all out of season as well as in it, has a double duty to perform, and must himself rouse, charm, and stimulate her to the local readiness which would have been to some extent naturally prepared for him had he waited till her own desire welled up. But here it is necessary to repeat what cannot be too vividly realised: woman's love is stirred *primarily* through her heart and mind, and the perfect lover need not lag awaiting her bodily and spontaneous help, but can rouse and raise it to follow their soaring minds.

To render a woman ready before uniting with her is not only the merest act of humanity to save her pain, but is of value from the man's point of view, for (unless he is one of those relatively few abnormal and diseased variants who delight only in rape) the man gains an immense increase of sensation from the mutuality thus attained, and the health of both the man and the woman is most beneficially affected.

Assuming now that the two are in the closest mental and spiritual, as well as sensory harmony: in what position should the act be consummated? Men and women, looking into each other's eyes, kissing tenderly on the mouth, with their arms round each other, meet face to face. And that position is symbolic of the coming together of the two who meet gladly.

It seems incredible that today educated men should be found who—apparently on theological grounds—refuse to countenance any other position. Yet one wife told me that she was crushed and nearly suffocated by her husband, so that it took her hours to recover after each union, but that "on principle" he refused to attempt any other position than the one he chose to consider normal, although he was ignorant of so obvious a requirement as that he should support his weight on his elbows. Mutual well-being should be the guide for each pair.

A rigidity of mental as well as physical capacity seems to characterise some excellent and well-meaning people, and among those whose marriages fail to reach that height of perfection in a physical sense which they intellectually desire are those who are either entirely ignorant that sex-union may be accomplished in many various positions, or those who consider any other position but the most usual one to be wrong.

Yet, curiously enough, it sometimes comes to light that a pair do not even know the usual position, and in my own experience several couples who have failed to have children, or have failed to obtain the complete delight of union, have revealed that the woman did not know that it is not only her arms which should embrace her lover. Consequently, entry was to him both difficult and sometimes impossible....

It is utterly impossible, organised as our bodies are at present, for us to obey the dictates of theologians and refrain from the destruction of potential life. The germ-[1]cells of the woman, though immeasurably less numerous than the male germ-cells (the sperm), yet develop uselessly over and over again in every celibate as well as in every married woman; while myriads of sperm-cells are destroyed even in the process of the act which does ensure fertilisation of the woman by the single favoured sperm. If the theologians really mean what they say, and demand the voluntary effort of complete celibacy for all men, save for the purpose of procreation, this will *not* achieve their end of preventing the destruction of all potential life; and the monthly loss of unfertilised egg-cell by women is beyond all the efforts of the will to curb. Nature, not man, arranged the destruction of potential life against which ascetic Bishops rage.

If then, throughout the greater part of their lives the germinal cells of both sexes inevitably disintegrate without creating an embryo, there can be nothing wrong in selecting the most favourable moment possible for the conception of the first of these germinal cells to be endowed with the supreme privilege of creating a new life.

What generally happens in marriage where this is not thought of is that one of the very earliest unions results in the fertilisation of the wife, so that the young pair have a baby nine months, or a little more, after

---

[1] *germ* I.e., in the sense of seed; the part of an organism that is capable of developing into a new organism.

marriage.

Whereas, were they wise and did they realise the full significance of what they were doing, they would allow at least six months or a year to elapse before beginning the supreme task of their lives, the burden of which falls mainly upon the woman.

For many reasons it is more ideal to have the children spontaneously and early; but if economic conditions are hard, as they so often are in "civilised" life, it may be better to marry and defer the children rather than not to marry....

The child, conceived in rapture and hope, should be given every material chance which the wisdom and love of the parents can devise. And the first and *most* vital condition of its health is that the mother should be well and happy and free from anxiety while she bears it.

The tremendous and far-reaching effects of marriage on the woman's whole organism make her less fitted to bear a child at the very commencement of marriage than later on, when the system will have adjusted itself to its new conditions.

Not only for the sake of the child, however, should the first conception be a little delayed, but also to secure the lasting happiness of the married lovers. It is generally (though perhaps not always) wise thoroughly to establish their relation to each other before introducing the inevitable dislocation and readjustment necessitated by the wife's pregnancy and the birth of a child.

from Virginia Woolf, *Orlando* (1928)

Virginia Woolf (1882–1941) wrote *Orlando*, a fantastical fictional biography, as a tribute to her friend (and, it has been speculated, her lover), Vita Sackville-West. The novel recounts the life of Orlando, whose life spans three hundred years and two sexes. The excerpt below, which falls midway through the novel, follows shortly after the narrator's revelation that Orlando—formerly a young nobleman—has woken from a deep slumber to discover that "he was a woman." Though unchanged in personality, Orlando must now, of course, adopt a woman's typical dress, habits, and lifestyle.

There is much to support the view that it is clothes that wear us and not we them; we may make them take the mould of arm or breast, but they mould our hearts, our brains, our tongues to their liking. So, having now worn skirts for a considerable time, a certain change was visible in Orlando.... If we compare the picture of Orlando as a man with that of Orlando as a woman we shall see that though both are undoubtedly one and the same person, there are certain changes. The man has his hand free to seize his sword, the woman must use hers to keep the satins from slipping from her shoulders. The man looks the world full in the face, as if it were made for his uses and fashioned to his liking. The woman takes a sidelong glance at it, full of subtlety, even of suspicion. Had they both worn the same clothes, it is possible that their outlook might have been the same.

That is the view of some philosophers and wise ones, but on the whole, we incline to another. The difference between the sexes is, happily, one of great profundity. Clothes are but a symbol of something hid deep beneath. It was a change in Orlando herself that dictated her choice of a woman's dress and of a woman's sex. And perhaps in this she was only expressing rather more openly than usual—openness indeed was the soul of her nature—something that happens to most people without being thus plainly expressed. For here again, we come to a dilemma. Different though the sexes are, they intermix. In every human being a vacillation from one sex to the other takes place, and often it is only the clothes that keep the male or female likeness, while underneath the sex is the very opposite of what it is above. Of the complications and confusions which thus result everyone has had experience; but here we leave the general question and note only the odd effect it had in the particular case of Orlando herself.

For it was this mixture in her of man and woman, one being uppermost and then the other, that often gave her conduct an unexpected turn. The curious of her own sex would argue, for example, if Orlando was a woman, how did she never take more than ten minutes to dress? And were not her clothes chosen rather at random, and sometimes worn rather shabby? And then they would say, still, she has none of the formality of a man, or a man's love of power. She is excessively tender-hearted. She could not endure to see a donkey beaten or a kitten drowned. Yet again, they noted, she detested household matters, was up at dawn and out among the fields in summer before the sun had risen. No farmer knew more about the crops than she did. She could drink with the best and liked games of hazard. She rode well and drove six horses at a gallop over London Bridge. Yet again, though bold and active as a man, it was remarked that the sight of another in danger brought on the most womanly palpitations. She would burst into tears on slight provocation. She was unversed in geography, found mathematics intolerable, and held some caprices which are more common among women than men, as for instance that to travel south is to travel downhill.

from George Orwell, "Boys' Weeklies" (*Horizon*, March 1940)

You never walk far through any poor quarter in any big town without coming upon a small news agent's shop. The general appearance of these shops is always very much the same: a few posters for the *Daily Mail* and the *News of the World* outside, a poky little window with sweet-bottles and packets of Players,[1] and a dark interior smelling of liquorice allsorts and festooned from floor to ceiling with vilely printed twopenny papers, most of them with lurid cover illustrations in three colours.

Except for the daily and evening papers, the stock of these shops hardly overlaps at all with that of the big newsagents. Their main selling line is the twopenny weekly, and the number and variety of these are almost unbelievable. Every hobby and pastime—cage-birds, fretwork, carpentering, bees, carrier-pigeons, home conjuring, philately, chess—has at least one paper devoted to it, and generally several....

Probably the contents of these shops is the best available indication of what the mass of the English people really feels and thinks. Certainly nothing half so revealing exists in documentary form....

Here I am only dealing with a single series of papers, the boys' twopenny weeklies, often inaccurately described as "penny dreadfuls." Falling strictly within this class there are at present ten papers, the *Gem*,

Magnet, *Modern Boy*, *Triumph* and *Champion*, all owned by the Amalgamated Press, and the *Wizard*, *Rover*, *Skipper*, *Hotspur* and *Adventure*, all owned by D. C. Thompson & Co. What the circulations of these papers are, I do not know.... But there is no question that the combined public of the ten papers is a very large one: They are on sale in every town in England, and nearly every boy who reads at all goes through a phase of reading one or more of them. The *Gem* and *Magnet*, which are much the oldest of these papers, are of rather different type from the rest, and they have evidently lost some of their popularity during the past few years. A good many boys now regard them as old-fashioned and "slow." Nevertheless I want to discuss them first, because they are more interesting psychologically than the others, and also because the mere survival of such papers into the nineteen-thirties is a rather startling phenomenon....

The *Gem* and *Magnet* are sister-papers (characters out of one paper frequently appear in the other), and were both started more than thirty years ago.... Each of them carries every week a fifteen- or twenty-thousand word school story, complete in itself, but usually more or less connected with the story of the week before....

Needless to say, these stories are fantastically unlike life at a real public school. They run in cycles of rather differing types, but in general they are the clean-fun, knockabout type of story, with interest centring round horseplay, practical jokes, ragging masters, fights, canings, football, cricket and food. A constantly recurring story is one in which a boy is accused of some misdeed committed by another and is too much of a sportsman to reveal the truth. The "good" boys are "good" in the clean-living Englishman tradition—they keep in hard training, wash behind their ears, never hit below the belt, etc. etc.—and by way of contrast there is a series of "bad" boys, Racke, Crooke, Loder and others, whose badness consists in betting, smoking cigarettes and frequenting public houses.[2] All these boys are constantly on the verge of expulsion, but as it would mean a change of personnel if any boy were actually expelled, no one is ever caught out in any really serious offence. Stealing, for instance, barely enters as a motif. Sex is completely taboo, especially in the form in which

---

[1] *Players* Brand of cigarettes.

[2] *public houses* Pubs, taverns.

it actually arises at public schools. Occasionally girls enter into the stories, and very rarely there is something approaching a mild flirtation, but it is always entirely in the spirit of clean fun. A boy and a girl enjoy going for bicycle rides together—that is all it ever amounts to. Kissing, for instance, would be regarded as "soppy." Even the bad boys are presumed to be completely sexless. When the *Gem* and *Magnet* were started, it is probable that there was a deliberate intention to get away from the guilty sex-ridden atmosphere that pervaded so much of the earlier literature for boys. In the nineties the *Boy's Own Paper*, for instance, used to have its correspondence columns full of terrifying warnings against masturbation, and books like *St. Winifred's* and *Tom Brown's Schooldays* were heavy with homosexual feeling, though no doubt the authors were not fully aware of it. In the *Gem* and *Magnet* sex simply does not exist as a problem....

Naturally the politics of the *Gem* and *Magnet* are Conservative, but in a completely pre-1914 style, with no Fascist tinge. In reality their basic political assumptions are two: nothing ever changes, and foreigners are funny. In the *Gem* of 1939 Frenchmen are still Froggies and Italians are still Dagoes. Mossoo, the French master at Greyfriars, is the usual comic-paper Frog, with pointed beard, pegtop trousers,[1] etc. Inky, the Indian boy, though a rajah, and therefore possessing snob-appeal, is also the comic babu of the *Punch*[2] tradition. ("'The rowfulness is not the proper caper, my esteemed Bob,' said Inky. 'Let dogs delight in the barkfulness and bitefulness, but the soft answer is the cracked pitcher that goes longest to a bird in the bush, as the English proverb remarks.'") Fisher T. Fish is the old-style stage Yankee ("'Waal, I guess,'" etc.) dating from a period of Anglo-American jealousy. Wun Lung, the Chinese boy (he has rather faded out of late, no doubt because some of the Magnet's readers are Straits Chinese),[3] is the nineteenth-century pantomime Chinaman, with saucer-shaped hat, pigtail and pidgin-English....

---

[1] *pegtop trousers* Pants that are cut wide at the hips and narrow at the ankles.

[2] *Punch* A satirical weekly magazine.

[3] *Straits Chinese* Chinese people from the Straits Settlements, on the Malay Peninsula.

from Frank Richard, "Frank Richard Replies to George Orwell" (*Horizon*, May 1940)

The Editor has kindly given me space to reply to Mr. Orwell, whose article on Boys' Weeklies appeared in *Horizon* No. 3. Mr. Orwell's article is a rather remarkable one to appear in a periodical of this kind. From the fact that *Horizon* contains a picture that does not resemble a picture, a poem that does not resemble poetry, and a story that does not resemble a story, I conclude that it must be a very high-browed paper indeed: and I was agreeable surprised, therefore, to find in it an article written in a lively and entertaining manner, and actually readable. I was still more interested as this article dealt chiefly with my work as an author for boys. Mr. Orwell perpetrates so many inaccuracies, however, and flicks off his condemnations with so careless a hand, that I am glad of the opportunity to set him right on a few points.

... "Sex," says Mr. Orwell, "is completely taboo." Mr. Noel Coward,[4] in his autobiography, is equally amused at the absence of the sex-motif in the *Magnet* series. But what would Mr. Orwell have? The *Magnet* is intended chiefly for readers up to sixteen; though I am proud to know that it has readers of sixty! It is read by girls as well as boys. Would it do these children good, or harm, to turn their thoughts to such matters? Sex, certainly, does enter uncomfortably into the experience of the adolescent. But surely the less he thinks about it, at an early age, the better. I am aware that, in these "modern" days, there are people who think that children should be told things of which in my own childhood no small person was ever allowed to hear. I disagree with this entirely. My own opinion is that such people generally suffer from disordered digestions, which cause their minds to take a nasty turn. They fancy that they are "realists," when they are only obscene. They go grubbing in the sewers for their realism, and refuse to believe in the grass and flowers above ground—which, nevertheless, are equally real! Moreover, this "motif" does not play so stupendous a part in real life, among healthy and wholesome people, as these "realists" imagine. If Mr. Orwell supposes that the average Sixth-form boy cuddles a parlour-maid as often as he handles

---

[4] *Mr. Noel Coward* English playwright (1899–1953).

UP, CLERKS, AND AT 'EM!

INSTEAD OF SITTING AT HIS DESK AND "DOING HIS DUTY IN THAT STATE OF LIFE ETC."—

WHY DOESN'T A CLERK—SUITABLY DRESSED FOR THE PART—HIT THE MANAGER ON THE HEAD WITH A RULER—

HOLD UP THE CASHIER WITH A GUN—

TRANSFER THE CONTENTS OF THE PETTY CASH BOX TO HIS HIP POCKET—

CARRY OFF THE LOVELY TYPIST—

AND—IGNORING BRIDGES—SWIM ACROSS THE THAMES!—SOME PEOPLE SEEM TO EXPECT SOMETHING OF THE SORT FROM HIM.

WHAT A MAN!

Some people appear to think that a clerk should be like a cinema "sheikh." The poor hard-worked fellows are accused of being "spineless."

"Up, Clerks, and At 'Em!" *Daily Mirror*, 13 May 1921. The term "sheikh" (used to mean "strong, romantic lover") became popular after the 1919 E.M. Hull novel *The Sheik* and the 1921 movie adaptation *The Sheikh*.[1]

a cricket-bat, Mr. Orwell is in error.

... As for foreigners being funny, I must shock Mr. Orwell by telling him that foreigners are funny. They lack the sense of humour which is the special gift to our own chosen nation: and people without a sense of humour are always unconsciously funny. Take Hitler, for example, with his swastika, his "good German sword," his fortifications named after characters from Wagner, his military coat that he will never take off till he marches home victorious: and the rest of his fripperies out of the property-box.[2] In Germany they lap

---

[1] *Sheikh* In the larger picture, this corruption of a word that, properly speaking, denotes the head of an Arabic group or a Muslim leader, is one of the cruder manifestations of Orientalism—the tendency among Westerners to represent those from the East as part of an exotic "other."

[2] *property-box* Box in which theatrical properties ("props") are kept.

this up like milk, with the most awful seriousness; in England, the play-acting ass would be laughed out of existence. Take Mussolini—can anyone imagine a fat man in London talking the balderdash that Benito talks in Rome to wildly-cheering audiences, without evoking, not wild cheers, but inextinguishable laughter? But is Il Duce regarded as a mountebank[1] in Italy? Very far from it. I submit to Mr. Orwell that people who take their theatricals seriously are funny. The fact that Adolf Hitler is deadly dangerous does not make him less comic.

from Robert Roberts, *The Classic Slum* (1971)

The Classic Slum, which Robert Roberts published to extensive critical claim, is his attempt to counteract what he saw as romanticized depictions of working-class communities by sociologists. Blending social history and autobiography, the memoir describes his hometown of Salford, Lancashire, in the years before World War I. The excerpt below addresses issues of gender, class, and sexual orientation.

In the forty years before 1915 the national birth rate itself had fallen from 35.5 per thousand of the population to 24. It seems most likely that the general decline was due to an increasing knowledge among the working classes of the use of contraceptives and the bolder practice of abortion. Artificial checks on conception could be bought as early as the 1820s and rubber vaginal caps from 1881. Increasing literacy no doubt went some way to spreading a knowledge of their existence; yet in the ordinary working-class bed, while coitus interruptus remained permissible, any artificial interference with the will of God aroused nothing but abhorrence. Still, among the "low," certain homely safeguards against conception had been known for generations, especially the small piece of oiled sponge with tapes hopefully attached[2] adopted by women.

Common, too, was the home-made pessary,[3] a compound of lard (later margarine) and flour. This, thoughtfully carried in the handbag and judiciously used, saved many a girl's honour. Bolder females had bolder methods, all designed for the same purpose. But by now the sheath, long bought discreetly by the middle classes, had become familiar to many manual workers. Even before 1914 several small societies were at work propagating methods of birth control, the most prominent perhaps being the "Liberator League," with its manual *What women ought to know on the subject of sex*. From 1919 on Marie Stopes's pamphlet *A letter to working mothers*, price 6d,[4] had a very wide sale. While such works would be read only by the more intelligent and liberal-minded in the working class, verbal instruction was undoubtedly passed on to those in the lower social layers. Here again the corner shop played its part. The fall in the bastardy rate seems to have been due more to newly acquired skills than to moral restraint or fear of father. By 1920 no youngster having gone from school into mine, mill or factory could remain ignorant for long of the existence of "rubber" stores and the uses of the goods they sold. By now "surgical" was a dirty word....

Men in the lower working class, aping their social betters, displayed virility by never performing any task in or about the home which was considered by tradition to be women's work. Some wives encouraged their partners in this and proudly boasted that they would never allow the "man of the house" to do a "hand's turn." Derisive names like "mop rag" and "diddy man" were used for those who did help. Nevertheless, kindlier husbands, especially when their wives were near exhaustion at the end of a day or in the last stages of a pregnancy, would willingly do housework, cooking, washing the children or scrubbing a floor, provided doors remained locked and neighbours uninformed....

The male weakling in certain households, often known even through manhood as "Sonny," could be a subject of whispered concern among neighbours. He was usually "delicate." In pub and workshop there was

---

[1] *mountebank* Charlatan.

[2] [Roberts's note] The method was said to have been introduced from France by Robert Owen of New Lanark in the early years of the nineteenth century. But many women scorn this theory; an artifice so obvious, they claim, must have been invented even before the wheel!

[3] *pessary* Vaginal suppository intended to provide a barrier to conception.

[4] *d* Pence.

plenty of talk, *sub rosa*,[1] about the unspeakable. The working class, always fascinated by the great criminal trials, had been stirred to its depths by the prosecution of Oscar Wilde in 1895. As late as the First World War the ribald cry heard in factories, "Watch out for oscarwile!" mystified raw young apprentices. The proletariat knew and marked what they considered to be sure signs of homosexuality, though the term was unknown. Any evidence of dandyism in the young was severely frowned on. One "mother-bound" youth among us, son of a widow and clerk in a city warehouse, strolled out on Sundays wearing of all things gloves, "low quarters"[2] and carrying an umbrella! The virile damned him at once—an incipient "nancy" beyond all doubt, especially since he was known to be learning to play the violin. Among ignorant men any interest in music, books or the arts in general, learning or even courtesy and intelligence could make one suspect. This linking of homosexuality with culture played some part, I believe, in keeping the lower working class as near-illiterate as they were.

from E.M. Forster "Terminal Note" to *Maurice* (1971)

E.M. Forster's novel *Maurice*, which was written in 1913–14 (although it was not published until after Forster's death, as a result of its then controversial subject matter), was, Forster claimed, "the direct result of a visit to Edward Carpenter at Milthorpe. Carpenter had a prestige which cannot be understood today." In the novel, the protagonist realizes his true nature through a love for another man that is "harmonious, immense, pouring into it the dignity as well as the richness of being." The novel challenges many of the entrenched values of early twentieth-century Britain; in the words of Maurice's lover, Clive, as long as "these people ... talk of the unspeakable vice of the Greeks they can't expect fair play." On the novel's dedication page appear the words "Begun 1913. Finished 1914. Dedicated to a happier year." Forster's "Terminal Note" was written in 1960.

---

[1] *sub rosa*   Latin: under the rose; i.e., secretly.

[2] *low quarters*   I.e., Oxford shoes, low-heeled shoes laced over the instep.

Note in conclusion on a word hitherto unmentioned. Since *Maurice* was written there has been a change in the public attitude here: the change from ignorance and terror to familiarity and contempt. It is not the change towards which Edward Carpenter had worked. He had hoped for the generous recognition of an emotion and for the reintegration of something primitive[3] into the common stock. And I, though less optimistic, had supposed that knowledge would bring understanding. We had not realized that what the public really loathes in homosexuality is not the thing itself but having to think about it. If it could be slipped into our midst unnoticed, or legalized overnight by a decree in small print, there would be few protests. Unfortunately it can only be legalized by Parliament, and Members of Parliament are obliged to think or to appear to think. Consequently, the Wolfenden recommendations[4] will be indefinitely rejected, police prosecutions will continue....

from Virginia Woolf, "Old Bloomsbury" (1976)

Virginia Woolf composed this autobiographical essay to be read aloud to the Memoir Club, a group that formed in 1920 and included most of the original members of the Bloomsbury group. Members would get together to dine and listen to one another's memoirs. "Old Bloomsbury" describes the period in the Bloomsbury group's history after the marriage of Woolf's sister Vanessa to the critic Clive Bell, in 1907.

Another scene has always lived in my memory—I do not know if I invented it or not—as the best illustration of Bloomsbury Chapter Two. It was a spring evening. Vanessa and I were sitting in the drawing room.... At any moment Clive might come in and he and

---

[3] *primitive*   Here, elemental, forceful.

[4] *Wolfenden recommendations*   The 1957 Report of the Departmental Committee on Homosexual Offences and Prostitution, chaired by Lord Wolfenden and informally known as the Wolfenden Report, put forward the then highly controversial recommendation that "homosexual behaviour between consenting adults in private should no longer be a criminal offence." A decade later that recommendation was finally implemented after the 1967 Sexual Offences Act narrowly passed a parliamentary vote.

I should begin to argue amicably, impersonally at first; soon we should be hurling abuse at each other and pacing up and down the room. Vanessa sat silent and did something mysterious with her needle or her scissors. I talked, egotistically, excitedly, about my own affairs no doubt. Suddenly the door opened and the long and sinister figure of Mr. Lytton Strachey stood on the threshold. He pointed his finger at a stain on Vanessa's white dress.

"Semen?" he said.

Can one really say it? I thought and we burst out laughing. With that one word all barriers of reticence and reserve went down. A flood of the sacred fluid seemed to overwhelm us. Sex permeated our conversation. The word bugger was never far from our lips. We discussed copulation with the same excitement and openness that we had discussed the nature of good. It is strange to think how reticent, how reserved we had been and for how long. It seems a marvel now that so late as the year 1908 or 9 Clive had blushed and I had blushed too when I asked him to let me pass to go to the lavatory on the French Express. I never dreamt of asking Vanessa to tell me what happened on her wedding night. Thoby and Adrian[1] would have died rather than discuss the love affairs of undergraduates. When all intellectual questions had been debated so freely, sex was ignored. Now a flood of light poured in upon that department too. We had known everything but we had never talked. Now we talked of nothing else. We listened with rapt interest to the love affairs of the buggers. We followed the ups and downs of their chequered histories; Vanessa sympathetically; I—had I not written in 1905, women are so much more amusing than men—frivolously, laughingly. "Norton tells me," Vanessa would say, "that James is in utter despair. Rupert has been twice to bed with Hobhouse" and I would cap her stories with some equally thrilling piece of gossip; about a divine undergraduate with a head like a Greek God—but alas his teeth were bad—called George Mallory.

All this had the result that the old sentimental views of marriage in which we were brought up were revolutionized. I should be sorry to tell you how old I was before I saw that there is nothing shocking in a man's having a mistress, or in a woman's being one. Perhaps the

46 Gordon Square, London.

fidelity of our parents was not the only or inevitably the highest form of married life. Perhaps indeed that fidelity was not so strict as one had supposed. "Of course Kitty Maxse has two or three lovers," said Clive—Kitty Maxse, the chaste, the exquisite, the devoted! Again, the whole aspect of life was changed.

So there was now nothing that one could not say, nothing that one could not do, at 46 Gordon Square. It was, I think, a great advance in civilisation. It may be true that the loves of buggers are not—at least if one is of the other persuasion—of enthralling interest or paramount importance. But the fact that they can be mentioned openly leads to the fact that no one minds if they are practised privately. Thus many customs and beliefs were revised. Indeed the future of Bloomsbury was to prove that many variations can be played on the theme of sex, and with such happy results that my father himself might have hesitated before he thundered out the one word which he thought fit to apply to a bugger or an adulterer; which was Blackguard![2]

---

[1] *Thoby and Adrian* Virginia and Vanessa's brothers.

[2] *Blackguard* A worthless character; a scoundrel.

JAMES JOYCE
1882 – 1941

Irish novelist James Joyce's prose style and subject matter were so innovative and influential that fellow writer T.S. Eliot was prompted to declare that Joyce had helped to make "the modern world possible for art" by discovering "a way of controlling, or ordering, of giving a shape and a significance to the panorama of futility and anarchy which is contemporary history." Joyce's works as a whole redefined realism as they sought to access reality as perceived by the mind—whether awake or dreaming. Although throughout his life Joyce battled publishers, critics, and readers who objected to his frank treatment of the more "vulgar" aspects of his characters' thoughts and actions, Joyce became a literary figure of the first magnitude during his lifetime, and has remained so since.

James Augustus Aloysius Joyce was born in the middle-class Dublin suburb of Rathgar and was the first surviving son in a family of twelve siblings. Through his father's fecklessness, Joyce's family situation would eventually devolve into poverty. John Joyce's increasing dependence on alcohol created strains both on the family's finances and on its morale. On the other hand, Joyce's mother, Mary Jane Joyce, exposed the young Joyce to the arts and to religion, as she was both accomplished in music and devout in her Catholicism. The former he would embrace with as much fervor as he rejected the latter.

At the age of 6, Joyce started his studies under the tutorship of the Jesuits. During the course of his schooling, however, he became increasingly cynical about the Church. His intellectual and spiritual rebelliousness grew so that by the time he entered university he had begun to believe that religion, family, and nation were all traps of conventionality that the true artist must avoid.

While at University College, Joyce attempted to write poetry and enjoyed writing articles parodying various literary styles. A penchant for experimentation with form stayed with him, from the economy of voice exhibited in *Dubliners*, to the variety of narrative expressions created for *A Portrait of the Artist as a Young Man* and *Ulysses*, to the radical linguistic experimentation of *Finnegan's Wake*. In political matters, he rejected the single-minded nationalism of his peers and wrote outspoken articles that were published privately after the school advisory board barred publication in the school newspaper. Meanwhile, he was very successful in his chosen field of study—modern languages.

Joyce originally moved to Paris in 1902 to study medicine, but it was not until about 1904 that he took up his artistic mission in earnest and decided to leave Ireland. Apart from some brief periods, Joyce remained an exile from the country about which he would spend his life writing. For Joyce, exile was a prerequisite for artistic objectivity and freedom; he believed that his self-imposed exile allowed him to see the truth of Ireland and Irishness with clarity, precision, and detachment.

In June 1904, Joyce was invited by the paper *The Irish Homestead* to submit a short story. In the end he wrote a series of fifteen stories that were published in 1914 under the title *Dubliners*. Along the way Joyce had a series of arguments with publishers that would also dog and delay the publication of *A Portrait of the Artist as a Young Man,* as editors objected to what they saw as the inappropriate subject matter and language of his work. In 1909, he wrote to London publisher Grant Richards, with whom he was in negotiations for *Dubliners,* "I seriously believe that you will retard the course of civilization in Ireland by preventing the Irish people from having one good look at themselves in my nicely polished looking-glass." Richards, however, was in no financial position to advance the course of Irish civilization, and the book was rejected, not to be published until 1914.

Joyce described *Dubliners* as "a chapter of the moral history of my country." The book is divided—according to a letter Joyce wrote to his publisher—into four sections, representing childhood, adolescence, maturity, and public life. The fifteenth story, "The Dead," was not part of Joyce's original manuscript. This story, the longest in the collection, became the showpiece of the book upon its publication. Thematically, each of the stories in *Dubliners* deals with the lives of ordinary people, many of whom suffer from a sort of emotional paralysis—as a result of internal or external forces or moral decay—that makes them unable to move forward.

Many of these stories have as their focus a moment of self-recognition on the part of a character, a moment Joyce referred to as an "epiphany." The triggers to an epiphany are often accidental, "little errors and gestures—mere straws in the wind," as Joyce described them in a letter to his brother Stanislaus. The sharp focus allowed by a sudden flash of clarity is fleeting but allows characters a moment in which to see above their particular circumstances.

1904 was also the year Joyce met the woman who would be his lifelong partner. As legend has it, it was on 16 June, or "Bloomsday" (the day on which the events in *Ulysses* take place), that James Joyce first went out walking with Nora Barnacle, a chambermaid from Galway. Uninterested in literature, but with a fresh charm and wit and, like Joyce, an interest in music, she followed Joyce to the city of Pola, in the Austro-Hungarian Empire, four months after their meeting. They lived there a short time, without the sanction of marriage, and later moved to Trieste, Italy, where Joyce continued to write and eked out a meager living teaching English. The couple produced two children, Lucia and Georgio, and ultimately married, in 1931.

During their time in Trieste, in the fall of 1907, Joyce started editing, cutting, and reshaping the almost 1,000 pages of *Stephen Hero,* a novel he had begun in 1904. The result would be *A Portrait of the Artist as a Young Man*, on which Joyce continued to work intermittently for the next nine years. The novel-in-progress began to be published serially in *The Egoist* in 1914. It was not published as a volume until 1916, by the New York publisher B.W. Huebsch. It had been rejected by every London publisher to whom Joyce had sent it, despite the support of some major literary figures of the day, including W.B. Yeats, H.G. Wells, and Ezra Pound.

The hero of *Portrait*, Stephen Dedalus, bears a striking similarity to Joyce himself. The novel details the artistic growth of a writer, from childhood to the age of twenty, and outlines Joyce's artistic mission in life: to "record … with extreme care" epiphanic moments of sublime self-awareness; it also extends Joyce's experiments with style. The voice of the implied narrator changes and develops in correspondence with the development of the central character.

Ulysses details a day in Dublin life. Events in the novel follow the comings and goings of Stephen Dedalus, continuing the artistic journey on which Joyce set him in *A Portrait of the Artist as a Young Man*, and Leo Bloom, the Jewish-Irish Everyman who is the hero of the novel. *Ulysses* takes as its model Homer's *Odyssey*; an everyday journey through the neighborhoods of Dublin becomes highly symbolic as Leo Bloom follows a path that parallels that of Homer's hero. Meanwhile, Stephen Dedalus plays the role of Homer's Telemachus; Joyce imagines him an artist and visionary cut off from society. Joyce believed that Odysseus was perhaps the most well-rounded character in Western literature, embodying the best and the worst in human behavior: he was both brave and cowardly, a liar and an intellectual. Joyce's endeavors to portray these traits in his hero make Leo Bloom one of the most warmly compelling characters in all of twentieth-century literature.

In form, each chapter is an ironic rewriting of a chapter from Homer's *Odyssey*, and is written in a broadly different literary style from the one that precedes it. The novel adopts a stream-of-consciousness approach that makes little or no distinction between what is happening externally and what takes place in a character's mind. Perspectives move fluidly from internal to external dialogue, from character to character, and from event to event, with little to indicate the change. The novel's central themes are those that recur in Joyce's work: the inner life of Dublin in all its beauty and hollowness, and the outsider status of Leo Bloom (because of his Jewishness) and Stephen Dedalus (because of his artistic mission). This shared experience of Leo and Stephen, and Stephen's figurative search for an absent father, link the two thematically throughout the story.

Ulysses began to be published serially in the *Little Review* beginning in 1918, but in 1920 publication ceased in the face of obscenity charges. Not until 1922 was *Ulysses* published, and even then it was printed in Paris, not Britain. An American edition was published in 1934, after a landmark court case decided the book was not pornography. The weary judge at the time acquiesced to the view that the book was a work of art, even if many readers would not understand it. A British edition of *Ulysses* finally appeared in 1937.

It was not until about 1920 that the Joyce family began to attain a modest level of financial security, largely the result of the support and patronage of a number of people who had as much faith in Joyce's genius as he himself did. The family moved from Trieste to Zurich in 1914, then to Paris in 1920, then back to Zurich in 1940, where Joyce died of a perforated ulcer, just after seeing the publication of his final—and perhaps least understood—novel, *Finnegan's Wake* (1939). In stylistic terms, the novel goes beyond the playful, self-conscious mode of *Ulysses* and enters a far more obscure territory. The title refers to a common folk song in which a laborer, Finnegan, falls and hits his head. His friends assume he is dead and hold a wake for him; he finally awakens after having whiskey spilled on him. *Finnegan's Wake* is ostensibly the dream of Finnegan's successor, a Dublin Everyman with the initials H.C.E. (which stand for a variety of names, including Humphrey Chimpden Earwicker and Here Comes Everybody), and also features H.C.E.'s wife, A.L.P. (Anna Livia Plurabelle, Amnis Limina Permanent) and their twin sons, Shem and Shaun. Everything that occurs, and all the characters present, belong at least partially to the realm of dream. The novel's form relies on the cyclical view of history set out by Italian philosopher Giambattista Vico (detailed in Samuel Beckett's essay "Dante … Bruno. Vico … Joyce," included here). The narrative is largely composed of multi-leveled puns that are fraught with symbolic meaning. Joyce used elements of English and seven other languages to create the texture of the novel, reinventing not just the form of the novel but the structure of language itself in order to escape the stifling traditions in which he felt conventional language was steeped.

During his lifetime Joyce promised his writing would "keep the professors busy," and in this he has succeeded, and continues to succeed, to an extent that even he might not have expected. For many years scholars were occupied with historical, cultural, and anthropological research into the background of Joyce's Dublin. While this research continues, developments in critical theory (such as postcolonialism) have also opened up many new ways to interpret Joyce's texts. During his lifetime much of his work was, as one of Joyce's friends said, "outside of literature"; "literature" has since shifted to accommodate Joyce.

⌘ ⌘ ⌘

Eveline

She sat at the window watching the evening invade the avenue. Her head was leaned against the window curtains and in her nostrils was the odour of dusty cretonne.[1] She was tired.

Few people passed. The man out of the last house passed on his way home; she heard his footsteps clacking along the concrete pavement and afterwards crunching on the cinder path before the new red houses. One time there used to be a field there in which they used to play every evening with other people's children. Then a man from Belfast bought the field and built houses in it—not like their little brown houses but bright brick houses with shining roofs. The children of the avenue used to play together in that field—the Devines, the Waters, the Dunns, little Keogh the cripple, she and her brothers and sisters. Ernest, however, never played: he was too grown up. Her father used often to hunt them in out of the field with his blackthorn stick but usually little Keogh used to keep nix[2] and call out when he saw her father coming. Still they seemed to have been rather happy then. Her father was not so bad then, and besides her mother was alive. That was a long time ago; she and her brothers and sisters were all grown up; her mother was dead. Tizzie Dunn was dead, too, and the Waters had gone back to England. Everything changes. Now she was going to go away like the others, to leave her home.

Home! She looked round the room reviewing all its familiar objects which she had dusted once a week for so many years, wondering where on earth all the dust came from. Perhaps she would never see again those familiar objects from which she had never dreamed of being divided. And yet during all those years she had never found out the name of the priest whose yellowing photograph hung on the wall above the broken harmonium[3] beside the coloured print of the promises made to Blessed Margaret Mary Alacoque.[4] He had been a school friend of her father's. Whenever he showed the photograph to a visitor her father used to pass it with a casual word:

—He is in Melbourne now.

She had consented to go away, to leave her home. Was that wise? She tried to weigh each side of the question. In her home anyway she had shelter and food; she had those whom she had known all her life about her. Of course she had to work hard both in the house and at business. What would they say of her in the stores when they found out that she had run away with a fellow? Say she was a fool, perhaps; and her place would be filled up by advertisement. Miss Gavan would be glad. She had always had an edge on her, especially whenever there were people listening.

—Miss Hill, don't you see these ladies are waiting?

—Look lively, Miss Hill, please.

She would not cry many tears at leaving the stores.

But in her new home, in a distant unknown country, it would not be like that. Then she would be married—she, Eveline. People would treat her with respect then. She would not be treated as her mother had been. Even now, though she was over nineteen, she sometimes felt herself in danger of her father's violence. She knew it was that that had given her the palpitations. When they were growing up he had never gone for her, like he used to go for Harry and Ernest, because she was a girl; but latterly he had begun to threaten her and say what he would do to her only for her dead mother's sake. And now she had nobody to protect her. Ernest was dead and Harry, who was in the church decorating business, was nearly always down somewhere in the country. Besides, the invariable squabble for money on Saturday nights had begun to weary her unspeakably. She always gave her entire wages—seven shillings—and Harry always sent up what he could but the trouble was to get any money from her father. He said she used to

---

[1] *cretonne* Thick, unglazed, cotton fabric often used for chair covers and curtains.

[2] *keep nix* Keep watch.

[3] *harmonium* Type of reed organ.

[4] *Blessed Margaret Mary Alacoque* Seventeenth-century French nun whose devotion led her to perform extreme acts of penance, such as drinking water in which laundry had been washed and carving the name of Jesus into her chest.

squander the money, that she had no head, that he wasn't going to give her his hard earned money to throw about the streets and much more for he was usually fairly bad of a Saturday night. In the end he would give her the money and ask her had she any intention of buying Sunday's dinner. Then she had to rush out as quickly as she could and do her marketing, holding her black leather purse tightly in her hand as she elbowed her way through the crowds and returning home late under her load of provisions. She had hard work to keep the house together and to see that the two young children who had been left to her charge went to school regularly and got their meals regularly. It was hard work—a hard life—but now that she was about to leave it she did not find it a wholly undesirable life.

She was about to explore another life with Frank. Frank was very kind, manly, openhearted. She was to go away with him by the night boat to be his wife and to live with him in Buenos Ayres where he had a home waiting for her. How well she remembered the first time she had seen him; he was lodging in a house on the main road where she used to visit. It seemed a few weeks ago. He was standing at the gate, his peaked cap pushed back on his head and his hair tumbled forward over a face of bronze. Then they had come to know each other. He used to meet her outside the stores every evening and see her home. He took her to see the *Bohemian Girl*[1] and she felt elated as she sat in an unaccustomed part of the theatre with him. He was awfully fond of music and sang a little. People knew that they were courting and when he sang about the lass that loves a sailor she always felt pleasantly confused. He used to call her Poppens out of fun. First of all it had been an excitement for her to have a fellow and then she had begun to like him. He had tales of distant countries. He had started as a deck boy at a pound a month on a ship of the Allan line[2] going out to Canada. He told her the names of the ships he had been on and the names of the different services. He had sailed through the Straits of Magellan and he told her stories of the terrible Patagonians.[3] He had fallen on his feet in Buenos Ayres, he said, and had come over to the old country just for a holiday. Of course, her father had found out the affair and had forbidden her to have anything to say to him:

—I know these sailor chaps, he said.

One day he had quarrelled with Frank and after that she had to meet her lover secretly.

The evening deepened in the avenue. The white of two letters in her lap grew indistinct. One was to Harry, the other was to her father. Ernest had been her favourite but she liked Harry too. Her father was becoming old lately, she noticed; he would miss her. Sometimes he could be very nice. Not long before, when she had been laid up for a day, he had read her out a ghost story and made toast for her at the fire. Another day, when their mother was alive, they had all gone for a picnic to the Hill of Howth.[4] She remembered her father putting on her mother's bonnet to make the children laugh.

Her time was running out but she continued to sit by the window, leaning her head against the window curtain, inhaling the odour of dusty cretonne. Down far in the avenue she could hear a street organ playing. She knew the air. Strange that it should come that very night to remind her of the promise to her mother, her promise to keep the home together as long as she could. She remembered the last night of her mother's illness; she was again in the close dark room at the other side of the hall and outside she heard a melancholy air of Italy. The organ player had been ordered to go away and given sixpence. She remembered her father strutting back into the sickroom saying:

—Damned Italians! coming over here!

As she mused the pitiful vision of her mother's life laid its spell on the very quick of her being—that life of commonplace sacrifices closing in final craziness. She trembled as she heard again her mother's voice saying constantly with foolish insistence:

---

[1] *Bohemian Girl* 1843 opera by Dubliner Michael Balfe (1808–70).

[2] *the Allan line* The Allan Steamship Company, founded in 1852 by Sir Hugh Allan, made weekly departures from Liverpool to the Western coast of Canada (with stops along the way, including at Cape Horn and Buenos Aires).

[3] *the terrible Patagonians* The tall stature of these South American natives was greatly exaggerated in the seventeenth and eighteenth centuries, and they were rumored to be fierce giants.

[4] *Hill of Howth* Located northeast of Dublin, on the Howth peninsula.

—Derevaun Seraun! Derevaun Seraun![1]

She stood up in a sudden impulse of terror. Escape! She must escape! Frank would save her. He would give her life, perhaps love too. But she wanted to live. Why should she be unhappy? She had a right to happiness. Frank would take her in his arms, fold her in his arms. He would save her.

She stood among the swaying crowd in the station at the North Wall. He held her hand and she knew that he was speaking to her, saying something about the passage over and over again. The station was full of soldiers with brown baggages. Through the wide doors of the sheds she caught a glimpse of the black mass of the boat lying in beside the quay wall, with illumined portholes. She answered nothing. She felt her cheek pale and cold and out of a maze of distress she prayed to God to direct her, to show her what was her duty. The boat blew a long mournful whistle into the mist. If she went, tomorrow she would be on the sea with Frank, steaming towards Buenos Ayres. Their passage had been booked. Could she still draw back after all he had done for her? Her distress awoke a nausea in her body and she kept moving her lips in silent fervent prayer.

A bell clanged upon her heart. She felt him seize her hand:

—Come!

All the seas of the world tumbled about her heart. He was drawing her into them: he would drown her. She gripped with both hands at the iron railing.

—Come!

No! No! No! It was impossible. Her hands clutched the iron in frenzy. Amid the seas she sent a cry of anguish.

—Eveline! Evvy!

He rushed beyond the barrier and called to her to follow. He was shouted at to go on but he still called to her. She set her white face to him, passive, like a helpless animal. Her eyes gave him no sign of love or farewell or recognition.

—1914

---

[1] *Derevaun Seraun* The meaning of this phrase, if there is one, is uncertain. While some scholars believe it to be garbled Irish, others assert it is gibberish.

Araby[2]

North Richmond Street, being blind,[3] was a quiet street except at the hour when the Christian Brothers' School set the boys free. An uninhabited house of two storeys stood at the blind end, detached from its neighbours in a square ground. The other houses of the street, conscious of decent lives within them, gazed at one another with brown imperturbable faces.

The former tenant of our house, a priest, had died in the back drawingroom. Air, musty from having been long enclosed, hung in all the rooms and the waste room behind the kitchen was littered with old useless papers. Among these I found a few papercovered books, the pages of which were curled and damp: *The Abbot* by Walter Scott, *The Devout Communicant* and *The Memoirs of Vidocq*.[4] I liked the last best because its leaves were yellow. The wild garden behind the house contained a central apple tree and a few straggling bushes under one of which I found the late tenant's rusty bicycle pump. He had been a very charitable priest; in his will he had left all his money to institutions and the furniture of his house to his sister.

When the short days of winter came dusk fell before we had well eaten our dinners. When we met in the street the houses had grown sombre. The space of sky above us was the colour of everchanging violet and towards it the lamps of the street lifted their feeble lanterns. The cold air stung us and we played till our bodies glowed. Our shouts echoed in the silent street. The career of our play brought us through the dark muddy lanes behind the houses where we ran the gantlet of the rough tribes from the cottages, to the back doors of the dark dripping gardens where odours arose from the ashpits, to the dark odorous stables where a coachman smoothed and combed the horse or shook music from the buckled harness. When we returned to the street light from the kitchen windows had filled the

---

[2] *Araby* Charity bazaar held in Dublin in 1894.

[3] *blind* A dead end.

[4] *The Devout Communicant* Catholic religious manual published in 1831; *The Memoirs of Viducq* Written by François-Eugène Vidocq (1775–1857), a career criminal who was appointed chief of a French detective force.

areas.[1] If my uncle was seen turning the corner we hid in the shadow until we had seen him safely housed. Or if Mangan's sister came out on the doorstep to call her brother in to his tea we watched her from our shadow peer up and down the street. We waited to see whether she would remain or go in and if she remained we left our shadow and walked up to Mangan's steps resignedly. She was waiting for us, her figure defined by the light from the half-opened door. Her brother always teased her before he obeyed and I stood by the railings looking at her. Her dress swung as she moved her body and the soft rope of her hair tossed from side to side.

Every morning I lay on the floor in the front parlour watching her door. The blind was pulled down to within an inch of the sash so that I could not be seen. When she came out on the doorstep my heart leaped. I ran to the hall, seized my books and followed her. I kept her brown figure always in my eye and when we came near the point at which our ways diverged I quickened my pace and passed her. This happened morning after morning. I had never spoken to her except for a few casual words and yet her name was like a summons to all my foolish blood.

Her image accompanied me even in places the most hostile to romance. On Saturday evenings when my aunt went marketing I had to go to carry some of the parcels. We walked through the flaring streets, jostled by drunken men and bargaining women, amid the curses of labourers, the shrill litanies of shop boys who stood on guard by the barrels of pigs' cheeks, the nasal chanting of street singers who sang a *come-all-you* about O'Donovan Rossa[2] or a ballad about the troubles in our native land. These noises converged in a single sensation of life for me: I imagined that I bore my chalice safely through a throng of foes. Her name sprang to my lips at moments in strange prayers and praises which I myself did not understand. My eyes were often full of tears (I could not tell why) and at times a flood from my heart seemed to pour itself out into my bosom. I thought little

of the future. I did not know whether I would ever speak to her or not or, if I spoke to her, how I could tell her of my confused adoration. But my body was like a harp and her words and gestures were like fingers running upon the wires.

One evening I went into the back drawingroom in which the priest had died. It was a dark rainy evening and there was no sound in the house. Through one of the broken panes I heard the rain impinge upon the earth, the fine incessant needles of water playing in the sodden beds. Some distant lamp or lighted window gleamed below me. I was thankful that I could see so little. All my senses seemed to desire to veil themselves and, feeling that I was about to slip from them, I pressed the palms of my hands together until they trembled, murmuring: *O love! O love!* many times.

At last she spoke to me. When she addressed the first words to me I was so confused that I did not know what to answer. She asked me was I going to *Araby*. I forget whether I answered yes or no. It would be a splendid bazaar, she said; she would love to go.

—And why can't you? I asked.

While she spoke she turned a silver bracelet round and round her wrist. She could not go, she said, because there would be a retreat that week in her convent.[3] Her brother and two other boys were fighting for their caps and I was alone at the railings. She held one of the spikes, bowing her head towards me. The light from the lamp opposite our door caught the white curve of her neck, lit up the hair that rested there and, falling, lit up the hand upon the railing. It fell over one side of her dress and caught the white border of a petticoat, just visible as she stood at ease.

—It's well for you, she said.

—If I go, I said, I will bring you something.

What innumerable follies laid waste my waking and sleeping thoughts after that evening! I wished to annihilate the tedious intervening days. I chafed against the work of school. At night in my bedroom and by day in the classroom her image came between me and the page I strove to read. The syllables of the word *Araby* were called to me through the silence in which my soul luxuriated and cast an eastern enchantment over me. I asked for leave to go to the bazaar on Saturday night.

---

[1] *areas* Spaces between the railings and the fronts of houses, below street level.

[2] *come-all-you* Ballad (so called because many ballads started with this phrase); *O'Donovan Rossa* Jeremiah Donovan, Irish nationalist who was sentenced to a lifetime of penal servitude but was granted amnesty and departed for America.

[3] *convent* I.e., convent school.

My aunt was surprised and hoped it was not some freemason affair.[1] I answered few questions in class. I watched my master's face pass from amiability to sternness; he hoped I was not beginning to idle. I could not call my wandering thoughts together. I had hardly any patience with the serious work of life which, now that it stood between me and my desire, seemed to me child's play, ugly monotonous child's play.

On Saturday morning I reminded my uncle that I wished to go to the bazaar in the evening. He was fussing at the hallstand, looking for the hatbrush, and answered me curtly:

—Yes, boy, I know.

As he was in the hall I could not go into the front parlour and lie at the window. I left the house in bad humour and walked slowly towards the school. The air was pitilessly raw and already my heart misgave me.

When I came home to dinner my uncle had not yet been home. Still it was early. I sat staring at the clock for some time and when its ticking began to irritate me I left the room. I mounted the staircase and gained the upper part of the house. The high cold empty gloomy rooms liberated me and I went from room to room singing. From the front window I saw my companions playing below in the street. Their cries reached me weakened and indistinct and, leaning my forehead against the cool glass, I looked over at the dark house where she lived. I may have stood there for an hour seeing nothing but the brownclad figure cast by my imagination, touched discreetly by the lamplight at the curved neck, at the hand upon the railings and at the border below the dress.

When I came downstairs again I found Mrs. Mercer sitting at the fire. She was an old garrulous woman, a pawnbroker's widow who collected used stamps for some pious purpose. I had to endure the gossip of the teatable. The meal was prolonged beyond an hour and still my uncle did not come. Mrs. Mercer stood up to go: she was sorry she couldn't wait any longer but it was after eight o'clock and she did not like to be out late as

the night air was bad for her. When she had gone I began to walk up and down the room, clenching my fists. My aunt said:

—I'm afraid you may put off your bazaar for this night of Our Lord.

At nine o'clock I heard my uncle's latchkey in the halldoor. I heard him talking to himself and heard the hallstand rocking when it had received the weight of his overcoat. I could interpret these signs. When he was midway through his dinner I asked him to give me the money to go to the bazaar. He had forgotten.

—The people are in bed and after their first sleep now, he said.

I did not smile. My aunt said to him energetically:

—Can't you give him the money and let him go? You've kept him late enough as it is.

My uncle said he was very sorry he had forgotten. He said he believed in the old saying: *All work and no play makes Jack a dull boy*. He asked me where I was going and when I had told him a second time he asked me did I know *The Arab's Farewell to his Steed*.[2] When I left the kitchen he was about to recite the opening lines of the piece to my aunt.

I held a florin tightly in my hand as I strode down Buckingham Street towards the station. The sight of the streets thronged with buyers and glaring with gas recalled to me the purpose of my journey. I took my seat in a third class carriage of a deserted train. After an intolerable delay the train moved out of the station slowly. It crept onward among ruinous houses and over the twinkling river. At Westland Row Station a crowd of people pressed at the carriage doors; but the porters moved them back, saying that it was a special train for the bazaar. I remained alone in the bare carriage. In a few minutes the train drew up beside an improvised wooden platform. I passed out on to the road and saw by the lighted dial of a clock that it was ten minutes to ten. In front of me was a large building which displayed the magical name.

I could not find any sixpenny entrance and, fearing that the bazaar would be closed, I passed in quickly through a turnstile, handing a shilling to a wearylooking man. I found myself in a big hall girdled at half its

---

[1] *freemason affair* Affiliated with the Freemasons, a secret society originally made up of skilled stone-workers. The society was said to be anti-Catholic, and the Archbishop of Dublin had decreed that any Catholics caught at a freemason bazaar could be excommunicated.

[2] *The Arab's ... Steed* Popular romantic poem by Caroline Norton (1808–77).

height by a gallery. Nearly all the stalls were closed and the greater part of the hall was in darkness. I recognised a silence like that which pervades a church after a service. I walked into the centre of the bazaar timidly. A few people were gathered about the stalls which were still open. Before a curtain over which the words *Café Chantant*[1] were written in coloured lamps two men were counting money on a salver. I listened to the fall of the coins.

Remembering with difficulty why I had come I went over to one of the stalls and examined porcelain vases and flowered teasets. At the door of the stall a young lady was talking and laughing with two young gentlemen. I remarked their English accents and listened vaguely to their conversation.

—O, I never said such a thing!

—O, but you did!

—O, but I didn't!

—Didn't she say that?

—She did. I heard her.

—O, there's a … fib!

Observing me the young lady came over and asked me did I wish to buy anything. The tone of her voice was not encouraging: she seemed to have spoken to me out of a sense of duty. I looked humbly at the great jars that stood like eastern guards at either side of the dark entrance to her stall and murmured:

—No, thank you.

The young lady changed the position of one of the vases and went back to the two young men. They began to talk of the same subject. Once or twice the young lady glanced at me over her shoulder.

I lingered before her stall, though I knew my stay was useless, to make my interest in her wares seem the more real. Then I turned away slowly and walked down the middle of the bazaar. I allowed the two pennies to fall against the sixpence in my pocket. I heard a voice call from one end of the gallery that the light was out. The upper part of the hall was now completely dark.

Gazing up into the darkness I saw myself as a creature driven and derided by vanity: and my eyes burned with anguish and anger.

—1914

---

[1] *Café Chantant* Café that provides musical entertainment.

The Dead

Lily, the caretaker's daughter, was literally run off her feet. Hardly had she brought one gentleman into the little pantry behind the office on the ground floor and helped him off with his overcoat when the wheezy hall-door bell clanged again and she had to scamper along the bare hallway to let in another guest. It was well for her she had not to attend to the ladies also. But Miss Kate and Miss Julia had thought of that and had converted the bathroom upstairs into a ladies' dressing-room. Miss Kate and Miss Julia were there, gossiping and laughing and fussing, walking after each other to the head of the stairs, peering down over the banisters and calling down to Lily to ask her who had come.

It was always a great affair, the Misses Morkan's annual dance. Everybody who knew them came to it, members of the family, old friends of the family, the members of Julia's choir, any of Kate's pupils that were grown up enough and even some of Mary Jane's pupils too. Never once had it fallen flat. For years and years it had gone off in splendid style as long as anyone could remember, ever since Kate and Julia, after the death of their brother Pat, had left the house in Stony Batter and taken Mary Jane, their only niece, to live with them in the dark gaunt house on Usher's Island, the upper part of which they had rented from Mr. Fullam, the corn factor[2] on the ground floor. That was a good thirty years ago if it was a day. Mary Jane, who was then a little girl in short clothes, was now the main prop of the household for she had the organ in Haddington Road. She had been through the academy[3] and gave a pupils' concert every year in the upper room of the Antient Concert Rooms. Many of her pupils belonged to better class families on the Kingstown and Dalkey line. Old as they were, her aunts also did their share. Julia, though she was quite grey, was still the leading soprano in Adam and Eve's[4] and Kate, being too feeble to go about much, gave music lessons to beginners on the old square piano in the back room. Lily, the caretaker's daughter, did housemaid work for them. Though their life was modest

---

[2] *corn factor* Grain merchant.

[3] *the academy* Royal Irish Academy of Music.

[4] *Adam and Eve's* Roman Catholic church in Dublin.

they believed in eating well, the best of everything: diamond bone sirloins, three shilling tea and the best bottled stout. But Lily seldom made a mistake in the orders so that she got on well with her three mistresses. They were fussy, that was all. But the only thing they would not stand was back answers.[1]

Of course they had good reason to be fussy on such a night. And then it was long after ten o'clock and yet there was no sign of Gabriel and his wife. Besides they were dreadfully afraid that Freddy Malins might turn up screwed.[2] They would not wish for worlds that any of Mary Jane's pupils should see him under the influence: and when he was like that it was sometimes very hard to manage him. Freddy Malins always came late but they wondered what could be keeping Gabriel: and that was what brought them every two minutes to the banisters to ask Lily had Gabriel or Freddy come.

—O, Mr. Conroy, said Lily to Gabriel when she opened the door for him, Miss Kate and Miss Julia thought you were never coming. Good night, Mrs. Conroy.

—I'll engage they did, said Gabriel, but they forget that my wife here takes three mortal hours to dress herself.

He stood on the mat, scraping the snow from his goloshes, while Lily led his wife to the foot of the stairs and called out:

—Miss Kate, here's Mrs. Conroy.

Kate and Julia came toddling down the dark stairs at once. Both of them kissed Gabriel's wife, said she must be perished alive and asked was Gabriel with her.

—Here I am as right as the mail, Aunt Kate! Go on up. I'll follow, called out Gabriel from the dark.

He continued scraping his feet vigorously while the three women went upstairs, laughing, to the ladies' dressingroom. A light fringe of snow lay like a cape on the shoulders of his overcoat and like toecaps on the toes of his goloshes; and, as the buttons of his overcoat slipped with a squeaking noise through the snow-stiffened frieze,[3] a cold fragrant air from out of doors escaped from crevices and folds.

—Is it snowing again, Mr. Conroy? asked Lily.

She had preceded him into the pantry to help him off with his overcoat. Gabriel smiled at the three syllables she had given his surname and glanced at her. She was a slim growing girl, pale in complexion and with haycoloured hair. The gas in the pantry made her look still paler. Gabriel had known her when she was a child and used to sit on the lowest step nursing[4] a rag doll.

—Yes, Lily, he answered, and I think we're in for a night of it. He looked up at the pantry ceiling which was shaking with the stamping and shuffling of feet on the floor above, listened for a moment to the piano and then glanced at the girl who was folding his overcoat carefully at the end of a shelf.

—Tell me, Lily, he said in a friendly tone, do you still go to school?

—O no, sir, she answered, I'm done schooling this year and more.

—O then, said Gabriel gaily, I suppose we'll be going to your wedding one of these fine days with your young man—eh?

The girl glanced back at him over her shoulder and said with great bitterness:

—The men that is now is only all palaver[5] and what they can get out of you.

Gabriel coloured as if he felt he had made a mistake and, without looking at her, kicked off his goloshes and flicked actively with his muffler at his patent leather shoes.

He was a stout tallish young man. The high colour of his cheeks pushed upwards even to his forehead where it scattered itself in a few formless patches of pale red; and on his hairless face there scintillated restlessly the polished lenses and bright gilt rims of the glasses which screened his delicate and restless eyes. His glossy black hair was parted in the middle and brushed in a long curve behind his ears where it curled slightly beneath the groove left by his hat.

When he had flicked lustre into his shoes he stood up and pulled his waistcoat down more tightly on his plump body. Then he took a coin rapidly from his pocket.

—O Lily, he said, thrusting it into her hand, it's

---

[1] *back answers* Rudeness; back-talk.

[2] *screwed* Drunk.

[3] *frieze* Coarse woolen cloth.

[4] *nursing* Here, taking care of.

[5] *palaver* Flattering talk.

Christmas time, isn't it? Just … here's a little …

He walked rapidly towards the door.

—O no, sir! cried the girl, following him. Really, sir, I wouldn't take it.

—Christmas time! Christmas time! said Gabriel, almost trotting to the stairs and waving his hand to her in deprecation.

The girl, seeing that he had gained the stairs, called out after him:

—Well, thank you, sir.

He waited outside the drawingroom door until the waltz should finish, listening to the skirts that swept against it and to the shuffling of feet. He was still discomposed by the girl's bitter and sudden retort. It had cast a gloom over him which he tried to dispel by arranging his cuffs and the bows of his tie. Then he took from his waistcoat pocket a little paper and glanced at the headings he had made for his speech. He was undecided about the lines from Robert Browning[1] for he feared they would be above the heads of his hearers. Some quotation that they could recognise from Shakespeare or from the Melodies[2] would be better. The indelicate clacking of the men's heels and the shuffling of their soles reminded him that their grade of culture differed from his. He would only make himself ridiculous by quoting poetry to them which they could not understand. They would think that he was airing his superior education. He would fail with them just as he had failed with the girl in the pantry. He had taken up a wrong tone. His whole speech was a mistake from first to last, an utter failure.

Just then his aunts and his wife came out of the ladies' dressingroom. His aunts were two small plainly dressed old women. Aunt Julia was an inch or so the taller. Her hair, drawn low over the tops of her ears, was grey; and grey also, with darker shadows, was her large flaccid face. Though she was stout in build and stood erect her slow eyes and parted lips gave her the appearance of a woman who did not know where she was or where she was going. Aunt Kate was more vivacious. Her face, healthier than her sister's, was all puckers and

creases like a shrivelled red apple and her hair, braided in the same oldfashioned way, had not lost its ripe nut colour.

They both kissed Gabriel frankly. He was their favourite nephew, the son of their dead elder sister Ellen who had married T. J. Conroy of the Port and Docks.[3]

—Gretta tells me you're not going to take a cab back to Monkstown tonight, Gabriel, said Aunt Kate.

—No, said Gabriel, turning to his wife, we had quite enough of that last year, hadn't we? Don't you remember, Aunt Kate, what a cold Gretta got out of it? Cab windows rattling all the way and the east wind blowing in after we passed Merrion. Very jolly it was. Gretta caught a dreadful cold.

Aunt Kate frowned severely and nodded her head at every word.

—Quite right, Gabriel, quite right, she said. You can't be too careful.

—But as for Gretta there, said Gabriel, she'd walk home in the snow if she were let.

Mrs. Conroy laughed.

—Don't mind him, Aunt Kate, she said. He's really an awful bother, what with green shades for Tom's eyes at night and making him do the dumbbells and forcing Lottie to eat the stirabout.[4] The poor child! And she simply hates the sight of it! … O, but you'll never guess what he makes me wear now!

She broke out into a peal of laughter and glanced at her husband whose admiring and happy eyes had been wandering from her dress to her face and hair. The two aunts laughed heartily too for Gabriel's solicitude was a standing joke with them.

—Goloshes! said Mrs. Conroy. That's the latest. Whenever it's wet underfoot I must put on my goloshes. Tonight even he wanted me to put them on but I wouldn't. The next thing he'll buy me will be a diving suit.

Gabriel laughed nervously and patted his tie reassuringly while Aunt Kate nearly doubled herself so heartily did she enjoy the joke. The smile soon faded from Aunt Julia's face and her mirthless eyes were directed towards her nephew's face. After a pause she asked:

—And what are goloshes, Gabriel?

---

[1] *Robert Browning* English poet (1812–89).

[2] *Melodies* Thomas Moore's collection of poetry and songs, *Irish Melodies*.

[3] *Port and Docks* Dublin Port and Docks Board, an essential part of Dublin's commercial life.

[4] *stirabout* Porridge.

—Goloshes, Julia! exclaimed her sister. Goodness me, don't you know what goloshes are? You wear them over your … over your boots, Gretta, isn't it?

—Yes, said Mrs. Conroy. Guttapercha[1] things. We both have a pair now. Gabriel says everyone wears them on the continent.[2]

—O, on the continent, murmured Aunt Julia, nodding her head slowly.

Gabriel knitted his brows and said, as if he were slightly angered:

—It's nothing very wonderful but Gretta thinks it very funny because she says the word reminds her of christy minstrels.[3]

—But tell me, Gabriel, said Aunt Kate with brisk tact. Of course you've seen about the room. Gretta was saying …

—O, the room is all right, replied Gabriel. I've taken one in the Gresham.[4]

—To be sure, said Aunt Kate, by far the best thing to do. And the children, Gretta, you're not anxious about them?

—O, for one night, said Mrs. Conroy. Besides Bessie will look after them.

—To be sure, said Aunt Kate again. What a comfort it is to have a girl like that, one you can depend on! There's that Lily, I'm sure I don't know what has come over her lately. She's not the girl she was at all.

Gabriel was about to ask his aunt some questions on this point but she broke off suddenly to gaze after her sister who had wandered down the stairs and was craning her neck over the banisters.

—Now, I ask you, she said almost testily, where is Julia going. Julia! Julia! Where are you going?

Julia who had gone half way down one flight came back and announced blandly:

—Here's Freddy!

At the same moment a clapping of hands and a final flourish of the pianist told that the waltz had ended. The drawingroom door was opened from within and some couples came out. Aunt Kate drew Gabriel aside hurriedly and whispered into his ear:

—Slip down, Gabriel, like a good fellow and see if he's all right and don't let him up if he's screwed. I'm sure he's screwed. I'm sure he is.

Gabriel went to the stairs and listened over the banisters. He could hear two persons talking in the pantry. Then he recognised Freddy Malins' laugh. He went down the stairs noisily.

—It's such a relief, said Aunt Kate to Mrs. Conroy, that Gabriel is here. I always feel easier in my mind when he's here …

—Julia, there's Miss Daly and Miss Power will take some refreshment. Thanks for your beautiful waltz, Miss Daly. It made lovely time.

A tall wizenfaced man with a stiff grizzled moustache and swarthy skin who was passing out with his partner said:

—And may we have some refreshment too, Miss Morkan?

—Julia, said Aunt Kate summarily, and here's Mr. Browne and Miss Furlong. Take them in, Julia, with Miss Daly and Miss Power.

—I'm the man for the ladies, said Mr. Browne, pursing his lips until his moustache bristled and smiling in all his wrinkles. You know, Miss Morkan, the reason they are so fond of me is …

He did not finish his sentence but, seeing that Aunt Kate was out of earshot, at once led the three young ladies into the back room. The middle of the room was occupied by two square tables placed end to end and on these Aunt Julia and the caretaker were straightening and smoothing a large cloth. On the sideboard were arrayed dishes and plates and glasses and bundles of knives and forks and spoons. The top of the closed square piano served also as a sideboard for viands and sweets. At a smaller sideboard in one corner two young men were standing, drinking hop bitters.[5]

Mr. Browne led his charges thither and invited them all, in jest, to some ladies' punch, hot, strong and sweet. As they said they never took anything strong he opened three bottles of lemonade for them. Then he asked one of the young men to move aside and, taking hold of the decanter, filled out for himself a goodly measure of

---

[1] *Guttapercha*   Substance similar to rubber and used for waterproofing.

[2] *continent*   I.e., Europe.

[3] *christy minstrels*   Minstrel show. From the nineteenth-century minstrel show founded by George Christy.

[4] *Gresham*   One of Dublin's top hotels.

[5] *hop bitters*   Unfermented liquor flavored with hops.

whisky. The young men eyed him respectfully while he took a trial sip.

—God help me, he said smiling, it's the doctor's orders.

His wizened face broke into a broader smile and the three young ladies laughed in musical echo to his pleasantry, swaying their bodies to and fro, with nervous jerks of their shoulders. The boldest said:

—O, now, Mr. Browne, I'm sure the doctor never ordered anything of the kind.

Mr. Browne took another sip of his whisky and said, with sidling mimicry:

—Well, you see, I'm like the famous Mrs. Cassidy who is reported to have said: *Now, Mary Grimes, if I don't take it make me take it for I feel I want it.*

His hot face had leaned forward a little too confidentially and he had assumed a very low Dublin accent so that the young ladies, with one instinct, received his speech in silence. Miss Furlong, who was one of Mary Jane's pupils, asked Miss Daly what was the name of the pretty waltz she had played; and Mr. Browne, seeing that he was ignored, turned promptly to the two young men who were more appreciative.

A redfaced young woman, dressed in pansy, came into the room, excitedly clapping her hands and crying:

—Quadrilles![1] Quadrilles!

Close on her heels came Aunt Kate, crying:

—Two gentlemen and three ladies, Mary Jane!

—O, here's Mr. Bergin and Mr. Kerrigan, said Mary Jane. Mr. Kerrigan, will you take Miss Power. Miss Furlong, may I get you a partner, Mr. Bergin. O, that'll just do now.

—Three ladies, Mary Jane, said Aunt Kate.

The two young gentlemen asked the ladies if they might have the pleasure and Mary Jane turned to Miss Daly.

—O, Miss Daly, you're really awfully good after playing for the last two dances but really we're so short of ladies tonight.

—I don't mind in the least, Miss Morkan.

—But I've a nice partner for you, Mr. Bartell D'Arcy, the tenor. I'll get him to sing later on. All Dublin is raving about him.

—Lovely voice, lovely voice! said Aunt Kate.

As the piano had twice begun the prelude to the first figure Mary Jane led her recruits quickly from the room. They had hardly gone when Aunt Julia wandered slowly into the room, looking behind her at something.

—What is the matter, Julia? asked Aunt Kate anxiously. Who is it?

Julia, who was carrying in a column of table-napkins, turned to her sister and said simply, as if the question had surprised her:

—It's only Freddy, Kate, and Gabriel with him.

In fact right behind her Gabriel could be seen piloting Freddy Malins across the landing. The latter, a young man of about forty, was of Gabriel's size and build with very round shoulders. His face was fleshy and pallid, touched with colour only at the thick hanging lobes of his ears and at the wide wings of his nose. He had coarse features, a blunt nose, a convex and receding brow, tumid and protruded lips. His heavylidded eyes and the disorder of his scanty hair made him look sleepy. He was laughing heartily in a high key at a story which he had been telling Gabriel on the stairs and at the same time rubbing the knuckles of his left fist backwards and forwards into his left eye.

—Good evening, Freddy, said Aunt Julia.

Freddy Malins bade the Misses Morkan good evening in what seemed an offhand fashion by reason of the habitual catch in his voice and then, seeing that Mr. Browne was grinning at him from the sideboard, crossed the room on rather shaky legs and began to repeat in an undertone the story he had just told to Gabriel.

—He's not so bad, is he? said Aunt Kate to Gabriel.

Gabriel's brows were dark but he raised them quickly and answered:

—O no, hardly noticeable.

—Now, isn't he a terrible fellow! she said. And his poor mother made him take the pledge[2] on New Year's Eve. But come on, Gabriel, into the drawingroom.

Before leaving the room with Gabriel she signalled to Mr. Browne by frowning and shaking her forefinger in warning to and fro. Mr. Browne nodded in answer and, when she had gone, said to Freddy Malins:

—Now then, Teddy, I'm going to fill you out a good glass of lemonade just to buck you up.

Freddy Malins, who was nearing the climax of his

---

[1]   *Quadrilles*   Type of square dance.

[2]   *take the pledge*   I.e., pledge to abstain from alcoholic beverages.

story, waved the offer aside impatiently but Mr. Browne, having first called Freddy Malins' attention to a disarray in his dress, filled out and handed him a full glass of lemonade. Freddy Malins' left hand accepted the glass mechanically, his right hand being engaged in the mechanical readjustment of his dress. Mr. Browne, whose face was once more wrinkling with mirth, poured out for himself a glass of whisky while Freddy Malins exploded, before he had well reached the climax of his story, in a kink of highpitched bronchitic laughter and, setting down his untasted and overflowing glass, began to rub the knuckles of his left fist backwards and forwards into his left eye, repeating words of his last phrase as well as his fit of laughter would allow him.

Gabriel could not listen while Mary Jane was playing her academy piece, full of runs and difficult passages, to the hushed drawingroom. He liked music but the piece she was playing had no melody for him and he doubted whether it had any melody for the other listeners though they had begged Mary Jane to play something. Four young men, who had come from the refreshment room to stand in the doorway at the sound of the piano, had gone away quietly in couples after a few minutes. The only persons who seemed to follow the music were Mary Jane herself, her hands racing along the keyboard or lifted from it at the pauses like those of a priestess in momentary imprecation, and Aunt Kate standing at her elbow to turn the page.

Gabriel's eyes, irritated by the floor which glittered with beeswax under the heavy chandelier, wandered to the wall above the piano. A picture of the balcony scene in *Romeo and Juliet* hung there and beside it was a picture of the two murdered princes in the tower[1] which Aunt Julia had worked[2] in red, blue and brown wools when she was a girl. Probably in the school they had gone to as girls that kind of work had been taught, for one year his mother had worked for him as a birthday present a waistcoat of purple tabinet[3] with little foxes' heads upon it, lined with brown satin and having round

mulberry buttons. It was strange that his mother had had no musical talent though Aunt Kate used to call her the brainscarrier of the Morkan family. Both she and Julia had always seemed a little proud of their serious and matronly sister. Her photograph stood before the pierglass.[4] She held an open book on her knees and was pointing out something in it to Constantine who, dressed in a man-o'-war suit,[5] lay at her feet. It was she who had chosen the names for her sons for she was very sensible of the dignity of family life. Thanks to her, Constantine was now senior curate in Balbriggan and, thanks to her, Gabriel himself had taken his degree in the Royal University. A shadow passed over his face as he remembered her sullen opposition to his marriage. Some slighting phrases she had used still rankled in his memory. She had once spoken of Gretta as being country cute and that was not true of Gretta at all. It was Gretta who had nursed her all during her last long illness in their house at Monkstown.

He knew that Mary Jane must be near the end of her piece for she was playing again the opening melody with runs of scales after every bar and while he waited for the end the resentment died down in his heart. The piece ended with a trill of octaves in the treble and a final deep octave in the bass. Great applause greeted Mary Jane as, blushing and rolling up her music nervously, she escaped from the room. The most vigorous clapping came from the four young men in the doorway who had gone away to the refreshment room at the beginning of the piece but had come back when the piano had stopped.

Lancers[6] were arranged. Gabriel found himself partnered with Miss Ivors. She was a frankmannered talkative young lady with a freckled face and prominent brown eyes. She did not wear a lowcut bodice and the large brooch which was fixed in the front of her collar bore on it an Irish device.

When they had taken their places she said abruptly:

—I have a crow to pluck with you.

—With me? said Gabriel.

She nodded her head gravely.

---

[1] *the two … tower* Edward IV's two sons were murdered in the Tower of London in about 1483–84, allegedly at the instigation of their uncle, the future Richard III.

[2] *worked* I.e., wrought; made.

[3] *tabinet* Fabric made of silk and wool, similar to poplin.

---

[4] *pierglass* Tall mirror.

[5] *man-o'-war suit* Sailor suit, frequently worn by children.

[6] *Lancers* Type of quadrille.

—What is it? asked Gabriel, smiling at her solemn manner.

—Who is G.C.? answered Miss Ivors turning her eyes upon him.

Gabriel coloured and was about to knit his brows as if he did not understand when she said bluntly:

—O, innocent Amy! I have found out that you write for the *Daily Express*. Now aren't you ashamed of yourself?

—Why should I be ashamed of myself? asked Gabriel blinking his eyes and trying to smile.

—Well, I'm ashamed of you, said Miss Ivors frankly. To say you'd write for a rag like that. I didn't think you were a west Briton.[1]

A look of perplexity appeared on Gabriel's face. It was true that he wrote a literary column every Wednesday in the *Daily Express* for which he was paid fifteen shillings. But that did not make him a west Briton surely. The books he received for review were almost more welcome than the paltry cheque. He loved to feel the covers and turn over the pages of newly printed books. Nearly every day when his teaching in the college was ended he used to wander down the quays to the secondhand booksellers, to Hickey's on Bachelor's Walk, to Webb's or Massey's on Aston's Quay or to Clohissey's in the bystreet. He did not know how to meet her charge. He wanted to say that literature was above politics. But they were friends of many years' standing and their careers had been parallel, first at the university and then as teachers: he could not risk a grandiose phrase with her. He continued blinking his eyes and trying to smile and murmured lamely that he saw nothing political in writing reviews of books.

When their turn to cross had come he was still perplexed and inattentive. Miss Ivors promptly took his hand in a warm grasp and said in a soft friendly tone:

—Of course, I was only joking. Come, we cross now. When they were together again she spoke of the university question[2] and Gabriel felt more at ease. A

friend of hers had shown her his review of Browning's poems. That was how she had found out the secret: but she liked the review immensely. Then she said suddenly:

—O, Mr. Conroy, will you come for an excursion to the Aran Isles[3] this summer? We're going to stay there a whole month. It will be splendid out in the Atlantic. You ought to come. Mr. Clancy is coming and Mr. Kilkelly and Kathleen Kearney. It would be splendid for Gretta too if she'd come. She's from Connacht,[4] isn't she?

—Her people are, said Gabriel shortly.

—But you will come, won't you? said Miss Ivors, laying her warm hand eagerly on his arm.

—The fact is, said Gabriel, I have already arranged to go …

—Go where? asked Miss Ivors.

—Well, you know, every year I go for a cycling tour with some fellows and so …

—But where? asked Miss Ivors.

—Well, we usually go to France or Belgium or perhaps Germany, said Gabriel awkwardly.

—And why do you go to France and Belgium, said Miss Ivors, instead of visiting your own land?

—Well, said Gabriel, it's partly to keep in touch with the languages and partly for a change.

—And haven't you your own language to keep in touch with, Irish? asked Miss Ivors.

—Well, said Gabriel, if it comes to that, you know, Irish is not my language.

Their neighbours had turned to listen to the cross-examination. Gabriel glanced right and left nervously and tried to keep his good humour under the ordeal which was making a blush invade his forehead.

—And haven't you your own land to visit, continued Miss Ivors, that you know nothing of, your own people and your own country?

—O, to tell you the truth, retorted Gabriel suddenly, I'm sick of my own country, sick of it!

—Why? asked Miss Ivors.

Gabriel did not answer for his retort had heated him.

—Why? repeated Miss Ivors.

[1] *west Briton* Colloquial term for an Irish person who sees Ireland as the western part of Great Britain, rather than as a separate nation.

[2] *university question* Concerning the establishment of an Irish national university, the representation of "Irish" values in universities, and the provision of equal access to education for Catholics (Trinity College was open only to Protestants).

[3] *Aran Isles* Three islands off the coast of Country Galway, on Ireland's west coast.

[4] *Connacht* Connaught, in west Ireland.

They had to go visiting[1] together and, as he had not answered her, Miss Ivors said warmly:

—Of course, you've no answer.

Gabriel tried to cover his agitation by taking part in the dance with great energy. He avoided her eyes for he had seen a sour expression on her face. But when they met in the long chain he was surprised to feel his hand firmly pressed. She looked at him from under her brows for a moment quizzically until he smiled. Then, just as the chain was about to start again, she stood on tiptoe and whispered into his ear:

—West Briton!

When the lancers were over Gabriel went away to a remote corner of the room where Freddy Malins' mother was sitting. She was a stout feeble old woman with white hair. Her voice had a catch in it like her son's and she stuttered slightly. She had been told that Freddy had come and that he was nearly all right. Gabriel asked her whether she had had a good crossing. She lived with her married daughter in Glasgow and came to Dublin on a visit once a year. She answered placidly that she had had a beautiful crossing and that the captain had been most attentive to her. She spoke also of the beautiful house her daughter kept in Glasgow and of the nice friends they had there. While her tongue rambled on Gabriel tried to banish from his mind all memory of the unpleasant incident with Miss Ivors. Of course the girl or woman or whatever she was was an enthusiast but there was a time for all things. Perhaps he ought not to have answered her like that. But she had no right to call him a west Briton before people, even in joke. She had tried to make him ridiculous before people, heckling him and staring at him with her rabbit's eyes.

He saw his wife making her way towards him through the waltzing couples. When she reached him she said into his ear:

—Gabriel, Aunt Kate wants to know won't you carve the goose as usual. Miss Daly will carve the ham and I'll do the pudding.

—All right, said Gabriel.

—She's sending in the younger ones first as soon as this waltz is over so that we'll have the table to ourselves.

—Were you dancing? asked Gabriel.

—Of course I was. Didn't you see me? What words had you with Molly Ivors?

—No words. Why! Did she say so?

—Something like that. I'm trying to get that Mr. D'Arcy to sing. He's full of conceit, I think.

—There were no words, said Gabriel moodily, only she wanted me to go for a trip to the west of Ireland and I said I wouldn't.

His wife clasped her hands excitedly and gave a little jump.

—O, do go, Gabriel, she cried. I'd love to see Galway again.

—You can go if you like, said Gabriel coldly.

She looked at him for a moment, then turned to Mrs. Malins and said:

—There's a nice husband for you, Mrs. Malins.

While she was threading her way back across the room Mrs. Malins, without adverting to the interruption, went on to tell Gabriel what beautiful places there were in Scotland and beautiful scenery. Her son-in-law brought them every year to the lakes and they used to go fishing. Her son-in-law was a splendid fisher. One day he caught a fish, a beautiful big big fish: and the man in the hotel boiled it for their dinner.

Gabriel hardly heard what she said. Now that supper was coming near he began to think again about his speech and about the quotation. When he saw Freddy Malins coming across the room to visit his mother Gabriel left the chair free for him and retired into the embrasure of the window. The room had already cleared and from the back room came the clatter of plates and knives. Those who still remained in the drawingroom seemed tired of dancing and were conversing quietly in little groups. Gabriel's warm trembling fingers tapped the cold pane of the window. How cool it must be outside! How pleasant it would be to walk out alone, first along by the river and then through the park! The snow would be lying on the branches of the trees and forming a bright cap on the top of the Wellington monument.[2] How much more pleasant it would be there than at the supper table!

---

[1] *go visiting* Reference to the part of the dance in which the partners cross the floor together and meet another couple.

[2] *Wellington monument* Monument to the Duke of Wellington, an English military hero born in Ireland.

He ran over the headings of his speech: Irish hospitality, sad memories, the Three Graces, Paris,[1] the quotation from Browning. He repeated to himself a phrase he had written in his review: *One feels that one is listening to a thought-tormented music.* Miss Ivors had praised the review. Was she sincere? Had she really any life of her own behind all her propagandism? There had never been any ill feeling between them until that night. It unnerved him to think that she would be at the supper table, looking up at him while he spoke with her critical quizzing eyes. Perhaps she would not be sorry to see him fail in his speech. An idea came into his mind and gave him courage. He would say, alluding to Aunt Kate and Aunt Julia: *Ladies and gentlemen, the generation which is now on the wane among us may have had its faults but for my part I think it had certain qualities of hospitality, of humour, of humanity, which the new and very serious and hypereducated generation that is growing up around us seems to me to lack.* Very good: that was one for Miss Ivors. What did he care that his aunts were only two ignorant old women?

A murmur in the room attracted his attention. Mr. Browne was advancing from the door, gallantly escorting Aunt Julia who leaned upon his arm, smiling and hanging her head. An irregular musketry of applause escorted her also as far as the piano and then, as Mary Jane seated herself on the stool and Aunt Julia, no longer smiling, half turned so as to pitch her voice fairly into the room, gradually ceased. Gabriel recognised the prelude. It was that of an old song of Aunt Julia's, *Arrayed for the Bridal.*[2] Her voice strong and clear in tone attacked with great spirit the runs which embellish the air and, though she sang very rapidly, she did not miss even the smallest of the grace notes. To follow the voice, without looking at the singer's face, was to feel

and share the excitement of swift and secure flight. Gabriel applauded loudly with all the others at the close of the song and loud applause was borne in from the invisible supper table. It sounded so genuine that a little colour struggled into Aunt Julia's face as she bent to replace in the music stand the old leatherbound songbook that had her initials on the cover. Freddy Malins, who had listened with his head perched sideways to hear the better, was still applauding when everyone else had ceased and talking animatedly to his mother who nodded her head gravely and slowly in acquiescence. At last, when he could clap no more, he stood up suddenly and hurried across the room to Aunt Julia, whose hand he seized and held in both his hands, shaking it when words failed him or the catch in his voice proved too much for him.

—I was just telling my mother, he said, I never heard you sing so well, never. No, I never heard your voice so good as it is tonight. Now! Would you believe that now? That's the truth. Upon my word and honour that's the truth. I never heard your voice sound so fresh and so ... so clear and fresh, never.

Aunt Julia smiled broadly and murmured something about compliments as she released her hand from his grasp. Mr. Browne extended his open hand towards her and said to those who were near him in the manner of a showman introducing a prodigy to an audience:

—Miss Julia Morkan, my latest discovery!

He was laughing very heartily at this himself when Freddy Malins turned to him and said:

—Well, Browne, if you're serious you might make a worse discovery. All I can say is I never heard her sing half so well as long as I am coming here. And that's the honest truth.

—Neither did I, said Mr. Browne. I think her voice has greatly improved.

Aunt Julia shrugged her shoulders and said with meek pride:

—Thirty years ago I hadn't a bad voice as voices go.

—I often told Julia, said Aunt Kate emphatically, that she was simply thrown away in that choir. But she never would be said by[3] me.

She turned as if to appeal to the good sense of the others against a refractory child while Aunt Julia gazed

---

[1] *Three Graces* In Greek mythology, the three daughters of Zeus and Eurynome who embodied the qualities of beauty and charm; *Paris* In Greek mythology, Paris was asked by the gods to judge a beauty contest between Hera, Athena, and Aphrodite. All three goddesses offered Paris a bribe. When he chose Aphrodite, she rewarded him by granting him the most beautiful woman in the world, who was Helen of Troy. Paris's abduction of Helen from her husband, Menelaus, is the putative cause of the Trojan War.

[2] *Arrayed ... Bridal* Popular and challenging song from Bellini's opera *I Puritani* (1835) that begins with the words "Arrayed for the bridal, in beauty behold her."

[3] *be said by* Be ruled by; submit to.

in front of her, a vague smile of reminiscence playing on her face.

—No, continued Aunt Kate, she wouldn't be said or led by anyone, slaving there in that choir night and day, night and day. Six o'clock on Christmas morning! And all for what?

—Well, isn't it for the honour of God, Aunt Kate? asked Mary Jane twisting round on the piano stool and smiling.

Aunt Kate turned fiercely on her niece and said:

—I know all about the honour of God, Mary Jane, but I think it's not at all honourable for the pope to turn out the women out of the choirs that have slaved there all their lives and put little whippersnappers of boys over their heads. I suppose it is for the good of the church if the pope does it. But it's not just, Mary Jane, and it's not right.[1]

She had worked herself into a passion and would have continued in defence of her sister for it was a sore subject with her but Mary Jane, seeing that all the dancers had come back, intervened pacifically:

—Now, Aunt Kate, you're giving scandal to Mr. Browne who is of the other persuasion.[2]

Aunt Kate turned to Mr. Browne, who was grinning at this allusion to his religion, and said hastily:

—O, I don't question the pope's being right. I'm only a stupid old woman and I wouldn't presume to do such a thing. But there's such a thing as common everyday politeness and gratitude. And if I were in Julia's place I'd tell that Father Healy straight up to his face …

—And besides, Aunt Kate, said Mary Jane, we really are all hungry and when we are hungry we are all very quarrelsome.

—And when we are thirsty we are also quarrelsome, added Mr. Browne.

—So that we had better go to supper, said Mary Jane, and finish the discussion afterwards.

On the landing outside the drawingroom Gabriel found his wife and Mary Jane trying to persuade Miss Ivors to stay for supper. But Miss Ivors, who had put on her hat and was buttoning her cloak, would not stay. She did not feel in the least hungry and she had already overstayed her time.

—But only for ten minutes, Molly, said Mrs. Conroy. That won't delay you.

—To take a pick itself,[3] said Mary Jane, after all your dancing.

—I really couldn't, said Miss Ivors.

—I am afraid you didn't enjoy yourself at all, said Mary Jane hopelessly.

—Ever so much, I assure you, said Miss Ivors, but you really must let me run off now.

—But how can you get home? asked Mrs. Conroy.

—O, it's only two steps up the quay. Gabriel hesitated a moment and said:

—If you will allow me, Miss Ivors, I'll see you home if you really are obliged to go.

But Miss Ivors broke away from them.

—I won't hear of it, she cried. For goodness' sake go in to your suppers and don't mind me. I'm quite well able to take care of myself.

—Well, you're the comical girl, Molly, said Mrs. Conroy frankly.

—*Beannacht libh*,[4] cried Miss Ivors with a laugh as she ran down the staircase.

Mary Jane gazed after her, a moody puzzled expression on her face, while Mrs. Conroy leaned over the banisters to listen for the hall door. Gabriel asked himself was he the cause of her abrupt departure. But she did not seem to be in ill humour: she had gone away laughing. He stared blankly down the staircase.

At that moment Aunt Kate came toddling out of the supper room, almost wringing her hands in despair.

—Where is Gabriel? she cried. Where on earth is Gabriel? There's everyone waiting in there, stage to let, and nobody to carve the goose!

—Here I am, Aunt Kate! cried Gabriel with sudden animation, ready to carve a flock of geese, if necessary.

A fat brown goose lay at one end of the table and at the other end, on a bed of creased paper strewn with sprigs of parsley, lay a great ham, stripped of its outer

---

1 *I know … right* On 22 November 1903, Pope Pius X issued a papal bull, in which he announced that the singing of Church music constituted a liturgical function for which women were ineligible and that, henceforth, soprano and alto voices would be produced by young boys.

2 *of the other persuasion* I.e., a Protestant.

3 *a pick itself* I.e., a little bit.

4 *Beannacht libh* Gaelic: blessing to you; goodbye.

skin and peppered over with crust crumbs, a neat paper frill round its shin, and beside this was a round of spiced beef. Between these rival ends ran parallel lines of side dishes: two little minsters of jelly, red and yellow, a shallow dish full of blocks of blancmange[1] and red jam, a large green leafshaped dish with a stalkshaped handle on which lay bunches of purple raisins and peeled almonds, a companion dish on which lay a solid rectangle of Smyrna figs, a dish of custard topped with grated nutmeg, a small bowl full of chocolates and sweets wrapped in gold and silver papers and a glass vase in which stood some tall celery stalks. In the centre of the table there stood, as sentries to a fruit stand which upheld a pyramid of oranges and American apples, two squat oldfashioned decanters of cut glass, one containing port and the other dark sherry. On the closed square piano a pudding in a huge yellow dish lay in waiting and behind it were three squads of bottles of stout and ale and minerals drawn up according to the colours of their uniforms, the first two black with brown and red labels, the third and smallest squad white, with transverse green sashes.

Gabriel took his seat boldly at the head of the table and, having looked to the edge of the carver, plunged his fork firmly into the goose. He felt quite at ease now for he was an expert carver and liked nothing better than to find himself at the head of a well laden table.

—Miss Furlong, what shall I send you? he asked. A wing or a slice of the breast?

—Just a small slice of the breast.

—Miss Higgins, what for you?

—O, anything at all, Mr. Conroy.

While Gabriel and Miss Daly exchanged plates of goose and plates of ham and spiced beef Lily went from guest to guest with a dish of hot floury potatoes wrapped in a white napkin. This was Mary Jane's idea and she had also suggested apple sauce for the goose but Aunt Kate had said that plain roast goose without any apple sauce had always been good enough for her and she hoped she might never eat worse. Mary Jane waited on her pupils and saw that they got the best slices and Aunt Kate and Aunt Julia opened and carried across from the piano bottles of stout and ale for the gentlemen and bottles of minerals for the ladies. There was a

great deal of confusion and laughter and noise, the noise of orders and counterorders, of knives and forks, of corks and glass stoppers. Gabriel began to carve second helpings as soon as he had finished the first round without serving himself. Everyone protested loudly so that he compromised by taking a long draught of stout for he had found the carving hot work. Mary Jane settled down quietly to her supper but Aunt Kate and Aunt Julia were still toddling round the table, walking on each other's heels, getting in each other's way and giving each other unheeded orders. Mr. Browne begged of them to sit down and eat their supper and so did Gabriel but they said they were time enough so that, at last, Freddy Malins stood up and, capturing Aunt Kate, plumped her down on her chair amid general laughter.

When everyone had been well served Gabriel said smiling:

—Now if anyone wants a little more of what vulgar people call stuffing let him or her speak.

A chorus of voices invited him to begin his own supper and Lily came forward with three potatoes which she had reserved for him.

—Very well, said Gabriel amiably as he took another preparatory draught, kindly forget my existence, ladies and gentlemen, for a few minutes.

He set to his supper and took no part in the conversation with which the table covered Lily's removal of the plates. The subject of talk was the opera company which was then at the Theatre Royal. Mr. Bartell D'Arcy, the tenor, a dark-complexioned young man with a smart moustache, praised very highly the leading contralto of the company but Miss Furlong thought she had a rather vulgar style of production. Freddy Malins said there was a negro chieftain singing in the second part of the Gaiety pantomime who had one of the finest tenor voices he had ever heard.

—Have you heard him? he asked Mr. Bartell D'Arcy across the table.

—No, answered Mr. Bartell D'Arcy carelessly.

—Because, Freddy Malins explained, now I'd be curious to hear your opinion of him. I think he has a grand voice.

—It takes Teddy to find out the really good things, said Mr. Browne familiarly to the table.

---

[1] *blancmange*   Milk jelly.

—And why couldn't he have a voice too? asked Freddy Malins sharply. Is it because he's only a black?

Nobody answered this question and Mary Jane led the table back to the legitimate opera. One of her pupils had given her a pass for *Mignon*.[1] Of course, it was very fine, she said, but it made her think of poor Georgina Burns.[2] Mr. Browne could go back farther still to the old Italian companies that used to come to Dublin, Tietjens, Trebelli, Ilma de Murzka, Campanini, the great Giuglini, Ravelli, Aramburo. Those were the days, he said, when there was something like singing to be heard in Dublin. He told too of how the top gallery of the old Royal used to be packed night after night, of how one night an Italian tenor had sung five encores to *Let Me Like a Soldier Fall*, introducing a high C every time, and of how the gallery boys would sometimes in their enthusiasm unyoke the horses from the carriage of some great *prima donna* and pull her themselves through the streets to her hotel. Why did they never play the grand old operas now, he asked. *Dinorah*, *Lucrezia Borgia*?[3] Because they could not get the voices to sing them: that was why.

—O, well, said Mr. Bartell D'Arcy, I presume there are as good singers today as there were then.

—Where are they? asked Mr. Browne defiantly.

—In London, Paris, Milan, said Mr. Bartell D'Arcy warmly. I suppose Caruso,[4] for example, is quite as good, if not better than any of the men you have mentioned.

—Maybe so, said Mr. Browne. But I may tell you I doubt it strongly.

—O, I'd give anything to hear Caruso sing, said Mary Jane.

—For me, said Aunt Kate, who had been picking a bone, there was only one tenor. To please me, I mean. But I suppose none of you ever heard of him.

—Who was he, Miss Morkan? asked Mr. Bartell D'Arcy politely.

—His name, said Aunt Kate, was Parkinson. I heard him when he was in his prime and I think he had then the purest tenor voice that was ever put into a man's throat.

—Strange, said Mr. Bartell D'Arcy. I never even heard of him.

—Yes, yes, Miss Morkan is right, said Mr. Browne. I remember hearing of old Parkinson but he's too far back for me.

—A beautiful pure sweet mellow English tenor, said Aunt Kate with enthusiasm.

Gabriel having finished, the huge pudding was transferred to the table. The clatter of forks and spoons began again. Gabriel's wife served out spoonfuls of the pudding and passed the plates down the table. Midway down they were held up by Mary Jane who replenished them with raspberry or orange jelly or with blancmange and jam. The pudding was of Aunt Julia's making and she received praises for it from all quarters. She herself said that it was not quite brown enough.

—Well, I hope, Miss Morkan, said Mr. Browne, that I'm brown enough for you because, you know, I'm all brown.

All the gentlemen, except Gabriel, ate some of the pudding out of compliment to Aunt Julia. As Gabriel never ate sweets the celery had been left for him. Freddy Malins also took a stalk of celery and ate it with his pudding. He had been told that celery was a capital thing for the blood and he was just then under doctor's care. Mrs. Malins, who had been silent all through the supper, said that her son was going down to Mount Melleray[5] in a week or so. The table then spoke of Mount Melleray, how bracing the air was down there, how hospitable the monks were and how they never asked for a penny-piece from their guests.

—And do you mean to say, asked Mr. Browne incredulously, that a chap can go down there and put up there as if it were a hotel and live on the fat of the land and then come away without paying a farthing?

—O, most people give some donation to the monastery when they leave, said Mary Jane.

—I wish we had an institution like that in our church, said Mr. Browne candidly.

[1] *Mignon* 1866 opera by Ambroise Thomas.
[2] *Georgina Burns* Famous soprano who made her Dublin début in 1878.
[3] *Dinorah* 1859 comic opera by Giacomo Meyerbeer; *Lucrezia Borgia* 1833 opera by Gaetano Donizetti.
[4] *Caruso* Tenor Enrico Caruso (1874–1921).
[5] *Mount Melleray* Site of the Abbey of St. Bernard de Trappe, founded in 1831 by the Cistercian monks.

He was astonished to hear that the monks never spoke, got up at two in the morning and slept in their coffins.[1] He asked what they did it for.

—That's the rule of the order, said Aunt Kate firmly.

—Yes, but why? asked Mr. Browne.

Aunt Kate repeated that it was the rule, that was all. Mr. Browne still seemed not to understand. Freddy Malins explained to him, as best he could, that the monks were trying to make up for the sins committed by all the sinners in the outside world. The explanation was not very clear for Mr. Browne grinned and said:

—I like that idea very much but wouldn't a comfortable spring bed do them as well as a coffin?

—The coffin, said Mary Jane, is to remind them of their last end.

As the subject had grown lugubrious it was buried in a silence of the table during which Mrs. Malins could be heard saying to her neighbour in an indistinct undertone:

—They are very good men, the monks, very pious men.

The raisins and almonds and figs and apples and oranges and chocolates and sweets were now passed about the table and Aunt Julia invited all the guests to have either port or sherry. At first Mr. Bartell D'Arcy refused to take either but one of his neighbours nudged him and whispered something to him upon which he allowed his glass to be filled. Gradually as the last glasses were being filled the conversation ceased. A pause followed, broken only by the noise of the wine and by unsettlings of chairs. The Misses Morkan, all three, looked down at the tablecloth. Someone coughed once or twice and then a few gentlemen patted the table gently as a signal for silence. The silence came and Gabriel pushed back his chair and stood up.

The patting at once grew louder in encouragement and then ceased altogether. Gabriel leaned his ten trembling fingers on the tablecloth and smiled nervously at the company. Meeting a row of upturned faces he raised his eyes to the chandelier. The piano was playing a waltz tune and he could hear the skirts sweeping against the drawingroom door. People perhaps were standing in the snow on the quay outside, gazing up at the lighted windows and listening to the waltz music. The air was pure there. In the distance lay the park where the trees were weighted with snow. The Wellington monument wore a gleaming cap of snow that flashed westward over the white field of Fifteen Acres.

He began:

—Ladies and gentlemen.

It has fallen to my lot this evening as in years past to perform a very pleasing task, but a task for which I am afraid my poor powers as a speaker are all too inadequate.

—No, no, said Mr. Browne.

—But, however that may be, I can only ask you tonight to take the will for the deed and to lend me your attention for a few moments while I endeavour to express to you in words what my feelings are on this occasion.

—Ladies and gentlemen. It is not the first time that we have gathered together under this hospitable roof, around this hospitable board. It is not the first time that we have been the recipients—or, perhaps I had better say, the victims—of the hospitality of certain good ladies.

He made a circle in the air with his arm and paused. Everyone laughed or smiled at Aunt Kate and Aunt Julia and Mary Jane who all turned crimson with pleasure. Gabriel went on more boldly:

—I feel more strongly with every recurring year that our country has no tradition which does it so much honour and which it should guard so jealously as that of its hospitality. It is a tradition that is unique so far as my experience goes (and I have visited not a few places abroad) among the modern nations. Some would say, perhaps, that with us it is rather a failing than anything to be boasted of. But granted even that, it is, to my mind, a princely failing and one that I trust will long be cultivated among us. Of one thing, at least, I am sure. As long as this one roof shelters the good ladies aforesaid—and I wish from my heart it may do so for many and many a long year to come—the tradition of genuine warmhearted courteous Irish hospitality, which our forefathers have handed down to us and which we in turn must hand down to our descendants, is still alive among us.

---

[1] *slept in their coffins* Though commonly believed, this is not a real custom of the Cistercians.

A hearty murmur of assent ran round the table. It shot through Gabriel's mind that Miss Ivors was not there and that she had gone away discourteously: and he said with confidence in himself:

—Ladies and gentlemen.

A new generation is growing up in our midst, a generation actuated by new ideas and new principles. It is serious and enthusiastic for these new ideas and its enthusiasm, even when it is misdirected, is, I believe, in the main sincere. But we are living in a sceptical and, if I may use the phrase, a thought-tormented age: and sometimes I fear that this new generation, educated or hypereducated as it is, will lack those qualities of humanity, of hospitality, of kindly humour which belonged to an older day. Listening tonight to the names of all those great singers of the past it seemed to me, I must confess, that we were living in a less spacious age. Those days might without exaggeration be called spacious days: and if they are gone beyond recall let us hope, at least, that in gatherings such as this we shall still speak of them with pride and affection, still cherish in our hearts the memory of those dead and gone great ones whose fame the world will not willingly let die.

—Hear! hear! said Mr. Browne loudly.

—But yet, continued Gabriel, his voice falling into a softer inflection, there are always in gatherings such as this sadder thoughts that will recur to our minds: thoughts of the past, of youth, of changes, of absent faces that we miss here tonight. Our path through life is strewn with many such sad memories: and were we to brood upon them always we could not find the heart to go on bravely with our work among the living. We have all of us living duties and living affections which claim, and rightly claim, our strenuous endeavours.

Therefore I will not linger on the past. I will not let any gloomy moralising intrude upon us here tonight. Here we are gathered together for a brief moment from the bustle and rush of our everyday routine. We are met here as friends, in the spirit of good fellowship, as colleagues also, to a certain extent, in the true spirit of camaraderie, and as the guests of—what shall I call them?—the three Graces of the Dublin musical world.

The table burst into applause and laughter at this sally. Aunt Julia vainly asked each of her neighbours in turn to tell her what Gabriel had said.

—He says we are the three Graces, Aunt Julia, said Mary Jane. Aunt Julia did not understand but she looked up, smiling, at Gabriel who continued in the same vein:

—Ladies and gentlemen.

I will not attempt to play tonight the part that Paris played on another occasion. I will not attempt to choose between them. The task would be an invidious one and one beyond my poor powers. For when I view them in turn, whether it be our chief hostess herself, whose good heart, whose too good heart, has become a byword with all who know her, or her sister, who seems to be gifted with perennial youth and whose singing must have been a surprise and a revelation to us all tonight, or, last but not least, when I consider our youngest hostess, talented, cheerful, hard-working and the best of nieces, I confess, ladies and gentlemen, that I do not know to which of them I should award the prize.

Gabriel glanced down at his aunts and, seeing the large smile on Aunt Julia's face and the tears which had risen to Aunt Kate's eyes, hastened to his close. He raised his glass of port gallantly while every member of the company fingered a glass expectantly and said loudly:

—Let us toast them all three together. Let us drink to their health, wealth, long life, happiness and prosperity and may they long continue to hold the proud and self-won position which they hold in their profession and the position of honour and affection which they hold in our hearts.

All the guests stood up, glass in hand and, turning towards the three seated ladies, sang in unison with Mr. Browne as leader:

—For they are jolly gay fellows,
For they are jolly gay fellows,
For they are jolly gay fellows
Which nobody can deny.

Aunt Kate was making frank use of her handkerchief and even Aunt Julia seemed moved. Freddy Malins beat time with his pudding fork and the singers turned towards one another as if in melodious conference, while they sang with emphasis:

—Unless he tells a lie,
Unless he tells a lie.

Then turning once more towards their hostesses they sang:

—For they are jolly gay fellows,
For they are jolly gay fellows,
For they are jolly gay fellows
Which nobody can deny.

The acclamation which followed was taken up beyond the door of the supper room by many of the other guests and renewed time after time, Freddy Malins acting as officer with his fork on high.

The piercing morning air came into the hall where they were standing so that Aunt Kate said:

—Close the door, somebody. Mrs. Malins will get her death of cold.

—Browne is out there, Aunt Kate, said Mary Jane.

—Browne is everywhere, said Aunt Kate lowering her voice.

Mary Jane laughed at her tone.

—Really, she said archly, he is very attentive.

—He has been laid on here like the gas, said Aunt Kate in the same tone, all during the Christmas.

She laughed herself this time good-humouredly and then added quickly:

—But tell him to come in, Mary Jane, and close the door. I hope to goodness he didn't hear me.

At that moment the hall door was opened and Mr. Browne came in from the doorstep, laughing as if his heart would break. He was dressed in a long green overcoat with mock astrakhan[1] cuffs and collar and wore on his head an oval fur cap. He pointed down the snowcovered quay whence the sound of shrill prolonged whistling was borne in.

—Teddy will have all the cabs in Dublin out, he said. Gabriel advanced from the little pantry behind the office, struggling into his overcoat and, looking round the hall, said:

—Gretta not down yet?

—She's getting on her things, Gabriel, said Aunt Kate.

—Who's playing up there? asked Gabriel.

—Nobody. They're all gone.

—O no, Aunt Kate, said Mary Jane. Bartell D'Arcy and Miss O'Callaghan aren't gone yet.

—Someone is strumming at the piano, anyhow, said Gabriel. Mary Jane glanced at Gabriel and Mr. Browne and said with a shiver:

—It makes me feel cold to look at you two gentlemen muffled up like that. I wouldn't like to face your journey home at this hour.

—I'd like nothing better this minute, said Mr. Browne stoutly, than a rattling fine walk in the country or a fast drive with a good spanking goer between the shafts.

—We used to have a very good horse and trap[2] at home, said Aunt Julia sadly.

—The never-to-be-forgotten Johnny, said Mary Jane laughing. Aunt Kate and Gabriel laughed too.

—Why, what was wonderful about Johnny? asked Mr. Browne.

—The late lamented Patrick Morkan, our grandfather that is, explained Gabriel, commonly known in his later years as the old gentleman, was a glue boiler.

—O now, Gabriel, said aunt Kate laughing, he had a starch mill.

—Well, glue or starch, said Gabriel, the old gentleman had a horse by the name of Johnny. And Johnny used to work in the old gentleman's mill walking round and round in order to drive the mill. That was all very well; but now comes the tragic part about Johnny. One fine day the old gentleman thought he'd like to drive out with the quality to a military review in the park.

—The Lord have mercy on his soul, said Aunt Kate compassionately.

—Amen, said Gabriel. So the old gentleman, as I said, harnessed Johnny and put on his very best tall hat and his very best stock collar and drove out in grand style from his ancestral mansion somewhere near Back Lane, I think.

Everyone laughed, even Mrs. Malins, at Gabriel's manner and Aunt Kate said:

---

[1] *astrakhan* Lambskin.

[2] *trap* Small, two-wheeled carriage on springs.

—O now, Gabriel, he didn't live in Back Lane really. Only the mill was there.

—Out from the mansion of his forefathers, continued Gabriel, he drove with Johnny. And everything went on beautifully until Johnny came in sight of King Billy's[1] statue: and whether he fell in love with the horse King Billy sits on or whether he thought he was back again in the mill, anyhow he began to walk round the statue.

Gabriel paced in a circle round the hall in his goloshes amid the laughter of the others.

—Round and round he went, said Gabriel, and the old gentleman, who was a very pompous old gentleman, was highly indignant. *Go on, sir! What do you mean, sir? Johnny! Johnny! Most extraordinary conduct! Can't understand the horse!*

The peals of laughter which followed Gabriel's imitation of the incident were interrupted by a resounding knock at the hall door. Mary Jane ran to open it and let in Freddy Malins. Freddy Malins, with his hat well back on his head and his shoulders humped with cold, was puffing and steaming after his exertions.

—I could only get one cab, he said.

—O, we'll find another along the quay, said Gabriel.

—Yes, said Aunt Kate. Better not keep Mrs. Malins standing in the draught.

Mrs. Malins was helped down the front steps by her son and Mr. Browne and, after many manoeuvres, hoisted into the cab. Freddy Malins clambered in after her and spent a long time settling her on the seat, Mr. Browne helping him with advice. At last she was settled comfortably and Freddy Malins invited Mr. Browne into the cab. There was a good deal of confused talk, then Mr. Browne got into the cab. The cabman settled his rug over his knees and bent down for the address. The confusion grew greater and the cabman was directed differently by Freddy Malins and Mr. Browne, each of whom had his head out through a window of the cab. The difficulty was to know where to drop Mr. Browne along the route and Aunt Kate, Aunt Julia and Mary Jane helped the discussion from the doorstep with cross-directions and contradictions and abundance of laughter. As for Freddy Malins he was speechless with

laughter. He popped his head in and out of the window every moment, to the great danger of his hat, and told his mother how the discussion was progressing till at last Mr. Browne shouted to the bewildered cabman above the din of everybody's laughter:

—Do you know Trinity College?

—Yes, sir, said the cabman.

—Well, drive bang up against Trinity College gates, said Mr. Browne, and then we'll tell you where to go. You understand now?

—Yes, sir, said the cabman.

—Make like a bird for Trinity College.

—Right, sir, cried the cabman.

The horse was whipped up and the cab rattled off along the quay amid a chorus of laughter and adieus.

Gabriel had not gone to the door with the others. He was in a dark part of the hall gazing up the staircase. A woman was standing near the top of the first flight in the shadow also. He could not see her face but he could see the terracotta and salmonpink panels of her skirt which the shadow made appear black and white. It was his wife. She was leaning on the banisters listening to something. Gabriel was surprised at her stillness and strained his ear to listen also. But he could hear little save the noise of laughter and dispute on the front steps, a few chords struck on the piano and a few notes of a man's voice singing.

He stood still in the gloom of the hall, trying to catch the air that the voice was singing and gazing up at his wife. There was grace and mystery in her attitude as if she were a symbol of something. He asked himself what is a woman standing on the stairs in the shadow, listening to distant music, a symbol of. If he were a painter he would paint her in that attitude. Her blue felt hat would show off the bronze of her hair against the darkness and the dark panels of her skirt would show off the light ones. *Distant Music* he would call the picture if he were a painter.

The hall door was closed and Aunt Kate, Aunt Julia and Mary Jane came down the hall, still laughing.

—Well, isn't Freddy terrible? said Mary Jane. He's really terrible.

Gabriel said nothing but pointed up the stairs towards where his wife was standing. Now that the hall door was closed the voice and the piano could be heard

---

[1] *King Billy* King William III (William of Orange), who took the British throne in the Glorious Revolution of 1688.

more clearly. Gabriel held up his hand for them to be silent. The song seemed to be in the old Irish tonality and the singer seemed uncertain both of his words and of his voice. The voice made plaintive by the distance and by the singer's hoarseness faintly illuminated the cadence of the air with words expressing grief:

> —O, the rain falls on my heavy locks
> And the dew wets my shin,
> My babe lies cold …

—O, exclaimed Mary Jane. It's Bartell D'Arcy singing and he wouldn't sing all the night. O, I'll get him to sing a song before he goes.

—O do, Mary Jane, said Aunt Kate.

Mary Jane brushed past the others and ran to the staircase but before she reached it the singing stopped and the piano was closed abruptly.

—O, what a pity! she cried. Is he coming down, Gretta? Gabriel heard his wife answer yes and saw her come down towards them. A few steps behind her were Mr. Bartell D'Arcy and Miss O'Callaghan.

—O, Mr. D'Arcy, cried Mary Jane, it's downright mean of you to break off like that when we were all in raptures listening to you.

—I have been at him all the evening, said Miss O'Callaghan, and Mrs. Conroy too, and he told us he had a dreadful cold and couldn't sing.

—O, Mr. D'Arcy, said Aunt Kate, now that was a great fib to tell.

—Can't you see that I'm as hoarse as a crow? said Mr. D'Arcy roughly.

He went into the pantry hastily and put on his overcoat. The others, taken aback by his rude speech, could find nothing to say. Aunt Kate wrinkled her brows and made signs to the others to drop the subject. Mr. D'Arcy stood swathing his neck carefully and frowning.

—It's the weather, said Aunt Julia after a pause.

—Yes, everybody has colds, said Aunt Kate readily, everybody.

—They say, said Mary Jane, we haven't had snow like it for thirty years: and I read this morning in the newspaper that the snow is general all over Ireland.

—I love the look of snow, said Aunt Julia sadly.

—So do I, said Miss O'Callaghan. I think Christmas is never really Christmas unless we have the snow on the ground.

—But poor Mr. D'Arcy doesn't like the snow, said Aunt Kate smiling.

Mr. D'Arcy came from the pantry, fully swathed and buttoned, and in a repentant tone told them the history of his cold. Everyone gave him advice and said it was a great pity and urged him to be very careful of his throat in the night air. Gabriel watched his wife who did not join in the conversation. She was standing right under the dusty fanlight and the flame of the gas lit up the rich bronze of her hair which he had seen her drying at the fire a few days before. She was in the same attitude and seemed unaware of the talk about her. At last she turned towards them and Gabriel saw that there was colour on her cheeks and that her eyes were shining. A sudden tide of joy went leaping out of his heart.

—Mr. D'Arcy, she said, what is the name of that song you were singing?

—It's called *The Lass of Aughrim*,[1] said Mr. D'Arcy, but I couldn't remember it properly. Why? Do you know it?

—*The Lass of Aughrim*, she repeated. I couldn't think of the name.

—It's a very nice air, said Mary Jane. I'm sorry you were not in voice tonight.

—Now, Mary Jane, said Aunt Kate, don't annoy Mr. D'Arcy. I won't have him annoyed.

Seeing that all were ready to start she shepherded them to the door where goodnight was said:

—Well, goodnight Aunt Kate, and thanks for the pleasant evening.

—Goodnight, Gabriel. Goodnight, Gretta!

—Goodnight, Aunt Kate, and thanks ever so much. Goodnight, Aunt Julia.

—O, goodnight, Gretta, I didn't see you.

—Goodnight, Mr. D'Arcy. Goodnight, Miss O'Callaghan.

—Goodnight, Miss Morkan.

—Goodnight again.

—Goodnight all. Safe home.

---

[1] *The Lass of Aughrim*   Irish ballad about a peasant girl who commits suicide when her noble seducer refuses to recognize her when she arrives at his door pregnant with his child.

—Goodnight. Goodnight.

The morning was still dark. A dull yellow light brooded over the houses and the river and the sky seemed to be descending. It was slushy underfoot and only streaks and patches of snow lay on the roofs, on the parapets of the quay and on the area railings. The lamps were still burning redly in the murky air and, across the river, the palace of the Four Courts[1] stood out menacingly against the heavy sky.

She was walking on before him with Mr. Bartell D'Arcy, her shoes in a brown parcel tucked under one arm and her hands holding her skirt up from the slush. She had no longer any grace of attitude but Gabriel's eyes were still bright with happiness. The blood went bounding along his veins and the thoughts went rioting through his brain, proud, joyful, tender, valorous.

She was walking on before him so lightly and so erect that he longed to run after her noiselessly, catch her by the shoulders and say something foolish and affectionate into her ear. She seemed to him so frail that he longed to defend her against something and then to be alone with her. Moments of their secret life together burst like stars upon his memory. A heliotrope envelope was lying beside his breakfast cup and he was caressing it with his hand. Birds were twittering in the ivy and the sunny web of the curtain was shimmering along the floor: he could not eat for happiness. They were standing on the crowded platform and he was placing a ticket inside the warm palm of her glove. He was standing with her in the cold, looking in through a grated window at a man making bottles in a roaring furnace. It was very cold. Her face, fragrant in the cold air, was quite close to his and suddenly she called out to the man at the furnace:

—Is the fire hot, sir?

But the man could not hear her with the noise of the furnace. It was just as well. He might have answered rudely.

A wave of yet more tender joy escaped from his heart and went coursing in warm flood along his arteries. Like the tender fire of stars moments of their life together, that no one knew of or would ever know of, broke upon and illumined his memory. He longed to recall to her

those moments, to make her forget the years of their dull existence together and remember only their moments of ecstasy. For the years, he felt, had not quenched his soul or hers. Their children, his writing, her household cares had not quenched all their souls' tender fire. In one letter that he had written to her then he had said: *Why is it that words like these seem to me so dull and cold? Is it because there is no word tender enough to be your name?*

Like distant music these words that he had written years before were borne towards him from the past. He longed to be alone with her. When the others had gone away, when he and she were in their room in the hotel, then they would be alone together. He would call her softly:

—Gretta!

Perhaps she would not hear at once: she would be undressing. Then something in his voice would strike her. She would turn and look at him …

At the corner of Winetavern Street they met a cab. He was glad of its rattling noise as it saved him from conversation. She was looking out of the window and seemed tired. The others spoke only a few words, pointing out some building or street. The horse galloped along wearily under the murky morning sky, dragging his old rattling box after his heels, and Gabriel was again in a cab with her galloping to catch the boat, galloping to their honeymoon.

As the cab drove across O'Connell bridge Miss O'Callaghan said:

—They say you never cross O'Connell bridge without seeing a white horse.

—I see a white man this time, said Gabriel.

—Where? asked Mr. Bartell D'Arcy.

Gabriel pointed to the statue[2] on which lay patches of snow. Then he nodded familiarly to it and waved his hand.

—Goodnight, Dan, he said gaily.

When the cab drew up before the hotel Gabriel jumped out and, in spite of Mr. Bartell D'Arcy's protest, paid the driver. He gave the man a shilling over his fare. The man saluted and said:

—A prosperous new year to you, sir.

---

[1] *palace … Courts* Judicial building; home of the four traditional divisions of the judicial system in Ireland.

[2] *the statue* The O'Connell Memorial, commemorating Irish nationalist Daniel O'Connell (1775–1847).

—The same to you, said Gabriel cordially.

She leaned for a moment on his arm in getting out of the cab and while standing at the kerbstone bidding the others goodnight. She leaned lightly on his arm, as lightly as when she had danced with him a few hours before. He had felt proud and happy then, happy that she was his, proud of her grace and wifely carriage. But now after the kindling again of so many memories, the first touch of her body, musical and strange and perfumed, sent through him a keen pang of lust. Under cover of her silence he pressed her arm closely to his side: and, as they stood at the hotel door, he felt that they had escaped from their lives and duties, escaped from home and friends and run away together with wild and radiant hearts to a new adventure.

An old man was dozing in a great hooded chair in the hall. He lit a candle in the office and went before them to the stairs. They followed him in silence, their feet falling in soft thuds on the thickly carpeted stairs. She mounted the stairs behind the porter, her head bowed in the ascent, her frail shoulders curved as with a burden, her skirt girt tightly about her. He could have flung his arms about her hips and held her still for his arms were trembling with desire to seize her and only the stress of his nails against the palms of his hands held the wild impulse of his body in check. The porter halted on the stairs to settle his guttering candle. They halted too on the steps below him. In the silence Gabriel could hear the falling of the molten wax into the tray and the thumping of his own heart against his ribs.

The porter led them along a corridor and opened a door. Then he set his unstable candle down on a toilet table and asked at what hour they were to be called in the morning.

—Eight, said Gabriel.

The porter pointed to the tap of the electric light and began a muttered apology but Gabriel cut him short.

—We don't want any light. We have light enough from the street. And, I say, he added pointing to the candle, you might remove that handsome article, like a good man.

The porter took up his candle again, but slowly, for he was surprised by such a novel idea. Then he mumbled goodnight and went out. Gabriel shot the lock to.

A ghostly light from the street lamp lay in a long shaft from one window to the door. Gabriel threw his overcoat and hat on a couch and crossed the room towards the window. He looked down into the street in order that his emotion might calm a little. Then he turned and leaned against a chest of drawers with his back to the light. She had taken off her hat and cloak and was standing before a large swinging mirror, unhooking her waist. Gabriel paused for a few moments, watching her, and then said:

—Gretta!

She turned away from the mirror slowly and walked along the shaft of light towards him. Her face looked so serious and weary that the words would not pass Gabriel's lips. No, it was not the moment yet.

—You look tired, he said.

—I am a little, she answered.

—You don't feel ill or weak?

—No, tired: that's all.

She went on to the window and stood there, looking out. Gabriel waited again and then, fearing that diffidence was about to conquer him, he said abruptly:

—By the way, Gretta!

—What is it?

—You know that poor fellow Malins? he said quickly.

—Yes, what about him?

—Well, poor fellow, he's a decent sort of chap after all, continued Gabriel in a false voice. He gave me back that sovereign I lent him and I didn't expect it really. It's a pity he wouldn't keep away from that Browne because he's not a bad fellow at heart.

He was trembling now with annoyance. Why did she seem so abstracted? He did not know how he could begin. Was she annoyed too about something? If she would only turn to him or come to him of her own accord! To take her as she was would be brutal. No, he must see some ardour in her eyes first. He longed to be master of her strange mood.

—When did you lend him the pound? she asked after a pause. Gabriel strove to restrain himself from breaking out into brutal language about the sottish Malins and his pound. He longed to cry to her from his soul, to crush her body against his, to overmaster her. But he said:

—O, at Christmas, when he opened that little Christmas card shop in Henry Street.

He was in such a fever of rage and desire that he did not hear her come from the window. She stood before him for an instant looking at him strangely. Then, suddenly raising herself on tiptoe and resting her hands lightly on his shoulders, she kissed him.

—You are a very generous person, Gabriel, she said.

—Gabriel, trembling with delight at her sudden kiss and at the quaintness of her phrase, put his hands on her hair and began smoothing it back, scarcely touching it with his fingers. The washing had made it fine and brilliant. His heart was brimming over with happiness. Just when he was wishing for it she had come to him of her own accord. Perhaps her thoughts had been running with his. Perhaps she had felt the impetuous desire that was in him and then the yielding mood had come upon her. Now that she had fallen to him so easily he wondered why he had been so diffident.

He stood, holding her head between his hands. Then, slipping one arm swiftly about her body and drawing her towards him, he said softly:

—Gretta dear, what are you thinking about?

She did not answer nor yield wholly to his arm. He said again softly:

—Tell me what it is, Gretta. I think I know what is the matter. Do I know?

She did not answer at once. Then she said in an outburst of tears:

—O, I am thinking about that song, *The Lass of Aughrim*.

She broke loose from him and ran to the bed and, throwing her arms across the bedrail, hid her face. Gabriel stood stockstill for a moment in astonishment and then followed her. As he passed in the way of the cheval glass he caught sight of himself in full length, his broad, wellfilled shirtfront, the face whose expression always puzzled him when he saw it in a mirror and his glimmering gilt-rimmed eyeglasses. He halted a few paces from her and said:

—What about the song? Why does that make you cry?

She raised her head from her arms and dried her eyes with the back of her hand like a child. A kinder note than he had intended went into his voice.

—Why, Gretta? he asked.

—I am thinking about a person long ago who used to sing that song.

—And who was the person long ago? asked Gabriel smiling.

—It was a person I used to know in Galway when I was living with my grandmother, she said.

The smile passed away from Gabriel's face. A dull anger began to gather again at the back of his mind and the dull fires of his lust began to glow angrily in his veins.

—Someone you were in love with? he asked ironically.

—It was a young boy I used to know, she answered, named Michael Furey. He used to sing that song, *The Lass of Aughrim*. He was very delicate.

Gabriel was silent. He did not wish her to think that he was interested in this delicate boy.

—I can see him so plainly, she said after a moment. Such eyes as he had, big dark eyes! And such an expression in them—an expression! …

—O, then you were in love with him? said Gabriel.

—I used to go out walking with him, she said, when I was in Galway.

A thought flew across Gabriel's mind.

—Perhaps that was why you wanted to go to Galway with that Ivors girl? he said coldly.

She looked at him and asked in surprise:

—What for?

Her eyes made Gabriel feel awkward. He shrugged his shoulders and said:

—How do I know? To see him, perhaps.

She looked away from him along the shaft of light towards the window in silence.

—He is dead, she said at length. He died when he was only seventeen. Isn't it a terrible thing to die so young as that?

—What was he? asked Gabriel, still ironically.

—He was in the gasworks, she said.

Gabriel felt humiliated by the failure of his irony and by the evocation of this figure from the dead, a boy in the gasworks. The irony of his mood soured into sarcasm. While he had been full of memories of their secret life together, full of tenderness and joy and desire, she had been comparing him in her mind with another.

A shameful consciousness of his own person assailed him. He saw himself as a ludicrous figure, acting as a pennyboy for his aunts, a nervous wellmeaning sentimentalist, orating to vulgarians and idealising his own clownish lusts, the pitiable fatuous fellow he had caught a glimpse of in the mirror. Instinctively he turned his back more to the light lest she might see the shame that burned upon his forehead.

He tried to keep up his tone of cold interrogation but his voice when he spoke was humble and indifferent.

—I suppose you were in love with this Michael Furey, Gretta, he said.

—I was great with him at that time, she said.

Her voice was veiled and sad. Gabriel, feeling now how vain it would be to try to lead her whither he had purposed, caressed one of her hands and said also sadly:

—And what did he die of so young, Gretta? Consumption, was it?

—I think he died for me, she answered.

A vague terror seized Gabriel at this answer as if, at that hour when he had hoped to triumph, some impalpable and vindictive being was coming against him, gathering forces against him in its vague world. But he shook himself free of it with an effort of reason and continued to caress her hand. He did not question her again for he felt that she would tell him of herself. Her hand was warm and moist: it did not respond to his touch but he continued to caress it just as he had caressed her first letter to him that spring morning.

—It was in the winter, she said, about the beginning of the winter when I was going to leave my grandmother's and come up here to the convent. And he was ill at the time in his lodgings in Galway and wouldn't be let out and his people in Oughterard were written to. He was in decline, they said, or something like that. I never knew rightly.

She paused for a moment and sighed.

—Poor fellow, she said, he was very fond of me and he was such a gentle boy. We used to go out together walking, you know, Gabriel, like the way they do in the country. He was going to study singing only for his health. He had a very good voice, poor Michael Furey.

—Well, and then? asked Gabriel.

—And then when it came to the time for me to leave Galway and come up to the convent he was much worse and I wouldn't be let see him so I wrote him a letter saying I was going up to Dublin and would be back in the summer and hoping he would be better then.

She paused for a moment to get her voice under control and then went on:

—Then the night before I left I was in my grandmother's house in Nun's Island, packing up, and I heard gravel thrown up against the window. The window was so wet I couldn't see so I ran downstairs as I was and slipped out the back into the garden and there was the poor fellow at the end of the garden shivering.

—And did you not tell him to go back? asked Gabriel.

—I implored of him to go home at once and told him he would get his death in the rain. But he said he did not want to live. I can see his eyes as well as well![1] He was standing at the end of the wall where there was a tree.

—And did he go home? asked Gabriel.

—Yes, he went home. And when I was only a week in the convent he died and he was buried in Oughterard where his people came from. O, the day I heard that, that he was dead! …

She stopped, choking with sobs and, overcome by emotion, flung herself face downward on the bed, sobbing in the quilt. Gabriel held her hand for a moment longer, irresolutely, and then, shy of intruding on her grief, let it fall gently and walked quietly to the window. She was fast asleep.

Gabriel, leaning on his elbow, looked for a few moments unresentfully at her tangled hair and half open mouth, listening to her deep drawn breath. So she had had that romance in her life: a man had died for her sake. It hardly pained him now to think how poor a part he, her husband, had played in her life. He watched her while she slept as though he and she had never lived together as man and wife. His curious eyes rested long upon her face and on her hair: and as he thought of what she must have been then, in that time of her first girlish beauty, a strange friendly pity for her entered his soul. He did not like to say even to himself that her face was no

---

[1]   *as well as well*   I.e., as well as well can be.

longer beautiful but he knew that it was no longer the face for which Michael Furey had braved death.

Perhaps she had not told him all the story. His eyes moved to the chair over which she had thrown some of her clothes. A petticoat string dangled to the floor. One boot stood upright, its limp upper fallen down: the fellow of it lay upon its side. He wondered at his riot of emotions of an hour before. From what had it proceeded? From his aunts' supper, from his own foolish speech, from the wine and dancing, the merrymaking when saying goodnight in the hall, the pleasure of the walk along the river in the snow. Poor Aunt Julia! She too would soon be a shade[1] with the shade of Patrick Morkan and his horse. He had caught that haggard look upon her face for a moment when she was singing *Arrayed for the Bridal*. Soon perhaps he would be sitting in that same drawingroom, dressed in black, his silk hat on his knees. The blinds would be drawn down and Aunt Kate would be sitting beside him, crying and blowing her nose and telling him how Julia had died. He would cast about in his mind for some words that might console her and would find only lame and useless ones. Yes, yes: that would happen very soon.

The air of the room chilled his shoulders. He stretched himself cautiously along under the sheets and lay down beside his wife. One by one they were all becoming shades. Better pass boldly into that other world, in the full glory of some passion, than fade and wither dismally with age. He thought of how she who lay beside him had locked in her heart for so many years that image of her lover's eyes when he had told her that he did not wish to live.

Generous tears filled Gabriel's eyes. He had never felt like that himself towards any woman but he knew that such a feeling must be love. The tears gathered more thickly in his eyes and in the partial darkness he imagined he saw the form of a young man standing under a dripping tree. Other forms were near. His soul had approached that region where dwell the vast hosts of the dead. He was conscious of, but could not apprehend, their wayward and flickering existence. His own identity was fading out into a grey impalpable world: the solid world itself which these dead had one time reared and lived in was dissolving and dwindling.

A few light taps upon the pane made him turn to the window. It had begun to snow again. He watched sleepily the flakes, silver and dark, falling obliquely against the lamplight. The time had come for him to set out on his journey westward. Yes, the newspapers were right: snow was general all over Ireland. It was falling on every part of the dark central plain, on the treeless hills, falling softly upon the Bog of Allen and, farther westward, softly falling into the dark mutinous Shannon waves. It was falling, too, upon every part of the lonely churchyard on the hill where Michael Furey lay buried. It lay thickly drifted on the crooked crosses and headstones, on the spears of the little gate, on the barren thorns. His soul swooned slowly as he heard the snow falling faintly through the universe and faintly falling, like the descent of their last end, upon all the living and the dead.

—1914

Ulysses

The chapter of *Ulysses* reprinted here follows Book 5 of Homer's *Odyssey*, in which Odysseus is beached on the land of the Phaeacians, where he hides in a thicket to sleep. He is awakened by Princess Nausicaa and her ladies-in-waiting, who have come to do their washing on the beach and are playing a ball game. He reveals himself and begs for their help in returning home to his wife, Penelope. In Joyce's version, Leopold Bloom is loitering on the beach, avoiding returning home to his unfaithful Penelope, Molly Bloom. In this episode it is not Bloom but Gerty (the Nausicaa figure) who reveals herself.

from *Ulysses*

CHAPTER 13 [NAUSICAA]

The summer evening had begun to fold the world in its mysterious embrace. Far away in the west the sun was setting and the last glow of all too fleeting day lingered lovingly on sea and strand,[2] on the proud

---

[1] *shade* Ghost.

[2] *strand* Shore.

promontory of dear old Howth[1] guarding as ever the waters of the bay, on the weedgrown rocks along Sandymount shore and, last but not least, on the quiet church whence there streamed forth at times upon the stillness the voice of prayer to her who is in her pure radiance a beacon ever to the stormtossed heart of man, Mary, star of the sea.[2]

The three girl friends were seated on the rocks, enjoying the evening scene and the air which was fresh but not too chilly. Many a time and oft were they wont to come there to that favourite nook to have a cosy chat beside the sparkling waves and discuss matters feminine, Cissy Caffrey and Edy Boardman with the baby in the push-car and Tommy and Jacky Caffrey, two little curlyheaded boys, dressed in sailor suits with caps to match and the name H.M.S. Belleisle printed on both. For Tommy and Jacky Caffrey were twins, scarce four years old and very noisy and spoiled twins sometimes but for all that darling little fellows with bright merry faces and endearing ways about them. They were dabbling in the sand with their spades and buckets, building castles as children do, or playing with their big coloured ball, happy as the day was long. And Edy Boardman was rocking the chubby baby to and fro in the pushcar while that young gentleman fairly chuckled with delight. He was but eleven months and nine days old and, though still a tiny toddler, was just beginning to lisp his first babyish words. Cissy Caffrey bent over him to tease his fat little plucks[3] and the dainty dimple in his chin.

—Now, baby, Cissy Caffrey said. Say out big, big. I want a drink of water.

And baby prattled after her:

—A jink a jink a jawbo.

Cissy Caffrey cuddled the wee chap for she was awfully fond of children, so patient with little sufferers and Tommy Caffrey could never be got to take his castor oil unless it was Cissy Caffrey that held his nose

and promised him the scatty[4] heel of the loaf or brown bread with golden syrup on. What a persuasive power that girl had! But to be sure baby was as good as gold, a perfect little dote in his new fancy bib. None of your spoilt beauties, Flora Mac Flimsy[5] sort, was Cissy Caffrey. A truerhearted lass never drew the breath of life, always with a laugh in her gipsylike eyes and a frolicsome word on her cherryripe red lips, a girl lovable in the extreme. And Edy Boardman laughed too at the quaint language of little brother.

But just then there was a slight altercation between Master Tommy and Master Jacky. Boys will be boys and our two twins were no exception to this golden rule. The apple of discord[6] was a certain castle of sand which Master Jacky had built and Master Tommy would have it right go wrong that it was to be architecturally improved by a frontdoor like the Martello tower[7] had. But if Master Tommy was headstrong Master Jacky was selfwilled too and, true to the maxim that every little Irishman's house is his castle, he fell upon his hated rival and to such purpose that the wouldbe assailant came to grief and (alas to relate!) the coveted castle too. Needless to say the cries of discomfited Master Tommy drew the attention of the girl friends.

—Come here, Tommy, his sister called imperatively, at once! And you, Jacky, for shame to throw poor Tommy in the dirty sand. Wait till I catch you for that.

His eyes misty with unshed tears Master Tommy came at her call for their big sister's word was law with the twins. And in a sad plight he was after his misadven-

---

[1] *Howth* Fishing port on the northeast headland of Dublin Bay. Howth Head overlooks Sandymount, on the shore of Dublin Bay.

[2] *Mary ... sea* The Roman Catholic Church of Mary, Star of the Sea, is located near Sandymount beach. *Stella Maris* is an attribute of the Virgin Mary.

[3] *plucks* Cheeks.

[4] *scatty* Crumbled.

[5] *Flora Mac Flimsey* Miss Flora MacFlimsey of Madison Square, a character in American poet William Allen Butler's "Nothing to Wear" (1857) who is mocked for her obsession with fashionable clothing.

[6] *apple of discord* Reference to the Greek myth in which Eris (goddess of discord) threw a golden apple into the midst of a wedding banquet and said that it belonged to the fairest goddess present. The subsequent argument between Athena, Aphrodite, and Hera as to its rightful owner and the resolution of the argument is the putative cause of the Trojan War.

[7] *Martello tower* Round, fortified tower near Sandymount, one of a series of such structures built by the British in the nineteenth century to deter a sea invasion.

ture. His little man-o'-war[1] top and unmentionables[2] were full of sand but Cissy was a past mistress in the art of smoothing over life's tiny troubles and and very quickly not one speck of sand was to be seen on his smart little suit. Still the blue eyes were glistening with hot tears that would well up so she kissed away the hurtness and shook her hand at Master Jacky the culprit and said if she was near him she wouldn't be far from him, her eyes dancing in admonition.

—Nasty bold Jacky! she cried.

She put an arm round the little mariner and coaxed winningly:

—What's your name? Butter and cream?[3]

—Tell us who is your sweetheart, spoke Edy Boardman. Is Cissy your sweetheart?

—Nao, tearful Tommy said.

—Is Edy Boardman your sweetheart? Cissy queried.

—Nao, Tommy said.

—I know, Edy Boardman said none too amiably with an arch glance from her shortsighted eyes. I know who is Tommy's sweetheart, Gerty is Tommy's sweetheart.

—Nao, Tommy said on the verge of tears.

Cissy's quick motherwit guessed what was amiss and she whispered to Edy Boardman to take him there behind the pushcar where the gentlemen couldn't see and to mind he didn't wet his new tan shoes.

But who was Gerty?

Gerty MacDowell who was seated near her companions, lost in thought, gazing far away into the distance was in very truth as fair a specimen of winsome Irish girlhood as one could wish to see. She was pronounced beautiful by all who knew her though, as folks often said, she was more a Giltrap than a MacDowell. Her figure was slight and graceful, inclining even to fragility but those iron jelloids[4] she had been taking of late had done her a world of good much better than the Widow Welch's female pills[5] and she was much better of those discharges she used to get and that tired feeling. The waxen pallor of her face was almost spiritual in its ivorylike purity though her rosebud mouth was a genuine Cupid's bow, Greekly perfect. Her hands were of finely veined alabaster with tapering fingers and as white as lemon juice and queen of ointments could make them though it was not true that she used to wear kid gloves in bed or take a milk footbath either. Bertha Supple told that once to Edy Boardman, a deliberate lie, when she was black out at daggers drawn with Gerty (the girl chums had of course their little tiffs from time to time like the rest of mortals) and she told her to not let on whatever she did that it was her that told her or she'd never speak to her again. No. Honour where honour is due. There was an innate refinement, a languid queenly *hauteur*[6] about Gerty which was unmistakably evidenced in her delicate hands and higharched instep. Had kind fate but willed her to be born a gentlewoman of high degree in her own right and had she only received the benefit of a good education Gerty MacDowell might easily have held her own beside any lady in the land and have seen herself exquisitely gowned with jewels on her brow and patrician suitors at her feet vying with one another to pay their devoirs[7] to her. Mayhap it was this, the love that might have been, that lent to her softlyfeatured face at whiles a look, tense with suppressed meaning, that imparted a strange yearning tendency to the beautiful eyes, a charm few could resist. Why have women such eyes of witchery? Gerty's were of the bluest Irish blue, set off by lustrous lashes and dark expressive brows. Time was when those brows were not so silkily seductive. It was Madame Vera Verity, directress of the Woman Beautiful page of the Princess novelette,[8] who had first advised her to try eyebrowleine which gave that haunting expression to the eyes, so becoming in leaders of fashion, and she had never regretted it. Then there was blushing scientifically cured and how to be tall increase your height and you

---

[1] *man-o'-war* Sailor suit, frequently worn by children.

[2] *unmentionables* Underwear.

[3] *What's your ... cream* From a popular rhyme: "What's your name? / Butter an' crame / All the way from / Dirty Lane."

[4] *iron jelloids* Gelatine lozenges containing iron and sold as a cure for anemia.

[5] *Widow ... pills* Brand of medicine advertised as a remedy for gynecological problems.

[6] *hauteur* Haughtiness, elevation of manner.

[7] *devoirs* Dues; respects.

[8] *Princess novelette* Weekly London magazine *The Princess Novelettes*.

have a beautiful face but your nose? That would suit Mrs. Dignam because she had a button one. But Gerty's crowning glory was her wealth of wonderful hair. It was dark brown with a natural wave in it. She had cut it that very morning on account of the new moon[1] and it nestled about her pretty head in a profusion of luxuriant clusters and pared her nails too, Thursday for wealth.[2] And just now at Edy's words as a telltale flush, delicate as the faintest rosebloom, crept into her cheeks she looked so lovely in her sweet girlish shyness that of a surety God's fair land of Ireland did not hold her equal.

For an instant she was silent with rather sad downcast eyes. She was about to retort but something checked the words on her tongue. Inclination prompted her to speak out: dignity told her to be silent. The pretty lips pouted a while but then she glanced up and broke out into a joyous little laugh which had in it all the freshness of a young May morning. She knew right well, no-one better, what made squinty Edy say that because of him cooling in his attentions when it was simply a lover's quarrel. As per usual somebody's nose was out of joint about the boy that had the bicycle always riding up and down in front of her window. Only now his father kept him in the evenings studying hard to get an exhibition in the intermediate[3] that was on and he was going to Trinity college to study for a doctor when he left the high school like his brother W. E. Wylie who was racing in the bicycle races in Trinity college university. Little recked[4] he perhaps for what she felt, that dull aching void in her heart sometimes, piercing to the core. Yet he was young and perchance he might learn to love her in time. They were protestants in his family and of course Gerty knew Who came first and after Him the blessed Virgin and then Saint Joseph.[5] But he was undeniably handsome with an exquisite nose and he was what he looked, every inch a gentleman, the shape of his head too at the back without his cap on that she would know anywhere something off the common and the way he turned the bicycle at the lamp with his hands off the bars and also the nice perfume of those good cigarettes and besides they were both of a size and that was why Edy Boardman thought she was so frightfully clever because he didn't go and ride up and down in front of her bit of a garden.

Gerty was dressed simply but with the instinctive taste of a votary of Dame Fashion for she felt that there was just a might that he might be out. A neat blouse of electric blue, selftinted by dolly dyes[6] (because it was expected in the *Lady's Pictorial* that electric blue would be worn), with a smart vee opening down to the division and kerchief pocket (in which she always kept a piece of cottonwool scented with her favourite perfume because the handkerchief spoiled the sit) and a navy threequarter skirt cut to the stride showed off her slim graceful figure to perfection. She wore a coquettish little love of a hat of wideleaved nigger straw contrast trimmed with an underbrim of eggblue chenille and at the side a butterfly bow to tone. All Tuesday week[7] afternoon she was hunting to match that chenille but at last she found what she wanted at Clery's[8] summer sales, the very it, slightly shopsoiled but you would never notice, seven fingers two and a penny. She did it up all by herself and what joy was hers when she tried it on then, smiling at the lovely reflection which the mirror gave back to her! And when she put it on the waterjug to keep the shape she knew that that would take the shine out of some people she knew. Her shoes were the newest thing in footwear (Edy Boardman prided herself that she was very *petite* but she never had a foot like Gerty Mac-Dowell, a five, and never would ash, oak or elm[9]) with patent toecaps and just one smart buckle at her high-arched instep. Her well-turned ankle displayed its perfect proportions beneath her skirt and just the proper amount and no more of her shapely limbs encased in finespun hose with highspliced heels and wide garter

---

[1] *She had ... moon* According to popular superstition, it was best to cut one's hair during a new moon.

[2] *Thursday for wealth* According to astrologists, Thursday (the day sacred to Jupiter) is a good day on which to transact business and to be courageous.

[3] *exhibition in the intermediate* Exams given at the end of the school year to determine the winners of various cash prizes.

[4] *recked* Cared or knew.

[5] *Who came ... Joseph* More polite version of the oath "Jesus, Mary and Joseph."

[6] *dolly dyes* Brand of dye.

[7] *Tuesday week* I.e., a week ago last Tuesday.

[8] *Clery's* Major Dublin department store.

[9] *ash, oak or elm* I.e., for the rest of time.

tops. As for undies they were Gerty's chief care and who that knows the fluttering hopes and fears of sweet seventeen (though Gerty would never see seventeen again) can find it in his heart to blame her? She had four dinky sets, with awfully pretty stitchery, three garments and nighties extra, and each set slotted with different coloured ribbons, rosepink, pale blue, mauve and peagreen and she aired them herself and blued[1] them when they came home from the wash and ironed them and she had a brickbat[2] to keep the iron on because she wouldn't trust those washerwomen as far as she'd see them scorching the things. She was wearing the blue for luck, hoping against hope, her own colour and the lucky colour too for a bride to have a bit of blue somewhere on her because the green she wore that day week brought grief because his father brought him in to study for the intermediate exhibition and because she thought perhaps he might be out because when she was dressing that morning she nearly slipped up the old pair on her inside out and that was for luck and lovers' meetings if you put those things on inside out so long as it wasn't of a Friday.

And yet and yet! That strained look on her face! A gnawing sorrow is there all the time. Her very soul is in her eyes and she would give worlds to be in the privacy of her own familiar chamber where, giving way to tears, she could have a good cry and relieve her pentup feelings. Though not too much because she knew how to cry nicely before the mirror. You are lovely, Gerty, it said. The paly light of evening falls upon a face infinitely sad and wistful. Gerty MacDowell yearns in vain. Yes, she had known from the first that her daydream of a marriage has been arranged and the weddingbells ringing for Mrs. Reggy Wylie T.C.D.[3] (because the one who married the elder brother would be Mrs. Wylie) and in the fashionable intelligence[4] Mrs. Gertrude Wylie was wearing a sumptuous confection of grey trimmed with expensive blue fox was not to be. He was too young to understand. He would not believe in love, a woman's birthright. The night of the party long ago in

Stoers' (he was still in short trousers) when they were alone and he stole an arm round her waist she went white to the very lips. He called her little one in a strangely husky voice and snatched a half kiss (the first!) but it was only the end of her nose and then he hastened from the room with a remark about refreshments. Impetuous fellow! Strength of character had never been Reggy Wylie's strong point and he who would woo and win Gerty MacDowell must be a man among men. But waiting, always waiting to be asked and it was leap year[5] too and would soon be over. No prince charming is her beau ideal to lay a rare and wondrous love at her feet but rather a manly man with a strong quiet face who had not found his ideal, perhaps his hair slightly flecked with grey, and who would understand, take her in his sheltering arms, strain her to him in all the strength of his deep passionate nature and comfort her with a long long kiss. It would be like heaven. For such a one she yearns this balmy summer eve. With all the heart of her she longs to be his only, his affianced bride for riches for poor, in sickness in health, till death us two part, from this to this day forward.

And while Edy Boardman was with little Tommy behind the pushcar she was just thinking would the day ever come when she could call herself his little wife to be. Then they could talk about her till they went blue in the face, Bertha Supple too, and Edy, the spitfire, because she would be twenty-two in November. She would care for him with creature comforts too for Gerty was womanly wise and knew that a mere man liked that feeling of hominess. Her griddlecakes done to a golden-brown hue and queen Ann's pudding of delightful creaminess had won golden opinions from all because she had a lucky hand also for lighting a fire, dredge in the fine selfraising flour and always stir in the same direction then cream the milk and sugar and whisk well the white of eggs though she didn't like the eating part when there were any people that made her shy and often she wondered why you couldn't eat something poetical like violets or roses and they would have a beautifully appointed drawingroom with pictures and engravings and the photograph of grandpapa Giltrap's lovely dog Garryowen that almost talked, it was so human, and

---

[1] *blued* Treated with bluing, a cleaning agent that helps keep colors bright.

[2] *brickbat* Piece of brick.

[3] *T.C.D.* Trinity College, Dublin.

[4] *fashionable intelligence* I.e., society columns.

[5] *a leap year* The only time, according to traditional belief, when it was permissible for a woman to propose to a man.

chintz covers for the chairs and that silver toastrack in Clery's summer jumble sales like they have in rich houses. He would be tall with broad shoulders (she had always admired tall men for a husband) with glistening white teeth under his carefully trimmed sweeping moustache and they would go on the continent[1] for their honeymoon (three wonderful weeks!) and then, when they settled down in a nice snug and cosy little homely house, every morning they would both have brekky,[2] simple but perfectly served, for their own two selves and before he went out to business he would give his dear little wifey a good hearty hug and gaze for a moment deep down into her eyes.

Edy Boardman asked Tommy Caffrey was he done and he said yes, so then she buttoned up his little knickerbockers for him and told him to run off and play with Jacky and to be good now and not to fight. But Tommy said he wanted the ball and Edy told him no that baby was playing with the ball and if he took it there'd be wigs on the green[3] but Tommy said it was his ball and he wanted his ball and he pranced on the ground, if you please. The temper of him! O, he was a man already was little Tommy Caffrey since he was out of pinnies.[4] Edy told him no, no and to be off now with him and she told Cissy Caffrey not to give in to him.

—You're not my sister, naughty Tommy said. It's my ball.

But Cissy Caffrey told baby Boardman to look up, look up high at her finger and she snatched the ball quickly and threw it along the sand and Tommy after it in full career, having won the day.

—Anything for a quiet life, laughed Ciss.

And she tickled tiny tot's two cheeks to make him forget and played here's the lord mayor, here's his two horses, here's his gingerbread carriage and here he walks in, chinchopper, chinchopper, chinchopper chin. But Edy got as cross as two sticks about him getting his own way like that from everyone always petting him.

—I'd like to give him something, she said, so I would, where I won't say.

—On the beeoteetom, laughed Cissy merrily.

Gerty MacDowell bent down her head and crimsoned at the idea of Cissy saying an unladylike thing like that out loud she'd be ashamed of her life to say, flushing a deep rosy red, and Edy Boardman said she was sure the gentleman opposite heard what she said. But not a pin cared Ciss.

—Let him! she said with a pert toss of her head and a piquant tilt of her nose. Give it to him too on the same place as quick as I'd look at him.

Madcap Ciss with her golliwog[5] curls. You had to laugh at her sometimes. For instance when she asked you would you have some more Chinese tea and jaspberry ram and when she drew the jugs too and the men's faces on her nails with red ink make you split your sides or when she wanted to go where you know she said she wanted to run and pay a visit to the Miss White. That was just like Cissycums. O, and will you ever forget the evening she dressed up in her father's suit and hat and the burned cork moustache and walked down Tritonville road, smoking a cigarette. There was none to come up to her for fun. But she was sincerity itself, one of the bravest and truest hearts heaven ever made, not one of your twofaced things, too sweet to be wholesome.

And then there came out upon the air the sound of voices and the pealing anthem of the organ. It was the men's temperance retreat conducted by the missioner, the reverend John Hughes S.J.[6] rosary, sermon and benediction of the Most Blessed Sacrament. They were there gathered together without distinction of social class (and a most edifying spectacle it was to see) in that simple fane[7] beside the waves, after the storms of this weary world, kneeling before the feet of the immaculate, reciting the litany of Our Lady of Loreto, beseeching her to intercede for them, the old familiar words, holy Mary, holy virgin of virgins. How sad to poor Gerty's ears! Had her father only avoided the clutches of the demon drink, by taking the pledge or those powders the drink habit cured in Pearson's Weekly, she might now be rolling in her carriage, second to none. Over and over had she told herself that as she mused by the dying

---

[1] *continent* I.e., Europe.

[2] *brekky* Breakfast.

[3] *wigs on the green* I.e., a brawl (Irish slang).

[4] *pinnies* Pinafores (babies' clothing).

[5] *golliwog* Black-faced male doll with frizzy hair.

[6] *S.J.* Society of Jesus (the Jesuits).

[7] *fane* Temple.

embers in a brown study[1] without the lamp because she hated two lights or oftentimes gazing out of the window dreamily by the hour at the rain falling on the rusty bucket, thinking. But that vile decoction which has ruined so many hearths and homes had cast its shadow over her childhood days. Nay, she had even witnessed in the home circle deeds of violence caused by intemperance and had seen her own father, a prey to the fumes of intoxication, forget himself completely for if there was one thing of all things that Gerty knew it was the man who lifts his hand to a woman save in the way of kindness deserves to be branded as the lowest of the low.

And still the voices sang in supplication to the Virgin most powerful, Virgin most merciful. And Gerty, rapt in thought, scarce saw or heard her companions or the twins at their boyish gambols[2] or the gentleman off Sandymount green that Cissy Caffrey called the man that was so like himself passing along the strand taking a short walk. You never saw him anyway screwed[3] but still and for all that she would not like him for a father because he was too old or something or on account of his face (it was a palpable case of doctor Fell)[4] or his carbuncly nose with the pimples on it and his sandy moustache a bit white under his nose. Poor father! With all his faults she loved him still when he sang *Tell me, Mary, how to woo thee* or *My love and cottage near Rochelle* and they had stewed cockles and lettuce with Lazenby's salad dressing for supper and when he sang *The moon hath raised* with Mr. Dignam that died suddenly and was buried, God have mercy on him, from a stroke. Her mother's birthday that was and Charley was home on his holidays and Tom and Mr. Dignam and Mrs. and Patsy and Freddy Dignam and they were to have had a group[5] taken. No-one would have thought the end was so near. Now he was laid to rest. And her mother said to him to let that be a warning to him for

the rest of his days and he couldn't even go to the funeral on account of the gout and she had to go into town to bring him the letters and samples from his office about Catesby's cork lino,[6] artistic standard designs, fit for a palace, gives tiptop wear and always bright and cheery in the home.

A sterling good daughter was Gerty just like a second mother in the house, a ministering angel too with a little heart worth its weight in gold. And when her mother had those raging splitting headaches who was it rubbed on the menthol cone[7] on her forehead but Gerty though she didn't like her mother taking pinches of snuff and that was the only single thing they ever had words about, taking snuff. Everyone thought the world of her for her gentle ways. It was Gerty who turned off the gas at the main every night and it was Gerty who tacked up on the wall of that place where she never forgot every fortnight the chlorate of lime[8] Mr. Tunney the grocer's christmas almanac the picture of halcyon days where a young gentleman in the costume they used to wear then with a threecornered hat was offering a bunch of flowers to his ladylove with oldtime chivalry through her lattice window. You could see there was a story behind it. The colours were done something lovely. She was in a soft clinging white in a studied attitude and the gentleman was in chocolate and he looked a thorough aristocrat. She often looked at them dreamily when she went there for a certain purpose and felt her own arms that were white and soft just like hers with the sleeves back and thought about those times because she had found out in Walker's pronouncing dictionary that belonged to grandpapa Giltrap about the halcyon days[9] what they meant.

The twins were now playing in the most approved brotherly fashion, till at last Master Jacky who was really as bold as brass there was no getting behind that deliberately kicked the ball as hard as ever he could down towards the seaweedy rocks. Needless to say poor Tommy was not slow to voice his dismay but luckily the gentleman in black who was sitting there by himself

---

[1] *in a brown study* Expression meaning lost in thought.
[2] *gambols* Merrymaking.
[3] *screwed* Drunk.
[4] *doctor Fell* John Fell was Dean of Christ Church, Oxford. When he supposedly threatened satirist Thomas Brown with expulsion from the college, Brown is said to have responded poetically: "I do not love thee, Dr. Fell / The reason why I cannot tell; / But this alone I know full well, / I do not love thee, Dr. Fell."
[5] *group* I.e., group photo.
[6] *lino* Linoleum.
[7] *menthol cone* Menthol, with its cooling effects, was a common home remedy for headaches.
[8] *chlorate of lime* Used to disinfect and deodorize outdoor toilets.
[9] *halcyon days* Calm, peaceful days.

came gallantly to the rescue and intercepted the ball. Our two champions claimed their plaything with lusty cries and to avoid trouble Cissy Caffrey called to the gentleman to throw it to her please. The gentleman aimed the ball once or twice and then threw it up the strand towards Cissy Caffrey but it rolled down the slope and stopped right under Gerty's skirt near the little pool by the rock. The twins clamoured again for it and Cissy told her to kick it away and let them fight for it so Gerty drew back her foot but she wished their stupid ball hadn't come rolling down to her and she gave a kick but she missed and Edy and Cissy laughed.

—If you fail try again, Edy Boardman said.

Gerty smiled assent and bit her lip. A delicate pink crept into her pretty cheek but she was determined to let them see so she just lifted her skirt a little but just enough and took good aim and gave the ball a jolly good kick and it went ever so far and the two twins after it down towards the shingle.[1] Pure jealousy of course it was nothing else to draw attention on account of the gentleman opposite looking. She felt the warm flush, a danger signal always with Gerty MacDowell, surging and flaming into her cheeks. Till then they had only exchanged glances of the most casual but now under the brim of her new hat she ventured a look at him and the face that met her gaze there in the twilight, wan and strangely drawn, seemed to her the saddest she had ever seen.

Through the open window of the church the fragrant incense was wafted and with it the fragrant names of her who was conceived without stain of original sin, spiritual vessel, pray for us, honourable vessel, pray for us, vessel of singular devotion, pray for us, mystical rose. And careworn hearts were there and toilers for their daily bread and many who had erred and wandered, their eyes wet with contrition but for all that bright with hope for the reverend father Hughes had told them what the great saint Bernard said in his famous prayer of Mary,[2] the most pious Virgin's intercessory power that it was not recorded in any age that those who implored her powerful protection were ever

abandoned by her.

The twins were now playing again right merrily for the troubles of childhood are but as fleeting summer showers. Cissy played with baby Boardman till he crowed with glee, clapping baby hands in air. Peep she cried behind the hood of the pushcar and Edy asked where was Cissy gone and then Cissy popped up her head and cried ah! and, my word, didn't the little chap enjoy that! And then she told him to say papa.

—Say papa, baby. Say pa pa pa pa pa pa pa.

And baby did his level best to say it for he was very intelligent for eleven months everyone said and big for his age and the picture of health, a perfect little bunch of love, and he would certainly turn out to be something great, they said.

—Haja ja ja haja.

Cissy wiped his little mouth with the dribbling bib and wanted him to sit up properly and say pa pa pa but when she undid the strap she cried out, holy saint Denis, that he was possing wet and to double the half blanket the other way under him. Of course his infant majesty was most obstreperous at such toilet formalities and he let everyone know it:

—Habaa baaaahabaaa baaaa.

And two great big lovely big tears coursing down his cheeks. It was all no use soothering him with no, nono, baby, no and telling him about the geegee and where was the puffpuff but Ciss, always, readywitted, gave him in his mouth the teat of the suckingbottle and the young heathen was quickly appeased.

Gerty wished to goodness they would take their squalling baby home out of that and not get on her nerves no hour to be out and the little brats of twins. She gazed out towards the distant sea. It was like the paintings that man used to do on the pavement with all the coloured chalks and such a pity too leaving them there to be all blotted out, the evening and the clouds coming out and the Bailey light on Howth[3] and to hear the music like that and the perfume of those incense they burned in the church like a kind of waft. And while she gazed her heart went pitapat. Yes, it was her he was looking at and there was meaning in his look. His eyes burned into her as though they would search her through and through, read her very soul. Wonderful

---

[1] *shingle* Pebbly beach.

[2] *his famous ... Mary* Reference to the "Memorare," a prayer frequently used by Saint Bernard of Clairvaux but not actually composed by him.

[3] *Bailey ... Howth* Lighthouse on Howth Head.

eyes they were, superbly expressive, but could you trust them? People were so queer. She could see at once by his dark eyes and his pale intellectual face that he was a foreigner the image of the photo she had of Martin Harvey, the matinee idol, only for the moustache which she preferred because she wasn't stagestruck like Winny Rippingham that wanted they two to always dress the same on account of a play but she could not see whether he had an aquiline nose or a slightly *retroussé*[1] from where he was sitting. He was in deep mourning,[2] she could see that, and the story of a haunting sorrow was written on his face. She would have given worlds to know what it was. He was looking up so intently, so still and he saw her kick the ball and perhaps he could see the bright steel buckles of her shoes if she swung them like that thoughtfully with the toes down. She was glad that something told her to put on the transparent stockings thinking Reggy Wylie might be out but that was far away. Here was that of which she had so often dreamed. It was he who mattered and there was joy on her face because she wanted him because she felt instinctively that he was like no-one else. The very heart of the girlwoman went out to him, her dreamhusband, because she knew on the instant it was him. If he had suffered, more sinned against than sinning, or even, even, if he had been himself a sinner, a wicked man, she cared not. Even if he was a protestant or methodist she could convert him easily if he truly loved her. There were wounds that wanted healing with heartbalm. She was a womanly woman not like other flighty girls, unfeminine, he had known, those cyclists showing off what they hadn't got and she just yearned to know all, to forgive all if she could make him fall in love with her, make him forget the memory of the past. Then mayhap he would embrace her gently, like a real man, crushing her soft body to him, and love her, his ownest girlie, for herself alone.

Refuge of sinners. Comfortress of the afflicted. *Ora pro nobis*.[3] Well has it been said that whosoever prays to her with faith and constancy can never be lost or cast away: and fitly is she too a haven of refuge for the afflicted because of the seven dolours which transpierced her own heart. Gerty could picture the whole scene in the church, the stained glass windows lighted up, the candles, the flowers and the blue banners of the blessed Virgin's sodality[4] and Father Conroy was helping Canon O'Hanlon at the altar, carrying things in and out with his eyes cast down. He looked almost a saint and his confessionbox was so quiet and clean and dark and his hands were just like white wax and if ever she became a Dominican nun in their white habit perhaps he might come to the convent for the novena of Saint Dominic. He told her that time when she told him about that in confession crimsoning up to the roots of her hair for fear he could see, not to be troubled because that was only the voice of nature and we were all subject to nature's laws, he said, in this life and that that was no sin because that came from the nature of woman instituted by God, he said, and that Our Blessed Lady herself said to the archangel Gabriel be it done unto me according to Thy Word. He was so kind and holy and often and often she thought and thought could she work a ruched teacosy with embroidered floral design for him as a present or a clock but they had a clock she noticed on the mantelpiece white and gold with a canary bird that came out of a little house to tell the time the day she went there about the flowers for the forty hours' adoration[5] because it was hard to know what sort of a present to give or perhaps an album of illuminated views of Dublin or some place.

The exasperating little brats of twins began to quarrel again and Jacky threw the ball out towards the sea and they both ran after it. Little monkeys common as ditch-water. Someone ought to take them and give them a good hiding for themselves to keep them in their places, the both of them. And Cissy and Edy shouted after them to come back because they were afraid the tide might come in on them and be drowned.

—Jacky! Tommy!

Not they! What a great notion they had! So Cissy said it was the very last time she'd ever bring them out. She jumped up and called them and she ran down the slope past him, tossing her hair behind her which had a

---

[1] *retroussé* Turned up.

[2] *in deep mourning* I.e., dressed in black, out of respect for a recently deceased friend or family member.

[3] *Ora pro nobis* Latin: pray for us.

[4] *sodality* Religious guild or society.

[5] *forty hours' adoration* Forty hours' prayer in memory of the time during which Jesus lay in His tomb before the Resurrection.

good enough colour if there had been more of it but with all the thingamerry she was always rubbing into it she couldn't get it to grow long because it wasn't natural so she could just go and throw her hat at it.[1] She ran with long gandery strides it was a wonder she didn't rip up her skirt at the side that was too tight on her because there was a lot of the tomboy about Cissy Caffrey and she was a forward piece[2] whenever she thought she had a good opportunity to show off and just because she was a good runner she ran like that so that he could see all the end of her petticoat running and her skinny shanks up as far as possible. It would have served her just right if she had tripped up over something accidentally on purpose with her high crooked French heels on her to make her look tall and got a fine tumble. *Tableau!*[3] That would have been a very charming exposé for a gentleman like that to witness.

Queen of angels, queen of patriarchs, queen of prophets, of all saints, they prayed, queen of the most holy rosary and then Father Conroy handed the thurible[4] to Canon O' Hanlon and he put in the incense and censed the Blessed Sacrament and Cissy Caffrey caught the two twins and she was itching to give them a ringing good clip on the ear but she didn't because she thought he might be watching but she never made a bigger mistake in all her life because Gerty could see without looking that he never took his eyes off of her and then Canon O'Hanlon handed the thurible back to Father Conroy and knelt down looking up at the Blessed Sacrament and the choir began to sing *Tantum ergo*[5] and she just swung her foot in and out in time as the music rose and fell to the *Tantumer gosa cramen turn*. Three and eleven she paid for those stockings in Sparrow's of George's street on the Tuesday, no the

Monday before Easter and there wasn't a brack[6] on them and that was what he was looking at, transparent, and not at her insignificant ones that had neither shape nor form (the cheek of her!) because he had eyes in his head to see the difference for himself.

Cissy came up along the strand with the two twins and their ball with her hat anyhow on her to one side after her run and she did look a streel[7] tugging the two kids along with the flimsy blouse she bought only a fortnight before like a rag on her back and a bit of her petticoat hanging like a caricature. Gerty just took off her hat for a moment to settle her hair and a prettier, a daintier head of nutbrown tresses was never seen on a girl's shoulders, a radiant little vision, in sooth, almost maddening in its sweetness. You would have to travel many a long mile before you found a head of hair the like of that. She could almost see the swift answering flush of admiration in his eyes that set her tingling in every nerve. She put on her hat so that she could see from underneath the brim and swung her buckled shoe faster for her breath caught as she caught the expression in his eyes. He was eyeing her as a snake eyes its prey. Her woman's instinct told her that she had raised the devil in him and at the thought a burning scarlet swept from throat to brow till the lovely colour of her face became a glorious rose.

Edy Boardman was noticing it too because she was squinting at Gerty, half smiling, with her specs, like an old maid, pretending to nurse the baby. Irritable little gnat she was and always would be and that was why no-one could get on with her, poking her nose into what was no concern of hers. And she said to Gerty:

—A penny for your thoughts.

—What? replied Gerty with a smile reinforced by the whitest of teeth. I was only wondering was it late.

Because she wished to goodness they'd take the snottynosed twins and their baby home to the mischief out of that so that was why she just gave a gentle hint about its being late. And when Cissy came up Edy asked her the time and Miss Cissy, as glib as you like, said it was half past kissing time, time to kiss again. But Edy wanted to know because they were told to be in early.

---

[1] *throw her ... it* When a woman could not attract a man's attention any other way (i.e., by her appearance), it was said that she might as well "throw her hat at him."

[2] *piece* Slang: attractive woman.

[3] *Tableau* French: picture. Name of a popular parlor game in which participants would strike poses to convey a particular scene, announcing "tableau!" to indicate their pose was ready to be interpreted.

[4] *thurible* Vessel for burning and disseminating incense.

[5] *Tantum ergo* Hymn beginning *Tantum ergo Sacramentum* (Latin: so great a sacrament).

[6] *brack* Flaw.

[7] *streel* Disreputable woman.

—Wait, said Cissy, I'll ask my uncle Peter over there what's the time by his conundrum.

So over she went and when he saw her coming she could see him take his hand out of his pocket, getting nervous, and beginning to play with his watchchain, looking at the church. Passionate nature though he was Gerty could see that he had enormous control over himself. One moment he had been there, fascinated by a loveliness that made him gaze and the next moment it was the quiet gravefaced gentleman, selfcontrol expressed in every line of his distinguishedlooking figure.

Cissy said to excuse her would he mind telling her what was the right time and Gerty could see him taking out his watch, listening to it and looking up and clearing his throat and he said he was very sorry his watch was stopped but he thought it must be after eight because the sun was set. His voice had a cultured ring in it and though he spoke in measured accents there was a suspicion of a quiver in the mellow tones. Cissy said thanks and came back with her tongue out and said uncle said his waterworks were out of order.

Then they sang the second verse of the *Tantum ergo* and Canon O'Hanlon got up again and censed the Blessed Sacrament and knelt down and he told Father Conroy that one of the candles was just going to set fire to the flowers and Father Conroy got up and settled it all right and she could see the gentleman winding his watch and listening to the works and she swung her leg more in and out in time. It was getting darker but he could see and he was looking all the time that he was winding the watch or whatever he was doing to it and then he put it back and put his hands back into his pockets. She felt a kind of a sensation rushing all over her and she knew by the feel of her scalp and that irritation against her stays that that thing must be coming on because the last time too was when she clipped her hair on account of the moon. His dark eyes fixed themselves on her again drinking in her every contour, literally worshipping at her shrine. If ever there was undisguised admiration in a man's passionate gaze it was there plain to be seen on that man's face. It is for you, Gertrude MacDowell, and you know it.

Edy began to get ready to go and it was high time for her and Gerty noticed that that little hint she gave had the desired effect because it was a long way along the strand to where there was the place to push up the pushcar and Cissy took off the twins' caps and tidied their hair to make herself attractive of course and Canon O'Hanlon stood up with his cope[1] poking up at his neck and Father Conroy handed him the card to read off and he read out *Panem de coelo praestitisti eis*[2] and Edy and Cissy were talking about the time all the time and asking her but Gerty could pay them back in their own coin and she just answered with scathing politeness when Edy asked her was she heartbroken about her best boy throwing her over. Gerty winced sharply. A brief cold blaze shone from her eyes that spoke volumes of scorn immeasurable. It hurt. O yes, it cut deep because Edy had her own quiet way of saying things like that she knew would wound like the confounded little cat she was. Gerty's lips parted swiftly to frame the word but she fought back the sob that rose to her throat, so slim, so flawless, so beautifully moulded it seemed one an artist might have dreamed of. She had loved him better than he knew. Lighthearted deceiver and fickle like all his sex he would never understand what he had meant to her and for an instant there was in the blue eyes a quick stinging of tears. Their eyes were probing her mercilessly but with a brave effort she sparkled back in sympathy as she glanced at her new conquest for them to see.

—O, responded Gerty, quick as lightning, laughing, and the proud head flashed up. I can throw my cap at who I like because it's leap year.

Her words rang out crystalclear, more musical than the cooing of the ringdove but they cut the silence icily. There was that in her young voice that told that she was not a one to be lightly trifled with. As for Mr. Reggy with his swank and his bit of money she could just chuck him aside as if he was so much filth and never again would she cast as much as a second thought on him and tear his silly postcard into a dozen pieces. And if ever after he dared to presume she could give him one look of measured scorn that would make him shrivel up on the spot. Miss puny little Edy's countenance fell to no slight extent and Gerty could see by her looking as black as thunder that she was simply in a towering rage

---

[1] *cope* Cloak-like ecclesiastical vestment.

[2] *Panem … eis* Latin: You have given them bread from Heaven.

though she hid it, the little kinnatt,[1] because that shaft had struck home for her petty jealousy and they both knew that she was something aloof, apart in another sphere, that she was not of them and there was somebody else too that knew it and saw it so they could put that in their pipe and smoke it.

Edy straightened up baby Boardman to get ready to go and Cissy tucked in the ball and the spades and buckets and it was high time too because the sandman was on his way for Master Boardman junior and Cissy told him too that Billy Winks was coming and that baby was to go deedaw and baby looked just too ducky, laughing up out of his gleeful eyes, and Cissy poked him like that out of fun in his wee fat tummy and baby, without as much as by your leave, sent up his compliments on to his brand-new dribbling bib.

—O my! Puddeny pie! protested Ciss. He has his bib destroyed.

The slight *contretemps*[2] claimed her attention but in two twos she set that little matter to rights.

Gerty stifled a smothered exclamation and gave a nervous cough and Edy asked what and she was just going to tell her to catch it while it was flying but she was ever ladylike in her deportment so she simply passed it off with consummate tact by saying that that was the benediction because just then the bell rang out from the steeple over the quiet seashore because Canon O'Hanlon was up on the altar with the veil that Father Conroy put round him round his shoulders giving the benediction with the Blessed Sacrament in his hands.

How moving the scene there in the gathering twilight, the last glimpse of Erin,[3] the touching chime of those evening bells and at the same time a bat flew forth from the ivied belfry through the dusk, hither, thither, with a tiny lost cry. And she could see far away the lights of the lighthouses so picturesque she would have loved to do with a box of paints because it was easier than to make a man and soon the lamplighter would be going his rounds past the presbyterian church grounds and along by shady Tritonville avenue where the couples walked and lighting the lamp near her window where

Reggy Wylie used to turn his freewheel like she read in that book *The Lamplighter*[4] by Miss Cummins, author of *Mabel Vaughan* and other tales. For Gerty had her dreams that no-one knew of. She loved to read poetry and when she got a keepsake from Bertha Supple of that lovely confession album with the coralpink cover to write her thoughts in she laid it in the drawer of her toilettable which, though it did not err on the side of luxury, was scrupulously neat and clean. It was there she kept her girlish treasures trove, the tortoiseshell combs, her child of Mary badge, the whiterose scent, the eyebrowleine, her alabaster pouncetbox and the ribbons to change when her things came home from the wash and there were some beautiful thoughts written in it in violet ink that she bought in Hely's of Dame Street for she felt that she too could write poetry if she could only express herself like that poem that appealed to her so deeply that she had copied out of the newspaper she found one evening round the potherbs. *Art thou real, my ideal?* it was called by Louis J. Walsh, Magherafelt,[5] and after there was something about twilight, *wilt thou ever?* and ofttimes the beauty of poetry, so sad in its transient loveliness, had misted her eyes with silent tears that the years were slipping by for her, one by one, and but for that one shortcoming she knew she need fear no competition and that was an accident coming down Dalkey hill and she always tried to conceal it. But it must end, she felt. If she saw that magic lure in his eyes there would be no holding back for her. Love laughs at locksmiths.[6] She would make the great sacrifice. Her every effort would be to share his thoughts. Dearer than the whole world would she be to him and gild his days with happiness. There was the allimportant question and she was dying to know was he a married man or a widower who had lost his wife or some tragedy like the nobleman with the foreign name from the land of song had to have her put into a madhouse, cruel only to be kind. But even if—what then? Would it make a very great difference? From everything in the least indelicate

---

[1] *kinnatt* Impudent puppy.

[2] *contretemps* Mishap.

[3] *Erin* Ireland.

[4] *The Lamplighter* Title of 1854 novel by American novelist Maria Cummins. Gerty is also the name of Cummins's protagonist.

[5] *Louis J. Walsh* Orator and versifier (1880–1942); *Magherafelt* Parish in northeastern Ireland.

[6] *Love … locksmiths* Title of an 1803 play by George Colman that then became a proverbial phrase.

her finebred nature instinctively recoiled. She loathed that sort of person, the fallen women off the accommodation walk beside the Dodder[1] that went with the soldiers and coarse men, with no respect for a girl's honour, degrading the sex and being taken up to the police station. No, no: not that. They would be just good friends like a big brother and sister without all that other in spite of the conventions of Society with a big ess. Perhaps it was an old flame he was in mourning for from the days beyond recall. She thought she understood. She would try to understand him because men were so different. The old love was waiting, waiting with little white hands stretched out, with blue appealing eyes. Heart of mine! She would follow her dream of love, the dictates of her heart that told her he was her all in all, the only man in all the world for her for love was the master guide. Nothing else mattered. Come what might she would be wild, untrammelled, free.

Canon O'Hanlon put the Blessed Sacrament back into the tabernacle[2] and the choir sang *Laudate Dominum omnes gentes*[3] and then he locked the tabernacle door because the benediction was over and Father Conroy handed him his hat to put on and crosscat Edy asked wasn't she coming but Jacky Caffrey called out:

—O, look, Cissy!

And they all looked was it sheet lightning but Tommy saw it too over the trees beside the church, blue and then green and purple.

—It's fireworks, Cissy Caffrey said.

And they all ran down the strand to see over the houses and the church, helterskelter, Edy with the pushcar with baby Boardman in it and Cissy holding Tommy and Jacky by the hand so they wouldn't fall running.

—Come on, Gerty, Cissy called. It's the bazaar fireworks.

But Gerty was adamant. She had no intention of being at their beck and call. If they could run like rossies[4] she could sit so she said she could see from where she was. The eyes that were fastened upon her set her pulses tingling. She looked at him a moment, meeting his glance, and a light broke in upon her. Whitehot passion was in that face, passion silent as the grave and it had made her his. At last they were left alone without the others to pry and pass remarks and she knew he could be trusted to the death, steadfast, a sterling man, a man of inflexible honour to his fingertips. His hands and face were working and a tremor went over her. She leaned back far to look up where the fireworks were and she caught her knee in her hands so as not to fall back looking up and there was no-one to see only him and her when she revealed all her graceful beautifully shaped legs like that, supply soft and delicately rounded, and she seemed to hear the panting of his heart, his hoarse breathing, because she knew about the passion of men like that, hotblooded, because Bertha Supple told her once in dead secret and made her swear she'd never about the gentleman lodger that was staying with them out of the Congested Districts Board[5] that had pictures cut out of papers of those skirtdancers and highkickers and she said he used to do something not very nice that you could imagine sometimes in the bed. But this was altogether different from a thing like that because there was all the difference because she could almost feel him draw her face to his and the first quick hot touch of his handsome lips. Besides there was absolution so long as you didn't do the other thing before being married and there ought to be women priests that would understand without your telling out and Cissy Caffrey too sometimes had that dreamy kind of dreamy look in her eyes so that she too, my dear, and Winny Rippingham so mad about actors' photographs and besides it was on account of that other thing coming on the way it did.

And Jacky Caffrey shouted to look, there was another and she leaned back and the garters were blue to match on account of the transparent and they all saw it and shouted to look, look there it was and she leaned back ever so far to see the fireworks and something queer was flying about through the air, a soft thing to and fro, dark. And she saw a long Roman candle going up over the trees up, up, and, in the tense hush, they were all breathless with excitement as it went higher and

---

[1] *Dodder* River in Ireland.

[2] *tabernacle* Receptacle for the consecrated Host.

[3] *Laudate ... gentes* Latin: Give praise to the Lord, O ye nations.

[4] *rossies* Unchaste women.

[5] *Congested Districts Board* Established in 1891 to deal with the perceived problems of overpopulation in poor rural areas.

higher and she had to lean back more and more to look up after it, high, high, almost out of sight, and her face was suffused with a divine, an entrancing blush from straining back and he could see her other things too, nainsook knickers, the fabric that caresses the skin, better than those other pettiwidth,[1] the green, four and eleven, on account of being white and she let him and she saw that he saw and then it went so high it went out of sight a moment and she was trembling in every limb from being bent so far back that he had a full view high up above her knee where no-one ever not even on the swing or wading and she wasn't ashamed and he wasn't either to look in that immodest way like that because he couldn't resist the sight of the wondrous revealment half offered like those skirtdancers behaving so immodest before gentlemen looking and he kept on looking, looking. She would fain have cried to him chokingly, held out her snowy slender arms to him to come, to feel his lips laid on her white brow, the cry of a young girl's love, a little strangled cry, wrung from her, that cry that has rung through the ages. And then a rocket sprang and bang shot blind blank and O! then the Roman candle burst and it was like a sigh of O! and everyone cried O! O! in raptures and it gushed out of it a stream of rain gold hair threads and they shed and ah! they were all greeny dewy stars falling with golden, O so lovely! O so soft, sweet, soft!

Then all melted away dewily in the grey air: all was silent. Ah! She glanced at him as she bent forward quickly, a pathetic little glance of piteous protest, of shy reproach under which he coloured like a girl. He was leaning back against the rock behind. Leopold Bloom (for it is he) stands silent, with bowed head before those young guileless eyes. What a brute he had been! At it again? A fair unsullied soul had called to him and, wretch that he was, how had he answered? An utter cad he had been! He of all men! But there was an infinite store of mercy in those eyes, for him too a word of pardon even though he had erred and sinned and wandered. Should a girl tell? No, a thousand times no. That was their secret, only theirs, alone in the hiding twilight and there was none to know or tell save the little bat that flew so softly through the evening to and fro and little bats don't tell.

Cissy Caffrey whistled, imitating the boys in the football field to show what a great person she was: and then she cried:

—Gerty! Gerty! We're going. Come on. We can see from farther up.

Gerty had an idea, one of love's little ruses. She slipped a hand into her kerchief pocket and took out the wadding and waved in reply of course without letting him and then slipped it back. Wonder if he's too far to. She rose. Was it goodbye? No. She had to go but they would meet again, there, and she would dream of that till then, tomorrow, of her dream of yester eve. She drew herself up to her full height. Their souls met in a last lingering glance and the eyes that reached her heart, full of a strange shining, hung enraptured on her sweet flowerlike face. She half smiled at him wanly, a sweet forgiving smile, a smile that verged on tears, and then they parted.

Slowly without looking back she went down the uneven strand to Cissy, to Edy, to Jacky and Tommy Caffrey, to little baby Boardman. It was darker now and there were stones and bits of wood on the strand and slippy seaweed. She walked with a certain quiet dignity characteristic of her but with care and very slowly because, because Gerty MacDowell was …

Tight boots? No. She's lame! O!

Mr. Bloom watched her as she limped away. Poor girl! That's why she's left on the shelf and the others did a sprint. Thought something was wrong by the cut of her jib.[2] Jilted beauty. A defect is ten times worse in a woman. But makes them polite. Glad I didn't know it when she was on show. Hot little devil all the same. Wouldn't mind. Curiosity like a nun or a negress or a girl with glasses. That squinty one is delicate. Near her monthlies, I expect, makes them feel ticklish. I have such a bad headache today.[3] Where did I put the letter? Yes, all right. All kinds of crazy longings. Licking pennies. Girl in Tranquilla convent that nun told me liked to smell rock oil. Virgins go mad in the end I suppose. Sister? How many women in Dublin have it

---

1   *pettiwidth*   Name of a brand of underwear.

2   *cut of her jib*   Originally a nautical term, referring to the configuration of a boat's sails. It was also commonly used to refer to a person's look or style.

3   *I have … today*   This sentence is from a letter Bloom received from his secret correspondent, Martha Clifford, earlier that morning.

today? Martha, she. Something in the air. That's the moon. But then why don't all women menstruate at the same time with same moon, I mean? Depends on the time they were born, I suppose. Or all start scratch then get out of step. Sometimes Molly and Milly[1] together. Anyhow I got the best of that. Damned glad I didn't do it in the bath this morning over her silly I will punish you letter. Made up for that tramdriver this morning. That gouger M'Coy stopping me to say nothing. And his wife engagement in the country valise, voice like a pickaxe. Thankful for small mercies. Cheap too. Yours for the asking. Because they want it themselves. Their natural craving. Shoals of them every evening poured out of offices. Reserve better. Don't want it they throw it at you. Catch em alive, O. Pity they can't see themselves. A dream of wellfilled hose. Where was that? Ah, yes. Mutoscope[2] pictures in Capel street: for men only. Peeping Tom. Willy's hat and what the girls did with it. Do they snapshot those girls or is it all a fake. *Lingerie* does it. Felt for the curves inside her *deshabillé*.[3] Excites them also when they're. I'm all clean come and dirty me. And they like dressing one another for the sacrifice. Milly delighted with Molly's new blouse. At first. Put them all on to take them all off. Molly. Why I bought her the violet garters. Us too: the tie he[4] wore, his lovely socks and turnedup trousers. He wore a pair of gaiters the night that first we met. His lovely shirt was shining beneath his what? of jet. Say a woman loses a charm with every pin she takes out. Pinned together. O Mairy lost the pin of her. Dressed up to the nines for somebody. Fashion part of their charm. Just changes when you're on the track of the secret. Except the east: Mary, Martha:[5] now as then. No reasonable offer refused. She wasn't in a hurry either. Always off to a fellow when they are. They never forget an appointment. Out on

spec probably. They believe in chance because like themselves. And the others inclined to give her an odd dig. Girl friends at school, arms round each other's necks or with ten fingers locked, kissing and whispering secrets about nothing in the convent garden. Nuns with whitewashed faces, cool coif and their rosaries going up and down, vindictive too for what they can't get. Barbed wire.[6] Be sure now and write to me. And I'll write to you. Now won't you? Molly and Josie Powell. Till Mr. Right comes along, then meet once in a blue moon. *Tableau!* O, look who it is for the love of God! How are you at all? What have you been doing with yourself? Kiss and delighted to, kiss, to see you. Picking holes in each other's appearance. You're looking splendid. Sister souls showing their teeth at one another. How many have you left? Wouldn't lend each other a pinch of salt.

Ah!

Devils they are when that's coming on them. Dark devilish appearance. Molly often told me feel things a ton weight. Scratch the sole of my foot. O that way! O, that's exquisite! Feel it myself too. Good to rest once in a way. Wonder if it's bad to go with them then. Safe in one way. Turns milk, makes fiddlestrings snap. Something about withering plants I read in a garden. Besides they say if the flower withers she wears she's a flirt. All are. Daresay she felt I. When you feel like that you often meet what you feel. Liked me or what? Dress they look at. Always know a fellow courting: collars and cuffs. Well cocks and lions do the same and stags. Same time might prefer a tie undone or something. Trousers? Suppose I when I was? No. Gently does it. Dislike rough and tumble. Kiss in the dark and never tell. Saw something in me. Wonder what. Sooner have me as I am than some poet chap with bearsgrease plastery hair, lovelock over his dexter optic.[7] To aid gentleman in literary. Ought to attend to my appearance my age. Didn't let her see me in profile. Still, you never know. Pretty girls and ugly men marrying. Beauty and the beast. Besides I can't be so if Molly. Took off her hat to show her hair. Wide brim bought to hide her face, meeting someone might know her, bend down or carry

[1] *Molly and Milly* Bloom's wife (Molly is short for Marion) and daughter.

[2] *Mutoscope* Device for viewing, in quick succession, a series of pictures of objects in motion.

[3] *deshabillé* Revealing undergarment. Here Bloom is remembering phrases from the pornographic book, *Sweets of Sin*, that he bought earlier that day.

[4] *he* Dublin singer Hugh "Blazes" Boylan, with whom Molly Bloom is having an affair.

[5] *Mary, Martha* Biblical sisters of Lazarus. See Luke 10.38–42.

[6] *Barbed wire* Reference to the fictitious belief that barbed wire was invented by nuns.

[7] *lovelock* Curl of particular shape or style; *dexter optic* Latin: right eye.

a bunch of flowers to smell. Hair strong in rut.[1] Ten bob I got for Molly's combings when we were on the rocks in Holies street. Why not? Suppose he gave her money. Why not? All a prejudice. She's worth ten, fifteen, more a pound. What? I think so. All that for nothing. Bold hand. Mrs. Marion.[2] Did I forget to write address on that letter like the postcard I sent to Flynn. And the day I went to Drimmie's[3] without a necktie. Wrangle with Molly it was put me off. No, I remember. Richie Goulding. He's another. Weighs on his mind. Funny my watch stopped at half past four. Dust. Shark liver oil[4] they use to clean could do it myself. Save. Was that just when he, she?

O, he did. Into her. She did. Done.

Ah!

Mr. Bloom with careful hand recomposed his wet shirt. O Lord, that little limping devil. Begins to feel cold and clammy. After effect not pleasant. Still you have to get rid of it someway. They don't care. Complimented perhaps. Go home to nicey bread and milky and say night prayers with the kiddies. Well, aren't they. See her as she is spoil all. Must have the stage setting, the rouge, costume, position, music. The name too. Amours[5] of actresses. Nell Gwynn, Mrs. Bracegirdle, Maud Branscombe.[6] Curtain up. Moonlight silver effulgence. Maiden discovered with pensive bosom. Little sweetheart come and kiss me. Still I feel. The strength it gives a man. That's the secret of it. Good job I let off there behind coming out of Dignam's. Cider that was. Otherwise I couldn't have. Makes you want to sing after. Lacaus esant taratara.[7] Suppose I spoke to her. What about? Bad plan however of you don't know how to end the conversation. Ask them a question they ask you another. Good idea if you're in a cart. Wonderful of course if you say: good evening, and you see she's on for it: good evening. O but the dark evening in the Appian way[8] I nearly spoke to Mrs. Clinch O thinking she was. Whew! Girl in Meath street that night. All the dirty things I made her say all wrong of course. My arks she called it. It's so hard to find one who. Aho! If you don't answer when they solicit must be horrible for them till they harden. And kissed my hand when I gave her the extra two shillings. Parrots. Press the button and the bird will squeak. Wish she hadn't called me sir. O, her mouth in the dark! And you a married man with a single girl! That's what they enjoy. Taking a man from another woman. Or even hear of it. Different with me. Glad to get away from other chap's wife. Eating off his cold plate. Chap in the Burton today spitting back gum-chewed gristle. French letter[9] still in my pocketbook. Cause of half the trouble. But might happen sometime, I don't think. Come in. All is prepared. I dreamt. What? Worst is beginning. How they change the venue when it's not what they like. Ask you do you like mushrooms because she once knew a gentleman who. Or ask you what someone was going to say when he changed his mind and stopped. Yet if I went the whole hog, say: I want to, something like that. Because I did. She too. Offend her. Then make it up. Pretend to want something awfully, then cry off for her sake. Flatters them. She must have been thinking of someone else all the time. What harm? Must since she came to the use of reason, he, he and he. First kiss does the trick. The propitious moment. Something inside them goes pop. Mushy like, tell by their eye, on the sly. First thoughts are best. Remember that till their dying day. Molly, lieutenant Mulvey that kissed her under the Moorish wall[10] beside the gardens. Fifteen she told me. But her breasts were developed. Fell asleep then. After Glencree dinner that was when we drove home the featherbed mountain. Gnashing her teeth in sleep. Lord mayor had his eye on her too. Val Dillon. Apoplectic.

There she is with them down there for the fireworks. My fireworks. Up like a rocket, down like a stick. And

---

[1] Hair … rut During mating season, the odor of an animal's skin changes. Here Bloom imagines similar changes occurring in women.

[2] Mrs. Marion Reference to the letter Blazes Boylan wrote to Marion Bloom.

[3] Drimmie's David Drimmie and Sons, the law office where Bloom used to work.

[4] Shark liver oil Used to lubricate machinery.

[5] Amours Love affairs.

[6] Nell … Branscombe Famous English actresses of the seventeenth, eighteenth, and nineteenth centuries, respectively.

[7] Lacaus esant taratara Bloom's rendition of a quote from Giacomo Meyerbeer's opera Les Huguenots (1836): La causa è santa (Italian: The cause is sacred).

[8] Appian way Street on the southern edge of Dublin.

[9] French letter Slang: condom.

[10] Moorish wall In Gibraltar, where Molly was raised.

the children, twins they must be, waiting for something to happen. Want to be grownups. Dressing in mother's clothes. Time enough, understand all the ways of the world. And the dark one with the mop head and the nigger mouth. I knew she could whistle. Mouth made for that. Like Molly. Why that high class whore in Jammet's wore her veil only to her nose. Would you mind, please, telling me the right time? I'll tell you the right time up a dark lane. Say prunes and prisms forty times every morning, cure for fat lips.[1] Caressing the little boy too. Onlookers see most of the game. Of course they understand birds, animals, babies. In their line.

Didn't look back when she was going down the strand. Wouldn't give that satisfaction. Those girls, those girls, those lovely seaside girls. Fine eyes she had, clear. It's the white of the eye brings that out not so much the pupil. Did she know what I? Course. Like a cat sitting beyond a dog's jump. Women never meet one like that Wilkins in the high school drawing a picture of Venus with all his belongings on show. Call that innocence? Poor idiot! His wife has her work cut out for her. Never see them sit on a bench marked *Wet Paint*. Eyes all over them. Look under the bed for what's not there. Longing to get the fright of their lives. Sharp as needles they are. When I said to Molly the man at the corner of Cuffe street was goodlooking, thought she might like, twigged at once he had a false arm. Had too. Where do they get that? Typist going up Roger Greene's stairs two at a time to show her understandings. Handed down from father to mother to daughter, I mean. Bred in the bone. Milly for example drying her handkerchief on the mirror to save the ironing. Best place for an ad to catch a woman's eye on a mirror.[2] And when I sent her for Molly's Paisley shawl to Presscott's, by the way that ad I must, carrying home the change in her stocking. Clever little minx! I never told her. Neat way she carries parcels too. Attract men, small thing like that. Holding up her hand, shaking it, to let the blood flow back when it was red. Who did you learn that from? Nobody.

Something the nurse taught me. O, don't they know? Three years old she was in front of Molly's dressingtable just before we left Lombard street west. Me have a nice pace. Mullingar. Who knows? Ways of the world. Young student. Straight on her pins anyway not like the other. Still she was game. Lord, I am wet. Devil you are. Swell of her calf. Transparent stockings, stretched to breaking point. Not like that frump today. A.E.[3] Rumpled stockings. Or the one in Grafton street. White. Wow! Beef to the heel.[4]

A monkey puzzle rocket burst, spluttering in darting crackles. Zrads and zrads, zrads, zrads. And Cissy and Tommy ran out to see and Edy after with the pushcar and then Gerty beyond the curve of the rocks. Will she? Watch! Watch! See! Looked round. She smelt an onion.[5] Darling, I saw your. I saw all.

Lord!

Did me good all the same. Off colour after Kiernan's, Dignam's. For this relief much thanks. In *Hamlet*,[6] that is. Lord! It was all things combined. Excitement. When she leaned back felt an ache at the butt of my tongue. Your head it simply swirls. He's right. Might have made a worse fool of myself however. Instead of talking about nothing. Then I will tell you all. Still it was a kind of language between us. It couldn't be? No, Gerty they called her. Might be false name however like my and the address Dolphin's barn a blind.

*Her maiden name was Jemima Brown
And she lived with her mother in Irishtown.*[7]

Place made me think of that I suppose. All tarred with the same brush. Wiping pens in their stockings. But the ball rolled down to her as if it understood. Every

---

[1] *Say prunes … lips*   See Dickens's *Little Dorrit* (1857): "Papa, potatoes, poultry, prunes, and prism are all very good words for the lips: especially prunes and prism."

[2] *Best place … mirror*   Bloom is in the advertising industry; he sells ad space in newspapers.

[3] *A.E.*   Pen name of Irish writer and artist George Russell (1865–1935).

[4] *Beef to the heel*   Said of women whose legs are very thick, right down to their feet.

[5] *smelt an onion*   Reference to a popular joke in which a man eats a raw onion whenever he will be around a woman so that she will not tempt him to become entangled in an affair. His plan is foiled when he meets a woman who finds the onion smell attractive.

[6] *In Hamlet*   See *Hamlet* 1.1.8, in which one of the guards thanks another for relieving him.

[7] *Her maiden … Irishtown*   From an Irish street ballad.

bullet has its billet.[1] Course I never could throw anything straight at school. Crooked as a ram's horn. Sad however because it lasts only a few years till they settle down to pot-walloping and papa's pants will soon fit Willy and fullers' earth[2] for the baby when they hold him out to do ah ah. No soft job. Saves them. Keeps them out of harm's way. Nature. Washing child, washing corpse.[3] Dignam. Children's hands always round them. Cocoanut skulls, monkeys, not even closed at first, sour milk in their swaddles and tainted curds. Oughtn't to have given that child an empty teat to suck. Fill it up with wind. Mrs. Beaufoy, Purefoy. Must call to the hospital.[4] Wonder is nurse Callan there still. She used to look over some nights when Molly was in the Coffee Palace. That young doctor O'Hare I noticed her brushing his coat. And Mrs. Breen and Mrs. Dignam once like that too, marriageable. Worst of all at night Mrs. Duggan told me in the City Arms. Husband rolling in drunk, stink of pub off him like a polecat. Have that in your nose in the dark, whiff of stale boose. Then ask in the morning: was I drunk last night? Bad policy however to fault the husband. Chickens come home to roost. They stick by one another like glue. Maybe the women's fault also. That's where Molly can knock spots off them.[5] It is the blood of the south. Moorish. Also the form, the figure. Hands felt for the opulent. Just compare for instance those others. Wife locked up at home, skeleton in the cupboard. Allow me to introduce my. Then they trot you out some kind of a nondescript, wouldn't know what to call her. Always see a fellow's weak point in his wife. Still there's destiny in it, falling in love. Have their own secrets between them. Chaps that would go to the dogs if some woman didn't take them in hand. Then little chits of girls, height of a shilling in coppers,[6] with little hubbies. As God made them He matched them. Sometimes children

turn out well enough. Twice nought makes one. Or old rich chap of seventy and blushing bride. Marry in May and repent in December. This wet is very unpleasant. Stuck. Well the foreskin is not back. Better detach.

Ow!

Other hand a sixfooter with a wifey up to his watchpocket. Long and the short of it. Big he and little she. Very strange about my watch. Wristwatches are always going wrong. Wonder is there any magnetic influence between the person because that was about the time he. Yes, I suppose at once. Cat's away the mice will play. I remember looking in Pill lane. Also that now is magnetism. Back of everything magnetism. Earth for instance pulling this and being pulled. That causes movement. And time? Well that's the time the movement takes. Then if one thing stopped the whole ghesabo[7] would stop bit by bit. Because it's all arranged. Magnetic needle tells you what's going on in the sun, the stars. Little piece of steel iron. When you hold out the fork. Come. Come. Tip. Woman and man that is. Fork and steel. Molly, he. Dress up and look and suggest and let you see and see more and defy you if you're a man to see that and, like a sneeze coming, legs, look, look and if you have any guts in you. Tip. Have to let fly.

Wonder how is she feeling in that region. Shame all put on before third person. More put out about a hole in her stocking. Molly, her underjaw stuck out, head back, about the farmer in the ridingboots and spurs at the horse show. And when the painters were in Lombard street west. Fine voice that fellow had. How Giuglini[8] began. Smell that I did, like flowers. It was too. Violets. Came from the turpentine probably in the paint. Make their own use of everything. Same time doing it scraped her slipper on the floor so they wouldn't hear. But lots of them can't kick the beam,[9] I think. Keep that thing up for hours. Kind of a general all round over me and half down my back.

Wait. Hm. Hm. Yes. That's her perfume. Why she waved her hand. I leave you this to think of me when I'm far away on the pillow. What is it? Heliotrope? No, Hyacinth? Hm. Roses, I think. She'd like scent of that kind. Sweet and cheap: soon sour. Why Molly likes

---

[1] *Every bullet … billet* Expression meaning everything has its place.

[2] *fullers' earth* Used for cleaning grease from clothing.

[3] *washing corpse* It was traditionally the women's job to prepare a body for burial.

[4] *Must call … hospital* The Blooms's family friend, Mina Purefoy, is in labor.

[5] *knock spots off them* Beat them; be much better than they are.

[6] *shilling … coppers* Equal to twelve pennies ("coppers").

[7] *whole ghesabo* I.e., whole show.

[8] *Giuglini* Italian tenor Antonio Giuglini (1827–65).

[9] *kick the beam* Experience orgasm.

opoponax. Suits her with a little jessamine mixed. Her high notes and her low notes. At the dance night she met him, dance of the hours.[1] Heat brought it out. She was wearing her black and it had the perfume of the time before. Good conductor, is it? Or bad? Light too. Suppose there's some connection. For instance if you go into a cellar where it's dark. Mysterious thing too. Why did I smell it only now? Took its time in coming like herself, slow but sure. Suppose it's ever so many millions of tiny grains blown across. Yes, it is. Because those spice islands, Cinghalese this morning, smell them leagues off. Tell you what it is. It's like a fine fine veil or web they have all over the skin, fine like what do you call it gossamer and they're always spinning it out of them, fine as anything, rainbow colours without knowing it. Clings to everything she takes off. Vamp of her stockings. Warm shoe. Stays. Drawers: little kick, taking them off. Byby till next time. Also the cat likes to sniff in her shift on the bed. Know her smell in a thousand. Bathwater too. Reminds me of strawberries and cream. Wonder where it is really. There or the armpits or under the neck. Because you get it out of all holes and corners. Hyacinth perfume made of oil or ether or something. Muskrat. Bag under their tails one grain pour off odour for years. Dogs at each other behind. Good evening. Evening, How do you sniff? Hm. Hm. Very well, thank you. Animals go by that. Yes now, look at it that way. We're the same. Some women for instance warn you off when they have their period. Come near. Then get a hogo[2] you could hang your hat on. Like what? Potted herrings gone stale or. Boof! Please keep off the grass.

Perhaps they get a man smell off us. What though? Cigary gloves Long John had on his desk the other. Breath? What you eat and drink gives that. No. Mansmell, I mean. Must be connected with that because priests that are supposed to be are different. Women buzz round it like flies round treacle. Railed off the altar get on to it at any cost. The tree of forbidden priest. O father, will you? Let me be the first to. That diffuses itself all through the body, permeates. Source of life and it's extremely curious the smell. Celery sauce. Let me.

Mr. Bloom inserted his nose. Hm. Into the. Hm.

Opening of his waistcoat. Almonds or. No. Lemons it is. Ah no, that's the soap.[3]

O by the by that lotion. I knew there was something on my mind. Never went back and the soap not paid. Dislike carrying bottles like that hag this morning. Hynes might have paid me that three shillings. I could mention Meagher's[4] just to remind him. Still if he works that paragraph. Two and nine. Bad opinion of me he'll have. Call tomorrow. How much do I owe you? Three and nine? Two and nine, sir. Ah. Might stop him giving credit another time. Lose your customers that way. Pubs do. Fellows run up a bill on the slate and then slinking around the back streets into somewhere else.

Here's this nobleman passed before. Blown in from the bay. Just went as far as turn back. Always at home at dinnertime. Looks mangled out: had a good tuck in.[5] Enjoying nature now. Grace after meals. After supper walk a mile. Sure he has a small bank balance somewhere, government sit.[6] Walk after him now make him awkward like those newsboys me today. Still you learn something. See ourselves as others see us. So long as women don't mock what matter? That's the way to find out. Ask yourself who is he now. *The Mystery Man on the Beach*, prize titbit story by Mr. Leopold Bloom. Payment at the rate of one guinea per column. And that fellow today at the graveside in the brown macintosh. Corns on his kismet[7] however. Healthy perhaps absorb all the. Whistle brings rain they say. Must be some somewhere. Salt in the Ormond damp. The body feels the atmosphere. Old Betty's joints are on the rack. Mother Shipton's prophecy that is about ships around they fly in the twinkling.[8] No. Signs of rain it is. The

---

[1] *dance of the hours* Ballet from Amilcare Ponchiellei's *La Gioconda*.

[2] *hogo* Scent.

[3] *the soap* Bloom bought lemon soap earlier, and is carrying it in his pocket. He has also ordered the hand lotion that he mentions in the following paragraph.

[4] *Meagher's* A pub.

[5] *tuck in* Meal.

[6] *sit* Position.

[7] *Corns on his kismet* I.e., he is having bad luck.

[8] *Mother Shipton's … twinkling* Mother Shipton was a famous prophetess of Tudor England. Here Bloom confuses two quotations from Charles Hindley's 1862 fictional work *The Wonderful History and Surprising Prophecies of Mother Shipton*. The first is a prediction of the telegraph ("Around the world thoughts shall fly / In the twinkling of an eye"), and the second is a prediction of steam locomotion ("Water shall yet more wonders do, / Now strange, yet

royal reader.[1] And distant hills seem coming nigh.

Howth. Bailey light. Two, four, six, eight, nine. See. Has to change or they might think it a house. Wreckers. Grace darling.[2] People afraid of the dark. Also glow-worms, cyclists: lightingup time. Jewels diamonds flash better. Light is a kind of reassuring. Not going to hurt you. Better now of course than long ago. Country roads. Run you through the small guts for nothing. Still two types there are you bob against. Scowl or smile. Pardon! Not at all. Best time to spray plants too in the shade after the sun. Some light still. Red rays are longest. Roygbiv Vance taught us: red, orange, yellow, green, blue, indigo, violet. A star I see. Venus? Can't tell yet. Two, when three it's night. Were those nightclouds there all the time? Looks like a phantom ship. No. Wait. Trees are they? An optical illusion. Mirage. Land of the setting sun this. Homerule sun setting in the southeast. My native land, goodnight.

Dew falling. Bad for you, dear, to sit on that stone. Brings on white fluxions. Never have little baby then less he was big strong fight his way up through. Might get piles myself. Sticks too like a summer cold, sore on the mouth. Cut with grass or paper worst. Friction of the position. Like to be that rock she sat on. O sweet little, you don't know how nice you looked. I begin to like them at that age. Green apples. Grab at all that offer. Suppose it's the only time we cross legs, seated. Also the library today: those girl graduates. Happy chairs under them. But it's the evening influence. They feel all that. Open like flowers, know their hours, sunflowers, Jerusalem artichokes, in ballrooms, chandeliers, avenues under the lamps. Nightstock in Mat Dillon's garden where I kissed her shoulder. Wish I had a full length oilpainting of her then. June that was too I wooed. The year returns. History repeats itself. Ye crags and peaks I'm with you once again. Life, love, voyage round your own little world. And now? Sad about her lame of course but must be on your guard not to feel too much pity. They take advantage.

All quiet on Howth now. The distant hills seem. Where we.[3] The rhododendrons. I am a fool perhaps. He gets the plums and I the plumstones. Where I come in. All that old hill has seen. Names change: that's all. Lovers: yum yum.

Tired I feel now. Will I get up? O wait. Drained all the manhood out of me, little wretch. She kissed me. My youth. Never again. Only once it comes. Or hers. Take the train there tomorrow. No. Returning not the same. Like kids your second visit to a house. The new I want. Nothing new under the sun. Care of P.O. Dolphin's barn. Are you not happy in your? Naughty darling. At Dolphin's barn charades in Luke Doyle's house. Mat Dillon and his bevy of daughters: Tiny, Atty, Floey, Maimy, Louy, Hetty. Molly too. Eighty-seven that was. Year before we. And the old major partial to his drop of spirits. Curious she an only child, I an only child. So it returns. Think you're escaping and run into yourself. Longest way round is the shortest way home. And just when he and she. Circus horse walking in a ring. Rip van Winkle we played. Rip: tear in Henny Doyle's overcoat. Van: breadvan delivering. Winkle: cockles and periwinkles. Then I did Rip van Winkle coming back. She leaned on the sideboard watching. Moorish eyes. Twenty years asleep in Sleepy Hollow. All changed. Forgotten. The young are old. His gun rusty from the dew.

Ba. What is that flying about? Swallow? Bat probably. Thinks I'm a tree, so blind. Have birds no smell? Metempsychosis.[4] They believed you could be changed into a tree from grief. Weeping willow. Ba. There he goes. Funny little beggar. Wonder where he lives. Belfry up there. Very likely. Hanging by his heels in the odour of sanctity. Bell scared him out, I suppose. Mass seems to be over. Could hear them all at it. Pray for us. And pray for us. And pray for us. Good idea the repetition. Same thing with ads. Buy from us. And buy from us. Yes, there's the light in the priest's house. Their frugal meal. Remember about the mistake in the valuation

---

shall be true").

[1]   *royal reader*   School textbook.

[2]   *Grace darling*   Grace Darling and her father, William, were lighthouse keepers who became national heroes after they braved dangerous waters to rescue the victims of a shipwreck in 1838.

[3]   *Where we*   Where Leopold courted Molly.

[4]   *Metempsychosis*   Belief that after death the soul moves into another body.

when I was in Thom's. Twentyeight it is.[1] Two houses they have. Gabriel Conroy's brother is curate. Ba. Again. Wonder why they come out at night like mice. They're a mixed breed. Birds are like hopping mice. What frightens them, light or noise? Better sit still. All instinct like the bird in drouth got water out of the end of a jar by throwing in pebbles.[2] Like a little man in a cloak he is with tiny hands. Weeny bones. Almost see them shimmering, kind of a bluey white. Colours depend on the light you see. Stare the sun for example like the eagle[3] then look at a shoe see a blotch blob yellowish. Wants to stamp his trademark on everything. Instance, that cat this morning on the staircase. Colour of brown turf. Say you never see them with three colours. Not true. That half tabbywhite tortoiseshell in the *City Arms* with the letter em on her forehead. Body fifty different colours. Howth a while ago amethyst. Glass flashing. That's how that wise man what's his name with the burning glass.[4] Then the heather goes on fire. It can't be tourists' matches. What? Perhaps the sticks dry rub together in the wind and light. Or broken bottles in the furze act as a burning glass in the sun. Archimedes. I have it! My memory's not so bad.

Ba. Who knows what they're always flying for. Insects? That bee last week got into the room playing with his shadow on the ceiling. Might be the one bit me, come back to see. Birds too never find out what they say. Like our small talk. And says she and says he. Nerve they have to fly over the ocean and back. Lots must be killed in storms, telegraph wires. Dreadful life sailors have too. Big brutes of oceangoing steamers floundering along in the dark, lowing out like seacows. *Faugh a ballagh.*[5] Out of that, bloody curse to you. Others in vessels, bit of a handkerchief sail, pitched about like snuff at a wake when the stormy winds do

blow. Married too. Sometimes away for years at the ends of the earth somewhere. No ends really because it's round. Wife in every port they say. She has a good job if she minds it till Johnny comes marching home again. If ever he does. Smelling the tail end of ports. How can they like the sea? Yet they do. The anchor's weighed. Off he sails with a scapular or a medal on him for luck. Well? And the tephilim[6] no what's this they call it poor papa's father had on his door to touch. That brought us out of the land of Egypt and into the house of bondage. Something in all those superstitions because when you go out never know what dangers. Hanging on to a plank or astride of a beam for grim life, lifebelt round round him, gulping salt water, and that's the last of his nibs till the sharks catch hold of him. Do fish ever get seasick?

Then you have a beautiful calm without a cloud, smooth sea, placid, crew and cargo in smithereens, Davy Jones' locker.[7] Moon looking down. Not my fault, old cockalorum.[8]

A lost long candle wandered up the sky from Mirus bazaar in search of funds for Mercer's hospital and broke, drooping, and shed a cluster of violet but one white stars. They floated, fell: they faded. The shepherd's hour: the hour of folding: hour of tryst. From house to house, giving his everwelcome double knock, went the nine o'clock postman, the glowworm's lamp at his belt gleaming here and there through the laurel hedges. And among the five young trees a hoisted lintstock[9] lit the lamp at Leahy's terrace. By screens of lighted windows, by equal gardens a shrill voice went crying, wailing: *Evening Telegraph, stop press edition! Result of the Gold Cup races!* and from the door of Dignam's house a boy ran out and called. Twittering the bat flew here, flew there. Far out over the sands the coming surf crept, grey. Howth settled for slumber tired of long days, of yumyum rhododendrons (he was old) and felt gladly the night breeze lift, ruffle his fell of ferns. He lay but opened a red eye unsleeping, deep and

---

[1] *Remember about … it is* Bloom seems to be referring to a mistake that was made while he was working for Thom's, in which the priest's house was evaluated at 28 pounds.

[2] *like the … pebbles* One of Aesop's Fables.

[3] *like the eagle* According to myth, eagles could stare at the sun, and by flying up toward the sun would rejuvenate their eyes.

[4] *wise man … glass* Greek mathematician Archimedes was said to have set the Roman fleet on fire by concentrating the sun's rays with mirrors.

[5] *Faugh a ballagh* Irish battle cry: clear the way.

[6] *tephilim* Jewish phyllactery. The words Bloom is thinking of is the Hebrew word "mezuzah," a piece of parchment containing Biblical passages that is placed in a case on the doorpost.

[7] *Davy Jones' locker* According to sailors' folklore, this locker at the bottom of the ocean was where all things lost at sea were stored.

[8] *cockalorum* Self-important person.

[9] *lintstock* Long staff with a forked head to hold a match.

slowly breathing, slumberous but awake. And far on Kish bank the anchored lightship twinkled, winked at Mr. Bloom.

Life those chaps out there must have, stuck in the same spot. Irish Lights board.[1] Penance for their sins. Coastguards too. Rocket and breeches buoy and life-boat. Day we went out for the pleasure cruise in the Erin's King,[2] throwing them the sack of old papers. Bears in the zoo. Filthy trip. Drunkards out to shake up their livers. Puking overboard to feed the herrings. Nausea. And the women, fear of God in their faces. Milly, no sign of funk. Her blue scarf loose, laughing. Don't know what death is at that age. And then their stomachs clean. But being lost they fear. When we hid behind the tree at Crumlin. I didn't want to. Mamma! Mamma! Babes in the wood. Frightening them with masks too. Throwing them up in the air to catch them. I'll murder you. Is it only half fun? Or children playing battle. Whole earnest. How can people aim guns at each other. Sometimes they go off. Poor kids. Only troubles wildfire and nettlerash. Calomel purge[3] I got her for that. After getting better asleep with Molly. Very same teeth she has. What do they love? Another themselves? But the morning she chased her with the umbrella. Perhaps so as not to hurt. I felt her pulse. Ticking. Little hand it was: now big. Dearest Papli.[4] All that the hand says when you touch. Loved to count my waistcoat buttons. Her first stays I remember. Made me laugh to see. Little paps to begin with. Left one is more sensitive, I think.[5] Mine too. Nearer the heart. Padding themselves out if fat is in fashion. Her growing pains at night, calling, wakening me. Frightened she was when her nature came on her first. Poor child! Strange moment for the mother too. Brings back her girlhood. Gibraltar. Looking from Buena Vista. O'Hara's tower. The seabirds screaming. Old Barbary ape that gobbled all his family. Sundown, gunfire for the men to cross the lines.

Looking out over the sea she told me. Evening like this, but clear, no clouds. I always thought I'd marry a lord or a gentleman with a private yacht. *Buenas noches, señorita. El hombre ama la muchaha hermosa.*[6] Why me? Because you were so foreign from the others.

Better not stick here all night like a limpet. This weather makes you dull. Must be getting on for nine by the light. Go home. Too late for *Leah, Lily of Killarney.*[7] No. Might be still up. Call to the hospital to see. Hope she's over. Long day I've had. Martha, the bath, funeral, house of keys, museum with those goddesses, Dedalus' song. Then that bawler in Barney Kiernan's. Got my own back there. Drunken ranters. What I said about his God made him wince. Mistake to hit back. Or? No. Ought to go home and laugh at themselves. Always want to be swilling in company. Afraid to be alone like a child of two. Suppose he hit me. Look at it other way round. Not so bad then. Perhaps not to hurt he meant. Three cheers for Israel. Three cheers for the sister-in-law he hawked about, three fangs in her mouth. Same style of beauty. Particularly nice old party for a cup of tea. The sister of the wife of the wild man of Borneo has just come to town. Imagine that in the early morning at close range. Everyone to his taste as Morris said when he kissed the cow. But Dignam's put the boots on it.[8] Houses of mourning so depressing because you never know. Anyhow she wants the money. Must call to those Scottish widows[9] as I promised. Strange name. Takes it for granted we're going to pop off first. That widow on Monday was is outside Cramer's that looked at me. Buried the poor husband but progressing favourably on the premium. Her widow's mite. Well? What do you expect her to do? Must wheedle her way along. Widower I hate to see. Looks so forlorn. Poor man O'Connor wife and five children poisoned by mussels here. The sewage. Hopeless. Some good matronly woman in a porkpie hat to mother him. Take him in tow, platter face and a large apron. Ladies' grey flannelette bloomers, three shillings a pair, astonishing bargain.

---

[1] *Irish Lights board* Board that maintained lighthouses and lightships.

[2] *Erin's King* Ship that took tourists around Dublin Bay.

[3] *Calomel purge* Calomel is used to relieve skin irritations.

[4] *Dearest Papli* The opening of Milly's letter to her father, which he received that morning.

[5] *paps* Breasts; *Left one ... think* A common belief, because the left breast is nearer to the heart.

[6] *Buenas ... hermosa* Spanish: Good evening, Miss. The man loves the beautiful young girl.

[7] *Leah ... Killarney* *Leah,* a popular play, and *Lily of Killarney,* an opera.

[8] *put the ... it* I.e., brought things to a head.

[9] *Scottish widows* Name of a life insurance company.

Plain and loved, loved for ever, they say. Ugly: no woman thinks she is. Love, lie and be handsome for tomorrow we die. See him sometimes walking about trying to find out who played the trick. U. p: up. Fate that is. He, not me. Also a shop often noticed. Curse seems to dog it. Dreamt last night? Wait. Something confused. She had red slippers on. Turkish. Wore the breeches. Suppose she does. Would I like her in pyjamas? Damned hard to answer. Nannetti's gone. Mailboat. Near Holyhead by now. Must nail that ad of Keyes's. Work Hynes and Crawford. Petticoats for Molly. She has something to put in them. What's that? Might be money.

Mr. Bloom stooped and turned over a piece of paper on the strand. He brought it near his eyes and peered. Letter? No. Can't read. Better go. Better. I'm tired to move. Page of an old copybook. All those holes and pebbles. Who could count them? Never know what you find. Bottle with story of a treasure in it thrown from a wreck. Parcels post. Children always want to throw things in the sea. Trust? Bread cast on the waters.[1] What's this? Bit of stick.

O! Exhausted that female has me. Not so young now. Will she come here tomorrow? Wait for her somewhere for ever. Must come back. Murderers do.[2] Will I?

Mr. Bloom with his stick gently vexed the thick sand at his foot. Write a message for her. Might remain. What?

I.

Some flatfoot tramp on it in the morning. Useless. Washed away. Tide comes here a pool near her foot. Bend, see my face there, dark mirror, breathe on it, stirs. All these rocks with lines and scars and letters. O, those transparent! Besides they don't know. What is the meaning of that other world. I called you naughty boy because I do not like.[3]

AM. A.

No room. Let it go.

Mr. Bloom effaced the letters with his slow boot. Hopeless thing sand. Nothing grows in it. All fades. No fear of big vessels coming up here. Except Guinness's barges. Round the Kish[4] in eighty days. Done half by design.

He flung his wooden pen away. The stick fell in silted sand, stuck. Now if you were trying to do that for a week on end you couldn't. Chance. We'll never meet again. But it was lovely. Goodbye, dear. Thanks. Made me feel so young.

Short snooze now if I had. Must be near nine. Liverpool boat long gone. Not even the smoke. And she can do the other. Did too. And Belfast.[5] I won't go. Race there, race back to Ennis.[6] Let him. Just close my eyes a moment. Won't sleep though. Half dream. It never comes the same. Bat again. No harm in him. Just a few.

O sweety all your little girlwhite up I saw dirty bracegirdle made me do love sticky we two naughty Grace darling she him half past the bed met him pike hoses frillies for Raoul to perfume your wife black hair heave under embon *señorita* young eyes Mulvey plump years dreams return tail end Agendath swoony lovey showed me her next year in drawers return next in her next her next.

A bat flew. Here. There. Here. Far in the grey a bell chimed. Mr. Bloom with open mouth, his left boot sanded sideways, leaned, breathed. Just for a few

Cuckoo
Cuckoo
Cuckoo.

The clock on the mantelpiece in the priest's house cooed where Canon O'Hanlon and Father Conroy and the reverend John Hughes S.J. were taking tea and sodabread and butter and fried mutton chops with catsup and talking about

---

1 *Bread ... waters* See Ecclesiastes 11.1: "Cast thy bread upon the waters: for thou shalt find it after many days."

2 *Must come ... do* Reference to the old adage that murderers always return to the scene of the crime.

3 *What is ... like* From Martha Clifford's letter.

4 *Kish* Southeast of Dublin Bay.

5 *Belfast* Bloom is thinking of the concert tour on which Molly will be embarking with Blazes Boylan.

6 *Ennis* Where Bloom's father committed suicide, and where Bloom will be returning for the anniversary of his father's death—June 27.

Cuckoo
Cuckoo
Cuckoo.

Because it was a little canarybird bird that came out of its little house to tell the time that Gerty MacDowell noticed the time she was there because she was as quick as anything about a thing like that, was Gerty Mac-

Dowell, and she noticed at once that that foreign gentleman that was sitting on the rocks looking was

Cuckoo
Cuckoo
Cuckoo.

—1922

In Context

Joyce's Dublin

The Custom House and the River Liffey, 1885.

Above: View from the O'Connell Bridge along what is now O'Connell Street (then Sackville Street), c. 1905. Daniel O'Connell (1775–1847), known as the Great Liberator, was a nationalist leader to whom Joyce claimed a family connection. The statue of O'Connell referred to in "The Dead" stands in front of Nelson's Pillar (in the background in this photograph).

Right: View of O'Connell Bridge and the Liffey, c. 1895.

IN CONTEXT

Beckett and Joyce

James Joyce and Samuel Beckett became friends while both were in Paris in the late 1920s. Joyce dictated to Beckett sections of the work he had begun shortly after completing *Ulysses*; for many years Joyce continued to refer to this work, which would eventually be published in 1939 as *Finnegan's Wake*, as "Work in Progress" (a seemingly nondescript title that nevertheless drew attention to the importance of process to the work itself). Beckett's own first published work was the essay excerpted below, which appeared as the opening piece in a 1929 volume devoted to a discussion of "Work in Progress" that was entitled *Our Exagimination Round His Factification for Incamination of Work in Progress*.

from Samuel Beckett, "Dante ... Bruno. Vico ... Joyce"[1] (1929)

The danger is in the neatness of identifications. The conception of Philosophy and Philology as a pair of nigger[2] not minstrels out of the Teatro dei Piccoli[3] is soothing, like the contemplation of a carefully folded ham-sandwich.... And now here am I, with my handful of abstractions, among which notably: a mountain, the coincidence of contraries, the inevitability of cyclic evolution, a system of poetics, and the prospect of self-extension in the world of Mr. Joyce's *Work in Progress*. There is the temptation to treat every concept like "a bass dropt neck fust in till a bung crate,"[4] and make a really tidy job of it. Unfortunately such an exactitude of application would imply distortion in one of two directions. Must we wring the neck of a certain system in order to stuff it into a contemporary pigeon-hole, or modify the dimensions of that pigeon-hole for the satisfaction of the analogymongers? Literary criticism is not book-keeping.

[Giambattista Vico's] division of the development of human society into three ages—Theocratic, Heroic, Human (civilized), with a corresponding classification of language: Hieroglyphic (sacred), Metaphorical (poetic), Philosophical (capable of abstraction and generalisation)—was by no means new, although it must have appeared so to his contemporaries. He derived this convenient classification from the Egyptians, via Herodotus.[5] At the same time it is impossible to deny the

---

[1] *Dante* Italian poet Dante Alighieri (1265–1321), author of the epic poem the *Divine Comedy*; *Bruno* Giordanno Bruno (1548–1600), Italian philosopher who was burned to death as a heretic by the Inquisition; *Vico* Giovanni Battista (known as Giambattista) Vico (1668–1744), Italian philosopher, historian, and professor of rhetoric. He is often seen as the first modern historian, having been the first to develop a systematic method of historical research.

[2] *nigger* The use of derogatory racial terms even in "serious" literature remained common until the middle of the nineteenth century.

[3] *Teatro di Piccoli* Founded by Vittorio Podrecca in Rome in 1914, this theater was the home of the Piccoli, a famous puppet company who toured Europe and briefly performed in London's West End in 1922.

[4] *"a bass ... crate"* From *Finnegan's Wake* 1.3.

[5] *Herodotus* Fifth-century BCE Greek historian.

originality with which he applied and developed its implications. His exposition of the ineluctable circular progression of society was completely new, although the germ of it was contained in Giordano Bruno's treatment of identified contraries. But it is in Book 2... that appears the unqualified originality of his mind; here he evolved a theory of the origins of poetry and language, the significance of myth, and the nature of barbaric civilization that must have appeared nothing less than an impertinent outrage against tradition. These two aspects of Vico have their reverberations, their reapplications—without however, receiving the faintest explicit illustration—in *Work in Progress*.

It is first necessary to condense the thesis of Vico, the scientific historian. In the beginning was the thunder: the thunder set free religion, in its most objective and unphilosophical form—idolatrous animism: religion produced society, and the first social men were the cave-dwellers, taking refuge from a passionate nature: this primitive family life receives its first impulse towards development from the arrival of terrified vagabonds: admitted, they are the first slaves: growing stronger, they exact agrarian concessions, and a despotism has evolved into a primitive feudalism: the cave becomes a city, and the feudal system a democracy: then an anarchy: this is corrected by a return to monarchy: the last stage is a tendency towards interdestruction: the nations are dispersed, and the phoenix of society arises out of their ashes. To this six-termed social progression corresponds a six-termed progression of human motives: necessity, utility, convenience, pleasure, luxury, abuse of luxury: and their incarnate manifestations: Polyphemus, Achilles, Caesar and Alexander, Tiberius, Caligula, and Nero.[1] At this point Vico applies Bruno—though he takes very good care not to say so—and proceeds from rather arbitrary data to philosophical abstraction. There is no difference, says Bruno, between the smallest possible chord and the smallest possible arc, no difference between the infinite circle and the straight line. The maxima and minima of particular contraries are one and indifferent. Minimal heat equals minimal cold. Consequently transmutations are circular. The principle (minimum) of one contrary takes its movement from the principle (maximum) of another. Therefore not only do the minima coincide with the minima, the maxima with the maxima, but the minima with the maxima in the succession of transmutations. Maximal speed is a state of rest. The maximum of corruption and the minimum of generation are identical: in principle, corruption is generation. And all things are ultimately identified with God, the universal monad,[2] Monad of monads. From these considerations Vico evolved a Science and Philosophy of History. It may be an amusing exercise to take an historical figure, such as Scipio,[3] and label him No. 3; it is of no ultimate importance. What is of ultimate importance is the recognition that the passage from Scipio to Caesar is as inevitable as the passage from Caesar to Tiberius, since the flowers of corruption in Scipio and Caesar are the seeds of vitality in Caesar and Tiberius. Thus we have the spectacle of a human progression that depends for its movement on individuals, and which at the same time is independent of individuals in virtue of what appears to be a preordained cyclicism. It follows that history is neither to be considered as a formless structure, due exclusively to the achievements of individual agents, nor as possessing reality apart from and independent of them, accomplished behind their backs in spite of them, the work of some superior force, variously known as Fate, Chance, Fortune, God. Both these views, the materialistic

---

[1] *Polyphemus* Cyclops of Greek mythology and of Homer's *Odyssey*; *Achilles* Greek hero of the Trojan War; *Caesar and Alexander* Great military leaders and rulers of Macedon and Rome, respectively; *Tiberius* Second Roman Emperor (14–37 CE); *Caligula* Third Roman Emperor (37–41 CE), notorious for his cruelty and reputed to have been insane; *Nero* Roman emperor (54–68 CE) who murdered his father and his wife, began the Roman persecution of the Christians, and committed suicide when the people revolted against him.

[2] *monad* According to Bruno, an irreducible metaphysical element of being.

[3] *Scipio* Second-century BCE Roman general who conquered Carthage.

and the transcendental, Vico rejects in favour of the rational. Individuality is the concretion of universality, and every individual action is at the same time superindividual. The individual and the universal cannot be considered as distinct from each other. History, then, is not the result of fate or chance—in both cases the individual would be separated from his product—but the result of a necessity that is not fate, of a liberty that is not chance. ... This force he called Divine Providence, with his tongue, one feels, very much in his cheek. And it is to this Providence that we must trace the three institutions common to every society: Church, Marriage, Burial. ... Humanity is its work in itself. God acts on her, but by means of her. Humanity is divine, but no man is divine. This social and historical classification is clearly adapted by Mr. Joyce as a structural convenience—or inconvenience. His position is in no way a philosophical one. ... By structural I do not mean a bold outward division, a bare-skeleton for the housing of material. I mean the endless substantial variations on these three beats, and interior intertwining of these three themes into a decoration of arabesques—decoration and more than decoration. Part 1 is a mass of past shadow, correspondent therefore to Vico's first human institution, religion, or to his Theocratic age, or simply to an abstraction—birth. Part 2 is the lovegame of the children, corresponding to the second institution, marriage, or to the Heroic age, or to an abstraction—maturity. Part 3 is passed in sleep, corresponding to the third institution, burial, or to the human age, or to an abstraction—corruption. Part 4 is the day beginning again, and corresponds to Vico's providence, or to the transition from the Human to the Theocratic, or to an abstraction—generation. Mr. Joyce does not take birth for granted, as Vico seems to have done. So much for the dry bones. The consciousness that there is a great deal of the unborn infant in the lifeless octogenarian, and a great deal of both in the man at the apogee of his life's curve, removes all the stiff interexclusiveness that is often the danger in neat construction. Corruption is not excluded from Part 1 nor maturity from Part 3. The four "lovedroyd curdinals" are presented on the same plane—"his element curdinal numen and his enement curdinal marrying and his epulent curdinal weisswasch and his eminent curdinal Kay o' Kay!" There are numerous references to Vico's four human institutions—Providence counting as one! "A good clap, a fore wedding, a bad wake, tell hell's well": "their weatherings and their marryings and their buryings and their natural selections": "the lightning look, the birding cry, awe from the grave, everflowing on our times": "by four hands of forethought the first babe of reconcilement is laid in its last cradle of hume sweet hume."

Apart from this emphasis on the tangible conveniences common to Humanity, we find frequent expressions of Vico's insistence on the inevitable character of every progression—or retrogression: "The Vico road goes round and round to meet where terms begin. Still onappealed to by the cycles and onappalled by the recoursers, we feel all serene, never you fret, as regards our dutyful cask ... before there was a man at all in Ireland there was a lord at Lucan. We only wish everyone was as sure of anything in this watery world as we are of everything in the newlywet fellow that's bound to follow." ... In a word, here is all humanity circling with fatal monotony about the Providential fulcrum—the "convoy wheeling encirculing abound the gigantig's lifetree." Enough has been said, or at least enough has been suggested, to show how Vico is substantially present in the *Work in Progress*. Passing to the Vico of the Poetics we hope to establish an even more striking, if less direct, relationship.

Vico rejected the three popular interpretations of the poetic spirit, which considered poetry as either an ingenious popular expression of philosophical conceptions, or an amusing social diversion, or an exact science within the reach of everyone in possession of the recipe. Poetry, he says, was born of curiosity, daughter of ignorance. The first men had to create matter by the force of their imagination, and "poet" means "creator."[1] Poetry was the first operation of the human mind, and without it thought could not exist. Barbarians, incapable of analysis and abstraction, must use their fantasy to explain what their reason cannot comprehend. Before articulation comes song; before abstract terms, metaphors. The figurative character of the oldest poetry must be regarded, not as sophisticated confectionery, but as evidence of a poverty-stricken vocabulary and of a disability to achieve abstraction. Poetry is essentially the antithesis of metaphysics: Metaphysics purge the mind of the senses and cultivate the disembodiment of the spiritual; poetry is all passion and feeling and animates the inanimate; metaphysics are most perfect when most concerned with universals; poetry, when most concerned with particulars. Poets are the sense, philosophers the intelligence of humanity.

    … His treatment of the origin of language proceeds along similar lines. Here again he rejected the materialistic and transcendental views: the one declaring that language was nothing but a polite and conventional symbolism; the other, in desperation, describing it as a gift from the Gods. As before, Vico is the rationalist, aware of the natural and inevitable growth of language. In its first dumb form, language was gesture. If a man wanted to say "sea," he pointed to the sea. With the spread of animism this gesture was replaced by the word: "Neptune."[2] He directs our attention to the fact that every need of life, natural, moral, and economic, has its verbal expression in one or other of the 30 000 Greek divinities. This is Homer's "language of the Gods." Its evolution through poetry to a highly civilized vehicle, rich in abstract and technical terms, was as little fortuitous as the evolution of society itself. Words have their progressions as well as social phases. "Forest-cabin-village-city-academy" is one rough progression. Another: "mountain-plain-riverbank." And ever word expands with psychological inevitability.

    The root of any word whatsoever can be traced back to some pre-lingual symbol. This early inability to abstract the general from the particular produced the Type-names. It is the child's mind over again. The child extends the names of the first familiar objects to other strange objects in which he is conscious of some analogy. … Thus Vico asserts the spontaneity of language and denies the dualism of poetry and language. Similarly, poetry is the foundation of writing. When language consisted of gesture, the spoken and the written were identical. Hieroglyphics, or sacred language, as he calls it, were not the invention of philosophers for the mysterious expression of profound thought, but the common necessity of primitive peoples. Convenience only begins to assert itself at a far more advanced stage of civilization, in the form of alphabetism. Here Vico, implicitly at least, distinguishes between writing and direct expression. In such direct expression, form and content are inseparable. Examples are the medals of the Middle Ages, which bore no inscription and were a mute testimony to the feebleness of conventional alphabetic writing: and the flags of our own day. As with poetry and language, so with myth. Myth, according to Vico, is neither an allegorical expression of general philosophical axioms (Conti, Bacon),[3] nor a derivative from particular peoples, as for instance the Hebrews or Egyptians, nor yet the work of isolated poets, but an historical statement of fact, of actual contemporary phenomena, actual in the sense that they were created out of necessity by primitive minds, and firmly believed. Allegory implies a threefold intellectual operation: the construction of a

---

[1] *"poet" means "creator"*   The Greek word "poet" is a variant of the word for "maker" or "creator."

[2] *Neptune*   Roman god of the sea.

[3] *Conti*   Armand de Bourbon, Prince de Conti (1629–66), who wrote several theological and moral treatises; *Bacon*   English philosopher Francis Bacon (1561–1626).

message of general significance, the preparation of a fabulous form, and an exercise of considerable technical difficulty in uniting the two, an operation totally beyond the reach of the primitive mind. Moreover, if we consider the myth as being essentially allegorical, we are not obliged to accept the form in which it is cast as a statement of fact. But we know that the actual creators of these myths gave full credence to their face-value. Jove[1] was no symbol: he was terribly real. It was precisely their superficial metaphorical character that made them intelligible to people incapable of receiving anything more abstract than the plain record of objectivity. …

On turning to the *Work in Progress* we find that the mirror is not so convex. Here is direct expression—pages and pages of it. And if you don't understand it, Ladies and Gentlemen, it is because you are too decadent to receive it. You are not satisfied unless form is so strictly divorced from content that you can comprehend the one almost without bothering to read the other. This rapid skimming and absorption of the scant cream of sense is made possible by what I may call a continuous process of copious intellectual salivation. The form that is an arbitrary and independent phenomenon can fulfil no higher function than that of stimulus for a tertiary or quartary conditioned reflex of dribbling comprehension. When Miss Rebecca West[2] clears her decks for a sorrowful deprecation of the Narcissistic element in Mr. Joyce by the purchase of 3 hats, one feels that she might very well wear her bib at all her intellectual banquets, or alternatively, assert a more noteworthy control over her salivary glands than is possible for Monsieur Pavlo[v]'s unfortunate dogs. … Mr. Joyce has a word to say to you on the subject: … "Yet to concentrate solely on the literal sense or even teh psychological content of any document to the sore neglect of the enveloping facts themselves circumstantiating it is just as harmful; etc." And another: "Who in his hearts doubts either that the facts of feminine clothiering are there all the time or that the feminine fiction, stranger than the facts, is there also at the same time, only a little to the rere? Or that one may be separated from the orther? Or that both may be contemplated simultaneously? Or that each may be taken up in turn and considered apart from the other?"

Here form *is* content, content *is* form. You complain that this stuff is not written in English. It is not written at all. It is not to be read—or rather it is not only to be read. It is to be looked at and listened to. His writing is not *about* something; *it is that something itself*. … When the sense is sleep, the words go to sleep. (See the end of *Anna Livia*.) When the sense is dancing, the words dance. Take the passage at the end of Shaun's pastoral: "To stirr up love's young fizz I tilt with this bridle's cup champagne, dimming douce from her peepair of hideseeks tight squeezed on my snowybreasted and while my pearlies in their sparkling wisdom are nippling her bubblets I swear (and let you swear) by the bumper round of my poor old snaggletooth's solidbowel I ne'er will prove I'm untrue to (theare!) you liking so long as my hole looks. Down." The language is drunk. The very words are tilted and effervescent. … There is one point to make clear: the beauty of *Work in Progress* is not presented in space alone, since its adequate apprehension depends as much on its visibility as on its audibility. There is a temporal as well as a spatial unity to be apprehended. … Mr. Joyce has desophisticated language. And it is worth while remarking that no language is so sophisticated as English. It is abstracted to death. Take the word "doubt": it gives us hardly any sensuous suggestion of hesitancy, of the necessity for choice, of static irresolution. Whereas the German "Zweifel" does, and, in lesser

---

[1] *Jove* Roman king of the gods.

[2] *Rebecca West* Writer and critic whose essay "Strange Necessity" (1928) spoke disparagingly of Joyce's *Ulysses*. He took his revenge by depicting her in an unflattering light in *Finnegan's Wake*.

degree, the Italian "dubitare." Mr. Joyce recognises how inadequate "doubt" is to express a state of extreme uncertainty, and replaces it by "in twosome twiminds." Nor is he by any means the first to recognize the importance of treating words as something more than mere polite symbols. Shakespeare uses fat, greasy words to express corruption: "Duller shouldst thou be than the fat weed that rots itself in death on Lethe wharf."[1] We hear the ooze squelching all through Dickens's description of the Thames in *Great Expectations*. This writing that you find so obscure is a quintessential extraction of language and painting and gesture, with all the inevitable clarity of the old inarticulation. Here is the savage economy of hieroglyphics. Here words are not the polite contortions of 20th century printer's ink. They are alive. They elbow their way on to the page, and glow and blaze and fade and disappear. "Brawn is my name and broad is my nature and I've breit on my brow and all's right with every feature and I'll brune this bird or Brown Bess's bung's gone bandy." ... There is an endless verbal germination, maturation, putrefaction, the cyclic dynamism of the intermediate. This reduction of various expressive media to their primitive economic directness, and the fusion of these primal essences into an assimilated medium for the exteriorisation of thought, is pure Vico, and Vico, applied to the problem of style. But Vico is reflected more explicitly than by a distillation of disparate poetic ingredients into a synthetical syrup. We notice that there is little or no attempt at subjectivism or abstraction, no attempt at metaphysical generalisation. We are presented with a statement of the particular. It is the old myth: the girl on the dirt track, the two washerwomen on the banks of the river. And there is considerable animism: the mountain "abhearing," the river puffing her old doudheen. (See the beautiful passage beginning: "First she let her hair fall and down it ffussed.") We have Type-names: Isolde—any beautiful girl: Earwigger—Guinness's Brewery, the Wellington monument, the Phoenix Park, anything that occupies an extremely comfortable position between the two stools. Anna Livia herself, mother of Dublin, but no more the only mother than Zoroaster was the only oriental stargazer. "Teems of times and happy returns. The same anew. Ordovico or viricordo. Anna was, Livia is, Plurabelle's to be. Northmen's thing made Southfolk's place, but howmultyplurators made eachone in person." Basta![2] Vico and Bruno are here, and more substantially than would appear from this swift survey of the question.

... [Dante and Joyce] both saw how worn out and threadbare was the conventional language of cunning literary artificers, both rejected an approximation to a universal language. If English is not yet so definitely a polite necessity as Latin was in the Middle Ages, at least one is justified in declaring that its position in relation to other European languages is to a great extent that of mediaeval Latin to the Italian dialects. Dante did not adopt the vulgar out of any kind of local jingoism nor out of any determination to assert the superiority of Tuscan to all its rivals as a form of spoken Italian.... His conclusion is that the corruption common to all the dialects makes it impossible to select one rather than another as an adequate literary form, and that he who would write in the vulgar must assemble the purest elements from each dialect and construct a synthetic language that would at least possess more than a circumscribed local interest: which is precisely what he did. He did not write in Florentine any more than in Neapolitan. He wrote a vulgar that *could* have been spoken by an ideal Italian who had assimilated what was best in all the dialects of his country, but which in fact was certainly not spoken nor ever had been. Which disposes of the capital objection that might be made against this attractive parallel between Dante and Mr. Joyce in the question of language, i.e., that at

---

[1] *Duller ... wharf* Misquote of *Hamlet* 1.5. 38–39: "And duller shouldst thou be than the fat weed that rots itself in ease on Lethe wharf."

[2] *Basta* Italian: enough.

least Dante wrote what was being spoken in the streets of his own town, whereas no creature in heaven or earth ever spoke the language of *Work in Progress*. ...

We may also compare, if we think it worth while, the storm of ecclesiastical abuse raised by Mr. Joyce's work, and the treatment that the *Divine Comedy* must certainly have received from the same source. ... Another point of comparison is the preoccupation with the significance of numbers. The death of Beatrice[1] inspired nothing less than a highly complicated poem dealing with the importance of the number 3 in her life. Dante never ceased to be obsessed by this number. Thus the poem is divided into three Cantiche, each composed of 33 Canti, and written in terza rima.[2] Why, Mr. Joyce seems to say, should there be four legs to a table, and four to a horse, and four seasons and four Gospels and four Provinces in Ireland? Why twelve Tables of the Law, and twelve Apostles and twelve months and twelve Napoleonic marshals and twelve men in Florence called Ottolenghi? Why should the Armistice be celebrated at the eleventh hour of the eleventh day of the eleventh month? He cannot tell you because he is not God Almighty, but in a thousand years he will tell you, and in the meantime must be content to know why horses have not five legs, nor three.

---

[1] *Beatrice*   The woman to whom Dante was devoted.

[2] *terza rima*   Verse form of iambic tercets with a rhyme scheme of aba, bcb, cdc, etc.

D.H. Lawrence
1885 – 1930

D.H. Lawrence declared that "one sheds one's sicknesses in books." That claim suggests not only the sufferings of a man whose fierce desire to live was helplessly incarcerated in a body wasting away from tuberculosis, but also the broader afflictions associated with British modernization: the rise of machine culture, the devastating loss of life in World War I, and the outmoded moral values governing relations between the sexes and the classes. A prolific writer, Lawrence "shed" a staggering array of novels, short stories, essays and poems that relentlessly—and usually scandalously—broke cultural prohibitions to pioneer a new language of sexual and social possibility.

Some critics claim that Lawrence's only lasting allegiance was to his mother, an omnipresent figure who haunted his thoughts long after her death from cancer when he was twenty-five. David Herbert Lawrence, the fourth of five children born in the English mining town of Eastwood, Nottinghamshire, was his mother's favorite. Lawrence's parents were miserably mismatched. Lydia Lawrence felt she had married beneath herself, and struggled to cultivate more than working-class sensibilities in her children. Arthur Lawrence, the miner father, felt belittled by his own family. Marital tensions remembered from childhood percolate through Lawrence's works. If at first he villainized his father in the guise of various literary characters, Lawrence slowly gained sympathy for his father's awkward role in the family and for his earthy vitality. Scenes of an educated woman being sexually liberated through a liaison with a virile working-class man—most controversially explicit in *Lady Chatterley's Lover* (1928)—are seen throughout the works of Lawrence. His early novel *Sons and Lovers* (1913), while often interpreted as an Oedipal tale of mother-love, has also been read as a story of matricide. Feminist critics have noted how his texts encode both adoration and dread of the primal power Lawrence imagined that the female held over the male.

Lawrence worked as a clerk and an elementary-school teacher to pay for his studies at Nottingham University College, and obtained his teacher's certificate in 1908. He secured a good teaching position at the Davidson Road School in Croydon, one of England's spacious new turn-of-the-century state schools. But two severe attacks of pneumonia, at ages sixteen and twenty-six, nearly killed Lawrence and led him to give up his teaching career. His close encounters with death left him, in the words of one critic, "with a heightened awareness of the physical world and a messianic tendency to preach." A suspected if not yet confirmed consumptive, Lawrence broke off an uninspired engagement to Louie Burrows on the grounds that his doctor advised against marriage.

Ford Madox Ford, editor of *The English Review* when the prestigious journal published Lawrence's first poems in 1909, introduced Lawrence to literati who were fascinated by the idea of meeting a young working-class genius in the flesh. A "primitivism" that at the time was prompting writers and artists to seek a remedy for European modernity in non-European cultures also supported fantasies about the curative raw talent of the working class. (Lawrence, romanticized for his class background, would himself exoticize Mexican culture in his 1926 novel, *The Plumed Serpent*.)

Though Lawrence castigated homosexual desire throughout his life (most sharply in his introduction to Maurice Magnus's steamy *Memoirs of the Foreign Legion*, 1924), a homoerotic element in his work makes its appearance in the first of his novels, *The White Peacock* (1910). The figure of "Cyril" in the novel, based upon his childhood friend Alan Chambers, may have represented one of the loves of Lawrence's life. Soon after his second illness, however, Lawrence was to have a fateful encounter with Frieda von Richthofen at the home of Ernest Weekley, one of Lawrence's favorite professors from college. Lawrence was by now rebelling against the universe of Christian guilt and glorifying an animal instinct in its place; he quickly came to worship the sensuality of Weekley's wife, a German baroness (and cousin of the WWI German flying ace Manfred von Richthofen, the "Red Baron"). Though Frieda left her husband and three children to be with Lawrence, she had little intention of re-marrying; it was Lawrence who pressured Frieda into marriage and cut her off from her young children, fearful that he could not compete with the force of maternal love which he himself knew so well.

Before meeting Lawrence, Frieda had been the lover of Otto Gross, a Freudian disciple who believed in sexually revolutionizing society to a degree never endorsed by Freud, and the indomitable Frieda continued to have countless lovers after marrying Lawrence. Lawrence's commitment to monogamy was in conflict with his goal of transcending sexual possessiveness. The Lawrences' many arguments were recorded by many visitors, yet the two remained together until Lawrence's death. To an acquaintance who asked what his ultimate message was, Lawrence wrote, "You shall love your wife completely and implicitly and in entire nakedness of body and spirit." Yet as one biographer dryly noted, "Lawrence's complete love included throttling her and covering her with bruises."

Lawrence's second major work of fiction, *The Rainbow*, was published in 1915, but its descriptions of sex and its coarse language led not only to its suppression, but also to legal difficulties for Lawrence. Persecuted, as well, during the war years, on account of his German wife and his provocative views, Lawrence felt exiled. Embracing a tramp-like lifestyle with Frieda, Lawrence set up house successively in Italy, Australia, the United States, Mexico, and France. World War I bred in Lawrence a fierce desire to form a community of the like-minded in tune with archetypal life forces, and the Lawrences' nomadic lifestyle was largely fueled by his restless utopian desires.

If Lawrence's sexual frankness created controversy, his radical dissolution of conventional narrative voice also disturbed many contemporaries. By the time he published *Women in Love* (1921), a story of two sisters who leave the countryside in pursuit of modern careers and sexual freedom, Lawrence no longer put any stock in individual subjectivity. His fiction strove to capture poetically the impersonal forces of nature that work through individuals but are in themselves vast and impersonal. To many minds, *Women in Love* succeeds magnificently in conveying a sense of individuals caught in the struggle with larger forces.

The publication of *Lady Chatterley's Lover* (1928) further scandalized the British public. The novel graphically depicts the primal sexuality awakened in Constance Chatterley by her working-class lover, Mellors. An anonymous critic who reviewed the novel in *John Bull* famously called it "a cesspool, the most obscene book in the English language." The publication of the book provoked censorship debates in the British Parliament in 1929, and the novel's label of "obscene" was not officially lifted until 1960.

Both Lawrence and his wife refused to admit that he was dying of tuberculosis until the disease was too advanced to deny. He died in 1930 at the age of 45 in the south of France.

⌘⌘⌘

Tortoise Shout

I thought he was dumb,
  I said he was dumb,
Yet I've heard him cry.

First faint scream,
5 Out of life's unfathomable dawn,
Far off, so far, like a madness, under the horizon's
      dawning rim,
Far, far off, far scream.

Tortoise *in extremis*.[1]

Why were we crucified into sex?
10 Why were we not left rounded off, and finished in
      ourselves,
As we began,
As he certainly began, so perfectly alone?

A far, was-it-audible scream,
Or did it sound on the plasm direct?

15 Worse than the cry of the new-born,
A scream,
A yell,
A shout,
A paean,
20 A death-agony,
A birth-cry,
A submission,
All tiny, tiny, far away, reptile under the first dawn.

War-cry, triumph, acute-delight, death-scream
      reptilian,
25 Why was the veil torn?[2]
The silken shriek of the soul's torn membrane?
The male soul's membrane
Torn with a shriek half music, half horror.

Crucifixion.
30 Male tortoise, cleaving behind the hovel-wall of that
      dense female,
Mounted and tense, spread-eagle, out-reaching out of
      the shell
In tortoise-nakedness,
Long neck, and long vulnerable limbs extruded,
      spread-eagle over her house-roof,
And the deep, secret, all-penetrating tail curved
      beneath her walls,
35 Reaching and gripping tense, more reaching anguish
      in uttermost tension
Till suddenly, in the spasm of coition, tupping° *copulating*
      like a jerking leap, and oh!
Opening its clenched face from his outstretched neck
And giving that fragile yell, that scream,
Super-audible,
40 From his pink, cleft, old-man's mouth,
Giving up the ghost,
Or screaming in Pentecost,[3] receiving the ghost.

His scream, and his moment's subsidence,
The moment of eternal silence,
45 Yet unreleased, and after the moment, the sudden,
      startling jerk of coition, and at once
The inexpressible faint yell—
And so on, till the last plasm of my body was melted
      back
To the primeval rudiments of life, and the secret.

So he tups, and screams
50 Time after time that frail, torn scream
After each jerk, the longish interval,
The tortoise eternity,
Age-long, reptilian persistence,
Heart-throb, slow heart-throb, persistent for the next
      spasm.

55 I remember, when I was a boy,
I heard the scream of a frog, which was caught with
      his foot in the mouth of an up-starting snake;

---

1 *in extremis* Latin: at the point of death.

2 *Why ... torn* See Matthew 27.50–51: "Jesus, when he had cried again with a loud voice, yielded up the ghost. And, behold, the veil of the temple was rent in twain, from the top to the bottom; and the earth did quake, and the rocks rent."

3 *Pentecost* Feast day commemorating the day on which the Holy Spirit descended on the twelve disciples and granted them the gift of speaking many languages.

I remember when I first heard bull-frogs break into
    sound in the spring;
I remember hearing a wild goose out of the throat of night
Cry loudly, beyond the lake of waters;
60 I remember the first time, out of a bush in the
    darkness, a nightingale's piercing cries and
    gurgles startled the depths of my soul;
I remember the scream of a rabbit as I went through a
    wood at midnight;
I remember the heifer in her heat, blorting and
    blorting through the hours, persistent and
    irrepressible;
I remember my first terror hearing the howl of weird,
    amorous cats;
I remember the scream of a terrified, injured horse,
    the sheet-lightning,
65 And running away from the sound of a woman in
    labour, something like an owl whooing,
And listening inwardly to the first bleat of a lamb,
The first wail of an infant,
And my mother singing to herself,
And the first tenor singing of the passionate throat of
    a young collier,[1] who has long since drunk
    himself to death,
70 The first elements of foreign speech
On wild dark lips.

And more than all these,
And less than all these,
This last,
75 Strange, faint coition yell
Of the male tortoise at extremity,
Tiny from under the very edge of the farthest far-off
    horizon of life.

The cross,
The wheel on which our silence first is broken,
80 Sex, which breaks up our integrity, our single
    inviolability, our deep silence,
Tearing a cry from us.

Sex, which breaks us into voice, sets us calling across
    the deeps, calling, calling for the complement,

Singing, and calling, and singing again, being
    answered, having found.

Torn, to become whole again, after long seeking for
    what is lost,
85 The same cry from the tortoise as from Christ, the
    Osiris[2]-cry of abandonment,
That which is whole, torn asunder,
That which is in part, finding its whole again
    throughout the universe.

—1921

Snake

A Snake came to my water-trough
  On a hot, hot day, and I in pyjamas for the heat,
To drink there.

In the deep, strange-scented shade of the great dark
    carob-tree
5 I came down the steps with my pitcher
And must wait, must stand and wait, for there he was
    at the trough before me.

He reached down from a fissure in the earth-wall in
    the gloom
And trailed his yellow-brown slackness soft-bellied
    down, over the edge of the stone trough
And rested his throat upon the stone bottom,
10 And where the water had dripped from the tap, in a
    small clearness,
He sipped with his straight mouth,
Softly drank through his straight gums, into his slack
    long body,
Silently.

Someone was before me at my water-trough,
15 And I, like a second comer, waiting.

He lifted his head from his drinking, as cattle do,
And looked at me vaguely, as drinking cattle do,

---

1 *collier* Coal miner.

2 *Osiris* Egyptian king, murdered by his brother Set, who scattered pieces of his body throughout the country. Osiris was then resurrected as god of the underworld.

And flickered his two-forked tongue from his lips, and
    mused a moment,
And stooped and drank a little more,
20 Being earth-brown, earth-golden from the burning
    bowels of the earth
On the day of Sicilian July, with Etna[1] smoking.

The voice of my education said to me
He must be killed,
For in Sicily the black, black snakes are innocent, the
    gold are venomous.

25 And voices in me said, If you were a man
You would take a stick and break him now, and finish
    him off.

But must I confess how I liked him,
How glad I was he had come like a guest in quiet, to
    drink at my water-trough
And depart peaceful, pacified, and thankless,
30 Into the burning bowels of this earth?

Was it cowardice, that I dared not kill him?
Was it perversity, that I longed to talk to him?
Was it humility, to feel so honoured?
I felt so honoured.

35 And yet those voices:
If you were not afraid, you would kill him!

And truly I was afraid, I was most afraid,
But even so, honoured still more
That he should seek my hospitality
40 From out the dark door of the secret earth.

He drank enough
And lifted his head, dreamily, as one who has
    drunken,
And flickered his tongue like a forked night on the
    air, so black,
Seeming to lick his lips,
45 And looked around like a god, unseeing, into the air,
And slowly turned his head,
And slowly, very slowly, as if thrice adream,

Proceeded to draw his slow length curving round
And climb again the broken bank of my wall-face.

50 And as he put his head into that dreadful hole,
And as he slowly drew up, snake-easing his shoulders,
    and entered farther,
A sort of horror, a sort of protest against his
    withdrawing into that horrid black hole,
Deliberately going into the blackness, and slowly
    drawing himself after,
Overcame me now his back was turned.

55 I looked round, I put down my pitcher,
I picked up a clumsy log
And threw it at the water-trough with a clatter.

I think it did not hit him,
But suddenly that part of him that was left behind
    convulsed in undignified haste,
60 Writhed like lightning, and was gone
Into the black hole, the earth-lipped fissure in the
    wall-front,
At which, in the intense still noon, I stared with
    fascination.

And immediately I regretted it.
I thought how paltry, how vulgar, what a mean act!
65 I despised myself and the voices of my accursed
    human education.

And I thought of the albatross,[2]
And I wished he would come back, my snake.

For he seemed to me again like a king,
Like a king in exile, uncrowned in the underworld,
70 Now due to be crowned again.

And so, I missed my chance with one of the lords
Of life.
And I have something to expiate;
A pettiness.
—1923

---

[1] *Etna* Volcano in Sicily.

[2] *albatross* Reference to Samuel Taylor Coleridge's *Rime of the Ancient Mariner* (1798), in which a sailor needlessly and thoughtlessly kills an albatross.

Bavarian Gentians

Not every man has gentians[1] in his house
in soft September, at slow, sad Michaelmas.[2]

Bavarian gentians, big and dark, only dark
darkening the day-time, torch-like with the smoking
    blueness of Pluto's[3] gloom,
5 ribbed and torch-like, with their blaze of darkness
    spread blue
down flattening into points, flattened under the sweep
    of white day
torch-flower of the blue-smoking darkness, Pluto's
    dark-blue daze,
black lamps from the halls of Dis, burning dark blue,
giving off darkness, blue darkness, as Demeter's pale
    lamps give off light,
10 lead me then, lead the way.

Reach me a gentian, give me a torch!
let me guide myself with the blue, forked torch of this
    flower
down the darker and darker stairs, where blue is
    darkened on blueness
even where Persephone goes, just now, from the
    frosted September
15 to the sightless realm where darkness is awake upon
    the dark
and Persephone herself is but a voice
or a darkness invisible enfolded in the deeper dark
of the arms Plutonic, and pierced with the passion of
    dense gloom,
among the splendour of torches of darkness, shedding
    darkness on the lost bride and her groom.[4]

—1933

---

[1] *gentians* Herb that bears blue flowers.

[2] *Michaelmas* Feast of St. Michael the Archangel, on September 29.

[3] *Pluto* Greek God of the underworld (Roman Dis). He abducted Persephone, daughter of Demeter (the goddess of agriculture), and brought her to Hades to be his queen. Her mother grieved for her loss, putting the earth into an eternal winter. Finally she was allowed to return to earth for half the year (the reason for spring and summer) if she returned to Hades for the other half (the reason for fall and winter).

[4] *among... groom* In another, longer version of the poem (thought to be an earlier version), the following three lines follow: "Give me a flower on a tall stem, and three dark flames, / for I will go to the

The Prussian[5] Officer

I

They had marched more than thirty kilometres since dawn, along the white, hot road where occasional thickets of trees threw a moment of shade, then out into the glare again. On either hand, the valley, wide and shallow, glittered with heat; dark green patches of rye, pale young corn, fallow and meadow and black pine woods spread in a dull, hot diagram under a glistening sky. But right in front the mountains ranged across, pale blue and very still, snow gleaming gently out of the deep atmosphere. And towards the mountains, on and on, the regiment marched between the rye fields and the meadows, between the scraggy fruit trees set regularly on either side the high road. The burnished, dark green rye threw off a suffocating heat, the mountains drew gradually nearer and more distinct. While the feet of the soldiers grew hotter, sweat ran through their hair under their helmets, and their knapsacks could burn no more in contact with their shoulders, but seemed instead to give off a cold, prickly sensation.

He walked on and on in silence, staring at the mountains ahead, that rose sheer out of the land, and stood fold behind fold, half earth, half heaven, the heaven, the barrier with slits of soft snow, in the pale, bluish peaks.

He could now walk almost without pain. At the start, he had determined not to limp. It had made him sick to take the first steps, and during the first mile or so, he had compressed his breath, and the cold drops of sweat had stood on his forehead. But he had walked it off. What were they after all but bruises! He had looked at them, as he was getting up: deep bruises on the backs of his thighs. And since he had made his first step in the morning, he had been conscious of them, till now he had a tight, hot place in his chest, with suppressing the pain, and holding himself in. There seemed no air when he breathed. But he walked almost lightly.

The Captain's hand had trembled at taking his coffee at dawn: his orderly[6] saw it again. And he saw the

---

wedding, and be wedding-guest / at the marriage of the living dark."

[5] *Prussian* Inhabitant of Prussia, a duchy or kingdom that was divided between East and West Germany, Poland, and the Soviet Union in 1947.

[6] *orderly* Soldier who acts as a servant for a superior officer.

fine figure of the Captain wheeling on horseback at the farm-house ahead, a handsome figure in pale blue uniform with facings of scarlet, and the metal gleaming on the black helmet and the sword-scabbard, and dark streaks of sweat coming on the silky bay horse. The orderly felt he was connected with that figure moving so suddenly on horseback: he followed it like a shadow, mute and inevitable and damned by it. And the officer was always aware of the tramp of the company behind, the march of his orderly among the men.

The Captain was a tall man of about forty, grey at the temples. He had a handsome, finely knit figure, and was one of the best horsemen in the West. His orderly, having to rub him down, admired the amazing riding-muscles of his loins.

For the rest, the orderly scarcely noticed the officer any more than he noticed himself. It was rarely he saw his master's face: he did not look at it. The Captain had reddish-brown, stiff hair, that he wore short upon his skull. His moustache was also cut short and bristly over a full, brutal mouth. His face was rather rugged, the cheeks thin. Perhaps the man was the more handsome for the deep lines in his face, the irritable tension of his brow, which gave him the look of a man who fights with life. His fair eyebrows stood bushy over light blue eyes that were always flashing with cold fire.

He was a Prussian aristocrat, haughty and overbearing. But his mother had been a Polish Countess. Having made too many gambling debts when he was young, he had ruined his prospects in the Army, and remained an infantry captain. He had never married: his position did not allow of it, and no woman had ever moved him to it. His time he spent riding—occasionally he rode one of his own horses at the races—and at the officers' club. Now and then he took himself a mistress. But after such an event, he returned to duty with his brow still more tense, his eyes still more hostile and irritable. With the men, however, he was merely impersonal, though a devil when roused; so that, on the whole, they feared him, but had no great aversion from him. They accepted him as the inevitable.

To his orderly he was at first cold and just and indifferent: he did not fuss over trifles. So that his servant knew practically nothing about him, except just what orders he would give, and how he wanted them obeyed. That was quite simple. Then the change gradually came.

The orderly was a youth of about twenty-two, of medium height, and well built. He had strong, heavy limbs, was swarthy, with a soft, black, young moustache. There was something altogether warm and young about him. He had firmly marked eyebrows over dark, expressionless eyes, that seemed never to have thought, only to have received life direct through his senses, and acted straight from instinct.

Gradually the officer had become aware of his servant's young, vigorous, unconscious presence about him. He could not get away from the sense of the youth's person, while he was in attendance. It was like a warm flame upon the older man's tense, rigid body, that had become almost unliving, fixed. There was something so free and self-contained about him, and something in the young fellow's movement, that made the officer aware of him. And this irritated the Prussian. He did not choose to be touched into life by his servant. He might easily have changed his man, but he did not. He now very rarely looked direct at his orderly, but kept his face averted, as if to avoid seeing him. And yet as the young soldier moved unthinking about the apartment, the elder watched him, and would notice the movement of his strong young shoulders under the blue cloth, the bend of his neck. And it irritated him. To see the soldier's young, brown, shapely peasant's hand grasp the loaf or the wine-bottle sent a flash of hate or of anger through the elder man's blood. It was not that the youth was clumsy: it was rather the blind, instinctive sureness of movement of an unhampered young animal that irritated the officer to such a degree.

Once, when a bottle of wine had gone over, and the red gushed out on to the tablecloth, the officer had started up with an oath, and his eyes, bluey like fire, had held those of the confused youth for a moment. It was a shock for the young soldier. He felt something sink deeper, deeper into his soul, where nothing had ever gone before. It left him rather blank and wondering. Some of his natural completeness in himself was gone, a little uneasiness took its place. And from that time an undiscovered feeling had held between the two men.

Henceforward the orderly was afraid of really meeting his master. His subconsciousness remembered those steely blue eyes and the harsh brows, and did not intend to meet them again. So he always stared past his master, and avoided him. Also, in a little anxiety, he waited for the three months to have gone, when his time would be up. He began to feel a constraint in the Captain's presence, and the soldier even more than the officer wanted to be left alone, in his neutrality as servant.

He had served the Captain for more than a year, and knew his duty. This he performed easily, as if it were natural to him. The officer and his commands he took for granted, as he took the sun and the rain, and he served as a matter of course. It did not implicate him personally.

But now if he were going to be forced into a personal interchange with his master he would be like a wild thing caught, he felt he must get away.

But the influence of the young soldier's being had penetrated through the officer's stiffened discipline, and perturbed the man in him. He, however, was a gentleman, with long, fine hands and cultivated movements, and was not going to allow such a thing as the stirring of his innate self. He was a man of passionate temper, who had always kept himself suppressed. Occasionally there had been a duel, an outburst before the soldiers. He knew himself to be always on the point of breaking out. But he kept himself hard to the idea of the Service. Whereas the young soldier seemed to live out his warm, full nature, to give it off in his very movements, which had a certain zest, such as wild animals have in free movement. And this irritated the officer more and more.

In spite of himself, the Captain could not regain his neutrality of feeling towards his orderly. Nor could he leave the man alone. In spite of himself, he watched him, gave him sharp orders, tried to take up as much of his time as possible. Sometimes he flew into a rage with the young soldier, and bullied him. Then the orderly shut himself off, as it were out of earshot, and waited, with sullen, flushed face, for the end of the noise. The words never pierced to his intelligence, he made himself, protectively, impervious to the feelings of his master.

He had a scar on his left thumb, a deep seam going across the knuckle. The officer had long suffered from it, and wanted to do something to it. Still it was there, ugly and brutal on the young, brown hand. At last the Captain's reserve gave way. One day, as the orderly was smoothing out the tablecloth, the officer pinned down his thumb with a pencil, asking:

"How did you come by that?"

The young man winced and drew back at attention.

"A wood axe, Herr Hauptmann," he answered.

The officer waited for further explanation. None came. The orderly went about his duties. The elder man was sullenly angry. His servant avoided him. And the next day he had to use all his will-power to avoid seeing the scarred thumb. He wanted to get hold of it and—A hot flame ran in his blood.

He knew his servant would soon be free, and would be glad. As yet, the soldier had held himself off from the elder man. The Captain grew madly irritable. He could not rest when the soldier was away, and when he was present, he glared at him with tormented eyes. He hated those fine, black brows over the unmeaning, dark eyes, he was infuriated by the free movement of the handsome limbs, which no military discipline could make stiff. And he became harsh and cruelly bullying, using contempt and satire. The young soldier only grew more mute and expressionless.

"What cattle were you bred by, that you can't keep straight eyes? Look me in the eyes when I speak to you."

And the soldier turned his dark eyes to the other's face, but there was no sight in them: he stared with the slightest possible cast, holding back his sight, perceiving the blue of his master's eyes, but receiving no look from them. And the elder man went pale, and his reddish eyebrows twitched. He gave his order, barrenly.

Once he flung a heavy military glove into the young soldier's face. Then he had the satisfaction of seeing the black eyes flare up into his own, like a blaze when straw is thrown on a fire. And he had laughed with a little tremor and a sneer.

But there were only two months more. The youth instinctively tried to keep himself intact: he tried to serve the officer as if the latter were an abstract authority and not a man. All his instinct was to avoid personal contact, even definite hate. But in spite of himself the hate grew, responsive to the officer's passion. However, he put it in the background. When he had left the Army he could dare acknowledge it. By nature he was active, and had many friends. He thought what amazing good fellows they were. But, without knowing it, he was alone. Now this solitariness was intensified. It would carry him through his term. But the officer seemed to be going irritably insane, and the youth was deeply frightened.

The soldier had a sweetheart, a girl from the mountains, independent and primitive. The two walked together, rather silently. He went with her, not to talk, but to have his arm round her, and for the physical contact. This eased him, made it easier for him to ignore the Captain; for he could rest with her held fast against his chest. And she, in some unspoken fashion, was there for him. They loved each other.

The Captain perceived it, and was mad with irritation. He kept the young man engaged all the evenings long, and took pleasure in the dark look that came on his face. Occasionally, the eyes of the two men met, those of the younger sullen and dark, doggedly unalterable, those of the elder sneering with restless contempt.

The officer tried hard not to admit the passion that had got hold of him. He would not know that his feeling for his orderly was anything but that of a man incensed by his stupid, perverse servant. So, keeping quite justified and conventional in his consciousness, he let the other thing run on. His nerves, however, were suffering. At last he slung the end of a belt in his servant's face. When he saw the youth start back, the pain-tears in his eyes and the blood on his mouth, he had felt at once a thrill of deep pleasure and of shame.

But this, he acknowledged to himself, was a thing he had never done before. The fellow was too exasperating. His own nerves must be going to pieces. He went away for some days with a woman.

It was a mockery of pleasure. He simply did not want the woman. But he stayed on for his time. At the end of it, he came back in an agony of irritation, torment, and misery. He rode all the evening, then came straight in to supper. His orderly was out. The officer sat with his long, fine hands lying on the table, perfectly still, and all his blood seemed to be corroding.

At last his servant entered. He watched the strong, easy young figure, the fine eyebrows, the thick black hair. In a week's time the youth had got back his old well-being. The hands of the officer twitched and seemed to be full of mad flame. The young man stood at attention, unmoving, shut off.

The meal went in silence. But the orderly seemed eager. He made a clatter with the dishes.

"Are you in a hurry?" asked the officer, watching the intent, warm face of his servant. The other did not reply.

"Will you answer my question?" said the Captain.

"Yes, sir," replied the orderly, standing with his pile of deep Army-plates. The Captain waited, looked at him, then asked again:

"Are you in a hurry?"

"Yes, sir," came the answer, that sent a flash through the listener.

"For what?"

"I was going out, sir."

"I want you this evening."

There was a moment's hesitation. The officer had a curious stiffness of countenance.

"Yes, sir," replied the servant, in his throat.

"I want you tomorrow evening also—in fact, you may consider your evenings occupied, unless I give you leave."

The mouth with the young moustache set close.

"Yes, sir," answered the orderly, loosening his lips for a moment.

He again turned to the door.

"And why have you a piece of pencil in your ear?"

The orderly hesitated, then continued on his way without answering. He set the plates in a pile outside the door, took the stump of pencil from his ear, and put it in his pocket. He had been copying a verse for his sweetheart's birthday card. He returned to finish clearing the table. The officer's eyes were dancing, he had a little, eager smile.

"Why have you a piece of pencil in your ear?" he asked. The orderly took his hands full of dishes. His master was standing near the great green stove, a little smile on his face, his chin thrust forward. When the young soldier saw him his heart suddenly ran hot. He felt blind. Instead of answering, he turned dazedly to the door. As he was crouching to set down the dishes, he was pitched forward by a kick from behind. The pots went in a stream down the stairs, he clung to the pillar of the banisters. And as he was rising he was kicked heavily again, and again, so that he clung sickly to the post for some moments. His master had gone swiftly into the room and closed the door. The maid-servant downstairs looked up the staircase and made a mocking face at the crockery disaster.

The officer's heart was plunging. He poured himself

a glass of wine, part of which he spilled on the floor, and gulped the remainder, leaning against the cool, green stove. He heard his man collecting the dishes from the stairs. Pale, as if intoxicated, he waited. The servant entered again. The Captain's heart gave a pang, as of pleasure, seeing the young fellow bewildered and uncertain on his feet, with pain.

"Schöner!" he said.

The soldier was a little slower in coming to attention.

"Yes, sir!"

The youth stood before him, with pathetic young moustache, and fine eyebrows very distinct on his forehead of dark marble.

"I asked you a question."

"Yes, sir."

The officer's tone bit like acid.

"Why had you a pencil in your ear?"

Again the servant's heart ran hot, and he could not breathe. With dark, strained eyes, he looked at the officer, as if fascinated. And he stood there sturdily planted, unconscious. The withering smile came into the Captain's eyes, and he lifted his foot.

"I—I forgot it—sir," panted the soldier, his dark eyes fixed on the other man's dancing blue ones.

"What was it doing there?"

He saw the young man's breast heaving as he made an effort for words.

"I had been writing."

"Writing what?"

Again the soldier looked up and down. The officer could hear him panting. The smile came into the blue eyes. The soldier worked his dry throat, but could not speak. Suddenly the smile lit like a flame on the officer's face, and a kick came heavily against the orderly's thigh. The youth moved a pace sideways. His face went dead, with two black, staring eyes.

"Well?" said the officer.

The orderly's mouth had gone dry, and his tongue rubbed in it as on dry brown-paper. He worked his throat. The officer raised his foot. The servant went stiff.

"Some poetry, sir," came the crackling, unrecognizable sound of his voice.

"Poetry, what poetry?" asked the Captain, with a sickly smile.

Again there was the working in the throat. The Captain's heart had suddenly gone down heavily, and he stood sick and tired.

"For my girl, sir," he heard the dry, inhuman sound.

"Oh!" he said, turning away. "Clear the table."

"Click!" went the soldier's throat; then again, "click!" and then the half-articulate:

"Yes, sir."

The young soldier was gone, looking old, and walking heavily.

The officer, left alone, held himself rigid, to prevent himself from thinking. His instinct warned him that he must not think. Deep inside him was the intense gratification of his passion, still working powerfully. Then there was a counter-action, a horrible breaking down of something inside him, a whole agony of reaction. He stood there for an hour motionless, a chaos of sensations, but rigid with a will to keep blank his consciousness, to prevent his mind grasping. And he held himself so until the worst of the stress had passed, when he began to drink, drank himself to an intoxication, till he slept obliterated. When he woke in the morning he was shaken to the base of his nature. But he had fought off the realization of what he had done. He had prevented his mind from taking it in, had suppressed it along with his instincts, and the conscious man had nothing to do with it. He felt only as after a bout of intoxication, weak, but the affair itself all dim and not to be recovered. Of the drunkenness of his passion he successfully refused remembrance. And when his orderly appeared with coffee, the officer assumed the same self he had had the morning before. He refused the event of the past night—denied it had ever been—and was successful in his denial. He had not done any such thing—not he himself. Whatever there might be lay at the door of a stupid, insubordinate servant.

The orderly had gone about in a stupor all the evening. He drank some beer because he was parched, but not much, the alcohol made his feeling come back, and he could not bear it. He was dulled, as if nine-tenths of the ordinary man in him were inert. He crawled about disfigured. Still, when he thought of the kicks, he went sick, and when he thought of the threat of more kicking, in the room afterwards, his heart went hot and faint, and he panted, remembering the one that had come. He had been forced to say, "For my girl." He was much too done even to want to cry. His mouth hung slightly open, like an idiot's. He felt vacant, and wasted. So, he wandered at his work, painfully, and very slowly and clumsily, fumbling blindly with the brushes, and finding it difficult, when he sat down, to summon the energy to move again. His limbs, his jaw, were slack and nerveless. But he was very tired. He got to bed at last, and slept inert, relaxed, in a sleep that was rather stupor than slumber, a dead night of stupefaction shot through with gleams of anguish.

In the morning were the manoeuvres. But he woke even before the bugle sounded. The painful ache in his chest, the dryness of his throat, the awful steady feeling of misery made his eyes come awake and dreary at once. He knew, without thinking, what had happened. And he knew that the day had come again, when he must go on with his round. The last bit of darkness was being pushed out of the room. He would have to move his inert body and go on. He was so young, and had known so little trouble, that he was bewildered. He only wished it would stay night, so that he could lie still, covered up by the darkness. And yet nothing would prevent the day from coming, nothing would save him from having to get up and saddle the Captain's horse, and make the Captain's coffee. It was there, inevitable. And then, he thought, it was impossible. Yet they would not leave him free. He must go and take the coffee to the Captain. He was too stunned to understand it. He only knew it was inevitable—inevitable, however long he lay inert.

At last, after heaving at himself, for he seemed to be a mass of inertia, he got up. But he had to force every one of his movements from behind, with his will. He felt lost, and dazed, and helpless. Then he clutched hold of the bed, the pain was so keen. And looking at his thighs, he saw the darker bruises on his swarthy flesh and he knew that, if he pressed one of his fingers on one of the bruises, he should faint. But he did not want to faint—he did not want anybody to know. No one should ever know. It was between him and the Captain. There were only the two people in the world now—himself and the Captain.

Slowly, economically, he got dressed and forced himself to walk. Everything was obscure, except just what he had his hands on. But he managed to get through his work. The very pain revived his dull senses. The worst remained yet. He took the tray and went up to the Captain's room. The officer, pale and heavy, sat at the table. The orderly, as he saluted, felt himself put out of existence. He stood still for a moment submitting to his own nullification—then he gathered himself, seemed to regain himself, and then the Captain began to grow vague, unreal, and the younger soldier's heart beat up. He clung to this situation—that the Captain did not exist—so that he himself might live. But when he saw his officer's hand tremble as he took the coffee, he felt everything falling shattered. And he went away, feeling as if he himself were coming to pieces, disintegrated. And when the Captain was there on horseback, giving orders, while he himself stood, with rifle and knapsack, sick with pain, he felt as if he must shut his eyes—as if he must shut his eyes on everything. It was only the long agony of marching with a parched throat that filled him with one single, sleep-heavy intention: to save himself.

2

He was getting used even to his parched throat. That the snowy peaks were radiant among the sky, that the whitey-green glacier-river twisted through its pale shoals, in the valley below, seemed almost supernatural. But he was going mad with fever and thirst. He plodded on uncomplaining. He did not want to speak, not to anybody. There were two gulls, like flakes of water and snow, over the river. The scent of green rye soaked in sunshine came like a sickness. And the march continued, monotonously, almost like a bad sleep.

At the next farm-house, which stood low and broad near the high road, tubs of water had been put out. The soldiers clustered round to drink. They took off their helmets, and the steam mounted from their wet hair. The Captain sat on horseback, watching. He needed to see his orderly. His helmet threw a dark shadow over his light, fierce eyes, but his moustache and mouth and chin were distinct in the sunshine. The orderly must move under the presence of the figure of the horseman. It was not that he was afraid, or cowed. It was as if he was disembowelled, made empty, like an empty shell. He felt himself as nothing, a shadow creeping under the sunshine. And, thirsty as he was, he could scarcely drink, feeling the Captain near him. He would not take off his helmet to wipe his wet hair. He wanted to stay in shadow, not to be forced into consciousness. Starting, he saw the light heel of the officer prick the belly of the horse; the Captain cantered away, and he himself could relapse into vacancy.

Nothing, however, could give him back his living place in the hot, bright morning. He felt like a gap among it all. Whereas the Captain was prouder, overriding. A hot flash went through the young servant's body. The Captain was firmer and prouder with life, he himself was empty as a shadow. Again the flash went through him, dazing him out. But his heart ran a little firmer.

The company turned up the hill, to make a loop for the return. Below, from among the trees, the farm-bell clanged. He saw the labourers, mowing barefoot at the thick grass, leave off their work and go downhill, their scythes hanging over their shoulders, like long, bright claws curving down behind them. They seemed like dream-people, as if they had no relation to himself. He felt as in a blackish dream: as if all the other things were there and had form, but he himself was only a consciousness, a gap that could think and perceive. The soldiers were tramping silently up the glaring hillside. Gradually his head began to revolve, slowly, rhythmically. Sometimes it was dark before his eyes, as if he saw this world through a smoked glass, frail shadows and unreal. It gave him a pain in his head to walk.

The air was too scented, it gave no breath. All the lush greenstuff seemed to be issuing its sap, till the air was deathly, sickly with the smell of greenness. There was the perfume of clover, like pure honey and bees. Then there grew a faint acrid tang—they were near the beeches; and then a queer clattering noise, and a suffocating, hideous smell; they were passing a flock of sheep, a shepherd in a black smock, holding his crook. Why should the sheep huddle together under this fierce sun? He felt that the shepherd would not see him, though he could see the shepherd.

At last there was the halt. They stacked rifles in a conical stack, put down their kit in a scattered circle around it, and dispersed a little, sitting on a small knoll high on the hillside. The chatter began. The soldiers were steaming with heat, but were lively. He sat still, seeing the blue mountains rising upon the land, twenty kilometers away. There was a blue fold in the ranges, then out of that, at the foot, the broad, pale bed of the river, stretches of whitey-green water between pinkish-grey shoals among the dark pine woods. There it was, spread out a long way off. And it seemed to come downhill, the river. There was a raft being steered, a mile away. It was a strange country. Nearer, a red-roofed, broad farm with white base and square dots of windows crouched beside the wall of beech foliage on the wood's edge. There were long strips of rye and clover and pale green corn. And just at his feet, below the knoll, was a darkish bog, where globe flowers stood breathless still on their slim stalks. And some of the pale gold bubbles were burst, and a broken fragment hung in the air. He thought he was going to sleep.

Suddenly something moved into this coloured mirage before his eyes. The Captain, a small, light-blue and scarlet figure, was trotting evenly between the strips of corn, along the level brow of the hill. And the man making flag-signals was coming on. Proud and sure moved the horseman's figure, the quick, bright thing, in which was concentrated all the light of this morning, which for the rest lay a fragile, shining shadow. Submissive, apathetic, the young soldier sat and stared. But as the horse slowed to a walk, coming up the last steep path, the great flash flared over the body and soul of the orderly. He sat waiting. The back of his head felt as if it were weighted with a heavy piece of fire. He did not want to eat. His hands trembled slightly as he moved them. Meanwhile the officer on horseback was approaching slowly and proudly. The tension grew in the orderly's soul. Then again, seeing the Captain ease himself on the saddle, the flash blazed through him.

The Captain looked at the patch of light blue and scarlet, and dark heads, scattered closely on the hillside. It pleased him. The command pleased him. And he was feeling proud. His orderly was among them in common subjection. The officer rose a little on his stirrups to look. The young soldier sat with averted, dumb face. The Captain relaxed on his seat. His slim-legged, beautiful horse, brown as a beech nut, walked proudly uphill. The Captain passed into the zone of the company's atmosphere: a hot smell of men, of sweat, of leather. He knew it very well. After a word with the lieutenant, he went a few paces higher, and sat there, a dominant figure, his sweat-marked horse swishing its tail, while he looked down on his men, on his orderly, a nonentity among the crowd.

The young soldier's heart was like fire in his chest, and he breathed with difficulty. The officer, looking downhill, saw three of the young soldiers, two pails of water between them, staggering across a sunny green field. A table had been set up under a tree, and there the slim lieutenant stood, importantly busy. Then the Captain summoned himself to an act of courage. He called his orderly.

The flame leapt into the young soldier's throat as he heard the command, and he rose blindly, stifled. He saluted, standing below the officer. He did not look up. But there was the flicker in the Captain's voice.

"Go to the inn and fetch me ..." the officer gave his commands. "Quick!" he added.

At the last word, the heart of the servant leapt with a flash, and he felt the strength come over his body. But he turned in mechanical obedience, and set off at a heavy run downhill, looking almost like a bear, his trousers bagging over his military boots. And the officer watched this blind, plunging run all the way.

But it was only the outside of the orderly's body that was obeying so humbly and mechanically. Inside had gradually accumulated a core into which all the energy of that young life was compact and concentrated. He executed his commission, and plodded quickly back uphill. There was a pain in his head, as he walked, that made him twist his features unknowingly. But hard there in the centre of his chest was himself, himself, firm, and not to be plucked to pieces.

The Captain had gone up into the wood. The orderly plodded through the hot, powerfully smelling zone of the company's atmosphere. He had a curious mass of energy inside him now. The Captain was less real than himself. He approached the green entrance to the wood. There, in the half-shade, he saw the horse standing, the sunshine and the flickering shadow of leaves dancing over his brown body. There was a clearing where timber had lately been felled. Here, in the gold-green shade beside the brilliant cup of sunshine, stood two figures, blue and pink, the bits of pink showing out plainly. The Captain was talking to his lieutenant.

The orderly stood on the edge of the bright clearing, where great trunks of trees, stripped and glistening, lay stretched like naked, brown-skinned bodies. Chips of wood littered the trampled floor, like splashed light, and the bases of the felled trees stood here and there, with their raw, level tops. Beyond was the brilliant, sunlit green of a beech.

"Then I will ride forward," the orderly heard his Captain say. The lieutenant saluted and strode away. He himself went forward. A hot flash passed through his belly, as he tramped towards his officer.

The Captain watched the rather heavy figure of the young soldier stumble forward, and his veins, too, ran hot. This was to be man to man between them. He yielded before the solid, stumbling figure with bent head. The orderly stooped and put the food on a level-sawn tree-base. The Captain watched the glistening, sun-inflamed, naked hands. He wanted to speak to the young soldier, but could not. The servant propped a bottle against his thigh, pressed open the cork, and poured out the beer into the mug. He kept his head bent. The Captain accepted the mug.

"Hot!" he said, as if amiably.

The flame sprang out of the orderly's heart, nearly suffocating him.

"Yes, sir," he replied, between shut teeth.

And he heard the sound of the Captain's drinking, and he clenched his fists, such a strong torment came into his wrists. Then came the faint clang of the closing pot-lid. He looked up. The Captain was watching him. He glanced swiftly away. Then he saw the officer stoop and take a piece of bread from the tree-base. Again the flash of flame went through the young soldier, seeing the stiff body stoop beneath him, and his hands jerked. He looked away. He could feel the officer was nervous. The bread fell as it was being broken. The officer ate the other piece. The two men stood tense and still, the master laboriously chewing his bread, the servant staring with averted face, his fist clenched.

Then the young soldier started. The officer had pressed open the lid of the mug again. The orderly watched the lid of the mug, and the white hand that clenched the handle, as if he were fascinated. It was raised. The youth followed it with his eyes. And then he saw the thin, strong throat of the elder man moving up and down as he drank, the strong jaw working. And the instinct which had been jerking at the young man's wrists suddenly jerked free. He jumped, feeling as if it were rent in two by a strong flame.

The spur of the officer caught in a tree-root, he went down backwards with a crash, the middle of his back thudding sickeningly against a sharp-edged tree-base, the pot flying away. And in a second the orderly, with serious, earnest young face, and underlip between his teeth, had got his knee in the officer's chest and was pressing the chin backward over the farther edge of the tree-stump, pressing, with all his heart behind in a passion of relief, the tension of his wrists exquisite with relief. And with the base of his palms he shoved at the chin, with all his might. And it was pleasant, too, to have that chin, that hard jaw already slightly rough with beard, in his hands. He did not relax one hair's breadth, but, all the force of all his blood exulting in his thrust, he shoved back the head of the other man, till there was a little "cluck" and a crunching sensation. Then he felt as if his head went to vapour. Heavy convulsions shook the body of the officer, frightening and horrifying the young soldier. Yet it pleased him, too, to repress them. It pleased him to keep his hands pressing back the chin, to feel the chest of the other man yield in expiration to the weight of his strong, young knees, to feel the hard twitchings of the prostrate body jerking his own whole frame, which was pressed down on it.

But it went still. He could look into the nostrils of the other man, the eyes he could scarcely see. How curiously the mouth was pushed out, exaggerating the full lips, and the moustache bristling up from them. Then, with a start, he noticed the nostrils gradually filled with blood. The red brimmed, hesitated, ran over, and went in a thin trickle down the face to the eyes.

It shocked and distressed him. Slowly, he got up. The body twitched and sprawled there, inert. He stood and looked at it in silence. It was a pity it was broken. It represented more than the thing which had kicked and bullied him. He was afraid to look at the eyes. They were hideous now, only the whites showing, and the blood running to them. The face of the orderly was drawn with horror at the sight. Well, it was so. In his heart he was satisfied. He had hated the face of the Captain. It was extinguished now. There was a heavy relief in the orderly's soul. That was as it should be. But he could not bear to see the long, military body lying broken over the tree-base, the fine fingers crisped. He wanted to hide it away.

Quickly, busily, he gathered it up and pushed it under the felled tree-trunks, which rested their beautiful, smooth length either end on logs. The face was horrible with blood. He covered it with the helmet.

Then he pushed the limbs straight and decent, and brushed the dead leaves off the fine cloth of the uniform. So, it lay quite still in the shadow under there. A little strip of sunshine ran along the breast, from a chink between the logs. The orderly sat by it for a few moments. Here his own life also ended.

Then, through his daze, he heard the lieutenant, in a loud voice, explaining to the men outside the wood, that they were to suppose the bridge on the river below was held by the enemy. Now they were to march to the attack in such and such a manner. The lieutenant had no gift of expression. The orderly, listening from habit, got muddled. And when the lieutenant began it all again he ceased to hear.

He knew he must go. He stood up. It surprised him that the leaves were glittering in the sun, and the chips of wood reflecting white from the ground. For him a change had come over the world. But for the rest it had not—all seemed the same. Only he had left it. And he could not go back. It was his duty to return with the beer-pot and the bottle. He could not. He had left all that. The lieutenant was still hoarsely explaining. He must go, or they would overtake him. And he could not bear contact with anyone now.

He drew his fingers over his eyes, trying to find out where he was. Then he turned away. He saw the horse standing in the path. He went up to it and mounted. It hurt him to sit in the saddle. The pain of keeping his seat occupied him as they cantered through the wood. He would not have minded anything, but he could not get away from the sense of being divided from the others. The path led out of the trees. On the edge of the wood he pulled up and stood watching. There in the spacious sunshine of the valley soldiers were moving in a little swarm. Every now and then, a man harrowing on a strip of fallow shouted to his oxen, at the turn. The village and the white-towered church was small in the sunshine. And he no longer belonged to it—he sat there, beyond, like a man outside in the dark. He had gone out from everyday life into the unknown, and he could not, he even did not want to go back.

Turning from the sun-blazing valley, he rode deep into the wood. Tree-trunks, like people standing grey and still, took no notice as he went. A doe, herself a moving bit of sunshine and shadow, went running through the flecked shade. There were bright green rents in the foliage. Then it was all pine wood, dark and cool. And he was sick with pain, he had an intolerable great pulse in his head, and he was sick. He had never been ill in his life. He felt lost, quite dazed with all this.

Trying to get down from the horse, he fell, astonished at the pain and his lack of balance. The horse shifted uneasily. He jerked its bridle and sent it cantering jerkily away. It was his last connection with the rest of things.

But he only wanted to lie down and not be disturbed. Stumbling through the trees, he came on a quiet place where beeches and pine trees grew on a slope. Immediately he had lain down and closed his eyes, his consciousness went racing on without him. A big pulse of sickness beat in him as if it throbbed through the whole earth. He was burning with dry heat. But he was too busy, too tearingly active in the incoherent race of delirium to observe.

3

He came to with a start. His mouth was dry and hard, his heart beat heavily, but he had not the energy to get up. His heart beat heavily. Where was he?—the barracks—at home? There was something knocking. And, making an effort, he looked round—trees, and litter of greenery, and reddish, bright, still pieces of sunshine on the floor. He did not believe he was himself, he did not believe what he saw. Something was knocking. He made a struggle towards consciousness, but relapsed. Then he struggled again. And gradually his surroundings fell into relationship with himself. He knew, and a great pang of fear went through his heart. Somebody was knocking. He could see the heavy, black rags of a fir tree overhead. Then everything went black. Yet he did not believe he had closed his eyes. He had not. Out of the blackness sight slowly emerged again. And someone was knocking. Quickly, he saw the blood-disfigured face of his Captain, which he hated. And he held himself still with horror. Yet, deep inside him, he knew that it was so, the Captain should be dead. But the physical delirium got hold of him. Someone was knocking. He lay perfectly still, as if dead, with fear. And he went unconscious.

When he opened his eyes again, he started, seeing something creeping swiftly up a tree-trunk. It was a little bird. And the bird was whistling overhead. Tap-tap-tap—it was the small, quick bird rapping the tree-trunk with its beak, as if its head were a little round hammer. He watched it curiously. It shifted sharply, in its creeping fashion. Then, like a mouse, it slid down the bare trunk. Its swift creeping sent a flash of revulsion through him. He raised his head. It felt a great weight. Then, the little bird ran out of the shadow across a still patch of sunshine, its little head bobbing swiftly, its white legs twinkling brightly for a moment. How neat it was in its build, so compact, with pieces of white on its wings. There were several of them. They were so pretty—but they crept like swift, erratic mice, running here and there among the beech-mast.

He lay down again exhausted, and his consciousness lapsed. He had a horror of the little creeping birds. All his blood seemed to be darting and creeping in his head. And yet he could not move.

He came to with a further ache of exhaustion. There was the pain in his head, and the horrible sickness, and his inability to move. He had never been ill in his life. He did not know where he was or what he was. Probably he had got sunstroke. Or what else?—he had silenced the Captain for ever—some time ago—oh, a long time ago. There had been blood on his face, and his eyes had turned upwards. It was all right, somehow. It was peace. But now he had got beyond himself. He had never been here before. Was it life, or not life? He was by himself. They were in a big, bright place, those others, and he was outside. The town, all the country, a big bright place of light: and he was outside, here, in the darkened open beyond, where each thing existed alone. But they would all have to come out there sometime, those others. Little, and left behind him, they all were. There had been father and mother and sweetheart. What did they all matter? This was the open land.

He sat up. Something scuffled. It was a little, brown squirrel running in lovely, undulating bounds over the floor, its red tail completing the undulation of its body—and then, as it sat up, furling arid unfurling. He watched it, pleased. It ran on again, friskily, enjoying itself. It flew wildly at another squirrel, and they were chasing each other, and making little scolding, chattering noises. The soldier wanted to speak to them. But only a hoarse sound came out of his throat. The squirrels burst away—they flew up the trees. And then he saw the one peeping round at him, half-way up a tree-trunk.

A start of fear went through him, though, in so far as he was conscious, he was amused. It still stayed, its little, keen face staring at him halfway up the tree-trunk, its little ears pricked up, its clawey little hands clinging to the bark, its white breast reared. He started from it in panic.

Struggling to his feet, he lurched away. He went on walking, walking, looking for something—for a drink. His brain felt hot and inflamed for want of water. He stumbled on. Then he did not know anything. He went unconscious as he walked. Yet he stumbled on, his mouth open.

When, to his dumb wonder, he opened his eyes on the world again, he no longer tried to remember what it was. There was thick, golden light behind golden-green glitterings, and tall, grey-purple shafts, and darknesses further off, surrounding him, growing deeper. He was conscious of a sense of arrival. He was amid the reality, on the real, dark bottom. But there was the thirst burning in his brain. He felt lighter, not so heavy. He supposed it was newness. The air was muttering with thunder. He thought he was walking wonderfully swiftly and was coming straight to relief—or was it to water?

Suddenly he stood still with fear. There was a tremendous flare of gold, immense—just a few dark trunks like bars between him and it. All the young level wheat was burnished gold glaring on its silky green. A woman, full-skirted, a black cloth on her head for head-dress, was passing like a block of shadow through the glistening, green corn, into the full glare. There was a farm, too, pale blue in shadow, and the timber black. And there was a church spire, nearly fused away in the gold. The woman moved on, away from him. He had no language with which to speak to her. She was the bright, solid unreality. She would make a noise of words that would confuse him, and her eyes would look at him without seeing him. She was crossing there to the other side. He stood against a tree.

When at last he turned, looking down the long, bare grove whose flat bed was already filling dark, he saw the mountains in a wonder-light, not far away, and radiant. Behind the soft, grey ridge of the nearest range the further mountains stood golden and pale grey, the snow all radiant like pure, soft gold. So still, gleaming in the sky, fashioned pure out of the ore of the sky, they shone in their silence. He stood and looked at them, his face illuminated. And like the golden, lustrous gleaming of the snow he felt his own thirst bright in him. He stood and gazed, leaning against a tree. And then everything slid away into space.

During the night the lightning fluttered perpetually, making the whole sky white. He must have walked again. The world hung livid round him for moments, fields a level sheen of grey-green light, trees in dark bulk, and the range of clouds black across a white sky. Then the darkness fell like a shutter, and the night was whole. A faint flutter of a half-revealed world, that could not quite leap out of the darkness!—Then there again stood a sweep of pallor for the land, dark shapes looming, a range of clouds hanging overhead. The world was a ghostly shadow, thrown for a moment upon the pure darkness, which returned ever whole and complete.

And the mere delirium of sickness and fever went on inside him—his brain opening and shutting like the night—then sometimes convulsions of terror from something with great eyes that stared round a tree—then the long agony of the march, and the sun decomposing his blood—then the pang of hate for the Captain, followed by a pang of tenderness and ease. But everything was distorted, born of an ache and resolving into an ache.

In the morning he came definitely awake. Then his brain flamed with the sole horror of thirstiness! The sun was on his face, the dew was steaming from his wet clothes. Like one possessed, he got up. There, straight in front of him, blue and cool and tender, the mountains ranged across the pale edge of the morning sky. He wanted them—he wanted them alone—he wanted to leave himself and be identified with them. They did not move, they were still soft, with white, gentle markings of snow. He stood still, mad with suffering, his hands crisping and clutching. Then he was twisting in a paroxysm on the grass.

He lay still, in a kind of dream of anguish. His thirst seemed to have separated itself from him, and to stand apart, a single demand. Then the pain he felt was another single self. Then there was the clog of his body, another separate thing. He was divided among all kinds of separate beings. There was some strange, agonized connection between them, but they were drawing further apart. Then they would all split. The sun, drilling down on him, was drilling through the bond. Then they would all fall, fall through the everlasting lapse of space. Then again, his consciousness reasserted itself. He roused on to his elbow and stared at the gleaming mountains. There they ranked, all still and wonderful between earth and heaven. He stared till his eyes went black, and the mountains, as they stood in their beauty, so clean and cool, seemed to have it, that which was lost in him.

4

When the soldiers found him, three hours later, he was lying with his face over his arm, his black hair giving off heat under the sun. But he was still alive. Seeing the open, black mouth the young soldiers dropped him in horror.

He died in the hospital at night, without having seen again.

The doctors saw the bruises on his legs, behind, and were silent.

The bodies of the two men lay together, side by side, in the mortuary, the one white and slender, but laid rigidly at rest, the other looking as if every moment it must rouse into life again, so young and unused, from a slumber.

—1914

Odour of Chrysanthemums

I

The small locomotive engine, Number 4, came clanking, stumbling down from Selston with seven full wagons. It appeared round the corner with loud threats of speed, but the colt that it startled from among the gorse,[1] which still flickered indistinctly in the raw afternoon, out-distanced it at a canter. A woman, walking up the railway line to Underwood, drew back into the hedge, held her basket aside, and watched the footplate of the engine advancing. The trucks thumped heavily past, one by one, with slow inevitable movement, as she stood insignificantly trapped between the jolting black wagons and the hedge; then they curved away towards the coppice[2] where the withered oak leaves dropped noiselessly, while the birds, pulling at the scarlet hips[3] beside the track, made off into the dusk that had already crept into the spinney.[4] In the open, the smoke from the engine sank and cleaved to the rough grass. The fields were dreary and forsaken, and in the marshy strip that led to the whimsey,[5] a reedy pit-pond, the fowls had already abandoned their run among the alders, to roost in the tarred fowl-house. The pit-bank loomed up beyond the pond, flames like red sores licking its ashy sides, in the afternoon's stagnant light. Just beyond rose the tapering chimneys and the clumsy black headstocks of Brinsley Colliery.[6] The two wheels were spinning fast up against the sky, and the winding engine rapped out its little spasms. The miners were being turned up.

The engine whistled as it came into the wide bay of railway lines beside the colliery, where rows of trucks stood in harbour.

Miners, single, trailing and in groups, passed like shadows diverging home. At the edge of the ribbed level of sidings squat a low cottage, three steps down from the cinder track. A large bony vine clutched at the house, as if to claw down the tiled roof. Round the bricked yard grew a few wintry primroses. Beyond, the long garden sloped down to a bush-covered brook course. There were some twiggy apple trees, winter-crack trees, and ragged cabbages. Beside the path hung dishevelled pink chrysanthemums, like pink cloths hung on bushes. A woman came stooping out of the felt-covered fowl-house, halfway down the garden. She closed and padlocked the door, then drew herself erect, having brushed some bits from her white apron.

She was a tall woman of imperious mien,[7] handsome, with definite black eyebrows. Her smooth black hair was parted exactly. For a few moments she stood steadily watching the miners as they passed along the railway: then she turned towards the brook course. Her face was calm and set, her mouth was closed with disillusionment. After a moment she called:

---

[1] *gorse* Prickly shrub.

[2] *coppice* Thicket of small trees.

[3] *hips* Berries of wild roses.

[4] *spinney* Small copse.

[5] *whimsey* Machine used to raise water or ore from a mine.

[6] *headstocks* Supports of revolving machine parts; *Colliery* Coal mine.

[7] *mien* Bearing.

"John!" There was no answer. She waited, and then said distinctly:

"Where are you?"

"Here!" replied a child's sulky voice from among the bushes. The woman looked piercingly through the dusk.

"Are you at that brook?" she asked sternly.

For answer the child showed himself before the raspberry-canes that rose like whips. He was a small, sturdy boy of five. He stood quite still, defiantly.

"Oh!" said the mother, conciliated. "I thought you were down at that wet brook—and you remember what I told you—"

The boy did not move or answer.

"Come, come on in," she said more gently, "it's getting dark. There's your grandfather's engine coming down the line!"

The lad advanced slowly, with resentful, taciturn movement. He was dressed in trousers and waistcoat of cloth that was too thick and hard for the size of the garments. They were evidently cut down from a man's clothes.

As they went slowly towards the house he tore at the ragged wisps of chrysanthemums and dropped the petals in handfuls among the path.

"Don't do that—it does look nasty," said his mother. He refrained, and she, suddenly pitiful, broke off a twig with three or four wan flowers and held them against her face. When mother and son reached the yard her hand hesitated, and instead of laying the flower aside, she pushed it in her apron-band. The mother and son stood at the foot of the three steps looking across the bay of lines at the passing home of the miners. The trundle of the small train was imminent. Suddenly the engine loomed past the house and came to a stop opposite the gate.

The engine-driver, a short man with round grey beard, leaned out of the cab high above the woman.

"Have you got a cup of tea?" he said in a cheery, hearty fashion.

It was her father. She went in, saying she would mash.[1] Directly, she returned.

"I didn't come to see you on Sunday," began the little grey-bearded man.

"I didn't expect you," said his daughter.

The engine-driver winced; then, reassuming his cheery, airy manner, he said:

"Oh, have you heard then? Well, and what do you think—?"

"I think it is soon enough," she replied.

At her brief censure the little man made an impatient gesture, and said coaxingly, yet with dangerous coldness:

"Well, what's a man to do? It's no sort of life for a man of my years, to sit at my own hearth like a stranger. And if I'm going to marry again it may as well be soon as late—what does it matter to anybody?"

The woman did not reply, but turned and went into the house. The man in the engine-cab stood assertive, till she returned with a cup of tea and a piece of bread and butter on a plate. She went up the steps and stood near the footplate of the hissing engine.

"You needn't 'a' brought me bread an' butter," said her father. "But a cup of tea"—he sipped appreciatively—"it's very nice." He sipped for a moment or two, then: "I hear as Walter's got another bout[2] on," he said.

"When hasn't he?" said the woman bitterly.

"I heerd tell of him in the 'Lord Nelson'[3] braggin' as he was going to spend that b—— afore he went: half a sovereign[4] that was."

"When?" asked the woman.

"A' Sat'day night—I know that's true."

"Very likely," she laughed bitterly. "He gives me twenty-three shillings."

"Aye, it's a nice thing, when a man can do nothing with his money but make a beast of himself!" said the grey-whiskered man. The woman turned her head away. Her father swallowed the last of his tea and handed her the cup.

"Aye," he sighed, wiping his mouth. "It's a settler,[5] it is—"

He put his hand on the lever. The little engine strained and groaned, and the train rumbled towards the crossing. The woman again looked across the metals. Darkness was settling over the spaces of the railway and trucks: the miners, in grey sombre groups, were still passing home. The winding engine pulsed hurriedly,

1   *mash*   Brew tea.

2   *bout*   I.e., of drinking.

3   *'Lord Nelson'*   I.e., the pub.

4   *sovereign*   Coin worth twenty shillings.

5   *settler*   Finishing or deciding blow.

with brief pauses. Elizabeth Bates looked at the dreary flow of men, then she went indoors. Her husband did not come.

The kitchen was small and full of firelight; red coals piled glowing up the chimney mouth. All the life of the room seemed in the white, warm hearth and the steel fender reflecting the red fire. The cloth was laid for tea; cups glinted in the shadows. At the back, where the lowest stairs protruded into the room, the boy sat struggling with a knife and a piece of white wood. He was almost hidden in the shadow. It was half-past four. They had but to await the father's coming to begin tea. As the mother watched her son's sullen little struggle with the wood, she saw herself in his silence and pertinacity; she saw the father in her child's indifference to all but himself. She seemed to be occupied by her husband. He had probably gone past his home, slunk past his own door, to drink before he came in, while his dinner spoiled and wasted in waiting. She glanced at the clock, then took the potatoes to strain them in the yard. The garden and fields beyond the brook were closed in uncertain darkness. When she rose with the saucepan, leaving the drain steaming into the night behind her, she saw the yellow lamps were lit along the high road that went up the hill away beyond the space of the railway lines and the field.

Then again she watched the men trooping home, fewer now and fewer.

Indoors the fire was sinking and the room was dark red. The woman put her saucepan on the hob, and set a batter-pudding near the mouth of the oven. Then she stood unmoving. Directly, gratefully, came quick young steps to the door. Someone hung on the latch a moment, then a little girl entered and began pulling off her outdoor things, dragging a mass of curls, just ripening from gold to brown, over her eyes with her hat.

Her mother chid her for coming late from school, and said she would have to keep her at home the dark winter days.

"Why, mother, it's hardly a bit dark yet. The lamp's not lighted, and my father's not home."

"No, he isn't. But it's a quarter to five! Did you see anything of him?"

The child became serious. She looked at her mother with large, wistful blue eyes.

"No, mother, I've never seen him. Why? Has he come up an' gone past, to Old Brinsley? He hasn't, mother, 'cos I never saw him."

"He'd watch that," said the mother bitterly, "he'd take care as you didn't see him. But you may depend upon it, he's seated in the 'Prince o' Wales.' He wouldn't be this late."

The girl looked at her mother piteously.

"Let's have our teas, mother, should we?" said she.

The mother called John to table. She opened the door once more and looked out across the darkness of the lines. All was deserted: she could not hear the winding-engines.

"Perhaps," she said to herself, "he's stopped to get some ripping[1] done."

They sat down to tea. John, at the end of the table near the door, was almost lost in the darkness. Their faces were hidden from each other. The girl crouched against the fender slowly moving a thick piece of bread before the fire. The lad, his face a dusky mark on the shadow, sat watching her who was transfigured in the red glow.

"I do think it's beautiful to look in the fire," said the child.

"Do you?" said her mother. "Why?"

"It's so red, and full of little caves—and it feels so nice, and you can fair smell it."

"It'll want mending directly," replied her mother, "and then if your father comes he'll carry on and say there never is a fire when a man comes home sweating from the pit. A public-house is always warm enough."

There was silence till the boy said complainingly: "Make haste, our Annie."

"Well, I am doing! I can't make the fire do it no faster, can I?"

"She keeps wafflin' it about so's to make 'er slow," grumbled the boy.

"Don't have such an evil imagination, child," replied the mother.

Soon the room was busy in the darkness with the crisp sound of crunching. The mother ate very little. She drank her tea determinedly, and sat thinking. When she rose her anger was evident in the stern unbending of her head. She looked at the pudding in the fender, and broke out:

"It is a scandalous thing as a man can't even come

_____

[1] *ripping* Cutting away coal.

home to his dinner! If it's crozzled[1] up to a cinder I don't see why I should care. Past his very door he goes to get to a public-house, and here I sit with his dinner waiting for him—"

She went out. As she dropped piece after piece of coal on the red fire, the shadows fell on the walls, till the room was almost in total darkness.

"I canna see," grumbled the invisible John. In spite of herself, the mother laughed.

"You know the way to your mouth," she said. She set the dust-pan outside the door. When she came again like a shadow on the hearth, the lad repeated, complaining sulkily:

"I canna see."

"Good gracious!" cried the mother irritably, "you're as bad as your father if it's a bit dusk!"

Nevertheless, she took a paper spill[2] from a sheaf on the mantelpiece and proceeded to light the lamp that hung from the ceiling in the middle of the room. As she reached up, her figure displayed itself just rounding with maternity.

"Oh, mother—!" exclaimed the girl.

"What?" said the woman, suspended in the act of putting the lamp-glass over the flame. The copper reflector shone handsomely on her, as she stood with uplifted arm, turning to face her daughter.

"You've got a flower in your apron!" said the child, in a little rapture at this unusual event.

"Goodness me!" exclaimed the woman, relieved. "One would think the house was afire." She replaced the glass and waited a moment before turning up the wick. A pale shadow was seen floating vaguely on the floor.

"Let me smell!" said the child, still rapturously, coming forward and putting her face to her mother's waist.

"Go along, silly!" said the mother, turning up the lamp. The light revealed their suspense so that the woman felt it almost unbearable. Annie was still bending at her waist. Irritably, the mother took the flowers out from her apron-band.

"Oh, mother—don't take them out!" Annie cried, catching her hand and trying to replace the sprig.

"Such nonsense!" said the mother, turning away.

The child put the pale chrysanthemums to her lips, murmuring:

"Don't they smell beautiful!"

Her mother gave a short laugh.

"No," she said, "not to me. It was chrysanthemums when I married him, and chrysanthemums when you were born, and the first time they ever brought him home drunk, he'd got brown chrysanthemums in his button-hole."

She looked at the children. Their eyes and their parted lips were wondering. The mother sat rocking in silence for some time. Then she looked at the clock.

"Twenty minutes to six!" In a tone of fine bitter carelessness she continued: "Eh, he'll not come now till they bring him. There he'll stick! But he needn't come rolling in here in his pit-dirt, for *I* won't wash him. He can lie on the floor—Eh, what a fool I've been, what a fool! And this is what I came here for, to this dirty hole, rats and all, for him to slink past his very door. Twice last week—he's begun now—"

She silenced herself, and rose to clear the table. While for an hour or more the children played, subduedly intent, fertile of imagination, united in fear of the mother's wrath, and in dread of their father's home-coming, Mrs. Bates sat in her rocking-chair making a "singlet"[3] of thick cream-coloured flannel, which gave a dull wounded sound as she tore off the grey edge. She worked at her sewing with energy, listening to the children, and her anger wearied itself, lay down to rest, opening its eyes from time to time and steadily watching, its ears raised to listen. Sometimes even her anger quailed and shrank, and the mother suspended her sewing, tracing the footsteps that thudded along the sleepers outside; she would lift her head sharply to bid the children "hush," but she recovered herself in time, and the footsteps went past the gate, and the children were not flung out of their play-world.

But at last Annie sighed, and gave in. She glanced at her wagon of slippers, and loathed the game. She turned plaintively to her mother.

"Mother!"—but she was inarticulate.

John crept out like a frog from under the sofa. His mother glanced up.

"Yes," she said, "just look at those shirt-sleeves!"

The boy held them out to survey them, saying

---

[1] *crozzled* Curled; burnt.

[2] *paper spill* Folded or twisted paper used for lighting candle, fire, lamp, etc.

[3] *singlet* Undershirt.

nothing. Then somebody called in a hoarse voice away down the line, and suspense bristled in the room, till two people had gone by outside, talking.

"It is time for bed," said the mother.

"My father hasn't come," wailed Annie plaintively. But her mother was primed with courage.

"Never mind. They'll bring him when he does come—like a log." She meant there would be no scene. "And he may sleep on the floor till he wakes himself. I know he'll not go to work tomorrow after this!"

The children had their hands and faces wiped with a flannel. They were very quiet. When they had put on their nightdresses, they said their prayers, the boy mumbling. The mother looked down at them, at the brown silken bush of intertwining curls in the nape of the girl's neck, at the little black head of the lad, and her heart burst with anger at their father, who caused all three such distress. The children hid their faces in her skirts for comfort.

When Mrs. Bates came down, the room was strangely empty, with a tension of expectancy. She took up her sewing and stitched for some time without raising her head. Meantime her anger was tinged with fear.

2

The clock struck eight and she rose suddenly, dropping her sewing on her chair. She went to the stair-foot door, opened it, listening. Then she went out, locking the door behind her.

Something scuffled in the yard, and she started, though she knew it was only the rats with which the place was over-run. The night was very dark. In the great bay of railway lines, bulked with trucks, there was no trace of light, only away back she could see a few yellow lamps at the pit-top, and the red smear of the burning pit-bank on the night. She hurried along the edge of the track, then, crossing the converging lines, came to the stile by the white gates, whence she emerged on the road. Then the fear which had led her shrank. People were walking up to New Brinsley; she saw the lights in the houses; twenty yards farther on were the broad windows of the "Prince of Wales," very warm and bright, and the loud voices of men could be heard distinctly. What a fool she had been to imagine that anything had happened to him! He was merely drinking over there at the "Prince of Wales." She faltered. She had never yet been to fetch him, and she never would go. So she continued her walk towards the long straggling line of houses, standing back on the highway. She entered a passage between the dwellings.

"Mr. Rigley?—Yes! Did you want him? No, he's not in at this minute."

The raw-boned woman leaned forward from her dark scullery and peered at the other, upon whom fell a dim light through the blind of the kitchen window.

"Is it Mrs. Bates?" she asked in a tone tinged with respect.

"Yes. I wondered if your Master was at home. Mine hasn't come yet."

"'Asn't 'e! Oh, Jack's been 'ome an' 'ad 'is dinner an' gone out. 'E's just gone for 'alf an hour afore bed-time. Did you call at the 'Prince of Wales'?"

"No—"

"No, you didn't like—! It's not very nice." The other woman was indulgent. There was an awkward pause. "Jack never said nothink about—about your Master," she said.

"No!—I expect he's stuck in there!"

Elizabeth Bates said this bitterly, and with recklessness. She knew that the woman across the yard was standing at her door listening, but she did not care. As she turned:

"Stop a minute! I'll just go an' ask Jack if 'e knows anythink," said Mrs. Rigley.

"Oh no—I wouldn't like to put——!"

"Yes, I will, if you'll just step inside an' see as th' childer doesn't come downstairs and set theirselves afire."

Elizabeth Bates, murmuring a remonstrance, stepped inside. The other woman apologised for the state of the room.

The kitchen needed apology. There were little frocks and trousers and childish undergarments on the squab[1] and on the floor, and a litter of playthings everywhere. On the black American cloth[2] of the table were pieces of bread and cake, crusts, slops, and a teapot with cold tea.

"Eh, ours is just as bad," said Elizabeth Bates, looking at the woman, not at the house. Mrs. Rigley put a shawl over her head and hurried out, saying:

---

[1] *squab* Sofa.

[2] *American cloth* Flexible enameled cloth used for covering furniture.

"I shanna be a minute."

The other sat, noting with faint disapproval the general untidiness of the room. Then she fell to counting the shoes of various sizes scattered over the floor. There were twelve. She sighed and said to herself: "No wonder!"—glancing at the litter. There came the scratching of two pairs of feet on the yard, and the Rigleys entered. Elizabeth Bates rose. Rigley was a big man, with very large bones. His head looked particularly bony. Across his temple was a blue scar, caused by a wound got in the pit, a wound in which the coal-dust remained blue like tattooing.

"'Asna 'e come whoam yit?" asked the man, without any form of greeting, but with deference and sympathy. "I couldna say wheer he is—'e's non ower theer!"—he jerked his head to signify the "Prince of Wales."

"'E's 'appen gone up to th' 'Yew,'" said Mrs. Rigley. There was another pause. Rigley had evidently something to get off his mind:

"Ah left 'im finishin' a stint," he began. "Loose-all[1] 'ad bin gone about ten minutes when we com'n away, an' I shouted: 'Are ter comin', Walt?' an' 'e said: 'Go on, Ah shanna be but a'ef a minnit,' so we com'n ter th' bottom, me an' Bowers, thinkin' as 'e wor just behint, an' 'ud come up i' th' next bantle[2]—"

He stood perplexed, as if answering a charge of deserting his mate. Elizabeth Bates, now again certain of disaster, hastened to reassure him:

"I expect 'e's gone up to th' 'Yew Tree,' as you say. It's not the first time. I've fretted myself into a fever before now. He'll come home when they carry him."

"Ay, isn't it too bad!" deplored the other woman.

"I'll just step up to Dick's an' see if 'e is theer," offered the man, afraid of appearing alarmed, afraid of taking liberties.

"Oh, I wouldn't think of bothering you that far," said Elizabeth Bates, with emphasis, but he knew she was glad of his offer.

As they stumbled up the entry, Elizabeth Bates heard Rigley's wife run across the yard and open her neighbour's door. At this, suddenly all the blood in her body seemed to switch away from her heart.

"Mind!" warned Rigley. "Ah've said many a time as Ah'd fill up them ruts in this entry, sumb'dy 'll be breakin' their legs yit."

She recovered herself and walked quickly along with the miner.

"I don't like leaving the children in bed, and nobody in the house," she said.

"No, you dunna!" he replied courteously. They were soon at the gate of the cottage.

"Well, I shanna be many minnits. Dunna you be frettin' now, 'e'll be all right," said the butty.[3]

"Thank you very much, Mr. Rigley," she replied.

"You're welcome!" he stammered, moving away. "I shanna be many minnits."

The house was quiet. Elizabeth Bates took off her hat and shawl, and rolled back the rug. When she had finished, she sat down. It was a few minutes past nine. She was startled by the rapid chuff of the winding-engine at the pit, and the sharp whirr of the brakes on the rope as it descended. Again she felt the painful sweep of her blood, and she put her hand to her side, saying aloud: "Good gracious!—it's only the nine o'clock deputy going down," rebuking herself.

She sat still, listening. Half an hour of this, and she was wearied out.

"What am I working myself up like this for?" she said pitiably to herself, "I s'll only be doing myself some damage."

She took out her sewing again.

At a quarter to ten there were footsteps. One person! She watched for the door to open. It was an elderly woman, in a black bonnet and a black woollen shawl—his mother. She was about sixty years old, pale, with blue eyes, and her face all wrinkled and lamentable. She shut the door and turned to her daughter-in-law peevishly.

"Eh, Lizzie, whatever shall we do, whatever shall we do!" she cried.

Elizabeth drew back a little, sharply.

"What is it, mother?" she said.

The elder woman seated herself on the sofa.

"I don't know, child, I can't tell you!"—she shook her head slowly. Elizabeth sat watching her, anxious and vexed.

"I don't know," replied the grandmother, sighing very deeply. "There's no end to my troubles, there isn't.

---

1 *Loose-all* Signal to finish working in the pits.

2 *bantle* Group.

3 *butty* Buddy; workmate.

The things I've gone through, I'm sure it's enough—!" She wept without wiping her eyes, the tears running.

"But, mother," interrupted Elizabeth, "what do you mean? What is it?"

The grandmother slowly wiped her eyes. The fountains of her tears were stopped by Elizabeth's directness. She wiped her eyes slowly.

"Poor child! Eh, you poor thing!" she moaned. "I don't know what we're going to do, I don't—and you as you are—it's a thing, it is indeed!"

Elizabeth waited.

"Is he dead?" she asked, and at the words her heart swung violently, though she felt a slight flush of shame at the ultimate extravagance of the question. Her words sufficiently frightened the old lady, almost brought her to herself.

"Don't say so, Elizabeth! We'll hope it's not as bad as that; no, may the Lord spare us that, Elizabeth. Jack Rigley came just as I was sittin' down to a glass afore going to bed, an' 'e said: ''Appen you'll go down th' line, Mrs. Bates. Walt's had an accident. 'Appen you'll go an' sit wi' 'er till we can get him home.' I hadn't time to ask him a word afore he was gone. An' I put my bonnet on an' come straight down, Lizzie. I thought to myself: 'Eh, that poor blessed child, if anybody should come an' tell her of a sudden, there's no knowin' what'll 'appen to 'er.' You mustn't let it upset you, Lizzie—or you know what to expect. How long is it, six months—or is it five, Lizzie? Ay!"—the old woman shook her head—"time slips on, it slips on! Ay!"

Elizabeth's thoughts were busy elsewhere. If he was killed—would she be able to manage on the little pension and what she could earn?—she counted up rapidly. If he was hurt—they wouldn't take him to the hospital—how tiresome he would be to nurse!—but perhaps she'd be able to get him away from the drink and his hateful ways. She would—while he was ill. The tears offered to come to her eyes at the picture. But what sentimental luxury was this she was beginning? She turned to consider the children. At any rate she was absolutely necessary for them. They were her business.

"Ay!" repeated the old woman, "it seems but a week or two since he brought me his first wages. Ay—he was a good lad, Elizabeth, he was, in his way. I don't know why he got to be such a trouble, I don't. He was a happy lad at home, only full of spirits. But there's no mistake

he's been a handful of trouble, he has! I hope the Lord'll spare him to mend his ways. I hope so, I hope so. You've had a sight o' trouble with him, Elizabeth, you have indeed. But he was a jolly enough lad wi' me, he was, I can assure you. I don't know how it is. ..."

The old woman continued to muse aloud, a monotonous irritating sound, while Elizabeth thought concentratedly, startled once, when she heard the winding-engine chuff quickly, and the brakes skirr with a shriek. Then she heard the engine more slowly, and the brakes made no sound. The old woman did not notice. Elizabeth waited in suspense. The mother-in-law talked, with lapses into silence.

"But he wasn't your son, Lizzie, an' it makes a difference. Whatever he was, I remember him when he was little, an' I learned to understand him and to make allowances. You've got to make allowances for them—"

It was half-past ten, and the old woman was saying: "But it's trouble from beginning to end; you're never too old for trouble, never too old for that—" when the gate banged back, and there were heavy feet on the steps.

"I'll go, Lizzie, let me go," cried the old woman, rising. But Elizabeth was at the door. It was a man in pit-clothes.

"They're bringin' 'im, Missis," he said. Elizabeth's heart halted a moment. Then it surged on again, almost suffocating her.

"Is he—is it bad?" she asked.

The man turned away, looking at the darkness:

"The doctor says 'e'd been dead hours. 'E saw 'im i' th' lamp-cabin."

The old woman, who stood just behind Elizabeth, dropped into a chair, and folded her hands, crying: "Oh, my boy, my boy!"

"Hush!" said Elizabeth, with a sharp twitch of a frown. "Be still, mother, don't waken th' children: I wouldn't have them down for anything!"

The old woman moaned softly, rocking herself. The man was drawing away. Elizabeth took a step forward.

"How was it?" she asked.

"Well, I couldn't say for sure," the man replied, very ill at ease. "'E wor finishin' a stint an' th' butties 'ad gone, an' a lot o' stuff come down atop 'n 'im."

"And crushed him?" cried the widow, with a shudder.

"No," said the man, "it fell at th' back of 'im. 'E wor under th' face, an' it niver touched 'im. It shut 'im in. It seems 'e wor smothered."

Elizabeth shrank back. She heard the old woman behind her cry:

"What?—what did 'e say it was?"

The man replied, more loudly: "'E wor smothered!"

Then the old woman wailed aloud, and this relieved Elizabeth.

"Oh, mother," she said, putting her hand on the old woman, "don't waken th' children, don't waken th' children."

She wept a little, unknowing, while the old mother rocked herself and moaned. Elizabeth remembered that they were bringing him home, and she must be ready. "They'll lay him in the parlour," she said to herself, standing a moment pale and perplexed.

Then she lighted a candle and went into the tiny room. The air was cold and damp, but she could not make a fire, there was no fireplace. She set down the candle and looked round. The candlelight glittered on the lustre-glasses, on the two vases that held some of the pink chrysanthemums, and on the dark mahogany. There was a cold, deathly smell of chrysanthemums in the room. Elizabeth stood looking at the flowers. She turned away, and calculated whether there would be room to lay him on the floor, between the couch and the chiffonier. She pushed the chairs aside. There would be room to lay him down and to step round him. Then she fetched the old red tablecloth, and another old cloth, spreading them down to save her bit of carpet. She shivered on leaving the parlour; so, from the dresser drawer she took a clean shirt and put it at the fire to air. All the time her mother-in-law was rocking herself in the chair and moaning.

"You'll have to move from there, mother," said Elizabeth. "They'll be bringing him in. Come in the rocker."

The old mother rose mechanically, and seated herself by the fire, continuing to lament. Elizabeth went into the pantry for another candle, and there, in the little pent-house[1] under the naked tiles, she heard them coming. She stood still in the pantry doorway, listening. She heard them pass the end of the house, and come awkwardly down the three steps, a jumble of shuffling footsteps and muttering voices. The old woman was silent. The men were in the yard.

Then Elizabeth heard Matthews, the manager of the pit, say: "You go in first, Jim. Mind!"

The door came open, and the two women saw a collier[2] backing into the room, holding one end of a stretcher, on which they could see the nailed pit-boots of the dead man. The two carriers halted, the man at the head stooping to the lintel[3] of the door.

"Wheer will you have him?" asked the manager, a short, white-bearded man.

Elizabeth roused herself and came from the pantry carrying the unlighted candle.

"In the parlour," she said.

"In there, Jim!" pointed the manager, and the carriers backed round into the tiny room. The coat with which they had covered the body fell off as they awkwardly turned through the two doorways, and the women saw their man, naked to the waist, lying stripped for work. The old woman began to moan in a low voice of horror.

"Lay th' stretcher at th' side," snapped the manager, "an' put 'im on th' cloths. Mind now, mind! Look you now—!"

One of the men had knocked off a vase of chrysanthemums. He stared awkwardly, then they set down the stretcher. Elizabeth did not look at her husband. As soon as she could get in the room, she went and picked up the broken vase and the flowers.

"Wait a minute!" she said.

The three men waited in silence while she mopped up the water with a duster.

"Eh, what a job, what a job, to be sure!" the manager was saying, rubbing his brow with trouble and perplexity. "Never knew such a thing in my life, never! He'd no business to ha' been left. I never knew such a thing in my life! Fell over him clean as a whistle, an' shut him in. Not four foot of space, there wasn't—yet it scarce bruised him."

He looked down at the dead man, lying prone, half naked, all grimed with coal-dust.

"'Sphyxiated,' the doctor said. It *is* the most terrible

---

1   *pent-house*   Subsidiary structure with a sloping roof, attached to the wall of the main building.

2   *collier*   Coal miner.

3   *lintel*   Horizontal support beam.

job I've ever known. Seems as if it was done o' purpose. Clean over him, an' shut 'im in, like a mouse-trap"—he made a sharp, descending gesture with his hand.

The colliers standing by jerked aside their heads in hopeless comment.

The horror of the thing bristled upon them all.

Then they heard the girl's voice upstairs calling shrilly:

"Mother, mother—who is it? Mother, who is it?"

Elizabeth hurried to the foot of the stairs and opened the door:

"Go to sleep!" she commanded sharply. "What are you shouting about? Go to sleep at once—there's nothing—"

Then she began to mount the stairs. They could hear her on the boards, and on the plaster floor of the little bedroom. They could hear her distinctly:

"What's the matter now?—what's the matter with you, silly thing?"—her voice was much agitated, with an unreal gentleness.

"I thought it was some men come," said the plaintive voice of the child. "Has he come?"

"Yes, they've brought him. There's nothing to make a fuss about. Go to sleep now, like a good child."

They could hear her voice in the bedroom, they waited whilst she covered the children under the bed-clothes.

"Is he drunk?" asked the girl, timidly, faintly.

"No! No—he's not! He—he's asleep."

"Is he asleep downstairs?"

"Yes—and don't make a noise."

There was silence for a moment, then the men heard the frightened child again:

"What's that noise?"

"It's nothing, I tell you, what are you bothering for?"

The noise was the grandmother moaning. She was oblivious of everything, sitting on her chair rocking and moaning. The manager put his hand on her arm and bade her "Sh—sh!!"

The old woman opened her eyes and looked at him. She was shocked by this interruption, and seemed to wonder.

"What time is it?" the plaintive thin voice of the child, sinking back unhappily into sleep, asked this last question.

"Ten o'clock," answered the mother more softly. Then she must have bent down and kissed the children.

Matthews beckoned to the men to come away. They put on their caps and took up the stretcher. Stepping over the body, they tiptoed out of the house. None of them spoke till they were far from the wakeful children.

When Elizabeth came down she found her mother alone on the parlour floor, leaning over the dead man, the tears dropping on him.

"We must lay him out," the wife said. She put on the kettle, then returning knelt at the feet, and began to unfasten the knotted leather laces. The room was clammy and dim with only one candle, so that she had to bend her face almost to the floor. At last she got off the heavy boots and put them away.

"You must help me now," she whispered to the old woman. Together they stripped the man.

When they arose, saw him lying in the naïve dignity of death, the woman stood arrested in fear and respect. For a few moments they remained still, looking down, the old mother whimpering. Elizabeth felt counter-manded. She saw him, how utterly inviolable he lay in himself. She had nothing to do with him. She could not accept it. Stooping, she laid her hand on him, in claim. He was still warm, for the mine was hot where he had died. His mother had his face between her hands, and was murmuring incoherently. The old tears fell in succession as drops from wet leaves; the mother was not weeping, merely her tears flowed. Elizabeth embraced the body of her husband, with cheek and lips. She seemed to be listening, inquiring, trying to get some connection. But she could not. She was driven away. He was impregnable.

She rose, went into the kitchen, where she poured warm water into a bowl, brought soap and flannel and a soft towel.

"I must wash him," she said.

Then the old mother rose stiffly, and watched Elizabeth as she carefully washed his face, carefully brushing the big blond moustache from his mouth with the flannel. She was afraid with a bottomless fear, so she ministered to him. The old woman, jealous, said:

"Let me wipe him!"—and she kneeled on the other side drying slowly as Elizabeth washed, her big black bonnet sometimes brushing the dark head of her daughter-in-law. They worked thus in silence for a long time. They never forgot it was death, and the touch of the man's dead body gave them strange emotions, different in each of the women; a great dread possessed them both, the mother felt the lie was given to her womb, she was denied; the wife felt the utter isolation of the human soul, the child within her was a weight apart from her.

At last it was finished. He was a man of handsome body, and his face showed no traces of drink. He was blond, full-fleshed, with fine limbs. But he was dead.

"Bless him," whispered his mother, looking always at his face, and speaking out of sheer terror. "Dear lad—bless him!" She spoke in a faint, sibilant ecstasy of fear and mother love.

Elizabeth sank down again to the floor, and put her face against his neck, and trembled and shuddered. But she had to draw away again. He was dead, and her living flesh had no place against his. A great dread and weariness held her: she was so unavailing. Her life was gone like this.

"White as milk he is, clear as a twelve-month baby, bless him, the darling!" the old mother murmured to herself. "Not a mark on him, clear and clean and white, beautiful as ever a child was made," she murmured with pride. Elizabeth kept her face hidden.

"He went peaceful, Lizzie—peaceful as sleep. Isn't he beautiful, the lamb? Ay—he must ha' made his peace, Lizzie. 'Appen he made it all right, Lizzie, shut in there. He'd have time. He wouldn't look like this if he hadn't made his peace. The lamb, the dear lamb. Eh, but he had a hearty laugh. I loved to hear it. He had the heartiest laugh, Lizzie, as a lad—"

Elizabeth looked up. The man's mouth was fallen back, slightly open under the cover of the moustache. The eyes, half shut, did not show glazed in the obscurity. Life with its smoky burning gone from him, had left him apart and utterly alien to her. And she knew what a stranger he was to her. In her womb was ice of fear, because of this separate stranger with whom she had been living as one flesh. Was this what it all meant—utter, intact separateness, obscured by heat of living? In dread she turned her face away. The fact was too deadly. There had been nothing between them, and yet they had come together, exchanging their nakedness repeatedly. Each time he had taken her, they had been two isolated beings, far apart as now. He was no more

responsible than she. The child was like ice in her womb. For as she looked at the dead man, her mind, cold and detached, said clearly: "Who am I? What have I been doing? I have been fighting a husband who did not exist. *He* existed all the time. What wrong have I done? What was that I have been living with? There lies the reality, this man." And her soul died in her for fear: she knew she had never seen him, he had never seen her, they had met in the dark and had fought in the dark, not knowing whom they met nor whom they fought. And now she saw, and turned silent in seeing. For she had been wrong. She had said he was something he was not; she had felt familiar with him. Whereas he was apart all the while, living as she never lived, feeling as she never felt.

In fear and shame she looked at his naked body, that she had known falsely. And he was the father of her children. Her soul was torn from her body and stood apart. She looked at his naked body and was ashamed, as if she had denied it. After all, it was itself. It seemed awful to her. She looked at his face, and she turned her own face to the wall. For his look was other than hers, his way was not her way. She had denied him what he was—she saw it now. She had refused him as himself. And this had been her life, and his life. She was grateful to death, which restored the truth. And she knew she was not dead.

And all the while her heart was bursting with grief and pity for him. What had he suffered? What stretch of horror for this helpless man! She was rigid with agony. She had not been able to help him. He had been cruelly injured, this naked man, this other being, and she could make no reparation. There were the children—but the children belonged to life. This dead man had nothing to do with them. He and she were only channels through which life had flowed to issue in the children. She was a mother—but how awful she knew it now to have been a wife. And he, dead now, how awful he must have felt it to be a husband. She felt that in the next world he would be a stranger to her. If they met there, in the beyond, they would only be ashamed of what had been before. The children had come, for some mysterious reason, out of both of them. But the children did not unite them. Now he was dead, she knew how eternally he was apart from her, how eternally he had nothing more to do with her. She saw this episode of her life closed. They had denied each other in life. Now he had withdrawn. An anguish came over her. It was finished then: it had become hopeless between them long before he died. Yet he had been her husband. But how little!

"Have you got his shirt, 'Lizabeth?"

Elizabeth turned without answering, though she strove to weep and behave as her mother-in-law expected. But she could not, she was silenced. She went into the kitchen and returned with the garment.

"It is aired," she said, grasping the cotton shirt here and there to try. She was almost ashamed to handle him; what right had she or anyone to lay hands on him; but her touch was humble on his body. It was hard work to clothe him. He was so heavy and inert. A terrible dread gripped her all the while: that he could be so heavy and utterly inert, unresponsive, apart. The horror of the distance between them was almost too much for her—it was so infinite a gap she must look across.

At last it was finished. They covered him with a sheet and left him lying, with his face bound. And she fastened the door of the little parlour, lest the children should see what was lying there. Then, with peace sunk heavy on her heart, she went about making tidy the kitchen. She knew she submitted to life, which was her immediate master. But from death, her ultimate master, she winced with fear and shame.

—1914

The Hopi Snake Dance[1]

The Hopi country is in Arizona, next the Navajo country, and some seventy miles north of the Santa Fé railroad. The Hopis are Pueblo Indians, village Indians, so their reservation is not large. It consists of a square track of greyish, unappetizing desert, out of which rise three tall arid mesas,[2] broken off in ragged pallid rock. On the top of the mesas perch the ragged, broken, greyish pueblos, identical with the mesas on which they stand.

The nearest village, Walpi, stands in half-ruin high, high on a narrow rock-top where no leaf of life ever was tender. It is all grey, utterly grey, utterly pallid stone and dust, and very narrow. Below it all the stark light of the dry Arizona sun.

Walpi is called the "first mesa." And it is at the far edge of Walpi you see the withered beaks and claws and bones of sacrificed eagles, in a rock-cleft under the sky. They sacrifice an eagle each year, on the brink, by rolling him out and crushing him so as to shed no blood. Then they drop his remains down the dry cleft in the promontory's farthest grey tip.

The trail winds on, utterly bumpy and horrible, for thirty miles, past the second mesa, where Chimopova is, on to the third mesa. And on the Sunday afternoon of 17th August black automobile after automobile lurched and crawled across the grey desert, where low, grey, sage-scrub was coming to pallid yellow. Black hood followed crawling after black hood, like a funeral cortège. The motor-cars, with all the tourists wending their way to the third and farthest mesa, thirty miles across this dismal desert where an odd water-windmill spun, and odd patches of corn blew in the strong desert wind, like dark-green women with fringed shawls blowing and fluttering, not far from the foot of the great, grey, up-piled mesa.

The snake dance (I am told) is held once a year, on each of the three mesas in succession. This year of grace 1924 it was to be held in Hotevilla, the last village on the farthest western tip of the third mesa.

On and on bumped the cars. The lonely second mesa lay in the distance. On and on, to the ragged ghost of the third mesa.

The third mesa has two main villages, Oraibi, which is on the near edge, and Hotevilla, on the far. Up scrambles the car, on all its four legs, like a black-beetle straddling past the school-house and store down below, up the bare rock and over the changeless boulders, with a surge and a sickening lurch to the sky-brim, where stands the rather foolish church. Just beyond, dry, grey, ruined, and apparently abandoned, Oraibi, its few ragged stone huts. All these cars come all this way, and apparently nobody at home.

You climb still, up the shoulder of rock, a few more miles, across the lofty, wind-swept mesa, and so you come to Hotevilla, where the dance is, and where already hundreds of motor-cars are herded in an official camping-ground, among the piñon bushes.

Hotevilla is a tiny little village of grey little houses, raggedly built with undressed stone and mud around a

---

[1] *The ... Dance* From *Mornings in Mexico* (1927), a series of essays about Lawrence's travels in Mexico.

[2] *mesas* Rock plateaus.

little oblong *plaza*, and partly in ruins. One of the chief two-storey houses on the small square is a ruin, with big square window-holes.

It is a parched, grey country of snakes and eagles, pitched up against the sky. And a few dark-faced, short, thickly built Indians have their few peach trees among the sand, their beans and squashes on the naked sand under the sky, their springs of brackish water.

Three thousand people came to see the little snake dance this year, over miles of desert and bumps. Three thousand, of all sorts, cultured people from New York, Californians, onward-pressing tourists, cowboys, Navajo Indians, even Negroes; fathers, mothers, children, of all ages, colours, sizes of stoutness, dimensions of curiosity.

What had they come for? Mostly to see men hold *live rattlesnakes* in their mouths. "*I never did see a rattlesnake and I'm crazy to see one!*" cried a girl with bobbed hair.[1]

There you have it. People trail hundreds of miles, avidly, to see this circus-performance of men handling live rattlesnakes that may bite them any minute—even do bite them. Some show, that!

There is the other aspect, of the ritual dance. One may look on from the angle of culture, as one looks on while Anna Pavlova[2] dances with the Russian Ballet.

Or there is still another point of view, the religious. Before the snake dance begins, on the Monday, and the spectators are packed thick on the ground round the square, and in the window-holes, and on all the roofs, all sorts of people greedy with curiosity, a little speech is made to them all, asking the audience to be silent and respectful, as this is a sacred religious ceremonial of the Hopi Indians, and not a public entertainment. Therefore, please, no clapping or cheering or applause, but remember you are, as it were, in a church.

The audience accepts the implied rebuke in good faith, and looks round with a grin at the "church." But it is a good-humoured, very decent crowd, ready to respect any sort of feelings. And the Indian with his "religion" is a sort of public pet.

From the cultured point of view, the Hopi snake dance is almost nothing, not much more than a circus turn, or the games that children play in the street. It has none of the impressive beauty of the Corn Dance at Santo Domingo, for example. The big pueblos of Zuni, Santo Domingo, Taos have a cultured instinct which is not revealed in the Hopi snake dance. This last is uncouth rather than beautiful, and rather uncouth in its touch of horror. Hence the thrill, and the crowd.

As a cultured spectacle, it is a circus turn: men actually dancing round with snakes, poisonous snakes, dangling from their mouths.

And as a religious ceremonial: well, you can either be politely tolerant like the crowd to the Hopis; or you must have some spark of understanding of the sort of religion implied.

"Oh, the Indians," I heard a woman say, "they believe we are all brothers, the snakes are the Indians' brothers, and the Indians are the snakes' brothers. The Indians would never hurt the snakes, they won't hurt any animal. So the snakes won't bite the Indians. They are all brothers, and none of them hurt anybody."

This sounds very nice, only more Hindoo than Hopi. The dance itself does not convey much sense of fraternal communion. It is not in the least like St. Francis preaching to the birds.[3]

The animistic religion, as we call it, is not the religion of the Spirit. A religion of spirits, yes. But not of Spirit. There is no One Spirit. There is no One God. There is no Creator. There is strictly no God at all: because all is alive. In our conception of religion there exists God and His Creation: two things. We are creatures of God, therefore we pray to God as the Father, the Saviour, the Maker.

But strictly, in the religion of aboriginal America, there is no Father, and no Maker. There is the great living source of life: say the Sun of existence: to which you can no more pray than you can pray to Electricity. And emerging from this Sun are the great potencies, the invincible influences which make shine and warmth and rain. From these great interrelated potencies of rain and heat and thunder emerge the seeds of life itself, corn, and creatures like snakes. And beyond these, men, persons. But all emerge separately. There is no oneness, no sympathetic identifying oneself with the rest. The

---

[1] *bobbed hair*   Fashionable short haircut for women in the 1920s.

[2] *Anna Pavlova*   World-famous Russian ballet dancer (1881–1931).

[3] *St. Francis … birds*   St. Francis of Assisi (c. 1182–1236), founder of the Franciscan Order and now the patron saint of animals and the environment. He often preached to birds (and other animals), exhorting them to love and praise their Creator.

law of isolation is heavy on every creature.

Now the Sun, the rain, the shine, the thunder, they are alive. But they are not persons or people. They are alive. They are manifestations of living activity. But they are not personal Gods.

Everything lives. Thunder lives, and rain lives, and sunshine lives. But not in the personal sense.

How is man to get himself into relation with the vast living convulsions of rain and thunder and sun, which are conscious and alive and potent, but like vastest of beasts, inscrutable and incomprehensible. How is man to get himself into relation with these, the vastest of cosmic beasts?

It is the problem of the ages of man. Our religion says the cosmos is Matter, to be conquered by the Spirit of Man. The yogi, the fakir,[1] the saint try conquest by abnegation and by psychic powers. The real conquest of the cosmos is made by science.

The American-Indian sees no division into Spirit and Matter, God and not-God. Everything is alive, though not personally so. Thunder is neither Thor nor Zeus.[2] Thunder is the vast living thunder asserting itself like some incomprehensible monster, or some huge reptile-bird of the pristine cosmos.

How to conquer the dragon-mouthed thunder! How to capture the feathered rain!

We make reservoirs, and irrigation ditches and artesian wells. We make lightning conductors, and build vast electric plants. We say it is a matter of science, energy, force.

But the Indian says No! It all lives. We must approach it fairly, with profound respect, but also with desperate courage. Because man must conquer the cosmic monsters of living thunder and live rain. The rain that slides down from its source, and ebbs back subtly, with a strange energy generated between its coming and going, an energy which, even to our science, is of life: this, man has to conquer. The serpent-striped, feathery Rain.

We made the conquest by dams and reservoirs and windmills. The Indian, like the old Egyptian, seeks to make the conquest from the mystic will within him,

pitted against the Cosmic Dragon.

We must remember, to the animistic vision there is no perfect God behind us, who created us from his knowledge, and foreordained all things. No such God. Behind lies only the terrific, terrible, crude Source, the mystic Sun, the well-head of all things. From this mystic Sun emanate the Dragons, Rain, Wind, Thunder Shine, Light. The Potencies of Powers. These bring forth Earth, then reptiles, birds, and fishes.

The Potencies are not Gods. They are Dragons. The Sun of Creation itself is a dragon most terrible, vast, and most powerful, yet even so, less in being than we. The only gods on earth are men. For gods, like man, do not exist beforehand. They are created and evolved gradually, with aeons of effort, out of the fire and smelting of life. They are the highest thing created, smelted between the furnace of the Life-Sun, and beaten on the anvil of the rain, with hammers or thunder and bellows of rushing wind. The cosmos is a great furnace, a dragon's den, where the heroes and demi-gods, men, forge themselves into being. It is a vast and violent matrix, where souls form like diamonds in earth, under extreme pressure.

So that gods are the outcome, not the origin. And the best gods that have resulted, so far, are men. But gods frail as flowers; which have also the godliness of things that have won perfection out of the terrific dragon-clutch of the cosmos. Men are frail as flowers. Man is as a flower, rain can kill him or succour him, heat can flick him with a bright tail, and destroy him: or, on the other hand, it can softly call him into existence, out of the egg of chaos. Man is delicate as a flower, godly beyond flowers, and his lordship is a ticklish business.

He has to conquer, and hold his own, and again conquer all the time. Conquer the powers of the cosmos. To us, science is our religion of conquest. Hence through science, we are the conquerors and resultant gods of our earth. But to the Indian, the so-called mechanical processes do not exist. All lives. And the conquest is made by the means of the living will.

This is the religion of all aboriginal America. Peruvian, Aztec, Athabascan: perhaps the aboriginal religion of all the word. In Mexico, men fell into horror of the crude, pristine gods, the dragons. But to the pueblo

---

[1] *yogi* Indian devotee; one who practices yoga; *fakir* Mohammedan ascetic religious devotee.

[2] *Thor ... Zeus* Norse and Greek gods of thunder, respectively.

Indian, the most terrible dragon is still somewhat gentle-hearted.

This brings us back to the Hopi. He has the hardest task, the stubbornest destiny. Some inward fate drove him to the top of these parched mesas, all rocks and eagles, sand and snakes, and wind and sun and alkali. These he had to conquer. Not merely, as we should put it, the natural conditions of the place. But the mysterious life-spirit that reigned there. The eagle and the snake.

It is a destiny as well as another. The destiny of the animistic soul of man, instead of our destiny of Mind and Spirit. We have undertaken the scientific conquest of forces, of natural conditions. It has been comparatively easy, and we are victors. Look at our black motor-cars like beetles working up the rock-face at Oraibi. Look at our three thousand tourists gathered to gaze at the twenty lonely men who dance in the tribe's snake dance!

The Hopi sought the conquest by means of the mystic, living will that is in man, pitted against the living will of the dragon-cosmos. The Egyptians long ago made a partial conquest by the same means. We have made a partial conquest by other means. Our corn doesn't fail us: we have no seven years' famine, and apparently need never have. But the other thing fails us, the strange inward sun of life; the pellucid monster of the rain never shows us his stripes. To us, heaven switches on daylight, or turns on the shower-bath. We little gods are gods of the machine only. It is our highest. Our cosmos is a great engine. And we die of *ennui*.[1] A subtle dragon stings us in the midst of plenty. *Quos vult perdere Deus, dementat prius.*[2]

On the Sunday evening is a first little dance in the plaza at Hotevilla, called the Antelope dance. There is the hot, sandy, oblong little place, with a tuft of green cotton-wood boughs stuck like a plume at the south end, and on the floor at the foot of the green, a little lid of a trap-door. They say the snakes are under there.

They say that the twelve officiating men of the snake clan of the tribe have for nine days been hunting snakes in the rocks. They have been performing the mysteries for nine days, in the kiva,[3] and for two days they have fasted completely. All these days they have tended the snakes, washed them with repeated lustrations, soothed them, and exchanged spirits with them. The spirit of man soothing and seeking and making interchange with the spirits of the snakes. For the snakes are more rudimentary, nearer to the great convulsive powers. Nearer to the nameless Sun, more knowing in the slanting tracks of the rain, the pattering of the invisible feet of the rain-monster from the sky. The snakes are man's next emissaries to the rain-gods. The snakes lie nearer to the source of potency, the dark, lurking, intense sun at the centre of the earth. For to the cultured animist, and the pueblo Indian is such, the earth's dark centre holds its dark sun, our source of isolated being, round which our world coils its folds like a great snake. The snake is nearer the dark sun, and cunning of it.

They say—people say—that rattlesnakes are not travellers. They haunt the same spots on earth, and die there. It is said also that the snake priest (so-called) of the Hopi probably capture the same snakes year after year.

Be that as it may. At sundown before the real dance, there is the little dance called the Antelope Dance. We stand and wait on a house-roof. Behind us is tethered an eagle; rather dishevelled he sits on the coping,[4] and looks at us in unutterable resentment. See him, and see how much "brotherhood" the Indian feels with animals—at best the silent tolerance that acknowledges dangerous difference. We wait without event. There are no drums, no announcements. Suddenly into the *plaza*, with rude, intense movements, hurried a little file of men. They are smeared all with grey and black, and are naked save for little kilts embroidered like the sacred dance-kilts in other pueblos, red and green and black on a white fibre-cloth. The fox-skins hangs behind. The feet of the dancers are pure ash-grey. Their hair is long.

The first is a heavy old man with heavy, long, wild grey hair and heavy fringe. He plods intensely forward in the silence, followed in a sort of circle by the other grey-smeared, longhaired, naked, concentrated men. The oldest men are first: the last is a short-haired boy of fourteen or fifteen. There are only eight men—the so-

---

[1] *ennui* French: boredom.

[2] *Quos ... prius* Latin: those whom God wishes to destroy, he first drives mad.

[3] *kiva* Partially underground chamber.

[4] *coping* Overhanging ledge.

called antelope priests. They pace round in a circle, rudely, absorbedly, till the first heavy, intense old man with his massive grey hair flowing, comes to the lid on the ground, near the tuft of kiva-boughs. He rapidly shakes from the hollow of his right hand a little white meal[1] on the lid, stamps heavily, with naked right foot, on the meal, so the wood resounds, and paces heavily forward. Each man, to the boy, shakes meal, stamps, paces absorbedly on in the circle, comes to the lid again, shakes meal, stamps, paces absorbedly on, comes a third time to the lid, or trap-door, and this time spits on the lid, stamps, and goes on. And this time the eight men file away behind the lid, between it and the tuft of green boughs. And there they stand in a line, their backs to the kiva-tuft of green; silent, absorbed, bowing a little to the ground.

Suddenly paces with rude haste another file of men. They are naked, and smeared with red "medicine," with big black lozenges of smeared paint on their backs. Their wild heavy hair hangs loose, the old, heavy, grey-haired men go first, then the middle-aged, then the young men, then last, two short-haired, slim boys, schoolboys. The hair of the young men, growing after school, is bobbed round.

The grown men are all heavily built, rather short, with heavy but shapely flesh, and rather straight sides. They have not the archaic slim waists of the Taos Indians. They have archaic squareness, and a sensuous heaviness. Their very hair is black, massive, heavy. These are the so-called snake-priests, men of the snake clan. And tonight they are eleven in number.

They pace rapidly round, with that heavy wild silence of concentration characteristic of them, and cast meal and stamp upon the lid, cast meal and stamp in the second round, come round and spit and stamp in the third. For to the savage, the animist, to spit may be a kind of blessing, a communion, a sort of embrace.

The eleven snake-priests form silently in a row, facing the eight grey smeared antelope-priests across the little lid, and bowing forward a little, to earth. Then the antelope-priests, bending forward, begin a low, sombre chant, or call, that sounds wordless, only a deep, low-toned, secret Ay-a! Ay-a! Ay-a! And they bend from right to left, giving two shakes to the little, flat, white rattle in

their left hand, at each shake, and stamping the right foot in heavy rhythm. In their right hand, that held the meal, is grasped a little skin bag, perhaps also containing meal.

They lean from right to left, two seed-like shakes of the rattle each time and the heavy rhythmic stamp of the foot, and the low, sombre, secretive chant-call each time. It is a strange low sound, such as we never hear, and it reveals how deep, how deep the men are in the mystery they are practising, how sunk deep below our world, to the world of snakes, and dark ways in the earth, where the roots of corn, and where the little rivers of unchannelled, uncreated life-passion run like dark, trickling lightning, to the roots of the corn and to the feet and loins of men, from the earth's innermost dark sun. They are calling in the deep, almost silent snake-language, to the snakes and the rays of dark emission from the earth's inward "Sun."

At this moment, a silence falls on the whole crowd of listeners. It is that famous darkness and silence of Egypt, the touch of the other mystery. The deep concentration of the "priests" conquers for a few seconds our white-faced flippancy, and we hear only the deep Hah-ha! Hah-ha! speaking to snakes and the earth's inner core.

This lasts a minute or two. Then the antelope-priests stand bowed and still, and the snake-priests take up the swaying and the deep chant, that sometimes is so low, it is like a mutter underground, inaudible. The rhythm is crude, the swaying unison is all uneven. Culturally, there is nothing. If it were not for that mystic, dark-sacred concentration.

Several times in turn, the two rows of daubed, long-haired, insunk men facing one another take up the swaying and the chant. Then that too is finished. There is a break in the formation. A young snake-priest takes up something that may be a corn-cob—perhaps an antelope-priest hands it to him—and comes forward, with an old, heavy, but still shapely snake-priest behind him dusting his shoulders with the feathers, eagle-feathers presumably, which are the Indians' hollow prayer-sticks. With the heavy, stamping hop they move round in the previous circle, the young priest holding the cob curiously, and the old priest prancing strangely at the young priest's back, in a sort of incantation, and brushing the heavy young shoulders delicately with the

---

[1] *meal* Flour, ground grain.

prayer-feathers. It is the God-vibration that enters us from behind, and is transmitted to the hands, from the hands to the corn-cob. Several young priests emerge, with the bowed heads and the cob in their hands and the heavy older priests hanging over them behind. They tread round the rough curve and come back to the kiva, take perhaps another cob, and tread round again.

That is all. In ten or fifteen minutes it is over. The two files file rapidly and silently away. A brief, primitive performance.

The crowd disperses. They were not many people. There were no Venomous snakes on exhibition, so the mass had nothing to come for. And therefore the curious immersed intensity of the priests was able to conquer the white crowd.

By afternoon of the next day the three thousand people had massed in the little *plaza*, secured themselves places on the roof and in the window-spaces, everywhere, till the small pueblo seemed built of people instead of stones. All sorts of people, hundreds and hundreds of white women, all in breeches like half-men, hundreds and hundreds of men who had been driving motor-cars, then many Navajos, the women in their full, long skirts and tight velvet bodices, the men rather lanky, long-waisted, real nomads. In the hot sun and the wind which blows the sand every day, every day in volumes round the corners, the three thousand tourists sat for hours, waiting for the show. The Indian policeman cleared the central oblong, in front of the kiva. The front rows of onlookers sat thick on the ground. And at last, rather early, because of the masses awaiting them, suddenly, silently, in the same rude haste, the antelope-priests filed absorbedly in, and made the rounds over the lid, as before. Today, the eight antelope-priests were very grey. Their feet ashed pure grey, like suède soft boots: and their lower jaw was pure suede grey, while the rest of their face was blackish. With that pale-grey jaw, they looked like corpse-faces with swathing-bands. And all their bodies ash-grey smeared, with smears of black, and a black cloth today at the loins.

They made their rounds, and took their silent position behind the lid, with backs to the green tuft: an unearthly grey row of men with little skin bags in their hands. They were the lords of shadow, the intermediate twilight, the place of afterlife and before-life, where house the winds of change. Lords of the mysterious,

fleeting power of change.

Suddenly, with abrupt silence, in paced the snake-priests, headed by the same heavy man with solid grey hair like iron. Today they were twelve men, from the old one, down to the slight, short-haired, erect boy of fourteen. Twelve men, two for each of the six worlds, or quarters: east, north, south, west, above, and below. And today they were in a queer ecstasy. Their faces were black, showing the whites of the eyes. And they wore small black loin-aprons. They were the hot living men of the darkness, lords of the earth's inner rays, the black sun of the earth's vital core, from which dart the speckled snakes, like beams.

Round they went, in rapid, uneven, silent absorption, the three rounds. Then in a row they faced the eight ash-grey men, across the lid. All kept their heads bowed towards earth, except the young boys.

Then, in the intense, secret, muttering chant the grey men began their leaning from right to left, shaking the hand, one-two, one-two, and bowing the body each time from right to left, left to right, above the lid in the ground, under which were the snakes. And their low, deep, mysterious voices spoke to the spirits under the earth, not to men above the earth.

But the crowd was on tenterhooks for the snakes, and could hardly wait for the mummery to cease. There was an atmosphere of inattention and impatience. But the chant and the swaying passed from the grey men to the black-faced men, and back again, several times.

This was finished. The formation of the lines broke up. There was a slight crowding to the centre, round the lid. The old antelope-priest (so called) was stooping. And before the crowd could realize anything else a young priest emerged, bowing reverently, with the neck of a pale, delicate rattlesnake held between his teeth, the little, naïve, bird-like head of the rattlesnake quite still, near the black cheek, and the long, pale, yellowish, spangled body of the snake dangling like some thick, beautiful cord. On passed the black-faced young priest, with the wondering snake dangling from his mouth, pacing in the original circle, while behind him, leaping almost on his shoulders, was the oldest heavy priest, dusting the young man's shoulders with the feather-prayer-sticks, in an intense, earnest anxiety of concentration such as I have only seen in the old Indian men during a religious dance.

Came another young black-faced man out of the confusion, with another snake dangling and writhing a little from his mouth, and an elder priest dusting him from behind with the feathers: and then another, and another: till it was all confusion, probably, of six, and then four young priests with snakes dangling from their mouths, going round, apparently, three times in the circle. At the end of the third round the young priest stooped and delicately laid his snake on the earth, waving him away, away, as it were, into the world. He must not wriggle back to the kiva bush.

And after wondering a moment, the pale, delicate snake steered away with a rattlesnake's beautiful movement, rippling and looping, with the small, sensitive head lifted like antennae, across the sand to the massed audience squatting solid on the ground around. Like soft, watery lightning went the wondering snake at the crowd. As he came nearer, the people began to shrink aside, half-mesmerized. But they betrayed no exaggerated fear. And as the little snake drew very near, up rushed one of the two black-faced young priests who held the snake-stick, poised a moment over the snake, in the prayer-concentration of reverence which is at the same time conquest, and snatched the pale, long creature delicately from the ground, waving him in a swoop over the heads of the seated crowd, then delicately smoothing down the length of the snake with his left hand, stroking and smoothing and soothing the long, pale, bird-like thing; and returning with it to the kiva, handed it to one of the grey-jawed antelope-priests.

Meanwhile, all the time, the other young priests were emerging with a snake dangling from their mouths. The boy had finished his rounds. He launched his rattlesnake on the ground, like a ship, and like a ship away it steered. In a moment, after it went one of those two black-faced priests who carried snake-sticks and were the snake-catchers. As it neared the crowd, very close, he caught it up and waved it dramatically, his eyes glaring strangely out of his black face. And in the interim that youngest boy had been given a long, handsome bull-snake, by the priest at the hole under the kiva boughs. The bull-snake is not poisonous. It is a constrictor. This one was six feet long, with a sumptuous pattern. It waved its pale belly, and pulled its neck out of the boy's mouth. With two hands he put it back. It pulled itself once more free. Again he got it back, and

managed to hold it. And then as he went round in his looping circle, it coiled its handsome folds twice round his knee. He stooped, quietly, and as quietly as if he were untying his garter, he unloosed the folds. And all the time, an old priest was intently brushing the boy's thin straight shoulders with the feathers. And all the time, the snakes seemed strangely gentle, naïve, wondering and almost willing, almost in harmony with the man. Which of course was the sacred aim. While the boy's expression remained quite still and simple, as it were candid, in a candour where he and the snake should be in unison. The only dancers who showed signs of being wrought-up were the two young snake-catchers, and one of these, particularly, seemed in a state of actor-like uplift, rather ostentatious. But the old priests had that immersed, religious intentness which is like a spell, something from another world.

The young boy launched his bull-snake. It wanted to go back to the kiva. The snake-catcher drove it gently forward. Away it went, towards the crowd, and at the last minute was caught up into the air. Then this snake was handed to an old man sitting on the ground in the audience, in the front row. He was an old Hopi of the Snake clan.

Snake after snake had been carried round in the circles, dangling by the neck from the mouths of one young priest or another, and writhing and swaying slowly, with the small, delicate snake-head held as if wondering and listening. There had been some very large rattlesnakes, unusually large, two or three handsome bull-snakes, and some racers, whipsnakes. All had been launched, after their circuits in the mouth, all had been caught up by the young priests with the snake-sticks, one or two had been handed to old-snake clan men in the audience, who sat holding them in their arms as men hold a kitten. The most of the snakes, however, had been handed to the grey antelope-men who stood in the row with their backs to the kiva bush. Till some of these ash-smeared men held armfuls of snakes, hanging over their arms like wet washing. Some of the snakes twisted and knotted round one another, showing pale bellies.

Yet most of them hung very still and docile. Docile, almost sympathetic, so that one was struck only by their clean, slim length of snake nudity, their beauty, like soft, quiescent lightning. They were so clean, because they had been washed and anointed and lustrated by the priests, in the days they had been in the kiva.

At last all the snakes had been mouth-carried in the circuits, and had made their little outrunning excursion to the crowd, and had been handed back to the priests in the rear. And now the Indian policemen, Hopi and Navajo, began to clear away the crowd that sat on the ground, five or six rows deep, around the small *plaza*. The snakes were all going to be set free on the ground. We must clear away.

We recoiled to the farther end of the *plaza*. There, two Hopi women were scattering white corn-meal on the sandy ground. And thither came the two snake-catchers, almost at once, with their arms full of snakes. And before we who stood had realized it, the snakes were all writhing and squirming on the ground, in the white dust of meal, a couple of yards from our feet. Then immediately, before they could writhe clear of each other and steer away, they were gently, swiftly snatched up again, and with their arms full of snakes, the two young priests went running out of the *plaza*.

We followed slowly, wondering, towards the western, or north-western edge of the mesa. There the mesa dropped steeply, and a broad trail wound down to the vast hollow of desert brimmed up with strong evening light, up out of which jutted a perspective of sharp rock and further mesas and distant sharp mountains: the great, hollow, rock-wilderness space of that part of Arizona, submerged in light.

Away down the trail, small, dark, naked, rapid figures with arms held close, went the two young men, running swiftly down to the hollow level, and diminishing, running across the hollow towards more stark rocks of the other side. Two small, rapid, intent, dwindling little human figures. The tiny, dark sparks of men. Such specks of gods.

They disappeared, no bigger than stones, behind rocks in shadow. They had gone, it was said, to lay down the snakes before a rock called the snake-shrine, and let them all go free. Free to carry the message and thanks to the dragon-gods who can give and withhold. To carry the human spirit, the human breath, the human prayer, the human gratitude, the human command which had been breathed upon them in the mouths of the priests, transferred into them from those feather-prayer-sticks which the old wise men swept

upon the shoulders of the young, snake-bearing men, to carry this back, into the vaster, dimmer, inchoate regions where the monsters of rain and wind alternated in beneficence and wrath. Carry the human prayer and will-power into the holes of the winds, down into the octopus heart of the rain-source. Carry the corn-meal which the women had scattered, back to that terrific, dread, and causeful dark sun which is at the earth's core, that which sends us corn out of the earth's nearness, sends us food or death, according to our strength of vital purpose, our power of sensitive will, our courage.

It is a battle, a wrestling all the time. The Sun, the nameless Sun, source of all things, which we call sun because the other name is too fearful, this, this vast dark protoplasmic sun from which issues all that feeds our life, this original One is all the time willing and unwilling. Systole, diastole, it pulses its willingness and its unwillingness that we should live and move on, from being to being, manhood to further manhood. Man, small, vulnerable man, the farthest adventurer from the dark heart of the first of suns, into the cosmos of creation. Man, the last god won into existence. And all the time, he is sustained and threated, menaced and sustained from the Source, the innermost sun-dragon. And all the time, he must submit and he must conquer. Submit to the strange beneficence from the Source, whose ways are past finding out. And conquer the strange malevolence of the Source, which is past comprehension also.

For the great dragons from which we draw our vitality are all the time willing and unwilling that we should have being. Hence only the heroes snatch manhood, little by little, from the strange den of the Cosmos.

Man, little man, with his consciousness and his will, must both submit to the great origin-powers of his life, and conquer them. Conquered by man who has overcome his fears, the snakes must go back into the earth with his messages of tenderness, of request, and of power. They go back as rays of love to the dark heart of the first of suns. But they go back also as arrows shot clean by man's sapience and courage, into the resistant, malevolent heart of the earth's oldest, stubborn core. In the core of the first of suns, whence man draws his vitality, lies poison as bitter as the rattlesnake's. This poison man must overcome, he must be master of its issue. Because from the first of suns come travelling the rays that make men strong and glad and gods who can range between the known and the unknown. Rays that quiver out of the earth as serpents do, naked with vitality. But each ray charged with poison for the unwary, the irreverent, and the cowardly. Awareness, wariness, is the first virtue in primitive man's morality. And his awareness must travel back and forth, back and forth, from the darkest origins out to the brightest edifices of creation.

And amid all its crudity, and the sensationalism which comes chiefly out of the crowd's desire for thrills, one cannot help pausing in reverence before the delicate, anointed bravery of the snake-priests (so called), with the snakes.

They say the Hopis have a marvellous secret cure for snakebites. They say the bitten are given an emetic drink, after the dance, by the old women, and that they must lie on the edge of the cliff and vomit, vomit, vomit. I saw none of this. The two snake-men who ran down into the shadow came soon running up again, running all the while, and steering off at a tangent, ran up the mesa once more, but beyond a deep, impassable cleft. And there, when they had come up to our level, we saw them across the cleft distance washing, brown and naked, in a pool; washing off the paint, the medicine, the ecstasy, to come back into daily life and eat food. Because for two days they had eaten nothing, it was said. And for nine days they had been immersed in the mystery of snakes, and fasting in some measure.

Men who have lived many years among the Indians say they do not believe the Hopi have any secret cure. Sometimes priests do die of bites, it is said. But a rattlesnake secretes his poison slowly. Each time he strikes he loses his venom, until if he strikes several times, he has very little wherewithal to poison a man. Not enough, not half enough to kill. His glands must be very full charged with poison, as they are when he merges from winter-sleep, before he can kill a man outright. And even then, he must strike near some artery.

Therefore, during the nine days of the kiva, when the snakes are bathed and lustrated, perhaps they strike their poison away into some inanimate object. And surely they are soothed and calmed with such things as the priests, after centuries of experience, know how to administer to them.

We dam the Nile and take the railway across America. The Hopi smooths the rattlesnake and carries him in his mouth, to send him back into the dark places of the earth, an emissary to the inner powers.

To each sort of man his own achievement, his own victory, his own conquest. To the Hopi, the origins are dark and dual, cruelty is coiled in the very beginnings of all things, and circle after circle creation emerges towards a flickering, revealed Godhead. With Man as the godhead so far achieved, waveringly and for ever incomplete, in this world.

To us and to the Orientals, the Godhead was perfect to start with, and man makes but a mechanical excursion into a created and ordained universe, an excursion of mechanical achievement, and of yearning for the return to the perfect Godhead of the beginning.

To us, God was in the beginning, Paradise and the Golden Age have been long lost, and all we can do is to win back.

To the Hopi, God is not yet, and the Golden Age lies far ahead. Out of the dragon's den of the cosmos, we have wrested only the beginnings of our being, the rudiments of our Godhead.

Between the two visions lies the gulf of mutual negations. But ours was the quickest way, so we are conquerors for the moment.

The American aborigines are radically, innately religious. The fabric of their life is religion. But their religion is animistic, their sources are dark and impersonal, their conflict with their "gods" is slow, and unceasing.

This is true of the settled pueblo Indian and the wandering Navajo, the ancient Maya, and the surviving Aztec. They are all involved at every moment, in their old, struggling religion.

Until they break in a kind of hopelessness under our cheerful, triumphant success. Which is what is rapidly happening. The young Indians who have been to school for many years are losing their religion, becoming discontented, bored, and rootless. An Indian with his own religion inside him *cannot* be bored. The flow of the mystery is too intense all the time, too intense, even, for him to adjust himself to circumstances which really are mechanical. Hence his failure. So he, in his great religious struggle for the Godhead of man, falls back beaten. The Personal God who ordained a mechanical cosmos gave the victory to his sons, a mechanical triumph.

Soon after the dance is over, the Navajo begin to ride down the Western trail, into the light. Their women, with velvet bodices and full, full skirts, silver and turquoise tinkling thick on their breasts, sit back on their horses and ride down the steep slope, looking wonderingly around from their pleasant, broad, no-madic, Mongolian faces. And the men, long, loose, thin, long-waisted, with tall hats on their brows and low-sunk silver belts on their hips, come down to water their horses at the spring. We say they look wild. But they have the remoteness of their religion, their animistic vision, in their eyes, they can't see as we see. And they cannot accept us. They stare at us as the coyotes stare at us: the gulf of mutual negation between us.

So in groups, in pairs, singly, they ride silently down into the lower strata of light, the aboriginal Americans riding into their shut-in reservations. While the white Americans hurry back to their motor-cars, and soon the air buzzes with starting engines, like the biggest of rattlesnakes buzzing.

—1927

Why the Novel Matters

We have curious ideas of ourselves. We think of ourselves as a body with a spirit in it, or a body with a soul in it, or a body with a mind in it. *Mens sana in corpore sano.*[1] The years drink up the wine, and at last throw the bottle away, the body, of course, being the bottle.

It is a funny sort of superstition. Why should I look at my hand, as it so cleverly writes these words, and decide that it is a mere nothing compared to the mind that directs it? Is there really any huge difference be-tween my hand and my brain? Or my mind? My hand is alive, it flickers with a life of its own. It meets all the strange universe in touch, and learns a vast number of things, and knows a vast number of things. My hand, as it writes these words, slips gaily along, jumps like a grasshopper to dot an *i*, feels the table rather cold, gets a little bored if I write too long, has its own rudiments of thought, and is just as much *me* as is my brain, my mind, or my soul. Why should I imagine that there is a *me* which is more *me* than my hand is? Since my hand is absolutely alive, me alive.

Whereas, of course, as far as I am concerned, my pen isn't alive at all. My pen *isn't me* alive. Me alive ends at my finger-tips.

Whatever is me alive is me. Every tiny bit of my hands is alive, every little freckle and hair and fold of skin. And whatever is me alive is me. Only my finger-nails, those ten little weapons between me and an inanimate universe, they cross the mysterious Rubicon[2] between me alive and things like my pen, which are not alive, in my own sense.

So, seeing my hand is all alive, and me alive, wherein is it just a bottle, or a jug, or a tin can, or a vessel of clay, or any of the rest of that nonsense? True, if I cut it it will bleed, like a can of cherries. But then the skin that is cut, and the veins that bleed, and the bones that should never be seen, they are all just as alive as the blood that flows. So the tin can business, or vessel of clay, is just bunk.

And that's what you learn, when you're a novelist. And that's what you are very liable *not* to know, if you're a parson, or a philosopher, or a scientist, or a stupid person. If you're a parson, you talk about souls in heaven. If you're a novelist, you know that paradise is in the palm of your hand, and on the end of your nose, because both are alive; and alive, and man alive, which is more than you can say, for certain, of paradise. Paradise is after life, and I for one am not keen on anything that is *after* life. If you are a philosopher, you talk about infinity, and the pure spirit which knows all things. But if you pick up a novel, you realize immedi-ately that infinity is just a handle to this self-same jug of a body of mine; while as for knowing, if I find my finger in the fire, I know that fire burns, with a knowledge so emphatic and vital, it leaves Nirvana merely a conjec-ture. Oh, yes, my body, me alive, *knows*, and knows intensely. And as for the sum of all knowledge, it can't be anything more than an accumulation of all the things I know in the body, and you, dear reader, know in the

[1] *Mens ... sano* Latin: a healthy mind in a healthy body.

[2] *Rubicon* Boundary. From the stream of that name that marked the southern boundary of Gaul. By crossing it, Caesar marked the beginning of the war with Pompey.

body.

These damned philosophers, they talk as if they suddenly went off in steam, and were then much more important than they are when they're in their shirts. It is nonsense. Every man, philosopher included, ends in his own finger-tips. That's the end of his man alive. As for the words and thoughts and sighs and aspirations that fly from him, they are so many tremulations in the ether, and not alive at all. But if the tremulations reach another man alive, he may receive them into his life, and his life may take on a new colour, like a chameleon creeping from a brown rock on to a green leaf. All very well and good. It still doesn't alter the fact that the so-called spirit, the message or teaching of the philosopher or the saint, isn't alive at all, but just a tremulation upon the ether, like a radio message. All this spirit stuff is just tremulations upon the ether. If you, as man alive, quiver from the tremulation of the ether into new life, that is because you are man alive, and you take sustenance and stimulation into your alive man in a myriad ways. But to say that the message, or the spirit which is communicated to you, is more important than your living body, is nonsense. You might as well say that the potato at dinner was more important.

Nothing is important but life. And for myself, I can absolutely see life nowhere but in the living. Life with a capital L is only man alive. Even a cabbage in the rain is cabbage alive. All things that are alive are amazing. And all things that are dead are subsidiary to the living. Better a live dog than a dead lion. But better a live lion than a live dog. *C'est la vie!*[1]

It seems impossible to get a saint, or a philosopher, or a scientist, to stick to this simple truth. They are all, in a sense, renegades. The saint wishes to offer himself up as spiritual food for the multitude. Even Francis of Assisi[2] turns himself into a sort of angel-cake, of which anyone may take a slice. But an angel-cake is rather less than man alive. And poor St. Francis might well apologize to his body, when he is dying: "Oh, pardon me, my body, the wrong I did you through the years!" It was no wafer, for others to eat.

The philosopher, on the other hand, because he can

think, decides that nothing but thoughts matter. It is as if a rabbit, because he can make little pills, should decide that nothing but little pills matter. As for the scientist, he has absolutely no use for me so long as I am man alive. To the scientist, I am dead. He puts under the microscope a bit of dead me, and calls it me. He takes me to pieces, and says first one piece, and then another piece, is me. My heart, my liver, my stomach have all been scientifically me, according to the scientist; and nowadays I am either a brain, or nerves, or glands, or something more up-to-date in the tissue line.

Now I absolutely flatly deny that I am a soul, or a body, or a mind, or an intelligence, or a brain, or a nervous system, or a bunch of glands, or any of the rest of these bits of me. The whole is greater than the part. And therefore, I, who am man alive, am greater than my soul, or spirit, or body, or mind, or consciousness, or anything else that is merely a part of me. I am a man, and alive. I am man alive, and as long as I can, I intend to go on being man alive.

For this reason I am a novelist. And being a novelist, I consider myself superior to the saint, the scientist, the philosopher, and the poet, who are all great masters of different bits of man alive, but never get the whole hog.

The novel is the one bright book of life. Books are not life. They are only tremulations on the ether. But the novel as a tremulation can make the whole man alive tremble. Which is more than poetry, philosophy, science, or any other book-tremulation can do.

The novel is the book of life. In this sense, the Bible is a great confused novel. You may say, it is about God. But it is really about man alive. Adam, Eve, Sarai, Abraham, Isaac, Jacob, Samuel, David, Bath-Sheba, Ruth, Esther, Solomon, Job, Isaiah, Jesus, Mark, Judas, Paul, Peter: what is it but man alive, from start to finish? Man alive, not mere bits. Even the Lord is another man alive, in a burning bush, throwing the tablets of stone at Moses's head.[3]

I do hope you begin to get my idea, why the novel is supremely important, as a tremulation on the ether. Plato makes the perfect ideal being tremble in me. But that's only a bit of me. Perfection is only a bit, in the strange make-up of man alive. The Sermon on the

---

[1] *C'est la vie!*   French: That is life!

[2] *Francis of Assisi*   Founder of the Franciscan Order and the patron saint of animals (c. 1182–1236).

[3] *Even ... head*   See Exodus 3.

Mount[1] makes the selfless spirit of me quiver. But that, too, is only a bit of me. The Ten Commandments set the old Adam shivering in me, warning me that I am a thief and a murderer, unless I watch it. But even the old Adam is only a bit of me.

I very much like all these bits of me to be set trembling with life and the wisdom of life. But I do ask that the whole of me shall tremble in its wholeness, some time or other.

And this, of course, must happen in me, living.

But as far as it can happen from a communication, it can only happen when a whole novel communicates itself to me. The Bible—but *all* the Bible—and Homer, and Shakespeare: these are the supreme old novels. These are all things to all men. Which means that in their wholeness they affect the whole man alive, which is the man himself, beyond any part of him. They set the whole tree trembling with a new access of life, they do not just stimulate growth in one direction.

I don't want to grow in any one direction any more. And, if I can help it, I don't want to stimulate anybody else into some particular direction. A particular direction ends in a *cul-de-sac*. We're in a *cul-de-sac* at present.

I don't believe in any dazzling revelation, or in any supreme Word. "The grass withereth, the flower fadeth, but the Word of the Lord shall stand for ever."[2] That's the kind of stuff we've drugged ourselves with. As a matter of fact, the grass withereth, but comes up all the greener for that reason, after the rains. The flower fadeth, and therefore the bud opens. But the Word of the Lord, being man-uttered and a mere vibration on the ether, becomes staler and staler, more and more boring, till at last we turn a deaf ear and it ceases to exist, far more finally than any withered grass. It is grass that renews its youth like the eagle, not any Word.

We should ask for no absolutes, or absolute. Once and for all and for ever, let us have done with the ugly imperialism of any absolute. There is no absolute good, there is nothing absolutely right. All things flow and change, and even change is not absolute. The whole is a strange assembly of apparently incongruous parts, slipping past one another.

Me, man alive, I am a very curious assembly of incongruous parts. My yea! of today is oddly different from my yea! of yesterday. My tears of tomorrow will have nothing to do with my tears of a year ago. If the one I love remains unchanged and unchanging, I shall cease to love her. It is only because she changes and startles me into change and defies my inertia, and is herself staggered in her inertia by my changing, that I can continue to love her. If she stayed put, I might as well love the pepper-pot.

In all this change, I maintain a certain integrity. But woe betide me if I try to put my finger on it. If I say of myself, I am this, I am that!—then, if I stick to it, I turn into a stupid fixed thing like a lamp-post. I shall never know wherein lies my integrity, my individuality, my me. I *can* never know it. It is useless to talk about my ego. That only means that I have made up an *idea* of myself, and that I am trying to cut myself out to pattern. Which is no good. You can cut your cloth to fit your coat, but you can't clip bits off your living body, to trim it down to your idea. True, you can put yourself into ideal corsets. But even in ideal corsets, fashions change. Let us learn from the novel. In the novel, the characters can do nothing but *live*. If they keep on being good, according to pattern, or bad, according to pattern, or even volatile, according to pattern, they cease to live, and the novel falls dead. A character in a novel has got to live, or it is nothing.

We, likewise, in life have got to live, or we are nothing.

What we mean by living is, of course, just as indescribable as what we mean by *being*. Men get ideas into their heads, of what they mean by Life, and they proceed to cut life out to pattern. Sometimes they go into the desert to seek God, sometimes they go into the desert to seek cash, sometimes it is wine, woman, and song, and again it is water, political reform, and votes. You never know what it will be next: from killing your neighbour with hideous bombs and gas that tears the lungs, to supporting a Foundlings Home and preaching infinite Love, and being co-respondent in a divorce.

In all this wild welter, we need some sort of guide. It's no good inventing Thou Shalt Nots!

What then? Turn truly, honourably to the novel, and see wherein you are man alive, and wherein you are dead man in life. You may love a woman as man alive, and you may be making love to a woman as sheer dead

---

[1]   *Sermon on the Mount*   See Matthew 5–7.

[2]   *The grass … ever*   Isaiah 40.7.

man in life. You may eat your dinner as man alive, or as a mere masticating corpse. As man alive you may have a shot at your enemy. But as a ghastly simulacrum of life you may be firing bombs into men who are neither your enemies nor your friends, but just things you are dead to. Which is criminal, when the things happen to be alive.

To be alive, to be man alive, to be whole man alive: that is the point. And at its best, the novel, and the novel supremely, can help you. It can help you not to be dead man in life. So much of a man walks about dead and a carcass in the street and house, today: so much of women is merely dead. Like a pianoforte with half the notes mute.

But in the novel you can see, plainly, when the man goes dead, the woman goes inert. You can develop an instinct for life, if you will, instead of a theory of right and wrong, good and bad.

In life, there is right and wrong, good and bad, all the time. But what is right in one case is wrong in another. And in the novel you see one man becoming a corpse, because of his so-called goodness, another going dead because of his so-called wickedness. Right and wrong is an instinct: but an instinct of the whole consciousness in a man, bodily, mental, spiritual at once. And only in the novel are *all* things given full play, or at least, they may be given full play, when we realize that life itself, and not inert safety, is the reason for living. For out of the full play of all things emerges the only thing that is anything, the wholeness of a man, the wholeness of a woman, man alive, and live woman.

—1936

WORK AND WORKING-CLASS LIFE

CONTEXTS

D.H. Lawrence presents a bleak picture of life in the mining communities of the English Midlands (in novels such as *Sons and Lovers* as well as stories such as "The Odour of Chysanthemums") but does not exaggerate the hardships of the working class. The materials in this section—chief among them excerpts from two of the most important non-fictional accounts of working-class life in northern England in the first half of the twentieth century (George Orwell's *The Road to Wigan Pier* and Robert Roberts's *The Classic Slum*)—provide a broader picture of such hardships.

⌘⌘⌘

Anonymous, "Armoured cars at Hyde Park Corner," 1926. A convoy of armored cars assembles at Hyde Park Corner in London. During the General Strike of 1926, troops were called on to maintain Britain's food supply—and no doubt to intimidate the strikers. The spark that set off the General Strike was the dissatisfaction coal miners' felt about their working conditions. When, following World War I, a reviving coal industry in Germany had caused the price of coal in Britain to tumble, mine owners had responded by reducing the already-low wages of their workers. On May 1, one million coal miners went on strike in protest, and the five-million-strong Trades Union Congress backed them; transport-ation, the steel industry, and many other sectors of the economy were paralyzed. The government, led by Prime Minister Stanley Baldwin and Chancellor of the Exchequer Winston Churchill, took a strong stand against the workers, and within twelve days the General Strike had ended. The miners continued to strike for several more months, but eventually acceded to the demands of the owners that they work longer hours for lower pay.

from George Orwell, *The Road to Wigan Pier* (1937)

George Orwell's *The Road to Wigan Pier* was commissioned by the Left Book Club as a report on the state of the unemployed in northern England. Characteristically, Orwell did not do exactly as he had been instructed or had expected to do; he wrote extensively about the conditions of workers as well as those of the unemployed, and he wrote frankly and not always flatteringly about the working class (as well as writing scathingly about the privileged classes).

Our civilization, *pace* Chesterton,[1] *is* founded on coal, more completely than one realises until one stops to think about it. The machines that keep us alive, and the machines that make the machines, are all

---

[1] *pace Chesterton*   Despite what Chesterton said. See the exchange below involving G.K. Chesterton, George Bernard Shaw, and Hilaire Belloc.

directly or indirectly dependent upon coal. In the metabolism of the Western world the coal-miner is second in importance only to the man who ploughs the soil. He is a sort of grimy caryatid[1] upon whose shoulders nearly everything that is *not* grimy is supported. For this reason the actual process by which coal is extracted is well worth watching, if you get the chance and are willing to take the trouble.

When you go down a coal-mine it is important to try and get to the coal face when the "fillers"[2] are at work.... On a Sunday, for instance, a mine seems almost peaceful. The time to go there is when the machines are roaring and the air is black with coal dust, and when you can actually see what the miners have to do. At those times the place is like hell, or at any rate like my own mental picture of hell. Most of the things one imagines in hell are there—heat, noise, confusion, darkness, foul air, and, above all, unbearably cramped space. Everything except the fire, for there is no fire down there except the feeble beams of Davy lamps[3] and electric torches which scarcely penetrate the clouds of coal dust.

When you have finally got there ... you crawl through the last line of pit props and see opposite you a shiny black wall three or four feet high. This is the coal face. Overhead is the smooth ceiling made by the rock from which the coal has been cut; underneath is the rock again, so that the gallery you are in is only as high as the ledge of coal itself, probably not much more than a yard. The first impression of all, overmastering everything else for a while, is the frightful, deafening din from the conveyor belt which carries the coal away. You cannot see very far, because the fog of coal dust throws back the beam of your lamp, but you can see on either side of you the line of half-naked kneeling men, one to every four or five yards, driving their shovels under the fallen coal and flinging it swiftly over their left shoulders. They are feeding it on to the conveyor belt, a moving rubber belt a couple of feet wide which runs a yard or two behind them. Down this belt a glittering river of coal races constantly. In a big mine it is carrying away several tons of coal every minute. It bears it off to some place in the main roads where it is shot into tubs holding half a ton, and thence dragged to the cages and hoisted to the outer air.

It is impossible to watch the "fillers" at work without feeling a pang of envy for their toughness. It is a dreadful job that they do, an almost superhuman job by the standards of an ordinary person. For they are not only shifting monstrous quantities of coal, they are also doing it in a position that doubles or trebles the work. They have got to remain kneeling all the while—they could hardly rise from their knees without hitting the ceiling—and you can easily see by trying it what a tremendous effort this means. Shovelling is comparatively easy when you are standing up, because you can use your knee and thigh to drive the shovel along; kneeling down, the whole of the strain is thrown upon your arm and belly muscles. And the other conditions do not exactly make things easier. There is the heat—it varies, but in some mines it is suffocating—and the coal dust that stuffs up your throat and nostrils and collects along your eyelids, and the unending rattle of the conveyor belt, which in that confined space is rather like the rattle of a machine gun. ...

It is not long since conditions in the mines were worse than they are now. There are still living a few very old women who in their youth have worked underground, with a harness round their waists and a chain that passed between their legs, crawling on all fours and dragging tubs of coal. They used to go on doing this even when they were pregnant....

The adjustments a miner's family have to make when he is changed from one shift to another must be tiresome in the extreme. If he is on the night shift he gets home in time for breakfast, on the morning shift he gets home in the middle of the afternoon, and on the afternoon shift he gets home in the middle of the night; and in each case, of course, he wants his principal meal of the day as soon as he returns. I notice that the Rev. W.R. Inge, in his book *England*, accuses the miners of gluttony. From my own observation I should say that they eat astonishingly little. Most of the miners I stayed with ate slightly less than I did. Many of them declare that they cannot do their day's work if they have had a

---

[1]   *caryatid*   Supporting column carved in the shape of a female.

[2]   *fillers*   Miners who load coal onto conveyor belts.

[3]   *Davy lamps*   Glass cylinder-shaped lamps. The flame in the lamps was encased in wire gauze, which allowed air in, but prevented the flame from escaping and igniting flammable gases in the mine.

heavy meal beforehand, and the food they take with them is only a snack, usually bread-and-dripping[1] and cold tea....

Every miner of long standing that I have talked to had either been in a fairly serious accident himself or had seen some of his mates killed, and in every mining family they tell you tales of fathers, brothers or uncles killed at work. ("And he fell seven hundred feet, and they wouldn't never have collected t'pieces only he were wearing a new suit of oilskins," etc., etc., etc.) ...

Anyone who wants to see the effects of the housing shortage at their very worst should visit the dreadful caravan-dwellings that exist in numbers in many of the northern towns. Ever since the war, in the complete impossibility of getting houses, parts of the population have overflowed into supposedly temporary quarters in fixed caravans.... One [caravan] measuring fourteen feet long, had seven people in it—seven people in about 450 cubic feet of space; which is to say that each person had for his entire dwelling a space *a good deal* smaller than one compartment of a public lavatory. The dirt and congestion of these places is such that you cannot well imagine it unless you have tested it with your own eyes and more particularly your nose....

Talking once with a miner I asked him when the housing shortage first became acute in his district; he answered, "When we were told about it," meaning that till recently people's standards were so low that they took almost any degree of overcrowding for granted. He added that when he was a child his family had slept eleven in a room and thought nothing of it, and that later, when he was grown-up, he and his wife had lived in one of the old-style back to back houses[2] in which you not only had to walk a couple of hundred yards to the lavatory but often had to wait in a queue when you got there, the lavatory being shared by thirty-six people....

[But nowadays] the middle classes—yes, even the bridge clubs in the country towns—are beginning to realise that there is such a thing as unemployment. The "My dear, I don't *believe* in all this nonsense about unemployment. Why, only last week we wanted a man to weed the garden, and we simply couldn't get one. They don't *want* to work, that's all it is!" which you heard at every decent tea-table five years ago, is growing perceptibly less frequent. As for the working class themselves, they have gained immensely in economic knowledge. I believe that the *Daily Worker* has accomplished a great deal here: its influence is out of all proportion to its circulation....

[Anywhere in the North] there is immense and systematic thieving of coal by the unemployed. I call it thieving because technically it is that, though it does no harm to anybody. In the "dirt" that is sent up from the pits there is a certain amount of broken coal, and unemployed people spend a lot of time in picking it out of the slag-heaps. All day long over those strange grey mountains you see people wandering to and fro with sacks and baskets among the sulphurous smoke (many slag-heaps are on fire under the surface), prising out the tiny nuggets of coal which are buried here and there. You meet men coming away, wheeling strange and wonderful homemade bicycles—bicycles made of rusty parts picked off refuse-tips, without saddles, without chains and almost always without tyres—across which are slung bags containing perhaps half a hundredweight of coal, fruit of half a day's searching. In times of strikes, when everybody is short of fuel, the miners turn out with pick and shovel and burrow into the slag-heaps, whence the hummocky appearance which most slag-heaps have. During long strikes, in places where there are outcrops of coal, they have sunk surface mines and carried them scores of yards into the earth.

---

[1]   *dripping*   Fat from cooked meat.

[2]   *back to back houses*   Terraced houses (with communal lavatories).

Coal Searchers (Illustration to *The Road to Wigan Pier*, 1937).

Caravan Dwellers Near a Durham Quarry
(Illustration to *The Road to Wigan Pier*, 1937).

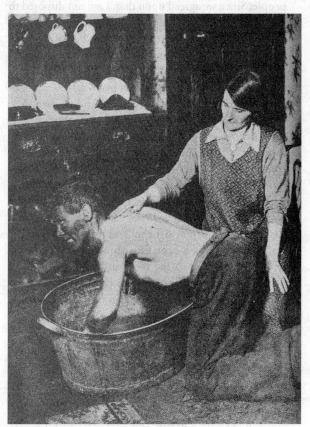

A South Wales Miner Takes His Bath
(Illustration to *The Road to Wigan Pier*, 1937).

Stepney, Shadwell District
(Illustration to *The Road to Wigan Pier*, 1937).

from "A Debate Between G.B. Shaw and G.K. Chesterton, Chaired by Hilaire Belloc" (1928)

As the following excerpts from this 1928 exchange illustrate, the exploitation of coal miners was sufficiently extreme as to motivate even some conservative thinkers (Chesterton notable among them) to advocate nationalization of the industry. Shaw, a longtime socialist, saw nationalization of the coal industry as a necessary first step towards a much broader program. Belloc, a renowned writer of humorous sketches, attempted to keep the tone light. Coal was one of several major industries nationalized by Clement Atlee's Labour Government when it took power after World War II.

SHAW. ... You have to begin with the question of the distribution of wealth. The other day a man died and the Government took four and a half million pounds as death duty on his property. That man made all his money by the labour of men who received twenty-six shillings a week after years of qualifying for their work. Was that a reasonable distribution of wealth between them?

... Let us come down to facts. Mr. Chesterton has formed the Distributist League[1] which organized this meeting. What was the very first thing the League said must be done? It said the coal-mines must be nationalized. Instead of saying that the miner's means of production must be made his own property, it was forced to advocate making national property of the coal mines. These coal-mines, when nationalized, will not be managed by the House of Commons: if they were you would very soon have no coal. But neither will they be managed by the miners. If you ask the man working in the mine to manage the mine he will say, "Not me, governor! That is your job." I would like Mr. Chesterton to consider what he understands by the means of production. He has spoken of them in rather a nineteenth-century manner. He has been talking as though the means of production were machines. I submit to you that the real means of production in this country are men and women, and that consequently you always have the maximum control of the individual over

the means of production, because it means self-control over his own person. But he must surrender that control to the manager of the mine because he does not know how to manage it himself. Under the present capitalistic system he has to surrender it to the manager appointed by the proprietors of the mine. Under Socialism he would have to surrender it to the manager appointed by the Coalmaster-General. That would not prevent the product of the mine being equally distributed among the people. There is no difficulty here. In a sense Mr. Chesterton really does not disagree with me in this matter, since he does see that in the matter of fuel in this country you have to come to nationalization. Fuel must be controlled equally for the benefit of all the people. Since we agreed upon that, I am not disposed to argue the matter further. Now that Mr. Chesterton agreed that the coal-mines will have to be nationalized he will be led by the same pressure of facts to agree to the nationalization of everything else. I have to allow for the pressure of facts because, as a playwright, I think of all problems in terms of actual men and women. Mr. Chesterton lets himself idealize them sometimes as virtuous peasant proprietors and self-managing petty capitalists. The capitalist and the landlord have their own particular ways of robbing the poor; but their legal rights are quite different. It is a very direct way on the part of the landlord. He may do exactly what he likes with the land he owns. If I own a large part of Scotland I can turn the people off the land practically into the sea, or across the sea. I can take women in child-bearing and throw them into the snow and leave them there. That has been done. I can do it for no better reason than I think it is better to shoot deer on the land than allow people to live on it....

CHESTERTON. ... We have said again and again that in our human state of society there must be a class of things called exceptions. We admit that upon the whole in the very peculiar case of coal it is desirable and about the best way out of the difficulty that it should be controlled by the officials of the State, just in the same way as postage stamps are controlled. No one says anything else about postage stamps. I cannot imagine that anyone wants to have his own postage stamps, of

---

[1] *Distributist League* Founded in 1926, the Distributist League advocated broad ownership of property and capital within society.

perhaps more picturesque design and varied colours. I can assure you that Distributists are perfectly sensible and sane people, and they have always recognized that there are institutions in the State in which it is very difficult to apply the principle of individual property, and that one of these cases is the discovery under the earth of valuable minerals. Socialists are not alone in believing this. Charles I, who, I suppose, could not be called a Socialist, pointed out that certain kinds of minerals ought to belong to the State, that is, to the Commons. We have said over and over again that we support the nationalization of the coal-mines, not as a general example of Distribution but as a common-sense admission of an exception. The reason why we make it an exception is because it is not very easy to see how the healthy principle of personal ownership can be applied. If it could we should apply it with the greatest pleasure. We consider personal ownership infinitely more healthy. If there were a way in which a miner could mark out one particular piece of coal and say, "This is mine, and I am proud of it," we should have made an enormous improvement upon State management. There are cases in which it is very difficult to apply the principle, and that is one of them. It is the reverse of the truth for Mr. Shaw to say that the logic of that fact will lead me to the application of the same principle to other cases, like the ownership of the land....

BELLOC. ... I was told when I accepted this onerous office that I was to sum up. I shall do nothing of the sort. In a very few years from now this debate will be antiquated. I will now recite you a poem: "Our civilization Is built upon coal. Let us chant in rotation Our civilization That lump of damnation Without any soul, Our civilization Is built upon coal. In a very few years, It will float upon oil. Then give three hearty cheers, In a very few years We shall mop up our tears And have done with our toil. In a very few years It will float upon oil." In I do not know how many years—five, ten, twenty—this debate will be as antiquated as crinolines are. I am surprised that neither of the two speakers pointed out that one of three things is going to happen. One of three things: not one of two. It is always one of three things. This industrial civilization which, thank God, oppresses only the small part of the world in which we are most inextricably bound up, will break down and therefore end from its monstrous wickedness, folly, ineptitude, leading to a restoration of sane, ordinary human affairs, complicated but based as a whole upon the freedom of the citizens. Or it will break down and lead to nothing but a desert. Or it will lead the mass of men to become contented slaves, with a few rich men controlling them. Take your choice. You will all be dead before any of the three things comes off. One of the three things is going to happen, or a mixture of two, or possibly a mixture of the three combined.

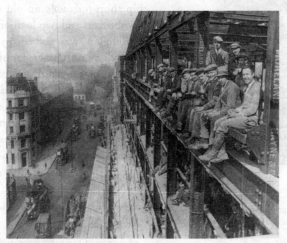

Construction workers, London, 1920s.

An English bedspring factory, unidentified location, 1920s.

Cleaning and maintenance for a steam engine, England, unidentified location, 1920s.

from Robert Roberts, *The Classic Slum* (1971)

> Though it was not published until 1971, *The Classic Slum* is a largely first-hand account of working class life in the early twentieth century; Robert Roberts (1905–74) had grown up in the same area of the northern English city of Salford that Frederic Engels had described in 1844 as "the classic slum."

Every industrial city, of course, folds within itself a clutter of loosely defined overlapping "villages." Those in the Great Britain of seventy years ago were almost self-contained communities. Our own consisted of some thirty streets and alleys locked along the north and south by two railway systems a furlong[1] apart. About twice that distance to the east lay another slum which turned on its farther side into a land of bonded warehouses and the city proper. West of us, well beyond the tramlines, lay the middle classes, bay-windowed and begardened. We knew them not.

In the city as a whole our village rated indubitably low. "The children of this school," wrote one of King Edward VII's inspectors, commenting on our only seat of learning, "are of the poorest class; so, too, is the teaching." With cash, or on tick,[2] our villagers, about three thousand in all, patronized fifteen beer-houses, a hotel and two off-licences,[3] nine grocery and general shops, three greengrocers (forever struggling to survive against the street hawker), two tripe shops, three barbers, three cloggers, two cook shops, one fish and chip shop *(déclassé),* an old clothes store, a couple of pawnbrokers and two loan offices.

Religion was served by two chapels (Primitive Methodist and Congregationalist), one "tin" mission (Church of England) and one sinister character who held spiritualist seances in his parlour and claimed from the window to cure "Female Bad Legs." (Through overwork innumerable women suffered from burst varicose veins.) Culture, pleasure and need found outlet through one theatre (and, later, three cinemas), a dancing room ("low"), two coy brothels, eight book-

---

[1] *furlong* Unit of distance. (One furlong equals 660 feet.)

[2] *on tick* On credit.

[3] *off-licences* Originally, permits that allowed the sale of alcoholic beverages; here, a shop at which alcohol is sold by permit.

makers, and a private moneylender. … Over one quarter of a mile industry stood represented by a dying brickworks and an iron foundry. Several gasholders on the south side polluted the air, sometimes for days together. Little would grow; even the valiant aspidistra pined. We possessed besides two coal yards, a corn[1] store, a cattle wharf and perhaps as closed an urban society as any in Europe.

In our community, as in every other of its kind, each street had the usual social rating; one side or one end of that street might be classed higher than another. Weekly rents varied from 2s 6d[2] for the back-to-back to 4s 6d for a "two up and two down."[3] End houses often had special status. Every family, too, had a tacit ranking, and even individual members within it; neighbours would consider a daughter in one household as "dead common" while registering her sister as "refined," a word much in vogue. (Young women with incipient consumption were often thought "refined.") Class divisions were of the greatest consequence, though their implications remained unrealized: the many looked upon social and economic inequality as the law of nature. Division in our own society ranged from an elite at the peak, composed of the leading families, through recognized strata to a social base whose members one damned as the "lowest of the low," or simply "no class." Shopkeepers, publicans[4] and skilled tradesmen occupied the premier positions, each family having its own sphere of influence. A few of these aristocrats, while sharing working-class culture, had aspirations. From their ranks the lower middle class, then clearly defined, drew most of its recruits—clerks and, in particular, schoolteachers (struggling hard at that time for social position). Well before translation those striving to "get on" tried to ape what they believed were "real" middle-class manners and customs. Publicans' and shopkeepers' daughters, for instance, set the fashion in clothes for a district. Some went to private commercial colleges in the city, took music lessons or perhaps studied elocution—that short cut, it was felt, to "culture"—at two shillings an hour,

their new "twang" tried out later over the bar and counter, earning them a deal of covert ridicule….

Many women and girls in the district worked in some branch of the textile industry. Of these, we accepted weavers as "top" in their class, followed by winders and drawers-in. Then came spinners. They lacked standing on several counts: first, the trade contained a strong Irish Catholic element, and wages generally were lower than in other sections. Again, because of the heat and slippery floors, women worked barefoot, dressed in little more than calico shifts. These garments, the respectable believed, induced in female spinners a certain moral carelessness. They came home, too, covered in dust and fluff; all things which combined to depress their social prestige. Women employees of dye works, however, filled the lowest bracket: their work was dirty, wet and heavy and they paid due penalty for it. Clogs and shawls were, of course, standard wear for all. The girl who first defied this tradition in one of Lancashire's largest mills remembered the "stares, skits and sneers" of fellow workers sixty years afterwards. Her parents, urgently in need of money, had put her to weaving, where earnings for girls were comparatively good. They lived, however, in one of the newer suburbs with its parloured houses and small back gardens. To be seen in such a district returning from a mill in clogs and shawl would have meant instant social demotion for the whole family. She was sent to the weaving shed wearing coat and shoes and thereby shocked a whole establishment. Here was a "forward little bitch," getting above herself. So clearly, in fact, did headwear denote class that, in Glasgow, separate clubs existed for "hat" girls and "shawl" girls. Nevertheless, before 1914 even, continued good wages in weaving and the consequent urge to bolster status had persuaded not a few to follow the lone teenager's example. By the end of the war, in the big town cotton mills at least, coats and shoes could be worn without comment. …

Position in our Edwardian community was judged not only by what one possessed but also by what one pawned. Through agreement with the local broker the back room of our corner shop served as a depot for those goods pledged by the week which owners had been unable to redeem before nine o'clock on Saturday, when

---

[1] *corn* I.e., grain.

[2] *2s 6d* Two shillings sixpence.

[3] *two up and two down* House consisting of two rooms downstairs and two upstairs.

[4] *publicans* Owners of pubs.

the local pawnshop closed. Our service gave women waiting on drunken or late-working husbands a few hours' grace in which to redeem shoes and clothing before the Sabbath, and so maintain their social stake in the English Sunday. Towards our closing time there was always a great scurrying shopwards to get the "bundle." Housewives after washday on Monday pledged what clean clothes could be spared until weekend and returned with cash to buy food. Often they stood in the shop and thanked God that *they* were not as certain others who, having no clothes but what they stood in, had sunk low enough to pawn ashpans, hearth rugs or even the "pots off the table." Other customers tut-tutted in disgust. News of domestic distress soon got around. Inability to redeem basic goods was a sure sign of a family's approaching destitution, and credit dried up fast in local tick shops. Naturally, the gulf between those households who patronized "Uncle," even if only occasionally, and those who did not gaped wide. Some families would go hungry rather than pledge their belongings.

The interest charged on articles pawned was usually a penny in the shilling per week, one half being paid at pledging time (Monday) and the other on redemption of the goods (Saturday). …

A working-class woman, if she went even a short distance from her own door, would slip on a shawl. In public without it she was said to be "in her figure," and to be seen that way too often caused comment. With their graceful hair styles, sweeping gowns, narrow waists and curving forms, women seem to have held more feminine allure then than at any time since. But realists among the old working class today remember, and with sadness, not King Edward's "lovely ladies" and tea on the lawn at Hurlingham, but the many women broken and aged with childbearing well before their own youth was done. They remember the spoiled complexions, the mouths full of rotten teeth, the varicose veins, the ignorance of simple hygiene, the intelligence stifled and the endless battle merely to keep clean. Unlike many in the middle and upper classes, fondly looking back, they see no "glory gleaming." They weep no tears for the past. What things the poor did own then, most made gallant use of. The tragedy was that in the most opulent country in the world so many possessed so little.…

Whenever status was being assessed in shop or street group, one marked with puzzlement that one or two households were dismissed with ominous brevity, and this not for any obvious reason, social or economic. Only in late teenage did we discover that the closed community, like the family, could hold skeletons in its cupboard. The damned houses were those where, neighbours knew, incestuous relationship had borne a fruit which walked the streets before their very eyes. Here stood a hazard that faced all poor parents of large adolescent families sleeping together, perhaps with older relatives, in two small bedrooms. In their hearts they harboured a dread of what seemed to a respectable household the ultimate disgrace. Such sin, of course, had to be recognized in whispered *tête à tête;* but I don't recall a single prosecution: strict public silence saved miscreants from the rigours of the law.

The matriarchy presided in judgement over the public behaviour of both children and young teenagers. Mothers round washing lines or going to the shop half a dozen times a day would inevitably hear of the peccadilloes of their offspring. Punishment followed, often unjustly, since the word of an adult was accepted almost always against that of a child. With some people a child had no "word"; only too often he was looked upon as an incomplete human being whose opinions and feelings were of little or no account—until he began to earn money! It is true that a much more indulgent attitude towards the young had already developed among the middle classes, but it had not yet spread far down the social scale. In the lower working class "manners" were imposed upon children with the firmest hand: adults recognized that if anything was to be got from "above" one should learn early to ask for it with a proper measure of humble politeness. There was besides, of course, the desire to imitate one's betters.…

Among women in shop talk the confinement of daily life was often a subject for bitter complaint. Some did manage an occasional visit to the cemetery, or an hour in a balding park on the edge of the village, but many were denied even this. One, I recall, spoke wearily of never having been more than five minutes' walk from her home in eighteen years of married life. Husbands were luckier: at least once a year a beer-house picnic would take them for a long boozing day in the country.

Children too got intense pleasure from the outings that charity or the Sunday school provided. Our top people paid annual visits to Blackpool, New Brighton and Southport and made sure that everybody knew, especially about their first ride in a motor car. At Southport quite early in the century an enterprising young man was doing excellent business with his Daimler open saloon,[1] taking half a dozen passengers a time for five-minute trips round the lake.

In general, slum life was far from being the jolly hive of communal activity that some romantics have claimed. They forget, perhaps, or never knew of the dirt that hung over all, of the rubbish that lay for months in the back alleys, of the "entries" or ginnels[2] with open middens[3] where starving cats and dogs roamed or died and lay for weeks unmoved. They did not know those houses that stank so badly through an open doorway that one stepped off the pavement to pass them by. That people stayed scrupulously clean in such surroundings— and many did—only proves the tenacity of the human spirit.

On the light evenings after a day's work many men, even if they had the desire, possessed no means of occupying body or mind. Ignorance and poverty combined to breed, for the most part, tedium, a dumb accidie[4] of the back streets to which only brawling brought relief. Summer evening leisure for men without the few coppers to go into a tavern meant long, empty hours lounging between kitchen chair and threshold. How familiar one grew in childhood with those silent figures leaning against door jambs, staring into vacancy waiting for bedtime.

---

[1] *saloon*   Here, a car with passenger room for four or more.

[2] *ginnels*   Narrow passages between homes.

[3] *open middens*   Garbage heaps.

[4] *accidie*   Sloth.

KATHERINE MANSFIELD
1888 – 1923

In her short life, Katherine Mansfield managed to secure a reputation as one of the world's most gifted writers of short fiction. Her later stories in particular are important for their experimentation with style and atmosphere. Instead of a conventional storyline, these stories present a series of loosely linked moments, portraying the small details of human life as a means of illuminating a specific character at a specific point of crisis or epiphany. Among Mansfield's favorite devices are internal monologues, daydreams, the flexible manipulation of time and tense, and the use of rhythm and sound to convey mood and meaning. Her stories also often feature a variety of viewpoints, with language and syntax specific to each. Mansfield also experimented with the short story cycle, linking character and/or setting and utilizing repeating images and motifs. In "The Garden Party," for instance, the Sheridan family maintains the ongoing family chronicle Mansfield created in her earlier works (using the name "Burnell").

Kathleen Mansfield Beauchamp was born in Wellington, New Zealand, the third of six children of Harold Beauchamp and Annie Burnell Dyer Beauchamp. Her father was of working-class origins, but became a successful industrialist and later chairman of the Bank of New Zealand; his rise in the financial and commercial world was rewarded with a knighthood in the year of Mansfield's death. Dyer Beauchamp was a genteel woman of delicate persuasion, for whom the regimens of household management and child rearing seemed both too taxing and beneath her social ambitions. As a result, Mansfield's memories of her mother were more frequently detached than affectionate.

Mansfield's school years were divided between the country village of Karori and the capital, Wellington, where the family moved to a mansion at Tinakori Road (the setting for "The Garden Party"). In 1903, she and her sisters entered Queen's College in London. She immersed herself in French and German while contemplating a career as a cellist. Mansfield also advanced her literary career as she became a contributor to and editor of the College's magazine. It was at Queen's College that she developed a close relationship with Ida Baker (to whom she referred as Leslie Moore)—a relationship Mansfield would depend upon for the rest of her life. By this time, the young author and musician Kathleen Beauchamp had decided to adopt the professional name of "Katherine Mansfield."

At the conclusion of her studies in London, Mansfield returned unwillingly to Wellington. Having flourished artistically in the cosmopolitan environment of London, she despised the provincial lifestyle of her home, and for nearly two years she exhausted her parents with constant pleas to return to England. In 1908, with the support of Baker, she was given leave to return to London and never saw New Zealand again.

Within weeks of returning, Mansfield fell in love with a fellow musician, Garnett Trowell. When their relationship collapsed within a few months, she impulsively married G.C. Bowden, a singing teacher whose name she bore for the next nine years, despite having left him on their wedding night. She returned to Trowell and traveled with his opera company until she became pregnant and was sent by her mother to an unfashionable Bavarian spa for the duration of her pregnancy, which ended in miscarriage. During her stay in Germany, she wrote a series of satirical sketches of German characters that were published individually in *The New Age*; they were later collected and published as *In a German Pension* (1911). On her return to London Mansfield was diagnosed with rheumatic fever; it was later discovered to be gonorrhea, a condition that contributed to her failing health for the rest of her life.

By late 1911, Mansfield had begun contributing to *Rhythm*, an avant-garde quarterly edited by John Middleton Murry. A year later she became *Rhythm*'s editor and began a lifelong, tumultuous love affair with Murry. The "Two Tigers," as they were known, cultivated several close relationships within literary circles, most notably with D.H. Lawrence (a friendship that would end bitterly in 1920), Virginia Woolf, and Aldous Huxley. In 1913, *Rhythm* became *The Blue Review* after the publisher absconded, leaving Mansfield and Murry with considerable debts. *The Blue Review* folded after only three months, despite an impressive list of contributors including Lawrence, H.G. Wells, Hugh Walpole, and T.S. Eliot.

In 1915, Mansfield's youngest brother Leslie was killed in France. Her profound grief sent her into self-imposed exile in that country, where in an effort to console herself she began writing stories about her childhood in New Zealand; thus began her most productive and successful period as a writer. That same year Mansfield finally divorced G.C. Bowden and married John Murry. Later in the year she was diagnosed with tuberculosis; for the remaining years of her life she traveled between London, Switzerland, and the French Riviera in search of modern treatments and salubrious climates.

In 1919 Mansfield began reviewing novels for the *Athenaeum*, the editor of which was Murry, and a year later she published *Bliss, and Other Stories*. In the next two years she wrote many of her most notable works, several of which are included in *The Garden Party and Other Stories* (1922). In October of that year she entered the Gurdjieff Institute in France for controversial therapy under the guidance of mystic George Ivanovich Gurdjieff. In early 1923, overexcited by a visit from her husband, Mansfield suffered a severe lung hemorrhage upon rapidly climbing the steps to her room; she died later that evening. Although Mansfield had requested in her will that Murry publish as little of her work as possible, two further collections of her stories were published, as well as a collection of poetry and other works.

The stories included here are representative of Mansfield's favorite themes: the evolution of the self, the terrors of childhood, the solitude of the outsider, and the reality of death. Malcolm Cowley, a contemporary of Mansfield, wrote that her stories "have a thesis: namely, that life is a very wonderful spectacle, but disagreeable for the actors."

⌘⌘⌘

Bliss

Although Bertha Young was thirty she still had moments like this when she wanted to run instead of walk, to take dancing steps on and off the pavement, to bowl a hoop, to throw something up in the air and catch it again, or to stand still and laugh at—nothing— at nothing, simply.

What can you do if you are thirty and, turning the corner of your own street, you are overcome, suddenly, by a feeling of bliss—absolute bliss!—as though you'd suddenly swallowed a bright piece of that late afternoon sun and it burned in your bosom, sending out a little shower of sparks into every particle, into every finger and toe?…

Oh, is there no way you can express it without being "drunk and disorderly"? How idiotic civilisation is! Why be given a body if you have to keep it shut up in a case like a rare, rare fiddle?

"No, that about the fiddle is not quite what I mean," she thought, running up the steps and feeling in her bag for the key—she'd forgotten it, as usual—and rattling the letterbox. "It's not what I mean, because—Thank you, Mary"—she went into the hall. "Is nurse back?"

"Yes, M'm."

"And has the fruit come?"

"Yes, M'm. Everything's come."

"Bring the fruit up to the dining room, will you? I'll arrange it before I go upstairs."

It was dusky in the dining room and quite chilly. But all the same Bertha threw off her coat; she could not bear the tight clasp of it another moment, and the cold air fell on her arms.

But in her bosom there was still that bright glowing place—that shower of little sparks coming from it. It was almost unbearable. She hardly dared to breathe for fear of fanning it higher, and yet she breathed deeply, deeply. She hardly dared to look into the cold mirror—but she did look, and it gave her back a woman, radiant, with smiling, trembling lips, with big, dark eyes and an air of listening, waiting for something … divine to happen … that she knew must happen … infallibly.

Mary brought in the fruit on a tray and with it a glass bowl, and a blue dish, very lovely, with a strange sheen on it as though it had been dipped in milk.

"Shall I turn on the light, M'm?"

"No, thank you. I can see quite well."

There were tangerines and apples stained with strawberry pink. Some yellow pears, smooth as silk, some white grapes covered with a silver bloom and a big cluster of purple ones. These last she had bought to tone in with the new dining room carpet. Yes, that did sound rather farfetched and absurd, but it was really why she had bought them. She had thought in the shop: "I must have some purple ones to bring the carpet up to the table." And it had seemed quite sense at the time.

When she had finished with them and had made two pyramids of these bright round shapes, she stood away from the table to get the effect—and it really was most curious. For the dark table seemed to melt into the dusky light and the glass dish and the blue bowl to float in the air. This, of course, in her present mood, was so incredibly beautiful. … She began to laugh.

"No, no. I'm getting hysterical." And she seized her bag and coat and ran upstairs to the nursery.

Nurse sat at a low table giving Little B her supper after her bath. The baby had on a white flannel gown and a blue woollen jacket, and her dark, fine hair was brushed up into a funny little peak. She looked up when she saw her mother and began to jump.

"Now, my lovey, eat it up like a good girl," said nurse, setting her lips in a way that Bertha knew, and that meant she had come into the nursery at another wrong moment.

"Has she been good, Nanny?"

"She's been a little sweet all the afternoon," whispered Nanny. "We went to the park and I sat down on a chair and took her out of the pram and a big dog came along and put its head on my knee and she clutched its ear, tugged it. Oh, you should have seen her."

Bertha wanted to ask if it wasn't rather dangerous to let her clutch at a strange dog's ear. But she did not dare to. She stood watching them, her hands by her side, like the poor little girl in front of the rich little girl with the doll.

The baby looked up at her again, stared, and then smiled so charmingly that Bertha couldn't help crying:

"Oh, Nanny, do let me finish giving her her supper while you put the bath things away."

"Well, M'm, she oughtn't to be changed hands while she's eating," said Nanny, still whispering. "It unsettles her; it's very likely to upset her."

How absurd it was. Why have a baby if it has to be kept—not in a case like a rare, rare fiddle—but in another woman's arms?

"Oh, I must!" said she.

Very offended, Nanny handed her over.

"Now, don't excite her after her supper. You know you do, M'm. And I have such a time with her after!"

Thank heaven! Nanny went out of the room with the bath towels.

"Now I've got you to myself, my little precious," said Bertha, as the baby leaned against her.

She ate delightfully, holding up her lips for the spoon and then waving her hands. Sometimes she wouldn't let the spoon go; and sometimes, just as Bertha had filled it, she waved it away to the four winds.

When the soup was finished Bertha turned round to the fire.

"You're nice—you're very nice!" said she, kissing her warm baby. "I'm fond of you. I like you."

And, indeed, she loved Little B so much—her neck as she bent forward, her exquisite toes as they shone transparent in the firelight—that all her feeling of bliss came back again, and again she didn't know how to express it—what to do with it.

"You're wanted on the telephone," said Nanny, coming back in triumph and seizing *her* Little B.

Down she flew. It was Harry.

"Oh, is that you, Ber? Look here. I'll be late. I'll take a taxi and come along as quickly as I can, but get dinner put back ten minutes—will you? Alright?"

"Yes, perfectly. Oh, Harry!"

"Yes?"

What had she to say? She'd nothing to say. She only wanted to get in touch with him for a moment. She couldn't absurdly cry: "Hasn't it been a divine day!"

"What is it?" rapped out the little voice.

"Nothing. *Entendu*"[1] said Bertha, and hung up the receiver, thinking how much more than idiotic civilisation was.

They had people coming to dinner. The Norman Knights—a very sound couple—he was about to start a theatre, and she was awfully keen on interior decoration, a young man, Eddie Warren, who had just published a little book of poems and whom everybody was asking to dine, and a "find" of Bertha's called Pearl Fulton. What Miss Fulton did, Bertha didn't know. They had met at the club and Bertha had fallen in love with her, as she always did fall in love with beautiful women who had something strange about them.

The provoking thing was that, though they had been about together and met a number of times and really talked, Bertha couldn't make her out. Up to a certain point Miss Fulton was rarely, wonderfully frank, but the certain point was there, and beyond that she would not go.

Was there anything beyond it? Harry said "No." Voted her dullish, and "cold like all blonde women,

with a touch, perhaps, of anæmia of the brain." But Bertha wouldn't agree with him; not yet, at any rate.

"No, the way she has of sitting with her head a little on one side, and smiling, has something behind it, Harry, and I must find out what that something is."

"Most likely it's a good stomach," answered Harry.

He made a point of catching Bertha's heels with replies of that kind … "liver frozen, my dear girl," or "pure flatulence," or "kidney disease," … and so on. For some strange reason Bertha liked this, and almost admired it in him very much.

She went into the drawing room and lighted the fire; then, picking up the cushions, one by one, that Mary had disposed so carefully, she threw them back onto the chairs and the couches. That made all the difference; the room came alive at once. As she was about to throw the last one she surprised herself by suddenly hugging it to her, passionately, passionately. But it did not put out the fire in her bosom. Oh, on the contrary!

The windows of the drawing room opened onto a balcony overlooking the garden. At the far end, against the wall, there was a tall, slender pear tree in fullest, richest bloom; it stood perfect, as though becalmed against the jade green sky. Bertha couldn't help feeling, even from this distance, that it had not a single bud or a faded petal. Down below, in the garden beds, the red and yellow tulips, heavy with flowers, seemed to lean upon the dusk. A grey cat, dragging its belly, crept across the lawn, and a black one, its shadow, trailed after. The sight of them, so intent and so quick, gave Bertha a curious shiver.

"What creepy things cats are!" she stammered, and she turned away from the window and began walking up and down. …

How strong the jonquils[2] smelled in the warm room. Too strong? Oh, no. And yet, as though overcome, she flung down on a couch and pressed her hands to her eyes.

"I'm too happy—too happy!" she murmured.

And she seemed to see on her eyelids the lovely pear tree with its wide open blossoms as a symbol of her own life.

Really—really—she had everything. She was young. Harry and she were as much in love as ever, and they

---

[1] *Entendu* Heard; understood.

[2] *jonquils* Daffodils.

got on together splendidly and were really good pals. She had an adorable baby. They didn't have to worry about money. They had this absolutely satisfactory house and garden. And friends—modern, thrilling friends, writers and painters and poets or people keen on social questions—just the kind of friends they wanted. And then there were books, and there was music, and she had found a wonderful little dressmaker, and they were going abroad in the summer, and their new cook made the most superb omelettes. …

"I'm absurd. Absurd!" She sat up; but she felt quite dizzy, quite drunk. It must have been the spring.

Yes, it was the spring. Now she was so tired she could not drag herself upstairs to dress.

A white dress, a string of jade beads, green shoes and stockings. It wasn't intentional. She had thought of this scheme hours before she stood at the drawing room window.

Her petals rustled softly into the hall, and she kissed Mrs. Norman Knight, who was taking off the most amusing orange coat with a procession of black monkeys round the hem and up the fronts.

"… Why! Why! Why is the middle-class so stodgy — so utterly without a sense of humour! My dear, it's only by a fluke that I am here at all—Norman being the protective fluke. For my darling monkeys so upset the train that it rose to a man and simply ate me with its eyes. Didn't laugh—wasn't amused—that I should have loved. No, just stared—and bored me through and through."

"But the cream of it was," said Norman, pressing a large tortoiseshell-rimmed monocle into his eye, "you don't mind me telling this, Face, do you?" (In their home and among their friends they called each other Face and Mug.) "The cream of it was when she, being full fed, turned to the woman beside her and said: 'Haven't you ever seen a monkey before?'"

"Oh yes!" Mrs. Norman Knight joined in the laughter. "Wasn't that too absolutely creamy?"

And a funnier thing still was that now her coat was off she did look like a very intelligent monkey—who had even made that yellow silk dress out of scraped banana skins. And her amber earrings: they were like little dangling nuts.

"This is a sad, sad fall!" said Mug, pausing in front of Little B's perambulator. "When the perambulator comes into the hall—"[1] and he waved the rest of the quotation away.

The bell rang. It was lean, pale Eddie Warren (as usual) in a state of acute distress.

"It *is* the right house, *isn't* it?" he pleaded.

"Oh, I think so—I hope so," said Bertha brightly.

"I have had such a *dreadful* experience with a taxi man; he was *most* sinister. I couldn't get him to *stop*. The *more* I knocked and called *the faster* he went. And *in* the moonlight this *bizarre* figure with the *flattened* head *crouching* over the *lit-tle* wheel …"

He shuddered, taking off an immense white silk scarf. Bertha noticed that his socks were white, too—most charming.

"But how dreadful!" she cried.

"Yes, it really was," said Eddie, following her into the drawing room. "I saw myself *driving* through Eternity in a *timeless* taxi."

He knew the Norman Knights. In fact, he was going to write a play for N.K. when the theatre scheme came off.

"Well, Warren, how's the play?" said Norman Knight, dropping his monocle and giving his eye a moment in which to rise to the surface before it was screwed down again.

And Mrs. Norman Knight: "Oh, Mr. Warren, what happy socks?"

"I *am* so glad you like them," said he, staring at his feet. "They seem to have got so *much* whiter since the moon rose." And he turned his lean sorrowful young face to Bertha. "There *is* a moon, you know."

She wanted to cry: "I am sure there is—often—often!"

He really was a most attractive person. But so was Face, crouched before the fire in her banana skins, and so was Mug, smoking a cigarette and saying as he flicked the ash: "Why doth the bridegroom tarry?"

"There he is, now."

Bang went the front door open and shut. Harry shouted: "Hullo, you people. Down in five minutes." And they heard him swarm up the stairs. Bertha couldn't help smiling; she knew how he loved doing

---

[1] *This is … hall* Quotation unidentified.

things at high pressure. What, after all, did an extra five minutes matter? But he would pretend to himself that they mattered beyond measure. And then he would make a great point of coming into the drawing room, extravagantly cool and collected.

Harry had such a zest for life. Oh, how she appreciated it in him. And his passion for fighting—for seeking in everything that came up against him another test of his power and of his courage—that, too, she understood. Even when it made him just occasionally, to other people, who didn't know him well, a little ridiculous perhaps.... For there were moments when he rushed into battle where no battle was.... She talked and laughed and positively forgot until he had come in (just as she had imagined) that Pearl Fulton had not turned up.

"I wonder if Miss Fulton has forgotten?"

"I expect so," said Harry. "Is she on the phone?"

"Ah! There's a taxi now." And Bertha smiled with that little air of proprietorship that she always assumed while her women finds were new and mysterious. "She lives in taxis."

"She'll run to fat if she does," said Harry coolly, ringing the bell for dinner. "Frightful danger for blonde women."

"Harry—don't," warned Bertha, laughing up at him.

Came another tiny moment, while they waited, laughing and talking, just a trifle too much at their ease, a trifle too unaware. And then Miss Fulton, all in silver, with a silver fillet binding her pale blonde hair, came in smiling, her head a little on one side.

"Am I late?"

"No, not at all," said Bertha. "Come along." And she took her arm and they moved into the dining room.

What was there in the touch of that cool arm that could fan—fan—start blazing—blazing—the fire of bliss that Bertha did not know what to do with?

Miss Fulton did not look at her; but then she seldom did look at people directly. Her heavy eyelids lay upon her eyes and the strange half-smile came and went upon her lips as though she lived by listening rather than seeing. But Bertha knew, suddenly, as if the longest, most intimate look had passed between them—as if they had said to each other: "You, too?"— that Pearl Fulton, stirring the beautiful red soup in the grey plate, was feeling just what she was feeling.

And the others? Face and Mug, Eddie and Harry, their spoons rising and falling—dabbing their lips with their napkins, crumbling bread, fiddling with the forks and glasses and talking.

"I met her at the Alpha show—the weirdest little person. She'd not only cut off her hair, but she seemed to have taken a dreadfully good snip off her legs and arms and her neck and her poor little nose as well."

"Isn't she very *liée* with[1] Michael Oat?"

"The man who wrote *Love in False Teeth*?"

"He wants to write a play for me. One act. One man. Decides to commit suicide. Gives all the reasons why he should and why he shouldn't. And just as he has made up his mind either to do it or not to do it— curtain. Not half a bad idea."

"What's he going to call it—'Stomach Trouble'?"

"I *think* I've come across the *same* idea in a lit-tle French review, *quite* unknown in England."

No, they didn't share it. They were dears—dears — and she loved having them there, at her table, and giving them delicious food and wine. In fact, she longed to tell them how delightful they were, and what a decorative group they made, how they seemed to set one another off and how they reminded her of a play by Chekhov![2]

Harry was enjoying his dinner. It was part of his—well, not his nature, exactly, and certainly not his pose—his—something or other—to talk about food and to glory in his "shameless passion for the white flesh of the lobster" and "the green of pistachio ices—green and cold like the eyelids of Egyptian dancers."

When he looked up at her and said: "Bertha, this is a very admirable *soufflé*!" she almost could have wept with childlike pleasure.

Oh, why did she feel so tender towards the whole world tonight? Everything was good—was right. All that happened seemed to fill again her brimming cup of bliss.

And still, in the back of her mind, there was the pear tree. It would be silver now, in the light of poor dear Eddie's moon, silver as Miss Fulton, who sat there

---

[1] *very liée with* Bound to, close to.

[2] *Chekhov* Anton Chekhov (1860–1904), Russian playwright and short story writer.

turning a tangerine in her slender fingers that were so pale a light seemed to come from them.

What she simply couldn't make out—what was miraculous—was how she should have guessed Miss Fulton's mood so exactly and so instantly. For she never doubted for a moment that she was right, and yet what had she to go on? Less than nothing.

"I believe this does happen very, very rarely between women. Never between men," thought Bertha. "But while I am making the coffee in the drawing room perhaps she will 'give a sign.'"

What she meant by that she did not know, and what would happen after that she could not imagine.

While she thought like this she saw herself talking and laughing. She had to talk because of her desire to laugh.

"I must laugh or die."

But when she noticed Face's funny little habit of tucking something down the front of her bodice—as if she kept a tiny, secret hoard of nuts there, too— Bertha had to dig her nails into her hands—so as not to laugh too much.

It was over at last. And: "Come and see my new coffee machine," said Bertha.

"We only have a new coffee machine once a fortnight," said Harry. Face took her arm this time; Miss Fulton bent her head and followed after.

The fire had died down in the drawing room to a red, flickering "nest of baby phoenixes," said Face.

"Don't turn up the light for a moment. It is so lovely."

And down she crouched by the fire again. She was always cold … "without her little red flannel jacket, of course," thought Bertha.

At that moment Miss Fulton "gave the sign."

"Have you a garden?" said the cool, sleepy voice.

This was so exquisite on her part that all Bertha could do was to obey. She crossed the room, pulled the curtains apart, and opened those long windows.

"There!" she breathed.

And the two women stood side by side looking at the slender, flowering tree. Although it was so still it seemed, like the flame of a candle, to stretch up, to point, to quiver in the bright air, to grow taller and

taller as they gazed—almost to touch the rim of the round, silver moon.

How long did they stand there? Both, as it were, caught in that circle of unearthly light, understanding each other perfectly, creatures of another world, and wondering what they were to do in this one with all this blissful treasure that burned in their bosoms and dropped, in silver flowers, from their hair and hands?

For ever—for a moment? And did Miss Fulton murmur:

"Yes. Just *that*." Or did Bertha dream it?

Then the light was snapped on and Face made the coffee and Harry said: "My dear Mrs. Knight, don't ask me about my baby. I never see her. I shan't feel the slightest interest in her until she has a lover," and Mug took his eye out of the conservatory for a moment and then put it under glass again and Eddie Warren drank his coffee and set down the cup with a face of anguish as though he had drunk and seen the spider.

"What I want to do is to give the young men a show. I believe London is simply teeming with first-chop,[1] unwritten plays. What I want to say to 'em is: 'Here's the theatre. Fire ahead.'"

"You know, my dear, I am going to decorate a room for the Jacob Nathans. Oh, I am so tempted to do a fried fish scheme, with the backs of the chairs shaped like frying pans and lovely chip potatoes embroidered all over the curtains."

"The trouble with our young writing men is that they are still too romantic. You can't put out to sea without being seasick and wanting a basin. Well, why won't they have the courage of those basins?"

"A *dreadful* poem about a *girl* who was *violated* by a beggar *without* a nose in a lit-tle wood.…"

Miss Fulton sank into the lowest, deepest chair and Harry handed round the cigarettes.

From the way he stood in front of her shaking the silver box and saying abruptly: "Egyptian? Turkish? Virginian? They're all mixed up," Bertha realised that she not only bored him; he really disliked her. And she decided from the way Miss Fulton said: "No, thank you, I won't smoke," that she felt it, too, and was hurt.

"Oh, Harry, don't dislike her. You are quite wrong about her. She's wonderful, wonderful. And, besides,

---

[1] *first-chop* First-class.

how can you feel so differently about someone who means so much to me. I shall try to tell you when we are in bed tonight what has been happening. What she and I have shared."

At those last words something strange and almost terrifying darted into Bertha's mind. And this something blind and smiling whispered to her: "Soon these people will go. The house will be quiet—quiet. The lights will be out. And you and he will be alone together in the dark room—the warm bed...."

She jumped up from her chair and ran over to the piano.

"What a pity someone does not play!" she cried. "What a pity somebody does not play."

For the first time in her life Bertha Young desired her husband.

Oh, she'd loved him—she'd been in love with him, of course, in every other way, but just not in that way. And equally, of course, she'd understood that he was different. They'd discussed it so often. It had worried her dreadfully at first to find that she was so cold, but after a time it had not seemed to matter. They were so frank with each other—such good pals. That was the best of being modern.

But now—ardently! ardently! The word ached in her ardent body! Was this what that feeling of bliss had been leading up to? But then, then—

"My dear," said Mrs. Norman Knight, "you know our shame. We are the victims of time and train. We live in Hampstead. It's been so nice."

"I'll come with you into the hall," said Bertha. "I loved having you. But you must not miss the last train. That's so awful, isn't it?"

"Have a whisky, Knight, before you go?" called Harry.

"No, thanks, old chap."

Bertha squeezed his hand for that as she shook it.

"Good night, goodbye," she cried from the top step, feeling that this self of hers was taking leave of them forever.

When she got back into the drawing room the others were on the move.

"... Then you can come part of the way in my taxi."

"I shall be *so* thankful *not* to have to face *another* drive *alone* after my *dreadful* experience."

"You can get a taxi at the rank just at the end of the street. You won't have to walk more than a few yards."

"That's a comfort. I'll go and put on my coat."

Miss Fulton moved towards the hall and Bertha was following when Harry almost pushed past.

"Let me help you."

Bertha knew that he was repenting his rudeness—she let him go. What a boy he was in some ways—so impulsive—so—simple.

And Eddie and she were left by the fire.

"I *wonder* if you have seen Bilks' *new* poem called *Table d'Hôte*,"[1] said Eddie softly. "It's *so* wonderful. In the last anthology. Have you got a copy? I'd *so* like to *show* it to you. It begins with an *incredibly* beautiful line: 'Why Must it Always be Tomato Soup?'"

"Yes," said Bertha. And she moved noiselessly to a table opposite the drawing room door and Eddie glided noiselessly after her. She picked up the little book and gave it to him; they had not made a sound.

While he looked it up she turned her head towards the hall. And she saw ... Harry with Miss Fulton's coat in his arms and Miss Fulton with her back turned to him and her head bent. He tossed the coat away, put his hands on her shoulders and turned her violently to him. His lips said: "I adore you," and Miss Fulton laid her moonbeam fingers on his cheeks and smiled her sleepy smile. Harry's nostrils quivered; his lips curled back in a hideous grin while he whispered: "Tomorrow," and with her eyelids Miss Fulton said: "Yes."

"Here it is," said Eddie. "'Why Must it Always be Tomato Soup?' It's so *deeply* true, don't you feel? Tomato soup is so *dreadfully* eternal."

"If you prefer," said Harry's voice, very loud, from the hall, "I can phone you a cab to come to the door."

"Oh, no. It's not necessary," said Miss Fulton, and she came up to Bertha and gave her the slender fingers to hold.

"Goodbye. Thank you so much."

"Goodbye," said Bertha.

Miss Fulton held her hand a moment longer.

"Your lovely pear tree!" she murmured.

[1] *Table d'Hôte* Set meal.

And then she was gone, with Eddie following, like the black cat following the grey cat.

"I'll shut up shop," said Harry, extravagantly cool and collected.

"Your lovely pear tree—pear tree—pear tree!"

Bertha simply ran over to the long windows.

"Oh, what is going to happen now?" she cried.

But the pear tree was as lovely as ever and as full of flower and as still.

—1920

The Garden Party

And after all the weather was ideal. They could not have had a more perfect day for a garden party if they had ordered it. Windless, warm, the sky without a cloud. Only the blue was veiled with a haze of light gold, as it is sometimes in early summer. The gardener had been up since dawn, mowing the lawns and sweeping them, until the grass and the dark flat rosettes where the daisy plants had been seemed to shine. As for the roses, you could not help feeling they understood that roses are the only flowers that impress people at garden parties, the only flowers that everybody is certain of knowing. Hundreds, yes, literally hundreds, had come out in a single night; the green bushes bowed down as though they had been visited by archangels.

Breakfast was not yet over before the men came to put up the marquee.

"Where do you want the marquee put, mother?"

"My dear child, it's no use asking me. I'm determined to leave everything to you children this year. Forget I am your mother. Treat me as an honoured guest."

But Meg could not possibly go and supervise the men. She had washed her hair before breakfast, and she sat drinking her coffee in a green turban, with a dark wet curl stamped on each cheek. Jose, the butterfly, always came down in a silk petticoat and a kimono jacket.

"You'll have to go, Laura; you're the artistic one."

Away Laura flew, still holding her piece of bread and butter. It's so delicious to have an excuse for eating out of doors and, besides, she loved having to arrange things; she always felt she could do it so much better than anybody else.

Four men in their shirt sleeves stood grouped together on the garden path. They carried staves[1] covered with rolls of canvas and they had big toolbags slung on their backs. They looked impressive. Laura wished now that she was not holding that piece of bread and butter, but there was nowhere to put it and she couldn't possibly throw it away. She blushed and tried to look severe and even a little bit shortsighted as she came up to them.

"Good morning," she said, copying her mother's voice. But that sounded so fearfully affected that she was ashamed, and stammered like a little girl, "Oh—er—have you come—is it about the marquee?"

"That's right, miss," said the tallest of the men, a lanky, freckled fellow, and he shifted his tool bag, knocked back his straw hat and smiled down at her. "That's about it."

His smile was so easy, so friendly, that Laura recovered. What nice eyes he had, small, but such a dark blue! And now she looked at the others, they were smiling too. "Cheer up, we won't bite," their smile seemed to say. How very nice workmen were! And what a beautiful morning! She mustn't mention the morning; she must be businesslike. The marquee.

"Well, what about the lily lawn? Would that do?"

And she pointed to the lily lawn with the hand that didn't hold the bread and butter. They turned, they stared in the direction. A little fat chap thrust out his underlip and the tall fellow frowned.

"I don't fancy it," said he. "Not conspicuous enough. You see, with a thing like a marquee"—and he turned to Laura in his easy way—"you want to put it somewhere where it'll give you a bang slap in the eye, if you follow me."

Laura's upbringing made her wonder for a moment whether it was quite respectful of a workman to talk to her of bangs slap in the eye. But she did quite follow him.

"A corner of the tennis court," she suggested. "But the band's going to be in one corner."

"H'm, going to have a band, are you?" said another of the workmen. He was pale. He had a haggard look as

---

[1] *staves* Rods.

his dark eyes scanned the tennis court. What was he thinking?

"Only a very small band," said Laura gently. Perhaps he wouldn't mind so much if the band was quite small. But the tall fellow interrupted.

"Look here, miss, that's the place. Against those trees. Over there. That'll do fine."

Against the karakas. Then the karaka trees would be hidden. And they were so lovely, with their broad, gleaming leaves, and their clusters of yellow fruit. They were like trees you imagined growing on a desert island, proud, solitary, lifting their leaves and fruits to the sun in a kind of silent splendour. Must they be hidden by a marquee?

They must. Already the men had shouldered their staves and were making for the place. Only the tall fellow was left. He bent down, pinched a sprig of lavender, put his thumb and forefinger to his nose and snuffed up the smell. When Laura saw that gesture she forgot all about the karakas in her wonder at him caring for things like that—caring for the smell of lavender. How many men that she knew would have done such a thing. Oh, how extraordinarily nice workmen were, she thought. Why couldn't she have workmen for friends rather than the silly boys she danced with and who came to Sunday night supper? She would get on much better with men like these.

It's all the fault, she decided, as the tall fellow drew something on the back of an envelope, something that was to be looped up or left to hang, of these absurd class distinctions. Well, for her part, she didn't feel them. Not a bit, not an atom.... And now there came the chock-chock of wooden hammers. Someone whistled, someone sang out, "Are you right there, matey?" "Matey!" The friendliness of it, the—the— Just to prove how happy she was, just to show the tall fellow how at home she felt, and how she despised stupid conventions, Laura took a big bite of her bread and butter as she stared at the little drawing. She felt just like a work girl.

"Laura, Laura, where are you? Telephone, Laura!" a voice cried from the house.

"Coming!" Away she skimmed, over the lawn, up the path, up the steps, across the veranda and into the porch. In the hall her father and Laurie were brushing their hats ready to go to the office.

"I say, Laura," said Laurie very fast, "you might just give a squiz[1] at my coat before this afternoon. See if it wants pressing."

"I will," said she. Suddenly she couldn't stop herself. She ran at Laurie and gave him a small, quick squeeze. "Oh, I do love parties, don't you?" gasped Laura.

"Ra–ther," said Laurie's warm, boyish voice, and he squeezed his sister too and gave her a gentle push. "Dash off to the telephone, old girl."

The telephone. "Yes, yes; oh yes. Kitty? Good morning, dear. Come to lunch? Do, dear. Delighted, of course. It will only be a very scratch[2] meal—just the sandwich crusts and broken meringue shells and what's left over. Yes, isn't it a perfect morning? Your white? Oh, I certainly should. One moment—hold the line. Mother's calling." And Laura sat back. "What, mother? Can't hear."

Mrs. Sheridan's voice floated down the stairs. "Tell her to wear that sweet hat she had on last Sunday."

"Mother says you're to wear that sweet hat you had on last Sunday. Good. One o'clock. Bye-bye."

Laura put back the receiver, flung her arms over her head, took a deep breath, stretched and let them fall. "Huh," she sighed, and the moment after the sigh she sat up quickly. She was still, listening. All the doors in the house seemed to be open. The house was alive with soft, quick steps and running voices. The green baize door[3] that led to the kitchen regions swung open and shut with a muffled thud. And now there came a long, chuckling absurd sound. It was the heavy piano being moved on its stiff castors. But the air! If you stopped to notice, was the air always like this? Little faint winds were playing chase in at the tops of the windows, out at the doors. And there were two tiny spots of sun, one on the inkpot, one on a silver photograph frame, playing too. Darling little spots. Especially the one on the inkpot lid. It was quite warm. A warm little silver star. She could have kissed it.

---

[1] *squiz* Glance.

[2] *scratch* Quickly thrown together.

[3] *baize door* Door, covered with a green felt-like material, that separates the kitchen from the rest of the house in large English homes.

The front door bell pealed and there sounded the rustle of Sadie's print skirt on the stairs. A man's voice murmured; Sadie answered, careless, "I'm sure I don't know. Wait. I'll ask Mrs. Sheridan."

"What is it, Sadie?" Laura came into the hall.

"It's the florist, Miss Laura."

It was, indeed. There, just inside the door, stood a wide, shallow tray full of pots of pink lilies. No other kind. Nothing but lilies—canna lilies, big pink flowers, wide open, radiant, almost frighteningly alive on bright crimson stems.

"O–oh, Sadie!" said Laura, and the sound was like a little moan. She crouched down as if to warm herself at that blaze of lilies; she felt they were in her fingers, on her lips, growing in her breast.

"It's some mistake," she said faintly. "Nobody ever ordered so many. Sadie, go and find mother."

But at that moment Mrs. Sheridan joined them.

"It's quite right," she said calmly. "Yes, I ordered them. Aren't they lovely?" She pressed Laura's arm. "I was passing the shop yesterday, and I saw them in the window. And I suddenly thought for once in my life I shall have enough canna lilies. The garden party will be a good excuse."

"But I thought you said you didn't mean to interfere," said Laura. Sadie had gone. The florist's man was still outside at his van. She put her arm round her mother's neck and gently, very gently, she bit her mother's ear.

"My darling child, you wouldn't like a logical mother, would you? Don't do that. Here's the man."

He carried more lilies still, another whole tray.

"Bank them up, just inside the door, on both sides of the porch, please," said Mrs. Sheridan. "Don't you agree, Laura?"

"Oh, I *do*, mother."

In the drawing room Meg, Jose and good little Hans had at last succeeded in moving the piano.

"Now, if we put this chesterfield against the wall and move everything out of the room except the chairs, don't you think?"

"Quite."

"Hans, move these tables into the smoking room, and bring a sweeper to take these marks off the carpet and—one moment, Hans—" Jose loved giving orders to the servants and they loved obeying her. She always made them feel they were taking part in some drama. "Tell mother and Miss Laura to come here at once."

"Very good, Miss Jose."

She turned to Meg. "I want to hear what the piano sounds like, just in case I'm asked to sing this afternoon. Let's try over 'This Life is Weary.'"

Pom! Ta-ta-ta *Tee*-ta! The piano burst out so passionately that Jose's face changed. She clasped her hands. She looked mournfully and enigmatically at her mother and Laura as they came in.

> This Life is *Wee*-ary,
> A Tear—a Sigh.
> A Love that *Chan*-ges,
>   This Life is *Wee*-ary,
> A Tear—a Sigh.
> A Love that *Chan*-ges,
> And then … Goodbye!

But at the word "Goodbye," and although the piano sounded more desperate than ever, her face broke into a brilliant, dreadfully unsympathetic smile.

"Aren't I in good voice, mummy?" she beamed.

> This Life is *Wee*-ary,
> Hope comes to Die.
> A Dream—a *Wa*-kening.

But now Sadie interrupted them. "What is it, Sadie?"

"If you please, m'm, cook says have you got the flags for the sandwiches?"

"The flags for the sandwiches, Sadie?" echoed Mrs. Sheridan dreamily. And the children knew by her face that she hadn't got them. "Let me see." And she said to Sadie firmly, "Tell cook I'll let her have them in ten minutes."

Sadie went.

"Now, Laura," said her mother quickly, "come with me into the smoking room. I've got the names somewhere on the back of an envelope. You'll have to write them out for me. Meg, go upstairs this minute and take that wet thing off your head. Jose, run and finish dressing this instant. Do you hear me, children, or shall I have to tell your father when he comes home tonight?

And—and, Jose, pacify cook if you do go into the kitchen, will you? I'm terrified of her this morning."

The envelope was found at last behind the dining room clock, though how it had got there Mrs. Sheridan could not imagine.

"One of you children must have stolen it out of my bag, because I remember vividly—cream cheese and lemon curd. Have you done that?"

"Yes."

"Egg and—" Mrs. Sheridan held the envelope away from her. "It looks like mice. It can't be mice, can it?"

"Olive, pet," said Laura, looking over her shoulder.

"Yes, of course, olive. What a horrible combination it sounds. Egg and olive."

They were finished at last, and Laura took them off to the kitchen. She found Jose there pacifying the cook, who did not look at all terrifying.

"I have never seen such exquisite sandwiches," said Jose's rapturous voice. "How many kinds did you say there were, cook? Fifteen?"

"Fifteen, Miss Jose."

"Well, cook, I congratulate you."

Cook swept up crusts with the long sandwich knife, and smiled broadly.

"Godber's has come," announced Sadie, issuing out of the pantry. She had seen the man pass the window.

That meant the cream puffs had come. Godber's were famous for their cream puffs. Nobody ever thought of making them at home.

"Bring them in and put them on the table, my girl," ordered cook.

Sadie brought them in and went back to the door. Of course Laura and Jose were far too grown up to really care about such things. All the same, they couldn't help agreeing that the puffs looked very attractive. Very. Cook began arranging them, shaking off the extra icing sugar.

"Don't they carry one back to all one's parties?" said Laura.

"I suppose they do," said practical Jose, who never liked to be carried back. "They look beautifully light and feathery, I must say."

"Have one each, my dears," said cook in her comfortable voice. "Yer ma won't know."

Oh, impossible. Fancy cream puffs so soon after breakfast. The very idea made one shudder. All the same, two minutes later Jose and Laura were licking their fingers with that absorbed inward look that only comes from whipped cream.

"Let's go into the garden, out by the back way," suggested Laura. "I want to see how the men are getting on with the marquee. They're such awfully nice men."

But the back door was blocked by cook, Sadie, Godber's man and Hans.

Something had happened.

"Tuk-tuk-tuk," clucked cook like an agitated hen. Sadie had her hand clapped to her cheek as though she had toothache. Han's face was screwed up in the effort to understand. Only Godber's man seemed to be enjoying himself; it was his story.

"What's the matter? What's happened?"

"There's been a horrible accident," said cook. "A man killed."

"A man killed! Where? How? When?"

But Godber's man wasn't going to have his story snatched from under his very nose.

"Know those little cottages just below here, miss?" Know them? Of course she knew them. "Well, there's a young chap living there, name of Scott, a carter. His horse shied at a traction engine, corner of Hawke Street this morning, and he was thrown out on the back of his head. Killed."

"Dead!" Laura stared at Godber's man.

"Dead when they picked him up," said Godber's man with relish. "They were taking the body home as I come up here." And he said to the cook, "He's left a wife and five little ones."

"Jose, come here." Laura caught hold of her sister's sleeve and dragged her through the kitchen to the other side of the green baize door. There she paused and leaned against it. "Jose!" she said, horrified, "however are we going to stop everything?"

"Stop everything, Laura!" cried Jose in astonishment. "What do you mean?"

"Stop the garden party, of course." Why did Jose pretend?

But Jose was still more amazed. "Stop the garden party? My dear Laura, don't be so absurd. Of course we can't do anything of the kind. Nobody expects us to. Don't be so extravagant."

"But we can't possibly have a garden party with a man dead just outside the front gate."

That really was extravagant, for the little cottages were in a lane to themselves at the very bottom of a steep rise that led up to the house. A broad road ran between. True, they were far too near. They were the greatest possible eyesore and they had no right to be in that neighbourhood at all. They were little mean dwellings painted a chocolate brown. In the garden patches there was nothing but cabbage stalks, sick hens and tomato cans. The very smoke coming out of their chimneys was poverty stricken. Little rags and shreds of smoke, so unlike the great silvery plumes that uncurled from the Sheridans' chimneys. Washerwomen lived in the lane and sweeps and a cobbler and a man whose house front was studded all over with minute birdcages. Children swarmed. When the Sheridans were little they were forbidden to set foot there because of the revolting language and of what they might catch. But since they were grown up Laura and Laurie on their prowls sometimes walked through. It was disgusting and sordid. They came out with a shudder. But still one must go everywhere; one must see everything. So through they went.

"And just think of what the band would sound like to that poor woman," said Laura.

"Oh, Laura!" Jose began to be seriously annoyed. "If you're going to stop a band playing every time someone has an accident, you'll lead a very strenuous life. I'm every bit as sorry about it as you. I feel just as sympathetic." Her eyes hardened. She looked at her sister just as she used to when they were little and fighting together. "You won't bring a drunken workman back to life by being sentimental," she said softly.

"Drunk! Who said he was drunk?" Laura turned furiously on Jose. She said just as they had used to say on those occasions, "I'm going straight up to tell mother."

"Do, dear," cooed Jose.

"Mother, can I come into your room?" Laura turned the big glass doorknob.

"Of course, child. Why, what's the matter? What's given you such a colour?" And Mrs. Sheridan turned round from her dressing table. She was trying on a new hat.

"Mother, a man's been killed," began Laura.

"*Not* in the garden?" interrupted her mother.

"No, no!"

"Oh, what a fright you gave me!" Mrs. Sheridan sighed with relief and took off the big hat and held it on her knees.

"But listen, mother," said Laura. Breathless, half choking, she told the dreadful story. "Of course, we can't have our party, can we?" she pleaded. "The band and everybody arriving. They'd hear us, mother; they're nearly neighbours!"

To Laura's astonishment her mother behaved just like Jose; it was harder to bear because she seemed amused. She refused to take Laura seriously.

"But, my dear child, use your common sense. It's only by accident we've heard of it. If someone had died there normally—and I can't understand how they keep alive in those poky little holes—we should still be having our party, shouldn't we?"

Laura had to say "yes" to that, but she felt it was all wrong. She sat down on her mother's sofa and pinched the cushion frill.

"Mother, isn't it really terribly heartless of us?" she asked.

"Darling!" Mrs. Sheridan got up and came over to her, carrying the hat. Before Laura could stop her she had popped it on. "My child!" said her mother, "the hat is yours. It's made for you. It's much too young for me. I have never seen you look such a picture. Look at yourself!" And she held up her hand-mirror.

"But, mother," Laura began again. She couldn't look at herself; she turned aside.

This time Mrs. Sheridan lost patience just as Jose had done.

"You are being very absurd, Laura," she said coldly. "People like that don't expect sacrifices from us. And it's not very sympathetic to spoil everybody's enjoyment as you're doing now."

"I don't understand," said Laura, and she walked quickly out of the room into her own bedroom. There, quite by chance, the first thing she saw was this charming girl in the mirror, in her black hat trimmed with gold daisies and a long black velvet ribbon. Never had she imagined she could look like that. Is mother right? she thought. And now she hoped her mother was right. Am I being extravagant? Perhaps it was extravagant. Just for a moment she had another glimpse of that poor woman and those little children and the body being carried into the house. But it all seemed blurred, unreal, like a picture in the newspaper. I'll remember it again after the party's over, she decided. And somehow that seemed quite the best plan....

Lunch was over by half-past one. By half-past two they were all ready for the fray. The green-coated band had arrived and was established in a corner of the tennis court.

"My dear!" trilled Kitty Maitland, "aren't they too like frogs for words? You ought to have arranged them round the pond with the conductor in the middle on a leaf."

Laurie arrived and hailed them on his way to dress. At the sight of him Laura remembered the accident again. She wanted to tell him. If Laurie agreed with the others, then it was bound to be all right. And she followed him into the hall.

"Laurie!"

"Hallo!" He was halfway upstairs, but when he turned round and saw Laura he suddenly puffed out his cheeks and goggled his eyes at her. "My word, Laura! You do look stunning," said Laurie. "What an absolutely topping hat!"

Laura said faintly "Is it?" and smiled up at Laurie and didn't tell him after all.

Soon after that people began coming in streams. The band struck up; the hired waiters ran from the house to the marquee. Wherever you looked there were couples strolling, bending to the flowers, greeting, moving on over the lawn. They were like bright birds that had alighted in the Sheridans' garden for this one afternoon, on their way to—where? Ah, what happiness it is to be with people who all are happy, to press hands, press cheeks, smile into eyes.

"Darling Laura, how well you look!"

"What a becoming hat, child!"

"Laura, you look quite Spanish. I've never seen you look so striking."

And Laura, glowing, answered softly, "Have you had tea? Won't you have an ice? The passion fruit ices really are rather special." She ran to her father and begged him: "Daddy darling, can't the band have something to drink?"

And the perfect afternoon slowly ripened, slowly faded, slowly its petals closed.

"Never a more delightful garden party ..." "The greatest success ..." "Quite the most ..."

Laura helped her mother with the goodbyes. They stood side by side in the porch till it was all over.

"All over, all over, thank heaven," said Mrs. Sheridan. "Round up the others, Laura. Let's go and have some fresh coffee. I'm exhausted. Yes, it's been very successful. But oh, these parties, these parties! Why will you children insist on giving parties!" And they all of them sat down in the deserted marquee.

"Have a sandwich, daddy dear. I wrote the flag."

"Thanks." Mr. Sheridan took a bite and the sandwich was gone. He took another. "I suppose you didn't hear of a beastly accident that happened today?" he said.

"My dear," said Mrs. Sheridan, holding up her hand, "we did. It nearly ruined the party. Laura insisted we should put it off."

"Oh, mother!" Laura didn't want to be teased about it.

"It was a horrible affair all the same," said Mr. Sheridan. "The chap was married too. Lived just below in the lane, and leaves a wife and half a dozen kiddies, so they say."

An awkward little silence fell. Mrs. Sheridan fidgeted with her cup. Really, it was very tactless of father....

Suddenly she looked up. There on the table were all those sandwiches, cakes, puffs, all uneaten, all going to be wasted. She had one of her brilliant ideas.

"I know," she said. "Let's make up a basket. Let's send that poor creature some of this perfectly good food. At any rate, it will be the greatest treat for the children. Don't you agree? And she's sure to have neighbours calling in and so on. What a point to have it all ready prepared. Laura!" She jumped up. "Get me the big basket out of the stairs cupboard."

"But, mother, do you really think it's a good idea?" said Laura.

Again, how curious, she seemed to be different from them all. To take scraps from their party. Would the poor woman really like that?

"Of course! What's the matter with you today? An hour or two ago you were insisting on us being sympathetic."

Oh well! Laura ran for the basket. It was filled, it was now heaped by her mother.

"Take it yourself, darling," said she. "Run down just as you are. No, wait, take the arum lilies too. People of that class are so impressed by arum lilies."

"The stems will ruin her lace frock," said practical Jose.

So they would. Just in time. "Only the basket, then. And, Laura!"—her mother followed her out of the marquee—"don't on any account—"

"What, mother?"

No, better not put such ideas into the child's head! "Nothing! Run along."

It was just growing dusky as Laura shut their garden gates. A big dog ran by like a shadow. The road gleamed white, and down below in the hollow the little cottages were in deep shade. How quiet it seemed after the afternoon. Here she was going down the hill to somewhere where a man lay dead, and she couldn't realise it. Why couldn't she? She stopped a minute. And it seemed to her that kisses, voices, tinkling spoons, laughter, the smell of crushed grass were somehow inside her. She had no room for anything else. How strange! She looked up at the pale sky, and all she thought was, "Yes, it was the most successful party."

Now the broad road was crossed. The lane began, smoky and dark. Women in shawls and men's tweed caps hurried by. Men hung over the palings; the children played in the doorways. A low hum came from the mean little cottages. In some of them there was a flicker of light, and a shadow, crab-like, moved across the window. Laura bent her head and hurried on. She wished now she had put on a coat. How her frock shone! And the big hat with the velvet streamer—if only it was another hat! Were the people looking at her? They must be. It was a mistake to have come; she knew all along it was a mistake. Should she go back even now?

No, too late. This was the house. It must be. A dark knot of people stood outside. Beside the gate an old, old woman with a crutch sat in a chair, watching. She had her feet on a newspaper. The voices stopped as Laura drew near. The group parted. It was as though she was expected, as though they had known she was coming here.

Laura was terribly nervous. Tossing the velvet ribbon over her shoulder, she said to a woman standing by, "Is this Mrs. Scott's house?" and the woman, smiling queerly, said, "It is, my lass."

Oh, to be away from this! She actually said, "Help me, God," as she walked up the tiny path and knocked. To be away from those staring eyes, or to be covered up in anything, one of those women's shawls even. I'll just leave the basket and go, she decided. I shan't even wait for it to be emptied.

Then the door opened. A little woman in black showed in the gloom.

Laura said, "Are you Mrs. Scott?" But to her horror the woman answered, "Walk in, please, miss," and she was shut in the passage.

"No," said Laura, "I don't want to come in. I only want to leave this basket. Mother sent—"

The little woman in the gloomy passage seemed not to have heard her. "Step this way, please, miss," she said in an oily voice, and Laura followed her.

She found herself in a wretched little low kitchen, lighted by a smoky lamp. There was a woman sitting before the fire.

"Em," said the little creature who had let her in. "Em! It's a young lady." She turned to Laura. She said meaningly, "I'm 'er sister, miss. You'll excuse 'er, won't you?"

"Oh, but of course!" said Laura. "Please, please don't disturb her. I—I only want to leave—"

But at that moment the woman at the fire turned round. Her face, puffed up, red, with swollen eyes and swollen lips, looked terrible. She seemed as though she couldn't understand why Laura was there. What did it mean? Why was this stranger standing in the kitchen with a basket? What was it all about? And the poor face puckered up again.

"All right, my dear," said the other. "I'll thenk the young lady."

And again she began, "You'll excuse her, miss, I'm sure," and her face, swollen too, tried an oily smile.

Laura only wanted to get out, to get away. She was back in the passage. The door opened. She walked straight through into the bedroom, where the dead man was lying.

"You'd like a look at 'im, wouldn't you?" said Em's sister, and she brushed past Laura over to the bed. "Don't be afraid, my lass"—and now her voice sounded fond and sly, and fondly she drew down the sheet—"'e looks a picture. There's nothing to show. Come along, my dear."

Laura came.

There lay a young man, fast asleep—sleeping so soundly, so deeply, that he was far, far away from them both. Oh, so remote, so peaceful. He was dreaming. Never wake him up again. His head was sunk in the pillow, his eyes were closed; they were blind under the closed eyelids. He was given up to his dream. What did garden parties and baskets and lace frocks matter to him? He was far from all those things. He was wonderful, beautiful. While they were laughing and while the band was playing, this marvel had come to the lane. Happy … happy…. All is well, said that sleeping face. This is just as it should be. I am content.

But all the same you had to cry, and she couldn't go out of the room without saying something to him. Laura gave a loud childish sob.

"Forgive my hat," she said.

And this time she didn't wait for Em's sister. She found her way out of the door, down the path past all those dark people. At the corner of the lane she met Laurie.

He stepped out of the shadow. "Is that you, Laura?"

"Yes."

"Mother was getting anxious. Was it all right?"

"Yes, quite, Oh, Laurie!" She took his arm, she pressed up against him.

"I say, you're not crying, are you?" asked her brother.

Laura shook her head. She was.

Laurie put his arm round her shoulder. "Don't cry," he said in his warm, loving voice. "Was it awful?"

"No," sobbed Laura. "It was simply marvellous. But, Laurie—" She stopped, she looked at her brother. "Isn't life," she stammered, "isn't life—" But what life was she couldn't explain. No matter. He quite understood.

"*Isn't* it, darling?" said Laurie.

—1922

Miss Brill

Although it was so brilliantly fine—the blue sky powdered with gold and the great spots of light like white wine splashed over the Jardins Publiques[1]—Miss Brill was glad that she had decided on her fur. The air was motionless, but when you opened your mouth there was just a faint chill, like a chill from a glass of iced water before you sip, and now and again a leaf came drifting—from nowhere, from the sky. Miss Brill put up her hand and touched her fur. Dear little thing! It was nice to feel it again. She had taken it out of its box that afternoon, shaken out the moth powder, given it a good brush, and rubbed the life back into the dim little eyes. "What has been happening to me?" said the sad little eyes. Oh, how sweet it was to see them snap at her again from the red eiderdown! … But the nose, which was of some black composition, wasn't at all firm. It must have had a knock, somehow. Never mind—a little dab of black sealing-wax when the time came—when it was absolutely necessary. … Little rogue! Yes, she really felt like that about it. Little rogue biting its tail just by her left ear. She could have taken it off and laid it on her lap and stroked it. She felt a tingling in her hands and arms, but that came from walking, she supposed. And when she breathed, something light and sad—no, not sad, exactly—something gentle seemed to move in her bosom.

There were a number of people out this afternoon, far more than last Sunday. And the band sounded louder and gayer. That was because the season had begun. For although the band played all the year round on Sundays, out of season it was never the same. It was like someone playing with only the family to listen; it didn't care how it played if there weren't any strangers present. Wasn't the conductor wearing a new coat, too? She was sure it was new. He scraped with his foot and flapped his arms like a rooster about to crow, and the bandsmen sitting in the green rotunda blew out their cheeks and glared at the music. Now there came a little "flutey" bit—very pretty!—a little chain of bright drops. She was sure it would be repeated. It was; she lifted her head and smiled.

---

[1] *Jardins Publiques* Public gardens.

Only two people shared her "special" seat: a fine old man in a velvet coat, his hands clasped over a huge carved walking-stick, and a big old woman, sitting upright, with a roll of knitting on her embroidered apron. They did not speak. This was disappointing, for Miss Brill always looked forward to the conversation. She had become really quite expert, she thought, at listening as though she didn't listen, at sitting in other people's lives just for a minute while they talked round her.

She glanced, sideways, at the old couple. Perhaps they would go soon. Last Sunday, too, hadn't been as interesting as usual. An Englishman and his wife, he wearing a dreadful Panama hat and she button boots. And she'd gone on the whole time about how she ought to wear spectacles; she knew she needed them; but that it was no good getting any; they'd be sure to break and they'd never keep on. And he'd been so patient. He'd suggested everything—gold rims, the kind that curved round your ears, little pads inside the bridge. No, nothing would please her. "They'll always be sliding down my nose!" Miss Brill had wanted to shake her.

The old people sat on the bench, still as statues. Never mind, there was always the crowd to watch. To and fro, in front of the flowerbeds and the band rotunda, the couples and groups paraded, stopped to talk, to greet, to buy a handful of flowers from the old beggar who had his tray fixed to the railings. Little children ran among them, swooping and laughing; little boys with big white silk bows under their chins; little girls, little French dolls, dressed up in velvet and lace. And sometimes a tiny staggerer came suddenly rocking into the open from under the trees, stopped, stared, as suddenly sat down "flop," until its small high-stepping mother, like a young hen, rushed scolding to its rescue. Other people sat on the benches and green chairs, but they were nearly always the same, Sunday after Sunday, and— Miss Brill had often noticed—there was something funny about nearly all of them. They were odd, silent, nearly all old, and from the way they stared they looked as though they'd just come from dark little rooms or even—even cupboards!

Behind the rotunda the slender trees with yellow leaves down drooping, and through them just a line of sea, and beyond the blue sky with gold-veined clouds.

Tum-tum-tum tiddle-um! tiddle-um! tum tiddley-um tum ta! blew the band.

Two young girls in red came by and two young soldiers in blue met them, and they laughed and paired and went off arm in arm. Two peasant women with funny straw hats passed, gravely, leading beautiful smoke-coloured donkeys. A cold, pale nun hurried by. A beautiful woman came along and dropped her bunch of violets, and a little boy ran after to hand them to her, and she took them and threw them away as if they'd been poisoned. Dear me! Miss Brill didn't know whether to admire that or not! And now an ermine toque and a gentleman in grey met just in front of her. He was tall, stiff, dignified, and she was wearing the ermine toque she'd bought when her hair was yellow. Now everything, her hair, her face, even her eyes, was the same colour as the shabby ermine, and her hand, in its cleaned glove, lifted to dab her lips, was a tiny yellowish paw. Oh, she was so pleased to see him—delighted! She rather thought they were going to meet that afternoon. She described where she'd been—everywhere, here, there, along by the sea. The day was so charming—didn't he agree? And wouldn't he, perhaps? ... But he shook his head, lighted a cigarette, slowly breathed a great deep puff into her face and, even while she was still talking and laughing, flicked the match away and walked on. The ermine toque was alone; she smiled more brightly than ever. But even the band seemed to know what she was feeling and played more softly, played tenderly, and the drum beat "The Brute! The Brute!" over and over. What would she do? What was going to happen now? But as Miss Brill wondered, the ermine toque turned, raised her hand as though she'd seen someone else, much nicer, just over there, and pattered away. And the band changed again and played more quickly, more gaily than ever, and the old couple on Miss Brill's seat got up and marched away, and such a funny old man with long whiskers hobbled along in time to the music and was nearly knocked over by four girls walking abreast.

Oh, how fascinating it was! How she enjoyed it! How she loved sitting here, watching it all! It was like a play. It was exactly like a play. Who could believe the sky at the back wasn't painted? But it wasn't till a little brown dog trotted on solemnly and then slowly trotted off, like a little "theatre" dog, a little dog that had been drugged, that Miss Brill discovered what it was that made it so exciting. They were all on the stage. They weren't only the audience, not only looking on; they were acting. Even she had a part and came every Sunday. No doubt somebody would have noticed if she hadn't been there; she was part of the performance, after all. How strange she'd never thought of it like that before! And yet it explained why she made such a point of starting from home at just the same time each week—so as not to be late for the performance—and it also explained why she had quite a queer, shy feeling at telling her English pupils how she spent her Sunday afternoons. No wonder! Miss Brill nearly laughed out loud. She was on the stage. She thought of the old invalid gentleman to whom she read the newspaper four afternoons a week while he slept in the garden. She had got quite used to the frail head on the cotton pillow, the hollowed eyes, the open mouth and the high pinched nose. If he'd been dead she mightn't have noticed for weeks; she wouldn't have minded. But suddenly he knew he was having the paper read to him by an actress! "An actress!" The old head lifted; two points of light quivered in the old eyes. "An actress—are ye?" And Miss Brill smoothed the newspaper as though it were the manuscript of her part and said gently: "Yes, I have been an actress for a long time."

The band had been having a rest. Now they started again. And what they played was warm, sunny, yet there was just a faint chill—a something, what was it?—not sadness—no, not sadness—a something that made you want to sing. The tune lifted, lifted, the light shone; and it seemed to Miss Brill that in another moment all of them, all the whole company, would begin singing. The young ones, the laughing ones who were moving together, they would begin, and the men's voices, very resolute and brave, would join them. And then she too, she too, and the others on the benches—they would come in with a kind of accompaniment—something low, that scarcely rose or fell, something so beautiful—moving.... And Miss Brill's eyes filled with tears

and she looked smiling at all the other members of the company. Yes, we understand, we understand, she thought—though what they understood she didn't know.

Just at that moment a boy and a girl came and sat down where the old couple had been. They were beautifully dressed; they were in love. The hero and heroine, of course, just arrived from his father's yacht. And still soundlessly singing, still with that trembling smile, Miss Brill prepared to listen.

"No, not now," said the girl. "Not here, I can't."

"But why? Because of that stupid old thing at the end there?" asked the boy. "Why does she come here at all—who wants her? Why doesn't she keep her silly old mug at home? "

"It's her fu-fur which is so funny," giggled the girl. "It's exactly like a fried whiting."[1]

"Ah, be off with you!" said the boy in an angry whisper. Then: "Tell me, ma petite chère—"

"No, not here," said the girl. "Not *yet*."

* * * * * *

On her way home she usually bought a slice of honey cake at the baker's. It was her Sunday treat. Sometimes there was an almond in her slice, sometimes not. It made a great difference. If there was an almond it was like carrying home a tiny present—a surprise—something that might very well not have been there. She hurried on the almond Sundays and struck the match for the kettle in quite a dashing way.

But today she passed the baker's by, climbed the stairs, went into the little dark room—her room like a cupboard—and sat down on the red eiderdown. She sat there for a long time. The box that the fur came out of was on the bed. She unclasped the necklet quickly; quickly, without looking, laid it inside. But when she put the lid on she thought she heard something crying.
—1924

---

[1] *whiting* Fish.

T.S. Eliot
1888 – 1965

The poetry and prose of T.S. Eliot probably did more than that of any other writer to transform the face of twentieth-century English writing. His Modernist poems of the 1910s and 1920s (*The Waste Land* chief among them) were revolutionary both in their form and in their content—yet Eliot himself, the most unlikely of revolutionaries, became an icon of the literary establishment. He voiced in unique fashion the bleakness and despair that was characteristically felt by many in the early twentieth century—yet he became a leading voice of traditional Christianity. He embraced difficulty as the literary strategy most consonant with the character of his era—yet he also wrote a succession of highly accessible plays for the popular stage. He strove for Christian virtue, but has been strongly criticized for alleged hostility towards women and towards Jews. In short, he is a central figure of the twentieth century not only because his works are central documents of its literature, but also because they embody many of the paradoxes of the age.

Thomas Stearns Eliot was born in St. Louis, Missouri, in 1888, the youngest son in a distinguished New England family that traced its roots back to the first Puritan settlers of

Massachusetts. Eliot followed his older brother to Harvard in 1906, where he joined the board of Harvard's literary magazine and started a lifelong friendship with Conrad Aiken, a fellow board member. In 1909. the year before he completed his M.A., Eliot began drafting the poems that would become "The Love Song of J. Alfred Prufrock," "Preludes," "Portrait of a Lady," and "Rhapsody on a Windy Night." He spent a postgraduate year at the Sorbonne in Paris and then began doctoral studies in philosophy at Harvard. His dissertation was on the ideas of the then-influential French philosopher Henri Bergson, whose emphasis on the intuitive and subjective aspects of reality and on the importance of change may have influenced Eliot's poetic explorations of the human psyche. Certainly a strong awareness of the subjectivity of perception, of the importance of the unconscious, and of alienation and social claustrophobia in an unpredictably changing world are all powerful elements in Eliot's early poetry.

While both Eliot and Aiken were in London in 1914, Aiken showed the manuscript of "Prufrock" to American poet and critic Ezra Pound (then living abroad), who immediately recognized it as extraordinary work. The alliance of Pound and Eliot marked the beginning not only of Eliot's career as a poet (Pound and his wife financed the 1917 publication of *Prufrock and Other Observations*), but of a literary collaboration that profoundly influenced the development of modern literature.

"The Love Song of J. Alfred Prufrock," as critic James F. Knapp said, changed "our conception of what kind of shape a poem might take." With little connecting or transitional material, the poem juxtaposes disparate thoughts and scenes and combines classical literary references with images of urban, industrial twentieth-century life. Eliot was heavily influenced by French Symbolist poets Charles Baudelaire and Jules Laforgue. Their powerful, disconnected imagery, their ironic, detached tones, and their themes of alienation helped Eliot discover his own poetic voice. With strong rhythms that blend formal and informal speech and striking metaphors, Eliot creates an ironic love song in the frustrated inner voice of "Prufrock"'s central figure, who, in the face of his bleak physical and spiritual life, is unable to act on his love.

Inspired by what he referred to as "the mind of Europe," and with some persuasion by Pound, Eliot chose England as his permanent home. His decision was solidified by an impulsive decision in 1915 to marry Vivien Haigh-Wood, an Englishwoman whom he had met that spring. In England, Eliot balanced writing and editorial work for the avant-garde magazine *The Egoist* with more reliable employment as a schoolteacher and then as a bank clerk at Lloyd's Bank in London.

Eliot's first book of criticism, *The Sacred Wood* (1920), established him as a discerning and erudite literary critic and introduced a new set of critical precepts that would become highly influential. Eliot placed a high value on "impersonality" in poetry, and on the idea of an "objective correlative" as a means of expressing emotion through a set of objects, circumstances, or chain of events. Eliot's introduction of these ideas to the literary world helped pave the way for the critical approach known as "New Criticism." In the writings of I.A. Richards and others of this school, the focus was on the work itself as an artefact independent of authorial intention. Eliot's essays also examined his sense of the necessary difficulty of modern writing, which he believed had the nearly impossible task of synthesizing the seemingly unrelated, chaotic experiences of modern citizens.

By 1921, affected by the strain of overwork and the increasing pressure of his wife's failing physical and mental health, Eliot had a nervous breakdown. During a three-month-long rest cure, he was finally able to complete *The Waste Land*, a project he had begun in 1914. Originally composed as a series of narrative poems, *The Waste Land* was considerably longer in its original version; Pound helped Eliot pare down and fuse the diverse materials into a rhythmically coherent whole. Published in 1922, *The Waste Land* deviated far more decisively than had "Prufrock" from accepted notions of what constituted poetry. Written in fragmented form, this poem of complex imagery, multiple voices, jazz rhythms, and dense literary and mythological allusions jumps between perspectives and scenes without connective or transitional passages. With its radical break from established conventions in structure, theme, and expression, and its blending of western and of non-western ideologies, *The Waste Land* can be disorienting for readers—so much so, in fact, that when the poem first appeared some writers and critics wondered if the poem was a hoax orchestrated by Eliot and his literary friends.

Much as *The Waste Land* was derided in some quarters, in others it established Eliot as a groundbreaking writer. Meanwhile, his critical writing in the international literary journal *The Criterion* (which Eliot founded in 1922) helped to round out his reputation as one of London's leading literary figures. In 1925, Eliot was recruited by the publishing firm Faber and Gwyer (later Faber and Faber) as a literary editor and board member. The position, which he held for many years, further extended Eliot's influence, as he was able to cultivate young writers—such as W.H. Auden—whose work he found promising.

Eliot's next long poem, *The Hollow Men* (1925), in some ways extends *The Waste Land*'s articulation of alienation and despair, but it also deals with more transcendent themes of what Eliot called "the salvation of the soul." Eliot's Christian faith continued to strengthen, and in 1927, the same year he was naturalized as a British citizen, Eliot was baptized into the Church of England. Religion thereafter became the focus of his life, and in 1933 he moved to Glenville Place presbytery, where he served as a church warden for seven years. There he wrote a series of poetic meditations on religious themes and scenarios, including *Journey of the Magi* (1927) and *Marina* (1930). Steeped in Eliot's studies of Shakespeare and Dante, these works meditate on spiritual growth while experimenting with more traditional dramatic forms. The dramatic monologue form in which *Journey of the Magi* is constructed, for example, is reminiscent of Robert Browning's work.

Much of Eliot's later career focused on dramatic writing. For many years he worked on *Sweeney Agonistes*, an unfinished experimental play of modern life, written in rhythmic prose accented by drum beats. He then published two ecclesiastical dramas, one of which was *Murder in the Cathedral* (1935), a ritual drama based on the murder of Thomas à Becket, before turning to clever West End social dramas like *The Cocktail Party* (1950). Though innovative in their attempts to reconcile classical drama with modern themes, these plays have not been successfully revived in recent decades. Ironically, however, a book of playful children's verse that Eliot wrote for his godchildren, *Old Possum's Book of Practical Cats* (1939), has been much more successful on the stage than any of Eliot's plays; it was adapted by British composer Andrew Lloyd Webber into the hit musical *Cats* (1980).

Despite a busy lecturing schedule and a marriage that was increasingly taxing (Vivien was institutionalized in 1938), Eliot produced four long poems in the late 1930s and early 1940s that together, published as *Four Quartets* (1943), he considered his crowning achievement. Comprising "Burnt Norton," "The Dry Salvages," "East Coker," and "Little Gidding," *Four Quartets* was in part inspired by the later string quartets of Beethoven. With its powerfully suggestive imagery and elaborate patterns of sound, it is among Eliot's most complex and technically masterful works. It also gives voice to Eliot's conviction that, in a world otherwise devoid of meaning, submission to God is essential. *Four Quartets* for a time took pride of place over *The Waste Land* as Eliot's most celebrated work.

The late years of Eliot's life were filled with personal happiness and public recognition of his contribution to modern literature. He was awarded eighteen honorary degrees, and in 1948 he was awarded both a Nobel Prize for Literature and the British Order of Merit. Vivien having died in 1947, in 1957 Eliot married Valerie Fletcher and enjoyed what he described as the only happy period of his life since childhood. He died in London in 1965 and was buried, according to his wishes, in his ancestors' parish church at East Coker. The plaque on the church wall bears his chosen epitaph, from *Four Quartets*: "In my beginning is my end, in my end is my beginning."

Near the end of his life Eliot commented, with sly irony, that he would "perhaps have a certain historical place in the literary history of our period." And indeed, he was lauded on his death as a unique literary figure; his obituary in *Life* magazine declared that "our age beyond any doubt has been, and will continue to be, the Age of Eliot." In subsequent decades the praise has been less effusive, and in two respects Eliot's work has been sharply criticized: most critics now acknowledge elements of misogyny and of anti-Semitism in his writing. But the impact of his poetic innovation is lasting, and a sense of the centrality of Eliot's work to the literary history of the twentieth century has remained constant. As Northrop Frye observed, "Whether he is liked or disliked is of no importance, but he must be read."

⌘ ⌘ ⌘

The Love Song of J. Alfred Prufrock [1]

S'io credesse che mia risposta fosse
A persona che mai tornasse al mondo,
Questa fiamma staria senza piu scosse.
Ma perciocche giammai di questo fondo

Non torno viva alcun, s'i'odo il vero,
Senza tema d'infamia ti rispondo. [2]

L et us go then, you and I,
  When the evening is spread out against the sky

---

[1] *J. Alfred Prufrock*   The name is likely taken from the The Prufrock-Littau Company, a furniture dealer located in St. Louis, Eliot's birthplace.

[2] *S'io credesse … ti rispondo*   Italian: "If I thought that my reply were given to anyone who might return to the world, this flame would stand forever still; but since never from this deep place has anyone ever returned alive, if what I hear is true, without fear of infamy I answer thee," Dante's *Inferno* 27.61–66; Guido da Montefeltro's speech as he burns in Hell.

Like a patient etherized upon a table;
Let us go, through certain half-deserted streets,
5   The muttering retreats
Of restless nights in one-night cheap hotels
And sawdust restaurants with oyster-shells:
Streets that follow like a tedious argument
Of insidious intent
10   To lead you to an overwhelming question …
Oh, do not ask, "What is it?"
Let us go and make our visit.

    In the room the women come and go
Talking of Michelangelo.

15   The yellow fog that rubs its back upon the
      window-panes,
The yellow smoke that rubs its muzzle on the
      window-panes
Licked its tongue into the corners of the evening,
Lingered upon the pools that stand in drains,
Let fall upon its back the soot that falls from chimneys,
20   Slipped by the terrace, made a sudden leap,
And seeing that it was a soft October night,
Curled once about the house, and fell asleep.

    And indeed there will be time
For the yellow smoke that slides along the street,
25   Rubbing its back upon the window panes;
There will be time, there will be time[1]
To prepare a face to meet the faces that you meet
There will be time to murder and create,
And time for all the works and days[2] of hands
30   That lift and drop a question on your plate;
Time for you and time for me,
And time yet for a hundred indecisions,
And for a hundred visions and revisions,
Before the taking of a toast and tea.

35   In the room the women come and go
Talking of Michelangelo.

    And indeed there will be time
To wonder, "Do I dare?" and, "Do I dare?"
Time to turn back and descend the stair,
40   With a bald spot in the middle of my hair—
(They will say: "How his hair is growing thin!")
My morning coat,[3] my collar mounting firmly to the
    chin,
My necktie rich and modest, but asserted by a simple
    pin—
(They will say: "But how his arms and legs are thin!")
45   Do I dare
Disturb the universe?
In a minute there is time
For decisions and revisions which a minute will reverse.

    For I have known them all already, known them
    all—
50   Have known the evenings, mornings, afternoons,
I have measured out my life with coffee spoons;
I know the voices dying with a dying fall[4]
Beneath the music from a farther room.
    So how should I presume?

55   And I have known the eyes already, known them
    all—
The eyes that fix you in a formulated phrase,
And when I am formulated, sprawling on a pin,
When I am pinned and wriggling on the wall,
Then how should I begin
60   To spit out all the butt-ends of my days and ways?
    And how should I presume?

    And I have known the arms already, known them
    all—
Arms that are braceleted and white and bare
(But in the lamplight, downed with light brown hair!)
65   Is it perfume from a dress
That makes me so digress?
Arms that lie along a table, or wrap about a shawl.

---

[1]   *there will be time*   See Ecclesiastes 3.1–8. "To everything there is a season, and a time to every purpose under heaven: A time to be born, and a time to die; a time to plant, and a time to pluck up that which is planted; a time to kill, and a time to heal …"

[2]   *works and days*   Title of a poem by eighth-century BCE Greek poet Hesiod.

[3]   *morning coat*   A formal coat with tails.

[4]   *with a dying fall*   In Shakespeare's *Twelfth Night* 1.1.1–15. Duke Orsino commands, "That strain again, it had a dying fall."

And should I then presume?
And how should I begin?

*   *   *

70   Shall I say, I have gone at dusk through narrow streets
And watched the smoke that rises from the pipes
Of lonely men in shirt-sleeves, leaning out of
        windows? ...[1]

I should have been a pair of ragged claws
Scuttling across the floors of silent seas.[2]

*   *   *

75   And the afternoon, the evening, sleeps so peacefully!
Smoothed by long fingers,
Asleep ... tired ... or it malingers,
Stretched on the floor, here beside you and me.
Should I, after tea and cakes and ices,
80   Have the strength to force the moment to its crisis?
But though I have wept and fasted, wept and prayed,
Though I have seen my head (grown slightly bald)
        brought in upon a platter,[3]
I am no prophet[4]—and here's no great matter;
I have seen the moment of my greatness flicker,
85   And I have seen the eternal Footman hold my coat,
        and snicker,
And in short, I was afraid.

And would it have been worth it, after all,
After the cups, the marmalade, the tea,
Among the porcelain, among some talk of you and me,

90   Would it have been worth while,
To have bitten off the matter with a smile,
To have squeezed the universe into a ball[5]
To roll it toward some overwhelming question,
To say: "I am Lazarus,[6] come from the dead,
95   Come back to tell you all, I shall tell you all"—
If one, settling a pillow by her head,
        Should say: "That is not what I meant at all;
        That is not it, at all."

And would it have been worth it, after all,
100   Would it have been worth while,
After the sunsets and the dooryards and the sprinkled
        streets,[7]
After the novels, after the teacups, after the skirts that
        trail along the floor—
And this, and so much more?—
It is impossible to say just what I mean!
105   But as if a magic lantern[8] threw the nerves in patterns
        on a screen:
Would it have been worth while
If one, settling a pillow or throwing off a shawl,
And turning toward the window, should say:
        "That is not it at all,
110   That is not what I meant, at all."

*   *   *

No! I am not Prince Hamlet, nor was meant to be;
Am an attendant lord, one that will do
To swell a progress,[9] start a scene or two,
Advise the prince; no doubt, an easy tool,
115   Deferential, glad to be of use,
Politic, cautious, and meticulous;
Full of high sentence,[10] but a bit obtuse;

---

[1]   ...   The ellipsis here makes note of a 38 line insertion written by Eliot, entitled *Prufrock's Pervigilium*. The subtitle and 33 of the lines were later removed.

[2]   *I should ... seas*   See Shakespeare's *Hamlet* 2.2, in which Hamlet tells Polonius, "for you yourself, sir, should be old as I am, if like a crab you could go backwards."

[3]   *brought in upon a platter*   Reference to Matthew 14.1–12, in which the prophet John the Baptist is beheaded at the command of Herod, and his head presented to Salomé upon a platter.

[4]   *I am no prophet*   See Amos 7.14. When commanded by King Amiziah not to prophesy, the Judean Amos answered; "I was no prophet, neither was I a prophet's son; but I was a herdsman, and a farmer of sycamore fruit."

[5]   *Squeezed ... ball*   See Andrew Marvell's "To His Coy Mistress" 41–2: "Let us roll our strength and all / Our sweetness up into one ball."

[6]   *Lazarus*   Raised from the dead by Jesus in John 11.1–44.

[7]   *sprinkled streets*   Streets sprayed with water to keep dust down.

[8]   *magic lantern*   In Victorian times, a device used to project images painted on glass onto a blank screen or wall.

[9]   *progress*   Journey made by royalty through the country.

[10]   *high sentence*   Serious, elevated sentiments or opinions.

At times, indeed, almost ridiculous—
Almost, at times, the Fool.

120   I grow old ... I grow old ...
I shall wear the bottoms of my trousers rolled.

     Shall I part my hair behind? Do I dare to eat a
         peach?
I shall wear white flannel trousers, and walk upon the
    beach.
I have heard the mermaids singing,[1] each to each.

125   I do not think that they will sing to me.

     I have seen them riding seaward on the waves
Combing the white hair of the waves blown back
When the wind blows the water white and black.

     We have lingered in the chambers of the sea
130 By sea-girls wreathed with seaweed red and brown
Till human voices wake us, and we drown.
         —1915, 1917

Preludes [2]

1

The winter evening settles down
  With smell of steaks in passageways.
Six o'clock.
The burnt-out ends of smoky days.
5 And now a gusty shower wraps
The grimy scraps
Of withered leaves about your feet
And newspapers from vacant lots;
The showers beat
10 On broken blinds and chimney-pots,
And at the corner of the street
A lonely cab-horse steams and stamps.
And then the lighting of the lamps.

2

The morning comes to consciousness
15 Of faint stale smells of beer
From the sawdust-trampled[3] street
With all its muddy feet that press
To early coffee-stands.
With the other masquerades
20 That time resumes,
One thinks of all the hands
That are raising dingy shades
In a thousand furnished rooms.

3

You tossed a blanket from the bed,
25 You lay upon your back, and waited;
You dozed, and watched the night revealing
The thousand sordid images
Of which your soul was constituted;
They flickered against the ceiling.
30 And when all the world came back
And the light crept up between the shutters,
And you heard the sparrows in the gutters,
You had such a vision of the street
As the street hardly understands;
35 Sitting along the bed's edge, where
You curled the papers from your hair,[4]
Or clasped the yellow soles of feet
In the palms of both soiled hands.

4

His soul stretched tight across the skies
40 That fade behind a city block,
Or trampled by insistent feet
At four and five and six o'clock;
And short square fingers stuffing pipes,
And evening newspapers, and eyes
45 Assured of certain certainties,
The conscience of a blackened street
Impatient to assume the world.

     I am moved by fancies that are curled
Around these images, and cling:

---

[1] *I have ... singing* See John Donne's "Song": "Teach me to hear the mermaids singing."

[2] *Preludes* In Parts 3 and 4 of this poem, many of the images and details of setting are taken from Charles-Louis Philippe's novel *Bubu-de-Montparnasse* (1898).

[3] *sawdust-trampled* Sawdust was placed on the floors of bars and restaurants to absorb dirt.

[4] *papers ... hair* I.e., "curl papers," used to curl hair.

50　The notion of some infinitely gentle
　　Infinitely suffering thing.

　　Wipe your hand across your mouth, and laugh;
　　The worlds revolve like ancient women
　　Gathering fuel in vacant lots.
　　　　—1915

Burbank with a Baedeker:
Bleistein with a Cigar[1]

Tra-la- la- la- la- la-laire—nil nisi divinum stabile est;
caetera fumus[2]—the gondola stopped, the old palace was
there, how charming its grey and pink[3]—goats and monkeys,
with such hair too![4]—so the countess passed on until she came
through the little park, where Niobe presented her with a
cabinet, and so departed.[5]

Burbank crossed a little bridge
　　Descending at a small hotel;
Princess Volupine arrived,
　　They were together, and he fell.[6]

5　Defunctive° music under sea　　　　　　　　　*dying*
　　Passed seaward with the passing bell

Slowly: the God Hercules
　　Had left him, that had loved him well.[7]

The horses, under the axletree
10　Beat up the dawn from Istria[8]
With even feet. Her shuttered barge
　　Burned on the water all the day.

But this or such was Bleistein's way:
　　A saggy bending of the knees
15 And elbows, with the palms turned out,
　　Chicago Semite Viennese.

A lustreless protrusive eye
　　Stares from the protozoic slime
At a perspective of Canaletto.[9]
20　The smoky candle end of time

Declines. On the Rialto[10] once.
　　The rats are underneath the piles.
The jew is underneath the lot.[11]
　　Money in furs.[12] The boatman smiles,

25 Princess Volupine extends
　　A meagre, blue-nailed, phthisic° hand　　*consumptive*
To climb the waterstair. Lights, lights,
　　She entertains Sir Ferdinand

---

[1] *Baedeker* Popular line of guide-books; *Bleistein* Jewish-German name literally meaning "Leadstone."

[2] *nil ... fumus* Latin: Nothing but the divine endures; all the rest is smoke.

[3] *the gondola ... pink* From Henry James's *Aspern Papers* (1888), Chapter 1. The passage is narrated by an American woman living in Venice who is giving her visiting friend a tour of the city: "The gondola stopped, the old palace was there.... 'How charming! It's grey and pink!' my companion exclaimed."

[4] *goats and monkeys* An exclamation made by Othello in Shakespeare's *Othello* 4.1 (set in Venice) when he becomes convinced his wife is having an affair; *with such hair too* From Robert Browning's "A Toccata of Galuppi's," about the eighteenth-century Venetian composer Baldassare Galuppi (1706–85).

[5] *so the ... departed* From the stage directions of *Entertainment of Alice, Dowager Countess of Derby* by John Marston (c.1575–1634); *Niobe* Mother in Greek myth who boasted that her children were better than those of Zeus.

[6] *They were ... fell* From Alfred Tennyson's "The Sisters" (Eliot has changed the pronoun from "she" to "he").

[7] *Defunctive music ... well* See Shakespeare's *Antony and Cleopatra* 4.3, in which Cleopatra's soldiers hear music just before they are defeated by Caesar's army. "'Tis the god Hercules, whom Antony lov'd, / Now leaves him," one soldier says.

[8] *Horses ... dawn* In classical myth, the sun is a chariot pulled across the sky; *Istria* Peninsula that juts into the northeast Adriatic.

[9] *Canaletto* Italian painter Antonio Canale (1697–1768), famous for his paintings of Venice and London.

[10] *Rialto* Island in Venice, containing the old mercantile quarter of the medieval city.

[11] *The jew ... lot* For a discussion of the controversy over Eliot's attitudes towards Jewish people, see the "In Context" section on "Eliot and Anti-Semitism" later in this volume.

[12] *Money in furs* Venice was a center for fur trade from the Black Sea.

Klein. Who clipped the lion's wings[1]
30   And flea'd his rump and pared his claws?
Thought Burbank, meditating on
    Time's ruins, and the seven laws.[2]
—1919

Gerontion[3]

> *Thou hast nor youth nor age*
> *But as it were an after dinner sleep*
> *Dreaming of both.*[4]

Here I am, an old man in a dry month,
Being read to by a boy, waiting for rain.[5]
I was neither at the hot gates[6]
Nor fought in the warm rain
5   Nor knee deep in the salt marsh, heaving a cutlass,
Bitten by flies, fought.
My house is a decayed house,
And the jew squats on the window sill, the owner,
Spawned in some estaminet[7] of Antwerp,
10   Blistered in Brussels, patched and peeled in London.[8]

The goat coughs at night in the field overhead;
Rocks, moss, stonecrop, iron, merds.[9]
The woman keeps the kitchen, makes tea,
Sneezes at evening, poking the peevish gutter.[10]
15   I an old man,
A dull head among windy spaces.

        Signs are taken for wonders. "We would see a
            sign!"
The word within a word, unable to speak a word,
Swaddled with darkness.[11] In the juvescence°   *youth*
    of the year
20   Came Christ the tiger

        In depraved May, dogwood and chestnut,
            flowering judas,[12]
To be eaten, to be divided, to be drunk
Among whispers; by Mr. Silvero
With caressing hands, at Limoges[13]
25   Who walked all night in the next room;

        By Hakagawa, bowing among the Titians;[14]
By Madame de Tornquist, in the dark room
Shifting the candles; Fraulein von Kulp
Who turned in the hall, one hand on the door.
30   Vacant shuttles
Weave the wind. I have no ghosts,
An old man in a draughty house
Under a windy knob.[15]

---

[1] *lion's wings* The winged lion was a symbol of the Venetian Republic.

[2] *seven laws* Either the seven laws of architecture that John Ruskin outlined in his *Seven Lamps of Architecture* (1849), which describes Venice's Gothic style as the ideal, or the Noachian Laws, the Seven Commandments of the Sons of Noah from the Jewish Talmud.

[3] *Gerontion* Greek: little old man. Eliot originally planned to print this poem as a prelude to *The Waste Land*, but when Ezra Pound advised against this he published it separately.

[4] *Thou hast ... both* From Shakespeare's *Measure for Measure* 3.1.32–34.

[5] *Here I ... rain* These two lines are based on a sentence in A.C. Benson's biography *Edward Fitzgerald* (1905), in which the poet is described as sitting "in a dry month, old and blind, being read to by a country boy, longing for rain."

[6] *hot gates* Literal translation of the Greek *Thermopylae*, a pass between northern and central Greece and the location of several historical battles, including that between the Greeks and the Persians in 480 BCE.

[7] *stonecrop* Herb with yellow flowers that grows on rocks or old walls; *estaminet* French: café.

[8] *the jew ... London* The association of Jews with images of squalor, decay, and disgusting physicality was one of the many ways in which anti-Semitism was expressed in British literary tradition. For more on the controversy over such elements as they appear in

Eliot's verse see the "In Context" section below.

[9] *merds* Feces.

[10] *gutter* Sputtering fire.

[11] *Signs are ... darkness* Reference to two Biblical passages. The first is Matthew 12.39: "An evil and adulterous generation seeketh after a sign; and there shall no sign be given to it, but the sign of the prophet Jonas," and the second is John 1.1: "In the beginning was the Word, and the Word was with God, and the Word was God." Both of these passages were sources for a Christmas sermon given by Anglican preacher Lancelot Andrewes in 1618.

[12] *judas* Purple-flowered tree of southern Europe named after Judas, who was said to have hanged himself from a tree of this type after betraying Jesus.

[13] *Limoges* French town known for its china of the same name.

[14] *Titians* Paintings by Venetian painter Titian (1485–1576).

[15] *Vacant shuttles ... knob* See Job 7.6–7: "My days are swifter than a weaver's shuttle, and are spent without hope. O remember that my life is wind: mine eye shall no more see good"; *knob* Knoll.

After such knowledge, what forgiveness? Think now
35 History has many cunning passages, contrived
corridors
And issues, deceives with whispering ambitions,
Guides us by vanities. Think now
She gives when our attention is distracted
And what she gives, gives with such supple confusions
40 That the giving famishes the craving. Gives too late
What's not believed in, or if still believed,
In memory only, reconsidered passion. Gives too soon
Into weak hands,[1] what's thought can be dispensed with
Till the refusal propagates a fear. Think
45 Neither fear nor courage saves us. Unnatural vices
Are fathered by our heroism. Virtues
Are forced upon us by our impudent crimes.
These tears are shaken from the wrath-bearing tree.

The tiger springs in the new year. Us he devours.
Think at last
50 We have not reached conclusion, when I
Stiffen in a rented house. Think at last
I have not made this show purposelessly
And it is not by any concitation°   stirring up
Of the backward devils.[2]
55 I would meet you upon this honestly.
I that was near your heart was removed therefrom
To lose beauty in terror, terror in inquisition.
I have lost my passion: why should I need to keep it
Since what is kept must be adulterated?
60 I have lost my sight, smell, hearing, taste and touch:
How should I use them for your closer contact?

These with a thousand small deliberations
Protract the profit of their chilled delirium,
Excite the membrane, when the sense has cooled,
65 With pungent sauces, multiply variety
In a wilderness of mirrors. What will the spider do,
Suspend its operations, will the weevil
Delay? De Bailhache, Fresca, Mrs. Cammel, whirled
Beyond the circuit of the shuddering Bear[3]

---

[1] *too soon ... hands* See Percy Shelley's *Adonais* (1821), in which he describes Keats's death: "Too soon, and with weak hands."

[2] *backward devils* In Dante's *Inferno*, tellers of the future were punished by being forced to walk backwards.

[3] *Bear* Constellation Ursa Major (the Great Bear).

---

70 In fractured atoms. Gull against the wind, in the
windy straits
Of Belle Isle, or running on the Horn,[4]
White feathers in the snow, the Gulf[5] claims,
And an old man driven by the Trades[6]
To a sleepy corner.

75   Tenants of the house,
Thoughts of a dry brain in a dry season.
—1920

The Waste Land

The title and plan of Eliot's groundbreaking poem *The Waste Land* were substantially influenced by Jessie Weston's *From Ritual to Romance* (1920), which details the various legends of the Holy Grail and explores the influence of pre-Christian religions on these legends. According to most accounts of the Grail, the sacred vessel lies in the heart of a (formerly fertile) Waste Land that is now stricken with drought and presided over by a Fisher King who is cursed with impotence. The land and its king can only be saved from permanent sterility by a knight who is able to pass several tests and attain the Grail, thus bringing about regeneration. Overlaying this myth with a modern setting and numerous cultural references, Eliot shows that a similar sterility plagues a contemporary society characterized by casual sexuality, blatant materialism, and industrial exploitation of nature.

With its disparate images, ever-shifting narrative events, and seemingly random structure, *The Waste Land* embraces the fragmented present while looking back to a more coherent past. Allusions to seventeenth-century poets, to Chaucer, to Shakespeare, to Dante, to pre-Socratic philosophers, and to works of history and anthropology, such as James Frazer's twelve-volume anthropological study *The Golden*

---

[4] *Belle Isle* Channel between Labrador and Newfoundland at the entrance to the Gulf of St. Lawrence; *the Horn* Cape Horn, the southernmost tip of South America.

[5] *Gulf* Gulf stream, a warm ocean current in the North Atlantic.

[6] *Trades* Trade winds, which blow, almost constantly, towards the equator.

Bough (1890–1915), gesture towards the presence of a recurring order beneath contemporary history and indicate the possibility of regeneration. The poem's disconnected and highly allusive character (which gives it a sense of difficulty more often heightened than alleviated by Eliot's copious notes) provoked charges of intentional obscurity upon the poem's publication, but Eliot maintained that any poetry developed out of such a complex and various society must itself be various and complex.

By its very nature, *The Waste Land* seems to resist order and any cohesive account of meaning; its complexity and ambiguity make possible a variety of interpretations. Even the identity of its narrator is unclear: are all the disparate voices filtered through any single voice? And, if so, is the voice that of the blind prophet Tiresias, or some other nameless narrator, or is the speaker Eliot himself? This very complexity may in large part be responsible for the continued vitality of the poem, however. Eliot's friend Conrad Aiken maintained that the poem was important primarily for its private "emotional value," and that readers should rely as much on their first responses to the diverse elements of the poem as on the copious and ever-expanding body of scholarship surrounding it. As much as *The Waste Land* has taken its place as a central document of the modernist movement, it retains as well the ability to speak directly to readers.

The Waste Land [1]

"Nam Sibyllam quidem Cumis ego ipse oculis meis vidi in ampulla pendere, et cum illi pueri dicerent: Σίβυλλα τί

θέλεις; respondebat illa: ἀποθανεῖν θέλω."[2]

For Ezra Pound
il miglior fabbro.[3]

I. THE BURIAL OF THE DEAD[4]

April is the cruellest month, breeding
Lilacs out of the dead land, mixing
Memory and desire, stirring
Dull roots with spring rain.
5   Winter kept us warm, covering
Earth in forgetful snow, feeding
A little life with dried tubers.
Summer surprised us, coming over the Starnbergersee[5]
With a shower of rain; we stopped in the colonnade,
And went on in sunlight, into the Hofgarten,[6]
And drank coffee, and talked for an hour.
Bin gar keine Russin, stamm' aus Litauen, echt deutsch.[7]
And when we were children, staying at the archduke's,
My cousin's, he took me out on a sled,
15   And I was frightened. He said, Marie,
Marie, hold on tight. And down we went.
In the mountains, there you feel free.
I read, much of the night, and go south in the winter.

What are the roots that clutch, what branches grow

---

[1] [Eliot's note]   Not only the title, but the plan and a good deal of the incidental symbolism of the poem were suggested by Miss Jessie L. Weston's book on the Grail legend: *From Ritual to Romance* (Cambridge). Indeed, so deeply am I indebted, Miss Weston's book will elucidate the difficulties of the poem much better than my notes can do; and I recommend it (apart from the great interest of the book itself) to any who think such elucidation of the poem worth the trouble. To another work of anthropology I am indebted in general, one which has influenced our generation profoundly; I mean [Sir James Frazer's 1890 to 1915 twelve-volume] *The Golden Bough*; I have used especially the two volumes *Adonis, Attis, Osiris*. Anyone who is acquainted with these works will immediately recognise in the poem certain references to vegetation ceremonies.

[2] *Nam ... θέλω*   Latin and Greek: "For once I saw with my own eyes the Sybil at Cumae hanging in a cage, and when the boys asked her, 'Sybil, what do you want?' she responded, 'I want to die.'" From the *Satyricon* of Petronius Arbiter (first-century CE Roman writer). The most famous of the prophetic Sibyls of Greek mythology, the Cumaean Sibyl received immortality from the god Apollo, but neglected to ask him for eternal youth.

[3] *il miglior fabbro*   Italian: the better craftsman. This compliment was originally paid by Dante, in his *Purgatorio* (26.117), to the Provençal poet, Arnaut Daniel. Eliot adopts it for his dedication to fellow expatriate and Modernist American poet, Ezra Pound (1885–1972), who played a key editorial role in the poem's production.

[4] *The Burial of the Dead*   Reference to the Anglican Order for the Burial of the Dead.

[5] *Starnbergersee*   Lake near Munich, Germany.

[6] *Hofgarten*   Public park in Munich.

[7] *Bin ... deutsch*   German: I'm not Russian at all, I come from Lithuania, a pure German.

[Handwritten annotations: "prophetic", "fragment of my world", "gender queer prophet for Huckleback. figure", "hermaphrodite", "Tiresias"]

20 Out of this stony rubbish? Son of man,[1]
    You cannot say, or guess, for you know only   *[Ecclesiastes]*
    A heap of broken images, where the sun beats,   *[allegory of old age]*
    And the dead tree gives no shelter, the cricket no
          relief,[2]
    And the dry stone no sound of water. Only
25 There is shadow under this red rock,[3]
    (Come in under the shadow of this red rock),
    And I will show you something different from either   *[passage of time]*
    Your shadow at morning striding behind you
    Or your shadow at evening rising to meet you;
30 I will show you fear in a handful of dust.   *[fear of death]*
          Frisch weht der Wind   *[lament of sailor for a companion he has left behind. Phoenician sailor?]*   *[fear of death or ? to girl]*
          Der Heimat zu   *[unrequited in love]*
          Mein Irisch Kind,
          Wo weilest du?[4]
35 "You gave me hyacinths first a year ago;
    They called me the hyacinth girl."
    —Yet when we came back, late, from the Hyacinth   *[Tiresias' blindness]*
          garden,   *[Dante]*
    Your arms full, and your hair wet, I could not
    Speak, and my eyes failed, I was neither
40 Living nor dead, and I knew nothing,
    Looking into the heart of light, the silence.
          Oed' und leer das Meer.[5]

    Madame Sosostris,[6] famous clairvoyante,
    Had a bad cold, nevertheless
45 Is known to be the wisest woman in Europe,
    With a wicked pack of cards.[7]   *[Tarot]* Here, said she,
    Is your card, the drowned Phoenician Sailor,
    (Those are pearls that were his eyes.[8] Look!)   *[Death by water]*
    Here is Belladonna, the Lady of the Rocks,[9]
50 The lady of situations.   *[Beautiful lady? poisonous flower]* *[sex worker?]*
    Here is the man with three staves, and here the Wheel,[10]
    And here is the one-eyed merchant, and this card,   *[change]*
    Which is blank, is something he carries on his back,   *[Mr. Eugenides]*
    Which I am forbidden to see. I do not find
55 The Hanged Man.[11] Fear death by water.   *[Does not see connection of fertility]*
    I see crowds of people, walking round in a ring.
    Thank you. If you see dear Mrs. Equitone,
    Tell her I bring the horoscope myself:
    One must be so careful these days.   *[decline of civilization]*

---

[1] *Son of man* Eliot's note cites Ezekiel 2.1, in which God addresses Ezekiel, whose mission will be to preach the coming of the Messiah to unbelievers, saying, "Son of man, stand upon thy feet, and I will speak unto thee."

[2] *cricket no relief* Eliot's note cites Ecclesiastes 12.5, in which the preacher speaks of the fearful deprivations of old age: "Also *when* they shall be afraid of *that which is* high, and fears *shall be* in the way, and the almond tree shall flourish, and the grasshopper shall be a burden, and desire shall fail: because man goeth to his long home, and the mourners go about the streets …"

[3] *There is shadow … rock* See Isaiah 32.2, in which the blessings of Christ's kingdom are described: "And a man shall be as an hiding place from the wind, and a covert from the tempest; as rivers of water in a dry place, as the shadow of a great rock in a weary land."

[4] *Frisch … du?* German: "Fresh blows the wind to the homeland—my Irish child, where do you tarry?" From Richard Wagner's opera *Tristan und Isolde* (1865), 1.5–8, this is a sailor's lament for the girl he has left behind in Ireland.

[5] *Oed' … Meer* German: "Desolate and empty is the sea." Eliot's note cites *Tristan und Isolde* 3.24, in which Tristan lies dying, waiting for his beloved, Isolde, to come to him, but there is no sign of her ship on the sea.

[6] *Madame Sosostris* This name is often thought to have been "unconsciously" borrowed by Eliot from the name of the fortune-teller Madame Sesostris in Aldous Huxley's novel *Crome Yellow* (1921). It may more plausibly have derived from the Greek word for saviour, *soteros*.

[7] [Eliot's note] I am not familiar with the exact constitution of the Tarot pack of cards, from which I have obviously departed to suit my own convenience. The Hanged Man, a member of the traditional pack, fits my purpose in two ways: because he is associated in my mind with the Hanged God of Frazer, and because I associate him with the hooded figure in the passage of the disciples to Emmaus in Part V. The Phoenician Sailor and the Merchant appear later; also the "crowds of people," and Death by Water is executed in Part IV. The Man with Three Staves (an authentic member of the Tarot pack) I associate, quite arbitrarily, with the Fisher King himself. [The Tarot pack, generally used for fortune-telling, consists of 78 cards in four suits—cups, wands, swords, and pentangles. It originated in France and Italy in the fourteenth century.]

[8] *Those are … eyes* From Ariel's song in Shakespeare's *The Tempest* 1.2.397–403: "Full fathom five thy father lies; / Of his bones are coral made; / Those are pearls that were his eyes; / Nothing of him that doth fade / But doth suffer a sea-change / Into something rich and strange: / Sea nymphs hourly ring his knell: / *Burden.* Ding-dong. / Hark! Now I hear them—ding-dong bell."

[9] *Belladonna* Italian: beautiful woman. Also another name for the poisonous plant deadly nightshade, once used for cosmetic purposes by Italian women; *Lady of the Rocks* Possible ironic reference to Leonardo da Vinci's painting *Madonna of the Rocks*.

[10] *Wheel* Wheel of Fortune.

[11] *Hanged Man* This man's self-sacrifice in the role of fertility god is necessary for the annual rejuvenation of the land.

England [handwritten]

60   Unreal City,[1]
Under the brown fog of a winter dawn,
A crowd flowed over London Bridge, so many, [*people going to work in the morning, look dead* — handwritten]
I had not thought death had undone so many.[2] [*at their feet* — handwritten]
Sighs, short and infrequent, were exhaled,
65   And each man fixed his eyes before his feet.
Flowed up the hill and down King William Street,
To where Saint Mary Woolnoth[3] kept the hours
With a dead sound on the final stroke of nine.[4]
There I saw one I knew, and stopped him, crying
    "Stetson![5]
70   You who were with me in the ships at Mylae![6]
That corpse you planted last year in your garden,
Has it begun to sprout? Will it bloom this year?
Or has the sudden frost disturbed its bed?
Oh keep the Dog far hence, that's friend to men,
75   Or with his nails he'll dig it up again![7] [*Dog will mess up fertility* — handwritten]
You! hypocrite lecteur!—mon semblable,—mon frère!"[8]

directly speaking to the reader [handwritten]

---

[1] *Unreal City* Eliot's note cites the following lines from the 1859 poem "Les sept vieillards" by poet Charles Baudelaire: "Fourmillante cité, cité pleine de rêves, / Où le spectre en plein jour raccroche le passant." (French: "Swarming city, city full of dreams, / Where the daylight spectre intercepts the passerby.") "The City" is the name for London's financial district, located north of London Bridge.

[2] *so many … so many* Eliot's note cites Dante's *Inferno* 3.55–57: "such a long stream / of people, that I would not have thought / that death had undone so many." This is spoken by Dante soon after he has entered the Gates of Hell in the company of Virgil, his guide through the underworld.

[3] *Saint Mary Woolnoth* Church in King William Street. Eliot joined a campaign to have this church, and others like it that were slated for demolition, preserved.

[4] [Eliot's note] A phenomenon which I have often noticed.

[5] *Stetson* Eliot, when questioned, maintained this was a reference to the average City clerk, and not, as some had suggested, to Ezra Pound, whose nickname was "Buffalo Bill."

[6] *Mylae* The Battle of Mylae (260 BCE) took place in the trade-based First Punic War between the Romans and the Carthaginians.

[7] *O keep … men* Eliot's note cites the dirge in John Webster's play *The White Devil* (1612) 5.4: "But keep the wolf far thence, that's foe to men, / For with his nails he'll dig them up again." Sirius, the Dog Star, heralded the annual flooding of the Nile in Egyptian mythology.

[8] *hypocrite … mon frère* French: "Hypocrite reader—my double—my brother!" Eliot's note cites the preface of Baudelaire's *Fleurs du Mal*.

---

2. A GAME OF CHESS [9]

The Chair she sat in, like a burnished throne,[10]
Glowed on the marble, where the glass
Held up by standards wrought with fruited vines
80   From which a golden Cupidon peeped out
(Another hid his eyes behind his wing)
Doubled the flames of sevenbranched candelabra
Reflecting light upon the table as
The glitter of her jewels rose to meet it,
85   From satin cases poured in rich profusion;
In vials of ivory and coloured glass
Unstoppered, lurked her strange synthetic perfumes,
Unguent, powdered, or liquid—troubled, confused
And drowned the sense in odours; stirred by the air
90   That freshened from the window, these ascended
In fattening the prolonged candle-flames,
Flung their smoke into the laquearia,[11]
Stirring the pattern on the coffered ceiling.
Huge sea-wood fed with copper
95   Burned green and orange, framed by the coloured
    stone,
In which sad light a carved dolphin swam.
Above the antique mantel was displayed
As though a window gave upon the sylvan scene[12]
The change of Philomel, by the barbarous king
100   So rudely forced;[13] yet there the nightingale
Filled all the desert with inviolable voice
And still she cried, and still the world pursues,

---

[9] *A Game of Chess* Title of Thomas Middleton's 1624 satirical political drama. In Middleton's play *Women Beware Women*, a game of chess distracts a mother-in-law, preventing her from noticing that her daughter-in-law is being seduced upstairs. Each move in the chess game mirrors a move in the seduction.

[10] [Eliot's note] Cf. Antony and Cleopatra, 2.2.190. [This is the beginning of Enorbarbus's description of the first meeting of Antony and Cleopatra: "The barge she sat in, like a burnished throne, / Burned on the water."]

[11] *laquearia* Latin: paneled ceiling. Eliot's note cites Virgil's *Aeneid* 1.726, describing a banquet given by Queen Dido of Carthage for her soon-to-be lover, Aeneas: "Burning lamps hang from the gold-paneled ceiling, and torches dispel the night with their flames."

[12] *sylvan scene* Eliot's note cites Milton's *Paradise Lost* 4.140, which describes the Garden of Eden seen through Satan's eyes.

[13] *The change … forced* Eliot's notes for this passage cite Greek poet Ovid's *Metamorphoses* 6, which tells the Greek myth of Philomela, who was raped by King Tereus of Thrace (her sister's husband) and had her tongue cut out before being changed into a nightingale.

*Song of nightingale
or Sex*

"Jug Jug"[1] to dirty ears.
And other withered stumps of time
105 Were told upon the walls; staring forms
Leaned out, leaning, hushing the room enclosed.
Footsteps shuffled on the stair.
Under the firelight, under the brush, her hair
Spread out in fiery points
110 Glowed into words, then would be savagely still.

"My nerves are bad to-night. Yes, bad. Stay with me.
Speak to me. Why do you never speak. Speak.
What are you thinking of? What thinking? What?
I never know what you are thinking. Think."

115 I think we are in rats' alley[2]
Where the dead men lost their bones.

"What is that noise?"
The wind under the door.[3]
"What is that noise now? What is the wind doing?"
120 Nothing again nothing.
"Do
You know nothing? Do you see nothing? Do you
remember
Nothing?"

I remember
125 Those are pearls that were his eyes.
"Are you alive, or not? Is there nothing in your head?"
But

O O O O that Shakespeherian Rag[4]—
It's so elegant
130 So intelligent
"What shall I do now? What shall I do?"
"I shall rush out as I am, and walk the street
With my hair down, so. What shall we do to-morrow?

What shall we ever do?"
135 The hot water at ten.
And if it rains, a closed car at four.
And we shall play a game of chess,
Pressing lidless eyes and waiting for a knock upon the
door.[5]

When Lil's husband got demobbed,[6] I said—
140 I didn't mince my words, I said to her myself,
HURRY UP PLEASE ITS TIME[7]
Now Albert's coming back, make yourself a bit smart.
He'll want to know what you done with that money he
gave you
To get yourself some teeth. He did, I was there.
145 You have them all out, Lil, and get a nice set,
He said, I swear, I can't bear to look at you.
And no more can't I, I said, and think of poor Albert,
He's been in the army four years, he wants a good time,
And if you don't give it him, there's others will, I said.
150 Oh is there, she said. Something o' that, I said.
Then I'll know who to thank, she said, and give me a
straight look.
HURRY UP PLEASE ITS TIME
If you don't like it you can get on with it, I said.
Others can pick and choose if you can't.
155 But if Albert makes off, it won't be for lack of telling.
You ought to be ashamed, I said, to look so antique.
(And her only thirty-one.)
I can't help it, she said, pulling a long face,
It's them pills I took, to bring it off, she said.
160 (She's had five already, and nearly died of young
George.)
The chemist° said it would be alright, but I've never
been the same.   *pharmacist*
You are a proper fool, I said.
Well, if Albert won't leave you alone, there it is, I said,
What you get married for if you don't want children?
165 HURRY UP PLEASE ITS TIME
Well, that Sunday Albert was home, they had a hot
gammon,°   *smoked ham*

---

[1] *Jug Jug* In Elizabethan poetry, a conventional representation of a nightingale's song. Also, a crude reference to sexual intercourse.

[2] [Eliot's note] Cf. part 3, line 195 [of *Metamorphoses* 6].

[3] *The wind … door* Eliot's note cites a line from John Webster's *The Devil's Law Case* (3.2.162). A patient who is believed to have been stabbed to death groans in pain, prompting the surgeon ask, "Is the wind in that door still?"

[4] *O … Rag* Reference to a popular American ragtime song performed in Ziegfield's Follies in 1912.

[5] [Eliot's note] Cf. the game of chess in Middleton's *Women Beware Women*.

[6] *demobbed* Demobilized; released from military service.

[7] *HURRY … TIME* Expression used by bartenders in Britain to announce closing time.

THE WASTE LAND   455

And they asked me in to dinner, to get the beauty of it
    hot—
HURRY UP PLEASE ITS TIME
HURRY UP PLEASE ITS TIME
170 Goonight Bill. Goonight Lou. Goonight May. Goonight.
Ta ta. Goonight. Goonight.
Good night, ladies, good night, sweet ladies, good night,
    good night.[1]

3. THE FIRE SERMON [2]

The river's tent is broken: the last fingers of leaf
Clutch and sink into the wet bank. The wind
175 Crosses the brown land, unheard. The nymphs are
    departed.
Sweet Thames, run softly, till I end my song.[3]
The river bears no empty bottles, sandwich papers,
Silk handkerchiefs, cardboard boxes, cigarette ends
Or other testimony of summer nights. The nymphs
    are departed.
180 And their friends, the loitering heirs of city directors;
Departed, have left no addresses.
By the waters of Leman I sat down and wept ...[4]
Sweet Thames, run softly till I end my song,
Sweet Thames, run softly, for I speak not loud or long.
185 But at my back in a cold blast I hear
The rattle of the bones, and chuckle spread from ear
    to ear.[5]

A rat crept softly through the vegetation
Dragging its slimy belly on the bank
While I was fishing in the dull canal
190 On a winter evening round behind the gashouse
Musing upon the king my brother's wreck
And on the king my father's death before him.[6]
White bodies naked on the low damp ground
And bones cast in a little low dry garret,
195 Rattled by the rat's foot only, year to year.
But at my back from time to time I hear
The sound of horns and motors, which shall bring
Sweeney[8] to Mrs. Porter in the spring.
O the moon shone bright on Mrs. Porter
200 And on her daughter
They wash their feet in soda water[9]
Et O ces voix d'enfants, chantant dans la coupole![10]

    Twit twit twit
Jug jug jug jug jug jug

---

[1] *Good night ... night* Ophelia's last words in Shakespeare's *Hamlet* (4.5.72–3) before she drowns herself. These words are taken by her father as evidence that she had been driven insane by Hamlet's seeming indifference to her.

[2] *The Fire Sermon* Sermon preached by the Buddha against passions (such as lust, anger, and envy) that consume people and prevent their regeneration.

[3] *Sweet Thames ... song* Eliot's note cites the refrain of Edmund Spenser's *Prothalamion* (1596), a poem that celebrates the ideals of marriage, written to commemorate the joint marriages of the two daughters of the Earl of Worcester.

[4] *By the ... wept* Reference to Psalm 137, in which the Hebrews lament their exile in Babylon and their lost homeland of Jerusalem: "By the rivers of Babylon, there sat we down, yea, we wept, when we remembered Zion." For Babylon Eliot substitutes "Leman," the French name for Lake Geneva. "Leman" is also a medieval word meaning sweetheart.

[5] *But at ... ear* Eliot's note cites Andrew Marvell's "To His Coy Mistress": "But at my back I always hear / Time's wingèd chariot hurrying near" (lines 21–22).

[6] *And on ... him* Eliot's note cites Shakespeare's *The Tempest* 1.2.388–93, in which Ferdinand, shipwrecked on the shore, is prompted by Ariel's music to ponder the supposed drowning of his father, King Alonso: "Sitting on a bank, / Weeping again the king my father's wrack / This music crept by me upon the waters, / Allaying both their fury and my passion / With its sweet air." Eliot also quotes from this passage on line 257.

[7] [Eliot's note] Cf. [John] Day, *Parliament of Bees*: "When of the sudden, listening, you shall hear, / A noise of horns and hunting, which shall bring / Actaeon to Diana in the spring, / Where all shall see her naked skin..." [According to classical myth, when the hunter Actaeon saw Diana, goddess of chastity and the hunt, bathing naked with her nymphs, she changed him into a stag and set his dogs upon him.]

[8] *Sweeney* Character in two earlier poems by Eliot, "Sweeney Erect" and "Sweeney Among the Nightingales."

[9] [Eliot's note] I do not know the origin of the ballad from which these are taken: it was reported to me from Sydney, Australia. [One version of this ballad, which was sung by Australian soldiers in World War I, is as follows: "O the moon shone bright on Mrs. Porter / And on the daughter / Of Mrs. Porter / They wash their feet in soda water / And so they oughter / To keep them clean."]

[10] *Et O ... coupole* French: "And O those children's voices singing under the cupola." Eliot's note indicates that this is the last line of French poet Paul Verlaine's sonnet "Parsifal" (1886). Verlaine refers to the opera *Parsifal* (1882) by Richard Wagner, in which a choir of children sings while the innocent knight Parsifal has his feet washed before entering the Castle of the Grail.

roped

205   So rudely forc'd.
Tereu[1]

Unreal City   *Tarot card,*
Under the brown fog of a winter noon   *cardother*
Mr. Eugenides, the Smyrna[2] merchant
210   Unshaven, with a pocket full of currants
C.i.f. London: documents at sight,[3]   *Sexually*
Asked me in demotic[4] French   *charged*
To luncheon at the Cannon Street Hotel[5]   *invitation*
Followed by a weekend at the Metropole.[6]

215   At the violet hour, when the eyes and back
Turn upward from the desk, when the human engine
waits   *End of work day*
Like a taxi throbbing waiting,
I Tiresias,[7] though blind, throbbing between two lives,

---

[1]   *Tereu* Latin vocative form of Tereus, who raped Philomela.

[2]   *Smyrna* Port city in western Turkey.

rep. [3]   *C.i.f. ... sight* Eliot's note explains that "C.i.f." means that the
of   price includes "cost, insurance, freight to London," and that
human   "documents on sight" indicates that "the Bill of Lading, etc., were
experience to be handed to the buyer upon payment of the sight draft."

past, [4]   *demotic* Popular; vulgar.
present,
future? [5]   *Cannon Street Hotel* Hotel near the Cannon Street train station,
        a terminus for travelers to and from the continent.
Border? [6]   *Metropole* Large hotel on the seashore at Brighton.

[7]   [Eliot's note] Tiresias, although a mere spectator and not indeed
a "character," is yet the most important personage in the poem,
uniting all the rest. Just as the one-eyed merchant, seller of currants,
melts into the Phoenician Sailor, and the latter is not wholly distinct
from Ferdinand Prince of Naples, so all the women are one woman,
and the two sexes meet in Tiresias. What Tiresias sees, in fact, is the
substance of the poem. The whole passage from Ovid is of great
anthropological interest. [Eliot then quotes in Latin the passage from
Metamorphoses that describes Tiresias's sex change. Jove, who had
drunk a great deal, "jested with Juno. He said, 'Your pleasure in love
is really greater than that enjoyed by men.' She denied it; so they
decided to seek the opinion of the wise Tiresias, for he knew both
aspects of love. For once, with a blow of his staff, he had committed
violence on two huge snakes as they copulated in the green forest;
and—wonderful to tell—was turned into a woman and thus spent
seven years. In the eighth year he saw the same snakes again and said:
'If a blow struck at you is so powerful that it changes the sex of the
giver, I will now strike at you again.' With these words she struck the
snakes, and again became a man. So he was appointed arbiter in the
playful quarrel, and supported Jove's statement. It is said that
Saturnia [Juno] was quite disproportionately upset, and condemned
the arbiter to perpetual blindness. But the almighty father (for no
god may undo what has been done by another god), in return for the

---

Old man with wrinkled female breasts, can see
220   At the violet hour, the evening hour that strives
Homeward, and brings the sailor home from sea,[8]
The typist home at teatime, clears her breakfast, lights
Her stove, and lays out food in tins.
Out of the window perilously spread
225   Her drying combinations[9] touched by the sun's last
rays,
On the divan are piled (at night her bed)
Stockings, slippers, camisoles, and stays.° *lingerie*   corset
I Tiresias, old man with wrinkled dugs°   breasts
Perceived the scene, and foretold the rest—
230   I too awaited the expected guest.
He, the young man carbuncular,° arrives,   *pimply*
A small house agent's clerk, with one bold stare,
One of the low on whom assurance sits   *self-conscious*
As a silk hat on a Bradford[10] millionaire.   *self insecure*
235   The time is now propitious, as he guesses,
The meal is ended, she is bored and tired,
Endeavours to engage her in caresses
Which still are unreproved, if undesired.
Flushed and decided, he assaults at once;
240   Exploring hands encounter no defence;
His vanity requires no response,
And makes a welcome of indifference.
(And I Tiresias have foresuffered all
Enacted on this same divan or bed;
245   I who have sat by Thebes below the wall
And walked among the lowest of the dead.)[11]

---

sight that was taken away, gave him the power to know the future
and so lightened the penalty paid by the honor."]

[8]   [Eliot's note] This may not appear as exact as Sappho's lines but
I had in mind the "longshore" or "dory" fisherman, who returns at
nightfall. [Eliot refers to seventh-century BCE Greek poet Sappho's
poem, known as Fragment 149, in which Hesperus, the evening star,
brings home "all things the bright dawn disperses," including "the
sheep, the goat, the child to its mother."]

[9]   *combinations* Undergarments that combined the chemise and
panties.

[10]   *Bradford* Textile center in industrial Yorkshire, many of whose
residents became extremely wealthy during the textile boom that
accompanied World War I.

[11]   *I who ... dead* In *Oedipus Rex*, by fifth-century BCE Greek
dramatist Sophocles, Tiresias perceives that the curse of infertility
that plagues the people and land of Thebes has been brought upon
them by the unwitting marriage of Oedipus to his mother, Queen
Jocasta. In book 9 of Homer's *Odyssey*, Odysseus journeys to the
underworld, where he consults Tiresias.

Bestows one final patronising kiss,
And gropes his way, finding the stairs unlit …

    She turns and looks a moment in the glass,
250 Hardly aware of her departed lover;
Her brain allows one half-formed thought to pass:
"Well now that's done: and I'm glad it's over."
When lovely woman stoops to folly and[1]
Paces about her room again, alone,
255 She smoothes her hair with automatic hand,
And puts a record on the gramophone.

    "This music crept by me upon the waters"[2]
And along the Strand, up Queen Victoria Street.
O City city, I can sometimes hear
260 Beside a public bar in Lower Thames Street,
The pleasant whining of a mandoline
And a clatter and a chatter from within
Where fishmen lounge at noon: where the walls
Of Magnus Martyr[3] hold
265 Inexplicable splendour of Ionian white and gold.[4]

    The river sweats[5]
    Oil and tar   *Modern*
    The barges drift   *post industrial*
    With the turning tide
270   Red sails

    Wide
    To leeward, swing on the heavy spar.
    The barges wash
    Drifting logs
275 Down Greenwich reach
    Past the Isle of Dogs.[6]
      Weialala leia   *lamentation*
      Wallala leialala[7]

    Elizabeth and Leicester[8]   *pre industrial*
280 Beating oars
    The stern was formed
    A gilded shell
    Red and gold
    The brisk swell
285 Rippled both shores
    Southwest wind
    Carried down stream
    The peal of bells
    White towers
290   Weialala leia   *R.*
      Wallala leialala

    "Trams and dusty trees.   *present*
Highbury bore me. Richmond and Kew
Undid me. By Richmond I raised my knees
295 Supine on the floor of a narrow canoe."[9]

---

[1] *When … and* Eliot's note cites Oliver Goldsmith's novel *The Vicar of Wakefield* (1762), in which Olivia, returning to the place where she was seduced, sings: "When lovely woman stoops to folly / And finds to late that men betray / What charm can soothe her melancholy, / What art can wash her guilt away? / The only art her guilt to cover, / To hide her shame from every eye, / To give repentance to her lover, / And wring his bosom—is to die."

[2] [Eliot's note] V. [I.e., "see," from the Latin *vide*.] *The Tempest*, as above.

[3] [Eliot's note] The interior of St. Magnus Martyr is to my mind one of the finest among [Sir Christopher] Wren's interiors. See *The Proposed Demolition of Nineteen City Churches* (P.S. King & Son, Ltd.).

[4] *Inexplicable … gold* Reference to the slender Ionic columns inside the church.

[5] [Eliot's note] The Song of the (three) Thames-daughters begins here. From line 292 to 306 inclusive they speak in turn. V. *Gotterdammerung*, 3.1: the Rhine-daughters. [Eliot refers to Wagner's opera *The Twilight of the Gods*, in which the Rhine maidens lament the theft of the Rhine's gold, which has also robbed the river of its beauty.]

[6] *Isle of Dogs* Peninsula formed by a bend in the river Thames. Opposite this peninsula, on the south side of the Thames, lies the London borough of Greenwich.

[7] *Weialala … leialala* In Wagner's opera, this is the ecstatic cry repeated by the maidens as they guard the lump of gold in the river.

[8] [Eliot's note] V. Froude, *Elizabeth*, Vol. 1, ch. 4, letter of De Quadra to Philip of Spain:
"In the afternoon we were in a barge, watching the games on the river. (The queen) was alone with Lord Robert and myself on the poop, when they began to talk nonsense, and went so far that Lord Robert at last said, as I was on the spot there was no reason why they should not be married if the queen pleased." [Eliot refers to *History of England from the Fall of Wolsey to the Death of Elizabeth* (1856–70), by James Anthony Froude. Froude quotes from a letter by Alvarez de Quadra, Bishop of Aquila and Spanish Ambassador to Queen Elizabeth's court. De Quadra believed the young queen would marry Lord Dudley.]

[9] *Trams and … canoe* Eliot's note cites the lines from Dante's *Purgatorio* (5.130–136) that he parodies: "Remember me, who am La Pia [Piety]; / Sienna made me and the Maremma undid me"; *Highbury* Middle-class suburb in north London; *Richmond and Kew* Areas of London located on the Thames in southwest London.

"My feet are at Moorgate,[1] and my heart
Under my feet. After the event
He wept. He promised 'a new start.'
I made no comment. What should I resent?"

300   "On Margate Sands.[2]
I can connect
Nothing with nothing.   *No meaningful conversations.*
The broken fingernails of dirty hands.
My people humble people who expect
305   Nothing."
                 la la

To Carthage then I came[3]   *St Augustine*

Burning burning burning burning[4] *b.*
O Lord Thou pluckest me out[5] *A*
310   O Lord Thou pluckest   *A*

burning *b*   *desire to give (physical).*

4. DEATH BY WATER

Phlebas the Phoenician, a fortnight dead,
Forgot the cry of gulls, and the deep sea swell
And the profit and loss.
315   A current under sea
Picked his bones in whispers. As he rose and fell
He passed the stages of his age and youth

Between them lies Kew Gardens.

[1] *Moorgate*   Area in the east of the City.

[2] *Margate Sands*   Primary beach in the Kent seaside resort of
Margate.

[3] *To Carthage ... came*   Eliot's note cites the opening of Book 3 of
The Confessions of Saint Augustine: "To Carthage then I came, where
a cauldron of unholy loves sang all about mine ears."

[4] [Eliot's note]   The complete text of the Buddha's Fire Sermon
(which corresponds in importance to the Sermon on the Mount)
from which these words are taken, will be found translated in the
late Henry Clarke Warren's *Buddhism in Translation* (Harvard
Oriental Series). Mr. Warren was one of the great pioneers of
Buddhist studies in the Occident.

[5] [Eliot's note]   From St. Augustine's *Confessions* again. The
collocation of these two representatives of eastern and western
asceticism, as the culmination of this part of the poem, is not an
accident. [Eliot refers to 10.237–38 of the Confessions: "I entangle
my steps with these outward beauties, but thou pluckest me out, O
Lord, thou pluckest me out."]

Entering the whirlpool.
                         Gentile or Jew
320   O you who turn the wheel and look to windward,
Consider Phlebas, who was once handsome and tall as
        you.

5. WHAT THE THUNDER SAID [6]

After the torchlight red on sweaty faces
After the frosty silence in the gardens
After the agony in stony places
325   The shouting and the crying
Prison and palace and reverberation
Of thunder of spring over distant mountains
He who was living is now dead[7]
We who were living are now dying   *Sybil*
330   With a little patience

        Here is no water but only rock
Rock and no water and the sandy road
The road winding above among the mountains
Which are mountains of rock without water
335   If there were water we should stop and drink
Amongst the rock one cannot stop or think
Sweat is dry and feet are in the sand
If there were only water amongst the rock
Dead mountain mouth of carious[8] teeth that cannot spit
340   Here one can neither stand nor lie nor sit
There is not even silence in the mountains
But dry sterile thunder without rain
There is not even solitude in the mountains
But red sullen faces sneer and snarl
345   From doors of mudcracked houses
                         If there were water

        And no rock
        If there were rock

[6] [Eliot's note]   In the first part of Part 5 three themes are employed: the journey to Emmaus, the approach to the Chapel Perilous
(see Miss Weston's book), and the present decay of eastern Europe.
[*journey to Emmaus* See Luke 24.13–31, in which Jesus, after being
resurrected, joins two of his disciples on the road to Emmaus, but
they do not recognize him; *Chapel Perilous* The final stage of the
Grail quest.]

[7] *After the torchlight ... dead*   References to the events from the
betrayal of Christ to His death.

[8] *carious*   Decayed.

And also water
350 And water
A spring
A pool among the rock
If there were the sound of water only
Not the cicada[1]
355 And dry grass singing
But sound of water over a rock
Where the hermit-thrush sings in the pine trees[2]
Drip drop drip drop drop drop drop
But there is no water

360 Who is the third who walks always beside you?[3]
When I count, there are only you and I together
But when I look ahead up the white road
There is always another one walking beside you
Gliding wrapt in a brown mantle, hooded
365 I do not know whether a man or a woman
—But who is that on the other side of you?

What is that sound high in the air
Murmur of maternal lamentation
Who are those hooded hordes swarming
370 Over endless plains, stumbling in cracked earth
Ringed by the flat horizon only
What is the city over the mountains
Cracks and reforms and bursts in the violet air
Falling towers

375 Jerusalem Athens Alexandria
Vienna London
Unreal[4]

A woman drew her long black hair out tight
And fiddled whisper music on those strings
380 And bats with baby faces in the violet light
Whistled, and beat their wings
And crawled head downward down a blackened wall
And upside down in air were towers
Tolling reminiscent bells, that kept the hours
385 And voices singing out of empty cisterns and exhausted
wells.

In this decayed hole among the mountains
In the faint moonlight, the grass is singing
Over the tumbled graves, about the chapel
There is the empty chapel, only the wind's home.[5]
390 It has no windows, and the door swings,
Dry bones can harm no one.
Only a cock stood on the rooftree
Co co rico co co rico[6]
In a flash of lightning. Then a damp gust
395 Bringing rain

Ganga[7] was sunken, and the limp leaves
Waited for rain, while the black clouds

---

[1] *cicada* Grasshopper. See Ecclesiastes 12.4: "Also when they shall be afraid of that which is high, and fears shall be in the way, and the almond tree shall flourish, and the grasshopper shall be a burden, and desire shall fail: because man goeth to his long home, and the mourners go about the streets."

[2] [Eliot's note] This is *Turdus aonalaschkae pallasii,* the hermit-thrush which I have heard in Quebec Province. Chapman says (*Handbook of Birds of Eastern North America*) "it is most at home in secluded woodland and thickety retreats. ... Its notes are not remarkable for variety or volume, but in purity and sweetness of tone and exquisite modulation they are unequalled." Its "water-dripping song" is justly celebrated.

[3] [Eliot's note] The following lines were stimulated by the account of one of the Antarctic expeditions (I forget which, but I think one of Shackleton's): it was related that the party of explorers, at the extremity of their strength, had the constant delusion that there was *one more member* than could actually be counted. [Eliot refers to Sir Ernest Shakleton's third journey to the Antarctic (1914–17), during which he and his men attempted to cross the Antarctic ice cap on foot. See *South: The Story of Shackleton's Last Expedition, 1914-1917* (1919).]

[4] *What is that ... unreal* Eliot's note for these lines quotes in German Herman Hesse, *Blick ins Chaos: Drei Aufsätze* (*A Glimpse into Chaos: Three Essays*). "Already half of Europe, already at least half of Eastern Europe, on the way to chaos, drives drunk in sacred infatuation along the edge of the precipice, singing drunkenly, as though singing hymns, as Dmitri Karamazov sang. The offended bourgeois laughs at the songs; the saint and the seer hear them with tears." Dmitri Karamazov is a character in Fyodor Dostoevsky's *The Brothers Karamazov* (1879–80).

[5] *There is ... home* The Chapel Perilous appeared to be surrounded by death and decay; these nightmare visions were meant to induce despair in the questing knight. Once inside the Chapel, the knight's courage would be tested with further horrors.

[6] *Only a ... rico* The crowing of the cock signals the coming of the morning and the departure of ghosts and evil spirits, as in *Hamlet* 1.1, when Hamlet's father's ghost disappears with its call. Also, in the Gospels Peter repents his repudiation of Christ after the cock crows.

[7] *Ganga* The Ganges, a sacred river in India.

Gathered far distant, over Himavant.[1]
The jungle crouched, humped in silence.
400   Then spoke the thunder
DA[2]
Datta: what have we given? ~emotional giving~
My friend, blood shaking my heart
The awful daring of a moment's surrender
405   Which an age of prudence can never retract
By this, and this only, we have existed
Which is not to be found in our obituaries   *epitaph*
Or in memories draped by the beneficent spider[3]
Or under seals broken by the lean solicitor   *officialibo*
410   In our empty rooms
DA
Dayadhvam: I have heard the key[4]
Turn in the door once and turn once only
We think of the key, each in his prison
415   Thinking of the key, each confirms a prison
Only at nightfall, aetherial rumours

Revive for a moment a broken Coriolanus[5]
DA
Damyata: The boat responded   *Contr.*
420   Gaily, to the hand expert with sail and oar
The sea was calm, your heart would have responded
Gaily, when invited, beating obedient
To controlling hands

I sat upon the shore
425   Fishing, with the arid plain behind me[6]
Shall I at least set my lands in order?[7]   *setting things in*
London Bridge is falling down falling down falling
down
Poi s'ascose nel foco che gli affina[8]   *cleansing fire*   *Shifted, now on the*
Quando fiam ceu chelidon[9]—O swallow swallow
430   *Le Prince d'Aquitaine a la tour abolie*[10]
These fragments I have shored against my ruins   *support.*

---

[1] *Himavant* Sanskrit: snowy. Adjective used to describe the Himalayas.

[2] [Eliot's note] "Datta, dayadhvam, damyata" (Give, sympathise, control). The fable of the meaning of the Thunder is found in the *Brihadaranyaka—Upanishad*, 5, 1. A translation is found in Deussen's *Sechzig Upanishads des Veda*, p. 489. [Eliot refers to the Hindu fable in which gods, men, and demons, each, in turn, ask the Lord of Creation, Prajapati, "Please instruct us, Sir." To each he utters the syllable "Da," and each group interprets the answer differently: "Damyata," practice self-control; "Datta," give alms; "Dayadhvam," have compassion. According to the fable, "This very thing is repeated even today by the heavenly voice, in the form of thunder, as 'Da,' 'Da,' 'Da,' which means: 'Control yourselves,' 'Give,' and 'Have compassion.'"]

[3] [Eliot's note] Cf. [John] Webster, *The White Devil*, 5, 6: "… they'll remarry / Ere the worm pierce your winding-sheet, ere the spider / Make a thin curtain for your epitaphs." [In this excerpt from the play, the villain Flamineo urges men never to trust their wives.]

[4] *I have … key* Eliot's note cites the passage in Dante's *Inferno* 33.46, in which Ugolino della Gherardesca remembers being locked up with his children in the tower, where they all starved to death. Eliot also quotes philosopher Francis Herbert Bradley's *Appearance and Reality: A Metaphysical Essay* (1893), p. 346: "My external sensations are no less private to myself than are my thoughts or my feelings. In either case my experience falls within my own circle, a circle closed on the outside; and, with all its elements alike, every sphere is opaque to the others which surround it.… In brief, regarded as an existence which appears in a soul, the whole world for each is peculiar and private to that soul."

[5] *Coriolanus* Roman general of Shakespeare's play of that name. A character who is motivated by pride rather than duty, Coriolanus leads the enemy against Rome, the city from which he has been exiled.

[6] *Fishing … me* Eliot's note refers readers to Weston's *From Ritual to Romance*, chapter 9, "The Fisher King." In this chapter, Weston comments upon the Fisher King's intimate relation with his people and his land, "a relation mainly dependent upon the identification of the King with the Divine principle of Life and Fertility." Weston also argues that "the Fish is a Life symbol of immemorial antiquity, and that the title of Fisher has, from the earliest ages, been associated with Deities who were held to be specially connected with the origin and preservation of life."

[7] *Shall I … order* See Isaiah 38.1, in which the prophet Isaiah counsels the sickly King Hezekiah, whose kingdom has been destroyed by the conquering Assyrians, "Thus saith the Lord, Set thine house in order: for thou shalt die, and not live."

[8] *Poi … affina* Italian: "Then he vanished into the fire that refines them" (Dante's *Purgatorio* 26.148). Eliot's note quotes, in Italian, the three lines of the *Purgatorio* immediately preceding, in which the poet Arnaut Daniel, who is in Purgatory for lust, says to Dante "Now I pray you, by the goodness that guides you to the top of the staircase [of purgatory], be mindful in time of my suffering."

[9] *Quando … chelidon* Latin: "When shall I be as the swallow?" Eliot's note cites an anonymous Latin poem about Venus and the spring, "The Vigil of Venus," as well as the story of Philomela, whose sister Procne (the wife of Tereus) was turned into a swallow. "The Vigil of Venus" refers to Philomela and Procne in its closing lines.

[10] *Le Prince … abolie* French: "The Prince of Aquitaine in the ruined tower." Eliot's note cites French poet Gerard de Nerval's sonnet "El Desdichado" (1853). One of the Tarot cards shows a tower struck by lightning.

method to madness

Why then Ile fit you. Hieronymo's mad againe.[1]
Datta. Dayadhvam. Damyata. *Control.*
Fire   Shantih \ shantih   shantih[2]
        —1922

Sympathize

Journey of the Magi [3]

"A cold coming we had of it,
        Just the worst time of the year
For a journey, and such a long journey:
The ways deep and the weather sharp,
5   The very dead of winter."[4]
And the camels galled, sore-footed, refractory,
Lying down in the melting snow.
There were times we regretted
The summer palaces on slopes, the terraces,
10 And the silken girls bringing sherbet.
Then the camel men cursing and grumbling
And running away, and wanting their liquor and
        women,
And the night-fires going out, and the lack of shelters,
And the cities hostile and the towns unfriendly
15 And the villages dirty and charging high prices:
A hard time we had of it.
At the end we preferred to travel all night,

Sleeping in snatches,
With the voices singing in our ears, saying
20 That this was all folly.

    Then at dawn we came down to a temperate valley,
Wet, below the snow line, smelling of vegetation;
With a running stream and a water-mill beating the
        darkness,
And three trees[5] on the low sky,
25 And an old white horse[6] galloped away in the meadow.
Then we came to a tavern with vine-leaves over the
        lintel,[7]
Six hands at an open door dicing for pieces of silver,[8]
And feet kicking the empty wine-skins.
But there was no information, and so we continued
30 And arrived at evening, not a moment too soon
Finding the place; it was (you may say) satisfactory.

    All this was a long time ago, I remember,
And I would do it again, but set down
This set down
35 This: were we led all that way for
Birth or Death? There was a Birth, certainly,
We had evidence and no doubt. I had seen birth and
        death,
But had thought they were different; this Birth was
Hard and bitter agony for us, like Death, our death.
40 We returned to our places, these Kingdoms,
But no longer at ease here, in the old dispensation,
With an alien people clutching their gods.
I should be glad of another death.

    —1927

---

1   *Why then ... againe*   Eliot's note cites Thomas Kyd's *The Spanish Tragedy: Hieronymo Is Mad Againe* (1592). In the play, Hieronymo, whose son has been murdered, is asked to write a play for the court. He responds "Why then Ile fit you (i.e., "I'll accommodate you," or "I'll give you your due"). He writes the play and persuades the murderers to act in it. During the course of the play, his son's murder is avenged.

2   [Eliot's note]   Shantih. Repeated as here, a formal ending to an Upanishad. "The Peace which passeth understanding" is our equivalent to this word. [The Upanishads are poetic dialogues that comment on the Vedas, the ancient Hindu Scriptures. Eliot's phrasing derives from Paul's letter to the early Christians in Philippians 4.7: "And the peace of God, which passeth all understanding, shall keep your hearts and minds through Jesus Christ."]

3   *Magi*   Three wise men who journeyed to Bethlehem to honor Jesus at His birth (see Matthew 2.1–12).

4   *A cold ... winter*   Adapted from a sermon given by Anglican preacher Lancelot Andrews on Christmas Day, 1622.

5   *three trees*   Suggests the three crosses on Calvary, on which Christ and two criminals were crucified (see Luke 23.32–43).

6   *white horse*   Ridden by Christ in Revelation 6.2 and 19.11–14.

7   *lintel*   Doorframe.

8   *dicing ... silver*   Allusion to Judas's betrayal of Jesus for thirty pieces of silver, and to the soldiers who dice for the robes of Christ at His crucifixion (Matthew 26.14 and 27.35).

Marina [1]

Quis hic locus, quae regio, quae mundi plaga? [2]

What seas what shores what grey rocks and what
    islands
What water lapping the bow
And scent of pine and the woodthrush singing
    through the fog
What images return
5   O my daughter.

    Those who sharpen the tooth of the dog, meaning
Death
Those who glitter with the glory of the humming-
    bird, meaning
Death
10 Those who sit in the stye of contentment, meaning
Death
Those who suffer the ecstasy of the animals, meaning
Death

    Are become unsubstantial, reduced by a wind,
15 A breath of pine, and the woodsong fog
By this grace dissolved in place

    What is this face, less clear and clearer
The pulse in the arm, less strong and stronger—
Given or lent? more distant than stars and nearer than
    the eye

20 Whispers and small laughter between leaves and
    hurrying feet
Under sleep, where all the waters meet.

Bowsprit [3] cracked with ice and paint cracked
    with heat.
I made this, I have forgotten
And remember.
25 The rigging weak and the canvas rotten
Between one June and another September.
Made this unknowing, half conscious, unknown, my
    own.
The garboard strake [4] leaks, the seams need caulking.
This form, this face, this life
30 Living to live in a world of time beyond me; let me
Resign my life for this life, my speech for that
    unspoken,
The awakened, lips parted, the hope, the new ships.

    What seas what shores what granite islands
    towards my timbers
And woodthrush calling through the fog
My daughter.
—1930

Burnt Norton

τοῦ λόλου δ' ἐόντος ξυνοῦ ζώουσιν οἱ πολλοί
ὡς ἰδίαν ἔχοντες φρόνησιν.

1. p. 77. Fr. 2

ὁδὸς ἄνω κάτω μία καὶ ὠυτή.

1. p. 89. Fr. 60

Diels: *Die Fragmente der der Vorsokratiker (Herakleitos).* [5]

---

[1] *Marina* In Shakespeare's *Pericles*, the daughter of the title character. She is born during a storm at sea and her mother dies giving birth to her. Pericles gives her to the governor of Tarsus and his wife to raise. Through a series of plot twists, Marina is believed, by age sixteen, to have died. Pericles, maddened by grief, becomes a wanderer. During his travels he finds Marina and they are restored to one another.

[2] *Quis hic ... plaga* Latin: "What place is this, what region, what corner of the world?" Spoken by Hercules in Seneca's *Hercules Furens (The Mad Hercules)* after he regains his senses following a period of madness during which he murders his children and wife.

[3] *Bowsprit* Large spar projecting from the front of a boat.

[4] *garboard strake* Thick wooden plank forming a ridge along the keel of a boat.

[5] *Burnt Norton* Name of a large country house in Gloucestershire, England, that was built on the site of an earlier home that had burned down in the seventeenth century. Eliot visited the home in 1934. This poem was first published in 1935, and then republished in 1943 as one of the *Four Quartets*. Eliot modeled the structure of this long poem on one of Beethoven's final quartets, particularly the A Minor Quartet (Beethoven's last), which Eliot found "quite inexhaustible to study. There is some sort of heavenly or at least more than human gaiety about some of his later things which one imagines must come to oneself as the fruit of reconciliation and relief after immense suffering; I should like to get something of that into verse before I die." The epigraphs are from the writings of sixth-century BCE philosopher Heraclites: τοῦ ... φρόνησιν Greek: "Although the Word governs all things, most people live as though they had wisdom of their own." ὁδὸς ... ὠυτή Greek: "The way up and the way down are the same."

1

Time present and time past
Are both perhaps present in time future,
And time future contained in time past.
If all time is eternally present
5 All time is unredeemable.
What might have been is an abstraction
Remaining a perpetual possibility
Only in a world of speculation.
What might have been and what has been
10 Point to one end, which is always present.
Footfalls echo in the memory
Down the passage which we did not take
Towards the door we never opened
Into the rose-garden. My words echo
15 Thus, in your mind.
           But to what purpose
Disturbing the dust on a bowl of rose-leaves
I do not know.
           Other echoes
20 Inhabit the garden. Shall we follow?
Quick, said the bird, find them, find them,
Round the corner. Through the first gate,
Into our first world, shall we follow
The deception of the thrush? Into our first world.
25 There they were, dignified, invisible,
Moving without pressure, over the dead leaves,
In the autumn heat, through the vibrant air,
And the bird called, in response to
The unheard music hidden in the shrubbery,
30 And the unseen eyebeam crossed, for the roses
Had the look of flowers that are looked at.
There they were as our guests, accepted and accepting.
So we moved, and they, in a formal pattern,
Along the empty alley, into the box circle,
35 To look down into the drained pool.
Dry the pool, dry concrete, brown edged,
And the pool was filled with water out of sunlight,
And the lotos[1] rose, quietly, quietly,
The surface glittered out of heart of light,
40 And they were behind us, reflected in the pool.
Then a cloud passed, and the pool was empty.
Go, said the bird, for the leaves were full of children,
Hidden excitedly, containing laughter.

Go, go, go, said the bird: human kind
45 Cannot bear very much reality.
Time past and time future
What might have been and what has been
Point to one end, which is always present.

2

Garlic and sapphires in the mud
50 Clot the bedded axle-tree.
The trilling wire in the blood
Sings below inveterate scars
And reconciles forgotten wars.
The dance along the artery
55 The circulation of the lymph
Are figured in the drift of stars
Ascend to summer in the tree
We move above the moving tree
In light upon the figured leaf
60 And hear upon the sodden floor
Below, the boarhound and the boar
Pursue their pattern as before
But reconciled among the stars.

      At the still point of the turning world. Neither
        flesh nor fleshless;
65 Neither from nor towards; at the still point, there the
      dance is,
But neither arrest nor movement. And do not call it
      fixity,
Where past and future are gathered. Neither
      movement from nor towards,
Neither ascent nor decline. Except for the point, the
      still point,
There would be no dance, and there is only the dance.
70 I can only say, *there* we have been: but I cannot say where.
And I cannot say, how long, for that is to place it in time.

      The inner freedom from the practical desire,
      The release from action and suffering, release from the
      inner
And the outer compulsion, yet surrounded
75 By a grace of sense, a white light still and moving,
Erhebung[2] without motion, concentration

---

[1] *lotos* Plant whose flowers, according to Greek myth, produced
dreamy forgetfulness in those who ate them.

[2] *Erhebung* German: lifting up. Term used by the German
philosopher Georg Wilhelm Friedrich Hegel (1770–1831) to denote
a new level of understanding.

Without elimination, both a new world
And the old made explicit, understood
In the completion of its partial ecstasy,
80   The resolution of its partial horror.
Yet the enchainment of past and future
Woven in the weakness of the changing body,
Protects mankind from heaven and damnation
Which flesh cannot endure.
85   Time past and time future
Allow but a little consciousness.
To be conscious is not to be in time
But only in time can the moment in the rose-garden,
The moment in the arbour where the rain beat,
90   The moment in the draughty church at smokefall
Be remembered; involved with past and future.
Only through time time is conquered.

3

Here is a place of disaffection
Time before and time after
95   In a dim light: neither daylight
Investing form with lucid stillness
Turning shadow into transient beauty
With slow rotation suggesting permanence
Nor darkness to purify the soul
100   Emptying the sensual with deprivation
Cleansing affection from the temporal.
Neither plenitude nor vacancy. Only a flicker
Over the strained time-ridden faces
Distracted from distraction by distraction
105   Filled with fancies and empty of meaning
Tumid apathy with no concentration
Men and bits of paper, whirled by the cold wind
That blows before and after time,
Wind in and out of unwholesome lungs
110   Time before and time after.
Eructation° of unhealthy souls   belching
Into the faded air, the torpid
Driven on the wind that sweeps the gloomy hills of
        London,
Hampstead and Clerkenwell, Campden and Putney,
115   Highgate, Primrose and Ludgate. Not here
Not here the darkness, in this twittering world.

Descend lower, descend only
Into the world of perpetual solitude,
World not world, but that which is not world,

120   Internal darkness, deprivation
And destitution of all property,
Desiccation of the world of sense,
Evacuation of the world of fancy,
Inoperancy of the world of spirit;
125   This is the one way, and the other
Is the same, not in movement
But abstention from movement; while the world moves
In appetency,[1] on its metalled ways
Of time past and time future.

4

130   Time and the bell have buried the day,
The black cloud carries the sun away.
Will the sunflower turn to us, will the clematis[2]
Stray down, bend to us; tendril and spray
Clutch and cling?
135   Chill
Fingers of yew be curled
Down on us? After the kingfisher's wing
Has answered light to light, and is silent, the light is still
At the still point of the turning world.

5

140   Words move, music moves
Only in time; but that which is only living
Can only die. Words, after speech, reach
Into the silence. Only by the form, the pattern,
Can words or music reach
145   The stillness, as a Chinese jar still
Moves perpetually in its stillness.
Not the stillness of the violin, while the note lasts,
Not that only, but the co-existence,
Or say that the end precedes the beginning,
150   And the end and the beginning were always there
Before the beginning and after the end.
And all is always now. Words strain,
Crack and sometimes break, under the burden,
Under the tension, slip, slide, perish,
155   Decay with imprecision, will not stay in place,
Will not stay still. Shrieking voices
Scolding, mocking, or merely chattering,
Always assail them. The Word in the desert
Is most attacked by voices of temptation,

---

[1]   *appetency* Instinctive inclination.
[2]   *clematis* Type of twining shrub.

160 The crying shadow in the funeral dance,
The loud lament of the disconsolate chimera.[1]

The detail of the pattern is movement,
As in the figure of the ten stairs.[2]
Desire itself is movement
165 Not in itself desirable;
Love is itself unmoving,
Only the cause and end of movement,
Timeless, and undesiring
Except in the aspect of time
170 Caught in the form of limitation
Between un-being and being.
Sudden in a shaft of sunlight
Even while the dust moves
There rises the hidden laughter
175 Of children in the foliage
Quick now, here, now, always—
Ridiculous the waste sad time
Stretching before and after.
—1935, 1943

Tradition and the Individual Talent

I

In English writing we seldom speak of tradition, though we occasionally apply its name in deploring its absence. We cannot refer to "the tradition" or to "a tradition"; at most, we employ the adjective in saying that the poetry of So-and-so is "traditional" or even "too traditional." Seldom, perhaps, does the word appear except in a phrase of censure. If otherwise, it is vaguely approbative, with the implication, as to the work approved, of some pleasing archaeological reconstruction. You can hardly make the word agreeable to English ears without this comfortable reference to the reassuring science of archaeology.

Certainly the word is not likely to appear in our appreciations of living or dead writers. Every nation, every race, has not only its own creative, but its own critical turn of mind; and is even more oblivious of the shortcomings and limitations of its critical habits than of those of its creative genius. We know, or think we know, from the enormous mass of critical writing that has appeared in the French language, the critical method or habit of the French; we only conclude (we are such unconscious people) that the French are "more critical than we," and sometimes even plume ourselves a little with the fact, as if the French were the less spontaneous. Perhaps they are; but we might remind ourselves that criticism is as inevitable as breathing, and that we should be none the worse for articulating what passes in our minds when we read a book and feel an emotion about it, for criticizing our own minds in their work of criticism. One of the facts that might come to light in this process is our tendency to insist, when we praise a poet, upon those aspects of his work in which he least resembles anyone else. In these aspects or parts of his work we pretend to find what is individual, what is the peculiar essence of the man. We dwell with satisfaction upon the poet's difference from his predecessors, especially his immediate predecessors; we endeavour to find something that can be isolated in order to be enjoyed. Whereas if we approach a poet without this prejudice we shall often find that not only the best, but the most individual parts of his work may be those in which the dead poets, his ancestors, assert their immortality most vigorously. And I do not mean the impressionable period of adolescence, but the period of full maturity.

Yet if the only form of tradition, of handing down, consisted in following the ways of the immediate generation before us in a blind or timid adherence to its successes, "tradition" should positively be discouraged. We have seen many such simple currents soon lost in the sand; and novelty is better than repetition. Tradition is a matter of much wider significance. It cannot be inherited, and if you want it you must obtain it by great labour. It involves, in the first place, the historical sense, which we may call nearly indispensable to anyone who would continue to be a poet beyond his twenty-fifth year; and the historical sense involves a perception, not only of the pastness of the past, but of its presence; the historical sense compels a man to write not merely with his own generation in his bones, but with a feeling that

---

[1] *chimera*   Fire-breathing monster of Greek mythology that was usually represented as part goat, part lion, and part serpent. Hence, any fantastic monster of disparate parts or fanciful illusion.

[2] *ten stairs*   According to Spanish poet and mystic St. John of the Cross (1542–91), there are ten steps on the mystical ladder of divine love.

the whole of the literature of Europe from Homer[1] and within it the whole of the literature of his own country has a simultaneous existence and composes a simultaneous order. This historical sense, which is a sense of the timeless as well as of the temporal and of the timeless and of the temporal together, is what makes a writer traditional. And it is at the same time what makes a writer most acutely conscious of his place in time, of his own contemporaneity.

No poet, no artist of any art, has his complete meaning alone. His significance, his appreciation is the appreciation of his relation to the dead poets and artists. You cannot value him alone; you must set him, for contrast and comparison, among the dead. I mean this as a principle of aesthetic, not merely historical, criticism. The necessity that he shall conform, that he shall cohere, is not one-sided; what happens when a new work of art is created is something that happens simultaneously to all the works of art which preceded it. The existing monuments form an ideal order among themselves, which is modified by the introduction of the new (the really new) work of art among them. The existing order is complete before the new work arrives; for order to persist after the supervention of novelty, the *whole* existing order must be, if ever so slightly, altered; and so the relations, proportions, values of each work of art toward the whole are readjusted; and this is conformity between the old and the new. Whoever has approved this idea of order, of the form of European, of English literature will not find it preposterous that the past should be altered by the present as much as the present is directed by the past. And the poet who is aware of this will be aware of great difficulties and responsibilities.

In a peculiar sense he will be aware also that he must inevitably be judged by the standards of the past. I say judged, not amputated, by them; not judged to be as good as, or worse or better than, the dead; and certainly not judged by the canons of dead critics. It is a judgement, a comparison, in which two things are measured by each other. To conform merely would be for the new work not really to conform at all; it would not be new, and would therefore not be a work of art. And we do not quite say that the new is more valuable because it fits in; but its fitting in is a test of its value—a test, it is

true, which can only be slowly and cautiously applied, for we are none of us infallible judges of conformity. We say: it appears to conform, and is perhaps individual, or it appears individual, and may conform; but we are hardly likely to find that it is one and not the other.

To proceed to a more intelligible exposition of the relation of the poet to the past: he can neither take the past as a lump, an indiscriminate bolus,[2] nor can he form himself wholly on one or two private admirations, nor can he form himself wholly upon one preferred period. The first course is inadmissible, the second is an important experience of youth, and the third is a pleasant and highly desirable supplement. The poet must be very conscious of the main current, which does not at all flow invariably through the most distinguished reputations. He must be quite aware of the obvious fact that art never improves, but that the material of art is never quite the same. He must be aware that the mind of Europe—the mind of his own country—a mind which he learns in time to be much more important than his own private mind—is a mind which changes, and that this change is a development which abandons nothing *en route*, which does not superannuate either Shakespeare, or Homer, or the rock drawing of the Magdalenian draughtsmen.[3] That this development, refinement perhaps, complication certainly, is not, from the point of view of the artist, any improvement. Perhaps not even an improvement from the point of view of the psychologist or not to the extent which we imagine; perhaps only in the end based upon a complication in economics and machinery. But the difference between the present and the past is that the conscious present is an awareness of the past in a way and to an extent which the past's awareness of itself cannot show.

Someone said: "The dead writers are remote from us because we *know* so much more than they did." Precisely, and they are that which we know.

I am alive to a usual objection to what is clearly part of my programme for the *métier* of poetry. The objection is that the doctrine requires a ridiculous amount of erudition (pedantry), a claim which can be rejected by appeal to the lives of poets in any pantheon. It will even be affirmed that much learning deadens or perverts

[1] *Homer* Greek poet (c. 700 BCE), author of the *Iliad* and the *Odyssey*.

[2] *bolus* Round mass.

[3] *Magdalenian draughtsmen* Magdalenian cave paintings of the Paleolithic period are among the first known works of art.

poetic sensibility. While, however, we persist in believing that a poet ought to know as much as will not encroach upon his necessary receptivity and necessary laziness, it is not desirable to confine knowledge to whatever can be put into a useful shape for examinations, drawing rooms, or the still more pretentious modes of publicity. Some can absorb knowledge, the more tardy must sweat for it. Shakespeare acquired more essential history from Plutarch[1] than most men could from the whole British Museum. What is to be insisted upon is that the poet must develop or procure the consciousness of the past and that he should continue to develop this consciousness throughout his career.

What happens is a continual surrender of himself as he is at the moment to something which is more valuable. The progress of an artist is a continual self-sacrifice, a continual extinction of personality.

There remains to define this process of depersonalization and its relation to the sense of tradition. It is in this depersonalization that art may be said to approach the condition of science. I therefore invite you to consider, as a suggestive analogy, the action which takes place when a bit of finely filiated[2] platinum is introduced into a chamber containing oxygen and sulphur dioxide.

2

Honest criticism and sensitive appreciation is directed not upon the poet but upon the poetry. If we attend to the confused cries of the newspaper critics and the susurrus[3] of popular repetition that follows, we shall hear the names of poets in great numbers; if we seek not Blue-book[4] knowledge but the enjoyment of poetry, and ask for a poem, we shall seldom find it. I have tried to point out the importance of the relation of the poem to other poems by other authors, and suggested the conception of poetry as a living whole of all the poetry that has ever been written. The other aspect of this Impersonal theory of poetry is the relation of the poem to its author. And I hinted, by an analogy, that the mind of the mature poet differs from that of the immature one not precisely in any valuation of "personality," not being necessarily more interesting, or having "more to say," but rather by being a more finely perfected medium in which special, or very varied, feelings are at liberty to enter into new combinations.

The analogy was that of the catalyst. When the two gases previously mentioned are mixed in the presence of a filament of platinum, they form sulphurous acid. This combination takes place only if the platinum is present; nevertheless, the newly formed acid contains no trace of platinum, and the platinum itself is apparently unaffected: has remained inert, neutral, and unchanged. The mind of the poet is the shred of platinum. It may partly or exclusively operate upon the experience of the man himself; but, the more perfect the artist, the more completely separate in him will be the man who suffers and the mind which creates; the more perfectly will the mind digest and transmute the passions which are its material.

The experience, you will notice, the elements which enter the presence of the transforming catalyst, are of two kinds: emotions and feelings. The effect of a work of art upon the person who enjoys it is an experience different in kind from any experience not of art. It may be formed out of one emotion, or may be a combination of several; and various feelings, inhering for the writer in particular words or phrases or images, may be added to compose the final result. Or great poetry may be made without the direct use of any emotion whatever: composed out of feelings solely. Canto XV of the *Inferno*[5] (Brunetto Latini) is a working up of the emotion evident in the situation; but the effect, though single as that of any work of art, is obtained by considerable complexity of detail. The last quatrain gives an image, a feeling attaching to an image, which "came," which did not develop simply out of what precedes, but which was probably in suspension in the poet's mind until the proper combination arrived for it to add itself to. The poet's mind is in fact a receptacle for seizing and storing up numberless feelings, phrases, images, which remain there until all the particles which can unite to form a new compound are present together.

---

[1] *Plutarch* Greek biographer of the first century CE who a strong influence on English literature; Shakespeare drew some of his characters in plays such as *Coriolanus, Antony and Cleopatra*, and *Julius Caesar* from Plutarch's biographies.

[2] *filiated* Made into filament, or fine thread.

[3] *susurrus* Whispering or muttering.

[4] *Blue-book* Official reports of the British Government.

---

[5] *Canto XV of the Inferno* In this canto, Dante meets an old acquaintance, Brunetto Latini, who is in Hell for being a Sodomite.

If you compare several representative passages of the greatest poetry you see how great is the variety of types of combination, and also how completely any semi-ethical criterion of "sublimity" misses the mark. For it is not the "greatness," the intensity, of the emotions, the components, but the intensity of the artistic process, the pressure, so to speak, under which the fusion takes place, that counts. The episode of Paolo and Francesca[1] employs a definite emotion, but the intensity of the poetry is something quite different from whatever intensity in the supposed experience it may give the impression of. It is no more intense, furthermore, than Canto XXVI, the voyage of Ulysses, which has not the direct dependence upon an emotion. Great variety is possible in the process of transmutation of emotion: the murder of Agamemnon,[2] or the agony of Othello,[3] gives an artistic effect apparently closer to a possible original than the scenes from Dante. In the *Agamemnon,* the artistic emotion approximates to the emotion of an actual spectator; in *Othello* to the emotion of the protagonist himself. But the difference between art and the event is always absolute; the combination which is the murder of Agamemnon is probably as complex as that which is the voyage of Ulysses. In either case there has been a fusion of elements. The ode of Keats contains a number of feelings which have nothing particular to do with the nightingale, but which the nightingale, partly perhaps because of its attractive name, and partly because of its reputation, served to bring together.

The point of view which I am struggling to attack is perhaps related to the metaphysical theory of the substantial unity of the soul: for my meaning is, that the poet has, not a "personality" to express, but a particular medium, which is only a medium and not a personality, in which impressions and experiences combine in peculiar and unexpected ways. Impressions and experiences which are important for the man may take no place in the poetry, and those which become important

in the poetry may play quite a negligible part in the man, the personality.

I will quote a passage which is unfamiliar enough to be regarded with fresh attention in the light—or darkness—of these observations:

> And now methinks I could e'en chide myself
> For doting on her beauty, though her death
> Shall be revenged after no common action.
> Does the silkworm expend her yellow labours
> For thee? For thee does she undo herself?
> Are lordships sold to maintain ladyships
> For the poor benefit of a bewildering minute?
> Why does yon fellow falsify highways,
> And put his life between the judge's lips,
> To refine such a thing—keeps horse and men
> To beat their valours for her?...[4]

In this passage (as is evident if it is taken in its context) there is a combination of positive and negative emotions: an intensely strong attraction toward beauty and an equally intense fascination by the ugliness which is contrasted with it and which destroys it. This balance of contrasted emotion is in the dramatic situation to which the speech is pertinent, but that situation alone is inadequate to it. This is, so to speak, the structural emotion, provided by the drama. But the whole effect, the dominant tone, is due to the fact that a number of floating feelings, having an affinity to this emotion by no means superficially evident, have combined with it to give us a new art emotion.

It is not in his personal emotions, the emotions provoked by particular events in his life, that the poet is in anyway remarkable or interesting. His particular emotions may be simple, or crude, or flat. The emotion in his poetry will be a very complex thing, but not with the complexity of the emotions of people who have very complex or unusual emotions in life. One error, in fact, of eccentricity in poetry is to seek for new human emotions to express; and in this search for novelty in the wrong place it discovers the perverse. The business of the poet is not to find new emotions, but to use the ordinary ones and, in working them up into poetry, to express feelings which are not in actual emotions at all.

---

[1] *episode of Paolo and Francesca* Two illicit lovers (Paolo is Francesca's husband's brother).

[2] *murder of Agamemnon* In Aeschylus's play, Clytemnestra kills her husband Agamemnon after he sacrifices their daughter to the god Artemis.

[3] *agony of Othello* In the play by Shakespeare, Othello mistakenly thinks that his wife is unfaithful, kills her, and then, upon learning the truth, commits suicide.

[4] *And now ... for her* From *The Revenger's Tragedy* (1607), a play variously ascribed to Cyril Tourneur and to Thomas Middleton.

And emotions which he has never experienced will serve his turn as well as those familiar to him. Consequently, we must believe that "emotion recollected in tranquillity"[1] is an inexact formula. For it is neither emotion, nor recollection, nor, without distortion of meaning, tranquillity. It is a concentration, and a new thing resulting from the concentration, of a very great number of experiences which to the practical and active person would not seem to be experiences at all; it is a concentration which does not happen consciously or of deliberation. These experiences are not "recollected," and they finally unite in an atmosphere which is "tranquil" only in that it is a passive attending upon the event. Of course this is not quite the whole story. There is a great deal, in the writing of poetry, which must be conscious and deliberate. In fact, the bad poet is usually unconscious where he ought to be conscious, and conscious where he ought to be unconscious. Both errors tend to make him "personal." Poetry is not a turning loose of emotion, but an escape from emotion; it is not the expression of personality, but an escape from personality. But, of course, only those who have personality and emotions know what it means to want to escape from these things.

3

ὁ δὲ νοῦς ἴσως θειότερόν τι καὶ ἀπαθές ἐστιν[2]

This essay proposes to halt at the frontier of metaphysics or mysticism, and confine itself to such practical conclusions as can be applied by the responsible person interested in poetry. To divert interest from the poet to the poetry is a laudable aim: for it would conduce to a juster estimation of actual poetry, good and bad. There are many people who appreciate the expression of sincere emotion in verse, and there is a smaller number of people who can appreciate technical excellence. But very

few know when there is an expression of *significant* emotion, emotion which has its life in the poem and not in the history of the poet. The emotion of art is impersonal. And the poet cannot reach this impersonality without surrendering himself wholly to the work to be done. And he is not likely to know what is to be done unless he lives in what is not merely the present, but the present moment of the past, unless he is conscious, not of what is dead, but of what is already living.

—1919

The Metaphysical Poets [3]

By collecting these poems from the work of a generation more often named than read, and more often read than profitably studied, Professor Grierson has rendered a service of some importance. Certainly the reader will meet with many poems already preserved in other anthologies, at the same time that he discovers poems such as those of Aurelian Townshend or Lord Herbert of Cherbury here included. But the function of such an anthology as this is neither that of Professor Saintsbury's admirable edition of Caroline poets nor that of *The Oxford Book of English Verse*. Mr. Grierson's book is in itself a piece of criticism, and a provocation of criticism; and we think that he was right in including so many poems of Donne, elsewhere (though not in many editions) accessible, as documents in the case of "metaphysical poetry." The phrase has long done duty as a term of abuse, or as the label of a quaint and pleasant taste. The question is to what extent the so-called metaphysicals formed a school (in our own time we should say a "movement"), and how far this so-called school or movement is a digression from the main current.

Not only is it extremely difficult to define metaphysical poetry, but difficult to decide what poets practise it and in which of their verses. The poetry of Donne (to whom Marvell and Bishop King are sometimes nearer than any of the other authors) is late Elizabethan, its feeling often very close to that of Chapman. The "courtly" poetry is derivative from Jonson, who bor-

---

[1] *"emotion... tranquillity"* From William Wordsworth's Preface to *Lyrical Ballads* (1800): "Poetry is the spontaneous overflow of powerful feelings: it takes its origin from emotion recollected in tranquillity: the emotion is contemplated till by a species of reaction the tranquillity gradually disappears, and an emotion, kindred to that which was before the subject of contemplation, is gradually produced, and does itself actually exist in the mind."

[2] ὁ δὲ ... ἐστιν Greek: "The mind is doubtless something more divine and unaffected." From Aristotle's *De Anima* (Latin: On the Soul) 1.4.

[3] *The Metaphysical Poets* Originally published in the *Times Literary Supplement* as a review of the Clarendon Press volume *Metaphysical Lyrics and Poems of the Seventeenth Century: Donne to Butler* (1921), edited by Herbert J.C. Grierson.

rowed liberally from the Latin; it expires in the next century with the sentiment and witticism of Prior. There is finally the devotional verse of Herbert, Vaughan, and Crashaw (echoed long after by Christina Rossetti and Francis Thompson); Crashaw, sometimes more profound and less sectarian than the others, has a quality which returns through the Elizabethan period to the early Italians. It is difficult to find any precise use of metaphor, simile, or other conceit, which is common to all the poets and at the same time important enough as an element of style to isolate these poets as a group. Donne, and often Cowley, employ a device which is sometimes considered characteristically "metaphysical"; the elaboration (contrasted with the condensation) of a figure of speech to the furthest stage to which ingenuity can carry it. Thus Cowley develops the commonplace comparison of the world to a chess-board through long stanzas ("To Destiny"),[1] and Donne, with more grace, in "A Valediction,"[2] the comparison of two lovers to a pair of compasses. But elsewhere we find, instead of the mere explication of the content of a comparison, a development by rapid association of thought which requires considerable agility on the part of the reader.

> On a round ball
> A workeman that hath copies by, can lay
> An Europe, Afrique, and an Asia,
> And quickly make that, which was nothing, All,
> So doth each teare,
> Which thee doth weare,
> A globe, yea world by that impression grow,
> Till thy tears mixt with mine doe overflow
> This world, by waters sent from thee, my heaven
> dissolved so.[3]

Here we find at least two connexions which are not implicit in the first figure, but are forced upon it by the poet: from the geographer's globe to the tear, and the tear to the deluge. On the other hand, some of Donne's most successful and characteristic effects are secured by brief words and sudden contrasts:

> A bracelet of bright hair about the bone,[4]

where the most powerful effect is produced by the sudden contrast of associations of "bright hair" and of "bone." This telescoping of images and multiplied associations is characteristic of the phrase of some of the dramatists of the period which Donne knew: not to mention Shakespeare, it is frequent in Middleton, Webster, and Tourneur, and is one of the sources of the vitality of their language.

Johnson, who employed the term "metaphysical poets," apparently having Donne, Cleveland, and Cowley chiefly in mind, remarks of them that "the most heterogeneous ideas are yoked by violence together."[5] The force of this impeachment lies in the failure of the conjunction, the fact that often the ideas are yoked but not united; and if we are to judge of styles of poetry by their abuse, enough examples may be found in Cleveland to justify Johnson's condemnation. But a degree of heterogeneity of material compelled into unity by the operation of the poet's mind is omnipresent in poetry. We need not select for illustration such a line as

> Notre ame est un trois-mats cherchant son Icarie;[6]

we may find it in some of the best lines of Johnson himself (*The Vanity of Human Wishes*):

> His fate was destined to a barren strand,
> A petty fortress, and a dubious hand;
> He left a name at which the world grew pale,
> To point a moral, or adorn a tale—

where the effect is due to a contrast of ideas, different in degree but the same in principle, as that which Johnson mildly reprehended. And in one of the finest poems of the age (a poem which could not have been written in any other age), the *Exequy* of Bishop King, the extended comparison is used with perfect success: the idea and the simile become one, in the passage in which the Bishop illustrates his impatience to see his dead wife, under the figure of a journey:

---

[1]   *"To Destiny"*   Abraham Cowley's "Destiny" (1656).

[2]   *"A Valediction"*   Donne's poem "A Valediction: Forbidding Mourning" (1633).

[3]   *On a round ... dissolved so*   From Donne's "A Valediction: Of Weeping," 10–18.

[4]   *A bracelet ... bone*   From "The Relic" (1633), 6.

[5]   *"the most ... together"*   Samuel Johnson in his "Life of Cowley" (1779).

[6]   *Notre ... Icarie*   French: "Our soul is a three-masted ship seeking its Icarie." From Charles Baudelaire's *Le Voyage*.

Stay for me there; I will not faile
To meet thee in that hollow Vale.
And think not much of my delay;
I am already on the way,
And follow thee with all the speed
Desire can make, or sorrows breed.
Each minute is a short degree,
And ev'ry houre a step towards thee.
At night when I betake to rest,
Next morn I rise nearer my West
Of life, almost by eight houres sail,
Than when sleep breath'd his drowsy gale. . . .
But heark! My Pulse, like a soft Drum
Beats my approach, tells Thee *I come;*
And slow howere my marches be,
I shall at last sit down by Thee.

(In the last few lines there is that effect of terror which is several times attained by one of Bishop King's admirers, Edgar Poe.) Again, we may justly take these quatrains from Lord Herbert's "Ode,"[1] stanzas which would, we think, be immediately pronounced to be of the metaphysical school:

So when from hence we shall be gone,
And be no more, nor you, nor I,
As one another's mystery,
Each shall be both, yet both but one.

This said, in her up-lifted face,
Her eyes, which did that beauty crown,
Were like two starrs, that having faln down,
Look up again to find their place:

While such a moveless silent peace
Did seize on their becalmed sense,
One would have thought some influence
Their ravished spirits did possess.

There is nothing in these lines (with the possible exception of the stars, a simile not at once grasped, but lovely and justified) which fits Johnson's general observations on the metaphysical poets in his essay on Cowley. A good deal resides in the richness of association which is at the same time borrowed from and given to the word

"becalmed"; but the meaning is clear, the language simple and elegant. It is to be observed that the language of these poets is as a rule simple and pure; in the verse of George Herbert this simplicity is carried as far as it can go—a simplicity emulated without success by numerous modern poets. The *structure* of the sentences, on the other hand, is sometimes far from simple, but this is not a vice; it is a fidelity to thought and feeling. The effect, at its best, is far less artificial than that of an ode by Gray. And as this fidelity induces variety of thought and feeling, so it induces variety of music. We doubt whether, in the eighteenth century, could be found two poems in nominally the same metre, so dissimilar as Marvell's "Coy Mistress" and Crashaw's "Saint Teresa"; the one producing an effect of great speed by the use of short syllables, and the other an ecclesiastical solemnity by the use of long ones:

Love, thou art absolute sole lord
Of life and death.

If so shrewd and sensitive (though so limited) a critic as Johnson failed to define metaphysical poetry by its faults, it is worthwhile to inquire whether we may not have more success by adopting the opposite method: by assuming that the poets of the seventeenth century (up to the Revolution)[2] were the direct and normal development of the precedent age; and, without prejudicing their case by the adjective "metaphysical," consider whether their virtue was not something permanently valuable, which subsequently disappeared, but ought not to have disappeared. Johnson has hit, perhaps by accident, on one of their peculiarities, when he observes that "their attempts were always analytic"; he would not agree that, after the dissociation, they put the material together again in a new unity.

It is certain that the dramatic verse of the later Elizabethan and early Jacobean poets expresses a degree of development of sensibility which is not found in any of the prose, good as it often is. If we except Marlowe, a man of prodigious intelligence, these dramatists were directly or indirectly (it is at least a tenable theory) affected by Montaigne. Even if we except also Jonson and Chapman, these two were notably erudite, and were notably men who incorporated their erudition into their

---

[1] *Lord Herbert's "Ode"* Edward Herbert, Lord Cherbury's "An Ode Upon a Question Moved, Whether Love Should Continue Forever?" (1664).

[2] *Revolution* I.e., the English Revolution, 1640–60.

sensibility: their mode of feeling was directly and freshly altered by their reading and thought. In Chapman especially there is a direct sensuous apprehension of thought, or a re-creation of thought into feeling, which is exactly what we find in Donne:

> in this one thing, all the discipline
> Of manners and of manhood is contained;
> A man to join himself with th' Universe
> In his main sway, and make in all things fit
> One with that All, and go on, round as it;
> Not plucking from the whole his wretched part,
> And into straits, or into nought revert,
> Wishing the complete Universe might be
> Subject to such a rag of it as he;
> But to consider great Necessity.[1]

We compare this with some modern passage:

> No, when the fight begins within himself,
> A man's worth something. God stoops o'er his head
> Satan looks up between his feet—both tug—
> He's left, himself, i' the middle; the soul wakes
> And grows. Prolong that battle through his life![2]

It is perhaps somewhat less fair, though very tempting (as both poets are concerned with the perpetuation of love by offspring), to compare with the stanzas already quoted from Lord Herbert's "Ode" the following from Tennyson:

> One walked between his wife and child,
> With measured footfall firm and mild,
> And now and then he gravely smiled.
>
> The prudent partner of his blood
> Leaned on him, faithful, gentle,
> Wearing the rose of womanhood.
>
> And in their double love secure,
> The little maiden walked demure,
> Pacing with downward eyelids pure.

> These three made unity so sweet,
> My frozen heart began to beat,
> Remembering its ancient beat.[3]

The difference is not a simple difference of degree between poets. It is something which had happened to the mind of England between the time of Donne or Lord Herbert of Cherbury and the time of Tennyson and Browning; it is the difference between the intellectual poet and the reflective poet. Tennyson and Browning are poets, and they think; but they do not feel their thought as immediately as the odour of a rose. A thought to Donne was an experience; it modified his sensibility. When a poet's mind is perfectly equipped for its work, it is constantly amalgamating disparate experience; the ordinary man's experience is chaotic, irregular, fragmentary. The latter falls in love, or reads Spinoza, and these two experiences have nothing to do with each other, or with the noise of the typewriter or the smell of cooking; in the mind of the poet these experiences are always forming new wholes.

We may express the difference by the following theory: The poets of the seventeenth century, the successors of the dramatists of the sixteenth, possessed a mechanism of sensibility which could devour any kind of experience. They are simple, artificial, difficult, or fantastic, as their predecessors were; no less nor more than Dante, Guido Cavalcanti, Guinicelli, or Cino. In the seventeenth century a dissociation of sensibility set in, from which we have never recovered; and this dissociation, as is natural, was aggravated by the influence of the two most powerful poets of the century, Milton and Dryden. Each of these men performed certain poetic functions so magnificently well that the magnitude of the effect concealed the absence of others. The language went on and in some respects improved; the best verse of Collins, Gray, Johnson, and even Goldsmith satisfies some of our fastidious demands better than that of Donne or Marvell or King. But while the language became more refined, the feeling became more crude. The feeling, the sensibility, expressed in the "Country Churchyard"[4] (to say nothing of Tennyson and

---

[1] in this one ... Necessity From The Revenge of Bussy d'Ambois (1613), 4.1.

[2] No ... life From Robert Browning's "Bishop Blougram's Apology" (1855), 693–97.

[3] One walked ... beat From "The Two Voices" (1833,) 412–33.

[4] "Country Churchyard" "Elegy Written in a Country Church-Yard," by Thomas Gray (1716–71).

Browning) is cruder than that in the "Coy Mistress."[1]

The second effect of the influence of Milton and Dryden followed from the first, and was therefore slow in manifestation. The sentimental age began early in the eighteenth century, and continued. The poets revolted against the ratiocinative, the descriptive; they thought and felt by fits, unbalanced; they reflected. In one or two passages of Shelley's "Triumph of Life," in the second *Hyperion*,[2] there are traces of a struggle toward unification of sensibility. But Keats and Shelley died, and Tennyson and Browning ruminated.

After this brief exposition of a theory—too brief, perhaps, to carry conviction—we may ask, what would have been the fate of the "metaphysical" had the current of poetry descended in a direct line from them, as it descended in a direct line to them? They would not, certainly, be classified as metaphysical. The possible interests of a poet are unlimited; the more intelligent he is the better; the more intelligent he is the more likely that he will have interests: our only condition is that he turn them into poetry, and not merely meditate on them poetically. A philosophical theory which has entered into poetry is established, for its truth or falsity in one sense ceases to matter, and its truth in another sense is proved. The poets in question have, like other poets, various faults. But they were, at best, engaged in the task of trying to find the verbal equivalent for states of mind and feeling. And this means both that they are more mature, and that they wear better, than later poets of certainly not less literary ability.

It is not a permanent necessity that poets should be interested in philosophy, or in any other subject. We can only say that it appears likely that poets in our civilization, as it exists at present, must be *difficult*. Our civilization comprehends great variety and complexity, and this variety and complexity, playing upon a refined sensibility, must produce various and complex results. The poet must become more and more comprehensive, more allusive, more indirect, in order to force, to dislocate if necessary, language into his meaning. (A brilliant and extreme statement of this view, with which it is not requisite to associate oneself, is that of M. Jean Epstein,[3] *La Poésie d'aujourd-hui*.) Hence we get something which looks very much like the conceit—we get, in fact, a method curiously similar to that of the "metaphysical poets," similar also in its use of obscure words and of simple phrasing.

> *O géraniums diaphanes, guerroyeurs sortilèges,*
> *Sacrilèges monomanes!*
> *Emballages, dévergondages, douches! O pressoirs*
> *Des vendanges des grands soirs!*
> *Layettes aux abois,*
> *Thyrses au fond des bois!*
> *Transfusions, représailles,*
> *Relevailles, compresses et l'éternel potion,*
> *Angélus! n'en pouvoir plus*
> *De débâcles nuptiales! de débâcles nuptiales!*[4]

The same poet could write also simply:

> *Elle est bien loin, elle pleure,*
> *Le grand vent se lamente aussi …*[5]

Jules Laforgue, and Tristan Corbière in many of his poems, are nearer to the "school of Donne" than any modern English poet. But poets more classical than they have the same essential quality of transmuting ideas into sensations, of transforming an observation into a state of mind.

> *Pour l'enfant, amoureux de cartes et d'estampes,*
> *L'univers est égal à son vaste appétit.*
> *Ah, que le monde est grand à la clarté des lampes!*
> *Aux yeux du souvenir que le monde est petit!*[6]

---

[1] *"Coy Mistress"* "To His Coy Mistress," by Andrew Marvell (1621–78).

[2] *Hyperion* John Keats began his epic fragment in 1818; in 1819 he revised the poem and wrote *The Fall of Hyperion, A Dream*.

[3] *M. Jean Epstein* French intellectual (1897–1953).

[4] *O géraniums … nuptiales* French: "O diaphanous geraniums, warrior magic spells, / Monomaniacal sacrileges! / Packing materials, licentiousness, showers! O presses / Of the great evening grape harvests! / Pressed baby clothes, / Thyrsis deep in the woods! / Transfusions, reprisals, / Reawakenings, compresses, and the eternal potion, / Angelus! No longer able / Marriage debacles! Marriage debacles!" From Jules Laforgue's *Derniers vers* (1890).

[5] *Elle est bien … aussi* French: "She is far away, she cries, / The high wind also laments." From *Derniers vers*.

[6] *Pour l'enfant … est petit* French: "For the child, loving maps and stamps, / The universe is his vast appetite. / Ah, how large the world is by the clear light of the lamps! / To eyes remembering that the world is small." From Baudelaire's *Le Voyage*.

In French literature the great master of the seventeenth century—Racine—and the great master of the nineteenth—Baudelaire—are in some ways more like each other than they are like anyone else. The greatest two masters of diction are also the greatest two psychologists, the most curious explorers of the soul. It is interesting to speculate whether it is not a misfortune that two of the greatest masters of diction in our language, Milton and Dryden, triumph with a dazzling disregard of the soul. If we continued to produce Miltons and Drydens it might not so much matter, but as things are it is a pity that English poetry has remained so incomplete. Those who object to the "artificiality" of Milton or Dryden sometimes tell us to "look into our hearts and write." But that is not looking deep enough; Racine or Donne looked into a good deal more than the heart. One must look into the cerebral cortex, the nervous system, and the digestive tracts.

May we not conclude, then, that Donne, Crashaw, Vaughan, Herbert and Lord Herbert, Marvell, King, Cowley at his best, are in the direct current of English poetry, and that their faults should be reprimanded by this standard rather than coddled by antiquarian affection? They have been enough praised in terms which are implicit limitations because they are "metaphysical" or "witty," "quaint" or "obscure," though at their best they have not these attributes more than other serious poets. On the other hand, we must not reject the criticism of Johnson (a dangerous person to disagree with) without having mastered it, without having assimilated the Johnsonian canons of taste. In reading the celebrated passage in his essay on Cowley we must remember that by wit he clearly means something more serious than we usually mean today; in his criticism of their versification we must remember in what a narrow discipline he was trained, but also how well trained; we must remember that Johnson tortures chiefly the chief offenders, Cowley and Cleveland. It would be a fruitful work, and one requiring a substantial book, to break up the classification of Johnson and exhibit these poets in all their difference of kind and of degree, from the massive music of Donne to the faint, pleasing tinkle of Aurelian Townshend.

—1921

IN CONTEXT

T.S. Eliot and Anti-Semitism

Considerable controversy occurred in the latter years of the twentieth century over the issue of T.S. Eliot and anti-Semitism. The issue had been raised here and there during Eliot's lifetime: J.V. Healy raised the matter in correspondence with Eliot in 1940; a letter of George Orwell's in 1948 reveals that some were then suggesting in conversation that Eliot was anti-Semitic, and so on. Orwell no doubt gave voice to a then-common view in dismissing the suggestion:

> It is nonsense what Fyvel said about Eliot being anti-Semitic. Of course you can find what would now be called antisemitic remarks in his early work, but who didn't say such things at that time? (Letter to Julian Symons, 29 October 1948)

That anti-Semitism was widespread in the 1910s and 1920s in both the USA and Britain is unquestionable, and to some extent Eliot's views on the question were no doubt those of the majority at the time. But few published literary works displayed the consistency of association that one finds in Eliot's early poetry between what is Jewish and what is squalid and distasteful. Still, leading critics and scholars did not begin to air the matter publicly until 1971, when the issue of anti-Semitism in Eliot's works was raised by a leading critic, George Steiner, in a letter to *The Listener*:

The obstinate puzzle is Eliot's uglier touches tend to occur at the heart of very good poetry (which is *not* the case with Pound). One thinks of the notorious "the Jew squats on the window-sill ... Spawned in some estaminet of Antwerp" in "Geron-tion"; of

> The rats are underneath the piles.
> The Jew is underneath the lot.

In "Burbank with a Baedeker: Bleistein with a Cigar"; of

> Rachel nee Rabinovich
> tears at the grapes with murderous paws

in "Sweeney among the Nightingales." (*The Listener*, 29 April 1971)

The question Steiner raised as to how the uglier touches in Eliot's work connected with the aesthetic quality of the whole is one that has continued to interest scholars and critics. In an important 1988 book, another leading scholar, Christopher Ricks, put forward an extended analysis of the ways in which various forms of prejudice may have animated both Eliot's work itself and responses to it. Ricks begins his study with a look at prejudice against women; he notes how the critics had picked up on the latent element of misogyny in two famous lines from "The Love Song of J. Alfred Prufrock":

John Crowe Ransom [puts a] rhetorical question: "How could they ['the women'] have had any inkling of that glory which Michaelangelo had put into his marbles and his paintings?"

Helen Gardner does not as a woman have any different sense of the women: "The absurdity of discussing his giant art, in high-pitched feminine voices, drifting through a drawing room, adds merely extra irony to the underlying sense of the lines."

[T]he critics miss ... one of the things that is salutory in the lines

> In the room the women come and go
> Talking of Michaelangelo.

What none of the critics will own is how much their sense of the lines is incited by prejudice.... Grover Smith [writes that] "the women meanwhile are talking, no doubt tediously and ignorantly, of Michaelangelo." For all we know, as against suspect (perhaps justifiably, but still), the women could be talking as invaluably as [renowned art historian] Kenneth Clark (*T.S. Eliot and Prejudice*, 10–11).

Ricks analyzes at length and with considerable subtlety the "uglier touches" in Eliot's poetry, noting how these are associative rather than unequivocally prejudicial or inciteful. A line such as "The Jew is underneath the lot," he comments, does not "come clean, since the effect of the article 'The Jew' is to disparage all Jews ... while nevertheless leaving open a bolt-hole for the disingenuous reply that a particular Jew only is meant" (35).

As Ricks pointed out, some of Eliot's other writings are at least as disturbing as the published poems. Particularly troubling are an unpublished poem, "Dirge," that was part of an early draft of *The Waste Land*, and a passage from *After Strange Gods*, a series of lectures given by Eliot in Virginia in 1933, and published in book form a year later. (Eliot never allowed the book to be reprinted.) In the passage Eliot is describing what he feels is to be striven for in a society that properly values tradition:

> The population should be homogenous.... What is still more important is unity of religious background; and reasons of race and religion combine to make any large number of free-thinking Jews undesirable. There must be a proper balance between urban and rural, industrial and agricultural development. And a spirit of excessive tolerance is to be deprecated (*After Strange Gods*, 20).

If Ricks's focus was primarily a literary one, that of Anthony Julius in his *T.S. Eliot, Anti-Semitism, and Literary Form* (1995) was more broadly social—and more clearly provocative. With his searing indictment both of the anti-Semitism of Eliot's age and its memorable expressions in Eliot's verse, Julius touched a raw nerve. Whereas Ricks's criticisms are often elliptical, and his tone generally reserved, Julius is direct and unrelenting:

> "Women," "jews," and "negroes" are not interchangeable "aliens" in Eliot's work. They are, respectively, intimidating, sightless, and transparent; their deaths are respectively longed for, delighted in, and noted without emotion....
> ... However, this does not amount to an argument for suppression. I censure; I do not wish to censor.... Eliot's anti-Semitic poems are integral to his oeuvre, an oeuvre which is to be valued and preserved.... One can teach anti-Semitism from such texts; one can also teach poetry. One reads them, appalled, and impressed.

Like Steiner a generation earlier, Julius concludes that Eliot is "able to place his anti-Semitism at the service of his art." A storm of controversy followed the publication of Julius's book, with many defending Julius but many others continuing to argue either that Eliot was not anti-Semitic or that anti-Semitism was irrelevant to his work. A further camp held that anti-Semitism was in fact a significant presence, but that the poetry succeeds despite such "uglier touches" rather than in any way because of them. Today there remains no consensus on these issues, but there can be no doubt that the controversy has left a mark; it is unlikely that extended discussion of Eliot's poetry will again be able to take place without any reference to this troubling issue.

ELIOT, POUND, AND THE VORTEX OF MODERNISM

CONTEXTS

According to Virginia Woolf's oft-quoted formulation (from a 1924 essay excerpted in this section), "on or about December 1910 human character changed." Woolf saw that date as marking the moment at which writers began smashing literary conventions in an effort to represent the complexity of human experience through "the spasmodic, the obscure, the fragmentary." At the same moment, painting and sculpture were breaking visual reality into fragments to express the reality of fragmented experience—or indeed to express the reality of what increasingly seemed a fragmented world. Such is now a conventional account of the birth of Modernism.

There was, of course, a mock-precision in Woolf's dating, but many others have linked the birth of Modernism to developments that occurred at *about* this time: in painting, the development of Cubism by Pablo Picasso and Georges Braque; in music, the development of strikingly discordant styles such as that of Schoenberg's *The Rite of Spring*; in poetry, the development of Imagism and its offshoots by Ezra Pound, H.D. and, a few years later, T.S. Eliot; in fiction, the development by Dorothy Richardson, James Joyce, Virginia Woolf, and others, of "stream of consciousness" techniques of narration; and, in the world of art as well as of ideas, the development of Futurism by F.T. Marinetti and others. Arguably, though, the birth of Modernism can be traced to developments that occurred in France considerably earlier—developments such as Arthur Rimbaud's wholesale rejection in 1871 of the conventions of Western poetry. In the 1880s and 90s the Symbolist aesthetic of poets Jules Laforgue and Stephane Mallarmé foreshadowed the coming of Modernism even more directly than had that of Rimbaud. In the 1891 interview excerpted below, Mallarmé asserted that "when a society is without stability, without unity, it cannot create a stable and definitive art," and suggested that we must not try to elude the intellectual work that is entailed in coming to terms with the appropriate obscurity of poetry. A generation later, T.S. Eliot declared (in his essay "The Metaphysical Poets") that "poets in our civilization must be *difficult*. Our civilization comprehends great variety and complexity, and this variety and complexity ... must produce various and complex results. The poet must become ... more allusive, more indirect, in order to force, to dislocate if necessary, language into his meaning."

The vortex of Modernism includes within it a wide variety of narrower "isms"—including not only post-Impressionism, Symbolism, Imagism, and Futurism, but also Vorticism, Absurdism, Dadaism, and a number of others. All shun the linear, the decorative, and the sentimental. All tend towards the presentation of reality fractured into its component pieces—and conversely, towards a rejection of all traditions within which reality is represented through the construction of conventionally unified wholes. Often, however, it was suggested that the fractured forms might represent the world as humans *perceive* it more realistically than other, seemingly more "realistic" forms of representation. Such was the case with stream of consciousness narration in fiction, for example, and also with Cubism; Picasso is famously reported to have said of his Cubist work, "I paint objects as I think them, not as I see them."

In the revolutionary ferment of the late eighteenth and early nineteenth centuries, there was a close correlation between literary or artistic positions and political ones; those who held radical political views tended also to hold radical aesthetic ones. In the revolutionary ferment of Modernism a century later, however, the lines of association between the aesthetic and the political are much more tangled; certainly it would be difficult to argue that Modernism was particularly friendly towards the political left. While Woolf and most of the Bloomsbury circle held progressive political views, Pound and many of the Futurists gravitated towards fascism, Eliot towards conservative High Anglicanism. Modernism's strong desire to recognize the force of often anarchic psychological impulse eventually found its most venomous expression in the racism and anti-Semitism of Pound ("Let us be done with Jews … / Let us spit on those who fawn on the Jews for their money"). Nor was Modernism on the whole friendly towards feminism—or, more generally, towards women. H.D., Richardson, and Woolf must be numbered among the major figures of Modernism—and in the long run, their writing on issues relating to gender has counted more than the less progressive pronouncements of some other Modernist figures. But in their own time, the virulent misogyny of such figures as Marinetti and Pound (and the much milder variety of Eliot) had a wide-ranging impact, on literature as in other contexts. The "modern woman" that had been so central to the cultural world at the turn of the century was of little interest to the major male figures of Modernism. (Paradoxically, though, the climate that Modernism helped to create may not, finally, have been hostile to women or to progressive causes, if only because Modernism promoted the belief that nothing is stable—and thus implicitly that change can occur in surprising directions, and with surprising speed.)

A particular focus in this section is placed on the reception of the Modernist poetry of T.S. Eliot, which was as influential upon later twentieth-century generations as it was controversial when first published.

⌘ ⌘ ⌘

from Jules Huret, "Interview with Stephane Mallarmé," *L'Echo de Paris* (1891)

… "We are taking part, at this moment," he told me, "in an extraordinary spectacle, unique in all the history of poetry…. Until now, poets had to have as accompaniment the grand organ notes of regular meter. Well, they have been played too much, and one gets tired of it. … When he was dying I'm sure the great [Victor] Hugo convinced himself that he had buried poetry for a century—yet even then, Paul Verlaine had already written 'Sagesse'; [Hugo] failed above all to realise that in a society without stability, without unity, it is not possible to create art that is stable, that is definitive…."

"So much for the form," I said to Mr. Mallarmé. "And the content?"

"I believe," he answered me, "that the young are closer to the poetic ideal than the old Parnassians,[1] who … try to present their subjects plainly and directly. I believe that

it is necessary to have nothing but allusion. The contemplation of objects, images flying dreamlike from the eyes—these are the song. The Parnassians take the thing as a whole and look at it, but they rob it of its mystery…. To name a thing is to take away three quarters of the enjoyment of a poem, which is to be found in divining little by little…."

"We come now," I said to him, "to a great objection that I am obliged to raise with you—the issue of *obscurity*."

"This is equally dangerous," he replied to me, "if the obscurity comes from the insufficiencies of the reader, or those of the poet—but it is deceitful to try to get away from this work [of unravelling the poem]…. There ought always to be an enigma in poetry, and it is the purpose of literature—there is no other—to *evoke* objects."

… "Is it you, sir," I now demanded of him, "who has created the new movement?"

---

[1] *Parnassians* School of French poetry whose members (which included Paul Verlaine, Catulle Mendes, and Pierre Louÿs) reacted against Romanticism, preferring instead the formal structure and emotional detachment of classicist poetry.

"I abhor schools," he said, "and all that they repre-sent: … literature, to the contrary, is entirely an individual matter. For me, the case of the poet in this society that does not allow one to live, resembles the situation of a man confined in isolation.…"

Pablo Picasso, *Les Demoiselles d'Avignon* (1907). The style of painting known as Cubism was developed by the Spanish painter Pablo Picasso and French painter Georges Braque in 1907. Braque had been much influenced by the landscapes of the French Impressionist Paul Cézanne, in which land, sea and sky are loosely broken up into soft blocks of color; by 1907 he was developing a style that fragmented landscape much more radically than had Cézanne. Meanwhile Picasso, influenced by traditions of African portraiture through mask, was developing a similarly radical approach to the depiction of the human body. When Braque visited Picasso's studio

in the spring of 1907, Picasso showed his ground-breaking painting *Les Demoiselles d'Avignon*, which depicts five women from a brothel in dramatically fragmented fashion. For the next few years, Braque and Picasso followed similar lines of development in their painting.

Though *Les Demoiselles d'Avignon* is now regarded as a landmark in the development of Cubism —and of Modernism generally—it was not well received initially. The leading Post-Impressionist painter Henri Matisse thought the painting represented an attack on "the modern movement," while Picasso's friend and patron Leo Stein is reported to have said sarcastically, "You have been trying to paint the fourth dimension; how amusing!" Picasso did not publicly exhibit the painting until 1925.

Imagist and Futurist Poetry: A Sampling

T.E. Hulme (1883–1917)

Art and literary critic, philosopher, and friend of T.S. Eliot, T.E. Hulme wrote some of the earliest "Modernist" poetry in English. He enlisted in the artillery when the First World War broke out, and was killed in battle in 1917.

"Autumn" (1912)

A touch of cold in the Autumn night—
Walked abroad,
And saw the ruddy moon lean over a hedge
Like a red-faced farmer.
5   I did not stop to speak, but nodded,
And round about were the wistful stars
With white faces like town children.

Ezra Pound (1885–1972)

Ezra Pound was an expatriate American in London when he became a leading force behind the poetic movement known as "Imagism" and subsequently behind the intellectual and artistic movement known as "Vorticism." He exerted a prolonged influence on the poetry of T.S. Eliot, and is himself reckoned among the most important of Modernist poets. Unlike Eliot, however, Pound did not develop a lifelong attachment to Britain; he spent years in Italy (where, notoriously, he broadcast propaganda for Mussolini's Fascist government during World War II), and after the war he returned to the United States. The critic Hugh Kenner, who wrote extensively on Pound and his work, said that when he met the poet "I knew that I was in the presence of the center of Modernism."

"In a Station of the Metro" (1916, written c. 1911)

The apparition   of these faces   in the crowd;
Petals   on a wet, black   bough.

"Alba" (1916)

As cool as the pale wet leaves
    of lily-of-the-valley
She lay beside me in the dawn.

"L'Art, 1910" (1916)

Green arsenic smeared on an egg-white cloth,
Crushed strawberries! Come, let us feast our eyes.

H.D. (1886–1961)

Like T.S. Eliot and Ezra Pound (to whom she was twice engaged), H.D. was an American expatriate whose work was central to Modernism. Born and educated in Pennsylvania as Hilda Doolittle, she left for Europe in 1911, and soon became known as an Imagist poet. She lived thereafter in England and later in Switzerland, identifying herself as "H.D." beginning in 1913. A writer of fiction as well as of poetry, she wrote the pioneering novel *HERmione*, exploring the tension between a woman's lesbian and heterosexual feelings, in 1927. Her long poem *Trilogy* (1944–46) is regarded by many as her most important work.

"Oread" (1914)

Whirl up, sea—
    whirl your pointed pines,
splash your great pines
on our rocks,
hurl your green over us,
cover us with your pools of fir.

"The Pool" (1915)

Are you alive?
    I touch you.
You quiver like a sea-fish.
I cover you with my net.
What are you—banded one?

Mina Loy (1882–1966)

Loy is often categorized as a Futurist poet, though she had a stormy relationship with many of the Futurists. She is also often discussed as an American poet, although she was 34 and had already composed most of the work for which she is now best remembered when she left Europe for America. She moved to the United States in 1916 and soon became a part of the New York avant-garde. Born and raised in England, Loy had by then also spent several years amidst the literary and artistic community in Paris, devoting considerable time to painting before turning to poetry in the 1910s. When her "Love Songs" was published in the debut issue of a New York magazine called *Others* in 1915, both the poem and its author immediately became notorious. In 1921, Ezra Pound (then living outside America) suggested that Loy, Marianne Moore, and William Carlos Williams were the only three writers then in the United States "who can write anything of interest in verse."

Recently, Loy has again become notorious, this

time for the *Feminist Manifesto* that she wrote in 1914, which includes such incendiary lines as "Men and women are enemies, with the enmity of the exploited for the parasite, the parasite for the exploited … The only point at which the interests of the sexes merge—is the sexual embrace." Loy drafted the manifesto as an angry response to the misogynist manifestos of the Italian Futurists and (earlier that same year) the BLAST manifesto of Pound, Wyndham Lewis, and others; Loy considered it merely a rough draft, however, and chose not to publish it; the manifesto did not appear in print until 1982.

There are numerous versions of many of Loy's poems; notably, a longer and more explicitly erotic version of "Love Songs" appeared in 1917 under the title "Love Songs to Joannes."

from "Three Moments in Paris" (1915, written 1914)

1. ONE O'CLOCK AT NIGHT

Though you have never possessed me
  I have belonged to you since the beginning of time
And sleepily I sit on your chair beside you
Leaning against your shoulder
5 And your careless arm across my back gesticulates
As your indisputable male voice   roars
Through my brain and my body
Arguing "Dynamic Decomposition"
Of which I understand nothing
10 Sleepily
And the only less male voice of your brother
      pugilist of the intellect
Booms   as it seems to me so sleepy
Across an interval of a thousand miles
An interim of a thousand years
15 But you who make more noise than any man
      in the world when you clear your throat
Deafening   wake me
And I catch the thread of the argument
Immediately assuming my personal mental attitude
And cease to be a woman

20 Beautiful halfhour of being a mere woman
The animal woman

Understanding nothing of man
But mastery   and the security of imparted
      physical heat
Indifferent to cerebral gymnastics
25 Or regarding them as the self-indulgent play of children
Or the thunder of alien gods
But you wake me up
Anyhow   who am I that I should criticize
      your theories of "Plastic Velocity"

"Let us go home   she is tired   and wants to go to
    bed."

from "Love Songs" (1915)

1

Spawn of Fantasies
  Sitting[1] the appraisable
Pig Cupid[2]   his rosy snout
Rooting erotic garbage
5 "Once upon a time"
Pulls a weed   white star-topped
Among wild oats sown in mucous-membrane
I would an eye in a Bengal light
Eternity in a sky-rocket
10 Constellations in an ocean
Whose rivers run no fresher
Than a trickle of saliver[3]

These are suspect places
I must live in my lantern
15 Trimming subliminal flicker
Virginal   to the bellows
Of Experience

  Coloured glass

---

[1] *Sitting* The handwritten original may read "silting."

[2] *Pig Cupid* The poem as a whole is often referred to as "Pig Cupid."

[3] *saliver* In most published versions this spelling is corrected to "saliva," but the handwritten original reads "-er," and it seems plausible that a connection with the "-er" ending of "fresher" is intended.

Imagism and Vorticism

The first two of the following selections appeared together in a 1913 issue of *Poetry* magazine: a short article by civil servant, poet, and translator F.S. Flint on Imagism was followed by a longer discussion of Imagism by Ezra Pound. In an article on Vorticism three years later Pound made further efforts to define Imagism and Vorticism—as well as to define and comment on Impressionism and Post-Impressionism, Symbolism, and various other of the component movements of Modernism.

from F.S. Flint, "Imagisme,"[1] *Poetry Magazine* (March 1913)

Some curiosity has been aroused concerning *Imagisme*, and as I was unable to find anything definite about it in print, I sought out an *Imagiste*, with intent to discover whether the group itself knew anything about the "movement." I gleaned these facts.

The *Imagists* admitted that they were contemporaries of the Post Impressionists and the Futurists; but they had nothing in common with these schools. They had not published a manifesto. ... They had a few rules, drawn up for their own satisfaction only, and they had not published them. They were:

1. Direct treatment of the "thing," whether subjective or objective.
2. To use absolutely no word that does not contribute to the presentation.
3. As regarding rhythm: to compose in sequence of the musical phrase, not in sequence of the metronome. By these standards they judged all poetry and found most of it wanting....

I found among them an earnestness that is amazing to one accustomed to the usual London air of poetic dilettantism. They consider that Art is all science, all religion, philosophy and metaphysic. It is true that

---

[1] [1913 note from the *Editors of Poetry* magazine.] In response to many requests for information regarding Imagism and the Imagistes, we publish this note by Mr. Flint, supplementing it with further exemplification by Mr. Pound. It will be seen from these that Imagism is not necessarily associated with Hellenic subjects, or with *vers libre* as a prescribed form.

snobisme may be urged against them; but it is at least *snobisme* in its most dynamic form, with a great deal of sound sense and energy behind it; and they are stricter with themselves than with any outsider.

from Ezra Pound, "A Few Don'ts By an Imagiste," *Poetry* (March 1913)

An "Image" is that which presents an intellectual and emotional complex in an instant of time. I use the term "complex" rather in the technical sense employed by the newer psychologists, such as Hart,[2] though we might not agree absolutely in our application.

It is the presentation of such a "complex" instantaneously which gives that sense of sudden liberation; that sense of freedom from time limits and space limits; that sense of sudden growth, which we experience in the presence of the greatest works of art.

It is better to present one Image in a lifetime than to produce voluminous works....

LANGUAGE

Use no superfluous word, no adjective, which does not reveal something.

Don't use such an expression as "dim lands of *peace.*" It dulls the image. It mixes an abstraction with the concrete. It comes from the writer's not realizing that the natural object is always the *adequate* symbol.

Go in fear of abstractions. Don't retell in mediocre verse what has already been done in good prose. Don't think any intelligent person is going to be deceived when you try to shirk all the difficulties of the unspeakably difficult art of good prose by chopping your composition into line lengths. What the expert is tired of today the public will be tired of tomorrow.

---

[2] *Hart* Bernard Hart (1880–1960), British psychologist who played a central role in promulgating and expanding on the ideas of Sigmund Freud and Carl Jung concerning the unconscious. As the concept was used by Jung, a "complex" was a set of mental patterns in the unconscious which might predispose an individual towards pathological patterns of thought and action. Hart broadened the notion to include any "emotionally toned system of ideas" that might predispose certain patterns of conscious behavior, including patterns that might shape, for example, political biases, but also benign patterns such as those involved in following a hobby.

Don't imagine that the art of poetry is any simpler than the art of music, or that you can please the expert before you have spent at least as much effort on the art of verse as the average piano teacher spends on the art of music. ...

RHYTHM AND RHYME

Let the candidate fill his mind with the finest cadences he can discover, preferably in a foreign language so that the meaning of the words may be less likely to divert his attention from the movement. ...

It is not necessary that a poem should rely on its music, but if it does rely on its music that music must be such as will delight the expert.

Let the neophyte know assonance and alliteration, rhyme immediate and delayed, simple and polyphonic, as a musician would expect to know harmony and counterpoint and all the minutiae of his craft. No time is too great to give to these matters or to any one of them, even if the artists seldom have need of them. ...

Don't chop your stuff into separate *iambs*. Don't make each line stop dead at the end, and then begin every next line with a heave. Let the beginning of the next line catch the rise of the rhythm wave, unless you want a definite longish pause.

In short, behave as a musician, a good musician, when dealing with that phase of your art which has exact parallels in music. The same laws govern, and you are bound by no others.

Naturally, your rhythmic structure should not destroy the shape of your words, or their natural sound, or their meaning. It is improbable that, at the start, you will be able to get a rhythm-structure strong enough to affect them very much, though you may fall a victim to all sorts of false stopping due to line ends and caesurae.

The musician can rely on pitch and the volume of the orchestra. You can not. The term harmony is misapplied to poetry; it refers to simultaneous sounds of different pitch. There is, however, in the best verse a sort of residue of sound which remains in the ear of the hearer and acts more or less as an organ-base. A rhyme must have in it some slight element of surprise if it is to give pleasure; it need not be bizarre or curious, but it must be well used if used at all. ...

The first three simple proscriptions will throw out nine-tenths of all the bad poetry now accepted as standard and classic; and will prevent you from many a crime of production. ...

from Ezra Pound, "Vorticism," *Gaudier-Brzeska* (1916)

"It is no more ridiculous that a person should receive or convey an emotion by means of an arrangement of shapes, or planes, or colours, than that they should receive or convey such emotion by an arrangement of musical notes."

I suppose this proposition is self-evident. Whistler[1] said as much, some years ago, and Pater[2] proclaimed that "All arts approach the condition of music."

Whenever I say this I am greeted with a storm of "Yes, but"s. "But why isn't this art futurism?" "Why isn't?" "Why don't?" and above all: "What, in Heaven's name, has it got to do with your Imagiste poetry?"

Let me explain at leisure, and in nice, orderly, old-fashioned prose. ...

"Futurism," when it gets into art, is, for the most part, a descendant of impressionism. It is a sort of accelerated impressionism.

There is another artistic descent *via* Picasso and Kandinsky;[3] *via* Cubism and Expressionism. One does not complain of neo-Impressionism or of accelerated Impressionism and "simultaneity," but one is not wholly satisfied by them. One has perhaps other needs.

... Vorticism has been announced as including such and such painting and sculpture and "Imagisme" in verse. I shall explain "Imagisme," and then proceed to show its inner relation to certain modern paintings and sculpture.

Imagisme, in so far as it has been known at all, has been known chiefly as a stylistic movement, as a movement of criticism rather than of creation. This is natural, for, despite all possible celerity of publication, the public is always, and of necessity, some years behind the artists' actual thought. ...

---

[1] *Whistler* American painter James Abbott McNeill Whistler (1834–1903).

[2] *Pater* English critic Walter Pater (1839–94).

[3] *Kandinsky* Russian abstract painter Wassily Kandinsky (1866–1944).

Imagisme is not Symbolism. The Symbolists dealt in "association," that is, in a sort of allusion, almost of allegory. They degraded the symbol to the status of a word. They made it a form of metonomy. One can be grossly "symbolic," for example, by using the term "cross" to mean "trial." The Symbolist's *symbols* have a fixed value, like numbers in arithmetic, like 1, 2, and 7. The Imagiste's images have a variable significance, like the signs *a*, *b*, and *x* in algebra.

Moreover, one does not want to be called a Symbolist, because Symbolism has usually been associated with mushy technique.

On the other hand, Imagisme is not Impressionism, though one borrows, or could borrow, much from the impressionist method of presentation. But this is only negative definition....

The image is the poet's pigment.[1] The painter should use his colour because he sees it or feels it. I don't much care whether he is representative or non-representative. He should *depend*, of course, on the creative, not upon the mimetic or representational part in his work. It is the same in writing poems, the author must use his *image* because he sees it or feels it, *not* because he thinks he can use it to back up some creed or some system of ethics or economics.

An *image*, in our sense, is real because we know it directly....

Any mind that is worth calling a mind must have needs beyond the existing categories of language, just as a painter must have pigments or shades more numerous than the existing names of the colours.

Perhaps this is enough to explain the words in my "Vortex":—

"Every concept, every emotion, presents itself to the vivid consciousness in some primary form. It belongs to the art of this form...."

What I have said of one Vorticist art can be transposed for another vorticist art. But let me go on then with my own branch of vorticism, about which I can probably speak with greater clarity. All poetic language is the language of exploration. Since the beginning of bad writing, writers have used images as ornaments. The point of Imagisme is that it does not use images *as*

ornaments. The image is itself the speech. The image is the word beyond formulated language.

I once saw a small child go to an electric light switch and say, "Mamma, can I *open* the light?" She was using the age-old language of exploration, the language of art. It was a sort of metaphor, but she was not using it as ornamentation.

One is tired of ornamentations, they are all a trick, and any sharp person can learn them.

The Japanese have had the sense of exploration. They have understood the beauty of this sort of knowing. A Chinaman said long ago that if a man can't say what he has to say in twelve lines he had better keep quiet. The Japanese have evolved the still shorter form of the *hokku*.[2]

> The fallen blossom flies back to its branch:
>   A butterfly.

That is the substance of a very well-known *hokku*. Victor Plarr[3] tells me that once, when he was walking over snow with a Japanese naval officer, they came to a place where a cat had crossed the path, and the officer said, "Stop, I am making a poem." Which poem was, roughly, as follows:—

> The footsteps of the cat upon the snow:
>   (are like) plum-blossoms.

The words "are like" would not occur in the original, but I add them for clarity.

The "one image poem" is a form of super-position, that is to say, it is one idea set on top of another. I found it useful in getting out of the impasse in which I had been left by my metro emotion. I wrote a thirty-line poem, and destroyed it because it was what we call work "of second intensity." Six months later I made a poem half that length; a year later I made the following *hokku*-like sentence:—

> The apparition of these faces in the crowd:
>   Petals on a wet, black bough.

---

[1] [Pound's note] The image has been defined as "that which presents an intellectual and emotional complex in an instant of time."

[2] *hokku*   I.e., haiku.

[3] *Victor Plarr*   English poet (1863–1929).

Cover of the second (and last) issue of *BLAST*, July 1915; the cover illustration is a Vorticist woodcut by Wyndham Lewis. The first issue (in 1914) included the famous Vorticist manifesto signed by Lewis, Pound, and others.

I dare say it is meaningless unless one has drifted into a certain vein of thought.[1] In a poem of this sort one is trying to record the precise instant when a thing outward and objective transforms itself, or darts into a thing inward and subjective.

… I see no reason why I, and various men who agree with me, should be expected to call ourselves Futurists. We do not desire to evade comparison with the past. We prefer that the comparison be made by some intelligent person whose idea of "the tradition" is not limited by the conventional taste of four or five centuries and one continent.

---

[1] [Pound's note] Mr. Flint and Mr. Rodker have made longer poems depending on a similar presentation of matter. So also have Richard Aldington, in his *In Via Sestina*, and "H.D." in her *Oread*, which latter poems express much stronger emotions than that in my lines here given. Mr Hueffer gives an interesting account of a similar adventure of his own in his review of the Imagiste anthology.

Vorticism is an intensive art. I mean by this, that one is concerned with the relative intensity, or relative significance of different sorts of expression. One desires the most intense, for certain forms of expression *are* "more intense" than others. They are more dynamic. …

The image is not an idea. It is a radiant node or cluster; it is what I can, and must perforce, call a VORTEX, from which, and through which, and into which, ideas are constantly rushing. In decency one can only call it a VORTEX. And from this necessity came the name "Vorticism."

from Virginia Woolf, "Character in Fiction" (1924)

Virginia Woolf's famous assertion that "on or about December 1910 human character changed" appears in the essay excerpted below, "Character in Fiction." Among the significant developments of 1910 in Britain were the death of Edward VII on 6 May, and the groundbreaking exhibition "Manet and the Post-Impressionists," curated by Roger Fry, which opened at the Grafton Galleries on 8 November, and which then unleashed a storm of controversy in the London press. (The term "Post-Impressionist" was invented by Fry before the show as an umbrella term to describe an exhibit that featured work in a variety of disparate styles, including Pointillism, Fauvism, and Symbolism.) As Woolf and Fry were both central figures in the Bloomsbury circle, Woolf may well have had the controversy surrounding this exhibition in mind in choosing December 1910 as a reference point—though she does not in fact mention the Post-Impressionists in her essay.

In the contrast Woolf draws immediately after making her assertion there is little to associate post-December 1910 human character with the changes wrought by what we now call Modernism (she first cites the work of Samuel Butler and of Bernard Shaw as having recorded "the signs of change"), but the later discussion comparing the aesthetic of Joyce and Eliot to that of novelists such as Arnold Bennett is clearly germane to the development of Modernism.

"Character in Fiction" was first published in the *Criterion* in July 1924. Early variants of much of the essay appeared in Woolf's 1923 essay "Mr. Bennett and Mrs. Brown," first published in the "Literary

Review" section of the *New York Evening Post*, 17 November 1923, and in a paper read to a group called the Cambridge Heretics on 18 May 1924. (A subsequent version appeared as a pamphlet in 1925, again using the title "Mr. Bennett and Mrs. Brown," published by the Hogarth Press.)

It seems to me possible, perhaps desirable, that I may be the only person in this room who has committed the folly of writing, trying to write, or failing to write, a novel. And when I asked myself, as your invitation to speak to you about modern fiction made me ask myself, what demon whispered in my ear and urged me to my doom, a little figure rose before me—the figure of a man, or of a woman, who said, "My name is Brown. Catch me if you can."

Most novelists have the same experience. Some Brown, Smith, or Jones comes before them and says in the most seductive and charming way in the world, "Come and catch me if you can." And so, led on by this will-o'-the-wisp, they flounder through volume after volume, spending the best years of their lives in the pursuit, and receiving for the most part very little cash in exchange. Few catch the phantom; most have to be content with a scrap of her dress or a wisp of her hair.

My belief that men and women write novels because they are lured on to create some character which has thus imposed itself upon them has the sanction of Mr. Arnold Bennett.[1] In an article from which I will quote[2] he says: "The foundation of good fiction is character-creating and nothing else ... Style counts; plot counts; originality of outlook counts. But none of these counts anything like so much as the convincingness of the characters. If the characters are real the novel will have a chance; if they are not, oblivion will be its portion...." And he goes on to draw the conclusion that we have no young novelists of first-rate importance at the present moment, because they are unable to create characters that are real, true, and convincing.

These are the questions that I want with greater boldness than discretion to discuss tonight. I want to make out what we mean when we talk about "character" in fiction; to say something about the question of reality which Mr. Bennett raises; and to suggest some reasons why the younger novelists fail to create characters, if, as Mr. Bennett asserts, it is true that fail they do. This will lead me, I am well aware, to make some very sweeping and some very vague assertions. For the question is an extremely difficult one. Think how little we know about character—think how little we know about art. But, to make a clearance before I begin, I will suggest that we range Edwardians and Georgians into two camps; Mr. Wells, Mr. Bennett, and Mr. Galsworthy I will call the Edwardians; Mr. Forster, Mr. Lawrence, Mr. Strachey, Mr. Joyce, and Mr. Eliot I will call the Georgians.[3] And if I speak in the first person, with intolerable egotism, I will ask you to excuse me. I do not want to attribute to the world at large the opinions of one solitary, ill-informed, and misguided individual.

My first assertion is one that I think you will grant—that every one in this room is a judge of character. Indeed it would be impossible to live for a year without disaster unless one practised character-reading and had some skill in the art. Our marriages, our friendships depend on it; our business largely depends on it; every day questions arise which can only be solved by its help. And now I will hazard a second assertion, which is more disputable perhaps, to the effect that on or about December 1910 human character changed.

I am not saying that one went out, as one might into a garden, and there saw that a rose had flowered, or that a hen had laid an egg. The change was not sudden and

---

[1] *Mr. Arnold Bennett* Arnold Bennett (1867–1931) was a leading novelist of the realistic tradition in the early twentieth century. He was the author of over 20 novels, including *The Old Wives' Tale* (1908), *Clayhanger* (1910), and *Riceyman Steps* (1923), as well as of non-fiction works such as *Literary Taste and How to Form It* (1909).

[2] *article ... quote* Arnold Bennett's article "Is the Novel Decaying?" appeared in *Cassell's Weekly*, 28 March 1923.

[3] *Mr. Wells* H.G. Wells (1866–1946), author of many realistic novels as well as numerous works of science fiction; *Mr. Galsworthy* John Galsworthy (1867–1933), leading realistic dramatist and novelist, best known for *The Forsyte Saga*; *Edwardian* Relating to or characteristic of the reign of Edward VII (1901–10); *Mr. Forster* E.M. Forster (1879–1970), fiction writer; *Mr. Lawrence* D.H. Lawrence (1885–1930), poet and novelist; *Mr. Strachey* Lytton Strachey (1880–1932), essayist; *Mr. Joyce* James Joyce (1882–1941), novelist and short story writer; *Mr. Eliot* T.S. Eliot (1888–1963), poet, essayist, and dramatist. In the draft of this essay as it was delivered to the Cambridge Heretics Society, 18 May 1924, Woolf included two more people in this list—referring to poet Edith Sitwell (1887–1964) and novelist Dorothy Richardson (1873–1957); *Georgians* Relating to or characteristic of the reign of George V, which had begun in 1910.

definite like that. But a change there was, nevertheless; and since one must be arbitrary, let us date it about the year 1910. The first signs of it are recorded in the books of Samuel Butler,[1] in *The Way of All Flesh* in particular; the plays of Bernard Shaw[2] continue to record it. In life one can see the change, if I may use a homely illustration, in the character of one's cook. The Victorian cook lived like a leviathan in the lower depths, formidable, silent, obscure, inscrutable; the Georgian cook is a creature of sunshine and fresh air; in and out of the drawing room, now to borrow the *Daily Herald*, now to ask advice about a hat. Do you ask for more solemn instances of the power of the human race to change? ... All human relations have shifted—those between masters and servants, husbands and wives, parents and children. And when human relations change there is at the same time a change in religion, conduct, politics and literature. Let us agree to place one of these changes about the year 1910.

I have said that people have to acquire a good deal of skill in character-reading if they are to live a single year of life without disaster. But it is the art of the young. In middle age and in old age the art is practised mostly for its uses, and friendships and other adventures and experiments in the art of reading character are seldom made. But novelists differ from the rest of the world because they do not cease to be interested in character when they have learnt enough about it for practical purposes. They go a step further; they feel that there is something permanently interesting in character in itself. When all the practical business of life has been discharged, there is something about people which continues to seem to them of overwhelming importance, in spite of the fact that it has no bearing whatever upon their happiness, comfort, or income. The study of character becomes to them an absorbing pursuit; to impart character an obsession. And this I find it very difficult to explain: what novelists mean when they talk about character, what the impulse is that urges them so powerfully every now and then to embody their view in writing.

---

[1] *Samuel Butler* Writer Samuel Butler (1835–1902), best known for his novel *The Way of All Flesh* (1903), a bitingly satirical vision of Victorian England that was written between 1873 and 1885 but not published until after Butler's death.

[2] *Bernard Shaw* Dramatist George Bernard Shaw (1856–1950).

... I am not going to deny that Mr. Bennett has some reason when he complains that our Georgian writers are unable to make us believe that our characters are real. I am forced to agree that they do not pour out three immortal masterpieces with Victorian regularity every autumn. But instead of being gloomy, I am sanguine. For this state of things is, I think, inevitable whenever from hoar old age or callow youth the convention ceases to be a means of communication between writer and reader, and becomes instead an obstacle and an impediment. At the present moment we are suffering, not from decay, but from having no code of manners which writers and readers accept as a prelude to the more exciting intercourse of friendship. The literary convention of the time is so artificial—you have to talk about the weather and nothing but the weather throughout the entire visit—that, naturally, the feeble are tempted to outrage, and the strong are led to destroy the very foundations and rules of literary society. Signs of this are everywhere apparent. Grammar is violated; syntax disintegrated, as a boy staying with an aunt for the weekend rolls in the geranium bed out of sheer desperation as the solemnities of the sabbath wear on. The more adult writers do not, of course, indulge in such wanton exhibitions of spleen. Their sincerity is desperate, and their courage tremendous; it is only that they do not know which to use, a fork or their fingers. Thus, if you read Mr. Joyce and Mr. Eliot you will be struck by the indecency of the one, and the obscurity of the other. Mr. Joyce's indecency in *Ulysses* seems to me the conscious and calculated indecency of a desperate man who feels that in order to breathe he must break the windows. At moments, when the window is broken, he is magnificent. But what a waste of energy! And, after all, how dull indecency is, when it is not the overflowing of a superabundant energy or savagery, but the determined and public-spirited act of a man who needs fresh air! Again, with the obscurity of Mr. Eliot. I think that Mr. Eliot has written some of the loveliest lines in modern poetry. But how intolerant he is of the old usages and politenesses of society—respect for the weak, consideration for the dull! As I sun myself upon the intense and ravishing beauty of one of his lines, and reflect that I must make a dizzy and dangerous leap to the next, and so on from line to line, like an acrobat flying precariously from bar to bar, I cry out, I confess, for the old decorums, and envy the indolence of my ancestors who, instead of spinning madly through mid-air, dreamt quietly in the shade with a book. Again, in Mr. Strachey's books, *Eminent Victorians* and *Queen Victoria*,[1] the effort and strain of writing against the grain and current of the times is visible too. It is much less visible, of course, for not only is he dealing with facts, which are stubborn things, but he has fabricated, chiefly from eighteenth-century material, a very discreet code of manners of his own, which allows him to sit at table with the highest in the land and to say a great many things under cover of that exquisite apparel which, had they gone naked, would have been chased by the menservants from the room. Still, if you compare *Eminent Victorians* with some of Lord Macaulay's[2] essays, though you will feel that Lord Macaulay is always wrong, and Mr. Strachey always right, you will also feel a body, a sweep, a richness in Lord Macaulay's essays which show that his age was behind him; all his strength went straight into his work; none was used for purposes of concealment or of conversion. But Mr. Strachey has had to open our eyes before he made us see; he has had to search out and sew together a very artful manner of speech; and the effort, beautifully though it is concealed, has robbed his work of some of the force that should have gone into it, and limited his scope.

For these reasons, then, we must reconcile ourselves to a season of failures and fragments. We must reflect that where so much strength is spent on finding a way of telling the truth the truth itself is bound to reach us in rather an exhausted and chaotic condition. Ulysses, Queen Victoria, Mr. Prufrock—to give Mrs. Brown some of the names she has made famous lately—is a little pale and dishevelled by the time her rescuers reach her. And it is the sound of their axes that we hear—a vigorous and stimulating sound in my ears—unless of course you wish to sleep, when in the bounty of his concern, Providence has provided a host of writers anxious and able to satisfy your needs.

---

[1] *Eminent Victorians and Queen Victoria* Both books (published in 1918 and 1921, respectively) adopt an ironical or satirical tone in presenting a largely critical portrayal of the Victorian era.

[2] *Macaulay* Thomas Babington Macaulay (1800–59), historian and essayist, known for shaping English history, in his work, as a story of progress and improvement.

Thus I have tried, at tedious length, I fear, to answer some of the questions which I began by asking. I have given an account of some of the difficulties which in my view beset the Georgian writer in all his forms. I have sought to excuse him. May I end by venturing to remind you of the duties and responsibilities that are yours as partners in this business of writing books, as companions in the railway carriage, as fellow travelers with Mrs. Brown? For she is just as visible to you who remain silent as to us who tell stories about her. In the course of your daily life this past week you have had far stranger and more interesting experiences than the one I have tried to describe. You have overheard scraps of talk that filled you with amazement. You have gone to bed at night bewildered by the complexity of your feelings. In one day thousands of ideas have coursed through your brains; thousands of emotions have met, collided, and disappeared in astonishing disorder. Nevertheless, you allow the writers to palm off upon you a version of all this, an image of Mrs. Brown, which has no likeness to that surprising apparition whatsoever. In your modesty you seem to consider that writers are of different blood and bone from yourselves; that they know more of Mrs. Brown than you do. Never was there a more fatal mistake. It is this division between reader and writer, this humility on your part, these professional airs and graces on ours, that corrupt and emasculate the books which should be the healthy offspring of a close and equal alliance between us. Hence spring those sleek, smooth novels, those portentous and ridiculous biographies, that milk and watery criticism, those poems melodiously celebrating the innocence of roses and sheep which pass so plausibly for literature at the present time.

Your part is to insist that writers shall come down off their plinths and pedestals, and describe beautifully if possible, truthfully at any rate, our Mrs. Brown. You should insist that she is an old lady of unlimited capacity and infinite variety; capable of appearing in any place; wearing any dress; saying anything and doing heaven knows what. But the things she says and the things she does and her eyes and her nose and her speech and her silence have an overwhelming fascination, for she is, of course, the spirit we live by, life itself.

But do not expect just at present a complete and satisfactory presentment of her. Tolerate the spasmodic, the obscure, the fragmentary, the failure. Your help is invoked in a good cause. For I will make one final and surpassingly rash prediction—we are trembling on the verge of one of the great ages of English literature. But it can only be reached if we are determined never, never to desert Mrs. Brown. ...

Reactions to the Poems of T.S. Eliot

As the pieces excerpted below demonstrate, *Prufrock and Other Observations* was recognized as groundbreaking both by those who praised and by those who attacked it. Five years later *The Waste Land* provoked similar reactions. In *The Guardian* Charles Powell wrote that "the ordinary reader" would "make nothing of it," and complained that "meaning, plan, and intention alike are massed behind a smoke-screen of literary and anthropological erudition." To all except "anthropologists and *literati*," he said, the poem was just "so much waste paper." In America the influential critic Louis Untermeyer savaged the poem as "a pompous parade of erudition ... a mingling of wilful obscurity and weak vaudeville." *Time* (with reference to Joyce's *Ulysses* as well as to *The Waste Land*) reported that there was "a new kind of literature abroad in the land, whose only obvious fault is that no one can understand it." A significant number of early responses, however, were extraordinarily positive; two of these are excerpted below. Also excerpted is I.A. Richards's influential 1926 discussion of the responses to and nature of Eliot's poetry.

from Arthur Waugh, "The New Poetry," *Quarterly Review* (October 1916)

Cleverness is, indeed, the pitfall of the New Poetry. There is no question about the ingenuity with which its varying moods are exploited, its elaborate symbolism evolved, and its sudden, disconcerting effects exploded upon the imagination. Swift, brilliant images break into the field of vision, scatter like rockets, and leave a trail of flying fire behind. But the general impression is momentary; there are moods and emotions, but no steady current of ideas behind them. Further, in their

determination to surprise and even to puzzle at all costs, these young poets are continually forgetting that the first essence of poetry is beauty; and that, however much you may have observed the world around you, it is impossible to translate your observation into poetry, without the intervention of the spirit of beauty, controlling the vision, and reanimating the idea. The temptations of cleverness may be insistent, but its risks are equally great ...

... Mr. Ezra Pound ['s poetry is in effect] wooden prose, cut into battens:

Come, my songs, let us express our baser passions.
    Let us express our envy for the man with a
        steady job and no worry about the future.
You are very idle, my songs,
I fear you will come to a bad end.
You stand about the streets. You loiter at the
    corners and bus-stops,
You do next to nothing at all.
You do not even express our inner nobility,
You will come to a very bad end.
And I? I have gone half cracked.

It is not for his audience to contradict the poet, who for once may be allowed to pronounce his own literary epitaph. But this, it is to be noted, is the "poetry" that was to say nothing that might not be said "actually in life—under emotion," the sort of emotion that settles down into the banality of a premature decrepitude:

I grow old ... grow old
I shall wear the bottoms of my trousers rolled.
Shall I part my hair behind? Do I dare to eat a peach?
I shall wear white flannel trousers, and walk upon
    the beach.
I have heard the mermaids singing, each to each.

I do not think that they will sing to me.

Here, surely, is the reduction to absurdity of that school of literary license which, beginning with the declaration "I knew my father well and he was a fool," naturally proceeds to the convenient assumption that everything which seemed wise and true to the father must inevitably be false and foolish to the son. Yet if the fruits of emancipation are to be recognised in the unmetrical, incoherent banalities of these literary "Cubists," the state of Poetry is indeed threatened with anarchy which will end in something worse even than "red ruin and the breaking up of laws." From such a catastrophe the humour, commonsense, and artistic judgment of the best of the new "Georgians" will assuredly save their generation; nevertheless, a hint of warning may not be altogether out of place. It was a classic custom in the family hall, when the feast was at its height, to display a drunken slave among the sons of the household, to the end that they, being ashamed at the ignominious folly of his gesticulations, might determine never to be tempted into such a pitiable condition themselves. The custom had its advantages; for the wisdom of the younger generation was found to be fostered more surely by a single example than by a world of homily and precept.

from Ezra Pound, "Drunken Helots[1] and Mr. Eliot," *The Egoist* (June 1917)

Genius has I know not what peculiar property, its manifestations are various, but however diverse and dissimilar they may be, they have at least one property in common. It makes no difference in what art, in what mode, whether the most conservative, or the most ribbald-revolutionary, or the most diffident; if in any land, or upon any floating deck over the ocean, or upon some newly contrapted craft in the nether, genius manifests itself, at once some elderly gentleman has a flux of bile from his liver; at once from the throne or the easy Cowperian sofa,[2] or from the gutter, or from the economical press room there bursts a torrent of elderly words, splenetic, irrelevant, they form themselves instinctively into large phrases denouncing the inordinate product.

This peculiar kind of rabbia[3] might almost be taken as the test of a work of art; mere talent seems incapable

of exciting it. "You can't fool me, sir, you're a scoundrel," bawls the testy old gentleman.

Fortunately the days when "that very fiery particle" could be crushed out by the *Quarterly* are over, but it interests me, as an archaeologist, to note that the firm which no longer produces Byron,[4] but rather memoirs, letters of the late Queen, etc., is still running a review, and that this review is still where it was in 1812, or whatever the year was; and that, not having an uneducated Keats[5] to condemn, a certain Mr. Waugh is scolding about Mr. Eliot.

All I can find out, by asking questions concerning Mr. Waugh, is that he is "a very old chap," "a reviewer." From internal evidence we deduce that he is, like the rest of his generation of English *gens-de-lettres*,[6] ignorant of Laforgue;[7] of his French contemporaries generally.... This is by no means surprising. We are used to it from his "bilin'."

However, he outdoes himself, he calls Mr. Eliot a "drunken helot." So called they Anacreon[8] in the days of his predecessors, but from the context in the *Quarterly* article I judge that Mr. Waugh does not intend the phrase as a compliment, he is trying to be abusive, and moreover, he in his limited way has succeeded.

Let us sample the works of the last "Drunken Helot." I shall call my next anthology "Drunken Helots" if I can find a dozen poems written half so well as the following:

[Quotes from Eliot's poems "Conversation Galante" and "La Figlia che Piange"]

---

[1] *Helots* Slaves. Pound alludes to Arthur Waugh's likening of the poetic displays of Eliot to the performances of a "drunken slave" (see above).

[2] *Cowperian sofa* "The Sofa" (1785), a work by poet William Cowper (1731–1800).

[3] *rabbia* Italian: rage.

[4] *the firm which no longer produces Byron* The publishing firm of John Murray, which had been founded in the eighteenth century by John Murray (1745–93) and which in the early nineteenth century published the works of such distinguished writers as Lord Byron, Sir Walter Scott, and Robert Southey, also founded the *Quarterly Review* in 1809. At the time Pound was writing, the firm remained an active book publisher, and still controlled the *Quarterly Review*, which had just published Waugh's article.

[5] *Keats* John Keats (1795–1821), whose poetry had famously been attacked in the pages of the *Quarterly Review* a century earlier.

[6] *gens-de-lettres* French: men of letters.

[7] *Laforgue* Jules Laforgue (1860–87), French Symbolist poet.

[8] *Anacreon* Greek poet (c. 572 BCE–448 BCE), noted for both his hymns and his drinking songs.

Since when have helots made a new music, a new refinement, a new method of turning old phrases into new by their aptness? However, the *Quarterly*, the century old, the venerable ... has pronounced this author a helot. They are all for an aristocracy made up of, possibly, Tennyson, Southey and Wordsworth, the flunkey, the dull and the duller. Let us sup with the helots.

I confess [Waugh's] type of mind puzzles me, there is no telling what he is up to. I do not wish to misjudge him, his theory may be the correct one. You never can tell when old gentlemen grow facetious. He does not mention Mr. Eliot's name; he merely takes his lines and abuses them. The artful dodger, he didn't (*sotto voce*[1] "he didn't want 'people' to know that Mr. Eliot was a poet"). The poem he chooses for malediction is the title poem, "Prufrock." It is too long to quote entire.

[Quotes "The Love Song of J. Alfred Prufrock": "For I have known them ... leaning out of windows"]

Let us leave the silly old Waugh. Mr. Eliot has made an advance on Browning. He has also made his dramatic personae contemporary and convincing. He has been an individual in his poems. I have read the contents of this book over and over, and with continued joy in the freshness, the humanity, the deep quiet culture. "I have tried to write of a few things that really have moved me" is so far as I know, the sum of Mr. Eliot's "poetic theory." His practice has been a distinctive cadence, a personal modus of arrangement, remote origins in Elizabethan English and in the modern French masters, neither origin being sufficiently apparent to affect the personal quality. It is writing without presence. Mr. Eliot at once takes rank with the five or six living poets whose English one can read with enjoyment.

The Egoist has published the best prose writer of my generation. It follows its publication of Joyce by the publication of a "new" poet who is at least unsurpassed by any of his contemporaries, either of his own age or his elders.

It is perhaps "unenglish" to praise a poet whom one can read with enjoyment. Carlyle's generation wanted

"improving" literature, Smiles's *Self-Help*[2] and the rest of it. Mr. Waugh dates back to that generation, the virus is in his blood, he can't help it. The exactitude of the younger generation gets on his nerves, and so on and so on. He will "fall into line in time" like the rest of the bread-and-butter reviewers. Intelligent people will read "J. Alfred Prufrock"; they will wait with some eagerness for Mr. Eliot's further inspirations.

from unsigned "Review," *Literary World* (5 July 1917)

Mr. Eliot is one of those clever young men who find it amusing to pull the leg of a sober reviewer. We can imagine his saying to his friends: "See me have a lark out of the old fogies who don't know a poem from a pea-shooter. I'll just put down the first thing that comes into my head, and call it 'The Love Song of J. Alfred Prufrock.' Of course it will be idiotic; but the fogies are sure to praise it, because when they don't understand a thing and yet cannot hold their tongues they find safety in praise." We once knew a clever musician who found a boisterous delight in playing that pathetic melody "Only a Jew" in two keys at once. At first the effect was amusing in its complete idiocy, but we cannot imagine that our friend would have been so foolish as to print the score. Among a few friends the man of genius is privileged to make a fool of himself. He is usually careful not to do so outside an intimate circle. Mr. Eliot has not the wisdom of youth. If the "Love Song" is neither witty nor amusing, the other poems are interesting experiments in the bizarre and violent. The subjects of the poems, the imagery, the rhythms have the wilful outlandishness of the young revolutionary idea. We do not wish to appear patronising, but we are certain that Mr. Eliot could do finer work on traditional lines. With him it seems to be a case of missing the effect by too much cleverness. All beauty has in it an element of strangeness, but here the strangeness overbalances the beauty.

---

[1] *sotto voce* Italian: under voice; i.e., in a subdued voice or in an aside, privately.

[2] *Smiles's Self-Help* The best known work of Samuel Smiles (1812–1904), *Self-Help* (1882) laid out Smiles's theories on developing, educating, and improving the self. Its title became a catchphrase shortly after its publication.

from unsigned "Review," *New Statesman* (18 August 1917)

Mr. Eliot may possibly give us the quintessence of twenty-first century poetry. Certainly much of what he writes is unrecognisable as poetry at present, but it is all decidedly amusing, and it is only fair to say that he does not call these pieces poems. He calls them "observations,"and the description seems exact, for he has a keen eye as well as a sharp pen, and draws wittily whatever his capricious glance descends on. We do not pretend to follow the drift of "The Love Song of J. Alfred Prufrock"…

from Conrad Aiken, "Diverse Realists," *Dial* (8 November 1917)

Mr. T.S. Eliot, whose book *Prufrock and Other Observations* is really hardly more than a pamphlet, is also a realist, but of a different sort. Like Mr. Gibson,[1] Mr. Eliot is a psychologist; but his intuitions are keener; his technique subtler. For the two semi-narrative psychological portraits which form the greater and better part of his book, "The Love Song of J. Alfred Prufrock" and the "Portrait of a Lady," one can have little but praise. This is psychological realism, but in a highly subjective or introspective vein; whereas Mr. Gibson, for example, gives us, in the third person, the reactions of an individual to a situation which is largely external (an accident, let us say), Mr. Eliot gives us, in the first person, the reactions of an individual to a situation for which to a large extent his own character is responsible. Such work is more purely autobiographic than the other—the field is narrowed, and the terms are idiosyncratic (sometimes almost blindly so). The dangers of such work are obvious: one must be certain that one's mental character and idiom are sufficiently close to the norm to be comprehensible or significant. In this respect, Mr. Eliot is near the border-line. His temperament is peculiar, it is sometimes, as remarked heretofore, almost bafflingly peculiar, but on the whole it is the average hyper-aesthetic one with a good deal of introspective curiosity; it will puzzle many, it will delight a few. Mr. Eliot writes pungently and sharply,

with an eye for unexpected and vivid details, and, particularly in the two longer poems and in the "Rhapsody on a Windy Night," he shows himself to be an exceptionally acute technician. Such free rhyme as this, with irregular line lengths, is difficult to write well, and Mr. Eliot does it well enough to make one wonder whether such a form is not what the adorers of free verse will eventually have to come to. In the rest of Mr. Eliot's volume one finds the piquant and the trivial in about equal proportions.

from May Sinclair, *"Prufrock and Other Observations*: A Criticism," *Little Review* (December 1917)

So far I have seen two and only two reviews of Mr. Eliot's poems: one by Ezra Pound in the *Egoist*, one by an anonymous writer in the *New Statesman*. I learn from Mr. Pound's review that there is a third, by Mr. Arthur Waugh, in the *Quarterly*. To Mr. Ezra Pound Mr. Eliot is a poet with genius as incontestable as the genius of Browning.[2] To the anonymous one he is an insignificant phenomenon that may be appropriately disposed of among the Shorter Notices. To Mr. Waugh, quoted by Mr. Pound, he is a "drunken Helot." I do not know what Mr. Pound would say to the anonymous one, but I can imagine. Anyhow, to him the *Quarterly* reviewer is "the silly old Waugh." And that is enough for Mr. Pound. It ought to be enough for me. Of course I know that genius does inevitably provoke these outbursts of silliness. I know that Mr. Waugh is simply keeping up the good old manly traditions of the *Quarterly*. And though the behaviour of the *New Statesman* puzzles me, since it has an editor who sometimes knows better, and really ought to have known better this time, still the *New Statesman* also can plead precedent. But when Mr. Waugh calls Mr. Eliot "a drunken Helot," it is clear that he thinks he is on the track of a tendency and is making a public example of Mr. Eliot.

I think it is something more than Mr. Eliot's genius that has terrified the *Quarterly* into exposing him in the full glare of publicity and the *New Statesman* into shoving him and his masterpieces away out of the public sight. For "The Love Song of J. Alfred Prufrock" and the "Portrait of a Lady" are masterpieces in the same

---

[1] *Mr. Gibson* Poet Wilfred Gibson (1878–1962).

[2] *Browning* English poet Robert Browning (1812–89).

sense and in the same degree as Browning's *Romances* and *Men and Women*.

But Mr. Eliot is dangerous. Mr. Eliot is associated with an unpopular movement and with unpopular people. His "Preludes" and his "Rhapsody" appeared in *Blast*. They stood out from the experimental violences of *Blast* with an air of tranquil and triumphant achievement; but, no matter; it was in *Blast* that they appeared. That circumstance alone was disturbing to the comfortable respectability of Mr. Waugh and the *New Statesman*. And apart from this purely extraneous happening, Mr. Eliot's genius is in itself disturbing. It is elusive; it is difficult; it demands a distinct effort of attention. Comfortable and respectable people could see, in the first moment after dinner, what Mr. Henley and Mr. Robert Louis Stevenson and Mr. Rudyard Kipling[1] would be at; for the genius of these three travelled, comfortably and fairly respectably, along the great high roads. They could even, with a little boosting, follow Francis Thompson's[2] flight in mid-air, partly because it was signalled to them by the sound and shining of his wings, partly because Thompson had hitched himself securely to some well-known starry team. He was in the poetic tradition all right. People knew where they were with him, just as they know now where they are with Mr. Davies[3] and his fields and flowers and birds. But Mr. Eliot is not in any tradition at all, not even in Browning's and Henley's tradition. His resemblances to Browning and Henley are superficial. His difference is twofold; a difference of method and technique; a difference of sight and aim. He does not see anything between him and reality, and he makes straight for the reality he sees; he cuts all his corners and his curves; and this directness of method is startling and upsetting to comfortable, respectable people accustomed to going superfluously in and out of corners and carefully round curves. Unless you are prepared to follow with the same nimbleness and straightness you will never arrive with Mr. Eliot at his meaning.

He insists on your seeing, very vividly, as he sees them, the streets of his "Preludes" and his "Rhapsody."

He insists on your smelling them. And these things are ugly. The comfortable mind turns away from them in disgust.

Instead of writing round and round about Prufrock, explaining that his tragedy is the tragedy of submerged passion, Mr. Eliot simply removes the covering from Prufrock's mind: Prufrock's mind, jumping quickly from actuality to memory and back again, like an animal, hunted, tormented, terribly and poignantly alive. It is nothing to the *Quarterly* and to the *New Statesman* that Mr. Eliot should have done this thing. But it is a great deal to the few people who care for poetry and insist that it should concern itself with reality. With ideas, if you like, but ideas that are realities and not abstractions.

from Review of the First Issue of *The Criterion, The Times Literary Supplement* (26 October 1922)

Mr. Eliot's poem is also a collection of flashes, but there is no effect of heterogeneity, since all these flashes are relevant to the same thing and together give what seems to be a complete expression of this poet's vision of modern life. We have here range, depth, and beautiful expression. What more is necessary to a great poem? This vision is singularly complex and in all its labyrinths utterly sincere. It is the mystery of life that it shows two faces, and we know of no other modern poet who can more adequately and movingly reveal to us the inextricable tangle of the sordid and the beautiful that make up life. Life is neither hellish nor heavenly; it has a purgatorial quality. And since it is purgatory, deliverance is possible. Students of Mr. Eliot's work will find a new note, and a profoundly interesting one, in the latter part of this poem.

from Gilbert Seldes, "Review," *The Nation* (6 December 1922)

In essence "The Waste Land" says something which is not new: that life has become barren and sterile, that man is withering, impotent, and without assurance that the waters which made the land fruitful will ever rise

[1] *Mr. Henley* English poet and critic William Henley (1849–1903); *Robert Louis Stevenson* Scottish poet and novelist (1850–94); *Rudyard Kipling* English author (1865–1936).

[2] *Francis Thompson* English poet (1859–1907).

[3] *Mr. Davies* British poet William Henry Davies (1871–1940).

again. (I need not say that "thoughtful" as the poem is, it does not "express an idea"; it deals with emotions, and ends precisely in that significant emotion, inherent in the poem, which Mr. Eliot has described.) The title, the plan, and much of the symbolism of the poem, the author tells us in his "Notes," were suggested by Miss Weston's remarkable book on the Grail legend, *From Ritual to Romance*; it is only indispensable to know that there exists the legend of a king rendered impotent, and his country sterile, both awaiting deliverance by a knight on his way to seek the Grail; it is interesting to know further that this is part of the Life or Fertility mysteries; but the poem is self-contained. It seems at first sight remarkably disconnected, confused, the emotion seems to disengage itself in spite of the objects and events chosen by the poet as their vehicle. The poem begins with a memory of summer showers, gaiety, joyful and perilous escapades; a moment later someone else is saying "I will show you fear in a handful of dust," and this is followed by the first lines of "Tristan und Isolde," and then again by a fleeting recollection of loveliness. The symbolism of the poem is introduced by means of the Tarot pack of cards; quotations, precise or dislocated, occur; gradually one discovers a rhythm of alternation between the visionary (so to name the memories of the past) and the actual, between the spoken and the unspoken thought. There are scraps, fragments; then sustained episodes; the poem culminates with the juxtaposition of the highest types of Eastern and Western asceticism, by means of allusions to St. Augustine and Buddha; and ends with a sour commentary on the injunctions "Give, sympathize, control" of the Upanishads,[1] a commentary which reaches its conclusion in a pastiche recalling all that is despairing and disinherited in the memory of man.

A closer view of the poem does more than illuminate the difficulties; it reveals the hidden form of the work, indicates how each thing falls into place, and to the reader's surprise shows that the emotion which at first seemed to come in spite of the framework and the detail could not otherwise have been communicated. For the theme is not a distaste for life, nor is it a disillusion, a romantic pessimism of any kind. It is specifically concerned with the idea of the Waste Land—that the land was fruitful and now is not, that life had been rich, beautiful, assured, organized, lofty, and now is dragging itself out in a poverty-stricken, and disrupted and ugly tedium, without health, and with no consolation in morality; there may remain for the poet the labor of poetry, but in the poem there remain only "these fragments I have shored against my ruins"—the broken glimpses of what was. The poem is not an argument and I can only add, to be fair, that it contains no romantic idealization of the past; one feels simply that even in the cruelty and madness which have left their record in history and in art, there was an intensity of life, a germination and fruitfulness, which are now gone, and that even the creative imagination, even hallucination and vision have atrophied, so that water shall never again be struck from a rock in the desert. Mr. Bertrand Russell has recently said that since the Renaissance the clock of Europe has been running down; without the feeling that it was once wound up, without the contrasting emotions as one looks at the past and at the present, "The Waste Land" would be a different poem, and the problem of the poem would have been solved in another way.

It will be interesting for those who have knowledge of another great work of our time, Mr. Joyce's "Ulysses," to think of the two together.[2] That "The Waste Land" is, in a sense, the inversion and the complement of "Ulysses" is at least tenable. We have in "Ulysses" the poet defeated, turning outward, savoring the ugliness which is no longer transmutable into beauty, and, in the end, homeless. We have in "The Waste Land" some indication of the inner life of such a poet. The contrast between the forms of these two works is not expressed in the recognition that one is among the longest and one among the shortest of works in its genre; the important thing is that in each the theme, once it is comprehended, is seen to have dictated the form. More important still, I fancy, is that each has expressed something of

---

[1] *Upanishads*   Mystical scriptures of Hinduism.

[2] *It will be interesting ... the two together*   Ezra Pound may have been the first to make this comparison; when Pound was lobbying for the publication of *The Waste Land* in the United States, he wrote to Scofield Thayer, editor of *The Dial*, claiming that Eliot's "poem is as good in its way as *Ulysses* is in its way." Seldes was then Managing Editor of *The Dial*, in the pages of which *The Waste Land* was published on 20 October 1922 (four days after its first British publication, in the first issue of *The Criterion*).

supreme relevance to our present life in the everlasting terms of art.

from I.A. Richards, *Principles of Literary Criticism* (1926)

Mr. Eliot's poetry has occasioned an unusual amount of irritated or enthusiastic bewilderment. The bewilderment has several sources. The most formidable is the unobtrusiveness, in some cases the absence, of any coherent intellectual thread upon which the items of the poem are strung. A reader of "Gerontion," of "Preludes," or of "The Waste Land," may, if he will, after repeated readings, introduce such a thread. Another reader after much effort may fail to contrive one. But in either case energy will have been misapplied. For the items are united by the accord, contrast, and interaction of their emotional effects, not by an intellectual scheme that analysis must work out. The value lies in the unified response which this interaction creates in the right reader. The only intellectual activity required takes place in the realisation of the separate items. We can, of course, make a "rationalisation" of the whole experience, as we can of any experience. If we do, we are adding something which does not belong to the poem. Such a logical scheme is, at best, a scaffolding that vanishes when the poem is constructed. But we have so built into our nervous systems a demand for intellectual coherence, even in poetry, that we find a difficulty in doing without it.

This point may be misunderstood, for the charge most usually brought against Mr. Eliot's poetry is that it is overintellectualised. One reason for this is his use of allusion. A reader who in one short poem picks up allusions to *The Aspern Papers, Othello,* "A Toccata of Galuppi's," *Marston, The Phoenix and the Turtle, Antony and Cleopatra* (twice), "The Extasie," *Macbeth, The Merchant of Venice,* and Ruskin, feels that his wits are being unusually well exercised. He may easily leap to the conclusion that the basis of the poem is in wit also. But this would be a mistake. These things come in, not that the reader may be ingenious or admire the writer's erudition (this last accusation has tempted several critics to disgrace themselves), but for the sake of the emotional aura which they bring and the attitudes they incite. Allusion in Mr. Eliot's hands is a technical device for compression. "The Waste Land" is the equivalent in content to an epic. Without this device twelve books would have been needed. But these allusions and the notes in which some of them are elucidated have made many a petulant reader turn down his thumb at once. Such a reader has not begun to understand what it is all about.

This objection is connected with another, that of obscurity. To quote a recent pronouncement upon "The Waste Land" from Mr. Middleton Murry: "The reader is compelled, in the mere effort to understand, to adopt an attitude of intellectual suspicion, which makes impossible the communication of feeling. The work offends against the most elementary canon of good writing: that the immediate effect should be unambiguous." Consider first this "canon." What would happen, if we pressed it, to Shakespeare's greatest sonnets or to *Hamlet*? The truth is that very much of the best poetry is necessarily ambiguous in its immediate effect. Even the most careful and responsive reader must reread and do hard work before the poem forms itself clearly and unambiguously in his mind. An original poem, as much as a new branch of mathematics, compels the mind which receives it to grow, and this takes time. Anyone who upon reflection asserts the contrary for his own case must be either a demigod or dishonest; probably Mr. Murry was in haste. His remarks show that he has failed in his attempt to read the poem, and they reveal, in part, the reason for his failure—namely, his own overintellectual approach. To read it successfully he would have to discontinue his present self-mystifications.

The critical question in all cases is whether the poem is worth the trouble it entails. For "The Waste Land" this is considerable. There is Miss Weston's *From Ritual to Romance* to read, and its "astral" trimmings to be discarded—they have nothing to do with Mr. Eliot's poem. There is Canto XXVI of the *Purgatorio* to be studied—the relevance of the close of that canto to the whole of Mr. Eliot's work must be insisted upon. It illuminates his persistent concern with sex, the problem of our generation, as religion was the problem of the last. There is the central position of Tiresias in the poem to be puzzled out—the cryptic form of the note which Mr. Eliot writes on this point is just a little tiresome. It is a way of underlining the fact that the poem is concerned with many aspects of the one fact of sex, a hint that is perhaps neither indispensable nor entirely successful.

When all this has been done by the reader, when the materials with which the words are to clothe themselves have been collected, the poem still remains to be read. And it is easy to fail in this undertaking. An "attitude of intellectual suspicion" must certainly be abandoned. But this is not difficult to those who still know how to give their feelings precedence to their thoughts, who can accept and unify an experience without trying to catch it in an intellectual net or to squeeze out a doctrine. One form of this attempt must be mentioned. Some, misled no doubt by its origin in a Mystery, have endeavoured to give the poem a symbolical reading. But its symbols are not mystical, but emotional. They stand, that is, not for ineffable objects, but for normal human experience. The poem, in fact, is radically naturalistic; only its compression makes it appear otherwise. And in this it probably comes nearer to the original Mystery which it perpetuates than transcendentalism does.

If it were desired to label in three words the most characteristic feature of Mr. Eliot's technique, this might be done by calling his poetry a "music of ideas." The ideas are of all kinds, abstract and concrete, general and particular, and, like the musician's phrases, they are arranged, not that they may tell us something, but that their effects in us may combine into a coherent whole of feeling and attitude and produce a peculiar liberation of the will. They are there to be responded to, not to be pondered or worked out....

How this technique lends itself to misunderstandings we have seen. But many readers who have failed in the end to escape bewilderment have begun by finding on almost every line that Mr. Eliot has written—if we except certain youthful poems on American topics— that personal stamp which is the hardest thing for the craftsman to imitate and perhaps the most certain sign that the experience, good or bad, rendered in the poem is authentic. Only those unfortunate persons who are incapable of reading poetry can resist Mr. Eliot's rhythms. The poem as a whole may elude us while every fragment, as a fragment, comes victoriously home. It is difficult to believe that this is Mr. Eliot's fault rather than his reader's, because a parallel case of a poet who so constantly achieves the hardest part of his task and yet

fails in the easier is not to be found. It is much more likely that we have been trying to put the fragments together on a wrong principle.

Another doubt has been expressed. Mr. Eliot repeats himself in two ways. The nightingale, Cleopatra's barge, the rats, and the smoky candle-end, recur and recur. Is this a sign of a poverty of inspiration? A more plausible explanation is that this repetition is in part a consequence of the technique above described, and in part something which many writers who are not accused of poverty also show. Shelley, with his rivers, towers, and stars, Conrad, Hardy, Walt Whitman, and Dostoevski spring to mind. When a writer has found a theme or image which fixes a point of relative stability in the drift of experience, it is not to be expected that he will avoid it. Such themes are a means of orientation. And it is quite true that the central process in all Mr. Eliot's best poems is the same; the conjunction of feelings which, though superficially opposed —as squalor, for example, is opposed to grandeur —yet tend as they develop to change places and even to unite. If they do not develop far enough the intention of the poet is missed. Mr. Eliot is neither sighing after vanished glories nor holding contemporary experience up to scorn.

Both bitterness and desolation are superficial aspects of his poetry. There are those who think that he merely takes his readers into the Waste Land and leaves them there, that in his last poem he confesses his impotence to release the healing waters. The reply is that some readers find in his poetry not only a clearer, fuller realization of their plight, the plight of a whole generation, than they find elsewhere, but also through the very energies set free in that realization a return of the saving passion.

from Douglas LePan, "Personality of the Poet: Some Recollections of T.S. Eliot" (1979)

Douglas LePan (1915–98), a poet, academic, and civil servant who lived in London in the 1940s, was introduced to Eliot through a letter from fellow-Canadian Wyndham Lewis. The account excerpted below describes conversations during and after World War II in which Eliot spoke of the composition of *The Waste Land*, of writing generally, and of his relationship with Ezra Pound. The excerpt is taken from LePan's *Bright Glass of Memory: A Set of Four Memoirs.*

When I returned from Italy towards the end of the War in Europe and was once again a civilian on the staff of Canada House, we picked up where we had left off. But now our meetings were more varied. We still sometimes met for tea in his office. Other times, though, he came to have lunch with me at the Carlton Grill. This was at the corner of the Haymarket and Pall Mall, and was the only part of the old Carlton Hotel that had been allowed to stay open, the rest having been taken for government offices. I had quickly fallen into the habit of having lunch there more often than I should, partly because it was so close to Canada House, partly because I now had diplomatic allowances and was supposed to spend them on reasonably civilized entertainment, and partly because it served such excellent dry martinis—cold and strong, with plenty of gin and not too much vermouth in them. I was pleased to find that Eliot was as fond of dry martinis as I was, and we always had two or three of them before having lunch.

It was there, amid hovering waiters and white-aproned busboys and trolleys being trundled about with joints and sweets, in a milieu of wealthy businessmen and senior civil servants and women of fashion, that we had some of our most interesting conversations about how to write poetry. I was usually there first. But in a few minutes Eliot would come in, looking tall and brisk and elegant. I was always faintly surprised by how worldly he looked in those surroundings, although more often than not our talk was far from worldly. It was there, I remember, that one day he gave me advice about cutting a poem. When you think you have finished a poem, he advised, look at it carefully to see what is best in it, always bearing in mind that those passages by themselves may convey everything you want to say. If they do, you can cut away all the rest and leave the poem much clearer and stronger. Or the best parts of the poem may need only slight additions to make them complete in themselves. Or they may only need to be linked by brief transitional passages. But always work towards highlighting what is best in the poem. In particular, he warned me against the danger of going on after the poem is really finished. Stop before yielding to the temptation of adding something unnecessary. I think it was at that point that I said that, for me at least, as great a temptation was to open with an unnecessary introduction. He agreed, but in a tone that suggested that for him it was a temptation he had completely outgrown. He did volunteer, though, that when he had first started writing reviews for the *Times Literary Supplement* he had been greatly impressed by some counsel given him by Desmond McCarthy,[1] who had advised him as a matter of routine always to strike out the first paragraph he had written so that the rest of the essay would stand out more sharply.

Naturally I don't remember the course or continuity of many of our conversations at the Carlton Grill. But something else I remember very vividly is his telling me one day at lunch that he wrote the last page of *The Waste Land* in an afternoon and hardly changed anything in it afterwards. It would have been too pedantic for me to have asked him what he meant by the last page of *The Waste Land*. Yet it is by no means clear. In none of the editions in print at that time is the last page a more or less self-contained unit which could plausibly have been written at a single sitting. Nor is that true of any of the manuscripts published much later by Valerie Eliot in her edition of the original drafts of the poem. All that is beyond question is that at least the last eleven lines of the poem, so heterogeneous, so strange, so learned, and yet so molten, were written in an afternoon and never afterwards altered. From the way Eliot spoke, I think it can also be safely added that, after all the trouble he had had with the poem, he took a kind of pride that the end of it was given to him so spontaneously and so quickly.

In speaking to me about cutting, Eliot didn't mention Ezra Pound, although what he was recommending was really a generalization to all poetry of what Pound had done for *The Waste Land*. But one afternoon when I was having tea with him in his office, he did speak to me at length about Pound in an entirely different connection. It was at a time when Pound's name was in all the newspapers as a result of his being charged with treason by the United States Government because of his support for Mussolini during the War; and Eliot was clearly in great distress over what had happened to his old friend. He said he had been going over in his

---

[1] *Desmond McCarthy* Editor, literary critic, and member of the Bloomsbury Group (1877–1952).

own mind what in Pound's character and nature might have brought him to the point where he could be charged with treason. He was still deeply perplexed and uncertain. But he had come to some tentative conclusions. All his life Pound had been extremely generous to writers and artists, particularly to writers and artists who were still unknown. He couldn't think of a single genuine new talent whom Pound had failed to recognize, or had failed to help, if help were required. In cases like that, his generosity had been unfailing and tireless. There he couldn't be faulted. But, on the other hand, he had had very little simple human kindliness of the undiscriminating kind that could go out to charwomen and sales clerks as well as to artists, simply because of irreducible human obligation. There, as Eliot went over

his memories of him, he seemed to be almost totally lacking—almost totally lacking in the common ties that are indispensable for holding a society together. Was it that lack that had led him into treason? He had one other lack, Eliot went on speculatively, that might have had something to do with his willingness to break the bonds of obligation to his own countrymen. It was an almost total lack of humour. Could that also have contributed to his downfall? So Eliot sat in obvious pain, sifting the possibilities, while I was unable to say a word about a problem that clearly came home to him with such intimacy and anguish. I never knew Eliot to speak with such passion and such open bewilderment as when he was speaking of what had happened to Ezra Pound.

JEAN RHYS
1890 – 1979

Jean Rhys, born Ella Gwendolyn Rees Williams, was a West Indies-born writer whose works are strongly marked by her cultural background and by her experience of life as a white Creole woman in the heavily colonized Caribbean and later in metropolitan London. Although she published four novels early in her career, she was not recognized as a major literary figure until the publication of *Wide Sargasso Sea* (1966), which won the prestigious WH Smith Literary Award and became one of the most widely-read novels of the late twentieth century. The novel is a "prequel" to Charlotte Brontë's *Jane Eyre* (1847), in which Rhys gives a voice to Rochester's insane and confined wife, Bertha Mason. Rhys made no secret of her motive for writing the book; as she remarked in an interview, "I was convinced Charlotte Brontë must have had something against the West Indies, and I was angry about it." She was thus led to explore the conflict of cultures between colonizer and colonized as she cast in a different light the central motif of *Jane Eyre*—that of a helpless female outsider, powerless and victimized, who relies on older European men for protection. In doing so, Rhys anticipated by a decade or more many of the insights of postcolonialism, the literary movement examining the repercussions of imperialism on subject nations and their citizens that became prevalent in the 1990s. She was one of the first to explicitly connect the marginalization of women with issues of race and class.

Rhys was born in 1890 in Roseau, Dominica, in the West Indies. Her father was a Welsh doctor, and her mother a Dominican Creole of Scottish lineage. She began her education in Roseau, in a convent school. As a white Creole in a predominantly black area, she often felt socially isolated, despite identifying with the black community from an early age. At sixteen she traveled to England, attending the prestigious Perse Prepatory girls' school in Cambridge. While there, Rhys excelled academically, taking first prize in Roman literature in the exams for Cambridge and Oxford. She attended one term at the Royal Academy of Dramatic Art in London in 1909, though she never made it to university; her father died in 1910, leaving Rhys in severely reduced circumstances. Alone and destitute in England, Rhys lived a drifter's life, taking on a variety of jobs: chorus girl (under the stage name Vivian Gray), actress, volunteer cook during World War I, secretary, and ghostwriter of a book about furniture.

In 1919 Rhys married the first of her three husbands. The pair had two children—a son who died as an infant and a daughter—and lived a largely itinerant existence, residing sporadically in Vienna, Budapest, and Paris. During this period she acquainted herself with works of modern art and literature, and began to suffer from the alcoholism that would plague her for the rest of her life. In Paris in 1922, she met Modernist novelist Ford Madox Ford (1873–1939) under whose patronage she began to write. She published her first short story, "Vienne," in Ford's magazine *The Transatlantic Review* in 1924, and followed this with her first collection, *The Left Bank and Other Stories*, in 1927. She continued to publish steadily during the 1930s. Her first novel, *Postures* (1928; *Quartet*, 1929, in the United States), further developed the typical Rhys heroine: sexually alluring, sensitive, and dependent. She followed this with a trio of critically acclaimed semi-autobiographical novels, *After*

Leaving Mr. Mackenzie (1930), *Voyage in the Dark* (1934), and *Good Morning, Midnight* (1939). For some time these publications allowed her to enjoy moderate literary recognition and financial security, but the late 1940s and 50s were marked for Rhys by near-poverty, continuing alcoholism, and trouble with the authorities. Her second husband was jailed in the 1950s for financial misdoing, and she herself spent time in London's Holloway Prison in 1949 after an altercation with neighbors. Rhys brings this period to vivid life in her story of the displaced black drifter, Selina, "Let Them Call It Jazz."

Rhys fell into relative obscurity during the 1940s and 50s, but interest in her work revived with the radio production of *Good Morning, Midnight* in 1958. She followed this with her 1966 masterpiece, *Wide Sargasso Sea*, which she had begun to write over twenty years earlier. The rest of her career was devoted to her memoirs, *Smile Please* (published posthumously in 1979), and her collections *Tigers are Better-Looking* (1968) and *Sleep It Off, Lady* (1976). Rhys died in Devonshire, England, in 1979, at the age of 88.

⌘ ⌘ ⌘

Let Them Call It Jazz

One bright Sunday morning in July I have trouble with my Notting Hill[1] landlord because he ask for a month's rent in advance. He tell me this after I live there since winter, settling up[2] every week without fail. I have no job at the time, and if I give the money he want there's not much left. So I refuse. The man drunk already at that early hour, and he abuse me—all talk, he can't frighten me. But his wife is a bad one—now she walk in my room and say she must have cash. When I tell her no, she give my suitcase one kick and it burst open. My best dress fall out, then she laugh and give another kick. She say month in advance is usual, and if I can't pay find somewhere else.

Don't talk to me about London. Plenty people there have heart like stone. Any complaint—the answer is "prove it." But if nobody see and bear witness for me, how to prove anything? So I pack up and leave, I think better not have dealings with that woman. She too cunning, and Satan don't lie worse.

I walk about till a place nearby is open where I can have coffee and a sandwich. There I start talking to a man at my table. He talk to me already, I know him, but I don't know his name. After a while he ask, "What's the matter? Anything wrong?" and when I tell

him my trouble he say I can use an empty flat[3] he own till I have time to look around.

This man is not at all like most English people. He see very quick, and he decide very quick. English people take long time to decide—you three-quarter dead before they make up their mind about you. Too besides, he speak very matter of fact, as if it's nothing. He speak as if he realize well what it is to live like I do—that's why I accept and go.

He tell me somebody occupy the flat till last week, so I find everything all right, and he tell me how to get there—three-quarters of an hour from Victoria Station,[4] up a steep hill, turn left, and I can't mistake the house. He give me the keys and an envelope with a telephone number on the back. Underneath is written "After 6 p.m. ask for Mr. Sims."

In the train that evening I think myself lucky, for to walk about London on a Sunday with nowhere to go—that take the heart out of you.

I find the place and the bedroom of the downstairs flat is nicely furnished—two looking glass, wardrobe, chest of drawers, sheets, everything. It smell of jasmine scent, but it smell strong of damp too.

I open the door opposite and there's a table, a couple chairs, a gas stove and a cupboard, but this room so big it look empty. When I pull the blind up I notice the

---

[1] *Notting Hill* At this time, an unfashionable and relatively cheap district in London.

[2] *settling up* Paying.

[3] *flat* Apartment.

[4] *Victoria Station* Major railway station in London.

paper peeling off and mushrooms growing on the walls—you never see such a thing.

The bathroom the same, all the taps rusty. I leave the two other rooms and make up the bed. Then I listen, but I can't hear one sound. Nobody come in, nobody go out of that house. I lie awake for a long time, then I decide not to stay and in the morning I start to get ready quickly before I change my mind. I want to wear my best dress, but it's a funny thing—when I take up that dress and remember how my landlady kick it I cry. I cry and I can't stop. When I stop I feel tired to my bones, tired like old woman. I don't want to move again—I have to force myself. But in the end I get out in the passage and there's a postcard for me. "Stay as long as you like. I'll be seeing you soon—Friday probably. Not to worry." It isn't signed, but I don't feel so sad and I think, "All right, I wait here till he come. Perhaps he know of a job for me."

Nobody else live in the house but a couple on the top floor—quiet people and they don't trouble me. I have no word to say against them.

First time I meet the lady she's opening the front door and she give me a very inquisitive look. But next time she smile a bit and I smile back—once she talk to me. She tell me the house very old, hundred and fifty year old, and she and her husband live there since long time. "Valuable property," she says, "it could have been saved, but nothing done of course." Then she tells me that as to the present owner—if he is the owner—well he have to deal with local authorities and she believe they make difficulties. "These people are determined to pull down all the lovely old houses—it's shameful."

So I agree that many things shameful. But what to do? What to do? I say it have an elegant shape, it make the other houses in the street look cheap trash, and she seem pleased. That's true too. The house sad and out of place, especially at night. But it have style. The second floor shut up, and as for my flat, I go in the two empty rooms once, but never again.

Underneath was the cellar, full of old boards and broken-up furniture—I see a big rat there one day. It was no place to be alone in I tell you, and I get the habit of buying a bottle of wine most evenings, for I don't like whisky and the rum here no good. It don't even *taste* like rum. You wonder what they do to it.

After I drink a glass or two I can sing and when I sing all the misery goes from my heart. Sometimes I make up songs but next morning I forget them, so other times I sing the old ones like *Tantalizin'* or *Don't Trouble Me Now.*

I think I go but I don't go. Instead I wait for the evening and the wine and that's all. Everywhere else I live—well, it doesn't matter to me, but this house is different—empty and no noise and full of shadows, so that sometimes you ask yourself what make all those shadows in an empty room.

I eat in the kitchen, then I clean up everything nice and have a bath for coolness. Afterwards I lean my elbows on the windowsill and look at the garden. Red and blue flowers mix up with the weeds and there are five-six apple trees. But the fruit drop and lie in the grass, so sour nobody want it. At the back, near the wall, is a bigger tree—this garden certainly take up a lot of room, perhaps that's why they want to pull the place down.

Not much rain all the summer, but not much sunshine either. More of a glare. The grass get brown and dry, the weeds grow tall, the leaves on the trees hang down. Only the red flowers—the poppies—stand up to that light, everything else look weary.

I don't trouble about money, but what with wine and shillings for the slot-meters,[1] it go quickly; so I don't waste much on food. In the evening I walk outside—not by the apple trees but near the street—it's not so lonely.

There's no wall here and I can see the woman next door looking at me over the hedge. At first I say good evening, but she turn away her head, so afterwards I don't speak. A man is often with her, he wear a straw hat with a black ribbon and goldrim spectacles. His suit hang on him like it's too big. He's the husband it seems and he stare at me worse than his wife—he stare as if I'm wild animal let loose. Once I laugh in his face because why these people have to be like that? I don't bother them. In the end I get that I don't even give them one single glance. I have plenty other things to worry about.

---

[1] *shillings* Coins used in the United Kingdom prior to 1971, each worth 1/20th of a pound; *slot-meters* Meters, here for hot water, operated by inserting a coin into a slot, often used to provide gas heating.

To show you how I felt. I don't remember exactly. But I believe it's the second Saturday after I come that when I'm at the window just before I go for my wine I feel somebody's hand on my shoulder and it's Mr Sims. He must walk very quiet because I don't know a thing till he touch me.

He says hullo, then he tells me I've got terrible thin, do I ever eat. I say of course I eat but he goes on that it doesn't suit me at all to be so thin and he'll buy some food in the village. (That's the way he talk. There's no village here. You don't get away from London so quick.)

It don't seem to me he look very well himself, but I just say bring a drink instead, as I am not hungry.

He come back with three bottles—vermouth, gin and red wine. Then he ask if the little devil who was here last smash all the glasses and I tell him she smash some, I find the pieces. But not all. "You fight with her, eh?"

He laugh, and he don't answer. He pour out the drinks then he says, "Now, you eat up those sandwiches."

Some men when they are there you don't worry so much. These sort of men you do all they tell you blindfold because they can take the trouble from your heart and make you think you're safe. It's nothing they say or do. It's a feeling they can give you. So I don't talk with him seriously—I don't want to spoil that evening. But I ask about the house and why it's so empty and he says:

"Has the old trout upstairs been gossiping?"

I tell him, "She suppose they make difficulties for you."

"It was a damn bad buy," he says and talks about selling the lease or something. I don't listen much.

We were standing by the window then and the sun low. No more glare. He puts his hand over my eyes. "Too big—much too big for your face," he says and kisses me like you kiss a baby. When he takes his hand away I see he's looking out at the garden and he says this—"It gets you. My God it does."

I know very well it's not me he means, so I ask him, "Why sell it then? If you like it, keep it."

"Sell what?" he says. "I'm not talking about this damned house."

I ask what he's talking about. "Money," he says. "Money. That's what I'm talking about. Ways of making it."

"I don't think so much of money. It don't like me and what do I care?" I was joking, but he turns around, his face quite pale and he tells me I'm a fool. He tells me I'll get push around all my life and die like a dog, only worse because they'd finish off a dog, but they'll let me live till I'm a caricature of myself. That's what he say, "Caricature of yourself." He say I'll curse the day I was born and everything and everybody in this bloody world before I'm done.

I tell him, "No I'll never feel like that," and he smiles, if you can call it a smile, and says he's glad I'm content with my lot. "I'm disappointed in you, Selina. I thought you had more spirit."

"If I contented that's all right," I answer him, "I don't see very many looking contented over here." We're standing staring at each other when the door bell rings. "That's a friend of mine," he says. "I'll let him in."

As to the friend, he's all dressed up in stripe pants and a black jacket and he's carrying a brief-case. Very ordinary looking but with a soft kind of voice.

"Maurice, this is Selina Davis," says Mr. Sims, and Maurice smiles very kind but it don't mean much, then he looks at his watch and says they ought to be getting along.

At the door Mr. Sims tells me he'll see me next week and I answer straight out, "I won't be here next week because I want a job and I won't get one in this place."

"Just what I'm going to talk about. Give it a week longer, Selina."

I say, "Perhaps I stay a few more days. Then I go. Perhaps I go before."

"Oh no you won't go," he says.

They walk to the gates quickly and drive off in a yellow car. Then I feel eyes on me and it's the woman and her husband in the next door garden watching. The man make some remark and she look at me so hateful, so hating I shut the front door quick.

I don't want more wine. I want to go to bed early because I must think. I must think about money. It's true I don't care for it. Even when somebody steal my savings—this happen soon after I get to the Notting Hill house—I forget it soon. About thirty pounds they steal. I keep it roll up in a pair of stockings, but I go to the drawer one day, and no money. In the end I have to tell the police. They ask me exact sum and I say I don't count it lately, about thirty pounds. "You don't know how much?" they say. "When did you count it last? Do you remember? Was it before you move or after?"

I get confuse, and I keep saying, "I don't remember," though I remember well I see it two days before. They don't believe me and when a policeman come to the house I hear the landlady tell him, "She certainly had no money when she came here. She wasn't able to pay a month's rent in advance for her room though it's a rule in this house." "These people terrible liars," she say and I think "it's you a terrible liar, because when I come you tell me weekly or monthly as you like." It's from that time she don't speak to me and perhaps it's she take it. All I know is I never see one penny of my savings again, all I know is they pretend I never have any, but as it's gone, no use to cry about it. Then my mind goes to my father, for my father is a white man and I think a lot about him. If I could see him only once, for I too small to remember when he was there. My mother is fair coloured woman, fairer than I am they say, and she don't stay long with me either. She have a chance to go to Venezuela when I three-four year old and she never come back. She send money instead. It's my grandmother take care of me. She's quite dark and what we call "country-cookie" but she's the best I know.

She save up all the money my mother send, she don't keep one penny for herself—that's how I get to England. I was a bit late in going to school regular, getting on for twelve years, but I can sew very beautiful, excellent—so I think I get a good job—in London perhaps.

However here they tell me all this fine handsewing take too long. Waste of time—too slow. They want somebody to work quick and to hell with the small stitches. Altogether it don't look so good for me, I must say, and I wish I could see my father. I have his name—Davis. But my grandmother tell me, "Every word that come out of that man's mouth a damn lie. He is certainly first class liar, though no class otherwise." So perhaps I have not even his real name.

Last thing I see before I put the light out is the postcard on the dressing table. "Not to worry."

Not to worry! Next day is Sunday, and it's on the Monday the people next door complain about me to the police. That evening the woman is by the hedge, and when I pass her she says in very sweet quiet voice, "*Must* you stay? *Can't* you go?" I don't answer. I walk out in the street to get rid of her. But she run inside her house to the window, she can still see me. Then I start to sing, so she can understand I'm not afraid of her. The husband call out: "If you don't stop that noise I'll send for the police." I answer them quite short. I say, "You go to hell and take your wife with you." And I sing louder.

The police come pretty quick—two of them. Maybe they just round the corner. All I can say about police, and how they behave is I think it all depend who they dealing with. Of my own free will I don't want to mix up with police. No.

One man says, you can't cause this disturbance here. But the other asks a lot of questions. What is my name? Am I tenant of a flat in No. 17? How long have I lived there? Last address and so on. I get vexed the way he speak and I tell him, "I come here because somebody steal my savings. Why you don't look for my money instead of bawling at me? I work hard for my money. All-you don't do one single thing to find it."

"What's she talking about?" the first one says, and the other one tells me, "You can't make that noise here. Get along home. You've been drinking."

I see that woman looking at me and smiling, and other people at their windows, and I'm so angry I bawl at them too. I say, "I have absolute and perfect right to be in the street same as anybody else, and I have absolute and perfect right to ask the police why they don't even look for my money when it disappear. It's because a dam' English thief take it you don't look," I say. The end of all this is that I have to go before a magistrate, and he fine me five pounds for drunk and disorderly, and he give me two weeks to pay.

When I get back from the court I walk up and down the kitchen, up and down, waiting for six o'clock because I have no five pounds left, and I don't know what to do. I telephone at six and a woman answers me very short and sharp, then Mr. Sims comes along and he don't sound too pleased either when I tell him what happen. "Oh Lord!" he says, and I say I'm sorry. "Well don't panic," he says, "I'll pay the fine. But look, I don't think … " Then he breaks off and talk to some other person in the room. He goes on, "Perhaps better not stay at No. 17. I think I can arrange something else. I'll call for you Wednesday—Saturday latest. Now behave till then." And he hang up before I can answer that I don't want to wait till Wednesday, much less Saturday. I want to get out of that house double quick and with no delay. First I think I ring back, then I think better not as he sound so vex.

I get ready, but Wednesday he don't come, and Saturday he don't come. All the week I stay in the flat. Only once I go out and arrange for bread, milk and eggs to be left at the door, and seems to me I meet up with a lot of policemen. They don't look at me, but they see me all right. I don't want to drink—I'm all the time listening, listening and thinking, how can I leave before I know if my fine is paid? I tell myself the police let me know, that's certain. But I don't trust them. What they care? The answer is Nothing. Nobody care. One afternoon I knock at the old lady's flat upstairs, because I get the idea she give me good advice. I can hear her moving about and talking, but she don't answer and I never try again.

Nearly two weeks pass like that, then I telephone. It's the woman speaking and she say, "Mr. Sims is not in London at present." I ask, "When will he be back—it's urgent," and she hang up. I'm not surprised. Not at all. I knew that would happen. All the same I feel heavy like lead. Near the phone box is a chemist's shop, so I ask him for something to make me sleep, the day is bad enough, but to lie awake all night—Ah no! He gives me a little bottle marked *One or two tablets only*" and I take three when I go to bed because more and more I think that sleeping is better than no matter what else. However, I lie there, eyes wide open as usual, so I take three more. Next thing I know the room is full of sunlight, so it must be late afternoon, but the lamp is still on. My head turn around and I can't think well at all. At first I ask myself how I get to the place. Then it comes to me, but in pictures—like the landlady kicking my dress, and when I take my ticket at Victoria Station, and Mr. Sims telling me to eat the sandwiches, but I can't remember everything clear, and I feel very giddy and sick. I take in the milk and eggs at the door, go in the kitchen, and try to eat but the food hard to swallow.

It's when I'm putting the things away that I see the bottles—pushed back on the lowest shelf in the cupboard.

There's a lot of drink left, and I'm glad I tell you. Because I can't bear the way I feel. Not any more. I mix a gin and vermouth and I drink it quick, then I mix another and drink it slow by the window. The garden looks different, like I never see it before. I know quite well what I must do, but it's late now—tomorrow. I have one more drink, of wine this time, and then a song come in my head, I sing it and I dance it, and more I sing, more I am sure this is the best tune that has ever come to me in all my life.

The sunset light from the window is gold colour. My shoes sound loud on the boards. So I take them off, my stockings too and go on dancing but the room feel shut in, I can't breathe, and I go outside still singing. Maybe I dance a bit too. I forget all about that woman till I hear her saying, "Henry, look at this." I turn around and I see her at the window. "Oh yes, I wanted to speak with you," I say, "Why bring the police and get me in bad trouble? Tell me that."

"And you tell *me* what you're doing here at all," she says. "This is a respectable neighbourhood."

Then the man come along. "Now young woman, take yourself off. You ought to be ashamed of this behaviour."

"It's disgraceful," he says, talking to his wife, but loud so I can hear, and she speaks loud too—for once. "At least the other tarts[1] that crook installed here were *white* girls," she says.

"You a dam' fouti[2] liar," I say. "Plenty of those girls in your country already. Numberless as the sands on the shore. You don't need me for that."

"You're not a howling success at it certainly." Her voice sweet sugar again. "And you won't be seeing much more of your friend Mr. Sims. He's in trouble too. Try somewhere else. Find somebody else. If you can, of course." When she say that my arm moves of itself. I pick up a stone and bam! through the window. Not the one they are standing at but the next, which is of coloured glass, green and purple and yellow.

I never see a woman look so surprise. Her mouth fall open she so full of surprise. I start to laugh, louder and louder—I laugh like my grandmother, with my hands on my hips and my head back. (When she laugh like that you can hear her to the end of our street.) At last I say, "Well, I'm sorry. An accident. I get it fixed tomorrow early." "That glass is irreplaceable," the man

---

[1] *tarts* Women considered sexually promiscuous.

[2] *fouti* Crazy.

says. "Irreplaceable." "Good thing," I say, "those colours look like they sea-sick to me. I buy you a better window-glass."

He shake his fist at me. "You won't be let off with a fine this time," he says. Then they draw the curtains. I call out at them. "You run away. Always you run away. Ever since I come here you hunt me down because I don't answer back. It's you shameless." I try to sing "Don't trouble me now."

> Don't trouble me now
> You without honour.
> Don't walk in my footstep
> You without shame.

But my voice don't sound right, so I get back indoors and drink one more glass of wine—still wanting to laugh, and still thinking of my grandmother for that is one of her songs.

It's about a man whose doudou[1] give him the go-by when she find somebody rich and he sail away to Panama. Plenty people die there of fever when they make that Panama canal so long ago. But he don't die. He come back with dollars and the girl meet him on the jetty, all dressed up and smiling. Then he sing to her, "You without honour, you without shame." It sound good in Martinique patois[2] too: "Sans honte."

Afterwards I ask myself, "Why I do that? It's not like me. But if they treat you wrong over and over again the hour strike when you burst out that's what."

Too besides, Mr. Sims can't tell me now I have no spirit. I don't care, I sleep quickly and I'm glad I break the woman's ugly window. But as to my own song it go *right* away and it never come back. A pity.

Next morning the doorbell ringing wake me up. The people upstairs don't come down, and the bell keeps on like fury self. So I go to look, and there is a policeman and a policewoman outside. As soon as I open the door the woman put her foot in it. She wear sandals and thick stockings and I never see a foot so big or so bad. It look like it want to mash up the whole world. Then she come in after the foot, and her face not so pretty either. The policeman tell me my fine is not

paid and people make serious complaints about me, so they're taking me back to the magistrate. He show me a paper and I look at it, but I don't read it. The woman push me in the bedroom, and tell me to get dress quickly, but I just stare at her, because I think perhaps I wake up soon. Then I ask her what I must wear. She say she suppose I had some clothes on yesterday. Or not? "What's it matter, wear anything," she says. But I find clean underclothes and stockings and my shoes with high heels and I comb my hair. I start to file my nails, because I think they too long for magistrate's court but she get angry. "Are you coming quietly or aren't you?" she says. So I go with them and we get in a car outside.

I wait for a long time in a room full of policemen. They come in, they go out, they telephone, they talk in low voices. Then it's my turn, and first thing I notice in the court room is a man with frowning black eyebrows. He sit below the magistrate, he dressed in black and he so handsome I can't take my eyes off him. When he see that he frown worse than before.

First comes a policeman to testify I cause disturbance, and then comes the old gentleman from next door. He repeat that bit about nothing but the truth so help me God. Then he says I make dreadful noise at night and use abominable language, and dance in obscene fashion. He says when they try to shut the curtains because his wife so terrify of me, I throw stones and break a valuable stain-glass window. He say his wife get serious injury if she'd been hit, and as it is she in terrible nervous condition and the doctor is with her. I think, "Believe me, if I aim at your wife I hit your wife—that's certain." "There was no provocation," he says. "None at all." Then another lady from across the street says this is true. She heard no provocation whatsoever, and she swear that they shut the curtains but I go on insulting them and using filthy language and she saw all this and heard it.

The magistrate is a little gentleman with a quiet voice, but I'm very suspicious of these quiet voices now. He ask me why I don't pay my fine, and I say because I haven't the money. I get the idea they want to find out all about Mr. Sims—they listen so very attentive. But they'll find out nothing from me. He ask how long I have the flat and I say I don't remember. I know they want to trip me up like they trip me up about my

---

[1] *doudou* Sweetheart.

[2] *Martinique* West Indian island colonized by the French; *patois* Regional dialect, in this case the Creole dialect of Martinique.

savings so I won't answer. At last he ask if I have anything to say as I can't be allowed to go on being a nuisance. I think, "I'm nuisance to you because I have no money that's all." I want to speak up and tell him how they steal all my savings, so when my landlord asks for month's rent I haven't got it to give. I want to tell him the woman next door provoke me since long time and call me bad names but she have a soft sugar voice and nobody hear—that's why I broke her window, but I'm ready to buy another after all. I want to say all I do is sing in that old garden, and I want to say this in decent quiet voice. But I hear myself talking loud and I see my hands wave in the air. Too besides it's no use, they won't believe me, so I don't finish. I stop, and I feel the tears on my face. "Prove it." That's all they will say. They whisper, they whisper. They nod, they nod.

Next thing I'm in a car again with a different policewoman, dressed very smart. Not in uniform. I ask her where she's taking me and she says "Holloway"[1] just that "Holloway."

I catch hold of her hand because I'm afraid. But she takes it away. Cold and smooth her hand slide away and her face is china face—smooth like a doll and I think, "This is the last time I ask anything from anybody. So help me God."

The car come up to a black castle and little mean streets are all round it. A lorry[2] was blocking up the castle gates. When it get by we pass through and I am in jail. First I stand in a line with others who are waiting to give up handbags and all belongings to a woman behind bars like in a post office. The girl in front bring out a nice compact, look like gold to me, lipstick to match and a wallet full of notes. The woman keep the money, but she give back the powder and lipstick and she half-smile. I have two pounds seven shillings and sixpence in pennies. She take my purse, then she throw me my compact (which is cheap) my comb and my handkerchief like everything in my bag is dirty. So I think, "Here too, here too." But I tell myself, "Girl, what you expect, eh? They all like that. All."

Some of what happen afterwards I forget, or perhaps better not remember. Seems to me they start by trying to frighten you. But they don't succeed with me for I don't care for nothing now, it's as if my heart hard like a rock and I can't feel.

Then I'm standing at the top of a staircase with a lot of women and girls. As we are going down I notice the railing very low on one side, very easy to jump, and a long way below there's the grey stone passage like it's waiting for you.

As I'm thinking this a uniform woman step up alongside quick and grab my arm. She say, "Oh no you don't."

I was just noticing the railing very low that's all—but what's the use of saying so.

Another long line waits for the doctor. It move forward slowly and my legs terrible tired. The girl in front is very young and she cry and cry. "I'm scared," she keeps saying. She's lucky in a way—as for me I never will cry again. It all dry up and hard in me now. That, and a lot besides. In the end I tell her to stop, because she doing just what these people want her to do.

She stop crying and start a long story, but while she is speaking her voice get very far away, and I find I can't see her face clear at all.

Then I'm in a chair, and one of those uniform women is pushing my head down between my knees, but let her push—everything go away from me just the same.

They put me in the hospital because the doctor say I'm sick. I have cell by myself and it's all right except I don't sleep. The things they say you mind I don't mind.

When they clang the door on me I think, "You shut me in, but you shut all those other dam' devils *out*. They can't reach me now."

At first it bothers me when they keep on looking at me all through the night. They open a little window in the doorway to do this. But I get used to it and get used to the night chemise[3] they give me. It very thick, and to my mind it not very clean either—but what's that matter to me? Only the food I can't swallow—especially the porridge. The woman ask me sarcastic, "Hunger striking?" But afterwards I can leave most of it, and she don't say nothing.

One day a nice girl comes around with books and she give me two, but I don't want to read so much. Beside one is about a murder, and the other is about a ghost and I don't think it's at all like those books tell you.

---

[1] *Holloway* Notorious women's prison in London.

[2] *lorry* Truck.

[3] *night chemise* Nightgown.

There is nothing I want now. It's no use. If they leave me in peace and quiet that's all I ask. The window is barred but not small, so I can see a little thin tree through the bars, and I like watching it.

After a week they tell me I'm better and I can go out with the others for exercise. We walk round and round one of the yards in that castle—it is fine weather and the sky is a kind of pale blue, but the yard is a terrible sad place. The sunlight fall down and die there. I get tired walking in high heels and I'm glad when that's over.

We can talk, and one day an old woman come up and ask me for dog-ends. I don't understand, and she start muttering at me like she very vexed. Another woman tell me she mean cigarette ends, so I say I don't smoke. But the old woman still look angry, and when we're going in she give me one push and I nearly fall down. I'm glad to get away from these people, and hear the door clang and take my shoes off.

Sometimes I think, "I'm here because I wanted to sing" and I have to laugh. But there's a small looking glass in my cell and I see myself and I'm like somebody else. Like some strange new person. Mr. Sims tell me I too thin, but what he say now to this person in the looking glass? So I don't laugh again.

Usually I don't think at all. Everything and everybody seem small and far away, that is the only trouble.

Twice the doctor come to see me. He don't say much and I don't say anything, because a uniform woman is always there. She look like she thinking, "Now the lies start." So I prefer not to speak. Then I'm sure they can't trip me up. Perhaps I there still, or in a worse place. But one day this happen.

We were walking round and round in the yard and I hear a woman singing—the voice come from high up, from one of the small barred windows. At first I don't believe it. Why should anybody sing here? Nobody want to sing in jail, nobody want to do anything. There's no reason, and you have no hope. I think I must be asleep, dreaming, but I'm awake all right and I see all the others are listening too. A nurse is with us that afternoon, not a policewoman. She stop and look up at the window.

It's a smoky kind of voice, and a bit rough sometimes, as if those old dark walls theyselves are complaining, because they see too much misery—too much. But it don't fall down and die in the courtyard; seems to me it could jump the gates of the jail easy and travel far, and nobody could stop it. I don't hear the words—only the music. She sing one verse and she begin another, then she break off sudden. Everybody starts walking again, and nobody says one word. But as we go in I ask the woman in front who was singing. "That's the Holloway song," she says. "Don't you know it yet? She was singing from the punishment cells, and she tell the girls cheerio and never say die." Then I have to go one way to the hospital block and she goes another so we don't speak again.

When I'm back in my cell I can't just wait for bed. I walk up and down and I think. "One day I hear that song on trumpets and these walls will fall and rest."[1] I want to get out so bad I could hammer on the door, for I know now that anything can happen, and I don't want to stay lock up here and miss it.

Then I'm hungry. I eat everything they bring and in the morning I'm still so hungry I eat the porridge. Next time the doctor come he tells me I seem much better. Then I say a little of what really happen in that house. Not much. Very careful.

He look at me hard and kind of surprised. At the door he shake his finger and says, "Now don't let me see you here again."

That evening the woman tells me I'm going, but she's so upset about it I don't ask questions. Very early, before it's light she bangs the door open and shouts at me to hurry up. As we're going along the passages I see the girl who gave me the books. She's in a row with others doing exercises. Up Down, Up Down, Up. We pass quite close and I notice she's looking very pale and tired. It's crazy, it's all crazy. This up down business and everything else too. When they give me my money I remember I leave my compact in the cell, so I ask if I can go back for it. You should see that policewoman's face as she shoo me on.

There's no car, there's a van and you can't see through the windows. The third time it stop I get out with one other, a young girl, and it's the same magistrates' court as before.

The two of us wait in a small room, nobody else there, and after a while the girl say, "What the hell are they doing? I don't want to spend all day here." She go

---

[1] *One day ... rest* Cf. Joshua 6, in which the sound of trumpets brings down the walls of Jericho.

to the bell and she keep her finger press on it. When I look at her she say, "Well, what are they *for?*" That girl's face is hard like a board—she could change faces with many and you wouldn't know the difference. But she get results certainly. A policeman come in, all smiling, and we go in the court. The same magistrate, the same frowning man sits below, and when I hear my fine is paid I want to ask who paid it, but he yells at me. "Silence."

I think I will never understand the half of what happen, but they tell me I can go, and I understand that. The magistrate ask if I'm leaving the neighbourhood and I say yes, then I'm out in the streets again, and it's the same fine weather, same feeling I'm dreaming.

When I get to the house I see two men talking in the garden. The front door and the door of the flat are both open. I go in, and the bedroom is empty, nothing but the glare streaming inside because they take the Venetian blinds away. As I'm wondering where my suitcase is, and the clothes I leave in the wardrobe, there's a knock and it's the old lady from upstairs carrying my case packed, and my coat is over her arm. She says she sees me come in. "I kept your things for you." I start to thank her but she turn her back and walk away. They like that here, and better not expect too much. Too besides, I bet they tell her I'm terrible person.

I go in the kitchen, but when I see they are cutting down the big tree at the back I don't stay to watch.

At the station I'm waiting for the train and a woman asks if I feel well. "You look so tired," she says. "Have you come a long way?" I want to answer, "I come so far I lose myself on that journey." But I tell her, "Yes, I am quite well. But I can't stand the heat." She says she can't stand it either, and we talk about the weather till the train come in.

I'm not frightened of them any more—after all what else can they do ? I know what to say and everything go like a clock works.

I get a room near Victoria where the landlady accept one pound in advance, and next day I find a job in the kitchen of a private hotel close by. But I don't stay there long. I hear of another job going in a big store—altering ladies' dresses and I get that. I lie and tell them I work in very expensive New York shop. I speak bold and smooth faced, and they never check up on me. I make a friend there—Clarice—very light coloured, very smart, she have a lot to do with the customers and she laugh at some of them behind their backs. But I say it's not their fault if the dress don't fit. Special dress for one person only—that's very expensive in London. So it's take in, or let out all the time. Clarice have two rooms not far from the store. She furnish them herself gradual and she gives parties sometimes Saturday nights. It's there I start whistling the Holloway Song. A man comes up to me and says, "Let's hear that again." So I whistle it again (I never sing now) and he tells me "Not bad." Clarice have an old piano somebody give her to store and he plays the tune, jazzing it up. I say, "No, not like that," but everybody else say the way he do it is first class. Well I think no more of this till I get a letter from him telling me he has sold the song and as I was quite a help he encloses five pounds with thanks.

I read the letter and I could cry. For after all, that song was all I had. I don't belong nowhere really, and I haven't money to buy my way to belonging. I don't want to either.

But when that girl sing, she sing to me, and she sing for me. I was there because I was *meant* to be there. It was *meant* I should hear it—this I *know.*

Now I've let them play it wrong, and it will go from me like all the other songs—like everything. Nothing left for me at all.

But then I tell myself all this is foolishness. Even if they played it on trumpets, even if they played it just right, like I wanted—no walls would fall so soon. "So let them call it jazz," I think, and let them play it wrong. That won't make no difference to the song I heard.

I buy myself a dusty pink dress with the money.

—1962

DAVID JONES
1895 – 1974

Poet, painter, illustrator, essayist, and engraver, David Jones was an accomplished artist whose work was highly regarded by his contemporaries. Although his poetry has never been widely read, few writers have garnered such high praise from their fellow poets. T.S. Eliot referred to Jones as a "figure of major importance" and called *In Parenthesis* (1937) "a work of genius," while W.H. Auden described *The Anathemata* (1952) as "one of the most important poems of our time," and W.B. Yeats saluted Jones for his tremendous poetic accomplishment. Like these poets, Jones looked to the past—to mythical, historical, literary, and religious sources—for material with which to understand and interpret the present. Using references to Welsh literature and legend, Norse and classical mythology, ancient history, and Catholic liturgy, Jones's poetry attempts to link the contemporary world to a past culture from which it appeared severed. Stylistically, these works are frequently epic in length, fragmented in nature, composed in a combination of prose and poetry, and accompanied by a plethora of Jones's own notes.

Born in Brockley, Kent, in 1895, of an English mother, Alice Ann Bradsawn, and a Welsh father, James Jones, David Jones developed a love for the history and culture of Wales that is evident throughout his work. As an adolescent he studied art at the Camberwell School of Art until the beginning of World War I, when he enlisted in the Royal Welch Fusiliers; he served as a private from 1915–18. Jones's experiences at war served as a basis for his first publication, the prose poem *In Parenthesis*. This highly allusive epic describes the experiences of a British infantry unit as it travels from training in England to the Battle of the Somme—a journey that mirrors that of the Royal Welch Fusiliers.

After the war Jones resumed his artistic education, first at the Westminster School of Art and then, following his conversion to Roman Catholicism in 1921, with a community of craftsmen run by Eric Gill, a stone carver and engraver whose religious convictions had influenced Jones's own decision to convert. References to Roman Catholicism occur in all Jones's poetry but are particularly significant in his religious poem *The Anathemata*, which centers on the ways in which Roman Catholic ritual and symbolism have shaped contemporary Western culture.

Jones died in a nursing home in 1974, the same year that *The Sleeping Lord and Other Fragments* was published. Though this work can be read as a collection of independent poems, recurring motifs link the pieces as they trace aspects of the contemporary world back to the worlds of the Roman Empire and of sixth-century Britain. *The Sleeping Lord* begins with a modern artist lamenting the futility of his work, but it concludes with a vision of faith in the ultimate triumph of the artist, a vision echoed in many of Jones's poems and essays. While Jones agreed with Eliot's statement that the modern poet was offered "very little assistance" by a society that appeared to rate scientific, technological, and commercial progress over cultural values or artistic achievement, Jones remained firm in his belief that the artist, as a perpetuator of culture, served a function that was fundamental to human experience.

⌘ ⌘ ⌘

from *In Parenthesis*

from "PREFACE"

This writing has to do with some things I saw, felt, &
was part of. The period covered begins early in
December 1915 and ends early in July 1916. The first
date corresponds to my going to France. The latter
roughly marks a change in the character of our lives in
the Infantry on the West Front. From then onward
things hardened into a more relentless, mechanical
affair, took on a more sinister aspect. The wholesale
slaughter of the later years, the conscripted levies filling
the gaps in every file of four, knocked the bottom out of
the intimate, continuing, domestic life of small con-
tingents of men, within whose structure Roland could
find, and, for a reasonable while, enjoy, his Oliver.[1] In
the earlier months there was a certain attractive
amateurishness, and elbow-room for idiosyncrasy that
connected one with a less exacting past. The period of
the individual rifle-man, of the "old sweat" of the Boer
campaign, the "Bairnsfather" war, seemed to terminate
with the Somme battle.[2] There were, of course, glimpses
of it long after—all through in fact—but it seemed
never quite the same.

... My companions in the war were mostly
Londoners with an admixture of Welshmen, so that the
mind and folk-life of those two differing racial groups
are an essential ingredient to my theme. Nothing could
be more representative. These came from London.
Those from Wales. Together they bore in their bodies
the genuine tradition of the Island of Britain, from
Bendigeid Vran to Jingle and Marie Lloyd.[3] These were
the children of Doll Tearsheet. Those are before

Sketch by David Jones.
Frontispiece to *In Parenthesis*, 1937.

Caractacus[4] was. Both speak in parables, the wit of both
is quick, both are natural poets; yet no two groups could
well be more dissimilar. It was curious to know them
harnessed together, and together caught in the toils of
"good order and military discipline"; to see them shape
together to the remains of an antique regimental
tradition, to see them react to the few things that united
us—the same jargon, the same prejudice against "other
arms" and against the Staff, the same discomforts, the
same grievances, the same maims, the same deep fears,
the same pathetic jokes; to watch them, oneself part of
them, respond to the war landscape; for I think the day
by day in the Waste Land, the sudden violences and the
long stillnesses, the sharp contours and unformed voids
of that mysterious existence, profoundly affected the
imaginations of those who suffered it. It was a place of

---

[1] *Roland ... Oliver* In the Old French epic *Chanson de Roland* (*The
Song of Roland*), Oliver is Roland's companion-at-arms.

[2] *Boer campaign* War between Great Britain and the South African
Republic and the Orange Free State (1899–1902); *"Bairnsfather"
war* I.e., World War I. Bruce Bairnsfather (1888–1959) served as an
infantryman in the war and typified the spirit of his fellow infantryman
in his cartoon "Old Bill"; *Somme battle* July–November 1916.

[3] *Bendigeid Vran* Heroic king of old Welsh legend; *Jingle* Alfred
Jingle, a notorious rascal in Charles Dickens's *Pickwick Papers*
(1836–37); *Marie Lloyd* Popular singer known as "Queen of the
music hall" (1870–1922).

[4] *Doll Tearsheet* Prostitute in Shakespeare's *Henry IV.II*;
Caractacus Caradoc, first-century CE British king who, after the
Roman invasion of England, led a rebellion against Emperor
Claudius.

enchantment. It is perhaps best described in Malory,[1] book 4, chapter 15—that landscape spoke "with a grimly voice."

… This writing is called "In Parenthesis" because I have written it in a kind of space between—I don't know between quite what—but as you turn aside to do something; and because for us amateur soldiers (and especially for the writer, who was not only amateur, but grotesquely incompetent, a knocker-over of piles, a parade's despair) the war itself was a parenthesis—how glad we thought we were to step outside its brackets at the end of '18—and also because our curious type of existence here is altogether in parenthesis.

D.J.

from PART 7: THE FIVE UNMISTAKABLE MARKS[2]

Across upon this undulated board of verdure chequered bright
when you look to left and right
small, drab, bundled pawns severally make effort
moved in tenuous line
and if you looked behind—the next wave came slowly,
as successive surfs creep in to dissipate on flat shore;
and to your front, stretched long laterally,
and receded deeply,
the dark wood.

And now the gradient runs more flatly toward the separate scarred saplings, where they make fringe for the interior thicket and you take notice.
　　There between the thinning uprights
at the margin
straggle tangled oak and flayed sheeny beech-bole, and fragile birch whose silver queenery is draggled and un-graced
and June shoots lopt
and fresh stalks bled
　　　　runs the Jerry° trench.　　　　*German*

And cork-screw stapled trip-wire
to snare among the briars
and iron warp with bramble weft[3]
with meadow-sweet and lady-smock[4]
for a fair camouflage.

Mr. Jenkins half inclined his head to them—he walked just barely in advance of his platoon and immediately to the left of Private Ball.

　　He makes the conventional sign
and there is the deeply inward effort of spent men who would make response for him,
and take it at the double.
He sinks on one knee
and now on the other,
his upper body tilts in rigid inclination
this way and back;
weighted lanyard[5] runs out to full tether,
　　　　swings like a pendulum
　　　　　　and the clock run down.
Lurched over, jerked iron saucer over tilted brow,
clampt unkindly over lip and chin
nor no ventaille[6] to this darkening
　　　　and masked face lifts to grope the air
and so disconsolate;
enfeebled fingering at a paltry strap—
buckle holds,
holds him blind against the morning.
　　Then stretch still where weeds pattern the chalk predella[7]
—where it rises to his wire[8]—and Sergeant T. Quilter takes over. …

It's difficult with the weight of the rifle.
Leave it—under the oak.
Leave it for a salvage-bloke

---

[1] *Malory*　Sir Thomas Malory's *Le Morte Darthur* (*The Death of Arthur*).

[2] [Jones's note]　Carroll's *Hunting of the Snark*, Fit the 2nd, verse 15. [In Lewis Carroll's poem *The Hunting of the Snark*, he describes a fictional animal, the snark, which can be identified by "five unmistakable marks."]

[3] *warp … weft*　Threads that run horizontally and vertically in woven cloth.

[4] *meadow-sweet*　Plant with fragrant white flowers that is found in damp areas; *lady-smock*　Cuckoo-flower, a type of wildflower.

[5] *lanyard*　Short rope or cord (from which the man's whistle hangs).

[6] *ventaille*　Ventail, the visor of a helmet.

[7] *predella*　Raised shelf behind an altar.

[8] [Jones's note]　The approach to the German trenches here rose slightly, in low chalk ridges.

let it lie bruised for a monument
dispense the authenticated fragments to the faithful.
It's the thunder-besom[1] for us
it's the bright bough borne
it's the tensioned yew for a Genoese jammed arbalest[2]
and a scarlet square for a mounted *mareschal*,[3] it's that
county-mob back to back.[4] Majuba mountain and Mons
Cherubim[5] and spreaded mats for Sydney Street East,[6]
and come to Bisley for a Silver Dish.[7] It's R. S. M.
O'Grady[8] says, it's the soldier's best friend if you care for
the working parts and let us be 'aving those springs released smartly in Company billets on wet forenoons and
clickerty-click and one up the spout and you men must
really cultivate the habit of treating this weapon with the
very greatest care and there should be a healthy rivalry
among you—it should be a matter of very proper pride
and
　　　Marry it man! Marry it!
Cherish her, she's your very own.
　　　Coax it man coax it—it's delicately and ingeniously
made—it's an instrument of precision—it costs us tax-
payers, money—I want you men to remember that.
　　　Fondle it like a granny—talk to it—consider it as

---

[1] *besom* Bundle of twigs bound together and used for sweeping;
figuratively, something that cleanses.

[2] *arbalest* Crossbow.

[3] *mareschal* French: marshal.

[4] [Jones's note] The Gloucestershire Regiment, during an action
near Alexandria, in 1801, about-turned their rear tank and engaged
the enemy back to back.

[5] *Majuba mountain* In the battle of Majuba Hill on 27 February
1881, the Boers won a convincing victory over British troops; *Mons
Cherubim* "Angels of Mons," said to be a troop of angels, led by
Saint George, that was observed in the sky by retreating British
troops in the Battle of Mons, on 23 August 1914. Many veterans say
these angels helped them to defeat the superior German forces.

[6] [Jones's note] It is said that in "The Battle of Sydney Street" under
Mr. Churchill's Home Secretaryship mats were spread on the pavement for troops firing from prone position. [In 1911, Churchill, as
home secretary, directed a military attack against a group of anarchists.
The conflict became known as the Battle of Sydney Street.]

[7] *Bisley … Dish* The Silver Dish is one of the trophies competed
for in an annual competition at Bisley.

[8] [Jones's note] Refers to mythological personage figuring in Army
exercises, the precise describing of which would be tedious. Anyway
these exercises were supposed to foster alertness in dull minds—and
were a curious blend of the parlour game and military drill. [*R.S.M.*
Regimental Sergeant Major.]

you would a friend—and when you ground these arms
she's not a rooky's gas-pipe for greenhorns to tarnish.[9]
　　　You've known her hot and cold.
You would choose her from among many.
You know her by her bias, and by her exact error at 300,
and by the deep scar at the small, by the fair flaw in the
grain, above the lower sling-swivel—but leave it under
the oak. . . .

　　　The secret princes between the leaning trees have
diadems given them.
　　　Life the leveller hugs her impudent equality—she
may proceed at once to less discriminating zones.

The Queen of the Woods has cut bright boughs of
various flowering.
　　　These knew her influential eyes. Her awarding
hands can pluck for each
their fragile prize.
　　　She speaks to them according to precedence. She
knows what's due to this elect society. She can choose
twelve gentle-men. She knows who is most lord between
the high trees and on the open down.
　　　Some she gives white berries
　　　　　　some she gives brown
Emil has a curious crown it's
　　　　　　made of golden saxifrage.
Fatty wears sweet-briar,
he will reign with her for a thousand years.
　　　For Balder she reaches high to fetch his.
　　　Ulrich smiles for his myrtle wand.
　　　That swine Lillywhite has daisies to his chain—
you'd hardly credit it.
　　　She plaits torques[10] of equal splendour for Mr.
Jenkins and Billy Crower.
　　　Hansel with Gronwy share dog-violets for a palm,
where they lie in serious embrace beneath the twisted
tripod.
　　　Siôn gets St. John's Wort—that's fair enough.
　　　Dai Great-coat,[11] she can't find him anywhere—she

---

[9] [Jones's note] I have employed here only such ideas as were
common to the form of speech affected by Instructors in Musketry.

[10] *torques* Collars, particularly those of precious metal worn by
ancient Gauls and Britons.

[11] *Dai Great-coat* Reference to La Cote Male Tayle, a knight in
Malory's *Morte Darthur* 9.1. "Dai" is a Welsh familiar form of
David.

calls both high and low, she had a very special one for him.

Among this July noblesse she is mindful of December wood—when the trees of the forest beat against each other because of him.

She carries to Aneirin-in-the-nullah[1] a rowan[2] sprig, or the glory of Guenedota.[3] You couldn't hear what she said to him, because she was careful for the Disciplines of the Wars.

At the gate of the wood you try a last adjustment, but slung so, it's an impediment, it's of detriment to your hopes, you had best be rid of it—the sagging webbing and all and what's left of your two fifty[4]—but it were wise to hold on to your mask.

You're clumsy in your feebleness, you implicate your tin-hat rim with the slack sling of it.

Let it lie for the dews to rust it, or ought you to decently cover the working parts.

Its dark barrel, where you leave it under the oak, reflects the solemn star that rises urgently from Cliff Trench.

It's a beautiful doll for us
it's the Last Reputable Arm.

But leave it—under the oak.
leave it for a Cook's tourist to the Devastated Areas and crawl as far as you can and wait for the bearers.[5]

Mrs. Willy Hartington has learned to draw sheets and so has Miss Melpomené; and on the south lawns,
men walk in red white and blue
under the cedars
and by every green tree
and beside comfortable waters.
But why dont the bastards come—

Bearers!—stret-cher bear-errs!
or do they divide the spoils at the Aid-Post.[6]

But how many men do you suppose could bear away a third of us:
drag just a little further—he yet may counter-attack.

Lie still under the oak
next to the Jerry
and Sergeant Jerry Coke.

The feet of the reserves going up tread level with your forehead; and no word for you; they whisper one with another; pass on, inward;
these latest succours:
green Kimmerii[7] to bear up the war.

Oeth and Annoeth's hosts they were
who in that night grew
younger men
younger striplings.[8]

The geste[9] says this and the man who was on the field ... and who wrote the book ... the man who does not know this has not understood anything.[10]

—1937

---

[1] *nullah* River-bed.

[2] *rowan* Mountain ash, a tree said in Celtic folklore to have magical properties.

[3] [Jones's note] The north-west part of Wales. [Llywelyn, the last king of Wales, was killed there in 1282.]

[4] *two fifty* I.e., 250 rounds of ammunition.

[5] [Jones's note] This may appear to be an anachronism, but I remember in 1917 discussing with a friend the possibilities of tourist activity if peace ever came. I remember we went into details wondering if the unexploded projectile lying near us would go up under a holiday-maker, and how people would stand to be photographed on our parapets. I recall feeling very angry about this, as you do if you think of strangers ever occupying a house you live in, and which has, for you, particular associations.

[6] [Jones's note] The R.A.M.C. was suspected by disgruntled men of the fighting units of purloining articles from the kit of the wounded and the dead. Their regimental initials were commonly interpreted: "Rob All My Comrades." [*R.A.M.C.* Royal Army Medical Corps.]

[7] *Kimmerii* Cimmerii, nomadic people who were the earliest known inhabitant of the Crimea.

[8] [Jones's note] Cf. Englyn 30 of the *Englynion y Beddeu*, "The Stanzas of the Graves." See Rhys, *Origin of the Englyn, Y Cymmrodor*, vol. xviii. Oeth and Annoeth's hosts occur in Welsh tradition as a mysterious body of troops that seem to have some affinity with the Legions. They were said to "fight as well in the covert as in the open." Cf. The Iolo MSS. ["Oeth and Annoeth" is often though to be a name for the Otherworld, and is also the name of a prison, said to be partially constructed from the bones of its victims, where King Arthur was kept.]

[9] *geste* Tale, history of notable deeds.

[10] [Jones's note] Cf. *Chanson de Roland*, lines 2095–8:
"Co dit la geste e cil el camp fut,
[Li ber Gilie por qui Deus fait vertuz]
E fist la chartre [el muster de Loüm].
Ki tant ne set, ne l'ad prod entendut."
I have used Mr. René Hague's translation.

ROBERT GRAVES
1895 – 1985

Unlike many poets who served in World War I, Robert Graves is not remembered for verses he wrote during the war, or for a career cut short by a tragic death in the trenches. Graves survived the war and reflected back upon it critically, used his experiences to fuel his literary development, and became a celebrated novelist and mythographer as well as poet.

Robert von Ranke Graves was born in London and educated at the prestigious Charterhouse School, where he prepared to attend Oxford on a classical scholarship. When war broke out, however, he enlisted in the Royal Welch Fusiliers, along with poet Siegfried Sassoon, where Graves became a captain. Graves's poetry from this time shows a range of forms, meters, and rhyme schemes; as a rule, it achieves greater economy and density when he conveys aspects of his war experience. In his work, a sense

Photo by Peter Stark.

of the awfulness of war is often coupled with a positive response to it, such as his pleasure in the bonds he formed with his fellow men. "Two Fusiliers" (1916), for example, celebrates his newfound friendship with Sassoon.

In July 1916, Graves was seriously injured in enemy fire and left for dead. He survived—though his obituary was mistakenly printed in *The Times*—but his injuries and shell shock kept him from active duty for the remainder of the war. In the following years Graves attempted to resume his life—marrying, obtaining a degree in Literature from Oxford, starting a family, and accepting a teaching position at the University of Cairo—but found he could not escape the lingering effects of his war trauma.

After several turbulent years and the dissolution of his marriage, Graves, then 33, embarked on his autobiography. *Goodbye to All That* (1929) details his experiences in the war and its aftermath. (An excerpt appears in the "War and Revolution" section elsewhere in this volume.) Like his poetry, Graves's prose is terse, sharp, and controlled, and in *Goodbye to All That* he analyzes as well as describes his experiences in the war, exploring his anger at its absurdity, his guilt at the part he played, and his undeniable pride in his Regiment. Graves also interrogates (and rejects) the bourgeois and Christian values according to which he was raised, finding them ultimately untenable in post-war society. *Goodbye* is not only the story of a war survivor, but a record of social change from Edwardian to post-war England—one characterized by disillusionment and a disintegration of values.

Having put into the book "all the frank answers to all the inquisitive questions people liked to ask," Graves felt he had finally paid his debt to the past. He said goodbye to his family, friends, and literary community, and retreated to the island of Majorca with American poet Laura Riding. From this point on Graves suppressed all his war poems from collected publications and concentrated on taking his writing in new directions. The most popular of his works were his numerous historical fictions, including *I, Claudius* (1934) and *Claudius the God* (1934), which were adapted into a successful BBC television series. Perhaps equally influential has been his wide-ranging study of mythology, *The White Goddess: A Historical Grammar of the Poetic Muse* (1948), which combines a wide-ranging mythological study with a theory of poetry and poetic inspiration. According to Graves, all poets compose in service to the White Goddess, a triple muse who is mother, lover, and crone and who presides over both the development and the destruction of the poet's creative energies. Graves devotedly served his Muse in the relative seclusion of Majorca until his death in 1985.

⌘ ⌘ ⌘

The Cool Web

Children are dumb to say how hot the day is,
    How hot the scent is of the summer rose,
How dreadful the black wastes of evening sky,
How dreadful the tall soldiers drumming by.

5   But we have speech, to chill the angry day,
And speech, to dull the rose's cruel scent.
We spell away the overhanging night,
We spell away the soldiers and the fright.

There's a cool web of language winds us in,
10 Retreat from too much joy or too much fear:
We grow sea-green at last and coldly die
In brininess and volubility.

But if we let our tongues lose self-possession,
Throwing off language and its watery clasp
15 Before our death, instead of when death comes,
Facing the wide glare of the children's day,
Facing the rose, the dark sky and the drums
We shall go mad no doubt and die that way.
    —1927

Down, Wanton, Down!

Down, wanton,[1] down! Have you no shame
    That at the whisper of Love's name,
Or Beauty's, presto! up you raise
Your angry head and stand at gaze?

5   Poor bombard-captain, sworn to reach
The ravelin[2] and effect a breach—

Indifferent what you storm or why,
So be that in the breach you die!

Love may be blind, but Love at least
10 Knows what is man and what mere beast;
Or Beauty wayward, but requires
More delicacy from her squires.

Tell me, my witless, whose one boast
Could be your staunchness at the post,
15 When were you made a man of parts
To think fine and profess the arts?

Will many-gifted Beauty come
Bowing to your bald rule of thumb,
Or Love swear loyalty to your crown?
20 Be gone, have done! Down, wanton, down!
    —1933

Recalling War

Entrance and exit wounds are silvered clean,
    The track aches only when the rain reminds.
The one-legged man forgets his leg of wood,
The one-armed man his jointed wooden arm.
5   The blinded man sees with his ears and hands
As much or more than once with both his eyes.
Their war was fought these twenty years ago
And now assumes the nature-look of time,
As when the morning traveller turns and views
10 His wild night-stumbling carved into a hill.

What, then, was war? No mere discord of flags
But an infection of the common sky
That sagged ominously upon the earth
Even when the season was the airiest May.
15 Down pressed the sky, and we, oppressed, thrust out

---
[1] *wanton* Ungoverned or uncontrollable person or thing; here, the speaker's penis.

[2] *ravelin* Outwork; a fortification.

Boastful tongue, clenched fist and valiant yard.
Natural infirmities were out of mode,
For Death was young again: patron alone
Of healthy dying, premature fate-spasm.

20 Fear made fine bed-fellows. Sick with delight
At life's discovered transitoriness,
Our youth became all-flesh and waived the mind.
Never was such antiqueness of romance,
Such tasty honey oozing from the heart.
25 And old importances came swimming back—
Wine, meat, log-fires, a roof over the head,
A weapon at the thigh, surgeons at call.
Even there was a use again for God—
A word of rage in lack of meat, wine, fire,
30 In ache of wounds beyond all surgeoning.

War was return of earth to ugly earth,
War was foundering of sublimities,

Extinction of each happy art and faith
By which the world had still kept head in air,
35 Protesting logic or protesting love,
Until the unendurable moment struck—
The inward scream, the duty to run mad.

And we recall the merry ways of guns—
Nibbling the walls of factory and church
40 Like a child, piecrust; felling groves of trees
Like a child, dandelions with a switch.
Machine-guns rattle toy-like from a hill,
Down in a row the brave tin-soldiers fall:
A sight to be recalled in elder days
45 When learnedly the future we devote
To yet more boastful visions of despair.
—1938

NANCY CUNARD
1896 – 1965

Known as the "Enfant Terrible of the Parisian Bohemia" and the "toast of the twenties," Nancy Cunard fought both for civil rights for refugees of the Spanish Civil War and for African-Americans during the 1930s. A published poet, she was equally known as a publisher, journalist, avant-garde Parisian figure, pamphleteer, and was one of the much-photographed women of the period. Her interest in African art, however, placed her in the ambiguous position of being both a promoter and purveyor of primitivism.

Cunard was born at her family's estate in England, Nevill Holt, and was only child of Sir Bache Cunard and Maud "Emerald" Burke. Her father was the heir to the Cunard shipping line and her mother was an American heiress. Cunard led a cloistered Edwardian childhood, raised primarily by

servants. She developed a lively imagination and began writing poetry while still a child. In 1911, her mother left her father and took up residence in London, where she filled the house with writers and artists. One of them, the philosopher George Moore, also Maud's (or "Emerald's") lover, made a point of encouraging Cunard's writing. Her work began to be published in 1916. She attended private schools in Germany and Paris to study music, and was there introduced to Dadaism and various other "unconventional" art forms. In 1916, she announced her engagement to an Australian Guards officer, Sidney Fairbairn. Her parents disapproved of the marriage, which did not last; the couple would separate 20 months later.

Cunard's first volume of poetry, *Outlaws*, was published in 1921. She soon became known as a member of the Paris avant-garde, bohemian set; she wore ivory African bracelets the full length of her arms and was often photographed by artists such as Man Ray. Like others of her set she asserted a woman's right to participate in male discourse and often dressed androgynously.

Leonard and Virginia Woolf, with whom Cunard was friendly, published her third volume of poetry, *Parallax*, in 1925. In 1928 she opened her own publishing house in a small farmhouse just outside of Paris. Cunard's firm, known as the Hours Press, published the work of poets such as Ezra Pound, Robert Graves, and Samuel Beckett. Sales were modest, however, and Cunard closed the press in 1931.

Paris was much more open-minded than Britain when it came to interracial relationships, and Cunard was able publicly to carry on an affair with Henry Crowder, an African-American jazz pianist. She also traveled with him, however, which caused a scandal when she returned to London. Her relationship with Crowder caused a rift between Cunard and her mother and prompted her to write the pamphlet *Black Man and White Ladyship* (1931), a thinly disguised attack on the racist attitudes of her mother and her friends. She later traveled with Crowder to the United States to gather material for an anthology of African-American art, called *Negro*. The anthology brought together many of the leading African-American artists of the time and was widely acclaimed, but Cunard's relationship with Crowder continued to provoke racist responses—including several death threats. She and Crowder would separate in 1933.

In the late 1930s Cunard volunteered to report on the Spanish Civil War. She wrote a number of anti-fascist poems while in Spain; on her return to Paris she asked many of her friends to set down their views of the war. This resulted in *Authors Take Sides* (1937), a volume of artists' responses to the war and to the refugee situation that it was creating in France.

After World War II, Cunard traveled extensively, working as a freelance journalist. She often wrote about the effects of colonialism while traveling to South America, the Caribbean, and Tunisia. The last decades of her life were adversely affected by a growing dependence on alcohol, by mental illness, and by poor physical health. In 1965 Cunard was discovered by the Parisian police lying unconscious in the street. She was unable to provide them with her name and they took her to a charity hospital. She died shortly thereafter at the age of 69.

⌘ ⌘ ⌘

from *Jamaica: The Negro Island*

And the Jamaica of today? Evidently and most essentially a land of black people. It is ridiculous and bound to strike any traveller there overpoweringly that this island should be anything but a black man's territory. Africa is peopled by Negroes. So is Jamaica. As clearly and categorically as that. Of Kingston, the capital, I cannot say otherwise than that I found it a very ugly town, contrived by that singular British spirit which is quite desperately without any concept of even the existence of plan, architecture, or form. Yes, totally in keeping with the administrative and official atmosphere, which in other words signifies no geographic or human atmosphere of any kind. Spanish Town[1] is different; the Latins made it, and though frequent earthquakes have shaken half of it down the sort of warm yellow sunset colouring on the lovely 18th century buildings gives an idea of what the white man's past must have looked like.

Of the black man's past ... observe his present. Those wattled[2] huts the slaves lived in, doing their cooking in still rougher shanties, or outside ... all this is swept away? Indeed no. In the north, at least in such parts as I saw, the description of the 17th and 18th century writers is exactly appropriate still. I went through the island in the hot July days. There are few inns for the tourist save along the sea-coast. In Mande-

ville, a large country town inland, there are one or two "white" hotels, and banks. The feeling of the rather tentative "luxuries" you visualise the white man in general, the British in particular, hazarding in lands wrested from the natives. But no white people visible. Not one. It was market day, a sea of black people, a most vivacious crowd. What are they selling? The fruits of the earth; akees,[3] yams, plantains, and various delicious exotic half-fruits, half-nuts. Twists of rough tobacco. And those superb "Jamaica cloths" at one shilling, six pence a square yard, which are made at Manchester in England. All the women wear them turbaned about their heads. You begin to wonder what these blue, red, and yellow striped squares cost to produce in Manchester, begin to suspect the profit made out of these rough cottons, but of course you will never see one in England; they are reserved for export to the West Indian colonies. They are not just kerchiefs, they have the standing of a dress, one shilling, six pence being a sum to the black worker. I looked for the indigenous goods that black Jamaicans might, in their turn, make a profit on in white markets. Sugar? No, she would not sell me less than that keg for one shilling; you could hardly carry one shilling-worth of the rich brown melting cane sugar that has to be searched for as a delicacy in England. Five or six bananas cost one shilling; we know what we pay for them here. Who gets the profits on that? Never the Jamaican peasant grower! Fruits and plantations are largely in the name of the United Fruit Company. The posters of the United Fruit Company are enthroned throughout Jamaica; they sit

---

[1] *Spanish Town*   Former capital of Jamaica when the island was under Spanish rule (1662–1872); located on the western outskirts of Kingston.

[2] *wattled*   Composed of woven branches.

[3] *akees*   Fruits from the *Blighia sapida*, a tropical tree.

on the eminent hills, and facing them on other feathery luxuriant heights are other inventions of white civilisation: tin or brick chapels. These and fine, not much travelled motor roads are the modernities of Jamaica inland. And in the valleys and gorges of Crooked River down comes the daily cloudburst in that season as the old washerwoman slams hurriedly together the dispersed items she has been trying to get clean "in all dese stones." Along the road there would suddenly be an expanse of English park land, not a palm or banana tree in sight. And then the rain made it all go black and dark green, as if one were looking up from under deep water at the low knotted hills of the old Maroon country. It is not possible to describe the rapid changes of this beautiful land; only a film will be able to give any sense of it. Black River, banana, plantain, and palm fronds fiercely tossing in the rain, deserted roads on completely empty mountains, and then the region where the huts are so frail you wonder if people can live in these. They do. They live life out in them, things a man would run up in a day or two, with the smoke coming out through the old pressed-down palm thatch at one corner. Maroon Town, St. James—it was some trouble to find it, for several of the roads that seemed to go there ended after a time in a flank of forest. There were cows' horns on one or two of the houses in that place, perhaps as Obeah[1] signs still, and the sense of the utter remoteness of a barely inhabited region, whose people though pay homage to Christian Sunday with tightly clasped Bibles, very much "dressed up" and with black buttoned shoes. The "progress" lies in the shoes; the wistful longing for shoes you meet with is a class distinction, to possess them constitutes a "rise" in the black labouring class. After Maroon Town there were no more huts even; the forests closed in the steep roads with immense trailing and dripping lianas.[2]

Montego Bay is a sharp contrast. You come down on to a flat sand-stretch. A white man's resort, a bathing beach and accessory hotels, at twenty-five shillings a day. But there were no white men. Again, that night, there was the dense, moving, vivacious black crowd, round a preacher in the open square. The whites have planted Christianity in Jamaica in such a way that it is as much *there* as the native vegetation. In Kingston the raucous

crashing of the Salvation Army is as inescapable as it is insufferable. Imagine a landscape of gravel, of glaring white concrete posts, railings, and flower-beds round an immense, exotic, though somewhat humanity-scarred tree, with a small arrogant statue of the good Queen[3] in whitest marble like the apex of the Victorian wedding cake—that is the centre of Kingston under a flaming sun. A vast number of tropical plants, and again they would be impossible to portray otherwise than by the film, has been gathered into a special garden nearby. This too is a pineapple farm. For working on it the descendant of the slave told me he got about two shillings a day. And it comes to about the same for the man who carries those full banana bunches onto the boats. A full bunch must have between 150 and 200 bananas. If there are less "we bruise them" (destroy them), said the young black worker who was coming down barefoot from the hills to Banana Day in Frankfield.

The English want this colony to progress, they say. Yet it was years before the banana agent, an ex-Justice and schoolmaster, was able to get permission to have the railway brought some eleven miles from its previous terminus to the banana centre, to transport the bi-weekly consignments. He had applied again and again. One day an official came from England. Asked to see the leading citizen of the place. My friend the banana agent is a pure Negro. The Englishman, said he, seemed very surprised at finding a Negro with education and who could explain the situation with detail and authority—very soon after we were allowed to have our railway. Is the ignorance of the white man really as simple as all that? However, what is lacking in ignorance is fully made up in prejudice.

To one coming direct from a distorted America where all coloured people are, governmentally and socially, labelled "niggers," Jamaica may at first seem without any of this social dementia. The colour question is more "subtly" handled by the English. It has the atmosphere of an orderly place. British Authority respected—an old-fashioned tempo, excessively so. But soon enough you notice there is a positive minimum of really black people "in office." By "in office" I mean the shops, all kinds of trading establishments, and all milieus of middle-class independent life. The pure black

---

[1] *Obeah*   Sorcery, witchcraft, medicine of the Caribbean.

[2] *lianas*   Climbing plants that twist around trees in tropical forests.

[3] *good Queen*   I.e., Queen Victoria.

people are on the land, an agricultural peasantry. Or in menial employ. The maids of the inn at which I stayed are black—and shoeless. The harbour workers, the market sellers are so. But in the newspaper offices, the shipping companies, banks, etc., and nearly all upper or middle class strata they are mulatto.[1] This is indeed the white man's doing. As there are so few whites they have established on the rock foundation of British Empire custom the "mulatto superiority" to fill the place of the "white superiority" which, from their very lack of numbers, they cannot operate with the same prestige here. From all times this has been used to divide the peoples of African and semi-African descent. White at the top, mulatto in the centre, and black at the bottom of the economic and social scale.

… We have noted already the tremendously dominant number of black and coloured over whites in Jamaica, and of pure Negro over coloured. There is hardly any middle class in the island. It is essentially, as are other West Indian islands, a place of black peasantry. One is apt to think of "slavery" as the name for the most frightful condition that can befall mankind. Yet the economic state of the mass of black Jamaicans is not far removed therefrom. One shilling a day for ten hours' work in a rope factory is one example of wages. The fruit packers of the United Fruit Company are almost as badly off. There is no other work to go to outside of the equally ill-paid forms of labour in an island which, though ample in proportion to population, cannot employ all its natives as it is. So that large numbers have been emigrating to America to settle, have been going to Cuba for plantation work and have been repatriated therefrom soon after, the conditions in Cuba being even worse. Of natural resources Jamaica has plenty, but insufficient capital to develop these. And it is logical that enterprise and effort will decline when constantly thwarted. Yet the Jamaican Negro peasant is particularly energetic; this comes out most visibly in any chance conversation, for instance, along the roads. In no sense ever an abruti[2] by the encompassment of the economic horizon. Jamaicans are as full of curiosity concerning the rest of the world as they are of talk, mother-wit, and logic. A most lovable and interesting people. They give you a great sense of the *justice* in them. They are subtle, their minds work at such a slant angle (and how apparent this is in the very shortest exchange of words, and in their famous proverbs) that you have the impression no other people in the least like them exist in the world. Probably this is true. And they are a beautiful race, or rather, blend of black races. The women's hair is done in a wealth of twists and knobs and knots and curls—a perfect series in which no two seem alike in style but all suggest direct parentage to Africa. Their manners are exquisite; a lusty, strong, and dignified people, without the least trace of any of the surface "inferiority" or exterior hesitancy that has been beaten and pumped into some of the American Negroes by the bestiality of the American whites.

I am walking along those blue winding macadam[3] roads after rain, when the steam rises through the indescribably lovely trees, through the whole outpouring of these tender and dark green tropics that were so fluid after the dry and tawny Cuba. The black women come out of their houses laughing. "Take us to Eng-land with you" (in a rich sing-song), "we want to go a-way from here" (scanning it, unforgettably). To England, "mother country" of so many plundered black peoples, to the brutality of colour bar and all the talk about "not wanting the damned niggers"? They know nothing about these things. "Oh we would like to see Eng-land so much." These are the loyalest subjects of Great Britain. I pass on wondering *how much longer* the roguery, insolence, and domination of the whites must last.

In a street near the harbour in Kingston an old majestic black cripple hobbles over to me, peers into my face. "English missie going away again, we people here are very poor, very *very* poor—don't forget that." That was all he said. Have I not indeed seen it … And the *busher* (property overseer), the only mulatto I met with in that inland region in ten days: "The poor people are the backbone of this country, and they have a shackle round their necks they cannot shake off." And the black boys in the harbour waters diving for money thrown from gaping passengers on shipboard, swimming miraculously right under the keel from side to side, cheeks bulging with coins, making a bit more maybe than the dockers and ship loaders on such days as

---

[1] *mulatto* Person with one black and one white parent.

[2] *abruti* French: brutalized or worn-down person.

[3] *macadam* I.e., covered with tarmac.

passenger steamers do come in …

That is the Jamaica I saw. It culminates into a certainty that comes like a voice out of the soil itself. "This island is the place of black peasantry, it must be unconditionally theirs. It belongs undividedly and by right to the black Jamaican on the land."
—1934

from *The White Man's Duty*[1]

from "PREFACE"

The logical feeling exists among coloured peoples: "Now Britain is in trouble she needs us, but when it is all over we shall be as before." This could be removed—but to do so would call for a change of heart, and of policy, toward coloured peoples on the part of many of the authorities and officials, *particularly in the Colonies*. In the United States the thirteen million Negroes see the call to the Colours translated for their race into a matter of segregated regiments and army service groups. One of their four hundred newspapers, commenting on a proposal made here in London during the worst air-raids to create separate shelters for coloured people, wrote: "If this is all that Britain is fighting for, the status quo, then to ask American Negroes to fight and die for Britain is like asking them to fight and die for Mississippi" (land of lynchings). True, civilians and soldiers of Great Britain are against treating the American coloured soldiers differently to the white, as they are requested to do. Yet is it possible to say that colour prejudice and colour bar are on the decline?

We salute the forceful article by our Minister of Information, Mr. Bracken,[2] "Colour bar Must Go" (*Sunday Express*, September 20th), but we firmly believe that an act of parliament making all colour bar manifestations an offence (as was the case, for instance, in France before Hitler) would be an efficacious and sensible basis for its eradication. Race prejudice (of Jew, Negro, or any people) belongs to Nazi-fascism and not to democracy. If the British government intends colour prejudice to end, as Mr. Bracken states it does, it will have gone a long way in initiating "the second freeing" of all coloured peoples in the world, over one hundred years, as this would be, after our abolition of slavery itself. The gratitude of those of colour and of those who understand the effects of race prejudice will be acquired in fullest measure.

What is said in this article of Brendan Bracken is today's parallel and continuation of the speeches of the great abolitionists during the twenty-year struggle in Parliament at the end of the 18th century. Let me quote some passages: "The barriers still standing in the way of the social equality of coloured people must be withdrawn." "This is a process which will take time, but responsible people in Britain are determined that it shall be carried through, and the sooner the better." "I should like to emphasise that the theory of equal rights is not a mere high-sounding phrase." "I wish to emphasise here only that we in Britain do not intend to stand fast upon theories of political equality and economic freedom without seeing to it that the victory for which we are striving will be as much theirs as ours."

Colour bar (*legally* non-existent in Great Britain, as says Mr. Bracken) all too often does exist in hotels, lodging-houses, restaurants, bars, public-houses and the minds of landlords. A new clause added to the legal regulations to which these places conform, punishing colour bar, as, say, disorderliness is punished, would be excellent. This outspoken article deals mainly with colour bar in our own country. It is Lord Samuel who throws a revealing light on the colonial situation. In a letter to *The Times* (August 8th), Lord Samuel says that several recent articles on the Colonial Empire "all stress the need for a forward colonial policy," and quotes from one: "Until an end is put to public indifference there is no hope of a truly dynamic policy for the Empire … The key is in the hands of the people at home." Lord Samuel then writes: "The fact is that, while Parliament and the public are becoming more and more uneasy about the Crown Colonies, they are still hardly alive to their own responsibilities." Further he states that the House of Commons "devotes *one day a year* (emphasis

---

[1] *The … Duty* Written in the autumn of 1942, the third anniversary of the declaration of World War II, this treatise examines the focus in both Great Britain and the United States not merely on the defeat of the Nazis, but on post-war reconstruction. In the opening of her "Preface" Cunard asks, "At the cost of this, the Second World War, what transformation of the social and economic world situation is being envisaged? Are the white peoples to be the sole beneficiaries?"

[2] *Mr. Bracken* Brendan Bracken (1901–58).

mine) to the colonial estimates ... There are useful discussions from time to time in the House of Lords. *But there is no normal agency, continuously at work* (emphasis mine), *which will link the democratic forces of the nation with the processes of colonial administration,* which will diffuse the spirit of British policy throughout the Colonial Empire."

What are the "democratic forces of the nation"?

Coloured people translate this, and logically enough, into those who understand and who will back up our plea for "equal rights." A year ago when I was in the British West Indies, black workers said to me constantly: "In England the government and the people talk a great deal now about 'democracy for all after the war.' Do they include *us* in this?" But back in England I was unable to find the slightest increase of interest, concern, or knowledge of our coloured subjects' lamentable conditions, although there was, and continues to be an immense amount of talk and of writing and of hope about the future instauration of "the better life for all."

Democracy is not a difficult idea, or theory, or concept, or state of being to understand, and the colonized peoples have a very clear sense of what it means. *It is exactly what they are asking for*: equal opportunities as the white people in all fields of life. Full equal rights are of course freedom, and freedom has been set down last of all in the words of Clause Three of the Atlantic Charter:[1] "The right of all peoples to choose the form of government under which they live."
—1942

---

[1] *Atlantic Charter* Product of the Atlantic Conference, the meeting of President Franklin D. Roosevelt and Winston Churchill in August of 1941, in which they discussed their strategy of war against the Axis Powers. The treaty became the basis of the United Nations Charter.

ELIZABETH BOWEN
_1899 – 1973_

One of the major writers of her time, Elizabeth Bowen produced numerous short stories and novels that examine the complexities of human relationships. Combining modernist themes of alienation and disillusionment with social comedy and psychological realism, Bowen analyzed the small dramas in the lives of her stuffy, upper middle-class characters. In her fiction, orphans and only children abound, as do hopelessly innocent and socially inept characters; Bowen uses the perspective of these outsiders to interrogate and dissect established social conventions.

Having been raised in an isolated, Anglo-Irish family, Bowen was sympathetic to outsiders. She described the Anglo-Irish—whose dual allegiance to Ireland and England made them outsiders both geographically and politically—as "only children who do not know how much they miss. Their existence, like those of only children, are singular, independent, secretive." An only child herself, Bowen (born Elizabeth Dorothea Cole) lived in her ancestral home, Bowen's Court, in County Cork, Ireland, until she was seven, when her father suffered a mental breakdown and she and her mother moved to England to stay with her mother's relatives. After her mother's death of cancer when Bowen was thirteen, Bowen spent her school years in England and her summers at Bowen's Court with her father. Bowen eventually moved to London to study art, but soon found herself publishing short stories instead—with the encouragement of fellow writer Rose Macaulay, who helped her make the necessary connections in the publishing world. Bowen's first short story collection, _Encounters_, appeared in 1923.

Bowen married Alan Cameron that same year, and the two moved to Oxford, where Bowen published her first novels, _The Hotel_ (1927), _The Last September_ (1929), _Friends and Relations_ (1931), and _To the North_ (1932). After these gained considerable notice, Bowen (who relocated with Cameron to London in 1935) began to move in established literary circles, counting Virginia Woolf, Rosamond Lehmann, William Plomer, Stephen Spender, Iris Murdoch, and literary critic David Cecil among her friends and acquaintances.

Bowen's work was frequently compared to Virginia Woolf's because of Bowen's use of layered narratives and varying points of view, and to the work of E.M. Forster and Henry James because of her detailed studies of individual behavior and societal demands. In Bowen's work, two contradictory worlds, one of moral values and the other of social conventions, often oppose one another, with the demands of the social world usually eclipsing those of the moral one. Ultimately, Bowen shows, any love or meaningful connection between people must be asocial in order to survive. She exposes the insincerities hidden behind conventions, using a disjointed writing style that accentuates her characters' sense of dislocation and disorientation. Narratives jump between past and present and move between various geographical locations, while peculiar turns of phrase and unusual syntax and sentence constructions reflect the characters' sense of unease.

While continuing to produce numerous short stories (in which she sought "an immediacy and purity of sensation," rather than extended character development), Bowen published two of her most successful and technically accomplished novels, _The House in Paris_ (1935) and _Death of the Heart_ (1938). Bowen also completed a memoir, _Bowen's Court_ (1942), which commemorated the family home she had inherited upon her father's death in 1930. Bowen sold the home, which she felt to be a burden both emotionally and financially, in 1959.

During World War II, Bowen worked as an air raid warden and a reporter on Ireland for the Ministry of Information, and it was in this period that she wrote her most enduring and critically acclaimed work. *The Demon Lover and Other Stories* (1945) and her novel *The Heat of the Day* (1949), though not often directly concerned with the war itself, convey the climate and mood of wartime England. As Bowen says in the preface to *Demon Lover*, "The violent destruction of solid things, the explosion of the illusion that prestige, power and permanence attach to bulk and weight, left all of us, equally, heady and disembodied. Walls went down; and we felt, if not knew, each other. We all lived in a state of lucid abnormality."

Though Bowen's reputation during her lifetime has been described as "towering," after her death her work was often overlooked. Lately, however, Bowen has again been recognized as a powerful and influential writer for her critique of class conventions, her unique prose style, and her contributions to the development of the short story.

⌘ ⌘ ⌘

Oh, Madam ...

Oh, madam ... Oh, *madam*, here you are! I don't know what you'll say. Look, sit down just for a minute, madam; I dusted this chair for you. Yes, the hall's all right really; you don't see so much at first—only, our beautiful fanlight gone. No, there's nothing in here to hurt: I swept up the glass. Oh, *do* sit a minute, madam; you look quite white ... This is a shock for you, isn't it! I was in half a mind to go out and meet you, but I didn't rightly like to leave everything. Not with the windows gone. They can see in.

Oh, *I'm* quite all right, madam. I made some tea this morning ... Do I? Oh well, that's natural, I suppose. I'd be quite all right if I wasn't feeling so bad. Well, you know how I always was—I don't like a cup to go. And now ... If you'll only sit still, madam, I'll go and get you something. I know you don't take tea, not in the regular way, but it really is wonderful what tea does for you ... Sherry? I'll go and try, but I really don't know—the dining-room door won't—I'm *afraid*, madam, I'm afraid it's the ceiling in there gone ... And as you know, Johnson's got the key to the cellar, and Johnson went off after the all clear. I said, "You did ought to stay till madam's with us." But he didn't seem quite himself—he *did* have a bad night, madam, and you know how men are, nervous ... I don't know where—back to his wife's, I daresay: he didn't vouchsafe ... The girls? Oh, *they're* quite well, I'm thankful to say. They were

very good through it, really, better than Johnson. They'll be back for their things, that is, if—Well, oh *dear*, madam, wait till you see....

No, I'm all *right*, madam, really ... Do I? Not more than you do, I'm sure. This *is* a home-coming for you—after that nice visit. I don't know what to say to you—your beautiful house! There usen't to be a thing wrong in it, used there, madam? I took too much pride in it, I daresay ... I *know*, madam, the stairs—all plaster. I took the dustpan and brush to them, but as fast as you work it keeps flaking down. It's all got in my hair, under my cap. I caught a sight of myself in Johnson's mirror and I said to myself, "Why, madam will think I've turned white in the night!" ... Yes, there it goes; watch it. It's the shock to the house. Like snow? The things you think of! You *are* brave!

Oh *no*, madam. No, you get through it somehow. You'd have been wonderful ... We'd have done what we could to make you comfortable, madam, but it would not have been fit for you—not last night. If I said once I said a dozen times, to the others, "Well, thank goodness *madam's* not here tonight; thank goodness madam's away." ... Yes, we all sat down in our sitting-room. It *is* a strong basement. It does rock, but not like the rest of the house. ... It was that one they dropped in the cinema that did our damage, madam. They say what went on the cinema weighed a ton. They should never have put a cinema, not in this neighbourhood. However—poor thing, it's not there now.... No, *I* haven't, madam; I haven't been out this morning. I only just saw what I saw from the back. And I'm only glad *you* didn't—it would only distress you. I expect your taxi brought you the other way. All I know I heard from the warden. He seemed to consider we'd had quite an escape.

Well, I suppose we did, madam—that's if you come to think of it. They did seem to have quite set their hearts on us. I don't know how many went in the park. When it was not the bangs it was the hums. ... Well, I don't know, really—what *could* we do? As I say, all things come to an end. It would have sickened you, madam, to hear our glass going. Well, you've *seen* the front. No wonder you came in white. Then that ceiling down. I know *I* thought, "Well, there does go the house!" Of course I ran up at once, but I couldn't do anything.... The wardens were nice; they were very nice gentlemen. I don't know how they think of it all, I'm sure.

You won't take *anything,* madam? ... You'll need your fur coat, excuse me, madam, you will. There's the draught right through the house. You don't want to catch cold, not on top of everything. ... No, it's useless; you *can't* move that dining-room door ... But the house has been wonderful, madam, really—you really have cause to be proud of it. Yes, it's all right here in the little telephone room—that is—well, you can see for yourself ... What is it—an ashtray, madam? ... No, I don't wonder, really: I'm sure if I were a smoker—you have to have *something,* don't you, to fall back on? I'll bring the ashtray upstairs with us for the rest of the stumps ... Yes, madam, I'll follow, madam. As you say, get it over.... Oh dear, madam, you *are* upset.

You can't help that; you can't but walk in the plaster. I'll have it all off in a day or two.

Airy? Well yes, if you call it that. I'd sooner our landing window, I must say. You see, what the warden said happened, the blast passed through. Well, I don't know, I'm sure: that was what he said. You have to have names for things, I suppose.

The drawing-room? Oh, *madam* ... Very well ... *There* !

I don't know what to say: really ... You know, madam, I'd rather last night again than have to show you all this. It's a piece in the Bible, isn't it, where they say not to set your heart on anything on this earth. But that's not nature, not when you care for things ...

Haven't you, madam? It's good of you to say so. I know how I'd have felt if I'd thought there ever *was* dust in here. It used to sort of sparkle, didn't it, in its way ... As it is—why, look, madam: just this rub with my apron and the cabinet starts to come up again, doesn't it? Like a mirror—look—as though nothing had happened ... If I could get started in here—but what am I talking about! The windows gone—it doesn't look decent, does it ... Oh, I *know,* madam, I know: your satin curtains, madam! Torn and torn, like a maniac been at them. Well, he *is* a maniac, isn't he? ... Yes, it did look worse—I swept up a bit in here. But I don't seem to have any head—I didn't know where to start.

That's right, madam, go on the balcony. You won't see so much different from there. To look at the park, you wouldn't hardly believe ... Sun shining ... Well, it may do good, I suppose. But this doesn't rightly feel like a day to me ... All that mess there? That was one of those last night. Yes, it *sounded* near us, all right: I hadn't properly looked ... Oh dear, madam, did that give you a turn?

No, I don't know yet, madam; I haven't heard. I didn't care to go asking out on the street. I expect I'd hear in good time, if—It doesn't do to meet trouble. No, not Kentish Town, madam, Camden Town. ... Well, I have been wondering, naturally. It did pass through my mind that my sister'd telephone me. ... Well, I would like to —just run up there for a minute? That is, if my sister doesn't telephone me. Just run up there for a minute this afternoon? That always has been my home.... It's very kind of you, madam: I hope so, too....

Little houses aren't strong, madam. You always worry a bit. When I looked out at the back this morning at some of those little houses, where the mews used to be—(no, don't *you* look out that way, madam; you can't do anything; better look at the park)—I thought, "Well, they're paper, aren't they." They're not built to stand up. That was the big bomb they got, the cinema bomb ... Yes, they always seemed to be nice people: the girls and I used to go through that way to shop. Very quiet; you wouldn't know they were there. I don't think this terrace has ever had to complain ... Didn't you, madam? No, I hardly suppose you did ... Well, perhaps they were, madam. Let's hope that they were.

That's right madam, turn up your coat collar. The draught comes right through.

What with you being so good about everything, and now I take another look—well, it might be worse, mightn't it! When we just get the windows back in again—why, madam, I'll have the drawing-room fit for you in no time! I'll sheet my furniture till we're thoroughly swept, then take the electro to the upholstery. Because, look, madam, I don't think anything's *stained* … The clock's going: listen—would you believe that? We mustn't go crying after the curtains, must we? … Well, I did, first thing this morning: I couldn't *but* cry. It all seemed to come over me all at once. But now *you're* back—such a difference I feel! Hitler can't beat you and me, madam, can he? If I can just get these glaziers—they expect you to whistle. It's not good for a trade to be too much in demand, is it? It makes the working people ever so slow.

No such great hurry?—I don't understand—I—you—why, madam? *Wouldn't* you wish—?

Why no, I suppose not, madam … I hadn't thought.

You feel you don't really … Not after all this.

But you couldn't ever, not this beautiful house! You couldn't ever … I know many ladies *are*. I know many ladies feel it is for the best. You can't but notice all those good houses shut. But, madam, this seemed so much your home —

You must excuse me, madam. I had no right—It was the shock, a minute. I should have thought. The whole thing come on so sudden … Why yes, madam; I've not doubt that you should. It will be nice for you down at her ladyship's. All that nice quiet country and everything. We should all wish you to be where it's safe, I'm sure … You mean, for the duration? … *I* see, madam. I am sure you'll only decide what's right. Only … this lovely house, madam. We've all cared for it so … I *am* a silly: I was upset this morning, but somehow I never saw us not starting again…

I suppose it might, yes. Happen another night…

All the same, I should like, if you didn't object, madam, to stay on here for the month and get things straight. I'd like to leave things as I found them—fancy, ten years ago! … That's very good of you, madam, but it's been my own satisfaction. If it has made any difference I'm only glad … I daresay I'm funny in ways, madam, but it's been quite my life here, really it has … I *should* prefer that, if it would suit you. I couldn't think of workmen round in here without me … I've been

through so much with this place … In *any* event, madam, I should rather be here.

Tonight? … *I* see, madam, I'm sure they'll be glad to see you. I'm sure you should lose no time, not after a shock like this.

We should think of your packing, then, shouldn't we? If we went up now to your room perhaps you'd just show me what … Oh, yes, I see. I hadn't properly thought. Of course you would need to take everything. When it's for so long, and—Well, good clothes should be where it's safe.

The plaster's worse on the second flight, I'm afraid.

Yes … I was really dreading bringing you up here, madam. But now you won't want to sleep here for some time. Your luck's not hurt—look; there's not a mirror got cracked … It was that old blast got the little lamp … I can't picture you, if I may say so, madam, waking up in the mornings anywhere not here. Oh, you've traveled, I know, but you have always been back. Still, nothing goes on for ever, does it … Your dresses, madam—I've been over them: not a speck. There must be some merciful Providence, mustn't there?

You won't find such good-fitting cupboards, not at her ladyship's.

Yes, look at the sun out there. Autumn's always the nicest season just around here, I think.

Excuse me, madam—Madam, it's nothing, really. I—I—I—I'm really not taking on. I daresay I—got a bit of dust in my eye … You're too kind—you make me ashamed, really … Yes, I daresay it's the lack of sleep … The sun out there … If you'll excuse me, madam—I'll give my nose a good blow—that clears a thing off … Yes, I will try, when I've just run up to my sister's. I'll try a good nap. But to tell you the truth, madam, I shan't truly sleep till I've started to get things straight … I'm quite myself now, really. Hope I didn't upset you … I'll just run up to the boxroom after the trunks and cases—they'll need some brushing, I *should* think….

That really is what I'd rather, if you have no objection. Johnson and the girls will be round tomorrow, and as you won't be here, madam, no doubt you would like me to … And I couldn't leave this house empty, the whole night … I know, madam; I know that must come in time … Lonely? No; no, *I* don't feel lonely. And this never did feel to me a lonely house.

—1941

STEVIE SMITH
1902 – 1971

The poetry Stevie Smith produced in the years surrounding World War II has been considered some of the most original of its time. Sharing elements with the work of such diverse poets as William Blake, Robert Browning, Edward Lear, and Ogden Nash, Smith's poetry fits into no established genres and follows no known conventions. So unusual is her work, with its weighty themes explored in deceptively simple tones, that for many years her critical reputation remained ambiguous—she was for the most part not regarded as a "serious" poet. Smith experienced immense popularity during her lifetime, but her writing has only recently received substantial critical attention.

Stevie Smith was born in Hull on 20 September 1902. (Christened Florence Margaret, Smith was many years later nicknamed Stevie—after the then-famous jockey Steve Donaghue—when horseback riding with friends one day.) Shortly after her birth, her father abandoned the family, and her mother took Smith and her sister to live with their unmarried aunt in Palmer's Green, a London suburb. After Smith's mother died in 1919 she was raised by her aunt, whom she affectionately called "The Lion Aunt of Hull." Smith and her aunt lived together in the house in Palmer's Green until the Lion Aunt's death in 1968, after which point Smith remained in the house alone.

After completing school, Smith pursued a secretarial course and acquired a position in 1922 as private secretary to Sir Neville Pearson, Chairman of the leading publishing firm of Pearson, Newness; she retained this position until her retirement in 1953. Smith had begun writing poetry in her twenties and in 1935 she collected several pieces and approached the publisher Chatto and Windus. The firm's editor turned down the poems, advising her to write a novel instead. The result, completed six weeks later, was *Novel on Yellow Paper* (1936), thus named because Smith had typed it while at work, on Pearson's yellow carbon-copy paper.

Novel on Yellow Paper was widely and favorably reviewed. Readers were astonished by the deft insights and frantic pace of its chatty-voiced narrator, who tells her story in a stream-of-consciousness style which many have compared to that of Virginia Woolf. Although Smith wrote two sequels to her first novel, *Over the Frontier* (1938) and *The Holiday* (1949), she preferred writing poetry to the novel. With the commercial success of *Novel on Yellow Paper*, Smith was able to ensure the publication of her first volume of poems, *A Good Time Was Had By All* (1937). This was soon followed by the collections *Tender Only to One* (1938) and *Mother, What Is Man?* (1942).

Readers appreciated the unique sense of humor that characterized Smith's neat, economical poems. The simple language, often-ridiculous rhymes, odd syntax, and repetitive, singsong rhythms conveyed the sense of a child-like sensibility—a sense that was accentuated by the bizarre doodles she published alongside the poems. When she began holding her own poetry readings after the war, Smith emphasized the nursery-rhyme quality of her poems; she would arrive in her customary schoolgirl's frocks and pageboy haircut and proceed to sing her poems in a loud, off-key voice to the tunes of well-known hymns or children's songs.

Underneath the apparent frivolity of Smith's poems, however, lie powerful themes. She frequently rewrote common myths and legends and satirized accepted ideas or conventions. In "The Blue From

Heaven" (1957), for example, she isolates and dissects one image from the myth of King Arthur, while in "The New Age" (1957) she mocks the often-heard lament over the decline of culture and civilization. Though she called herself an agnostic, Smith had a lifelong attachment to the Church of England, and many of her poems deal with Christian themes; she once called the main business of her life "death, loneliness, God, and the devil." Her fascination with death—a subject of many of her poems—has been much commented upon. She claimed to find comfort in the knowledge that death was always an option, and in poems such as "Thoughts About a Person from Porlock" (1962) and "Is It Wise?" (1937) she contemplates the release that death would bring. But Smith's poetry also celebrates life, even at its most bizarre and unpleasant. She possessed a remarkable ability to see the comic in tragic events, as is evident in the black humor of "Not Waving But Drowning"(1957).

By the 1960s Stevie Smith had published numerous collections of poetry and was something of a cult figure, idolized by her younger peers for her indifference to established conventions, her cynicism, and her fierce honesty. When she died in 1971 she was at the height of her popularity, having recently been honored with the Cholmondeley Award for Poetry (1966) and the Queen's Medal for Poetry (1969). Smith herself did not believe that poets should occupy a privileged position in society. On the contrary, she said a poet should "be just made to get on with his writing: put in a room with pencils and pen or a typewriter; and then if his poems are no good, then he must just be thrown out."

⌘ ⌘ ⌘

Mother, Among the Dustbins

Mother, among the dustbins and the manure
I feel the measure of my humanity, an allure
As of the presence of God. I am sure

In the dustbins, in the manure, in the cat at play,
5 Is the presence of God, in a sure way
He moves there. Mother, what do you say?

I too have felt the presence of God in the broom
I hold, in the cobwebs in the room,
But most of all in the silence of the tomb.

10 Ah! but that thought that informs the hope of our kind
Is but an empty thing, what lies behind?—
Naught but the vanity of a protesting mind

That would not die. This is the thought that bounces
Within a conceited head and trounces
15 Inquiry. Man is most frivolous when he pronounces.

Well Mother, I shall continue to feel as I do,
And I think you would be wise to do so too,

Can you question the folly of man in the creation of God?
Who are you?
—1938

The River God

I may be smelly, and I may be old,
Rough in my pebbles, reedy in my pools,
But where my fish float by I bless their swimming
And I like the people to bathe in me, especially women.
5 But I can drown the fools
Who bathe too close to the weir,[1] contrary to rules.
And they take a long time drowning
As I throw them up now and then in a spirit of clowning.
Hi yih, yippity-yap, merrily I flow,
10 O I may be an old foul river but I have plenty of go.
Once there was a lady who was too bold
She bathed in me by the tall black cliff where the
     water runs cold,
So I brought her down here
To be my beautiful dear.
15 Oh will she stay with me will she stay
This beautiful lady, or will she go away?

[1] *weir* Barrier or dam to hold back water.

She lies in my beautiful deep river bed with many a weed
To hold her, and many a waving reed.
Oh who would guess what a beautiful white face lies there
20 Waiting for me to smooth and wash away the fear
She looks at me with. Hi yih, do not let her
Go. There is no one on earth who does not forget her
Now. They say I am a foolish old smelly river
But they do not know of my wide original bed
25 Where the lady waits, with her golden sleepy head.
If she wishes to go I will not forgive her.
—1950

Not Waving but Drowning

Nobody heard him, the dead man,
  But still he lay moaning:
I was much further out than you thought
And not waving but drowning.

5   Poor chap, he always loved larking
And now he's dead
It must have been too cold for him his heart gave way,
They said.

Oh, no no no, it was too cold always
10 (Still the dead one lay moaning)
I was much too far out all my life
And not waving but drowning.
—1957

The New Age

Shall I tell you the signs of a New Age coming?
  It is a sound of drubbing and sobbing
Of people crying, We are old, we are old
And the sun is going down and becoming cold
5   Oh sinful and sad and the last of our kind
If we turn to God now do you think He will mind?
Then they fall on their knees and begin to whine
That the state of Art itself presages decline
As if Art has anything or ever had
10 To do with civilization whether good or bad.

Art is wild as a cat and quite separate from civilization
But that is another matter that is not now under
    consideration.
Oh these people are fools with their sighing and sinning
Why should Man be at an end? he is hardly beginning.
15 This New Age will slip in under cover of their cries
And be upon them before they have opened their eyes.
Well, say geological time is a one-foot rule
Then Man's only been here about half an inch to play
    the fool
Or be wise if he likes, as he often has been
20 Oh heavens how these crying people spoil the
    beautiful geological scene.
—1957

Away, Melancholy

Away, melancholy,
  Away with it, let it go.

Are not the trees green,
The earth as green?
5   Does not the wind blow,
Fire leap and the rivers flow?
Away melancholy.

The ant is busy
He carrieth his meat,
10 All things hurry
To be eaten or eat.
Away, melancholy.

Man, too, hurries,
Eats, couples, buries,
15 He is an animal also
With a hey ho melancholy,
Away with it, let it go.

Man of all creatures
Is superlative
20 (Away melancholy)
He of all creatures alone
Raiseth a stone
(Away melancholy)
Into the stone, the god

25 Pours what he knows of good
Calling, good, God.
Away melancholy, let it go.

Speak not to me of tears,
Tyranny, pox, wars,
30 Saying, Can God
Stone of man's thought, be good?

Say rather it is enough
That the stuffed
Stone of man's good, growing,
35 By man's called God.
Away, melancholy, let it go.

Man aspires
To good,
To love
40 Sighs;

Beaten, corrupted, dying
In his own blood lying
Yet heaves up an eye above
Cries, Love, love.
45 It is his virtue needs explaining,
Not his failing.

Away, melancholy,
Away with it, let it go.
—1957

The Blue from Heaven

A legend of King Arthur of Britain.

King Arthur rode in another world
And his twelve knights rode behind him
And Guinevere was there
Crying: Arthur, where are you dear?

5 Why is the King so blue
Why is he this blue colour?
It is because the sun is shining
And he rides under the blue cornflowers.

High wave the cornflowers
10 That shed the pale blue light
And under the tall cornflowers
Rides King Arthur and his twelve knights.

And Guinevere is there
Crying: Arthur, where are you dear?

15 First there were twelve knights riding
And then there was only one
And King Arthur said to the one knight,
Be gone.

All I wish for now, said Arthur,
20 Is the beautiful colour blue
And to ride in the blue sunshine
And Guinevere I do not wish for you.

Oh Lord, said Guinevere
I do not see the colour blue
25 And I wish to ride where our knights rode,
After you.

Go back, go back, Guinevere,
Go back to the palace, said the King.
So she went back to the palace
30 And her grief did not seem to her a small thing.

The Queen has returned to the palace
Crying: Arthur, where are you dear?
And every day she speaks of Arthur's grandeur
To the knights who are there.

35 That Arthur has fallen from the grandeur
Of his powers all agree
And the falling off of Arthur
Becomes their theme presently.

As if it were only temporarily
40 And it was not for ever
They speak, but the Queen knows
He will come back never.

Yes, Arthur has passed away
Gladly he has laid down his reigning powers

45 He has gone to ride in the blue light
Of the peculiar towering cornflowers.
—1957

Pretty

Why is the word pretty so underrated?
    In November the leaf is pretty when it falls
The stream grows deep in the woods after rain
And in the pretty pool the pike stalks

5 He stalks his prey, and this is pretty too,
The prey escapes with an underwater flash
But not for long, the great fish has him now
The pike is a fish who always has his prey

And this is pretty. The water rat is pretty
10 His paws are not webbed, he cannot shut his nostrils
As the otter can and the beaver, he is torn between
The land and water. Not "torn," he does not mind.

The owl hunts in the evening and it is pretty
The lake water below him rustles with ice
15 There is frost coming from the ground, in the air mist
All this is pretty, it could not be prettier.

Yes, it could always be prettier, the eye abashes
It is becoming an eye that cannot see enough,
Out of the wood the eye climbs. This is prettier
20 A field in the evening, tilting up.

The field tilts to the sky. Though it is late
The sky is lighter than the hill field
All this looks easy but really it is extraordinary
Well, it is extraordinary to be so pretty.

25 And it is careless, and that is always pretty
This field, this owl, this pike, this pool are careless,
As Nature is always careless and indifferent
Who sees, who steps, means nothing, and this is pretty.

So a person can come along like a thief—pretty!—
30 Stealing a look, pinching the sound and feel,
Lick the icicle broken from the bank
And still say nothing at all, only cry pretty.

Cry pretty, pretty, pretty and you'll be able
Very soon not even to cry pretty
35 And so be delivered entirely from humanity
This is prettiest of all, it is very pretty.
—1962

GEORGE ORWELL
1903 – 1950

George Orwell struggled throughout his life to live his convictions as well as to write from them. His most famous novels, *Animal Farm* (1945) and *1984* (1949), have been translated into more than sixty languages and have sold over forty million copies. While his writerly craftsmanship and strongly articulated views on the importance of linguistic integrity (most directly expressed in his 1946 essay "Politics and the English Language") are admired and respected, he is recognized even more widely for his moral integrity, independence of mind, and scope of vision.

Born Eric Arthur Blair in Motihari, India on 25 June 1903, Orwell came from a family with strong colonial ties on both sides. His father, Richard Blair, worked as an opium agent for the British Imperial government; his mother, Ida Limouzin, grew up in Burma surrounded by a large staff of native servants, taking work as a governess in India when her father lost his wealth. Although the baby Eric returned to England with his mother and older sister in 1904, his sense of identity was moulded by the colonial experience. He was also strongly marked by his experiences as an economically poor but culturally middle-class student in English boarding schools, first at St. Cyprian's School (an experience later immortalized in his 1953 *Such, Such Were the Joys*) and then as a scholarship student at Eton.

Despite his evident abilities as a scholar, Eric did not apply himself while at Eton and was ultimately discouraged from pursuing university-level studies; in fact, he was himself more interested in returning to his colonial roots and pursuing a more adventurous career. After sitting eight days of qualifying examinations, he was selected to travel to Burma to join the Imperial Police. He served there from 1922 to 1927 in an array of posts around the country before deciding that the work was not suited to his character or his ideals; it had also taken its toll physically. His experiences left him feeling profoundly ambivalent about the colonial presence of the British, and about the nature of imperialist authority in general. He resigned his assignment upon his return to England, filled with a profound sense of guilt.

Although he was at this point determined to become a writer, he had not written much of anything while in Burma, nor published any adult work. Nevertheless, he decided that living in poverty, first in the East End of London, then in Paris, taking various low-paying jobs here and there, would help provide him with suitable material and would also condition his mind for the task of writing. He spent the years 1928–29 in Paris, taking menial jobs in restaurants and hotels and contracting pneumonia in the process, and then returned to England where he spent some time living as a tramp. His first book, *Down and Out in Paris and London*, appeared in 1933 under the pseudonym of George Orwell, chosen to protect his family and to distance himself from them and from his own earlier life.

Orwell spent nine months in 1934 living with his parents while he finished his second book, the novel *A Clergyman's Daughter* (1935). He then moved out, took work in a bookshop, and continued to write; his *Burmese Days*, which drew on his experiences in Burma and expressed his sense of indignation about imperialism, appeared in 1934. *A Clergyman's Daughter* was published the following year; in it Orwell attempted to use his tramping experiences as material for fiction, but was himself dissatisfied with the results. In later years he did his best to keep this and his next autobiographical novel, *Keep the Aspidistra Flying* (1936), out of view, preventing their reissues; the latter did not appear in the United States until 1956.

In 1936, emboldened by an advance for his next, nonfictional project, Orwell married Eileen O'Shaughnessy. Eileen abandoned her graduate studies in Educational Psychology at University College in London to move with Orwell into a tiny, isolated, and primitive cottage in Wallington, Hertfordshire, where they kept a garden, goats, and chickens, and managed a small shop, and where Orwell continued to write. His study of the dismal lives of the poor and unemployed in the industrial towns of the north of England took him tramping once again; *The Road to Wigan Pier* (1937) gave voice to his socialist views and established his reputation as a political writer.

Orwell's political idealism was severely tested when he fought for the Republicans in the Spanish Civil War. He witnessed first-hand the intense in-fighting amongst the various factions of the Left, and he became an intense critic of all political orthodoxies as a result. His next book, *Homage to Catalonia*, combined personal recollection with biting political analysis; it was as critical of the Soviet-influenced Communist faction in Spain as it was of Franco's Fascists. It received a mixed reception when it appeared in 1938. Today, however, it is recognized as an eloquent illustration of Orwell's passionate intellectual and political independence of mind.

World War II broke out three months after the publication of Orwell's next novel, *Coming Up for Air* (1939); unable to join the army due to his poor health, Orwell worked for two years for the BBC's Eastern Service, in addition to writing various essays and reviews. In 1944, Orwell and his wife adopted a son, Richard Horatio Blair, to whom they were both deeply devoted. But in 1945, Orwell's life changed: Eileen died (and her death devastated Orwell), and *Animal Farm* was published and brought overnight literary and financial success. This short novel is a fable that satirizes the corruption of socialist ideals that had by then occurred in the Soviet Union under Joseph Stalin; everyone was supposedly equal but "some animals are more equal than others," in Orwell's famous phrase.

Orwell spent most of the last years of his life in an isolated cottage on the island of Jura, off the coast of Scotland, with Richard, a nanny, and his sister Avril for company. As he gradually succumbed to tuberculosis, he wrote *1984*, widely considered his most ambitious and important work. This dark novel imagines a totalitarian future in which absolute conformity is rigidly enforced; "Big Brother is watching you" is the catchword of a society in which privacy and individual freedom have all but disappeared. In 1949 that book was published, and Orwell entered a sanatorium in England. Three months before his death on 21 January 1950, he married Sonia Brownell.

⌘ ⌘ ⌘

from *Homage to Catalonia*

It must have been three days after the Barcelona fighting[1] ended that we returned to the front. After

---

[1] *the Barcelona fighting*   The Spanish Civil War officially broke out in 1936, after a period of turmoil following the collapse of the monarchy in 1931. A leftist Popular Front government, elected in February of 1936, promised substantial land reforms to a nation made up of large agricultural estates on which peasants worked for little money. A conservative military uprising, led by Francisco Franco, attempted to thwart the Popular Front, but the Spanish people united and initially defeated these forces. Franco then

the fighting—more particularly after the slanging-match in the newspapers—it was difficult to think about this war in quite the same naively idealistic manner as before. I suppose there is no one who spent more than a few weeks in Spain without being in some degree

---

appealed to other fascist leaders for support. Troops from Italy, Germany, and Portugal arrived. Meanwhile, as the war continued, volunteers from all over Europe and North America formed International Brigades and came to Spain to fight against fascism. Orwell, a committed socialist, was among them. The "Barcelona fighting" referred to here occurred from May 3 to 7, 1937—five days referred to as the "May Days."

disillusioned. My mind went back to the newspaper correspondent whom I had met my first day in Barcelona, and who said to me: "This war is a racket the same as any other." The remark had shocked me deeply, and at that time (December) I do not believe it was true; it was not true even now, in May; but it was becoming truer. The fact is that every war suffers a kind of progressive degradation with every month that it continues, because such things as individual liberty and a truthful press are simply not compatible with military efficiency.

One could begin now to make some kind of guess at what was likely to happen. It was easy to see that the Caballero Government[1] would fall and be replaced by a more Right-wing Government with a stronger Communist influence (this happened a week or two later), which would set itself to break the power of the trade unions once and for all. And afterwards, when Franco was beaten—and putting aside the huge problems raised by the reorganization of Spain—the prospect was not rosy. As for the newspaper talk about this being a "war for democracy," it was plain eyewash. No one in his senses supposed that there was any hope of democracy, even as we understand it in England or France, in a country so divided and exhausted as Spain would be when the war was over. It would have to be a dictatorship, and it was clear that the chance of a working-class dictatorship had passed. That meant that the general movement would be in the direction of some kind of Fascism. Fascism called, no doubt, by some politer name, and—because this was Spain—more human and less efficient than the German or Italian varieties. The only alternatives were an infinitely worse dictatorship by Franco, or (always a possibility) that the war would end with Spain divided up, either by actual frontiers or into economic zones.

Whichever way you took it it was a depressing outlook. But it did not follow that the Government was not worth fighting for as against the more naked and developed Fascism of Franco and Hitler. Whatever faults the post-war Government might have, Franco's regime would certainly be worse. To the workers—the town proletariat—it might in the end make very little

difference who won, but Spain is primarily an agricultural country and the peasants would almost certainly benefit by a Government victory. Some at least of the seized lands would remain in their possession, in which case there would also be a distribution of land in the territory that had been Franco's, and the virtual serfdom that had existed in some parts of Spain was not likely to be restored. The Government in control at the end of the war would at any rate be anti-clerical and anti-feudal. It would keep the Church in check, at least for the time being, and would modernize the country—build roads, for instance, and promote education and public health; a certain amount had been done in this direction even during the war. Franco, on the other hand, in so far as he was not merely the puppet of Italy and Germany, was tied to the big feudal landlords and stood for a stuffy clerico-military reaction.

The Popular Front might be a swindle, but Franco was an anachronism. Only millionaires or romantics could want him to win....

There was not much happening at the front. The battle round the Jaca road had died away and did not begin again till mid-June. In our position the chief trouble was the snipers. The Fascist trenches were more than a hundred and fifty yards away, but they were on higher ground and were on two sides of us, our line forming a right-angle salient. The corner of the salient was a dangerous spot; there had always been a toll of sniper casualties there. From time to time the Fascists let fly at us with a rifle-grenade or some similar weapon. It made a ghastly crash—unnerving, because you could not hear it coming in time to dodge—but was not really dangerous; the hole it blew in the ground was no bigger than a wash-tub. The nights were pleasantly warm, the days blazing hot, the mosquitoes were becoming a nuisance, and in spite of the clean clothes we had brought from Barcelona we were almost immediately lousy. Out in the deserted orchards in no man's land the cherries were whitening on the trees. For two days there were torrential rains, the dugouts flooded and the parapet sank a foot; after that there were more days of digging out the sticky clay with the wretched Spanish spades which have no handles and bend like tin spoons.

They had promised us a trench-mortar for the company; I was looking forward to it greatly. At nights

[1] *Caballero Government* The Republican government was led by Largo Caballero from 4 September 1936 to 17 May 1937, when a new government was formed under Dr. Juan Negrin, a Socialist with Communist sympathies.

we patrolled as usual—more dangerous than it used to be, because the Fascist trenches were better manned and they had grown more alert; they had scattered tin cans just outside their wire and used to open up with the machine-guns when they heard a clank. In the daytime we sniped from no man's land. By crawling a hundred yards you could get to a ditch, hidden by tall grasses, which commanded a gap in the Fascist parapet. We had set up a rifle-rest in the ditch. If you waited long enough you generally saw a khaki-clad figure slip hurriedly across the gap. I had several shots. I don't know whether I hit anyone—it is most unlikely; I am a very poor shot with a rifle. But it was rather fun, the Fascists did not know where the shots were coming from, and I made sure I would get one of them sooner or later. However, the dog it was that died[1]—a Fascist sniper got me instead. I had been about ten days at the front when it happened. The whole experience of being hit by a bullet is very interesting and I think it is worth describing in detail.

It was at the corner of the parapet, at five o'clock in the morning. This was always a dangerous time, because we had the dawn at our backs, and if you stuck your head above the parapet it was clearly outlined against the sky. I was talking to the sentries preparatory to changing the guard. Suddenly, in the very middle of saying something, I felt—it is very hard to describe what I felt, though I remember it with the utmost vividness.

Roughly speaking it was the sensation of being at the centre of an explosion. There seemed to be a loud bang and a blinding flash of light all round me, and I felt a tremendous shock—no pain, only a violent shock, such as you get from an electric terminal; with it a sense of utter weakness, a feeling of being stricken and shrivelled up to nothing. The sand-bags in front of me receded into immense distance. I fancy you would feel much the same if you were struck by lightning. I knew immediately that I was hit, but because of the seeming bang and flash I thought it was a rifle nearby that had gone off accidentally and shot me. All this happened in a space of time much less than a second. The next moment my knees crumpled up and I was falling, my head hitting

the ground with a violent bang which, to my relief, did not hurt. I had a numb, dazed feeling, a consciousness of being very badly hurt, but no pain in the ordinary sense.

The American sentry I had been talking to had started forward. "Gosh! Are you hit?" People gathered round. There was the usual fuss—"Lift him up! Where's he hit? Get his shirt open!" etc., etc. The American called for a knife to cut my shirt open. I knew that there was one in my pocket and tried to get it out, but discovered that my right arm was paralysed. Not being in pain, I felt a vague satisfaction. This ought to please my wife, I thought; she had always wanted me to be wounded, which would save me from being killed when the great battle came. It was only now that it occurred to me to wonder where I was hit, and how badly; I could feel nothing, but I was conscious that the bullet had struck me somewhere in the front of the body. When I tried to speak I found that I had no voice, only a faint squeak, but at the second attempt I managed to ask where I was hit. In the throat, they said. Harry Webb, our stretcher-bearer, had brought a bandage and one of the little bottles of alcohol they gave us for field-dressings. As they lifted me up a lot of blood poured out of my mouth, and I heard a Spaniard behind me say that the bullet had gone clean through my neck. I felt the alcohol, which at ordinary times would sting like the devil, splash on to the wound as a pleasant coolness.

They laid me down again while somebody fetched a stretcher. As soon as I knew that the bullet had gone clean through my neck I took it for granted that I was done for. I had never heard of a man or an animal getting a bullet through the middle of the neck and surviving it. The blood was dribbling out of the corner of my mouth. "The artery's gone," I thought. I wondered how long you last when your carotid artery is cut; not many minutes, presumably. Everything was very blurry. There must have been about two minutes during which I assumed that I was killed. And that too was interesting—I mean it is interesting to know what your thoughts would be at such a time. My first thought, conventionally enough, was for my wife. My second was a violent resentment at having to leave this world which, when all is said and done, suits me so well. I had time to feel this very vividly. The stupid mischance infuriated me. The meaninglessness of it! To be bumped off, not

---

[1] *the dog ... died* Reference to Oliver Goldsmith's poem "An Elegy on the Death of a Mad Dog" (1766), in which a mad dog bites a man, who is expected to die from the wound. However, "the man recovered of the bite, / the dog it was that died" (21–22).

even in battle, but in this stale corner of the trenches, thanks to a moment's carelessness! I thought, too, of the man who had shot me—wondered what he was like, whether he was a Spaniard or a foreigner, whether he knew he had got me, and so forth. I could not feel any resentment against him. I reflected that as he was a Fascist I would have killed him if I could, but that if he had been taken prisoner and brought before me at this moment I would merely have congratulated him on his good shooting. It may be, though, that if you were really dying your thoughts would be quite different.

They had just got me on to the stretcher when my paralysed right arm came to life and began hurting damnably. At the time I imagined that I must have broken it in falling; but the pain reassured me, for I knew that your sensations do not become more acute when you are dying. I began to feel more normal and to be sorry for the four poor devils who were sweating and slithering with the stretcher on their shoulders. It was a mile and a half to the ambulance, and vile going, over lumpy, slippery tracks. I knew what a sweat it was, having helped to carry a wounded man down a day or two earlier. The leaves of the silver poplars which, in places, fringed our trenches brushed against my face; I thought what a good thing it was to be alive in a world where silver poplars grow. But all the while the pain in my arm was diabolical, making me swear and then try not to swear, because every time I breathed too hard the blood bubbled out of my mouth.

The doctor re-bandaged the wound, gave me a shot of morphia, and sent me off to Sietamo.[1] The hospitals at Sietamo were hurriedly constructed wooden huts where the wounded were, as a rule, only kept for a few hours before being sent on to Barbastro or Lerida.[2] I was dopey from morphia but still in great pain, practically unable to move and swallowing blood constantly. It was typical of Spanish hospital methods that while I was in this state the untrained nurse tried to force the regulation hospital meal—a huge meal of soup, eggs, greasy stew and so forth—down my throat and seemed surprised when I would not take it. I asked for a cigarette, but this was one of the periods of tobacco famine and there was not a cigarette in the place. Presently two comrades who had got permission to leave the line for a few hours appeared at my bedside.

"Hullo! You're alive, are you? Good. We want your watch and your revolver and your electric torch. And your knife, if you've got one."

They made off with all my portable possessions. This always happened when a man was wounded—everything he possessed was promptly divided up; quite rightly, for watches, revolvers, and so forth were precious at the front and if they went down the line in a wounded man's kit they were certain to be stolen somewhere on the way.

By the evening enough sick and wounded had trickled in to make up a few ambulance-loads, and they sent us on to Barbastro. What a journey! It used to be said that in this war you got well if you were wounded in the extremities, but always died of a wound in the abdomen. I now realized why. No one who was liable to bleed internally could have survived those miles of jolting over metal roads that had been smashed to pieces by heavy lorries and never repaired since the war began. Bang, bump, wallop! It took me back to my early childhood and a dreadful thing called the Wiggle-Woggle at the White City[3] Exhibition. They had forgotten to tie us into the stretchers. I had enough strength in my left arm to hang on, but one poor wretch was spilt on to the floor and suffered God knows what agonies. Another, a walking case who was sitting in the corner of the ambulance, vomited all over the place. The hospital in Barbastro was very crowded, the beds so close together that they were almost touching. Next morning they loaded a number of us on to the hospital train and sent us down to Lerida.

I was five or six days in Lerida. It was a big hospital, with sick, wounded, and ordinary civilian patients more or less jumbled up together. Some of the men in my ward had frightful wounds. In the next bed to me there was a youth with black hair who was suffering from some disease or other and was being given medicine that made his urine as green as emerald. His bed-bottle was one of the sights of the ward. An English-speaking Dutch Communist, having heard that there was an Englishman in the hospital, befriended me and brought me English newspapers. He had been terribly wounded in the October fighting, and had somehow managed to

---

[1] *Sietamo* Town in the Huesca region, in the province of Aragón.

[2] *Barbastro or Lerida* Two larger towns south of Sietamo.

[3] *White City* Area of greater London, site of a Franco-British Exhibition and the Olympic Games in 1908.

settle down at Lerida hospital and had married one of the nurses. Thanks to his wound, one of his legs had shrivelled till it was no thicker than my arm. Two militiamen on leave, whom I had met my first week at the front, came in to see a wounded friend and recognized me. They were kids of about eighteen. They stood awkwardly beside my bed, trying to think of something to say, and then, as a way of demonstrating that they were sorry I was wounded, suddenly took all the tobacco out of their pockets, gave it to me, and fled before I could give it back. How typically Spanish! I discovered afterwards that you could not buy tobacco anywhere in the town and what they had given me was a week's ration.

After a few days I was able to get up and walk about with my arm in a sling. For some reason it hurt much more when it hung down. I also had, for the time being, a good deal of internal pain from the damage I had done myself in falling, and my voice had disappeared almost completely, but I never had a moment's pain from the bullet wound itself. It seems this is usually the case. The tremendous shock of a bullet prevents sensation locally; a splinter of shell or bomb, which is jagged and usually hits you less hard, would probably hurt like the devil. There was a pleasant garden in the hospital grounds, and in it was a pool with gold-fishes and some small dark grey fish—bleak, I think. I used to sit watching them for hours. The way things were done at Lerida gave me an insight into the hospital system on the Aragon front—whether it was the same on other fronts I do not know. In some ways the hospitals were very good. The doctors were able men and there seemed to be no shortage of drugs and equipment. But there were two bad faults on account of which, I have no doubt, hundreds or thousands of men have died who might have been saved.

One was the fact that all the hospitals anywhere near the front line were used more or less as casualty clearing-stations. The result was that you got no treatment there unless you were too badly wounded to be moved. In theory most of the wounded were sent straight to Barcelona or Tarragona, but owing to the lack of transport they were often a week or ten days in getting there. They were kept hanging about at Sietamo, Barbastro, Monzon, Lerida, and other places, and meanwhile they were getting no treatment except an occasional clean bandage, sometimes not even that. Men with dreadful shell wounds, smashed bones and so forth, were swathed in a sort of casing made of bandages and plaster of Paris; a description of the wound was written in pencil on the outside, and as a rule the casing was not removed till the man reached Barcelona or Tarragona ten days later. It was almost impossible to get one's wound examined on the way; the few doctors could not cope with the work, and they simply walked hurriedly past your bed, saying: "Yes, yes, they'll attend to you at Barcelona." There were always rumours that the hospital train was leaving for Barcelona *mañana*.[1] The other fault was the lack of competent nurses. Apparently there was no supply of trained nurses in Spain, perhaps because before the war this work was done chiefly by nuns. I have no complaint against the Spanish nurses, they always treated me with the greatest kindness, but there is no doubt that they were terribly ignorant. All of them knew how to take a temperature, and some of them knew how to tie a bandage, but that was about all. The result was that men who were too ill to fend for themselves were often shamefully neglected. The nurses would let a man remain constipated for a week on end, and they seldom washed those who were too weak to wash themselves. I remember one poor devil with a smashed arm telling me that he had been three weeks without having his face washed. Even beds were left unmade for days together. The food in all the hospitals was very good—too good, indeed. Even more in Spain than elsewhere it seemed to be the tradition to stuff sick people with heavy food. At Lerida the meals were terrific. Breakfast, at about six in the morning, consisted of soup, an omelette, stew, bread, white wine, and coffee, and lunch was even larger—this at a time when most of the civil population was seriously underfed. Spaniards seem not to recognize such a thing as a light diet. They give the same food to sick people as to well ones—always the same rich, greasy cookery, with everything sodden in olive oil.

One morning it was announced that the men in my ward were to be sent down to Barcelona today. I managed to send a wire to my wife, telling her that I was coming, and presently they packed us into buses and took us down to the station. It was only when the train was actually starting that the hospital orderly who

---

[1] *mañana* Spanish: tomorrow.

travelled with us casually let fall that we were not going to Barcelona after all, but to Tarragona. I suppose the engine-driver had changed his mind. "Just like Spain!" I thought. But it was very Spanish, too, that they agreed to hold up the train while I sent another wire, and more Spanish still that the wire never got there.

They had put us into ordinary third-class carriages with wooden seats, and many of the men were badly wounded and had only got out of bed for the first time that morning. Before long, what with the heat and the jolting, half of them were in a state of collapse and several vomited on the floor. The hospital orderly threaded his way among the corpse-like forms that sprawled everywhere, carrying a large goat-skin bottle full of water which he squirted into this mouth or that. It was beastly water; I remember the taste of it still. We got into Tarragona as the sun was getting low. The line runs along the shore a stone's throw from the sea. As our train drew into the station a troop-train full of men from the International Column was drawing out, and a knot of people on the bridge were waving to them. It was a very long train, packed to bursting-point with men, with field-guns lashed on the open trucks and more men clustering round the guns. I remember with peculiar vividness the spectacle of that train passing in the yellow evening light; window after window full of dark, smiling faces, the long tilted barrels of the guns, the scarlet scarves fluttering—all this gliding slowly past us against a turquoise-coloured sea.

"Estranjeros—foreigners," said someone. "They're Italians."

Obviously they were Italians. No other people could have grouped themselves so picturesquely or returned the salutes of the crowd with so much grace—a grace that was none the less because about half the men on the train were drinking out of up-ended wine bottles. We heard afterwards that these were some of the troops who won the great victory at Guadalajara in March; they had been on leave and were being transferred to the Aragon front. Most of them, I am afraid, were killed at Huesca only a few weeks later. The men who were well enough to stand had moved across the carriage to cheer the Italians as they went past. A crutch waved out of the window; bandaged forearms made the Red Salute. It was like an allegorical picture of war; the trainload of fresh men gliding proudly up the line, the maimed men sliding slowly down, and all the while the guns on the open trucks making one's heart leap as guns always do, and reviving that pernicious feeling, so difficult to get rid of, that war *is* glorious after all.

The hospital at Tarragona was a very big one and full of wounded from all fronts. What wounds one saw there! They had a way of treating certain wounds which I suppose was in accordance with the latest medical practice, but which was peculiarly horrible to look at. This was to leave the wound completely open and unbandaged, but protected from flies by a net of butter-muslin, stretched over wires. Under the muslin you would see the red jelly of a half-healed wound. There was one man wounded in the face and throat who had his head inside a sort of spherical helmet of butter-muslin; his mouth was closed up and he breathed through a little tube that was fixed between his lips. Poor devil, he looked so lonely, wandering to and fro, looking at you through his muslin cage and unable to speak. I was three or four days at Tarragona. My strength was coming back, and one day, by going slowly, I managed to walk down as far as the beach. It was queer to see the seaside life going on almost as usual; the smart cafes along the promenade and the plump local bourgeoisie bathing and sunning themselves in deck-chairs as though there had not been a war within a thousand miles. Nevertheless, as it happened, I saw a bather drowned, which one would have thought impossible in that shallow and tepid sea.

Finally, eight or nine days after leaving the front, I had my wound examined. In the surgery where newly-arrived cases were examined, doctors with huge pairs of shears were hacking away the breast-plates of plaster in which men with smashed ribs, collar-bones and so forth had been cased at the dressing-stations behind the line; out of the neck-hole of the huge clumsy breastplate you would see protruding an anxious, dirty face, scrubby with a week's beard. The doctor, a brisk, handsome man of about thirty, sat me down in a chair, grasped my tongue with a piece of rough gauze, pulled it out as far as it would go, thrust a dentist's mirror down my throat and told me to say "Eh!" After doing this till my tongue was bleeding and my eyes running with water, he told me that one vocal cord was paralysed.

"When shall I get my voice back?" I said.

"Your voice? Oh, you'll never get your voice back,"

he said cheerfully.

However, he was wrong, as it turned out. For about two months I could not speak much above a whisper, but after that my voice became normal rather suddenly, the other vocal cord having "compensated." The pain in my arm was due to the bullet having pierced a bunch of nerves at the back of the neck. It was a shooting pain like neuralgia, and it went on hurting continuously for about a month, especially at night, so that I did not get much sleep. The fingers of my right hand were also semi-paralysed. Even now, five months afterwards, my forefinger is still numb—a queer effect for a neck wound to have.

The wound was a curiosity in a small way and various doctors examined it with much clicking of tongues and "Que suerte! Que suerte!"[1] One of them told me with an air of authority that the bullet had missed the artery by "about a millimetre." I don't know how he knew. No one I met at this time—doctors, nurses, *practicantes*,[2] or fellow-patients—failed to assure me that a man who is hit through the neck and survives it is the luckiest creature alive. I could not help thinking that it would be even luckier not to be hit at all.

—1938

Politics and the English Language

Most people who bother with the matter at all would admit that the English language is in a bad way, but it is generally assumed that we cannot by conscious action do anything about it. Our civilization is decadent and our language—so the argument runs—must inevitably share in the general collapse. It follows that any struggle against the abuse of language is a sentimental archaism, like preferring candles to electric light or hansom cabs to aeroplanes. Underneath this lies the half-conscious belief that language is a natural growth and not an instrument which we shape for our own purposes.

Now, it is clear that the decline of a language must ultimately have political and economic causes: it is not due simply to the bad influence of this or that individ-

ual writer. But an effect can become a cause, reinforcing the original cause and producing the same effect in an intensified form, and so on indefinitely. A man may take to drink because he feels himself to be a failure, and then fail all the more completely because he drinks. It is rather the same thing that is happening to the English language. It becomes ugly and inaccurate because our thoughts are foolish, but the slovenliness of our language makes it easier for us to have foolish thoughts. The point is that the process is reversible. Modern English, especially written English, is full of bad habits which spread by imitation and which can be avoided if one is willing to take the necessary trouble. If one gets rid of these habits one can think more clearly, and to think clearly is a necessary first step towards political regeneration: so that the fight against bad English is not frivolous and is not the exclusive concern of professional writers. I will come back to this presently, and I hope that by that time the meaning of what I have said here will have become clearer. Meanwhile, here are five specimens of the English language as it is now habitually written.

These five passages have not been picked out because they are especially bad—I could have quoted far worse if I had chosen—but because they illustrate various of the mental vices from which we now suffer. They are a little below the average, but are fairly representative samples. I number them so that I can refer back to them when necessary:

1. I am not, indeed, sure whether it is not true to say that the Milton who once seemed not unlike a seventeenth-century Shelley had not become, out of an experience ever more bitter in each year, more alien (*sic*) to the founder of that Jesuit sect which nothing could induce him to tolerate.

Professor Harold Laski

(Essay in *Freedom of Expression*).

2. Above all, we cannot play ducks and drakes with a native battery of idioms which prescribes such egregious collocations of vocables as the Basic *put up with* for *tolerate* or *put at a loss* for *bewilder*.

Professor Lancelot Hogben (*Interglossa*).

3. On the one side we have the free personality: by definition it is not neurotic, for it has neither

---

[1] *Que suerte* Spanish: What luck!

[2] *practicantes* Spanish: practitioners.

conflict nor dream. Its desires, such as they are, are transparent, for they are just what institutional approval keeps in the forefront of consciousness; another institutional pattern would alter their number and intensity; there is little in them that is natural, irreducible, or culturally dangerous. But *on the other side*, the social bond itself is nothing but the mutual reflection of these self-secure integrities. Recall the definition of love. Is not this the very picture of a small academic? Where is there a place in this hall of mirrors for either personality or fraternity?

Essay on psychology in *Politics* (New York).

4. All the "best people" from the gentlemen's clubs, and all the frantic Fascist captains, united in common hatred of Socialism and bestial horror of the rising tide of the mass revolutionary movement, have turned to acts of provocation, to foul incendiarism, to medieval legends of poisoned wells, to legalise their own destruction to proletarian organisations, and rouse the agitated petty-bourgeoisie to chauvinistic fervour on behalf of the fight against the revolutionary way out of the crisis.

Communist pamphlet.

5. If a new spirit *is* to be infused into this old country, there is one thorny and contentious reform which must be tackled, and that is the humanisation and galvanisation of the BBC.[1] Timidity here will bespeak canker and atrophy of the soul. The heart of Britain may be sound and of strong beat, for instance, but the British lion's roar at present is like that of Bottom in Shakespeare's *Midsummer Night's Dream*—as gentle as any sucking dove. A virile new Britain cannot continue indefinitely to be traduced in the eyes, or rather ears, of the world by the effete languors of Langham Place,[2] brazenly masquerading as "standard English." When the Voice of Britain is heard at nine o'clock, better far and infinitely less ludicrous to hear aitches honestly dropped than the present priggish, inflated, inhibited, school-ma'amish arch braying of blameless bashful mewing maidens!

Letter in *Tribune*.

Each of these passages has faults of its own, but, quite apart from avoidable ugliness, two qualities are common to all of them. The first is staleness of imagery: the other is lack of precision. The writer either has a meaning and cannot express it, or he inadvertently says something else, or he is almost indifferent as to whether his words mean anything or not. This mixture of vagueness and sheer incompetence is the most marked characteristic of modern English prose, and especially of any kind of political writing. As soon as certain topics are raised, the concrete melts into the abstract and no one seems able to think of turns of speech that are not hackneyed: prose consists less and less of *words* chosen for the sake of their meaning, and more of *phrases* tacked together like the sections of a prefabricated hen-house. I list below, with notes and examples, various of the tricks by means of which the work of prose construction is habitually dodged:

Dying metaphors. A newly invented metaphor assists thought by evoking a visual image, while on the other hand a metaphor which is technically "dead" (e.g., *iron resolution*) has in effect reverted to being an ordinary word and can generally be used without loss of vividness. But in between these two classes there is a huge dump of worn-out metaphors which have lost all evocative power and are merely used because they save people the trouble of inventing phrases for themselves. Examples are: *Ring the changes on, take up the cudgels for, toe the line, ride roughshod over, stand shoulder to shoulder with, play into the hands of, no axe to grind, grist to the mill, fishing in troubled waters, rift within the lute, on the order of the day, Achilles' heel, swan song, hotbed*. Many of these are used without knowledge of their meaning (What is a "rift," for instance?), and incompatible metaphors are frequently mixed, a sure sign that the writer is not interested in what he is saying. Some metaphors now current have been twisted out of their original meaning without those who use them even being aware of the fact. For example, *toe the line* is sometimes written *tow the line*. Another example is *the hammer and the anvil*, now always used with the implication that the anvil gets the worst of it. In real life it is always the anvil that breaks the hammer, never the other way about: a writer who stopped to think what he was

---

[1] *BBC*   British Broadcasting Corporation.

[2] *Langham Place*   Location of the main office of the BBC.

saying would be aware of this, and would avoid perverting the original phrase.

Operators, or *verbal false limbs*. These save the trouble of picking out appropriate verbs and nouns, and at the same time pad each sentence with extra syllables which give it an appearance of symmetry. Characteristic phrases are: *render inoperative, militate against, prove unacceptable, make contact with, be subjected to, give rise to, give grounds for, have the effect of, play a leading part (role) in, make itself felt, take effect, exhibit a tendency to, serve the purpose of,* etc etc. The keynote is the elimination of simple verbs. Instead of being a single word, such as *break, stop, spoil, mend, kill,* a verb becomes a *phrase*, made up of a noun or adjective tacked on to some general-purposes verb such as *prove, serve, form, play, render.* In addition, the passive voice is wherever possible used in preference to the active, and noun constructions are used instead of gerunds (*by examination of* instead of *by examining*). The range of verbs is further cut down by means of the *-ise* and *de-* formations, and banal statements are given an appearance of profundity by means of the *not un-* formation. Simple conjunctions and prepositions are replaced by such phrases as *with respect to, having regard to, the fact that, by dint of, in view of, in the interests of, on the hypothesis that;* and the ends of sentences are saved from anticlimax by such resounding commonplaces as *greatly to be desired, cannot be left out of account, a development to be expected in the near future, deserving of serious consideration, brought to a satisfactory conclusion,* and so on and so forth.

Pretentious diction. Words like *phenomenon, element, individual* (as noun), *objective, categorical, effective, virtual, basic, primary, promote, constitute, exhibit, exploit, utilise, eliminate, liquidate,* are used to dress up simple statements and give an air of scientific impartiality to biassed judgements. Adjectives like *epoch-making, epic, historic, unforgettable, triumphant, age-old, inevitable, inexorable, veritable,* are used to dignify the sordid processes of international politics, while writing that aims at glorifying war usually takes on an archaic colour, its characteristic words being: *realm, throne, chariot, mailed fist, trident, sword, shield, buckler, banner, jackboot, clarion.* Foreign words and expressions such as *cul de sac, ancien régime, deus ex machina, mutatis mutandis, status quo, Gleichschaltung, Weltanschauung,*[1] are used to give an air of culture and elegance. Except for the useful abbreviation *i.e., e.g.,* and *etc.*, there is no real need for any of the hundreds of foreign phrases now current in English. Bad writers, and especially scientific, political, and sociological writers, are nearly always haunted by the notion that Latin or Greek words are grander than Saxon ones, and unnecessary words like *expedite, ameliorate, predict, extraneous, deracinated, clandestine, subaqueous* and hundreds of others constantly gain ground from their Anglo-Saxon opposite numbers.[2] The jargon peculiar to Marxist writing (*hyena, hangman, cannibal, petty bourgeois, these gentry, lacquey, flunkey, mad dog, White Guard,* etc.) consists largely of words and phrases translated from Russian, German, or French; but the normal way of coining a new word is to use a Latin or Greek root with the appropriate affix and, where necessary, the *-ise* formation. It is often easier to make up words of this kind (*deregionalise, impermissible, extramarital, non-fragmentatory* and so forth) than to think up the English words that will cover one's meaning. The result, in general, is an increase in slovenliness and vagueness.

Meaningless words. In certain kinds of writing, particularly in art criticism and literary criticism, it is normal to come across long passages which are almost completely lacking in meaning.[3] Words like *romantic, plastic, values, human, dead, sentimental, natural, vitality,* as used in art

---

[1] *ancien ... Weltanschauung* Phrases meaning, respectively, old system of government (French), god from the machine (Latin), the necessary changes being made (Latin), the state of things (Latin), enforced political conformity (German), philosophy of life (German).

[2] [Orwell's note] An interesting illustration of this is the way in which the English flower names which were in use till very recently are being ousted by Greek ones, *snapdragon* becoming *atirrhinum, forget-me-not* becoming *myosotis,* etc. It is hard to see any practical reason for this change in fashion: it is probably due to an instinctive turning-away from the more homely word and a vague feeling that the Greek word is scientific.

[3] [Orwell's note] Example: "Comfort's catholicity of perception and image, strangely Whitmanesque in range, continues to evoke that trembling atmospheric accumulative hinting at a cruel, an inexorably serene timelessness ... Wrey Gardiner scores by aiming at simple bullseyes with precision. Only they are not so simple, and through this contented sadness runs more than the surface bittersweet of resignation" (*Poetry Quarterly*).

criticism, are strictly meaningless, in the sense that they not only do not point to any discoverable object, but are hardly even expected to do so by the reader.

When one critic writes, "The outstanding features of Mr. X's work is its living quality," while another writes, "The immediately striking thing about Mr. X's work is its peculiar deadness," the reader accepts this as a simple difference of opinion. If words like *black* and *white* were involved, instead of the jargon words *dead* and *living*, he would see at once that language was being used in an improper way. Many political words are similarly abused. The word *Fascism* has now no meaning except in so far as it signifies "something not desirable." The words *democracy, socialism, freedom patriotic, realistic, justice*, have each of them several different meanings which cannot be reconciled with one another. In the case of a word like *democracy*, not only is there no agreed definition, but the attempt to make one is resisted from all sides. It is almost universally felt that when we call a country democratic we are praising it: consequently the defenders of every kind of regime claim that it is a democracy, and fear that they might have to stop using the word if it were tied down to any one meaning. Words of this kind are often used in a consciously dishonest way. That is, the person who uses them has his own private definition, but allows his hearer to think he means something quite different. Statements like *Marshal Pétain[1] was a true patriot, The Soviet press is the freest in the world, The Catholic Church is opposed to persecution*, are almost always made with intent to deceive. Other words used in variable meanings, in most cases more or less dishonestly, are: *class, totalitarian, science, progressive, reactionary, bourgeois, equality*.

Now that I have made this catalogue of swindles and perversions, let me give another example of the kind of writing that they lead to. This time it must of its nature be an imaginary one. I am going to translate a passage of good English into modern English of the worst sort. Here is a well-known verse from *Ecclesiastes*:

I returned and saw under the sun, that the race is not to the swift, nor the battle to the strong, neither yet bread to the wise, nor yet riches to men of

understanding, nor yet favour to men of skill; but time and chance happeneth to them all.

Here it is in modern English:

Objective considerations of contemporary phenomena compels the conclusion that success or failure in competitive activities exhibits no tendency to be commensurate with innate capacity, but that a considerable element of the unpredictable must invariably be taken into account.

This is a parody, but not a very gross one. Exhibit 3, above, for instance, contains several patches of the same kind in English. It will be seen that I have not made a full translation. The beginning and ending of the sentence follow the original meaning fairly closely, but in the middle the concrete illustrations— race, battle, bread—dissolve into the vague phrase "success or failure in competitive activities." This had to be so, because no modern writer of the kind I am discussing—no one capable of using phrases like "objective consideration of contemporary phenomena"—would ever tabulate his thoughts in that precise and detailed way. The whole tendency of modern prose is away from concreteness. Now analyse these two sentences a little more closely. The first contains forty-nine words but only sixty syllables, and all its words are those of everyday life. The second contains thirty-eight words of ninety syllables: eighteen of its words are from Latin roots, and one from Greek. The first sentence contains six vivid images, and only one phrase ("time and chance") that could be called vague. The second contains not a single fresh, arresting phrase, and in spite of its ninety syllables it gives only a shortened version of the meaning contained in the first. Yet without a doubt it is the second kind of sentence that is gaining ground in modern English. I do not want to exaggerate. This kind of writing is not yet universal, and outcrops of simplicity will occur here and there in the worst-written page. Still, if you or I were told to write a few lines on the uncertainty of human fortunes, we should probably come much nearer to my imaginary sentence than to the one from *Ecclesiastes*.

As I have tried to show, modern writing at its worst does not consist in picking out words for the sake of their meaning and inventing images in order to make the meaning clearer. It consists in gumming together

---

[1] *Marshal Pétain*   French general (1856–1951) who was appointed head of the Vichy government, which ruled Occupied France during World War II in collaboration with the Nazis.

long strips of words which have already been set in order by someone else, and making the results presentable by sheer humbug. The attraction of this way of writing is that it is easy. It is easier—even quicker, once you have the habit—to say *In my opinion it is a not unjustifiable assumption that* than to say *I think*. If you use ready-made phrases, you not only don't have to hunt about for words; you also don't have to bother with the rhythms of your sentences, since these phrases are generally so arranged as to be more or less euphonious. When you are composing in a hurry—when you are dictating to a stenographer, for instance, or making a public speech—it is natural to fall into a pretentious, Latinized style. Tags like *a consideration which we should do well to bear in mind* or *a conclusion to which all of us would readily assent* will save many a sentence from coming down with a bump. By using stale metaphors, similes, and idioms, you save much mental effort, at the cost of leaving your meaning vague, not only for your reader but for yourself. This is the significance of mixed metaphors. The sole aim of a metaphor is to call up a visual image. When these images clash—as in *The Fascist octopus has sung its swan song, the jackboot is thrown into the melting pot*—it can be taken as certain that the writer is not seeing a mental image of the objects he is naming; in other words he is not really thinking.

Look again at the examples I gave at the beginning of this essay. Professor Laski (1) uses five negatives in 53 words. One of these is superfluous, making nonsense of the whole passage, and in addition there is the slip *alien* for akin, making further nonsense, and several avoidable pieces of clumsiness which increase the general vagueness. Professor Hogben (2) plays ducks and drakes with a battery which is able to write prescriptions, and, while disapproving of the everyday phrase *put up with*, is unwilling to look *egregious* up in the dictionary and see what it means. (3), if one takes an uncharitable attitude towards it, is simply meaningless: probably one could work out its intended meaning by reading the whole of the article in which it occurs. In (4) the writer knows more or less what he wants to say, but an accumulation of stale phrases chokes him like tea-leaves blocking a sink. In (5) words and meaning have almost parted company. People who write in this manner usually have a general emotional meaning—they dislike one thing and want to express solidarity with another—but they are not interested in the detail of what they are saying. A scrupulous writer, in every sentence that he writes, will ask himself at least four questions, thus: What am I trying to say? What words will express it? What image or idiom will make it clearer? Is this image fresh enough to have an effect? And he will probably ask himself two more: Could I put it more shortly? Have I said anything that is avoidably ugly? But you are not obliged to go to all this trouble. You can shirk it by simply throwing your mind open and letting the ready-made phrases come crowding in. They will construct your sentences for you—even think your thoughts for you, to a certain extent—and at need they will perform the important service of partially concealing your meaning even from yourself. It is at this point that the special connection between politics and the debasement of language becomes clear.

In our time it is broadly true that political writing is bad writing. Where it is not true, it will generally be found that the writer is some kind of rebel, expressing his private opinions, and not a "party line." Orthodoxy, of whatever colour, seems to demand a lifeless, imitative style. The political dialects to be found in pamphlets, leading articles, manifestos, White Papers,[1] and the speeches of Under-Secretaries do, of course, vary from party to party, but they are all alike in that one almost never finds in them a fresh, vivid, homemade turn of speech. When one watches some tired hack on the platform mechanically repeating the familiar phrases—*bestial atrocities, iron heel, blood-stained tyranny, free peoples of the world, stand shoulder to shoulder*—one often has a curious feeling that one is not watching a live human being but some kind of dummy: a feeling which suddenly becomes stronger at moments when the light catches the speaker's spectacles and turns them into blank discs which seem to have no eyes behind them. And this is not altogether fanciful. A speaker who uses that kind of phraseology has gone some distance towards turning himself into a machine. The appropriate noises are coming out of his larynx, but his brain is not involved as it would be if he were choosing his words for himself. If the speech he is making is one that he is accustomed to make over and over again, he may be almost unconscious of what he is saying, as one is when one utters the responses in church. And this reduced

---

[1] *White Papers* Parliamentary documents.

state of consciousness, if not indispensable, is at any rate favourable to political conformity.

In our time, political speech and writing are largely the defence of the indefensible. Things like the continuance of British rule in India, the Russian purges and deportations, the dropping of the atom bombs on Japan, can indeed be defended, but only by arguments which are too brutal for most people to face, and which do not square with the professed aims of political parties. Thus political language has to consist largely of euphemism, question-begging and sheer cloudy vagueness. Defenceless villages are bombarded from the air, the inhabitants driven out into the countryside, the cattle machinegunned, the huts set on fire with incendiary bullets: this is called *pacification*. Millions of peasants are robbed of their farms and sent trudging along the roads with no more than they can carry: this is called *transfer of population* or *rectification of frontiers*. People are imprisoned for years without trial, or shot in the back of the neck, or sent to die of scurvy in Arctic lumber camps: this is called *elimination of unreliable elements*. Such phraseology is needed if one wants to name things without calling up mental pictures of them. Consider for instance some comfortable English professor defending Russian totalitarianism. He cannot say outright, "I believe in killing off your opponents when you can get good results by doing so." Probably, therefore, he will say something like this:

> While freely conceding that the Soviet regime exhibits certain features which the humanitarian may be inclined to deplore, we must, I think, agree that a certain curtailment of the right to political opposition is an unavoidable concomitant of transitional periods, and that the rigours which the Russian people have been called upon to undergo have been amply justified in the sphere of concrete achievement.

The inflated style is itself a kind of euphemism. A mass of Latin words falls upon the facts like soft snow, blurring the outlines and covering up all the details. The great enemy of clear language is insincerity. When there is a gap between one's real and one's declared aims, one turns as it were instinctively to long words and exhausted idioms, like a cuttlefish[1] squirting out ink. In our age there is no such thing as "keeping out of politics." All issues are political issues, and politics itself is a mass of lies, evasions, folly, hatred and schizophrenia. When the general atmosphere is bad, language must suffer. I should expect to find—this is a guess which I have not sufficient knowledge to verify—that the German, Russian, and Italian languages have all deteriorated in the last ten or fifteen years, as a result of dictatorship.

But if thought corrupts language, language can also corrupt thought. A bad usage can spread by tradition and imitation, even among people who should and do know better. The debased language that I have been discussing is in some ways very convenient. Phrases like *a not unjustifiable assumption, leaves much to be desired, would serve no good purpose, a consideration which we should do well to bear in mind*, are a continuous temptation, a packet of aspirins always at one's elbow. Look back through this essay, and for certain you will find that I have again and again committed the very faults I am protesting against. By this morning's post I have received a pamphlet dealing with conditions in Germany. The author tells me that he "felt impelled" to write it. I open it at random, and here is almost the first sentence that I see: "(The Allies) have an opportunity not only of achieving a radical transformation of Germany's social and political structure in such a way as to avoid a nationalistic reaction in Germany itself, but at the same time of laying the foundations of a co-operative and unified Europe." You see, he "feels impelled" to write—feels, presumably, that he has something new to say—and yet his words, like cavalry horses answering the bugle, group themselves automatically into the familiar dreary pattern. This invasion of one's mind by readymade phrases (*lay the foundations, achieve a radical transformation*) can only be prevented if one is constantly on guard against them, and every such phrase anaesthetises a portion of one's brain.

I said earlier that the decadence of our language is probably curable. Those who deny this would argue, if they produced an argument at all, that language merely reflects existing social conditions, and that we cannot influence its development by any direct tinkering with words and constructions. So far as the general tone or spirit of a language goes, this may be true, but it is not true in detail. Silly words and expressions have often

---

[1] *cuttleefish* Octopus.

disappeared, not through any evolutionary process but owing to the conscious action of a minority. Two recent examples were *explore every avenue* and *leave no stone unturned*, which were killed by the jeers of a few journalists. There is a long list of flyblown metaphors which could similarly be got rid of if enough people would interest themselves in the job; and it should also be possible to laugh the *not un-* formation out of existence,[1] to reduce the amount of Latin and Greek in the average sentence, to drive out foreign phrases and strayed scientific words, and, in general, to make pretentiousness unfashionable. But all these are minor points. The defence of the English language implies more than this, and perhaps it is best to start by saying what it does *not* imply.

To begin with it has nothing to do with archaism, with the salvaging of obsolete words and turns of speech, or with the setting up of a "standard English" which must never be departed from. On the contrary, it is especially concerned with the scrapping of every word or idiom which has outworn its usefulness. It has nothing to do with correct grammar and syntax, which are of no importance so long as one makes one's meaning clear, or with the avoidance of Americanisms, or with having what is called a "good prose style." On the other hand it is not concerned with fake simplicity and the attempt to make written English colloquial. Nor does it even imply in every case preferring the Saxon word to the Latin one, though it does imply using the fewest and shortest words that will cover one's meaning. What is above all needed is to let the meaning choose the word, and not the other way about. In prose, the worst thing one can do with words is to surrender to them. When you think of a concrete object, you think wordlessly, and then, if you want to describe the thing you have been visualizing you probably hunt about till you find the exact words that seem to fit it. When you think of something abstract you are more inclined to use words from the start, and unless you make a conscious effort to prevent it, the existing dialect will come rushing in and do the job for you, at the expense of blurring or even changing your meaning. Probably it is better to put off using words as long as possible and get

one's meaning as clear as one can through pictures or sensations. Afterwards one can choose—not simply accept—the phrases that will best cover the meaning, and then switch round and decide what impression one's words are likely to make on another person. This last effort of the mind cuts out all stale or mixed images, all prefabricated phrases, needless repetitions, and humbug and vagueness generally. But one can often be in doubt about the effect of a word or a phrase, and one needs rules that one can rely on when instinct fails. I think the following rules will cover most cases:

(i) Never use a metaphor, simile, or other figure of speech which you are used to seeing in print.

(ii) Never use a long word where a short one will do.

(iii) If it is possible to cut a word out, always cut it out.

(iv) Never use the passive where you can use the active.

(v) Never use a foreign phrase, a scientific word, or a jargon word if you can think of an everyday English equivalent.

(vi) Break any of these rules sooner than say anything outright barbarous.

These rules sound elementary, and so they are, but they demand a deep change of attitude in anyone who has grown used to writing in the style now fashionable. One could keep all of them and still write bad English, but one could not write the kind of stuff that I quoted in those five specimens at the beginning of this article.

I have not here been considering the literary use of language, but merely language as an instrument for expressing and not for concealing or preventing thought. Stuart Chase and others have come near to claiming that all abstract words are meaningless, and have used this as a pretext for advocating a kind of political quietism. Since you don't know what Fascism is, how can you struggle against Fascism? One need not swallow such absurdities as this, but one ought to recognise that the present political chaos is connected with the decay of language, and that one can probably bring about some improvement by starting at the verbal end. If you simplify your English, you are freed from the worst follies of orthodoxy. You cannot speak any of the necessary dialects, and when you make a stupid remark

---

[1] [Orwell's note]   One can cure oneself of the *not un-* formation by memorizing this sentence: *A not unblack dog was chasing a not unsmall rabbit across a not ungreen field.*

its stupidity will be obvious, even to yourself. Political language—and with variations this is true of all political parties, from Conservatives to Anarchists—is designed to make lies sound truthful and murder respectable, and to give an appearance of solidity to pure wind. One cannot change this all in a moment, but one can at least change one's own habits, and from time to time one can even, if one jeers loudly enough, send some worn-out and useless phrase—some *jackboot, Achilles' heel, hotbed, melting pot, acid test, veritable inferno* or other lump of verbal refuse—into the dustbin where it belongs.

—1946

Shooting an Elephant

In Moulmein, in Lower Burma, I was hated by large numbers of people—the only time in my life that I have been important enough for this to happen to me. I was sub-divisional police officer of the town, and in an aimless, petty kind of way anti-European feeling was very bitter. No one had the guts to raise a riot, but if a European woman went through the bazaars alone somebody would probably spit betel juice over her dress. As a police officer I was an obvious target and was baited whenever it seemed safe to do so. When a nimble Burman tripped me up on the football field and the referee (another Burman) looked the other way, the crowd yelled with hideous laughter. This happened more than once. In the end the sneering yellow faces of young men that met me everywhere, the insults hooted after me when I was at a safe distance, got badly on my nerves. The young Buddhist priests were the worst of all. There were several thousands of them in the town and none of them seemed to have anything to do except stand on street corners and jeer at Europeans.

All this was perplexing and upsetting. For at that time I had already made up my mind that imperialism was an evil thing and the sooner I chucked up my job and got out of it the better. Theoretically—and secretly, of course—I was all for the Burmese and all against their oppressors, the British. As for the job I was doing, I hated it more bitterly than I can perhaps make clear. In a job like that you see the dirty work of Empire at close quarters. The wretched prisoners huddling in the stinking cages of the lock-ups, the grey, cowed faces of the long-term convicts, the scarred buttocks of the men who had been flogged with bamboos—all these oppressed me with an intolerable sense of guilt. But I could get nothing into perspective. I was young and ill-educated and I had had to think out my problems in the utter silence that is imposed on every Englishman in the East. I did not even know that the British Empire is dying, still less did I know that it is a great deal better than the younger empires that are going to supplant it. All I knew was that I was stuck between my hatred of the empire I served and my rage against the evil-spirited little beasts who tried to make my job impossible. With one part of my mind I thought of the British Raj as an unbreakable tyranny, as something clamped down, *in saecula saeculorum*,[1] upon the will of prostrate peoples; with another part I thought that the greatest joy in the world would be to drive a bayonet into a Buddhist priest's guts. Feelings like these are the normal by-products of imperialism; ask any Anglo-Indian official, if you can catch him off duty.

One day something happened which in a round-about way was enlightening. It was a tiny incident in itself, but it gave me a better glimpse than I had had before of the real nature of imperialism—the real motives for which despotic governments act. Early one morning the sub-inspector at a police station the other end of the town rang me up on the 'phone and said that an elephant was ravaging the bazaar. Would I please come and do something about it? I did not know what I could do, but I wanted to see what was happening and I got on to a pony and started out. I took my rifle, an old .44 Winchester and much too small to kill an elephant, but I thought the noise might be useful *in terrorem*.[2] Various Burmans stopped me on the way and told me about the elephant's doings. It was not, of course, a wild elephant, but a tame one which had gone "must."[3] It had been chained up, as tame elephants always are when their attack of "must" is due, but on the previous night it had broken its chain and escaped. Its mahout,[4] the only person who could manage it when it was in that state, had set out in pursuit, but had taken

---

[1] *in saecula saeculorum* Latin: for centuries upon centuries; forever.

[2] *terrorem* Latin: in fright, terror, or alarm.

[3] *"must"* I.e., condition characterized by aggressive behavior brought on by a surge in testosterone.

[4] *mahout* Elephant trainer or keeper.

the wrong direction and was now twelve hours' journey away, and in the morning the elephant had suddenly reappeared in the town. The Burmese population had no weapons and were quite helpless against it. It had already destroyed somebody's bamboo hut, killed a cow, and raided some fruit-stalls and devoured the stock; also it had met the municipal rubbish van, and, when the driver jumped out and took to his heels, had turned the van over and inflicted violences upon it.

The Burmese sub-inspector and some Indian constables were waiting for me in the quarter where the elephant had been seen. It was a very poor quarter, a labyrinth of squalid bamboo huts, thatched with palm-leaf, winding all over a steep hillside. I remember that it was a cloudy, stuffy morning at the beginning of the rains. We began questioning the people as to where the elephant had gone, and, as usual, failed to get any definite information. That is invariably the case in the East; a story always sounds clear enough at a distance, but the nearer you get to the scene of events the vaguer it becomes. Some of the people said that the elephant had gone in one direction, some said that he had gone in another, some professed not even to have heard of any elephant. I had almost made up my mind that the whole story was a pack of lies, when we heard yells a little distance away. There was a loud, scandalized cry of "Go away, child! Go away this instant!" and an old woman with a switch in her hand came round the corner of a hut, violently shooing away a crowd of naked children. Some more women followed, clicking their tongues and exclaiming; evidently there was something that the children ought not to have seen. I rounded the hut and saw a man's dead body sprawling in the mud. He was an Indian, a black Dravidian coolie, almost naked, and he could not have been dead many minutes. The people said that the elephant had come suddenly upon him round the corner of the hut, caught him with its trunk, put its foot on his back and ground him into the earth. This was the rainy season and the ground was soft, and his face had scored a trench a foot deep and a couple of yards long. He was lying on his belly with arms crucified and head sharply twisted to one side. His face was coated with mud, the eyes wide open, the teeth bared and grinning with an expression of unendurable agony. (Never tell me, by the way, that the dead look peaceful. Most of the corpses I have seen looked devil-ish.) The friction of the great beast's foot had stripped the skin from his back as neatly as one skins a rabbit. As soon as I saw the dead man I sent an orderly to a friend's house nearby to borrow an elephant rifle. I had already sent back the pony, not wanting it to go mad with fright and throw me if it smelt the elephant.

The orderly came back in a few minutes with a rifle and five cartridges, and meanwhile some Burmans had arrived and told us that the elephant was in the paddy fields below, only a few hundred yards away. As I started forward practically the whole population of the quarter flocked out of the houses and followed me. They had seen the rifle and were all shouting excitedly that I was going to shoot the elephant. They had not shown much interest in the elephant when he was merely ravaging their homes, but it was different now that he was going to be shot. It was a bit of fun to them, as it would be to an English crowd; besides they wanted the meat. It made me vaguely uneasy. I had no intention of shooting the elephant—I had merely sent for the rifle to defend myself if necessary—and it is always unnerving to have a crowd following you. I marched down the hill, looking and feeling a fool, with the rifle over my shoulder and an ever-growing army of people jostling at my heels. At the bottom, when you got away from the huts, there was a metalled road and beyond that a miry waste of paddy fields a thousand yards across, not yet ploughed but soggy from the first rains and dotted with coarse grass. The elephant was standing eight yards from the road, his left side towards us. He took not the slightest notice of the crowd's approach. He was tearing up bunches of grass, beating them against his knees to clean them and stuffing them into his mouth.

I had halted on the road. As soon as I saw the elephant I knew with perfect certainty that I ought not to shoot him. It is a serious matter to shoot a working elephant—it is comparable to destroying a huge and costly piece of machinery—and obviously one ought not to do it if it can possibly be avoided. And at that distance, peacefully eating, the elephant looked no more dangerous than a cow. I thought then and I think now that his attack of "must" was already passing off; in which case he would merely wander harmlessly about until the mahout came back and caught him. Moreover, I did not in the least want to shoot him. I decided that I would watch him for a little while to make sure that he did not turn savage again, and then go home.

But at that moment I glanced round at the crowd that had followed me. It was an immense crowd, two thousand at the least and growing every minute. It blocked the road for a long distance on either side. I looked at the sea of yellow faces above the garish clothes—faces all happy and excited over this bit of fun, all certain that the elephant was going to be shot. They were watching me as they would watch a conjurer about to perform a trick. They did not like me, but with the magical rifle in my hands I was momentarily worth watching. And suddenly I realized that I should have to shoot the elephant after all. The people expected it of me and I had got to do it; I could feel their two thousand wills pressing me forward, irresistibly. And it was at this moment, as I stood there with the rifle in my hands, that I first grasped the hollowness, the futility of the white man's dominion in the East. Here was I, the white man with his gun, standing in front of the unarmed native crowd—seemingly the leading actor of the piece; but in reality I was only an absurd puppet pushed to and fro by the will of those yellow faces behind. I perceived in this moment that when the white man turns tyrant it is his own freedom that he destroys. He becomes a sort of hollow, posing dummy, the conventionalized figure of a sahib. For it is the condition of his rule that he shall spend his life in trying to impress the "natives," and so in every crisis he has got to do what the "natives" expect of him. He wears a mask, and his face grows to fit it. I had got to shoot the elephant. I had committed myself to doing it when I sent for the rifle. A sahib has got to act like a sahib; he has got to appear resolute, to know his own mind and do definite things. To come all that way, rifle in hand, with two thousand people marching at my heels, and then to trail feebly away, having done nothing—no, that was impossible. The crowd would laugh at me. And my whole life, every white man's life in the East, was one long struggle not to be laughed at.

But I did not want to shoot the elephant. I watched him beating his bunch of grass against his knees, with that preoccupied grandmotherly air that elephants have. It seemed to me that it would be murder to shoot him. At that age I was not squeamish about killing animals, but I had never shot an elephant and never wanted to. (Somehow it always seems worse to kill a *large* animal.)

Besides, there was the beast's owner to be considered. Alive, the elephant was worth at least a hundred pounds; dead, he would only be worth the value of his tusks, five pounds, possibly. But I had got to act quickly. I turned to some experienced-looking Burmans who had been there when we arrived, and asked them how the elephant had been behaving. They all said the same thing: he took no notice of you if you left him alone, but he might charge if you went too close to him.

It was perfectly clear to me what I ought to do. I ought to walk up to within, say, twenty-five yards of the elephant and test his behaviour. If he charged I could shoot, if he took no notice of me it would be safe to leave him until the mahout came back. But also I knew that I was going to do no such thing. I was a poor shot with a rifle and the ground was soft mud into which one would sink at every step. If the elephant charged and I missed him, I should have about as much chance as a toad under a steam-roller. But even then I was not thinking particularly of my own skin, only of the watchful yellow faces behind. For at that moment, with the crowd watching me, I was not afraid in the ordinary sense, as I would have been if I had been alone. A white man mustn't be frightened in front of "natives"; and so, in general, he isn't frightened. The sole thought in my mind was that if anything went wrong those two thousand Burmans would see me pursued, caught, trampled on and reduced to a grinning corpse like that Indian up the hill. And if that happened it was quite probable that some of them would laugh. That would never do. There was only one alternative. I shoved the cartridges into the magazine and lay down on the road to get a better aim.

The crowd grew very still, and a deep, low, happy sigh, as of people who see the theatre curtain go up at last, breathed from innumerable throats. They were going to have their bit of fun after all. The rifle was a beautiful German thing with cross-hair sights. I did not then know that in shooting an elephant one would shoot to cut an imaginary bar running from ear-hole to ear-hole. I ought, therefore, as the elephant was sideways on, to have aimed straight at his ear-hole; actually I aimed several inches in front of this, thinking the brain would be further forward.

When I pulled the trigger I did not hear the bang or feel the kick—one never does when a shot goes home

—but I heard the devilish roar of glee that went up from the crowd. In that instant, in too short a time, one would have thought, even for the bullet to get there, a mysterious, terrible change had come over the elephant. He neither stirred nor fell, but every line of his body had altered. He looked suddenly stricken, shrunken, immensely old, as though the frightful impact of the bullet had paralysed him without knocking him down. At last, after what seemed a long time—it might have been five seconds, I dare say—he sagged flabbily to his knees. His mouth slobbered. An enormous senility seemed to have settled upon him. One could have imagined him thousands of years old. I fired again into the same spot. At the second shot he did not collapse but climbed with desperate slowness to his feet and stood weakly upright, with legs sagging and head drooping. I fired a third time. That was the shot that did for him. You could see the agony of it jolt his whole body and knock the last remnant of strength from his legs. But in falling he seemed for a moment to rise, for as his hind legs collapsed beneath him he seemed to tower upwards like a huge rock toppling, his trunk reaching skywards like a tree. He trumpeted, for the first and only time. And then down he came, his belly towards me, with a crash that seemed to shake the ground even where I lay.

I got up. The Burmans were already racing past me across the mud. It was obvious that the elephant would never rise again, but he was not dead. He was breathing very rhythmically with long rattling gasps, his great mound of a side painfully rising and falling. His mouth was wide open—I could see far down into caverns of pale pink throat. I waited a long time for him to die, but his breathing did not weaken. Finally I fired my two remaining shots into the spot where I thought his heart must be. The thick blood welled out of him like red velvet, but still he did not die. His body did not even jerk when the shots hit him, the tortured breathing continued without a pause. He was dying, very slowly and in great agony, but in some world remote from me where not even a bullet could damage him further. I felt that I had got to put an end to that dreadful noise. It seemed dreadful to see the great beast lying there, powerless to move and yet powerless to die, and not even to be able to finish him. I sent back for my small rifle and poured shot after shot into his heart and down his throat. They seemed to make no impression. The tortured gasps continued as steadily as the ticking of a clock.

In the end I could not stand it any longer and went away. I heard later that it took him half an hour to die. Burmans were bringing dahs[1] and baskets even before I left, and I was told they had stripped his body almost to the bones by the afternoon.

Afterwards, of course, there were endless discussions about the shooting of the elephant. The owner was furious, but he was only an Indian and could do nothing. Besides, legally I had done the right thing, for a mad elephant has to be killed, like a mad dog, if its owner fails to control it. Among the Europeans opinion was divided. The older men said I was right, the younger men said it was a damn shame to shoot an elephant for killing a coolie, because an elephant was worth more than any damn Coringhee coolie. And afterwards I was very glad that the coolie had been killed; it put me legally in the right and it gave me a sufficient pretext for shooting the elephant. I often wondered whether any of the others grasped that I had done it solely to avoid looking a fool.

—1950

---

[1] *dahs* Short swords or knives.

IN CONTEXT

Elephants in Asia

There are two types of elephant: the African elephant is by definition a wild animal, but the smaller Asian (or Indian) elephant may be tamed. The latter has long been employed as a beast of burden in many parts of Asia, used for transport, logging, and various other tasks—including hunting, as in the photograph below, of a royal expedition to India in 1912, illustrates.

SAMUEL BECKETT
1906 – 1989

Though Samuel Beckett was a prolific writer of poetry, prose fiction, and criticism, he remains best known for two of his plays, *Waiting for Godot* and *Endgame*, which are credited with having revolutionized theater, and which continue to be performed worldwide today. Fragmented, filled with absences and silences, and sparing of plot, characterization, and setting, Beckett's work is broadly innovative; it attempts to dispense with elements previously thought to be essential to dramatic productions. By paring down his writing to the bare necessities, Beckett created new possibilities of form and produced works whose brevity and lack of structure leaves them open to a variety of critical interpretations.

Beckett was born on 13 April 1906 in Foxrock, an upper-class, Protestant suburb of Dublin. He attended a boarding school in Northern Ireland and from there continued on (in 1923) to Trinity College, Dublin, where he studied French and Italian. Upon graduation, having excelled academically, Beckett was offered a two-year position as an exchange lecturer in Paris, and it was there that his writing career began. Within months of arriving in Paris he had been introduced to fellow Dublin writer James Joyce, whose writing Beckett greatly admired. Beckett established himself as part of Joyce's circle of literary friends in Paris, and in 1928 was commissioned to write an essay on Joyce's *Finnegan's Wake*, which was still a work in progress at the time. That essay (excerpts from which are included in this anthology as contextual material relating to Joyce's work) and a short story of Beckett's were published simultaneously in the Paris literary magazine *transition*. Shortly thereafter his first poem, *Whoroscope* (1930), was published by Nancy Cunard's Hours Press. Beckett had been encouraged by a friend to submit a poem to Cunard's competition for the best short poem on the subject of time. Using existing notes, he composed the prize-winning poem about French philosopher René Descartes in one night.

After living in Paris for two years, Beckett was loath to return to Ireland. He found the atmosphere and literary community in Paris far more conducive to his writing, but largely as a result of financial pressures, he spent the following seven years (1930–37) in Ireland, moving between his family home in Foxtrot and Dublin, where he taught at Trinity College for two years immediately following his departure from Paris. Beckett also spent some time in London undergoing therapy for recurring panic attacks and bouts of depression. During these seven years he worked on several projects, including his first novel, *Dream of Fair to Middling Women*; the series of short stories *More Pricks than Kicks* (1970); the novel *Murphy*; and a small collection of poems. This early work was not well received: his collection of poetry barely sold, *Dream* (1992) was not published during his lifetime, *More Pricks* received mixed reviews, and *Murphy* was rejected dozens of times before finally being accepted in 1938, two years after its completion.

In October 1937 Beckett returned to Paris, intending to settle there permanently and devote himself to his writing. This writer's life, however, was not without incident. Walking home late one night in January 1938, Beckett was stabbed in the chest and spent months recovering in hospital. There he was visited by Suzanne Deschevaux-Dumesnil, the woman who eventually became his wife.

(Though the two were living together less than a year later, they did not marry until 1961.) Beckett and Deschevaux-Dumesnil were forced to leave Paris twice during World War II. The first time, in 1940, they escaped the city days before it fell to German forces. Upon returning to Paris a few months later, Beckett began working for the French Resistance (for which service he was decorated by the French government after the war). In 1942 the two had to flee Paris again when Beckett's Resistance cell was betrayed. They escaped their apartment only hours before the Gestapo arrived.

Though Beckett was able to do some writing while in hiding in the south of France, his most prolific period occurred after his return to his Paris flat in 1945. Between 1946 and 1950 he underwent what he referred to as "the siege in the room," composing four novellas, two plays, and four novels. Three of these novels—*Molloy* (1951), *Malone Dies* (*Malone meurt*, 1951), and *The Unnamable* (*L'innommable*, 1953)—comprise a trilogy and are perhaps his most highly regarded prose works. All the prose from this period departs from his earlier work in several ways. First, Beckett had decided to write entirely in French, translating his work back into English once it was completed. This helped him to avoid lyricism and enhanced the distinctive sparseness of his writing style. He also abandoned the omniscient narration of his earlier novels in favor of a first-person point of view. Frequently, as in *Texts for Nothing* (*Textes pour rien*, 1955) these narratives are more like fragmented meditations or monologues than stories. In fact, Beckett's prose, like his plays, tended towards monologue as his writing career progressed, to the point where the distinction between the two sometimes becomes blurred; many of his later works of short prose, such as *Imagination Dead Imagine* (*Imagination morte imaginez*, 1965), have been given stage performances.

To take a break from his trilogy, Beckett began working on *Waiting for Godot* (*En attendant Godot*, 1952), the two-act play in which, as Irish critic Vivian Mercier famously said, "Nothing happens, twice." The lack of progression in this play about two men waiting for someone called Godot (who never arrives) is characteristic of the majority of Beckett's drama. Set on practically bare stages, lacking significant character development, and consisting of plots with neither climax nor resolution, Beckett's plays have been referred to as more "anti-theater" than theater. The spareness of the setting of *Godot* ("A country road. A tree.") is exceeded by that of the setting of *Endgame* (*Fin de partie*, 1957)—a nearly empty room. In *Endgame*, which Beckett called "more inhuman than *Godot*," the characters are also waiting, though for nothing in particular, except the inevitable end. The frequently nonsensical dialogue of this play, like that of Beckett's others, often doubles back on itself and is interrupted by long silences; Beckett believed the role of theater was not to give "meaning" but to provide an "experience" from which audience members could generate their own meaning if they so desired.

Beckett's characters are largely of a piece. They tend to be aging, homeless, in mental and physical pain, and isolated from those around them yet desperately trying to maintain a sense of connection. Their bodies are sources of anguish, and they are constantly plagued by some difficulty or other. Their sense of disconnection from the outside world and from one another is a source of anxiety, as is the seemingly tenuous nature of their sterile existence. They attempt to alleviate this anxiety and give meaning to their existence through action, but to little avail. The dialogue, movements, and choices of these characters are rarely shown to have logic or consequence, and the result is by turns painful and funny to watch. Beckett's plays, like those of Eugène Ionesco and Jean Genet, are central texts to any discussion of absurdist theater—they present the absurdity and futility of the human condition as a given. Though often bleak, absurdist drama can also be highly comic; as Nell says in *Endgame*, "Nothing is funnier than unhappiness."

At no point in his career did Beckett demonstrate any concern for audience expectations, or feel the need to write in any currently popular style. Perhaps as a result, his work pushed the limits of what was thought possible. His willingness to experiment with new ideas, new media, and new technology resulted in a remarkably rich and diverse body of work. In 1958, shortly after reel-to-reel tape recorders were invented, Beckett incorporated one into a ground-breaking short play, *Krapp's Last*

Tape (*La dernière bande*, 1958), in which a man conducts a "conversation" with a recording of his own voice from years before. In 1964 Beckett forayed into the world of film, writing a script for a film (titled simply *Film*) and travelling to New York to assist in making it.

As he aged, Beckett increasingly despaired of the ability of language to express anything meaningful about the nature of human existence. His 1969 play *Breath* is the most extreme manifestation of such feelings; it lasts less than one minute and includes sounds but no articulated words.

The extraordinary importance of Beckett's work was acknowledged in 1969 when he was awarded the Nobel Prize for Literature. He continued to direct many of his plays and to assist in their production for television up until only a few years before his death in 1989.

⌘ ⌘ ⌘

Whoroscope

What's that?
      An egg?[1]
By the brothers Boot[2] it stinks fresh.
Give it to Gillot.[3]

5   Galileo how are you
      and his consecutive thirds![4]
    The vile old Copernican[5] lead-swinging son of a
            sutler![6]
    We're moving he said we're off—Porca Madonna![7]
    the way a boatswain would be, or a sack-of-potatoey
            charging Pretender.
10 That's not moving, that's *moving*.

What's that?
A little green fry or a mushroomy one?
Two lashed ovaries with prostisciutto?
How long did she womb it, the feathery one?
15 Three days and four nights?
Give it to Gillot.

Faulhaber, Beeckman and Peter the Red,[8]
come now in the cloudy avalanche or Gassendi's[9] sun-
            red crystally cloud
and I'll pebble you all your hen-and-a-half ones
20 or I'll pebble a lens under the quilt in the midst of day.

To think he was my own brother, Peter the Bruiser,[10]
and not a syllogism out of him
no more than if Pa were still in it.
Hey! pass over those coppers,
25 sweet millèd sweat of my burning liver!
Them were the days I sat in the hot-cupboard
            throwing Jesuits[11] out of the skylight.

Who's that? Hals?[12]

---

[1] *egg* René Descartes (1596–1650), the French philosopher and mathematician who is the subject of this poem, was reportedly fussy about his omelets. He believed that a hen needed to brood on an egg for between eight and ten days before it could be eaten; any more or less, according to Descartes, was disgusting.

[2] *brothers Boot* Irish philosophers who disputed various claims of Aristotle.

[3] *Gillot* Jean Gillot, Descartes's servant, who was said to have done some of Descartes's less difficult calculations.

[4] *Galileo … thirds* The famous scientist Galileo Galilei (1564–1642), but somewhat confused with his father, Vincenzo Galilei (1520–1591), who was a mathematician and also a musician.

[5] *Copernican* Follower of Nicolaus Copernicus (1473–1543), Polish mathematician and astronomer, who rejected Aristotle's model of the solar system.

[6] *sutler* One who follows an army, selling provisions to soldiers.

[7] *Porca Madonna* Italian: the Madonna is a pig (vulgar expression of surprise).

[8] *Faulhaber … Red* Three mathematicians, Descartes's contemporaries.

[9] *Gassendi's* Pierre Gassendi (1592–1655), French philosopher, scientist and mathematician, who also rejected Aristotle's teachings about the order of the solar system.

[10] *Peter the Bruiser* Descartes's brother, Pierre Descartes de la Bretaillière (1591–1660).

[11] *Jesuits* Members of the Society of Jesus, an order of the Roman Catholic priesthood.

[12] *Hals* Frans Hals (c. 1580–1666), Dutch painter.

Let him wait.

My squinty doaty!°   dear
30   I hid and you sook.
And Francine[1] my precious fruit of a house-and-
        parlour foetus!
What an exfoliation!
Her little grey flayed epidermis and scarlet tonsils!
My one child
35   scourged by a fever to stagnant murky blood—
blood!
Oh Harvey[2] belovèd
how shall the red and white, the many in the few,
(dear bloodswirling Harvey)
40   eddy through that cracked beater?
And the fourth Henry[3] came to the crypt of the arrow.

What's that?
How long?
Sit on it.

45   A wind of evil flung my despair of ease
against the sharp spires of the one
lady:
not once or twice but ….
(Kip of Christ hatch it!)
50   in one sun's drowning
(Jesuitasters please copy).
So on with the silk hose over the knitted, and the
        morbid leather—
what am I saying! the gentle canvas—
and away to Ancona on the bright Adriatic,
55   and farewell for a space to the yellow key of the
        Rosicrucians.[4]
They don't know what the master of them that do did,
that the nose is touched by the kiss of all foul and
        sweet air,

and the drums, and the throne of the faecal inlet,
and the eyes by its zig-zags.
60   So we drink Him and eat Him
and the watery Beaune[5] and the stale cubes of Hovis[6]
because He can jig
near or as far from His Jigging Self
and as sad or lively as the chalice or the tray asks.
65   How's that, Antonio?

In the name of Bacon will you chicken me up that egg.
Shall I swallow cave-phantoms?

Anna Maria![7]
She reads Moses and says her love is crucified.
70   Leider!° Leider! she bloomed and withered,   alas!
a pale abusive parakeet in a mainstreet window.

No I believe every word of it I assure you.
Fallor, ergo sum![8]
The coy old frôleur!°   groper
75   He tolle'd° and legge'd°   enticed / bowed
and he buttoned on his redemptorist[9] waistcoat.
No matter, let it pass.
I'm a bold boy I know
so I'm not my son
80   (even if I were a concierge)
nor Joachim my father's[10]
but the chip of a perfect block that's neither old nor
        new,
the lonely petal of a great high bright rose.

Are you ripe at last,
85   my slim pale double-breasted turd ?
How rich she smells,

---

[1] *Francine* Francine Descartes (1635–1640), Descartes's daughter, who died of scarlet fever.

[2] *Harvey* William Harvey (1578–1657), English medical doctor who described the circulatory system.

[3] *fourth Henry* In 1610 Descartes participated in a ceremony in which the heart of Henry IV of France (who had recently been assassinated) was placed in the cathedral of La Flèche (French: the arrow).

[4] *Rosicrucians* Famous secret society founded in 1407 by Christian Rosenkreuz (1378–1484). Many famous cultural figures, including Francis Bacon (1561–1626) are thought to have been Rosicrucians.

[5] *Beaune* Type of red wine.

[6] *Hovis* Bread made from the Hovis brand of flour.

[7] *Anna Maria* Anna Maria van Schurman (1607–1678), Dutch philosopher. Her friendship with Descartes dissolved after he published religious ideas in his *Discourse on Method* (1637) that she found distasteful.

[8] *Fallor … sum!* Latin: I deceive, therefore I am! Descartes famously asserted as part of his refutation of scepticism in *Meditations on First Philosophy*, "Cogito ergo sum" (Latin: I think, therefore I am).

[9] *redemptorist* Belonging to a member of the Congregation of the Most Holy Redeemer, an order of the Roman Catholic priesthood.

[10] *Joachim my father* Joachim Descartes, Descartes's father.

this abortion of a fledgling!
I will eat it with a fish fork.
White and yolk and feathers.
90 Then I will rise and move moving
toward Rahab[1] of the snows,
the murdering matinal[2] pope-confessed amazon,
Christina[3] the ripper.
Oh Weulles[4] spare the blood of a Frank[5]
95 who has climbed the bitter steps,
(René du Perron[6] ....!)
and grant me my second
starless inscrutable hour.
—1930

from *Texts For Nothing*

I

Suddenly, no, at last, long last, I couldn't any more, I couldn't go on. Someone said, You can't stay here. I couldn't stay there and I couldn't go on. I'll describe the place, that's unimportant. The top, very flat, of a mountain, no, a hill, but so wild, so wild, enough. Quag,[7] heath up to the knees, faint sheeptracks, troughs scooped deep by the rains. It was far down in one of these I was lying, out of the wind. Glorious prospect, but for the mist that blotted out everything, valleys, loughs,[8] plain and sea. How can I go on, I shouldn't have begun, no, I had to begin. Someone said, perhaps the same, What possessed you to come? I could have stayed in my den, snug and dry, I couldn't. My den, I'll describe it, no, I can't. It's simple, I can do nothing any

more, that's what you think. I say to the body, Up with you now, and I can feel it struggling, like an old hack foundered in the street, struggling no more, struggling again, till it gives up. I say to the head, Leave it alone, stay quiet, it stops breathing, then pants on worse than ever. I am far from all that wrangle, I shouldn't bother with it, I need nothing, neither to go on nor to stay where I am, it's truly all one to me, I should turn away from it all, away from the body, away from the head, let them work it out between them, let them cease, I can't, it's I would have to cease. Ah yes, we seem to be more than one, all deaf, not even, gathered together for life. Another said, or the same, or the first, they all have the same voice, the same ideas, All you had to do was stay at home. Home. They wanted me to go home. My dwelling-place. But for the mist, with good eyes, with a telescope, I could see it from here. It's not just tiredness, I'm not just tired, in spite of the climb. It's not that I want to stay here either. I had heard tell, I must have heard tell of the view, the distant sea in hammered lead, the so-called golden vale so often sung, the double valleys, the glacial loughs, the city in its haze, it was all on every tongue. Who are these people anyway? Did they follow me up here, go before me, come with me? I am down in the hole the centuries have dug, centuries of filthy weather, flat on my face on the dark earth sodden with the creeping saffron waters it slowly drinks. They are up above, all round me, as in a graveyard. I can't raise my eyes to them, what a pity, I wouldn't see their faces, their legs perhaps, plunged in the heath. Do they see me, what can they see of me? Perhaps there is no one left, perhaps they are all gone, sickened. I listen and it's the same thoughts I hear, I mean the same as ever, strange. To think in the valley the sun is blazing all down the ravelled sky. How long have I been here, what a question, I've often wondered. And often I could answer, An hour, a month, a year, a century, depending on what I meant by here, and me, and being, and there I never went looking for extravagant meanings, there I never much varied, only the here would sometimes seem to vary. Or I said, I can't have been here long, I wouldn't have held out. I hear the curlews,[9] that means close of day, fall of night, for that's the way with curlews, silent all day, then crying when the darkness gathers, that's the way with those wild creatures and so short-

---

[1] *Rahab* Prostitute of Jericho who assisted Israelite spies. See Joshua 2.1–7.

[2] *matinal* Early-rising.

[3] *Christina* Christina of Sweden (1626–1689), queen of Sweden. Descartes came to Sweden to be her teacher, but found that her early-rising tendencies conflicted with his practice of studying in bed until noon.

[4] *Weulles* Dutch physician also at the court of Christina of Sweden, an adversary of Descartes.

[5] *Frank* Frenchman (i.e., Descartes).

[6] *René du Perron* Descartes was a minor noble, the Seigneur du Perron.

[7] *Quag* Quagmire.

[8] *loughs* Lakes.

[9] *curlews* Brown, long-legged shore birds.

lived, compared with me. And that other question I know so well too, What possessed you to come? unanswerable, so that I answered, To change, or, It's not me, or Chance, or again, To see, or again, years of great sun, Fate, I feel that other coming, let it come, it won't catch me napping. All is noise, unending suck of black sopping peat, surge of giant ferns, heathery gulfs of quiet where the wind drowns, my life and its old jingles. To change, to see, no, there's no more to see, I've seen it all, till my eyes are blear, nor to get away from harm, the harm is done, one day the harm was done, the day my feet dragged me out that must go their ways, that I let go their ways and drag me here, that's what possessed me to come. And what I'm doing, all-important, breathing in and out and saying, with words like smoke, I can't go, I can't stay, let's see what happens next. And in the way of sensation? My God I can't complain, it's himself all right, only muffled, like buried in snow, less the warmth, less the drowse, I can follow them well, all the voices, all the parts, fairly well, the cold is eating me, the wet too, at least I presume so, I'm far. My rheumatism in any case is no more than a memory, it hurts me no more than my mother's did, when it hurt her. Eye ravening[1] patient in the haggard vulture face, perhaps it's carrion time. I'm up there and I'm down here, under my gaze, foundered, eyes closed, ear cupped against the sucking peat, we're of one mind, all of one mind, always were, deep down, we're fond of one another, we're sorry for one another, but there it is, there's nothing we can do for one another. One thing at least is certain, in an hour it will be too late, in half-an-hour it will be night, and yet it's not, not certain, what is not certain, absolutely certain, that night prevents what day permits, for those who know how to go about it, who have the will to go about it, and the strength, the strength to try again. Yes, it will be night, the mist will clear, I know my mist, for all my distraction, the wind freshen and the whole nightsky open over the mountain, with its lights, including the Bears, to guide me once again on my way, let's wait for night. All mingles, times and tenses, at first I only had been here, now I'm here still, soon I won't be here yet, toiling up the slope, or in the bracken by the wood, it's larch, I don't try to understand, I'll never try

to understand any more, that's what you think, for the moment I'm here, always have been, always shall be, I won't be afraid of the big words any more, they are not big. I don't remember coming, I can't go, all my little company, my eyes are closed and I feel the wet humus harsh against my cheek, my hat is gone, it can't be gone far, or the wind has swept it away, I was attached to it. Sometimes it's the sea, other times the mountains, often it was the forest, the city, the plain too, I've flirted with the plain too, I've given myself up for dead all over the place, of hunger, of old age, murdered, drowned, and then for no reason, of tedium, nothing like breathing your last to put new life in you, and then the rooms, natural death, tucked up in bed, smothered in household gods, and always muttering, the same old mutterings, the same old stories, the same old questions and answers, no malice in me, hardly any, stultior stultissimo,[2] never an imprecation,[3] not such a fool, or else it's gone from mind. Yes, to the end, always muttering, to lull me and keep me company, and all ears always, all ears for the old stories, as when my father took me on his knee and read me the one about Joe Breem, or Breen, the son of a lighthouse-keeper, evening after evening, all the long winter through. A tale, it was a tale for children, it all happened on a rock, in the storm, the mother was dead and the gulls came beating against the light, Joe jumped into the sea, that's all I remember, a knife between his teeth, did what was to be done and came back, that's all I remember this evening, it ended happily, it began unhappily and it ended happily, every evening, a comedy, for children. Yes, I was my father and I was my son, I asked myself questions and answered as best I could, I had it told to me evening after evening, the same old story I knew by heart and couldn't believe, or we walked together, hand in hand, silent, sunk in our worlds, each in his worlds, the hands forgotten in each other. That's how I've held out till now. And this evening again it seems to be working, I'm in my arms, I'm holding myself in my arms, without much tenderness, but faithfully, faithfully. Sleep now, as under that ancient lamp, all twined together, tired out with so much talking, so much listening, so much toil and play. . . .

---

[1]   *ravening* Seeking prey.

[2]   *stultior stultissimo* Latin: More stupid than the most stupid person.

[3]   *imprecation* Curse.

4

Where would I go, if I could go, who would I be, if I could Be, what would I say, if I had a voice, who says this, saying it's me? Answer simply, someone answer simply. It's the same old stranger as ever, for whom alone accusative I exist, in the pit of my existence, of his, of ours, there's a simple answer. It's not with thinking he'll find me, but what is he to do, living and bewildered, yes, living, say what he may. Forget me, know me not, yes, that would be the wisest, none better able than he. Why this sudden affability after such desertion, it's easy to understand, that's what he says, but he doesn't understand. I'm not in his head, nowhere in his old body, and yet I'm there, for him I'm there, with him, hence all the confusion. That should have been enough for him, to have found me absent, but it's not, he wants me there, with a form and a world, like him, in spite of him, me who am everything, like him who is nothing. And when he feels me void of existence it's of his he would have me void, and vice versa, mad, mad, he's mad. The truth is he's looking for me to kill me, to have me dead like him, dead like the living. He knows all that, but it's no help his knowing it, I don't know it, I know nothing. He protests he doesn't reason and does nothing but reason, crooked, as if that could improve matters. He thinks words fail him, he thinks because words fail him he's on his way to my speechlessness, to being speechless with my speechlessness, he would like it to be my fault that words fail him, of course words fail him. He tells his story every five minutes, saying it is not his, there's cleverness for you. He would like it to be my fault that he has no story, of course he has no story, that's no reason for trying to foist one on me. That's how he reasons, wide of the mark, but wide of what mark, answer us that. He has me say things saying it's not me, there's profundity for you, he has me who say nothing say it's not me. All that is truly crass. If at least he would dignify me with the third person, like his other figments, not he, he'll be satisfied with nothing less than me, for his me. When he had me, when he was me, he couldn't get rid of me quick enough, I didn't exist, he couldn't have that, that was no kind of life, of course I didn't exist, any more than he did, of course it was no kind of life, now he has it, his kind of life, let him lose it, if he wants to be in peace, with a bit of luck. His life, what a mine, what a life, he can't have that, you can't fool him, ergo it's not his, it's not him, what a thought, treat him like that, like a vulgar Molloy, a common Malone,[1] those mere mortals, happy mortals, have a heart, land him in that shit, who never stirred, who is none but me, all things considered, and what things, and how considered, he had only to keep out of it. That's how he speaks, this evening, how he has me speak, how he speaks to himself, how I speak, there is only me, this evening, here, on earth, and a voice that makes no sound because it goes towards none, and a head strewn with arms laid down and corpses fighting fresh, and a body, I nearly forgot. This evening, I say this evening, perhaps it's morning. And all these things, what things, all about me, I won't deny them any more, there's no sense in that any more. If it's nature perhaps it's trees and birds, they go together, water and air, so that all may go on, I don't need to know the details, perhaps I'm sitting under a palm. Or it's a room, with furniture, all that's required to make life comfortable, dark, because of the wall outside the window. What am I doing, talking, having my figments talk, it can only be me. Spells of silence too, when I listen, and hear the local sounds, the world sounds, see what an effort I make, to be reasonable. There's my life, why not, it is one, if you like, if you must, I don't say no, this evening. There has to be one, it seems, once there is speech, no need of a story, a story is not compulsory, just a life, that's the mistake I made, one of the mistakes, to have wanted a story for myself, whereas life alone is enough. I'm making progress, it was time, I'll learn to keep my foul mouth shut before I'm done, if nothing foreseen crops up. But he who somehow comes and goes, unaided from place to place, even though nothing happens to him, true, what of him? I stay here, sitting, if I'm sitting, often I feel sitting, sometimes standing, it's one or the other, or lying down, there's another possibility, often I feel lying down, it's one of the three, or kneeling. What counts is to be in the world, the posture is immaterial, so long as one is on earth. To breathe is all that is required, there is no obligation to ramble, or receive company, you may even believe yourself dead on condition you make no bones about it, what more liberal regimen could be imagined, I don't know, I don't

---

[1] *Molloy ... Malone* Beckett had completed two novels, *Molloy* and *Malone Meurt* (*Malone Dies*) a few years before writing *Texts for Nothing*. (Neither novel was published until many years later.)

imagine. No point under such circumstances in saying I am somewhere else, someone else, such as I am I have all I need to hand, for to do what, I don't know, all I have to do, there I am on my own again at last, what a relief that must be. Yes, there are moments, like this moment, when I seem almost restored to the feasible. Then it goes, all goes, and I'm far again, with a far story again, I wait for me afar for my story to begin, to end, and again this voice cannot be mine. That's where I'd go, if I could go, that's who I'd be, if I could be....

8

Only the words break the silence, all other sounds have ceased. If I were silent I'd hear nothing. But if I were silent the other sounds would start again, those to which the words have made me deaf, or which have really ceased. But I am silent, it sometimes happens, no, never, not one second. I weep too without interruption. It's an unbroken flow of words and tears. With no pause for reflection. But I speak softer, every year a little softer. Perhaps. Slower too, every year a little slower. Perhaps. It is hard for me to judge. If so the pauses would be longer, between the words, the sentences, the syllables, the tears, I confuse them, words and tears, my words are my tears, my eyes my mouth. And I should hear, at every little pause, if it's the silence I say when I say that only the words break it. But nothing of the kind, that's not how it is, it's for ever the same murmur, flowing unbroken, like a single endless word and therefore meaningless, for it's the end gives the meaning to words. What right have you then, no, this time I see what I'm up to and put a stop to it, saying, None, none. But get on with the stupid old threne[1] and ask, ask until you answer, a new question, the most ancient of all, the question were things always so. Well I'm going to tell myself something (if I'm able), pregnant I hope with promise for the future, namely that I begin to have no very clear recollection of how things were before (I was!), and by before I mean elsewhere, time has turned into space and there will be no more time, till I get out of here. Yes, my past has thrown me out, its gates have slammed behind me, or I burrowed my way out alone, to linger a moment free in a dream of days and nights, dreaming of me moving, season after season, towards the last, like the living, till suddenly I was here, all

memory gone. Ever since nothing but fantasies and hope of a story for me somehow, of having come from somewhere and of being able to go back, or on, somehow, some day, or without hope. Without what hope, haven't I just said, of seeing me alive, not merely inside an imaginary head, but a pebble sand to be, under a restless sky, restless on its shore, faint stirs day and night, as if to grow less could help, ever less and less and never quite be gone. No truly, no matter what, I say no matter what, hoping to wear out a voice, to wear out a head, or without hope, without reason, no matter what, without reason. But it will end, a desinence[2] will come, or the breath fail better still, I'll be silence, I'll know I'm silence, no, in the silence you can't know, I'll never know anything. But at least get out of here, at least that, no? I don't know. And time begin again, the steps on the earth, the night the fool implores at morning and the morning he begs at evening not to dawn. I don't know, I don't know what all that means, day and night, earth and sky, begging and imploring. And I can desire them? Who says I desire them, the voice, and that I can't desire anything, that looks like a contradiction, it may be for all I know. Me, here, if they could open, those little words, open and swallow me up, perhaps that is what has happened. If so let them open again and let me out, in the tumult of light that sealed my eyes, and of men, to try and be one again. Or if I'm guilty let me be forgiven and graciously authorized to expiate,[3] coming and going in passing time, every day a little purer, a little deader. The mistake I make is to try and think, even the way I do, such as I am I shouldn't be able, even the way I do. But whom can I have offended so grievously, to be punished in this inexplicable way, all is inexplicable, space and time, false and inexplicable, suffering and tears, and even the old convulsive cry, It's not me, it can't be me. But am I in pain, whether it's me or not, frankly now, is there pain? Now is here and here there is no frankness, all I say will be false and to begin with not said by me, here I'm a mere ventriloquist's dummy, I feel nothing, say nothing, he holds me in his arms and moves my lips with a string, with a fish-hook, no, no need of lips, all is dark, there is no one, what's the matter with my head, I must have left it in Ireland, in a saloon, it must be there still, lying on the bar, it's all

---

[1] *threne* Lamentation.

[2] *desinence* Termination.

[3] *expiate* Atone.

it deserved. But that other who is me, blind and deaf and mute, because of whom I'm here, in this black silence, helpless to move or accept this voice as mine, it's as him I must disguise myself till I die, for him in the meantime do my best not to live, in this pseudo-sepulture[1] claiming to be his. Whereas to my certain knowledge I'm dead and kicking above, somewhere in Europe probably, with every plunge and suck of the sky a little more overripe, as yesterday in the pump of the womb. No, to have said so convinces me of the contrary, I never saw the light of day, any more than he, ah if no were content to cut yes's throat and never cut its own. Watch out for the right moment then not another word, is that the only way to have being and habitat? But I'm here, that much at least is certain, it's in vain I keep on saying it, it remains true. Does it? It's hard for me to judge. Less true and less certain in any case than when I say I'm on earth, come into the world and assured of getting out, that's why I say it, patiently, variously, trying to vary, for you never know, it's perhaps all a question of hitting on the right aggregate. So as to be here no more at last, to have never been here, but all this time above, with a name like a dog to be called up with and distinctive marks to be had up with, the chest expanding and contracting unaided, panting towards the grand apnoea.[2] The right aggregate, but there are four million possible, nay probable, according to Aristotle, who knew everything. But what is this I see, and how, a white stick and an ear-trumpet, where, Place de la République,[3] at pernod[4] time, let me look closer at this, it's perhaps me at last. The trumpet, sailing at ear level, suddenly resembles a steam-whistle, of the kind thanks to which my steamers forge fearfully through the fog. That should fix the period, to the nearest half-century or so. The stick gains ground, tapping with its ferrule[5] the noble bassamento of the United Stores, it must be winter, at least not summer. I can also just discern, with a final effort of will, a bowler hat which seems to my sorrow a sardonic synthesis of all those that

never fitted me and, at the other extremity, similarly suspicious, a complete pair of brown boots lacerated and gaping. These insignia, if I may so describe them, advance in concert, as though connected by the traditional human excipient,[6] halt, move on again, confirmed by the vast show windows. The level of the hat, and consequently of the trumpet, hold out some hope for me as a dying dwarf or at least hunchback. The vacancy is tempting, shall I enthrone my infirmities, give them this chance again, my dream infirmities, that they may take flesh and move, deteriorating, round and round this grandiose square which I hope I don't confuse with the Bastille,[7] until they are deemed worthy of the adjacent Père Lachaise[8] or, better still, prematurely relieved trying to cross over, at the hour of night's young thoughts. No, the answer is no. For even as I moved, or when the moment came, affecting beyond all others, to hold out my hand, or hat, without previous song, or any other form of concession to self-respect, at the terrace of a café, or in the mouth of the underground, I would know it was not me, I would know I was here, begging in another dark, another silence, for another alm, that of being or of ceasing, better still, before having been. And the hand old in vain would drop the mite[9] and the old feet shuffle on, towards an even vainer death than no matter whose.

—1950

The Calmative

I don't know when I died. It always seemed to me I died old, about ninety years old, and what years, and that my body bore it out, from head to foot. But this evening, alone in my icy bed, I have the feeling I'll be older than the day, the night, when the sky with all its lights fell upon me, the same I had so often gazed on since my first stumblings on the distant earth. For I'm too frightened this evening to listen to myself rot, waiting for the great red lapses of the heart, the tearings

---

[1] *sepulture*   Tomb.

[2] *apnoea*   Cessation of breath.

[3] *Place de la République*   Square in Paris.

[4] *pernod*   Anise-flavored liquor.

[5] *ferrule*   Metal cap placed on the end of a wooden pole to protect it.

[6] *excipient*   Medium to which pigment is added, in the making of paint.

[7] *Bastille*   Place de la Bastille (another Parisian square).

[8] *Père Lachaise*   Cimetière du Père Lachaise, the largest cemetery in Paris.

[9] *mite*   Small coin.

at the caecal walls, and for the slow killings to finish in my skull, the assaults on unshakable pillars, the fornications with corpses. So I'll tell myself a story, I'll try and tell myself another story, to try and calm myself, and it's there I feel I'll be old, old, even older than the day I fell, calling for help, and it came. Or is it possible that in this story I have come back to life, after my death? No, it's not like me to come back to life, after my death.

What possessed me to stir when I wasn't with anybody? Was I being thrown out? No, I wasn't with anybody. I see a kind of den littered with empty tins. And yet we are not in the country. Perhaps it's just ruins, a ruined folly, on the skirts of the town, in a field, for the fields come right up to our walls, their walls, and the cows lie down at night in the lee of the ramparts. I have changed refuge so often, in the course of my rout, that now I can't tell between dens and ruins. But there was never any city but the one. It is true you often move along in a dream, houses and factories darken the air, trams go by and under your feet wet from the grass there are suddenly cobbles. I only know the city of my childhood, I must have seen the other, but unbelieving. All I say cancels out, I'll have said nothing. Was I hungry itself? Did the weather tempt me? It was cloudy and cool, I insist, but not to the extent of luring me out. I couldn't get up at the first attempt, nor let us say at the second, and once up, propped against the wall, I wondered if I could go on, I mean up, propped against the wall. Impossible to go out and walk. I speak as though it all happened yesterday. Yesterday indeed *is* recent, but not enough. For what I tell this evening is passing this evening, at this passing hour. I'm no longer with these assassins, in this bed of terror, but in my distant refuge, my hands twined together, my head bowed, weak, breathless, calm, free, and older than I'll have ever been, if my calculations are correct. I'll tell my story in the past none the less, as though it were a myth, or an old fable, for this evening I need another age, that age to become another age in which I became what I was.

But little by little I got myself out and started walking with short steps among the trees, oh look, trees! The paths of other days were rank with tangled growth. I leaned against the trunks to get my breath and pulled myself forward with the help of boughs. Of my last passage no trace remained. They were the perishing oaks

immortalized by d'Aubigné.[1] It was only a grove. The fringe was near, a light less green and kind of tattered told me so, in a whisper. Yes, no matter where you stood, in this little wood, and were it in the furthest recess of its poor secrecies, you saw on every hand the gleam of this pale light, promise of God knows what fatuous eternity. Die without too much pain, a little, that's worth your while. Under the blind sky close with your own hands the eyes soon sockets, then quick into carrion not to mislead the crows. That's the advantage of death by drowning, one of the advantages, the crabs never get there too soon. But here a strange thing, I was no sooner free of the wood at last, having crossed unminding the ditch that girdles it, than thoughts came to me of cruelty, the kind that smiles. A lush pasture lay before me, nonsuch[2] perhaps, who cares, drenched in evening dew or recent rain. Beyond this meadow to my certain knowledge a path, then a field and finally the ramparts, closing the prospect. Cyclopean[3] and crenellated,[4] standing out faintly against a sky scarcely less sombre, they did not seem in ruins, viewed from mine, but were, to my certain knowledge. Such was the scene offered to me, in vain, for I knew it well and loathed it. What I saw was a bald man in a brown suit, a comedian. He was telling a funny story about a fiasco. Its point escaped me. He used the word snail, or slug, to the delight of all present. The women seemed even more entertained than their escorts, if that were possible. Their shrill laughter pierced the clapping and, when this had subsided, broke out still here and there in sudden peals even after the next story had begun, so that part of it was lost. Perhaps they had in mind the reigning penis sitting who knows by their side and from that sweet shore launched their cries of joy towards the comic vast, what a talent. But it's to me this evening something has to happen, to my body as in myth and metamorphosis, this old body to which nothing ever happened, or so little, which never met with anything, loved anything, wished for anything, in its tarnished universe, except for the mirrors to shatter, the plane, the curved, the magni-

---

[1] *d'Aubigné* Théodore-Agrippa d'Aubigné (1552–1630), French baroque poet. Beckett refers to d'Aubigné's poem "Stanzas" (1571).

[2] *nonsuch* A low-lying clover-like plant, also called black medic.

[3] *Cyclopean* Made of large, irregularly shaped stones.

[4] *crenellated* Notched or indented usually for the purpose of facilitating the defense of battlements.

fying, the minifying, and to vanish in the havoc of its images. Yes, this evening it has to be as in the story my father used to read to me, evening after evening, when I was small, and he had all his health, to calm me, evening after evening, year after year it seems to me this evening, which I don't remember much about, except that it was the adventures of one Joe Breem, or Breen, the son of a lighthouse-keeper, a strong muscular lad of fifteen, those were the words, who swam for miles in the night, a knife between his teeth, after a shark, I forget why, out of sheer heroism. He might have simply told me the story, he knew it by heart, so did I, but that wouldn't have calmed me, he had to read it to me, evening after evening, or pretend to read it to me, turning the pages and explaining the pictures that were of me already, evening after evening the same pictures till I dozed off on his shoulder. If he had skipped a single word I would have hit him, with my little fist, in his big belly bursting out of the old cardigan and unbuttoned trousers that rested him from his office canonicals. For me now the setting forth, the struggle and perhaps the return, for the old man I am this evening, older than my father ever was, older than I shall ever be. I crossed the meadow with little stiff steps at the same time limp, the best I could manage. Of my last passage no trace remained, it was long ago. And the little bruised stems soon straighten up again, having need of air and light, and as for the broken their place is soon taken. I entered the town by what they call the Shepherds' Gate without having seen a soul, only the first bats like flying crucifixions, nor heard a sound except my steps, my heart in my breast and then, as I went under the arch, the hoot of an owl, that cry at once so soft and fierce which in the night, calling, answering, through my little wood and those nearby, sounded in my shelter like a tocsin.[1] The further I went into the city the more I was struck by its deserted air. It was lit as usual, brighter than usual, although the shops were shut. But the lights were on in their windows with the object no doubt of attracting customers and prompting them to say, I say, I like that, not dear[2] either, I'll come back tomorrow, if I'm still alive. I nearly said, Good God it's Sunday. The trams were running, the buses too, but few, slow, empty, noiseless, as if under water. I didn't

see a single horse! I was wearing my long green greatcoat with the velvet collar, such as motorists wore about 1900, my father's, but that day it was sleeveless, a vast cloak. But on me it was still the same great dead weight, with no warmth to it, and the tails swept the ground, scraped it rather, they had grown so stiff, and I so shrunken. What would, what could happen to me in this empty place? But I felt the houses packed with people, lurking behind the curtains they looked out into the street or, crouched far back in the depths of the room, head in hands, were sunk in dream. Up aloft my hat, the same as always, I reached no further. I went right across the city and came to the sea, having followed the river to its mouth. I kept saying, I'll go back, unbelieving. The boats at anchor in the harbour, tied up to the jetty, seemed no less numerous than usual, as if I knew anything about what was usual. But the quays were deserted and there was no sign or stir of arrival or departure. But all might change from one moment to the next and be transformed like magic before my eyes. Then all the bustle of the people and things of the sea, the masts of the big craft gravely rocking and of the small more jauntily, I insist, and I'd hear the gulls' terrible cry and perhaps the sailors' cry. And I might slip unnoticed aboard a freighter outward bound and get far away and spend far away a few good months, perhaps even a year or two, in the sun, in peace, before I died. And without going that far it would be a sad state of affairs if in that unscandalizable throng I couldn't achieve a little encounter that would calm me a little, or exchange a few words with a navigator for example, words to carry away with me to my refuge, to add to my collection. I waited sitting on a kind of topless capstan,[3] saying, The very capstans this evening are out of order. And I gazed out to sea, out beyond the breakwaters, without sighting the least vessel. I could see lights flush with the water. And the pretty beacons at the harbour mouth I could see too, and others in the distance, flashing from the coast, the islands, the headlands. But seeing still no sign or stir I made ready to go, to turn away sadly from this dead haven, for there are scenes that call for strange farewells. I had merely to bow my head and look down at my feet, for it is in this attitude I always drew the strength to, how shall I say, I don't know, and it was always from the earth, rather than

---

[1] *tocsin* Alarm bell.

[2] *dear* Expensive.

[3] *capstan* Mechanism used for winding up cable.

from the sky, notwithstanding its reputation, that my help came in time of trouble. And there, on the flagstone, which I was not focussing, for why focus it, I saw haven afar, where the black swell was most perilous, and all about me storm and wreck. I'll never come back here, I said. But when with a thrust of both hands against the rim of the capstan I heaved myself up I found facing me a young boy holding a goat by a horn. I sat down again. He stood there silent looking at me without visible fear or revulsion. Admittedly the light was poor. His silence seemed natural to me, it befitted me as the elder to speak first. He was barefoot and in rags. Haunter of the waterfront he had stepped aside to see what the dark hulk could be abandoned on the quayside. Such was my train of thought. Close up to me now with his little guttersnipe's eye there could be no doubt left in his mind. And yet he stayed. Can this base thought be mine? Moved, for after all that is what I must have come out for, in a way, and with little expectation of advantage from what might follow, I resolved to speak to him. So I marshalled the words and opened my mouth, thinking I would hear them. But all I heard was a kind of rattle, unintelligible even to me who knew what was intended. But it was nothing, mere speechlessness due to long silence, as in the wood that darkens the mouth of hell, do you remember, I only just. Without letting go of his goat he moved right up against me and offered me a sweet out of a twist of paper such as you could buy for a penny. I hadn't been offered a sweet for eighty years at least, but I took it eagerly and put it in my mouth, the old gesture came back to me, more and more moved since that is what I wanted. The sweets were stuck together and I had my work cut out to separate the top one, a green one, from the others, but he helped me and his hand brushed mine. And a moment later as he made to move away, hauling his goat after him, with a great gesticulation of my whole body I motioned him to stay and I said, in an impetuous murmur, Where are you off to, my little man, with your nanny? The words were hardly out of my mouth when for shame I covered my face. And yet they were the same I had tried to utter but a moment before. Where are you off to, my little man, with your nanny! If I could have blushed I would have, but there was not enough blood left in my extremities. If I had had a penny in my pocket I would have given it to him, for him to forgive me, but I did not have a penny in my pocket, nor anything resembling it. Nothing that could give pleasure to a little unfortunate at the mouth of life. I suspect I had nothing with me but my stone, that day, having gone out as it were without premeditation. Of his little person I was fated to see no more than the black curly hair and the pretty curve of the long bare legs all muscle and dirt. And the hand, so fresh and keen, I would not forget in a hurry either. I looked for better words to say to him, I found them too late, he was gone, oh not far, but far. Out of my life too he went without a care, not one of his thoughts would ever be for me again, unless perhaps when he was old and, delving in his boyhood, would come upon that gallows night and hold the goat by the horn again and linger again a moment by my side, with who knows perhaps a touch of tenderness, even of envy, but I have my doubts. Poor dear dumb beasts, how you will have helped me. What does your daddy do? that's what I would have said to him if he had given me the chance. Soon they were no more than a single blur which if I hadn't known I might have taken for a young centaur. I was nearly going to have the goat dung, then pick up a handful of the pellets so soon cold and hard, sniff and even taste them, no, that would not help me this evening. I say this evening as if it were always the same evening, but are there two evenings? I went, intending to get back as fast as I could, but it would not be quite empty-handed, repeating, I'll never come back here. My legs were paining me, every step would gladly have been the last, but the glances I darted towards the windows, stealthily, showed me a great cylinder sweeping past as though on rollers on the asphalt. I must indeed have been moving fast, for I overhauled more than one pedestrian, there are the first men, without extending myself, I who in the normal way was left standing by cripples, and then I seemed to hear the footfalls die behind me. And yet each little step would gladly have been the last. So much so that when I emerged on a square I hadn't noticed on the way out, with a cathedral looming on the far side, I decided to go in, if it was open, and hide, as in the Middle Ages, for a space. I say cathedral, it may not have been, I don't know, all I know is it would vex me in this story that aspires to be the last, to have taken refuge in a common church. I remarked the Saxon Stützenwechsel.[1] Charming effect, but it didn't charm me. The brilliantly lit nave appeared deserted. I walked round it several times without seeing a soul. They were hiding perhaps, under the choir-stalls, or dodging behind the pillars, like woodpeckers. Suddenly close to where I was, and without my having heard the long preliminary rumblings, the organ began to boom. I sprang up from the mat on which I lay before the altar and hastened to the far end of the nave as if on my way out. But it was a side aisle and the door I disappeared through was not the exit. For instead of being restored to the night I found myself at the foot of a spiral staircase which I began to climb at top speed, mindless of my heart, like one hotly pursued by a homicidal maniac. This staircase faintly lit by I know not what means, slits perhaps, I mounted panting as far as the projecting gallery[2] in which it culminated and which, separated from the void by a cynical parapet, encompassed a smooth round wall capped by a little dome covered with lead or verdigrised copper, phew, if that's not clear. People must have come here for the view, those who fall die on the way. Flattening myself against the wall I started round, clockwise. But I had hardly gone a few steps when I met a man revolving in the other direction, with the utmost circumspection. How I'd love to push him, or him to push me, over the edge. He gazed at me wild-eyed for a moment and then, not daring to pass me on the parapet side and surmising correctly that I would not relinquish the wall just to oblige him, abruptly turned his back on me, his head rather, for his back remained glued to the wall, and went back the way he had come so that soon there was nothing left of him but a left hand. It lingered a moment, then slid out of sight. All that remained to me was the vision of two burning eyes starting out of their sockets under a check cap. Into what nightmare thingness am I fallen? My hat flew off, but did not get far thanks to the string. I turned my head towards the staircase and lent an eye. Nothing. Then a little girl came into view followed by a man holding her by the hand, both pressed against the wall. He pushed her into the stairway, disappeared after her, turned and raised towards me a face that made me

recoil. I could only see his bare head above the top step. When they were gone I called. I completed in haste the round of the gallery. No one. I saw on the horizon, where sky, sea, plain and mountain meet, a few low stars, not to be confused with the fires men light, at night, or that go alight alone. Enough. Back in the street I tried to find my way in the sky, where I knew the Bears so well. If I had seen someone I would have stopped him to ask, the most ferocious aspect would not have daunted me. I would have said, touching my hat, Pardon me your honour, the Shepherds' Gate for the love of God. I thought I could go no further, but no sooner had the impetus reached my legs than on I went, believe it or not, at a very fair pace. I wasn't returning empty-handed, not quite, I was taking back with me the virtual certainty that I was still of this world, of that world too, in a way. But I was paying the price. I would have done better to spend the night in the cathedral, on the mat before the altar, I would have continued on my way at first light, or they would have found me stretched out in the rigor of death, the genuine bodily article, under the blue eyes fount of so much hope, and put me in the evening papers. But suddenly I was descending a wide street, vaguely familiar, but in which I could never have set foot, in my lifetime. But soon realizing I was going downhill I turned about and set off in the other direction. For I was afraid if I went downhill of returning to the sea where I had sworn never to return. When I say I turned about I mean I wheeled round in a wide semi-circle without slowing down, for I was afraid if I stopped of not being able to start again, yes, I was afraid of that too. And this evening too I dare not stop. I was struck more and more by the contrast between the brightly lit streets and their deserted air. To say it distressed me, no, but I say it all the same, in the hope of calming myself. To say there was no one abroad, no, I would not go that far, for I remarked a number of shapes, male and female, strange shapes, but not more so than usual. As to what hour it might have been I had no idea, except that it must have been some hour of the night. But it might have been three or four in the morning just as it might have been ten or eleven in the evening, depending no doubt on whether one wondered at the scarcity of passers-by or at the extraordinary radiance shed by the street-lamps and traffic-lights. For at one or other of these no one could fail to wonder,

---

[1] *Saxon Stützenwechsel*   Architectural feature which utilizes alternating support columns.

[2] *projecting gallery*   Balcony.

unless he was out of his mind. Not a single private car, but admittedly from time to time a public vehicle, slow sweep of light silent and empty. It is not my wish to labour these antinomies,[1] for we are needless to say in a skull, but I have no choice but to add the following few remarks. All the mortals I saw were alone and as if sunk in themselves. It must be a common sight, but mixed with something else I imagine. The only couple was two men grappling, their legs intertwined. I only saw one cyclist! He was going the same way as I was. All were going the same way as I was, vehicles too, I have only just realized it. He was pedalling slowly in the middle of the street, reading a newspaper which he held with both hands spread open before his eyes. Every now and then he rang his bell without interrupting his reading. I watched him recede till he was no more than a dot on the horizon. Suddenly a young woman perhaps of easy virtue, dishevelled and her dress in disarray, darted across the street like a rabbit. That is all I had to add. But here a strange thing, yet another, I had no pain whatever, not even in my legs. Weakness. A good night's nightmare and a tin of sardines would restore my sensitivity. My shadow, one of my shadows, flew before me, dwindled, slid under my feet, trailed behind me the way shadows will. This degree of opacity appeared to me conclusive. But suddenly ahead of me a man on the same side of the street and going the same way, to keep harping on the same thing lest I forget. The distance between us was considerable, seventy paces at least, and fearing he might escape me I quickened my step with the result I swept forward as if on rollers. This is not me, I said, let us make the most of it. Finding myself in an instant a bare ten paces in his rear I slowed down so as not to burst in on him and so heighten the aversion my person inspired even in its most abject and obsequious attitudes. And a moment later, keeping humbly in step with him, Excuse me your honour, the Shepherds' Gate for the love of God! At close quarters he appeared normal apart from that air already noted of ebbing inward. I drew a few steps ahead, turned, cringed, touched my hat and said, The right time for mercy's sake! I might as well not have existed. But what about the sweet? A light! I cried. Given my need of help I can't think why I did not bar his path. I couldn't have, that's all, I couldn't have touched him. Seeing a stone seat by

the kerb I sat down and crossed my legs, like Walther.[2] I must have dozed off, for the next thing was a man sitting beside me. I was still taking him in when he opened his eyes and set them on me, as if for the first time, for he shrank back unaffectedly. Where did you spring from? he said. To hear myself addressed again so soon impressed me greatly. What's the matter with you? he said. I tried to look like one with whom that only is the matter which is native to him. Forgive me your honour, I said, gingerly lifting my hat and rising a fraction from the seat, the right time for the love of God! He said a time, I don't remember which, a time that explained nothing, that's all I remember, and did not calm me. But what time could have done that? Oh I know, I know, one will come that will. But in the meantime? What's that you said? he said. Unfortunately I had said nothing. But I wriggled out of it by asking him if he could help me find my way which I had lost. No, he said, for I am not from these parts and if I am sitting on this slab it is because the hotels were full or would not let me in, I have no opinion. But tell me the story of your life, then we'll see. My life! I cried. Why yes, he said, you know, that kind of—what shall I say? He brooded for a time, no doubt trying to think of what life could well be said to be a kind. In the end he went on, testily, Come now, everyone knows that. He jogged me in the ribs. No details, he said, the main drift, the main drift. But as I remained silent he said, Shall I tell you mine, then you'll see what I mean. The account he then gave was brief and dense, facts, without comment. That's what I call a life, he said, do you follow me now? It wasn't bad, his story, positively fairy-like in places. But that Pauline, I said, are you still with her? I am, he said, but I'm going to leave her and set up with another, younger and plumper. You travel a lot, I said. Oh widely, widely, he said. Words were coming back to me, and the way to make them sound. All that's a thing of the past for you no doubt, he said. Do you think of spending some time among us? I said. This sentence struck me as particularly well turned. If it's not a rude question, he said, how old are you? I don't know, I said. You don't know! he cried. Not exactly, I said. Are thighs much in your thoughts, he said, arses, cunts and envi-

---

1   *antinomies* Paradoxes.

rons? I didn't follow. No more erections naturally, he said. Erections? I said. The penis, he said, you know what the penis is, there, between the legs. Ah that! I said. It thickens, lengthens, stiffens and rises, he said, does it not? I assented, though they were not the terms I would have used. That is what we call an erection, he said. He pondered, then exclaimed, Phenomenal! No? Strange right enough, I said. And there you have it all, he said. But what will become of her? I said. Who? he said. Pauline, I said. She will grow old, he said with tranquil assurance, slowly at first, then faster and faster, in pain and bitterness, pulling the devil by the tail. The face was not full, but I eyed it in vain, it remained clothed in its flesh instead of turning all chalky and channelled as with a gouge. The very vomer[1] kept its cushion. It is true discussion was always bad for me. I longed for the tender nonsuch, I would have trodden it gently, with my boots in my hand, and for the shade of my wood, far from this terrible light. What are you grinning and bearing? he said. He held on his knees a big black bag, like a midwife's I imagine. It was full of glittering phials. I asked him if they were all alike. Oho no, he said, for every taste. He took one and held it out to me, saying, One and six. What did he want? To sell it to me? Proceeding on this hypothesis I told him I had no money. No money! he cried. All of a sudden his hand came down on the back of my neck, his sinewy fingers closed and with a jerk and a twist he had me up against him. But instead of dispatching me he began to murmur words so sweet that I went limp and my head fell forward in his lap. Between the caressing voice and the fingers rowelling[2] my neck the contrast was striking. But gradually the two things merged in a devastating hope, if I dare say so, and I dare. For this evening I have nothing to lose that I can discern. And if I have reached this point (in my story) without anything having changed, for if anything had changed I think I'd know, the fact remains I have reached it, and that's something, and with nothing changed, and that's something too. It's no excuse for rushing matters. No, it must cease gently, as gently cease on the stairs the steps of the loved one, who could not love and will not come back, and whose steps say so, that she could not love and will not come back. He suddenly shoved me away and showed me the phial again. There you have it all, he said. It can't have been the same all as before. Want it? he said. No, but I said yes, so as not to vex him. He proposed an exchange. Give me your hat, he said. I refused. What vehemence! he said. I haven't a thing, I said. Try in your pockets, he said. I haven't a thing, I said, I came out without a thing. Give me a lace, he said. I refused. Long silence. And if you gave me a kiss, he said finally. I knew there were kisses in the air. Can you take off your hat? he said. I took it off. Put it back, he said, you look nicer with it on. I put it back. Come on, he said, give me a kiss and let there be an end to it. Did it not occur to him I might turn him down? No, a kiss is not a boot-lace, he must have seen from my face that all passion was not quite spent. Come, he said. I wiped my mouth in its tod[3] of hair and advanced it towards his. Just a moment, he said. My mouth stood still. You know what a kiss is? he said. Yes yes, I said. If it's not a rude question, he said, when was your last? Some time ago, I said, but I can still do them. He took off his hat, a bowler, and tapped the middle of his forehead. There, he said, and there only. He had a noble brow, white and high. He leaned forward, closing his eyes. Quick, he said. I pursed up my lips as mother had taught me and brought them down where he had said. Enough, he said. He raised his hand to the spot, but left the gesture unfinished and put on his hat. I turned away and looked across the street. It was then I noticed we were sitting opposite a horse-butcher's. Here, he said, take it. I had forgotten. He rose. Standing he was quite short. One good turn, he said, with radiant smile. His teeth shone. I listened to his steps die away. How tell what remains? But it's the end. Or have I been dreaming, am I dreaming? No no, none of that, for dream is nothing, a joke, and significant what is worse. I said, Stay where you are till day breaks, wait sleeping till the lamps go out and the streets come to life. But I stood up and moved off. My pains were back, but with something untoward which prevented my wrapping them round me. But I said, Little by little you are coming to. From my gait alone, slow, stiff and which seemed at every step to solve a stato-dynamic problem never posed before, I would have been known again, if I had been known. I crossed over and stopped before the butcher's. Behind the grille the curtains were drawn, rough canvas curtains striped

---

[1]   *vomer*   Thin bone that separates the nostrils.

[2]   *rowelling*   Pricking (as with a spur).

[3]   *tod*   Bushy mass.

blue and white, colours of the Virgin, and stained with great pink stains. They did not quite meet in the middle, and through the chink I could make out the dim carcasses of the gutted horses hanging from hooks head downwards. I hugged the walls, famished for shadow. To think that in a moment all will be said, all to do again. And the city clocks, what was wrong with them, whose great chill clang even in my wood fell on me from the air? What else? Ah yes, my spoils. I tried to think of Pauline, but she eluded me, gleamed an instant and was gone, like the young woman in the street. So I went in the atrocious brightness, bedded in my old flesh, straining towards an issue and passing them by to left and right and my mind panting after this and that and always flung back to where there was nothing. I succeeded however in fastening briefly on the little girl, long enough to see her a little more clearly than before, so that she wore a kind of bonnet and clasped in her hand a book, of common prayer perhaps, and to try and have her smile, but she did not smile, but vanished down the staircase without having yielded me her little face. I had to stop. At first nothing, then little by little, I mean rising up out of the silence till suddenly no higher, a kind of massive murmur coming perhaps from the house that was propping me up. That reminded me that the houses were full of people, besieged, no, I don't know. When I stepped back to look at the windows I could see, in spite of shutters, blinds and muslins, that many of the rooms were lit. The light was so dimmed by the brilliancy flooding the boulevard that short of knowing or suspecting it was not so one might have supposed everyone sleeping. The sound was not continuous, but broken by silences possibly of consternation. I thought of ringing at the door and asking for shelter and protection till morning. But suddenly I was on my way again. But little by little, in a slow swoon, darkness fell about me. I saw a mass of bright flowers fade in an exquisite cascade of paling colours. I found myself admiring, all along the housefronts, the gradual blossoming of squares and rectangles, casement and sash, yellow, green, pink, according to the curtains and blinds, finding that pretty. Then at last, before I fell, first to my knees, as cattle do, then on my face, I was in a throng. I didn't lose consciousness, when I lose consciousness it will not be to recover it. They paid no heed to me, though careful not to walk on me, a cour-

tesy that must have touched me, it was what I had come out for. It was well with me, sated with dark and calm, lying at the feet of mortals, fathom deep in the grey of dawn, if it was dawn. But reality, too tired to look for the right word, was soon restored, the throng fell away, the light came back and I had no need to raise my head from the ground to know I was back in the same blinding void as before. I said, Stay where you are, down on the friendly stone, or at least indifferent, don't open your eyes, wait for morning. But up with me again and back on the way that was not mine, on uphill along the boulevard. A blessing he was not waiting for me, poor old Breem, or Breen. I said, The sea is east, it's west I must go, to the left of north. But in vain I raised without hope my eyes to the sky to look for the Bears.[1] For the light I stepped in put out the stars, assuming they were there, which I doubted, remembering the clouds.
—1950

Imagination Dead Imagine

No trace anywhere of life, you say, pah, no difficulty there, imagination not dead yet, yes, dead, good, imagination dead imagine. Islands, waters, azure, verdure, one glimpse and vanished, endlessly, omit. Till all white in the whiteness the rotunda. No way in, go in, measure. Diameter three feet, three feet from ground to summit of the vault. Two diameters at right angles AB CD divide the white ground into two semicircles ACB BDA. Lying on the ground two white bodies, each in its semicircle. White too the vault and the round wall eighteen inches high from which it springs. Go back out, a plain rotunda, all white in the whiteness, go back in, rap, solid throughout, a ring as in the imagination the ring of bone. The light that makes all so white no visible source, all shines with the same white shine, ground, wall, vault, bodies, no shadow. Strong heat, surfaces hot but not burning to the touch, bodies sweating. Go back out, move back, the little fabric vanishes, ascend, it vanishes, all white in the whiteness, descend, go back in. Emptiness, silence, heat, whiteness, wait, the light goes down, all grows dark together, ground, wall, vault, bodies, say twenty seconds, all the

---

[1] *the Bears* Constellations Ursa Major and Ursa Minor (Latin: Great Bear and Little Bear).

greys, the light goes out, all vanishes. At the same time the temperature goes down, to reach its minimum, say freezing-point, at the same instant that the black is reached, which may seem strange. Wait, more or less long, light and heat come back, all grows white and hot together, ground, wall, vault, bodies, say twenty seconds, all the greys, till the initial level is reached whence the fall began. More or less long, for there may intervene, experience shows, between end of fall and beginning of rise, pauses of varying length, from the fraction of the second to what would have seemed, in other times, other places, an eternity. Same remark for the other pause, between end of rise and beginning of fall. The extremes, as long as they last, are perfectly stable, which in the case of the temperature may seem strange, in the beginning. It is possible too, experience shows, for rise and fall to stop short at any point and mark a pause, more or less long, before resuming, or reversing, the rise now fall, the fall rise, these in their turn to be completed, or to stop short and mark a pause, more or less long, before resuming, or again reversing, and so on, till finally one or the other extreme is reached. Such variations of rise and fall, combining in countless rhythms, commonly attend the passage from white and heat to black and cold, and vice versa. The extremes alone are stable as is stressed by the vibration to be observed when a pause occurs at some intermediate stage, no matter what its level and duration. Then all vibrates, ground, wall, vault, bodies, ashen or leaden or between the two, as may be. But on the whole, experience shows, such uncertain passage is not common. And most often, when the light begins to fail, and along with it the heat, the movement continues unbroken until, in the space of some twenty seconds, pitch black is reached and at the same instant say freezing-point. Same remark for the reverse movement, towards heat and whiteness. Next most frequent is the fall or rise with pauses of varying length in these feverish greys, without at any moment reversal of the movement. But whatever its uncertainties the return sooner or later to a temporary calm seems assured, for the moment, in the black dark or the great whiteness, with attendant temperature, world still proof against enduring tumult. Rediscovered miraculously after what absence in perfect voids it is no longer quite the same, from this point of view, but there is no other. Externally all is as before and the sighting of the little fabric quite as much a matter of chance, its whiteness merging in the surrounding whiteness. But go in and now briefer lulls and never twice the same storm. Light and heat remain linked as though supplied by the same source of which still no trace. Still on the ground, bent in three, the head against the wall at B, the arse against the wall at A, the knees against the wall between B and C, the feet against the wall between C and A, that is to say inscribed in the semicircle ACB, merging in the white ground were it not for the long hair of strangely imperfect whiteness, the white body of a woman finally. Similarly inscribed in the other semicircle, against the wall his head at A, his arse at B, his knees between A and D, his feet between D and B, the partner. On their right sides therefore both and back to back head to arse. Hold a mirror to their lips, it mists. With their left hands they hold their left legs a little below the knee, with their right hands their left arms a little above the elbow. In this agitated light, its great white calm now so rare and brief, inspection is not easy. Sweat and mirror notwithstanding they might well pass for inanimate but for the left eyes which at incalculable intervals suddenly open wide and gaze in unblinking exposure long beyond what is humanly possible. Piercing pale blue the effect is striking, in the beginning. Never the two gazes together except once, when the beginning of one overlapped the end of the other, for about ten seconds. Neither fat nor thin, big nor small, the bodies seem whole and in fairly good condition, to judge by the surfaces exposed to view. The faces too, assuming the two sides of a piece, seem to want nothing essential. Between their absolute stillness and the convulsive light the contrast is striking, in the beginning, for one who still remembers having been struck by the contrary. It is clear however, from a thousand little signs too long to imagine, that they are not sleeping. Only murmur ah, no more, in this silence, and at the same instant for the eye of prey the infinitesimal shudder instantaneously suppressed. Leave them there, sweating and icy, there is better elsewhere. No, life ends and no, there is nothing elsewhere, and no question now of ever finding again that white speck lost in whiteness, to see if they still lie still in the stress of that storm, or of a worse storm, or in the black dark for good, or the great whiteness unchanging, and if not what they are doing.

—1966

Krapp's Last Tape

A late evening in the future.

Krapp's den.

Front centre a small table, the two drawers of which open towards audience.

Sitting at the table, facing front, i.e. across from the drawers, a wearish old man: Krapp.

Rusty black narrow trousers too short for him. Rusty black sleeveless waistcoat, four capacious pockets. Heavy silver watch and chain. Grimy white shirt open at neck, no collar. Surprising pair of dirty white boots, size ten at least, very narrow and pointed.

White face. Purple nose. Disordered grey hair. Unshaven.

Very near-sighted (but unspectacled). Hard of hearing.

Cracked voice. Distinctive intonation.

Laborious walk.

On the table a tape-recorder with microphone and a number of cardboard boxes containing reels of recorded tapes.

Table and immediately adjacent area in strong white light. Rest of stage in darkness.

Krapp remains a moment motionless, heaves a great sigh, looks at his watch, fumbles in his pockets, takes out an envelope, puts it back, fumbles, takes out a small bunch of keys, raises it to his eyes, chooses a key, gets up and moves to front of table. He stoops, unlocks first drawer, peers into it, feels about inside it, takes out a reel of tape, peers at it, puts it back, locks drawer, unlocks second drawer, peers into it, feels about inside it, takes out a large banana, peers at it, locks drawer, puts keys back in his pocket. He turns, advances to edge of stage, halts, strokes banana, peels it, drops skin at his feet, puts end of banana in his mouth and remains motionless, staring vacuously before him. Finally he bites off the end, turns aside and begins pacing to and fro at edge of stage, in the light, i.e. not more than four or five paces either way, meditatively eating banana. He treads on skin, slips, nearly falls, recovers himself, stoops and peers at skin and finally pushes it, still stooping, with his foot over the edge of stage into pit. He resumes his pacing, finishes banana, returns to table, sits down, remains a moment motionless, heaves a great sigh, takes keys from his pockets, raises them to his eyes, chooses key, gets up and moves to front of table, unlocks second drawer, takes out a second large banana, peers at it, locks drawer, puts back keys in his pocket, turns, advances to edge of stage, halts, strokes banana, peels it, tosses skin into pit, puts end of banana in his mouth and remains motionless, staring vacuously before him. Finally he has an idea, puts banana in his waistcoat pocket, the end emerging, and goes with all the speed he can muster backstage into darkness. Ten seconds. Loud pop of cork. Fifteen seconds. He comes back into light carrying an old ledger and sits down at table. He lays ledger on table, wipes his mouth, wipes his hands on the front of his waistcoat, brings them smartly together and rubs them.

KRAPP. (*Briskly.*) Ah! (*He bends over ledger, turns the pages, finds the entry he wants, reads.*) Box … thrree … spool … five. (*He raises his head and stares front. With relish.*) Spool! (*Pause.*) Spooool! (*Happy smile. Pause. He bends over table, starts peering and poking at the boxes.*) Box … thrree … thrree … four … two … (*With surprise.*) nine! good God! … seven … ah! the little rascal! (*He takes up box, peers at it.*) Box thrree. (*He lays it on table, opens it and peers at spools inside.*) Spool … (*He peers at ledger.*) … five … (*He peers at spools.*) … five … five … ah! the little scoundrel! (*He takes out a spool, peers at it.*) Spool five. (*He lays it on table, closes box three, puts it back with the others, takes up the spool.*) Box thrree, spool five. (*He bends over the machine, looks up. With relish.*) Spooool! (*Happy smile. He bends, loads spool on machine, rubs his hands.*) Ah! (*He peers at ledger, reads entry at foot of page.*) Mother at rest at last … Hm … The black ball … (*He raises his head, stares blankly front. Puzzled.*) Black ball? … (*He peers again at ledger, reads.*) The dark nurse … (*He raises his head, broods, peers again at ledger, reads.*) Slight improvement in bowel condition … Hm … Memorable … what? (*He peers closer.*) Equinox, memorable equinox. (*He raises his head, stares blankly front. Puzzled.*) Memorable equinox? … (*Pause.*

He shrugs his shoulders, peers again at ledger, reads.) Farewell to—(*He turns the page.*—) love.

(*He raises his head, broods, bends over machine, switches on and assumes listening posture, i.e. leaning forward, elbows on table, hand cupping ear towards machine, face front.*)

TAPE. (*Strong voice, rather pompous, clearly Krapp's at a much earlier time.*) Thirty-nine today, sound as a—(*Settling himself more comfortably he knocks one of the boxes off the table, curses, switches off, sweeps boxes and ledger violently to the ground, winds tape back to beginning, switches on, resumes posture.*) Thirty-nine today, sound as a bell, apart from my old weakness, and intellectually I have now every reason to suspect at the … (*Hesitates.*) … crest of the wave—or thereabouts. Celebrated the awful occasion, as in recent years, quietly at the Winehouse. Not a soul. Sat before the fire with closed eyes, separating the grain from the husks. Jotted down a few notes, on the back of an envelope. Good to be back in my den, in my old rags. Have just eaten I regret to say three bananas and only with difficulty refrained from a fourth. Fatal things for a man with my condition. (*Vehemently.*) Cut 'em out! (*Pause.*) The new light above my table is a great improvement. With all this darkness round me I feel less alone. (*Pause.*) In a way. (*Pause.*) I love to get up and move about in it, then back here to … (*Hesitates.*) … me. (*Pause.*) Krapp.

(*Pause.*)

The grain, now what I wonder do I mean by that, I mean … (*Hesitates.*) … I suppose I mean those things worth having when all the dust has—when all *my* dust has settled. I close my eyes and try and imagine them.

(*Pause. Krapp closes his eyes briefly.*)

Extraordinary silence this evening, I strain my ears and do not hear a sound. Old Miss McGlome always sings at this hour. But not tonight. Songs of her girlhood, she says. Hard to think of her as a girl. Wonderful woman though. Connaught,[1] I fancy. (*Pause.*) Shall I sing when I am her age, if I ever am? No. (*Pause.*) Did I sing as a boy? No. (*Pause.*) Did I ever sing? No.

(*Pause.*)

Just been listening to an old year, passages at random. I did not check in the book, but it must be at least ten or twelve years ago. At that time I think I was still living on and off with Bianca in Kedar Street. Well out of that, Jesus yes! Hopeless business. (*Pause.*) Not much about her, apart from a tribute to her eyes. Very warm. I suddenly saw them again. (*Pause.*) Incomparable! (*Pause.*) Ah well … (*Pause.*) These old P.M.s are gruesome, but I often find them—(*Krapp switches off, broods, switches on.*) —a help before embarking on a new … (*Hesitates.*) … retrospect. Hard to believe I was ever that young whelp. The voice! Jesus! And the aspirations! (*Brief laugh in which Krapp joins.*) And the resolutions! (*Brief laugh in which Krapp joins.*) To drink less, in particular. (*Brief laugh of Krapp alone.*) Statistics. Seventeen hundred hours, out of the preceding eight thousand odd, consumed on licensed premises alone. More than 20%, say 40% of his waking life. (*Pause.*) Plans for a less … (*Hesitates.*) … engrossing sexual life. Last illness of his father. Flagging pursuit of happiness. Unattainable laxation.[2] Sneers at what he calls his youth and thanks to God that it's over. (*Pause.*) False ring there. (*Pause.*) Shadows of the opus … magnum. Closing with a—(*Brief laugh.*)—yelp to Providence. (*Prolonged laugh in which Krapp joins.*) What remains of all that misery? A girl in a shabby green coat, on a railway-station platform? No?

(*Pause.*)

When I look—

(*Krapp switches off, broods, looks at his watch, gets up, goes backstage into darkness. Ten seconds. Pop of cork. Ten seconds. Second cork. Ten seconds. Third cork. Ten seconds. Brief burst of quavering song.*)

KRAPP. (*Sings.*)   Now the day is over,
                Night is drawing nigh-igh,

---

1 *Connaught* Western province of Ireland.

2 *laxation* Relaxed state.

Shadows—[1]

(*Fit of coughing. He comes back into light, sits down, wipes his mouth, switches on, resumes his listening posture.*)

90 TAPE.   —back on the year that is gone, with what I hope is perhaps a glint of the old eye to come, there is of course the house on the canal where mother lay a-dying, in the late autumn, after her long viduity (*Krapp gives a start.*), and the—(*Krapp switches off, winds back tape a*

95 *little, bends his ear closer to machine, switches on.*) —a-dying, after her long viduity, and the—

(*Krapp switches off, raises his head, stares blankly before him. His lips move in the syllables of "viduity." No sound. He gets up, goes backstage into darkness, comes back with an enormous dictionary, lays it on table, sits down and looks up the word.*)

KRAPP.   (*Reading from dictionary.*) State—or condition of being—or remaining—a widow—or widower. (*Looks up. Puzzled.*) Being—or remaining? … (*Pause. He peers*

100 *again at dictionary. Reading.*) "Deep weeds of viduity" … Also of an animal, especially a bird … the vidua or weaver-bird … Black plumage of male … (*He looks up. With relish.*) The vidua-bird!

(*Pause. He closes dictionary, switches on, resumes listening posture.*)

TAPE.   —bench by the weir from where I could see her

105 window. There I sat, in the biting wind, wishing she were gone. (*Pause.*) Hardly a soul, just a few regulars, nursemaids, infants, old men, dogs. I got to know them quite well—oh by appearance of course I mean! One dark young beauty I recollect particularly, all white and

110 starch, incomparable bosom, with a big black hooded perambulator, most funereal thing. Whenever I looked in her direction she had her eyes on me. And yet when I was bold enough to speak to her—not having been introduced—she threatened to call a policeman. As if I

115 had designs on her virtue! (*Laugh. Pause.*) The face she had! The eyes! Like … (*Hesitates.*) … chrysolite![2]

---

[1] *Now … Shadows* From an old hymn, words by Sabine Baring-Gould (1865).

[2] *chrysolite* Green gem.

(*Pause.*) Ah well … (*Pause.*) I was there when—(*Krapp switches off, broods, switches on again.*) —the blind went down, one of those dirty brown roller affairs, throwing

120 a ball for a little white dog, as chance would have it. I happened to look up and there it was. All over and done with, at last. I sat on for a few moments with the ball in my hand and the dog yelping and pawing at me. (*Pause.*) Moments. Her moments, my moments.

125 (*Pause.*) The dog's moments. (*Pause.*) In the end I held it out to him and he took it in his mouth, gently, gently. A small, old, black, hard, solid rubber ball. (*Pause.*) I shall feel it, in my hand, until my dying day. (*Pause.*) I might have kept it. (*Pause.*) But I gave it to the dog.

(*Pause.*)

130 Ah well …

(*Pause.*)

Spiritually a year of profound gloom and indigence until that memorable night in March, at the end of the jetty, in the howling wind, never to be forgotten, when suddenly I saw the whole thing. The vision, at last. This

135 I fancy is what I have chiefly to record this evening, against the day when my work will be done and perhaps no place left in my memory, warm or cold, for the miracle that … (*Hesitates.*) … for the fire that set it alight. What I suddenly saw then was this, that the

140 belief I had been going on all my life, namely—(*Krapp switches off impatiently, winds tape forward, switches on again.*)—great granite rocks the foam flying up in the light of the lighthouse and the wind-gauge spinning like a propeller, clear to me at last that the dark I have always

145 struggled to keep under is in reality my most—(*Krapp curses, switches off, winds tape forward, switches on again.*)—unshatterable association until my dissolution of storm and night with the light of the understanding and the fire—(*Krapp curses louder, switches off, winds*

150 *tape forward, switches on again.*) —my face in her breasts and my hand on her. We lay there without moving. But under us all moved, and moved us, gently, up and down, and from side to side.

(*Pause.*)

Past midnight. Never knew such silence. The earth might be uninhabited.

(*Pause.*)

Here I end—

(*Krapp switches off, winds tape back, switches on again.*)

—upper lake, with the punt,[1] bathed off the bank, then pushed out into the stream and drifted. She lay stretched out on the floorboards with her hands under her head and her eyes closed. Sun blazing down, bit of a breeze, water nice and lively. I noticed a scratch on her thigh and asked her how she came by it. Picking gooseberries, she said. I said again I thought it was hopeless and no good going on, and she agreed, without opening her eyes. (*Pause.*) I asked her to look at me and after a few moments—(*Pause.*)—after a few moments she did, but the eyes just slits, because of the glare. I bent over her to get them in the shadow and they opened. (*Pause. Low.*) Let me in. (*Pause.*) We drifted in among the flags[2] and stuck. The way they went down, sighing, before the stem! (*Pause.*) I lay down across her with my face in her breasts and my hand on her. We lay there without moving. But under us all moved, and moved us, gently, up and down, and from side to side.

(*Pause.*)

Past midnight. Never knew—

(*Krapp switches off, broods. Finally he fumbles in his pockets, encounters the banana, takes it out, peers at it, puts it back, fumbles, brings out the envelope, fumbles, puts back envelope, looks at his watch, gets up and goes backstage into darkness. Ten seconds. Sound of bottle against glass, then brief siphon. Ten seconds. Bottle against glass alone. Ten seconds. He comes back a little unsteadily into light, goes to front of table, takes out keys, raises them to his eyes, chooses key, unlocks first drawer, peers into it, feels about inside, takes out reel, peers at it, locks drawer, puts keys back in his pocket, goes and sits down, takes reel off machine, lays it on*)

dictionary, loads virgin reel on machine, takes envelope from his pocket, consults back of it, lays it on table, switches on, clears his throat and begins to record.)

KRAPP. Just been listening to that stupid bastard I took myself for thirty years ago, hard to believe I was ever as bad as that. Thank God that's all done with anyway. (*Pause.*) The eyes she had! (*Broods, realizes he is recording silence, switches off, broods. Finally.*) Everything there, everything, all the—(*Realizes this is not being recorded, switches on.*) Everything there, everything on this old muckball, all the light and dark and famine and feasting of … (*Hesitates.*) … the ages! (*In a shout.*) Yes! (*Pause.*) Let that go! Jesus! Take his mind off his homework! Jesus! (*Pause. Weary.*) Ah well, maybe he was right. (*Pause.*) Maybe he was right. (*Broods. Realizes. Switches off. Consults envelope.*) Pah! (*Crumples it and throws it away. Broods. Switches on.*) Nothing to say, not a squeak. What's a year now? The sour cud and the iron stool. (*Pause.*) Revelled in the word spool. (*With relish.*) Spooool! Happiest moment of the past half million. (*Pause.*) Seventeen copies sold, of which eleven at trade price to free circulating libraries beyond the seas. Getting known. (*Pause.*) One pound six and something, eight I have little doubt. (*Pause.*) Crawled out once or twice, before the summer was cold. Sat shivering in the park, drowned in dreams and burning to be gone. Not a soul. (*Pause.*) Last fancies. (*Vehemently.*) Keep 'em under! (*Pause.*) Scalded the eyes out of me reading *Effie*[3] again, a page a day, with tears again. Effie … (*Pause.*) Could have been happy with her, up there on the Baltic, and the pines, and the dunes. (*Pause.*) Could I? (*Pause.*) And she? (*Pause.*) Pah! (*Pause.*) Fanny came in a couple of times. Bony old ghost of a whore. Couldn't do much, but I suppose better than a kick in the crutch. The last time wasn't so bad. How do you manage it, she said, at your age? I told her I'd been saving up for her all my life. (*Pause.*) Went to Vespers[4] once, like when I was in short trousers. (*Pause. Sings.*)

> Now the day is over,
> Night is drawing nigh-igh,
> Shadows—(*Coughing, then almost* inaudible.)—of

---

[1] *punt* Shallow, flat-bottomed boat.

[2] *flags* Irises.

[3] *Effie* *Effi Briest* (1895), a sentimental novel by Theodor Fontane about a failed love affair.

[4] *Vespers* Evening prayer service.

the evening
Steal across the sky.

215 (*Gasping.*) Went to sleep and fell off the pew. (*Pause.*)
Sometimes wondered in the night if a last effort
mightn't—(*Pause.*) Ah finish your booze now and get to
your bed. Go on with this drivel in the morning. Or
leave it at that. (*Pause.*) Leave it at that. (*Pause.*) Lie
220 propped up in the dark—and wander. Be again in the
dingle[1] on a Christmas Eve, gathering holly, the red-
berried. (*Pause.*) Be again on Croghan[2] on a Sunday
morning, in the haze, with the bitch, stop and listen to
the bells. (*Pause.*) And so on. (*Pause.*) Be again, be again.
225 (*Pause.*) All that old misery. (*Pause.*) Once wasn't
enough for you. (*Pause.*) Lie down across her.

(*Long pause. He suddenly bends over machine, switches off,
wrenches off tape, throws it away, puts on the other, winds
it forward to the passage he wants, switches on, listens
staring front.*)

TAPE.   —gooseberries, she said. I said again I thought it
was hopeless and no good going on, and she agreed,
without opening her eyes. (*Pause.*) I asked her to look at
230 me and after a few moments—(*Pause.*) —after a few
moments she did, but the eyes just slits, because of the
glare. I bent over her to get them in the shadow and
they opened. (*Pause. Low.*) Let me in. (*Pause.*) We
drifted in among the flags and stuck. The way they went
235 down, sighing, before the stem! (*Pause.*) I lay down
across her with my face in her breasts and my hand on
her. We lay there without moving. But under us all
moved, and moved us, gently, up and down, and from
side to side.

(*Pause. Krapp's lips move. No sound.*)

240 Past midnight. Never knew such silence. The earth
might be uninhabited.

(*Pause.*)

Here I end this reel. Box—(*Pause.*)—three, spool—
(*Pause.*)—five. (*Pause.*) Perhaps my best years are gone.
When there was a chance of happiness. But I wouldn't
245 want them back. Not with the fire in me now. No, I
wouldn't want them back.

(*Krapp motionless staring before him. The tape runs on in
silence.*)

CURTAIN
—1958

---

[1] *dingle* Valley.

[2] *Croghan* Croghan Hill in County Wicklow, Ireland.

W.H. Auden
1907 – 1973

W.H. Auden's poetry documents the changing political, social, and psychological landscape of his time, using language firmly rooted in the world around him. In describing the physical and spiritual ills of society and seeking order and clarity in human existence, he developed a poetry that couples contemporary speech with more traditional, structured verse forms. "Auden was an epoch-making poet on public themes," Seamus Heaney said, "the register of a new sensibility."

hipster

Born in York, England, in 1907, Wystan Hugh Auden was the youngest of three sons. His chief childhood interests were scientific: he was fascinated by engineering, mineralogy, and geology, and won a scholarship to study natural science at Oxford. A developing passion for poetry, however, led him to transfer to English, although his interest in science—and his experiences growing up in industrial England (he spent his childhood in Birmingham)—remain evident in the themes that permeate his poetry. He became a central member of a group of writers known as the "Oxford Group," which included Cecil Day Lewis, Stephen Spender, and Louis MacNeice. Auden published numerous poems in undergraduate magazines, and when he had assembled a first volume, he sent it to T.S. Eliot at the publishing house of Faber and Gwyer (later Faber and Faber). The volume was rejected, and Auden had it printed privately on Spender's handpress. Eliot had expressed interest in Auden's work, however, and in 1930 he published Auden's *Poems*. Heavily colored by a sense of political commitment, *Poems* addresses concrete social problems, such as the poverty in depressed areas of industrial England. Many poems are experiments with tone and form—for example, Auden melded Anglo-Saxon sound patterns with modern subject matter.

After graduating from Oxford, Auden spent a year in Germany with a university friend, Christopher Isherwood, and was influenced by German music, literature, and theater—particularly the leftist political theater of Bertolt Brecht and Kurt Weill. When he returned to England, Auden worked variously as a schoolmaster, a university lecturer, a writer of experimental drama, and a verse commentator on documentary films. In this last position he worked with composer Benjamin Britten, who became a close friend and artistic collaborator. Collaborative work appealed to Auden, who went on to co-write three plays with Isherwood: *The Dog Beneath the Skin* (1935), *The Ascent of F6* (1936), and *On the Frontier* (1938). A trip to Iceland with MacNeice, funded by Auden's publishers, resulted in the collaborative travel book *Letters from Iceland* (1937), an unconventional collection of essays, poems, letters, and notes on everything from touring the country to contemporary politics.

Although Auden was openly homosexual, he agreed in 1935 to marry German novelist Thomas Mann's daughter Erika, whose passport was about to be revoked by the Nazis. When the Spanish Civil War began a year later, he volunteered for the Spanish Republic as a medical worker, but the authorities instead gave him work in the censor's office, writing government propaganda. He was disturbed by the extent to which Stalin's government controlled the Republic and also by the fact that the government had forced the churches to close. Although Auden had abandoned his religious beliefs after childhood, the experience caused him to reconsider the importance of spirituality.

Auden later traveled with Isherwood to China and Japan to observe the Sino-Japanese war. There they wrote *Journey to a War* (1939), largely about the complexity of political writing. In his poems of this period Auden developed his characteristically sparse, terse, and often fragmented style, relying on concrete images and colloquial language to create a sense of immediacy and intensity. His explicitly political poems of this period, such as "Spain, 1937," had helped to establish his reputation as a poet, but in 1939, the year he moved to New York, he decided he would never again write anything that resembled propaganda, regardless of cause. In fact, in later years he often rewrote and even suppressed his earlier, more left-wing poems.

In New York, where Auden settled for most of his later life, he devoted himself to his poetry with renewed energy. He became involved in a serious relationship with Chester Kallman, a nineteen-year-old student who would become his lifelong companion and an important literary collaborator. The 1940 volume *Another Time* signals his desire to move on to explore new subjects and modes of expression. *Another Time* meticulously measures the social pulse of the thirties—which Auden characterized as "the age of anxiety"—and includes some of his best-known works, including "Musée des Beaux Arts," "September 1, 1939" (his response to the declaration of war), and elegies to poets Matthew Arnold, A.E. Housman, and W.B. Yeats, all of whom had been significant influences on his poetic development.

From then on, Auden's poetry began to take on more intimate and subjective overtones, often with religious themes. In 1941 he began attending the Anglican church regularly and experienced a renewal of religious faith. While his earlier poetry examined concrete social ills, his later poetry developed a more complex worldview, often focusing on spiritual aspects of society and casting social problems in terms of personal responsibility. His next major collection, *For the Time Being* (1944), includes the Christmas Oratorio "For the Time Being" and "The Sea and the Mirror," a poetic commentary on Shakespeare's *The Tempest* that explored Auden's ideas of poetry in the light of Christianity. With *The Collected Poetry* (1945), Auden began revising and retitling his earlier work, a task he would continue, almost compulsively, throughout his life.

In 1948, Auden was awarded the Pulitzer Prize for *The Age of Anxiety* (1947), a verse dialogue between four people in a New York bar. *The Shield of Achilles* (1955), which won the National Book Award, displays the influence of Anglo-Catholic theology and rituals, which Auden increasingly explored in verse. During these years he also wrote a considerable body of criticism and taught at various universities. In 1956 he became a Professor of Poetry at Oxford, where he gave three lectures per year for five years. These lectures, together with numerous reviews and essays, were collected in *The Dyer's Hand* (1962).

In his later years, with volumes such as *About the House* (1965) and *City Without Walls* (1969), Auden cemented his reputation as one of the leading poets of his day. After awarding him the National Medal for Literature in 1967, the National Book Committee declared that Auden's poetry "has illuminated our lives and times with grace, wit, and vitality. His work, branded by the moral and ideological fires of our age, breathes with eloquence, perception, and intellectual power." In 1972, seeking to return to a small community in which he could live peacefully as a writer, Auden accepted an honorary studentship at Christ Church, Oxford, his alma mater. He died there the following year. A final volume of poetry, *Thank You, Fog*, was published posthumously in 1974. Auden's careful attention to poetic form and meter, his sensitivity to language and to the music of words, and his concern with eternal questions of spirituality, love, and humanity's place in the world have all served to secure his current standing as one of the twentieth century's most significant poetic voices.

⌘⌘⌘

[O what is that sound]

O what is that sound which so thrills the ear
    Down in the valley drumming, drumming?
Only the scarlet soldiers, dear,
    The soldiers coming.

5 O what is that light I see flashing so clear
    Over the distance brightly, brightly?
Only the sun on their weapons, dear,
    As they step lightly.

O what are they doing with all that gear,
10   What are they doing this morning, this morning?
Only their usual manoeuvres, dear,
    Or perhaps a warning.

O why have they left the road down there,
    Why are they suddenly wheeling, wheeling?
15 Perhaps a change in their orders, dear.
    Why are you kneeling?

O haven't they stopped for the doctor's care,
    Haven't they reined their horses, their horses?
Why, they are none of them wounded, dear,
20   None of these forces.

O is it the parson they want, with white hair,
    Is it the parson, is it, is it?
No, they are passing his gateway, dear,
    Without a visit.

25 O it must be the farmer who lives so near.
    It must be the farmer so cunning, so cunning?
They have passed the farmyard already, dear,
    And now they are running.

O where are you going? Stay with me here!
30   Were the vows you swore deceiving, deceiving?
No, I promised to love you, dear,
    But I must be leaving.

O it's broken the lock and splintered the door,
    O it's the gate where they're turning, turning;

35 Their boots are heavy on the floor
    And their eyes are burning.
—1934, 1945

[At last the secret is out]

At last the secret is out, as it always must come in
    the end,
The delicious story is ripe to tell to the intimate friend;
Over the tea-cups and into the square the tongue has
    its desire;
Still waters run deep, my dear, there's never smoke
    without fire.

5 Behind the corpse in the reservoir, behind the ghost
    on the links,[1]
Behind the lady who dances and the man who madly
    drinks,
Under the look of fatigue the attack of migraine and
    the sigh
There is always another story, there is more than
    meets the eye.

For the clear voice suddenly singing, high up in the
    convent wall,
10 The scent of the elder bushes, the sporting prints in
    the hall,
The croquet matches in summer, the handshake, the
    cough, the kiss,
There is always a wicked secret, a private reason for this.
—1936

[Funeral Blues][2]

Stop all the clocks, cut off the telephone,
  Prevent the dog from barking with a juicy bone,
Silence the pianos and with muffled drum
Bring out the coffin, let the mourners come.

---

[1] *links* Undulating, sandy ground near a shore.

[2] [*Funeral Blues*] This poem first appeared, along with "At last the secret is out," in *The Ascent of F6*, a play co-written by Auden and Christopher Isherwood. It then appeared, in a revised version and with this present title, in Auden's 1940 collection *Another Time*.

5   Let aeroplanes circle moaning overhead
Scribbling on the sky the message He Is Dead,
Put crêpe bows[1] round the white necks of the public
   doves,
Let the traffic policemen wear black cotton gloves.

He was my North, my South, my East and West,
10   My working week and my Sunday rest,
My noon, my midnight, my talk, my song;
I thought that love would last for ever: I was wrong.

The stars are not wanted now: put out every one;
Pack up the moon and dismantle the sun;
15   Pour away the ocean and sweep up the wood;
For nothing now can ever come to any good.
   —1936, 1940

Spain 1937[2]

Yesterday all the past. The language of size
   Spreading to China along the trade-routes; the
     diffusion

Of the counting-frame and the cromlech;[3]
Yesterday the shadow-reckoning in the sunny climates.

5   Yesterday the assessment of insurance by cards,
The divination of water; yesterday the invention
   Of cart-wheels and clocks, the taming of
Horses; yesterday the bustling world of the navigators.

Yesterday the abolition of fairies and giants;
10   The fortress like a motionless eagle eyeing the valley,
   The chapel built in the forest;
Yesterday the carving of angels and of frightening
   gargoyles.

The trial of heretics among the columns of stone;
Yesterday the theological feuds in the taverns
15   And the miraculous cure at the fountain;
Yesterday the Sabbath of Witches.[4] But today the
   struggle.

Yesterday the installation of dynamos[5] and turbines;
The construction of railways in the colonial desert;
   Yesterday the classic lecture
20   On the origin of Mankind. But today the struggle.

Yesterday the belief in the absolute value of Greek;
The fall of the curtain upon the death of a hero;
   Yesterday the prayer to the sunset,
And the adoration of madmen. But today the struggle.

25   As the poet whispers, startled among the pines
Or, where the loose waterfall sings, compact, or upright
   On the crag by the leaning tower:
"O my vision. O send me the luck of the sailor."

And the investigator peers through his instruments
30   At the inhuman provinces, the virile bacillus
   Or enormous Jupiter finished:
"But the lives of my friends. I inquire, I inquire."

---

[1] *crêpe bows*   Black crepe, a woven fabric with a wrinkled surface, is the traditional fabric of mourning clothes.

[2] *Spain, 1937*   In the 1930s, Spain was a nation in which wealthy landowners and a conservative Roman Catholic Church hierarchy controlled much of society, and much inequality existed. The election of a left-of-center government in 1936 signaled a break with the past; the new government promised to enact a substantial program of land reform and a variety of other progressive changes. Almost immediately following the government's election, conservative forces began to plan its overthrow. An attempted coup was launched by army factions on 18 July 1936, but faced stiff resistance. This was the beginning of the Spanish Civil War, which ended with the victory of Francisco Franco's Nationalists—a Fascist party—and the installation of Franco as commander-in-chief and Head of State. Progressives, liberal democrats, communists, and anarchists from around the world were drawn to the Republican cause, and many came to Spain to fight with the forces loyal to the democratically elected government. On the other side the fascist dictatorships of Hitler in Germany, Mussolini in Italy, and Salazar in Portugal all provided support for Franco's army. Sympathetic to the Republicans, Auden went to Spain in January 1937 with a medical unit. He wrote this poem in March 1937, after he had returned to Britain, and had it printed as a separate pamphlet, the proceeds of which went to aid Spanish medical work.

[3] *cromlech*   Ancient Celtic stone structure.

[4] *Sabbath of Witches*   Nocturnal gathering of witches believed by medieval Christians to be a demonic orgy or a heretical parody of the Mass.

[5] *dynamos*   Machines that rotate copper wire coils in a magnetic field to convert mechanical into electrical energy.

And the poor in their fireless lodgings dropping the
    sheets
Of the evening paper: "Our day is our loss. O show us
35   History the operator, the
Organiser, Time the refreshing river."

And the nations combine each cry, invoking the life
That shapes the individual belly and orders
    The private nocturnal terror:
40 "Did you not found once the city state of the sponge,

"Raise the vast military empires of the shark
And the tiger, establish the robin's plucky
    canton?°   *territory*
Intervene. O descend as a dove or
A furious papa or a mild engineer: but descend."

45 And the life, if it answers at all, replies from the heart
And the eyes and the lungs, from the shops and
    squares of the city:
        "O no, I am not the Mover,
Not today, not to you. To you I'm the

"Yes-man, the bar-companion, the easily-duped:
50 I am whatever you do; I am your vow to be
        Good, your humorous story;
I am your business voice; I am your marriage.

"What's your proposal? To build the Just City?[1] I will.
I agree. Or is it the suicide pact, the romantic
55   Death? Very well, I accept, for
I am your choice, your decision: yes, I am Spain."

Many have heard it on remote peninsulas,
On sleepy plains, in the aberrant fishermen's islands,
    In the corrupt heart of the city;
60 Have heard and migrated like gulls or the seeds of a
    flower.

They clung like burrs to the long expresses that lurch
Through the unjust lands, through the night, through
    the alpine tunnel;

    They floated over the oceans;
They walked the passes: they came to present their lives.

65 On that arid square, that fragment nipped off from hot
Africa, soldered so crudely to inventive Europe,
    On that tableland scored by rivers,
Our fever's menacing shapes are precise and alive.

To-morrow, perhaps, the future: the research on fatigue
70 And the movements of packers; the gradual exploring
    of all the
        Octaves of radiation;
To-morrow the enlarging of consciousness by diet and
    breathing.

To-morrow the rediscovery of romantic love;
The photographing of ravens; all the fun under
        Liberty's masterful shadow;
75 To-morrow the hour of the pageant-master and the
    musician.

To-morrow, for the young, the poets exploding like
    bombs,
The walks by the lake, the winter of perfect communion;
    To-morrow the bicycle races
80 Through the suburbs on summer evenings: but today
    the struggle.

To-day the inevitable increase in the chances of death;
The conscious acceptance of guilt in the fact of murder;
    To-day the expending of powers
On the flat ephemeral pamphlet and the boring meeting.

85 To-day the makeshift consolations; the shared cigarette;
The cards in the candle-lit barn and the scraping concert,
    The masculine jokes; today the
Fumbled and unsatisfactory embrace before hurting.

The stars are dead; the animals will not look:
90 We are left alone with our day, and the time is short and
    History to the defeated
May say Alas but cannot help or pardon.
    —1937

---

[1] *the Just City* In Plato's *Republic*, Socrates discusses what is required to make a just city, and recommends rule by a "philosopher-king."

[Lullaby]

Lay your sleeping head, my love,
　Human on my faithless arm;
Time and fevers burn away
Individual beauty from
5　Thoughtful children, and the grave
Proves the child ephemeral:
But in my arms till break of day
Let the living creature lie,
Mortal, guilty, but to me
10　The entirely beautiful.

Soul and body have no bounds:
To lovers as they lie upon
Her tolerant enchanted slope
In their ordinary swoon,
15　Grave the vision Venus[1] sends
Of supernatural sympathy,
Universal love and hope;
While an abstract insight wakes
Among the glaciers and the rocks
20　The hermit's carnal ecstasy.

Certainty, fidelity
On the stroke of midnight pass
Like vibrations of a bell,
And fashionable madmen raise
25　Their pedantic boring cry:
Every farthing of the cost,
All the dreaded cards foretell,
Shall be paid, but from this night
Not a whisper, not a thought,
30　Not a kiss nor look be lost.

Beauty, midnight, vision dies:
Let the winds of dawn that blow
Softly round your dreaming head
Such a day of sweetness show
35　Eye and knocking heart may bless,
Find the mortal world enough;
Noons of dryness see you fed
By the involuntary powers,
Nights of insult let you pass

40　Watched by every human love.
—1937

[As I walked out one evening]

As I walked out one evening,
　Walking down Bristol Street,
The crowds upon the pavement
　Were fields of harvest wheat.

5　And down by the brimming river
　I heard a lover sing
Under an arch of the railway:
　"Love has no ending.

"I'll love you, dear, I'll love you
10　Till China and Africa meet,
And the river jumps over the mountain
　And the salmon sing in the street,

"I'll love you till the ocean
　Is folded and hung up to dry
15　And the seven stars[2] go squawking
　Like geese about the sky.

"The years shall run like rabbits,
　For in my arms I hold
The Flower of the Ages,
20　And the first love of the world."

But all the clocks in the city
　Began to whirr and chime:
"O let not Time deceive you,
　You cannot conquer Time.

25　"In the burrows of the Nightmare
　Where Justice naked is,
Time watches from the shadow
　And coughs when you would kiss.

"In headaches and in worry
30　Vaguely life leaks away,

---

[1] *Venus* Roman goddess of beauty and love, mother of Cupid.

[2] *seven stars* Pleiades, seven daughters of Atlas who, according to Greek mythology, were transformed into stars by Zeus.

And Time will have his fancy
　　To-morrow or to-day.

"Into many a green valley
　　Drifts the appalling snow;
35　Time breaks the threaded dances
　　And the diver's brilliant bow.

"O plunge your hands in water,
　　Plunge them in up to the wrist;
Stare, stare in the basin
40　　And wonder what you've missed.

"The glacier knocks in the cupboard,
　　The desert sighs in the bed,
And the crack in the tea-cup opens
　　A lane to the land of the dead.

45　"Where the beggars raffle the banknotes
　　And the Giant is enchanting to Jack,[1]
And the Lily-white Boy is a Roarer,[2]
　　And Jill goes down on her back.

"O look, look in the mirror,
50　　O look in your distress:
Life remains a blessing
　　Although you cannot bless.

"O stand, stand at the window
　　As the tears scald and start;
55　You shall love your crooked neighbour
　　With your crooked heart."

It was late, late in the evening,
　　The lovers they were gone;
The clocks had ceased their chiming,
60　　And the deep river ran on.
　　—1938

---

[1]　*Giant ... Jack* Auden alters the story of Jack and the Beanstalk.

[2]　*Lily-white ... Roarer* Allusion to the English folk song, "Green Grow the Rushes, O": "Two, two lily-white boys / Clothèd all in green, O." A "roarer" is a riotous or disorderly person.

Musée des Beaux Arts[3]

About suffering they were never wrong,
　The Old Masters: how well they understood
Its human position; how it takes place
While someone else is eating or opening a window or
　　just walking dully along;
5　How, when the aged are reverently, passionately waiting
For the miraculous birth, there always must be
Children who did not specially want it to happen,
　　skating
On a pond at the edge of the wood:
They never forgot
10　That even the dreadful martyrdom must run its course
Anyhow in a corner, some untidy spot
Where the dogs go on with their doggy life and the
　　torturer's horse
Scratches its innocent behind on a tree.

In Brueghel's *Icarus*, for instance: how everything
　　turns away
15　Quite leisurely from the disaster;[4] the ploughman may
Have heard the splash, the forsaken cry,
But for him it was not an important failure; the sun
　　shone
As it had to on the white legs disappearing into the
　　green
Water; and the expensive delicate ship that must have
　　seen
20　Something amazing, a boy falling out of the sky,
Had somewhere to get to and sailed calmly on.
　　—1939, 1940

---

[3]　*Musée des Beaux Arts* The Royal Museum of Fine Arts in Brussels owns several paintings by Flemish painter Pieter Brueghel (1525–69), including *Landscape with the Fall of Icarus*. According to Greek myth, Icarus and his father, Daedalus, escaped from the island of Crete, where they were imprisoned, by constructing wings with feathers and wax. Icarus flew too close to the sun, however, and the wax of his wings melted, causing him to plummet into the sea.

[4]　*how everything ... disaster* In Brueghel's painting, a shepherd, a farmer, and a fisher carry on with their respective jobs, ignoring Icarus's legs disappearing into the water in the picture's lower right corner.

In Memory of W.B. Yeats[1]
(d. Jan. 1939)

1

He disappeared in the dead of winter:
The brooks were frozen, the airports almost
        deserted,
And snow disfigured the public statues;
The mercury sank in the mouth of the dying day.
5   O all the instruments agree[2]
The day of his death was a dark cold day.

Far from his illness
The wolves ran on through the evergreen forests,
The peasant river was untempted by the fashionable
        quays;
10   By mourning tongues
The death of the poet was kept from his poems.

But for him it was his last afternoon as himself,
An afternoon of nurses and rumours;
The provinces of his body revolted,
15   The squares of his mind were empty,
Silence invaded the suburbs,
The current of his feeling failed: he became his
        admirers.

Now he is scattered among a hundred cities
And wholly given over to unfamiliar affections;
20   To find his happiness in another kind of wood
And be punished under a foreign code of conscience.
The words of a dead man
Are modified in the guts of the living.

But in the importance and noise of to-morrow
25   When the brokers are roaring like beasts on the floor
        of the Bourse,[3]
And the poor have the sufferings to which they are
        fairly accustomed,
And each in the cell of himself is almost convinced of
        his freedom;

A few thousand will think of this day
As one thinks of a day when one did something
        slightly unusual.

30   O all the instruments agree
The day of his death was a dark cold day.

2

You were silly like us: your gift survived it all;
The parish of rich women, physical decay,
Yourself. Mad Ireland hurt you into poetry.
35   Now Ireland has her madness and her weather still,
For poetry makes nothing happen: it survives
In the valley of its saying where executives
Would never want to tamper, flows on south
From ranches of isolation and the busy griefs,
40   Raw towns that we believe and die in; it survives,
A way of happening, a mouth.

3

Earth, receive an honoured guest;
William Yeats is laid to rest:
Let the Irish vessel lie
45   Emptied of its poetry.

Time that is intolerant
Of the brave and innocent,
And indifferent in a week
To a beautiful physique,

50   Worships language and forgives
Everyone by whom it lives;
Pardons cowardice, conceit,
Lays its honours at their feet.

Time that with this strange excuse
55   Pardoned Kipling and his views,[4]
And will pardon Paul Claudel,[5]
Pardons him for writing well.

In the nightmare of the dark
All the dogs of Europe bark,

---

[1] *W.B. Yeats* Irish poet William Butler Yeats (1865–1939).

[2] *O all … agree* Auden later changed this line to read "What instruments we have agree."

[3] *Bourse* Paris Stock Exchange.

[4] *Kipling … views* Rudyard Kipling (1865–1936) was an Indian-born English writer whose work often celebrated imperialism.

[5] *Paul Claudel* French-Catholic poet, playwright, and diplomat (1868–1955) who was widely criticized for supporting Franco's fascist insurgency in the Spanish Civil War.

60 And the living nations wait,
   Each sequestered in its hate;

   Intellectual disgrace
   Stares from every human face,
   And the seas of pity lie
65 Locked and frozen in each eye.

   Follow, poet, follow right
   To the bottom of the night,
   With your unconstraining voice
   Still persuade us to rejoice;

70 With the farming of a verse
   Make a vineyard of the curse,
   Sing of human unsuccess
   In a rapture of distress;

   In the deserts of the heart
75 Let the healing fountain start,
   In the prison of his days
   Teach the free man how to praise.

   —1939

September 1, 1939[1]

I sit in one of the dives
  On Fifty-Second Street
Uncertain and afraid
As the clever hopes expire
5 Of a low dishonest decade:
Waves of anger and fear
Circulate over the bright
And darkened lands of the earth,
Obsessing our private lives;
10 The unmentionable odour of death
Offends the September night.

Accurate scholarship can
Unearth the whole offence
From Luther[2] until now

15 That has driven a culture mad,
Find what occurred at Linz,[3]
What huge imago[4] made
A psychopathic god:
I and the public know
20 What all schoolchildren learn,
Those to whom evil is done
Do evil in return.

Exiled Thucydides[5] knew
All that a speech can say
25 About Democracy,
And what dictators do,
The elderly rubbish they talk
To an apathetic grave;
Analysed all in his book,
30 The enlightenment driven away,
The habit-forming pain,
Mismanagement and grief:
We must suffer them all again.

Into this neutral air
35 Where blind skyscrapers use
Their full height to proclaim
The strength of Collective Man,
Each language pours its vain
Competitive excuse:
40 But who can live for long
In an euphoric dream;
Out of the mirror they stare,
Imperialism's face
And the international wrong.

---

1 *September 1, 1939* Date of Hitler's invasion of Poland; Britain and France declared war on Germany two days later. Auden had moved to New York in January 1939.

2 *Luther* Martin Luther (1483–1546), German monk whose attempts to reform the Catholic Church were instrumental in bringing about the Protestant Reformation. Luther's writings grew

markedly more anti-Semitic as he aged; in *Mein Kampf,* Hitler ranks Martin Luther as one of three great German cultural heroes, along with Frederick the Great and Richard Wagner.

3 *Linz* Town in Austria in which Hitler grew up; he returned in 1938 to announce Germany's annexation of Austria.

4 *imago* According to psychiatrist and founder of analytical psychology C.G. Jung (1875–1961), an idealized image of a person formed in childhood.

5 *Thucydides* Greek historian and general (c. 460–c. 400 BCE) and author of *The History of the Peloponnesian War* who was exiled at the war's end for failing to prevent the surrender of Amphipolis to the Spartans. One of the speeches in Thucydides's *History,* Pericles's funeral oration for the dead Athenian soldiers, outlines the dangers and benefits of democracy. Elected 16 times to the position of general, Pericles instituted many democratic reforms while retaining a significant degree of personal power.

45 Faces along the bar
Cling to their average day:
The lights must never go out,
The music must always play,
All the conventions conspire
50 To make this fort assume
The furniture of home;
Lest we should see where we are,
Lost in a haunted wood,
Children afraid of the night
55 Who have never been happy or good.

The windiest militant trash
Important Persons shout
Is not so crude as our wish:
What mad Nijinsky wrote
60 About Diaghilev[1]
Is true of the normal heart;
For the error bred in the bone
Of each woman and each man
Craves what it cannot have,
65 Not universal love
But to be loved alone.

From the conservative dark
Into the ethical life
The dense commuters come,
70 Repeating their morning vow,
"I *will* be true to the wife,
I'll concentrate more on my work,"
And helpless governors wake
To resume their compulsory game:
75 Who can release them now,
Who can reach the deaf,
Who can speak for the dumb?

All I have is a voice
To undo the folded lie,
80 The romantic lie in the brain
Of the sensual man-in-the-street

And the lie of Authority
Whose buildings grope the sky:
There is no such thing as the State
85 And no one exists alone;
Hunger allows no choice
To the citizen of the police;
We must love one another or die.[2]

Defenceless under the night
90 Our world in stupor lies;
Yet, dotted everywhere,
Ironic points of light
Flash out wherever the Just
Exchange their messages:
95 May I, composed like them
Of Eros[3] and of dust,
Beleaguered by the same
Negation and despair,
Show an affirming flame.
—1939

from *The Sea and the Mirror*

[Song of the Master and Boatswain][4]

At Dirty Dick's and Sloppy Joe's
We drank our liquor straight,
Some went upstairs with Margery,
And some, alas, with Kate;

1 *Nijinsky … Diaghilev* Vaslav Nijinsky (1890–1950), Russian ballet dancer and choreographer who was diagnosed with schizophrenia in 1919. In 1936, Nijinsky's wife published a heavily edited version of her husband's 1919 diary, in which he said of his former lover, founder of the Ballets Russes Sergei Pavlovich Diaghilev, "Some politicians are hypocrites like Diaghilev, who does not want universal love, but to be loved alone."

2 *All I have … die* In a revised edition of this poem, printed in *The Collected Poetry of W.H. Auden* (1945), this stanza is removed.

3 *Eros* In contrast to The New Testament *agape*, or Christian love, *eros* represents earthly, or sexual love. In Greek myth, the winged Eros, son of Aphrodite, is the god of love.

4 *Song … Boatswain* Auden's *The Sea and the Mirror* is a poetic response to Shakespeare's *The Tempest*. "The Master and Boatswain" refers to the prostitutes mentioned by a drunken Stephano in 2.2.46–54:
The master, the swabber, the boatswain, and I,
The gunner and his mate,
Loved Mall, Meg, and Marian, and Margery,
But none of us cared for Kate;
For she had a tongue with a tang,
Would cry to a sailor, "Go hang!"
She loved not the savour of tar nor of pitch,
Yet a tailor might scratch her where e'er she did itch.
Then to sea, boys, and let her go hang!

And two by two like cat and mouse
5   The homeless played at keeping house.

There Wealthy Meg, the Sailor's Friend,
  And Marion, cow-eyed,
Opened their arms to me but I
10   Refused to step inside;
I was not looking for a cage
In which to mope in my old age.

The nightingales[1] are sobbing in
  The orchards of our mothers,
15 And hearts that we broke long ago
  Have long been breaking others;
Tears are round, the sea is deep:
Roll them overboard and sleep.
—1944

The Shield of Achilles[2]

She looked over his shoulder
  For vines and olive trees,
Marble well-governed cities
  And ships upon untamed seas,
5 But there on the shining metal
  His hands had put instead
An artificial wilderness
  And a sky like lead.

A plain without a feature, bare and brown,
10   No blade of grass, no sign of neighborhood,
Nothing to eat and nowhere to sit down,

Yet, congregated on its blankness, stood
  An unintelligible multitude,
A million eyes, a million boots in line,
15 Without expression, waiting for a sign.

Out of the air a voice without a face
  Proved by statistics that some cause was just
In tones as dry and level as the place:
  No one was cheered and nothing was discussed;
20   Column by column in a cloud of dust
They marched away enduring a belief
Whose logic brought them, somewhere else, to grief.

She looked over his shoulder
  For ritual pieties,
25 White flower-garlanded heifers,
  Libation and sacrifice,[3]
But there on the shining metal
  Where the altar should have been,
She saw by his flickering forge-light
30   Quite another scene.

Barbed wire enclosed an arbitrary spot
  Where bored officials lounged (one cracked a joke)
And sentries sweated for the day was hot:
  A crowd of ordinary decent folk
35   Watched from without and neither moved nor spoke
As three pale figures were led forth and bound
To three posts driven upright in the ground.

The mass and majesty of this world, all
  That carries weight and always weighs the same
40 Lay in the hands of others; they were small
  And could not hope for help and no help came:
  What their foes liked to do was done, their shame
Was all the worst could wish; they lost their pride
And died as men before their bodies died.

45 She looked over his shoulder
  For athletes at their games,
Men and women in a dance
  Moving their sweet limbs

---

1 *nightingales* In Greek myth, Philomela, the daughter of the king of Athens, was transformed into a nightingale after being raped by her brother-in-law, Tereus, King of Thrace, who had cut out her tongue to prevent her from talking. A "nightingale" is also a slang term for a prostitute.

2 *The Shield of Achilles* Achilles, a Greek hero in Homer's *Iliad*, was a fierce warrior who chose the glory of an honourable death at Troy instead of a long and comfortable life. Book 18 of the Iliad recounts the story of Achilles's shield, wrought by Hephaestus, the lame god of fire and metals, at the request of Achilles's sea-nymph mother, Thetis. Achilles had lost his armor after lending it to Patroclus, who was later killed by the Trojan commander, Hector. Achilles's new shield depicted the earth, heavens, sun, moon, and stars, as well as scenes of agriculture, a bountiful harvest, and two cities, all encircled by the ocean.

3 *She looked … sacrifice* See John Keats's "Ode on a Grecian Urn" 31-4: "Who are these coming to the sacrifice? / To what green altar, o mysterious priest, / Lead'st thou that heifer lowing at the skies, / And all her silken flanks with garlands drest?"

Quick, quick, to music,
    But there on the shining shield
50 His hands had set no dancing-floor
    But a weed-choked field.

A ragged urchin, aimless and alone,
    Loitered about that vacancy; a bird
55 Flew up to safety from his well-aimed stone:
    That girls are raped, that two boys knife a third,
    Were axioms to him, who'd never heard
Of any world where promises were kept,
Or one could weep because another wept.

60   The thin-lipped armourer,
        Hephaestos, hobbled away,
    Thetis of the shining breasts
        Cried out in dismay
    At what the god had wrought
65   To please her son, the strong
    Iron-hearted man-slaying Achilles
        Who would not live long.

—1952

"The Truest Poetry is the Most Feigning"
(for Edgar Wind)[1]

By all means sing of love but, if you do,
  Please make a rare old proper hullabaloo:
When ladies ask *How much do you love me?*
The Christian answer is *così-così*;[2]
5 But poets are not celibate divines:
Had Dante[3] said so, who would read his lines?
Be subtle, various, ornamental, clever,
And do not listen to those critics ever
Whose crude provincial gullets crave in books
10 Plain cooking made still plainer by plain cooks,[4]

As though the Muse[5] preferred her half-wit sons;
Good poets have a weakness for bad puns.

Suppose your Beatrice be, as usual, late,
And you would tell us how it feels to wait,
15 You're free to think, what may be even true,
You're so in love that one hour seems like two,
But write—*As I sat waiting for her call,*
Each second longer darker seemed than all
(Something like this but more elaborate still)
20 *Those raining centuries it took to fill*
That quarry whence Endymion's[6] *Love was torn;*
From such ingenious fibs are poems born.
Then, should she leave you for some other guy,
Or ruin you with debts, or go and die,
25 No metaphor, remember, can express
A real historical unhappiness;
Your tears have value if they make us gay;
O Happy Grief! is all sad verse can say.

The living girl's your business (some odd sorts
30 Have been an inspiration to men's thoughts):
Yours may be old enough to be your mother,
Or have one leg that's shorter than the other,
Or play Lacrosse or do the Modern Dance,
To you that's destiny, to us it's chance;
35 We cannot love your love till she take on,
Through you, the wonders of a paragon.
Sing her triumphant passage to our land,
The sun her footstool, the moon in her right hand,
And seven planets blazing in her hair,
40 Queen of the Night and Empress of the Air;
Tell how her fleet by nine king swans is led,
Wild geese write magic letters overhead
And hippocampi[7] follow in her wake

---

[1] *The Truest ... Feigning* Touchstone's words to Audrey in Shakespeare's *As You Like It*, 3.3.19–20; *Edgar Wind* Renaissance scholar and friend of Auden's.

[2] *così-così* Italian: so-so.

[3] *Dante* Dante Alighieri (1265–1321), Italian poet famed in part for the depth of his devotion to his muse, Beatrice.

[4] *Plain cooking ... cooks* Auden reworks a quotation by the well-known British cookery writer of the 1930s and 1940s, Countess Morphy: "Plain cooking cannot be entrusted to plain cooks."

[5] *Muse* One of nine daughters of Zeus and Mnemosyne, each of whom presided over and provided inspiration for an aspect of the arts and sciences.

[6] *Endymion* Beautiful shepherd youth who attracted the attention of the moon goddess, Selene; she begged Zeus to grant her lover one wish. Endymion chose eternal sleep, by which he would remain forever youthful. Endymion is the subject of Keats's long poem *Endymion: A Poetic Romance* (1818).

[7] *hippocampi* Fish-tailed horses of the ocean who carried the sea gods.

With Amphisboene,[1] gentle for her sake;
45 Sing her descent on the exulting shore
To bless the vines and put an end to war.

If half-way through such praises of your dear,
Riot and shooting fill the streets with fear,
And overnight as in some terror dream
50 Poets are suspect with the New Regime,
Stick at your desk and hold your panic in,
What you are writing may still save your skin:
Re-sex the pronouns, add a few details,
And, lo, a panegyric ode which hails
55 (How is the Censor, bless his heart, to know?)
The new pot-bellied Generalissimo.
Some epithets, of course, like *lily-breasted*
Need modifying to, say, *lion-chested*,
A title *Goddess of wry-necks[2] and wrens*
60 To *Great Reticulator[3] of the fens*,
But in an hour your poem qualifies
For a State pension or His annual prize,

And you will die in bed (which He will not:
That public nuisance will be hanged or shot).
65 Though honest Iagos,[4] true to form, will write
Shame! in your margins, *Toady! Hypocrite!*
True hearts, clear heads will hear the note of glory
And put inverted commas round the story.
Thinking—*Old Sly-boots! We shall never know*
70 *Her name or nature. Well, it's better so.*

For given Man, by birth, by education,
Imago Dei[5] who forgot his station,
The self-made creature who himself unmakes,
The only creature ever made who fakes,
75 With no more nature in his loving smile
Than in his theories of a natural style,
What but tall tales, the luck of verbal playing,
Can trick his lying nature into saying
That love, or truth in any serious sense,
80 Like orthodoxy, is a reticence?
—1954

---

[1] *Amphisboene* Winged Greek serpents with two legs, glowing eyes, and heads on either ends of their bodies, who were known for swiftness and cunning.

[2] *wry-necks* Members of the woodpecker family.

[3] *Reticulator* One who divides or marks in such a way as to render a network.

[4] *honest Iagos* In Shakespeare's *Othello* the spiteful and jealous "honest Iago" convinces Othello that his innocent wife, Desdemona, is having an affair.

[5] *Imago Dei* Latin: image of God.

In Context

Auden on the Nature and Craft of Poetry

Auden's writings about poetry—many of which are collected in *The Dyer's Hand and Other Essays*—offer a remarkable range of insights into the nature of poetry as well as into his own work. The following passages are excerpted from one of the most wide-ranging of those essays.

from "Writing" (1962)

... The intellect of man is forced to choose
Perfection of the life or of the work. (YEATS)

This is untrue; perfection is possible in neither. All one can say is that a writer who, like all men, has his personal weaknesses and limitations, should be aware of them and try his best to keep them out of his work. For every writer, there are certain subjects which, because of defects in his character and his talent, he should never touch.

What makes it difficult for a poet not to tell lies is that, in poetry, all facts and all beliefs cease to be true or false and become interesting possibilities. The reader does not have to share the beliefs expressed in a poem in order to enjoy it. Knowing this, a poet is constantly tempted to make use of an idea or a belief, not because he believes it to be true, but because he sees it has interesting poetic possibilities. It may not, perhaps, be absolutely necessary that he *believe* it, but it is certainly necessary that his emotions be deeply involved, and this they can never be unless, as a man, he takes it more seriously than as a mere poetic convenience.

The integrity of a writer is more threatened by appeals to his social conscience, his political or religious convictions, than by appeals to his cupidity.[1] It is morally less confusing to be goosed by a traveling salesman than by a bishop. Some writers confuse authenticity, which they ought always to aim at, with originality, which they should never bother about. There is a certain kind of person who is so dominated by the desire to be loved for himself alone that he has constantly to test those around him by tiresome behavior; what he says and does must be admired, not because it is intrinsically admirable, but because it is *his* remark, *his* act. Does not this explain a good deal of avant-garde art?

... Rhymes, meters, stanza forms, etc., are like servants. If the master is fair enough to win their affection and firm enough to command their respect, the result is an orderly happy household. If he is too tyrannical, they give notice; if he lacks authority, they become slovenly, impertinent, drunk and dishonest.

The poet who writes "free" verse is like Robinson Crusoe on his desert island: he must do all his cooking, laundry, and darning for himself. In a few exceptional cases, this manly independence produces something original and impressive, but more often the result is squalor—dirty sheets on the unmade bed and empty bottles on the unswept floor.

There are some poets, Kipling[2] for example, whose relation to language reminds one of a drill sergeant: the words are taught to wash behind their ears, stand properly at attention and execute complicated maneuvers, but at the cost of never being allowed to think for themselves. There are

---

[1] *cupidity*   Desire for wealth.

[2] *Kipling*   English author Rudyard Kipling (1865–1936).

others, Swinburne, for example, who remind one more of Svengali:[1] under their hypnotic suggestion, an extraordinary performance is put on, not by raw recruits, but by feeble-minded schoolchildren. . . .

The difference between verse and prose is self-evident but it is a sheer waste of time to look for a definition of the difference between poetry and prose. Frost's[2] definition of poetry as the untranslatable element in language looks plausible at first sight but, on closer examination, will not quite do. In the first place, even in the most rarefied poetry, there are some elements which are translatable. The sound of the words, their rhythmical relations, and all meanings and association of meanings which depend upon sound, like rhymes and puns, are, of course, untranslatable, but poetry is not, like music, pure sound. Any elements in a poem which are not based on verbal experience are, to some degree, translatable into another tongue, for example, images, similes, and metaphors which are drawn from sensory experience. . . .

Poetry is not magic. In so far as poetry, or any other of the arts, can be said to have an ulterior purpose, it is, by telling the truth, to disenchant and disintoxicate.

"The unacknowledged legislators of the world"[3] describes the secret police, not the poets.

Catharsis is properly effected, not by works of art, but by religious rites. It is also effected, usually improperly, by bullfights, professional football matches, bad movies, military bands, and monster rallies at which ten thousand Girl Guides form themselves into a model of the national flag.

The condition of mankind is, and always has been, so miserable and depraved that, if anyone were to say to the poet: "For God's sake stop singing and do something useful like putting on the kettle or fetching bandages," what just reason could he give for refusing? But nobody says this. The self-appointed unqualified nurse says: "You are to sing the patient a song which will make him believe that I, and I alone, can cure him. If you can't or won't, I shall confiscate your passport and send you to the mines." And the poor patient in his delirium cries: "Please sing me a song which will give me sweet dreams instead of nightmares. If you succeed, I will give you a penthouse in New York or a ranch in Arizona."

---

[1]   *Swinburne*   Victorian poet Algernon Charles Swinburne (1837–1909); *Svengali*   Notorious hypnotist in George Du Maurier's novel *Trilby* (1894).

[2]   *Frost*   American poet Robert Frost (1874–1963).

[3]   *The unacknowledged ... world*   From Percy Shelley's description of poets in his *Defense of Poetry* (1820).

WORLD WAR II

CONTEXTS

World War II officially began with Hitler's invasion of Poland on 1 September 1939 (the origins of which can be traced back to the peace treaties of World War I). After Poland, Hitler took Denmark, Luxemburg, Norway, the Netherlands, and Belgium. With the fall of these last two nations, British troops were surrounded on land by German forces and were forced to flee by sea from Dunkirk. Then, in June 1940, France surrendered, making a separate peace with Germany. With England as his next goal, Hitler deployed the German Luftwaffe (Air Force) on England. The Blitz, during which the Royal Air Force battled the German bombers nightly over the skies of England, began in August 1940.

While World War I had been defined for the British by trench warfare and by grueling casualties with little movement on either side, World War II was the war of the bomb, and it was a war that, unlike trench warfare, took place on England's soil as well as on the Continent's. The Blitz, eight months of nearly nightly bombings of England's metropolitan centers, caused great destruction to England; 30,000 civilians were killed between 7 September and 2 November 1940, with half of those being inhabitants of London, and half a million people were left homeless. In London, landmarks such as Buckingham Palace and the House of Commons were destroyed or severely damaged. Amidst this assault, England's citizens were tested to the limits of their courage and patience. While most faced their daily tribulations with courage, the possibility of a potentially successful invasion could never be far from their minds. Some had plans to commit suicide rather than submit to Hitler, should such an invasion occur; writer Vita Sackville-West and her husband, diplomat Harold Nicholson, discuss their plans to take a lethal pill in the excerpts from their letters below. Virginia Woolf, whose diary is also excerpted here, made it clear in her correspondence that the sound of the bombs falling on London was a contributing factor in the despair that caused her to take her own life in March 1941. (Woolf and her husband, who was Jewish, had also decided to take their own lives should Hitler invade.)

It was largely through the efforts of Prime Minister Winston Churchill that the nation remained unified and optimistic even in the dark months before Germany gave up its attempt to conquer Britain from the air, in May 1941, and the United States entered the war, in December 1941, allowing the Allies to mount a major offensive on the European mainland. Churchill was a powerful orator, as well as an experienced journalist and essayist, and his speeches (some of the most famous of which are excerpted here) gave his people hope and pride and reminded them of their common cause. For the duration of the war, party politics were largely laid aside, and many found that the war provided them with an exhilarating sense of strength and purpose.

There is little naive idealism in the literature of the war, however; World War II has no Rupert Brooke or John McCrae. Most of the nation had lived through the previous war and the subsequent economic depression of the '30s, and many writers had documented the struggle against fascism in the Spanish Civil War (1936–39). World War II writers documented the grim realities of war as they appeared. But their devotion to realism did not preclude patriotic sentiment. The work of writers such as Keith Douglas, for example, whose poem "Vergissmeinnicht" appears below, manages to celebrate the gallantry and heroism of soldiers while simultaneously acknowledging the folly that is an inevitable part of war. Poets such as Douglas and Henry Reed (whose work is also represented below) were often influenced by the more realistic war poets of the previous generation, such as Wilfred Owen and Edward Thomas. And, as the two poems by Douglas LePan, published in 1987, demonstrate, the war remained alive in the minds of those who participated in it for decades after its official end.

One notable fact about the literature that emerged during and after the war was, as John Lehmann points out in his introduction to *The Penguin New Writing*, excerpted below, is that subjects in Britain's colonies began to develop their own voices and their own pride in national identity, defined separately from that of Britain. Campbell's well-known poem about paratroopers in New Guinea, reprinted here, is just one of many examples. This trend continued after the war, when Britain lacked both the resources and the will to maintain control over its colonial possessions. (India, Burma, and Ceylon all gained independence shortly after the war.)

In nearly all the works excerpted here, one senses clearly that the fate of Europe and of most of the rest of the world was felt to be hanging in the balance during the war. Many of these writers felt that, regardless of the outcome of the war, their lives and homes would never be the same. In this battle of democracy versus fascism, the war also prompted many writers to examine their views on fascism (and anti-Semitism) and to stand up for their beliefs. Particularly interesting in this connection is the article written by Bernard Shaw for broadcast on the B.B.C., which was never aired. Examinations of war crimes and fascism continued long after the war, particularly during the Nuremberg Trials, on which Rebecca West (the pen name of Cicily Fairfield) reported in "Greenhouse with Cyclamens," excerpted below.

⌘ ⌘ ⌘

Advertisement issued by the British Ministry of Fuel and Power.

Posters erected by the British Ministry of Information.

Winston Churchill, Speeches to the House of Commons

from "Blood, Toil, Tears, and Sweat" (13 May 1940)

At the beginning of May 1940, after the failure of the British operations in Norway, Neville Chamberlain resigned as Prime Minister, and the subsequent debate in the Commons resulted in a drastic reduction in the Government's majority. Churchill, who was then First Lord of the Admiralty (a position he had also held during World War I), replaced him as Prime Minister. In this, his first speech in the new position, Churchill introduces the House to the new administration he has formed to lead the nation through the war.

… To form an Administration of this scale and complexity is a serious undertaking in itself, but it must be remembered that we are in the preliminary stage of one of the greatest battles in history, that we are in action at many other points in Norway and in Holland, that we have to be prepared in the Mediterranean, that the air battle is continuous and that many preparations, such as have been indicated by my Honorable Friend below the Gangway,[1] have to be made here at home. In this crisis I hope I may be pardoned if I do not address the House at any length today. I hope that any of my friends and colleagues, or former colleagues, who are affected by the political reconstruction, will make allowance, all allowance, for any lack of ceremony with which it has been necessary to act. I would say to the House, as I said to those who have joined this government: "I have nothing to offer but blood, toil, tears and sweat."

We have before us an ordeal of the most grievous kind. We have before us many, many long months of struggle and of suffering. You ask, what is our policy? I can say: It is to wage war, by sea, land and air, with all our might and with all the strength that God can give us; to wage war against a monstrous tyranny, never surpassed in the dark, lamentable catalogue of human crime. That is our policy. You ask, what is our aim? I

can answer in one word: It is victory, victory at all costs, victory in spite of all terror, victory, however long and hard the road may be; for without victory, there is no survival. Let that be realised; no survival for the British Empire, no survival for all that the British Empire has stood for, no survival for the urge and impulse of the ages, that mankind will move forward towards its goal. But I take up my task with buoyancy and hope. I feel sure that our cause will not be suffered to fail among men. At this time I feel entitled to claim the aid of all, and I say, "Come then, let us go forward together with our united strength."

from "We Shall Fight on the Beaches" (4 June 1940)

This rallying speech was delivered shortly after the demoralizing defeat of the French and British armies in April and May of 1940. However, through the heroism of the Royal Air Force, who protected the Dunkirk evacuees from attacks by air, over 330,000 Allied troops had been successfully evacuated. In the midst of this national effort, Churchill here warns that Britain might soon be forced to fight alone, and on her own soil.

… We have found it necessary to take measures of increasing stringency, not only against enemy aliens and suspicious characters of other nationalities, but also against British subjects who may become a danger or a nuisance should the war be transported to the United Kingdom. I know there are a great many people affected by the orders which we have made who are the passionate enemies of Nazi Germany. I am very sorry for them, but we cannot, at the present time and under the present stress, draw all the distinctions which we should like to do. If parachute landings were attempted and fierce fighting attendant upon them followed, these unfortunate people would be far better out of the way, for their own sakes as well as for ours. There is, however, another class, for which I feel not the slightest sympathy. Parliament has given us the powers to put down

---

[1] *Gangway* In the House of Commons, the cross-passage about half-way down, located in front of the rear benches.

Fifth Column[1] activities with a strong hand, and we shall use those powers subject to the supervision and correction of the House, without the slightest hesitation until we are satisfied, and more than satisfied, that this malignancy in our midst has been effectively stamped out.

Turning once again, and this time more generally, to the question of invasion, I would observe that there has never been a period in all these long centuries of which we boast when an absolute guarantee against invasion, still less against serious raids, could have been given to our people. In the days of Napoleon the same wind which would have carried his transports across the Channel might have driven away the blockading fleet. There was always the chance, and it is that chance which has excited and befooled the imaginations of many Continental tyrants. Many are the tales that are told. We are assured that novel methods will be adopted, and when we see the originality of malice, the ingenuity of aggression, which our enemy displays, we may certainly prepare ourselves for every kind of novel stratagem and every kind of brutal and treacherous manoeuvre. I think that no idea is so outlandish that it should not be considered and viewed with a searching, but at the same time, I hope, with a steady eye. We must never forget the solid assurances of sea power and those which belong to air power if it can be locally exercised.

I have, myself, full confidence that if all do their duty, if nothing is neglected, and if the best arrangements are made, as they are being made, we shall prove ourselves once again able to defend our Island home, to ride out the storm of war, and to outlive the menace of tyranny, if necessary for years, if necessary alone. At any rate, that is what we are going to try to do. That is the resolve of His Majesty's Government—every man of them. That is the will of Parliament and the nation. The British Empire and the French Republic, linked together in their cause and in their need, will defend to the death their native soil, aiding each other like good comrades to the utmost of their strength. Even though large tracts of Europe and many old and famous States

Winston Churchill relaxing in a shelter during an RAF-Luftwaffe battle over Dover.

have fallen or may fall into the grip of the Gestapo[2] and all the odious apparatus of Nazi rule, we shall not flag or fail. We shall go on to the end, we shall fight in France, we shall fight on the seas and oceans, we shall fight with growing confidence and growing strength in the air, we shall defend our Island, whatever the cost may be, we shall fight on the beaches, we shall fight on the landing grounds, we shall fight in the fields and in the streets, we shall fight in the hills; we shall never surrender, and even if, which I do not for a moment believe, this island or a large part of it were subjugated and starving, then our Empire beyond the seas, armed and guarded by the British Fleet, would carry on the struggle, until, in God's good time, the New World, with all its power and might, steps forth to the rescue and the liberation of the old.

from "Their Finest Hour" (18 June 1940)

With French resistance crumbling, the French government fled Paris on 10 June 1940, and although Churchill made two visits to Paris to try to

---

[1] *Fifth Column* I.e., treasonous. The term originated in the Spanish Civil War, when a fascist general led four columns of troops in an attack against Madrid, and later claimed he was helped by a "fifth column" of secret supporters inside the city.

[2] *Gestapo* Secret police of Nazi Germany.

persuade the nation not to surrender, six days later Marshal Henri Philippe Pétain formed a new government, which then sued for peace. In this speech Churchill discusses these recent events and reaffirms the nation's resolve to continue fighting alone.

… During the first four years of the last war the Allies experienced nothing but disaster and disappointment. That was our constant fear: one blow after another, terrible losses, frightful dangers. Everything miscarried. And yet at the end of those four years the morale of the Allies was higher than that of the Germans, who had moved from one aggressive triumph to another, and who stood everywhere triumphant invaders of the lands into which they had broken. During that war we repeatedly asked ourselves the question: How are we going to win? and no one was able ever to answer it with much precision, until at the end, quite suddenly, quite unexpectedly, our terrible foe collapsed before us, and we were so glutted with victory that in our folly we threw it away.

We do not yet know what will happen in France or whether the French resistance will be prolonged, both in France and in the French Empire overseas. The French Government will be throwing away great opportunities and casting adrift their future if they do not continue the war in accordance with their Treaty obligations, from which we have not felt able to release them. The House will have read the historic declaration in which, at the desire of many Frenchmen—and of our own hearts—we have proclaimed our willingness at the darkest hour in French history to conclude a union of common citizenship in this struggle. However matters may go in France or with the French Government, or other French Governments, we in this Island and in the British Empire will never lose our sense of comradeship with the French people. If we are now called upon to endure what they have been suffering, we shall emulate their courage, and if final victory rewards our toils they shall share the gains, aye, and freedom shall be restored to all. We abate nothing of our just demands; not one jot or tittle[1] do we recede. Czechs, Poles, Norwegians, Dutch, Belgians have joined their causes to our own. All these shall be restored.

What General Weygand[2] called the Battle of France is over. I expect that the Battle of Britain is about to begin. Upon this battle depends the survival of Christian civilization. Upon it depends our own British life, and the long continuity of our institutions and our Empire. The whole fury and might of the enemy must very soon be turned on us. Hitler knows that he will have to break us in this Island or lose the war. If we can stand up to him, all Europe may be free and the life of the world may move forward into broad, sunlit uplands. But if we fail, then the whole world, including the United States, including all that we have known and cared for, will sink into the abyss of a new Dark Age made more sinister, and perhaps more protracted, by the lights of perverted science. Let us therefore brace ourselves to our duties, and so bear ourselves that, if the British Empire and its Commonwealth last for a thousand years, men will still say, "This was their finest hour."

Winston Churchill inspects the damage done to the Debating Chamber of the House of Commons.

---

[1] *jot or tittle* Minute amount.

[2] *General Weygand* Maxime Weygand, French general (1867–1965), who served as Supreme Allied Commander until the fall of France.

from Harold Nicholson, *The War Years: 1939–1945* (Volume 2 of *The Diaries and Letters of Harold Nicholson*, 1972)

Harold Nicholson was a Member of Parliament throughout the war, and served briefly in Churchill's government as Parliamentary Secretary to the Ministry of Information, from May 1940 until July 1941. As a result of his position, he was frequently forced to be in London, away from his home and his wife, Vita Sackville-West. Their letters to one another demonstrate their concern for one another's safety, as well as their conviction that their world could never be the same after the war. They were serious in their determination to commit suicide ingesting a lethal dose of drugs (referred to in their correspondence as "the bare bodkin," or unsheathed dagger) should Hitler invade and should it appear that either of them might be taken by the Germans. While Sackville-West's letters give a sense of the war experienced by those left helplessly watching from home, Nicholson's letters, and particularly his diary entries, often give a sense of the exhilarating patriotism that motivated others.

H.N. to V.S-W.

27 May 1940
Ministry of Information

I am afraid that the news this afternoon is very bad indeed, and that we must expect the Germans to surround a large proportion of our Army and to occupy the whole area of Belgium and Northern France. We must also face the possibility that the French may make a separate peace, especially if Italy joins in the conflict. I warn you of this so that you will prepare your mind for the bad news when it comes and be ready to summon all the courage that is in you. I think you had better keep this to yourself for the moment.

V.S-W to H.N.

28 May 1940
Sissinghurst

God help us, I have just heard about the Belgians! Well, we must wait. In the meantime, how deeply I agree with you about love and also about the bodkin. I promise you never to do anything rash or impetuous with the latter, but I should like to have it by me. So see Pierre Lansel[1] as soon as you can, for both our sakes, and get it for yourself and also post me a little parcel. There must be something quick and painless and portable. Oh my dear, my dearest, that we should come to this! Anyhow, we have had our lives, or at any rate more than half of them, so let us never repine. I won't write more. I know you are busy, and it is not necessary for me to say more than that I have loved you more than anyone or anything in all my life.

V.S-W. To H.N.

5 June 1940
Sissinghurst

I wish I had heard Winston making that magnificent speech![2] Even repeated by the announcer it sent shivers (not of fear) down my spine. I think that one of the reasons why one is stirred by his Elizabethan phrases is that one feels the whole massive backing of power and resolve behind them, like a great fortress: they are never words for words' sake.

How strange it is to have no knowledge of what is about to befall us. In ordinary times one seldom thinks how odd it is to have no knowledge of what may happen even within the next hour, but now the consciousness of this ignorance becomes acute. I see the future only in terms of colour: scarlet and black. But as you say, courage and hope. And there is always the bare bodkin.

H.N. To V.S-W.

19 June 1940
4 King's Bench Walk, E.C.4

I think it practically certain that the Americans will enter the war in November, and if we can last till then, all is well. Anyhow, as a precaution, I have got the bare bodkin. I shall bring down your half on Sunday. It all looks very simple.

How I wish Winston would not talk on the wireless[3] unless he is feeling in good form. He hates the micro-

---

[1] *Pierre Lansel*   Nicholson's doctor.

[2] *That magnificent speech*   The "We Shall Fight on the Beaches" speech of June 4.

[3] *wireless*   Radio.

phone, and when we bullied him into speaking last night, he just sulked and read his House of Commons speech[1] over again. Now, as delivered in the House of Commons, that speech was magnificent, especially the concluding sentences. But it sounded ghastly on the wireless. All the great vigour he put into it seemed to evaporate....

Harold Nicholson, *Diary*

12 July 1940

At the Policy Committee I bring up my draft of War Aims. I say that we are about to be faced by a dual problem, one international and the other national. The international problem is this. Hitler may call a European Economic Conference, announce the economic consolidation of Europe, and say, "Here is a vast purchasing organisation. The Americans wish to sell us their consolidated stocks. What prevents the suppliers from sending their stuff to the consumers? The British blockade. Great Britain is thus imposing famine and pestilence on Europe, and ruin upon the two Americas." The national problem is this. When bombing begins on a large scale, people will ask, "What are we fighting for? Would we not be better off with peace plus Hitler?" In order to combat the first, we must have Free Trade and pooled resources. In order to combat the second we must have Socialism. I suggest that I should draft in leaflet form a manifesto promising the world free trade and our own country equality of opportunity. They agree. But it will be difficult to get Duff[2] to put it to the War Cabinet. Will it not be felt that we had better leave this sleeping tiger to sleep in its own way?

Harold Nicholson, *Diary*

20 July 1940

I think that Hitler will probably invade us within the next few days. He has 6,000 aeroplanes ready for the job. How strange it all is! We know that we are faced

King George VI and Queen Elizabeth walk through the wreckage of the north side of Buckingham Palace, which was hit by a bomb on 10 September 1940.

with a terrific invasion. We half-know that the odds are heavily against us. Yet there is a sort of exhilaration in the air. If Hitler were to postpone invasion and fiddle about in Africa and the Mediterranean, our morale might weaken. But we are really proud to be the people who will not give way. The reaction to Hitler's speech yesterday[3] is a good reaction. Yet I know well that we shall be exposed to horrible punishment. It is so strange that in this moment of anxiety there is no hatred of Hitler or the Germans. Opinion slides off into oblique animosities such as criticism of the Old Gang and rage that the L.D.V.[4] are not better equipped. All this is dangerous, since it is in essence a form of escapism and appeasement. We are really frightened of Hitler, and

---

[1] *his House ... speech* The "Their Finest Hour" speech that he had delivered to the House the previous day (June 18).

[2] *Duff* Politician (Alfred) Duff Cooper (1890–1954), who was then serving as Minister of Information. Nicholson served on Cooper's Committee on German Refugees.

[3] *Hitler's speech yesterday* Hitler's speech to the Reichstag, the parliament of Germany until 1945, in which he implied that he might be willing to discuss peace terms with the British.

[4] *L.D.V.* Local Defence Volunteers.

avoid the dynamic resistance to him which is uniform hatred. 130 years ago all this hatred was concentrated against [Napoleon] Bonaparte. We flinch today from central enmity. If we are invaded we may become angry.

V.S-W. To H.N.

4 September 1940
Sissinghurst

Whenever the siren[1] goes, I wonder where you are: in the Ministry, in the streets, in King's Bench Walk, in a theatre? It is bloody. Meanwhile we have found machine-gun bullets, one in the lake-field and one came through the roof of the garden shed. So, you see, I am right to tell you to keep indoors when they fight just overhead. They are nasty pointed things.

We had a fine pyrotechnical display after dinner last night, when a German got caught in our searchlights and fired tracer-bullets. Blood-red they streamed down the sky. The rest of the night was quiet here.

V.S-W. To H.N.

8 October 1940
Sissinghurst

Lord! we have had a lot of raids this morning. They began at 8.30 and are still going on at 11. There was a most lovely sight: ten white machines climbed absolutely sheer, leaving perfectly regular white streaks of smoke like furrows in a cloudless blue sky, while a machine lower down looped smoke like gigantic spectacles before shooting up to join its friends. We saw one catch fire and fall. "That's one less to go after Hadji,"[2] I thought.

from Charles Ritchie, *The Siren Years* (1972)

The Siren Years is the first volume of Canadian diplomat Charles Ritchie's diary. During the war years, Ritchie was in London in the Canadian foreign service, posted to the Office of the High Commissioner for Canada.

---

[1] *siren* Used to warn of impending air-raids.

[2] *Hadji* Sackville-West's nickname for Nicholson.

2 June 1940

Went with Mike Pearson[3] to Dover. There we really had the feeling of being in an extension of the actual war zone. Destroyers were coming in and out of the harbour, going to Dunkirk to embark the remains of the British Expeditionary Force and the French Army of the North. As we walked along the pier we saw one of the destroyers returning, its stem had been blown clean off by a bomb. It was limping home with flags still flying. We went alongside two more destroyers, one English and one French. They began landing French soldiers who were herded into a troop train by a thin young officer in riding breeches. Looking down on the decks of the British destroyer we could see a bearded sailor lying asleep beside his gun. On the French destroyer the sailors were clustered in a chattering group —one was showing the others a postcard of a nude woman and they were gossiping and laughing. Soon a tug drew up alongside and began to debouch German prisoners. They were pallid and grimy and looked as if they had been kept underground for a year, the result I suppose of being packed together under the hatches while they were being bombed by their own people from the air. They came shambling out on to the deck in the sunshine and began running up the companion-way as if they had the devil behind them. There they formed into a file waiting to be taken away in buses. I remember the German prisoners-of-war at Calais, when I was a boy after the last war, carrying slop-pails around the British camps. They had shaven heads. These men had long hair which fell over their eyes as they stumbled along the gangplank. Some were aviators, and these had an air of arrogance. The privates ran and huddled like sheep. Prisoners without their guns and helmets have the look of having suffered an amputation, as if they were deprived of a vital limb or had been castrated. Then came the German wounded. They were swung from the decks of the ship by a crane. None of them moved or cried out but lay in waxen immobility as if they were already dead. While the procession of prisoners and wounded moved by, the Tommies[4] who were

---

[3] *Mike Pearson* Lester B. Pearson (1897–1972), then a senior diplomat, later a winner of the Nobel Peace Prize (1957) and Prime Minister of Canada (1963–68).

[4] *Tommies* Nickname for privates in the British Army.

guarding the pier remained silent. Anyone who spoke spoke in lowered tones. Out in the harbour a mist hung over the smooth sea and dozens of craft lay there at anchor after coming and going to Dunkirk time after time. About the cliffs the eternal gulls circled. Two little girls were shrilly calling to each other from their bicycles as they rode in and out of the small gardens in front of a row of houses at the foot of the great bluff of cliff behind the docks. These docks, and in fact the whole of Dover, are now within range of German shell-fire from Boulogne. But the life of the town is going on just the same....

From Dover they can see Boulogne at night burning across the Channel and hear bombs as they fall. Why the Germans do not bomb the small inner harbour at Dover, so crowded with shipping, one cannot guess....

26 August 1940. London
There go the sirens again! I do not know what will be left of our nerves after a winter of this. First the wail announcing impending doom. Then the city holds its breath as the last dying sound of the siren fades and we wait. Of course everyone is calm on the surface, but one gets jumpy at sudden noises. At first raids were exciting and frightening. Now they are getting unpleasant, risky and tiring.

13 September 1940
A week of air raids. Our ears have grown sharp for the sounds of danger—the humming menace that sweeps from the sky, the long whistle like an indrawn breath as the bomb falls. We are as continually alive to danger as animals in the jungle.

During a raid the silent empty streets wait for the shock like "a patient etherised upon a table."[1] The taxis race along carrying their fares to the shelters. A few pedestrians caught out in the streets make their way with as much restraint as possible to the nearest shelter, keeping an eye open for protection—for friendly archways. They try to saunter but long to run.

In the parks the fallen leaves lie thick upon the paths. No one has time to collect them into bonfires and burn them. The paint is beginning to peel off the great

cream coloured houses in Carlton House Terrace and the grand London squares. The owners will do nothing about it until "after the war." London is beginning to look down-at-heel and a bit battered. Every now and then one comes upon a gap in a row of houses or a façade of shops. In the gap is a pile of rubble where the bomb has hit. I suppose gradually there will be more and more such gaps until the face of London is pitted and furrowed with them.

The other night I was caught on my way home from Chelsea in a heavy barrage with falling shrapnel and turned into a public shelter to wait until things were quieter. There were half a dozen old women ... two conversational old men in battered bowlers and a drunken Irish maid-servant who kept mocking the English for their credulity and stupidity, "You English, sure you're the dumbest nation on earth. Now do you believe all this you read in the papers about how many German planes were shot down. Don't you see it is all propaganda now." Her harangues were greeted with sardonic amusement. These people were all cold and all sleepless. They had spent three nights in this shelter and outside was the recurrent roar of the barrage. Their homes in Chelsea have been badly pasted. The shelter itself was a feeble affair giving no protection from bombs. But their stolidity was unshaken. Their retort was the Englishman's immemorial reply to danger—irony. The kind of joke which hinges on the thought, "Well it ain't the Ritz[2] exactly." They were not afraid but they did want one thing—"a cup of tea."

14 September 1940
The attacks on London have only been going on for ten days. So far people are steady, there has been no panic. But they are depressed. Everyone is suffering from lack of sleep and nervous tension. There is some feeling that the poor are taking it the hardest and many complaints about lack of shelters. The ideal thing from Hitler's point of view would be to continue this all winter and then to attack in the spring. Is he strong enough to wait? That is the question hanging over us. His raids certainly have not been a spectacular success, but they're making a dent all right....

---

[1] *a patient ... table* From T.S. Eliot, "The Love Song of J. Alfred Prufrock" (1915), line 3.

[2] *Ritz* Luxury hotel in London.

6 November 1940

Things one will forget when this is over—fumbling in the dark of the black-out for one's front key while bits of shrapnel fall on the pavement beside one—the way shrapnel seems to drift—almost like snow-flakes through the air in an aimless, leisurely way and the clink of it landing on the pavement.

16 November 1940

I came back from spending the night at Aldershot to find my flat a heap of rubble from a direct hit, and I have lost everything I own. That is no tragedy but a bore—and doubtless a cash loss, as the Department of External Affairs will never approve replacing suits from Sackville Street at twenty pounds per suit. I am most annoyed at losing my new "woodsy" tweed suit, the picture of the Rose that Anne gave me, volume two of the book I am reading, my edition of Rimbaud and the little green book of my own chosen quotations. I do not much regret all the pigskin which used to jar on her so much.

I am enjoying the publicity attendant on this disaster, particularly the idea which I have put abroad that if it had not been for a chance decision to go to Aldershot for the night I should have been killed. I should probably only have been cut about or bruised. The rest of the people living in the flats were in the cellar and escaped unhurt. Hart and I went to see the ruins, and the youth next door was full of the fact that Lord A and Lady A too had had to be pulled out of the débris—so had fourteen other people, but what struck him was that even a lord had not been spared by the bomb. A further fascinating detail was that Lord A's naval uniform was still hanging on the hook on the open surviving wall for all the world to see. Now I know that the *Evening Standard* is right when it prints those items "Baronet's kinswoman in a bus smash" etc.

I feel like a tramp having only one suit and shirt and in particular only *one pair of shoes*.

Last week when I wrote this diary I was sitting on my sofa in front of my electric fire in my perfectly real and solid flat with my books at arm's length—the furniture had that false air of permanence which chairs and tables take on so readily—the drawn curtains shut out the weather. Now that is a pile of dirty rubble, with bits of my suits, wet and blackened, visible among the bricks. On top of the pile my sofa is perched (quite the most uncomfortable and useless article in the flat but it has survived)—this violent, meaningless gesture like a slap from a drunken giant has smashed my shell of a living into a heap.

27 November 1940

I am living at Brooks's Club,[1] a combination of discomfort and old-fashioned comfort. Magnificent coal fires in the living-rooms, icy bedrooms, the kind of confidential valeting that you get in a good country house, the superb bath towels, yards of them, impossible to manoeuvre—the only thing to do is to wrap yourself up in one and sit down until you dry.

As I write I hear the ever-menacing throb of a bomber coming out of the fog. Tonight there is an old-fashioned London fog. Fumbling my way along Piccadilly I could hardly—as they say—"see my hand before me." I hear the hall porter saying in a grieved tone, "There is no air-raid warning gone." This is one of the nights when I feel interested in life, when I should much resent a bomb removing me from the scene. There are other nights when I feel it could not matter less.

Came back last night in the tube[2] from Earl's Court. I hear that the drunks quite often fight it out by throwing each other on to the live wire, which contrary to superstition does not always kill you. If the toughs in the shelter tube do not like a chap they wait for him and throw him on to the wire. I must say that I saw nothing of this—just people sleeping,[3] and not the poorest of the poor. They were all fully dressed and looked clean and quite prosperous, some pretty girls who might be serving in a big store, quite a lot of men and children. I have never seen so many different ages and types of people asleep before. Their sprawled attitudes, arms flung out, etc. made me think of photographs of the dead in

---

[1] *Brooks's Club*   Club-house originally founded in 1764 as a gaming club. It was rebuilt in 1779 at the expense of a wine merchant and money-lender by the name of Brooks.

[2] *tube*   The London Underground, or subway.

[3] *people sleeping*   During the war, the Underground stations were used as bomb shelters.

battlefields—their stark and simplified faces. What one misses in the sleeping and the dead are the facial posturings prompted by perpetual vanity....

24 September 1941
Dinner with Elizabeth Bowen and her husband Alan Cameron[1] and a few writers and critics. So far in my excursions into High Bloomsbury I have not encountered, except for Elizabeth, any striking originality of thought, phrase or personality but rather a group of cultivated, agreeable people who think and feel very much alike....

25 September 1941
Dinner at a dining club got up by Berkeley Gage of the Foreign Office. I sat between Archduke Robert of Austria and de Selliers of the Belgian Embassy, the former rather someone seen in a distorted mirror. His head seems preternaturally shallow, his neck elongated. He has the romantic Austrian charm which springs from an inveterate superficiality. He never asserts himself, but he is a Hapsburg[2] and one cannot help knowing it. His mother, Empress Zita, and younger children are living near Quebec.

6 June 1944
D-Day[3] has come. It had become a hallucination—something like the Second Coming or the End of the World.... The soldiers who have been left behind in London look forlorn and subdued. The town seems empty. The gaiety and sense of pressure and excitement have gone. There is a morning after feeling abroad. The taxis have become plentiful again and the drivers are beginning to be quite polite now that the American debauch[4] is over.

---

[1] *Elizabeth Bowen* Modernist novelist and short-story writer (1899–1973); *Alan Cameron* Cameron (1893–1952) was at this time the Secretary to the Central Council for Schools Broadcasting.

[2] *a Hapsburg* I.e., a member of the Royal Family of the Imperial House of Hapsburg, a dynasty that can be traced to the tenth century.

[3] *D-Day* Reference to the 6 June 1944 Allied invasion of Normandy.

[4] *American debauch* American soldiers were eyed with some suspicion by the British, who famously characterized them as "overpaid, oversexed, and over here."

During the Blitz came an outpouring of patriotic and defiant songs—such as this song, "There'll Always be an England"—that were played on the radio and in pubs and music halls.

Ross Parker and Hughie Charles, "We'll Meet Again" (1939)

This song, like "The White Cliffs of Dover," which is also excerpted below, was made famous by the British singer Vera Lynn.

We'll meet again

We'll meet again,
    Don't know where,
Don't know when,
But I know we'll meet again some sunny day.
5 Keep smiling through,

Just like you always do,
Till the blue skies drive the dark clouds far away.

So will you please say "Hello"
To the folks that I know.
10 Tell them I won't be long;
They'll be happy to know
That as you saw me go,
I was singing this song.

We'll meet again,
15 Don't know where,
Don't know when
But I know we'll meet again some sunny day.

Nat Burton and Walter Kent, "The White Cliffs of Dover" (1941)

I'll never forget the people I met
Braving those angry skies;
I remember well as the shadows fell,
The light of hope in their eyes.
5 And tho' I'm far away,
I still can hear them say "Thumbs up!"
For when the dawn comes up:

There'll be bluebirds over the white cliffs of Dover
Tomorrow, just you wait and see.
10 There'll be love and laughter and peace ever after,
Tomorrow, when the world is free.

The shepherd will tend his sheep,
The valley will bloom again,
And Jimmy will go to sleep,
15 In his own little room again.

There'll be bluebirds over the white cliffs of Dover
Tomorrow, just you wait and see.
There'll be love and laughter and peace ever after,
Tomorrow, when the world is free.

20 When night shadows fall I always recall,
Out there across the sea,
Twilight falling down a little town—
It's fresh in my memory.
I hear a mother pray,
25 And to her baby say "Don't Cry";
This is her lullaby:

There'll be bluebirds over the white cliffs of Dover
Tomorrow, just you wait and see.
There'll be love and laughter and peace ever after,
30 Tomorrow, when the world is free.

War savings poster.

from John Lehmann, "Foreword" to *The Penguin New Writing* (April 1941)

There was a time, many months past now, when it seemed as if the war was going to make all serious literary activity impossible in this country. Since then, it has proved itself tougher and more independent than most people imagined, and even the blitz and the paper-shortage and the rapid spread of the call-up[1] have failed to interrupt it drastically. Writers have gone on producing poems and stories and articles—and also indulging in their squabbles with one another; and, perhaps even more surprising, the reading public has shown an undiminished appetite for it all.

It was when things looked their gloomiest that I received a letter from a friend on the other side of the world. He spoke of the heavy responsibility that lay on English-speaking writers in the further parts of the Empire to keep our literary tradition alive. He pictured us involved for years in the stresses of the actual battle and in war-restrictions of every sort, reduced to silence except for necessary propaganda; and he expressed something that was obviously stirring in the minds of many of the people he knew, when he said that Canada, Australia, and New Zealand had the chance and the duty to become centres of English art and writing while England herself was wholly transformed for war.

Luckily, these fears have not yet been realised, and recent months have even shown a remarkable revival of writing. Nevertheless, it seems inevitable, whatever happens to us here, that one of the results of the war will be that the Dominions will become more independent of us, and, relying on their own talent and tradition to a far greater degree than before, will gradually develop a civilization with its own special character in each country. It is an attractive vision of the future, this flowering of poetry and drama and fiction in lands where men's energies have for generations been poured into farming and mining and business. Till now, artistically, they have been too much under the enormous shadows of England and America; New Zealand, to take one example, seems to have been impeded in her creative growth by too insistent a backward-looking towards the English Channel; and yet in New Zealand there are already signs of a new self-consciousness emerging, of new poets and novelists who think of themselves as New Zealanders and not merely stranded Britishers. In this issue a story by one of the most gifted of these writers, Frank Sargeson,[2] is printed, and it is *New Writing*'s aim to introduce other Dominion authors in course of time. They may have learnt a great deal from us, but it will be surprising if they have nothing to teach us on their side....

David Campbell, "Men in Green" (1943)

Australian poet David Campbell served in the RAAF during World War II and fought in New Guinea against the Japanese, an experience upon which he draws in the following poem. Campbell was awarded the Distinguished Flying Cross and Bar for his service.

There were fifteen men in green,
Each with a tommy-gun,[3]
Who leapt into my plane at dawn;
We rose to meet the sun.

5 We set our course towards the east
And climbed into the day
Till the ribbed jungle underneath
Like a giant fossil lay.

We climbed towards the distant range
10 Where two white paws of cloud
Clutched at the shoulders of the pass;
The green men laughed aloud.

They did not fear the ape-like cloud
That climbed the mountain crest
15 And hung from twisted ropes of air
With thunder in its breast.

---

[1]   *call-up* Conscription.

[2]   *Frank Sargeson* Author who is considered one of New Zealand's first and foremost short-story writers (1903–82). Sargeson was born Norris Frank Davey.

[3]   *tommy-gun* Type of sub-machine gun, named after its inventor, the American general J.T. Thompson.

They did not fear the summer's sun
In whose hot centre lie
A hundred hissing cannon shells
20   For the unwatchful eye.

And when on Dobadura's field[1]
We landed, each man raised
His thumb towards the open sky;
But to their right I gazed.

25   For fifteen men in jungle green
Rose from the kunai grass[2]
And came towards the plane. My men
In silence watched them pass;
It seemed they looked upon themselves
30   In Time's prophetic glass.

Oh, there were some leaned on a stick
And some on stretchers lay,
But few walked on their own two feet
In the early green of day.
35   They had not feared the ape-like cloud
That climbed the mountain crest;
They had not feared the summer's sun
With bullets for their breast.

Their eyes were bright, their looks were dull,
40   Their skin had turned to clay.
Nature had met them in the night
And stalked them in the day.

And I think still of men in green
On the Soputa[3] track
45   With fifteen spitting tommy-guns
To keep a jungle back.

---

[1] *Dobadura's field* Clearing made in the Dobadura jungle, in New Guinea.

[2] *kunai grass* High, coarse grass.

[3] *Soputa* In Papua New Guinea; it was the location of an Allied drop zone during the Battle of Buna.

Keith Douglas, "Vergissmeinnicht"[4] (1944)

A student at Oxford when war broke out, Keith Douglas enlisted in a cavalry regiment (which was soon outfitted with tanks instead of horses) and was sent to the Egyptian desert in 1942. He was later killed in the assault on the Normandy beaches in 1944.

Three weeks gone and the combatants gone
returning over the nightmare ground
we found the place again, and found
the soldier sprawling in the sun.

5   The frowning barrel of his gun
overshadowing. As we came on
that day, he hit my tank with one
like the entry of a demon.

Look. Here in the gunpit spoil
10   the dishonoured picture of his girl
who has put: *Steffi. Vergissmeinnicht*
in a copybook gothic script.

We see him almost with content,
abased, and seeming to have paid
15   and mocked at by his own equipment
that's hard and good when he's decayed.

But she would weep to see today
how on his skin the swart° flies move;   *black*
the dust upon the paper eye
20   and the burst stomach like a cave.

For here the lover and killer are mingled
who had one body and one heart.
And death who had the soldier singled
has done the lover mortal hurt.

---

[4] *Vergissmeinnicht* German: forget me not.

from Henry Reed, *Lessons of War* (1945)

During World War II, Henry Reed was conscripted into the Royal Army Ordnance Corps. In *Lessons of War* (from which "Naming of Parts" is the best known individual poem) Reed plays upon the rhythms he noticed in the speech of his weapons instructor, the lulling patterns of which contrast sharply with the military-manual vocabulary.

Vixi duellis nuper idoneus
Et militavi non sine gloria[1]

1. NAMING OF PARTS

Today we have naming of parts. Yesterday,
We had daily cleaning. And tomorrow morning,
We shall have what to do after firing. But today,
Today we have naming of parts. Japonica[2]
5   Glistens like coral in all of the neighbouring gardens,
    And today we have naming of parts.

This is the lower sling swivel. And this
Is the upper sling swivel, whose use you will see,
When you are given your slings. And this is the piling
    swivel,
10   Which in your case you have not got. The branches
Hold in the gardens their silent, eloquent gestures,
    Which in our case we have not got.

This is the safety-catch, which is always released
With an easy flick of the thumb. And please do not let
    me
15   See anyone using his finger. You can do it quite easy
If you have any strength in your thumb. The blossoms
Are fragile and motionless, never letting anyone see
    Any of them using their finger.

And this you can see is the bolt. The purpose of this
20   Is to open the breech, as you see. We can slide it
Rapidly backwards and forwards: we call this

---

[1] *Vixi ... gloria* Latin: "Lately I have lived in the midst of battles, credibly enough, / And have soldiered, not without glory." (An adaptation of Horace, *Odes* 3.261–2, with the word *puellis* ("girls") changed to *duellis* ("battles.")

[2] *Japonica* Spring-flowering plant.

Easing the spring. And rapidly backwards and forwards
The early bees are assaulting and fumbling the flowers:
    They call it easing the Spring.

25   They call it easing the Spring: it is perfectly easy
If you have any strength in your thumb; like the bolt,
And the breech, and the cocking-piece, and the point of
    balance,
Which in our case we have not got; and the almond-
    blossom
Silent in all of the gardens and the bees going backwards
    and forwards,
    For today we have naming of parts.

Douglas LePan

In World War II Douglas LePan (1914–98) served in the Canadian army during the Italian campaign in 1943. His poetry about the war includes work published in the 1940s and 1950s (notably in *The Net and the Sword*, winner of the Governor General's Award for poetry) as well as poems such as those below, written some forty years after LePan's battlefield experiences.

"Below Monte Cassino" (1987)

Having had too much sex the night before for a man
    over sixty, he feels a dull ache in the small of his
    back
about the size of a pie-plate, and suddenly remembers
(as he urinates into the toilet-bowl) dead
5   American boys in a field below Monte Cassino
and how surprised he had been as he picked his way
forward (avoiding the bodies as best as he could,
scared shitless of trip-mines and shoe-mines and glass-
    mines)
by one dead boy lying face down in the mud
10 with his arms and his legs flung wide and one big
    wound
in the small of his back about the size of a pie-plate,
having been caught there by a fragment of mortar-fire—
surprised then, and still surprised now, that what was
oozing from the wide wound was, not blood, but shit.

"The Haystack" (1987)

It doesn't take a Hiroshima[1] to burn a man to a crisp.
A haystack will do. And what could be more bucolic
than that? And you get tired of sleeping in cellars or slit-
trenches,
so why not behind a haystack that has simmered all day
in the warmth of an Italian September sun? But at night
5 the jackals are ready to spring, the German eighty-
eights,
with their high muzzle-velocities and their low
trajectories,
so that the haystack ignites like a torch and a gunner is
burnt
to a crisp. How far back was that? thirty years? forty
years?
10 He doesn't remember. He only remembers the stench
of fear, his own fear, and a grey army blanket, and a
young
sunburned back alive on the banks of the Volturno,[2]
then burning, burning. By dire subtleties such as these
he was being prepared for the carbonization of cities.

St. Paul's Cathedral, London, during the Blitz.

---

[1] *Hiroshima* Japanese city that was the first city to ever be a target of a nuclear weapon. The United States dropped an atomic bomb on Hiroshima on 6 August 1945, killing approximately 130,000 people and leveling 90 per cent of the city.

[2] *Volturno* River in south-central Italy, the bank of which formed the Volturno line, a German defensive position in World War II.

Life at Home

During the war, the Ministry of Information re-corded and reported on the attitudes and actions of British residents, and particularly Londoners, in the face of the threat of invasion. From most reports, people coped with the war and the Blitz with sto-icism, courage, and patience. During the heaviest raids, the government was on the look-out for signs of panic, but incidents were rare and isolated. Confronted with the nightly danger of bombings, the loss of belongings, and the privations of wartime restrictions, the English people responded with resignation or even cheerful acceptance. Virginia Woolf understood such loss and privation at first hand; the Woolfs retreated to the relative safety of their country home in Sussex after their Bloomsbury home, where they had kept their press, was bombed in September 1940. In a diary entry dated 19 De-cember 1940, Virginia Woolf stepped back and examined the daily privations endured by people in even the most comfortable situations:

It would be interesting if I could take today, Thursday, and say exactly how the war changes it. It changes it when I order dinner. Our ration of margarine is so small that I cant think of any pudding save milk pudding. We have no sugar to make sugar puddings: no pastry, unless I buy it ready made. The shops don't fill till midday. Things are bought fast. In the afternoon they are often gone. Meat ration diminishes this week. Milk is so cut that we have to consider even the cat's saucer. I spent an hour making butter from our skim of cream—a week's takings provides about ½ lb. Petrol changes the day too. Nessa[3] can only come here when she goes to Lewes[4] shopping. All prices rise steadily. The screw is much increased since the summer. We buy no clothes but make do with the old. These are inconveniences rather than hardships. We don't go hungry or cold. But luxury is nipped off, & hospitality. It takes thought & trouble to feed one extra.... The pinch is said to be worse than last war. If it increases much we shall be hungry, I suppose.... Then the black out—that's half an hour

---

[3] *Nessa* Woolf's sister, Vanessa Bell.

[4] *Lewes* Large market town in East Sussex.

daily drudgery. We can't use the dining room after dark.....

In a December 1940 letter to her friend, American editor Irita Van Doren, journalist and writer Rebecca West described some of the emotional and physical difficulties of the war:

This is a beastly war—like the stage of seasickness when you are not sure you are seasick but realise that everything but seasickness has ceased to exist. ... We are all working like dogs, indeed, because in an odd way the connective tissue of life has gone. Everybody is living miles away from where they usually do and has shut up their house and if anybody gets ill the relevant doctors and surgeons aren't to be found, so if you have stayed in London life goes in endless odd jobs. If it weren't for the sailors being drowned one could stand it, and of course it's a disappointment about the Finns. It did seem that once we had declared war we wouldn't have this awful business of being comparatively safe and seeing the smaller peoples being butchered.

Many people left London for safety, as the Woolfs did, and those who stayed sought shelter during air raids in the safest places they could. For many, the best shelter was London's Underground, or subway system. Here they could sleep without fear of bombing. In another diary entry, dated 20 October 1940, and written on a visit to London, Virginia Woolf described the long lines of people waiting to take shelter in the Underground:

The most—what?—impressive, no, that's not it— sight in London on Friday was the queue, mostly children with suitcases, outside Warren Street tube.[1] This was about 11.30. We thought they were evacuees waiting for a bus. But there they were, in a much longer line, with women, men, more bags, blankets, sitting still at 3. Lining up for the shelter in the night's raid—which came of course. Thus, if they left the tube at 6 (a bad raid on Thursday) they were back again at 11.

Despite the courage exhibited across the nation, the stress of the nightly air raids did take its toll. Sleep

was constantly interrupted, and people lived under the threat of death. It was impossible not to contemplate the worst, as Woolf did in this diary entry from 2 October 1940:

Should I think of death? Last night a great heavy plunge of bomb under the window. So near we both started. A plane had passed dropping this fruit.... I said to L.[2]: I don't want to die yet. The chances are against it. But they're aiming at the railway and the power works. They get closer every time. Caburn[3] was crowned with what looked like a settled moth, wings extended—a Messerschmitt[4] it was, shot down on Sunday.... Oh I try to imagine how one's killed by a bomb. I've got it fairly vivid—the sensation: but can't see anything but suffocating nonentity following after. I shall think—oh I wanted another 10 years—not this—and shan't, for once, be able to describe it. It—I mean death; no, the scrunching and scrambling, the crushing of my bone shade in on my very active eye and brain: the process of putting out the light—painful? Yes. Terrifying. I suppose so. Then a swoon; a drain; two or three gulps attempting consciousness—and then dot dot dot.

During the Blitz the citizens of London proved that it was not only soldiers who could become accustomed to death and destruction, and learn to remain calm in the face of danger. Women, children, and ordinary shopkeepers and workers were equally capable of this courage. A woman in her thirties who had just returned from Scotland, where she had fled when the war began, described her feelings around the air raids:

Sweated with fear at the mere idea of being woken in the night by sirens, let alone at that of bombs and shells; was constantly imagining car and other noises were sirens or guns. Convinced of being most utter and complete coward—very ashamed. Sure I was bound to panic and lose control if things got hot.... Now I find

---

[1] *tube* I.e., Underground station.

[2] *L.* Leonard Woolf, Virginia's husband.

[3] *Caburn* Mount Caburn, an isolated peak that is East Sussex's highest landmark.

[4] *Messerschmitt* German aircraft.

Women workers make aircraft components in a disused section of the London Underground.
Many such tunnels were pressed into service for the war industry.

myself almost completely proof against fear and jumpiness ... am the most fearless among my own circle of friends. ...

As this woman's testimony demonstrates, bombings could often be an exhilarating experience when citizens realized they had reserves of courage of which they had never been aware. There was a sense of excitement associated with the air raids in that they gave civilians a sense of life on the "front line," as part of the action. They were no longer idle observers, helplessly hearing about the war from the safety of their homes. Their daily struggles, and their determination to cope with them, became essential to the success of the war effort. Here a young woman described a narrow escape she had during a bombing in Hampstead:

"Are you all right?" ... people kept asking; and it was only then—silly though it sounds—that it occurred to me that I might have been hurt! That I had been in actual danger, really! Somehow, right up to that minute I had taken everything for granted, in a queer, brainless

way, as if it was all perfectly ordinary. I never even thought about injury or death, for any of us. ...

I lay there feeling indescribably happy and triumphant. "I've been bombed!" I kept on saying to myself, over and over again—trying the phrase on, like a new dress, to see how it fitted. "I've been bombed!" ... "I've been bombed—me!"

It seems a terrible thing to say, when many people were killed and injured last night; but never in my whole life have I ever experienced such pure and flawless happiness.

Richard Titmuss, a historian and advisor to the Ministry of Economic Warfare at the time, attempted to explain this exhilaration:

What this period of the war meant to a great many people was less social disparagement. There was nothing to be ashamed of in being "bombed out" by the enemy. Public sympathy with, and approval of, families who suffered in the raids was in sharp contrast to the low social evaluation accorded to those who lost in material standards through being unemployed during the nineteen-thirties. The civilian war of 1939–45, with its many opportunities for service in civil defence and other schemes, also helped to satisfy an often inarticulate need; the need to be a wanted member of society. Circumstances were thus favourable to fuller self-expression, for there was plenty of scope for relieving a sense of inferiority and failure.

The war effort gave civilians a sense of purpose in other ways as well, and allowed them to lead lives very different from those they would have led in peacetime. Many women who would have moved directly from their parents's homes to those of their husbands left the house to find work in munitions factories or as nurses or civil servants. Whether driven by loneliness while their husbands were away, by economic need, or by patriotism, many of these women reveled in their new-found independence. For many women, this was the first time that they had had money of their own—even if they were generally receiving just over half of the remuneration made to men for the same work.

One other result of the war, however, was that teenaged girls tended not to be very strictly supervised—particularly if their fathers were at war and their mothers were working—and there was widespread concern that morals were becoming looser. A particular concern was the rise in teenaged prostitution. A patrolling officer of the Public Morality Council expressed anxiety concerning the moral climate:

I must again refer to the very large proportion of girls of about 16 to 18 years of age, always looking for a good time at somebody else's expense. These girls, a large number of whom travel from the East End and usually in couples, throng the amusement and sports arcades, often undoubtedly for the warmth and light offered, but principally to get off with the American troops who seem to use these places for a like purpose. There is no solicitation, but they easily get into conversation whilst playing with the various machines, and then they are on a very slippery slope, which in many instances ends in disaster.

Just before D-Day (6 June 1944, when the Allies invaded Normandy) there were nearly one and a half million troops in Britain, with many of them (particularly the Americans) staying in London. These soldiers were often looking to have a good time, particularly in the face of the uncertainties awaiting them in battle. They could be very persuasive with young women, and for many British

British women jitterbug with American GIs at the American Red Cross Club, 1945.

women, Americans held a particular appeal, as one Briton explained:

To girls brought up on the cinema, who copied the dress, hair styles and manners of Hollywood stars, the sudden influx of Americans, speaking like the films, who actually lived in the magic country, and who had plenty of money, at once went to the girls' heads. The American attitude to women, their proneness to spoil a girl, to build up, exaggerate, talk big, and to act with generosity and flamboyance, helped to make them the most attractive boy friends. In addition, they "picked up" easily, and even a comparatively plain and unattractive girl stood a chance.

During the war the incidence of venereal disease skyrocketed, prompting the Ministry of Health to launch a campaign to educate the public on this topic (which had rarely been publicly discussed). Efforts to stop the spread of disease were hampered by a shortage of contraceptives until the Chief Medical Officer gave the relevant companies the necessary rubber allocation. While many soldiers engaged in illicit sexual activity on the front, their wives were often up to the same thing at home. Illicit sexual activity was certainly on the rise, but so too was the marriage rate. (After the war the divorce rates would also climb.) A large number of British women married soldiers from the colonies or dominions. They also married American Gis, after having known them for only a few days. After the war, these young brides were frequently met with hostility when they attempted to get the visas necessary to emigrate, and they faced further challenges when they arrived in a foreign country to live with men they hardly knew.

These GI brides received a great deal of publicity, but the even greater number of war widows in England received very little attention or support. One woman recalled the utter hopelessness of her situation after the death of her husband:

As a young war widow, I was among the ranks of the "walking wounded." Almost ignored, as if one had a dread disease that no one wanted to know about. War widows were disregarded. You couldn't get accommodation easily. War Widows' Pensions were treated as "unearned income" for tax purposes and, therefore, taxed at the highest rate possible. How about that for losing my husband, three brothers, my home and a baby?

In general, when the war was over, England's citizens were emotionally and physically exhausted. Dr. Anthony Weymouth noted that, while most women were able to face the stresses and hardships of war with bravery, the prospect of such trials continuing for a length of time after the war made them despair:

Most people are agreed that women have had an extremely hard time in this war. Have I not seen dozens of women patients in the last two years who have told me that they are mentally and physically exhausted by the cooking, cleaning, and queuing? Only the other day one explained to me that she was able to carry on her life while the war was on only because she believed that it was "for the duration." Now, she added, she can see no end to her life of hardship and the hope which buoyed her up during the war years has left her.

In addition, for those couples who were reunited at the war's end, many challenges awaited. Many articles were written to women on how to best greet their husbands when they returned and how to help them adjust to life at home after their experiences on the front. Women had their own adjustments to make, however, particularly after they had become accustomed to living independently. In an October 1945 article from the *Daily Mirror* entitled "Advice to the Nervous Returning Serviceman from the Wife of One of Them," the author attempted to alert husbands to the difficulties their wives were facing:

So, servicemen, you're coming home. You and 320,000 like you are being demobbed this month, and the next and the next. Many of you married ones may be feeling rather scared about the homecoming, because you know it isn't going to be so easy to pick up the threads of married life again. Many people have taken it upon themselves to tell your wives how to welcome you. I think it's about time someone gave you a word of advice.

Be glad to be back. Say so as often as you can. You simply cannot overdo this, however much you repeat yourself.

Be prepared for civilian restrictions. Many of you will have little idea of what has been going on in English homes. So don't expect too liberal a welcome—in material things at any rate. If your wife greets you in a new dress, be surprised and delighted, and, if she produces a home-made cake or a roast dinner, ask her how on earth she managed to do it. Do the shopping for her one morning, too, and decide for yourself whether a piece of fish for supper is worth all the queuing.

Be appreciative. Life has just dragged on, becoming harder and more lonely with each successive month. So tell her she's wonderful, that you're proud of her, and all the rest of it.

Take over some of the family responsibility. Don't forget that for a long time she's been mother and father in the home, and maybe part breadwinner too. She may have been tied to the home and the children day and night for years, perhaps without a chance of an occasional evening out. Take over your fatherhood at once and help a little with the mothering too. See that young Tommy toes the line and doesn't play his mother up too much.

Be prepared for changes in her. I don't mean in her looks. In fact you should be prepared not to notice any war-weary lines in her face or her clothes. But you should expect to find a more independent woman, who has matured in the hard school of war.

Be affectionate. She'll be shy, the same as you. Don't rush her off her feet, or try to woo her too ardently at first. Don't forget that however much she's changed, however self-sufficient she may seem, she's darn glad to have you back.

Anti-Semitism and World War II

In hindsight, the Holocaust—the systematic murder by the Nazi regime of over 6,000,000 human beings, the vast majority of them Jewish—is for many the central event of the war; this was the horror that other nations were fighting to overthrow. At the time, however, the persecution of Jewish people was for most people of much less central importance.

It was widely known by the mid-1930s that German Jews were subject to severe and escalating levels of oppression, but the decision to attempt the systematic murder of all Jewish people was not taken until some time in 1941; the outbreak of war in 1939 had been sparked primarily by Hitler's taking over the territory of other nations. By the end of 1942, enough evidence of the Holocaust had emerged to make it clear that mass murder was occurring, and the Allies issued a widely-publicized condemnation of "this bestial policy" in December of that year. That, however, was the only such declaration made prior to 1944, and the Allies did not back up their words with concrete action; they did not bomb the gas chambers or the train tracks leading to them (even when they were already bombing nearby factories); they did not lift restrictions on Jewish immigration.

To be sure, details of the operation of the camps and of the gas chambers were not available until the spring of 1944, and the full import of the Nazi atrocities did not begin to sink fully into the consciousness of the world until photographic depictions of the liberation of the camps and of the condition of the survivors were published early in 1945. (To some extent it may be said that the full impact did not sink home even until years after that.) Yet it would be difficult to argue that the lack of information was all that prevented the Allies from making a stronger response to the horror of the Holocaust. The inescapable fact is that, even towards the end of World War II, many in Britain, the United States, Canada, Australia and elsewhere who were not otherwise Nazi sympathizers shared with many Germans, Italians, and Poles a strong anti-Semitic prejudice. The case of Ezra Pound is one of the best-known and most extreme cases—the pioneering poet of Modernism had always displayed an anti-Semitic streak, and during the war the streak widened. He moved to Italy and began broadcasting hate propaganda on behalf of the fascist government. (Below is an excerpt from one of Pound's speeches.)

> There can be no doubt that most Britons and North Americans in the 1940s were repelled by the help that Pound was giving to the Axis cause. But nor can there be any doubt that a remarkably high level of anti-Semitism remained prevalent throughout these years. The excerpt reprinted below from a 1945 essay by George Orwell is a striking reminder of the extent to which ordinary citizens remained in the habit of "blaming the victim." But, as the selection from Bernard Shaw's essay below illustrates, there were also those who were clear from the outset as to the particular sort of evil that Hitler represented.

from Ezra Pound, "Speech to the English" (Broadcast on Radio Rome, 15 March 1942)

… Your enemy is not Germany, your enemy is money on loan. And it would be better for you to be infected with typhus, and dysentery, and Bright's disease,[1] than to be infected with this blindness which prevents you from understanding HOW you are undermined, how you are ruined.

The big Jew is so bound up with this Leihkapital[2] that no one is able to unscramble that omelet. It would be better for you to retire to Derbyshire and defy New Jerusalem, better for you to retire to Gloucester and find one spot that is England than to go on fighting for Jewry and ignoring the process.

It is an outrage that any clean lad from the country—I suppose there are STILL a few ENGLISH lads from the country—it is an outrage that any nice young man from the suburbs should be expected to die for Victor Sassoon, it is an outrage that any drunken footman's byblow[3] should be asked to die for Sassoon.

As to your Empire, it was not all of it won by clean fighting. But however you got it, you did for a time more or less justify keeping it, on the ground that you exported good government or better government than the natives would have had without England.

You let in the Jew and the Jew rotted your Empire. … And the big Jew has rotted EVERY nation he has wormed into. A millstone. Well, an exceptionally good swimmer MIGHT conceivably be cast into the sea with a stone tied round his neck. He might perhaps untie it. …

WHAT is their system? Unvarying, cheap goods, sweated out of cheap labor, dung dust hurled on the world, the WORLD conceived as sweat shop, to hell with the eight-hour day, down with abundance. DUMPING sweated goods, dumped against any and every nation that pays a just price for labor. That is your ALLY. …

Is there a RACE left in England? Has it ANY will left to survive? You can carry slaughter to Ireland. Will that save you? I doubt it. Nothing can save you, save a purge. Nothing can save you, save an affirmation that you are English. …

In the year 1942 Anno Domini, there is only one start you can make. And that is a start toward being England. A refusal to be a province of Israel, or an outpost of Yankee-Judaea.

---

[1] *Bright's disease* Generic term for kidney disease.
[2] *Leihkapital* Pound's term for what he calls "Loan Capital."
[3] *byblow* I.e., illegitimate child.

from George Orwell, "Anti-Semitism in Britain"
(1945)

... It is generally admitted that anti-Semitism is on the
increase, that it has been greatly exacerbated by the war,
and that humane and enlightened people are not
immune to it.... Here are some samples of anti-Semitic
remarks that have been made to me during the past year
or two:

> Middle-aged office employee: "I generally come to
> work by bus. It takes longer, but I don't care about
> using the Underground from Golders Green[1]
> nowadays. There's too many of the Chosen Race
> travelling on that line."

> Young intellectual, Communist or near-Commu-
> nist: "No, I do *not* like Jews. I've never made any
> secret of that. I can't stick them. Mind you, I'm not
> anti-Semitic, of course."

> Middle-class woman: "Well, no one could call me
> anti-Semitic, but I do think the way these Jews
> behave is too absolutely stinking. The way they
> push their way to the head of queues, and so on.
> They're so abominably selfish. I think they're
> responsible for a lot of what happens to them."

> Milk roundsman: "A Jew don't do no work, not
> the same as what an Englishman does. 'E's too
> clever. We work with this 'ere" (flexes his biceps).
> "They work with that there" (taps his forehead).

> Chartered accountant, intelligent, left-wing in an
> undirected way: "These bloody Yids are all pro-
> German. They'd change sides tomorrow if the
> Nazis got here. I see a lot of them in my business.
> They admire Hitler at the bottom of their hearts.
> They'll always suck up to anyone who kicks them."

> Intelligent woman, on being offered a book dealing
> with anti-Semitism and German atrocities: "Don't
> show it me, *please* don't show it to me. It'll only
> make me hate the Jews more than ever."

I could fill pages with similar remarks, but these will do
to go on with. Two facts emerge from them. One—
which is very important and which I must return to in
a moment—is that above a certain intellectual level
people are ashamed of being anti-Semitic and are careful
to draw a distinction between "anti-Semitism" and
"disliking Jews." The other is that anti-Semitism is an
irrational thing. The Jews are accused of specific offences (for instance, bad behaviour in food queues)
which the person speaking feels strongly about, but it is
obvious that these accusations merely rationalize some
deep-rooted prejudice. To attempt to counter them with
facts and statistics is useless, and may sometimes be
worse than useless. As the last of the above-quoted
remarks shows, people can remain anti-Semitic, or at
least anti-Jewish, while being fully aware that their
outlook is indefensible. If you dislike somebody, you
dislike him and there is an end of it: your feelings are
not made any better by a recital of his virtues.

It so happens that the war has encouraged the
growth of anti-Semitism and even, in the eyes of many
ordinary people, given some justification for it. To
begin with, the Jews are one people of whom it can be
said with complete certainty that they will benefit by an
Allied victory. Consequently the theory that "this is a
Jewish war" has a certain plausibility, all the more so
because the Jewish war effort seldom gets its fair share of
recognition. The British Empire is a huge heterogeneous
organization held together largely by mutual consent,
and it is often necessary to flatter the less reliable elements at the expense of the more loyal ones. To publi-
cize the exploits of Jewish soldiers, or even to admit the
existence of a considerable Jewish army in the Middle
East, rouses hostility in South Africa, the Arab countries
and elsewhere: it is easier to ignore the whole subject
and allow the man in the street to go on thinking that
Jews are exceptionally clever at dodging military service....

There has been a perceptible anti-Semitic strain in
English literature from Chaucer onwards, and without
even getting up from this table to consult a book I can
think of passages which if written now would be stigma-
tized as anti-Semitism, in the works of Shakespeare,

---

[1] *Golders Green*   Suburban area in northeast London that has been
the site of a thriving Jewish community since the early 1900s.

Floodlights illuminate London on VE Day (8 March 1945),
lighting London for the first time in years.

Smollett, Thackeray,[1] Bernard Shaw, H. G. Wells, T. S.
Eliot, Aldous Huxley, and various others. Offhand, the
only English writers I can think of who, before the days
of Hitler, made a definite effort to stick up for Jews are
Dickens and Charles Reade.[2] And however little the
average intellectual may have agreed with the opinions
of Belloc and Chesterton,[3] he did not acutely disapprove
of them. Chesterton's endless tirades against Jews, which
he thrust into stories and essays upon the flimsiest
pretexts, never got him into trouble—indeed Chesterton
was one of the most generally respected figures in
English literary life. Anyone who wrote in that strain
now would bring down a storm of abuse upon himself,
or more probably would find it impossible to get his
writings published. ....

[1] *Smollett, Thackeray* Novelists Tobias Smollett (1721–71) and
William Makepeace Thackeray (1811–63).

[2] *Charles Reade* Novelist and playwright (1814–84).

[3] *Belloc* Hilaire Belloc (1870–1953), poet and author who was a
devout Roman Catholic, and whose book *The Jews* (1922) argues
that Jewish people cannot successfully be assimilated into Christian
society; *Chesterton* Novelist and journalist G.K. Chesterton (1874-
1936), who was known for his anti-Semitism and whose views were,
in the late twentieth century, closely associated with those of Belloc.
(Bernard Shaw referred to them as "the Chesterbelloc.")

from Rebecca West, "Greenhouse with Cyclamens" (1946)

Writer and journalist Rebecca West and her husband, Henry Andrews, provided shelter for wartime
refugees, particularly Jewish people and former
residents of Yugoslavia (where West had traveled
extensively before the war in order to report on the
threat Germany posed to that nation). Immediately
after the war, West wrote extensively on the psychology of espionage and treason, and gained a
reputation as a reporter on the Nuremberg Trials,
the topic of the article excerpted here. These trials
lasted from 1945 until 1949.

The Bavarian city of Nuremberg was made a
national shrine by the Nazis when Hitler came to
power. It was the center of anti-Semitic propaganda
throughout the war, and in 1935 it was the site of
the party congress that set out the so-called Nuremberg Laws, which stripped German Jews of their
civic rights. Nearly half of all airplanes, tanks, and
submarines produced during the war were made in
Nuremberg. After the war, Nuremberg's Palace of
Justice was the site of the international tribunal for
war crimes.

In the excerpt below, West notes the very ordinary appearance of the defendants—a fact that surprised many spectators of the trials. Of the 21 defendants, West mentions below Hermann Göring, commander of the Luftwaffe and several SS departments, who was sentenced to death (but committed suicide the night before his execution); Hjalmar Schacht, the pre-war president of the Reichsbank, who was acquitted; Albert Speer, Reichsminister of Armaments and Munitions and friend of Hitler's, who expressed repentance and was sentenced to twenty years in prison; and Rudolf Hess, Nazi Party leader, who was sentenced to life in prison.

… It seemed ridiculous for the defendants to make any effort to stave off the end, for they admitted by their appearance that nothing was to go well with them again on this earth. These Nazi leaders, self-dedicated to the breaking of all rules, broke last of all the rule that the verdict of a court must not be foretold. Their appearance announced what they believed. The Russians had asked for the death penalty for all of them, and it was plain that the defendants thought that wish would be granted. Believing that they were to lose everything, they forgot what possession had been. Not the slightest trace of their power and their glory remained; none of them looked as if he could ever have exercised any valid authority. Göring still used imperial gestures, but they were so vulgar that they did not suggest that he had really filled any great position; it merely seemed probable that in certain bars the frequenters had called him by some such nick-name as "The Emperor." These people were also surrendering physical characteristics which might have been thought inalienable during life, such as the colour and texture of their skins and the moulding of their features. Most of them, except Schacht, who was white-haired, and Speer, who was black like a monkey, were neither dark nor fair any more; and there was amongst them no leanness that did not sag and no plumpness that seemed more than inflation by some thin gas. So diminished were their personalities that it was hard to keep in mind which was which, even after one had sat and looked at them for days; and those who stood out defined themselves by oddity rather than character.

Hess was noticeable because he was so plainly mad: so plainly mad that it seemed shameful that he should be tried. His skin was ashen, and he had that odd faculty, peculiar to lunatics, of falling into strained positions which no normal person could maintain for more than a few minutes, and staying fixed in contortion for hours. He had the classless air characteristic of asylum inmates; evidently his distracted personality had torn up all clue to his past. He looked as if his mind had no surface, as if every part of it had been blasted away except the depth where the nightmares live. …

As these men gave up the effort to be themselves, they joined to make a common pattern which simply reiterated the plea of not guilty. All the time they made quite unidiosyncratic gestures expressive of innocence and outraged common sense, and in the intervals they stood up and chatted among themselves, forming little protesting groups, each one of which, painted as a mural, would be instantly recognized as a holy band that had tried to save the world but had been frustrated by mistaken men. But this performance they rendered more weakly every day. They were visibly receding from the field of existence and were, perhaps, no longer conscious of the recession. It is possible that they never thought directly of death or even of imprisonment, and there was nothing positive in them at all except their desire to hold time still. They were all praying with their sharp-set nerves: "Let this trial never finish, let it go on for ever and ever, without end." The nerves of all others present in the Palace of Justice were sending out a counter-prayer: the eight judges on the bench, who were plainly dragging the proceedings over the threshold of their consciousness by sheer force of will; the lawyers and the secretaries who sat sagged in their seats at the tables in the well of the court; the interpreters twittering unhappily in their glass box like cage-birds kept awake by a bright light, feeding the microphones with French and Russian and English versions of the proceedings for the spectators' earphones; the guards who stood with their arms gripping their white truncheons behind their backs, all still and hard as metal save their childish faces, which were puffy with boredom. All these people wanted to leave Nuremberg as urgently as a dental patient enduring the drill wants to up and leave the chair. …

So the Germans listened to the closing speeches made by Mr. Justice Jackson and Sir Hartley Shawcross, and were openly ashamed by their new-minted indignation. When Mr. Justice Jackson brought his speech to an end by pointing a forefinger at each of the defendants in turn and denouncing his specific share in the Nazi crime, all of them winced.... The speech showed the civilized good sense against which they had conspired, and it was patently admirable, patently a pattern of the material necessary to the salvation of peoples. ...

[Sir Hartley Shawcross's] speech was not so shapely and so decorative as Mr. Justice Jackson's, for English rhetoric has crossed the Atlantic in this century and is now more at home in the United States than on its native ground, and he spoke at greater length and stopped more legal holes. But his words were full of a living pity, which gave the men in the box their worst hour.... And when Sir Hartley quoted the deposition of a witness who had described a Jewish father who, standing with his little son in front of a firing squad, "pointed to the sky, stroked his head, and seemed to explain something to the boy," all the defendants wriggled on their seats, like children rated by a schoolmaster, while their faces grew old.

There was a mystery there: that [they] should have committed such a huge, cold crime. But it was a mystery that girt all Nuremberg. It was most clearly defined in a sentence spoken by the custodian of the room in the Palace of Justice that housed all the exhibits relating to atrocities. Certain of these were unconvincing; some, though not all, of the photographs purporting to show people being shot and tortured had a posed and theatrical air. This need not have indicated conscious fraud. It might well have been that these photographs represented attempts to reconstruct incidents which had really occurred, made at the instigation of officials as explanatory glosses to evidence provided by eye-witnesses, and that they had found their way into the record by error. But there was much stuff that was authentic. Somebody had been collecting tattooed human skin, and it is hard to think where such a connoisseur could find his pieces unless he had power over a concentration camp. Some of these pelts were infinitely pathetic, because of their obscenity. Through the years came the memory of the inconveniently high-pitched voice of an English child among a crowd of tourists watching a tournament of water-jousting in a French port: "Mummy, come and look, there's a sailor who's got no shirt on, and he has the funniest picture on his back—there's a lady with no clothes on upside down on a St. Andrew's Cross, and there's a snake crawling all over her and somebody with a whip." There had been men who had thought they could make a pet of cruelty, and the grown beast had flayed them.

But it was astonishing that there had been so much sadism. The French doctor in charge of these exhibits pondered, turning in his hand a lampshade made of tattooed human skin. "These people where I live send me in my breakfast tray strewn with pansies, beautiful pansies. I have never seen more beautiful pansies, arranged with exquisite taste. I have to remind myself that they belong to the same race that supplied me with my exhibits, the same race that tortured me month after month, year after year, at Mauthausen."[1] And, indeed, flowers were the visible sign of that mystery, flowers that were not only lovely but beloved. In the windowboxes of the high-gabled houses the pink and purple petunias were bright like lamps. In the gardens of the cottages bordering a road which was no longer there, which was a tom trench, the phloxes shone white and clear pink and mauve, as under harsh heat they will not do, unless they are well watered. It is tedious work, training clematis over low posts, so that its beauty does not stravaig[2] up the walls but lies open under the eye; but on the edge of the town many gardeners grew it thus. The countryside beyond continued this protestation of innocence. A path might mount the hillside, through the lacework of light and shadow the pine trees cast over the soft reddish bed of the pine needles, to the upland farm where the wedding party poured out of the door, riotous with honest laughter, but freezing before a camera into honest solemnity; it might fall to the valley and follow the trout stream, where the dragonflies drew iridescent patterns just above the cloudy green water, to the edge of the millpond, where the miller's flax-haired little son played with the grey kittens among the meadow-sweet; it would not lead to any place where it seemed other than plain that Germany was a beautiful country, inhabited by a people who loved all pleasant things and meant no harm.

[1]   *Mauthausen*   Concentration camp near Linz, Austria.

[2]   *stravaig*   Wander aimlessly.

from George Bernard Shaw, "The Unavoidable Subject" (1948)

Shaw wrote the following essay for a B.B.C. broadcast in early June, 1940. He is forthright in his call to resist Hitler and the Nazis, and far more steadfast than were most British people in 1940 in his opposition to Nazi racism and anti-Semitism. But he does not shy away from sardonic references to atrocities committed by Stalin (then Britain's ally), or from likening capitalist bosses to dictators, and the B.B.C. was not pleased. The broadcast was cancelled by the Ministry of Information and Shaw was banned from broadcasting on the B.B.C. But on June 10 of that year, when Italy entered the war, Shaw felt his concerns became obsolete, as the war was suddenly transformed "from a scrap between the Reich and the Allies to the European scale."

The other day a young man from Scotland told me that he was going to be a conscientious objector. I asked him why. He replied, "Because this is a silly war." I quite agreed with him. All wars are silly wars nowadays between civilized peoples. I pointed out, however, that this will not stop the onset of Mr. Hitler's tanks, nor turn his bombs into picnic baskets. I took it that my conscientious friend did not desire a triumphant victory for us. Not he; he thought that such a victory would go to our heads and we should abuse it. But did he desire a triumphant victory for Mr. Hitler? Certainly not; for that would be still worse, because the English would only come into the streets and maffick[1] for a fortnight and then forget all about it; but the Germans would make a philosophy of it and try to follow it up by a conquest of Europe. We agreed that our business is to reduce Mr. Hitler and his philosophy to absurdity. So I asked, is there any other way of doing this now except putting up such a devil of a fight that Germany will at last say to Mr. Hitler, What hast thou done with my legions? and turn on him as the French turned on Napoleon.

The young Caledonian was open to reason. He immediately borrowed £2 from me, and joined up. If he had been an Englishman he would have quoted the Scriptures to me or said he did not hold with Churchill and that lot. I should not have argued with him. I should have taken a hint from my friend Priestley[2] and just reminded him that the Germans have sunk the Gracie Fields. That would have sent him to the front like a thunderbolt. I have not forgotten the sinking of the Lusitania.[3] ...

When Mr. Hitler reconquered Poland, and had half his conquest immediately taken from him by Russia, there was peace for the moment, because Europe was terrified by his victory. The nations trembled and said, What will he do now? Who will be the next victim? Which of us dare bell this wild cat?[4] Thereupon we, the British Commonwealth, on our own single responsibility deliberately punched Mr. Hitler on the nose and told him in the plainest terms that his notions of humanity are not compatible with ours, and that we are going to abolish his rule by shot and shell, bayonet and blockade; and what had he to say to that? What could he do but take off his coat and come on? As to what he had to say he was explicit enough. He assured us that our view of the Hitleristic German Reich was exactly his view of the Imperialist British Empire; and that though *he* would be fighting with a rope round his neck, he would give us ten shots and shells for our one, and sink, burn, and destroy until he had done unto us what he had already done to Poland. And so we are at it hammer and tongs; and as it was we who asked for it, it is up to us to make good. I have no patience with the journalists and the tub thumpers[5] who are breaking our spirits by snivelling about our being the victims of a foul and treacherous

---

[1]   *maffick*   Rejoice uproariously.

[2]   *Priestley*   Celebrated writer J.B. Priestley (1894–1984), who served in World War I and whose series *Postscripts* (which often compared World War II to the previous war), broadcast weekly on the B.B.C. between June and October 1940, became an international institution.

[3]   *Lusitania*   British passenger ship that was sunk by a German submarine off the coast of Ireland on 17 May 1915. Of the 1,150 passengers on board who lost their lives, 128 were American, and the event marked a turn in the Americans' attitude towards Germany. When the United States entered World War I two years later, many recruitment poster urged young men to "Remember the Lusitania!"

[4]   *bell this wild cat*   I.e., undertake this hazardous feat, or agree to be the ringleader in this dangerous operation (literally, the expression refers to the act of hanging a bell around a cat's neck).

[5]   *tub thumpers*   Preachers or speakers who thump the pulpit for emphasis; declamatory orators.

aggression. We are the challengers and the champion fighters for humanity.

The British people, the real British people, feel this instinctively. But they are puzzled by the intellectuals and the politicians and journalists. They want to know exactly why we hit Mr. Hitler on the nose, when he had his hands in his pockets—and in some of his neighbours' pockets as well. And they are told officially what fine fellows we are, and that we are sure to win because God is on our side, and that a trumpery scrap in which three British warships drove one German one[1] into the River Plate was a greater victory than Jutland or Trafalgar or Lepanto.[2] That is not good enough. God has rebuked it in Belgium promptly and sharply. The people still ask, What exactly is the Big Idea that we must risk our lives for? …

Let us come down to brass tacks. What am I, a superannuated non-combatant, encouraging young men to fight against? It is not German national socialism: I was a National Socialist before Mr. Hitler was born. I hope we shall emulate and surpass his great achievement in that direction. I have no prejudices against him personally; much that he has written and spoken echoes what I myself have written and spoken. He has adopted even my diet. I am interested in him as one of the curiosities of political history; and I fully appreciate his physical and moral courage, his diplomatic sagacity, and his triumphant rescue of his country from the yoke the Allies imposed on it in 1918. I am quite aware of the fact that his mind is a twentieth-century mind, and that our governing class is mentally in the reign of Edward the Third, six centuries out of date. In short, I can pay him a dozen compliments which I could not honestly pay to any of our present rulers.

My quarrel with him is a very plain one. I happen to be what he calls a Nordic. In stature, in colour, in length of head, I am the perfect blond beast whom Mr. Hitler classes as the salt of the earth, divinely destined to rule over all lesser breeds. Trace me back as far as you can; and you will not find a Jew in my ancestry. Well, I have a friend who is a Jew. His name is Albert Einstein; and he is a far greater human prodigy than Mr. Hitler and myself rolled into one. The nobility of his character has made his genius an unmixed benefit to his fellow creatures. Yet Adolf Hitler would compel me, the Nordic Bernard Shaw, to insult Albert Einstein; to claim moral superiority to him and unlimited power over him; to rob him, drive him out of his house, exile him, be punished if I allow a relative of mine to marry a relative of his; and finally to kill him as part of a general duty to exterminate his race. Adolf has actually done these things to Albert, bar the killing, as he carelessly exiled him first and thus made the killing impossible. Since then he has extended the list of reprobates from Semites to Celts and from Poles to Slavs; in short, to all who are not what he calls Nordics and Nazis. If he conquers these islands he will certainly add my countrymen, the Irish, to the list, as several authorities have maintained that the Irish are the lost tribes of Israel.

Now, this is not the sort of thing that sane men can afford to argue with. It is on the face of it pernicious nonsense; and the moment any ruler starts imposing it on his nation or any other nation by physical force there is nothing for it but for the sane men to muster their own physical forces and go for him. We ought to have declared war on Germany the moment Mr. Hitler's police stole Einstein's violin. When the work of a police force consists not of *suppressing* robbery with violence but actually *committing* it, that force becomes a recruiting ground for the most infernal blackguards,[3] of whom every country has its natural-born share. Unless such agents are disciplined and controlled, their heads are turned by the authority they possess as a State police; and they resort to physical torture as the easiest way to do their work and amuse themselves at the same time. How is that discipline and control to be maintained? Not by an autocrat, because, as Napoleon said when he heard about Nelson and Trafalgar, an autocrat cannot be everywhere. When his police get out of hand and give his prisons and concentration camps a bad name, he has

---

[1] *one German one* The Graf Spee, a German battleship that sunk many British cargo ships on the Atlantic in the beginning of World War II, until it was taken down by three British cruisers in December 1939.

[2] *Jutland or Trafalgar or Lepanto* Shaw mentions three famous naval battles: the Battle of Jutland was the only engagement of the British and German fleets during World War I; in the Battle of Trafalgar the British navy, led by Horatio Nelson, won a victory over the French and Spanish fleets (21 October 1805); the Battle of Lepanto (7 October 1571) was the first major defeat of the Ottomans by the Christian powers.

[3] *blackguards* Scoundrels.

to back them up because he cannot do without them, and thus he becomes their slave instead of their master.

And this reminds me that we must stop talking nonsense about dictators. Practically the whole business of a modern civilized country is run by dictators and people who obey their orders. We call them bosses; but their powers are greater than those of any political dictator. To prevent them abusing those powers we have Factory Acts which have made short work of our employers' liberty to sacrifice the nation's interests to their own. It is true that we cannot get on without dictators in every street; but we can impose on them a discipline and a code of social obligations that remind them continually that their authority is given to them for the benefit of the commonwealth and not for their private gain. Well, one of our aims in this war is to impose a stiff international Factory Act on Mr. Hitler, one that will deal not with wages and hours of labour, but with the nature of the work done, for peace or war.

When I say that we must stop talking nonsense about the war what I mean is that we must be careful not to go on throwing words about that we do not understand. Could anything be more ridiculous than people who were terrified the other day when Sir William Beveridge[1] very properly used the word "Socialist" to describe our war organization? They flooded the B.B.C. with letters asking whether all their property was going to be taken away from them. Whilst they were writing, the Government in two hours and twenty minutes placed the country under the most absolute Military Communism. Everything we possess—our properties, our liberties, our lives—now belong to our country and not to ourselves. To say a word against Socialism or Communism is now treason. Without them we should soon have no property or liberty at all,

and would be lucky if we were alive. Therefore I beg you, if you must talk, to confine yourself to what the lawyers call vulgar abuse, which will relieve your feelings and hurt nobody. I hope you are too much of a gentleman (or a lady) to call the Germans swine; but if you want to blow off steam by calling Mr. Hitler a blood-stained monster do so by all means: it won't hurt him, nor need you worry if it does. But be careful; if you call Stalin a bloodstained monster you must be shot as the most dangerous of Fifth Columnists;[2] for the friendship of Russia is vitally important to us just now. Russia and America may soon have the fate of the world in their hands; that is why I am always so civil to Russia.

Remember that the really dangerous Fifth Column consists of the people who believe that Fascism is a better system of government than ours, and that what we call our democracy is a sham. They are not altogether wrong; but the remedy is for us to adopt all the good points of Fascism or Communism or any other Ism, not to allow Mr. Hitler and his Chosen Race to impose it on us by his demoralized police. We are fighting him, not for his virtues, but for his persecutions and dominations, which have no logical connection whatever with Fascism and which I hope we will not put up with from Mr. Hitler or anyone else. He is as sure that God is on his side as Lord Halifax[3] is that God is on ours. If so, then we shall have to fight God as well as Mr. Hitler. But as most of us believe that God made both Mr. Hitler and Lord Halifax, we must reasonably believe that God will see fair. And the rest is up to us.

---

[1] *Sir William Beveridge* Economist and social reformer (1879–1963).

[2] *Fifth Columnists* The term originated in the Spanish Civil War, when a fascist general led four columns of troops in an attack against Madrid, and later claimed he was helped by a "fifth column" of secret supporters inside the city.

[3] *Lord Halifax* British statesman who served as Foreign Secretary (1938–40) and as Ambassador to the United States (1941–46).

Reading Poetry

WHAT IS A POEM?

Most of us know what a poem is when we see one. Still, even poets find it difficult to define a poem, or poetry. In a lecture on "The Name and Nature of Poetry" (1933), the English poet A.E. Housman stated that he could "no more define poetry than a terrier can define a rat"; however, he added, "we both recognize the object by the symptoms which it provokes in us." Housman knew he was in the presence of poetry if he experienced a shiver down the spine, or "a constriction of the throat and a precipitation of water to the eyes." Implicit in Housman's response is a recognition that we have to go beyond mere formal characteristics—stanzas, rhymes, rhythms—if we want to know what poetry is, or why it differs from prose. Poetry both represents and *creates* emotions in a highly condensed way. Therefore, any definition of the genre needs to consider, as much as possible, the impact of poetry on us as readers or listeners.

Worth consideration too is the role of the listener or reader not only as passive recipient of a poem, but also as an active participant in its performance. Poetry is among other things the locus for a communicative exchange. A section below deals with the sub-genre of performance poetry, but in a very real sense all poetry is subject to performance. Poems are to be read aloud as well as on the page, and both in sensing meaning and in expressing sound the reader plays a vital role in bringing a poem to life, no matter how long dead its author may be; as W.H. Auden wrote memorably of his fellow poet W.B. Yeats, "the words of a dead man / Are modified in the guts of the living."

For some readers, poetry is, in William Wordsworth's phrase, "the breath and finer spirit of all knowledge" ("Preface" to the *Lyrical Ballads*). They look to poetry for insights into the nature of human experience, and expect elevated thought in carefully-wrought language. In contrast, other readers distrust poetry that seems moralistic or didactic. "We hate poetry that has a palpable design upon us," wrote John Keats to his friend J.H. Reynolds; rather, poetry should be "great & unobtrusive, a thing which enters into one's soul, and does not startle it or amaze it with itself but with its subject." The American poet Archibald MacLeish took Keats's idea a step further: in his poem "Ars Poetica" he suggested that "A poem should not mean / But be." MacLeish was not suggesting that a poem should lack meaning, but rather that meaning should inhere in the poem's expressive and sensuous qualities, not in some explicit statement or versified idea.

Whatever we look for in a poem, the infinitude of forms, styles, and subjects that make up the body of literature we call "poetry" is, in the end, impossible to capture in a definition that would satisfy all readers. All we can do, perhaps, is to agree that a poem is a discourse that is characterized by a heightened attention to language, form, and rhythm, by an expressiveness that works through figurative rather than literal modes, and by a capacity to stimulate our imagination and arouse our feelings.

THE LANGUAGE OF POETRY

To speak of "the language of poetry" implies that poets make use of a vocabulary that is somehow different from the language of everyday life. In fact, all language has the capacity to be "poetic," if by poetry we understand a use of language to which some special importance is attached. The ritualistic utterances of religious ceremonies sometimes have this force; so do the skipping rhymes of children in the schoolyard. We can distinguish such uses of language from the kind of writing we find in, say, a computer user's manual: the author of the manual can describe a given function in a variety of ways, whereas the magic of the skipping rhyme can be invoked only by getting the right words in the right order. So with the poet: he or she chooses particular words in a particular order; the *way* the poet speaks is as important to our understanding as what is said. This doesn't mean that an instruction manual couldn't have poetic qualities—indeed, modern poets have created "found" poems from even less likely materials—but it does mean that in poetry there is an intimate relation amongst language, form, and meaning, and that the writer deliberately structures and manipulates language to achieve very particular ends.

THE BEST WORDS IN THE BEST ORDER

Wordsworth provides us with a useful example of the way that poetry can invest quite ordinary words with a high emotional charge:

> No motion has she now, no force,
> She neither hears nor sees;
> Rolled round in earth's diurnal course
> With rocks, and stones, and trees.

To paraphrase the content of this stanza from "A Slumber Did My Spirit Seal," "she" is dead and buried. But the language and structures used here give this prosaic idea great impact. For example, the regular iambic meter of the two last lines conveys something of the inexorable motion of the earth and of Lucy embedded in it; the monosyllabic last line is a grim reminder of her oneness with objects in nature; the repeated negatives in the first two lines drive home the irreparable destructiveness of death; the alliteration in the third and fourth lines gives a tangible suggestion of roundness, circularity, repetition in terms of the earth's shape and motion, suggesting a cycle in which death is perhaps followed by renewal. Even the unusual word "diurnal" (which would not have seemed so unusual to Wordsworth's readers) seems "right" in this context; it lends more weight to the notion of the earth's perpetual movement than its mundane synonym "daily" (which, besides, would not scan here). It is difficult to imagine a change of any kind to these lines; they exemplify another attempted definition of poetry, this time by Wordsworth's friend Samuel Taylor Coleridge: "the best words in the best order" (*Table Talk*, 1827).

POETIC DICTION AND THE ELEVATED STYLE

Wordsworth's diction in the "Lucy" poem cited above is a model of clarity; he has chosen language that, in its simplicity and bluntness, conveys the strength of the speaker's feelings far more strongly than an elaborate description of grief in more conventionally "poetic" language might have done. Wordsworth, disturbed by what he felt was a deadness and artificiality in the poetry of his day, sought to "choose incidents and situations from common life" and to describe them in "a selection of language really used by men" ("Preface" to *Lyrical Ballads*). His plan might seem an implicit reproach of the "raised" style, the elevated diction of epic poetry we associate with John Milton's *Paradise Lost*:

> Anon out of the earth a fabric huge
> Rose like an exhalation, with the sound
> Of dulcet symphonies and voices sweet,

Built like a temple, where pilasters round
Were set, and Doric pillars overlaid
With golden architrave; nor did there want
Cornice or frieze, with bossy sculptures graven;
The roof was fretted gold.
                    (*Paradise Lost* I.710–17)

At first glance this passage, with its Latinate vocabulary and convoluted syntax, might seem guilty of inflated language and pretentiousness. However, Milton's description of the devils' palace in Hell deliberately seeks to distance us from its subject in order to emphasize the scale and sublimity of the spectacle, far removed from ordinary human experience. In other words, language and style in *Paradise Lost* are well adapted to suit a particular purpose, just as they are in "A Slumber Did My Spirit Seal," though on a wholly different scale. Wordsworth criticized the poetry of his day, not because of its elevation, but because the raised style was too often out of touch with its subject; in his view, the words did not bear any significant relation to the "truths" they were attempting to depict.

"PLAIN" LANGUAGE IN POETRY

Since Wordsworth's time, writers have been conscious of a need to narrow the apparent gap between "poetic" language and the language of everyday life. In much of the poetry of the past century, especially free verse, we can observe a growing approximation to speech—even to conversation—in the diction and rhythms of poetry. This may have something to do with the changed role of the poet, who today has discarded the mantle of teacher or prophet that was assumed by poets of earlier times, and who is ready to admit all fields of experience and endeavor as appropriate for poetry. The modern poet looks squarely at life, and can often find a provoking beauty in even the meanest of objects.

We should not assume, however, that a greater concern with the "ordinary," with simplicity, naturalness, and clarity, means a reduction in complexity or suggestiveness. A piece such as Stevie Smith's "Mother, Among the Dustbins," for all the casual and playful domesticity of some of its lines, skilfully evokes a range of emotions and sense impressions defying simple paraphrase.

IMAGERY, SYMBOLISM, AND FIGURES OF SPEECH

The language of poetry is grounded in the objects and phenomena that create sensory impressions. Sometimes the poet renders these impressions quite literally, in a series of *images* that seek to recreate a scene in the reader's mind:

Only a man harrowing clods
In a slow silent walk
With an old horse that stumbles and nods
Half asleep as they stalk.

Only thin smoke without flame
From the heaps of couch-grass;
Yet this will go onward the same
Though Dynasties pass.

> Yonder a maid and her wight
> Come whispering by:
> War's annals will cloud into night
> Ere their story die.
>
> (Thomas Hardy, "In Time of 'The Breaking of Nations'")

Here, the objects of everyday life are re-created with sensory details designed to evoke in us the sensations or responses felt by the speaker viewing the scene. At the same time, the writer invests the objects with such significance that the poem's meaning extends beyond the literal to the symbolic: that is, the images come to stand for something much larger than the objects they represent. Hardy's poem moves from the presentation of stark images of rural life to a sense of their timelessness. By the last stanza we see the ploughman, the burning grass, and the maid and her companion as symbols of recurring human actions and motives that defy the struggles and conflicts of history.

IMAGISM

The juxtaposition of clear, forceful images is associated particularly with the Imagist movement that flourished at the beginning of the twentieth century. Its chief representatives (in their early work) were the American poets H.D. and Ezra Pound, who defined an image as "that which represents an intellectual and emotional complex in an instant of time." Pound's two-line poem "In a Station of the Metro" provides a good example of the Imagists' goal of representing emotions or impressions through the use of concentrated images:

> The apparition of these faces in the crowd,
> Petals on a wet, black bough.

As in a Japanese *haiku,* a form that strongly influenced the Imagists, the poem uses sharp, clear, concrete details to evoke both a sensory impression and the emotion or the atmosphere of the scene. Though the Imagist movement itself lasted only a short time (from about 1912 to 1917), it had a far-reaching influence on modern poets such as T. S. Eliot, and William Carlos Williams.

FIGURES OF SPEECH

Imagery often works together with figurative expression to extend and deepen the meaning or impact of a poem. "Figurative" language means language that is metaphorical, not literal or referential. Through "figures of speech" such as metaphor and simile, metonymy, synecdoche, and personification, the writer may alter the ordinary, denotative meanings of words in order to convey greater force and vividness to ideas or impressions, often by showing likenesses between unlike things.

With *simile,* the poet makes an explicit comparison between the subject (called the *tenor*) and another object or idea (known as the *vehicle*), using "as" or "like":

> It is a beauteous evening, calm and free,
> The holy time is quiet as a Nun
> Breathless with adoration. ...

In this opening to a sonnet, Wordsworth uses a visual image of a nun in devout prayer to convey in concrete terms the less tangible idea of evening as a "holy time." The comparison also introduces an emotional dimension, conveying something of the feeling that the scene induces in the poet. The simile can thus illuminate and expand meaning in a compact way. The poet may also extend the simile to elaborate at length on any points of likeness.

In *metaphor*, the comparison between tenor and vehicle is implied: connectives such as "like" are omitted, and a kind of identity is created between the subject and the term with which it is being compared. Thus in John Donne's "The Good-Morrow," a lover asserts the endless joy that he and his beloved find in each other:

> My face in thine eye, thine in mine appears,
> And true plain hearts do in the faces rest;
> Where can we find two better hemispheres,
> Without sharp north, without declining west?

Here the lovers are transformed into "hemispheres," each of them a half of the world not subject to the usual natural phenomena of wintry cold ("sharp north") or the coming of night ("declining west"). Thus, they form a perfect world in balance, in which the normal processes of decay or decline have been arrested. Donne renders the abstract idea of a love that defies change in pictorial and physical terms, making it more real and accessible to us. The images here are all the more arresting for the degree of concentration involved; it is not merely the absence of "like" or "as" that gives the metaphor such direct power, but the fusion of distinct images and emotions into a new idea.

Personification is the figure of speech in which the writer endows abstract ideas, inanimate objects, or animals with human characteristics. In other words, it is a type of implied metaphorical comparison in which aspects of a non-human subject are compared to the feelings, appearance, or actions of a human being. In the second stanza of his ode "To Autumn," Keats personifies the concept of autumnal harvesting in the form of a woman, "sitting careless on a granary floor, / Thy hair soft-lifted by the winnowing wind." Personification may also help to create a mood, as when Thomas Gray attributes human feelings to a hooting owl in "Elegy Written in a Country Church-Yard"; using such words as "moping" and "complain," Gray invests the bird's cries with the quality of human melancholy:

> … from yonder ivy-mantled tow'r
> The moping owl does to the moon complain
> Of such, as wand'ring near her secret bow'r,
> Molest her ancient solitary reign.

In his book *Modern Painters* (1856), the English critic John Ruskin criticized such attribution of human feelings to objects in nature. Calling this device the "pathetic fallacy," he objected to what he saw as an irrational distortion of reality, producing "a falseness in all our impressions of external things." Modern criticism, with a distrust of any notions of an objective "reality," tends to use Ruskin's term as a neutral label simply to describe instances of extended personification of natural objects.

Apostrophe, which is closely related to personification, has the speaker directly addressing a non-human object or idea as if it were a sentient human listener. Blake's "The Sick Rose," Shelley's "Ode to the West Wind" and his ode "To a Sky-Lark" all employ apostrophe, personifying the object addressed. Keats's "Ode on a Grecian Urn" begins by apostrophizing the urn ("Thou still unravish'd bride of quietness"), then addresses it in a series of questions and reflections through which the speaker attempts to unravel the urn's mysteries.

Apostrophe also appeals to or addresses a person who is absent or dead. W. H. Auden's lament "In Memory of W. B. Yeats" apostrophizes both the earth in which Yeats is to be buried ("Earth, receive an honoured guest") and the dead poet himself ("Follow, poet, follow right / To the bottom of the night ..."). Religious prayers offer an illustration of the usefulness of apostrophe, since they are direct appeals from an earth-bound suppliant to an invisible god. The suggestion of strong emotion associated with such appeals is a common feature of apostrophe in poetry also, especially poetry with a religious theme, like Donne's "Holy Sonnets" (e.g., "Batter My Heart, Three-Personed God").

Metonymy and *synecdoche* are two closely related figures of speech that further illustrate the power of metaphorical language to convey meaning more intensely and vividly than is possible with prosaic statement. *Metonymy* (from the Greek, meaning "change of name") involves referring to an object or concept by substituting the name of another object or concept with which it is usually associated: for example, we might speak of "the Crown" when we mean the monarch, or describe the U.S. executive branch as "the White House." When the writer uses only part of something to signify the whole, or an individual to represent a class, we have an instance of *synecdoche*. T. S. Eliot provides an example in "The Love Song of J. Alfred Prufrock" when a crab is described as "a pair of ragged claws." Similarly, synecdoche is present in Milton's contemptous term "blind mouths" to describe the "corrupted clergy" he attacks in "Lycidas."

Dylan Thomas employs both metonymy and synecdoche in his poem "The Hand That Signed the Paper":

The hand that signed the paper felled a city;
Five sovereign fingers taxed the breath,
Doubled the globe of dead and halved a country;
These five kings did a king to death.

The mighty hand leads to a sloping shoulder,
The finger joints are cramped with chalk;
A goose's quill has put an end to murder
That put an end to talk.

The hand that signed the treaty bred a fever,
And famine grew, and locusts came;
Great is the hand that holds dominion over
Man by a scribbled name.

The five kings count the dead but do not soften
The crusted wound nor stroke the brow;
A hand rules pity as a hand rules heaven;
Hands have no tears to flow.

The "hand" of the poem is evidently a synecdoche for a great king who enters into treaties with friends and foes to wage wars, conquer kingdoms, and extend his personal power—all at the expense of his suffering subjects. The "goose quill" of the second stanza is a metonymy, standing for the pen used to sign the treaty or the death warrant that brings the war to an end.

Thomas's poem is an excellent example of the power of figurative language, which, by its vividness and concentrated force, can add layers of meaning to a poem, make abstract ideas concrete, and intensify the poem's emotional impact.

THE POEM AS PERFORMANCE: WRITER AND PERSON

Poetry is always dramatic. Sometimes the drama is explicit, as in Robert Browning's monologues, in which we hear the voice of a participant in a dialogue; in "My Last Duchess" we are present as the Duke reflects on the portrait of his late wife for the benefit of a visitor who has come to negotiate on behalf of the woman who is to become the Duke's next wife. Or we listen with amusement and pity as the dying Bishop addresses his venal and unsympathetic sons and tries to bargain with them for a fine burial ("The Bishop Orders His Tomb at St. Praxed's"). In such poems, the notion of a speaking voice is paramount: the speaker is a personage in a play, and the poem a means of conveying plot and character.

Sometimes the drama is less apparent, and takes the form of a plea, or a compliment, or an argument addressed to a silent listener. In Donne's "The Flea" we can infer from the poem the situation that has called it forth: a lover's advances are being rejected by his beloved, and his poem is an argument intended to overcome her reluctance by means of wit and logic. We can see a similar example in Marvell's "To His Coy Mistress": here the very shape of the poem, its three-paragraph structure, corresponds to the stages of the speaker's argument as he presents an apparently irrefutable line of reasoning. Much love poetry has this kind of background as its inspiration; the yearnings or lamentations of the lover are part of an imagined scene, not merely versified reflections about an abstraction called "love."

Meditative or reflective poetry can be dramatic too. Donne's "Holy Sonnets" are pleas from a tormented soul struggling to find its god; Tennyson's "In Memoriam" follows the agonized workings of a mind tracing a path from grief and anger to acceptance and renewed hope.

We should never assume that the speaker, the "I" of the poem, is simply a voice for the writer's own views. The speaker in W. H. Auden's "To an Unknown Citizen," presenting a summary of the dead citizen's life, appears to be an official spokesperson for the society which the citizen served ("Our report on his union"; "Our researchers ..." etc.). The speaker's words are laudatory, yet we perceive immediately that Auden's own views of this society are anything but approving. The speaker seems satisfied with the highly regimented nature of his society, one in which every aspect of the individual's life is under scrutiny and subject to correction. The only things necessary to the happiness of the "Modern Man," it seems, are "A phonograph, a radio, a car, and a frigidaire." The tone here is subtly ironic, an irony created by the gap between the imagined speaker's perception and the real feelings of the writer.

PERFORMANCE POETRY

Poetry began as an oral art, passed on in the form of chants, myths, ballads, and legends recited to an audience of listeners rather than readers. Even today, the dramatic qualities of a poem may extend beyond written text. "Performance poets" combine poetry and stagecraft in presenting their work to live audiences. Dramatic uses of voice, rhythm, body movement, music, and sometimes other visual effects make the "text" of the poem multi-dimensional. For example, Edith Sitwell's poem-sequence *Façade* (1922) was originally set to music: Sitwell read from behind a screen, while a live orchestra played. This performance was designed to enhance the verbal and rhythmic qualities of her poetry:

> Beneath the flat and paper sky
> The sun, a demon's eye
> Glowed through the air, that mask of glass;
> All wand'ring sounds that pass
>
> Seemed out of tune, as if the light
> Were fiddle-strings pulled tight.
> The market-square with spire and bell
> Clanged out the hour in Hell.
> (from *Façade*)

By performing their poetry, writers can also convey cultural values and traditions. The cultural aspect of performance is central to Black poetry, which originates in a highly oral tradition of folklore and storytelling. From its roots in Africa, this oral tradition has been manifested in the songs and stories of slaves, in spirituals, in the jazz rhythms of the Twenties and the Thirties and in the rebelliousness of reggae and of rap. Even when it remains "on the page," much Black poetry written in the oral tradition has a compelling rhythmic quality. The lines below from Linton Kwesi Johnson's "Mi Revalueshanary Fren," for example, blur the line between spoken poetry and song. Johnson often performs his "dub poetry" against reggae or hip-hop musical backings.

> yes, people powa jus a showa evry howa
> an evrybady claim dem democratic
> but some a wolf an some a sheep
> an dat is problematic

The chorus of Johnson's poems, with its constant repetitions, digs deeply into the roots of African song and chant. Its performance qualities become clearer when the poem is read aloud:

> Husak
> e ad to go
> Honnicka
> e ad to go
> Chowcheskhu
> e ad to go
> Just like apartied
> will av to go

To perform a poem is one way to see and hear poetry as multi-dimensional, cultural, historical, and often also political. Performance is also another way to discover how poetic "meaning" can be constructed in the dynamic relation between speaker and listener.

TONE: THE SPEAKER'S ATTITUDE

In understanding poetry, it is helpful to imagine a poem as having a "voice." The voice may be close to the poet's own, or that of an imagined character, a *persona* adopted by the poet. The tone of the voice will reveal the speaker's attitude to the subject, thus helping to shape our understanding and response. In speech we can indicate our feelings by raising or lowering our voices, and we can accompany words with physical actions. In writing, we must try to convey the tonal inflections of the speaking voice through devices of language and rhythm, through imagery and figures of speech, and through allusions and contrasts.

THE IRONIC TONE

Housman's poem "Terence, This Is Stupid Stuff" offers a useful example of ways in which manipulating tone can reinforce meaning. When Housman, presenting himself in the poem as "Terence," imagines himself to be criticized for writing gloomy poems, his response to his critics takes the form of an ironic alternative: perhaps they should stick to drinking ale:

> Oh, many a peer of England brews
> Livelier liquor than the Muse,
> And malt does more than Milton can
> To justify God's ways to man.

The tone here is one of heavy scorn. The speaker is impatient with those who refuse to look at the realities of life and death, and who prefer to take refuge in simple-minded pleasure. The ludicrous comparisons, first between the brewers who have been made peers of England and the classical Muse of poetry, then between malt and Milton, create a sense of disproportion and ironic tension; the explicit allusion to *Paradise Lost* ("To justify God's ways to man") helps to drive home the poet's bitter recognition that his auditors are part of that fallen world depicted by Milton, yet unable or unwilling to acknowledge their harsh condition. The three couplets that follow offer a series of contrasts: in each case, the first line sets up a pleasant expectation and the second dashes it with a blunt reminder of reality:

> Ale, man, ale's the stuff to drink
> For fellows whom it hurts to think:
> Look into the pewter pot
> To see the world as the world's not.
> And faith, 'tis pleasant till 'tis past:
> The mischief is that 'twill not last.

These are all jabs at the "sterling lads" who would prefer to lie in "lovely muck" and not think about the way the world is. Housman's sardonic advice is all the more pointed for its sharp and ironic tone.

POETIC FORMS

In poetry, language is intimately related to form, which is the structuring of words within identifiable patterns. In prose we speak of phrases, sentences, and paragraphs; in poetry, we identify structures by lines, stanzas, or complete forms such as the sonnet or the ode (though poetry in complete or blank verse has paragraphs of variable length, not formal stanzas: see below).

Rightly handled, the form enhances expression and meaning, just as a frame can define and enhance a painting or photograph. Unlike the photo frame, however, form in poetry is an integral part of the whole work. At one end of the scale, the term "form" may describe the *epic,* the lengthy narrative governed by such conventions as division into books, a lofty style, and the interplay between human and supernatural characters. At the other end lies the *epigram*, a witty and pointed saying whose distinguishing characteristic is its brevity, as in Alexander Pope's famous couplet,

> I am his Highness' dog at Kew;
> Pray tell me sir, whose dog are you?

Between the epic and the epigram lie many other poetic forms, such as the sonnet, the ballad, or the ode. "Form" may also describe stanzaic patterns like *couplets* and *quatrains*.

"FIXED FORM" POEMS

The best-known poetic form is probably the sonnet, the fourteen-line poem inherited from Italy (the word itself is from the Italian *sonetto*, little song or sound). Within those fourteen lines, whether the poet chooses the "Petrarchan" rhyme scheme or the "English" form (see below in the section on "Rhyme"), the challenge is to develop an idea or situation that must find its statement and its resolution within the strict confines of the sonnet frame. Typically, there is an initial idea, description, or statement of feeling, followed by a "turn" in the thought that takes the reader by surprise, or that casts the situation in an unexpected light. Thus in Sonnet 130, "My Mistress' Eyes Are Nothing Like the Sun," William Shakespeare spends the first three quatrains apparently disparaging his lover in a series of unfavorable comparisons—"If snow be white, why then her breasts are dun"—but in the closing couplet his point becomes clear:

> And yet, by heaven, I think my love as rare
> As any she belied with false compare.

In other words, the speaker's disparaging comparisons have really been parodies of sentimental clichés which falsify reality; his mistress has no need of the exaggerations or distortions of conventional love poetry.

Other foreign forms borrowed and adapted by English-language poets include the *ghazal* and the *pantoum*. The *ghazal*, strongly associated with classical Urdu literature, originated in Persia and Arabia and was brought to the Indian subcontinent in the twelfth century. It consists of a series of couplets held together by a refrain, a simple rhyme scheme (a/a, b/a, c/a, d/a…), and a common rhythm, but only loosely related in theme or subject. Some English-language practitioners of the form have captured the epigrammatic quality of the ghazal, but most do not adhere to the strict pattern of the classical form.

The *pantoum*, based on a Malaysian form, was imported into English poetry via the work of nineteenth-century French poets. Typically it presents a series of quatrains rhyming *abab*, linked by a pattern of repetition in which the second and fourth lines of a quatrain become the first and third lines of the stanza that follows. In the poem's final stanza, the pattern is reversed: the second line repeats the third line of the first stanza, and the last line repeats the poem's opening line, thus creating the effect of a loop.

Similar to the pantoum in the circularity of its structure is the *villanelle,* originally a French form, with five *tercets* and a concluding *quatrain* held together by only two rhymes (aba, aba, aba, aba, aba, abaa) and by a refrain that repeats the first line at lines 6, 12, and 18, while the third line of the first tercet reappears as lines 9, 15, and 19. With its interlocking rhymes and elaborate repetitions, the villanelle can create a variety of tonal effects, ranging from lighthearted parody to the sonorous and earnest exhortation of Dylan Thomas's "Do Not Go Gentle Into That Good Night."

STANZAIC FORMS

Recurring formal groupings of lines within a poem are usually described as "stanzas." Both the recurring and the formal aspects of stanzaic forms are important; it is a common misconception to think that any group of lines in a poem, if it is set off by line spaces, constitutes a stanza. If such a group of lines is not patterned as one of a recurring group sharing similar formal characteristics, however, then it may be more appropriate to refer to such irregular groupings in the way we do for prose—as paragraphs. A ballad is typically divided into stanzas; a prose poem or a poem written in free verse, on the other hand, will rarely be divided into stanzas.

A stanza may be identified by the number of lines and the patterns of rhyme repeated in each grouping. One of the simpler traditional forms is the *ballad stanza*, with its alternating four and three-foot lines and its *abcb* rhyme scheme. Drawing on this form's association with medieval ballads and legends, Keats produces the eerie mystery of "La Belle Dame Sans Merci":

> I saw pale kings and princes too,
> Pale warriors, death-pale were they all;
> They cried—"La Belle Dame sans Merci
> Hath thee in thrall!"

Such imitations are a form of literary allusion; Keats uses a traditional stanza form to remind us of poems like "Sir Patrick Spens" or "Barbara Allen" to dramatize the painful thralldom of love by placing it within a well-known tradition of ballad narratives with similar forms and themes.

The four-line stanza, or *quatrain*, may be used for a variety of effects: from the elegiac solemnity of Gray's "Elegy Written in a Country Churchyard" to the apparent lightness and simplicity of some of Emily Dickinson's poems. Tennyson used a rhyming quatrain to such good effect in *In Memoriam* that the form he employed (four lines of iambic tetrameter rhyming *abba*) is known as the "In Memoriam stanza."

Other commonly used forms of stanza include the *rhyming couplet, terza rima, ottava rima, rhyme royal*, and the *Spenserian stanza*. Each of these is a rhetorical unit within a longer whole, rather like a paragraph within an essay. The poet's choice among such forms is dictated, at least in part, by the effects that each may produce. Thus the *rhyming couplet* often expresses a complete statement within two lines, creating a sense of density of thought, of coherence and closure; it is particularly effective where the writer wishes to set up contrasts, or to achieve the witty compactness of epigram:

> Of all mad creatures, if the learn'd are right,
> It is the slaver kills, and not the bite.
> A fool quite angry is quite innocent:
> Alas! 'tis ten times worse when they repent.
>
> (from Pope, "Epistle to Dr. Arbuthnot")

Ottava rima, as its Italian name implies, is an eight-line stanza, with the rhyme scheme *abababcc*. Like the sonnet, it is long enough to allow the development of a single thought in some detail and complexity, with a concluding couplet that may extend the central idea or cast it in a wholly unexpected light. W.B. Yeats uses this stanza form in "Sailing to Byzantium" and "Among Schoolchildren." Though much used by Renaissance poets, it is particularly associated with George Gordon, Lord Byron's *Don Juan*, in which the poet exploits to the full its potential for devastating irony and bathos. It is long enough to allow the development of a single thought in some detail and complexity; the concluding couplet can then, sonnet-like, turn that thought upon its head, or cast it in a wholly unexpected light:

Sagest of women, even of widows, she
  Resolved that Juan should be quite a paragon,
And worthy of the noblest pedigree
  (His sire was of Castile, his dam from Aragon).
Then for accomplishments of chivalry,
  In case our lord the king should go to war again,
He learned the arts of riding, fencing, gunnery,
And how to scale a fortress—or a nunnery.
          (*Don Juan* I.38)

FREE VERSE

Not all writers want the order and symmetry—some might say the restraints and limitations—of traditional forms, and many have turned to *free verse* as a means of liberating their thoughts and feelings. Deriving its name from the French "vers libre" made popular by the French Symbolistes at the end of the nineteenth century, free verse is characterized by irregularity of metre, line length, and rhyme. This does not mean that it is without pattern; rather, it tends to follow more closely than other forms the unforced rhythms and accents of natural speech, making calculated use of spacing, line breaks, and "cadences," the rhythmic units that govern phrasing in speech.

Free verse is not a modern invention. Milton was an early practitioner, as was Blake; however, it was the great modern writers of free verse—first Walt Whitman, then Pound, Eliot, and William Carlos Williams (interestingly, all Americans, at least originally)—who gave this form a fluidity and flexibility that could free the imagination to deal with any kind of feeling or experience. Perhaps because it depends so much more than traditional forms upon the individual intuitions of the poet, it is the form of poetic structure most commonly found today. The best practitioners recognize that free verse, like any other kind of poetry, demands clarity, precision, and a close connection between technique and meaning.

PROSE POETRY

At the furthest extreme from traditional forms lies poetry written in prose. Contradictory as this label may seem, the two have much in common. Prose has at its disposal all the figurative devices available to poetry, such as metaphor, personification, or apostrophe; it may use structuring devices such as verbal repetition or parallel syntactical structures; it can draw on the same tonal range, from pathos to irony. The difference is that prose poetry accomplishes its ends in sentences and paragraphs, rather than lines or stanzas. First given prominence by the French poet Charles Baudelaire (*Petits Poèmes en prose*, 1862), the form is much used to present fragments of heightened sensation, conveyed through vivid or impressionistic description. It draws upon such prosaic forms as journal entries, lists, even footnotes. Prose poetry should be distinguished from "poetic prose," which may be found in a variety of settings (from the King James Bible to the fiction of Jeanette Winterson); the distinction—which not all critics would accept—appears to lie in the writer's intention.

Christan Bok's *Eunoia* is an interesting example of the ways in which a writer of prose poetry may try to balance the demands of each medium. *Eunoia* is an avowedly experimental work in which each chapter is restricted to the use of a single vowel. The text is governed by a series of rules described by the author in an afterword; they include a requirement that all chapters "must allude to the art of writing. All sentences must accent internal rhyme through the use of syntactical parallelism. The text must exhaust the lexicon for each vowel, citing at least 98% of the available repertoire...." Having imposed such constraints upon the language and form of the work, Bok then sets himself the task of showing that "even under such improbable conditions of duress, language can still express an uncanny, if not sublime, thought." The result is a surrealistic narrative that blends poetic and linguistic devices to almost hypnotic effect.

THE POEM AS A MATERIAL OBJECT

Both free verse and prose poetry pay attention in different ways to the poem as a living thing on the printed page. But the way in which poetry is presented in material form is an important part of the existence of almost any form of poetry. In the six volumes of this anthology the material form of the poem is highlighted by the inclusion of a number of facsimile reproductions of poems of other eras in their earliest extant material form.

RHYTHM AND SCANSION

When we read poetry, we often become aware of a pattern of rhythm within a line or set of lines. The formal analysis of that rhythmic pattern, or "metre," is called *scansion*. The verb "to scan" may carry different meanings, depending upon the context: if the *critic* "scans" a line, he or she is attempting to determine the metrical pattern in which it is cast; if the *line* "scans," we are making the observation that the line conforms to particular metrical rules. Whatever the context, the process of scansion is based on the premise that a line of verse is built on a pattern of stresses, a recurring set of more or less regular beats established by the alternation of light and heavy accents in syllables and words. The rhythmic pattern so distinguished in a given poem is said to be the "metre" of that poem. If we find it impossible to identify any specific metrical pattern, the poem is probably an example of free verse.

QUANTITATIVE, SYLLABIC, AND ACCENTUAL-SYLLABIC VERSE

Although we owe much of our terminology for analyzing or describing poetry to the Greeks and Romans, the foundation of our metrical system is quite different from theirs. They measured a line of verse by the duration of sound ("quantity") in each syllable, and by the combination of short and long syllables. Such poetry is known as *quantitative* verse.

Unlike Greek or Latin, English is a heavily accented language. Thus poetry of the Anglo-Saxon period, such as *Beowulf*, was *accentual:* that is, the lines were based on a fixed number of accents, or stresses, regardless of the number of syllables in the line:

> Oft Scyld Scefing   sceapena þreatum
> monegum maegþum   meodosetla ofteah.

Few modern poets have written in the accentual tradition. A notable exception was Gerard Manley Hopkins, who based his line on a pattern of strong stresses that he called "sprung rhythm." Hopkins experimented with rhythms and stresses that approximate the accentual quality of natural speech; the result is a line that is emphatic, abrupt, even harsh in its forcefulness:

> I caught this morning morning's minion, kingdom of daylight's dauphin, dapple-dawn-drawn
>   Falcon, in his riding

Of the rolling level underneath him steady air ....

(from "The Windhover")

Under the influence of French poetry, following the Norman invasion of the eleventh century, English writers were introduced to *syllabic* prosody: that is, poetry in which the number of syllables is the determining factor in the length of any line, regardless of the number of stresses or their placement. A few modern writers have successfully produced syllabic poetry.

However, the accentual patterns of English, in speech as well as in poetry, were too strongly ingrained to disappear. Instead, the native accentual practice combined with the imported syllabic conventions to produce the *accentual-syllabic* line, in which the writer works with combinations of stressed and unstressed syllables in lines of equal syllabic length. Geoffrey Chaucer was the first great writer to employ the accentual-syllabic line in English poetry:

Ther was also a Nonne, a Prioresse,
That of hir smiling was ful simple and coy.
Hir gretteste ooth was but by sainté Loy,
And she was clepéd Madame Eglantine.

(from *The Canterbury Tales*)

The fundamental pattern here is the ten-syllable line (although the convention of sounding the final "e" at the end of a line in Middle English verse sometimes produces eleven syllables). Each line contains five stressed syllables, each of which alternates with one or two unstressed syllables. This was to become the predominant metre of poetry in English until the general adoption of free verse in the twentieth century.

IDENTIFYING POETIC METER

Conventionally, meter is established by dividing a line into roughly equal parts, based on the rise and fall of the rhythmic beats. Each of these divisions, conventionally marked by a bar, is known as a "foot," and within the foot there will be a combination of stressed and unstressed syllables, indicated by the prosodic symbols / (stressed) and x (unstressed).

I know | that I | shall meet | my fate
Somewhere | among | the clouds | above ...

(from *Yeats*, "An Irish Airman Foresees His Death")

To describe the meter used in a poem, we must first determine what kind of foot predominates, and then count the number of feet in each line. To describe the resultant meter we use terminology borrowed from classical prosody. In identifying the meter of English verse we commonly apply the following labels:

iambic (x /): a foot with one weak stress followed by one strong stress

("Look home | ward, Ang | el, now, | and melt | with ruth")

trochaic (/ x): strong followed by weak

("Ty | ger! Ty | ger! bur | ning bright")

anapaestic (x x /): two weak stresses, followed by a strong

    ("I have passed | with a nod | of the head")

dactylic (/ x x): strong stress followed by two weak

    ("Hickory | dickory | dock")

spondaic (/ /): two strong stresses

    ("If hate | killed men,| Brother | Lawrence,
      God's blood,| would not | mine kill | you?")

We also use classical terms to describe the number of feet in a line. Thus, a line with one foot is *monometer*; with two feet, *dimeter*; three feet, *trimeter*; four feet, *tetrameter*; five feet, *pentameter*; and six feet, *hexameter*.

Scansion of the two lines from Yeats's "Irish Airman" quoted above shows that the predominant foot is iambic (x /), that there are four feet to each line, and that the poem is therefore written in *iambic tetrameters*. The first foot of the second line, however, may be read as a trochee ("Somewhere"); the variation upon the iambic norm here is an example of *substitution*, a means whereby the writer may avoid the monotony that would result from adhering too closely to a set rhythm. We very quickly build up an expectation about the dominant meter of a poem; the poet will sometimes disturb that expectation by changing the beat, and so through substitution create a pleasurable tension in our awareness.

The prevailing meter in English poetry is iambic, since the natural rhythm of spoken English is predominantly iambic. Nonetheless, poets may employ other rhythms where it suits their purpose. Thus W.H. Auden can create a solemn tone by the use of a trochaic meter(/ x):

    Earth, receive an honoured guest;
    William Yeats is laid to rest:
    Let the Irish vessel lie
    Emptied of its poetry.

The same meter may be much less funereal, as in Ben Jonson's song "*To Celia*":

    Come, my Celia, let us prove,
    While we may, the sports of love.
    Time will not be ours forever;
    He, at length, our good will sever.

The sense of greater pace in this last example derives in part from the more staccato phrasing, and also from the greater use of monosyllabic words. A more obviously lilting, dancing effect is obtained from anapaestic rhythm (x x /):

    I sprang to the stirrup, and Joris, and he;
    I galloped, Dirck galloped, we galloped all three.
    "Good speed!" cried the watch, as the gatebolts undrew;
    "Speed!" echoed the wall to us galloping through.
        (from *Browning*, "How They Brought the Good News from Ghent to Aix")

Coleridge wittily captured the varying effects of different meters in "Metrical Feet: Lesson for a Boy," which the poet wrote for his sons, and in which he marked the stresses himself:

> Trochee trips from long to short;
> From long to long in solemn sort
> Slow Spondee stalks; strong foot! yet ill able
> Ever to come up with Dactyl trisyllable.
> Iambics march from short to long:—
> With a leap and a bound the swift Anapaests throng....

A meter which often deals with serious themes is unrhymed iambic pentameter, also known as *blank verse*. This is the meter of Shakespeare's plays, notably his great tragedies; it is the meter, too, of Milton's *Paradise Lost*, to which it lends a desired sonority and magnificence; and of Wordsworth's "Lines Composed a Few Miles above Tintern Abbey," where the flexibility of the meter allows the writer to move by turns from description, to narration, to philosophical reflection.

RHYME, CONSONANCE, ASSONANCE, AND ALLITERATION

Perhaps the most obvious sign of poetic form is rhyme: that is, the repetition of syllables with the same or similar sounds. If the rhyme words are placed at the end of the line, they are known as *end-rhymes*. The opening stanza of Housman's "To an Athlete Dying Young" has two pairs of end-rhymes:

> The time you won your town the *race*
> We chaired you through the market-*place*;
> Man and boy stood cheering *by*,
> And home we brought you shoulder-*high*.

Words rhyming within a line are *internal rhymes*, as in the first and third lines of this stanza from Coleridge's "The Rime of the Ancient Mariner":

> The fair breeze *blew*, the white foam *flew*
> The furrow followed free;
> We were the *first* that ever *burst*
> Into that silent sea.

When, as is usually the case, the rhyme occurs in a stressed syllable, it is known as a *masculine rhyme*; if the rhyming word ends in an unstressed syllable, it is referred to as *feminine*. The difference is apparent in the opening stanzas of Alfred Tennyson's poem "The Lady of Shalott," where the first stanza establishes the basic iambic meter with strong stresses on the rhyming words:

> On either side the river *lie*
> Long fields of barley and of *rye*,
> That clothe the wold and meet the *sky*;
> And through the field the road runs *by*
> To many-towered Camelot ...

In the second stanza Tennyson changes to trochaic lines, ending in unstressed syllables and feminine rhymes:

> Willows whiten, aspens *quiver*,
> Little breezes dusk and *shiver*
> Through the wave that runs *forever*
> By the island in the *river*
> Flowing down to Camelot.

Not only does Tennyson avoid monotony here by his shift to feminine rhymes, he also darkens the mood by using words that imply a contrast with the bright warmth of day—"quiver," "dusk," "shiver"—in preparation for the introduction of the "silent isle" that embowers the Lady.

NEAR RHYMES

Most of the rhymes in "The Lady of Shalott" are exact, or "*perfect*" rhymes. However, in the second of the stanzas just quoted, it is evident that "forever" at the end of the third line is not a "perfect" rhyme; rather, it is an instance of "*near*" or "*slant*" rhyme. Such "*imperfect*" rhymes are quite deliberate; indeed, two stanzas later we find the rhyming sequence "early," "barley," "cheerly," and "clearly," followed by the rhymes "weary," "airy," and "fairy." As with the introduction of feminine rhymes, such divergences from one dominant pattern prevent monotony and avoid a too-mechanical sing-song effect.

More importantly, near-rhymes have an oddly unsettling effect, perhaps because they both raise and frustrate our expectation of a perfect rhyme. Their use certainly gives added emphasis to the words at the end of these chilling lines from Wilfred Owen's "*Strange Meeting*":

> For by my glee might many men have laughed,
> And of my weeping something had been left,
> Which must die now. I mean the truth untold,
> The pity of war, the pity war distilled.
> Now men will go content with what we spoiled,
> Or, discontent, boil bloody, and be spilled.

CONSONANCE AND ASSONANCE

In Owen's poem, the near-rhymes "laughed / left" and "spoiled / spilled" are good examples of *consonance*, which pairs words with similar consonants but different intervening vowels. Other examples from Owen's poem include "groined / groaned," "hall / Hell," "years / yours," and "mystery / mastery."

Related to consonance as a linking device is *assonance*, the echoing of similar vowel sounds in the stressed syllables of words with differing consonants (lane/hail, penitent/reticence). A device favored particularly by descriptive poets, it appears often in the work of the English Romantics, especially Shelley and Keats, and their great Victorian successor Tennyson, all of whom had a good ear for the musical quality of language. In the following passage, Tennyson makes effective use of repeated "o" and "ow" sounds to suggest the soft moaning of the wind as it spreads the seed of the lotos plant:

> The Lotos blooms below the barren peak,
> The Lotos blows by every winding creek;

All day the wind breathes low with mellower tone;
Through every hollow cave and alley lone
Round and round the spicy downs the yellow Lotos dust is blown.

(from "The Lotos-Eaters")

ALLITERATION

Alliteration connects words which have the same initial consonant. Like consonance and rhyme, alliteration adds emphasis, throwing individual words into strong relief, and lending force to rhythm. This is especially evident in the work of Gerard Manley Hopkins, where alliteration works in conjunction with the heavy stresses of *sprung rhythm*:

Brute beauty and valour and act, oh, air, pride, plume, here
Buckle! AND the fire that breaks from thee then, a billion
Times told lovelier, more dangerous, O my chevalier!

(from "The Windhover")

Like assonance, alliteration is useful in descriptive poetry, reinforcing an impression or mood through repeated sounds:

Thou on whose stream, 'mid the steep sky's commotion,
Loose clouds like Earth's decaying leaves are shed,
Shook from the tangled boughs of Heaven and Ocean ....

(from Percy Shelley, "Ode to the West Wind")

The repetition of "s" and "sh" sounds conveys the rushing sound of a wind that drives everything before it. This effect is also an example of *onomatopoeia*, a figure of speech in which the sound of the words seems to echo the sense.

RHYME AND POETIC STRUCTURE

Rhyme may play a central role in the structure of a poem. This is particularly apparent in the *sonnet* form, where the expression of the thought is heavily influenced by the poet's choice of rhyme-scheme. The "English" or "Shakespearean" sonnet has three quatrains rhyming *abab, cdcd, efef,* and concludes with a rhyming couplet, *gg*. This pattern lends itself well to the statement and restatement of an idea, as we find, for example, in Shakespeare's sonnet "That time of year thou mayst in me behold." Each of the quatrains presents an image of decline or decay—a tree in winter, the coming of night, a dying fire; the closing couplet then relates these images to the thought of an impending separation and attendant feelings of loss.

The organization of the "Italian" or "Petrarchan" sonnet, by contrast, hinges on a rhyme scheme that creates two parts, an eight-line section (the *octave*) typically rhyming *abbaabba*, and a concluding six-line section (the *sestet*) rhyming *cdecde* or some other variation. In the octave, the writer describes a thought or feeling; in the sestet, the writer may elaborate upon that thought, or may introduce a sudden "turn" or change of direction. A good example of the Italian form is Donne's "Batter My Heart, Three-Personed God."

The rhyming pattern established at the beginning of a poem is usually followed throughout; thus the opening sets up an expectation in the reader, which the poet may sometimes play on by means of an unexpected or surprising rhyme. This is especially evident in comic verse, where peculiar or unexpected rhymes can contribute a great deal to the comic effect:

> I shoot the Hippopotamus
> with bullets made of platinum,
>   Because if I use leaden ones
> his hide is sure to flatten 'em.
>   (*Hilaire Belloc,* "The Hippopotamus")

Finally, one of the most obvious yet important aspects of rhyme is its sound. It acts as a kind of musical punctuation, lending verse an added resonance and beauty. And as anyone who has ever had to learn poetry by heart will testify, the sound of rhyme is a powerful aid to memorization and recall, from helping a child to learn numbers—

> One, two,
> Buckle my shoe,
> Three, four,
> Knock at the door—

—to selling toothpaste through an advertising jingle in which the use of rhyme drives home the identity of a product:

> You'll wonder where the yellow went,
> When you brush your teeth with Pepsodent.

OTHER FORMS WITH INTERLOCKING RHYMES

Other forms besides the sonnet depend upon rhyme for their structural integrity. These include the *rondeau*, a poem of thirteen lines in three stanzas, with two half lines acting as a refrain, and having only two rhymes. The linking effect of rhyme is also essential to the three-line stanza called *terza rima*, the form chosen by Shelley for his "Ode to the West Wind," where the rhyme scheme (*aba, bcb, cdc* etc.) gives a strong sense of forward movement. But a poet need not be limited to particular forms to use interlocking rhyme schemes.

THE POET'S TASK

The poet's task, in Sir Philip Sidney's view, is to move us to virtue and well-doing by coming to us with

words set in delightful proportion, either accompanied with, or prepared for, the well-enchanting skill of music; and with a tale forsooth he cometh unto you, with a tale which holdeth children from play, and old men from the chimney corner; and pretending no more,

doth intend the winning of the mind from wickedness to virtue: even as the child is often
brought to take most wholesome things by hiding them in such other as have a pleasant taste.

(*The Defence of Poesy*, 1593)

Modern poets have been less preoccupied with the didactic or moral force of poetry, its capacity to win
the mind to virtue; nonetheless, like their Renaissance counterparts, they view poetry as a means to
understanding, a point of light in an otherwise dark universe. To Robert Frost, a poem "begins in delight
and ends in wisdom":

It begins in delight, it inclines to the impulse, it assumes direction with the first line laid down,
it runs a course of lucky events, and ends in a clarification of life—not necessarily a great
clarification, such as sects and cults are founded on, but in a momentary stay against confusion.

("The Figure a Poem Makes," *Collected Poems*, 1939)

Rhyme and metre are important tools at the poet's disposal, and can be valuable aids in developing
thought as well as in creating rhythmic or musical effects. However, the technical skills needed to turn
a good line or create metrical complexities should not be confused with the ability to write good poetry.
Sidney wryly observes in his *Defence of Poesy* that "there have been many excellent poets that never
versified, and now swarm many versifiers that need never answer to the name of poets.…it is not
rhyming and versing that maketh a poet, no more than a long gown maketh an advocate." Technical
virtuosity may arouse our admiration, but something else is needed to bring that "constriction of the
throat and … precipitation of water to the eyes" that A.E. Housman speaks about. What that
"something" is will always elude definition, and is perhaps best left for readers and listeners to determine
for themselves through their own encounters with poetry.

Maps

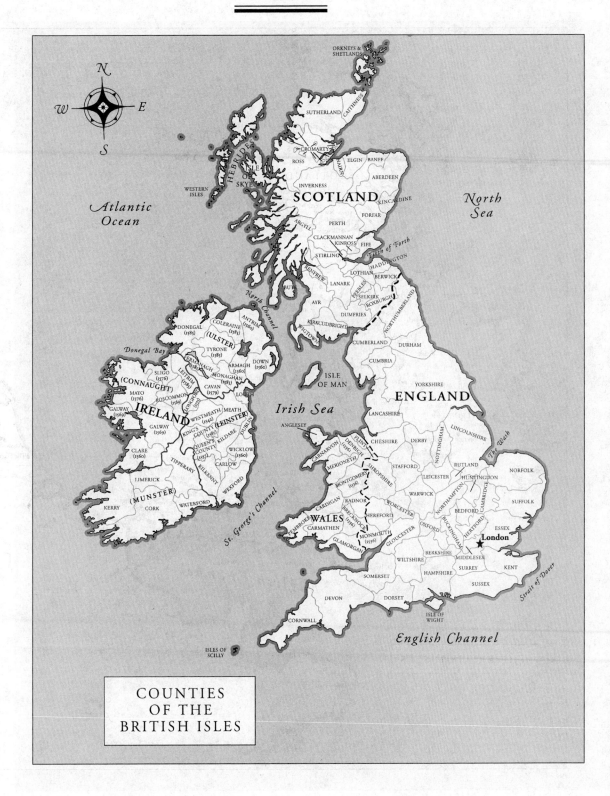

COUNTIES
OF THE
BRITISH ISLES

THE BRITISH ISLES

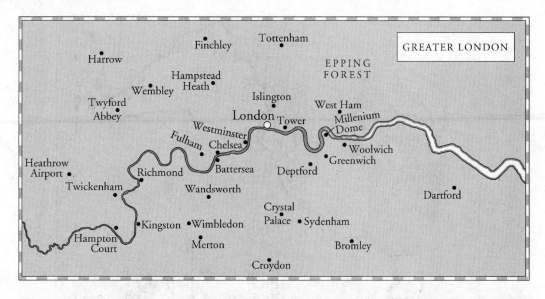

GREATER LONDON

Tottenham · Finchley · Harrow · EPPING FOREST · Hampstead Heath · Wembley · Islington · Twyford Abbey · London · Tower · West Ham · Millenium Dome · Westminster · Woolwich · Fulham · Chelsea · Greenwich · Heathrow Airport · Richmond · Battersea · Deptford · Twickenham · Wandsworth · Dartford · Kingston · Wimbledon · Crystal Palace · Sydenham · Hampton Court · Merton · Bromley · Croydon

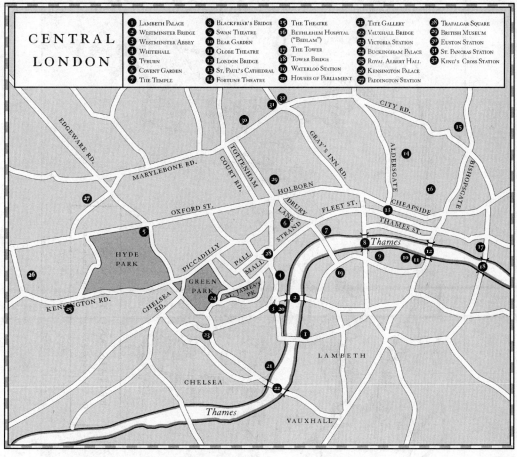

CENTRAL LONDON

1. Lambeth Palace
2. Westminster Bridge
3. Westminster Abbey
4. Whitehall
5. Tyburn
6. Covent Garden
7. The Temple
8. Blackfriar's Bridge
9. Swan Theatre
10. Bear Garden
11. Globe Theatre
12. London Bridge
13. St. Paul's Cathedral
14. Fortune Theatre
15. The Theatre
16. Bethlehem Hospital ("Bedlam")
17. The Tower
18. Tower Bridge
19. Waterloo Station
20. Houses of Parliament
21. Tate Gallery
22. Vauxhall Bridge
23. Victoria Station
24. Buckingham Palace
25. Royal Albert Hall
26. Kensington Palace
27. Paddington Station
28. Trafalgar Square
29. British Museum
30. Euston Station
31. St. Pancras Station
32. King's Cross Station

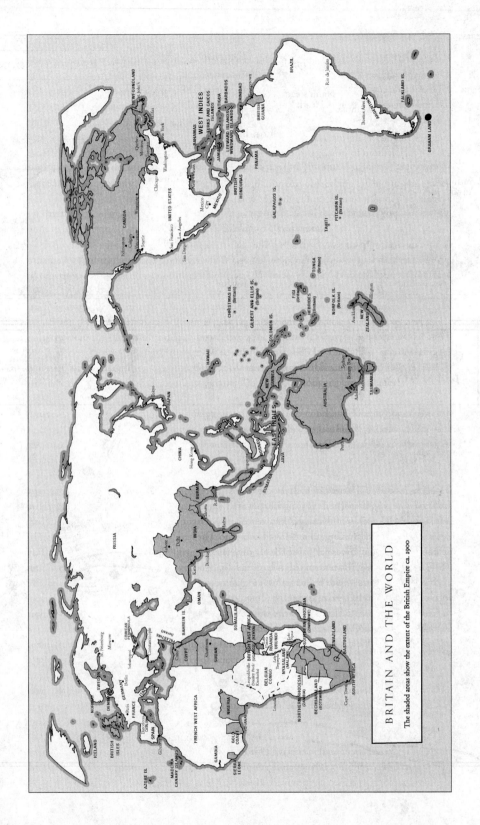

BRITAIN AND THE WORLD

The shaded areas show the extent of the British Empire ca. 1900

MONARCHS AND PRIME MINISTERS
OF GREAT BRITAIN

MONARCHS

HOUSE OF WESSEX

Egbert (Ecgberht)	829–39
Æthelwulf	839–58
Æthelbald	858–60
Æthelbert	860–66
Æthelred I	866–71
Alfred the Great	871–99
Edward the Elder	899–924
Athelstan	924–40
Edmund I	940–46
Edred (Eadred)	946–55
Edwy (Eadwig)	955–59
Edgar	959–75
Edward the Martyr	975–78
Æthelred II (the Unready)	978–1016
Edmund II (Ironside)	1016

DANISH LINE

Canute (Cnut)	1016–35
Harold I (Harefoot)	1035–40
Hardecanute	1040–42

WESSEX LINE, RESTORED

Edward the Confessor	1042–66
Harold II	1066

NORMAN LINE

William I (the Conqueror)	1066–87
William II (Rufus)	1087–1100
Henry I (Beauclerc)	1100–35
Stephen	1135–54

MONARCHS

PLANTAGENET,
ANGEVIN LINE

Henry II	1154–89
Richard I (Coeur de Lion)	1189–99
John (Lackland)	1199–1216
Henry III	1216–72
Edward I (Longshanks)	1272–1307
Edward II	1307–27
Edward III	1327–77
Richard II	1377–99

PLANTAGENET,
LANCASTRIAN LINE

Henry IV	1399–1413
Henry V	1413–22
Henry VI	1422–61

PLANTAGENET,
YORKIST LINE

Edward IV	1461–83
Edward V	1483
Richard III	1483–85

HOUSE OF TUDOR

Henry VII	1485–1509
Henry VIII	1509–47
Edward VI	1547–53
Mary I	1553–58
Elizabeth I	1558–1603

HOUSE OF STUART

James I	1603–25
Charles I	1625–49
(The Commonwealth)	1649–60
Oliver Cromwell	1649–58
Richard Cromwell	1658–59

Henry VIII

Mary I

MONARCHS

HOUSE OF STUART, RESTORED

Charles II	1660–85
James II	1685–88

HOUSE OF ORANGE AND STUART

William III and Mary II	1689–94
William III	1694–1702

HOUSE OF STUART

Anne	1702–14

HOUSE OF BRUNSWICK, HANOVER LINE

George I	1714–27
George II	1727–60
George III	1760–1820

George, Prince of Wales,
Prince Regent

PRIME MINISTERS

George III

Sir Robert Walpole (Whig)	1721–42
Earl of Wilmington (Whig)	1742–43
Henry Pelham (Whig)	1743–54
Duke of Newcastle (Whig)	1754–56
Duke of Devonshire (Whig)	1756–57
Duke of Newcastle (Whig)	1757–62
Earl of Bute (Tory)	1762–63
George Grenville (Whig)	1763–65
Marquess of Rockingham (Whig)	1765–66
William Pitt the Elder (Earl of Chatham) (Whig)	1766–68
Duke of Grafton (Whig)	1768–70
Frederick North (Lord North) (Tory)	1770–82
Marquess of Rockingham (Whig)	1782
Earl of Shelburne (Whig)	1782–83
Duke of Portland	1783
William Pitt the Younger (Tory)	1783–1801
Henry Addington (Tory)	1801–04
William Pitt the Younger (Tory)	1804–06
William Wyndham Grenville (Baron Grenville) (Whig)	1806–07

MONARCHS		PRIME MINISTERS	
		Duke of Portland (Whig)	1807–09
George, Prince of Wales, Prince Regent	1811–20	Spencer Perceval (Tory)	1809–12
		Earl of Liverpool (Tory)	1812–27
George IV	1820–30		
		George Canning (Tory)	1827
		Viscount Goderich (Tory)	1827–28
		Duke of Wellington (Tory)	1828–30
William IV	1830–37		
		Earl Grey (Whig)	1830–34
		Viscount Melbourne (Whig)	1834
Victoria	1837–1901		
		Sir Robert Peel (Tory)	1834–35
		Viscount Melbourne (Whig)	1835–41
		Sir Robert Peel (Tory)	1841–46
		Lord John Russell (later Earl) (Liberal)	1846–52
		Earl of Derby (Con.)	1852
		Earl of Aberdeen (Tory)	1852–55
		Viscount Palmerston (Lib.)	1855–58
		Earl of Derby (Con.)	1858–59
		Viscount Palmerston (Lib.)	1859–65
		Earl Russell (Liberal)	1865–66
		Earl of Derby (Con.)	1866–68
		Benjamin Disraeli (Con.)	1868
		William Gladstone (Lib.)	1868–74
		Benjamin Disraeli (Con.)	1874–80
		William Gladstone (Lib.)	1880–85
		Marquess of Salisbury (Con.)	1885–86
		William Gladstone (Lib.)	1886
HOUSE OF SAXE-COBURG-GOTHA		Marquess of Salisbury (Con.)	1886–92
Edward VII	1901–10	William Gladstone (Lib.)	1892–94
		Earl of Rosebery (Lib.)	1894–95
		Marquess of Salisbury (Con.)	1895–1902
		Arthur Balfour (Con.)	1902–05
		Sir Henry Campbell-Bannerman (Lib.)	1905–08
HOUSE OF WINDSOR		Herbert Asquith (Lib.)	1908–15
George V	1910–36		
		Herbert Asquith (Lib.)	1915–16

Victoria

MONARCHS		PRIME MINISTERS	
		Andrew Bonar Law (Con.)	1922–23
		Stanley Baldwin (Con.)	1923–24
		James Ramsay MacDonald (Labour)	1924
		Stanley Baldwin (Con.)	1924–29
		James Ramsay MacDonald (Labour)	1929–31
		James Ramsay MacDonald (Labour)	1931–35
		Stanley Baldwin (Con.)	1935–37
Edward VIII	1936	Neville Chamberlain (Con.)	1937–40
George VI	1936–52	Winston Churchill (Con.)	1940–45
		Winston Churchill (Con.)	1945
		Clement Attlee (Labour)	1945–51
		Sir Winston Churchill (Con.)	1951–55
Elizabeth II	1952–	Sir Anthony Eden (Con.)	1955–57
		Harold Macmillan (Con.)	1957–63
		Sir Alex Douglas-Home (Con.)	1963–64
		Harold Wilson (Labour)	1964–70
		Edward Heath (Con.)	1970–74
		Harold Wilson (Labour)	1974–76
		James Callaghan (Labour)	1976–79
		Margaret Thatcher (Con.)	1979–90
		John Major (Con.)	1990–97
		Tony Blair (Labour)	1997–

GLOSSARY OF TERMS

Accent: the natural emphasis (stress) speakers place on a syllable.

Accentual Verse: poetry in which a line is measured only by the number of accents or stresses, not by the number of syllables.

Accentual-Syllabic Verse: the most common metrical system in traditional English verse, in which a line is measured by the number of syllables and by the pattern of accented (stressed) and unaccented (unstressed) syllables.

Aesthetes: members of a late nineteenth-century movement that valued "art for art's sake"—for its purely aesthetic qualities, as opposed to valuing art for the moral content it may convey, for the intellectual stimulation it may provide, or for a range of other qualities.

Alexandrine: a line of verse that is 12 syllables long. In English verse, the alexandrine is always an iambic hexameter: that is, it has six iambic feet. The most-often quoted example is the second line in a couplet from Alexander Pope's "Essay on Criticism" (1711): "A needless Alexandrine ends the song / That, like a wounded snake, drags its slow length along." See also *Spenserian stanza*.

Allegory: a narrative with both a literal meaning and secondary, often symbolic meaning or meanings. Allegory frequently employs personification to give concrete embodiment to abstract concepts or entities, such as feelings or personal qualities. It may also present one set of characters or events in the guise of another, using implied parallels for the purposes of satire or political comment, as in John Dryden's poem "Absalom and Achitophel."

Alliteration: the grouping of words with the same initial consonant (e.g., "break, blow, burn, and make me new"). The repetition of sound acts as a connector. See also *assonance* and *consonance*.

Alliterative Verse: poetry that employs alliteration of stressed syllables in each line as its chief structural principle.

Allusion: a reference, often indirect or unidentified, to a person, thing, or event. A reference in one literary work to another literary work, whether to its content or its form, also constitutes an allusion.

Ambiguity: an "opening" of language created by the writer to allow for multiple meanings or differing interpretations. In literature, ambiguity may be deliberately employed by the writer to enrich meaning; this differs from any unintentional, unwanted, ambiguity in non-literary prose.

Amphibrach: a metrical foot with three syllables, the second of which is stressed: x / x (e.g., sensation).

Analogy: a broad term that refers to our processes of noting similarities among things or events. Specific forms of analogy in poetry include *simile* and *metaphor* (see below).

Anapaest: a metrical foot containing two unstressed syllables followed by one stressed syllable: xx / (e.g., underneath, intervene).

Anglican Church / Church of England: formed after Henry VIII's break with Rome in the 1530s, the Church of England had acquired a permanently Protestant cast by the 1570s. There has remained considerable variation within the Church, however, with distinctions often drawn among High Church, Broad Church, and Latitudinarian. At one extreme High Church Anglicans (some of whom prefer to be known as "Anglo-Catholics") prefer relatively elaborate church rituals not dissimilar in form to those of the Roman Catholic Church and place considerable emphasis on church hierarchy, while in the other direction Latitudinarians prefer relatively informal religious services and tend far more towards egalitarianism.

Antistrophe: from Greek drama, the chorus's countermovement or reply to an initial movement (strophe). See *ode* below.

Apostrophe: a figure of speech (a trope; see figures of speech below) in which a writer directly addresses an object—or a dead or absent person—as if the imagined audience were actually listening.

Archetype: in literature and mythology, a recurring idea, symbol, motif, character, or place. To some scholars and psychologists, an archetype represents universal human thought-patterns or experiences.

Assonance: the repetition of identical or similar vowel sounds in stressed syllables in which the surrounding consonants are different: for example, "shame" and "fate"; "gale" and "cage"; or the long "i" sounds in "Beside the pumice isle..."

Aubade: a lyric poem that greets or laments the arrival of dawn.

Ballad: a folk song, or a poem originally recited to an audience, which tells a dramatic story based on legend or history.

Ballad Stanza: a quatrain with alternating four-stress and three-stress lines, rhyming *abcb*. A variant is "common measure," in which the alternating lines are strictly iambic, and rhyme *abab*.

Ballade: a fixed form most commonly characterized by only three rhymes, with an 8-line stanza rhyming *ababbcbc* and an envoy rhyming *bcbc*. Both Chaucer and Dante Gabriel Rossetti ("Ballad of the Dead Ladies") adopted this form.

Baroque: powerful and heavily ornamented in style. "Baroque" is a term from the history of visual art and of music that is sometimes also used to describe certain literary styles, such as that of Richard Crashaw.

Bathos: an anticlimactic effect brought about by a writer's descent from an elevated subject or tone to the ordinary or trivial.

Benedictine Rule: set of instructions for monastic communities, composed by Saint Benedict of Nursia (died c. 457).

Blank Verse: unrhymed lines written in iambic pentameter, a form introduced to English verse by Henry Howard, Earl of Surrey, in his translation of parts of Virgil's *Aeneid* in 1547.

Bombast: inappropriately inflated or grandiose language.

Broadside: individual sheet of paper printed on only one side. From the sixteenth through to the eighteenth centuries broadsides of a variety of different sorts (e.g., ballads, political tracts, short satires) were sold on the streets.

Broken Rhyme: in which a multi-syllable word is split at the end of a line and continued onto the next, to allow an end-rhyme with the split syllable.

Burlesque: satire of a particularly exaggerated sort, particularly that which ridicules its subject by emphasising its vulgar or ridiculous aspects.

Caesura: a pause or break in a line of verse occurring where a phrase, clause, or sentence ends, and indicated in scansion by the mark II. If it occurs in the middle of the line, it is known as a "medial" caesura.

Canon: in literature, those works that are commonly accepted as possessing authority or importance. In practice, "canonical" texts or authors are those that are discussed most frequently by scholars and taught most frequently in university courses.

Canto: a sub-section of a long (usually epic) poem.

Canzone: a short song or poem, with stanzas of equal length and an envoy.

Carpe Diem: Latin (from Horace) meaning "seize the day." The idea of enjoying the moment is a common one in Renaissance love poetry. See, for example, Marvell's "To His Coy Mistress."

Catalexis: the omission of unstressed syllables from a line of verse (such a line is referred to as "catalectic"). In iambic verse it is usually the first syllable of the line that is omitted; in trochaic, the last. For example, in the first stanza of Housman's "To an Athlete Dying Young" the third line is catalectic: i.e., it has dropped the first, unstressed syllable called for by the poem's iambic tetrameter form: "The time you won your town the race / We chaired you through the market-place; / Man and boy stood cheering by, / And home we brought you shoulder-high."

Catharsis: the arousal through the performance of a dramatic tragedy of "emotions of pity and fear" to a point where "purgation" or "purification" occurs and the feelings are released or transformed. The concept was developed by Aristotle in his *Poetics* from an ancient Greek medical concept, and adapted by him into an aesthetic principle.

Chiasmus: a figure of speech (a scheme) that reverses word order in successive parallel clauses. If the word order is A-B-C in the first clause, it becomes C-B-A in the second: for example, Donne's line "She is all states, and all princes, I" ("The Sun Rising") incorporates this reversal (though with an ellipsis).

Classical: originating in or relating to ancient Greek or Roman culture. As commonly conceived, *classical* implies a strong sense of formal order. The term *neoclassical* is often used with reference to literature of the Restoration and eighteenth century that was strongly influenced by ancient Greek and Roman models.

Closet Drama: a play (typically in verse) written for private performance. The term came into use in the first half of the nineteenth century.

Colored Narrative: alternative term for *free indirect discourse.*

Comedy: as a literary term, used originally to denote that class of ancient Greek drama in which the action ends happily. More broadly the term has been used to describe a wide variety of literary forms of a more or less light-hearted character.

Commedia dell'arte: largely improvised comic performances conducted by masked performers and involving considerable physical activity. The genre of *commedia dell'arte* originated in Italy in the sixteenth century; it was influential throughout Europe for more than two centuries thereafter.

Commonwealth: from the fifteenth century, a term roughly equivalent to the modern "state," but tending to emphasize the commonality of interests among all citizens. In the seventeenth century Britain was named a commonwealth under Oliver Cromwell. In the twentieth century, the term came to be applied to associations of many nations; the British Commonwealth became the successor to the British Empire.

Conceit: an unusually elaborate metaphor or simile that extends beyond its original tenor and vehicle, sometimes becoming a "master" analogy for the entire poem (see, for example, Donne's "The Flea," and Robert Frost's sonnet "She is as in a field a silken tent"). Ingenious or fanciful images and comparisons were especially popular with the metaphysical poets of the seventeenth century, giving rise to the term "metaphysical conceit."

Concrete Poetry: an experimental form, most popular during the 1950s and 60s, in which the printed type itself forms a visual image of the poem's key words or ideas. See also *pattern poetry, assonance.*

Connotation: the implied, often unspoken meaning(s) of a given word, as distinct from its denotation, or literal meaning. Connotations may have highly emotional undertones and are usually culturally specific.

Conservative Party: See *Political Parties.*

Consonance: the pairing of words with similar initial and ending consonants, but with different vowel sounds (live/love, wander/wonder). See also *alliteration.*

Convention: aesthetic approach, technique, or practice accepted as characteristic and appropriate for a particular form. It is a convention of certain sorts of plays, for example, that the characters speak in blank verse, of other sorts of plays that characters speak in rhymed couplets, and of still other sorts of dramatic performances that characters frequently break into song to express their feelings.

Couplet: a pair of rhyming lines, usually in the same meter. If they form a complete unit of thought and are grammatically complete, the lines are known as a closed couplet. See also *heroic couplet* below.

Dactyl: a metrical foot containing one strong stress followed by two weak stresses: / xx (e.g., muttering, helplessly). A minor form known as "double dactyls" makes use of this meter for humorous purposes, e.g., "Jiggery pokery" or "Higgledy Piggledy."

Denotation: See *connotation* above.

Devolution: process through which a degree of political power was transferred in the late twentieth and early twenty-first centuries from the British government to assemblies in Scotland and in Wales.

Dialogue: words spoken by characters to one another. (When a character is addressing him or her self or the audience directly, the words spoken are referred to as a *monologue*.)

Diction: word choice. Whether the diction of a literary work (or of a literary character) is colloquial, conversational, formal, or of some other type contributes significantly to the tone of the text as well as to characterization.

Didacticism: aesthetic approach emphasizing moral instruction.

Dimeter: a poetic line containing two metrical feet.

Dirge: a song or poem that mourns someone's death. See also *elegy* and *lament* below.

Disestablishmentarianism: movement opposing an official state-supported religion, in particular the Church of England in that role.

Dissonance: harsh, unmusical sounds or rhythms which poets may use deliberately to achieve certain effects.

Dramatic Irony: this form of irony occurs when the audience's reception of a speech by a character on the stage is affected by the possession by the audience of information not available to the character.

Dramatic Monologue: a lyric poem that takes the form of an utterance by a single person addressing a silent listener. The speaker may be an historical personage (as in some of Robert Browning's dramatic monologues), a figure drawn from myth or legend (as in some of Tennyson's), or an entirely imagined figure, as in Webster's "A Castaway."

Dub Poetry: a form of protest poetry originating in Jamaica, with its roots in dance rhythms, especially reggae, and often accompanied in performance by drums and music. See also *rap* and *hip-hop*.

Duple Foot: A duple foot of poetry has two syllables. The possible duple forms are iamb (in which the stress is on the second of the two syllables), trochee (in which the stress is on the first of the two syllables), spondee (in which both are stressed equally), and pyrrhic (in which both syllables are unstressed).

Eclogue: now generally used simply as an alternative name for a pastoral poem. In classical times and in the early modern period, however, an *eclogue* (or *idyll*) was a specific type of pastoral poem—a dialogue or dramatic monologue involving rustic characters. (The other main sub-genre of the pastoral was the *georgic*.)

Elegiac Stanza: a quatrain of iambic pentameters rhyming *abab*, often used in poems meditating on death or sorrow. The best-known example is Thomas Gray's "Elegy Written in a Country Churchyard."

Elegy: a poem which formally mourns the death of a particular person (e.g., Tennyson's "In Memoriam") or in which the poet meditates on other serious subjects (e.g., Gray's "Elegy"). See also *dirge*.

Elision: omitting or suppressing a letter or an unstressed syllable at the beginning or end of a word, so that a line of verse may conform to a given metrical scheme. For example, the three syllables at the beginning of Shakespeare's sonnet 129 are reduced to two by the omission of the first vowel: "Th' expense of spirit in a waste of shame." See also *syncope*.

Ellipsis: the omission of a word or words necessary for the complete grammatical construction of a sentence, but not necessary for our understanding of the sentence.

End-Rhyme: See *rhyme*.

End-stopped: a line of poetry is said to be end-stopped when the end of the line coincides with a natural pause in the syntax, such as the conclusion of a sentence; e.g., in this couplet from Pope's "Essay on Criticism," both lines are end-stopped: "A little learning is a dangerous thing; / Drink deep, or taste not the Pierian spring." Compare this with *enjambement*.

Enjambement: the "running-on" of the sense from one line of poetry to the next, with no pause created by punctuation or syntax. (The more commonly found alternative is referred to as an *end-stopped line*.)

Envoy (Envoi): a stanza or half-stanza that forms the conclusion of certain French poetic forms, such as the *sestina* or the *ballade*. It often sums up or comments upon what has gone before.

Epic: a lengthy narrative poem, often divided into books and sub-divided into cantos. It generally celebrates heroic deeds or events, and the style tends to be lofty and grand. Examples in English include Spenser's *The Faerie Queene* and Milton's *Paradise Lost*.

Epic Simile: an elaborate simile, developed at such length that the vehicle of the comparison momentarily displaces the primary subject with which it is being compared.

Epigram: a very short poem, sometimes in closed couplet form, characterized by pointed wit.

Epigraph: a quotation placed at the beginning of a discourse to indicate or foreshadow the theme.

Epiphany: a moment at which matters of significance are suddenly illuminated for a literary character (or for the reader), typically triggered by something small and seemingly of little import. The term first came into wide currency in connection with the fiction of James Joyce.

Episodic Plot: plot comprising a variety of episodes that are only loosely connected by threads of story material (as opposed to plots that present one or more continually unfolding narratives where successive episodes build one on another).

Epithalamion: a poem celebrating a wedding. The best-known example in English is probably Edmund Spenser's "Epithalamion" (1595).

Eulogy: text expressing praise, especially for a distinguished person recently deceased.

Euphemism: mode of expression through which aspects of reality considered to be vulgar, crudely physical, or unpleasant are referred to indirectly rather than named explicitly. A variety of euphemisms exist for the processes of urination and defecation; *passed away* is often used as a euphemism for *died*. (The word *euphemism* has the same root as *Euphuism* (see below), but has taken on a different meaning.)

Euphony: pleasant, musical sounds or rhythms—the opposite of dissonance.

Euphuism: In the late sixteenth century John Lyly published a prose romance, *Euphues*, which employed a style that featured long sentences filled with balanced phrases and clauses, many of them adding little to the content. This highly mannered style was popular in the court of Elizabeth I for a few years following the publication of Lyly's famous work, and the style became known as *Euphuism*.

European Union: (EU) Group of nations formed in 1993 as the successor to the European Economic Community (Common Market). Britain first applied for membership in the latter in 1961; at first its efforts to join were blocked by the French government, but in 1973 Prime Minister Edward Heath successfully negotiated Britain's entry into the group. Britain has resisted some moves towards full integration with the European community, in particular retaining its own currency when other European nations adopted the Euro on 1 January 2002.

Exchequer: In earlier eras, the central royal financial office, responsible for receiving and keeping track of crown revenues. In later eras, part of the bureaucracy equivalent to the Ministry of Finance in Canada or the Treasury in the United States (the modern post of Chancellor of the Exchequer is equivalent to the American post of Secretary of the Treasury, the Canadian post of Minister of Finance or the Australian post of Treasurer).

Exposition: the setting out of material in an ordered form, either in speech or in writing. In a play those parts of the action that do not occur on stage but are rather recounted by the characters are frequently described as being presented in exposition. Similarly, when the background narrative is filled in near the beginning of a novel, such material is often described as having been presented in exposition. Somewhat confusingly, however, the term "expository prose" is usually used with reference not to fiction but to the setting forth of arguments or descriptions in the context of essays or other works of prose non-fiction.

Eye-Rhyme: See *rhyme* below.

Feminine Ending: the ending of a line of poetry on an "extra," and, especially, on an unstressed syllable. See, for example, the first line of Keat's "Ode on a Grecian Urn": "A thing of beauty is a joy forever," a line of iambic pentameter in which the final foot is an amphibrach rather than an iamb.

Feminine Rhyme: See *rhyme* below.

Figures of Speech: deliberate, highly concentrated uses of language to achieve particular purposes or effects on an audience. There are two kinds of figures: schemes and tropes. Schemes involve changes in word-sound and word-order, such as *alliteration* and *chiasmus*. Tropes play on our understandings of words to extend, alter, or transform meaning, as in *metaphor* and *personification*.

First-Person Narrative: narrative recounted using *I* and *me*. See also *narrative perspective*.

Fixed Forms: the term applied to a number of poetic forms and stanzaic patterns, many derived from French models, such as *ballade, rondeau, sestina, triolet,* and *villanelle*. Other "fixed forms" include the *sonnet, rhyme royal, haiku,* and *ottava rima*.

Folio: largest of several sizes of book page commonly used in the first few centuries after the introduction of the printing press. A folio size results from sheets of paper of at least 14 inches by 20 inches being folded in half (a folio page size will thus be at least 7 inches by 10 inches). When the same sheet is folded twice a quarto is produced, and when it is folded 3 times an octavo.

Foot: a unit of a line of verse which contains a particular combination of stressed and unstressed syllables. Dividing a line into metrical feet (*iambs, trochees,* etc.), then counting the number of feet per line, is part of *scansion*. See also *meter*.

Franklin: in the late medieval period, a landholder of free status, but ranking below the gentry.

Free Indirect Discourse: in prose fiction, commentary in which a seemingly objective and omniscient narrative voice assumes the point of view of one or more characters. When we hear through the third person narrative voice of Jane Austen's *Pride and Prejudice*, for example, that Mr. Darcy "was the proudest, most disagreeable man in the world, and every body hoped that he would never come there again," the narrative voice has assumed the point of view of "every body" in the community; we as readers are not meant to take it that Mr. Darcy is indeed the most disagreeable man in the world. Similarly, in the following passage from the same novel, we are likely to take it to read it as being the view of the character Charlotte that marriage is "the only honourable provision for well-educated young women of small fortune," not to take it to be an objective statement of perceived truth on the part of the novel's third person narrative voice:

> [Charlotte's] reflections were in general satisfactory. Mr. Collins to be sure was neither sensible nor agreeable; his society was irksome, and his attachment to her must be imaginary. But still he would be her husband. Without thinking highly either of men or of matrimony, marriage had always been her object; it was the only honourable provision for well-educated young women of small fortune, and however uncertain of giving happiness, must be their pleasantest preservative from want.

The term free indirect discourse may also be applied to situations in which it may not be entirely clear if the thoughts expressed emanate from the character, the narrator, or some combination of the two. (In the above-quoted passage expressing Charlotte's thoughts, indeed, some might argue that the statement concerning marriage should be taken as the expression of a belief that the narrative voice shares, at least in part.)

Free Verse: poetry that does not follow any regular meter, line length, or rhyming scheme. In many respects, though, free verse follows the complex natural "rules" and rhythmic patterns (or cadences) of speech.

Gaelic: Celtic language, variants of which are spoken in Ireland and Scotland.

Genre: a particular literary form. The concept of genre may be used with different levels of generality. At the most general, poetry, drama, and prose fiction are distinguished as separate genres. At a lower level of generality various sub-genres are frequently distinguished, such as (within drama) comedy and tragedy, or, at a still lower level of generality, Elizabethan domestic tragedy, Edwardian drawing-room comedy, and so on.

Georgic: (from Virgil's *Georgics*) a poem that celebrates the natural wealth of the countryside and advises how to cultivate and live in harmony with it. Pope's *Windsor Forest* and James Thomson's *Seasons* are classed as georgics. They were often said to make up, with eclogues, the two alliterative forms of pastoral poetry.

Ghazal: derived from Persian and Indian precedents, the ghazal presents a series of thoughts in closed couplets joined by a simple rhyme-scheme: *ab bb cb eb fb*, etc.

Gothic: in architecture and the visual arts, a term used to describe styles prevalent from the twelfth to the fourteenth centuries, but in literature a term used to describe work with a sinister or grotesque tone that seeks to evoke a sense of terror on the part of the reader or audience. Gothic literature originated as a genre in the eighteenth century with works such as Horace Walpole's *The Castle of Otranto*. To some extent the notion of the medieval itself then carried with it associations of the dark and the grotesque, but from the beginning an element of intentional exaggeration (sometimes verging on self-parody) attached itself to the genre. The Gothic trend of youth culture that began in the late twentieth century is less clearly associated with the medieval, but shares with the various varieties of Gothic literature (from Walpole in the eighteenth century, to Bram Stoker in the early twentieth, to Stephen King and Anne Rice in the late twentieth) a fondness for the sensational and the grotesque, as well as a propensity to self-parody.

Guilds: non-clerical associations that arose in the late Anglo-Saxon period, devoted both to social purposes (such as the organization of feasts for the members) and to piety. In the later medieval period guilds developed strong associations with particular occupations.

Haiku: a Japanese form, using three unrhymed lines of five, seven, and five syllables. Conventionally, it uses precise, concentrated images to suggest states of feeling.

Heptameter: a line containing seven metrical feet.

Heroic Couplet: a pair of rhymed iambic pentameters, so called because the form was much used in seventeenth and eighteenth-century poems and plays on heroic subjects.

Hexameter: a line containing six metrical feet.

Home Rule: movement dedicated to making Ireland politically independent from Britain.

Horatian Ode: inspired by the work of the Roman poet Horace, an ode that is usually calm and meditative in tone, and homostrophic (i.e., having regular stanzas) in form. Keats's odes are English examples.

House of Commons: elected legislative body, in Britain currently consisting of six hundred and fifty-nine members of Parliament. See also *Parliament.*

House of Lords: the "Upper House" of the British Houses of Parliament. Since the nineteenth century the House of Lords has been far less powerful than the elected House of Commons. The House of Lords is currently made up of both hereditary peers (Lords whose title is passed on from generation to generation) and life peers. As a result of legislation enacted by the Labour government of Tony Blair, the role of hereditary peers in Parliament is being phased out.

Humors: The four humors were believed in until the sixteenth and seventeenth centuries to be elements in the makeup of all humans; a person's temperament was thought to be determined by the way in which the humors were combined. When the *choleric* humor was dominant, the person would tend towards anger; when the *sanguine* humor was dominant, towards pleasant affability; when the *phlegmatic* humor was dominant, towards a cool and calm attitude and/or a lack of feeling or enthusiasm; and when the *melancholic* humor was dominant, towards withdrawal and melancholy.

Hymn: a song whose theme is usually religious, in praise of divinity. Literary hymns may praise more secular subjects.

Hyperbole: a *figure of speech* (a trope) that deliberately exaggerates or inflates meaning to achieve particular effects, such as the irony in A.E. Housman's claim (from "Terence, this is stupid stuff") that "malt does more than Milton can / To justify God's ways to man."

Iamb: the most common metrical foot in English verse, containing one unstressed syllable followed by a stressed syllable: x / (e.g., between, achieve).

Idyll: traditionally, a short pastoral poem that idealizes country life, conveying impressions of innocence and happiness.

Image: the recreation in words of objects perceived by the senses, sometimes thought of as "pictures," although other senses besides sight are involved. Besides this literal application, the term also refers more generally to the descriptive effects of figurative language, especially in *metaphor* and *simile*.

Imagism: a poetic movement that was popular mainly in the second decade of the twentieth century. The goal of Imagist poets (such as H.D. and Ezra Pound in their early work) was to represent emotions or impressions through highly concentrated imagery.

In Memoriam Stanza: a four-line stanza in iambic tetrameter, rhyming *abba*: the type of stanza used by Tennyson in *In Memoriam*.

Incantation: a chant or recitation of words that are believed to have magical power. A poem can achieve an "incantatory" effect through a compelling rhyme scheme and other repetitive patterns.

Interlocking Rhyme: See *rhyme*.

Internal Rhyme: See *rhyme*.

Irony: a subtle form of humor in which a statement is understood to convey a quite different (and often entirely opposite) meaning. A writer achieves this by carefully making sure that the statement occurs in a context which undermines or twists the statement's "literal" meaning. *Hyperbole* and *litotes* are often used for ironic effect. *Sarcasm* is a particularly strong or crude form of irony (usually spoken), in which the meaning is conveyed largely by the tone of voice adopted; something said sarcastically is meant clearly to imply its opposite.

Labour Party: See *Political Parties*.

Lament: a poem which expresses profound regret or grief either because of a death, or because of the loss of a former, happier state.

Language Poetry: a movement that defies the usual lyric and narrative conventions of poetry, and that challenges the structures and codes of everyday language. Often seen as both politically and aesthetically subversive, its roots lie in the works of modernist writers like Ezra Pound and Gertrude Stein.

Liberal Party: See *Political Parties*.

Litotes: a *figure of speech* (a trope) in which a writer deliberately uses understatement to highlight the importance of an argument, or to convey an ironic attitude.

Liturgical Drama: drama based on and/or incorporating text from the liturgy—the text recited during religious services.

Lollard: member of the group of radical Christians that took its inspiration from the ideas of John Wyclif (c. 1330–84). The Lollards, in many ways precursors of the Protestant Reformation, advocated making the Bible available to all, and dedication to the principles of evangelical poverty in imitation of Christ.

Luddites: protestors against the mechanization of industry on the grounds that it was leading to the loss of employment and to an increase in poverty. In the years 1811 to 1816 there were several Luddite protests in which machines were destroyed.

Lyric: a poem, usually short, expressing an individual speaker's feelings or private thoughts. Originally a song performed with accompaniment on a lyre, the lyric poem is often noted for musicality of rhyme and rhythm. The lyric genre includes a variety of forms, including the *sonnet*, the *ode*, the *elegy*, the *madrigal*, the *aubade*, the *dramatic monologue*, and the *hymn*.

Madrigal: a lyric poem, usually short and focusing on pastoral or romantic themes. A madrigal is often set to music.

Masculine Ending: a metrical line ending on a stressed syllable. *Masculine Rhyme*: see *rhyme*.

Masque: an entertainment typically combining music and dance, with a limited script, extravagant costumes and sets, and often incorporating spectacular special effects. Masques, which were performed before court audiences in the early seventeenth century, often focused on royal themes and frequently drew on classical mythology.

Mass: Within Christianity, a church service that includes the sacrament of the Eucharist (Holy Communion), in which bread and wine are consumed which are believed by those of many Christian denominations to have been transubstantiated into the body and blood of Christ. Anglicans (Episcopalians) are more likely to believe the bread and wine merely symbolizes the body and blood.

Melodrama: originally a term used to describe nineteenth-century-plays featuring sensational story lines and a crude separation of characters into moral categories, with the pure and virtuous pitted against evil villains. Early melodramas employed background music throughout the action of the play as a means of heightening the emotional response of the audience. By extension, certain sorts of prose fictions or poems are often described as having melodramatic elements.

Metaphor: a *figure of speech* (in this case, a trope) in which a comparison is made or identity is asserted between two unrelated things or actions without the use of "like" or "as." The primary subject is known as the *tenor*; to illuminate its nature, the writer links it to wholly different images, ideas, or actions referred to as the *vehicle*. Unlike a *simile*, which is a direct comparison of two things, a metaphor "fuses" the separate qualities of two things, creating a new idea. For example, Shakespeare's "Let slip the dogs of war" is a metaphorical statement. The tenor, or primary subject, is "war"; the vehicle of the metaphor is the image of hunting dogs released from their leash. The line fuses the idea of war with the qualities of ravening bloodlust associated with hunting dogs.

Metaphysical Poets: a group of seventeenth-century English poets, notably Donne, Cowley, Marvell, and Herbert, who employed unusual difficult imagery and *conceits* (see above) in order to develop intellectual and religious themes. The term was first applied to these writers to mark as far-fetched their use of philosophical and scientific ideas in a poetic context.

Meter: the pattern of stresses, syllables, and pauses that constitutes the regular rhythm of a line of verse. The meter of a poem written in the English accentual-syllabic tradition is determined by identifying the stressed and unstressed syllables in a line of verse, and grouping them into recurring units known as feet. See *accent, accentual-syllabic, caesura, elision*, and *scansion*. For some of the better known meters, see *iamb, trochee, dactyl, anapaest*, and *spondee*. See also *monometer, dimeter, trimeter, tetrameter, pentameter*, and *hexameter*.

Methodist: Protestant denomination formed in the eighteenth century as part of the religious movement led by John and Charles Wesley. Originally a movement within the Church of England, Methodism entailed enthusiastic evangelism, a strong emphasis on free will, and a strict regimen of Christian living.

Metonymy: a *figure of speech* (a trope), meaning "change of name," in which a writer refers to an object or idea by substituting the name of another object or idea closely associated with it: for example, the substitution of "crown" for monarchy, "the press" for journalism, or "the pen" for writing. *Synecdoche* (see below) is a kind of metonymy.

Mock-heroic: a style applying the elevated diction and vocabulary of epic poetry to low or ridiculous subjects. An example is Alexander Pope's "The Rape of the Lock."

Monologue: words spoken by a character to him or herself or to an audience directly.

Monometer: a line containing one metrical foot.

Mood: This can describe the writer's attitude, implied or expressed, towards the subject (see *tone* below); or it may refer to the atmosphere that a writer creates in a passage of description or narration.

Motif: an idea, image, action, or plot element that recurs throughout a literary work, creating new levels of meaning and strengthening structural coherence. The term is taken from music, where it describes recurring melodies or themes. See also *theme*.

Narrative Perspective: in fiction, the point of view from which the story is narrated. A first-person narrative is recounted using *I* and *me*, whereas a third person narrative is recounted using *he, she, they,* and so on. When a narrative is written in the third person and the narrative voice evidently "knows" all that is being done and thought, the story is typically described as being recounted by an "omniscient narrator."

Neoclassical: adapted from or substantially influenced by the cultures of ancient Greece and Rome. The term *neoclassical* is often used to describe the ideals of Restoration and eighteenth-century writers and artists who looked to ancient Greek and Roman civilization for models.

Nobility: privileged class, the members of which are distinguished by the holding of titles. Dukes, Marquesses, Earls, Viscounts, and Barons (in that order of precedence) are all holders of hereditary titles—that is to say, in the British patrilineal tradition, titles passed on from generation to generation to the eldest son. The title of Baronet, also hereditary, was added to this list by James I. Holders of non-hereditary titles include Knights and Dames.

Nonconformist: general term used to describe one who does subscribe to the Church of England.

Nonsense Verse: light, humorous poetry which contradicts logic, plays with the absurd, and invents words for amusing effects. Lewis Carroll is one of the best-known practitioners of nonsense verse.

Octave: also known as "octet," the first eight lines in an Italian/Petrarchan sonnet, rhyming *abbaabba*. See also *sestet* and *sonnet*.

Octosyllabic: a line of poetry with eight syllables, as in iambic tetrameter.

Ode: originally a classical poetic form, used by the Greeks and Romans to convey serious themes. English poetry has evolved three main forms of ode: the Pindaric (imitative of the odes of the Greek poet Pindar); the Horatian (modeled on the work of the Roman writer Horace); and the irregular ode.

The Pindaric ode was an irregular stanza in English, has a tripartite structure of "strophe," "antistrophe," and "epode" (meaning turn, counterturn, and stand), modeled on the songs and movements of the Chorus in Greek drama. The Horatian ode is more personal, reflective, and literary, and employs a pattern of repeated stanzas. The irregular ode, as its name implies, avoids a recurrent stanza pattern, and is sometimes irregular in line length also (see, for example, Wordsworth's "Ode: Intimations of Immortality").

Onomatopoeia: a *figure of speech* (a scheme) in which a word "imitates" a sound, or in which the sound of a word seems to reflect its meaning.

Ottava Rima: an 8-line stanza, usually in iambic pentameter, with the rhyme scheme *abababcc*. For an example, see Byron's *Don Juan*, or Yeats's "Sailing to Byzantium."

Oxymoron: a *figure of speech* (a trope) in which two words whose meanings seem contradictory are placed together, a paradox: for example, the phrase "darkness visible," from Milton's *Paradise Lost*.

Paean: a triumphant, celebratory song, often associated with a military victory.

Pale: in the medieval period, term for a protective zone around a fortress. As of the year 1500 three of these had been set up to guard frontiers of territory controlled by England—surrounding Calais in France, Berwick-upon-Tweed on the Scottish frontier, and Dublin in Ireland. The Dublin Pale was the largest of the three, and the term remained in use for a longer period there.

Pantoum: a poem in linked quatrains that rhyme *abab*. The second and fourth lines of one stanza are repeated as the first and third lines of the stanza that follows. In the final stanza the pattern is reversed: the second line repeats the third line of the first stanza, the fourth and final line repeats the first line of the first stanza.

Parliament: in Britain, the legislative body, comprising both the House of Commons and the House of Lords. Since the eighteenth century, the most powerful figure in the British government has been the Prime Minister rather than the monarch, the House of Commons has been the dominant body in Parliament, and members of the House of Commons have been organized in political parties. Since the mid-nineteenth century the effective executive in the British Parliamentary system has been the Cabinet, each member of which is typically in charge of a department of government. Unlike the American system, the British Parliamentary system (sometimes called the "Westminster system," after the location of the Houses of Parliament) brings together the executive and legislative functions of government, with the Prime Minister leading the government party in the House of Commons as well as directing the cabinet. By convention it is understood that the House of Lords will not contravene the wishes of the House of Commons in any fundamental way, though the "Upper House," as it is often referred to, may sometimes modify or reject legislation.

Parody: a close, usually mocking imitation of a particular literary work, or of the well-known style of a particular author, in order to expose or magnify weaknesses. Parody is a form of satire—that is, humor that may ridicule and scorn its object.

Pastiche: a discourse which borrows or imitates other writers' characters, forms, style, or ideas. Unlike a parody, a pastiche is usually intended as a compliment to the original writer.

Pastoral: in general, pertaining to country life; in prose, drama, and poetry, a stylized type of writing that idealizes the lives and innocence of country people, particularly shepherds and shepherdesses. Also see *eclogue, georgic, idyll*, above.

Pastoral Elegy: a poem in which the poet uses the pastoral style to lament the death of a friend, usually represented as a shepherd. Milton's "Lycidas" provides a good example of the form, including its use of such conventions as an invocation of the muse and a procession of mourners.

Pathetic Fallacy: a form of personification in which inanimate objects are given human emotions: for example, rain clouds "weeping." The word "fallacy" in this connection is intended to suggest the distortion of reality or the false emotion that may result from an exaggerated use of personification.

Pathos: the emotional quality of a discourse; or the ability of a discourse to appeal to our emotions. It is usually applied to the mood conveyed by images of pain, suffering, or loss that arouse feelings of pity or sorrow in the reader.

Pattern Poetry: a predecessor of modern concrete poetry, in which the shape of the poem on the page is intended to suggest or imitate an aspect of the poem's subject. George Herbert's "Easter Wings" is an example of pattern poetry.

Penny Dreadful: Victorian term for a cheap and poorly produced work of short fiction, usually of a sensational nature.

Pentameter: a line of verse containing five metrical feet.

Performance Poetry: poetry composed primarily for oral performance, often very theatrical in nature. See also *dub poetry* and *rap*.

Persona: the assumed identity or "speaking voice" that a writer projects in a discourse. The term "persona" literally means "mask." Even when a writer speaks in the first person, we should be aware that the attitudes or opinions we hear may not necessarily be those of the writer in real life.

Personification: a *figure of speech* (a trope), also known as "prosopopoeia," in which a writer refers to inanimate objects, ideas, or animals as if they were human, or creates a human figure to represent an abstract entity such as Philosophy or Peace.

Petrarchan Sonnet: the earliest form of the sonnet, also known as the Italian sonnet, with an 8-line octave and a 6-line sestet. The Petrarchan sonnet traditionally focuses on love and descriptions of physical beauty.

Phoneme: a linguistic term denoting the smallest unit of sound that it is possible to distinguish. The words *fun* and *phone* each have three phonemes, though one has three letters and one has five. (Each makes up a single syllable.)

Pindaric: See *ode*.

Plot: the organization of story materials within a literary work. The order in which story material is presented (especially causes and consequences); the inclusion of elements that allow or encourage the reader or audience to form expectations as to what is likely to happen; the decision to present some story material through exposition rather than in more extended form as part of the main action of the narrative—all these are matters of plotting.

Political Parties: The party names "Whig" and "Tory" began to be used in the late seventeenth century; before that time members of the House of Commons acted individually or through shifting and very informal factions. At first the Whigs and Tories had little formal organization either, but by the mid-eighteenth century parties had acknowledged leaders, and the leader of the party with the largest number of members in the House of Commons had begun to be recognized as the Prime Minister. The Tories evolved into the modern Conservative Party, and the Whigs into the Liberal Party. In the late nineteenth century the Labour Party was formed in an effort to provide better representation in Parliament for the working class, and since the 1920s Labour and the Conservatives have alternated as the party of government, with the Liberals reduced to third-party status. (Since 1988, when the Liberals merged with a breakaway faction from Labour known as the Social Democrats, this third party has been named the Liberal Democrats.)

Pre-Raphaelites: originally a group of Victorian artists and writers, formed in 1848. Their goal was to revive what they considered the simpler, fresher, more natural art that existed before Raphael (1483-1520). The poet Dante Gabriel Rossetti was one of the founders of the group.

Presbyterian: term applied to a group of Protestants (primarily English and Scottish) who advocated replacing the traditional hierarchical church in which bishops and archbishops governed lower level members of the clergy with a system in which all presbyters (or ministers) would be equal. The Presbyterians, originally led by John Knox, were strongly influenced by the ideas of John Calvin.

Prose Poem: a poetic discourse that uses prose formats (e.g., it may use margins and paragraphs rather than line breaks or stanzas) yet is written with the kind of attention to language, rhythm and cadence that characterizes verse.

Prosody: the study and analysis of meter, rhythm, rhyme, stanzaic pattern, and other devices of versification.

Protagonist: the central character in a literary work.

Prothalamion: a wedding song; a term coined by the poet Edmund Spenser, adapted from "epithalamion" (see above).

Public School: See *schools* below.

Pun: a play on words, in which a word with two or more distinct meanings, or two words with similar sounds, may create humorous ambiguities. Also known as *paranomasia*.

Puritan: term, originally applied only in a derogatory fashion but later widely accepted as descriptive, referring to those in England who favored religious reforms that went beyond those instituted as part of the Protestant Reformation, or, more generally, who were more forceful and uncompromising in pressing for religious purity both within the Church and in society as a whole.

Pyrrhic: a metrical foot containing two weak stresses: xx.

Quadrivium: group of four academic subjects (arithmetic, astronomy, geometry, and music) that made up part of the university coursework in the Middle Ages. There were studied after the more basic subjects of the *Trivium*.

Quantitative Meter: a metrical system used by Greek and Roman poets, in which a line of verse was measured by the "quantity," or length of sound of each syllable. A foot was measured in terms of syllables classed as long or short.

Quantity: duration of syllables in poetry. The line "There is a Garden in her face" (the first line from the poem of the same name by Thomas Campion) is characterized by the short quantities of the syllables. The last line of Thomas Hardy's "During Wind and Rain" has the same number of syllables as the line by Campion, but the quantities of the syllables are much longer—in other words, the line take much longer to say: "Down their carved names the rain drop ploughs."

Quatrain: a four-line stanza, usually rhymed.

Quintet: a five-line stanza. Sometimes given as *quintain*.

Rap: originally coined to describe informal conversation, "rap" now usually describes a style of performance poetry in which a poet will chant rhymed verse, sometimes improvised and usually with musical accompaniment that has a heavy beat.

Realism: as a literary term, the presentation through literature of material closely resembling real life. As notions both of what constitutes "real life" and of how it may be most faithfully represented in literature have varied widely, "realism" has taken a variety of meanings. The term *naturalistic* has sometimes been used a synonym for *realistic*; *naturalism* originated in the nineteenth century as a term denoting a form of realism focusing in particular on grim, unpleasant, or ugly aspects of the real.

Refrain: one or more words or lines repeated at regular points throughout a poem, often at the end of each stanza or group of stanzas. Sometimes a whole stanza may be repeated to create a refrain, like the chorus in a song.

Reggae: a style of heavily-rhythmic music from the West Indies with lyrics that are colloquial in language and often anti-establishment in content and flavor. First popularized in the 1960s and 1970s, reggae has had a lasting influence on performance poetry, rap, and dub.

Rhetoric: in classical Greece and Rome, the art of persuasion and public speaking. From the Middle Ages onwards, the study of rhetoric gave greater attention to style, particularly figures of speech. Today in poetics, the term rhetoric may encompass not only figures of speech, but also the persuasive effects of forms, sounds and word choices.

Rhyme: the repetition of identical or similar sounds, usually in pairs and generally at the ends of metrical lines.

End-rhyme: a rhyming word or syllable at the end of a line.

Eye Rhyme: rhyming that pairs words whose spellings are alike but whose pronunciations are different: for example, though/slough.

Feminine Rhyme: a two-syllable (also known as "double") rhyme. The first syllable is stressed and the second unstressed: for example, hasty/tasty. See also *triple rhyme* below.

Interlocking Rhyme: the repetition of rhymes from one stanza to the next, creating links that add to the poem's continuity and coherence. Examples may be found in Shelley's use of *terza rima* in "Ode to the West Wind" and in Dylan Thomas's villanelle "Do Not Go Gentle Into That Good Night."

Internal Rhyme: the placement of rhyming words within lines so that at least two words in a line rhyme with each other.

Masculine Rhyme: a correspondence of sound between the final stressed syllables at the end of two or more lines, as in grieve/leave, arr-ive/sur-vive.

Slant Rhyme: an imperfect or partial rhyme (also known as "near" or "half" rhyme) in which the final consonants of stressed syllables match but the vowel sounds do not. E.g., spoiled / spilled, taint / stint.

Triple Rhyme: a three-syllable rhyme in which the first syllable of each rhyme-word is stressed and the other two unstressed (e.g., lottery / coterie).

True Rhyme: a rhyme in which everything but the initial consonant matches perfectly in sound and spelling.

Rhyme Royal: a stanza of seven iambic pentameters, with a rhyme-scheme of *ababbcc*. This is also known as the Chaucerian stanza, as Chaucer was the first English poet to use this form. See also *septet*.

Rhythm: in speech, the arrangement of stressed and unstressed syllables creates units of sound. In song or verse, these units usually form a regular rhythmic pattern, a kind of beat, described in prosody as *meter*.

Romanticism: a major social and cultural movement, originating in Europe, that shaped much of Western artistic thought in the late eighteenth and nineteenth centuries. Opposing the ideal of controlled, rational order of the Enlightenment, Romanticism emphasizes the importance of spontaneous self-expression, emotion, and personal experience in producing art. In Romanticism, the "natural" is privileged over the conventional or the artificial.

Rondeau: a fifteen-line poem, generally octosyllabic, with only two rhymes throughout its three stanzas, and an unrhymed refrain at the end of the ninth and fifteenth lines, repeating part of the opening line.

Sarcasm: See *irony*.

Satire: literary work designed to make fun of or seriously criticize its subject. According to many literary theories of the Renaissance and neoclassical periods, the ridicule through satire of a certain sort of behavior may function for the reader or audience as a corrective of such behavior.

Scansion: the formal analysis of patterns of rhythm and rhyme in poetry. Each line of verse will have a certain number of fairly regular "beats" consisting of alternating stressed and unstressed syllables. To "scan" a poem is to count the beats in each line, to mark stressed and unstressed syllables and indicate their combination into "feet," to note pauses, and to identify rhyme schemes with letters of the alphabet.

Scheme: See *figures of speech*.

Schools: In the sixteenth and seventeenth centuries the different forms of school in England included Cathedral schools (often founded with a view to the education of members of the choir); grammar schools (often founded by towns or by guilds, and teaching a much broader curriculum than the modern sense of "grammar" might suggest, private schools, operated by private individuals out of private residences; and public schools, which (like the private schools and the grammar schools) operated independent of any church authority, but unlike the grammar schools and private schools were organized as independent charities, and often offered free education. Over the centuries certain of these public schools, while remaining not-for-profit institutions, began to accept fee-paying students and to adopt standards that made them more and more exclusive. In the eighteenth and nineteenth century attendance at such prestigious public boarding schools as Eton, Westminster, and Winchester had become almost exclusively the preserve of the upper classes; by the nineteenth century such "public" schools were the equivalent of private schools in North America. Though a few girls attended some early grammar schools, the greater part of this educational system was for boys only. Though a number of individuals of earlier periods were concerned to increase the number of private schools for girls, the movement to create a parallel girls' system of public schools and grammar schools dates from the later nineteenth century.

Septet: a stanza containing seven lines.

Serf: in the medieval period, a person of unfree status, typically engaged in working the land.

Sestet: a six-line stanza that forms the second grouping of lines in an Italian / Petrarchan sonnet, following the octave. See *sonnet* and *sestina*.

Sestina: an elaborate unrhymed poem with six 6-line stanzas and a 3-line envoy.

Shire: originally a multiple estate; since the late medieval period a larger territory forming an administrative unit—also referred to as a county.

Simile: a *figure of speech* (a trope) which makes an explicit comparison between a particular object and another object or idea that is similar in some (often unexpected) way. A simile always uses "like" or "as" to signal the connection. Compare with *metaphor* above.

Sonnet: a highly structured lyric poem, which normally has fourteen lines of iambic pentameter. We can distinguish four major variations of the sonnet.

Italian/Petrarchan: named for the 14th-century Italian poet Petrarch, has an octave rhyming *abbaabba*, and a sestet rhyming *cdecde*, or *cdcdcd* (other arrangements are possible here). Usually, a turn in argument takes place between octave and sestet.

Miltonic: developed by Milton and similar to the Petrarchan in rhyme scheme, but eliminating the turn after the octave, thus giving greater unity to the poem's structure of thought.

Shakespearean: often called the English sonnet, this form has three quatrains and a couplet. The quatrains rhyme internally but do not interlock: *abab cdcd efef gg*. The turn may occur after the second quatrain, but is usually revealed in the final couplet. Shakespeare's sonnets are the best-known examples of this form.

Spenserian: after Edmund Spenser, who developed the form in his sonnet cycle *Amoretti*. This sonnet form has three quatrains linked through interlocking rhyme, and a separately rhyming couplet: *abab bcbc cdcd ee*.

Speaker: in the late medieval period, a member of the Commons in Parliament who spoke on behalf of that entire group. (The Commons first elected a Speaker in 1376.) In later eras the role of Speaker became one of chairing debates in the House of Commons and arbitrating disputes over matters of procedure.

Spenserian Stanza: a nine-line stanza, with eight iambic pentameters and a concluding alexandrine, rhyming *ababbcbcc*.

Spondee: a metrical foot containing two strong stressed syllables: // (e.g., blind mouths).

Sprung Rhythm: a modern variation of accentual verse, created by the English poet Gerard Manley Hopkins, in which rhythms are determined largely by the number of strong stresses in a line, without regard to the number of unstressed syllables. Hopkins felt that sprung rhythm more closely approximated the natural rhythms of speech than did conventional poetry.

Stanza: any lines of verse that are grouped together in a poem and separated from other similarly-structured groups by a space. In metrical poetry, stanzas share metrical and rhyming patterns; however, stanzas may also be formed on the basis of thought, as in irregular odes. Conventional stanza forms include the *tercet*, the *quatrain*, *rhyme royal*, the *Spenserian stanza*, the *ballad stanza*, and *ottava rima*.

Stream of Consciousness: narrative technique that attempts to convey in prose fiction a sense of the progression of the full range of thoughts and sensations occurring within a character's mind. Twentieth-century pioneers in the use of the stream of consciousness technique include Dorothy Richardson, Virginia Woolf, and James Joyce.

Stress: See *accent*.

Strophe: the first stanza in a Pindaric ode. This is followed by an *antistrophe* (see above), which presents the same metrical pattern and rhyme scheme, and finally by an *epode*, differing in meter from the preceding stanzas. Upon completion of this "triad," the entire sequence can recur. *Strophe* may also describe a stanza or other subdivision in other kinds of poem.

Sublime: a concept, most popular in eighteenth-century England, of the qualities of grandeur, power, and awe that may be inherent in or produced by undomesticated nature or great art. The sublime was thought of as higher and loftier than something that is merely beautiful.

Subplot: a line of story that is subordinate to the main storyline of a narrative. (Note that properly speaking a subplot is a category of story material, not of plot.)

Substitution: a deliberate change from the dominant pattern of stresses in a line of verse to create emphasis or variation. Thus the first line of Shakespeare's sonnet "'Shall I compare thee to a summer's day?' is decidedly iambic in meter (x / x / x / x / x /), whereas the second line substitutes a trochee (/ x) in the opening foot: "Thou art more lovely and more temperate."

Subtext: implied or suggested meaning of a passage of text, or of an entire work.

Syllabic Verse: poetry in which the length of a line is measured solely by the number of syllables, regardless of accents or patterns of stress.

Syllable: vocal sound or group of sounds forming a unit of speech; a syllable may be formed with a single effort of articulation. Some syllables consist of a single phoneme (e.g., the word *I*, or the first syllable in the word *u*-ni-ty) but others may be made up of several phonemes (as with one-syllable words such as *lengths*, *splurged*, and *through*). By contrast, the much shorter words *ago*, *any*, and *open* each have two syllables.

Symbol: a word, image, or idea that represents something more, or other, than for what it at first appears to stand. Like metaphor, the symbol extends meaning; but while the tenor and vehicle of metaphor are bound in a specific relationship, a symbol may have a range of connotations. For example, the image of a rose may call forth associations of love, passion, transience, fragility, youth and beauty, among others. Depending upon the context, such an image could be interpreted in a variety of ways, as in Blake's lyric, "The Sick Rose." Though this power of symbolic representation characterizes all language, poetry most particularly endows the concrete imagery evoked through language with a larger meaning. Such meaning is implied rather than explicitly stated; indeed, much of the power of symbolic language lies in the reader's ability to make meaningful sense of it.

Syncope: in poetry, the dropping of a letter or syllable from the middle of a word, as in "trav'ler." Such a contraction allows a line to stay within a metrical scheme. See also *catalexis* and *elision*.

Synecdoche: a kind of *metonymy* in which a writer substitutes the name of a part of something to signify the whole: for example, "sail" for ship or "hand" for a member of the ship's crew.

Tercet: a group, or stanza, of three lines, often linked by an interlocking rhyme scheme as in *terza rima*. See also *triplet*.

Terza Rima: an arrangement of tercets interlocked by a rhyme scheme of *aba bcb cdc ded*, etc., and ending with a couplet that rhymes with the second-last line of the final tercet (for example, *efe, ff*). See, for example, Percy Shelley's "Ode to the West Wind."

Tetrameter: a line of poetry containing four metrical feet.

Theme: the governing idea of a discourse, conveyed through the development of the subject, and through the recurrence of certain words, sounds, or metrical patterns. See also *motif*.

Third-Person Narrative: See *narrative perspective*.

Tone: the writer's attitude toward a given subject or audience, as expressed though an authorial persona or "voice." Tone can be projected through particular choices of wording, imagery, figures of speech, and rhythmic devices. Compare *mood*.

Tories: See *Political Parties*.

Tragedy: in the traditional definition originating in discussions of ancient Greek drama, a serious narrative recounting the downfall of the protagonist. More loosely, the term has been applied to a wide variety of literary forms in which the tone is predominantly a dark one and the narrative does not end happily.

Transcendentalism: a philosophical movement that influenced such Victorian writers as Thomas Carlyle and Robert Browning. Also a mode of Romantic thought, Transcendentalism places the supernatural and the natural within one great Unity and believes that each individual person embodies aspects of the divine.

Trimeter: a line of poetry containing three metrical feet.

Triolet: a French form in which the first line appears three times in a poem of only eight lines. The first line is repeated at lines 4 and 7; the second line is repeated in line 8. The triolet has only two rhymes: *abaaabab*.

Triple Foot: poetic foot of three syllables. The possible varieties of triple foot are the anapest (in which two unstressed syllables are followed by a stressed syllable), the dactyl (in which a stressed syllable is followed by two unstressed lines), and the mollossus (in which all three syllables are stressed equally). English poetry tends to use duple rhythms far more frequently than triple rhythms.

Triplet: a group of three lines with the same end-rhyme, much used by eighteenth-century poets to vary or punctuate the flow of couplets. See also *tercet*.

Trivium: group of three academic subjects (dialectic, grammar, and rhetoric) that were part of the university curriculum in the Middle Ages. Their study precedes that of the more advanced subjects of the *quadrivium*.

Trochee: a metrical foot containing one strong stress followed by one weak stress: / x (heaven, lover).

Trope: any figure of speech that plays on our understandings of words to extend, alter, or transform "literal" meaning. Common tropes include *metaphor, simile, personification, hyperbole, metonymy, oxymoron, synecdoche,* and *irony*. See also *figures of speech*, above.

Turn (Italian "volta"): the point in a *sonnet* where the mood or argument changes. The turn may occur between the octave and sestet, i.e., after the eighth line, or in the final couplet, depending on the kind of sonnet.

Unities: Many literary theorists of the late sixteenth through late eighteenth centuries held that a play should ideally be presented as representing a single place, and confining the action to a single day and a single dominant event. They disapproved of plots involving gaps or long periods of time, shifts in place, or subplots. These concepts, which came to be referred to as the unities of space, time, and action, were based on a misreading of classical authorities (principally of Aristotle).

Vers de societé: French: literally, "verse about society." The term originated with poetry written by aristocrats and upper-middle-class poets that specifically disavows the ambition of creating "high art" while treating the concerns of their own group in verse forms that demonstrate a high degree of formal control (e.g., artful rhymes, surprising turns of diction).

Vers libre (French):   See *free verse* above.

Verse: a general term for works of poetry, usually referring to poems that incorporate some kind of metrical structure. The term may also describe a line of poetry, though more frequently it is applied to a stanza.

Villanelle: a poem usually consisting of 19 lines, with five 3-line stanzas (tercets) rhyming *aba*, and a concluding quatrain rhyming *abaa*. The first and third lines of the first tercet are repeated at fixed intervals throughout the rest of the poem. See, for example, Dylan Thomas's "Do Not Go Gentle Into That Good Night."

Whigs: See *Political Parties*.

Workhouse: public institution in which the poor were provided with a minimal level of sustenance and with lodging in exchange for work performed. Early workhouses were typically administered by individual parishes. In 1834 a unified system covering all of England and Wales was put into effect.

Zeugma: a *figure of speech* (trope) in which one word links or "yokes" two others in the same sentence, often to comic or ironic effect. For example, a verb may govern two objects, as in Pope's line "Or stain her honour, or her new brocade."

Permissions Acknowledgments

Achebe, Chinua. "The Sacrificial Egg," from GIRLS AT WAR AND OTHER STORIES. New York: Anchor, 1990. Copyright © 1972, 1973 by Chinua Achebe. Used by permission of Doubleday, a division of Random House, Inc., of the Emma Sweeney Agency and of Harold Ober Associates Incorporated; "An Image of Africa," from HOPES AND IMPEDIMENTS. New York: Anchor, 1990. Copyright © 1988 by Chinua Achebe. Used by permission of Doubleday, a division of Random House, Inc. and of the Emma Sweeney Agency.

Aiken, Conrad. "Diverse Realists." Originally printed in *The Dial*, 8 November, 1917.

Allain, Marie-Françoise. Excerpts from THE OTHER MAN: CONVERSATIONS WITH GRAHAM GREENE. Trans. from the French by Guido Waldman. London: The Bodley Head, 1983. English translation copyright © 1983 by the Bodley Head and Simon and Schuster. Reprinted by permission of The Random House Group Ltd. and Simon and Schuster.

Alvi, Moniza. "And If," from CARRYING MY WIFE. Northumberland: Bloodaxe Books, 2000; "How the World Split in Two," from HOW THE STONE FOUND ITS VOICE. Northumberland: Bloodaxe Books, 2005. Copyright © Bloodaxe Books.

Armitage, Simon. "The English" and "It Could Be You," from THE UNIVERSAL HOME DOCTOR. London: Faber, 2002. Reprinted by permission of Faber and Faber Ltd.

Armstrong, J.A. "Another Reply to Flanders Fields," from THE BEST LOVED POEMS OF THE AMERICAN PEOPLE. Ed. Hazel Felleman. New York: Doubleday, 1936.

Atwood, Margaret. "Further Arrivals," "Death of a Young Son by Drowning," "The Immigrants," "Later in Belleville: Career," "Thoughts From Underground," "Daguerreotype Taken in Old Age" and "A Bus Along St. Clair: December," from THE JOURNALS OF SUSANNA MOODIE. Toronto: Oxford University Press, 1970. Copyright © Oxford University Press Canada 1973, 1976. Reprinted by permission of the publisher and of Houghton Mifflin Company. All rights reserved; "We Are Hard" and "You Fit into Me," from POWER POLITICS. Toronto: House of Anansi Press, 1996. Copyright © 1971, 1996 by Margaret Atwood. Reprinted by permission of the publisher; "*The Handmaid's Tale* and *Oryx and Crake* in Context." PMLA, 119.3 (2004): 513-517. Reprinted by permission of Margaret Atwood. Originally published in PMLA, copyright © 2004 by O.W. Toad Ltd.

Auden, W. H. "O What is that Sound," from COLLECTED POEMS. New York: Vintage, 1991. Copyright © by W.H. Auden 1951; "At Last Our Secret is Out" and excerpts from "The Sea and The Mirror," from COLLECTED POEMS. New York: Vintage, 1991. Copyright © 1976 by Edward Mendelson, William Meredith and Monroe K. Spears, Executors of the Estate of W.H. Auden; "Stop All The Clocks," "Spain 1937," "Lullaby," "As I Walked Out One Evening," "Musée des Beaux Arts," "In Memory of W.B. Yeats" and "September 1, 1939," from COLLECTED POEMS. New York: Vintage, 1991. Copyright © by W.H. Auden 1940 and renewed 1968. Reprinted by permission of Faber and Faber Ltd; "The Shield of Achilles," from COLLECTED POEMS. New York: Vintage, 1991. Copyright © by W.H. Auden 1937 and renewed 1965; "The Truest Poet is the Most

Chapman, Graham, et al. "Dead Parrot Sketch" and "Pet Conversion," from MONTY PYTHONS FLYING CIRCUS: JUST THE WORDS, VOL. ONE. London: Methuen, 1999. Copyright © Python (Monty) Pictures Ltd, 1989; "Dirty Hungarian Phrasebook" and "Spam," from MONTY PYTHONS FLYING CIRCUS: JUST THE WORDS, VOL. TWO. London: Methuen, 1999. Copyright © Python (Monty) Pictures Ltd, 1989.

Charles, Hughie, and Ross Parker. "We'll Meet Again." Words and Music by Hughie Charles and Ross Parker. Copyright © 1939 (Renewed) by Irwin Dash Music Co., Ltd. All Rights for the Western Hemisphere controlled by Music Sales Corporation (ASCAP). International copyright secured. All right reserved. Reprinted by permission.

Churchill, Caryl. TOP GIRLS. London: Methuen, 1982. This play is fully protected by copyright. All rights reserved. All enquiries concerning the rights for professional or amateur stage productions must be made to: Casarotto Ramsay & Associates Ltd. 60-66 Wardour Street London, W1V 4ND. Tel: (0) 20 7287 4450. Fax: (0) 20 7287 9128. Email: agents@casarotto.uk.com. Website: www.casarotto.uk.com.

Cunard, Nancy. Excerpts from "Jamaica – The Negro Island" and "The White Man's Duty: An Analysis of the Colonial Question in Light of the Atlantic Charter," from ESSAYS ON RACE AND EMPIRE. Ed. Maureen Moynagh. Peterborough: Broadview, 2002. Reprinted by permission of A.R.A. Hobson.

Dabydeen, David. "Slave Song," "Coolie Odyssey," "Preface" and "Turner I-VI," from TURNER: NEW AND SELECTED POEMS. Leeds: Peepal, 2002. Copyright © David Dabydeen 1995, 2002.

Doolittle, Hilda (HD). "Oread" and "The Pool," from COLLECTED POEMS, 1912-1944. New York: New Directions, 1983. Copyright © 1982 by The Estate of Hilda Doolittle. Reprinted by permission of the publisher.

Douglas, Keith. "Vergissmeinnicht," from THE COMPLETE POEMS. London: Faber, 2000. Copyright © 1978, 1998 by the Estate of Keith Douglas. Reprinted by permission of Faber and Faber Ltd, an affiliate of Farrar, Straus and Giroux, LLC.

Duffy, Carol Ann. "Stealing," from SELLING MANHATTAN. London: Anvil Press Poetry, 1988; "Adultery," "The Good Teachers," "Drunk" and "Mean Time," from MEAN TIME. London: Anvil Press Poetry, 1993. Reprinted by permission of the publisher; "Wish" "Mrs. Lazarus," from THE WORLD'S WIFE. London: Faber, 1999. Reprinted by permission of Macmillan, London, UK; "Rapture," from RAPTURE. London: Picador, 2005. Reprinted by permission of Macmillan, London, UK.

Eliot, T.S. "Journey of the Magi," "Marina" and "Burnt Norton," from COMPLETE POEMS AND PLAYS, 1909-1950. New York: Harcourt, 1952. Reprinted by permission of Faber and Faber Ltd.

Ellis, Havelock. "Sexual Inversion," from STUDIES IN THE PSYCHOLOGY OF SEX: VOLUME 2. Philadelphia: F.A. Davis, 1918. Reprinted by permission of the publisher.

Evaristo, Bernardine. Excerpts from LARA. Reproduced by permission of Curtis Brown Group Ltd., London on behalf of Bernardine Evaristo. Copyright © Bernardine Evaristo, 1997.

Fenton, James. "A German Requiem," from THE MEMORY OF WAR. Edinburgh: Salamander, 1980. Reprinted by permission of PFD on behalf of James Fenton.

Fitzgerald, Penelope. "The Axe," from THE TIMES ANTHOLOGY OF GHOST STORIES. London: Jonathan Cape, 1975. Used by permission of the Random House Group Limited.

Flint, F.S. "Imagisme." Originally published in *Poetry Magazine*, March 1913.

Forrest-Thomson, Veronica. "Identikit" and "Phrase-Book," from COLLECTED POEMS AND TRANSLATIONS. Lewes, East Sussex: Allardyce, Barnett, 1990. Copyright © Jonathan Culler and the Estate of Veronica-Forrest Thomson 1990 and Allardyce, Barnett, Publishers 1990. Reprinted by permission of Allardyce, Barnett Publishers.

Forster, E.M. "The Road from Colonus," from THE COLLECTED TALES OF E.M. FORSTER. New York: Knopf, 1947. Copyright © Alfred A. Knopf, a division of Random House Inc., 1947. Used by permission of publisher and of The Provost and Scholars of King's College, Cambridge and The Society of Authors as the Literary Representatives of the Estate of E.M. Forster; "What I Believe," from TWO CHEERS FOR DEMOCRACY. New York: Harcourt, 1951. Copyright © 1951 by E.M. Forster and renewed 1979 by Donald Parry. Reprinted by permission of Harcourt Inc., of The Provost and Scholars of King's College, Cambridge and of The Society of Authors as the Literary Representatives of the Estate of E.M. Forster; Excerpts from "Terminal Note," from MAURICE. Toronto: Macmillan, 1971. Copyright © 1971 by the trustees of the late E.M. Forster. Used by permission of W.W. Norton & Company, Inc., and by The Provost and Scholars of King's College, Cambridge and The Society of Authors as the Literary Representatives of the Estate of E.M. Forster.

Graves, Robert. "The Cool Web," "Down, Wanton, Down!" and "Recalling War," from COMPLETE POEMS IN ONE VOLUME. Ed. Patrick Quinn. Manchester: Carcanet, 2000. Reprinted by permission of the publisher; Excerpts from GOODBYE TO ALL THAT. New York: Doubleday, 1929.

Greene, Graham. "The Basement Room," from COLLECTED STORIES. New York: Penguin Books, 1992. Reprinted by permission of David Higham Associates; "Preface," from THE FALLEN IDOL. London: Penguin, 1992. Copyright © 1950 by Graham Greene. Reprinted by permission of International Creative Management, Inc.

Gunn, Thom. "The Wound," "Tamer and Hawk," "To His Cynical Mistress," "The Hug" and "The Missing," from COLLECTED POEMS. New York: Farrar, Straus & Giroux, 1995. Copyright © 1994 by Thom Gunn. All poems reprinted by permission of the publisher and of Faber and Faber Ltd.

Harrison, Tony. "Them & [uz]" and "t'Ark," from SELECTED POEMS. London: Penguin, 1987. Copyright © Tony Harrison; Excerpts from "v.," from v. Northumberland: Bloodaxe Books, 1985. Copyright © Bloodaxe Books; "Sonnets for August 1945 (I)," from v. AND OTHER POEMS. New York: Farrar, Straus & Giroux, 1990.

Harsnet, David. "Art," from LEGION. London, Faber, 2005. Reprinted by permission of Faber and Faber Ltd.

& White., 20 Powis Mews, London W11 1JN and of Scribner, an imprint of Simon and Schuster Adult Publishing Group.

Larkin, Phillip. "Church Going," from THE LESS DECEIVED. Yorkshire: Marvel Press, 1955; "Days," "Dockery and Son," "Annus Mirabilis," "High Window," "This Be The Verse," "Vers de Société," "The Old Fools" and "Aubade," from COLLECTED POEMS. London: Faber, 2003. Copyright © 1988, 2003 by the Estate of Philip Larkin. Reprinted by permission of Faber and Faber Ltd and of Farrar, Straus & Giroux, LLC.

Lawrence, D.H. "Tortoise Shout" and "Bavarian Gentians," from THE COMPLETE POEMS OF D.H. LAWRENCE. Eds. Vivian De Sola Pinto and Warren Roberts. New York: Penguin, 1964. Reproduced by permission of Pollinger Limited and the proprietor; "Snake," from BIRDS, BEASTS AND FLOWERS: POEMS BY D.H. LAWRENCE. New York: Haskell House Publishers Ltd., 1974. Reproduced by permission of Pollinger Limited and the proprietor; "The Hopi Snake Dance," from MORNINGS IN MEXICO AND ETRUSCAN PLACES. London: Martin Secker, 1927. Reproduced by permission of Pollinger Limited and the proprietor; "Why the Novel Matters," from PHOENIX: THE POSTHUMOUS PAPERS OF D.H. LAWRENCE. Ed. Edward McDonald. London: William Heinemann Ltd., 1961. Reproduced by permission of Pollinger Limited and the proprietor.

Lehmann, John. Excerpts from "Foreword," from PENGUIN NEW WRITING NO. 5. Middlesex: Penguin, 1941. Reprinted by permission of David Higham Associates.

LePan, Douglas. "Below Monte Cassino" and "The Haystack," from WEATHERING IT: COMPLETE POEMS 1948-1987. Toronto: McClelland and Stewart, 1987. Copyright © 1987 The Estate of Douglas LePan. (Don LePan, literary executor, c/o Broadview Press); "Personality of the Poet: Some Recollections of T.S. Eliot," from BRIGHT GLASS OF MEMORY. Toronto: McGraw Hill, 1979. Copyright © 1979 The Estate of Douglas LePan. (Don LePan, literary executor, c/o Broadview Press).

Lessing, Doris. "To Room Nineteen," from A MAN AND TWO WOMEN. New York: Simon and Schuster, 1984. Copyright © 1963 Doris Lessing. Reprinted by kind permission of Jonathan Clowes Ltd., London, on behalf of Doris Lessing; Excerpts from "Preface," from THE GOLDEN NOTEBOOK. New York: Simon and Schuster, 1962. Copyright © 1972 by Doris Lessing. Reprinted by kind permission of Jonathan Clowes Ltd., London, on behalf of Doris Lessing.

Lewis, Gwyneth. "Mother Tongue," from CHAOTIC ANGELS. Northumberland: Bloodaxe Books, 2005. Copyright © Bloodaxe Books.

Loy, Mina. "Three Moments in Paris – One O'Clock at Night" and "Love Songs 1, 2 and 3," from THE LAST LUNAR BAEDEKER. Highlands: Jargon, 1982. Copyright © 1982 by The Jargon Society. Reprinted by permission of Roger L. Conover, Mina Loy's editor and literary executor.

McEwan, Ian. "Last Day of Summer," from FIRST LOVE, LAST RIGHTS. London: Jonathan Cape, 1975. Copyright © 1975 Ian McEwan. Reproduced by permission of the author, c/o Rogers, Coleridge & White Ltd., 20 Powis Mews, London W11 1JN.

McGuckian, Medbh. "Slips" and "The Sofa," from THE FLOWER MASTER AND OTHER POEMS. Loughcrew: The Gallery Press, 1993. Reprinted by kind permission of the author and of

The Gallery Press, Loughcrew, Oldcastle, County Meath, Ireland; "The Dream-Language of Fergus," from ON BALLYCASTLE BEACH. North Carolina: Wake Forest University Press, 1995. Reprinted by kind permission of the author, of the publisher, and of The Gallery Press, Loughcrew, Oldcastle, County Meath, Ireland.

Mitchell, John. "Reply to Flanders Fields," from THE BEST LOVED POEMS OF THE AMERICAN PEOPLE. Ed. Hazel Felleman. New York: Doubleday, 1936.

Muldoon, Paul. "Good Friday, 1971. Driving Westward," "Our Lady of Ardboe," "The Sightseers," "Cherish The Ladies," "Milkweed and Monarch," "The Plot" and "Anonymous: Myself and Pangur.," from POEMS 1968-1998. London, Faber, 2001. Copyright © 2001 by Paul Muldoon. Reprinted by permission of Faber and Faber Ltd and of Farrar, Straus & Giroux, LLC.

Munro, Alice. "The View from Castle Rock." Originally published in *The New Yorker*, 29 August 2005. Copyright © 2005 Alice Munro. Reprinted by permission of William Morris Agency, LLC on behalf of the Author.

Murray, Les. "An Absolutely Ordinary Rainbow," "Bent Water in the Tasmanian Highland" and "The Quality of Sprawl," from THE RABBITER'S BOUNTY. New York: Farrar, Straus & Giroux, 1991. Copyright 1992 by Les Murray; "Pigs," from TRANSLATIONS FROM THE NATURAL WORLD: POEMS. New York: Farrar, Straus & Giroux, 1994. All poems reprinted by permission of the pubisher and of Faber and Faber Ltd.; "The Mare Out On the Road." Originally published in *The New Yorker*, 13 & 20 June 1995.

Nichols, Grace. "Skanking Englishman Between Trains," from THE FAT BLACK WOMAN'S POEMS. London: Virago, 1984. Copyright © Grace Nichols 1984. Reproduced by permission of Curtis Brown Group Ltd, London on behalf of Grace Nichols; "Epilogue," from I IS A LONG MEMORIED WOMAN. London: Virago, 1983. Copyright © Grace Nichols 1983. Reproduced by permission of Curtis Brown Group Ltd, London on behalf of Grace Nichols; "Love," from LAZY THOUGHTS OF A LAZY WOMAN. London: Virago, 1989. Copyright © Grace Nichols 1989. Reproduced by permission of Curtis Brown Group Ltd, London on behalf of Grace Nichols; "White," from SUNRIS. London: Virago, 1996. Copyright © Grace Nichols 1996. Reproduced by permission of Curtis Brown Group Ltd, London on behalf of Grace Nichols.

Nicolson, Harold. Excerpts from HAROLD NICOLSON DIARIES AND LETTERS 1907-1964. Ed. Nigel Nicolson. New York: Anthenuem, 1967. Reprinted by permission of Weidenfeld & Nicolson, an imprint of The Orion Publishing Group.

Ondaatje, Michael. "Letters and Other Worlds," from THE CINNAMON PEELER. Toronto: McClelland & Stewart, 1989. Copyright © 1989 by permission of Ellen Levine Literary Agency / Trident Media Group; "Travels in Ceylon," from RUNNING IN THE FAMILY. New York: Vintage, 1993. Copyright © 1993 by Michael Ondaajte. Used by permission of Alfred A. Knopf, a division of Random House, Inc.

O'Reilly, Caitriona. "Hide" and "A Brief History of Light," from NOWHERE BIRDS. Northumberland: Bloodaxe Books, 2001. Copyright © Bloodaxe Books.

Publishing Corp; Excerpts from "A Few Don'ts," from "A Retrospect," from THE LITERARY ESSAYS OF EZRA POUND. New York: New Directions, 1954. Copyright © 1935 by Ezra Pound. Reprinted by permission of the publisher; Excerpts from "Vorticism.," from GAUDIER-BRZESKA: A MEMOIR. London: Bodley Head, 1916. Copyright © 1980 by New Directions Publishing Corp. Reprinted by permission of New Directions Publishing Corp; "Drunken Helots and Mr. Eliot." Originally published in *The Egoist*, June 1917. Copyright © 1926 by Ezra Pound. Reprinted by permission of New Directions Publishing Corp.

Raine, Craig. "A Martian Sends a Postcard Home," from A MARTIAN SENDS A POSTCARD HOME. Oxford: Oxford University Press, 1979. Copyright © 1979 by Craig Raine.

Raworth, Tom. "Out of a Sudden," from CLEAN AND WELL LIT. New York: Roof Books, 1996; "Looking For Language," from COLLECTED POEMS. Manchester: Carcanet, 2003. Reprinted by permission of the publisher.

Reed, Henry. "I: Naming of Parts," from LESSONS OF WAR. New York: Chilmark Press, 1970. Reprinted by kind permission of The Estate of Henry Reed.

Rhys, Jean. "Let Them Call it Jazz," from TIGERS ARE BETTER - LOOKING. London: Penguin, 1972. Copyright © Jean Rhys 1972.

Richardson, Dorothy. "About Punctuation." Originally published in *The Adelphi*, 1 April, 1924. Reprinted by permission of Paterson Marsh Ltd on behalf of The Estate of Dorothy Richardson; "Journey to Paradise," from JOURNEY TO PARADISE. London: Virago, 1989. By permission of Paterson Marsh Ltd on behalf of The Estate of Dorothy Richardson; "Foreword," from PILGRIMAGE. London: Virago, 1979. By permission of Paterson Marsh Ltd on behalf of The Estate of Dorothy Richardson.

Ritchie, Charles. Excerpts from THE SIREN YEARS: A CANADIAN DIPLOMAT ABROAD 1937-1945. Toronto: McClelland & Stewart, 2001. Used by permission of the publisher.

Roberts, Robert. Excerpts from THE CLASSIC SLUM. London: Penguin, 1990. Reprinted by kind permission of Mr. G. Roberts.

Rushdie, Salman. "Is Nothing Sacred?," from IMAGINARY HOMELANDS. New York: Viking, 1991. Copyright © Salman Rushdie 1991. Used by permission of Viking Penguin, a division of Penguin Group (USA) Inc.

Sassoon, Siegfried. "They," "Glory of Women" and "Everyone Sang," from COLLECTED POEMS OF SIEGFRIED SASSOON. London: Faber, 1961. Copyright © 1918, 1920 by EP Dutton. Copyright © 1936, 1946, 1947, 1948 by Siegfried Sassoon. Used by kind permission of George Sassoon and Viking Penguin, a division of Penguin Group (USA) Inc; Excerpts from "Part II," from MEMOIRS OF AN INFANTRY OFFICER. London: Faber, 1930. Copyright © Siegfried Sassoon by kind permission of George Sassoon.

Shaw, Bernard. "Mrs. Warren's Profession," from PLAYS UNPLEASANT. London: Penguin, 1988. The Society of Authors on behalf of the Estate of Bernard Shaw, Copyright © 1898, 1913, 1926, 1930, 1933, 1941 by George Bernard Shaw. Copyright © 1905 Brentano's. Copyright © 1957 by

permission of PFD (www.pfd.co.uk) on behalf of the Estate of Rebecca West; "To Irita Van Doren, Dec. 1940," from SELECTED LETTERS OF REBECCA WEST. Ed. Bonnie Kime. London: Yale, 2000. Reprinted by permission of Sll/sterling Lord Literistic, Inc.

Winterson, Jeanette. "Lives of Saints," from THE WORLD AND OTHER PLACES. London: Vintage, 2000. Copyright © 1998 by Jeanette Winterson. Used by permission of Alfred A. Knopf, a division of Random House, Inc.

Wodehouse, P.G. "Honeysuckle Cottage," from THE WORLD OF MR. MULLINER. New York: Taplinger, 1974. Used by permission of Random House Group Limited.

Woolf, Virginia. "The Mark on the Wall," "Kew Gardens" and "Mrs. Dalloway In Bond Street," from THE MARK ON THE WALL AND OTHER SHORT FICTION. Ed. David Bradshaw. New York: Oxford University Press, 2001. The Society of Authors as the Literary Representatives of the Estate of Virginia Woolf; A ROOM OF ONE'S OWN. London: Hogarth, 1931. Copyright © 1929 by Harcourt Brace & Company and renewed 1957 by Leonard Woolf, reprinted by permission of the publisher; "Modern Fiction," from THE COMMON READER. London: Hogarth, 1968. The Society of Authors as the Literary Representatives of the Estate of Virginia Woolf; "A Sketch of the Past," from MOMENTS OF BEING. New York: Harvest, 1985. Copyright © 1976 by Quentin Bell and Angelica Garnett. Reprinted by permission of publisher; Excerpts from THE DIARY OF VIRGINIA WOOLF: VOLUME V, 1936-1941. London: Hogarth, 1959. Copyright © 1984 Quentin Bell and Angelica Garnett. Reprinted by permission of Harcourt, Inc; Excerpts from THE DIARY OF VIRGINIA WOOLF: VOLUME V, 1936-1941. London: Hogarth, 1959. Copyright © 1984 Quentin Bell and Angelica Garnett. Reprinted by permission of Harcourt, Inc; Excerpts from ORLANDO. London: Hogarth, 1928. Copyright © 1928 by Virginia Woolf and renewed 1956 by Leonard Woolf. Reprinted by permission of Harcourt Inc; Excerpts from A WRITER'S DIARY. London: Hogarth, 1959. Copyright 1954 by Leonard Woolf and renewed 1982 by Quentin Bell and Angelica Garnett. Reprinted by permission of Harcourt Inc; Excerpts from "Character in Fiction," from THE ESSAYS OF VIRGINIA WOOLF: VOL III, 1919-1924. London: Hogarth, 1988.

Wright, Judith. "Woman to Man," "The Bull," Woman to Child," "At Cooloola," "Introduction," "Sports Field" and "Two Dreamtimes," from A HUMAN PATTERN: SELECTED POEMS. Sydney: ETT Imprint, 1996.

Yeats, W.B. Meditations in Time of Civil War," Leda and the Swan," "Among School Children," "Sailing to Byzantium" and "The Tower," from THE COLLECTED WORKS OF W.B. YEATS, VOLUME I: THE POEMS, REVISED. New York: Scribner, 1997. Ed. Richard J. Finneran. Reprinted with permission of Scribner, an imprint of Simon & Schuster Adult Publishing Group, copyright © 1928 by The Macmillan Company; copyright renewed © by Georgie Yeats; "Dialogue of Self and Soul," "Byzantium," "For Anne Gregory" and "Crazy Jane Talks With the Bishop," from THE COLLECTED WORKS OF W.B. YEATS, VOLUME I: THE POEMS, REVISED. New York: Scribner, 1997. Ed. Richard J. Finneran. Reprinted with permission of Scribner, an imprint of Simon & Schuster Adult Publishing Group, copyright © 1933 by The Macmillan Company; copyright renewed © by Bertha Georgie Yeats; "Lapis Lazuli," "The Circus Animals' Desertion" and "Under Ben Bulben," from THE COLLECTED WORKS OF W.B. YEATS, VOLUME I: THE POEMS, REVISED. New York: Scribner, 1997. Ed. Richard J. Finneran. Reprinted with permission of Scribner, an imprint of Simon & Schuster Adult Publishing Group, copyright © 1940 by Georgie Yeats; copyright renewed © 1968 b Bertha Georgie Yeats, Michael Butler Yeats and Anne Yeats;

Picture Credits

permission by Unionsverlag. Page 859: Reproduced by permission of the National Portrait Gallery, London. Page 866: © Jess Atwood Gibson. Page 877: Courtesy of Michael Ondaatji and Trident Media. Page 833: Photo – Mark Gerson. Page 914: Reproduced by permission of the National Portrait Gallery, London. Page 952: Portrait by Lisa Brawn. Page 981: Portrait by Lisa Brawn. Page 990: Photo courtesy of Neil Wilder/www.wilderwilder.net. Page 999: Reproduced by permission of the National Portrait Gallery, London. Page 1004: Portrait by Lisa Brawn. Page 1012: Portrait by Lisa Brawn. Page 1020: With kind permission of David Dabydeen. Page 1027: Reprinted by permission of Anvil Press Poetry.   Page 1087: Reproduced by permission of the National Portrait Gallery, London. Page 1057: Reproduced by permission of the National Portrait Gallery, London. Page 1065: Portrait by Lisa Brawn.

INDEX OF FIRST LINES

INDEX OF AUTHORS AND TITLES